Florida Constitutional Law

Florida Constitutional Law

Cases and Materials

SIXTH EDITION

Tishia A. Dunham
Founder and Chief Executive Officer
Agape Christian Bar Preparation Services, Inc.

Carlos L. Woody
Chief Deputy General Counsel, Orlando Utilities Commission
Board Certified in City, County, and Local Government Law
Adjunct Professor of Law, Florida A&M University College of Law

Carolina Academic Press
Durham, North Carolina

Copyright © 2023
Carolina Academic Press, LLC
All Rights Reserved

ISBN: 978-1-5310-2467-3
eISBN: 978-1-5310-2468-0
LCCN: 2022946143

Carolina Academic Press
700 Kent Street
Durham, NC 27701
(919) 489-7486
www.cap-press.com

Printed in the United States of America

To my exceeding great reward, Jesus Christ,

for His abundant grace,

immense love, and enduring help.
—Tishia A. Dunham

I dedicate this edition to my hero, my father, Mr. W.W. Woody, Sr., who passed away during the writing of this edition. May your memory continue to be a blessing to all those you have touched with your kind and gentle spirit. You truly were one of the finest human beings to ever grace this planet. I am forever grateful to my Heavenly Father for blessing me with you as my earthly father.
(01/05/31–11/26/2021)
—Carlos L. Woody

To borrow freely from the *Holy Bible*[1]—

State governments have only inherent power. This is the first and great commandment and the second is like unto it: state constitutions can thus be nothing other than limitations on state power.

---

1. 35 Then one of them, *which was* a lawyer, asked *him* a *question*, tempting him, and saying,

36 Master, which *is* the great commandment in the law?

37 Jesus said unto him, Thou shalt love the Lord thy God with all thy heart, and with all thy soul, and with all thy mind.

38 This is the first and great commandment.

39 And the second *is* like unto it, Thou shalt love thy neighbour as thyself.

The Gospel according to St. Matthew, Chapter 22.

Contents

Table of Cases	xxiii
Preface to the First Edition	xxxiii
Preface to the Second Edition	xxxv
Preface to the Third Edition	xxxvii
Preface to the Fourth Edition	xxxix
Preface to the Fifth Edition	xli
Preface to the Sixth Edition	xliii

Chapter 1 · An Introduction to Studying the Florida Constitution — 3

A. Introduction	3
1. The Social Contract	3
2. Governmental Power in the American System	5
3. The Modern View of the State's Inherent Power	6
B. The Concept of the State Constitution	7
1. The State Constitution as a Limitation on Inherent State Governmental Power	7
a. In General	7
Peters v. Meeks	7
b. Constitutional Language that Looks Like a Grant of Power	9
(1) Constitutional Language as a Legitimate Limitation on Power	9
(2) Constitutional Language as a Reaffirmation of Existing Inherent Power	10
(3) Constitutional Language as an Allocation of Inherent Power	11
c. State Constitution as a Limitation on All Branches of State Government	12
2. Self-Executing and Non-Self-Executing Provisions	13
Florida Hospital Waterman, Inc. v. Buster	13
3. The Formal Amending Process	17
a. In General	17
b. The Single Subject Problem and the Ballot Summary Substance Problem	22
Advisory Opinion to the Attorney General re Rights of Electricity Consumers Regarding Solar Energy Choice	22
c. The Integration of the Formal Amendment with the Then-Existing Constitution	34

CONTENTS

State v. Division of Bond Finance of the
    Department of General Services — 35
Folks v. Marion County — 36
d. Amendment by Interpretation — 38
4. Aids in Interpreting the Constitution — 38
   Edwards v. Thomas — 39
   Ford v. Browning — 46
   Graham v. Haridopolos — 53
   Nichols v. State ex rel. Bolon — 57
   Greater Loretta Improvement Association v. State ex rel. Boone — 58

Chapter 2 · Separation of Powers — 63
A. In General — 63
   Fla. Const. art. II, § 3 — 63
B. Encroachment by One Branch of Government on the Powers
  of Another Branch — 66
   1. Encroachment by the Judicial Branch on the Power of
     the Legislative Branch — 66
     a. Judicial Modification of the Common Law — 66
     Shands Teaching Hospital and Clinics, Inc. v. Smith — 68
     Connor v. Southwest Florida Regional Medical Center, Inc. — 69
     b. Statutory Construction — 72
     Brown v. State — 72
     Westphal v. City of St. Petersburg — 75
     State v. Stalder — 80
     Dade County Classroom Teachers Association, Inc. v. Legislature — 85
     c. The Legislative Privilege — 87
     *League of Women Voters of Florida v. Florida House
       of Representatives* — 87
   2. Encroachment by the Executive Branch on the Power of
     the Legislative Branch — 95
     Florida House of Representatives v. Crist — 95
   3. Encroachment by the Judicial Branch on the Power of
     the Executive Branch — 103
     Florida Department of Children & Families v. J.B. — 103
   4. Encroachment by the Legislative Branch on the Power of
     the Executive Branch — 106
     Jones v. Chiles — 106
   5. Encroachment by the Executive Branch on the Power of
     the Judicial Branch — 109
     McNeil v. Canty — 109
   6. Encroachment by the Legislative Branch on the Power of
     the Judicial Branch — 112
     DeLisle v. Crane Co. — 112

CONTENTS xi

C. Delegation of Power as a Separation of Powers Problem	119
1. Legislative Delegation of Legislative Power	119
Florida Department of State v. Martin	119
2. Judicial Delegation of Judicial Power	124
Pearce v. State	124
Chapter 3 · The Legislature	127
A. In General	127
Fla. Const. art. III, § 1	127
B. Constitutional Limitations	128
1. Subject Matter and Title Requirement	128
Fla. Const. art. III, § 6	128
a. Single Subject Limitation	128
Franklin v. State	129
b. The "Window Period" for Asserting Single Subject Violations	136
Salters v. State	137
Santos v. State	143
State v. Combs	145
c. The Title Requirement	146
North Ridge General Hospital, Inc. v. City of Oakland Park	146
2. Appropriation Bills	148
Fla. Const. art. III, § 12	148
Department of Education v. Lewis	148
3. General Laws, Special Laws, and General Laws of Local Application	150
Fla. Const. art. III, § 10	150
Fla. Const. art. III, § 11	151
a. General Laws	153
Florida Department of Health v. Florigrown, LLC	153
b. Special Laws	159
Pinellas County Veterinary Medical Society, Inc. v. Chapman	159
c. General Laws of Local Application	160
State ex rel. Cotterill v. Bessenger	160
d. Prohibited Special Laws	164
Venice HMA, LLC v. Sarasota County	164
e. Precedence Between General and Special Laws	174
Town of Palm Beach v. Palm Beach Local 1866 of the International Association of Fire Fighters	174
4. Governor's Veto Power	176
Fla. Const. art. III, § 8	176
International Association of Firefighters Local S-20 v. State	178
5. When Laws Take Effect	180
Fla. Const. art. III, § 9	180
In re Advisory Opinion to the Governor Request of June 29, 1979	181

CONTENTS

Chapter 4 · The Courts	185
A. In General	185
Fla. Const. art. V, § 1	185
B. Constitutional Jurisdiction of Florida Courts	187
1. Supreme Court	187
a. "Shall hear appeals from final judgments of trial courts imposing the death penalty . . ." Fla. Const. art. V, § 3(b)(1)	187
Robertson v. State	188
b. "Shall hear appeals from . . . decisions of district courts of appeal declaring invalid a state statute or a provision of the state constitution." Fla. Const. art. V, § 3(b)(1)	191
Jackson v. State	193
c. "When provided by general law, shall hear appeals from final judgments entered in proceedings for the validation of bonds or certificates of indebtedness and shall review action of statewide agencies relating to rates or service of utilities providing electric, gas, or telephone service." Fla. Const. art. V, § 3(b)(2)	198
d. Discretionary Review	199
(1) In General	199
(2) "May review any decision of a district court of appeal that expressly declares valid a state statute, or that expressly construes a provision of the state or federal constitution, . . ." Fla. Const. art. V, § 3(b)(3)	200
(3) "May review any decision of a district court of appeal that . . . expressly affects a class of constitutional or state officers . . ." Fla. Const. art. V, § 3(b)(3)	201
Florida State Board of Health v. Lewis	201
Spradley v. State	203
(4) "May review any decision of a district court of appeal . . . that expressly and directly conflicts with a decision of another district court of appeal or of the supreme court on the same question of law." Fla. Const. art. V, § 3(b)(3)	205
City of Jacksonville v. Florida First National Bank of Jacksonville	206
Niemann v. Niemann	208
Skinner v. State	209
Bailey v. Hough	210
Jenkins v. State	210
Dodi Publishing Co. v. Editorial America, S. A.	213
Stevens v. Jefferson	214
Ford Motor Co. v. Kikis	216
Jollie v. State	217
Harrison v. Hyster Co.	221
Wells v. State	221

Jenkins v. State	226
Ogden Aviation Services v. Dar	226
O'Neal v. State	226

(5) "May review any decision of a district court of appeal that passes upon a question certified by it to be of great public importance . . ." Fla. Const. art. V, § 3(b)(4) — 227

Petrik v. New Hampshire Insurance Co. — 228

Floridians for a Level Playing Field v. Floridians Against Expanded Gambling — 229

(6) "May review any decision of a district court of appeal . . . that is certified by it to be in direct conflict with a decision of another district court of appeal." Fla. Const. art. V, § 3(b)(4) — 232

Davis v. Mandau — 232

State v. Vickery — 233

Curry v. State — 235

(7) "May review any order or judgment of a trial court certified by the district court of appeal in which an appeal is pending to be of great public importance, or to have a great effect on the proper administration of justice throughout the state, and certified to require immediate resolution by the supreme court." Fla. Const. art. V, § 3(b)(5) — 235

Department of Insurance, State of Florida v. Teachers Insurance Co. — 236

(8) "May review a question of law certified by the Supreme Court of the United States or a United States Court of Appeals which is determinative of the cause and for which there is no controlling precedent of the supreme court of Florida." Fla. Const. art. V, § 3(b)(6) — 240

e. Writs — 242

(1) "May issue writs of prohibition to courts . . ." Fla. Const. art. V, § 3(b)(7) — 242

Moffitt v. Willis — 242

English v. McCrary — 245

(2) "May issue . . . all writs necessary to the complete exercise of its jurisdiction." Fla. Const. art. V, § 3(b)(7) — 248

Besoner v. Crawford — 248

St. Paul Title Insurance Corp. v. Davis — 249

(3) "May issue writs of mandamus and quo warranto to state officers and state agencies." Fla. Const. art. V, § 3(b)(8) — 253

(4) "May, or any justice may, issue writs of habeas corpus returnable before the supreme court or any justice, a district court of appeal or any judge thereof, or any circuit judge." Fla. Const. art. V, § 3(b)(9) — 255

Florida Parole & Probation Commission v. Baker — 256

xiv CONTENTS

2. District Courts of Appeal 258
    Fla. Const. art V, § 4(b) 258
    a. In General 258
    b. "District courts of appeal shall have jurisdiction to hear appeals, that may be taken as a matter of right, from final judgments or orders of trial courts including those entered on review of administrative action, not directly appealable to the supreme court or a circuit court. . . ." Fla. Const. art. V, § 4(b)(1) (emphasis added) 259
    City of Deerfield Beach v. Vaillant 261
    Seminole County Board of County Commissioners v. Long 263
    Education Development Center, Inc. v. City of West Palm Beach Zoning Board of Appeals 265
    Cherokee Crushed Stone, Inc. v. City of Miramar 269
    Central Florida Investments, Inc. v. Orange County 274
    c. ". . . [District courts of appeal] may review interlocutory orders in such cases to the extent provided by rules adopted by the Supreme Court." Fla. Const. art. V, § 4(b)(1) 277
    d. "District courts of appeal shall have the power of direct review of administrative action, as prescribed by general law." Fla. Const. art. V, § 4(b)(2) 277
    Decker v. University of West Florida 278
    Sweetwater Utility Corp. v. Hillsborough County 280
    State Commission on Ethics v. Sullivan 282
    e. "A district court of appeal or any judge thereof may issue writs of habeas corpus returnable before the court or any judge thereof or before any circuit judge within the territorial jurisdiction of the court. . . ." Fla. Const. art. V, § 4(b)(3) 288
    f. ". . . A district court of appeal may issue writs of mandamus, certiorari, prohibition, quo warranto, and other writs necessary to the complete exercise of its jurisdiction. . . ." Fla. Const. art. V, § 4(b)(3) 288
    Haines City Community Development v. Heggs 289
    State v. Pettis 299
    Nader v. Florida Department of Highway Safety & Motor Vehicles 311
3. Circuit Courts and County Courts 318
    Fla. Const. art. V, § 5(b) 318
    Fla. Const. art. V, § 6(b) 318
    a. Common Law Certiorari 320
    G-W Development Corp. v. Village of North Palm Beach Zoning Board of Adjustment 320
    b. Legislative or Quasi-Judicial? 322
    Board of County Commissioners of Hillsborough County v. Casa Development, Ltd. 323

CONTENTS

Martin County v. Yusem — 326

Grace v. Town of Palm Beach — 336

C. Other Limitations on the Exercise of Judicial Power — 338

  1. Case or Controversy and Separation of Powers — 338

    a. In General — 338

    b. Mootness — 339

    Southeastern Utilities Service Co. v. Redding — 339

    Montgomery v. Department of Health and Rehabilitative Services — 341

    c. Ripeness — 344

    Bryant v. Gray — 344

    d. Taxpayer Standing — 350

    North Broward Hospital District v. Fornes — 350

    School Board of Volusia County v. Clayton — 355

    Clayton v. School Board of Volusia County — 358

    e. Citizen Standing — 362

    United States Steel Corp. v. Save Sand Key, Inc. — 362

    f. Associational Standing — 366

    g. Standing to Challenge Administrative Action — 367

    h. Third Party Standing — 367

Chapter 5 · Local Government — 369

A. In General — 369

B. Counties — 369

  1. In General — 369

    Fla. Const. art. VIII, § 1(a) — 369

    Fla. Const. art. VIII, § 1(f) — 370

    Fla. Const. art. VIII, § 1(g) — 370

  2. Non-Charter Counties — 371

    a. "... [S]hall have such power of self-government as is provided
by general or special law." Fla. Const. art. VIII, §1(f) — 371

    Speer v. Olson — 371

    b. "... [M]ay enact county ordinances not inconsistent with general
or special law, but an ordinance in conflict with a municipal
ordinance shall not be effective within the municipality to the
extent of such conflict." Fla. Const. art. VIII, §1(f) — 374

    Misty's Cafe, Inc. v. Leon County — 374

  3. Charter Counties — 376

    a. In General — 376

    b. "... [S]hall have all powers of local self-government not
inconsistent with general law, or with special law approved
by vote of the electors." Fla. Const. art. VIII, §1(g) — 377

    Hollywood, Inc. v. Broward County — 377

    c. "... [M]ay enact county ordinances not inconsistent with
general law." Fla. Const. art. VIII, §1(g) — 380

    McLeod v. Orange County — 380

xvi CONTENTS

d. "... The charter shall provide which shall prevail in the event
of conflict between county and municipal ordinances."
Fla. Const. art. VIII, §1(g)   383
Broward County v. City of Fort Lauderdale   383
C. Municipal Corporations   387
Fla. Const. art. VIII, § 2   387
1. In General   388
State ex rel. Lee v. City of Cape Coral   388
2. Municipal Home Rule Power   392
City of Boca Raton v. State   393
Basic Energy Corp. v. Hamilton County   397
3. Creation and Merger of Municipal Corporations and Annexation
by Municipal Corporations   400
Sullivan v. Volusia County Canvassing Board   400
a. "... Merger of municipalities, and exercise of extra-territorial
powers by municipalities shall be as provided by general or
special law." Fla. Const. art. VIII, §2(c)   401
City of Long Beach Resort v. Collins   401
(1) Annexation Under the Provisions of General Law   404
SCA Services of Florida, Inc. v. City of Tallahassee   404
(2) Annexation by Special Law   407
North Ridge General Hospital, Inc. v. City of Oakland Park   407
(3) Voluntary Annexation   409
City of Center Hill v. McBryde et al.   409
D. Special Districts   411
Halifax Hospital Medical Center v. State   412
E. Other Units of Local Government   418
Lederer v. Orlando Utilities Commission   419
Eldred v. North Broward Hospital District   423
F. State-Local Relationships   426
1. Preemption by the State   427
Hillsborough County v. Florida Restaurant Association, Inc.   427
2. Non-Preemption Type Conflict Between State and Local Government 432
*City of Temple Terrace v. Hillsborough Association
for Retarded Citizens, Inc.*   432
G. Local-Local Relationships   441
Fla. Const. art. VIII, § 3   441
Fla. Const. art. VIII, § 4   441
1. Consolidation   442
Albury v. City of Jacksonville Beach   442
Town of Baldwin v. Consolidated City of Jacksonville   445
2. The Tension Between Fla. Const. art. VIII, § 4, Transfer of Powers
and the Preemption Power of Charter Counties   448
City of New Smyrna Beach v. County of Volusia   448

CONTENTS xvii

Chapter 6 · Taxation and Finance 455
  A. Taxation 455
    1. What Is a Tax? 455
      a. Impact Fees and User Service Charges 456
      Contractors & Builders Association of Pinellas County
        v. City of Dunedin 456
      b. Special Assessments 460
        (1) Special Benefit Requirement 461
      Lake County v. Water Oak Management Corp. 461
        (2) Fair and Reasonable Apportionment Requirement 468
      City of Boca Raton v. State 468
    2. Constitutional Limitations: Who Is Allowed to Tax? 472
      Fla. Const. art. VII, § 1 472
      Fla. Const. art. VII, § 9 472
      Alachua County v. Adams 474
      McGrath v. City of Miami 481
      Gallant v. Stephens 482
      State v. City of Daytona Beach 487
    3. Constitutional Limitations on How Those Taxing May Tax 489
      a. Ad Valorem Taxation 489
        (1) Rate 489
      Fla. Const. art. VII, § 2 489
      Hayes v. Walker 490
        (2) Assessments of Value for Purposes of Ad Valorem Taxation 494
      Fla. Const. art. VII, § 4 494
      Miami Atlantic Development Corp. v. Blake 499
      Schultz v. TM Florida-Ohio Realty Ltd. Partnership 500
      Appleby v. Nolte 504
      Oyster Pointe Resort Condominium Association, Inc. v. Nolte 507
      Straughn v. GAC Properties, Inc. 513
      Straughn v. K & K Land Management, Inc. 515
      Orange County Property Appraiser v. Sommers 518
    4. Constitutional Limitations: Exemptions and Who Cannot Be
      Taxed or Taxed Beyond a Certain Point 523
      a. Ad Valorem Tax Exemption 523
      Fla. Const. art. VII, § 3 523
      Canaveral Port Authority v. Department of Revenue 525
      Markham v. Broward County 535
      City of Sarasota v. Mikos 537
      Capital City Country Club, Inc., v. Tucker 540
      Colding v. Herzog 544
      Saint Andrew's School of Boca Raton, Inc. v. Walker 548
      Underhill v. Edwards 551
      Crapo v. Gainesville Area Chamber of Commerce, Inc. 555

b. Restrictions on Estate, Inheritance, and Income Taxes	558
Fla. Const. art. VII, § 5	558
Department of Revenue v. Golder	559
Department of Revenue v. Leadership Housing, Inc.	561
c. Homestead Exemption from the Ad Valorem Tax	564
Fla. Const. art. VII, § 6	564
(1) "Every person who has the legal or equitable title to real estate and maintains thereon the permanent residence of the owner . . . shall be exempt from taxation thereon . . ." Fla. Const. art. VII, § (6)(a)	567
Robbins v. Welbaum	567
(2) "Every person who has he legal or equitable title to real estate and maintains thereon the permanent residence of the owner, or another legally or naturally dependent upon the owner, shall be exempt from taxation thereon . . ." Fla. Const. art. VII, § (6)(a)	568
Garcia v. Andonie	568
(3) "Not more than one exemption shall be allowed any individual or family unit or with respect to any residential unit." Fla. Const. art. VII, § (6)(b)	577
Wells v. Haldeos	577
(4) "By general law and subject to conditions and limitations specified therein, the Legislature may provide ad valorem tax relief equal to the total amount or a portion of the ad valorem tax otherwise owed on homestead property to: (1) The surviving spouse of a veteran who died from service-connected causes while on active duty as a member of the United States Armed Forces. . . ." Fla. Const. art. VII, § (6)(f)	581
Department of Revenue v. Bell	581
Fla. Const. art. VII, § 4	585
Smith v. Krosschell	586
Zingale v. Powell	591
d. Limitation on Which Property Can Be Taxed to Provide Services in Unincorporated Areas	598
Fla. Const. art. VIII, § 1(h)	598
City of St. Petersburg v. Briley, Wild & Associates, Inc.	599
Alsdorf v. Broward County	602
Alsdorf v. Broward County	607
B. Finance	611
1. Limitations on State and Local Aid to the Private Sector	614
Fla. Const. art. VII, § 10	614
Nohrr v. Brevard County Educational Facilities Authority	616
State v. Jacksonville Port Authority	620

Orange County Industrial Development Authority v. State	623
Linscott v. Orange County Industrial Development Authority	625
Northern Palm Beach County Water Control District v. State	628
2. Controls on the Pledging of the Credit of the State	638
Fla. Const. art. VII, § 11	638
State v. Division of Bond Finance of Department of General Services	639
Division of Bond Finance v. Smathers	641
3. Local Bonds	642
Fla. Const. art. VII, § 12	642
County of Volusia v. State	643
Murphy v. City of Port St. Lucie	647
Wilson v. Palm Beach County Housing Authority	649
4. Tax Increment Financing (TIF) Bonds	650
Strand v. Escambia County	651
5. Arbitrage Bonds	660
State v. City of Orlando	660
Chapter 7 · The Declaration of Rights and the Taking of Property	665
A. Introduction	665
Traylor v. State	666
Florida v. Powell	671
B. Basic Rights	674
Fla. Const. art. I, § 2	674
1. Introduction	674
2. "To Acquire, Possess and Protect Property"	674
Shriners Hospitals for Crippled Children v. Zrillic	675
3. "No Person Shall be Deprived of Any Right Because of Race, Religion, National Origin, or Physical Disability"	681
Schreiner v. McKenzie Tank Lines, Inc.	681
4. "All Natural Persons, Female and Male Alike, Are Equal Before the Law"	685
State v. J.P.	685
Jackson v. State	693
C. Florida Rational Basis Test	696
Estate of McCall v. United States	696
Shriners Hospital for Crippled Children v. Zrillic	704
D. Right to Assemble	707
Fla. Const. art. I, § 5	707
E. The Right to Work and the Right to Bargain Collectively	707
Fla. Const. art. I, § 6	707
Headley v. City of Miami	708
F. Prohibited Laws	715
Fla. Const. art. I, § 10	715
1. Obligation of Contract	716

Pomponio v. Claridge of Pompano Condominium, Inc.	716
Searcy, Denney, Scarola, Barnhart & Shipley, Etc. v. State	726
2. Ex Post Facto Laws	733
Shenfeld v. State	733
G. Substantive Due Process	737
Fla. Const. art. I, § 9	737
1. In General	737
L. Maxcy, Inc. v. Mayo	738
State v. Saiez	744
State v. Adkins	747
Jackson v. State	757
2. A Higher Level of Scrutiny	757
3. Due Process and Conclusive Presumptions	758
Castellanos v. Next Door Co.	758
4. Distinguishing Substantive from Procedural Due Process	766
H. Imprisonment for Debt	768
Fla. Const. art. I, § 11	768
Del Valle v. State	768
I. Search and Seizure	774
Fla. Const. art. I, § 12	774
Jardines v. State	776
J. Administrative Penalties	789
Fla. Const. art. I, § 18	789
Florida Elections Commission v. Davis	789
K. Access to Courts	792
Fla. Const. art. I, § 21	792
Kluger v. White	793
Westphal v. City of St. Petersburg	797
L. Privacy	803
1. In General	803
Fla. Const. art. I, § 23	803
Winfield v. Division of Pari-Mutuel Wagering, Department of Business Regulation	804
2. The Existence of a Reasonable Expectation of Privacy	807
City of North Miami v. Kurtz	808
Green v. Alachua County	812
3. Privacy and Public Trials	818
Barron v. Florida Freedom Newspapers, Inc.	818
4. Privacy and Abortion	824
In re T.W.	825
Gainesville Woman Care, LLC v. State	835
5. Privacy and the Refusal of Medical Treatment	843
In re Guardianship of Browning	843
Burton v. State	855

CONTENTS xxi

6. Privacy and Physician Assisted Suicide 857
   Krischer v. McIver 857
7. Privacy, Statutory Rape, and Sexual Misconduct with a Minor 869
   J.A.S. v. State 869
   A.H. v. State 877
8. Privacy and Grandparent Visitation Statutes 883
   Ledoux-Nottingham v. Downs 885
M. The Taking of Property 892
   Fla. Const. art. X, § 6 892
   City of Hollywood Community Redevelopment Agency
      v. 1843, LLC 893

Chapter 8 · Homestead 899
   Fla. Const. art. X, § 4 899
A. Introduction 899
B. Establishment of a Homestead 900
   1. Natural Person Requirement 900
   2. Permanent Residence Requirement 901
   3. Owner Requirement 901
   4. Size and Contiguity Requirements 902
C. Duration of and Protection Afforded to a Homestead 902
   1. Duration of Protection from Creditors 902
      Yost-Rudge v. A to Z Props., Inc. 903
      Orange Brevard Plumbing & Heating Co. v. La Croix 906
   2. Extent of Protection from Creditors 908
      Havoco of America, LTD v. Hill 908
D. Exceptions to Homestead Exemption 917
E. Inured Homestead Exemptions — Who Is an Heir? 918
   Public Health Trust of Dade County v. Lopez 919
   Snyder v. Davis 922
F. Restrictions on Inter Vivos Transfers of Homestead Property 931
   Jameson v. Jameson 932
   Clemons v. Thornton 936
G. Restrictions on the Devise of Homestead Property 938
   1. Homestead Owner Is Survived by Spouse and Minor Children 939
   2. Homestead Owner Is Survived by Spouse and No Minor Children 939
      In re Estate of Finch 940
   3. Homestead Owner Is Not Survived by Spouse or Minor Children 942
      Webb v. Blue 942
H. Jointly Held Property 945
   Marger v. DeRosa 945
I. Termination of Homestead 947
   In re Estate of Scholtz 948
J. Homestead Summary 950

Constitution of the State of Florida   953

Article I   954
Article II   964
Article III   971
Article IV   984
Article V   990
Article VI   1009
Article VII   1011
Article VIII   1029
Article IX   1040
Article X   1044
Article XI   1067
Article XII   1071

Index   1101

Table of Cases

A.H. v. State, 877–883

A Community Health, Inc. v. Department of Health & Rehabilitative Services, 190

Achord v. Osceola Farms Co., 793

Adams v. Gunter, 21

Admiral Development Corp. v. City of Maitland, 460

Advisory Opinion to the Attorney General re Rights of Electricity Consumers Regarding Solar Energy Choice, 22–34

Aetna Insurance Company v. LaGasse, 902

Agency for Health Care Administration v. Mount Sinai Medical Center of Greater Miami, 253

Alachua County v. Adams, 474–481, 482

Albury v. City of Jacksonville Beach, 442–444

Allen v. Butterworth, 254

Allstate Insurance Company v. Kaklamanos, 318

Alsdorf v. Broward County (Fla. 1976), 602–607

Alsdorf v. Broward County (Fla. 4th Dist. App. 1979), 607–611

American Bankers Insurance Company v. Chiles, 601

AmeriSteel Corp. v. Clark, 199

Amos v. Matthews, 370

Anderson v. Anderson, 917

Anoll v. Pomerance, 254

Appleby v. Nolte, 504–507

Armstrong v. City of Tampa, 192

Armstrong v. Harris, 34

Bailey v. Hough, 210–213

Bainter v. League of Women Voters of Florida, 823

Barron v. Florida Freedom Newspapers, Inc., 818–823

Bartelt v. Bartelt, 927, 928

Basic Energy Corporation v. Hamilton County, 397–399

Beagle v. Beagle, 838, 868, 883

Beaty v. State, 215

Belair v. Drew, 885

Beltran v. Kalb, 948

Bemis v. State, 215

Besoner v. Crawford, 248–249, 252

Bessemer Props., Inc. v. Gamble, 901

Board of County Commissioners of Hillsborough County v. Casa Development, Ltd., 323–326, 259

Bowen v. Bowen, 768

Broward County v. City of Fort Lauderdale, 383–387

Brown v. Lewis, 947

Brown v. State, 72–75

Bryant v. Gray, 344–348, 349

Burns v. State, 209

Burton v. State, 855–857

Butterworth v. Caggiano, 908

Byrd v. State, 197

Caldwell v. Mann, 163

Canaveral Port Authority v. Department of Revenue, 525–535

Cannery, Citrus, Drivers, Warehousemen & Allied Employees of Local 444 v. Winter Haven Hospital, Inc., 708

Capital City Country Club, Inc., v. Tucker, 540–544

Carlile v. Game & Fresh Water Fish Commission, 67

Carroll v. State, 4, 6

Carter v. Sparkman, 792

Castellanos v. Next Door Co., 758–766

Cawthon v. Town of De Funiak Springs, 12

Cent. Florida Investments, Inc. v. Orange Cnty, 274–276

Cherokee Crushed Stone, Inc. v. City of Miramar, 269–273, 268, 326

Chiles v. Children A, B, C, D, E, & F, 65

Chiles v. United Faculty of Florida, 725

City National Bank of Florida v. Tescher, 939, 942

City of Boca Raton v. State, 392, 393–397, 460, 468–471

City of Center Hill V. McBryde, et al., 409–411

City of Cleburne, Texas v. Cleburne Living Center, Inc., 707

City of Cooper v. Joliff, 461

City of Deerfield Beach v. Vaillant, 261–262

City of Hollywood Community Redevelopment Agency v. 1843, LLC, 893–897

City of Jacksonville v. Continental Can Co., 62

City of Jacksonville v. Florida First National Bank of Jacksonville, 206–207

City of Long Beach Resort v. Collins, 402–404

City of Miami Beach v. Frankel, 160, 163

City of Miami v. Lewis, 369

City of New Smyrna Beach v. County of Volusia, 448–453

City of North Miami v. Kurtz, 617, 808–811

City of Ormond Beach v. County of Volusia, 376

City of Sarasota v. Mikos, 537–539

City of Sarasota v. Windom, 361

City of St. Petersburg v. Briley, Wild & Associates, Inc., 599–602

City of Tallahassee v. Florida Public Service Commission, 198

City of Tallahassee v. Mann, 253

City of Tampa v. Tampa Waterworks Co., 11

City of Temple Terrace v. Hillsborough Association for Retarded Citizens, Inc., 432–441

Clayton v. School Board of Volusia County, 354, 358–361

Clemons v. Thornton, 936–938

Coastal Petroleum Company v. Chiles, 724

Cochran v. Harris, 681

Colding v. Herzog, 544–547

Commission on Ethics v. Barker, 192

Connor v. Southwest Florida Regional Medical Center, Inc., 69–71

Contractors & Builders Association of Pinellas County v. City of Dunedin, 456–461

Corn v. State, 674

County of Volusia v. State, 643–647

Couse v. Canal Authority, 236, 249, 253

Crapo v. Gainesville Area Chamber of Commerce, Inc., 555–557

Curry v. State, 235

Dade County Classroom Teachers Association, Inc. v. Legislature, 16, 85–86

Daniels v. Katz, 931

Davis v. State, 254

Davis v. Mandau, 232–233

Dean v. Heimbach, 950

TABLE OF CASES

Decker v. University of West Florida, 278–280

Del Valle v. State, 768–774

Delano v. Dade County, 192

Delisle v. Crane Co., 112–117

Deltona Corporation v. Bailey, 507

Department of Education v. Lewis, 148–150

Department of Environmental Protection v. Millender, 62

Department of Highway Safety and Motor Vehicles v. Nader, 310

Department of Insurance, State of Florida v. Teachers Insurance Company, 236–242

Department of Law Enforcement v. Real Property, 766

Department of Revenue of State v. GTE Mobilnet of Tampa, Inc., 473

Department of Revenue v. Bell, 581–585

Department of Revenue v. Golder, 559–561

Department of Revenue v. Kuhnlein, 338

Department of Revenue v. Leadership Housing Inc., 561–564

Diamond v. E. R. Squibb & Sons, Inc. 793

Division of Bond Finance v. Smathers, 641–642

Dodi Publishing Company v. Editorial America, S.A., 213

Dresner v. City of Tallahassee, 289

Dreyer v. Illinois, 9, 64

Eastern Air Lines, Inc. v. Department of Revenue, 473

Eberle v. Nielson, 8

Education Development Center, Inc. v. City of West Palm Beach Zoning Board of Appeals, 265–267

Edwards v. Thomas, 39–46

Eldred v. North Broward Hospital District, 423–426

Engelke v. Estate of Engelke, 901

English v. McCrary, 245–247

Estate of McCall v. United States, 696–704

Estate of Murphy, 941

Ex parte Smith, 254

Finley v. State, 257

Fitzsimmons v. City of Pensacola, 205

Flannery v. Green, 900

Flast v. Cohen, 365

Florida Association of Professional Lobbyists, Inc. v. Division of Legislative Information Services, 65

Florida Department of Business and Professional Regulation v. Gulfstream Park Racing Association, Inc., 158

Florida Department of Health v. Florigrown, LLC, 153–158

Florida Department of Children & Families v. J.B., 103–106

Florida Department of State v. Martin, 119–124

Florida Department of Highway Safety and Motor Vehicles v. Critchfield, 128

Florida Elections Commission v. Davis, 789–792

Florida Elks Children's Hospital v. Stanley, 680

Florida Home Builders Association v. Department of Labor & Employment Security, 365

Florida Hospital Waterman, Inc. v. Buster, 13–16

Florida House of Representatives v. Crist, 95–103

Florida Insurance Guaranty Association, Inc. v. Devon Neighborhood Association, Inc., 208

Florida Parole & Probation Commission v. Baker, 256

Florida Power & Light Co. v. Canal Authority of the State of Florida, 12

Florida Power Corporation v. Pinellas Utility Board, 38

Florida Senate v. Graham, 252

Florida Society of Ophthalmology v. Florida Optometric Association, 38

Florida State Board of Health v. Lewis, 201–202

Florida v. Powell, 671–673

Florida Welding & Erection Service, Inc. v. American Mutual Insurance Company of Boston, 127

Floridians Against Casino Takeover v. Let's Help Florida, 21

Floridians For A Level Playing Field v. Floridians Against Expanded Gambling, 229–232

Folks v. Marion County, 36–37

Ford Motor Company v. Kikis, 216

Ford v. Browning, 21, 46–53

Franklin v. State, 129–137

Frase v. Branch, 900

Friends of the Everglades, Inc. v. Board of Trustees of the Internal Improvement Trust Fund, 365

G.B.B. Investments, Inc. v. Hinterkopf, 793

Gainesville Woman Care, LLC v. State, 835–842

Gallant v. Stephens, 482–486

Garcia v. Andonie, 568–577

Geary Distributing Company, Inc. v. All Brand Importers, Inc., 725

Geraci v. Sunstar EMS, 902

Gilreath v. Westgate Daytona, LTD, 500

Godales v. Y.H. Investments, Inc., 67

Grace v. Town of Palm Beach, 334, 335–336

Graham v. Haridopolos, 53–56

Graham v. Vann, 253

Gray v. Bryant, 16

Greater Loretta Improvement Association v. State ex rel. Boone, 58–61

Green v. Alachua County, 812–818

Grisolia v. Pfeffer, 901

GTE Florida, Inc. v. Clark, 198

Gulf Coast Electric Cooperative, Inc. v. Johnson, 198

Gulf Oil Co. v. Bevis, 146

Gulf Power Company v. Bevis, 674

G-W Development Corporation v. Village of North Palm Beach Zoning Board of Adjustment, 199, 320–322

Haines City Community Development v. Heggs, 289–299, 310

Halifax Hosp. Med. Ctr. v. State, 412–418

Hancock v. Board of Public Instruction of Charlotte County, 34

Hanft v. Phelan, 197

Harrell's Candy Kitchen, Inc. v. Sarasota-Manatee Airport Authority, 191

Harrison v. Hyster Company, 221

Harvard v. Singletary, 254

Hayes v. Walker, 490–494

Havoco of America, LTD v. Hill, 908–916

Headley v. City of Miami, 708–713

Heiman v. Capital Bank, 901

Henry v. Santana, 255

Hill v. First National Bank of Marianna, 901

Hillsborough County Hospital & Welfare Board v. Taylor, 426

Hillsborough County v. Florida Restaurant Association, Inc., 366, 371, 427–432

Hoffman v. Jones, 205

Holley v. Adams, 348

Hollywood, Inc. v. Broward County, 377–379, 460

TABLE OF CASES

In re Advisory Opinion to the Governor, 10

In Re Advisory Opinion to the Governor Request of June 29, 1979, 180–183

In re Cooke, 901

In re Dubreuil, 854

In re Emergency Amendments to the Rules of Appellate Procedure, 186, 191, 198, 200, 227, 235, 240

In re Estate of Cleeves, 942

In re Estate of Finch, 940–941

In re Estate of Kant, 200

In re Estate of Scholtz, 948–950

In re Estate of Van Meter, 901

In re Fla. Evidence Code, 117

In re Guardianship of Browning, 843–854

In re T.A.C.P., 67

In re T.W., 825–835, 642

In re V, 17

International Association of Firefighters Local S-20 v. State (Fla. 1st Dist. App. 2017), 178–180

International Association of Firefighters Local S-20 v. State (Fla. 2018), 713

Irvine v. Duval County Planning Commission, 268

J.A.S. v. State, 869–872

Jackson v. Consolidated Government of the City of Jacksonville, 442, 445, 447

Jackson v. State (Fla. 2006), 193–197, 198

Jackson v. State (Fla. 2016), 693–695

Jameson v. Jameson, 932–936, 937

Jardines v. State, 776–788

JBK Associates, Inc. v. Sill Bros., Inc., 908

Jenkins v. State (Fla. 1980), 194, 195, 196, 197, 220, 222, 223, 224, 225, 233, 238, 249, **210–213**, 463, 464, 465, 466

Jenkins v. State (Fla. 3d Dist. App. 1994), 226

Johnson v. United States, 127

Jollie v. State, 215, 217–220, 221, 223, 224, 233

Jones v. Chiles, 106–109

Jones v. Jones, 942

Kansas v. Colorado, 5

Kelo v. City of New London, 892, 893

Kennedy v. Guarantee Management Services, Inc., 796

Key Haven Associated Enterprises, Inc. v. Board of Trustees of the Internal Improvement Fund, 281, 282, 285, 286, 287, 288

Kitchen v. K–Mart Corp., 67

Kluger v. White, 793–796, 797, 798, 799, 801, 802

Kohn v. Coats, 905

Krischer v. McIver, 857–869

Krivanek v. Take Back Tampa Political Committee, 707

L. Maxcy, Inc. v. Mayo, 738–743, 745

Lake County v. Water Oak Management Corporation, 461–468

Lake v. Lake, 211, 212, 220, 258

Lawrence v. Florida East Coast Railway Company, 199, 200

League of Women Voters of Fla. v. Fla. House or Representatives, 87–94

Lederer v. Orlando Utilities Commission, 419–423

Ledoux-Nottingham v. Downs, 885–891

Legal Environmental Assistance Foundation, Inc. v. Clark, 198, 367

Lehman Brothers v. Schein, 241

Leichtman v. Singletary, 256

Levine v. Whalen, 127

Linscott v. Orange County Industrial Development Authority, 614, 615, **625–627**, 628, 630, 637

Loan Assn. v. Topeka, 4

Lonon v. Ferrell, 885

TABLE OF CASES

Lowe v. Broward County, 382

Loxahatchee River Environmental Control District v. School Board of Palm Beach County, 139, 140, 142

M.O. Logue Sod Service, Inc. v. Logue, 947

Marger v. DeRosa, 945–947

Markham v. Broward County, 535–536

Martin County v. Yusem, 326–335

Massey v. David, 115

Mathieu v. City of Lauderdale Lakes, 917

McCulloch v. Maryland, 3, 6

McGowan v. Maryland, 706

McGrath v. City of Miami, 481–482

McGraw v. State, 776

McKean v. Warburton, 931, 944

McLeod v. Orange County, 380–381

McNamara v. State, 200

McNeil v. Canty, 109–111

Menendez v. Rodriguez, 901

Miami Atlantic Development Corp. v. Blake, 499–500

Miller v. Higgs, 472, 542, 544

Miller v. Highlands Insurance Company, 205

Mirzataheri v. FM East Developers, LLC, 938

Missouri, Kansas & Texas Railway Company of Texas v. May, 63

Misty's Cafe, Inc. v. Leon County, 374–376

Mizrahi v. North Miami Medical Center, Ltd., 757–758

Moffitt v. Willis, 93, 242–245

Montgomery v. Department of Health & Rehabilitative Services, 341–344

Mosher v. Speedstar Division of AMCA International, Inc., 241

Murphy v. City of Port St. Lucie, 466, 647–648

Nader v. Florida Dept. of Highway Safety and Motor Vehicles, 273, 311–317

Nelson P. v. Goss, 681

Nichols v. State ex rel, Bolon, 57–58

Niemann v. Niemann, 208–209

Nohrr v. Brevard County Educational Facilities Authority, 616–620, 622–627, 630–631, 636, 649–650

North Broward Hospital District v. Fornes, 350–354, 355–361

North Ridge General Hospital, Inc. v. City of Oakland Park, 132, 146–147, 401, 404, **407–408**

Northern Palm Beach County Water Control District v. State, 628–638

O'Neal v. State, 226

Ogden Aviation Services v. Dar, 226

Ogle v. Pepin, 191

Olive v. Maas, 348

Orange Brevard Plumbing & Heating Company v. La Croix, 903, 905, 906–908

Orange County Industrial Development Authority v. State, 623–625, 630, 636, 661

Oregon v. Hass, 665–666, 672

Oyster Pointe Resort Condominium Assoc., Inc. v. Nolte, 502–503, 507–512

Palm Beach Savings & Loan Ass'n v. Fishbein, 913–917

Partridge v. Partridge, 917

Pearce v. State, 124–125

Pesci v. Maistrellis, 367

Peters v. Meeks, 7–8, 10–11

Petrik v. New Hampshire Insurance Company, 228–229

Pinellas County Veterinary Medical Society, Inc. v. Chapman, 159–160

TABLE OF CASES

Pleasures II Adult Video, Inc. v. City of Sarasota, 338

Poe v. Hillsborough County, 627

Pomponio v. Claridge of Pompano Condominium, Inc., 716–724, 730

Price v. State, 227

Psychiatric Associates v. Siegel, 793, 797

Public Health Trust of Dade County v. Lopez, 900, 919–922, 948–949, 925

Putnam County Environmental Council, Inc. v. Board of County Commissioners of Putnam County, 365

Raulerson v. Peeples, 901

Rich v. Ryals, 192

Ricketts v. Village of Miami Shores, 680–681

Riddoch v. State, 6

Roberts v Brown, 253

Robertson v. State, 188–190

Robbins v. Welbaum, 567–568

Rollins v. Pizzarelli, 40–41, 415

Rosen v. Fla. Ins. Guar. Ass'n, 208

Ross v. State, 138

Saint Andrew's Sch. of Boca Raton, Inc. v. Walker, 548–550

Salters v. State, 137–142

Santos v. State, 139, 142, 143–144, 145

Sas v. Postman, 248

Saul v. Brunetti, 885, 891

SCA Services of Florida, Inc. v. City of Tallahassee, 404–406

School Board of Volusia County v. Clayton, 355–357

Schreiner v. McKenzie Tank Lines, Inc., 681–684

Schultz v. Crystal River Three Participants, 614

Schultz v. TM Florida-Ohio Realty Ltd. Partnership, 500–503

Seaboard Air Line R.R. v. Branham, 209

Searcy, Denney, Scarola, Barnhart & Shipley, Etc. v. State, 726–733

Seminole County Board of County Commissioners v. Long, 263–265

Shands Teaching Hospital & Clinics, Inc. v. Smith, 66, 68–69, 862

Shevin ex rel. State v. Public Service Commission, 249, 251–252

Shriners Hospitals For Crippled Children v. Zrillic, 28, 675–680, 694, 704–707

Simmons v. Faust, 186

Skinner v. State, 209

Smith v. Fisher, 793

Smith v. Krosschell, 586–591

Smith v. State, 162

Smith v. Unkefer, 902

Snyder v. Board of County Commissioners of Brevard County, 681

Snyder v. Davis, 922–931, 943

Sockol v. Kimmins Recycling Corp., 467

Southeastern Utilities Service Company v. Redding, 339–340

Southern Bell Telephone and Telegraph Company v. Broward County, 507

Southern Bell Telephone & Telegraph Company v. Markham, 507

Speer v. Olson, 371–374

Spradley v. State, 203–206

Springer v. Government of the Philippine Islands, 63

St. Johns County v. Northeast Florida Builders Association, Inc., 460

St. Paul Title Insurance Corporation v. Davis, 249

State Commission on Ethics v. Sullivan, 282–289

State ex rel. Bruce v. Kiesling, 254

State ex rel. Chiles v. Pub. Employees Rel. Commn., 252

State ex rel. Cotterill v. Bessenger, 160–162

State ex rel. Dade County v. Dickinson, 38, 484–485

State ex rel. Gibbs v. Couch, 392

State ex rel. Lee v. City of Cape Coral, 388–392

State ex rel. Municipal Bond & Investment Company, Inc. v. Knott, 4

State ex rel. Peacock v. Latham, 251

State ex rel. Pettigrew v. Kirk, 255

State ex rel. Reynolds v. Roan, 34

State ex rel. Vance v. Wellman, 254

State v. Adkins, 747–756

State v. Allen, 232, 259

State v. Ashley, 66

State v. Atlantic Coast Line R.R., 65, 99

State v. Barquet, 102, 685, 767

State v. City of Daytona Beach, 487–489, 650

State v. City of Miami, 408, 624, 627, 669

State v. City of Orlando, 399, 636, **660–663**

State v. Combs, 139, 142–143, **145,** 289, 294–299, 303, 313, 316

State v. Conforti, 807, 880

State v. Creighton, 232, 259, 300, 304

State v. Division of Bond Finance of Department of General Services (Fla. 1971), 639–642

State v. Division of Bond Finance of Department of General Services (Fla. 1973), 35–36

State v. Furen, 259, 264–265, 272, 325

State v. Grawien, 186

State v. Hamilton, 68

State v. Housing Finance Authority of Polk County, 624, 626, 627

State v. J.P., 685–692, 710, 837

State v. Jacksonville Port Authority, 615, 618, **620–623**

State v. Lee, 128, 144, 251–252

State v. Markus, 776

State v. Osceola County, 613

State v. Palmer, 66

State v. Pettis, 289, 295, 299–311

State v. Saiez, 744–746, 751

State v. Sarasota, 613

State v. Sarmiento, 775, 806, 814

State v. Stalder, 80–84

State v. Thompson, 130–132, 135–136, 139, 141–142

State v. Vickery, 233–234

Stevens v. Jefferson, 214–215

Strand v. Escambia County, 651–660

Straughn v. GAC Properties, Inc., 513–514

Straughn v. K & K Land Management, Inc., 515–518

Sturdivant v. Blanchard, 253

Sullivan v. Volusia County Canvassing Board, 400–401

Sun Ins. Office v. Clay, 65, 99

Sunbeam Television Corporation v. State, 340

Sunspan Engineering and Construction Company v. Spring-Lock Scaffolding Company, 199–200

Sweetwater Utility Corp. v. Hillsborough County, 280–281, 323

Tallahassee Mem'l Reg'l Med. Ctr., Inc. v. Tallahassee Med. Ctr., Inc., 382

Taylor v. Dorsey, 56

The Florida Star v. B.J.F., 215, 222

Thornber v. City of Ft. Walton Beach, 67

Town of Baldwin v. Consolidated City of Jacksonville, 445–447

Town of Palm Beach v. Palm Beach Local 1886 of International Association Fire Fighters, 174–176

Town of Palm Beach v. Vlahos, 174

Tribune Co. v. School Bd. of Hillsborough County, 127

Trapp v. State, 137

Traylor v. State, 666–670, 687, 714, 728, 865

Tucker v. Underdown, 373, 483, 487, 656–657

Tullis v. Tullis, 915, 947

TABLE OF CASES

Underhill v. Edwards, 551–555
United States Steel Corporation v. Save Sand Key, Inc., 351, 362–364, 365
United States v. Curtiss-Wright Export Corporation, 3
Upper Keys Citizens Association, Inc. v. Wedel, 365

Valdez v. Chief Judge of Eleventh Judicial Circuit of Florida, 340
Venice HMA, LLC v. Sarasota County, 164–174
Von Eiff v. Azicri, 885, 891

Wald Corporation v. Metropolitan Dade County, 459–460
Wale v. Barnes, 207
Walker v. Bentley, 8, 12, 16, 66
Wallace v. Dean, 208
Warning Safety Lights of Georgia, Inc. v. State Department of Revenue, 473
Warren v. State Farm Mutual Automobile Insurance Company, 699, 796
Weaver v. Myers, 796, 803
Webb v. Blue, 942–944
Weber v. Smathers, 21
Weinberger v. Board of Public Instruction of St. Johns County, 9
Weitzner v. United States, 917

Wells v. Haldeos, 577–580
Wells v. State, 187, 221–225
Werner v. State Department of Insurance and Treasurer, 103
Westphal v. City of St. Petersburg, 75–79, 797–803
Williston Highlands Development Corporation v. Hogue, 192
Wilson v. Florida Nat. Bank & Trust Co. at Miami, 900, 902
Wilson v. Hillsborough County Aviation Authority, 476, 478
Wilson v. Palm Beach County Housing Authority, 649–650
Wilson v. Sandstrom, 252
Winfield v. Division of Pari-Mutuel Wagering, Department of Business Regulation, 804–807, 808, 810, 813–815, 817, 827–829, 833–834, 837–839, 846, 859, 866, 873

Y.H. Investments, Inc. v. Godales, 67
Yost-Rudge v. A To Z Props., Inc., 903–905

Zerquera v. Centennial Homeowners' Assn., Inc., 917
Zorc v. City of Vero Beach, 432

Preface to the First Edition

This book is designed to serve as an introduction of the Florida Constitution to the law student. Although state constitutional law has always been important, it has recently assumed a more prominent role. In recent years the federal courts have reduced or restricted expansive interpretations of the Federal Constitution. This has resulted, particularly in the area of individual rights, with the state courts expanding their state constitutional provisions beyond federal minimums. Florida has been a leader in the area, particularly in regards to the right of privacy guaranteed by the state constitution.

In addition, this work can be valuable to the practitioner. As Florida constitutional law increases in importance, the competent practitioner must be familiar with this expanding area. This book contains most all important cases, currently available, in this area.

The current Florida Constitution was adopted by the electorate in 1968. Prior to that time Florida was governed by 5 separate constitutions enacted respectively in 1838, 1861, 1865, 1868, and 1885. Although the 1885 Constitution is occasionally referenced in the text, all references to the Florida Constitutions are intended to be references to the 1968 Constitution unless otherwise specifically indicated.

We wish to express our appreciation to the people who have helped to make these teaching materials a reality: to Harold L. Sebring and Everett Cushman who pioneered work in this field at Stetson; to our colleagues whose friendship and support nurtured this work; to our research assistants, whose conscientious and enthusiastic efforts have improved the quality of this work; to our students who have made helpful suggestions; to the faculty secretaries, who put up with us during the production of this work and without whom it could not have been accomplished; and to our wives and families for their love and understanding throughout the preparation of this manuscript. Special thanks go to Louise Petren who bore the primary responsibility for manuscript preparation.

John F. Cooper
Thomas C. Marks, Jr.
St. Petersburg, FL
October 1991

Preface to the Second Edition

The theory and organization of the Second Edition remains basically unchanged. New cases have been added and, in some instances, old cases deleted. Also, there does appear some new subject matter e.g., 1) the relationship between judicial review of agency action and an original action for declaratory and injunctive relief and 2) evolving material concerning the right of privacy guaranteed by the state constitution.

The names have changed to some extent. Our appreciation of the efforts of our research assistants would now include Michael J. Bertolini, Tabatha Liebert, and Shawn C. Nagel. The same appreciation to faculty secretaries would now include Choung-Mi Akehurst, Connie Evans, Sharon Gisclair, Barbara Lernihan, Marge Masters, Shad Mullins, and Sue Stinson. While our students have changed, our appreciation of their interest in the Florida Constitution remains the same. As before, special thanks to Louise Petren for preparation of most of the manuscript. And finally, what should have been in the original preface, to our friends at Carolina Academic Press. Better late than never.

The book remains dedicated to our wives in the terms expressed in the First Edition.

John F. Cooper
Thomas C. Marks, Jr.
St. Petersburg and Gulfport, FL
April 1996

Preface to the Third Edition

Close to ten years have passed since the publication of the first edition of this text. During this decade the Florida Constitution has been frequently amended, and the Florida appellate courts have repeatedly found the need to interpret and construe the provisions of the organic law of Florida.

While these developments have caused a lengthening of the text, the theory and organization of the first and second editions remain unchanged. While all chapters of the text have evolved, the materials involving the courts, individual rights, and the legal sufficiency of initiative petitions have experienced the greatest expansion and evolution.

There is one significant change in the way the text is organized. In earlier versions, brackets were placed around footnotes that accompanied cases included in the material. This was done to distinguish these footnotes from footnotes prepared by the authors. In this edition that distinction was not possible. As a result, occasionally author footnotes are commingled with footnotes in cases. These instances can be identified where footnotes do not appear sequentially, and the footnotes can be distinguished by context.

Once again we wish to express our appreciation for the outstanding efforts of our research assistants Joelle Aboytes, David Blum, Victoria Cecil, Dennis Hudson, Carol McCrory, Shakonda McDaniel, Susan Mitchell, Neil Morales, Patrice Parker, Thomas Townsend, and Lisa Wilcox.

We would also like to acknowledge the outstanding administrative and secretarial support we have received from the Faculty Support Staff at Stetson University College of Law. We would particularly like to thank Connie Evans, the director of the faculty support staff, for her thoroughness, efficiency, diligence, and good humor. We would also like to thank Sharon Gisclair who was responsible for the preparation of most of the text of the third edition. Through endless changes, rewrites, and edits, Sharon remained even tempered and committed to the completion of the project. Once again, our thanks to the folks at Carolina Academic Press for their support.

Finally, and certainly not least, this book remains dedicated to our spouses, as expressed in the First and Second Editions.

John F. Cooper
Thomas C. Marks
St. Petersburg, FL
December 2000

Preface to the Fourth Edition

As one who compares the Fourth Edition to the Third will see, our attempt to shorten the book met with some success, but not as much as we had hoped for. Some cases were more heavily edited to make them easier to deal with. Some duplicative cases were left out and several new cases were added.

The main function of this Preface is to thank people. First and foremost, our gratitude goes to what we call our team of editors. Pamela Buha, a Stetson student, was our Editor-in-Chief, and did a fantastic job. She was ably assisted by Shannon Mullins, Petra Risco-Adam, and Stephanie Jones. Petra and Stephanie are also Stetson students. Shannon, Coordinator of the Faculty Support Services, typed the manuscript in her usual flawless way. She could also be described as a co-Editor-in-Chief. With the retirement of Connie Evans in May, Louise Petren became Director of Faculty Support Services. Both Connie and Louise deserve worlds of credit for heading up the world class group of people who make up Stetson Law School's Faculty Support Services. We would like to thank our colleague, Brooke J. Bowman, Assistant Professor of Legal Skills and Special Assistant to the Dean, and her team of student Teaching Fellows, Erick Cruz, Katherine Jane Hurst, Jennifer Tanck, and Wilnar Jeanne Paul, for their assistance with checking the citations. Thanks is also due to so many fine people in the Stetson Law Library that it would be impossible to name them all. We could not conclude the list of people at Stetson without thanking our students for their suggestions. Finally, last but certainly not least, our thanks go to Dean Darby Dickerson for her unfaltering support.

Outside the Stetson family, thanks is due to Tom's friend, Professor Vin Bonventre of the Albany Law School for the permission to reprint the article found in Chapter 7. Thanks is also due to Tom's friends, Tom Graves and Charles Reischmann, who explained the change in the federal tax code that affected Florida's estate tax as discussed in Chapter 6. And, we cannot forget our friends at Carolina Academic Press. Last, but far from least, our thanks to Rohan Kelley, Esq. for his kind permission to use the Kelley's Homestead Paradigm diagram.

The book remains gratefully dedicated to our wives, Denise and Nancy, as has been the case since the First Edition.

John F. Cooper
Thomas C. Marks, Jr.
Gulfport, FL
July 2006

Preface to the Fifth Edition

The theory and organization of the Fifth Edition remains basically unchanged from the Fourth Edition. It has been seven years since the publication of the Fourth Edition and our primary goal in writing this edition was to update the book, while at the same time, make it more user friendly. In doing so, the authors have added more explanatory commentary; used a blend of lengthy and short cases to emphasize significant state constitutional principles and concepts; and re-edited select cases. While all chapters of the text have evolved, there have been important constitutional and statutory amendments to the materials involving the takings clause, homestead, taxation, and finance.

This project could not have been completed without the assistance of many people. We wish to express our sincere thanks and appreciation for the exceptional efforts of our research assistants Margaret Carland, Rebecca Csikos, Zouzouko Doualehi, Shaquana Harper, Courtney Norris, and Howard Williams, all of whom are either current or former students at Stetson University College of Law ("Stetson").

Further, we would like to acknowledge the outstanding administrative and secretarial support we received from the Faculty Support Staff at Stetson, especially Shannon Edgar, Janice Strawn, and Jessica Fehr. We particularly would like to thank members of the departments of Academic Success and Bar Preparation Services at Stetson and Florida A&M University College of Law (""FAMU"") and the legal staff at Orlando Utilities Commission for their suggestions and support. We further wish to express our sincere gratitude to Stetson University College of Law Dean Christopher Pietruszkiewicz, former Dean Darby Dickerson, and former Interim Dean Royal Gardner. We also would like to thank the Faculty and Associate Deans at Stetson and FAMU for their support.

We could not conclude without thanking Carolina Academic Press for their guidance and support. We also would like to thank Rohan Kelley, Esq. for his kind permission to use the Kelley's Homestead Paradigm diagram.

Finally, but certainly not least, Tishia and Carlos especially thank John Cooper and Thomas Marks, Jr., for the opportunity to continue the legacy of the preeminent casebook on Florida Constitutional Law.

Tishia A. Dunham
Carlos L. Woody
July 2013

Preface to the Sixth Edition

More than 30 years have passed since the publication of the first edition of this text. During these 30 years, the Florida Constitution has been frequently amended, and the Florida Supreme Court has had repeated opportunities to interpret and construe these amendments.

While the book has changed authors over the years, the theory and organization of the Sixth Edition remains basically unchanged from previous editions. In this edition we continue our goal of making the text more user friendly. All chapters of the text have evolved, but the materials involving the courts and individual rights have experienced the greatest revolution. Although developments in these areas have caused a lengthening of the text, we endeavored to restrict the text's expansion as much as possible by adding a balance of explanatory commentary and short and lengthy cases while removing some old cases.

We wish to express our sincere appreciation to the people who have helped make the Sixth Edition a reality: to our research assistants, Mykoll Finikin-Roumain, Esq. and Courtney Shannon, Esq. whose conscientious and enthusiastic efforts have improved the quality of this work; to our colleagues who have made helpful suggestions; to our editors, Debra Woody and Lotaya Wright, Esq. whose recommendations have helped improve the clarity, readability and flow of this text; and to our families for their love, understanding, and support throughout the preparation of this manuscript.

Carlos would like to personally express sincere gratitude and thanks to Wayne A. Morris, Esq. for his inspiration, wise counsel, and abiding support to take on this endeavor.

As always, Tishia and Carlos remain grateful to John Cooper and Thomas Marks, Jr., for the opportunity to continue the legacy of the preeminent casebook on Florida Constitutional Law.

Tishia A. Dunham
Carlos L. Woody
October 2022

Florida Constitutional Law

Chapter 1

An Introduction to Studying the Florida Constitution

A. Introduction

The basic consideration in any course dealing with the constitutional law of a state is the fact that although the governmental power of the United States flows either directly or impliedly from its Constitution,[1] the governmental power of a state does not flow from its constitution. The source of a state's governmental power is, rather, inherent. The state's constitution is, therefore, essentially a limitation on that inherent power. Accordingly, some knowledge about inherent power is necessary to any consideration of a state constitution. The Florida Constitution is no exception. And, since we have a federal system of government, the relationships between the two levels of government, federal and state, must also be mentioned.

1. The Social Contract

The origin of government is unclear. Philosophers have explained it in a number of different ways. However, the most common explanation is that, in any society, the personal security and property of individuals must be protected from those other individuals who would interfere with either or both.

In primitive societies, so one theory goes, a person was at liberty to do pretty much as he chose unless another person decided to challenge his right to do a particular thing. If such a challenge occurred, the dispute would be settled between the disputants themselves, not infrequently by force. Such a system, in addition to the possibility of being unpleasant, if not fatal, to at least one of the persons involved, frequently produced a result that had very little relationship to the rights and wrongs of the situation. The concept of "might makes right" was the rule rather than the exception. At least in part, as a result of this situation, philosophers tell us that man first banded together into social groupings to protect himself from the will of those stronger than himself. Thomas Hobbes described the existence of primitive man as

---

1. See *McCulloch v. Maryland*, 17 U.S. (4 Wheaton) 316 (1819). This rule may not apply to the power over foreign affairs which, it has been suggested, is inherent in the United States government. *See United States v. Curtiss-Wright Export Corp.*, 299 U.S. 304 (1936).

"solitary, poor, nasty, brutish, and short."[2] Therefore, theorized Hobbes, man came to form the ancient forerunners of our present-day governments. Man did so by what has been called "the social contract."[3] By this he meant that man surrendered some of his freedom in order to gain the protection of society.[4] It is from this "contract" that government derives its inherent power to govern.

As a result of the social contract, or perhaps whatever else may have been the true origin of its power, government has a certain amount of control over the lives of those within its borders. It is this control, given to government, presumably in exchange for a relatively safe and orderly environment, that is supposedly the essence of the social contract. Whatever its original source, this power is considered to be inherent in government. A government possessing this inherent power does not have to look for it in a document such as a constitution. Government possesses it because of the very fact that it is a government.

This inherent power of the state may be divided roughly into three areas: (1) the power to organize to achieve its purposes, (2) the power to raise the money necessary to achieve its purposes, and (3) the power necessary to provide a relatively safe and orderly environment within its territory. A great deal of this third type of power is encompassed within the rather vague term "police power."[5]

---

2. T. Hobbes, *The Leviathan* (1651), D. P. Sutton 1950, Part I, 104. Plato, nearly two thousand years earlier, had described that existence as being "as bad as that of the most savage beast." Plato, *The Laws*, reprinted in 7 *Great Books of the Western World* 754 (R. Hutchins ed. 1952).

3. Hobbes is not the only philosopher who espoused the social contract theory. Jean Jacques Rousseau recognized that primitive humans had:

> [R]eached the point at which the obstacles in the way of their preservation in the state of nature show their power of resistance to be greater than the resources at the disposal of each individual for his maintenance in that state. That primitive condition can then subsist no longer; the human race would perish unless it changed its manner of existence.

J. Rousseau, *The Social Contract* (1762), reprinted in 38 *Great Books of the Western World* 391 (R. Hutchins ed. 1952).

4. As John Locke explained, "The great and chief end, therefore, of uniting into commonwealths, and putting themselves under government, is the preservation of their property; to which in the state of nature there are many things wanting." J. Locke, *An Essay Concerning the True Original Extent and End of Civil Government* (1690), reprinted in 35 *Great Books of the Western World* 53 (R. Hutchins ed. 1952). Rousseau also recognized this concept of banding together for self-preservation.

> [Men] have no other means of preserving themselves than the formation, by aggregation, of a sum of forces great enough to overcome [the obstacles that exist in the state of nature]. These they have to bring into play by means of a single motive power, and cause to act in concert.

J. Rousseau, *The Social Contract* (1762), reprinted in 38 *Great Books of the Western World* 391 (R. Hutchins ed. 1952). The United States Supreme Court has recognized the theory of the social contract. *See Loan Ass'n v. Topeka*, 87 U.S. (20 Wallace) 655, 663 (1875).

5. Although there is no truly complete definition of "police power," frequently a definition like the one attempted by the Florida Supreme Court in *Carroll v. State*, 361 So. 2d 144, 146 (Fla. 1978), is used. "Police power is the sovereign right of the state to enact laws for the protection of lives, health, morals, comfort, and general welfare." (citing *State ex rel. Mun. Bond & Inv. Co. Inc. v. Knott*, 114 Fla. 120, 154 So. 143, 145 (1934).

2. Governmental Power in the American System

In the United States there exists a federal system of government. That is, governmental power is divided between the state and national levels of government. The United States Constitution determines how the governmental power is divided between these two levels of government.

It is the states of the United States that possess the inherent governmental power previously discussed. When the thirteen colonies gained their independence from Great Britain, this governmental power over their territory passed to them from the British government. This happened automatically when the colonies became independent states,[6] and not because the British Parliament, the Continental Congress, or anyone else decided to give them this power.

When the newly independent states entered into a loosely knit union, calling themselves the United States, the central government was given a very small amount of each state's inherent power. But less than five years after the end of the American Revolution, it became obvious that if the union of states were to continue, the central government would have to have enough power to ensure that the states worked together well enough for the union to survive. Without such national power, the states were raising interstate trade barriers, refusing to cooperate with each other, and generally squabbling among themselves.[7] Something within this new family of states had to have enough authority to ensure that the degree of interstate cooperation necessary for a union was maintained.

Therefore, a convention was called in Philadelphia in 1787. The members of the convention, whatever may have been their original purpose, decided to revise the relationship between the states and the central government of the United States. This new relationship was expressed in a document written by the Convention and called the Constitution of the United States. Through the Constitution all the people of the United States — not the people of each state, not the states themselves — gave the government of the United States the specific powers needed to overcome the earlier problems and to make the union work. The proposed Constitution was ratified by the people of the United States and went into effect in 1789.

Unlike state governments which have inherent power, the government of the United States is a government of delegated powers having only those specific powers given to it in the Constitution and other powers derived by implication from those powers specifically given.[8] Thus, the federal government has, with the exception of foreign affairs, only the powers delegated to it in the United States Constitution and

---

6. At the same time that they gained their independence or perhaps earlier, however, the colonies, loosely at first, bound themselves together as the United States of America. It was at this point that the power over foreign affairs passed from Great Britain to the United States. *See supra* n. 1.

7. *See, e.g., Proceedings of Commissioners to Remedy Defects in the Federal Government*, reprinted in *Documents Illustrative of the Formation of the Union of American States* (1927).

8. *See Kansas v. Colorado*, 206 U.S. 46 (1907).

3. The Modern View of the State's Inherent Power

The best judicial statement of the inherent nature of state power that the authors have seen is that of Justice Ellis of the Supreme Court of Washington in *Riddoch v. State*:[10]

> [T]he state is inherently sovereign at all times and in every capacity. It is the organized embodiment of the sovereign power of the whole people. By reason of this sovereignty it possesses all powers, but only such powers as are within the limitations of the state Constitution and without the prohibitions of the federal Constitution. It can do no act except in the exercise of this sovereign power and within these constitutional limitations.

The Florida Supreme Court has expressed the same general idea in *Carroll v. State*.[11] In fact, it is difficult to see how a state could take a different view of its inherent power.

In this book, references to the United States Constitution will be kept to a minimum and will be utilized only where needed to fully explore an element of the Florida Constitution. In part, and to a very limited extent, the views of other state courts will be compared to Florida's with regard to similar questions involving their respective constitutions.

Before proceeding to the great issues that begin with Chapter 2, it is necessary to briefly consider a few equally important miscellaneous matters: (1) the concept of the Florida Constitution; (2) the ways in which the Florida Constitution can be formally amended;[12] (3) the distinction between those of its provisions that are and those of its provisions that are not, self-executing; and (4) some of the rules of constitutional interpretation.

---

9. *McCulloch v. Maryland*, 17 U.S. (4 Wheaton) 316 (1819).
10. 123 P. 450, 452–453 (Wash. 1912).
11. 361 So. 2d 144 (Fla. 1978).
12. The significance of the word "formally" should become apparent.

B. The Concept of the State Constitution

1. The State Constitution as a Limitation on Inherent State Governmental Power

a. In General

Peters v. Meeks

163 So. 2d 753 (Fla. 1964)

THOMAS, Justice.

In determining this dispute, appropriately described by the appellees as a "massive" attack on the 1961 tax roll of Broward County, we go first to the decree of the chancellor to ascertain what was decreed that vested jurisdiction in this court to review the case. . . .

In the decree the chancellor held pointblank that Chapters 125, 127, 128, 129, 130, 131, 135, 137, 153, and Secs. 193.111, 193.25, 193.27, 193.28, 193.29, 193.30, 193.31, 193.32, 193.67, and 193.671, Florida Statutes, F.S.A., were constitutional thereby rejecting the appellants' contention that they were invalid because of the deletion at an election in 1944 of the clause in Sec. 5, Art. VIII, of the Constitution, F.S.A. before then existing: "The powers, duties, and compensation of such county commissioners shall be prescribed by law."

* * *

As we understand, then, the prime problem is whether county commissioners were stripped of any power that was vested in them by the sections of the statute we have listed, or to put it in the language of the appellants . . . by the deletion of the quoted clause there was withdrawn from the legislature the authority to enact any laws investing the county commissioners, all of them, of course, with power. Therefore, reason the appellants, all the [legislative] acts subsequent to the effective date of the [1944] constitutional amendment [which] undertak[e] to clothe them [the county commissioners] with power are of no effect and, to draw upon our recollection of the oral argument, such commissions could do little more than meet for a sort of social occasion, without compensation, no doubt.

* * *

We think the appellees have a ready reply to the challenge when they remind us that the State, as distinguished from the Federal, Constitution is a limitation of the power inherent in the people, or as it was specified in Sun Insurance Office, Limited v. Clay, Fla., 133 So.2d 735, "[S]tate constitutions . . . are limitations upon the power of the state legislature." A further pronouncement in that case sheds light on our problem, "It is a fundamental principle of constitutional law that each department of government . . . has, without any express grant, the inherent right to accomplish all *objects naturally within the orbit of that department*. . . ." Pertinent to these comments we refer to Sec. 5, Art. IX of the Constitution expressly providing for authority on the part of the legislature to empower the counties to assess and impose taxes for county purposes and enjoining them to do so on the principles governing State taxation. [The Emphasis is the Court's in *Sun Insurance Office.*]

The whole method of securing tax money to finance operation of the counties from the time the amount needed is fixed until the equalization and settlement of challenges of individual owners is vicariously or directly under supervision and control of the county commissioners. And afterward the expenditure of the money gathered for myriads of county purposes is directed by the Boards of County Commissioners. It would, in our view, be unrealistic and illogical to hold that the county commissioners were but holders of a naked title to office simply because of the omission of the quoted portion of the original Sec. 5, Art. VIII. And we believe we can adopt that attitude without any violence to the remainder of the Constitution or any of the rules by which it is to be construed.

[The Court then considers and rejects the remaining arguments of the appellants.]

The decree of the chancellor is affirmed.

DREW, C. J., ROBERTS, THORNAL, O'CONNELL and CALDWELL, JJ., and FITZPATRICK, Circuit Judge, concur.

This issue was addressed by the Second District Court of Appeal in an important case involving the inherent contempt power of the judiciary, *Walker v. Bentley.*[13]

The reader will encounter this case again in Chapter 2.

> [I]t is readily apparent that although the legislature at one point purported to vest the circuit courts with the power of indirect criminal contempt to enforce compliance with a domestic violence injunction, its attempt to do so constituted mere statutory surplusage because such courts already had the inherent constitutional authority, independent of any specific statutory grant, to invoke this power for willful disobedience of any of their orders. It follows, therefore, that the legislature had no authority at a later point to withdraw the power of indirect criminal contempt because a power the legislature cannot confer in the first instance cannot be taken away.[14]

As the reader should be able to understand, even though *Peters v. Meeks* was not cited as authority for this statement, it easily could have been.

Compare the views of the Supreme Court of Idaho in *Eberle v, Nielson:*[15]

> In construing our State Constitution there are also certain fundamental principles which must be recognized and given effect. Unlike the Federal Constitution, the State Constitution is a limitation, not a grant of power.

---

13. 660 So. 2d 313 (Fla. 2d Dist. Ct. App. 1995), *aff'd*, 678 So. 2d 1265 (Fla. 1996).
14. *Id.* at 318.
15. 306 P. 2d 1083, 1086 (Idaho 1957).

1 · AN INTRODUCTION TO STUDYING THE FLORIDA CONSTITUTION

We look to the State Constitution, not to determine what the legislature may do, but to determine what it may not do. If an act of the legislature is not forbidden by the state or federal constitutions, it must be held valid.

b. Constitutional Language that Looks Like a Grant of Power

(1) Constitutional Language as a Legitimate Limitation on Power

Some of the language in the 1968 Florida Constitution (as indeed was the case in earlier Florida constitutions) resembles more closely a grant of power than a limitation of power. Take for example, the following language from the Legislative Article of the 1968 Florida Constitution: "The legislative power of the state shall be vested in a legislature of the State of Florida, consisting of a Senate ... and a House of Representatives...."[16] While this language looks like a grant of power, in reality it is a limitation on inherent governmental power in that it requires: (1) a republican form of government (no doubt as much in deference to our traditions, as to the Guarantee Clause of the United States Constitution)[17] and (2) a bicameral legislature, in the face of undoubted inherent power to form a unicameral one. It might also be considered an allocation of inherent power to the legislature. See the section on allocation later in this chapter.

The Florida Supreme Court discussed this type of constitutional language in *Weinberger v. Board of Public Instruction of St. Johns County*:[18]

> The principle is well established that, where the Constitution expressly provides the manner of doing a thing, it impliedly forbids its being done in a substantially different manner. Even though the Constitution does not in terms prohibit the doing of a thing in another manner, the fact that it has prescribed the manner in which the thing shall be done is itself a prohibition against a different manner of doing it. Holland v. State, 15 Fla. 455 ... (citations omitted). Therefore, when the Constitution prescribes the manner of doing an act, the manner prescribed is exclusive, and it is beyond the power of the Legislature to enact a statute that would defeat the purpose of the constitutional provision.

This principle, frequently described as the rule of interpretation, or *expressio unius est exclusio alterius*, should be used with considerable caution. In regard to a constitutional provision reaffirming power, it is incorrect to say that a constitutional provision couched in granting language is always an implied limitation. Quite the opposite is true. See the discussion of *expressio unius est exclusio alterius* later in this chapter.

---

16. Fla. Const. art. III, § 1.

17. U.S. Const. art. IV, § 4. *See Dreyer v. Illinois*, 187 U.S. 71 (1902).

18. 112 So. 253, 256 (Fla. 1927). The same quote from *Weinberger* was used by Judge Benton in *Bush v. Holmes*, 886 So. 2d 340, 368 (Fla. 1st Dist. Ct. App. 2004) (en banc) (Benton, J., concurring.). The Florida Supreme Court version of *Bush v. Holmes* appears in Chapter 7 of this book.

(2) Constitutional Language as a Reaffirmation of Existing Inherent Power

Many constitutional provisions which resemble grants of power cannot be explained as limitations. Take, for example, the constitutional provision under consideration in *Peters v. Meeks*, Section 5 of Article IX of the 1885 Florida Constitution. It "expressly provid[ed] for authority on the part of the legislature to empower the counties to assess and impose taxes for county purposes. . . ."[19]

It is difficult to view that kind of constitutional provision as a limitation and it was not treated as such in *Peters v. Meeks*. It is probably best explained by Professor Thomas Dye in *Politics in States and Communities*:[20]

> Unlike the U.S. Congress, state legislatures do not need specific constitutional delegations of power to pass particular kinds of laws. Congress must justify every law it passes as part of its enumerated powers, according to Article I, Section 8 of the Constitution; but the states originated as governments of general sovereignty, and therefore did not need to enumerate their powers. *Yet as state constitutions have grown more lengthy and complex, thus giving state courts greater opportunity to limit legislative power, the practice of inserting constitutional authorization for specific state programs has grown. In other words, although state legislatures have **general** rather than **enumerated** powers, the practice of specific constitutional authorization for state power has grown as a safeguard against court interpretations limiting legislative authority.* (Emphasis added.)

Professor Dye's view of this type of state constitutional provision was apparently shared by the Florida Supreme Court in *In re Advisory Opinion to the Governor*,[21] where it made the following characterization of Article XVI, Section 30 of the 1885 Florida Constitution:[22]

> This section was not a grant of power to the Legislature, nor was it a limitation upon the power of the Legislature. It was simply an expressed recognition of a power existing in the legislative department of the state government. (Citation omitted.) The Legislature had inherent authority to create and empower a Public Utilities Commission. . . .

---

19. 163 So. 2d 753, 755 (Fla. 1964). See the edited version of the opinion earlier in this chapter.

20. Thomas R. Dye, *Politics in States and Communities*. Copyright © 1969. Reprinted by permission of Prentice-Hall, Inc., Englewood Cliffs, New Jersey. (Emphasis, other than "general" and "enumerated," supplied.)

21. 223 So. 2d 35, 37 (Fla. 1969).

22. "The Legislature is invested with full power to pass laws for the correction of abuses and to prevent unjust discrimination and excessive charges by persons and corporations engaged as common carriers in transporting persons and property, or performing other services of a public nature; and shall provide for enforcing such laws by adequate penalties or forfeitures."

As is illustrated by *Peters v. Meeks*,[23] courts do at times recognize constitutional reaffirmations of power as doing no more than that, reaffirming already existent state power. However, courts sometimes mistakenly read such language as a limitation. Thus, Article XVI, Section 30[24] was subsequently interpreted to work as a limitation of sorts. The Supreme Court, in considering the effect of this provision on legislative power, made the following comments in *City of Tampa v. Tampa Waterworks Co.*:[25]

> The power mentioned in this section is full power; a continuing, ever-present power. Being irrevocably vested by this section, the Legislature cannot divest itself of it. Neither can it bind itself by contract, nor authorize a municipality—one of its creatures—to bind it by contract, so as to preclude the exercise of this power whenever in its judgment the public exigencies demand its exercise. Full power cannot exist, if by contract that power can be curtailed or impaired. Without this section the power to regulate rates would exist under the general grant of legislative power in section 1, art. 3; but such power could be surrendered by a contract made by the state or by a municipality by its authority. With this section in force, the power to surrender by contract the right to regulate rates is taken away; for the authority to surrender cannot co-exist with the ever-present, continuing power to regulate, which is declared by this section to exist in the Legislature. The section in question does not operate to prevent the Legislature from making contracts itself, nor from authorizing municipalities to make them, and in and by such contracts stipulating for certain rates, which will be valid and binding obligations so long as the Legislature does not exercise or authorize municipalities to exercise, the power to prevent excessive charges, which is declared by the section to be vested in the Legislature. But every charter granted and every contract made by the Legislature, or by a municipality under its authority, are accepted and made subject to and in contemplation of the possibility of the subsequent exercise of the power to prevent excessive charges, which by this section is unalterably and irrevocably vested in the Legislature. . . .

(3) Constitutional Language as an Allocation of Inherent Power

In spite of the fact that a state constitution is useless as a granting document (since there is nothing to grant, the state's power being inherent) Florida courts continue to carelessly describe the state constitution as a granting document. As has already been discussed, constitutional language phrased in granting terms is best treated very cautiously as a limitation (*expressio unius est exclusio alterius*) or,

---

23. The case appears earlier in this chapter.
24. See n. 22, *supra*, for the text of this constitutional provision.
25. 34 So. 631, 639 (Fla. 1903). The reader will note that the Court wrongly considered the legislative article of the 1885 Constitution to be a "general grant of legislative power."

perhaps more frequently, as simply a reaffirmation of power that is already inherent in the state. Nevertheless, opinions discussing the granting of power by constitutional provisions continue to appear.

Consider, for example, *Florida Power & Light Co. v. Canal Authority of the State of Florida*,[26] where the District Court of Appeal described a court's subject matter jurisdiction as "that sovereign authority, *conferred* upon a court by constitution[27] either directly or by authorized statute, to make adjudications, or binding decisions, as to controversies within a certain class of cases or causes. . . ." (Emphasis added.)

In the authors' opinion, the correct view is that the judicial power, like all state power, is inherent and that the sections of the judicial article referred to in the *Florida Power & Light Co.* case merely allocate this inherent judicial power among those courts to which the state is limited by the constitution.[28] An allocation of inherent judicial power among those courts that share it is not a grant in any true sense of the word; it is a form of limitation.

This unfortunate use of "granting" language continues. In *Walker v. Bentley*, the court stated that "many years ago the Florida Supreme Court made it clear that under the power *vested in* the judicial branch of government by article V, section 1 of the Florida Constitution. . . ."[29] (Emphasis added.) In the authors' opinion it would have been more accurate to say, "power *allocated to* the judicial branch."

c. State Constitution as a Limitation on All Branches of State Government

Perhaps because much of the state's inherent power is exercised by the legislative branch of government, many of the Florida cases speak of the Constitution as a limitation only on legislative power. This is simply too narrow a view. Consider the following from *Cawthon v. Town of De Funiak Springs*:[30]

> Governments are not formed to sanction either official assumptions of power not conferred or the abuse of powers that are conferred, but to provide for limited governing functions to conserve the public welfare, and to establish safeguards to protect the people from unauthorized action by officials. The Constitution affords limitations upon the powers of the Legislature as well as upon the executive and judicial departments.

In other words, the state constitution is a document of limitation on all state power.

The general relationship of the state constitution to the governmental power of local governmental units could be discussed here but it will be more convenient to do so when these governmental entities are discussed in Chapter 5.

---

26. 423 So. 2d 421, 423 (Fla. 5th Dist. Ct. App. 1982).
27. *Id.* n. 7 (citing Fla. Const. art. V, §§ 3(b), 4(b), 5(b), 6(b)).
28. *See* Chapter 4 of this book.
29. 660 So. 2d 313, 317 (Fla. 2d Dist. Ct. App. 1995).
30. 102 So. 250, 251 (Fla. 1924).

2. Self-Executing and Non-Self-Executing Provisions

Florida Hospital Waterman, Inc. v. Buster

984 So. 2d 478 (Fla. 2008)

PER CURIAM.

These cases are before the Court for review of the decisions of the First and Fifth District Courts of Appeal in *Notami Hospital of Florida, Inc. v. Bowen,* 927 So.2d 139 (Fla. 1st DCA 2006), and *Florida Hospital Waterman, Inc. v. Buster,* 932 So.2d 344 (Fla. 5th DCA 2006). Both decisions address the scope of article X, section 25 of the Florida Constitution, a ballot initiative passed by the voters in November 2004 and known as amendment 7, the Patients' Right to Know About Adverse Medical Incidents.[1] The Fifth District in *Buster* certified three questions of great public importance to this Court, and the First District in *Notami Hospital* held a statute unconstitutional and certified conflict with *Buster.* We have jurisdiction. *See* art. V, § 3(b)(1), § 3(b)(4), Fla. Const.

For the reasons expressed below, we approve in part the decision of the Fifth District holding amendment 7 to be self-executing and we affirm the First District's holdings that the amendment is self-executing and retroactive and its provisions apply to records existing prior to its passage. We also conclude that several subsections of section 381.028, Florida Statutes (2005), conflict with amendment 7 and are therefore unconstitutional, but we sever those provisions and hold that the remainder of the statute is valid.

I. Facts and Procedural History

Each of these cases addresses amendment 7, approved by the voters on November 2, 2004, and codified as article X, section 25 of the Florida Constitution. . . .

* * *

The effective date and severability provision provides that "[t]his amendment shall be effective on the date it is approved by the electorate." *Advisory Opinion to the Att'y Gen. re Patients' Right to Know About Adverse Med. Incidents,* 880 So.2d 617, 619 (Fla.2004) ("*Patients' Right to Know* ").[2] The ballot title for the proposed amendment was "Patients' Right to Know About Adverse Medical Incidents," and the ballot summary accompanying the proposed amendment read as follows:

> Current Florida law restricts information available to patients related to investigations of adverse medical incidents, such as medical malpractice.

---

1. The amendment was passed by a vote of 81.2 percent in favor and 18.8 percent against. Fla. Dep't of State, Div. of Elections, Nov. 2, 2004 General Election, *Official Results,* http://election.dos .state.fl.us/elections/resultsarchive/ (select "2004 General" election from dropdown menu; then select "Const. Amendments" from dropdown menu).

2. Amendment 7, as proposed to the Secretary of State and to this Court, included an "Effective Date and Severability" section. That section was not officially added to the Florida Constitution. *See* art. X, § 25, Fla. Const.; *Patients' Right to Know,* 880 So.2d at 619.

This amendment would give patients the right to review, upon request, records of health care facilities' or providers' adverse medical incidents, including those which could cause injury or death. Provides that patients' identitie [sic] should not be disclosed.

Id.

After the passage of the amendment, the Legislature enacted chapter 2005–265, Laws of Florida, effective June 20, 2005, dealing with the same subject as amendment 7. [Footnote omitted.] This is now codified at section 381.028 in the Florida Statutes.

* * *

II. This Appeal

The primary areas of overlap between the two decisions on review involve whether amendment 7 is self-executing and whether it can be applied retroactively, and whether the provisions of section 381.028, Florida Statutes (2005), are constitutional. Accordingly, we address only those issues.

III. Governing Law and Analysis

Since all of the issues we consider are ones of constitutional or statutory interpretation, this Court's review is *de novo. See Zingale v. Powell,* 885 So.2d 277, 280 (Fla.2004) ("Although we take into consideration the district court's analysis on the issue, constitutional interpretation, like statutory interpretation, is performed *de novo.*"). In *Zingale,* while recognizing the fundamental nature of a constitutional edict, we emphasized that the principles governing constitutional interpretation largely parallel those of statutory interpretation. *Id.* at 282 (citing *Coastal Fla. Police Benev. Ass'n v. Williams,* 838 So.2d 543, 548 (Fla.2003)).

A. Self-Execution

Both the First and the Fifth Districts below agreed that amendment 7 is self-executing. The Fifth District in *Buster* cited the definitions provided in the amendment, its relatively narrow purpose to override existing statutory law, and an expressed intent gleaned from its provisions that "existing law was sufficient to implement the provisions of the amendment and that no further legislation was necessary." 932 So.2d at 355. The court also concluded that a contrary decision, finding that the amendment was not self-executing, would frustrate the will of the people, especially since the amendment states it was to be effective upon passage, leaving no time for the enactment of implementing legislation. *Id.* The First District's reasoning in *Notami Hospital* largely mirrors that of the Fifth District. The First District cited a presumption that constitutional provisions are self-executing and noted that the amendment "defines, in detail, what records are discoverable, who is entitled to discovery, and states it is effective on the date it is approved by the voters." *Notami Hosp.,* 927 So.2d at 144. We agree with both district courts that amendment 7 is self-executing.

This Court explained the appropriate standard for determining whether constitutional provisions are self-executing in *Gray v. Bryant,* 125 So.2d 846 (Fla.1960):

The basic guide, or test, in determining whether a constitutional provision should be construed to be self-executing, or not self-executing, is whether or not the provision lays down a sufficient rule by means of which the right or purpose which it gives or is intended to accomplish may be determined, enjoyed, or protected without the aid of legislative enactment. *State ex rel. City of Fulton v. Smith,* 1946, 355 Mo. 27, 194 S.W.2d 302. If the provision lays down a sufficient rule, it speaks for the entire people and is self-executing. *City of Shawnee v. Williamson,* Okl.1959, 338 P.2d 355. The fact that the right granted by the provision may be supplemented by legislation, further protecting the right or making it available, does not of itself prevent the provision from being self-executing. *People v. Carroll,* 1958, 3 N.Y.2d 686, 171 N.Y.S.2d 812, 148 N.E.2d 875.

Id. at 851. In *Gray,* the Court found self-executing a constitutional provision providing a formula to determine the number of judges in the judicial circuits, noting the provision laid down "a sufficient rule by which the number of circuit judges which the people have dictated shall be furnished to them may be readily determined without enabling action of the legislature." *Id.* In reaching this conclusion, we emphasized:

The will of the people is paramount in determining whether a constitutional provision is self-executing and the modern doctrine favors the presumption that constitutional provisions are intended to be self-operating. This is so because in the absence of such presumption the legislature would have the power to nullify the will of the people expressed in their constitution, the most sacrosanct of all expressions of the people.

Id. The importance of ascertaining and abiding by the intent of the framers was emphasized, so that "a provision must never be construed in such manner as to make it possible for the will of the people to be frustrated or denied." *Id.* at 852. Consistent with our precedent in *Gray,* we hold that amendment 7 is self-executing and its terms enforceable as of the date of its passage.

We agree with the district courts that the amendment provides a "sufficient rule" by which patients can gain access to records of a health care provider's adverse medical incidents. For example, all key terms are defined within the amendment, including "health care facility," "health care provider," "patient," "adverse medical incident," and "have access to any records." *See* art. X, §25, Fla. Const. In addition, the definition provided for the term "have access to any records" indicates that it is to encompass current document production procedures as provided "by general law." *Id.* Further, as noted above and as emphasized by both district courts, the amendment expressly declares that it is to be effective on passage, indicating that its effectiveness in overriding prior statutory law was not to be dependent upon the enactment of implementing legislation.

The amendment's language makes evident that it was intended to effect an immediate change in the law governing access to medical records without the need for legislative action. While the hospitals contend that a number of relevant and unanswered questions remain regarding the reach of the amendment, we emphasized in *Gray* that simply because the right conferred by the amendment could be supplemented by legislation does not prevent the provision from being self-executing. 125 So.2d at 851.

* * *

IV. Conclusion

Based upon the circumstances presented by the two decisions below regarding the scope of amendment 7, we find that the amendment is self-executing. . . .

* * *

It is so ordered.

LEWIS, C.J., and ANSTEAD, PARIENTE, and QUINCE, JJ., concur.

WELLS, J., concurs in part and dissents in part with an opinion, in which CANTERO and BELL, JJ., concur.

[The concurring and dissenting opinion of Justice Wells is omitted.]

———————

Gray v. Bryant, cited in the *Buster* opinion, is frequently cited for the definition of self-executing constitutional provisions. This definition seems clear, but the application of it may not be as easy as it sounds. Involved in *Gray* was Art. V, Sec. 6(2) of the 1885 Florida Constitution, which provided in pertinent part, "The legislature shall provide for one circuit judge in each circuit for each fifty thousand inhabitants or major fraction thereof according to the last courts authorized by law."

Refer to the *Gray* definition as found in *Buster*. Section 6(2) requires legislative action to "aid" it. It actually resembles a type of constitutional provision that is sometimes described as being "directory."[31] How can a "directory" be self-executing? Furthermore, a directory provision is there to require the legislature to do something; its enforcement can potentially cause problems. See *Dade County Classroom Teachers Assoc., Inc. v. Legislature*[32] found in Chapter 2. This being the case, it may be that the Supreme Court in *Gray* finessed the problem by calling the constitutional provision self-executing and supporting its decision by several of the familiar rules of constitutional interpretations, some of which are found later in this chapter.

Thus, the *Gray* question, taking the *Gray* definition, appears to boil down to this: Is a provision self-executing even though ancillary legislation is needed if the legislature is told by the constitutional provision exactly what to enact, or does the need for ancillary legislation itself keep the constitutional provision from being self-executing?

———————

31. *See, e.g., Walker v. Bentley*, 660 So. 2d 313, 320–321 (Fla. 2d Dist. Ct. App. 1995), *aff'd*, 678 So. 2d 1265 (Fla. 1996).

32. 269 So. 2d 684 (Fla. 1972).

See also the following analysis by the Supreme Court of Missouri in *In re V.*:[33]

> A constitutional provision is self-executing when it appears it was intended to have immediate effect and ancillary legislation is not necessary to the enjoyment of the right given or the enforcement of the duty imposed. When, however, general principles or powers are declared and specific legislation is contemplated or is necessary to make such principles or powers operative within the scope of their fair intendment and meaning, they are not and cannot be self-executing. [Citations omitted.] And, obviously, if the provision is so vague as not to admit of an understanding of its intended scope, it cannot be self-executing. [Citation omitted.] Especially is this true if to construe it to be self-executing would work confusion and mischief. [Citation omitted.]

It has apparently proved possible to circumvent the self-executing characteristics of a constitutional provision. That is what appears to have happened in regard to Article VIII, Section 2(b) of the Constitution. This problem is discussed in Chapter 5.

3. The Formal Amending Process

a. In General

Fla. Const. art. XI

SECTION 1. Proposal by legislature. — Amendment of a section or revision of one or more articles, or the whole, of this constitution may be proposed by joint resolution agreed to by three-fifths of the membership of each house of the legislature. The full text of the joint resolution and the vote of each member voting shall be entered on the journal of each house.

SECTION 2. Revision commission. —

(a) Within thirty days before the convening of the 2017 regular session of the legislature, and each twentieth year thereafter, there shall be established a constitution revision commission composed of the following thirty-seven members:

(1) the attorney general of the state;

(2) fifteen members selected by the governor;

(3) nine members selected by the speaker of the house of representatives and nine members selected by the president of the senate; and

(4) three members selected by the chief justice of the supreme court of Florida with the advice of the justices.

---

33. 306 S.W. 2d 461, 463 (Mo. 1957).

(b) The governor shall designate one member of the commission as its chair. Vacancies in the membership of the commission shall be filled in the same manner as the original appointments.

(c) Each constitution revision commission shall convene at the call of its chair, adopt its rules of procedure, examine the constitution of the state, hold public hearings, and, not later than one hundred eighty days prior to the next general election, file with the custodian of state records its proposal, if any, of a revision of this constitution or any part of it.

SECTION 3. Initiative. — The power to propose the revision or amendment of any portion or portions of this constitution by initiative is reserved to the people, provided that, any such revision or amendment, except for those limiting the power of government to raise revenue, shall embrace but one subject and matter directly connected therewith. It may be invoked by filing with the custodian of state records a petition containing a copy of the proposed revision or amendment, signed by a number of electors in each of one half of the congressional districts of the state, and of the state as a whole, equal to eight percent of the votes cast in each of such districts respectively and in the state as a whole in the last preceding election in which presidential electors were chosen.

SECTION 4. Constitutional convention. —

(a) The power to call a convention to consider a revision of the entire constitution is reserved to the people. It may be invoked by filing with the custodian of state records a petition, containing a declaration that a constitutional convention is desired, signed by a number of electors in each of one half of the congressional districts of the state, and of the state as a whole, equal to fifteen per cent of the votes cast in each such district respectively and in the state as a whole in the last preceding election of presidential electors.

(b) At the next general election held more than ninety days after the filing of such petition there shall be submitted to the electors of the state the question: "Shall a constitutional convention be held?" If a majority voting on the question votes in the affirmative, at the next succeeding general election there shall be elected from each representative district a member of a constitutional convention. On the twenty-first day following that election, the convention shall sit at the capital, elect officers, adopt rules of procedure, judge the election of its membership, and fix a time and place for its future meetings. Not later than ninety days before the next succeeding general election, the convention shall cause to be filed with the custodian of state records any revision of this constitution proposed by it.

SECTION 5. Amendment or revision election. —

(a) A proposed amendment to or revision of this constitution, or any part of it, shall be submitted to the electors at the next general election held more than ninety days after the joint resolution or report of revision commission, constitutional convention or taxation and budget reform commission proposing it is filed with the custodian of state records, unless, pursuant to law enacted by the affirmative vote of three-fourths of the membership of each house of the legislature and limited to a single amendment or revision, it is submitted at an earlier special election held more than ninety days after such filing.

(b) A proposed amendment or revision of this constitution, or any part of it, by initiative shall be submitted to the electors at the general election provided the initiative petition is filed with the custodian of state records no later than February 1 of the year in which the general election is held.

(c) The legislature shall provide by general law, prior to the holding of an election pursuant to this section, for the provision of a statement to the public regarding the probable financial impact of any amendment proposed by initiative pursuant to section 3.

(d) Once in the tenth week, and once in the sixth week immediately preceding the week in which the election is held, the proposed amendment or revision, with notice of the date of election at which it will be submitted to the electors, shall be published in one newspaper of general circulation in each county in which a newspaper is published.

(e) Unless otherwise specifically provided for elsewhere in this constitution, if the proposed amendment or revision is approved by vote of at least sixty percent of the electors voting on the measure, it shall be effective as an amendment to or revision of the constitution of the state on the first Tuesday after the first Monday in January following the election, or on such other date as may be specified in the amendment or revision.

SECTION 6. Taxation and budget reform commission. —

(a) Beginning in 2007 and each twentieth year thereafter, there shall be established a taxation and budget reform commission composed of the following members:

(1) eleven members selected by the governor, none of whom shall be a member of the legislature at the time of appointment.

(2) seven members selected by the speaker of the house of representatives and seven members selected by the president of the senate, none of whom shall be a member of the legislature at the time of appointment.

(3) four non-voting ex officio members, all of whom shall be members of the legislature at the time of appointment. Two of these members, one of whom shall be a member of the minority party in the house of representatives, shall be selected by the speaker of the house of representatives, and two of these members, one of whom shall be a member of the minority party in the senate, shall be selected by the president of the senate.

(b) Vacancies in the membership of the commission shall be filled in the same manner as the original appointments.

(c) At its initial meeting, the members of the commission shall elect a member who is not a member of the legislature to serve as chair and the commission shall adopt its rules of procedure. Thereafter, the commission shall convene at the call of the chair. An affirmative vote of two thirds of the full commission shall be necessary for any revision of this constitution or any part of it to be proposed by the commission.

(d) The commission shall examine the state budgetary process, the revenue needs and expenditure processes of the state, the appropriateness of the tax structure of the state, and governmental productivity and efficiency; review policy as it relates to the ability of state and local government to tax and adequately fund governmental operations and capital facilities required to meet the state's needs during the next twenty year period; determine methods favored by the citizens of the state to fund the needs of the state, including alternative methods for raising sufficient revenues for the needs of the state; determine measure that could be instituted to effectively gather funds from existing tax sources; examine constitutional limitations on taxation and expenditures at the state and local level; and review the state's comprehensive planning, budgeting and needs assessment processes to determine whether the resulting information adequately supports a strategic decision-making process.

(e) The commission shall hold public hearings as it deems necessary to carry out its responsibilities under this section. The commission shall issue a report of the results of the review carried out, and propose to the legislature any recommended statutory changes related to the taxation or budgetary laws of the state. Not later than one hundred eighty days prior to the general election in the second year following the year in which the commission is established, the commission shall file with the custodian of state records its proposal, if any, of a revision of this constitution or any part of it dealing with taxation or the state budgetary process.

[Section 7 omitted.]

––––––––––

Fla. Const. art. XI thus sets out five specific ways in which it may be amended. All proposals ultimately require approval by the electorate of this state. Legislative proposals[34] appear on the ballot fairly frequently. There have now been three sets of revision commission[35] proposals on the ballot. No convention[36] has been called under the 1968 Florida Constitution. The Taxation and Budget Reform Commission has

––––––––––

34. Fla. Const. art. XI, § 1.
35. Fla. Const. art. XI, § 2.
36. Fla. Const. art. XI, § 4.

proposed one set of revisions.[37] The citizens initiative provision[38] has caused, by far, the most controversy.

As originally enacted in 1968, the initiative provision allowed "any section" of the constitution to be amended. In *Adams v. Gunter*, the Supreme Court decided that this provision "include[d] only the power to amend any section in such a manner that such amendment if approved would be complete within itself, relate to one subject and not substantially affect any other section or article of the Constitution or require further amendments to the Constitution to accomplish its purpose."[39] As so interpreted a proposed amendment to create a unicameral legislature was not a proper subject to be placed on the ballot by initiative.

In 1972, the Legislature proposed an amended initiative provision. It was ratified by the voters and allows a change in more than one part of the constitution to be proposed by initiative so long as only "one subject and matter directly connected therewith" is involved.[40]

In two major cases, *Weber v. Smathers*[41] and *Floridians Against Casino Takeover v. Let's Help Florida*,[42] the Supreme Court found that the amended initiative provision should be broadly interpreted as being "functional" rather than "locational" so that the right of the people to propose changes by initiative would be expanded using the single subject requirement for legislation[43] as a guide.[44]

---

37. Fla. Const. art. XI, § 6. In 2008, the commission proposed a total of seven revisions to the Florida Constitution, two of which were struck down by the Florida Supreme Court in *Ford v. Browning*, 992 So. 2d 132 (Fla. 2008), excerpted later in this chapter.

38. Fla. Const. art. XI, § 3.

39. 238 So. 2d 824, 831 (Fla. 1970) (quoted in *Floridians Against Casino Takeover v. Let's Help Florida*, 363 So. 2d 337, 339–340 (Fla. 1978)).

40. Fla. Const. art. XI, § 3.

41. 338 So. 2d 819, 823 (Fla. 1976).

42. 363 So. 2d 337, 340 (Fla. 1978).

43. Fla. Const. art. III, § 6.

44. See generally the discussion in *Floridians Against Casino Takeover v. Let's Help Florida*, 363 So. 2d at 340–341.

b. The Single Subject Problem and the Ballot Summary Substance Problem

Advisory Opinion to the Attorney General re Rights of Electricity Consumers Regarding Solar Energy Choice

188 So. 3d 822 (Fla. 2016)

PER CURIAM.

The Attorney General of Florida has petitioned this Court for an advisory opinion as to the validity of a proposed citizen initiative amendment to the Florida Constitution titled "Rights of Electricity Consumers Regarding Solar Energy Choice" and the corresponding Financial Impact Statement submitted by the Financial Impact Estimating Conference. Consumers for Smart Solar, Inc., (the "sponsor"), submitted the proposed amendment under article XI, section 3 of the Florida Constitution. We have jurisdiction. *See* art. IV, § 10, art. V, § 3(b)(10), Fla. Const.

This Court's review of the proposed amendment is limited to three issues. First, we must determine whether the proposed amendment satisfies the single-subject requirement of article XI, section 3 of the Florida Constitution. Second, we must determine whether the ballot title and summary satisfy the requirements of section 101.161(1), Florida Statutes (2015). And third, this Court must determine whether the Financial Impact Statement complies with the requirements of section 100.371(5), Florida Statutes (2015). *See* § 101.161(1), Fla. Stat. (2015).

. . .

I. Background

On November 24, 2015, the Attorney General petitioned this Court for an opinion as to the validity of an initiative petition sponsored by Consumers for Smart Solar, Inc., and circulated under article XI, section 3 of the Florida Constitution. . . .

The amendment proposed by Consumers for Smart Solar, Inc., would add the following new section 29 to article X of the Florida Constitution:

Section 29 — Rights of electricity consumers regarding solar energy choice. —

(a) ESTABLISHMENT OF CONSTITUTIONAL RIGHT. Electricity consumers have the right to own or lease solar equipment installed on their property to generate electricity for their own use.

(b) RETENTION OF STATE AND LOCAL GOVERNMENTAL ABILITIES. State and local governments shall retain their abilities to protect consumer rights and public health, safety and welfare, and to ensure that consumers who do not choose to install solar are not required to subsidize the costs of backup power and electric grid access to those who do.

. . .

The ballot title for the proposed amendment is "Rights of Electricity Consumers Regarding Solar Energy Choice." The ballot summary for the proposed amendment states:

> This amendment establishes a right under Florida's constitution for consumers to own or lease solar equipment installed on their property to generate electricity for their own use. State and local governments shall retain their abilities to protect consumer rights and public health, safety and welfare, and to ensure that consumers who do not choose to install solar are not required to subsidize the costs of backup power and electric grid access to those who do. . . .

II. Standard of Review

"This Court has traditionally applied a deferential standard of review to the validity of a citizen initiative petition and 'has been reluctant to interfere' with 'the right of self-determination for *all* Florida's citizens' to formulate 'their own organic law.'" *In re Advisory Op. to Att'y Gen. re Use of Marijuana for Certain Med. Conditions (Medical Marijuana I)*, 132 So.3d 786, 794 (Fla.2014) (quoting *Advisory Op. to Att'y Gen. re Right to Treatment & Rehab. for Non–Violent Drug Offenses*, 818 So.2d 491, 494 (Fla.2002)). This Court does "not consider or address the merits or wisdom of the proposed amendment" and must "act with extreme care, caution, and restraint before it removes a constitutional amendment from the vote of the people." *In re Advisory Op. to Att'y Gen. re Limits or Prevents Barriers to Local Solar Elec. Supply*, 177 So.3d 235, 242 (Fla.2015) (quoting *In re Advisory Op. to Att'y Gen. re Fairness Initiative Requiring Legis. Determination that Sales Tax Exemptions & Exclusions Serve a Pub. Purpose (Fairness Initiative)*, 880 So.2d 630, 633 (Fla.2004)). Accordingly, it is this Court's duty to uphold a proposal unless it can be shown to be clearly and conclusively defective. *Limits or Prevents Barriers*, 177 So.3d at 246; *Medical Marijuana I*, 132 So.3d at 795.

III. Single–Subject Requirement

Article XI, section 3 of the Florida Constitution establishes the general requirement that a proposed citizen initiative amendment "shall embrace but one subject and matter directly connected therewith." Art. XI, § 3, Fla. Const. "In evaluating whether a proposed amendment violates the single-subject requirement, the Court must determine whether it has a logical and natural oneness of purpose." *In re Advisory Op. to Att'y Gen. re Use of Marijuana for Debilitating Medical Conditions (Medical Marijuana II)*, 181 So.3d 471, 477 (Fla.2015) (internal citations omitted). The single-subject requirement applies to the citizen initiative method of amending the Florida Constitution because the citizen initiative process does not afford the same opportunity for public hearing and debate that accompanies other constitutional proposal and drafting processes. *See Advisory Op. to the Att'y Gen. re 1.35% Prop. Tax Cap, Unless Voter Approved*, 2 So.3d 968, 972 (Fla.2009).

The single-subject rule prevents an amendment from (1) engaging in "logrolling" or (2) "substantially altering or performing the functions of multiple aspects of government." *Advisory Op. to Att'y Gen. re Fla. Transp. Initiative for Statewide High Speed Monorail, Fixed Guideway or Magnetic Levitation Sys.,* 769 So.2d 367, 369 (Fla.2000). The term logrolling refers to a practice whereby an amendment is proposed which contains unrelated provisions, some of which electors might wish to support, in order to get an otherwise disfavored provision passed. *Advisory Op. to Att'y Gen. re: Protect People, Especially Youth, from Addiction, Disease, & Other Health Hazards of Using Tobacco,* 926 So.2d 1186, 1191 (Fla.2006).

We conclude that the initiative has a logical and natural oneness of purpose. The logical and natural oneness of purpose of the proposed amendment is to establish a constitutional right for electricity consumers "to own or lease solar equipment installed on their property to generate electricity for their own use" while simultaneously ensuring that "State and local governments shall retain their abilities to protect consumer rights and public health, safety and welfare, and to ensure that consumers who do not choose to install solar are not required to subsidize the costs of backup power and electric grid access to those who do."

The opponents of the initiative contend that the proposed amendment violates the single-subject requirement by combining three disjointed subjects into one initiative. We disagree. Provision (b) of the proposed amendment is directly related to provision (a). The subparts of this amendment have a natural relation and connection as component parts or aspects of a single dominant plan or scheme. *See Advisory Op. to Att'y Gen. re Standards for Establishing Leg. Dist. Boundaries,* 2 So.3d 175, 181–82 (Fla.2009).

Combining a constitutional right with the government's authority to regulate that right represents two sides of the same coin, and we have approved ballot initiatives that similarly have created constitutional rights and allowed the government to regulate the right. *See, e.g., Medical Marijuana II,* 181 So.3d 471. While the amendment establishes a constitutional right, that right would not be unfettered. Instead, the right would be limited to the extent that State and local governments find necessary to protect consumer rights and public health, safety, and welfare, and to prevent the exercise of the constitutional right from infringing upon the rights of others, specifically, in the form of a subsidy. The components of the amendment are therefore naturally related and connected to the amendment's oneness of purpose.

The amendment does not engage in impermissible logrolling. It does not involve a popular, desirable provision combined with one that is undesirable, such as asking that solar consumers pay more than their fair share relative to non-solar consumers. Again, the provisions represent two sides of the same coin: individual rights and regulation related to those rights. *See State ex rel. Hosack v. Yocum,* 136 Fla. 246, 186 So. 448, 451 (1939) ("The fundamental right of a person to pursue a calling cannot be taken away by special legislative enactment, but the same is subject to proper and reasonable police regulations. This reasonable regulation may be imposed within proper limits without invading the fundamental right to engage in a lawful business or occupation.").

The opponents of the initiative assert that this case involves single-subject violations similar to those in *Evans v. Firestone*, 457 So.2d 1351 (Fla.1984), and *Fairness Initiative*, cases in which this Court determined the proposed amendment violated the single-subject requirement of article XI, section 3 of the Florida Constitution. We disagree.

In *Evans*, the proposed amendment sought to accomplish three things: (1) limit potential payment of damages by a party to a civil action to his or her percentage of liability; (2) require a court to grant summary judgment on the motion of any party when the court finds that no genuine dispute exists concerning material facts of the case; and (3) limit the award of non-economic damages to a maximum of $100,000 against any party. 457 So.2d at 1353. However, this Court determined that the proposed amendment failed the functional test for the single-subject requirement because it substantially performed the function of multiple branches of government. *See id.* at 1354. This Court also determined that proposed amendment failed the single-subject requirement because the summary judgment provision was not "directly connected" to the other two provisions. *Id.* Unlike the proposed amendment in *Evans*, the proposed amendment in this case does not substantially perform the function of multiple branches of government. Furthermore, unlike the proposed amendment in *Evans*, all of the provisions of the proposed amendment in this case are directly connected to each other.

In *Fairness Initiative*, the proposed amendment "contain[ed] three disparate subjects: (1) a scheme for the Legislature to review existing exemptions to the sales tax under chapter 212; (2) the creation of a sales tax on services that currently does not exist; and (3) limitations on the Legislature's ability to create or continue exemptions and exclusions from the sales tax." 880 So.2d at 634. This Court reasoned that

> [w]hile all of these three goals arguably relate to sales taxes, and any one of these three goals might be the permissible subject of a constitutional amendment under the initiative process, we conclude that together they constitute impermissible logrolling and violate the single-subject requirement of article XI, section 3, of the Florida Constitution because of the substantial, yet disparate, impact they may have.

Id. at 635. Unlike the proposed amendment in *Fairness Initiative*, the proposed amendment in this case does not contain disparate subjects. Rather, it involves one express right and addresses the related ability of State and local governments to regulate that right.

Additionally, we conclude that the proposed amendment does not substantially alter or perform the functions of multiple branches of government. The opponents of the initiative contend that the proposed amendment violates the single-subject requirement by removing the ability of the State to delegate its regulatory powers to its political subdivisions and prohibiting the State from revoking any powers it delegated to local governments before the adoption of the proposed amendment. However, nothing within the proposed amendment implicitly or explicitly abrogates the power of preemption "retain[ed]" by the State under the amendment. As this Court has long recognized, "[w]hile the authority given to cities and counties [and administrative bodies] in Florida is broad, both the constitution and statutes recognize that cities and counties [and administrative bodies] have no authority to act in areas that the legislature has preempted." *Florida Power Corp. v. Seminole Cty.,* 579 So.2d 105, 107 (Fla.1991) ; *see, e.g.,* art. VIII, § 1(f), 1(g), 2(b), Fla. Const.; §§ 125.01, 166.021, Fla. Stat. (2015) ; *City of Cape Coral v. GAC Utilities, Inc., of Florida,* 281 So.2d 493, 495–96 (Fla.1973) ("All administrative bodies created by the Legislature are not constitutional bodies, but, rather, simply mere creatures of statute. . . . As such, the [Public Service] Commission's powers, duties and authority are those and only those that are conferred expressly or impliedly by statute of the State."). Moreover, "the opponents do not indicate how this amendment will interfere with or take over the state's energy policy." *Limits or Prevents Barriers,* 177 So.3d at 244.

The proposed amendment would have a possible effect on the operation of the executive and legislative branches, but it does so only in the general sense that any constitutional provision does. The proposed amendment does not require any of the branches of government to perform any specific functions. Instead, it maintains the regulatory authority of State and local governments, but limited such that it does not violate the constitutional right that the proposed amendment seeks to establish. Requiring a branch of the government to comply with a provision of the Florida Constitution does not necessarily constitute the usurpation of the government branch's function within the meaning of the single-subject requirement. *See Protect People, Especially Youth,* 926 So.2d at 1192.

As this Court has recognized, "it [is] difficult to conceive of a constitutional amendment that would not affect other aspects of government to some extent." *Advisory Op. to Att'y Gen. re Ltd. Casinos,* 644 So.2d 71, 74 (Fla.1994). Accordingly, an initiative may affect the government without substantially altering or performing the functions of multiple aspects of government. For example, this Court approved an initiative in *Medical Marijuana I* that would require the Department of Health to "register and regulate centers that produce and distribute marijuana for medical purposes and . . . issue identification cards to patients and caregivers." 132 So.3d at 794, 796–97. Although the initiative in that case provided new, specific responsibilities for the Department of Health, this Court determined that the regulatory oversight did not constitute usurpation of a branch of government's function within the meaning of the single-subject rule and "the Department of Health would not be empowered under this amendment to make the types of primary policy decisions that are prohibited under the doctrine of nondelegation of legislative power." *Id.* at 797; *see also Medical Marijuana II,* 181 So.3d at 477–78 (coming to the same conclusion with respect to a similar ballot initiative).

The initiative at issue here simply provides that State and local governments "shall retain their abilities to protect consumer rights and public health, safety and welfare, and to ensure that consumers who do not choose to install solar are not required to subsidize the costs of backup power and electric grid access to those who do." This initiative does not specify the branches of government affected and does not detail specific functions in the manner that the initiatives in *Medical Marijuana I* and *Medical Marijuana II* had. Although the proposed amendment would *affect* the government in a literal sense by requiring State and local governments to comply with a provision of the Florida Constitution while retaining their existing abilities, it does not cause the "precipitous" or "cataclysmic" changes to the government structure indicative of substantially altering or performing the functions of multiple branches of government. *See Advisory Op. to Att'y Gen. re Prohibiting State Spending for Experimentation That Involves the Destruction of a Live Human Embryo,* 959 So.2d 210, 213 (Fla.2007).

Finally, because the proposed amendment is written so generally, one might argue that it requires unspecified legislation to be enacted in order to fully effectuate its purpose. However, this Court has rejected similar arguments before because the amendment did not mandate any legislation, and it would be premature to speculate as to how the amendment might interact with other portions of the Florida Constitution even though it is possible that, if passed, the amendment could have broad ramifications. *See, e.g., Leg. Dist. Boundaries,* 2 So.3d at 181; *Advisory Op. to Att'y Gen. English — the Official Language of Florida,* 520 So.2d 11, 12–13 (Fla.1988).

For the reasons set forth above, we hold that the proposed citizen initiative amendment does not violate the single-subject requirement of article XI, section 3 of the Florida Constitution.

IV. Ballot Title and Summary

Under section 101.161(1), Florida Statutes (2015), "[t]he ballot summary of the amendment or other public measure shall be an explanatory statement, not exceeding 75 words in length, of the chief purpose of the measure" and "[t]he ballot title shall consist of a caption, not exceeding 15 words in length, by which the measure is commonly referred to or spoken of." Moreover, "a ballot summary of such amendment or other public measure shall be printed in clear and unambiguous language." § 101.161(1), Fla. Stat. (2015). The basic purpose of section 101.161 is "to provide fair notice of the content of the proposed amendment so that the voter will not be misled as to its purpose, and can cast an intelligent and informed ballot." *Advisory Op. to Att'y Gen. — Fee on Everglades Sugar Prod.,* 681 So.2d 1124, 1127 (Fla.1996). Accordingly, in reviewing the ballot title and summary, this Court asks two questions: (1) whether the ballot title and summary fairly inform the voter of the chief purpose of the amendment; and (2) whether the language of the ballot title and summary misleads the public. *Prop. Tax Cap, Unless Voter Approved,* 2 So.3d at 974–75. "While the ballot title and summary must state in clear and unambiguous language the chief purpose of the measure, they need not explain every detail or ramification of the proposed amendment." *Id.* at 974.

After careful scrutiny of the text of the ballot title and summary, and the text of the amendment, and after consideration of all the arguments of counsel, we conclude that the ballot title and summary in this case do not run afoul of these requirements. Without considering the merits of the measure, we find that the title and summary clearly and unambiguously inform the voter that the amendment will establish a constitutional right for electricity consumers "to own or lease solar equipment installed on their property to generate electricity for their own use" while simultaneously retaining the government's ability to regulate that right. Neither the ballot title nor the summary misleads the public by suggesting that the amendment is necessary for consumers to be able to own or lease solar equipment installed on their property to generate electricity for their own use. Rather, the ballot title accurately identifies the proposed amendment as creating a framework of "Rights of Electricity Consumers *Regarding* Solar Energy Choice" and the ballot summary accurately tells the voter that "[t]his amendment establishes a right under Florida's constitution[,]" not that it allows solar energy use by consumers for the first time. In addition, the ballot summary accurately tells the voter that "State and local governments shall *retain* their abilities to protect consumer rights and public health, safety and welfare, and to ensure that consumers who do not choose to install solar are not required to subsidize the costs of backup power and electric grid access to those who do."

The opponents contend that the ballot title and summary mislead the voter by giving the false impression that he or she must vote for the amendment to maintain a right that already exists under article I, section 2 of the Florida Constitution. We disagree. Nothing within the Florida Constitution currently provides electricity consumers with the specific right "to own or lease solar equipment installed on their property to generate electricity for their own use." Although the Florida Constitution provides a general right to "acquire, possess and protect property[,]" this Court has recognized that it does not secure the right to own any specific good or asset. Art. I, § 2, Fla. Const.; *see Shriners Hosps. for Crippled Children v. Zrillic,* 563 So.2d 64, 68 (Fla.1990) (recognizing that "even constitutionally protected property rights are not absolute, and 'are held subject to the fair exercise of the power inherent in the State to promote the general welfare of the people through regulations that are reasonably necessary to secure the health, safety, good order, [and] general welfare.'" (quoting *Golden v. McCarty,* 337 So.2d 388, 390 (Fla.1976))). It follows that nothing within article I, section 2 of the Florida Constitution necessarily precludes the State under its inherent police powers from entirely barring electricity consumers from owning or leasing solar equipment installed on their property to generate electricity for their own use.

It is undeniable that a constitutional right to a specific type of property — by virtue of its enumeration and in the absence of language within the Florida Constitution to the contrary — necessarily receives greater protection than a general constitutional right to property. *Compare* art. I, § 2, Fla. Const. (establishing a general right to acquire, possess, and protect property), *and Haire v. Florida Dept. of Agric. & Consumer Servs.,* 870 So.2d 774, 783 (Fla.2004) (recognizing that this Court uses the "reasonable relationship test . . . to evaluate statutes and regulations that infringe on property rights"), *with* art. I, § 8, Fla. Const. (establishing a specific constitutional right to keep and bear arms), and *Norman v. State,* 159 So.3d 205, 222 (Fla. 4th DCA 2015) (applying a heightened level of scrutiny to a statute implicating the right to keep and bear arms), *review granted,* 182 So.3d 634 (Fla.2015). Any other conclusion would render the enumeration of a constitutional right to a specific type of property superfluous.

Accordingly, by enshrining a constitutional right "to own or lease solar equipment installed on their property to generate electricity for their own use" in the Florida Constitution, the proposed amendment provides stronger protection for solar energy consumers than previously existed under the Florida Constitution. Although State and local governments retain their abilities under the proposed amendment to protect public health, safety and welfare, the establishment of this specific constitutional right precludes State and local governments from entirely barring electricity consumers from "own[ing] or leas[ing] solar equipment installed on their property to generate electricity for their own use" under their retained police powers. No language within the proposed amendment indicates otherwise.

The opponents also contend that the proposed amendment is misleading under *Evans* because the ballot title and summary purport to establish a right that already exists without informing the voter that the amendment elevates an existing right to a constitutional level. We disagree. In *Evans,* this Court explained as follows:

> The summary states that it "establishes" citizen's rights in civil actions. This is clearly inaccurate as applied to provision b, relating to summary judgment. This provision has long been established in Florida. The effect of the amendment is to elevate this procedural rule to the status of a constitutional right, protected in the same manner and to the same degree as are other constitutional rights. We do not pass on the merits of the effect nor do we question the citizens' right to do exactly this. We do find, however, that the voter must be told clearly and unambiguously that this is what the amendment does.

457 So.2d at 1355. We concluded that the ballot summary in *Evans* was misleading because it claimed to "establish[ ]" a citizen's rights in civil actions, thereby implying that it was creating an entirely new right that would not exist otherwise, without disclosing that the provision relating to summary judgment already existed under the Florida Rules of Procedure. In contrast, the ballot summary in this case is not misleading because it explicitly claims to "establish[ ] a right *under Florida's constitution*" and no constitutional provision currently provides electricity consumers with the specific right "to own or lease solar equipment installed on their property to generate electricity for their own use." Moreover, no statute or rule in Florida currently provides electricity consumers with the specific right "to own or lease solar equipment installed on their property to generate electricity for their own use." *See, e.g.,* § 163.04, Fla. Stat. (2015) (limiting the power of local governments and homeowner associations to prohibit the installation of "solar collectors, clotheslines, or

other energy devices" without addressing the ownership or lease of solar equipment or the use of solar electricity); Fla. Admin. Code R. 25–6.065 (delineating the conditions that a customer must satisfy in order to be eligible for expedited grid interconnection and net-metering without creating a right for consumers to own or lease solar equipment or addressing the installation of solar equipment).

The opponents assert that the ballot title and summary contain misleading terms, some of which purportedly constitute political or emotional rhetoric. However, when read within the full context of the ballot title and summary, none of the terms contained within the ballot title and summary are misleading and none of the terms constitute political or emotional rhetoric. The opponents also claim that the ballot summary is misleading with respect to the current abilities of State and local governments to regulate the use of solar energy. We disagree. The ballot summary clearly states that both "State and local governments shall retain their abilities" — whatever they are — "to protect consumer rights and public health, safety and welfare, and to ensure that consumers who do not choose to install solar are not required to subsidize the costs of backup power and electric grid access to those who do." Additionally, nothing in the proposed amendment requires State or local governments to take any specific action — or adopt any particular policy — regarding their retained abilities. The proposed amendment leaves such decisions to government policymakers.

This Court has long explained that our duty is to uphold the proposal unless it can be shown to be clearly and conclusively defective. *Medical Marijuana I,* 132 So.3d at 795. The proposal has not been shown to be clearly and conclusively defective in any respect. Accordingly, the ballot title and summary are approved for placement on the ballot.

* * *

VI. Conclusion

For the reasons set forth above, we conclude that the initiative petition and ballot title and summary meet the legal requirements of article XI, section 3 of the Florida Constitution, and section 101.161(1), Florida Statutes (2015). Further, the Financial Impact Statement complies with section 100.371(5), Florida Statutes (2015). Therefore, we approve the proposed amendment and Financial Impact Statement for placement on the ballot.

It is so ordered.

LABARGA, C.J., and LEWIS, CANADY, and POLSTON, JJ., concur.

PARIENTE, J., dissents with an opinion, in which QUINCE and PERRY, JJ., concur.

PARIENTE, J., dissenting.

Let the pro-solar energy consumers beware. Masquerading as a pro-solar energy initiative, this proposed constitutional amendment, supported by some of Florida's major investor-owned electric utility companies, actually seeks to constitutionalize the status quo.[1] The ballot title is affirmatively misleading by its focus on "Solar Energy Choice," when no real choice exists for those who favor expansion of solar energy. The ballot language is further defective for purporting to grant rights to solar energy consumers that are illusory; and failing, as required, to clearly and unambiguously set forth the chief purpose of the proposed amendment — to maintain the status quo favoring the very electric utilities who are the proponents of this amendment.

As I more fully explain, the biggest problem with the proposed amendment "lies not with what the [ballot] summary says, but rather, with what it does not say." *Askew v. Firestone,* 421 So.2d 151, 156 (Fla.1982). What the ballot summary does not say is that there is already a right to use solar equipment for individual use afforded by the Florida Constitution and existing Florida statutes and regulations. It does not explain that the amendment will elevate the existing rights of the government to regulate solar energy use and establish that regulatory power as a constitutional right in Florida. This is a glaring omission, especially since rights enshrined in the Constitution are generally intended to limit, rather than grant, governmental power. *Bush v. Holmes,* 919 So.2d 392, 414 (Fla.2006) (citing *Chiles v. Phelps,* 714 So.2d 453, 458 (Fla.1998)). This ballot initiative is the proverbial "wolf in sheep's clothing."

The ballot initiative is titled "Rights of Electricity Consumers Regarding Solar Energy Choice," and is sponsored by "Consumers for Smart Solar" and supported by Duke Energy Florida, Florida Power & Light Co., Gulf Power Co., and Tampa Electric Company. At only eight words in length, the ballot title is affirmatively misleading because it focuses only on alleged rights related to a consumer's choice to use solar energy. But it does not illuminate the real purpose, namely, to place a critical restriction on those rights through elevating state and local governments' police powers to regulate solar energy to the constitutional level. In other words, what "rights" are purportedly given to consumers are severely limited by constitutionally protecting the local and state governments' ability to fully regulate individual consumers' solar energy use as part of their power to protect "public health, safety and welfare," and by preventing "subsidi[es]" on non- solar users.

The second part of the amendment acts as a significant restriction on the expansion of solar energy rights and "choice[s]" by embedding in the Constitution the government's unbridled discretion to regulate private solar energy use. Yet, any indication of this restriction is glaringly excluded from the ballot title, making it affirmatively misleading.

---

1. Due to the use and definitions of certain terms within the proposed amendment, it may actually have the effect of *diminishing* some rights of solar energy consumers. For example, a group of environmental groups who filed a brief in opposition assert that this amendment will eliminate "pay-by-the-watt" leases by narrowly defining "lease," rendering many ordinary consumers unable to afford the "tens of thousands of dollars to purchase solar panels." They explain that "pay-by-the-watt leases" obligate a homeowner to pay only for the electricity actually provided by the solar panels. *See* Answer Brief of Progress Florida, Inc., Environment Florida, Inc., and the Environmental Confederation of Southwest Florida, Inc., at 2–6.

In addition, the ballot title was artfully drafted to emphasize "choice." But what "choice" is being provided through this amendment? At one point, the "choice" intended by the ballot title appears to have been between this amendment and the amendment in *Advisory Opinion to the Att'y Gen. re Limits or Prevents Barriers to Local Solar Electricity Supply,* 177 So.3d 235 (Fla.2015), sponsored by "Floridians for Solar Choice." The *Limits or Prevents Barriers* amendment, which was intended to remove legal and regulatory barriers to local solar-generated electricity users who seek to sell a limited amount of solar-generated electricity to neighboring properties, *id.* at 243, was a driving force for the present ballot initiative. But that amendment, which we approved, will not appear on the November 2016 ballot because the sponsor did not obtain the necessary signatures.[2] In other words, with only this solar energy amendment appearing on the ballot, there really is no "choice" other than to preserve the status quo.

The language of the amendment does not appear to provide any "choice" or provide for the "rights" of electricity consumers who make the "choice" to install solar. For those electricity consumers, the amendment provides only *one* narrow right: to own or lease solar equipment for their own use. The only "choice" is whether to accept this narrow right or reject it.

At the same time, the ballot summary uses a term that the amendment does not define: "subsidize." It appears that the amendment's lack of a definition was intentional, especially since definitions are provided for every other substantive term, including the commonly understood term "consumer." The sponsor of the amendment asserts that the term "subsidize" was intended to refer to the concern that non-solar consumers could be faced with a higher proportion of the fixed costs associated with maintaining the power grid, as a result of solar consumers' reduced, but still existent, reliance on the power grid for backup power. Putting aside that this concern is speculative and not borne out in any present reality, the use of the term "subsidize" suggests that consumers who use solar energy necessarily impose a financial burden on non-solar consumers and implies that this undesirable consequence of the right to own or lease solar equipment must be remedied through the proposed amendment.

Further, the average voter's understanding of what "subsidize" means is highly unlikely to conform to what the sponsor claims the undefined term means. In common parlance, the term "subsid[y]" is often understood as government programs such as subsidized housing and food stamps, as well as tax breaks, corporate subsidies, and agricultural subsidies—often controversial topics with sometimes

---

2. While the identity of the sponsors and supporters of a given amendment is not a factor in determining if the ballot title and summary are misleading, the supporters of this amendment, such as Duke Energy Florida, Gulf Power Company, and Tampa Electric Company, that were among the opponents of the *Limits or Prevents Barriers* amendment, acknowledge that the *Limits or Prevents Barriers* amendment was an "impetus of sorts" for the present ballot initiative. Corrected Ans. Br. of Duke Energy Fla., et al. at 1.

negative connotations. The ballot summary's use of the undefined term "subsidize" allows the potential for broad and shifting interpretations by the state and local governments empowered to regulate and prevent these "subsidi[es]." It is therefore misleading.

Beyond my specific concerns with the affirmatively misleading use of the terms "choice" and "subsidize" in the ballot title and summary, the major flaw in the ballot title and summary is that they fail to accurately inform the voter of the chief purpose and effect of the proposed amendment. In evaluating a proposed amendment:

> The proper analysis to assess whether [the] ballot title and summary meet this requirement focuses on two questions: (1) whether the ballot title and summary, in clear and unambiguous language, fairly inform the voter of the chief purpose of the amendment; and (2) whether the language of the title and summary, as written, misleads the public. *Advisory Op. to Att'y Gen. re Prohibiting State Spending for Experimentation That Involves the Destruction of a Live Human Embryo*, 959 So.2d 210, 213–14 (Fla.2007) (citing *Advisory Op. to Att'y Gen. re Fla. Marriage Prot. Amend.*, 926 So.2d 1229, 1236 (Fla.2006)).

Even though the language of the ballot summary is consistent with and nearly verbatim to the language used in the amendment, the problem is with what the ballot summary (and actual language of the amendment) *fails* to say. *See Advisory Op. to Att'y Gen. re Casino Authorization, Taxation and Regulation*, 656 So.2d 466, 469 (Fla.1995) (concluding language of the ballot summary suggesting the amendment was necessary to prohibit casinos in the state was "misleading not because of what it says, but what it fails to say").

The ballot summary does not make clear that the right of homeowners to own solar equipment for their own use already exists. As a result, it creates a false impression that a vote in favor of the amendment is necessary for the voter to be afforded the right at all. Many voters may indeed believe that there is no existing right to the use of solar energy equipment since, by the end of 2014, only 8,500 Florida consumers — a miniscule percentage of all Florida electricity consumers — were using solar power to generate electricity. Initial Br. of Fla. Solar Energy Indus. Ass'n, at 22.[3]

The ballot title and summary plainly fail to acknowledge that consumers already have a right to own solar equipment for individual use by virtue of article I, section 2, of the Florida Constitution, which provides the right to own property generally. The right to own solar equipment is also afforded to consumers through other statutes and regulations. *See* § 366.91, Fla. Stat. (2015); Fla. Admin. Code R. 25–6.065. If the amendment is passed, it would elevate this existing right to a constitutional level.

---

3. As the opponents explain, this is an extremely small percentage of consumers in the "Sunshine State," as compared, for example, to the state of New Jersey, which has over 40,000 solar energy consumers. *See* Initial Br. of Fla. Solar Energy Indus. Ass'n, at 22.

The problem with the amendment in this ballot initiative is not that a specific property right cannot be placed in the Florida Constitution. Nor is it that the placement of a specific property right in the Constitution would not afford that right greater protection than would be afforded by the general right to property. Rather, the problem lies in the fact that the ballot title and summary fail to fairly inform voters that this is what the amendment does. This Court has held ballot summaries defective for failing to inform the voter of an existing right or prohibition or that the amendment would elevate the right or prohibition to a constitutional level. When that failure has existed in amendments, we have struck them from the ballot. *See, e.g., Casino Authorization,* 656 So.2d 466; *Evans v. Firestone,* 457 So.2d 1351 (Fla.1984).

* * *

Armstrong v. Harris[45] contains an extensive discussion of the ballot summary/ substance problem, including a review of a number of the earlier cases. It also covers in colorful detail the defects of "flying under false colors" and "hiding the ball," as well as what to do when a ballot summary/substance problem that turned out to be defective could not, because of time constraints, be considered by the Court before the proposed amendment was approved by the electorate.[46] It does this in the context of a legislatively proposed amendment that made Article I, Section 17, which had, among other things, prohibited cruel *or* unusual punishments, conform to United States Supreme Court interpretations of the Eighth Amendment (cruel *and* unusual punishments). *Armstrong* is highly recommended reading.

c. The Integration of the Formal Amendment with the Then-Existing Constitution

A constitutional amendment should be construed so as to be in harmony with the existing constitution, if at all possible. However, where this is not possible, the amendment, being the latest expression of the will of the electorate, takes precedence.[47] Constitutional provisions are not retroactive in application, unless the intent to make them retroactive is apparent from the provisions themselves.[48] [49] Thus, the general rule is that state constitutional amendments are to be given prospective application unless it is clear that the amendment was specifically intended to be retroactive in application.

As the second of the two following cases reflects, these rather straight-forward principles are not always easy to apply.

---

45. 773 So. 2d 7 (Fla. 2000).
46. *Id.* at 16.
47. *Jackson v. Consol. Gov't of Jacksonville,* 225 So. 2d 497 (Fla. 1969).
48. *Hancock v. Bd. of Pub. Instruction of Charlotte Cty,* 158 So. 2d 519 (Fla. 1963).
49. *State ex rel. Reynolds v. Roan,* 213 So. 2d 425 (Fla. 1968).

State v. Division of Bond Finance of the Department of General Services

278 So. 2d 614 (Fla. 1973)

ROBERTS, Acting Chief Justice.

[The issue was whether bonds to which were pledged the full faith and credit of the state could be validated without an authorizing vote of the electors concerned — in this case the statewide electorate. The bonds were for funding certain pollution control projects. The validation of such bonds without an election was authorized by Article VII, Section 14, a 1970 amendment to the Florida Constitution. With certain limitations and requirements (which were met by the bonds in question) it authorized the issuance of bonds to "finance the construction of air and water pollution control and abatement and solid waste disposal facilities" and the pledging thereto of the full faith and credit of the state and the full faith and credit and taxing power of local governmental agencies, (if they were involved in the project) without an authorizing election.]

* * *

Against this background, appellant poses two objections to the validation of the bonds in question. These objections relate to the requirement of elections when pledging the full faith and credit of the State and of local political subdivisions. The essence of both points on appeal advanced by appellant is that Article VII, Sections 11(a) and 12(a), Florida Constitution, generally require a vote of the electors to pledge the full faith and credit of the State or of local political subdivisions. [Footnote omitted.] Article VII, Section 14, Florida Constitution, being enacted subsequent to the enaction of Article VII, Section 11(a) and 12(a), is a specific exception thereto. It is a fundamental rule of construction that, if possible, amendments to the Constitution should be construed so as to harmonize with other constitutional provisions, but if this cannot be done, the amendment being the last expression of the will of the people will prevail. An amendment to the Constitution, duly adopted, is the last expression of the will and intent of the law-making power and prior provisions inconsistent therewith or repugnant to the amendment are modified or superseded to the extent of inconsistency or repugnancy. Advisory Opinion to Governor, 152 Fla. 686, 12 So.2d 876 (1943), Sylvester v. Tindall, 154 Fla. 633, 18 So.2d 892 (1944), Board of Public Instruction of Polk County v. Board of Commissioner's of Polk County, 58 Fla. 391, 50 So. 574, Jackson et al. v. Consolidated Government of City of Jacksonville, 225 So.2d 497 (Fla. 1969).

Furthermore, we note that all provisions of the Constitution bearing upon a particular subject matter are to be brought into view and to be so interpreted as to effectuate the great purpose of the instrument. A constitutional amendment becomes a part of the Constitution and must be construed in para materia with all of those portions of the Constitution which have a bearing on the same subject. Advisory Opinion to Governor, supra, Sylvester v. Tindall, supra, Lewis v. Florida State Board of Health, 143 So.2d 867 (Fla.App. 1962).

Article VII, Section 14, modified Sections 11(a) and 12(a) (requiring a vote of electors) so as to create a special exception thereto. In Gray v. Golden, 89 So.2d 785 (Fla.1956) which involved a proposed constitutional amendment providing home rule for Dade County in local affairs, this Court opined that where an amendment limits or modifies other provisions of the Constitution, it does so only to the extent defined in the amendment, and that ". . . such limitations are in harmony with constitutional amendments generally and except as to the 'purpose' of the amendment, the parent provision continues in force." It is obvious that in adopting Article VII, Section 14, by a statewide election, the sovereign people of this State intended to provide an alternative method of financing state bonds without a referendum in certain particular instances. The people of this State created a specific exception to the requirement of an election in this type of bond validation proceeding.

* * *

Having carefully examined the record in this case, and it appearing that the trial court was correct in validating the bonds, his judgment is —

Affirmed.

ERVIN, ADKINS, BOYD, and McCAIN, JJ., concur.

Folks v. Marion County

163 So. 298 (Fla. 1935)

BROWN, Justice.

This is an appeal from a decree of the circuit court for Marion County rendered on March 25, 1935, validating an issue of county refunding bonds.

The question involved on this appeal, stated in general terms, is whether or not 'homesteads,' as defined by article 10, §7, of the Constitution, being the constitutional amendment adopted on November 6, 1934, are subject to taxation for the payment of county refunding bonds authorized and issued after the adoption of said homestead exemption amendment; such refunding bonds being in renewal or extension of the obligation evidenced by county bonds issued prior to the adoption of said amendment, at a time when 'homesteads,' as so defined, were subject to taxation for the payment of such original obligation.

* * *

In order to determine the extent of the taxing power which may be exerted in order to provide for the payment of the proposed refunding bonds, it is necessary to determine what taxing power existed at the time the refunding resolution was adopted on February 19, 1935, and still exists, as security for the payment of the original bonds which were issued some fourteen years before the homestead exemption amendment of November 6, 1934, was adopted. In other words, did said constitutional amendment withdraw the power to levy taxes on homestead property if necessary to provide for the payment of the bonds which had been issued prior to the adoption of said amendment?

This question must be answered in the negative. Section 10 of article 1 of the Constitution of the United States provides that: 'no state shall * * * pass any * * * Law impairing the Obligation of Contracts.' The construction and application of this section of the National Constitution is primarily a federal question, upon which the decisions of the Supreme Court of the United States are controlling. That court has held that a state constitutional provision is a law within the meaning of this inhibitory clause of the Federal Constitution, and that 'a state can no more impair the obligation of a contract by her organic law than by legislative enactment.' *See* New Orleans Gas-Light Co. v. Louisiana Light, etc., Co., 115 U. S. 650, 6 S. Ct. 252, 264, 29 L. Ed. 516; Edwards v. Kearzey, 96 U. S. 595, 24 L. Ed. 793; Gunn v. Barry, 15 Wall. 610, 616, 21 L. Ed. 212.

[Here appears an extensive discussion on the Contract Clause of the United States Constitution.]

The foregoing opinion, representing the views of the writer, is concurred in by Mr. Chief Justice WHITFIELD, Mr. Justice TERRELL, and Mr. Justice DAVIS in so far as it holds that the Homestead Exemption Amendment of November 6, 1934, could not affect or impair the taxing power which had been pledged as security for the payment of the bonds already issued and outstanding at the time said amendment was adopted, and that therefore homestead property remains subject to taxation for that purpose just the same as before the adoption of the amendment. They also agree with the writer in holding that the same protection in the way of taxing power would extend to refunding bonds which are exchanged for a like amount of the original bonds which are being refunded; but they go a step further than the writer, and hold, as did the court below in this case, that the same protection would also extend to the entire issue of refunding bonds — those *sold* and the proceeds used to retire the old bonds, as well as those *exchanged* for the old bonds. In other words, they adhere to the principles expressed in the opinion of Mr. Chief Justice DAVIS in his opinion in the case of Boatright v. City of Jacksonville, 117 Fla. 477, 158 So. 42. Mr. Justice BUFORD dissents in part, his view being that all bonds issued after the adoption of the Homestead Exemption Amendment, whether refunding or original bonds, fall within the full operative effect of that amendment, and that no taxes can be levied on homesteads as therein defined for the payment of bonds of any character issued after the adoption of said amendment, excepting of course "special assessments for benefits," which exception is contained in the amendment itself. The court regrets that Mr. Justice ELLIS, who is unavoidably absent on account of illness, cannot participate in the decision of this case.

The result of these views is that the decree of validation appealed from should be, and is hereby,

Affirmed.

WHITFIELD, C. J., and TERRELL, BUFORD, and DAVIS, JJ., concur.

d. Amendment by Interpretation

Although the phrase "formal amending" was used as the heading of this subsection, the Constitution may also be amended through the less formal method of judicial interpretation. In effect, the Florida Constitution is interpreted by all branches and levels of government[50] and is, in effect, at times changed by such interpretations. This process is at least inferentially recognized in *Florida Power Corporation v. Pinellas Utility Board:*[51]

> ... It may be said that each generation should possess the right to construe or interpret our Constitution in the light of his daily needs in a complex society rather than in the light of now obsolete conditions and circumstances of the past. It is unjust to chain modern society to the views and opinions of eminent jurists of former generations not acquainted with our present day problems....

4. Aids in Interpreting the Constitution

It often becomes necessary to construe or interpret a constitutional provision to determine its applicability in a given situation. The same rules that apply in interpreting or construing statutes, the canons of construction, are generally applicable when interpreting or construing constitutions. Nonetheless, constitutions are said to receive a broader and more liberal interpretation or construction than statutes because they are living documents, not easily amended, which demand greater flexibility than statutes.[52]

The primary rule when interpreting or construing a constitutional provision is to ascertain and give effect to the intent of the drafters and the electorate that adopted the provision.[53] Constitutional provisions must be interpreted in such a manner as to fulfill this intention rather than to defeat it.[54]

The canons of construction have been criticized for their subjectivity.[55] Nonetheless, they remain the primary tools that the courts utilize to construe or interpret constitutional provisions.

A complete discussion of the canons would require considerably more space than has been allocated to this topic in this text. The following cases are merely intended to be illustrative of the approach courts utilize when interpreting or construing a constitutional provision. The following two cases are examples of the primary rules

---

50. The Florida Supreme Court, of course, has the final authority to interpret it. *See* Fla. Const. art. V and Chapter 4.

51. 40 So. 2d 350, 355 (Fla. 1949).

52. *Fla. Soc'y of Ophthalmology v. Fla. Optometric Ass'n*, 489 So. 2d 1118 (Fla. 1986).

53. *State ex rel. Dade Cnty. v. Dickinson*, 230 So. 2d 130 (Fla. 1969).

54. *Id.*

55. *See* Karl N. Llewellyn, *Remarks on the Theory of Appellate Decision and the Rules or Canons About How Statutes Are to Be Construed*, 3 Vand. L. Rev. 395 (1950).

that constitutional provisions are to be interpreted and construed by, thus giving effect to the intent of the drafters.

Edwards v. Thomas

229 So. 3d 277 (Fla. 2017)

LEWIS, J.

On November 2, 2004, the citizens of Florida voted to amend their constitution, adding in part the "right to have access to any records made or received in the course of business by a health care facility or provider relating to any adverse medical incident." Art. X, § 25(a), Fla. Const. This language was tested in the decision of the Second District Court of Appeal in *Bartow HMA, LLC v. Edwards*, 175 So.3d 820 (Fla. 2d DCA 2015). Because the district court expressly construed a provision of the Florida Constitution, this Court has jurisdiction to review the decision. *See* art. V, § 3(b)(3), Fla. Const. We accept that jurisdiction and analyze the significance of that constitutional provision in this case.

Factual and Procedural Background

While in Florida, Amber Edwards developed stomach pain and was diagnosed with having gallstones. A laparoscopic cholecystectomy was scheduled and performed at Bartow Regional Medical Center (Bartow) on May 9, 2011. Bartow assigned Dr. Larry D. Thomas, M.D., to perform the surgery. During the procedure, Thomas failed to identify Edwards's common bile duct, cut her common bile duct during surgery, and failed to timely recognize that he had done so. After suffering from severe stomach pain for multiple days post-operation, Edwards returned to Bartow's emergency room, where Thomas's error was discovered. Upon discovering the severed common bile duct, Edwards was transferred to Tampa General Hospital for emergency corrective surgery. Edwards ultimately sued Bartow and Thomas for medical negligence, including negligent hiring and retention. Edwards served a Request to Produce on Bartow on July 30, 2013, pursuant to article X, section 25 of the Florida Constitution, which is commonly referred to as Amendment 7, requesting a number of records relating to adverse medical incidents that occurred at Bartow. Bartow objected to the requested discovery, maintaining "that certain requested records did not relate to 'adverse medical incidents,' were not 'made or received in the course of business,' were protected by attorney-client privilege, and were protected as opinion work product." Pet'r's Br. 3–4. Edwards then filed a motion to compel Bartow to file better responses, which the trial court granted, and Bartow again attempted to frustrate compliance with that court order by asserting the same objections and attaching privilege logs.

. . .

After being ordered on two occasions to produce the redacted documents that Edwards requested, Bartow then only provided Edwards with its internal peer review documents and filed a petition for writ of certiorari in the Second District Court of Appeal challenging the trial court's order requiring the production of the external peer review reports at issue, which had been reviewed by the external company, M.D. Review. *See id.*

The Second District granted Bartow's petition and quashed, in part, the trial court's order on the basis that the external reports were not "made or received in the course of business" per Amendment 7's requirements and that they did not relate to an "adverse medical incident." *Id.* at 824–26. . . .

. . .

Edwards petitioned this Court to review the Second District's decision based on its express construction of a constitutional provision.[1] This review follows.

Amendment 7

The language of article X, section 25 of the Florida Constitution states in full:

(a) In addition to any other similar rights provided herein or by general law, *patients have a right to have access to any records made or received in the course of business by a health care facility or provider relating to any adverse medical incident.*

* * *

Analysis

Amendment 7's Scope

We must first determine the intended scope of Amendment 7's reach. The Second District asserts, and Bartow naturally agrees, that Amendment 7 was only intended to abrogate the specific *statutory* limitations on discovery of adverse medical incidents that were in place prior to the amendment's passage in 2004. *Edwards*, 175 So.3d at 824. Edwards, on the other hand, maintains that the intent of the Florida voters was to do away with *all* limitations on the discovery of adverse medical incidents. To properly address this issue, we look to both the language of the provision itself and the manner in which courts across the State of Florida have interpreted and applied Amendment 7.

> Statutory and constitutional construction are questions of law subject to a de novo review. *See Zingale v. Powell*, 885 So.2d 277, 280 (Fla. 2004) ("[C]onstitutional interpretation, like statutory interpretation, is performed de novo."). The polestar of a statutory construction analysis is legislative intent. *See Borden v. East — European Ins. Co.*, 921 So.2d 587, 595 (Fla. 2006). To discern legislative intent, this Court looks first to the plain and obvious meaning of the statute's text, which a court may discern from a dictionary. *See Rollins v. Pizzarelli*, 761 So.2d 294, 297–98 (Fla. 2000). If that language is clear and unambiguous and conveys a clear and definite meaning, this

---

1. Edwards also petitioned this Court for review, alleging that the Second District's decision below conflicts with the decision of the Fifth District in *Florida Eye Clinic, P.A. v. Gmach*, 14 So.3d 1044 (Fla. 5th DCA 2009). See art. V, § 3(b)(3), Fla. Const.

1 · AN INTRODUCTION TO STUDYING THE FLORIDA CONSTITUTION 41

> Court will apply that unequivocal meaning and not resort to the rules of statutory interpretation and construction. *See Holly v. Auld*, 450 So.2d 217, 219 (Fla. 1984). If, however, an ambiguity exists, this Court should look to the rules of statutory construction to help interpret legislative intent, which may include the examination of a statute's legislative history and the purpose behind its enactment. See, e.g., *Gulfstream Park Racing Ass'n v. Tampa Bay Downs*, Inc., 948 So.2d 599, 606–07 (Fla. 2006).
>
> Similarly, when this Court construes a constitutional provision, it will follow construction principles that parallel those of statutory interpretation. *See Ford v. Browning*, 992 So.2d 132, 136 (Fla. 2008) (quoting *Zingale v. Powell*, 885 So.2d 277, 282 (Fla. 2004)). As with statutory construction, a question with regard to the meaning of a constitutional provision must begin with the examination of that provision's explicit language. *See id*. If that language is "clear, unambiguous, and addresses the matter at issue," it is enforced as written. *Id*. If, however, the provision's language is ambiguous or does not address the exact issue, a court "must endeavor to construe the constitutional provision in a manner consistent with the intent of the framers and the voters." *Id*.

W. Fla. Reg'l Med. Ctr., Inc. v. See, 79 So.3d 1, 8–9 (Fla. 2012). "The importance of ascertaining and abiding by the intent of the framers was emphasized, so that 'a provision must never be construed in such manner as to make it possible for the will of the people to be frustrated or denied.'" *Buster*, 984 So.2d at 486 (quoting *Gray v. Bryant*, 125 So.2d 846, 852 (Fla. 1960)).

First, the language of Amendment 7 provides that "patients have a right to have access to *any records* made or received in the course of business by a health care facility or provider relating to *any adverse medical incident*." Art. X, § 25(a), Fla. Const. (emphasis added). As stated above, when interpreting a constitutional provision, we must look at the plain language of the provision. *See Rollins*, 761 So.2d at 297. Tellingly, the language in Amendment 7 contains no limitation on the types of adverse medical incident reports that are now discoverable.[4] There is also no quali-

---

4. In fact, in determining the applicability of Amendment 7 to adverse medical incident records created before the amendment's passage, we specifically noted the intentionally broad language of Amendment 7:

> Here, the plain language of the amendment permits patients to access any record relating to any adverse medical incident. . . . The use of the word "any" to define the scope of discoverable records relating to *adverse medical incidents* . . . expresses a clear intent that the records subject to disclosure include those created prior to the effective date of the amendment.

Buster, 984 So.2d at 487 (quoting *Notami Hosp. of Fla., Inc. v. Bowen*, 927 So.2d 139, 145 (Fla. 1st DCA 2006), aff'd sub nom. *Buster*, 984 So.2d 478) (emphasis in original). While Amendment 7's intentionally broad construction was being discussed in terms of its applicability to records created before the amendment's passage, this language nonetheless sheds light on the issue before the Court today. The use of "any record" relating to "any adverse medical incident" expresses a clear

fying provision in Amendment 7 that limits the scope of discoverable records to those previously barred by the Legislature and this Court will not read language into Amendment 7 that was not expressly included. Instead, we apply the unequivocal meaning of the plain language in Amendment 7, because "that language is clear and unambiguous and conveys a clear and definite meaning." *See*, 79 So.3d at 9 (citing *Holly*, 450 So.2d at 219). Additionally,

> Statutory interpretation is a "holistic endeavor," and when engaged in the task of discerning the meaning of a statute, we "'will not look merely to a particular clause in which general words may be used, but will take in connection with it the whole statute. . . .'" Adverting to our catalogue of rules of statutory construction,
>
> > [w]e are required to give effect to "every word, phrase, sentence, and part of the statute, if possible, and words in a statute should not be construed as mere surplusage." Moreover, "a basic rule of statutory construction provides that the Legislature does not intend to enact useless provisions, and courts should avoid readings that would render part of a statute meaningless." "[R]elated statutory provisions must be read together to achieve a consistent whole, and . . . '[w]here possible, courts must give full effect to all statutory provisions and construe related statutory provisions in harmony with one another.'"
>
> *Goode v. State*, 50 Fla. 45, 39 So. 461, 463 (1905) ("It is the general rule, in construing statutes, 'that construction is favored which gives effect to every clause and every part of the statute, thus producing a consistent and harmonious whole. A construction which would leave without effect any part of the language used should be rejected, if an interpretation can be found which will give it effect.'").

Quarantello v. Leroy, 977 So.2d 648, 651–52 (Fla. 5th DCA 2008) (some citations omitted).

We also note the plain language contained in Amendment 7's definition of an "adverse medical incident."[5] Namely, the language "including, but not limited to, those incidents that are required by state or federal law to be reported to any governmental agency or body" provides meaningful context as to Amendment 7's

---

intent to abrogate any and all previously- existing restrictions on the discoverability of these types of records.

    5. Amendment 7 defines the phrase "adverse medical incident" to mean

> medical negligence, intentional misconduct, and any other act, neglect, or default of a health care facility or health care provider that caused or could have caused injury to or death of a patient, *including, but not limited to, those incidents that are required by state or federal law to be reported to any governmental agency or body*, and incidents that are reported to or reviewed by any health care facility peer review, risk management, quality assurance, credentials, or similar committee, or any representative of any such committees.

Art. X, § 25(c)(3), Fla. Const. (emphasis added).

intended broad application. Rather than shed light on Bartow's and the Second District's assertion that Amendment 7 was only intended to eliminate previously statutorily-protected adverse medical incident reports, this language actually reinforces the opposite conclusion. Bartow voices the assertion, "The previously protected records were ones that the statutes required a facility's own risk management programs or internal review and quality assurance committees to create as a condition of licensure." Answer Br. at 15. It is only these "previously protected records," Bartow maintains, that were intended to become discoverable after Amendment 7's enactment.

Reading Amendment 7's language as a whole, and taking into account the definition of an "adverse medical incident," however, suggests that the newfound right to access *"any record"* under Amendment 7 relating to *"any* adverse medical incident" necessarily includes, *but is not limited to,* those adverse medical incident records required to be reported by state or federal law. Bartow's and the Second District's interpretation of Amendment 7's scope, on the other hand, would render the language of "including, *but not limited to,"* as "mere surplusage" — a result that is directly contrary to the rules of statutory and constitutional construction in this State. See *Quarantello,* 977 So.2d at 651–52. Thus, it could not have been the intent of the Florida voters to enact Amendment 7 with such broadly-worded language, while simultaneously extremely limiting its scope and application only to those records previously protected under the licensing statutes. Therefore, we hold that Amendment 7's application was not intended to be limited only to those adverse medical incident records previously protected by statute.

* * *

Adverse Medical Incident Reports

Next, we address whether the external peer review reports at issue here contain information on adverse medical incidents that fall within the purview of Amendment 7 — namely, by determining whether the external peer review committee itself constitutes a "similar committee" as enunciated in the constitutional provision. Amendment 7 defines the phrase "adverse medical incident" to mean

> medical negligence, intentional misconduct, and any other act, neglect, or default of a health care facility or health care provider that caused or could have caused injury to or death of a patient, *including, but not limited to,* those incidents that are required by state or federal law to be reported to any governmental agency or body, and incidents that are reported to or reviewed by any health care facility peer review, risk management, credentials, quality assurance, *or similar committee, or any representative of any such committees.*

Art. X, § 25(c)(3), Fla. Const. (emphasis added).

The Second District determined that the reports at issue were not created by a "similar committee," as contemplated by the language in Amendment 7, noting the distinction discussed in *Neely* "between incident reports prepared in accordance with Florida Statutes and those 'documents prepared or produced at the specific request of the client's attorney for use in litigation.'" *Edwards*, 175 So.3d at 826 (quoting *Neely*, 8 So.3d at 1270 n.2). This distinction, however, necessarily presumes that Amendment 7's application was intended only to reach those records previously protected by the Legislature before the amendment's passage — a presumption that, as explained above, we find to be erroneous. Importantly, Bartow concedes that the reports at issue do, in fact, contain information relating to adverse medical incidents, but nonetheless asserts that they are not the types of reports contemplated by Amendment 7 because they were not made pursuant to Bartow's statutory reporting obligations. Conversely, Edwards maintains that the external peer review committee that reviewed the reports at issue is the exact type of "similar committee" referenced in Amendment 7.

We must again employ the rules of statutory and constitutional construction in answering this question. First, in looking to the plain language quoted above, it must be noted again that the language of Amendment 7 contains *no limitation* on the definition of "adverse medical incidents" based on a health care facility's statutory reporting obligations.

In fact, as discussed above, the phrase "including, but not limited to" when referencing the reports required by state or federal law to be reported requires a directly contrary meaning. Furthermore, reading the entire provision logically, directly mentioning reports generated pursuant to state or federal law presumes that these reports are generated by statutorily-mandated risk management committees. The provision then goes on to *expressly include* an additional and entirely separate category of incidents — namely, those "that are reported to or reviewed by *any* health care facility peer review, risk management, quality assurance, credentials, or similar committee, or any representative of any such committees." Art. X, § 25(c)(3), Fla. Const. (emphasis added). Presumably, reading the provision as written in its entirety, the incident reports generated pursuant to state or federal law (which are incident reports generated pursuant to statutorily-mandated internal risk management or peer review committees) are a different category of reports from those created by any similar health care facility committee. Moreover, we often apply rules of grammar during our constitutional construction to determine the drafters' intent. *See State v. Bodden*, 877 So.2d 680, 685–86 (Fla. 2004). By making the language in this provision two separate clauses, the drafters of Amendment 7 signaled that these two clauses were intended to be read disjunctively.

Bartow and the Second District, however, read this provision to require only the production of incident reports generated pursuant to the statutory reporting obligations. This reading seemingly conflates the reports generated pursuant to a statutory obligation and those other reports generated pursuant to any similar health care facility committee. Rather than give the entire provision a reasonable and logical meaning, Bartow and the Second District's interpretation renders the language in the provision concerning incidents generated in accordance with state or federal law meaningless because it presumes that the second half of the language in the provision, including any "similar committees," refers only to those same statutorily-mandated committees. *See Quarantello*, 977 So.2d at 651–52 (stating that a statutory interpretation cannot render portions of the provision meaningless or "mere surplusage").

Additionally, as with the use of "*any* records" relating to "*any* adverse medical incident," the provision defining "adverse medical incident" also contains similarly broad wording with regard to the incidents reviewed by health care facility committees. *See* art. X, § 25(c)(3), Fla. Const. ("[A]nd incidents that are reported to or reviewed by *any* health care facility peer review, risk management, quality assurance, credentials, or similar committee, or any representative of any such committees." (emphasis added)). Rather than limiting its application, the use of "any" repeatedly throughout the language of Amendment 7 yet again indicates its broadly designed and intended nature. There is no mention in the provision of its applicability only to "any internal" committee or to "any statutorily-mandated" committee, and this Court will not read that language into Amendment 7. Therefore, we conclude that the committees specifically listed in article X, section 25(c)(3) of the Florida Constitution are not limited only to those required by a statutory obligation.

The meaning of "similar committees" is both clear and unambiguous as we delve further into the rules of constitutional analysis to ascertain the intended meaning behind the phrase. We conclude that the phrase "similar committees" was intended to apply to both risk management committees similar to those specifically listed, and also to those beyond what are statutorily required of health care facilities.

Tellingly, "[t]he Florida Legislature enacted these peer review statutes in an effort to control the escalating cost of health care by encouraging self-regulation by the medical profession through peer review and evaluation." *Cruger v. Love*, 599 So.2d 111, 113 (Fla. 1992). These statutes, however, are the floor, rather than the ceiling for health care facilities' self-regulation. *See* § 395.0197(3), Fla. Stat. (2017) ("In addition to the programs mandated by this section, other innovative approaches intended to reduce the frequency and severity of medical malpractice and patient injury claims shall be encouraged and their implementation and operation facilitated."). In addition to those required by statute, health care facilities can participate in and seek out additional voluntary committees and programs that provide additional resources on how to improve the quality of care rendered to patients. *Id.*; *see generally Charles*, 209 So.3d 1199 (discussing the Federal Patient Safety and Quality Improvement Act and how it relates to patients' rights under Amendment 7). These additional programs and reviews cannot logically be excluded from Amendment 7's application simply because they are in addition to the base-level, statutorily-required risk management committees. Such a result would be directly contrary to the intent and express words of Florida voters to have greater access to adverse medical incident records than they did before the passage of Amendment 7. Moreover, the result asserted by Bartow would provide a trap door through which hospitals could totally avoid their discovery obligations by outsourcing their adverse medical incident reporting to external, voluntary risk management committees separate from those required by the Florida statutory scheme.

Therefore, we hold that, based on the express language and the principles of constitutional analysis, the external peer review committee at issue in this case does qualify as a "similar committee" under Amendment 7.

* * *

Conclusion

Accordingly, we hold that the external peer review reports are discoverable under Amendment 7, and we quash the Second District's decision in *Edwards*.

It is so ordered.

LABARGA, C.J., and PARIENTE, and QUINCE, JJ., concur.

POLSTON, J., concurs in result.

LAWSON, J., dissents with an opinion, in which CANADY, J., concurs. [The dissenting opinion of Justice Lawson is omitted.]

Ford v. Browning

992 So. 2d 132 (Fla. 2008)

WELLS, J.

Appellants filed a complaint in the Circuit Court of the Second Judicial Circuit for Leon County, challenging two proposed constitutional amendments submitted by the Taxation and Budget Reform Commission (TBRC) on the ground that TBRC does not have the authority to propose constitutional revisions on these subjects. The first constitutional proposal would amend the freedom of religion provision found in article I, section 3 of the Florida Constitution by eliminating the restriction on state funds being used in aid of any religion and adding a provision that an individual or entity cannot be barred from participating in a public program based on religion. The second constitutional proposal would amend the public education provision found in article IX, section 1, by directing school districts to spend at least sixty-five percent of their funding on classroom instruction and providing that the duty to provide for public education is not exclusively limited to free public schools. The appellants further alleged in their complaint that the ballot title and summary language accompanying one of the proposals did not accurately inform voters as to the true effect of the proposed amendment. They sought an injunction barring the Secretary of State from placing Proposed Amendments 7 and 9 on the ballot for the November 2008 general election.[1] Appellants filed a motion for temporary injunc-

---

1. The ballot title and summary for Proposed Amendment 7 state:
RELIGIOUS FREEDOM

> Proposing an amendment to the State Constitution to provide that an individual or entity may not be barred from participating in any public program because of religion and to delete the prohibition against using revenues from the public treasury directly or

1 · AN INTRODUCTION TO STUDYING THE FLORIDA CONSTITUTION   47

tion, which was treated as a motion for final summary judgment. Following briefing and oral argument, the circuit court denied the appellants' motion for summary judgment and granted the cross-motions filed by the appellees and the intervenors, finding that TBRC had the authority to propose the amendments and that the challenged ballot title and summary were not misleading. Appellants appealed the judgment to the First District Court of Appeal, which certified to this Court that this case presents a question of great public importance requiring immediate resolution by this Court in light of the upcoming election. We have jurisdiction under article V, section 3(b)(5), of the Florida Constitution.

Analysis

As an initial matter, it is important to stress that the wisdom or merits of the proposed amendments are not issues before the Court. *See Advisory Op. to the Att'y Gen. re Fla. Marriage Protection Amendment,* 926 So.2d 1229, 1233 (Fla.2006). Rather, the question before the Court is to determine the extent of the authority provided to TBRC by article XI, section 6(e) of the Florida Constitution to propose constitutional amendments and whether the authority extends to Proposed Amendments 7 and 9. Our standard of review is *de novo. See Zingale v. Powell,* 885 So.2d 277, 280 (Fla.2004) ("[C]onstitutional interpretation, like statutory interpretation, is performed *de novo.*").

When reviewing constitutional provisions, this Court "follows principles parallel to those of statutory interpretation." *Zingale,* 885 So.2d at 282. Any question regarding the meaning of a constitutional provision must begin with examining that provision's explicit language. *See Fla. Soc'y of Ophthalmology v. Fla. Optometric Ass'n,* 489 So.2d 1118, 1119 (Fla.1986). If the constitutional language is clear, unambiguous, and addresses the matter at issue, it must be enforced as written, and courts do not turn to rules of constitutional construction. *Id.* If the explicit language is ambiguous or does not address the exact issue before the court, the court must endeavor to construe the constitutional provision in a manner consistent with the intent of the framers and the voters. *Crist v. Fla. Ass'n of Criminal Defense Lawyers, Inc.,* 978 So.2d 134, 140 (Fla.2008). As this Court has held:

> The fundamental object to be sought in construing a constitutional provision is to ascertain the intent of the framers and the provision must be

---

indirectly in aid of any church, sect, or religious denomination or in aid of any sectarian institution.

The ballot title and summary for Proposed Amendment 9 state:

REQUIRING 65 PERCENT OF SCHOOL FUNDING FOR CLASSROOM INSTRUCTION; STATE'S DUTY FOR CHILDREN'S EDUCATION

Requires at least 65 percent of school funding received by school districts be spent on classroom instruction, rather than administration; allows for differences in administrative expenditures by district. Provides the constitutional requirement for the state to provide a "uniform, efficient, safe, secure, and high quality system of free public schools" is a minimum, nonexclusive duty. Reverses legal precedent prohibiting public funding of private school alternatives to public school programs without creating an entitlement.

construed or interpreted in such manner as to fulfill the intent of the people, never to defeat it. Such a provision must never be construed in such manner as to make it possible for the will of the people to be frustrated or denied.

Id. (quoting *Caribbean Conservation Corp. v. Fla. Fish & Wildlife Conservation Comm'n,* 838 So.2d 492, 501 (Fla.2003)) (emphasis omitted). A constitutional provision should be "construed as a whole in order to ascertain the general purpose and meaning of each part; each subsection, sentence, and clause must be read in light of the others to form a congruous whole so as not to render any language superfluous." *Dep't of Envtl. Prot. v. Millender,* 666 So.2d 882, 886 (Fla.1996).

With these principles in mind, we turn to the language involved in the constitutional provision at issue. TBRC was created in 1988 via article XI, section 6, of the Florida Constitution. Subsection 6(d) sets forth TBRC's power to review and study matters; and subsection 6(e) sets forth TBRC's authority to act. Specifically, article XI, section 6(d)-(e), states as follows:

(d) The commission shall examine the state budgetary process, the revenue needs and expenditure processes of the state, the appropriateness of the tax structure of the state, and governmental productivity and efficiency; review policy as it relates to the ability of state and local government to tax and adequately fund governmental operations and capital facilities required to meet the state's needs during the next twenty year period; determine methods favored by the citizens of the state to fund the needs of the state, including alternative methods for raising sufficient revenues for the needs of the state; determine measures that could be instituted to effectively gather funds from existing tax sources; examine constitutional limitations on taxation and expenditures at the state and local level; and review the state's comprehensive planning, budgeting and needs assessment processes to determine whether the resulting information adequately supports a strategic decisionmaking process.

(e) The commission shall hold public hearings as it deems necessary to carry out its responsibilities under this section. The commission shall issue a report of the results of the review carried out, and propose to the legislature any recommended statutory changes related to the taxation or budgetary laws of the state. Not later than one hundred eighty days prior to the general election in the second year following the year in which the commission is established, *the commission shall file with the custodian of state records its proposal, if any, of a revision of this constitution or any part of it dealing with taxation or the state budgetary process.*

Art. XI, § 6(d)-(e), Fla. Const. (emphasis added).

The question to be resolved is the meaning of the limitation of TBRC's authority to propose constitutional amendments where that authority is limited to dealing with taxation or the state budgetary process. According to the appellees, TBRC's authority to propose constitutional revisions under subsection 6(e) must be read in conjunction with its powers to review and study matters under subsection 6(d). In support, the appellees point out that under section 6(d), TBRC is directed to "examine constitutional limitations on taxation and expenditures at the state and local level" and allege that it would be illogical for TBRC to examine this issue if it does not have the power to propose constitutional revisions to the voters in respect to both taxation and expenditures. The appellees do not contend that these proposed amendments deal with taxation, but according to the appellees, construing subsections 6(d) and 6(e) together, TBRC has the power to propose constitutional amendments regarding state revenue expenditures because expenditures are encompassed within the state budgetary process. The circuit court agreed and entered its judgment for the appellees.

We disagree. We find the appellees' and the circuit court's construction of section 6(e) to be contrary to the plain and unambiguous language of the constitutional provision. While we recognize that sub section 6(d) sets forth numerous subjects for TBRC to review and study, including "the state budgetary process, the revenue needs and expenditure processes of the state, the appropriateness of the tax structure of the state, *and* governmental productivity and efficiency," *see* art. XI, § 6(d), Fla. Const. (emphasis added), we do not conclude that subsection 6(d) can be construed to authorize TBRC to propose constitutional amendments on these subjects. Rather, based on the review authorized by subsection 6(d), subsection 6(e) sets forth four duties that TBRC is authorized to perform: (1) holding public hearings as necessary; (2) issuing a report relative to results of its review; (3) proposing to the Legislature "recommended statutory changes related to the taxation or *budgetary laws of the state* "; and (4) filing proposed constitutional revisions "dealing with taxation or *the state budgetary process.*" Art. XI, § 6(e), Fla. Const. (emphasis added). The review and study mandated by section 6(d) are for use in performing these four distinct duties.

In construing the authority given to the Commission in respect to its duties, it is important to recognize that subsection 6(e) expressly draws a distinction between TBRC's authority to propose to the Legislature recommendations of statutory changes related to "taxation or budgetary laws," which could include budgetary expenditures, and TBRC's authority to propose constitutional amendments, which is limited to dealing with "the state budgetary process." It is likewise important to note that subsection 6(e) does not use the phrase "deal with taxation or the state budget." We find that the phrase "the state budgetary process" has a meaning distinct from "budgetary laws of the state" and from "state budget." We construe "state budgetary process" to mean the process by which the state budget is developed. Our rules of construction require us to give all words their plain meaning. *Fla. Dep't of Bus. & Prof'l Regulation, Div. of Pari-Mutuel Wagering v. Inv. Corp. of Palm Beach,* 747 So.2d 374, 382 (Fla.1999) ("This Court consistently has adhered to the plain meaning rule in applying statutory and constitutional provisions.").

If this Court were to accept the appellee's view that the term "state budgetary process" includes any matter that addresses either raising revenue or any State expenditure, this definition would read out the word "process." The ordinary meaning of the word "process" is "a series of actions or operations conducing to an end." *Merriam Webster's Collegiate Dictionary* 929 (10th ed.1994). As this term is applied to "state budgetary process," it means the series of steps and actions that are necessary to producing a budget for the state. In other words, as the appellants suggest, it refers to "the structural and procedural aspects of developing and implementing the state budget." Additionally, if we were to accept the appellees' view that "state budgetary process" includes any matter that either raises revenue or involves any state expenditure, it would also render the term "taxation" superfluous since taxation is the raising of revenue.

We conclude that this construction is also consistent with TBRC's rule 1.005 (Functions and Duties), which provides in pertinent part:

> The "state budgetary process" means *the manner in which* every level of government in the state expends funds, incurs debt, assesses needs, acquires financial information, and administers its fiscal affairs, and includes the legislative appropriation process and the budgetary practices and principles of all agencies and subdivisions of the state involved in financial planning, determining, implementing, administering, and reviewing governmental programs and services.

See TBRC Rule 1.005 (2008) (emphasis added). The phrase "the manner in which" modifies the rest of TBRC's own definition of the term.

This plain meaning definition is also consistent with how "state budgeting process" is used in article III, section 19 of the Florida Constitution (entitled "State Budgeting, Planning and Appropriations Processes"), and Chapter 216, Florida Statutes, which sets forth various planning and budgeting processes. Article III, section 19, sets forth a detailed process whereby the State can ensure better fiscal responsibility, including provisions that: (a) direct an annual budget and planning process; (b) provide for the format for appropriations bills; (c) require agencies to submit planning documents and budget requests for legislative review; (d) mandate a seventy-two-hour public review period for appropriations bills; (e) require a final budget report; (f) impose further regulations on the creation of trust funds; and (g) direct the creation of a reserve fund to be used for revenue shortfalls and emergencies, among numerous other provisions. Pursuant to article III, section 19(a), which provides that "[g]eneral law shall prescribe the adoption of annual state budgetary . . . processes," the Legislature set out the general state budget process in chapter 216 of the Florida Statutes. Perusal of the detailed provisions of both article III, section 19, and chapter 216 of the statutes makes clear that the phrase "budgetary process" refers to the structural and procedural aspects of budget development. For example, section 216.015(3) sets forth the capital facilities planning and budgeting process and provides that "the process" includes:

> (a) An inventory of current facilities owned, leased, rented, or otherwise occupied by any agency of the state or the judicial branch;

1 · AN INTRODUCTION TO STUDYING THE FLORIDA CONSTITUTION

(b) An assessment of current population, economic, social, physical, and environmental trends and conditions that relate to public facilities;

(c) A determination of future demographic conditions deemed most appropriate and likely for this state and of a set of goals and objectives;

(d) A determination of unmet needs by comparing existing facilities to goals and objectives;

(e) A strategic matching of funding options and facility needs to ensure the most effective development strategy; and

(f) A management structure that maintains, operates, repairs, renovates, and replaces capital facilities to obtain the maximum value for each public dollar spent.

§ 216.015(3), Fla. Stat. (2007).

TBRC is a constitutional body that has only those powers which were specifically designated to it. If certain powers are not explicitly provided to the Commission, this Court cannot add to the constitutional limitations by expanding its authority beyond the provisions stated. *See Southern Armored Serv., Inc. v. Mason,* 167 So.2d 848, 850 (Fla.1964) (holding that a commission is a body with special and limited power and "[i]t can only exercise the power expressly or impliedly granted to it and any reasonable doubt of existence of any power must be resolved against the exercise thereof").

We find that the plain reading of the term "state budgetary process" is clear and unambiguous-TBRC's jurisdiction to propose constitutional amendments does not extend to a subject solely because the State will expend funds on that subject or because it could affect the State's expenditures. TBRC's authority to propose constitutional amendments directly to the voters is constitutionally limited to two scenarios: if the proposal addresses taxation or the process by which the State's budget is procedurally composed and considered by the Legislature. This interpretation does not render the Commission powerless. In fact, providing TBRC with the authority to propose constitutional amendments addressing taxation alone is a significant ability, in addition to its authority to directly propose constitutional amendments relating to the state budgetary process. Furthermore, TBRC has the authority to issue a report addressing any of its findings, including recommendations that the constitution be revised relative to expenditure issues and to recommend that the Legislature make statutory changes related to the taxation or budgetary laws of the state, which could include budgetary expenditures.

In the first challenged proposed amendment, Amendment 7 would amend article I, section 3, of the Florida Constitution, as follows:

SECTION 3. Religious freedom. — There shall be no law respecting the establishment of religion or prohibiting or penalizing the free exercise thereof. Religious freedom shall not justify practices inconsistent with public morals, peace or safety. *An individual or entity may not be barred from participating in any public program because of religion.* ~~No revenue of the state or any political subdivision or agency thereof shall ever be taken from the public treasury directly or indirectly in aid of any church, sect, or religious denomination or in aid of any sectarian institution.~~

(New language is indicated by underlining, and deleted language is struck through.) This proposal clearly does not address taxation or the state budgetary process as we have construed that provision.

In the next proposal, Amendment 9 would modify article IX, regarding education, by modifying article IX, section 1(a) to state as follows:

SECTION 1: Public *funding of* education. —

(a) The education of children is a fundamental value of the people of the State of Florida. It is, therefore, a paramount duty of the state to make adequate provision for the education of all children residing within its borders. *This duty shall be fulfilled, at a minimum and not exclusively, through adequate* provision ~~shall be made~~ by law for a uniform, efficient, safe, secure, and high quality system of free public schools that allows students to obtain a high quality education and for the establishment, maintenance, and operation of institutions of higher learning and other public education programs that the needs of the people may require. *Nothing in this subsection creates an entitlement to a publicly-financed private program.*

Proposed Amendment 9 would also add a new section 8 to article IX:

SECTION 8. Requiring sixty-five percent of school funding for classroom instruction. — At least sixty-five percent of the school funding received by school districts shall be spent on classroom instruction, rather than on administration. Classroom instruction and administration shall be defined by law. The legislature may also address differences in administrative expenditures by district for necessary services, such as transportation and food services. Funds for capital outlay shall not be included in the calculation required by this section.

Again, the appellees assert that TBRC has the authority to propose this constitutional amendment because it addresses a constitutional limitation on expenditures and is thus part of the state budgetary process since expenditures are a part of the process. For the reasons addressed above, as this amendment involves merely specific expenditures and not the budgetary process, we hold that TBRC exceeded its constitutional authority in proposing Amendment 9.

Conclusion

For the reasons set forth above, we conclude that the Taxation and Budget Reform Commission exceeded its authority in proposing these two amendments. Accordingly, we reverse the final judgment entered by the circuit court. The Secretary of State and all persons and entities acting under his direction are hereby enjoined from placing proposed Amendments 7 and 9 on the November 2008 general election ballot. We direct that no later than September 4, 2008, the trial court enter final judgment for appellants. No motion for rehearing will be entertained.

It is so ordered.

QUINCE, C.J., ANSTEAD, PARIENTE, LEWIS, and BELL, JJ., and CANTERO, Senior Justice, concur.

LEWIS, J., concurs with an opinion, in which ANSTEAD and PARIENTE, JJ., concur.

[The concurring opinion of Justice Lewis is omitted.]

The canons of construction are generally applicable in interpreting statutes or construing constitutional provisions. One such rule is the doctrine of *ejusdem generis*. Under this doctrine, where a general term is found in conjunction with a series of very specific terms, the meaning of the general term will be considered as restricted by the more specific terms.

Graham v. Haridopolos

108 So. 3d 597 (Fla. 2013)

PARIENTE, J.

The issue presented to the Court in this case is one of constitutional construction: whether the Legislature or the constitutionally created Board of Governors has the power to control the setting of and appropriating for the expenditure of tuition and fees for the Florida university system under article IX, section 7(d), of the Florida Constitution. . . .

. . .

Facts and Background

Prior to 2001, the Board of Regents, a statutorily created entity, managed the state university system under the control and supervision of the State Board of Education. The Board of Regents was abolished as of July 1, 2001, by the Legislature and its powers were transferred to a new entity known as the Florida Board of Education. [Footnote omitted.]

In apparent response to the Legislature's actions, a constitutional amendment was proposed by citizen initiative that "sought to amend the Florida Constitution to create a system of governance for the state university system." *In re Advisory Op. to Atty. Gen. ex rel. Local Trustees,* 819 So.2d 725, 727 (Fla.2002). In November 2002, the voters approved the proposed amendment to article IX of the Florida Constitution, establishing "a system of governance for the state university system of Florida" and creating the Board of Governors to "operate, regulate, control, and be fully responsible for the management of the whole university system." *See* art. IX, § 7(a), (d), Fla. Const.

* * *

Analysis

. . .

The sole issue presented in this case is whether the 2002 constitutional amendment creating the Board of Governors transferred authority over the setting of and appropriating for the expenditure of tuition and fees from the Legislature to the Board, and whether the challenged statutes exercising control over tuition and fees are therefore facially unconstitutional. "Because the issue before the Court involves the determination of a statute's constitutionality and the interpretation of a provision of the Florida Constitution, it is a question of law subject to de novo review." *Crist v. Fla. Ass'n of Criminal Def. Lawyers, Inc. (FACDL)*, 978 So.2d 134, 139 (Fla.2008). Although the Court's review is de novo, "statutes come clothed with a presumption of constitutionality and must be construed whenever possible to effect a constitutional outcome." *Id.*

"When reviewing constitutional provisions, this Court follows principles parallel to those of statutory interpretation. First and foremost, this Court must examine the actual language used in the Constitution. If that language is clear, unambiguous, and addresses the matter in issue, then it must be enforced as written." *Id.* at 139–40 (internal quotation marks and citations omitted). "When interpreting constitutional provisions, this Court endeavors to ascertain the will of the people in passing the amendment." *In re Senate Joint Resolution of Legislative Apportionment 1176*, 83 So.3d 597, 599 (Fla.2012). "In accord with those tenets of constitutional construction, this Court 'endeavors to construe a constitutional provision consistent with the intent of the framers and the voters.'" *Id.* at 614 (quoting *Zingale v. Powell*, 885 So.2d 277, 282 (Fla.2004)). "Moreover, in construing multiple constitutional provisions addressing a similar subject, the provisions 'must be read in pari materia to ensure a consistent and logical meaning that gives effect to each provision.'" *Caribbean Conservation Corp. v. Fla. Fish & Wildlife Conservation Comm'n*, 838 So.2d 492, 501 (Fla.2003) (quoting *Advisory Op. to the Gov.–1996 Amend. 5 (Everglades)*, 706 So.2d 278, 281 (Fla.1997)).

Both parties agree that the amendment at issue did not alter the Legislature's article VII, section 1, appropriations power. "Appropriation" is defined as a "legal authorization to make expenditures for specific purposes within the amounts authorized by law." § 216.011, Fla. Stat. (2007). The Florida Constitution in article VII, section 1, vests in the Legislature the constitutional duty and power to raise and appropriate state funds:

> (c) No money shall be drawn from the treasury except in pursuance of appropriation made by law.

> (d) Provision shall be made by law for raising sufficient revenue to defray the expenses of the state for each fiscal period.

Art. VII, § 1, Fla. Const.; *see also Chiles v. Children A, B, C, D, E, & F*, 589 So.2d 260, 265 (Fla.1991) (stating that based on article VII, sections 1(c) and 1(d), "this Court has long held that the power to appropriate state funds is legislative and is to be exercised only through duly enacted statutes"). Article VII, section 1(c), of the Florida Constitution gives the Legislature "the exclusive power of deciding how, when, and for what purpose the public funds shall be applied in carrying on the government." *Republican Party of Fla. v. Smith,* 638 So.2d 26, 28 (Fla.1994) (quoting *State ex rel. Kurz v. Lee,* 121 Fla. 360, 384, 163 So. 859, 868 (1935)).

. . .

Because the issue presented in this case involves constitutional construction, we begin with the actual language of the constitutional provision. *Caribbean Conservation Corp.,* 838 So.2d at 501 ("[A]ny inquiry into the proper interpretation of a constitutional provision must begin with an examination of that provision's explicit language." (citation and internal quotation marks omitted)). Article IX, section 7, of the Florida Constitution states that its purpose is to "establish a system of governance for the state university system of Florida." Art. IX, § 7(a), Fla. Const. It provides for the Board of Governors, which "shall operate, regulate, control, and be fully responsible for the management of the whole university system." Art. IX, § 7(d), Fla. Const. The provision then lists examples: "These responsibilities shall include, but not be limited to, defining the distinctive mission of each constituent university and its articulation with free public schools and community colleges, ensuring the well-planned coordination and operation of the system, and avoiding wasteful duplication of facilities or programs." *Id.* The provision also expressly states that the Board's "management shall be subject to the powers of the legislature to appropriate for the expenditure of funds, and the board shall account for such expenditures as provided by law." *Id.*

The Petitioners contend that the language of the amendment constituted an "all-inclusive" transfer of power to the Board, transferring control over every aspect of universities, with the exception of the Legislature's power of appropriations over the general revenue portion of university funding. However, contrary to the Petitioners' position, the language of article IX, section 7, does not plainly transfer to the Board the Legislature's control over tuition and fees, but instead grants to the Board the responsibility to "operate," "regulate," "control," and "be fully responsible for the management of the whole university system." Art. IX, § 7(d), Fla. Const. Nothing within the language of article IX, section 7, indicates that it was intended to transfer power over tuition and fees to the Board. Simply put, the language of article IX, section 7, is not "clear" or "unambiguous" and does not expressly "address[ ] the matter in issue." *FACDL,* 978 So.2d at 140. We therefore turn to principles of construction, always endeavoring to construe the constitutional provision "in a manner consistent with the intent of the framers and voters." *W. Fla. Reg'l Med. Ctr., Inc. v. See,* 79 So.3d 1, 9 (Fla.2012); *FACDL,* 978 So.2d at 140.

The canon of construction known as *ejusdem generis* is instructive in construing the meaning of "operate, regulate, control, and be fully responsible for the management of the whole university system." Art. IX, § 7(d), Fla. Const. Under this canon, "when a general phrase follows a list of specifics, the general phrase will be interpreted to include only items of the same type as those listed." *State v. Hearns,* 961

So.2d 211, 219 (Fla.2007). Employing this canon of constitutional construction, the Board's responsibilities in operating, regulating, controlling, and being responsible for the management of the university system include responsibilities that are executive and administrative in nature, such as "defining the distinctive mission of each constituent university" and "avoiding wasteful duplication of facilities or programs." Art. IX, §7(d), Fla. Const. The ability to set and appropriate for the expenditure of tuition and fees is of a wholly different nature than the executive and administrative functions delineated in the constitutional provision and therefore is not included in the meaning of "operate, regulate, control, and be fully responsible for the management of the whole university system." Art. IX, §7(d), Fla. Const.

* * *

Conclusion

For the foregoing reasons, we hold that the constitutional source of the Legislature's authority to set and appropriate for the expenditure of tuition and fees derives from its power to raise revenue and appropriate for the expenditure of state funds. Nothing within the language of article IX, section 7, of the Florida Constitution indicates an intent to transfer this quintessentially legislative power to the Board of Governors. Accordingly, we conclude that the challenged statutes by which the Legislature has exercised control over these funds are facially constitutional and approve the First District's decision.

It is so ordered.

QUINCE, LABARGA, and PERRY, JJ., concur.

LABARGA, J., concurs with an opinion. [The opinion of Justice Labarga is omitted.]

POLSTON, C.J., and LEWIS and CANADY, JJ., concur in result.

———————

Another rule of construction and interpretation is the doctrine of *expressio unius est exclusio alterius*. Literally, this means the expression of one thing is the exclusion of another. Although the doctrine is perhaps a mainstay of the rules of statutory construction, it has a more limited application when a constitutional provision is being construed or interpreted.[56] The following case is an application of the doctrine (or perhaps more accurately, a refusal to apply the doctrine).

———————

56. *Taylor v. Dorsey*, 19 So. 2d 876, 881 (Fla. 1944) (by inference).

Nichols v. State ex rel. Bolon

177 So. 2d 467 (Fla. 1965)

O'CONNELL, Justice.

In this interlocutory appeal we are asked to declare unconstitutional that portion of Chapter 29279, Special Acts of 1953, which requires that the City Commissioners of the City of Melbourne shall have been "* * * freeholder electors of the city for at least one year immediately preceding their qualifying for office * * *."

Appellant, Ted Nichols, and appellee, Leslie Bolon, were opposing candidates for the office of City Commissioner of the City of Melbourne. Nichols was elected, but before he was seated Bolon brought suit in circuit court challenging Nichols' qualifications. On petition of Bolon the circuit court issued a temporary order enjoining the City from administering the oath of office to Nichols. Nichols moved to dissolve the injunction on the ground that the provision of the city charter, inserted therein by ch. 29279, supra, was unconstitutional. The chancellor denied the motion, holding the statute to be valid. This appeal followed.

It is not disputed here that Nichols had not been a freeholder elector of the City for one year prior to his qualifying for office.

Mr. Nichols' argument seems to be that Section 5, Article VI of the Florida Constitution, F.S.A., which directs the Legislature to exclude from "every office of honor, power, trust or profit" all persons who have been convicted of certain crimes, operates, by the principle of *expressio unius est exclusio alterius*, to prohibit the legislature from establishing any other qualifications for any office, including municipal offices.

This contention is not sound. Neither precedent nor reason supports it. This court dealt with the precise question in the early case of State ex rel. Moodie v. Bryan, 1905, 50 Fla. 293, 39 So. 929. This court there said:

> "Section 5 of Article 6 of the Constitution * * * does not deal with the general subject of disqualifications of persons for office, but it simply makes it the duty of the Legislature to enact the necessary laws to exclude from every office within the state the persons falling within the classes therein named. It does not undertake to make such enumerated persons the only persons who may be excluded from offices to be established by the Legislature. * * * [This section] grants no power or authority, but simply prescribes a duty, requiring the Legislature to enact laws excluding from every office the persons enumerated therein; but the language used cannot be said to forbid the Legislature from enacting laws excluding other persons than those named from statutory offices. The principle of the maxim, 'Expressio unius est exclusio alterius,' should be applied with great caution to the provisions of an organic law relating to the legislative department, and we are of the opinion that it is not applicable here."

* * *

The chancellor was correct in holding that the legislature has the power to impose qualifications for municipal office. The qualification in question is not unreasonable.

The order appealed from is affirmed.

THORNAL, C. J., and THOMAS, ROBERTS, DREW, CALDWELL and ERVIN, JJ., concur.

A Constitution should be interpreted in its entirety, with each provision being interpreted so as to harmonize, if possible, with each other provision of the Constitution. Further, amendments should be construed so as to harmonize with existing constitutional provisions.[57] However, where this is not possible, the amendment, being the latest expression of the will of the electorate, must be given priority.

Frequently, a court will look to how another branch of government has interpreted or applied a constitutional provision and then defer to the interpretation of the coordinate branch of government. The following case is a classic illustration of the court deferring to both contemporaneous and non-contemporaneous interpretations by the Legislature of constitutional provisions.

Greater Loretta Improvement Association v. State ex rel. Boone

234 So. 2d 665 (Fla. 1970)

ADKINS, Justice.

This is a direct appeal from a summary final judgment declaring Fla.Stat., §849.093, F.S.A. (Bingo Statute) to be unconstitutional and void and enjoining appellant from conducting bingo games. [This statute was repealed in 1992.]

This case involves the meaning of the word "lottery" as used in Sec. 23, art. 3, Fla .Const. (1885), F.S.A. so as to determine whether the Bingo statute is compatible or in conflict with the Constitution.

* * *

In 1832, only four years after a lottery had been authorized for [raising funds for] Union Academy, the Florida Legislature banned all gaming. Sec. 1, Acts of the Legislative Council (1839); modified Ch. 75, Laws of Florida (1846); Ch. 542, Acts of Florida (1868).

In 1868, the anti-lottery provision was inserted in the new Constitution. Immediately after, the Legislature enacted new laws outlawing lotteries and related activities. Ch. X of Ch. 1637, Acts of Florida (1868).

---

57. *State v. Div. of Bond Fin. of the Dep't of Gen. Servs.*, 278 So. 2d 614 (1973). This case appears earlier in this chapter and illustrates these principles.

1 · AN INTRODUCTION TO STUDYING THE FLORIDA CONSTITUTION

Ten years later, the Legislature imposed a license tax on certain gambling games, including "keno." Ch. 3099, Sec. 11, Laws of Florida (1879). The act of 1868 forbidding lotteries was not disturbed.

* * *

It is clear that the Legislature, in 1879, considered that the bingo-like game of Keno was not forbidden under the Florida anti-lottery provision of the Constitution.

In 1881, this Court faced the question whether the Legislature had power to impose a license on this game resembling bingo. Overby v. State, 18 Fla. 178 (1881). The case arose when a Jacksonville licensee was arrested for violating the anti-gambling law.

The Court held that keno is a gambling game, but went on to say (at page 183) that the Legislature by authorizing licenses to operate keno games "legalized this game of 'keno' and made it, by the license tax imposed, a source of revenue to the State * * *." No constitutional arguments were presented. Overby's conviction was set aside, as were the convictions of three other licensees. Hazen v. State, 18 Fla. 184 (1881).

The correctness of this decision was verified by the Legislature in the same year, when it expressly repealed all laws in conflict with its licensing statute for gambling. Ch. 3277, Acts of Florida, 1881.

In 1885, four years after *Overby, supra,* the exact language of the anti-lottery provision of the 1868 Constitution was written into a new Constitution (Sec. 23, Art. III, Const. (1885)). By establishing rules of construction, the Overby decision retained its authority under the new Constitution.

Therefore, since the Florida Legislature was empowered in 1879 to legalize and license the bingo-like game of keno, it was empowered in 1967 to legalize bingo. Precedent commands this conclusion.

* * *

The situation then, as it presents itself in connection with our constitutional provision, is at least that by the decisions of the courts of Florida and other jurisdiction the word "lottery" may have either of several meanings, and that either is reasonable and possible. In such a situation, where a constitutional provision may well have either or several meanings, it is a fundamental rule of constitutional construction that, if the Legislature has by statute adopted one, its action in this respect is well-nigh, if not completely, controlling. As stated in *Fargo v. Powers (D.C.),* 220 F. 697, 709, it is said:

> "If the constitutional provisions in question are susceptible of two constructions — one being that contended for by complainants, the other that taken by the Legislature — the action of the Legislature in adopting one of those constructions and enacting a statute carrying it into effect, as thus construed, must be deemed conclusive. That rule is: 'That the acts of a state Legislature are to be presumed constitutional until the contrary is shown; and it is only when they manifestly infringe some provision of the Constitution that they can be declared void for that reason. In case of doubt,

every presumption, not clearly inconsistent with the language or subject-matter, is to be made in favor of the constitutionality of the act. The power of declaring laws unconstitutional should be exercised with extreme caution and never where serious doubt exists as to the conflict.'"

In *Jasper v. Mease Manor, Inc.* (Fla. 1968), 208 So.2d 821, this Court sustained a statute defining the word "charitable" as used in the Florida Constitution even though such definition conflicted with earlier decisions by this Court. Similarly, in *Ammerman v. Markham* (Fla.1969), 222 So.2d 423, this Court upheld a legislative definition of the terms "real property" and "dwelling house" as used in the Constitution even though such definitions were in conflict with earlier decisions of this Court.

* * *

When the Legislature has once construed the Constitution, for the courts then to place a different construction upon it means that they must declare void the action of the Legislature. It is no small matter for one branch of the government to annul the formal exercise by another of power committed to the latter. The courts should not and must not annul, as contrary to the Constitution, a statute passed by the Legislature, unless it can be said of the statute that it positively and certainly is opposed to the Constitution. This is elementary.

The Bingo law under attack was enacted by the Legislature in 1967, during the regular session of the Legislature. A proposed Constitution was under consideration at the time, and during the special session of June 24–July 3, 1968, the Legislature passed a joint resolution proposing a new Constitution. This Constitution, which was adopted by the people in 1968, contained the following provision as Art. X, §7:

> "*Lotteries*, other than the types of pari-mutuel pools authorized by law as of the effective date of this constitution, are hereby prohibited in this state." (emphasis supplied)

Although this provision has no application to the case *sub judice*, the Bingo law may be considered as a contemporaneous construction of the word "lottery" as used in the Constitution. There is a strong presumption that such contemporaneous construction rightly interprets the meaning and intention of a constitutional provision. 16 Am.Jur.2d, Constitutional Law, §85. In doubtful cases such a Legislative construction should, and ordinarily will, be followed, unless it is manifestly erroneous. 16 C.J.S. Constitutional Law §33.

* * *

Although this case was filed under the 1885 Constitution, the 1967 Legislature which passed the "Bingo" statute also functioned under that Constitution and many of the members of that Legislature were instrumental in the writing and passage of the 1969 Constitution. It appears that when the "Lottery" section was placed under the general section entitled "Miscellaneous" in the new Constitution, that Bingo, together with horse racing and jai alai, was an exception to the prohibition of lotteries.

Sec. 7, art. X, Fla.Const. (1968) reads:

1 · AN INTRODUCTION TO STUDYING THE FLORIDA CONSTITUTION

"Lotteries, other than types of pari-mutuel pools authorized by law as of the effective date of this constitution, are hereby prohibited in this state."

* * *

Although the term pari-mutuel is usually considered a method of betting on horse racing, it should be noted that this form of betting has been authorized for dog racing and Jai Alai. At the horse tracks, dog tracks and frontons, all the money paid for gambling tickets are placed in a common fund and paid to the winners less certain portions reserved for taxes to the State and fees due the track or fronton for operating expenses and for profit. The greater amount invested in tickets, the greater amounts one may win if his choice is correct.

Bingo is similar. The player may usually purchase and play on as many cards as may be desired. The greater amount invested in cards the greater the chance of winning. In both racing events and in Bingo games the hope of winning money prizes is not the only motive for attendance. In both instances entertainment, recreation, and social relations are factors of concern to many and just as important as the process of participating in the betting.

* * *

In view of the fact that Bingo could be considered the same type of gambling as described in the definition of pari-mutuel, the game of Bingo was "authorized by law as of the effective date of the Constitution of 1968."

* * *

The Legislature, in its wisdom, has seen fit to permit this form of recreation for those unable to participate in the uncertainties of the authorized pari-mutuel pools, and, at the same time, has allowed worthy organizations to receive the benefits. We should abide by the will of the Legislature in the construction of the Constitution.

The judgment and order of the Circuit Court is reversed and the cause is remanded with instructions to enter final judgment for the defendant.

ROBERTS and BOYD, JJ., concur.

ERVIN, C. J., concurs with opinion.

CARLTON, J., dissents with opinion.

DREW and THORNAL, JJ., dissent and concur with CARLTON, J.

[The opinions of Chief Justice Ervin, Justice Carlton, and Justice Thornal, are omitted.]

———————

In *American Bankers Insurance Company v. Chiles*,[58] the Supreme Court found that when a constitutional change became effective in one year and the legislature in the next year amended a statute in a subject area controlled by the amended

———————

58. 675 So. 2d 922, 924 (Fla. 1996).

constitutional provision, "contemporaneous construction" had occurred. Referring back to the *Greater Loretta* bingo case, the *Chiles* case appears to broaden the scope of contemporaneous interpretation or construction.

In *Department of Environmental Protection v. Millender*,[59] the Supreme Court provided a summary, of sorts, on how constitutional provisions are interpreted. Although it is not complete, the reader may find it helpful:

> ... In construing article X, section 16, the trial judge was obviously attempting to ascertain and give effect to the intent of the drafters and those who voted on the amendment. Intent is traditionally discerned
>
>> from historical precedent, from the present facts, from common sense, and from an examination of the purpose the provision was intended to accomplish and the evils sought to [be] prevented. Furthermore, we may look to the explanatory materials available to the people as predicate for their decision as persuasive of their intent.
>
> *Plante v. Smathers*, 372 So.2d 933, 936 (Fla. 1979) (citation omitted). The amendment should also be construed as a whole in order to ascertain the general purpose and meaning of each part; each subsection, sentence, and clause must be read in light of the others to form a congruous whole so as not to render any language superfluous. Less latitude is permitted when construing constitutional provisions because it is presumed that they have been more carefully and deliberately framed than statutes. *City of Jacksonville v. Continental Can Co.*, 113 Fla. 168, 172, 151 So. 488, 489 (1933).

---

59. 666 So. 2d 882, 885–886 (Fla. 1996).

Chapter 2

Separation of Powers

A. In General

Fla. Const. art. II, § 3

Branches of government. — The powers of the state government shall be divided into legislative, executive and judicial branches. No person belonging to one branch shall exercise any powers appertaining to either of the other branches unless expressly provided herein.

The concept of separation of powers as a check on overall governmental power is traditional in the American system of government. Consider the words of Justices Sutherland (majority opinion) and Holmes (dissenting opinion) in *Springer v. Government of the Philippine Islands:*[1]

Mr. Justice SUTHERLAND delivered the opinion of the Court.

* * *

It may be stated then, as a general rule inherent in the American constitutional system, that, unless otherwise expressly provided or incidental to the powers conferred, the Legislature cannot exercise either executive or judicial power; the executive cannot exercise either legislative or judicial power; the judiciary cannot exercise either executive or legislative power. The existence in the various Constitutions of occasional provisions expressly giving to one of the departments powers which by their nature otherwise would fall within the general scope of the authority of another department emphasizes, rather than casts doubt upon, the generally inviolate character of this basic rule.

* * *

Mr. Justice HOLMES (dissenting).[2] The great ordinances of the Constitution do not establish and divide fields of black and white. Even the more specific of them are found to terminate in a penumbra shading gradually from one extreme to the other. Property must not be taken without compensation, but with the help of a phrase (the police power), some property may be

---

1. 277 U.S. 189 (1928).

2. Speaking in another context in *Missouri, Kansas & Texas Railway Company of Texas v. May*, 194 U.S. 267, 270 (1904), Justice Holmes said that while recognizing the basic rule, he would allow considerable leeway because, "[s]ome play must be allowed for the joints of the machine . . ."

taken or destroyed for public use without paying for it, if you do not take too much. When we come to the fundamental distinctions it is still more obvious that they must be received with a certain latitude or our government could not go on.

To make the rule of conduct applicable to an individual who but for such action would be free from it is to legislate — yet it is what the judges do whenever they determine which of two competing principles of policy shall prevail. . . .

[Here Justice Holmes lists a number of additional exceptions to the rule of separation of powers.]

It does not seem to need argument to show that however we may disguise it by veiling words we do not and cannot carry out the distinction between legislative and executive action with mathematical precision and divide the branches into watertight compartments, were it ever so desirable to do so, which I am far from believing that it is, or that the Constitution requires.

Consider also the following from *Dreyer v. Illinois*:[3]

. . . 'When we speak,' said Story, 'of a separation of the three great departments of government, and maintain that that separation is indispensable to public liberty, we are to understand this maxim in a limited sense. It is not meant to affirm that they must be kept wholly and entirely distinct, and have no common link of connection or dependence, the one upon the other, in the slightest degree. The true meaning is, that the whole power of one of these departments should not be exercised by the same hands which possess the whole power of either of the other departments; and that such exercise of the whole would subvert the principles of a free Constitution.' Story, Const. 5th ed. 393. Again: 'Indeed, there is not a single constitution of any state in the Union, which does not practically embrace some acknowledgment of the maxim, and at the same time some admixture of powers constituting an exception to it.' *Id.* 395.

The Holmes dissent points out the inherent dilemma in separation of powers. This dilemma has continued to cause problems. At the same time, this uncertainty is a potential source of power for the judicial branch of government in the exercise of judicial review.

Unlike the United States Constitution, the Florida Constitution does not totally rely on inferences of separation of powers from other constitutional provisions. Article II, Section 3, of the Florida Constitution specifically creates three branches of government and prohibits one branch from exercising the powers of the other two branches but recognizes that exceptions to the general rule can be created.

---

3. 187 U.S. 71, 84 (1902).

The separation of powers doctrine remains viable in Florida and encompasses two fundamental prohibitions: (1) that no branch may encroach upon the powers of another, and (2) that no branch may delegate to another branch its constitutionally assigned powers.[4] Because the Florida Constitution does not contain an exhaustive list of each branch's powers, frequently the single most difficult issue confronting the court is characterizing a particular power as appertaining to one branch of government. Consequently, the characterization of a power as belonging to a particular branch of government is outcome-determinative of the separations of power issue. In *Florida Association of Professional Lobbyists, Inc. v. Division of Legislative Information Services*,[5] the Florida Supreme Court addressed the issue of unassigned powers in the context of a statute enacted by the Legislature regulating and disciplining lobbyists. The Florida Supreme Court stated:

> The Florida Constitution does not explicitly prohibit any of the functions set out in the Act. Although the constitution does not give the Legislature the exclusive power to discipline lobbyists, it also does not prevent it from doing so. As this Court has noted, "the state constitution does not exhaustively list each branch's powers." *Fla. House of Representatives v. Crist*, 999 So.2d 601, 611 (Fla. 2008). Rather,
>
> > the powers of the respective branches "are those so defined . . . or such as are inherent or so recognized by immemorial governmental usage, and which involve the exercise of primary and independent will, discretion, and judgment, subject not to the control of another department, but only to the limitations imposed by the state and federal Constitutions." [Each branch has] "the inherent right to accomplish all objects naturally within the orbit of that department, not expressly limited by the fact of the existence of a similar power elsewhere or the express limitations in the constitution."

Id. at 611 (citation omitted) (quoting *State v. Atlantic Coast Line R.R.*, 47 So. 969, 974 (Fla.1908); *Sun Ins. Office v. Clay*, 133 So. 2d 735, 742 (Fla.1961)). Therefore, since the regulation, discipline, and licensing of lobbyists is not subject to the control of any branch or office, the Legislature is not prohibited from using its own discretion and judgment to accomplish the task. *See State v. Palmer*, 791 So. 2d 1181, 1183 (Fla. 1st DCA 2001) ("[A] branch of government is prohibited from exercising a power only when that power has been constitutionally assigned exclusively to another branch; and the separation of powers doctrine does not contemplate that every governmental activity must be classified as belonging exclusively to a single branch."). . . .

---

4. *Chiles v. Children A, B, C, D, E, & F*, 589 So. 2d 260, 264 (Fla. 1991).

5. 7 So. 3d 511 (Fla. 2009).

B. Encroachment by One Branch of Government on the Powers of Another Branch

In *Walker v. Bentley*,[6] Judge Lazzara opined:

> The citizens of this state have expressly codified this doctrine [separation of powers] in article II, section 3 of the Florida Constitution, thereby adopting one of the doctrine's fundamental prohibitions that "no branch may encroach upon the powers of another." *Chiles v. Children A, B, C, D, E, and F*, 589 So.2d 260, 264 (Fla.1991). To achieve this constitutional goal of separation of governmental powers, the courts of this state are charged with diligently safeguarding the powers vested in one branch from encroachment by another. *Pepper v. Pepper*, 66 So.2d 280 (Fla.1953).

Simple math would indicate that there being three branches of government, and since each branch may in a given set of circumstances infringe upon the power of the others, there are six general types of infringement. The cases that follow in this section are organized into those six categories. The case or cases presented in each category are *not exhaustive* of that category, but merely illustrative.

1. Encroachment by the Judicial Branch on the Power of the Legislative Branch

a. Judicial Modification of the Common Law

The Florida Supreme Court in *State v. Ashley*[7] said:

> Under Florida's constitutional form of government, no branch of state government can arrogate to itself powers that properly inhere in a separate branch. [Footnote omitted.] ... This Court cannot abrogate willy-nilly a centuries-old principle of the common law—which is grounded in the wisdom of experience and has been adopted by the legislature—and install in its place a contrary rule bristling with red flags and followed by no other court in the nation. As we have said time and again, the making of social policy is a matter within the purview of the legislature—not this Court:
>
>> [O]f the three branches of government, the judiciary is the least capable of receiving public input and resolving broad public policy questions based on a societal consensus.
>
> *Shands Teaching Hospital & Clinics, Inc. v. Smith*, 497 So.2d 644, 646 (Fla.1986).

---

6. 660 So. 2d 313, 320 (Fla. 2d Dist. Ct. App. 1995), *aff'd*, 678 So. 2d 1265 (Fla. 1996).
7. 701 So. 2d 338, 342–343 (Fla. 1997).

In another case, *In re T.A.C.P.*,[8] the Florida Supreme Court wrote:

> ... Alterations of the common law, while rarely entertained or allowed, are within this Court's prerogative. *E.g., Hoffman v. Jones*, 280 So.2d 431 (Fla.1973). However, the rule we follow is that the common law will not be altered or expanded unless demanded by public necessity, *Coastal Petroleum Co. v. Mobil Oil Corp.*, 583 So.2d 1022, 1025 (Fla.1991), or where required to vindicate fundamental rights. *Haag v. State*, 591 So.2d 614, 618 (Fla.1992). ...

The Courts of Florida have also held:

> (1) A statute passed in derogation of the common law must be narrowly construed in favor of the broadest possible retention of the pre-existing common law rule. *Thornber v. City of Ft. Walton Beach*, 568 So.2d 914 (Fla.1990); *Graham v. Edwards*, 472 So.2d 803 (Fla. 3d DCA 1985), *reviewed denied*, 482 So. 2d 348 (Fla.1986)."[9]

and

> (2) Under our rules of statutory construction, a statute will not displace the common law unless the legislature expressly indicates an intention to do so. *Carlile v. Game & Fresh Water Fish Commission*, 354 So.2d 362 (Fla.1977). As we have explained:
>
>> Statutes ... will not be interpreted to displace the common law further than is clearly necessary. Rather, the courts will infer that such a statute was not intended to make any alteration other than was specified and plainly pronounced. A statute, therefore, designed to change the common law rule must speak in clear, unequivocal terms, for the presumption is that no change in the common law is intended unless the statute is explicit in this regard.
>
> *Carlile*, 354 So.2d at 364 (quoting 30 Fla. Jur. *Statutes*, § 130 (1974))."[10]

Thus, in *K-Mart*, the Supreme Court found that a common law theory of negligent entrustment of a dangerous instrumentality would support a cause of action against K-Mart because the legislature had not legislated in this area except for criminal statutes which the Court felt did not weaken the common law rule referred to above but actually made it stronger.[11] This situation was distinguished from cases where the legislature had actually precluded by statute the creation of common law causes of action where they did not already exist.[12]

---

8. 609 So. 2d 588, 594 (Fla. 1992).

9. *Godales v. Y.H. Investments, Inc.*, 667 So. 2d 871, 872 (Fla. 3d Dist. Ct. App. 1996) (decision quashed on other grounds, *Y.H. Investments, Inc. v. Godales*, 690 So. 2d 1273 (Fla. 1997)).

10. *Kitchen v. K-Mart Corp.*, 697 So. 2d 1200, 1207–1208 (Fla. 1997).

11. *Id.* at 1202.

12. *Id.* at 1202 and 1203.

However, once the legislature has adopted or at least seems to have adopted a common law definition, the judiciary has taken the position that it cannot modify that definition.

> We acknowledge that the legislature is vested with full authority to amend the burglary statute and to give curtilage any definition believed appropriate, including eliminating the requirement of an enclosure for certain areas, as has been done in other jurisdictions. Just as the legislature has redefined the common-law crime of burglary, it may redefine the concept of curtilage. That is the prerogative of the legislature. *See* Art. III, § 1, Fla. Const. However, we simply do not have the prerogative to redefine curtilage as it was treated under the common law, and, in effect, judicially amend the burglary statute ourselves.[13]

It would then seem that creation of new common law is somewhat rare, but where common law rules exist the legislature may modify or abolish them. However, legislative intent to interfere must be clear and will be narrowly construed. Of course, once a common law rule has been codified, it is beyond the judiciary's power to change it.

Shands Teaching Hospital and Clinics, Inc. v. Smith

480 So. 2d 1366 (Fla. 1st Dist. Ct. App. 1985), *aff'd*, 497 So. 2d 644 (Fla. 1986)

PER CURIAM.

Shands Teaching Hospital appeals the trial court's dismissal of its complaint against Rebecca Smith for payment of medical bills incurred by her husband, now deceased. Although appellee's husband entered into an agreement with the hospital which bound him as guarantor for all charges which were not paid by his insurance company, appellee never agreed in writing to pay for the services provided to her husband. In its order, the trial court conceded that *Manatee Convalescent Center, Inc. v. McDonald*, 392 So.2d 1356 (Fla. 2d DCA 1980) and *Parkway General Hospital, Inc. v. Stern*, 400 So.2d 166 (Fla. 3d DCA 1981), both hold that a wife is responsible for her husband's medical bills, even in the absence of a written contract, but declined to follow that authority because it found that the common law imposes no liability on a wife for the necessaries of her husband; therefore the only way that a wife can be held responsible for the medical bills of her husband is by contract.

The common law doctrine of necessaries, judicially countenanced in this state by our Supreme Court, *Phillips v. Sanchez*, 35 Fla. 187, 17 So. 363 (1895), has never been explicitly altered by constitution, Court or statutes, to require a wife to be subject to an action by a facility which has provided medical services to her husband without her contractual assumption; *see* specifically Article I, Section 2, and Article X, Section 5, Chapters 61 and 708 of the Florida Statutes, and *Gates v. Foley*, 247 So.2d 40 (Fla.1971) (despite the reliance on such authorities by the courts in

---

13. *State v. Hamilton*, 660 So. 2d 1038, 1045 (Fla. 1995).

Manatee Convalescent Center and *Parkway General Hospital*). The lesson to be learned from *Hoffman v. Jones*, 280 So.2d 431, 434 (Fla.1973), is that in the absence of constitutional or statutory authority reflecting a change in established law, the district courts of appeal do not enjoy the prerogative of overruling controlling precedent of the Florida Supreme Court. We also view the issue here as one which is most appropriate for legislative concern.

We therefore affirm the trial court's order, certifying conflict with *Manatee Convalescent Center* and *Parkway General Hospital.*

ERVIN and WENTWORTH, JJ., concur.

BARFIELD, J., concurs with opinion. [This opinion is omitted.]

Connor v. Southwest Florida Regional Medical Center, Inc.

668 So. 2d 175 (Fla. 1995)

GRIMES, Chief Justice.

We have for review *Southwest Florida Regional Medical Center, Inc. v. Connor*, 643 So.2d 681 (Fla. 2d DCA 1994), which certified conflict with the following district court decisions: *Waite v. Leesburg Regional Medical Center, Inc.*, 582 So.2d 789 (Fla. 5th DCA), *review denied*, 592 So.2d 683 (Fla.1991); *Heinemann v. John F. Kennedy Memorial Hospital*, 585 So.2d 1162 (Fla. 4th DCA 1991); *Faulk v. Palm Beach Gardens Community Hospital, Inc.*, 589 So.2d 1029 (Fla. 4th DCA 1991); and *Halifax Hospital Medical Center v. Ryals*, 526 So.2d 1022 (Fla. 5th DCA 1988). We have jurisdiction. Art. V, § 3(b)(4), Fla. Const.

Southwest Florida Regional Medical Center sued Kenneth Connor and his wife Barbara Connor in 1993 for payment of medical services the hospital had rendered to Kenneth. The trial court dismissed the hospital's complaint against Barbara Connor on the ground that she had not executed an agreement to pay for the services rendered to Kenneth Connor. In so doing, the trial court declined to expand the doctrine of necessaries to hold the wife responsible for her husband's medical bills. The district court of appeal reversed and remanded, thereby giving the hospital a cause of action against Barbara Connor.

This case involves what is known as the doctrine of necessaries. At common law, a married woman's legal identity merged with that of her husband, a condition known as coverture. She was unable to own property, enter into contracts, or receive credit. A married woman was therefore dependent upon her husband for maintenance and support, and he was under a corresponding legal duty to provide his wife with food, clothing, shelter, and medical services. The common law doctrine of necessaries mitigated the possible effects of coverture in the event a woman's husband failed to fulfill his support obligation. Under the doctrine, a husband was liable to a third party for any necessaries that the third party provided to his wife. Because the duty of support was uniquely the husband's obligation, and because coverture restricted the wife's access to the economic realm, the doctrine did not impose a similar liability upon married women.

This state recognized the doctrine of necessaries in *Phillips v. Sanchez*, 35 Fla. 187, 17 So. 363 (1895). However, the disability of coverture was later abrogated. Ch. 21977, Laws of Fla. (1943); *see* § 708.08, Fla. Stat. (1993). Further, the responsibilities for alimony between husband and wife are now reciprocal. § 61.08, Fla. Stat. (1993).

The first case to address the question of whether the obligations under the doctrine of necessaries should run both ways was *Manatee Convalescent Center, Inc. v. McDonald*, 392 So.2d 1356 (Fla. 2d DCA 1980). In holding a wife liable for the necessaries of her husband, the court stated:

> Changing times demand reexamination of seemingly unchangeable legal dogma. Equality under law and even handed treatment of the sexes in the modern market place must also carry the burden of responsibility which goes with the benefits.

Id. at 1358. *Accord Parkway Gen. Hosp., Inc. v. Stern*, 400 So.2d 166 (Fla. 3d DCA 1981). However, in *Shands Teaching Hospital & Clinics, Inc. v. Smith*, 497 So.2d 644 (Fla.1986), this Court declined to hold a wife liable for the husband's hospital bills and disapproved *Parkway General Hospital and Manatee Convalescent Center*. In reaching our decision, we first stated that it was an anachronism to hold the husband responsible for the necessaries of the wife without also holding the wife responsible for the necessaries of her husband. We also acknowledge that the respective arguments of both parties had merit. However, we concluded that because the issue had broad social implications and the judiciary was the branch of government least capable of resolving the question, it was best to leave to the legislature the decision of whether to modify the common law doctrine of necessaries. In a footnote we stated that the issue of whether it was a denial of equal protection to hold a husband liable for a wife's necessaries when a wife was not liable for a husband's necessaries was not before us.

Following our opinion in *Shands*, an equal protection issue was raised by a husband who suffered a judgment which required him to pay his wife's hospital bill. *Webb v. Hillsborough County Hosp. Auth.*, 521 So.2d 199 (Fla. 2d DCA 1988). The court ruled that the doctrine of necessaries remained viable so as to obligate a husband to pay for his wife's necessaries and went on to hold that the duty was reciprocal between spouses. In two subsequent decisions, the Fourth District Court of Appeal disagreed with *Webb* and held that a wife could not be held responsible for her husband's necessaries. *Faulk*; *Heinemann*. In the meantime, the Fifth District Court of Appeal held that a husband continues to be liable for his wife's necessaries. *Waite*; *Ryals*.

The case before us today is in essentially the same posture as *Shands*. Yet, we are faced with a series of cases in which the parties agree that husbands and wives must be treated alike but disagree over whether the doctrine of necessaries should be applied to both spouses or simply abolished. Therefore, we have concluded that we must now address this issue in the context of equal protection considerations. Mrs. Connor contends that with the removal of coverture, the doctrine of necessaries is no longer justifiable because wives are now freely able to enter into contracts and obtain their own necessaries. Southwest posits that while the initial reason for the doctrine has disappeared, it now serves the important function of promoting the partnership theory of marriage and should be expanded so that both men and women are liable to third-party creditors who provide necessaries to their respective spouses.

* * *

The fact that courts and other legislatures have treated this problem in different ways illustrates the lack of consensus regarding the doctrine's place in modern society and reinforces position we took in *Shands*. Yet, our legislature has not chosen to address this issue, and we know of no circumstances occurring since our decision in *Shands* which would suggest that we were wrong in refusing to hold the wife liable for the husband's necessaries. Because constitutional considerations demand equality between the sexes, it follows that a husband can no longer be held liable for his wife's necessaries. We therefore abrogate the common law doctrine of necessaries, thereby leaving it to the legislature to determine the policy of the state in this area. We do not make a judgment as to which is the better policy for the state to adopt. We merely leave it to the appropriate branch to decide this question.

We quash the decision below. We approve the decisions in *Faulk* and *Heinemann* and disapprove those in *Webb*, *Waite*, and *Ryals*.

It is so ordered.

SHAW, KOGAN, HARDING and ANSTEAD, JJ., concur.

OVERTON, J., dissents with an opinion, in which WELLS, J., concurs.

OVERTON, Justice, dissenting.

I dissent. The common law doctrine of necessaries was born of the need to provide a legal means to protect and enforce the moral terms of the marital obligation. I find that the doctrine is just as important today, under the partnership theory of marriage, as it was when the doctrine was created under the unity theory of marriage. In this day and age, we should not weaken the obligations of marriage by eliminating the spousal duty to care for one another. However, that is exactly what the majority opinion does, and, by doing so, it places this Court in the minority of state supreme courts that have addressed this issue.

I agree that the common law doctrine of necessaries in its present form violates the equal protection clause by imposing a duty of spousal support only on the husband. However, unlike the majority, I conclude that this Court, as a matter of policy, should extend the doctrine to apply to both spouses rather than abrogate it entirely. In doing so, I would make the spouse who incurred the debt primarily liable.

* * *

b. Statutory Construction

Brown v. State

358 So. 2d 16 (Fla. 1978)

SUNDBERG, Justice.

[Brown was charged with "open profanity", a violation of Florida Statute 847.04.[10] He challenged the constitutionality of that section on First Amendment grounds.]

... While we agree today with [the court in *Mayhew v. State*, 288 So.2d 243 (Fla.1973] that in appropriate instances a court may authoritatively construe a statute so that it does not conflict with the federal or state constitution, we cannot condone judicial excision of statute's overbreadth or clarification of its ambiguities where, as here, there is no statutory language to support judicial restructuring. ...

* * *

In *Chaplinsky v. New Hampshire*, [315 U.S. 568, 62 S.Ct. 766, 86 L.Ed. 1031 (1942)] the statute in issue read as follows:

> No person shall address any offensive, derisive or annoying word to any other person who is lawfully in any street or other public place, nor call him by any offensive or derisive name, nor make any noise or exclamation in his presence and hearing with intent to deride, offend or annoy him, or to prevent him from pursuing his lawful business or occupation.

Ch. 378, § 2, of the Public Laws of New Hampshire.

The New Hampshire Supreme Court severed the statute and considered only the first part of it. That Court stated:

> The section of the statute involved has two provisions. The first relates to words and names applied by one directly to another in a public place. The second refers to noises or exclamations, possibly not directed to the person derided, but with the intent expressed. The two provisions are distinct. One may stand separately from the other. Assuming, without holding, that the second were unconstitutional, the first could stand if constitutional.

State v. Chaplinsky, 91 N.H. 310, 312, 18 A.2d 754, 757 (1941).

Thus, that portion of the New Hampshire statute before the New Hampshire Supreme Court and later the United States Supreme Court provided:

> No person shall address any offensive, derisive or annoying word to any other person who is lawfully in any street or other public place, nor call him by any offensive or derisive name. ...

---

10. This statute in pertinent part read: "... Whoever having arrived at the age of discretion, uses profane, vulgar and indecent language, in any public place; or upon the private premises of another, or so near there to as to be heard by another, shall be guilty of a misdemeanor of the second degree, ..."

The statute could be interpreted to prohibit only the "face-to-face words plainly likely to cause a breach of the peace by the addressee, words whose speaking constitute a breach of the peace by the speaker . . ." *State v. Chaplinsky*, supra. This narrow interpretation [which was found not to violate the First Amendment] was justified because the statute specifically proscribed offensive, derisive, or annoying language *addressed to another person* which could cause that person to fight. . . .

In Gooding v. Wilson, [405 U.S. 518, 92 S.Ct. 1103, 31 L.Ed 2d 408 (1972)] the Georgia statute under review stated:

> Any person who shall without provocation, use to or of another, and in his presence . . . opprobrious words or abusive language, tending to cause a breach of the peace . . . shall be guilty of a misdemeanor.

Georgia Code Ann. § 26-6303.

On its face, this statute was even more specific than the statute examined in *Chaplinsky* in limiting the prohibited speech to "fighting words." It suggested that the conduct sought to be proscribed was language directed either directly or indirectly to a person tending to cause a breach of the peace. While the United States Supreme Court found that past Georgia decisions had not given the statue the requisite narrow construction, it stated, understandably, that an authoritative construction could have redeemed the Georgia act. Again, the statutory language necessary to support an authoritative construction was present had the Georgia courts chosen to so construe the statute.

Unlike the statutes examined in *Chaplinsky* and *Gooding*, Section 847.04, Florida Statutes (1975), contains no language to support the restrictive interpretation placed on the statute by the *Mayhew* Court. Our statute seeks to punish only spoken words, whether they be directed to a particular person or not. Pursuant to the provisions of our statute, a person could shout profanities alone in an open field, and if those words were heard by another person, he could be subject to criminal prosecution. As Justice Ervin stated eloquently in dissenting from the majority opinion in *Mayhew*:

> There are no saving words in our statute upon which this Court can honestly state it is inoffensive to the First and Fourteenth amendments. There was such a basis in the New Hampshire and Georgia statutes. Only by a bald judicial amendment similar to a legislative enactment can the statute be said not to violate freedom of speech. There is nothing in the statute to indicate it is limited to "fighting" words.

State v. Mayhew, 288 So. 2d at 252.

While we recognize that the state has an important interest in proscribing face-to-face encounters which are likely to cause a breach of the peace, we cannot endorse legislative regulation of mere spoken words when the freedom to speak one's beliefs is valued so preciously in our society.

This Court has traditionally adhered to the policy that all doubts as to the validity of a statute are to be resolved in favor of constitutionality when reasonably possible. *Carter v. Sparkman*, 335 So.2d 802 (Fla.1976); *State v. Aiuppa*, 298 So.2d 391 (Fla.1974). However, it has also been wary of transcending its constitutional authority by invading the province of the legislature. *State v. Wershow*, 343 So.2d 605 (Fla.1977); *State v. Egan*, 287 So.2d 1 (Fla. 1973). When the subject statute in no way suggests a saving construction, we will not abandon judicial restraint and effectively rewrite the enactment. The Florida Constitution requires a certain precision defined by the legislature, not legislation articulated by the judiciary. *See* Article II, Section 3, Florida Constitution. This constitutional mandate obtains for two reasons. First, if legislative intent is not apparent from the statutory language, judicial reconstruction of vague or overbroad statutes could frustrate the true legislative intent. Second, in some circumstances, doubts about judicial competence to authoritatively construe legislation are warranted. Often a court has neither the legislative fact-finding machinery nor experience with the particular statutory subject matter to enable it to authoritatively construe a state. *See Kunz v. New York*, 340 U.S. 290, 71 S. Ct. 312, 95 L.Ed. 280 (1951) (Frankfurter, J., concurring). The judicial body might question with justification whether its interpretation is workable or whether it is consistent with legislative policy which is, as yet, undetermined.

A court is not so restricted where the statute describes activity which the state can control even though its coverage is too sweeping. In this case, the perils enunciated above are not so ominous. In accordance with the court's duty to construe a statute so as not to conflict with the Constitution, the overbroad language might be excised instead of the entire statute being declared facially invalid. In the case *sub judice*, however, judicial excision will not produce a statute of constitutional dimension because excision cannot limit the law to fighting words directed to another as mandated by *Chaplinsky v. New Hampshire*, supra. We can only conclude that "[t]he separation of legitimate from illegitimate speech calls for more sensitive tools than [the legislature in §847.04, F.S. (1975)] has supplied." *Speiser v. Randall*, 357 U.S. 513, 525, 78 S.Ct. 1332, 1342, 2 L.Ed.2d 1460 (1958). This is so because the freedom to speak one's thoughts is the matrix, the indispensable condition of nearly every other form of freedom, *Palko v. Connecticut*, 302 U.S. 319, 58 S.Ct. 149, 82 L.Ed. 288 (1937). "Because First Amendment freedoms need breathing space to survive, government may regulate in the area only with narrow specificity." *NAACP v. Button*, 371 U.S. 415, 433, 83 S.Ct. 328, 338, 9 L.Ed.2d 405 (1963); *accord, Spears v. State*, 337 So.2d 977 (Fla.1976).

Accordingly, we are constrained to recede from our earlier holding in *State v. Mayhew*, supra, and find Section 847.04, Florida Statutes (1975), unconstitutional under the Florida Constitution because it seeks to punish pure speech.

The judgment of the county court is reversed with directions that appellant be discharged.

It is so ordered.

ENGLAND, HATCHETT and KARL, JJ., concur.

OVERTON, C. J., and ADKINS and BOYD, JJ., dissent [without opinion].

Considerable conflict exists between the idea that courts should not usurp the role of the legislature by legislating rather than interpreting and what courts frequently do. While it is clear that courts should not correct defective legislation under the guise of construction or interpretation, judicial self-restraint in the exercise of judicial review can be pushed to the extreme of rewriting a law so that it will neither offend the constitution nor reach an absurd result. The following cases are illustrative.

Westphal v. City of St. Petersburg

194 So. 3d 311 (Fla. 2016)

PARIENTE, J.

In this case, we consider the constitutionality of section 440.15(2)(a), Florida Statutes (2009) — part of the state's workers' compensation law — which cuts off disability benefits after 104 weeks to a worker who is totally disabled and incapable of working but who has not yet reached maximum medical improvement. . . .

In *Westphal v. City of St. Petersburg/City of St. Petersburg Risk Management,* 122 So.3d 440, 442 (Fla. 1st DCA 2013), an en banc majority of the First District Court of Appeal valiantly attempted to save the statute from unconstitutionality by interpreting section 440.15(2)(a) so that the severely injured worker who can no longer receive temporary total disability benefits, but who is not yet eligible for permanent total disability benefits, would not be cut off from compensation after 104 weeks. [Footnote omitted] The judiciary, however, is without power to rewrite a plainly written statute, even if it is to avoid an unconstitutional result. *See Brown v. State,* 358 So.2d 16, 20 (Fla.1978) ("When the subject statute in no way suggests a saving construction, we will not abandon judicial restraint and effectively rewrite the enactment."). We accordingly quash the First District's decision.

* * *

I. Facts and Procedural History

In December 2009, Bradley Westphal, then a fifty-three-year-old firefighter in St. Petersburg, Florida, suffered a severe lower back injury caused by lifting heavy furniture in the course of fighting a fire. As a result of the lower back injury, Westphal experienced extreme pain and loss of feeling in his left leg below the knee and required multiple surgical procedures, including an eventual spinal fusion.

Shortly after his workplace injury, Westphal began receiving benefits pursuant to the workers' compensation law set forth in chapter 440, Florida Statutes (2009). Specifically, the City of St. Petersburg began to provide both indemnity benefits, in the form of temporary total disability benefits pursuant to section 440.15(2), Florida Statutes, and medical benefits.

Under section 440.15(2)(a), entitlement to temporary total disability benefits ends when a totally disabled injured worker reaches the date of maximum medical improvement or after 104 weeks, whichever occurs earlier. § 440.15(2)(a), Fla. Stat. The "date of maximum medical improvement" is defined in section 440.02(10), Florida Statutes (2009), as "the date after which further recovery from, or lasting improvement to, an injury or disease can no longer reasonably be anticipated, based upon reasonable medical probability." Westphal did not reach maximum medical improvement prior to the expiration of the 104–week limitation on temporary total disability benefits.

At the expiration of temporary total disability benefits, Westphal was still incapable of working or obtaining employment, based on the advice of his doctors and the vocational experts that examined him. In an attempt to replace his pre-injury wages of approximately $1,500 per week that he was losing because of his injuries, Westphal filed a petition for benefits, claiming either further temporary disability or permanent total disability pursuant to section 440.15(1), Florida Statutes (2009).

II. Analysis

. . .

We thus begin our analysis by interpreting section 440.15 to determine if the First District's en banc opinion — eliminating the statutory gap — provides a permissible statutory construction, or if the First District's prior opinions in *Hadley* and *Oswald* — recognizing the statutory gap created by the Legislature — provided the correct interpretation. After concluding that the First District's en banc opinion is an impermissible judicial rewrite of the Legislature's plainly written statute, we are forced to confront the constitutional issue of whether the statute, as applied to Westphal and other similarly situated severely injured workers, is unconstitutional. Concluding that the statute, as applied, violates the access to courts provision of the Florida Constitution, we conclude by considering the appropriate remedy.

A. Section 440.15, Florida Statutes

Section 440.15, Florida Statutes (2009), governs the payment of disability benefits to injured workers. As of the 1968 adoption of the Florida Constitution, permanent total disability benefits were determined "in accordance with the facts," and the term "maximum medical improvement" was not included in the workers' compensation law. § 440.15(1), Fla. Stat. (1968). Nevertheless, the phrase "maximum medical improvement" was part of this Court's lexicon because it assisted in determining the permanence of the injury. Indeed, in 1969, this Court noted that "[t]he date of maximum medical improvement marks the end of temporary disability and the beginning of permanent disability." *Corral v. McCrory Corp.*, 228 So.2d 900, 903 (Fla.1969). At that time, section 440.15(2) provided for the payment of temporary total disability benefits for a duration not to exceed 350 weeks. § 440.15(2), Fla. Stat. (1967).

In 1979, the Legislature added the term "date of maximum medical improvement" to the statute, defining it consistently with this Court's prior 1969 construction in *Corral* and requiring that the date be "based upon reasonable medical probability." § 440.02(22), Fla. Stat. (1979). That statutory definition has remained unchanged to this day.

In 1990, the Legislature reduced the duration of temporary total disability benefits from 350 weeks to 260 weeks. § 440.15(2), Fla. Stat. (1990). Then, just four years later, and as part of an extensive statutory overhaul, the Legislature further reduced the duration of temporary total disability benefits from 260 weeks to 104 weeks. § 440.15(2)(a), Fla. Stat. (1994).

Accordingly, in 2009, at the time of the events giving rise to this case, section 440.15(1) provided in part:

> (a) In case of total disability adjudged to be permanent, 66 ⅔ percent of the average weekly wages shall be paid to the employee during the continuance of such total disability. No compensation shall be payable under this section if the employee is engaged in, or is physically capable of engaging in, at least sedentary employment.

> (b) In the following cases, an injured employee is presumed to be permanently and totally disabled unless the employer or carrier establishes that the employee is physically capable of engaging in at least sedentary employment within a 50–mile radius of the employee's residence:

> . . . .

> In all other cases, in order to obtain permanent total disability benefits, the employee must establish that he or she is not able to engage in at least sedentary employment, within a 50–mile radius of the employee's residence, due to his or her physical limitation. . . . Only claimants with catastrophic injuries or claimants who are incapable of engaging in employment, as described in this paragraph, are eligible for permanent total benefits. In no other case may permanent total disability be awarded.

Under the plain language of this provision, permanent total disability benefits are expressly limited to "claimants with catastrophic injuries or claimants who are incapable of engaging in employment." § 440.15(1)(b), Fla. Stat. (2009). "In no other case may permanent total disability be awarded." *Id.*

Section 440.15(2)(a), which governs temporary total disability benefits, provided in part as follows:

> Subject to subsection (7), in case of disability total in character but temporary in quality, 66 ⅔ percent of the average weekly wages shall be paid to the employee during the continuance thereof, not to exceed 104 weeks except as provided in this subsection, s. 440.12(1), and s. 440.14(3). [Footnote omitted.] Once the employee reaches the maximum number of weeks allowed, or the employee reaches the date of maximum medical improvement,

whichever occurs earlier, temporary disability benefits shall cease and the injured worker's permanent impairment shall be determined.

Under the plain language of this provision, temporary total disability benefits are payable for no more than 104 weeks, after which the worker's permanent impairment rating must be determined. "The permanent impairment rating is used to pay 'impairment income benefits,'" as distinguished from permanent total disability benefits, "commencing on 'the day after the employee reaches [maximum medical improvement] or after the expiration of temporary benefits, whichever occurs earlier,' and continuing for a period determined by the employee's percentage of impairment." *Hadley,* 78 So.3d at 624 (quoting § 440.15(3)(g), Fla. Stat.).

As the First District recognized in *Hadley,* "[t]he statutory scheme in section 440.15 works seamlessly when the injured employee reaches [maximum medical improvement] prior to the expiration of the 104 weeks of temporary disability benefits." *Id.* But where "the employee is not at [maximum medical improvement] at the expiration of the 104 weeks, there is the potential for a 'gap' in disability benefits because [temporary total disability] benefits cease by operation of law after 104 weeks and entitlement to [permanent total disability] benefits is generally not ripe until the employee reaches [maximum medical improvement]." *Id.*

Analyzing these statutory provisions, and in an apparent effort to avoid the statutory gap, the First District in *Westphal* ultimately concluded that the Legislature's use of the term "permanent impairment" in section 440.15(2)(a) signifies that the disabled worker has attained maximum medical improvement by operation of law. *See Westphal,* 122 So.3d at 445. The First District therefore held that "a worker who is totally disabled as a result of a workplace accident and remains totally disabled by the end of his or her eligibility for temporary total disability benefits is deemed to be at maximum medical improvement by operation of law and is therefore eligible to assert a claim for permanent and total disability benefits." *Id.* at 442.

Although this Court's review of the First District's statutory interpretation is de novo, "statutes come clothed with a presumption of constitutionality and must be construed whenever possible to effect a constitutional outcome." *Crist v. Fla. Ass'n of Crim. Def. Lawyers, Inc.,* 978 So.2d 134, 139 (Fla.2008). While we are confident that the First District en banc majority was attempting to save the statute's constitutionality by interpreting it so as to avoid a draconian result for severely injured workers, the clear language of the statute simply does not allow us to agree with the First District's interpretation.

Rather, the previous interpretation provided by the First District in *Oswald,* and adhered to in *Hadley,* is consistent with the Legislature's plainly stated intent, which nowhere indicates that the Legislature sought to equate the expiration of temporary total disability benefits with maximum medical improvement. As stated in *Oswald,* under the plain language of the statute, "an employee whose temporary benefits have run out — or are expected to do so imminently — must be able to show not only total disability upon the cessation of temporary benefits but also that total disability will be existing after the date of maximum medical improvement" in order to be eligible to receive permanent total disability benefits. 710 So.2d at 98 (internal citation omitted).

Specifically, section 440.15(2)(a) requires an injured worker's "permanent impairment," [footnote omitted] as opposed to permanent total disability, to be determined. In addition, section 440.15(3), which pertains to "permanent impairment benefits," is the only section that discusses an "evaluation" for permanent impairment of the employee, with entitlement to such benefits to commence the day after the employee reaches maximum medical improvement or his or her temporary total disability benefits expire. Permanent impairment benefits are distinct from, and not a substitute for, total disability benefits. Thus, the plain language of the statute provides for permanent impairment to be determined for purposes of impairment benefits as opposed to permanent total disability benefits.

It is clear from the statute that the Legislature intended to limit the duration of temporary total disability benefits to a maximum of 104 weeks. It is further clear that the Legislature intended to limit the class of individuals who are entitled to permanent total disability benefits to those with catastrophic injuries and those who are able to demonstrate a permanent inability to engage in even sedentary employment within a fifty-mile radius of their home. In other words, these provisions "create a gap in disability benefits for those injured workers who are totally disabled upon the expiration of temporary disability benefits but fail to prove prospectively that total disability will exist after the date of [maximum medical improvement]." *Hadley,* 78 So.3d at 626 (quoting *Crum v. Richmond,* 46 So.3d 633, 637 n. 3 (Fla. 1st DCA 2010)).

Although this Court must, whenever possible, construe statutes to effect a constitutional outcome, we may not salvage a plainly written statute by rewriting it. *See Sult v. State,* 906 So.2d 1013, 1019 (Fla.2005) ("Courts may not go so far in their narrowing constructions so as to effectively rewrite legislative enactments."). The gap in benefits caused by the Legislature's decision to reduce the duration of entitlement to temporary total disability benefits may be an unintentional, unanticipated, and unfortunate result. But even if potentially unwise and unfair, it is not the prerogative of the courts to rewrite a statute to overcome its shortcomings. *See Clines v. State,* 912 So.2d 550, 558 (Fla.2005) ("A court's function is to interpret statutes as they are written and give effect to each word in the statute." (quoting *Fla. Dep't of Revenue v. Fla. Mun. Power Agency,* 789 So.2d 320, 324 (Fla.2001))); *Metro. Dade Cty. v. Bridges,* 402 So.2d 411, 414 (Fla.1981), *receded from on other grounds by Makemson v. Martin Cty.,* 491 So.2d 1109 (Fla.1986) (explaining that "courts may not vary the intent of the legislature with respect to the meaning of the statute in order to render the statute constitutional").

Because we hold that the statute is clear in creating a statutory gap in benefits, and thus not susceptible to the rules of statutory construction, we turn to Westphal's constitutional challenge — ...

* * *

80   2 · SEPARATION OF POWERS

State v. Stalder

630 So. 2d 1072 (Fla. 1994)

SHAW, Justice.

We have for review a trial court order declaring section 775.085, Florida Statutes (1989), commonly referred to as Florida's Hate Crimes Statute, unconstitutional. The order was certified by the district court as passing on an issue of great public importance requiring immediate resolution by this Court. We have jurisdiction. Art. V, § 3(b)(5), Fla. Const. We quash the order.

Herbert Cohen went to Richard Stalder's home on April 14, 1991, to retrieve the earrings of a friend. Stalder then assaulted Cohen and maligned his Jewish heritage ...

* * *

The State noted as additional proof of Stalder's commission of a "hate crime" the fact that he denounced Cohen during the initial encounter at Stalder's home as a "Jewish lawyer": "Jew boy, you fat Jewish lawyer get the hell off my property. . . ." and "Jewish kike, come on Jewish lawyer . . . I'm going to kick your ass. . . ."

Stalder was charged with violating section 784.03(1), Florida Statutes (1989) (simple battery) for pushing Cohen, and the penalty was subject to reclassification pursuant to section 775.085(1) from a first-degree misdemeanor to a third-degree felony. The trial court granted Stalder's pretrial motion to dismiss the enhancement charge, adopting Stalder's argument that the statute violates the Free Speech Clause of the United States Constitution. The State appealed and the district court certified the matter as requiring immediate resolution by this Court.[1]

Stalder contends that the statute is both vague and overbroad and punishes pure thought and expression in violation of the First Amendment. The State, on the other hand, contends that section 775.085 is neither unconstitutionally vague nor overbroad—the statute simply enhances punishment for those crimes that are committed because the victim has one of several identified characteristics. It is the State's position that the statute punishes criminal action, not speech, and thus does not implicate the First Amendment.

* * *

---

1. The record before us in *State v. Leatherman,* No. 80,126, contains scant facts. Leatherman was charged with aggravated assault for pointing a handgun at and threatening the victim. He also was charged with violating section 775.085(1), Florida Statutes (1989), for evidencing prejudice during the assault. The same trial judge that presided over the Stalder case granted Leatherman's pretrial motion to dismiss the hate crimes charge for the same reasons. The district court certified the case here and the two cases were consolidated. The State has submitted essentially the same brief in both cases and Leatherman has chosen to take no action pending our ruling in *State v. Stalder,* No. 79, 924.

Section 775.085 requires penalty enhancement where the commission of any felony or misdemeanor evidences prejudice based on certain characteristics of the victim:

775.085 Evidencing prejudice while committing offense; enhanced penalties. —

(1) The penalty for any felony or misdemeanor shall be reclassified as provided in this subsection if the commission of such felony or misdemeanor evidences prejudice based on the race, color, ancestry, ethnicity, religion, or national origin of the victim:

(a) A misdemeanor of the second degree shall be punishable as if it were a misdemeanor of the first degree.

(b) A misdemeanor of the first degree shall be punishable as if it were a felony of the third degree.

(c) A felony of the third degree shall be punishable as if it were a felony of the second degree.

(d) A felony of the second degree shall be punishable as if it were a felony of the first degree.

Section 775.085(1), Fla. Stat. (1989).[2]

Giving plain meaning to the statute's text and title, the provision punishes all who "evidence," or demonstrate, prejudice in the commission of a crime based on an enumerated characteristic of the victim. The statute has three requirements: 1) The perpetrator must demonstrate prejudice, or bias; 2) the bias must be evidenced in the commission of a crime; and 3) the bias must be based on one or more of the enumerated characteristics of the victim. . . .

* * *

A bias-evidencing crime as set out in the statute's title and text is any crime wherein the perpetrator "evidences prejudice" based on one or more of the enumerated characteristics of the victim "while committing [the] offense." This category of conduct has been viewed as embracing two broad classes of offenses. [Citations omitted.]

First are those offenses committed because of prejudice. For instance, A beats B because B is a member of a particular racial group. This class of offense is virtually identical to the bias-motivated crimes proscribed by the valid Wisconsin statute in [*Wisconsin v. Mitchell,* 508 U.S. 476, 113 S.Ct. 2194, 124 L.Ed.2d 436 (1993)]. The targeted activity — the selection of a victim — is an integral part of the underlying

---

2. Section 775.085 has since been amended to include "sexual orientation" in its list of proscribed factors and to provide:

(3) It shall be an essential element of this section that the record reflect that the defendant perceived, knew, or had reasonable grounds to know or perceive that the victim was within the class delineated herein.

§ 775.085, Fla. Stat. (1991).

crime. As such, the conduct is not protected speech at all, but rather falls outside the First Amendment and may be banned.

Second are those offenses committed for some reason other than prejudice but that nevertheless show bias in their commission. For example, A beats B because of jealousy, but in the course of the battery calls B a racially derogatory term. The targeted conduct here — the expression of bias — is related to the underlying crime in only the most tangential way: The expression and crime share the same temporal framework, nothing more. This tenuous nexus, which amounts to mere temporal coincidence, is irrelevant for constitutional purposes. The proscribed conduct consists of pure expression indistinguishable from the bias-inspired expression targeted by the St. Paul ordinance in [*R.A.V. v. City of St. Paul*, 505 U.S. 377, 112 S.Ct. 2538, 120 L.Ed.2d 305 (1992)] and cannot be selectively banned.

The question before us is whether section 775.085 can pass constitutional muster by being read narrowly as proscribing the first class of conduct. We note that in assessing a statute's constitutionality, this Court is bound "to resolve all doubts as to the validity of [the] statute in favor of its constitutionality, provided the statute may be given a fair construction that is consistent with the federal and state constitutions as well as with the legislative intent." *State v. Elder,* 382 So.2d 687, 690 (Fla.1980). Further, "[w]henever possible, a statute should be construed so as not to conflict with the constitution. Just as federal courts are authorized to place narrowing constructions on acts of Congress, this Court may, under the proper circumstances, do the same with a state statute when to do so does not effectively rewrite the enactment." *Firestone v. News-Press Publishing Co.,* 538 So.2d 457, 459–60 (Fla.1989) (citations omitted).

Here, our legislature has determined that prejudice resulting in criminal acts against members of particular groups inflicts great individual and societal harm and is thus deserving of enhanced punishment. The legislature's apparent intent is to discourage criminal acts directed against groups that have historically been subjected to prejudicial acts. A reading of section 775.085 as embracing only bias-motivated crimes is entirely consistent with this intent. We note that the Fifth District Court of Appeal has so read the statute:

> Appellant first contends that the statute is vague and overbroad. He contends the statute is susceptible of applying to protected speech because it does not require that the prejudice alleged have any specific relationship to the commission of the crime.
>
> This argument seems to concede that if the statute permits enhancement only upon proof, beyond a reasonable doubt, that appellant committed the battery motivated in whole or in part, because Daly was Jewish, the enhanced penalty would be appropriate.
>
> That is precisely the way we read the statute. . . .

Appellant urges that the language can be read to apply to a situation in which the defendant commits a race, color or religious neutral crime (for example, resisting arrest because he thinks he's innocent), but during the commission of the offense makes a racial slur. We do not agree. The statute requires that it is the *commission of the crime* that must evidence the prejudice; the fact that racial prejudice may be exhibited during the commission of the crime is itself insufficient.

Dobbins, 605 So.2d at 923.

Based on the foregoing, we hold that section 775.085, Florida Statute (1989), applies only to bias-motivated crimes. So read, the statute is constitutional. A bias-motivated crime for purposes of this statute is any crime wherein the perpetrator intentionally selects the victim because of the victim's "race, color, ethnicity, religion, or national origin."

It may seem doubly vile to members of our legal community to denigrate another for being a "Jewish lawyer," as Mr. Stalder allegedly did, but such an act standing alone is every citizen's right — so long as the First Amendment breathes. To assault another solely because he or she is a "Jewish lawyer," on the other hand, is no one's right. When protected speech translates into criminal conduct, even the Free Speech Clause balks. "While the First Amendment confers on each citizen a powerful right to express oneself, it gives the [citizen] no boon to jeopardize the health, safety, and rights of others." *Operation Rescue v. Women's Health Center, Inc.*, 626 So.2d 664, 675 (Fla.1993).

We quash the trial court's order finding section 775.085, Florida Statutes (1989), unconstitutional and remand for proceedings consistent with this opinion.[4] We approve *Dobbins* and disapprove *Richards*.

It is so ordered.

OVERTON, McDONALD and GRIMES, JJ., concur.

KOGAN, J., concurs with an opinion. [This opinion is omitted.]

HARDING, J., dissents with an opinion, in which BARKETT, C.J., concurs.

HARDING, Justice, dissenting:

I respectfully dissent from the majority opinion in this cause. I find the majority's analysis crosses the line we have consistently drawn prohibiting the courts from rewriting legislation. *Brown v. State*, 358 So.2d 16, 20 (Fla.1978) ("The Florida Constitution requires a certain precision defined by the legislature, not legislation articulated by the judiciary."); *see also* art. II, § 3, Fla. Const.

The apparent goals of section 775.085, Florida Statutes (1989) are laudable, and I firmly believe that bias-motivated conduct is reprehensible and deserving of enhanced punishment. Yet no matter how commendable I find an enhanced penalty for bias-motivated criminal conduct, section 775.085 — by design or by unartful wording — also imposes an enhanced penalty for conduct that "evidences prejudice

---

4. We quash the corresponding order in consolidated case *State v. Leatherman,* No. 80,126. *See supra* note 1.

while committing [an] offense."[9] The Legislature's use of the verb "evidence" indicates that the statute applies not only to offenses motivated by bias, but also to displays of bias that happen to occur during the commission of a crime.

* * *

In my judgment, the majority reaches its conclusion by engaging in judicial legislation. A court may, under proper circumstances, adopt a narrowing construction when to do so does not effectively rewrite the statute. *Firestone v. News-Press Publishing Co.*, 538 So.2d 457, 459–60 (Fla.1989). In this case, the majority has gone too far in trying to give an unconstitutional statute a constitutional meaning. The Legislature spoke clearly when it chose the word "evidence" for the statute's text and title. In holding the statute constitutional, the majority ignores the plain meaning of "evidence" and narrows the verb to mean "motivated." While this Court should, when possible, construe statutes to avoid conflict with the Constitution, we have held that "courts may not vary the intent of the legislature with respect to the meaning of the statute in order to render the statute constitutional." *Metropolitan Dade County v. Bridges,* 402 So.2d 411, 414 (Fla.1981), *receded from on other grounds by Makemson v. Martin County,* 491 So.2d 1109 (Fla.1986), *cert. denied,* 479 U.S. 1043, 107 S.Ct. 908, 93 L.Ed.2d 857 (1987). The majority has impermissibly narrowed section 775.085 and now puts its own legislative gloss on the statute.

The Legislature could easily rewrite this statute in a constitutional manner. This would respect the separation of powers embodied in our constitution and would save the Court from legislating from the bench.

What is probably one of the most extreme, if not the most extreme, examples of potential judicial encroachment on legislative power in Florida is the threat (which was never carried out because the legislature acted) found in the following case.

---

9. As noted in the majority opinion, the title of section 775.085, Florida Statutes (1989) reads: "*Evidencing* prejudice while committing offense; enhanced penalties." (Emphasis added.) Subsection (1) says: "The penalty for any felony or misdemeanor shall be reclassified as provided in this subsection if the commission of such felony or misdemeanor *evidences* prejudice based on the race, color, ancestry, ethnicity, religion, or national origin of the victim. . . ." (Emphasis added.)

Dade County Classroom Teachers Association, Inc. v. Legislature

269 So. 2d 684 (Fla. 1972)

ROBERTS, Chief Justice.

This cause is before the Court in original mandamus proceedings filed by the Dade County Classroom Teachers' Association, Inc., in an attempt to compel the Legislature of the State of Florida to enact standards or guidelines regulating the right of collective bargaining by public employees of this state, as guaranteed by Section 6, Article I, 1968 Constitution of Florida, F.S.A. The petition for the constitutional writ was filed as a class action on behalf of the 7,500 classroom teachers employed by the District School Board of Dade County, and on behalf of all the public employees of this state — its counties, municipalities, school districts, and all other governmental agencies.

The petition complains of inaction on the part of the Legislature through three legislative sessions following the decision of this Court in *Dade County Classroom Teachers' Association v. Ryan*, 225 So.2d 903 (Fla.1969), in which this Court made clear that, except for the right to strike, our State Constitution guarantees to public employees the same rights of collective bargaining as are granted to private employees. We emphasized, however, that appropriate legislation setting out standards and guidelines and otherwise regulating "the sensitive area of labor relations between public employees and public employer" should be adopted by the Legislature. . . .

* * *

The petition for the writ must, of course, be denied. Florida's Constitution, like those of most other states, divides the state's sovereign powers into three coordinate branches — legislative, executive and judicial — and prohibits a person belonging to one of such branches from exercising any powers "appertaining to either of the other branches unless expressly provided herein." Section 3, Article II, 1968 Constitution. And it is too well settled to need any citation of authority that the judiciary cannot compel the Legislature to exercise a purely legislative prerogative. . . .

* * *

We think it is appropriate to observe here that one of the exceptions to the separation-of-powers doctrine is in the area of constitutionally guaranteed or protected rights. The judiciary is in a lofty sense the guardian of the law of the land and the Constitution is the highest law. A constitution would be a meaningless instrument without some responsible agency of government having authority to enforce it. As Chief Justice Charles Evans Hughes once stated,

> "We are under a constitution, but the constitution is what the judges say it is, and the judiciary is the safeguard of our liberty and of our property under the constitution."

When the people have spoken through their organic law concerning their basic rights, it is primarily the duty of the legislative body to provide the ways and means of enforcing such rights; however, in the absence of appropriate legislative action, it is the responsibility of the courts to do so.

* * *

We take judicial notice that the 1972 Legislature had many problems to deal with and we must assume that the weight of their labors in other matters precluded the establishing of guidelines for public employees other than the firefighters [who already enjoyed them]. And it is fair to assume that many Legislators, like the then Governor, may be opposed to the principle of collective bargaining for public employees and to incorporating this principle into our State constitution, as was the author of this opinion at the time when a member of the Florida Constitutional Revision Commission. But the people of this State have now spoken on this question in adopting Section 6 of Article I, supra. The question of the right of public employees to bargain collectively is no longer open to debate. It is a constitutionally protected right which may be enforced by the courts, if not protected by other agencies of government. It is a right which should be exercised in accordance with appropriate guidelines in order to make sure that there may be no denial of the right and, at the same time, that the *prohibition against strikes by public employees will not be violated*, either directly or indirectly, and with appropriate penalties for doing so.

The Legislature, having thus entered the field, we have confidence that within a reasonable time it will extend its time and study into this field and, therefore, judicial implementation of the rights in question would be premature at this time. If not, this Court will, in an appropriate case, have no choice but to fashion such guidelines by judicial decree in such manner as may seem to the Court best adapted to meet the requirements of the constitution, and comply with our responsibility.

The petition for the writ is denied and the cause is dismissed.

It is so ordered.

ERVIN, CARLTON, BOYD and DEKLE, JJ., concur.

c. The Legislative Privilege

League of Women Voters of Florida v. Florida House of Representatives

132 So. 3d 135 (Fla. 2013)

PARIENTE, J.

* * *

Facts and Background

In February 2012, the Florida Legislature approved the decennial plan apportioning Florida's twenty-seven congressional districts, based on population data derived from the 2010 United States Census. Soon after its adoption, two separate groups of plaintiffs filed civil complaints in circuit court, which were later consolidated, challenging the constitutionality of the plan under new state constitutional redistricting standards approved by the Florida voters in 2010 and now enumerated in article III, section 20, of the Florida Constitution. Those standards, governing the congressional reapportionment process, appeared on the 2010 general election ballot as "Amendment 6" and, together with their identical counterparts that apply to legislative reapportionment ("Amendment 5"), were generally referred to as the "Fair Districts" amendments.[1] All together, these "express new standards imposed by the voters clearly act as a restraint on legislative discretion in drawing apportionment plans." *Apportionment I,* 83 So.3d at 599.

* * *

In the consolidated circuit court lawsuit challenging the validity of the 2012 congressional apportionment plan under the Florida Constitution's redistricting standards, the challengers[3] allege that the congressional apportionment plan and numerous individual districts violate the article III, section 20, standards by impermissibly favoring Republicans and incumbents, by intentionally diminishing the ability of racial and language minorities to elect representatives of their choice, and by failing to adhere to the requirement that districts be compact and follow existing political and geographical boundaries where feasible. The challengers seek both a declaratory judgment invalidating the entire plan, or at least the specific districts challenged, as well as a permanent injunction against conducting any future elections using the congressional district boundaries established by the 2012 apportionment plan.

As part of ongoing pretrial civil discovery — and ... to further develop and discover evidence concerning their claim of unconstitutional legislative intent in

---

1. Amendment 5 is now codified in article III, section 21, of the Florida Constitution. The standards in article III, section 20 — governing congressional reapportionment — and those in article III, section 21 — governing legislative reapportionment — are identical.

3. The challengers collectively include the League of Women Voters of Florida, Common Cause Florida, named plaintiff Rene Romo, and ten other individually named plaintiffs.

violation of article III, section 20(a), the challengers served a notice of taking depositions of the then-state Senate Majority Leader, an administrative assistant to the Senate Reapportionment Committee, and the staff director of the House Redistricting Committee. Thereafter, the Legislature filed a "Motion for Protective Order Based on Legislative Privilege," in which it requested the circuit court to enter an order "declaring that (i) no legislators or legislative staff may be deposed, and (ii) unfiled legislative draft maps and supporting documents are not discoverable." The Legislature's motion for a protective order was filed in direct response to the challengers' notice of taking depositions; however, the Legislature sought to more generally prevent the depositions of *any* legislators and legislative staff, as well as the "discovery of legislatively drawn draft redistricting plans that were never filed as bills."

The circuit court granted in part and denied in part the Legislature's motion for a protective order. The circuit court determined that, although a legislative privilege exists in Florida, the privilege is not absolute and "must be balanced against other compelling government interests."

* * *

... [A]fter both groups of challengers in the consolidated litigation below sought review, we exercised our discretion to accept jurisdiction to review the First District's decision because that decision expressly affects a class of constitutional officers — namely, legislators — and because this Court has never considered whether a legislative privilege exists, which is clearly an important issue to resolve. *See* art. V, § 3(b)(3), Fla. Const.

Analysis

The questions we confront require this Court to interpret the Florida Constitution to determine whether a legislative privilege exists and to define the parameters of that privilege as applied in this case. These are pure questions of law that are subject to de novo review.

We hold, first, that a legislative privilege exists in Florida, based on the principle of separation of powers codified in article II, section 3, of the Florida Constitution. However, we conclude that this privilege is not absolute and may yield to a compelling, competing interest. We then proceed to review whether a compelling, competing interest exists in this case. Finally, we explain why we embrace the circuit court's balancing approach at this stage of the litigation, which determined that the compelling, competing constitutional interest present here outweighs the purposes underlying the privilege, therefore allowing discovery but retaining the right of an individual legislator or legislative staff member to assert the privilege as to his or her thoughts or impressions or the thoughts or impressions shared with legislators by staff or other legislators.

I. Florida's Legislative Privilege

The challengers contend that this Court should not recognize a legislative privilege because the Florida Constitution lacks a Speech or Debate Clause, which is the constitutional provision upon which the legislative privilege is traditionally premised. This clause, which generally states that legislators shall in all cases except treason, felony, or breach of the peace, not be questioned in any other place for any speech or debate in either legislative chamber,[4] is the general justification that the federal courts and other states with a state-specific clause have utilized in recognizing the legislative privilege. *See City of Pompano Beach v. Swerdlow Lightspeed Mgmt. Co.,* 942 So.2d 455, 457 (Fla. 4th DCA 2006) ("The federal courts which have acknowledged and applied the privilege have done so based largely on the Speech and Debate Clause in Article I, section 6, of the United States Constitution, which protects federal legislators from suits."); *Kerttula v. Abood,* 686 P.2d 1197, 1205 (Alaska 1984) (applying Alaska's state constitutional version of the Speech or Debate Clause to preclude the deposition of a state legislator).

In contrast to the vast majority of states, the Florida Constitution does not include a Speech or Debate Clause and has not included one since the clause was omitted during the 1868 constitutional revision.[5] In fact, Florida is one of only two states in the country that lacks either a state constitutional Speech or Debate Clause or a provision protecting legislators from arrest during legislative session.[6]

Coupled with the absence of a Speech or Debate Clause in the Florida Constitution is the presence of Florida's broad constitutional right of access to public records, set forth in article I, section 24, and right to transparency in the legislative process, codified in article III, section 4. Specifically regarding the Legislature, the Florida Constitution mandates as follows:

> [A]ll prearranged gatherings, between more than two members of the legislature, or between the governor, the president of the senate, or the speaker of the house of representatives, the purpose of which is to agree upon formal legislative action that will be taken at a subsequent time, or at which formal legislative action is taken, regarding pending legislation or amendments, shall be reasonably open to the public.

Art. III, § 4(e), Fla. Const.

Further, article I, section 24(a), which "specifically includes the legislative" branch, provides that "[e]very person has the right to inspect or copy any public record made or received in connection with the official business of any public body" of the state. Art. I, § 24(a), Fla. Const.

---

4. *See* art. IV, § 11, Fla. Const. (1865); *see also* U.S. Const. art. I, § 6, cl. 1.

5. *See Girardeau v. State,* 403 So.2d 513, 515 n. 3 (Fla. 1st DCA 1981) ("Florida's 1865 Constitution contained a speech and debate clause in language substantially similar to that found in the United States Constitution; however, the clause was omitted from the 1868, 1885, and the current (1968) Florida Constitutions.").

6. North Carolina is the other state. Forty- three states have a state constitutional Speech or Debate Clause and five other state constitutions contain an arrest exemption without explicitly conferring a speech or debate privilege. Many states have both provisions.

Thus, the absence of a Speech or Debate Clause and the strong public policy, as codified in our state constitution, favoring transparency and public access to the legislative process, are factors weighing against recognizing a legislative privilege in Florida. Florida statutes also do not provide for a legislative privilege.[7] Further, any common law legislative privilege has been abolished by a provision in the Florida Evidence Code providing that Florida law recognizes only privileges set forth by statute or in the state or federal constitutions.[8]

These factors, however, are not conclusive because there is another important factor that weighs in favor of recognizing the privilege — the doctrine of separation of powers. It is through this separate and important constitutional principle, which is codified in article II, section 3, of the Florida Constitution, that we recognize a legislative privilege under Florida law.

Forty states, including Florida, have a specific state constitutional provision recognizing the separation of powers between the three branches of government. [Footnote omitted.] Article II, section 3, of the Florida Constitution, which is Florida's separation of powers provision, provides as follows:

> The powers of the state government shall be divided into legislative, executive and judicial branches. No person belonging to one branch shall exercise any powers appertaining to either of the other branches unless expressly provided herein.

Art. II, § 3, Fla. Const.

* * *

... [B]ecause of the role that the principle of separation of powers plays in the structure of Florida's state government, as embodied in article II, section 3, of our state constitution, we reject the challengers' contention that there is no legislative privilege in Florida and hold that state legislators and legislative staff members do possess a legislative privilege under Florida law. This privilege is based on the principle that "no branch may encroach upon the powers of another," *Chiles*, 589 So.2d at 264, and on inherent principles of comity that exist between the coequal branches of government. In other words, "the privilege can be said to derive from the supremacy of each branch within its own assigned area of constitutional duties." *United States v. Nixon*, 418 U.S. 683, 705, 94 S.Ct. 3090, 41 L.Ed.2d 1039 (1974).

Several reasons support recognition of a legislative privilege. The most obvious is the practical concern of protecting the integrity of the legislative process by not unnecessarily interfering with the Legislature's business. As the circuit court

---

7. *See Swerdlow Lightspeed Mgmt. Co.*, 942 So.2d at 457 ("No Florida legislative testimonial privilege has been recognized in the Evidence Code, statutes, or Florida constitution.").

8. *See Marshall v. Anderson*, 459 So.2d 384, 387 (Fla. 3d DCA 1984) (stating that the adoption of section 90.501, Florida Statutes (1981), "abolishe[d] all common-law privileges existing in Florida," making "the creation of privileges dependent upon legislative action or pursuant to the Supreme Court's rule-making power" (quoting Law Revision Council Note)).

cogently articulated, "[l]egislators could not properly do their job if they had to sit for depositions every time someone thought they had information that was relevant to a particular court case or administrative proceeding." In addition, other reasons for recognizing a privilege include the "historical policy . . . of protecting disfavored legislators from intimidation by a hostile executive" and protecting legislators "from the burdens of forced participation in private litigation." *Kerttula,* 686 P.2d at 1202. These other policies undergirding the legislative privilege aim to ensure that the separation of powers is maintained so that the Legislature can accomplish its role of enacting legislation in the public interest without undue interference.

Although separation of powers principles require deference to the Legislature in refusing to provide compelled testimony in a judicial action, we emphasize that the legislative privilege is not absolute. As the United States Supreme Court has noted in determining that the President of the United States does not enjoy an absolute privilege of immunity from judicial process in all circumstances, "when the privilege depends solely on the broad, undifferentiated claim of public interest . . . a confrontation with other values arises." *Nixon,* 418 U.S. at 706, 94 S.Ct. 3090. This public interest component is especially true in Florida, where one of our state constitutional values is a strong and well-established public policy of transparency and public access to the legislative process, which is enshrined in the Florida Constitution.

Indeed, the proposition that a legislative privilege is not absolute, particularly where another compelling, competing interest is at stake, is not a novel one. For example, in *United States v. Gillock,* 445 U.S. 360, 369, 372, 100 S.Ct. 1185, 63 L.Ed.2d 454 (1980), the Supreme Court acknowledged the need to avoid unnecessary intrusion by the executive or judicial branches into the "affairs of a coequal branch," as well as the Court's "sensitivity to interference with the functioning of state legislators." However, the Court concluded nevertheless that "although principles of comity command careful consideration, . . . where important federal interests are at stake, as in the enforcement of federal criminal statutes, comity yields." *Id.* at 373, 100 S.Ct. 1185. . . .

As the First District itself has recognized, there may be a compelling, competing interest in a particular case that outweighs the purposes underlying the privilege. *See Expedia,* 85 So.3d at 525. When the legislative privilege is asserted, therefore, courts must engage in an inquiry to determine both if the privilege applies to protect the particular information being sought and the reason the information is being sought.[11] This inquiry is a two-step process.

---

11. This case does not involve legislative immunity, nor does it involve the liability of any individual legislator. We note that the legislative privilege (that is, an evidentiary privilege against compelled judicial process) is different than legislative immunity from suit, even though federal courts have held that the legislative privilege is derived from the principles underlying legislative immunity. *See Gravel v. United States,* 408 U.S. 606, 615, 92 S.Ct. 2614, 33 L.Ed.2d 583 (1972). These principles are based on the United States Constitution's Speech or Debate Clause, *see* U.S. Const. art. I, § 6, cl. 1, and arise out of "the Parliamentary struggles of the Sixteenth and Seventeenth Centuries." *Tenney v. Brandhove,* 341 U.S. 367, 372, 71 S.Ct. 783, 95 L.Ed. 1019 (1951).

The first step is to determine whether the information sought falls within the scope of the privilege. This is an important determination because, for example, information concerning evidence of a crime would not be covered by the legislative privilege. For purposes of our analysis in this case, however, we assume that all of the information being sought by the challengers, which relates to functions undertaken by legislators and legislative staff during the course of their legitimate legislative duties, would fall within the scope of the privilege. We therefore proceed to the next step.

Once a court determines that the information being sought is within the scope of the legislative privilege, the court then must determine whether the purposes underlying the privilege — namely, the deference owed by each coequal branch of government to the others and the practical concerns of legislators' abilities to perform their legislative functions free from the burdens of forced participation in private litigation — are outweighed by a compelling, competing interest.

* * *

Conclusion

Based on the foregoing, we conclude that Florida law should recognize a legislative privilege, but that this privilege is not absolute in this case, where the violations alleged are of an explicit state constitutional provision prohibiting partisan political gerrymandering and improper discriminatory intent in redistricting. We further conclude that the circuit court determined the proper balance of interests by protecting the thoughts or impressions of individual legislators and legislative staff members at this stage of the litigation, but recognizing the compelling, competing interest in ensuring that the Legislature complies with the constitutional mandate regarding redistricting by permitting discovery of all other information and communications pertaining to the constitutional validity of the challenged apportionment plan. Accordingly, we quash the First District's decision under review, approve the circuit court's order, and remand for further proceedings in accordance with this opinion.

It is so ordered.

LEWIS, QUINCE, LABARGA, and PERRY, JJ., concur.

LABARGA, J., concurs with an opinion in which LEWIS, J., concurs.

PERRY, J., concurs with an opinion in which QUINCE, J., concurs.

[The concurring opinions of Justice Labarga and Justice Perry are omitted.]

CANADY, J., dissents with an opinion in which POLSTON, C.J., concurs.

CANADY, J., dissenting.

In this case, for the first time in the recorded history of our Republic, a court has ruled that state legislators are required to submit to interrogation in a civil case concerning their legislative activities. I dissent from this unprecedented decision — a decision which effectively abrogates the well-established common law legislative privilege and grievously violates the constitutional separation of powers. I would approve the First District Court of Appeal's cogent decision.

I

* * *

The autonomy of the core internal operations of the legislative branch is a bulwark of the separation of powers. That autonomy is violated by the intrusion of the judicial branch into the internal operations of the legislative process. When the constitutional autonomy of one branch is breached by another branch, the separation of powers is violated. Florida law has recognized that

the judicial branch should not intrude into the internal operations of the legislative branch. "Florida courts have full authority to review the final product of the legislative process, but they are without authority to review the internal workings of [the Legislature]." *Fla. Senate v. Fla. Pub. Emps. Council 79,* 784 So.2d 404, 409 (Fla.2001); *see also Moffitt v. Willis,* 459 So.2d 1018, 1022 (Fla.1984) (rejecting judicial inquiry into "the propriety and constitutionality of certain internal activities of members of the legislature").

Due respect for the separation of powers precludes the judicial branch from requiring that legislators and legislative employees submit to an inquisition conducted to ferret out evidence of an improper purpose in the legislative process. As the Supreme Court stated in *Tenney,* the view that it is "not consonant with our scheme of government for a court to inquire into the motives of legislators, has remained unquestioned." 341 U.S. at 377, 71 S.Ct. 783 (citing *Fletcher v. Peck,* 10 U.S. (6 Cranch) 87, 130, 3 L.Ed. 162 (1810)). Courts are highly sensitive to the fact that "judicial inquiries into legislative . . . motivation represent a substantial intrusion into the workings of [an]other branch[ ] of government." *Vill. of Arlington Heights v. Metro. Hous. Dev. Corp.,* 429 U.S. 252, 268 n. 18, 97 S.Ct. 555, 50 L.Ed.2d 450 (1977).

* * *

II

The majority recognizes "that a legislative privilege exists in Florida, based on the principle of separation of powers codified in article II, section 3, of the Florida Constitution" but concludes "that this privilege is not absolute and may yield to a compelling, competing interest." Majority op. at 143. The majority holds that a compelling, competing interest is operative here because with the passage of article III, section 20, Florida Constitution, "'the framers and the voters clearly desired more judicial scrutiny' of the [redistricting] plans, 'not less.'" Majority op. at 148 (quoting *Fla. House of Representatives v. League of Women Voters of Fla.,* 118 So.3d 198, 205 (Fla.2013)). The majority adopts a "balancing approach" — applicable to both depositions and document production — under which "most information or communications regarding the congressional [redistricting] process" are discoverable, but the "thoughts or impressions of individual legislators and legislative staff members" are not subject to discovery "at this stage of the litigation." Majority op. at 151. The majority also holds that "any common law legislative privilege has been abolished by" the Florida Evidence Code. Majority op. at 144.

The majority's conclusion that the common law legislative privilege has been abolished is unwarranted. Section 90.501, Florida Statutes (2013), which the majority relies on to support this conclusion, simply provides that no evidentiary privilege exists other than those "provided by [chapter 90], any other statute, or the Constitution of the United States or of the State of Florida." The English common law legislative privilege, however, is given the force of law in Florida by the terms of another statute. Section 2.01, Florida Statutes (2013), provides that the general "common and statute laws of England . . . down to the 4th day of July, 1776, are declared to be in force in this state" to the extent they are "not inconsistent with the Constitution and laws of the United States and the acts of the Legislature of this state." Section 90.501 does nothing to abolish any privilege established in Florida law by section 2.01. By the plain terms of section 2.01, the legislative privilege contained in the Bill of Rights of 1689 is in force under Florida law.

The majority is correct in acknowledging that the legislative privilege is inherent in the separation of powers under Florida's Constitution. But the majority errs in reducing the constitutional legislative privilege to a matter of unfettered judicial discretion. . . .

The majority's balancing approach boils down to the exercise of unfettered judicial discretion: the legislative privilege inherent in the separation of powers will give way to the extent that an entirely subjective judicial determination requires that the privilege must give way. This is not the way that one branch of government should approach the acknowledged constitutional privilege of an equal and coordinate branch of government. When the judicial branch is called on to consider the scope of a privilege granted by the Constitution to another branch of government, it is incumbent upon the judicial branch to articulate clearly grounded, objective rules that can be applied without the suggestion that the coordinate branch's privilege is subject to diminishment or abrogation through the unfettered discretion of judges. At no time would it be more appropriate to pay heed to the maxim that "he is the best judge who leaves the least to his own discretion."[16] In a context such as this — where the internal functioning of a coordinate branch of government is at issue — due respect for the separation of powers requires that judicial restraint be at its zenith. Unfortunately, the balancing approach adopted by the majority represents the nadir of judicial restraint.

* * *

---

16. From the Latin maxim *Optimus judex qui minimum sibi*. *Black's Law Dictionary* 1858 (9th ed. 2009).

2. Encroachment by the Executive Branch on the Power of the Legislative Branch

Florida House of Representatives v. Crist

999 So. 2d 601 (Fla. 2008)

CANTERO, J.

After almost sixteen years of sporadic negotiations with four governors, in November 2007 the Seminole Indian Tribe of Florida signed a gambling "compact" (a contract between two sovereigns) with Florida Governor Charles Crist. The compact significantly expands casino gambling, also known as "gaming," on tribal lands. For example, it permits card games such as blackjack and baccarat that are otherwise prohibited by law. In return, the compact promises substantial remuneration to the State.

The Florida Legislature did not authorize the Governor to negotiate the compact before it was signed and has not ratified it since. To the contrary, shortly after the compact was signed, the Florida House of Representatives and its Speaker, Marco Rubio, filed in this Court a petition for a writ of quo warranto disputing the Governor's authority to bind the State to the compact. We have exercised our discretion to consider such petitions, *see* art. V, § 3(b)(8), Fla. Const., and now grant it on narrow grounds. We hold that the Governor does not have the constitutional authority to bind the State to a gaming compact that clearly departs from the State's public policy by legalizing types of gaming that are illegal everywhere else in the state.

* * *

B. The Negotiations Between the Tribe and the State

* * *

The Seminole Indian Tribe is a federally recognized Indian tribe whose reservations and trust lands are located in the State. The Tribe currently operates Class II gaming facilities, offering low stakes poker games and electronically aided bingo games. The Tribe first sought a compact allowing it to offer Class III gaming in 1991. That January, the Tribe and Governor Lawton Chiles began negotiations, but they ultimately proved fruitless. That same year, the Tribe filed suit in federal court alleging that the State had failed to negotiate in good faith. As noted earlier, the Supreme Court ultimately ruled that the State could assert immunity, and it did. *See Seminole Tribe,* 517 U.S. at 47, 116 S.Ct. 1114, *aff'g Seminole Tribe of Fla. v. Fla.,* 11 F.3d 1016 (11th Cir.1994).

Over the next several years, the Tribe repeatedly petitioned the [United States Department of the Interior] to establish Class III gaming procedures. In 1999, the Department did so. It found the Tribe eligible for the procedures and called an informal conference, which was held in Tallahassee that December. At the State's suggestion, however, the Tribe agreed to suspend the conference, though only temporarily. In January 2001, the Secretary issued a twenty-page decision allowing the

Tribe to offer a wide range of Class III games. When the State requested clarification, however, the Secretary withdrew the decision. The delay continued. Finally, five years later — in May 2006 — the Department reconvened the conference in Hollywood, Florida, and in September of that year warned that if the Tribe and the State did not execute a compact within 60 days, the Department would issue Class III gaming procedures. Despite the parties' failure to negotiate a compact, however, the Department never issued procedures.

Apparently exasperated with the slow progress of the procedures, in March 2007 the Tribe sued the Department in federal court. *See Seminole Tribe of Fla. v. United States,* No. 07-60317-CIV, 2007 WL 5077484 (S.D. Fla. filed Mar. 6, 2007). The Department then urged Governor Crist to negotiate a compact, warning that if a compact was not signed by November 15, 2007, the Department would finally issue procedures. Under the proposed procedures, the State would not receive any revenue and would have no control over the Tribe's gaming operations. The Tribe would be authorized to operate slot machines and "card games," defined as "a game or series of games of poker (other than Class II games) which are played in a *nonbanking* manner." (Emphasis added.) Notably, the alternative procedures would *not* have permitted the Tribe to operate banked card games such as blackjack.[1]

On November 14 — the day before the deadline — the Governor agreed to a compact with the Tribe (Compact). Five days later, the House and its Speaker, Marco Rubio, filed this petition disputing the Governor's authority to bind the State to the Compact without legislative authorization or ratification. We allowed the Tribe to join the action as a respondent.[2]

On January 7, 2008, upon publication of the Secretary's approval, the Compact went into effect. *See* Notice of Deemed Approved Tribal-State Class III Gaming Compact, 73 Fed.Reg. 1229 (Jan. 7, 2008). The parties agree, however, that the Secretary's approval does not render the petition moot.[3]

C. The Compact

The Compact recites that the Governor "has the authority to act for the State with respect to the negotiation and execution of this Compact." It covers a period of twenty-five years and allows the Tribe to offer specified Class III gaming at seven

---

1. During this period, two separate but identical bills designating the Governor to negotiate and execute a compact and submit it for ratification by the legislature were not voted on by the House of Representatives. *See* Fla. SB 160 (2007); Fla. HB 209 (2007).

2. We also allowed other organizations to file briefs as amici curiae in support of the House: the Florida Senate, the Gulfstream Park Racing Association, and the City of Hallandale Beach.

3. The federal district court, however, concluded that such approval did render the Tribe's suit moot. *Seminole Tribe of Fla. v. United States,* No. 07-60317-CIV (S.D. Fla. order filed June 20, 2008). The court dismissed the Tribe's case and noted that the Tribe already had begun operating under the Compact's terms.

casinos in the State. It establishes the terms, rights, and responsibilities of the parties regarding such gaming. We discuss only its more relevant provisions.

The Compact authorizes the Tribe to conduct "covered gaming," which includes several types of Class III gaming: slot machines; any banking or banked card game, including baccarat, blackjack (twenty-one), and *chemin de fer;* high stakes poker games; games and devices authorized for the state lottery; and any new game authorized by Florida law. The Compact expressly does *not* authorize roulette- or craps-style games. The gaming is limited to seven casinos on tribal lands in six areas of the state: Okeechobee, Coconut Creek, Hollywood (two), Clewiston, Immokalee, and Tampa. Compact pt. IV.B., at 7–8.

The Compact grants the Tribe the exclusive right to conduct certain types of gaming. That is, the Tribe may conduct some Class III gaming, such as banked card games, that is prohibited under state law. Based on that "partial but substantial exclusivity," the Tribe must pay the State a share of the gaming revenue. That share is based in part on amounts that increase at specified thresholds: when the Compact becomes effective, the State receives $50 million. Over the first twenty-four months of operation, it will receive another $175 million. Thereafter, for the third twelve months of operation the State will receive $150 million, and for each twelve-month cycle after that, a minimum of $100 million. If the State breaches the exclusivity provision, however — by legalizing any Class III gaming currently prohibited under state law — the Tribe may cease its payments. The Compact (attached as an appendix to this opinion) is thirty-seven pages long and contains several other provisions we need not detail here. [Footnote omitted.]

* * *

III. Discussion of Law

We now discuss the law that applies to this inter-branch dispute. In deciding whether the Governor or the Legislature has the authority to execute a compact, we first define a "compact" and its historical use in Florida. We then discuss how other jurisdictions have resolved this issue. Next, we review the relevant provisions of our own constitution. Finally, we explain our conclusion that the Governor lacked authority under our state's constitution to execute the Compact because it changes the state's public policy as expressed in the criminal law and therefore infringes on the Legislature's powers.

A. Compacts and their Use in Florida

A compact is essentially a contract between two sovereigns. *Texas v. New Mexico,* 482 U.S. 124, 128, 107 S.Ct. 2279, 96 L.Ed.2d 105 (1987); *see Black's Law Dictionary* 298 (8th ed.1999) (defining a compact as "[a]n agreement or covenant between two or more parties, esp[ecially] between governments or states"). The United States Supreme Court has described compacts as "a supple device for dealing with interests confined within a region." *State ex rel. Dyer v. Sims,* 341 U.S. 22, 27, 71 S.Ct. 557, 95 L. Ed. 713 (1951). The United States Constitution provides that "[n]o State shall, without the Consent of Congress . . . enter into any Agreement or Compact with another

State, or with a foreign Power." U.S. Const, art. I, §10. IGRA establishes the consent of Congress to execute gaming compacts, but requires federal approval before they become effective. *See* 25 U.S.C. §2710(d)(8).

Like many states, Florida has executed compacts on a range of subjects, including environmental control, water rights, energy, and education — more than thirty in all. The vast majority were executed with other states. In most cases, the Legislature enacted a law. *See, e.g.,* §372.831, Fla. Stat. (2007) ("The Wildlife Violator Compact is created and entered into with all other jurisdictions legally joining therein in the form substantially as follows[.]"); §257.28 (Interstate Library Compact); §252.921 (Emergency Management Assistance Compact); §322.44 (Driver License Compact). In others, the Legislature authorized the Governor to execute a compact in the form provided in a statute. *See, e.g.,* §370.19, Fla. Stat. (2007) ("The Governor of this state is hereby authorized and directed to execute a compact on behalf of the State of Florida with any one or more of [the following states] . . . legally joining therein in the form substantially as follows [.]"); §370.20 (containing the same authorization and establishing the terms for the Gulf States Marine Fisheries Compact); §403.60 (using the same authorization language for the Interstate Environmental Control Compact, establishing its terms, and "signi[fying] in advance" the Legislature's "approval and ratification of such compact"). In a few — including a compact among the State, the Tribe, and the South Florida Water Management District regulating water use on Tribal lands — the Legislature by statute approved and ratified the compact. §285.165, Fla. Stat. (2007). Thus, by tradition at least, it is the Legislature that has consistently either exercised itself or expressly authorized the exercise of the power to bind the State to compacts. We have found no instance in which the governor has signed a compact without legislative involvement.

Although tradition bears some relevance, it does not resolve the question of which branch actually has the constitutional authority to execute compacts in general and gaming compacts in particular. As explained above, the Compact here governs Class III gaming on certain tribal lands in Florida. The issue is whether, regardless of whether the Governor bucked tradition, he had constitutional authority to execute the Compact without the Legislature's prior authorization or, at least, subsequent ratification.

* * *

C. Florida Constitutional Provisions

The House contends that several of the Compact's provisions encroach on the Legislature's law- and policy-making powers. To answer the question, we first review the separation-of-powers provisions of the Florida Constitution and our interpretations of it. We then discuss one specific provision on which the Governor relies: the "necessary business" clause.

1. The Florida Constitution's Delegation and Separation of Powers

The Florida Constitution generally specifies the relative powers of the three branches of government. Article II, section 3 provides innocuously that "[t]he powers of the state government shall be divided into legislative, executive and judicial branches. No person belonging to one branch shall exercise any powers appertaining to either of the other branches unless expressly provided herein." In construing our constitution, we have "traditionally applied a strict separation of powers doctrine." *Bush v. Schiavo,* 885 So.2d 321, 329 (Fla.2004) (quoting *State v. Cotton,* 769 So.2d 345, 353 (Fla.2000)).

These provisions are not specific, however. In fact, as we first noted 100 years ago, the state constitution does not exhaustively list each branch's powers. *State v. Atlantic Coast Line R.R. Co.,* 56 Fla. 617, 47 So. 969, 974 (1908). Both the Governor and the House concede that the state constitution does not expressly grant *either* branch the authority to execute compacts.

We must therefore expand our analysis beyond the plain language of the constitution. We have held that the powers of the respective branches "are those so defined . . . or such as are inherent or so recognized by immemorial governmental usage, and which involve the exercise of primary and independent will, discretion, and judgment, subject not to the control of another department, but only to the limitations imposed by the state and federal Constitutions." *Id.* at 974. A branch has "the inherent right to accomplish all objects naturally within the orbit of that department, not expressly limited by the fact of the existence of a similar power elsewhere or the express limitations in the constitution." *Sun Ins. Office, Ltd. v. Clay,* 133 So.2d 735, 742 (Fla.1961) (quoting *In re Integration of Neb. State Bar Ass'n,* 275 N.W. 265, 266 (1937)). As we noted over seventy-five years ago, what determines whether a particular function is legislative, executive, or judicial "so that it may be exercised by appropriate officers of the proper department" is not "the name given to the function or to the officer who performs it" but the "essential nature and effect of the governmental function to be performed." *Florida Motor Lines v. Railroad Comm'rs,* 100 Fla. 538, 129 So. 876, 881 (1930).

The House argues that, precisely because the state constitution does not expressly grant the governor authority to execute compacts, such authority belongs to the Legislature. In other words, the "residual" power — that is, powers not specifically assigned to the governor — belongs to the Legislature. Albeit many years ago and under different circumstances, we have implied as much. *See State ex rel. Green v. Pearson,* 153 Fla. 314, 14 So.2d 565, 567 (1943) ("The legislative branch looks to the Constitution not for sources of power but for limitations upon power. But if such limitations are not found to exist, its discretion reasonably exercised may not be disturbed by the judicial branch of the government."); *State ex rel. Cunningham v. Davis,* 123 Fla. 41, 166 So. 289, 297 (1936) ("The test of legislative power is constitutional restriction; what the people have not said in their organic law their representatives shall not do, they may do."). And, as we noted above, other state courts have ascribed to their legislatures any residual power on which the state constitutions were silent. *See Clark,* 904 P.2d at 25; *Pataki,* 766 N.Y.S.2d at 668, n. 11, 798 N.E.2d at 1061 n. 11.

We need not decide, however, whether the authority to bind the state to compacts always resides in the legislature. Although the line of demarcation is not always clear, we have noted that "the legislature's exclusive power encompasses questions of fundamental policy and the articulation of reasonably definite standards to be used in implementing those policies." *B.H. v. State,* 645 So.2d 987, 993 (Fla.1994); *see also Askew v. Cross Key Waterways,* 372 So.2d 913, 925 (Fla.1978) (stating that under the nondelegation doctrine, "fundamental and primary policy decisions shall be made by members of the legislature"). Therefore, even if the Governor has authority to execute compacts, its terms cannot contradict the state's public policy, as expressed in its laws.

* * *

D. The Compact Violates the Separation of Powers

The House claims that the Compact violates the separation of powers on a number of grounds.[8] We find one of them dispositive. The Compact permits the Tribe to conduct certain Class III gaming that is prohibited under Florida law. Therefore, the Compact violates the state's public policy about the types of gambling that should be allowed. We hold that, whatever the Governor's authority to execute compacts, it does not extend so far. The Governor does not have authority to agree to legalize in some parts of the state, or for some persons, conduct that is otherwise illegal throughout the state.

We first discuss whether state laws in general, and gaming laws in particular, apply to Indian tribes. We next discuss Florida law on gaming. We then address the House's argument that IGRA prohibits compacts from expanding the gaming allowed under state law. Finally, we explain why the Governor lacked authority to bind the State to a compact, such as this one, that contradicts state law.

1. State Gaming Laws Apply to the Tribe

Generally, state laws do not apply to tribal Indians on Indian reservations unless Congress so provides. *McClanahan v. State Tax Comm'n of Ariz.,* 411 U.S. 164, 170, 93 S.Ct. 1257, 36 L.Ed.2d 129 (1973). Therefore, the extent to which a state may enforce its criminal laws on tribal land depends on federal authorization. *See Seminole Tribe of Fla. v. Butterworth,* 658 F.2d 310, 312 (5th Cir.1981). Congress has, however, conferred on the states the authority to assume jurisdiction over crimes committed on

---

8. The House argues that the Compact significantly changes Florida law and policy in a number of ways: it authorizes Class III slot machines outside of Broward County; it allows blackjack and other banked card games that are currently illegal throughout Florida; it provides for collection of funds from tribal casinos for State purposes under a revenue-sharing agreement and penalizes the State for any expansion of non-tribal gaming; it allows an exception to Florida's substantive right of access to public records for information dealing with Indian gaming; it changes the venue of litigation dealing with individual disputes with the tribal casinos; it sets procedures for tort remedies occurring in certain circumstances; it waives sovereign immunity to the extent that it creates enforceable contract rights between the State and the Tribe; and it establishes a regulatory mechanism to be undertaken by the Governor or his designee. Because of our resolution of this case, we need not consider whether these other provisions encroach on the legislature's policy-making authority.

tribal land, *see* Act of Aug. 15, 1953, Pub.L. No. 280 § 6, 67 Stat. 588, 590 (1953), and Florida has assumed such jurisdiction. *See* ch. 61-252, §§ 1–2, at 452–53, Laws of Fla. (codified at § 285.16, Fla. Stat. (2007)); *see also* § 285.16(2), Fla. Stat. (2007) ("The civil and criminal laws of Florida shall obtain on all Indian reservations in this state and shall be enforced in the same manner as elsewhere throughout the state."); Op. Att'y Gen. Fla. 94-45 (1994) (discussing the state's jurisdiction over Indian reservations). The state's law is therefore enforceable on tribal lands to the extent it does not conflict with federal law. *See* Op. Att'y Gen. Fla. 94-45 (1994); *see also Hall v. State*, 762 So.2d 936, 936–38 (Fla. 2d DCA 2000) (holding that the circuit court had jurisdiction over a vehicular homicide on an Indian reservation); *State v. Billie*, 497 So.2d 889, 892–95 (Fla. 2d DCA 1986) (holding that a Seminole Indian was properly charged under state criminal law with killing a Florida panther on tribal land). In regard to gambling in particular, federal law provides that, except as provided in a tribal-state compact, state gambling laws apply on tribal lands. *See* 18 U.S.C. § 1166(a) (2000).

Based on these state and federal provisions, what is legal in Florida is legal on tribal lands, and what is illegal in Florida is illegal there. Absent a compact, any gambling prohibited in the state is prohibited on tribal land.

2. Florida's Gaming Laws

It is undisputed that Florida permits limited forms of Class III gaming. The state's constitution authorizes the state lottery, which offers various Class III games, and now permits slot machines in Miami-Dade and Broward Counties. *See* art. X, §§ 7, 15, Fla. Const. For a long time, the State also has regulated pari-mutuel wagering — for example, on dog and horse racing. *See* ch. 550, Fla. Stat. (2007) (governing pari-mutuel wagering).

It is also undisputed, however, that the State prohibits all other types of Class III gaming, including lotteries not sponsored by the State and slot machines outside Miami-Dade and Broward Counties. Florida law distinguishes between nonbanked (Class II) card games and banked (Class III) card games.[9] A "banking game" is one "in which the house is a participant in the game, taking on players, paying winners, and collecting from losers or in which the cardroom establishes a bank against which participants play." § 849.086(2)(b); *see* § 849.086(1), Fla. Stat. (deeming banked games to be "casino gaming"). Florida law authorizes cardrooms at pari-mutuel facilities for games of "poker or dominoes," but only if they are played "in a non-banking manner." § 849.086(2), Fla. Stat.; *see* § 849.086(1)-(3). Florida law prohibits

---

9. Chapter 849, Florida Statutes (2007), regulates most gaming. It prohibits playing "any game at cards, keno, roulette, faro or other game of chance, at any place, by any device whatever, for money or other thing of value," designating it a second-degree misdemeanor. § 849.08, Fla. Stat. (2007). Certain "penny-ante games" are exempted when "conducted strictly in accordance" with the law. § 849.085, Fla. Stat. (2007) ("'Penny-ante game' means a game or series of games of poker, pinochle, bridge, rummy, canasta, hearts, dominoes, or mah-jongg in which the winnings of any player in a single round, hand, or game do not exceed $10 in value.").

banked card games, however. *See* § 849.086(12)(a), (15)(a). Blackjack, baccarat, and *chemin de fer* are banked card games. They are therefore illegal in Florida.

3. Does IGRA Permit Compacts to Expand Gaming?

* * *

Whether the Compact violates IGRA, however, is a question we need not and do not resolve. Given our narrow scope of review on a writ of quo warranto, the issue here is only whether the Florida Constitution grants the Governor the authority to unilaterally bind the State to a compact that violates public policy. We conclude that *even if* the Governor is correct that IGRA permits the expansion of gaming on tribal lands beyond what state law permits, such an agreement represents a significant change in Florida's public policy. It is therefore precisely the type of action particularly within the Legislature's power. We now discuss that issue.

4. The Compact Violates Florida's Public Policy on Gaming

Article II, section 3 of the Florida Constitution prohibits the executive branch from usurping the powers of another branch. Enacting laws — and especially criminal laws — is quintessentially a legislative function. *See State v. Barquet,* 262 So.2d 431, 433 (Fla.1972) ("The lawmaking function is the chief legislative power."). By authorizing the Tribe to conduct "banked card games" that are illegal throughout Florida — and thus illegal for the Tribe — the Compact violates Florida law. *See Chiles v. Children A, B, C, D, E, & F,* 589 So.2d 260, 264 (Fla.1991) ("This Court has repeatedly held that, under the doctrine of separation of powers, the legislature may not delegate the power to enact laws or to declare what the law shall be to any other branch."). The Governor's action therefore encroaches on the legislative function and was beyond his authority. Nor does it matter that the Compact is a contract between the State and the Tribe. Neither the Governor nor anyone else in the executive branch has the authority to execute a contract that violates state criminal law. *Cf. Local No. 234, United Assoc. of Journeymen & Apprentices of Plumbing & Pipefitting Industry v. Henley & Beckwith, Inc.,* 66 So.2d 818, 821 (Fla.1953) ("[A]n agreement that is violative of a provision of a constitution or a valid statute, or an agreement which cannot be performed without violating such a constitutional or statutory provision, is illegal and void."); *City of Miami v. Benson,* 63 So.2d 916, 923 (Fla.1953) ("The contract in question, that is, the acceptance by the City of the proposal made by its agent, employee or advisor, to purchase the bonds, is contrary to public policy and is, therefore, void.").

IV. Conclusion

We conclude that the Governor's execution of a compact authorizing types of gaming that are prohibited under Florida law violates the separation of powers. The Governor has no authority to change or amend state law. Such power falls exclusively to the Legislature. Therefore, we hold that the Governor lacked authority to bind the State to a compact that violates Florida law as this compact does. We need not resolve the broader issue of whether the Governor ever has the authority to execute compacts without either the Legislature's prior authorization or, at least, its subsequent ratification. Because we believe the parties will fully comply with the dictates of this opinion, we grant the petition but withhold issuance of the writ.

It is so ordered.

WELLS, ANSTEAD, PARIENTE, and BELL, JJ., concur.

QUINCE, C.J., concurs in result only.

LEWIS, J., concurs in result only with an opinion.

[The concurring opinion of Justice Lewis is omitted.]

Agencies that are part of the executive branch of government interpret the legislative statutes under which they operate. Courts defer to the agency's interpretation of those statutes that pertain to it unless the interpretation is contrary to the statute's "plain meaning."[14] We suppose it could be argued that this deference is to some extent a judicially approved intrusion by the executive branch, the agency, into the province of the legislative branch. If this is indeed the case, its impact on the doctrine of separation of powers is modest at best because the agency interpretation cannot depart from the statute's "plain meaning" and still be accepted by the judiciary.

3. Encroachment by the Judicial Branch on the Power of the Executive Branch

Florida Department of Children & Families v. J.B.

154 So. 3d 479 (Fla. 3d Dist. Ct. App. 2015)

LOGUE, J.

Florida Department of Children and Families appeals an order directing it to pay the travel costs of the pro bono Attorney Ad Litem to assist in the therapy of her client, a child in the custody of the Department and placed in a North Carolina residential treatment facility. We treat the appeal as a petition for writ of certiorari, grant the petition, and quash the order because it violates the doctrine of separation of powers.

Facts

J.B. is a minor child in the custody of the Department. Based on the recommendation of J.B.'s psychiatrist, both the Guardian Ad Litem and the Department concluded that J.B. required mental health treatment in a residential treatment facility. They further determined that the Alexander Youth Network, a residential program in North Carolina, provided the therapeutic treatment that best suited J.B.'s needs.

---

14. *See Werner v. State Department of Insurance and Treasurer,* 689 So. 2d 1211, 1214 (Fla. 1st Dist. Ct. App. 1997).

The Department and the Guardian Ad Litem moved the trial court to approve the placement. Based on the evidence submitted, the trial court agreed that the placement was in J.B.'s best interest. It ultimately entered an order which authorized the placement.

Afterwards, the pro bono Attorney Ad Litem filed a motion to require the Department to pay her travel costs to visit J.B. at the facility in North Carolina, arguing that personal visits were necessary to maintain a meaningful attorney-client relationship.[1] The trial court denied the request to require the Department to pay travel costs that "are made to foster the attorney/client relationship." Although not requested by the Attorney Ad Litem, the court ordered the Department to "fund any visits [by the pro bono Attorney Ad Litem] that are therapeutically recommended by the therapeutic staff of the Alexander Youth Network." The Department appealed.

Analysis

The issue presented is whether the trial court's order violated the separation of powers doctrine by requiring the Department, an executive agency, to pay for the travel of the pro bono Attorney Ad Litem for the purpose of facilitating the minor child's therapy. We have jurisdiction. *See Fla. Dep't of Children & Families v. Y.C.,* 82 So.3d 1139, 1141 n. 6 (Fla. 3d DCA 2012) (holding, in a similar case, that certiorari was the proper vehicle for review); *Dep't of Corrs. v. Harrison,* 896 So.2d 868, 869 (Fla. 5th DCA 2005) ("[T]he Department of Children and Families has successfully sought certiorari review in cases where a trial court allegedly exceeded its judicial authority by encroaching on the powers of the executive branch by ordering it to take some action not permitted under the law.").

Florida's Constitution provides for the separation of powers between the three branches of state government:

> The powers of the state government shall be divided into legislative, executive and judicial branches. No person belonging to one branch shall exercise any powers appertaining to either of the other branches unless expressly provided herein.

Art. II, § 3, Fla. Const.

---

1. This court takes this opportunity to thank the Attorney Ad Litem, Angela Vigil, Esquire, for her professionalism in providing representation to J.B. on a pro bono basis. Her representation benefits the child, our community, and the courts, and exemplifies the ideals of service in our profession. By advocating the child's point of view, Ms. Vigil not only contributed an important viewpoint to aid the court's deliberation, but also enabled the child to feel that her voice was heard, considered, and respected as part of the judicial process. The child's perception that she was treated with good faith is important, our Supreme Court has noted, because "a child who feels that he or she has been treated fairly in the course of the commitment proceedings will likely be more willing to accept hospitalization and treatment." *Amendment to the Rules of Juvenile Procedure, Fla. R. Juv. P. 8.350,* 804 So.2d 1206, 1211 (Fla.2001).

Under this doctrine, "the judicial branch must not interfere with the discretionary functions of the legislative or executive branches of government absent a violation of constitutional or statutory rights." *Detournay v. City of Coral Gables,* 127 So.3d 869, 873 (Fla. 3d DCA 2013) (quoting *Trianon Park Condo. Ass'n, Inc. v. City of Hialeah,* 468 So.2d 912, 918 (Fla.1985)). "When a court interferes with an executive agency's discretion in spending its appropriate[d] funds, it is encroaching on the powers of the agency." *Office of State Attorney for Eleventh Judicial Circuit v. Polites,* 904 So.2d 527, 532 (Fla. 3d DCA 2005).

A court may order an executive department to spend funds when a statute or constitution authorizes a court to do so. Courts, however, have rejected the idea that there is a "doctrine of inherent judicial power" that allows a court to direct how an executive department exercises its discretion to spend funds appropriated to the department. *Dep't of Children & Families v. J.H.,* 831 So.2d 782, 783 (Fla. 4th DCA 2002) (holding, absent statutory authority, a trial court could not order the Department to pay for long-term therapy by a specific therapist and any and all necessary evaluations for the dependent child). Instead, courts have repeatedly held that "[t]he judicial branch may not either interfere with the legislative branch by requiring funds to be spent by an executive agency *in a manner not authorized by statute,* nor interfere with an executive agency's discretion in the spending of appropriated funds." *Dep't of Children & Families v. K.R.,* 946 So.2d 106, 107–08 (Fla. 5th DCA 2007) (emphasis added).

Accordingly, unless a statute or a constitution authorizes the court to do so, it is a violation of the doctrine of separation of powers for a court to direct an executive department on how to expend funds appropriated to the department.[2] Turning to the instant case, because no statute authorized the trial court to order the Department to pay for the travel of the pro bono Attorney Ad Litem for the purpose of facilitating J.B.'s therapy, the order violates the doctrine of separation of powers.

The pro bono Attorney Ad Litem attempted to defend the trial court's order by citing to general law regarding the need to foster attorney-client relationships in this

---

2. *See, e.g., Polites,* 904 So.2d at 532 (holding the trial court violated the separation of powers doctrine when it ordered the Office of the State Attorney to pay for the costs of mental health experts evaluating the defendant); *Harrison,* 896 So.2d at 870 (holding the trial court violated the separation of powers doctrine when it ordered the Department of Corrections to pay for an interpreter for a defendant who was hearing impaired); *Dep't of Corr. v. Grubbs,* 884 So.2d 1147, 1148 (Fla. 2d DCA 2004) (holding the trial court violated the separation of powers doctrine when it ordered the Department of Corrections to pay for a convicted sex offender's treatment program); *Dep't of Children & Family Servs. v. Birchfield,* 718 So.2d 202 (Fla. 4th DCA 1998) (reversing a trial court order that held the Department in contempt for failing to place the appellee in a specific program); *Dep't of Juvenile Justice v. C.M.,* 704 So.2d 1123, 1125 (Fla. 4th DCA 1998) ("[T]he court cannot direct a particular placement for a child and order the expenditure of funds for such placement by an executive agency."); *Dep't of Health & Rehabilitative Servs. v. V.L.,* 583 So.2d 765, 767 (Fla. 5th DCA 1991) ("[I]t is not the judiciary's role to revise legislative appropriations or to interfere with an agency's discretionary budgetary decisions").

context. That issue is not before us. The order under review excluded travel costs relating to attorney-client matters.

Petition granted; order quashed.

---

4. Encroachment by the Legislative Branch on the Power of the Executive Branch

Jones v. Chiles

638 So. 2d 48 (Fla. 1994)

OVERTON, Justice.

John Paul Jones, Jr., a compensation claims judge, petitions for a writ of mandamus, asking this Court to require Lawton M. Chiles, Governor of the State of Florida, to reappoint him to office as required by the reappointment procedure set forth in section 440.45, Florida Statutes (1991). We have jurisdiction under article V, section 3(b)(8), of the Florida Constitution. We find that the portion of section 440.45(2) that eliminates the Governor's choice in the reappointment of a compensation claims judge is invalid, because it unconstitutionally encroaches on the power of the Governor to appoint executive branch officers. For the reasons expressed, we deny the petition.

The undisputed facts of this case are as follows. In 1972, Jones was appointed to a four-year term as a compensation claims judge to hear workers' compensation cases. Shortly thereafter, the legislature created a process for the merit selection and retention of compensation claims judges. *See* § 440.45, Fla. Stat. (1975). Under this process, each appellate district had a judicial nominating commission. For initial appointments, the commission submitted to the Governor a list containing the names of three lawyers, and the Governor appointed one of those lawyers to serve a four-year term as a compensation claims judge. Before the expiration of a judge's four-year term, the commission voted whether to retain the judge for another term. If the commission voted not to retain the judge, then the Governor could not reappoint the judge. If the commission voted to retain the judge, then the Governor was required to reappoint the judge to another four-year term. Under this process, Jones has been reappointed to five four-year terms since his initial appointment and was last reappointed by Governor Martinez in 1988.

In 1990, the legislature created a statewide nominating commission to replace the existing district judicial nominating commissions for workers' compensation judges. The retention process remained the same. *See* § 440.45, Fla. Stat. (1991). In 1992, the new statewide nominating commission voted 8–6 to retain Jones. Governor Chiles, however, has not reappointed Jones to office and has advised that he will not do so. At this time, Jones remains in office, is still performing his duties, and is being paid his state salary. He now files this petition for a writ of mandamus, asking this Court to require the Governor to reappoint him to office as mandated by section 440.45.

* * *

As the [applicable] portion of section 440.45 indicates, "if the statewide nominating commission votes to retain the judge of compensation claims in office then the governor *shall* reappoint the judge of compensation claims for a term of four years." (Emphasis added.) Because of this language in the statute, Jones maintains that the Governor must perform the ministerial act of reappointing him given that the nominating commission has voted to retain him in office. The Governor, on the other hand, argues that he need not reappoint Jones to office as required by section 440.45 because the statute violates the separation of powers doctrine by unconstitutionality depriving him of his gubernatorial prerogative to appoint executive branch officers.

* * *

... The question, then, is whether the statute is unconstitutional as asserted by the Governor. A number of provisions of the Florida Constitution are applicable in answering this question.

By law, compensation claims judges fall under the Workers' Compensation Division of the Department of Labor and Employment Security. *See* §§ 20.171(d), 440.45, Fla. Stat. (1991). The Department of Labor and Employment Security is one of the twenty-five *executive departments* provided for in article VI, section 6, of the Florida Constitution. As the chief executive officer in whom the supreme executive power is vested,[1] the Governor has direct supervision over all executive departments unless the legislature places that supervision in the hands of one of the following other executive officers: the lieutenant governor, the governor and cabinet, a cabinet member, or an officer or board appointed by and serving at the pleasure of the governor. *See* art. IV, §§ 1(a), 6, Fla. Const. Inherent in that direct supervisory authority is the power to appoint executive officers to public office.

Under Section 20.171, the Department of Labor and Employment Security comes under the direct supervision of the Secretary of Labor and Employment Security, an officer who is appointed by and serves at the pleasure of the Governor. As such, only the Governor or the Secretary of Labor and Employment Security, subject to the Governor's approval, would have the power to appoint judges of compensation claims. The legislature, under section 440.45, directs the Governor to "appoint as many full-time judges of compensation claims to the workers' compensation trial courts as may be necessary to effectually perform the duties prescribed for them." Consequently, the Governor alone is the executive officer in whom the power of appointment of compensation claims judges is vested. The only restriction that may be placed on that appointment power is that confirmation by the senate or the approval of three members of the cabinet may be required by law. Art. IV, § 6(a),

---

1. *See* art. IV, § 1(a), Fla. Const.

Fla. Const.[2] Additionally, because article III, section 13, of the Florida Constitution, expressly limits the terms of public officers to four years unless otherwise specified in the constitution, and because the Governor is the chief executive officer in whom the power to appoint compensation claims judges is vested, a new appointment by the Governor is required for compensation claims judges every four years. Under the reappointment provisions of section 440.45(2), however, the legislature has provided that reappointment of compensation claims judges is to be by majority vote of the statewide nominating commission. Because under section 440.45 the Governor *must* reappoint a judge of compensation claims if the statewide nominating commission votes to retain such judge, the Governor's act in reappointing a judge of compensation claims is purely ministerial. This procedure effectively eliminates the power of the Governor to reappoint compensation claims judges as officers of the executive branch.

Jones, nevertheless, maintains that the Governor has no constitutional right to appoint compensation claims judges because, although compensation claims judges are technically executive branch officers, they are, in reality, judicial officers inasmuch as they exercise quasi-judicial powers; they function exclusively as judicial officers; and they are governed by Supreme Court rules. Consequently, Jones asserts, the Governor has no constitutional appointment power in the reappointment of compensation claims judges.

As noted above, in Florida, the legislature has chosen to place compensation claims judges within the executive branch as part of the Department of Labor. Although, in the past, this Court has acknowledged that judges of compensation claims perform a quasi-judicial function, we have repeatedly acknowledged that those judges are still members of the executive branch. . . . We thus find that compensation claims judges are executive branch officials, not judicial branch officials. Having determined that judges of compensation claims fall within the authority of the executive branch, we conclude that section 440.45(2) violates the separation of powers doctrine to the extent that it deprives the Governor of his power to appoint and reappoint.

* * *

---

2. Article IV, section 6, of the Florida Constitution, provides in pertinent part:

Executive Departments. — All functions of the executive branch of state government shall be allotted among not more than twenty-five departments, exclusive of those specifically provided for or authorized in this constitution. The administration of each department, unless otherwise provided in this constitution, shall be placed by law under the direct supervision of the governor, the lieutenant governor, the governor and cabinet, a cabinet member, or an officer or board appointed by and serving at the pleasure of the governor, except:

(a) When provided by law, confirmation by the senate or the approval of three members of the cabinet shall be required for appointment to or removal from any designated statutory office.

In conclusion, we find the portion of section 440.45(2) that eliminates the Governor's choice in the reappointment of a compensation claims judge to be invalid because it unconstitutionally encroaches on the power of the Governor to appoint executive branch officers. Having made this determination, we find that the Governor is free to proceed under the new appointment procedure set forth in chapter 93-415, section 40, Laws of Florida, in filling Jones' position. The Governor has made no objection to the new appointment process set forth in that provision and, under that process, he is allowed to make the final choice in filling Jones' position by choosing from the qualified individuals submitted to him by the nominating commission. Further, under the unique circumstances of this case, we find that Jones and like-situated compensation claims judges should continue to serve as compensation claims judges in a de facto capacity until the Governor fills their positions under the provisions of chapter 93-415. [Footnote omitted.]

Accordingly, for the reasons expressed, the petition for a writ of mandamus is denied.

It is so ordered.

GRIMES, C.J., SHAW, KOGAN and HARDING, JJ., and McDONALD, Senior Justice, concur.

---

5. Encroachment by the Executive Branch on the Power of the Judicial Branch

McNeil v. Canty

12 So. 3d 215 (Fla. 2009)

PER CURIAM.

We review the decision of the First District Court of Appeal in *Canty v. McNeil*, 995 So.2d 998 (Fla. 1st DCA 2008), a case in which the First District certified a question of great public importance.[1] We rephrase the certified question as follows:

> Upon revocation of conditional release, can the Department of Corrections (DOC) calculate an inmate's new release date by using the gain time forfeited on the release eligible sentence with the most accrued gain time, even if this method requires the inmate to be incarcerated beyond the concurrent sentences imposed by the trial judge?

We answer the rephrased question in the negative and approve the result of the First District's decision. We also disapprove the Fifth District Court of Appeal's conflicting decision in *Crosby v. McNeal*, 865 So.2d 617 (Fla. 5th DCA 2004). We

---

1. We have jurisdiction. *See* art. V, § 3(b)(4), Fla. Const.

hold that DOC cannot require an inmate to serve more incarceration time than imposed by the trial judge.

I. Background

In 1992, Edison Canty was sentenced to serve multiple sentences concurrently. *Canty*, 995 So.2d at 998. Three of Canty's fifteen-year concurrent sentences were eligible for conditional release; however, these sentences were not subject to the same accrual of gain time. In April 2002, Canty was conditionally released. *Id.* His conditional release eligible sentence with the least accrued gain time, which mandated the longest incarceration, determined his release date.

In December 2005, Canty was returned to custody after he violated the conditions of his supervision. *Id.* Upon revocation of his conditional release, DOC declared a forfeiture of the previously accrued gain time on Canty's three conditional release eligible offenses. Then, DOC determined Canty's new release date by using the forfeited gain time on the conditional release eligible sentence that had accrued the greatest amount of gain time. Specifically, DOC calculated Canty's new tentative release date as follows: August 24, 2005 (date of revocation of supervision) + 2847 days (forfeited gain time on the sentence with the most accrued gain time) — 94 days (Florida Parole Commission credit) — 481 days (gain time awarded since revocation date) = January 15, 2012.

Canty challenged DOC's calculation of his new release date, arguing that "the new release date effectively extends his sentence from 15 years to over 17 years, a period beyond the statutory limits and the authority of [DOC]." *Id.* at 999. After being denied administrative relief as well as relief in the trial court, Canty filed a petition for a writ of certiorari in the First District. *Id.* The First District concluded that "[t]he court set the length of sentence, and [DOC] does not have the authority to increase it." *Id.* Accordingly, the First District granted Canty's petition and remanded to the trial court for further proceedings. *Id.*

II. Analysis

The Conditional Release Program Act provides that, upon revocation of conditional release, an inmate is returned to prison to serve the sentence imposed upon him by the sentencing judge, while the gain time the inmate earned prior to conditional release is forfeited. *See* § 947.141(3)-(4), Fla. Stat. (1991). Further, the Florida Corrections Code states that "forfeitures of gain-time, when ordered, shall be applied to make the tentative release date proportionately later." § 944.275(3)(a), Fla. Stat. (1991). Combined, these statutes appear to instruct DOC to calculate an inmate's new release date by using the gain time that is forfeited upon revocation. In most circumstances, such a calculation would not pose a problem.

But here, if the forfeited gain time on Canty's sentence with the most accrued gain time is applied to make his new tentative release date proportionately later, Canty would be required to serve more incarceration time than originally imposed by the sentencing judge. Specifically, Canty would have to serve approximately seventeen years in prison, rather than the fifteen-year concurrent sentences originally imposed. Such a result would be unconstitutional. "Sentencing is a power, obligation, and prerogative of the courts, not DOC." *Pearson v. Moore,* 767 So.2d 1235, 1239 (Fla. 1st DCA 2000), *approved,* 789 So.2d 316 (Fla.2001). And article II, section 3 of the Florida Constitution provides that "[n]o person belonging to one branch shall exercise any powers appertaining to either of the other branches unless expressly provided herein." *See also* art. I, § 18, Fla. Const. ("No administrative agency . . . shall impose a sentence of imprisonment, nor shall it impose any other penalty except as provided by law."); *Moore v. Pearson,* 789 So.2d 316, 319 (Fla.2001) ("DOC violates the separation of power doctrine when it refuses to carry out the sentence imposed by the court.").

To avoid this unconstitutional result, we hold that DOC, upon revocation of conditional release, must *retroactively* credit prison time served on any concurrent sentence as prison time served on all concurrent sentences. *See Crosby v. Bolden,* 867 So.2d 373, 378–79 (Fla.2004) (Wells, J., dissenting); *State v. Rabedeau,* 2 So.3d 191, 192 (Fla.2009). We are not receding from our decision in *Evans v. Singletary,* 737 So.2d 505 (Fla.1999).

III. Conclusion

For the above reasons, we answer the rephrased certified question in the negative and hold that DOC cannot require an inmate to serve more incarceration time than imposed by the trial judge. Upon revocation of conditional release, DOC must retroactively credit prison time served on any concurrent sentence as prison time served on all concurrent sentences. Accordingly, we approve the result of the First District's decision in *Canty* and disapprove the Fifth District's conflicting decision in *Crosby.*

It is so ordered.

PARIENTE, LEWIS, POLSTON, LABARGA, and PERRY, JJ., concur.

CANADY, J., specially concurs with an opinion.

QUINCE, C.J., concurs in result only with an opinion.

[The concurring opinions of Chief Justice Quince and Justice Canady are omitted.]

6. Encroachment by the Legislative Branch on the Power of the Judicial Branch

DeLisle v. Crane Co.

258 So. 3d 1219 (Fla. 2018)

QUINCE, J.

* * *

Court have worked in tandem for nearly forty years to enact and maintain codified rules of evidence. This arrangement between the branches to avoid constitutional questions of separation of powers continued uninterrupted from the Evidence Code's inception until 2000. In the instant case, we are asked to determine whether chapter 2013-107, section 1, Laws of Florida, which revised section 90.702, Florida Statutes (2015), and which we previously declined to adopt, to the extent it was procedural, infringes on this Court's rulemaking authority. We find that it does. Therefore, we reverse the Fourth District and remand for reinstatement of the final judgment.

The Florida Legislature enacted the first codified rules of evidence in 1976. Ch. 76-237, at 556, Laws of Florida. In 1979, we adopted the Florida Evidence Code, to the extent that the code was procedural. *See In re Fla. Evidence Code,* 372 So.2d 1369 (Fla.), *clarified, In re Fla. Evidence Code,* 376 So.2d 1161 (Fla. 1979). We recognized that "[r]ules of evidence may in some instances be substantive law and, therefore, the sole responsibility of the legislature. In other instances, evidentiary rules may be procedural and the responsibility of this Court." *Id.* at 1369. We therefore chose to adopt the rules, "[t]o avoid multiple appeals and confusion in the operation of the courts caused by assertions that portions of the evidence code are procedural and, therefore, unconstitutional because they had not been adopted by this Court under its rule-making authority." *Id.* Since then, we have traditionally continued to adopt the code, to the extent it is procedural, to avoid the issue of whether the Evidence Code is substantive in nature and therefore within the province of the Legislature or procedural in nature and therefore within the province of this Court. [Citations omitted.]

Until 2000, the working arrangement between the Legislature and the Florida Supreme Court remained intact. However, in *In re Amendments to the Florida Evidence Code,* 782 So.2d 339 (Fla. 2000), this Court for the first time declined to adopt, to the extent they were procedural, amendments to section 90.803, Florida Statutes (1997). *Id.* (declining to adopt chapter 98-2, section 1, Laws of Florida, amending section 90.803(22), Florida Statutes, which allows the admission of former testimony although the declarant is available as a witness, in part because of concerns about its constitutionality). We then considered the constitutionality of the provision in *State v. Abreu,* 837 So.2d 400 (Fla. 2003), determining that the revised statute was unconstitutional because it infringed on a defendant's right to confront witnesses. *Id.* at 406.

Since then, we have only rarely declined to adopt a statutory revision to the Evidence Code. *See, e.g., In re Amends. to the Fla. Evidence Code,* 210 So.3d 1231 (Fla. 2017) (declining to adopt chapter 2013-107, sections 1-2, Laws of Florida); *In re Amends. to the Fla. Evidence Code,* 144 So.3d 536 (Fla. 2014) (declining to adopt chapter 2011-183, section 1, Laws of Florida, creating section 90.5021, Florida Statutes (2012), which establishes a "fiduciary lawyer-client privilege," and declining to adopt chapter 2011-233, section 10, Laws of Florida, creating section 766.102(12), Florida Statutes (2012), which pertains to a medical malpractice expert witness provision). Since its inception, therefore, the Florida Evidence Code has been considered neither purely substantive nor purely procedural. *See In re Fla. Evidence Code,* 372 So.2d 1369, 1369 (Fla.), *clarified,* 376 So.2d 1161 (Fla. 1979) ("Rules of evidence may in some instances be substantive law and, therefore, the sole responsibility of the legislature. In other instances, evidentiary rules may be procedural and the responsibility of this Court.").

Generally, the Legislature has the power to enact substantive law while this Court has the power to enact procedural law. *See Allen v. Butterworth,* 756 So.2d 52, 59 (Fla. 2000). Substantive law has been described as that which defines, creates, or regulates rights — "those existing for their own sake and constituting the normal legal order of society, i.e., the rights of life, liberty, property, and reputation." *In re Fla. Rules of Criminal Procedure,* 272 So.2d 65, 65 (Fla. 1972) (Adkins, J., concurring). Procedural law, on the other hand, is the form, manner, or means by which substantive law is implemented. *Id.* at 66 (Adkins, J., concurring). Stated differently, procedural law "includes all rules governing the parties, their counsel and the Court throughout the progress of the case from the time of its initiation until final judgment and its execution." *Allen v. Butterworth,* 756 So.2d 52, 60 (Fla. 2000) (quoting *In re Rules of Criminal Procedure,* 272 So.2d at 66 (Adkins, J., concurring)). "It is the method of conducting litigation involving rights and corresponding defenses." *Haven Federal Savings & Loan Ass'n v. Kirian,* 579 So.2d 730, 732 (Fla. 1991) (citing *Skinner v. City of Eustis* , 147 Fla. 22, 2 So.2d 116 (1941)).

The distinction between substantive and procedural law, however, is not always clear. For example, a law is considered to be substantive when it both creates and conditions a right. *See State v. Raymond* , 906 So.2d 1045, 1049 (Fla. 2005); *Jackson v. Fla. Dep't of Corr.,* 790 So.2d 381, 383-84 (Fla. 2000) (holding that the Legislature could properly limit the right of indigents to proceed without payment of costs); *Caple v. Tuttle's Design-Build, Inc.,* 753 So.2d 49, 54 (Fla. 2000) (holding that a statute creating the right to petition for mortgage payment receipts during foreclosure proceedings and establishing the grounds for granting such a petition was constitutional); *School Bd. of Broward Cty. v. Price,* 362 So.2d 1337 (Fla. 1978) (holding that section 230.23(9)(d)(2), Florida Statutes (1977), set the bounds of a substantive right conditioned on a waiver and was therefore not an unconstitutional infringement of the Court's power to set procedural rules). However, when procedural aspects overwhelm substantive ones, the law may no longer be considered substantive. *Raymond,* 906 So.2d at 1049.

Here, the Legislature sought to adopt *Daubert* and cease the application of *Frye* to expert testimony. In *Frye v. United States,* 293 F. 1013 (D.C. Cir. 1923), a short opinion, the Court of Appeals for the District of Columbia pronounced that the line between when a scientific discovery or principle crosses from experimental to demonstrable is indiscernible so that courts would do better "admitting expert testimony deduced from a well- recognized scientific principle or discovery." *Id.* at 1014. Further, the Court explained, "the thing from which the deduction is made must be sufficiently established to have gained general acceptance in the particular field in which it belongs." *Id.* This rule — that expert testimony should be deduced from generally accepted scientific principles — has been the standard in Florida cases and, today, we reaffirm that it is still the standard. *See, e.g., Kaminski v. State,* 63 So.2d 339, 340 (Fla. 1952) (recognizing *Frye* 's rejection of systolic blood pressure deception tests as having "not yet gained such standing and scientific recognition among physiological and psychological authorities as would justify the courts in admitting expert testimony deduced from the discovery, development, and experiments thus far made.") (quoting *Frye,* 293 F. at 1014); *Bundy v. State,* 471 So.2d 9, 13 (Fla. 1985) (describing the *Frye* test as one in which "the results of mechanical or scientific testing are not admissible unless the testing has developed or improved to the point where experts in the field widely share the view that the results are scientifically reliable as accurate").

* * *

After decades of the federal courts' applying *Frye,* Congress revised the Federal Rules of Evidence. The revision was addressed by the United States Supreme Court in 1993. In *Daubert v. Merrell Dow Pharmaceuticals,* 509 U.S. 579, 113 S.Ct. 2786, 125 L.Ed.2d 469 (1993), the United States Supreme Court determined the appropriate standard for admitting expert scientific testimony in a federal trial. *Id.* at 582, 113 S.Ct. 2786. The Supreme Court ultimately agreed with the petitioners that *Frye* had been superseded by the adoption of the revised Federal Rules of Evidence. *Id.* at 587, 113 S.Ct. 2786.

The Court explained its decision, stating, "[I]n order to qualify as 'scientific knowledge,' an inference or assertion must be derived by the scientific method." *Daubert,* 509 U.S. at 590, 113 S.Ct. 2786. The inquiry derived from *Daubert* is a flexible one, as emphasized by the Supreme Court. *Id.* at 594, 113 S.Ct. 2786. "The focus, of course, must be solely on principles and methodology, not on the conclusions that they generate." *Id.* at 595, 113 S.Ct. 2786. The Supreme Court in *Daubert* opined that the change in rule 702 was necessary to permit scientifically valid and relevant evidence, summarizing:

> "General acceptance" is not a necessary precondition to the admissibility of scientific evidence under the Federal Rules of Evidence, but the Rules of Evidence — especially Rule 702 — do assign to the trial judge the task of ensuring that an expert's testimony both rests on a reliable foundation and is relevant to the task at hand. Pertinent evidence based on scientifically valid principles will satisfy those demands.

Id. at 597, 113 S.Ct. 2786. In short, in *Daubert,* the United States Supreme Court found that otherwise probative and scientifically valid evidence was being excluded under the *Frye* standard and the change in rule 702 was necessary to permit additional relevant evidence to be considered even if it was based on scientific methods or principles that were not yet generally accepted.

Nevertheless, in *Brim v. State,* 695 So.2d 268 (Fla. 1997), we unanimously emphasized that we continue to apply *Frye* to "guarantee the reliability of new or novel scientific evidence." *Id.* at 271 90.702 Testimony by experts. — If (citing *Stokes v. State,* 548 So.2d 188 (Fla. 1989) scientific, technical, or other specialized). We opined: knowledge will assist the trier of fact in

> Despite the federal adoption of a more lenient standard in *Daubert v. Merrell Dow*
>
> *Pharmaceuticals, Inc.,* 509 U.S. 579, 113 S.Ct. 2786, 125 L.Ed.2d 469 (1993), we have maintained the higher standard of reliability as dictated by *Frye. E.g., Ramirez v. State,* 651 So.2d 1164 (Fla.1995). This standard requires a determination, by the judge, that the basic underlying principles of scientific evidence have been sufficiently tested and accepted by the relevant scientific community. To that end, we have expressly held that the trial judge must treat new or novel scientific evidence as a matter of admissibility (for the judge) rather than a matter of weight (for the jury).

Brim, 695 So.2d at 271-72 (footnote omitted).

Following our repeated affirmations of the *Frye* rule, in 2013 the Legislature amended section 90.702 to incorporate *Daubert* in the Florida Rules of Evidence....

Article II, section 3 of the Florida Constitution prohibits one branch of government from exercising any of the powers of the other branches. Further, article V, section 2(a) provides this Court the exclusive authority to "adopt rules for the practice and procedure in all courts." Art. V, § 2(a), Fla. Const. The Legislature may only repeal the rules of this Court by "general law enacted by two-thirds vote of the membership of each house of the legislature." *Id.* First, the amendment was not written to repeal *Frye* or *Marsh* but to overrule this Court's decision. *See* Fla. HB 7015, preamble (2013) (available at www.flsenate.gov/Session/Bill/2013/7015) ("the Florida Legislature intends to prohibit in the courts of this state pure opinion testimony as provided in *Marsh . . .*". The vote here did not meet the requirement. The House passed the bill with a majority, 70 to 41 (or 58.3% of the membership). The Senate passed the bill with more than the necessary two-thirds vote, 30 to 9 (or 75% of the membership). *Id.* We have previously found that the Legislature exceeded its authority in adopting statutes we found to infringe on the authority of this Court to determine matters of practice or procedure. For example, in *Massey v. David,* 979 So.2d 931 (Fla. 2008), we considered the constitutionality of section 57.071(2), Florida Statutes (1999), finding that the section was purely procedural because the substantive right it purported to create existed in a different section of the statutes. *Id.* at 935-36. We determined that "because section 57.071(2) only delineates the steps that a party must fulfill (i.e., the proverbial hoops through which a party must jump) to be entitled to an award of expert witness fees as costs, the statute is unquestionably a procedural one which conveys no substantive right at all." *Id.* at 940 (citing *Raymond,* 906 So.2d at 1049). Likewise, we found the time requirements established by the Legislature in section 44.102, Florida Statutes (1993), to be unconstitutional, finding that the section "sets forth only procedural requirements, [and therefore] intrudes upon the rule-making authority of the Supreme Court." *Knealing v. Puleo,* 675 So.2d 593, 596 (Fla. 1996) (citing art. V, § 2(a), Fla. Const.).

In *Jackson v. Florida Department of Corrections* , 790 So.2d 381 (Fla. 2000), we explained that a statute can have both substantive provisions and procedural requirements and "[i]f the procedural requirements conflict with or interfere with the procedural mechanisms of the court system, they are unconstitutional under both a separation of powers analysis, and because [they intrude upon] the exclusive province of the Supreme Court pursuant to the rulemaking authority vested in it by the Florida Constitution." *Id.* at 384 (citing art. II, § 3, art. V, § 2, Fla. Const.; *State v. Garcia,* 229 So.2d 236, 238 (Fla. 1969)). We noted that the copy requirement contained in the rule provided an extra and unnecessary burden on the operation of this Court. *Id.* at 386.

In *State v. Raymond,* 906 So.2d 1045 (Fla. 2005), we determined that section 907.041(4)(b), Florida Statutes (2000), providing that a person charged with a dangerous crime was prohibited from receiving a nonmonetary pretrial release, was purely procedural and, therefore, an unconstitutional violation of the separation of powers clause. "It is a well-established principle that a statute which purports to create or modify a procedural rule of court is constitutionally infirm." *Id.* at 1048 (citing *Markert v. Johnston,* 367 So.2d 1003 (Fla. 1978)). Further, "where there is no substantive right conveyed by the statute, the procedural aspects are not incidental; accordingly, such a statute is unconstitutional." *Id.* at 1049 (citing *Knealing,* 675 So.2d 593).

. . .

Our consideration of the constitutionality of the amendment does not end with our determination that the provision was procedural. For this Court to determine that the amendment is unconstitutional, it must also conflict with a rule of this Court. *See Haven Fed. Sav. & Loan Ass'n v. Kirian,* 579 So.2d 730, 732–33 (Fla. 1991) ("Where this Court promulgates rules relating to the practice and procedure of all courts and a statute provides a contrary practice or procedure, the statute is unconstitutional to the extent of the conflict.") (citing *Sch. Bd. v. Surette,* 281 So.2d 481 (Fla. 1973), *receded from on other grounds* by *Sch. Bd. v. Price,* 362 So.2d 1337 (Fla. 1978)); *see also Leapai v. Milton* , 595 So.2d 12, 14 (Fla. 1992) (holding that section 45.061, Florida Statutes (1987), was not unconstitutional to the extent it did not conflict with Florida Rule of Civil Procedure 1.442 and stating that "statutes should be construed to effectuate the express legislative intent and all doubt as to the validity of any statute should be resolved in favor of its constitutionality" (quoting *McKibben v. Mallory* , 293 So.2d 48 (Fla. 1974))). A procedural rule of this Court may be pronounced in caselaw. *See Sch. Bd. of Broward Cty. v. Surette,* 281 So.2d 481, 483 (Fla. 1973), *receded from on other grounds* by *Sch. Bd. of Broward Cty. v. Price,* 362 So.2d 1337 (Fla. 1978) ("Where rules and construing opinions have been promulgated by this Court relating to the practice and procedure of all courts and a statutory provision provides a contrary practice or procedure . . . the statute must fall.") While the Legislature purports to have pronounced public policy in overturning *Marsh,* we hold that the rule announced in *Stokes* and reaffirmed in *Marsh* was a procedural rule of this Court that the Legislature could not repeal by simple majority.

We recognize that *Frye* and *Daubert* are competing methods for a trial judge to determine the reliability of expert testimony before allowing it to be admitted into evidence. Both purport to provide a trial judge with the tools necessary to ensure that only reliable evidence is presented to the jury. *Frye* relies on the scientific community to determine reliability whereas *Daubert* relies on the scientific savvy of trial judges to determine the significance of the methodology used. With our decision today, we reaffirm that *Frye,* not *Daubert,* is the appropriate test in Florida courts.[3]

* * *

For the foregoing reasons, we quash the Fourth District's decision. Furthermore, because the causation of mesothelioma is neither new nor novel, the trial court's acceptance of the expert testimony was proper. We therefore remand to the Fourth District with instructions to remand to the trial court to reinstate the final judgment. We decline to address the remaining issues.

It is so ordered.

PARIENTE, LEWIS, and LABARGA, JJ., concur.

PARIENTE, J., concurs with an opinion, in which LABARGA, J., concurs.

LABARGA, J., concurs with an opinion, in which PARIENTE, J., concurs.

[The concurring opinions of Justice Pariente and Justice Labarga are omitted.]

CANADY, C.J., dissents with an opinion, in which POLSTON and LAWSON, JJ., concur. [The dissenting opinion of Chief Justice Canady is omitted.]

In *In re Florida Evidence Code,*[15] the Florida Supreme Court, on its own initiative, rescinded its prior decision not to adopt the Legislature's *Daubert* amendments to the Florida Evidence Code and to retain the *Frye* standard. In deciding to adopt the Legislature's *Daubert* amendment, the Florida Supreme Court found Justice Polston's observations instructive:

> [T]he United States Supreme Court decided *Daubert v. Merrell Dow Pharmaceuticals, Inc.,* 509 U.S. 579, 113 S.Ct. 2786, 125 L.Ed.2d 469 (1993), in 1993,

---

3. We also note our concern that the amendment would affect access to courts much in the same way expressed by Justice Shaw in *VanBibber* by imposing an additional burden on the courts. The amici in this case have described the additional length and expense *Daubert* proceedings create.

15. 278 So. 3d 551 (Fla. 2019).

and the standard has been routinely applied in federal courts ever since. The clear majority of state jurisdictions also adhere to the *Daubert* standard. *See* 1 *McCormick on Evidence* § 13 (7th ed. June 2016 Supp.). In fact, there are 36 states that have rejected *Frye* in favor of *Daubert* to some extent. *See* Charles Alan Wright & Victor Gold, 29 *Federal Practice and Procedure* § 6267, at 308-09 n.15 (2016). Has the entire federal court system for the last 23 years as well as 36 states denied parties' rights to a jury trial and access to courts? Do only Florida and a few other states have a constitutionally sound standard for the admissibility of expert testimony? Of course not.

As a note to the federal rule of evidence explains, "[a] review of the caselaw after *Daubert* shows that the rejection of expert testimony is the exception rather than the rule." Fed. R. Evid. 702 advisory committee's note to 2000 amendment. "*Daubert* did not work a 'seachange over federal evidence law,' and 'the trial court's role as gatekeeper is not intended to serve as a replacement for the adversary system.'" *Id.* (quoting *United States v. 14.38 Acres of Land,* 80 F.3d 1074, 1078 (5th Cir. 1996)).

Furthermore, I know of no reported decisions that have held that the *Daubert* standard violates the constitutional guarantees of a jury trial and access to courts. To the contrary, there is case law holding that the *Daubert* standard does not violate the constitution. *See, e.g., Junk v. Terminix Int'l Co.* , 628 F.3d 439, 450 (8th Cir. 2010) (rejecting legal merit of the constitutional claim "that the district court violated [appellant's] Seventh Amendment right to a jury trial by improperly weighing evidence in the course of its *Daubert* rulings" and explaining that "*Junk* does not cite any case for the notion that a proper *Daubert* ruling violates a party's right to a jury trial"); *E.I. du Pont de Nemours & Co. v. Robinson* , 923 S.W.2d 549, 558 (Tex. 1995) (rejecting claim "that allowing the trial judge to assess the reliability of expert testimony violates [the parties'] federal and state constitutional rights to a jury trial by infringing upon the jury's inherent authority to assess the credibility of witnesses and the weight to be given their testimony"); *see also Gen. Elec. Co. v. Joiner* , 522 U.S. 136, 142-43, 118 S.Ct. 512, 139 L.Ed.2d 508 (1997) (rejecting "argument that because the granting of summary judgment in this case was 'outcome determinative,' it should have been subjected to a more searching standard of review" and explaining that, while "disputed issues of fact are resolved against the moving party[,] . . . the question of admissibility of expert testimony is not such an issue of fact").

Accordingly, the . . . "grave constitutional concerns" regarding the *Daubert* standard are unfounded.

In re Amends. to Fla. Evidence Code, 210 So. 3d 1231, 1242-43 (Fla. 2017) (Polston, J., concurring in part and dissenting in part).

C. Delegation of Power as a Separation of Powers Problem

1. Legislative Delegation of Legislative Power

Florida Department of State v. Martin

916 So. 2d 763 (Fla. 2005)

PARIENTE, C.J.

We have on appeal *Department of State, Division of Elections v. Martin*, 885 So.2d 453 (Fla. 1st DCA 2004), in which the First District Court of Appeal declared section 101.253(2), Florida Statutes (2004), unconstitutional. We have mandatory jurisdiction. *See* art. V, § 3(b)(1), Fla. Const. The issue in this case is whether section 101.253(2), which gives the Department of State absolute discretion to allow a candidate to withdraw after the forty-second day before an election, violates the separation of powers principle set forth in article II, section 3 of the Florida Constitution. We affirm the First District and hold that section 101.253(2) is an unconstitutional violation of the separation of powers under article II, section 3 because the Legislature has impermissibly delegated to the executive branch absolute, unfettered discretion to determine whether to grant or deny a candidate's request to withdraw after the forty-second day before an election.

Facts and Procedural History

James R. Stork qualified with the Department of State, Division of Elections (the Department) as the Democratic Party candidate for the Florida Congressional District 22 seat in the November 2, 2004, general election. On September 23, 2004, forty days before the election, the Department received a sworn notice from Stork seeking to withdraw as a candidate. On September 29, 2004, the Department, relying on section 101.253(2), notified Stork that "in the interest of avoiding disruption and confusion," his request to withdraw would be denied. *Martin*, 885 So.2d at 454. This in effect left the Democratic Party without the ability to substitute a candidate in his place prior to the election. Thereafter, members of the Congressional District 22 Democratic Party Executive Committee (Executive Committee), the appellees in this case, sought a mandatory injunction requiring the Department to declare that a vacancy had been created by Stork's withdrawal and to comply with section 100.111(4)(b), Florida Statutes (2004). This provision requires the Department to place on the ballot the name of a replacement candidate that is provided by the party's executive committee at least twenty-one days before the election.

At the hearing on the Executive Committee's request for injunctive relief, the Department acknowledged that on or before the forty-second day prior to an election, withdrawal of a candidate is a matter of right under section 101.253(2). The Department argued, however, that when a candidate seeks to withdraw after the forty-second day before an election, it has the absolute discretion under section 101.253(2) to grant or deny a request for withdrawal. In rejecting the Department's arguments, the trial court stated that "[t]o read Section 101.253(2) as the Department urges would essentially render Section 100.111(4) (b) meaningless." *Martin v. Dep't of State, Div. of Elections*, No. 04CA2400, order at 9 (Fla. 2d Cir. Ct. order filed Oct. 8, 2004). Because section 100.111(4)(b) was enacted after section 101.253(2), the trial court concluded that the Legislature intended that section 100.111(4)(b) control the procedure for allowing a candidate's withdrawal and filling a vacancy in nomination. The trial court therefore entered a final order granting injunctive relief in favor of the Executive Committee.

The Department appealed the trial court's order to the First District.[1] In affirming the trial court's order, the First District held that section 101.253(2) unconstitutionally delegates legislative authority in violation of article II, section 3. The First District concluded that section 101.253(2) does not provide any criteria or standards to guide the Department in the exercise of the power delegated under the statute, but rather "vests unbridled discretion in the Department" to determine whether a candidate should be permitted to withdraw where the sworn notice was received fewer than forty-two days before a general election. *Martin*, 885 So.2d at 458.

* * *

II. Separation of Powers

A. Article II, Section 3 of the Florida Constitution

Having concluded that section 101.253(2) intended to give the Department discretion, we must determine whether the grant of the discretion is so broad as to violate the separation of powers doctrine of article II, section 3. Article II, section 3 creates the three branches of government and prohibits one branch from exercising the powers of the other two branches:

> **Branches of government.**—The powers of the state government shall be divided into legislative, executive and judicial branches. No person belonging to one branch shall exercise any powers appertaining to either of the other branches unless expressly provided herein.

This Court has traditionally applied a "strict separation of powers doctrine," *State v. Cotton*, 769 So.2d 345, 353 (Fla. 2000), which "encompasses two fundamental prohibitions." *Chiles v. Children A, B, C, D, E, F*, 589 So.2d 260, 264 (Fla. 1991). "The first is that no branch may encroach upon the powers of another. The second is that no branch may delegate to another branch its constitutionally assigned power." *Id.* (citation omitted). In *Bush v. Schiavo*, 885 So.2d 321 (Fla. 2004), *cert. denied*, 543 U.S. 1121, 125 S.Ct. 1086, 160 L.Ed.2d 1069 (2005), we recently addressed this second prohibition and explained:

---

1. Upon suggestion of the Executive Committee, the First District certified the case to this Court as a matter of great public importance. This Court entered an order declining to exercise jurisdiction and remanded the case to the First District. *See Fla. Dep't of State, Div. of Elections v. Martin*, No. SC04-1980 (Fla. Oct. 13, 2004).

The Legislature is permitted to transfer subordinate functions "to permit administration of legislative policy by an agency with the expertise and flexibility to deal with complex and fluid conditions." *Microtel, Inc. v. Fla. Public Serv. Comm'n*, 464 So.2d 1189, 1191 (Fla. 1985). However, under article II, section 3 of the constitution the Legislature "may not delegate the power to enact a law or the right to exercise unrestricted discretion in applying the law." *Sims v. State*, 754 So.2d 657, 668 (Fla. 2000). This prohibition, known as the nondelegation doctrine, requires that "fundamental and primary policy decisions . . . be made by members of the legislature who are elected to perform those tasks, and [that the] administration of legislative programs must be pursuant to some minimal standards and guidelines ascertainable by reference to the enactment establishing the program." *Askew v. Cross Key Waterways*, 372 So.2d 913, 925 (Fla. 1978); *see also Avatar Dev. Corp. v. State;* 723 So.2d 199, 202 (Fla. 1998) (citing *Askew* with approval). In other words, statutes granting power to the executive branch "must clearly announce adequate standards to guide . . . in the execution of the powers delegated. The statute must so clearly define the power delegated that the [executive] is precluded from acting through whim, showing favoritism, or exercising unbridled discretion." *Lewis v. Bank of Pasco County*, 346 So.2d 53, 55- 56 (Fla. 1976).

Id. at 332 (alterations in original). The requirement that the Legislature delineate adequate standards enables courts to perform their constitutional duties. The failure to set forth adequate standards precludes a court from determining whether the executive branch is acting in accord with the Legislature's intent. *See Askew*, 372 So.2d at 918-19 ("When legislation is so lacking in guidelines that neither the agency nor the courts can determine whether the agency is carrying out the intent of the legislature in its conduct, then, in fact, the agency becomes the lawgiver rather than the administrator of the law.").

* * *

C. The Constitutionality of Section 101.253(2)

Similar to the statutes and proviso at issue in *Lewis, Orr,* and *Schiavo,* section 101.253(2) does not delineate any standards or criteria to guide the Department in exercising the authority delegated under the statute. This provision merely states that the Department "may in its discretion allow such a candidate to withdraw after the 42nd day before an election." Section 101.253(2) does not articulate any factors to be considered in determining whether withdrawal should be granted or denied, nor does it indicate the legislative purpose to be served in granting or denying a candidate's request to withdraw. *Cf. Avatar Dev. Corp.,* 723 So.2d at 207 ("While chapter 403 grants [the Department of Environmental Protection] the authority to determine conditions upon which permits may be issued, that power is limited to conditions necessary to effectuate the Legislature's specific policy."); *Microtel, Inc.,* 464 So.2d at 1191 (concluding that statute that required commission to determine whether to issue certificate and guided commission's discretion by providing that certification must be in the public interest evidenced sufficient standards and guidelines under article II, section 3); *Straughn v. O'Riordan*, 338 So.2d 832, 833-34 (Fla. 1976) (concluding that statute directing the Department of Revenue to require a bond from sales tax registrants "in all cases where it is necessary to insure compliance with the provisions of this chapter" was a constitutional delegation of legislative authority under article II, section 3).

The Department concedes that section 101.253(2) does not set forth any standards or guidelines to limit or regulate the decision to grant or deny a candidate's request to withdraw after the forty-second day before an election. The Department asserts, however, that section 97.012, Florida Statutes (2004), which delineates the responsibilities of the Secretary of State, limits the Department's discretion under section 101.253(2). Specifically, the Department asserts that section 97.012 appoints the Secretary of State as the chief elections officer and obligates the Secretary to obtain and maintain uniformity in the application, operation, and interpretation of the election laws. The Department asserts that its discretion is therefore guided by the stated goal of, and requirement for, orderly elections.

We reject the Department's assertions. Section 101.253(2) affords discretion to determine whether to permit a candidate to withdraw solely to the Department, not the Secretary of State. Thus, the responsibilities imposed on the Secretary by section 97.012 are inapplicable to the Department in the exercise of its discretion under section 101.253(2). Even assuming that the Department's discretion is limited by the requirement for orderly elections provided in section 97.012, this requirement does not set forth adequate standards to guide the Department under article II, section 3. According to the Department, allowing withdrawal after the forty-second day before an election jeopardizes an orderly election because at that point, "it would be extremely difficult to change the ballots so close to the election, and . . . any request to do so would be disruptive." *Martin*, 885 So.2d at 455. However, the Department acknowledges that these same problems exist when a request to withdraw is timely received. *See id.*

The Department also asserts that section 101.253(2) should be read *in pari materia* with the Florida Election Code, chapters 97 through 106, Florida Statutes (2004) (Code). According to the Department, the Code provides the standards by which the Department determines whether a request to withdraw is reasonable and does not interfere with legislative intent by jeopardizing an orderly election or imposing an undue burden on the Department in ensuring an orderly election. In support of this assertion, the Department cites *Brown v. Apalachee Regional Planning Council*, 560 So.2d 782 (Fla. 1990), in which the Court analyzed related statutes in discerning whether an administrative rule contained sufficient criteria to assist the agency in levying fees.

In *Brown*, the Court upheld the constitutionality of an administrative rule that allowed an agency to levy fees against an applicant seeking a development of regional impact review (DRI). The Court explained that the statutes upon which the rule was based set forth, in considerable detail specific criteria to be used by the [administrative agency] in conducting DRI reviews: which development projects must be reviewed, when review is to occur, who is to conduct review, and how review is to be performed. Under these circumstances, given the highly technical nature of the DRI review process, details relating to the imposition of a cost-based review fee can be viewed as a technical matter of implementation rather than a fundamental policy decision.

Brown, 560 So.2d at 785 (citation omitted).

In contrast to the statutory provisions in *Brown*, the Florida Election Code relates generally to Florida's election process and does not provide standards and criteria to be utilized by the Department in exercising its discretion under section 101.253(2). The Code does not set forth any restrictions or specific criteria governing the Department's response to requests to withdraw after the forty-second day before an election. Nor does section 101.253(2) require that the Department's decision be made in conformity with the legislative scheme and purpose of the Code. In fact, there is nothing in section 101.253(2) that indicates that the Legislature intended to limit the Department's discretion in any way.

Further, unlike the administrative rule at issue in *Brown*, section 101.253(2) cannot be viewed as a "technical matter of implementation rather than a fundamental policy decision." *Id.* Although the election process in general is subject to technical procedures, there is nothing "technical" about determining whether to permit a candidate to withdraw under section 101.253(2). The Department's decision concerning withdrawal is more akin to a policy decision, and we therefore conclude that *Brown* is inapplicable to this case. . . .

Although it would be impossible for the Legislature to specify every circumstance under which the Department may permit a candidate to withdraw after the forty-second day before an election, the Legislature must provide adequate standards to guide the Department in making a decision concerning whether withdrawal will be permitted. Otherwise, there is nothing to prevent the Department from making an arbitrary decision under section 101.253(2). We conclude that the second sentence of section 101.253(2) violates article II, section 3 because the statute is currently "drafted in terms so general and unrestrictive that [the Department is] left without standards for the guidance of [its] official acts." *Id.* (quoting *Griffin*, 239 So.2d at 581).

* * *

Conclusion

For the foregoing reasons, we conclude that section 101.253(2) vests the Department with absolute, unfettered discretion to decide whether to grant or deny a candidate's request to withdraw after the forty-second day before an election. Thus, we hold that section 101.253(2) is an unconstitutional delegation of legislative authority in violation of the separation of powers set forth in article II, section 3. We affirm the First District's decision below holding section 101.253(2) unconstitutional.

It is so ordered.

WELLS, ANSTEAD, LEWIS, QUINCE, CANTERO, and BELL, JJ., concur.

* * *

2. Judicial Delegation of Judicial Power

While less common, questions do arise as to whether a court has unconstitutionally delegated its judicial power to another branch of government. The following case illustrates an instance in which a court has been found to have unconstitutionally delegated its judicial power to the executive branch of government.

Pearce v. State

968 So. 2d 92 (Fla. 2d Dist. Ct. App. 2007)

WALLACE, J.

Kelvin Pearce challenges a restitution order imposed after he pleaded guilty to petit theft, a first-degree misdemeanor. § 812.014(2)(e), Fla. Stat. (2000). He argues — and the State concedes — that the trial court erred when it authorized Mr. Pearce's probation officer to establish a payment schedule for the restitution amount. We agree and reverse the restitution order in part with directions.

The Restitution Order & Subsequent Orders

At Mr. Pearce's April 26, 2006, sentencing and restitution hearing, the trial court withheld adjudication on the petit theft offense. The trial court imposed a sentence of twelve months' probation, and it ordered Mr. Pearce to pay $10,515 in restitution to the victim. Notably, the trial court delegated the matter of establishing a payment schedule to Mr. Pearce's probation officer. Mr. Pearce timely filed his notice of appeal.

On November 20, 2006, Mr. Pearce filed a motion to correct sentencing error under Florida Rule of Criminal Procedure 3.800(b)(2). Mr. Pearce did not contest the amount of the restitution award, but he argued that the trial court erred when it authorized his probation officer to determine a schedule for the restitution payments. The trial court agreed, and on January 25, 2007, it filed an order granting Mr. Pearce's motion and awarding him a new restitution hearing. On February 7, 2007, the circuit court set a restitution payment schedule at $250 per month. Finally, on April 12, 2007, the circuit court entered an order modifying the terms of Mr. Pearce's probation so that any restitution amount outstanding at the end of his one-year probationary term would be converted to a lien.

Analysis

As the State concedes, the trial court erred in its original restitution order when it delegated to Mr. Pearce's probation officer the authority for determining the restitution payment schedule. Florida courts have long held that the determination of a restitution payment schedule is a judicial responsibility that cannot be delegated. *Lewellen v. State,* 685 So.2d 1367, 1368 (Fla. 2d DCA 1996); *Douglas v. State,* 664 So.2d 1099, 1099 (Fla. 2d DCA 1995); *Guinn v. State,* 652 So.2d 902, 902 (Fla. 2d DCA 1995); *Briggs v. State,* 647 So.2d 182, 182 (Fla. 1st DCA 1994); *see also Thomas v. State,* 635 So.2d 1009, 1010 (Fla. 1st DCA 1994) (finding error where the trial court revoked probation based on the defendant's failure "to follow a payment schedule established, not by the trial court, but by the probation officer"). In addition, while the trial court clearly intended to correct its error when it granted Mr. Pearce's rule 3.800(b)(2) motion, we note that sixty-six days had elapsed from November 20, 2006 (the day Mr. Pearce filed his motion) to January 25, 2007 (the day the order granting the motion was filed). Consequently, Mr. Pearce's motion was deemed denied by rule when the trial court failed to dispose of it within sixty days — i.e., by January 19, 2007. *See* Fla. R. Crim. P. 3.800(b)(1)(B).

For these reasons, we affirm the restitution order to the extent that it established the restitution amount, but we reverse the restitution order to the extent that it delegated to the probation officer the determination of the payment schedule.

* * *

Conclusion

To summarize, we affirm Mr. Pearce's judgment and sentence, and we affirm the portion of the restitution order that establishes the restitution amount. We reverse the restitution order to the extent that it delegates authority to Mr. Pearce's probation officer to determine the restitution payment schedule. We vacate the three orders entered after January 19, 2007, and we remand with directions to conduct a new restitution hearing to determine the appropriate method for Mr. Pearce to satisfy the remainder of his restitution obligation.

Affirmed in part, reversed in part, and remanded with directions.

CASANUEVA and CANADY, JJ., Concur.

Chapter 3

The Legislature

A. In General

Fla. Const. art. III, §1

Composition. — The legislative power of the state shall be vested in the legislature of the State of Florida, ...

There is probably no better description of legislative power than that of Oliver Wendell Holmes, Jr., who, when sitting as a circuit justice, said, "The Legislature has the power to decide what the policy of the law shall be, ..."[1] The Supreme Court of Florida recognizes the same notion, as do courts throughout Florida's judicial system, with its separation of powers doctrine. "The constitutional provision vesting legislative power (Fla. Const. art. III, §1) requires of course that only the legislature shall establish the legislative policies and standards of the state."[2]

This, however, is not as simple as it may seem. Recall the distinction drawn in Chapter 2 between the Florida Legislature's role in making substantive law and the Florida Supreme Court's role in making procedural law, as set out in Fla. Const. art. V, §2(a). Also, contrast legislative power with the somewhat coordinate role of administrative agencies, as discussed in Chapter 2. It is important, although probably not completely possible, to distinguish the role of the Florida Legislature from that of an administrative agency. In theory the dividing line may be clear, but in practice, it is not. This is discussed in more detail in Chapter 2, but consider the following statement by the Court of Appeals of New York in *Levine v. Whalen*:[3]

> Because of the constitutional provision that "[t]he legislative power of this State shall be vested in the Senate and Assembly" (N.Y. Const., art. III, §1), the Legislature cannot pass on its law-making functions to other bodies [citation omitted], but there is no constitutional prohibition against the delegation of power, with reasonable safeguards and standards, to an agency or commission to administer the law as enacted by the Legislature [citations omitted]. The delegation of power to make the law, which necessarily

---

1. *Johnson v. United States*, 163 F. 30, 32 (1st Cir. 1908).
2. *Fla. Welding & Erection Serv., Inc. v. Am. Mut. Ins. Co. of Boston*, 285 So. 2d 386, 388 (Fla. 1973).
3. 349 N.E.2d 820, 822 (N.Y. 1976).

involves a discretion as to what it shall be, cannot be done, but there is no valid objection to the conferring of authority or discretion as to a law's execution, to be exercised under and in pursuance of it.

B. Constitutional Limitations

1. Subject Matter and Title Requirement

Fla. Const. art. III, § 6

Laws. — Every law shall embrace but one subject and matter properly connected therewith, and the subject shall be briefly expressed in the title. No law shall be revised or amended by reference to its title only. Laws to revise or amend shall set out in full the revised or amended act, section, subsection or paragraph of a subsection. The enacting clause of every law shall read: "Be It Enacted by the Legislature of the State of Florida".

a. Single Subject Limitation

In *Florida Department of Highway Safety and Motor Vehicles v. Critchfield*,[4] the Florida Supreme Court discussed the purpose of the single subject rule. "The purpose of this constitutional prohibition against a plurality of subjects in a single legislative act is to prevent 'logrolling' where a single enactment becomes a cloak for dissimilar legislation having no necessary or appropriate connection with the subject matter."[5] At issue in *Critchfield* was a law enacted by the Florida Legislature in 1998 that permanently revoked the driver's license and driving privileges of anyone who received four convictions for driving under the influence.[6] The law's "subject matter" was driver's licenses, vehicle registrations, and operation of motor vehicles. However, the law also included a provision allowing the assignment of bad checks to a private debt collector. The Court found this to be a second subject and found the entire law unconstitutional for that reason.[7]

In *State v. Lee*,[8] the Florida Supreme Court noted that the single subject limitation "is not designed to deter or impede legislation by requiring laws to be unnecessarily restrictive in their scope and operation" and stressed that the Florida Legislature must be given "wide latitude" in determining the subject of legislation. The question of what is meant by "wide latitude" is disputed by the majority and dissenting opinions in the following case.

---

4. 842 So. 2d 782 (Fla. 2003).
5. *Id.* at 785.
6. *Id.* at 783–784.
7. *Id.* at 786.
8. 356 So. 2d 276, 282 (Fla. 1978).

Franklin v. State

887 So. 2d 1063 (Fla. 2004)

PARIENTE, C.J.

The issue in this case is the constitutionality of chapter 99-188, Laws of Florida (the "Act"), designated by the Legislature as the "Three-Strike Violent Felony Offender Act." The specific constitutional question presented is whether the fourteen provisions of the Act "embrace but one subject and matter properly connected therewith" as mandated by article III, section 6 of the Florida Constitution, the single subject clause.[1] We have jurisdiction based on certified conflict among the district courts of appeal.[2] For the reasons expressed in this opinion, we conclude that the Act does not violate the single subject clause of the Florida Constitution.

* * *

II. Facts and Procedural Background

Franklin was convicted of armed robbery and resisting arrest based on acts that occurred after the effective date of chapter 99-188. He received a sentence of forty years in prison as a habitual felony offender, pursuant to section 775.084, Florida Statutes (1999), which had been amended by section 3 of the Act. Franklin's prior criminal history consisted of one felony conviction (possession of cocaine) and one felony for which adjudication of guilt was withheld (burglary of a dwelling). Prior to the Act's amendment to section 775.084, an offense for which adjudication of guilt had been withheld would not have qualified as a predicate for habitual offender sentencing unless the subsequent offenses pending for sentencing was committed while the offender was on probation or community control after the withhold of adjudication. *See* § 775.084(1)(a)(2)(b), Fla. Stat. (Supp.1998).

Franklin appealed. While his appeal was pending, the Second District held in *Taylor v. State,* 818 So.2d 544 (Fla. 2d DCA 2002), that the Act violated the single subject requirement of article III, section 6. Relying on *Taylor,* Franklin filed a motion to correct illegal sentence pursuant to Florida Rule of Criminal Procedure 3.800(b). The trial court granted the motion and the State appealed to the Third District. In *State v. Franklin,* 836 So.2d 1112 (Fla. 3d DCA 2003), the Third District held that the Act did not violate the constitutional requirement of a single subject. The Third District also certified conflict with *Taylor* on whether the Act violates the single subject requirement.

* * *

---

1. "Every law shall embrace but one subject and matter properly connected therewith, and the subject shall be briefly expressed in the title." Art. III, § 6, Fla. Const.

2. *See* art. V, § 3(b)(4), Fla. Const.

IV. Single Subject Rule Analysis

A. Applicable Law

1. The Purpose of the Single Subject Clause

Currently, forty-three states have some form of single subject clause applicable to legislation contained in their state constitutions.[13] In Florida, the single subject clause has been part of our state constitution since 1868, *see Canova,* 94 So.2d at 182, and is presently set forth in article III, section 6. This provision mandates:

> Every law shall embrace but one subject and matter properly connected therewith, and the subject shall be briefly expressed in the title.

Art. III, § 6, Fla. Const.

Thus, the single subject clause contains three requirements. First, each law shall "embrace" only "one subject." Second, the law may include any matter that is "properly connected" with the subject. The third requirement, related to the first, is that the subject shall be "briefly expressed in the title." In *State v. Thompson,* 750 So.2d 643, 646 (Fla.1999), this Court reaffirmed the purposes of the single subject provision:

> (1) to prevent hodgepodge or "log rolling" legislation, i.e. putting two unrelated matters in one act; (2) to prevent surprise or fraud by means of provisions in bills of which the title gave no intimation, and which might therefore be overlooked and carelessly and unintentionally adopted; and (3) to fairly apprise the people of the subjects of legislation that are being considered, in order that they may have opportunity of being heard thereon.

Id. (quoting *Canova,* 94 So.2d at 184).

* * *

3. Defining the Single Subject

The key to determining whether a legislative enactment violates the single subject clause of the Florida Constitution is the method by which the court defines the "single subject" of the legislation and the analysis employed to determine matters "properly connected therewith." An analysis of our prior case law reveals that, while maintaining fidelity to the mandate of our citizens expressed in our constitution, we have given considerable deference to the Legislature to determine the single subject.[15]

---

13. The treatise relied on by Judge Cope in his dissent cites forty-one states. *See Franklin,* 836 So.2d at 1124 (citing 1A Norman J. Singer, *Statutes and Statutory Construction* 17:1 at 2 (6th ed.2002 rev.)). In fact, forty-three states have some type of single subject clause in their constitutions. The treatise does not include Arkansas or Mississippi, whose constitutions contain a single subject requirement solely for appropriations bills. Most of the constitutional single subject clauses of the forty-one states referenced in the treatise are substantially similar to article III, section 6.

15. Starting with *Gibson v. State,* 16 Fla. 291 (1877), this Court has addressed the single subject clause approximately 135 times. In approximately seventy-five percent of the cases, we have upheld the legislation against attacks based on asserted single subject violations.

In determining the single subject, we start with the basic principle that "the subject is the one that is expressed in the title of the act." *Knight*, 41 So. at 788; *see also Colonial Inv. Co.*, 131 So. at 178. Indeed, the constitutional provision requires that the subject be briefly expressed in the title.

For purposes of single subject analysis, every law published in the Laws of Florida has both a short title, i.e. "An act relating to . . . ," and a full title, which begins with the chapter law number and ends with "providing an effective date," and encompasses the short title. *Cf. State v. Kaufman*, 430 So.2d 904, 907 (Fla.1983). "[F]ormerly the title of an act was not considered a part of it and, anciently, acts had no title prefixed at all but . . . titles [have] come to possess very great importance by reason of" the single subject clause contained in the constitution. *Canova*, 94 So.2d at 183–84.[16] Consistent with our earliest jurisprudence and the actual wording of our constitution, we reiterate that a court generally need look no further than the title of the act in question when defining the single subject.

Our determination that the single subject of an act can be found in the short title is subject to the following caveat: the title of an act may be general, "so long as it is not made a cover to legislation incongruous in itself." *State ex rel. Attorney General v. Green*, 36 Fla. 154, 18 So. 334, 338 (1895). In other words, the short title of the legislation cannot be so broad as to purportedly cover unrelated topics, and thus provide no real guidance as to what the body of the act contains. Indeed, allowing an overly broad short title to become the single subject runs the risk of permitting logrolling and hodgepodge or omnibus legislation.

An example of an overly broad short title can be found in *State v. Thompson*, 750 So.2d 643 (Fla.1999). In that case, the short title of the act was, "An act relating to [the] justice system." *Id.* at 648. The State argued that the reference to the "justice system" in the title encompassed provisions that addressed both career criminals and domestic violence. *See id.* Because the short title was so broad as to encompass the entire justice system, this Court looked beyond the short title to determine whether the act encompassed a single subject that was briefly stated in the title. We noted that the act was originally titled more narrowly as "an act relating to career criminals" before it was changed to refer to the "justice system" when the domestic violence provisions were added shortly before the bill passed. *See id.* Noting that nothing in the career criminal provisions addressed any facet of domestic violence, we determined that it was "clear" that the "various sections of [the chapter law] . . . address two different subjects: career criminals and domestic violence." *Id.* at 648.

---

16. Titles are also constitutionally important under article III, section 7 of the Florida Constitution, which requires that prior to passage every bill shall be read by its title "in each house on three separate days." In *Kaufman*, this Court held that the requirements of article III, section 7 were satisfied by a reading of the bill number or short title. According to the Court,

> [t]he obvious purpose of reading a bill's title is to inform the legislators and the public as to what bill is being voted on. Given the widespread publication of copies of bills, reading a bill's number or short title identifies which bill is being considered.

430 So.2d at 907.

132   3 · THE LEGISLATURE

Therefore, we hold here, as we did in *Thompson,* that if the Legislature's short title is suspect for being overly broad, a court should look to the remainder of the act and the history of the legislative process to determine if the act actually contains a single subject or violates the constitution by encompassing more than one subject.

Ordinarily, determining the single subject of an act by reference to the short title will be a straightforward process. The more difficult analysis is whether the various provisions are "properly connected" to the single subject. We now turn to the analysis to be used when evaluating the "properly connected" question.

4. Properly Connected

As stated above, the second requirement of the single subject clause in article III, section 6 mandates that all provisions in the body of the act be "properly connected" to the single subject.

* * *

A connection between a provision and the subject is proper (1) if the connection is natural or logical, or (2) if there is a reasonable explanation for how the provision is (a) necessary to the subject or (b) tends to make effective or promote the objects and purposes of legislation included in the subject.

In setting forth this test, we clarify that there is a difference between the subject of the act that is briefly stated in the title and the object of the act. Simply stated, "The subject is the matter to which an act relates; the object, the purpose to be accomplished." *Nichols v. Yandre,* 151 Fla. 87, 9 So.2d 157, 158 (1942). In this regard, we caution that the "accomplishment of several 'purposes' may be logically embraced in one 'subject' so long as all such purposes are germane to . . . the expressed general subject." *State ex rel. Crump v. Sullivan,* 99 Fla. 1070, 128 So. 478, 480 (1930); *see also North Ridge General Hosp., Inc. v. City of Oakland Park,* 374 So.2d 461, 463–64 (Fla.1979) ("The term 'subject' is broader than the word 'object,' as one subject may contain many objects."). The purposes of an act may be instructive in determining whether there is a reasonable explanation for the inclusion of a specific provision in the chapter law. However, the purposes of an act cannot be used to either define or expand the single subject. The single subject clause contained in article III, section 6 "refers to the subject-matter of the legislation, and not to a single purpose or end sought to be accomplished." *Gibson v. State,* 16 Fla. 291, 299 (1877).

* * *

B. Chapter 99-188

* * *

The short title of the Act is "An act relating to sentencing." The citation name is the "Three-Strike Violent Felony Offender Act." The full title is lengthy, running two pages and almost one thousand words. As we have explained, the constitution requires that the subject be briefly expressly in the title and we give considerable deference to the Legislature's selection of the title. Based on our determination that ordinarily the subject will be found in the short title, we conclude that the subject of chapter 99-188 is sentencing. In so holding, we agree with the majority analysis in *Hernandez-Molina* that the subject of the Act is not defined by either its purpose as expressed in the preamble or its citation name in section one — the "Three-Strike Violent Felony Offender Act."

* * *

We now turn to the controverted issue of whether sections 11 and 13 are properly connected to sentencing. The Second District in *Taylor* determined that sections 11 and 13 lack a proper connection. The test we utilize is whether there is a natural or logical connection to sentencing, or whether a reasonable explanation exists for how these provisions are either necessary to sentencing or tend to make effective or promote the purposes of the sentencing legislation. *Cf. Grant*, 770 So.2d at 657; *Canova*, 94 So.2d at 184.

We first address section 11, which provides that the clerk of the court shall furnish to the INS officers the charging document, judgment, and sentence "in every case in which an alien is convicted of a felony or misdemeanor or enters a plea of guilty or nolo contendre to any felony or misdemeanor charge." Under the language of the provision, this shall be done after the alien offender's sentencing proceeding.

We conclude that there is a natural or logical and thus proper connection between the requirements of section 11 that sentences of non-citizen offenders be provided to INS and the Act's subject of sentencing, in that section 11 is a post-sentencing measure. Our conclusion that the connection is proper is buttressed by the fact that in requiring the transmission of sentences to the INS, section 11 also promotes the Act's purpose of protecting the public from persons sentenced as serious or repeat violent offenders. As stated by the Third District in *Franklin* and the Fourth District in *Hernandez-Molina*, section 11 aids in the removal of violent alien offenders from the country after sentence completion. *See Franklin*, 836 So.2d at 1114; *Hernandez-Molina*, 860 So.2d at 489. Thus, there is also a reasonable explanation why the Legislature would include a provision that facilitates the removal of non-citizens who are serious or repeat violent offenders after sentence completion in an Act whose subject is sentencing and whose purposes include the use of sentencing to protect the public from this class of criminals.

In reaching this conclusion, we are not persuaded by Franklin's argument that the fact that the section applies to all persons who receive a criminal sentence, whether felony or misdemeanor, violent or nonviolent, first offense or fiftieth, renders this provision in violation of article III, section 6. The inquiry is not whether the section solely relates to the purpose of protecting the public from violent and repeat offenders, but rather whether the section is properly connected to the single subject of sentencing. Accordingly, the inclusion of section 11 does not result in a violation of the single subject clause of article III, section 6.

We next turn to section 13, which expands the substantive crime of burglary to specifically add "railroad vehicle" to the definition of conveyance. The Second District found the relationship between the substantive crime of burglary and sentencing too "tenuous, so dependent on the happenstance of individual cases, that it simply cannot be characterized as natural or logical." *Taylor*, 818 So.2d at 549. In contrast, the Third and Fourth Districts determined that including section 13 does not violate the single subject clause because the section expands the definition of the crime of armed burglary, which is an offense included in section 775.084, the habitual offender sentencing statute. *See Franklin*, 836 So.2d at 1113–1114; *Hernandez-Molina*, 860 So.2d at 490.

We agree with the Third and Fourth Districts. The proper connection between the expanded definition of burglary and sentencing is found in the fact that armed burglary is one of the qualifying offenses for a harsher *sentence* in the Act. In broadening the definition of conveyance in section 810.11, Florida Statutes, which previously encompassed a "railroad car" but not a "railroad vehicle," the Legislature ensured that a serious crime against a person inside a railroad vehicle (to wit, a locomotive) will be punished accordingly. *See Hernandez-Molina*, 860 So.2d at 490.[28] Thus, there is a proper connection to sentencing in that section 13 makes effective one of the purposes included within the subject-imposing harsher *sentences* on violent offenders. Considering that the purpose of the Act is to protect the public from serious and repeat violent offenders, a reasonable explanation exists for including this substantive section within an Act whose subject is sentencing.

In determining that section 13 did not relate to sentencing and therefore violates article III, section 6, the Second District in *Taylor* and Judge Cope in his dissenting opinion in *Franklin* relied, in part, on the fact that section 13 substantively amended the criminal law. *See Taylor*, 818 So.2d at 549; *Franklin*, 836 So.2d at 1120 (Cope, J., dissenting). However, we do not consider this fact to be determinative in this case.

* * *

For the reasons stated above, we conclude that sections 11 and 13 are properly connected to the single subject of sentencing. Chapter 99-188 does not violate the single subject clause of article III, section 6 of the Florida Constitution. Accordingly, we approve the Third District's decision in *Franklin*, which is before us for review. We also approve the Fourth District's decision in *Hernandez-Molina* and disapprove the Second District's decision in *Taylor*.

It is so ordered.

---

28. Burglary of a conveyance with an assault or battery is a first-degree felony punishable by life. *See* § 810.02(2)(a), Fla. Stat. (2003). Section 810.011 previously referenced railroad cars within the definition of conveyance. As noted by the Fourth District in *Hernandez-Molina*, the legislative history of section 13 reveals that "vehicle" was added to the definition of conveyance due to a perceived ambiguity in the statute. By previously covering only railroad "cars," the statute had apparently prevented some burglary prosecutions of persons entering railroad locomotives to commit violent offenses against conductors. *See Hernandez-Molina*, 860 So.2d at 490.

WELLS, CANTERO and BELL, JJ., concur.

QUINCE, J., dissents with an opinion, in which ANSTEAD and LEWIS, JJ., concur.

[Appendices A and B are omitted.]

QUINCE, J., dissenting.

I dissent from the majority's determination that chapter 99-188, Laws of Florida, does not violate the single subject rule of article III, section 6, of the Florida Constitution because the subject is not accurately reflected in the title and because sections 11 and 13 are not properly connected with the subject of the chapter. Therefore, contrary to the majority, I would approve the holding in *Taylor v. State,* 818 So.2d 544 (Fla. 2d DCA 2002), quash the decision in *State v. Franklin,* 836 So.2d 1112 (Fla. 3d DCA 2003), and disapprove the decision in *Hernandez-Molina v. State,* 860 So.2d 483 (Fla. 4th DCA 2003).

Chapter 99-188 contains several sections, most of which deal with either enhanced sentences for repeat criminal offenders or the imposition of minimum mandatory sentences for violent felons. Two sections, section 11 and section 13, however, do not involve sentencing issues at all. As the majority explains, article III, section 6, of the Florida Constitution contains three requirements: (1) each law shall embrace only one subject; (2) the law may include any matter properly connected with that subject; and (3) the subject must be expressed in the title. *See* majority op. at 1071–72 (citing *State v. Thompson,* 750 So.2d 643, 646 (Fla.1999)). While I agree with the majority that the broad subject of the chapter is sentencing and that this broad subject is expressed in the title, that is not the complete or specific subject of this chapter. As pointed out by Judge Hazouri in his concurring in part and dissenting in part opinion in *Hernandez-Molina v. State,* 860 So.2d 483, 491 (Fla. 4th DCA 2003), the more specific subject of chapter 99-188 is "enhanced sentencing for repeat violent felony offenders." All but two of the sections of the chapter pertain to this subject. As we have done on other occasions, we must look beyond the introductory phrase of the chapter, which in this case merely says "an act relating to sentencing," to discern its true subject. *See Tormey v. Moore,* 824 So.2d 137 (Fla.2002) (rejecting the State's argument that the subject of chapter 89-100, Laws of Florida, was simply "an act relating to criminal penalties"); *Heggs v. State,* 759 So.2d 620 (Fla.2000); *State v. Thompson,* 750 So.2d 643 (Fla.2000). Because the true subject of the chapter is not expressed in the title, I would find that there is a violation of the single subject requirement in chapter 99-188.

Additionally, this chapter does not satisfy the requirement of article III, section 6, because sections 11 and 13 are not properly connected to the subject and objective of chapter 99-188. "A connection between a provision and the subject is proper *if the connection is natural or logical, or* if there is a reasonable explanation for how *the provision is necessary to the subject or tends to make effective or promote the objects and purposes of legislation* included in the subject." Majority op. at 1078 (emphasis added). Neither section 11 nor section 13 is naturally or logically connected to the subject of the Act, which is enhanced sentencing for serious offenses.[30] Since neither section is naturally or logically connected to the subject of enhanced sentencing, or to sentencing in general, it is quite evident that neither section is "necessary to the subject" of sentencing. Furthermore, neither section tends to make effective or promote the object and purpose of the chapter, i.e., to protect the public from serious and repeat violent offenders. *See* majority op. at 1082 ("[T]he purpose of the Act is to protect the public from serious and repeat violent offenders. . . .").

Section 11 requires the clerk of the court to furnish to the appropriate United States immigration officer any records pertaining to any alien who is convicted of a felony or misdemeanor or who pleads guilty or no contest to any felony or misdemeanor charge. Section 11 cannot and does not relate to the chapter's subject of enhanced sentencing for serious felons; rather, "section 11 addresses a purely administrative subject that is far afield of the act's other provisions." *Taylor,* 818 So.2d at 549. The majority states that section 11 is "a provision that facilitates the removal of non-citizens who are serious or repeat violent offenders after sentence completion." Majority op. at 1081. However, the language in section 11 does not limit the transmission of criminal records for repeat offenders or those convicted of serious crimes. Because section 11 pertains to aliens who are convicted of, or plead guilty or no contest to, misdemeanors as well as all felonies, whether violent or nonviolent, it does not make effective or promote the Act's object of protecting the public from serious and repeat violent offenders.

Section 13 is likewise not connected to the purpose of chapter 99-188. Section 13 adds "railroad vehicle" to the definition of "conveyance" for purposes of the enforcement of Florida's burglary statutes. This provision does not address a minimum or enhanced sentencing requirement for violent or repeat offenders. In fact, the only connection between section 13 and the other provisions in the chapter is that both involve criminal law. Such a connection is insufficient. *See, e.g., State v. Johnson,* 616 So.2d 1 (Fla.1993) (rejecting the State's argument that chapter 89-280, Laws of Florida, did not violate the single subject requirement because the single subject was controlling crime). Therefore, I would also find that, like section 11, section 13 violates the single subject rule because it is not logically connected to the subject of the chapter.

* * *

b. The "Window Period" for Asserting Single Subject Violations

A brief "window period" during which a law may be challenged because of an alleged violation of the single subject limitation has evolved.[9] Generally, the "window period" commences on the effective date of the challenged law and closes on the

---

30. Even assuming the title of the chapter is sentencing, sections 11 and 13 are not properly connected to this broader topic.

9. *See State v. Thompson,* 750 So. 2d 643, 645 (Fla. 1999).

effective date of the Legislature's *biennial* adoption of the Florida Statutes.[10] When a legislative act is incorporated in the Florida Statutes, any single subject defect is deemed cured.[11] While it is unclear how the placement of a defective law in the Florida Statutes "cures" a single subject violation, the following Florida Supreme Court decision further explains this rule.

Salters v. State

758 So. 2d 667 (Fla. 2000)

PER CURIAM.

We have for review *Salters v. State,* 731 So.2d 826 (Fla. 4th DCA 1999), in which the Fourth District Court of Appeal certified conflict with the Second District Court of Appeal's decision in *Thompson v. State,* 708 So.2d 315 (Fla. 2d DCA 1998), *approved,* 750 So.2d 643 (Fla.1999), regarding the class of persons having standing to challenge a violent career criminal sentence on the basis that chapter 95-182, Laws of Florida, violates the single subject rule contained in article III, section 6 of the Florida Constitution. We have jurisdiction. *See* Art. V, § 3(b)(4), Fla. Const. As explained in more detail below, we quash that portion of the decision below that affirmed Salters' violent career criminal sentence.

I. Facts and Procedural History in this Case

On May 15, 1997, the State of Florida (the State) filed an information charging Leo Salters (Salters)[1] with strong-arm robbery in connection with the removal of eight bottles of Pepto-Bismol from a Winn Dixie Store, with such offense occurring on April 27, 1997. Salters' case proceeded to trial in July 1997, and the jury found him guilty as charged.[2] The trial court adjudicated Salters guilty and deferred sentencing to a later date.

Prior to sentencing, the State filed a request that the trial court, pursuant to section 775.084, Florida Statutes (Supp.1996), declare Salters to be a habitual felony offender, a habitual violent felony offender, or a violent career criminal. According to the guidelines scoresheet prepared in Salters' case, the sentencing range for

---

10. *Trapp v. State,* 760 So. 2d 924, 927 (Fla. 2000).

11. *Id.*

1. The name listed on the information was actually Willie Kyles, which is an alias name used by Leo Salters. The trial court later granted the State's oral motion to amend the information to reflect Salters' true name.

2. The evidence presented at trial showed that Esaak Mohamed, an assistant manager at a Winn Dixie store, observed Salters exiting that store with a protruding bulge in the back of his windbreaker jacket. Mohamed followed Salters outside the store, and when he spoke to Salters, Salters began to run. Mohamed chased Salters, and Mohamed was injured during the chase when Salters thrust a bicycle into Mohamed's path. A Winn Dixie customer apprehended Salters soon thereafter, at which time Salters stated that he had stolen from the store. The police recovered eight bottles of Pepto-Bismol from Salters' person. After considering these facts, the jury found Salters guilty of strong-arm robbery as charged, rejecting the lesser included offenses of resisting a merchant and petit theft.

the offense would have been from twenty-seven to forty-five months in prison. However, after conducting a sentencing hearing on August 15, 1997, the trial court sentenced Salters as a violent career criminal to thirty-five years in prison with a thirty-year mandatory minimum term pursuant to section 775.084(c), Florida Statutes (Supp.1996).[3] Salters filed a timely motion to correct sentencing error pursuant to rule 3.800(b) of the Florida Rule of Criminal Procedure (1997), arguing that the State had failed to prove that Salters qualified to be sentenced as a violent career criminal, but the trial court denied that motion. Salters appealed.

On appeal, the Fourth District affirmed Salters' conviction for strong-arm robbery. *See Salters,* 731 So.2d at 826. The Fourth District also affirmed Salters' violent career criminal sentence, stating, "We hold that appellant's opportunity to challenge his sentence, based upon the constitutionality of the statute, ended on October 1, 1996. Consequently, appellant lacked standing to challenge this issue, since his offenses occurred on April 27, 1997." *Id.* (citing *State v. Johnson,* 616 So.2d 1, 2 (Fla.1993), and *Scott v. State,* 721 So.2d 1245 (Fla. 4th DCA 1998)).[4] In so holding, the Fourth District certified conflict with the Second District's decision in *Thompson* regarding the close of the window period, and that certified conflict is now before us for consideration.[5]

---

3. In a written order, the trial court detailed Salters' relevant criminal record:

> On November 7, 1985, the Defendant was convicted of Uttering a Forged Instrument and placed on probation. On January 30, 1987, the probation was revoked, and the Defendant was also convicted of Burglary, and he was sentenced to eighteen (18) months in prison. On February 1, 1991, the Defendant was convicted of Robbery and sentenced to two (2) years in prison. On January 16, 1996, the Defendant was convicted of Burglary and sentenced to time served. On April 2, 1997, the Defendant was convicted of Burglary, and he was placed on supervision. On May 28, 1997, that supervision was revoked, and he was sentenced to two (2) years in prison. . . .

Based on Salters' criminal record, the trial court found it necessary for the protection of the public to sentence Salters as a violent career criminal.

4. Even though Salters failed to challenge chapter 95-182 on single subject rule grounds in the trial court, we find that such challenge may be properly addressed in this case for the first time on appeal. *Cf. Heggs v. State,* 759 So.2d 620, 623, 624 n. 4 (Fla.2000); *Nelson v. State,* 748 So.2d 237, 241–42 (Fla.1999), *cert. denied,* 528 U.S. 1123, 120 S.Ct. 950, 145 L.Ed.2d 825 (2000); *State v. Johnson,* 616 So.2d 1, 3–4 (Fla.1993). However, for those defendants who have available the procedural mechanism of our recently amended rule 3.800(b), *see Amendments to Rules of Criminal Procedure 3.111(e) & 3.800 & Rules of Appellate Procedure 9.010(h), 9.140, & 9.600,* 24 Fla. L. Weekly S530, 761So.2d 1015, 1999 WL 1029285 (Fla. Nov.12, 1999), we would require that such defendants in the future raise a single subject rule challenge in the trial court prior to filing the first appellate brief. *See Maddox v. State,* 760 So.2d 89, 98 (Fla.2000).

5. Salters makes the following three additional claims in an attempt to challenge his strong arm robbery conviction: (1) the evidence was insufficient to support the conviction; (2) the trial court erroneously allowed the State to exercise peremptory challenges in a racially discriminatory manner; and (3) the trial court erroneously denied various defense motions for mistrial. These additional claims are clearly outside the scope of the certified conflict issue, and we decline to address them. *See, e.g., Ross v. State,* 601 So.2d 1190, 1193 (Fla.1992).

II. Window Period Analysis

In *State v. Thompson*, 750 So.2d 643, 649 (Fla.1999), we held chapter 95-182, Laws of Florida, to be unconstitutional as violative of the single subject rule contained in article III, section 6 of the Florida Constitution. Prior to announcing that holding, however, we noted the conflict between the Second District's decision in *Thompson* and the Fourth District's decision in *Salters* as to when the window period closed for persons claiming a violent career criminal sentence to be invalid due to the amendments made by chapter 95-182. *See Thompson*, 750 So.2d at 646. As noted in *Thompson, see id.*, the *Salters* court apparently accepted an argument discussed by the Fourth District in *Scott*, in which the State argued that the Legislature's enactment of chapter 96-388, Laws of Florida, portions of which became effective on October 1, 1996, cured any alleged single subject rule problems in chapter 95-182. *See Scott*, 721 So.2d at 1246 n. 1. We declined to make a determination in *Thompson* regarding the close of the window period because the defendant in that case had standing to raise a single subject rule challenge even if the window period closed on October 1, 1996, as determined by the Fourth District in *Salters. See Thompson*, 750 So.2d at 646. It is clear in this case, however, that Salters would not have standing to challenge chapter 95-182 on single subject rule grounds if the window period for raising such a challenge closed on October 1, 1996, and we therefore must determine the window period issue here. In determining this issue, we consider this Court's prior decisions in the single subject rule context, the contents of chapter 96-388, Laws of Florida, as well as the arguments asserted by the parties in Thompson[6] and this case.

In *Loxahatchee River Environmental Control District v. School Board of Palm Beach County*, 515 So.2d 217 (Fla.1987), this Court explained how laws that violate the single subject rule generally are "cured":

> At every odd-year regular session, the legislature, as part of its program of continuing revision, adopts the laws passed in the preceding odd year as official statute laws and directs that they take effect immediately under the title of "Florida Statutes" dated the current year. In *Santos v. State*, 380 So.2d 1284 (Fla.1980), this Court held that when laws passed by the legislature are adopted and codified in this manner, the restrictions of article III, section 6, pertaining to one subject matter and notice in the title no longer apply. *Accord State v. Combs*, 388 So.2d 1029 (Fla.1980). . . .
>
> . . . .

---

6. We received supplemental briefs from the parties in *Thompson* regarding the window period issue, *see State v. Thompson*, 750 So.2d 643, 646 (Fla.1999), and we granted Salters' "Request to Take Judicial Notice" of those supplemental briefs in this case.

> ... A law passed in violation of the requirements of article III, section 6, is invalid until such time as it is reenacted for codification into the Florida Statutes. *See Thompson v. Intercounty Tel. & Tel. Co.*, 62 So.2d 16 (Fla.1952).

Loxahatchee, 515 So.2d at 218–19 (emphasis added) (footnote omitted); *see also Johnson*, 616 So.2d at 2. The Preface to the official Florida Statutes illustrates how the biennial adoption process works. Linda S. Jessen, Preface to Florida Statutes at vi (1999); *see also Loxahatchee*, 515 So.2d at 218 n. *. In essence, the Preface explains that, during the biennial adoption process, the Legislature amends sections 11.2421, 11.2422, 11.2424, and 11.2425, Florida Statutes, to prospectively adopt as the official statutory law of Florida those portions of the statutes that are carried forward from the preceding regular edition of the Florida Statutes. Thus, it is clear that the general rule for "curing" laws that violate the single subject rule is through the biennial adoption process.

Without discussing the general rule, this Court essentially recognized an exception to that rule in *Martinez v. Scanlan*, 582 So.2d 1167 (Fla.1991). In that case, the trial court held unconstitutional chapter 90-201, Laws of Florida, as violative of the single subject rule. *See id.* at 1169. Subsequent to the trial court's ruling but prior to this Court's decision, the Legislature convened a special session during which it (1) separated into two distinct bills the international trade and workers' compensation provisions contained in chapter 90-201; and (2) reenacted those two distinct bills into law. *See id.* at 1172 (citing the passage of chapters 91-1 and 91-5, Laws of Florida). On review, this Court agreed with the trial court that chapter 90-201 violated the single subject rule because "the subjects of workers' compensation and international trade are simply too dissimilar and lack the necessary logical and rational relationship to the legislature's stated purpose of comprehensive economic development to pass constitutional muster." *Id.* This Court also found, however, that the Legislature's separation and reenactment of the dissimilar provisions originally contained in chapter 90-201 "clearly cured the single subject objection and demonstrated the legislature's intent to amend the preexisting workers' compensation act without the appendage of the international trade legislation." *Id.* Thus, this Court clearly recognized in *Scanlan* that a single subject rule violative chapter law may be cured by means other than the biennial adoption process.

With the above exception in mind, we must determine whether the general rule or the exception applies in this case. The State asserts that the Legislature's passage of chapter 96-388 has the same effect in this case as did the Legislature's curative actions in *Scanlan*, while Salters argues that the Legislature's actions in *Scanlan* and this case are distinguishable. After reviewing the contents of chapter 96-388, we agree with Salters regarding the violent career criminal sentencing provisions addressed in chapter 96-388.

In sections 44, 45, and 46 of chapter 96-388, the Legislature addressed several statutory provisions that previously were addressed in chapter 95-182; specifically, sections 775.084, 775.0842, and 790.235, Florida Statutes. *Compare* Ch. 95-182,

§§ 2, 5, 7, at 1667–73, *with* Ch. 96-388, §§ 44–46, at 2330–37.[7] In section 44 of chapter 96-388, the Legislature amended section 775.084, Florida Statutes, by (1) adding language to provide that a defendant qualifies for enhanced sentencing if the offense at issue was committed "[w]hile the defendant was serving a prison sentence or other commitment imposed as a result of a prior conviction of [a qualifying] felony;" (2) deleting several references to the term "on parole or otherwise;" (3) deleting gender-specific language; (4) revising language relating to enhanced sentencing procedures; and (5) revising language regarding gain-time eligibility. *See* Ch. 96-388, § 44, at 2330–36. Also in section 44 of chapter 96-388, the Legislature reenacted subsection (6) of section 775.084, which states: "The purpose of this section is to provide uniform punishment for those crimes made punishable under this section, and to this end, a reference to this section constitutes a general reference under the doctrine of incorporation by reference." In section 45 of chapter 96-388, the Legislature reenacted section 790.235, Florida Statutes, which is the statutory section establishing the crime of unlawful possession of a firearm by a violent career criminal. *See* Ch. 96-388, § 45, at 2336. Finally, in section 46 of chapter 96-388, the Legislature amended section 775.0842, Florida Statutes, by deleting the word "or" from the statute in one instance. *See* Ch. 96-388, § 46, at 2337.[8]

After considering the relevant provisions of chapter 96-388 in light of the general rule and exception discussed above, we hold that the window period for challenging the violent career criminal sentencing provisions created by chapter 95-182, Laws of Florida, opened on October 1, 1995, when chapter 95-182 became effective, and closed on May 24, 1997, when chapter 97-97, Laws of Florida, reenacted the amendments contained in chapter 95-182 as part of the biennial adoption process. Stated another way, we hold that individuals such as Salters who are challenging the violent career criminal sentencing provisions enacted by chapter 95-182 have standing to do so if the relevant criminal offense or offenses occurred on or after October 1,

---

7. As noted in *State v. Thompson*, 750 So.2d 643, 647 (Fla.1999), in section 2 of chapter 95-182, the Legislature substantially amended section 775.084, Florida Statutes, by (1) creating and defining a new "violent career criminal" sentencing category; (2) adding "aggravated stalking" to the list of qualifying offenses for the habitual violent felony offender sentencing category; (3) establishing sentencing procedures for violent career criminals and modifying the sentencing procedures for habitual felony and habitual violent felony offenders; and (4) limiting the amount and types of gain-time for which violent career criminals are eligible. In section 5 of chapter 95-182, the Legislature added the phrase "or a violent career criminal" to section 775.0842, Florida Statutes, the statute establishing which persons that are subject to career criminal prosecution. *See* Ch. 95-182, § 5 at 1671; *see also Thompson*, 750 So.2d at 647. Finally, in section 7 of chapter 95-182, the Legislature created section 790.235, Florida Statutes, which sets forth the substantive crime of unlawful possession of a firearm by a violent career criminal. *See* Ch. 95-182, § 7, at 1673; *see also Thompson*, 750 So.2d at 647.

8. Because section 46 of chapter 96-388 did not specifically provide an effective date, *see* chapter 96-388, section 46, at 2337, the amendment to section 775.0842, Florida Statutes, made by that section actually became effective on July 1, 1996. *See* Ch. 96-388, § 74, at 2384 ("Except as otherwise provided herein, this act shall take effect July 1, 1996."). It is clear, however, that the Legislature's deletion of the word "or" in one instance had no substantive effect on the statute.

1995, and before May 24, 1997.[9] We reach this holding because other than reenacting the "general purpose" provision contained in section 775.084(6), Florida Statutes, the Legislature's passage of the relevant provisions of chapter 96-388 only amended various enhanced sentencing provisions contained in sections 775.084 and 775.0842. Unlike the situation in *Scanlan*, the Legislature here did not cure the single subject problems implicated in chapter 95-182 by separating the dissimilar provisions and reenacting those provisions into law separately. Based on this analysis and determination, we do not address Salters' argument that chapter 96-388, Laws of Florida, itself violates the single subject rule.

Accordingly, based on the foregoing, we quash that part of the decision below that affirmed Salters' sentence and approve the result reached by the Second District in *Thompson* regarding the applicable window period. Further, we reverse Salters' violent career criminal sentence and remand for resentencing in accordance with the valid laws in effect on April 27, 1997, the date on which Salters committed the underlying offense in this case. *See Thompson*, 750 So.2d at 649 (remanding for resentencing in accordance with the valid laws in effect at the time the defendant committed her offenses).

It is so ordered.

HARDING, C.J., and SHAW, ANSTEAD, PARIENTE, LEWIS and QUINCE, JJ., concur.

WELLS, J., dissents with an opinion.

WELLS, J., dissenting.

For the reasons stated in my dissent in *State v. Thompson*, 750 So.2d 643 (Fla.1999), I dissent from the majority decision in this case. I do not reach the window issue.

———————

It can be strongly argued that the entire "window period" limitation on asserting a claim of a violation of the single subject began when the Florida Supreme Court in *State v. Combs*[12] misread its earlier decision in *Santos v. State*.[13] The Court's opinions in these cases will be found at the conclusion of this section. The subject appears to be next (after *Santos*) discussed in *Loxahatchee River Environmental Control District v. School Board of Palm Beach County*.[14] The following brief quote from the Florida Supreme Court's opinion will give further proof of what we believe to be error:

———————

9. Because the offense of possession of a firearm by a violent career criminal is not involved here, we do not determine when the window period closed for persons attempting to challenge a conviction for such offense by raising a single subject rule challenge to chapter 95-182, Laws of Florida.

12. 388 So. 2d 1029 (Fla. 1980).

13. 380 So. 2d 1284 (Fla. 1980).

14. 515 So. 2d 217 (Fla. 1987).

3 · THE LEGISLATURE

... [T]he [district] court held that once the challenged law had been reenacted as a portion of the Florida Statutes, it was not subject to challenge under article III, section 6.

At every odd-year regular session, the legislature, as part of its program of continuing revision, adopts the laws passed in the preceding odd year as official statute laws and directs that they take effect immediately under the title of "Florida Statutes" dated the current year. [Footnote referring the reader to the Preface to the official Florida Statutes omitted.] In *Santos v. State*, 380 So.2d 1284 (Fla.1980), this Court held that when laws passed by the legislature [session laws] are adopted and codified in this manner, the restrictions of article III, section 6, pertaining to one subject and notice in the title no longer apply. *Accord State v. Combs*, 388 So.2d 1029 (Fla. 1980). . . .[15]

The Court further explained that "A law passed in violation of the requirements of article III, section 6, is invalid until such time as it is reenacted for codification into the Florida Statutes."[16]

It is our belief that *Santos* holds no more than that the single subject rule does *not* apply to the organizational structure of the Florida Statutes. It is our further belief that the Court in *Combs* misread *Santos*, leading to the creation of a "window period" that was never intended to exist.

Santos v. State

380 So. 2d 1284 (Fla. 1980)

BOYD, Justice.

This cause is before the Court on appeal from a judgment of the County Court of Orange County. The trial court passed upon the constitutionality of a state statute. We have jurisdiction. Art. V, § 3(b)(1), Fla. Const.

The appellant was charged with the crimes of driving while intoxicated and driving with unlawful blood alcohol level in violation of section 316.193, subsections (1) and (3) respectively, Florida Statutes (1977). . . .

* * *

. . . [Appellant] contends that section 316.193, Florida Statutes (1977), violates article III, section 6 of the Florida Constitution. . . .

* * *

Article III, section 6 provides in pertinent part: "Every law shall embrace but one subject and matter properly connected therewith, and the subject shall be briefly expressed in the title." The appellant contends that section 316.193 embraces more

---

15. *Id.* at 218.
16. *Id.* at 219.

than one subject and therefore violates the single-subject requirement for laws. In support of this contention, he asserts that it is improper for section 316.193(1) and (3) to create two separate and distinct offenses. This argument is without merit.

The quoted portion of article III, section 6 contains two essential requirements. The requirement that the subject of a law be briefly expressed in the title serves the purpose of providing notice to interested persons of the contents of an enactment. *State v. McDonald*, 357 So.2d 405 (Fla. 1978); *Knight & Wall Co. v. Bryant*, 178 So.2d 5 (Fla. 1965). The purpose of the requirement that each law embrace only one subject and matter properly connected with it is to prevent subterfuge, surprise, "hodge-podge" and log rolling in legislation. *State v. Lee*, 356 So.2d 276 (Fla. 1978); *Lee v. Bigby Electric Co.*, 136 Fla. 305, 186 So. 505 (1939). The purposes sought to be achieved by these constitutional restrictions are satisfied if each enactment of the legislature embraces "but one subject and matter properly connected therewith" and the subject is "briefly expressed in the title." Art. III, §6, Fla. Const. When laws passed by the legislature are being codified for publication in the Florida Statutes, these restrictions do not apply. The legislature is free to use whatever classification system it chooses. Article III, section 6 does not require sections of the Florida Statutes to conform to the single-subject requirement. The requirement applies to "laws" in the sense of acts of the legislature.

The offense proscribed by section 316.193(1), Florida Statutes (1977), was established by chapter 71-135, Laws of Florida. This act of the legislature is called the Florida Uniform Traffic Control Law. It regulates the use of the public roads of the state. It embraces only that subject and matters properly connected therewith. The offense proscribed by section 316.193(3) was created by chapter 74-384, Laws of Florida. That law embraces the subject of driving while under the influence of alcohol and matters properly connected therewith.

We hold that neither of the laws at issue here violates article III, section 6. The judgment of the county court is affirmed.

It is so ordered.

ENGLAND, C.J., and ADKINS, OVERTON, SUNDBERG, ALDERMAN and McDONALD, JJ., concur.

State v. Combs

388 So. 2d 1029 (Fla. 1980)

ADKINS, Justice.

The State brings this appeal from an order of the Circuit Court of the Twentieth Judicial Circuit in and for Lee County dismissing an indictment on the grounds that the statute on which it was based was unconstitutional. We have jurisdiction pursuant to article V, section 3(b)(1), Florida Constitution (1972).

Count II of the indictment in this case charged appellee, hereinafter defendant, with attempted first degree murder, section 777.04 Florida Statutes (1977). Section 777.04 is entitled "Attempts, solicitation, conspiracy, generally." The first three subsections define the crimes and the fourth provides the appropriate punishment. [Footnote omitted.] The defendant successfully argued to the trial court that the statute violates the single subject requirement of article III, section 6 of the Florida Constitution, "Every law shall embrace but one subject and matter properly connected therewith, and the subject shall be briefly expressed in the title."

In *Santos v. State*, 380 So.2d 1284 (Fla. 1980), we held that "article III, section 6, does not require sections of the Florida Statutes to conform to the single subject requirement. The requirement applies to 'laws' in the sense of acts of the legislature." *Id.* at 1285. Section 777.04 was enacted as chapter 74-383, Laws of Florida, and adopted or re-enacted in chapter 77-266, Laws of Florida. Article III, section 6 of our constitution applied only to chapter 74-383, Laws of Florida, and only so long as it remained a "law." Once re-enacted as a portion of the Florida Statutes it was not subject to challenge under article III, section 6. There have been no subsequent pertinent amendments to justify a challenge at this point.

The order of the trial court is reversed and the cause remanded for proceedings consistent with this opinion.

It is so ordered.

SUNDBERG, C. J., and BOYD, OVERTON, ENGLAND, ALDERMAN and McDONALD, JJ., concur.

Since *Santos* appears to do nothing more than state the apparent truism that the single subject limitation applies to session laws and not the contents of the Florida Statutes, and *Combs* takes, without a citation of authority, the giant step of expanding the *Santos* holding to reach the result that "reenactment cures," it can be argued with considerable force that the whole "window of opportunity" argument resembles a house of cards.

This is not to suggest that as a practice matter the rule is a bad one. However, the reader should note that a new system of "annual adoption" would substantially shorten the "window period."

c. The Title Requirement

North Ridge General Hospital, Inc. v. City of Oakland Park

374 So. 2d 461 (Fla. 1979)

SUNDBERG, Justice.

This cause is before us on direct appeal from an order of the Circuit Court for Broward County upholding the constitutionality of chapter 75-452, Laws of Florida, a special law annexing appellants' property to the City of Oakland Park, Florida. We have jurisdiction pursuant to article V, section 3(b)(1), Florida Constitution. On June 3, 1975, appellant North Ridge General Hospital, Inc. was notified by a city official that its property had been annexed to appellee City of Oakland Park by act of the legislature, chapter 75-452, Laws of Florida. Appellants immediately filed a declaratory judgment action in circuit court, seeking an injunction to prevent appellees from enforcing this law. Appellants asserted that chapter 75-452 is unconstitutional in that it denied them equal protection of the law and because the notice of intent to seek enactment[1] and the title[2] of the act were insufficient to inform appellants of the annexation. On appellants' motion for summary judgment the circuit court rejected the constitutional challenges and dismissed the action.

We disagree with appellants' contention that the title of chapter 75-452 and the notice of intention to seek its enactment are insufficient to give adequate notice as required by article III, sections 6 and 10, Florida Constitution.[3] The rule with respect to the notice required by each of these constitutional provisions was set forth by this Court in *Coldewey v. Board of Public Instruction*, 189 So.2d 878, 880 (Fla.1966):

---

1. "NOTICE OF PROPOSED LEGISLATION
TO WHOM IT MAY CONCERN:
Notice is hereby given of intention to apply to the 1975 session of the Legislature of the State of Florida for the passage of an act relating to the enlarging and extending of the corporate limits of the city of Oakland Park by including previously unincorporated land into said corporate limits; providing an effective date.
BROWARD COUNTY
LEGISLATIVE DELEGATION
By: (s) PETER B. TIERNAN
Attorney for the Delegation.
April 14, 1975"
2. "A bill to be entitled An act relating to the City of Oakland Park, Broward County; extending and enlarging the corporate limits of the City of Oakland Park by including previously unincorporated land into said corporate limits; providing an effective date."
3. These sections, in pertinent part, provide:
SECTION 6. — Laws. Every law shall embrace but one subject and matter properly connected therewith, and the subject shall be briefly expressed in the title. . . .
SECTION 10. — Special laws. No special law shall be passed unless notice of intention to seek enactment thereof has been published in the manner provided by general law. . . .

> [T]he purpose of both of these constitutional requirements is to assure that proper notice will be given of the subject matter of proposed legislation. *King Kole, Inc. v. Bryant*, Fla.1965, 178 So.2d 2; *State ex rel. Watson v. City of Miami*, 1943, 153 Fla. 653, 15 So.2d 481. Therefore, the measure of the violation of these constitutional requirements must be whether such published notice or title, as the case may be, confuses as to the subject matter of the proposed legislation.

Thus, the constitution requires only that notice be given of the *subject* of proposed legislation, not that the *object* of such legislation be defined in the notice. "The subject is the matter to which an act relates; the object, the purpose to be accomplished." *Wright v. Board of Public Instruction*, 48 So.2d 912, 915 (Fla.1950). The term "subject" is broader than the word "object," as one subject may contain many objects. *Spencer v. Hunt*, 109 Fla. 248, 147 So. 282 (1933). Therefore, the terms of both the notice of intention to seek enactment and the title of an act must be broad enough to include all matters contained in the body of the proposed legislation, but the specific contents of the act need not be listed in detail in either form of notice. *City of Naples v. Moon*, 269 So.2d 355 (Fla.1972); *King Kole v. Bryant*, 178 So.2d 2 (Fla.1965). The function of both the notice of intention to seek enactment and the title of a special legislative act is to provide reasonable notice to a person whose interests may be directly affected by the proposed legislation, so that he may inquire further into the details thereof and, if he so desires, seek to prevent its enactment or to persuade the legislature to change its substance. *City of Naples v. Moon*; *State ex rel. Watson v. City of Miami*, 153 Fla. 653, 15 So.2d 481 (1943). If the terms of the notice are broad enough so that an average person can reasonably foresee that his interests might be affected by the proposed legislation, the notice given is constitutionally sufficient.

In the instant case, we find that the terms of the notice of intention to seek enactment and the title of chapter 75-452, Laws of Florida, meet constitutional requirements. Both clearly state that the subject of the act is the annexation of property to the City of Oakland Park. Appellants' property is contiguous to the municipal boundaries and is situated in such a manner that its inclusion within the city is a logical extension of such boundaries. Therefore, it is clear that the notice given was reasonably sufficient to notify appellants that their property might be included in the proposed annexation.

* * *

ENGLAND, C.J., and ADKINS, BOYD, OVERTON, HATCHETT and ALDERMAN, JJ., concur.

2. Appropriation Bills

Fla. Const. art. III, § 12

Appropriation bills. — Laws making appropriations for salaries of public officers and other current expenses of the state shall contain provisions on no other subject.

An appropriation bill is a legislative act that authorizes the spending of public funds for a particular purpose.[17] Special constitutional restrictions are applicable to appropriation bills which are not applicable to other types of legislation. Specifically, appropriation bills are subject to a special "one subject" requirement which provides that they can only deal with the payment of salaries of public officers and other current state expenses.

This requirement is apparently based upon the assumption that appropriating funds is a function distinct from the general legislative process. As such these two legislative functions should not be intermixed.

While the principle appears straightforward, it is not always easy to apply. The courts have developed judicial tests to apply the provision. The following case is one of the judicial pronouncements on this requirement.

Department of Education v. Lewis

416 So. 2d 455 (Fla. 1982)

BOYD, Justice.

* * *

With both the appropriations act restriction issue and the freedom of expression issue properly presented by proper parties, we now turn to the merits.

Article III, section 12, Florida Constitution, provides:

Laws making appropriations for salaries of public officers and other current expenses of the state shall contain provisions on no other subject.

This provision is a corollary of article III, section 6, which requires that all laws be limited to a single subject and matters properly related to that subject. *Brown v. Firestone*, 382 So.2d 654 (Fla.1980). An extensive body of constitutional law teaches that the purpose of article III, section 6 is to ensure that every proposed enactment is considered with deliberation and on its own merits. A lawmaker must not be placed in the position of having to accept a repugnant provision in order to achieve adoption of a desired one. [Citations omitted.]

Through a number of cases decided over many years this Court has attempted to make clear to the Legislature that under our constitutional plan for the lawful

---

17. Fla. Stat. § 216.011.

exercise of governmental powers an appropriations act is not the proper place for the enactment of general public policies on matters other than appropriations. *Brown v. Firestone*, 382 So.2d 654 (Fla.1980); [citations omitted]. In *Brown v. Firestone*, the Court said:

> The enactment of laws providing for general appropriations involves different considerations and indeed different procedures than does the enactment of laws on other subjects. Our state constitution demands that each bill dealing with substantive matters be scrutinized separately through a comprehensive process which will ensure that all considerations prompting legislative action are fully aired. Provisions on substantive topics should not be ensconced in an appropriations bill in order to logroll or to circumvent the legislative process normally applicable to such action. Similarly, general appropriations bills should not be cluttered with extraneous matters which might cloud the legislative mind when it should be focused solely upon appropriations matters.

382 So.2d at 664.

The opinion in *Brown v. Firestone* went on to establish two principles by which to test restrictions and provisos in appropriations bills to determine whether they violate article III, section 12. First, if a provision in an appropriations bill changes existing law on any subject other than appropriations, it is invalid. Second, a qualification or restriction must directly and rationally relate to the purpose of the appropriation to which it applies. The opinion elaborated on this second principle as follows:

> That is to say, has the legislature in the appropriations process determined that the appropriation is worthwhile or advisable only if contingent upon a certain event or fact, or is the qualification or restriction being used merely as a device to further a legislative objective unrelated to the fund appropriated? This test possesses the dispositive virtue of permitting the legislature reasonably to direct appropriation use without hampering the gubernatorial veto power or abusing the legislative process.

382 So.2d at 664.

We now proceed to an analysis of the proviso according to the above-discussed principles. The portion or portions of chapter 81-206 to which the proviso, by its terms, logically relates includes all state funds to be expended on postsecondary education or granted to postsecondary educational institutions or students. The proviso directs that funds appropriated to such purposes shall be withheld from institutions in violation of the proviso and from students attending institutions that are in violation of the proviso. In order to avoid having state funds withheld, a postsecondary institution is required by the proviso to refrain from chartering, giving official recognition to, knowingly giving assistance to, or providing meeting facilities to, any group or organization that engages in a certain variety of expression or communication as broadly defined in the proviso. The proviso attempts to make substantive policy on the governance of postsecondary educational institutions.

Thus it amends a whole host of statutes pertaining to the operation of public colleges and universities and the regulation of private colleges and universities. By effecting such a de facto amendment of existing substantive law, the proviso violates the first principle announced in *Brown v. Firestone.*

One of the qualifications at issue in *Brown v. Firestone* was a requirement that the inmate count at a particular prison be phased back to design capacity. The restriction was connected to the appropriation for salaries, expenses, and capital outlay for major institutions of the state prison system. We held that the restriction was not rationally related to the funding of the state's correctional institutions but rather was "designed to further a legislative objective . . . unrelated to the funding of all the major institutions." 382 So.2d at 669.

Applying the second of the principles announced in *Brown v. Firestone*, we reach a similar conclusion in the present case. The proviso is not directly and rationally related to the appropriation of state funds to postsecondary institutions and students. It is, rather, designed to further a legislative objective unrelated to such funding.

Brown v. Firestone, decided over a year and a half ago, announced a new and useful formulation of principles, but the principles themselves were by no means new. They have been part of Florida constitutional law for decades. In *Brown v. Firestone*, some of the questions were close ones. In this case the question is clear-cut. We are simply following constitutional construction well known in Florida legal and governmental circles. We hold that the proviso violates article III, section 12.

* * *

. . . [The trial court] erred in holding that . . . it does not violate article III, section 12 of the Florida Constitution. The judgment is reversed. The proviso quoted at the beginning of this opinion is unconstitutional and void. The Comptroller is directed to disregard it. The Secretary of State is directed to strike it from chapter 81-206.

It is so ordered.

SUNDBERG, C.J., and ADKINS, OVERTON, ALDERMAN, McDONALD and EHRLICH, JJ., concur.

3. General Laws, Special Laws, and General Laws of Local Application

Fla. Const. art. III, § 10

Special laws. — No special law shall be passed unless notice of intention to seek enactment thereof has been published in the manner provided by general law. Such notice shall not be necessary when the law, except the provision for referendum, is conditioned to become effective only upon approval by vote of the electors of the area affected.

Fla. Const. art. III, § 11

Prohibited Special Laws. —

(a) There shall be no special law or general law of local application pertaining to:

(1) election, jurisdiction or duties of officers, except officers of municipalities, chartered counties, special districts or local governmental agencies;

(2) assessment or collection of taxes for state or county purposes, including extension of time therefor, relief of tax officers from due performance of their duties, and relief of their sureties from liability;

(3) rules of evidence in any court;

(4) punishment for crime;

(5) petit juries, including compensation of jurors, except establishment of jury commissions;

(6) change of civil or criminal venue;

(7) conditions precedent to bringing any civil or criminal proceedings, or limitations of time therefor;

(8) refund of money legally paid or remission of fines, penalties or forfeitures;

(9) creation, enforcement, extension or impairment of liens based on private contracts, or fixing of interest rates on private contracts;

(10) disposal of public property, including an interest therein, for private purposes;

(11) vacation of roads;

(12) private incorporation or grant of privilege to a private corporation;

(13) effectuation of invalid deeds, wills or other instruments, or change in the law of descent;

(14) change of name of any person;

(15) divorce;

(16) legitimation or adoption of persons;

(17) relief of minors from legal disabilities;

(18) transfer of any property interest of persons under legal disabilities or of estates of decedents;

(19) hunting or fresh water fishing;

(20) regulation of occupations which are regulated by state agency; or

(21) any subject when prohibited by general law passed by a three-fifths vote of the membership of each house. Such law may be amended or repealed by like vote.

(b) In the enactment of general laws on other subjects, political subdivisions or other governmental entities may be classified only on a basis reasonably related to the subject of the law.

All newly enacted laws are subject to the one subject and title requirements prescribed by art. III, §6. In addition to these basic requirements, additional restrictions exist which apply to special laws and general laws of local application, which are not applicable to general laws. It should be noted that in the 1885 Florida Constitution, the term "special law" as used in the 1968 Florida Constitution was divided into "special laws" and "local laws" (*see* art. V, §12(g)).

Under art. III, §10, in order for a special law to be valid, certain pre-enactment publication requirements must be satisfied (*see* Fla. Stat. §11.02) or the law must be conditioned upon approval by vote of the electors in the affected area. This restriction is not applicable to either a general law or a general law of local application.

Article III, §11 deprives the Florida Legislature of the ability to enact special laws or general laws of local application in certain enumerated areas. This provision presumably reflects the belief of the drafters of the Florida Constitution that the Florida Legislature should only be able to enact generally applicable legislation in the enumerated areas.

To summarize, special laws are only valid if statutorily provided pre-enactment notice is given or the laws are conditioned on a referendum in the affected area. However, no special law or general law of local application can be enacted at all if its subject matter is one of the categories enumerated in art. III, §11.

In a very broad sense, a general law is one which has statewide applicability and treats all objects coming within the operation of a statute in a uniform manner. A local law, which by definition now qualifies as a special law, was traditionally a law which singled out a particular geographic location, such as a county or municipality, for special treatment. A special law is a law confined to a particular person, object, or class. A general law of local application is often referred to as a population act and is defined in more detail below.

While these general definitions may appear clear, the courts have struggled to differentiate the different categories of laws. The following cases reflect a few of the many struggles in which the Florida courts have wrestled with these distinctions.

3 · THE LEGISLATURE

a. General Laws

Florida Department of Health v. Florigrown, LLC

317 So. 3d 1101 (Fla. 2021)

PER CURIAM.

We have for review the First District Court of Appeal's decision in *Florida Department of Health v. Florigrown, LLC* (*Florigrown I*), No. 1D18-4471, 320 So.3d 195 (Fla. 1st DCA July 9, 2019). The First District partially upheld a temporary injunction that prohibits enforcement of certain statutory provisions relating to the regulation of medical marijuana treatment centers (MMTCs). We have jurisdiction because the district court passed upon and certified a question to this Court as one of great public importance. *Fla. Dep't of Health v. Florigrown* (*Florigrown II*), No. 1D18-4471, —— So.3d ——, ——, 2019 WL 4019919, at *1 (Fla. 1st DCA Aug. 27, 2019); *see* art. V, § 3(b)(4), Fla. Const.

* * *

Background

In November 2016, the people of Florida amended our state constitution to mandate the development of a carefully regulated system for providing access to marijuana for certain patients suffering from debilitating medical conditions. Art. X, § 29, Fla. Const. The Amendment requires the Department to "issue reasonable regulations necessary for the implementation and enforcement of" its provisions, for the purpose of "ensur[ing] the availability and safe use of medical marijuana by qualifying patients." *Id.* § 29(d). At the same time, the Amendment contemplates that the Legislature may "enact[ ] laws consistent with" its provisions. *Id.* § 29(e).

Among the regulations the Department is required to issue are "[p]rocedures for the registration of MMTCs that include procedures for the issuance, renewal, suspension and revocation of registration, and standards to ensure proper security, record keeping, testing, labeling, inspection, and safety." *Id.* § 29(d)(1)c. The Amendment required the Department to issue these procedures within six months of the Amendment's effective date, January 3, 2017, and to begin registering MMTCs within nine months of that date. *Id.* § 29(d)(1) (2).

. . .

[This proceeding is based on a challenge to a statute enacted in light of the Amendment and to the Department's deference to that statute. Florigrown's lawsuit challenges some of these [statutory] provisions . . . as invalid special laws granting privileges to private corporations.]

* * *

Special-Law Challenge

Florigrown's last claim on the merits is that subparagraph 1, sub-subparagraph 2.a, and subparagraph 3 of section 381.986(8)(a) are unconstitutional under article

III, section 11(a)(12) of the Florida Constitution because they are special laws granting privileges to private corporations. . . .

The statutory provisions that Florigrown challenges as special laws granting privileges to private corporations are the following:

> 1. As soon as practicable, but no later than July 3, 2017, the department shall license as a medical marijuana treatment center any entity that holds an active, unrestricted license to cultivate, process, transport, and dispense low-THC cannabis, medical cannabis, and cannabis delivery devices, under former s. 381.986, Florida Statutes 2016, before July 1, 2017, and which meets the requirements of this section. . . .
>
> 2. The department shall license as medical marijuana treatment centers 10 applicants that meet the requirements of this section, under the following parameters:
>
>> a. As soon as practicable, but no later than August 1, 2017, the department shall license any applicant whose application was reviewed, evaluated, and scored by the department and which was denied a dispensing organization license by the department under former s. 381.986, Florida Statutes 2014; which had one or more administrative or judicial challenges pending as of January 1, 2017, or had a final ranking within one point of the highest final ranking in its region under former s. 381.986, Florida Statutes 2014; which meets the requirements of this section; and which provides documentation to the department that it has the existing infrastructure and technical and technological ability to begin cultivating marijuana within 30 days after registration as a medical marijuana treatment center.
>>
>> . . .
>>
>> c. As soon as practicable, but no later than October 3, 2017, the department shall license applicants that meet the requirements of this section in sufficient numbers to result in 10 total licenses issued under this subparagraph, while accounting for the number of licenses issued under sub subparagraphs a. and b.

3. For up to two of the licenses issued under subparagraph 2., the department shall give preference to applicants that demonstrate in their applications that they own one or more facilities that are, or were, used for the canning, concentrating, or otherwise processing of citrus fruit or citrus molasses and will use or convert the facility or facilities for the processing of marijuana.

§ 381.986(8)(a).

Article III, section 11(a)(12) of the Florida Constitution provides that "[t]here shall be no special law or general law of local application pertaining to . . . private incorporation or grant of privilege to a private corporation." Thus, to violate this provision, a statute must have two features: (1) it must be either a special law or a general law of local application, and (2) it must grant a privilege to a private corporation. We conclude that the challenged provisions are parts of a general law implementing a statewide regulatory scheme and, accordingly, do not violate article III, section 11(a)(12) of the Florida Constitution.

The Florida Constitution defines "special law" as "a special or local law." Art. X, §12(g), Fla. Const. A "special law" is "one relating to, or designed to operate upon, particular persons or things, or one that purports to operate upon classified persons or things when classification is not permissible or the classification adopted is illegal." *State ex rel. Landis v. Harris*, 120 Fla. 555, 163 So. 237, 240 (1934) (citation omitted). Additionally, in consideration of the constitutional requirement that a special law not be passed without either notice or a referendum, *see* art. III, §10, Fla. Const., this Court has made the following observation:

> The terms "special or local laws" as used in the Constitution refer ordinarily to law relating to entities, interests, rights, and functions other than those of the State since the organic law does not contemplate or require previous publication of notice of proposed laws for the exercise of State powers and functions though they may be more or less local or special in their operations or objects.

State ex rel. Gray v. Stoutamire, 131 Fla. 698, 179 So. 730, 733 (1938).

A law that addresses state interests and operates to protect those interests using valid classifications "based upon proper differences which are inherent in or peculiar to the class[es]" is a general law. *Schrader v. Fla. Keys Aqueduct Auth.*, 840 So. 2d 1050, 1055 (Fla. 2003) (citing *Dep't of Legal Affairs v. Sanford-Orlando Kennel Club, Inc.*, 434 So. 2d 879, 881 (Fla. 1983)); *see also Fla. Dep't of Bus. & Prof'l Regulation v. Gulfstream Park Racing Ass'n, Inc.*, 967 So. 2d 802, 806 (Fla. 2007). Even if the law is limited in direct application, it is still a general law as long as the limitation on its application bears a reasonable relationship to its statewide purpose. *See R.J. Reynolds Tobacco Co. v. Hall*, 67 So. 3d 1084, 1090-92 (Fla. 1st DCA 2011) (finding a law general where it applied to five tobacco companies in such a way as to protect funds used for statewide programs). The law at issue here appears to satisfy these criteria, and Florigrown has no substantial likelihood of proving otherwise.

Florigrown contends that the challenged provisions constitute special laws because they operate on closed classes. Indeed, we have often held that the closed nature of a class affected by a particular law indicated that the law was special. *E.g., Ocala Breeders' Sales Co. v. Fla. Gaming Ctrs., Inc.*, 793 So. 2d 899, 901 (Fla. 2001) (holding that a statute was a special law because it "created an impenetrable barrier to all intertrack wagering applicants except [one]"); *Dep't of Bus. Regulation v. Classic Mile, Inc.*, 541 So. 2d 1155, 1159 (Fla. 1989) ("In determining if a reasonable relationship exists [between the statute's purpose and the classification it uses], '[t]he fact that matters is that the classification is potentially open to other tracks.'" (quoting *Sanford-Orlando Kennel Club*, 434 So. 2d at 882). However, we have not held that every statute operating on a closed class constitutes a special law. *See, e.g., Schrader,*

840 So. 2d at 1056 (upholding a law that operated only in Monroe County but served to protect a "vital natural resource" of the entire state); *State v. Fla. State Turnpike Auth.*, 80 So. 2d 337, 343-44 (Fla. 1955) (upholding as general a law establishing the Florida State Turnpike Authority).

Regardless, we conclude that the statute at issue creates an open class of entities that may be eligible for MMTC licensure and, within that open class, creates sub-classifications "based upon proper distinctions and differences that inhere in or are peculiar or appropriate to the class," *Sanford-Orlando Kennel Club*, 434 So. 2d at 881, making it a general law. Florigrown's contrary argument is based on a myopic view of the subparagraphs and sub-subparagraph that it pulls out of the entire statutory scheme and fails to read the statute as a whole.

Read as a whole, and in light of the constitutional imperative for medical marijuana to be made available in a safe manner within nine months, the statute creates a licensure scheme designed to ensure regulated access to medical marijuana throughout the state within a short time frame, as contemplated by the Amendment. *See* art. X, § 29(d)(2), Fla. Const. (requiring the Department to begin registering MMTCS and issuing patient and caregiver identification cards within nine months). The statute does so by giving essentially immediate licensure to each licensed dispensing organization — which are spread across five regions encompassing the entire state — as long as those entities meet the current statutory criteria governing MMTCs. § 381.986(8)(a)11. (requiring licensure of dispensing organizations that meet the statutory criteria); § 381.986(5)(b), Fla. Stat. (2014) (requiring the Department to authorize the establishment of one dispensing organization in each of five regions in the state, consisting of the northwest, northeast, central, southeast, and southwest). Those licenses had to be issued by July 3, 2017. § 381.986(8)(a)11. The statute also required the licensure by August 1, 2017, of certain other entities that had already been through the application process for becoming dispensing organizations — as long as those entities met the statutory criteria governing MMTCs and provided "documentation . . . that [they had] the existing infrastructure and technical and technological ability to begin cultivating marijuana within 30 days after registration." § 381.986(8)(a)2.a. These provisions essentially "grandfather" the dispensing organizations and prior applicants into the current licensure scheme.

This grandfathering is accomplished with valid classifications that bear a "reasonable relation to the subject matter" of the statute. *See Sanford-Orlando Kennel Club*, 434 So. 2d at 881. Namely, these classifications describe entities that had already been engaged in, or had made a substantial effort to be engaged in, the pre-Amendment medical marijuana industry in Florida. They were applicants who were more likely than most to be prepared to join the industry efficiently, and they were applicants the Department was already familiar with.

The grandfathering provisions of section 381.986(8) are analogous to the statute upheld as a general law in *St. Johns River Water Management District v. Deseret Ranches of Florida, Inc.*, 421 So. 2d 1067, 1069 (Fla. 1982). That statute, read in isolation, applied to a limited geographical area of the state. *Id.* at 1067-68. It was nevertheless a general law because it was one part of a statewide system of water management contained within the Florida Statutes. *Id.* at 1068-69. Thus, focusing on one statute within a chapter of the Florida Statutes addressing a comprehensive legislative scheme was an improper approach to the question of whether a law was special or general. *See id.*

Similarly, when analyzing whether a law is special or general, it is improper to isolate subparagraphs of a statutory section embodying a broad regulatory scheme. The provisions of section 381.986 requiring the MMTC licensure of all dispensing organizations and certain prior applicants for dispensing-organization licensure — specifically, subparagraph (a)1. and sub-subparagraph (a)2.a. — are components of a statewide system of medical marijuana management. As in *St. Johns River Water Management District*, those provisions, though limited in direct application, "materially affect[ ] the people of the state" as part of a comprehensive approach to a statewide concern. 421 So. 2d at 1069.

Importantly, the statute as a whole does not limit MMTC licensure to the applicants that were eligible to receive licensure by July and August of 2017 based on their participation in the process for becoming dispensing organizations. Section 381.986(8)(a)2.c. provides for licensure by October 3, 2017, of additional applicants beyond those that participated in the prior process, until a total of ten licenses have been issued under section 381.986(8)(a)22., including those issued to prior dispensing organization applicants and another group identified in section 381.986(8)(a)2.b., which is not at issue in this proceeding. In addition, any other entity that wishes to apply for a license in the future may do so, and may potentially receive one, as the number of available licenses expands under section 381.986(8)(a) 4. to meet the needs of the state.

All future licensees will receive licenses equal to the ones initially issued during this early stage of Florida's medical marijuana industry. The fact that other entities may join the class of licensed MMTCs in the future as circumstances in the state change means that the class is open and the law general. *Cf. City of Coral Gables v. Crandon*, 157 Fla. 71, 25 So. 2d 1, 2–3 (1946) (holding that a law was not special where it was applicable to only one county when it was enacted but where other counties were expected to meet the criteria to join the class in the future); *Classic Mile*, 541 So. 2d at 1158 n.4 (finding a law special because its "classification scheme . . . [was] fixed so as to preclude additional parties from satisfying the requirements for inclusion within the statutory classification at some future point in time").

Thus far in our special-law analysis, we have addressed only two of the three challenged provisions. In addition to challenging the grandfathering provisions of section 381.986(8)(a)11. and 2.a., Florigrown challenges section 381.986(8)(a) 3., which provides a licensure preference to an open class of entities that intend to convert a citrus processing facility into a marijuana-processing facility. The basis for this classification in relation to the purpose of the statute is unclear. However, even assuming (without deciding) that this portion of the statute does not operate on a valid classification and that its existence within a broader scheme allowing the licensure of an ever-expanding open class does not defeat Florigrown's challenge, we conclude that this subclassification itself is open. This provision does not appear to be limited to entities who owned citrus facilities at the time of the statute's enactment, and we are aware of no reason to conclude that, even though the class is technically open, it applies to and was designed to apply to a narrow set of entities for no reason rationally related to the statute's purpose. *Cf. Knight v. Bd. of Pub. Instr. for Hillsborough Cty.*, 102 Fla. 922, 136 So. 631, 631 (1931). Therefore, we have no reason to believe this portion of the statute, even if properly viewed in isolation, is a special law enacted in the guise of a general law.[3]

For the foregoing reasons, we hold that Florigrown does not have a substantial likelihood of success on the merits of its constitutional challenge to section 381.986(8)(a)11, 2.a., and 3. as special laws granting privileges to private corporations in violation of article III, section 11(a)(12) of the Florida Constitution.

Conclusion

Florigrown does not have a substantial likelihood of success on the merits of its constitutional challenges to section 381.986(8). Accordingly, Florigrown's request for a temporary injunction should have been denied. We quash the First District's decision and remand this case to the First District with instructions to further remand to the trial court for vacation of the temporary injunction.

It is so ordered.

CANADY, C.J., and POLSTON, LABARGA, MUÑIZ, COURIEL, and GROSSHANS, JJ., concur.

LAWSON, J., concurs in part and dissents in part with an opinion.

[The dissenting opinion of Justice Lawson is omitted.]

———————

In determining the validity of general laws with special law characteristics, i.e., general laws that when enacted apply to only one area of the state, courts apply a "reasonableness" standard to determine whether a reasonable possibility exists that the challenged law will operate in other areas of the state in the future. For example, in *Florida Department of Business and Professional Regulation v. Gulfstream Park Racing Association, Inc.*,[18] the Florida Supreme Court found a law prohibiting thoroughbred permitholders from engaging intertrack wagering in any "area of the state where there were three or more horserace permitholders within 25 miles of each other" an unconstitutional special law enacted under the guise of a general law. In

———————

3. We understand that the citrus preference is the subject of separate litigation. Accordingly, we note that this opinion is not intended to announce a final conclusion on whether the citrus preference is an invalid special law or has any other constitutional infirmities. Our conclusions as to the citrus preference, like all of our conclusions on the merits of Florigrown's claims, should be understood as limited to the point that Florigrown has not established a substantial likelihood of success on the merits of its claims, based on the arguments and evidence presented in this proceeding.

18. 967 So. 2d 802 (Fla. 2007).

reaching its decision, the court reasoned, "Both the trial court and the district court concluded that at the time the statute was amended in 1996, these conditions existed only in the area where Gulfstream was located, and there was no reasonable possibility that they would ever exist in another part of the state. We concur in the findings of the trial court and the conclusion of the district court."[19]

b. Special Laws

A special law, by definition, is a law that singles out a particular person, object, location, or class for special treatment. It is often argued that the use of special laws violates federal and state constitutional guarantees of equal protection of the laws. Generally, this argument has been rejected by the courts.

Pinellas County Veterinary Medical Society, Inc. v. Chapman

224 So. 2d 307 (Fla. 1969)

BOYD, Justice.

This cause is before us on appeal from the Pinellas County Circuit Court. The judgment of that Court rendered May 7, 1968, held Chapter 67-1925, Laws of Florida, unconstitutional and enjoined Pinellas County from expending any funds or otherwise proceeding thereunder. . . .

* * *

The special act in question applies only to Pinellas County. It requires vaccination and licensing of dogs and the establishment of impounding agencies. Other provisions of the act prohibit mistreatment of various animals and provide that certain animals allowed to wander on public streets or roads may be impounded.

* * *

The Florida Constitution, Article III, Section 21, provides for the enactment of special or local laws subject to certain exceptions not applicable here. Special acts regulating animals within a county have been upheld.[2] The Legislature may do by special or local act that which it may not do by general act. Safeguards for persons within the locality to be affected are provided by the requirements of notice or referendum.[3] Appellees do not contend that Chapter 67-1925 was not properly enacted.

We cannot agree with the trial court's determination that the special act in question violates equal protection of the law. The act applies equally to all persons within Pinellas County. Special or local legislation, by definition, need not apply uniformly

---

19. *Id.* at 809.

2. *In re Barber*, 130 Fla. 342, 177 So. 708 (1938); *Harris v. Baden*, 154 Fla. 373, 17 So. 2d 608 (1944).

3. *State ex rel. Gray v. Stoutamire*, 131 Fla. 698, 179 So. 730 (1938).

160   3 · THE LEGISLATURE

throughout the State. In *West Flagler Kennel Club v. Florida State Racing Commission*, 153 So.2d 5 (Fla.1963), this Court stated:

> "The issue of classification for purposes of equal protection is one which applies, of course, to both general and special legislation, *although the requirement of equality or uniformity among those in like situation pertains, in the case of special acts* properly passed on a subject not required to be governed by general law, *only to those in the area where the special act is made applicable.*" (Emphasis supplied.)

* * *

For the reasons above stated, the judgment here reviewed, holding the statute invalid, should be and is hereby, reversed.

It is so ordered.

ERVIN, C. J., ROBERTS, DREW, CARLTON and ADKINS, JJ., and MASON, Circuit Judge, concur.

c. General Laws of Local Application

A general law of local application is "a law that uses a classification scheme based on population or some other criterion" to restrict its application to a particular locality.[20] For a general law of local application to be constitutional, the subject matter of the law must be reasonably related to the population classification (art. III, §11(b)). Additionally, the law cannot pertain to any of the twenty forbidden categories in art. III, §11(a), or to any subsequently added by the Florida Legislature under art. III, §11(a)(21).

State ex rel. Cotterill v. Bessenger
133 So. 2d 409 (Fla. 1961)

THOMAS, Justice.

The relator secured a writ of habeas corpus from this court commanding the respondent, Sheriff of Pasco County, Florida, to reveal by what authority he was restraining relator of his liberty.

The respondent filed his return stating that the petitioner was being held on a warrant for operating a nudist colony and sunbathers association in Pasco County, a county having a population of not less than 36,700 and not more than 38,000, in violation of the provisions of Chapter 61-1433, Laws of Florida, Acts of 1961.

The petition and writ bring into focus the constitutionality of 61-1433, supra, which according to its title and its terms is an act to regulate nudist colonies, but only in those counties having a population within the restricted number of 1300 persons.

---

20. *City of Miami Beach v. Frankel*, 363 So. 2d 555, 558 (Fla. 1978).

According to the certificate of the Secretary of State there is not on file in his office any proof of publication or notice with reference to the act, and the act itself carries no provision for a referendum. So the question arises whether it is a general act making the requirement of notice or referendum unnecessary to its validity or a local act in the guise of a general one inasmuch as it would be effective only in a county attaining a population of 36,700 and then become ineffective if that county should increase in population by 1301 persons. We are advised that the act presently applies only to Pasco County.

The pertinent provisions of Art. III, Sec. 21, F.S.A. are: "No local or special bill shall be passed * * * unless notice of intention to apply therefor shall have been published in the manner provided by law" but no such notice is necessary "when such law contains a provision to the effect that the same shall not become operative * * * until ratified or approved at a referendum election * * *." Since there is a total want of compliance with either requirement, of notice or referendum, we have skeletonized the constitutional language.

In the view of the stark constitutional question posed by the petition and return, it seems unnecessary to delve into the details of regulation contained in the act, so we content ourselves merely with the general statement that the law purportedly confines the practice of nudism to persons of respectability, in the interest of the public good, health, morals and welfare, but only in counties within the restricted population limits.

In the absence of compliance with the constitutional restrictions the law cannot withstand the attack upon it unless it is in truth a general act despite its application only to counties with the floor and ceiling in population we have set out.

And, of course, the thought immediately occurs whether there is a genuine reason to be concerned with health, morals, and welfare of the public as affected by nudist colonies once a certain population is reached, then to consider these elements inconsequential if the population increases beyond the higher limitation, only to become concerned over them again should a slump reduce the population to the bracketed number.

This is but another way of approaching the determinative point in the case, i.e., the relationship of the object of the act to the population range.

It is impossible for us to find any such distinction between this act and the one with which we dealt in *Ex parte Porter*, 141 Fla. 711, 193 So. 750 [1940], as would justify a different ruling here. In the cited case this court held unconstitutional an act prohibiting the operation of a nudist colony in counties having populations of not less than 155,000 and not more than 165,000 on the ground that there was no reasonable relationship between the attempted classification and the subject matter.

The Attorney General undertakes to distinguish the cases because the act described in the cited one prohibited while the act now challenged only restricts.

Bearing in mind the criterion of relationship between the classification and the subject, there seems to be no merit to the position.

As we did in *Ex parte Porter*, supra, we hold that the present law cannot endure for the simple reasons that prerequisites to the valid enactment of special acts were ignored, and that the want of reasonable relationship between the subject and the population precludes it from operating as a general law.

There must be a reasonable basis for the classification in order for a law of this kind, based on population, to be categorized as general, *Waybright v. Duval County, et al.*, 142 Fla. 875, 196 So. 430, and none is found here. And, of course, classification by population to avoid compliance with the constitutional requirements will not be sanctioned. *Shelton et al. v. Reeder, Fla.*, 121 So.2d 145 [(1960)].

The prisoner is discharged.

ROBERTS, C. J., and TERRELL, HOBSON, DREW, THORNAL and O'CONNELL, JJ., concur.

————

Population acts must also be open ended. That is, they must not be tied to a particular census, but rather must allow local governmental units to grow into and sometimes out of the designated population bracket or brackets. The reason for this should be obvious; if subject matter is reasonably related to population, then all those local governmental units meeting the requisite population should be included.

It is interesting to note that it is theoretically possible to circumvent the "open ended" requirement by amending the applicable population figures after each census that affects the classification desired. For example, consider the situation discussed in the Texas case, *Smith v. State*.[21]

In 1929 a certain law created a population classification for "every county in the state having a population of not less than 78,000 and not more than 85,000"[22] according to the latest United States census. The 1920 United States census listed McLennan County as having a population of 82,921. It was the only county in the state that fitted the above population bracket. The 1930 United States census listed McLennan County as having a population of 98,682 and thus no longer within the above population bracket. On January 13, 1931, the Texas legislature amended the 1929 law to change the population bracket to "not less than 95,000 and not more than 125,000."[23] No other change was made in the 1929 law. After the amendment, McLennan was again the only county within the new population bracket. The Court of Criminal Appeals of Texas held that the actions of the Texas legislature showed "a purpose, by a pretended classification, to evade the constitutional inhibition, and, under the guise of such classification, to enact a law designed for McLennan County alone."[24]

————

21. 49 S.W.2d 739 (Tex. Crim. App. 1932).
22. *Id.* at 740.
23. *Id.* at 739.
24. *Id.* at 743–744.

There is a problem in that art. III, § 11 uses the words "general law of local application" rather than the words "population act." The former obviously includes the latter, but does it include anything else? In other words, can there be general laws of local application other than population acts? It appears that at the present time this question is unanswered in Florida. In *City of Miami Beach v. Frankel*,[25] the Florida Supreme Court defined a general law of local application as follows:

> A general law of local application is a law that uses a classification scheme — based on population or some other criterion — so that its application is restricted to particular localities. *See*, e.g., *Lewis v. Mathis*, 345 So.2d 1066 (Fla.1977); *Vance v. Ruppel*, 215 So.2d 309 (Fla.1968); *County of Dade v. City of North Miami Beach*, 109 So.2d 362 (Fla.1959).

Unfortunately, the three cases cited by *Frankel* are all population act cases.[26] However, *Caldwell v. Mann*[27] may provide a partial answer. This case involved Fla. Stat. § 374.23 (1941), which, when originally enacted in 1925, provided a period of roughly two months when mullet (a saltwater fish) could not be caught or possessed in any county of the state.[28] By the time of the litigation in *Caldwell*, the Florida Legislature had removed the ban in fourteen coastal counties and sixteen non-coastal counties.[29] The ban remained intact in twenty-one coastal counties and sixteen non-coastal counties.[30] The Florida Supreme Court affirmed the order of the trial court striking down the law in those non-coastal counties still within the ban and involved in the litigation because the classification as to non-coastal counties not under the ban violated the equal protection clause.[31] The Florida Supreme Court, however, reversed the trial court's order as to the coastal counties still under the ban and involved in the litigation, and also upheld § 374.23 as it pertained to them.[32] The reason was that while the ban in non-coastal counties was "required as incidental to the accomplishment of the primary purpose . . . the protection of the mullet fish industry in the coastal counties"[33] and would thus be equally applicable to all the non-coastal counties, there might be some basis for distinguishing between some coastal counties and other coastal counties. In addition, there was apparently no challenge to the constitutionality of the laws that had, over the years, eliminated some of the coastal counties from the ban. In any event § 374.23 was, after the decision voiding its operation in non-coastal counties, arguably a general law of local application based on two non-population criteria of classification: geography and (presumably) the peculiarities of the mullet fishing industry in some of the coastal counties. For

---

25. 363 So. 2d 555, 558 (Fla. 1978).
26. *Id.*
27. 26 So. 2d 788 (Fla. 1946).
28. *Id.* at 789.
29. *Id.* at 789–790.
30. *Id.* at 790.
31. *Id.* at 791.
32. *Id.*
33. *Id.* at 790.

an excellent discussion of this problem and the problems surrounding population acts in general, see the Revised Edition of Jefferson Fordham's *Local Government Law*, referred to earlier.

Special laws and general laws of local application may not be enacted in any of the forbidden areas enumerated in art. III, §11. The Florida Constitution also includes two other ways in which special laws may be banned from certain subject areas. First, the Florida Legislature, by a three-fifths vote of each house, may, by general law, add to the list of banned categories. Of course, those do not become a part of art. III, §11, but are banned by law. Second, the Florida Constitution contains a number of non-self-executing provisions which require that legislation in a given area be enacted by general law.[34]

d. Prohibited Special Laws

The Florida judiciary has expressed extreme reluctance to interfere with the manner in which the Florida Legislature decides to enact laws. While art. III, §11 contains a number of restrictions on the Florida Legislature, the courts historically have extended wide latitude to the Florida Legislature when applying these provisions. The following case is illustrative.

Venice HMA, LLC v. Sarasota County

228 So. 3d 76 (Fla. 2017)

POLSTON, J.

These consolidated cases are before the Court on appeal from the decision of the Second District Court of Appeal in *Venice HMA, LLC v. Sarasota County*, 198 So.3d 23 (Fla. 2d DCA 2015), which held that the indigent care provision of the special law applicable only to Sarasota County constitutes an unconstitutional privilege because it provides for reimbursement to the public and private hospitals only in Sarasota County rather than in the entire State of Florida.[1] However, because a special law by definition operates only in a defined subdivision of the State, we reverse the Second District's decision. The indigent care provision does not grant a privilege to a private corporation in violation of article III, section 11(a)(12) of the Florida Constitution because it applies equally to all hospitals in Sarasota County, whether public or private.

Background

The Second District described the background of the statutory provision at issue and the factual history of these cases as follows:

> [B]y special law in 1949, the legislature established the Sarasota County Public Hospital

---

34. *See, e.g.,* Fla. Const. art. V, §3(b)(2).

1. We have jurisdiction. *See* art. V, §3(b)(1), Fla. Const.

District, one of thirty four special hospital districts. The special law granted the hospital district its own taxing authority separate from Sarasota County. *See* ch. 26468, Laws of Fla. (1949). Sarasota County voters approved the special act in a 1950 referendum.

Almost a decade later, in 1959, the legislature amended the special law. The legislature added an indigent care provision requiring Sarasota County to reimburse the hospital district for medical services provided to indigent patients at hospital district facilities. *See* ch. 59–1839, § 8(i), at 3884–85, Laws of Fla. Significantly, the indigent care provision also required reimbursement to any other hospital in Sarasota County providing indigent care. *See id.*

The indigent care provision was not submitted for voter approval. Our record does not contain documentation of public notice; presumably, such notice was published pursuant to article III, section 20 of the 1885 Constitution as an alternative to a referendum. The parties do not claim otherwise.

. . . .

[I]n 2003, the legislature repealed the 1959 special law. *See* ch. 03–359, § 2, at 316, Laws

of Fla. It enacted a 2003 special law for "the codification of all special acts relating to [the] Sarasota County Public Hospital District" to provide "a single, comprehensive special act charter for the District including all current legislative authority granted to the District by its several legislative enactments." *See id.* § 1. The 1959 indigent care provision, with only minor nonsubstantive changes, remained a part of this 2003 comprehensive legislation. *Compare* 1959 Laws of Fla. § 8(i), 3884–85 *with* ch. 03–359, § 8(9), at 321, Laws of Fla. Notice of the 2003 special law was published in compliance with article III, section 10 of the 1968 Constitution. *See* Fla. H.R. Comm. on Local Gov't & Veterans Affairs HB 1113 (2003) Staff Analysis 5 (Mar. 7, 2003).

. . . .

Beginning in November 2008, and monthly thereafter, the Private Hospitals[2] submitted to the County a list of costs associated with providing hospital care to the indigent in Sarasota County. The Private Hospitals requested reimbursement for these costs pursuant to section 8(9) of the 2003 special law[.] The County refused to pay. *Venice HMA*, 198 So.3d at 25–28 (footnotes omitted).

In 2011, the Private Hospitals "sought a declaration establishing their right to reimbursement from the County for providing indigent care under the indigent care provision of the 2003 special law." *Id.* at 28. However, "[t]he County maintained that such reimbursement would provide an unconstitutional privilege to private

---

2. Sarasota Doctors Hospital, Inc., Englewood Community Hospital, Inc., and Venice HMA, LLC d/b/a Venice Regional Medical Center are collectively referred to as "the Private Hospitals." *See Venice HMA*, 198 So.3d at 24.

corporations" in violation of article III, section 11(a)(12). *Id.* The trial court entered summary judgment agreeing with the County. *Id.* at 29.

On appeal, the Second District affirmed, stating that "[t]he correct analysis is whether the 2003 special act gives the Private Hospitals in Sarasota County a privilege that private hospitals elsewhere in the state do not share." *Id.* at 30 (quoting and agreeing with the County). The Second District explained that "[b]efore addition of the indigent care provision in the 1959 special law, no non-District hospital was entitled to reimbursement for providing medical care to the indigent" and that "[t]he Private Hospitals, if they prevail, certainly would have an advantageous position relative to other private hospitals in Florida, indeed, even as to those that may exist in adjacent counties." *Id.* at 29–30.[3]

Analysis

"The constitutionality of a statute is a pure question of law subject to de novo review." *City of Fort Lauderdale v. Dhar*, 185 So.3d 1232, 1234 (Fla. 2016). "[A] determination that a statute is facially unconstitutional means that no set of circumstances exists under which the statute would be valid." *Pub. Defender, Eleventh Jud. Cir. v. State*, 115 So.3d 261, 280 (Fla. 2013).

Article X, section 12(g) of the Florida Constitution explains that "'[s]pecial law' means a special or local law." And this Court has described special and local laws as follows:

> [A] special law is one relating to, or designed to operate upon, particular persons or things, or one that purports to operate upon classified persons or things when classification is not permissible or the classification adopted is illegal; *a local law is one relating to, or designed to operate only in, a specifically indicated part of the state, or one that purports to operate within classified territory when classification is not permissible or the classification adopted is illegal.*

Florida Dep't of Bus. & Prof'l Reg. v. Gulfstream Park Racing Ass'n, 967 So.2d 802, 807 (Fla. 2007) (quoting *State ex rel. Landis v. Harris*, 120 Fla. 555, 163 So. 237, 240 (1934)) (emphasis added). In contrast, "[a] general law operates universally throughout the state, or uniformly upon subjects as they may exist throughout the state, or uniformly within permissible classifications by population of counties or otherwise, or is a law relating to a state function or instrumentality." *Id.* No one disputes that

---

3. The brief filed in this Court by Sarasota Doctor's Hospital, Inc. and Englewood Community Hospital, Inc. states that there are 33 special hospital districts created by special law in Florida, and "[f]ully one-third of [those] authorize reimbursement for the delivery of medical care to indigent patients by nonpublic providers." Initial Brief at 12–13 (citing special laws involving the Health Care District of Palm Beach County, the West Volusia Hospital Authority, the Lakeshore Hospital Authority in Columbia County, the North Broward Hospital District, and the Citrus County Hospital District, among others).

the law at issue here is a local law (which is included in the constitutional definition of special law) in that it operates only in Sarasota County.

Article III, section 10 of the Florida Constitution provides that "[n]o special law shall be passed unless notice of intention to seek enactment thereof has been published in the manner provided by general law;" however, such notice is unnecessary if the special law is "conditioned to become effective only upon approval by vote of the electors of the area affected." As the Second District explained, no one is claiming that the provision at issue in this case was not properly noticed as a special law. *See Venice HMA*, 198 So.3d at 26.

Furthermore, article III, section 11 provides a list of subjects that may not be addressed by special law. Specifically, according to article III, section 11(a) (emphasis added), "[t]here shall be no special law or general law of local application pertaining to:"

(1) election, jurisdiction or duties of officers, except officers of municipalities, chartered counties, special districts or local governmental agencies;

(2) assessment or collection of taxes for state or county purposes, including extension of time therefor, relief of tax officers from due performance of their duties, and relief of their sureties from liability;

(3) rules of evidence in any court;

(4) punishment for crime;

(5) petit juries, including compensation of jurors, except establishment of jury commissions;

(6) change of civil or criminal venue;

(7) conditions precedent to bringing any civil or criminal proceedings, or limitations of time therefor;

(8) refund of money legally paid or remission of fines, penalties or forfeitures;

(9) creation, enforcement, extension or impairment of liens based on private contracts, or fixing of interest rates on private contracts;

(10) disposal of public property, including any interest therein, for private purposes;

(11) vacation of roads;

(12) *private incorporation or grant of privilege to a private corporation;*

(13) effectuation of invalid deeds, wills or other instruments, or change in the law of descent;

(14) change of name of any person;

(15) divorce;

(16) legitimation or adoption of persons;

(17) relief of minors from legal disabilities;

(18) transfer of any property interest of persons under legal disabilities or of estates of decedents;

(19) hunting or fresh water fishing;

(20) regulation of occupations which are regulated by a state agency; or

(21) any subject when prohibited by general law passed by a three-fifths vote of the membership of each house. Such law may be amended or repealed by like vote.

The Private Hospitals argue that the indigent care provision of the special law at issue here does not grant a privilege to a private corporation in violation of article III, section 11(a)(12) because it applies equally to all hospitals in Sarasota County, whether public or private. We agree.

In *Lawnwood Medical Center, Inc. v. Seeger*, 990 So.2d 503, 517–18 (Fla. 2008), this Court held that a special law affecting two private hospitals in St. Lucie County, which were both owned by the same private corporation, provided an unconstitutional privilege because it granted the corporation "almost absolute power in running the affairs of the hospital, essentially without meaningful regard for the recommendations or actions of the medical staff." In its analysis, this Court considered whether the "privilege" prohibited by section 11(a)(12) is "economic favoritism over other entities similarly situated" or whether "'privilege' encompasses more than a financial benefit." *Id.* at 510. This Court "conclude[d] that a broad reading of the term 'privilege' as used in article III, section 11(a)(12), — one not limiting the term to any particular type of benefit or advantage — is required." *Id.* at 512.

In determining the plain meaning of the constitutional text "grant of privilege to a private corporation," this Court in *Lawnwood* considered dictionary definitions of "privilege" from the time when the text was adopted, noting that "[t]he definitions have not substantially changed from those that existed at the time of the 1968 constitutional revision." *Id.* at 511 n.10; *see Myers v. Hawkins*, 362 So.2d 926, 930 (Fla. 1978) ("[W]e initially consult widely circulated dictionaries, to see if there exists some plain, obvious, and ordinary meaning for the words or phrases approved for placement in the Constitution."). Specifically, we referenced *Black's Law Dictionary*, which defined "privilege" as "a particular and peculiar benefit or advantage enjoyed by a person, company, or class, beyond the common advantage of other citizens." *Lawnwood*, 990 So.2d at 511 (quoting *Black's Law Dictionary* 1359 (4th ed. 1968)). We also considered *Webster's Seventh New Collegiate Dictionary*, which defined "privilege" as "a right or immunity granted as a peculiar benefit, advantage, or favor." *Id.* at 511 (quoting *Webster's Seventh New Collegiate Dictionary* 677 (7th ed. 1967)). Further, this Court in *Lawnwood* explained that "definitions from other state supreme courts construing similar provisions in their constitutions parallel the dictionary definitions as well as the common sense understanding of a 'privilege' as connoting a special benefit, advantage, or right enjoyed by a person or corporation." *Id.* at 512. In other words, in common parlance, a privilege is having something that others do not have.

3 · THE LEGISLATURE

Here, the indigent care provision provides for reimbursement to all hospitals in Sarasota County for expenses related to care for indigent patients:

> To certify to the Board of County Commissioners of Sarasota County, on or before the 15th day of each month commencing with the month of November 1959, a list of all the medically indigent persons who have been hospitalized in any of the hospitals which are operated by the Hospital Board during the preceding month, together with the itemized charges for the hospital services and care for each of said medically indigent persons which have been rendered in such preceding month by the said hospital. The Board of County Commissioners of Sarasota County shall, within 45 days after the receipt of such certified list of medically indigent patients with the hospital charges, make remittance to the treasurer of the Hospital Board of the sum total of the amount shown on the certified list to be the amount owing to the Hospital Board for the hospital services and care rendered to the medically indigent persons during the month embraced in said certification.
>
> . . . .
>
> *The said Board of County Commissioners shall in like manner reimburse any other hospital in Sarasota County*, approved by the State Board of Health, for hospital services rendered to medically indigent persons as herein defined, *upon like certification by such hospital and at such rates as shall not exceed those prescribed for such patients by hospitals owned and operated by said Hospital Board.*

Ch. 2003–359, § 3, at 321, Laws of Fla. (emphasis added). Therefore, because the provision provides for reimbursement to all hospitals in Sarasota County (private and public), it is not providing a "particular and peculiar benefit or advantage" to a private corporation that is "beyond the common advantage of other citizens." *Lawnwood*, 990 So.2d at 511 (quoting *Black's Law Dictionary* 1359 (4th ed. 1968)). Accordingly, the indigent care provision does not violate the plain meaning of article III, section 11(a)(12) of the Florida Constitution.

Importantly, we reach this holding based upon the plain meaning of the text in the Florida Constitution, including the plain meaning of the term "privilege." And we reject the dissent's accusation that our decision adds words to the text of our state's foundational document. We believe that the language "grant of privilege to a private corporation" contained in section 11(a)(12) reasonably means providing a benefit to a private corporation that others do not receive. This special law neither singles out private corporations as a class or any particular private corporations for any privilege.

The County argues, and the Second District agreed, that "[t]he correct analysis is whether the 2003 special act gives the Private Hospitals in Sarasota County a privilege that private hospitals elsewhere in the state do not share." *Venice HMA*, 198 So.3d at 30 (quoting and agreeing with the County). However, this argument conflates the definition of "privilege" with the very nature of special laws, which by definition only operate in a defined subdivision of the State. *See* article X, § 12(g), Fla. Const. (providing that "'[s]pecial law' means a special or local law"); *Gulfstream Park Racing Ass'n*, 967 So.2d at 807 (explaining that "a local law is one relating to, or designed to operate only in, a specifically indicated part of the state" (quoting *State ex rel. Landis*, 163 So. at 240)); *see also State v. Leavins*, 599 So.2d 1326, 1331 n.10 (Fla. 1st DCA 1992). Because the special law only applies to Sarasota County, we must limit our comparisons to Sarasota County.

The dissent observes that the special law in *Lawnwood* — the St. Lucie County Hospital Governance Law — "was a local law that applied only to hospitals in St. Lucie County." Dissenting op. at 84. Because this Court in *Lawnwood* invalidated such a local law (by ruling that it "impermissibly provide[d] a privilege to a private corporation"), the dissent contends that "*Lawnwood* made clear that the appropriate analysis is between the hospitals affected by the local law and other similarly situated hospitals in the State of Florida." *Id.* Based on this understanding of *Lawnwood*, the dissent asserts that our "resolution of this case is . . . directly and irreconcilably in conflict with *Lawnwood* on the facts." *Id.* at 85.

But our opinion in *Lawnwood* repeatedly makes the point that the special law affected only *privately* owned hospitals in St. Lucie County. And that fact was central to our reasoning in support of the conclusion that the special law at issue in *Lawnwood* impermissibly granted a corporate privilege. In reciting the facts in *Lawnwood*, we observed that "[i]t is uncontroverted that the special law affected only the two private hospitals in St. Lucie County, which are both owned by the same private parent corporation." 990 So.2d at 508. In our analysis, we stated that an express provision of the special law "makes clear that the hospitals affected by the law are only those whose licenses are held by corporations," and we observed that "[i]t is apparent from the express language in the [special law] that the law was intended to affect only those privately operated hospitals located in St. Lucie County." *Id.* at 510. From this we concluded that the special law "is unquestionably a special law affecting a private corporation." *Id.* We reiterated that the special act "was passed as a special law and specifically enacted to affect only private, corporately owned hospitals in St. Lucie County." *Id.*

Contrary to the dissent's apparent interpretation, all of this in the *Lawnwood* opinion cannot reasonably be understood as designed to make the obvious point that hospitals outside St. Lucie County were not affected by the St. Lucie County Hospital Governance Act. Rather, the point the *Lawnwood* opinion turned on was that only hospitals owned by private corporations were affected — that is, granted a privilege — by the special law. And that is what distinguishes *Lawnwood* from the present case. In other words, the special law was invalidated in *Lawnwood* because it affected only private hospitals, whereas the special law is permissible here because it affects both public and private hospitals.

. . .

Conclusion

Accordingly, because the indigent care provision of the special law applies to all hospitals (public and private) in Sarasota County, it does not grant a privilege to a private corporation in violation of the plain meaning of article III, section 11(a)(12). We reverse the Second District's decision affirming the invalidation and severance of the indigent care provision.

It is so ordered.

LABARGA, C.J., and LEWIS, QUINCE, and CANADY, JJ., concur.

LAWSON, J., dissents with an opinion, in which PARIENTE, J., concurs.

LAWSON, J., dissenting.

In my view, our decision in *Lawnwood Medical Center, Inc. v. Seeger*, 990 So.2d 503 (Fla. 2008), applies the unambiguous language of article III, section 11(a)(12), and article X, section 12(g), of the Florida Constitution and is controlling here. Staying the constitutional course charted by our precedent, I would approve the decision of the Second District Court of Appeal. Therefore, I respectfully dissent.

In *Lawnwood*, we defined "privilege" in the context of article III, section 11(a) (12)'s prohibition against a "special law" — which pursuant to article X, section 12(g), includes a "local law" of the type at issue here — as "a right, a special benefit [including "a financial benefit"], or an advantage."[5] *Lawnwood*, 990 So.2d at 511. The law at issue in *Lawnwood* was a local law that applied only to hospitals in St. Lucie County. *Id.* at 506 ("The parties do not dispute that the HGL is a special law applicable to private corporations only in St. Lucie County. . . ."). Our Court held the act to be invalid because it "impermissibly provide[d] a privilege to . . . a private corporation" in St. Lucie County not granted to other hospitals in the state. *Id.* After recognizing that the Florida Constitution defines "a special law as 'a special or local law,'" our Court clearly stated: "It is apparent from the express language in the HGL that the law was intended to affect only those privately operated hospitals *located in St. Lucie County*. Therefore, the HGL is unquestionably a special law affecting a private corporation." *Id.* at 510 (emphasis added). Thus, *Lawnwood* made clear that the appropriate analysis is between the hospitals affected by the local law and other similarly situated hospitals in the State of Florida.

I would apply *Lawnwood* the same way here and thereby stay the constitutional course. Specifically, the payment of local government funds to private hospital corporations mandated by the special law at issue here is a financial benefit and therefore a privilege as defined by *Lawnwood*. Because this financial benefit was conferred by special law, it violates article III, section 11(a)(12). Mandating these

---

5. Article X, section 12(g), of the Florida Constitution defines "[s]pecial law" as "a special *or local law*." (Emphasis added.) The law at issue here is a local law, meaning that it is a special law. *Id.* Article III, section 11(a)(12), prohibits any "special law" that "pertain[s] to . . . private incorporation or grant of privilege to a private corporation."

payments to private corporations from local tax dollars may constitute sound public policy that should be implemented on a statewide basis by general law. But, article III, section 11(a) (12), unambiguously bars the grant of this type of benefit to private corporations by special law.

Instead of applying the straightforward language of the Constitution in this straightforward manner, the majority focuses on the fact that the word "privilege" connotes a benefit not enjoyed by others. In my view, it makes no sense to ask whether the benefit conferred is "enjoyed by others" when that concept is a structural part of the constitutional provision. In other words, granting a benefit by special law means that the benefit is not extended to other similarly situated private corporations in the state. This is especially apparent when considering a non-local special law.

For example, if the special law at issue here had granted this very same financial benefit to one or more private hospital corporations by name, petitioners readily and properly concede that the financial benefit would constitute an unauthorized privilege because other private hospital corporations operating in Florida would be excluded from the same financial benefit. This same straightforward application should apply to local laws because the Constitution uses the exact same language for all special laws. Instead of applying the Constitution as written — to prohibit this local law "pertaining to . . . private incorporation or grant of privilege to a private corporation," article III, section 11(a)(12), Florida Constitution — the majority has effectively rewritten the Constitution to differentiate between local laws and other special laws as follows:

> The legislature shall not enact either: (1) special laws that pertain to private incorporation or grant of privilege to a private corporation or (2) local laws that pertain to private incorporation or grant of privilege to a private corporation *where the privilege is not also granted to other similar private and public corporations within the same locality.*

My first observation regarding this judicially reworked constitutional language is that it appears to *always* permit the grant of a privilege by local law because, by definition, "a local law is one relating to, or designed to operate only in, a specially indicated part of the state. . . ." *Lawnwood*, 990 So.2d at 509 (quoting *Florida Dep't of Bus. & Prof'l Regulation v. Gulfstream Park Racing Ass'n*, 967 So.2d 802, 807 (Fla. 2007). Therefore, a local law directed at hospitals, like the law at issue here and in *Lawnwood*, by definition necessarily applies to *all* hospitals in the locality (because that is the very nature of a local law). If the law were drawn more narrowly, to apply to only specified hospitals in the area, it would be a non-local special law.

My second observation is that this rewrite of the Constitution directly contradicts the acknowledgment in *Lawnwood* that "we are not at liberty to add words to article III, section 11(a)(12), which were not placed there by the drafters of the Florida Constitution." *Id.* at 512. Ironically, not only is this addition of language to article III, section 11(a)(12), expressly prohibited by *Lawnwood*, but the majority's resolution of this case is also directly and irreconcilably in conflict with *Lawnwood* on the facts.

My third observation about the majority's judicial rewrite of this constitutional provision is that it makes no logical sense to treat local laws differently than non-local special laws because it allows the Legislature to grant the exact same corporate privilege by local law that would clearly be barred by non-local special law. For example, take a county with one public hospital (say, the "Local Hospital") and one private hospital (the "ABC Hospital Corp."). Clearly, the Legislature could not pass a special law requiring millions of local tax dollars to be paid to the Local Hospital and the ABC Hospital Corp. by name, and no other hospital in the state. There is no rational argument that this non-local special law would not violate article III, section 11(a)(12). But, under the majority's interpretation of article III, section 11(a)(12), the Legislature could provide the exact same corporate privilege to the same private hospital by local law. That makes no sense where the language prohibits the grant of this type of privilege by any type of special law. Of course, I could come up with any number of hypotheticals involving counties with no private hospitals or multiple public and private hospitals where a non-local special law granting the privilege would be barred under the majority's interpretation but a local law granting the same corporate privilege would be upheld as constitutional. This odd anomaly of the majority's interpretation is really just another way of pointing out that the majority's reading of the language barring special law corporate privileges actually allows the Legislature to grant a corporate privilege by local law.

Finally, it seems worth reflecting upon the obvious policy concerns underlying this particular provision of the Florida Constitution, as written. Some relate to all special laws. For example, it seems that granting special benefits to private corporations by any type of special law would be subject to criticism as an improper use of taxpayer money or as unfair in a free market system or as rife with the potential for graft. Again, if it is good public policy to give taxpayer money to a class of private corporations (such as hospital corporations) in the state, then it should be good public policy throughout the state. Otherwise, the special treatment begins to look like legislative largess to particularly connected corporations in that class instead of just good public policy. But, at least the enactment of a non-local special law privilege (to a private corporation) would be consistent with the underlying structure of our representative form of government. That is, if a non-local special law privilege were permitted by the Constitution and the Florida Legislature voted to directly grant a significant financial benefit to a select group of named for-profit private hospitals in the state from general revenue, the citizens of this state would have recourse at the ballot box if they disagreed with the action.

But, with a local law like the one at issue here, legislators from other parts of the state could force the citizens of a single county to bear a significant financial burden flowing to a few private corporations in their county even if their local representatives voted against the measure and even if the electorate never had an opportunity to ratify the action by a local vote, as happened here. That, to me, seems like the most troublesome type of special law privilege because it could be enacted entirely by legislators not accountable to the local citizens on whom they placed the burden of financing the corporate privilege.[6] Unfortunately, the majority has now written the protection against granting a corporate privilege by local law out of our Constitution. Therefore, I dissent.

e. Precedence Between General and Special Laws

When the provisions of general and special laws can be read together and harmonized, courts generally do so.[35] However, questions have arisen as to whether a general or special law takes precedence when a conflict exists. The special law usually takes precedence as a more specific expression of legislative will, but consider the following case.

Town of Palm Beach v. Palm Beach Local 1866 of the International Association of Fire Fighters
275 So. 2d 247 (Fla. 1973)

ROBERTS, Justice.

This case is before us on direct appeal from a decision of the Circuit Court of the Fifteenth Judicial Circuit which directly passed upon the validity of a state statute. We have jurisdiction under Article V, section 3(b), Fla.Const., F.S.A.

Pursuant to published notice which first appeared in *The Palm Beach Post* newspaper, on March 13, 1970, House Bill 5233 was introduced as a local bill in the Florida Legislature. That notice was as follows:

No. 787

A bill to be entitled

> An Act relating to professional negotiations for firemen in Palm Beach County; defining certain terms; establishing the right to organize and bargain collectively; providing for recognition of bargaining agents; providing for arbitration board; providing for composition of hearings by and expenses of the board; providing that the decision of the board shall be advisory; defining collective bargaining contract; providing that firemen under the act shall not strike; providing for requests for collective bargaining; providing a savings clause, repealing conflicting laws; providing an effective date.
>
> > Palm Beach County Council of Firefighters Legislature Chairman L. E. Hoffman

---

6. In this case, it is estimated that the citizens of Sarasota County will owe $300 million to the private hospital corporations in their county.

35. *Tribune Co. v. School Bd. of Hillsborough County*, 367 So. 2d 627, 629 (Fla. 1979).

Pub. March 13, 1970

The published notice failed to state whether House Bill 5233 was general or special legislation, or whether there was any intention to seek enactment thereof.

On October 9, 1970, at a Special Session the Legislature, enacted into law, over the veto of the Governor, House Bill 5233, entitled as follows:

> "An Act authorizing firemen employed by any municipality, fire district, port authority or other governmental entity in Palm Beach County to organize and collectively bargain through an agent selected by them with respect to wages; working conditions; containing definitions; providing that firemen shall not strike; providing a savings clause, providing for judicial relief; providing an effective date."

and which became chapter 70-1004, Special Acts, Extraordinary Session, 1970.

The appellee then petitioned the town to recognize it (appellee) as the sole and exclusive bargaining agent for the firemen of the Town of Palm Beach. The town replied that it did not consider ch. 70-1004 to be valid law because, among other things it would require the town to recognize the appellee as the sole bargaining agent for all personnel of the fire department.

Controversy then arose and as a result, the town was in doubt as to its rights and obligations and initiated a suit for declaratory judgment. A final judgment adverse to the appellee was entered on November 30, 1971, wherein the trial court found that the published notice relating to the special act designated as House Bill 5233 failed to conform with and meet the requirements of §10 of Article III of the Florida Constitution (1968) and §11.02, Fla. Stat., F.S.A. Appellee moved for a rehearing and as a result of the rehearing, the trial court reversed the final judgment, in its order of April 7, and held the act to be constitutional. That judgment is brought here for review.

By this appeal we are asked to decide: (1) Whether the notice published prior to the adoption of ch. 70-1004 was sufficiently definite to comply with the requirements of Art. 3, §10, Fla.Const. (1968); (2) Whether ch. 70-1004 violates Art. I, §6, Fla.Const. (1968) by allegedly allowing a majority of the firefighters to select the bargaining agent for all the firefighters; (3) Whether ch. 70-1004 violates Art. III, §11(a)(10), Fla.Const. (1968) by regulating an occupation already regulated by a state agency.

During the pendency of this litigation and in 1972 the Legislature enacted as a general law ch. 72-275, Laws of Florida, (now Fla.Stat. §§447.20–447.35, F.S.A.) known as the Fire Fighters Bargaining Act. By the terms of this act

> "...any full-time permanently employed classified member of any fire department or fire fighting unit of any municipality, county, metropolitan government, or fire district, employed to engage in the extinguishment, prevention or suppression of fires.... shall have the right to bargain collectively with their respective ... counties. ..."

This language of 72-275 is clearly intended to replace the provision of ch. 70-1004,

"... uniformed and permanent paid members of any fire department of any municipality corporation, fire district, port authority or other governmental entity in Palm Beach County whose primary function is to extinguish fires...."

An examination of both acts reveals such extensive duplication that we cannot rationally attribute to the legislature an intent to enact the general law and not include Palm Beach County within its provisions.

Normally, the maxim *generalia specialibus non derogant* would apply, thereby retaining the effectiveness of the special act notwithstanding a subsequent general act on the same subject. However, where the general act is an overall revision or general restatement of the law on the same subject, the special act will be presumed to have been superseded and repealed. *See* Sanders v. Howell, 73 Fla. 563, 74 So. 802 (1917), Stewart v. DeLand-Lake Helen Special Road and Bridge District, 71 Fla. 158, 71 So. 42 (1916), Apalachicola v. State, 93 Fla. 921, 112 So. 618 (1927).

Thus we have before us a general act that is such an overall revision and re-enactment that the legislature must have intended for the later general act to govern. *See* also Turner v. State, 135 Fla. 380, 185 So. 831 (1938).

Because of the enactment of ch. 72-275, Laws of Florida, which is a general law of restatement the constitutional questions presented in this appeal, become moot in that they relate only to special acts.

Involved also is the question of whether a bargaining agent represents *all* of the firemen or only those who make the selection. By caveat we point to the direct answer found in chapter 72-275 which says:

"The association.... selected by the majority.... shall be recognized.... as the bargaining agent *for those members of the said fire department who, without restraint or coercion so affirmatively choose.*" (italics supplied).

Therefore, it is our opinion and we hold that chapter 72-275, Laws of Florida 1972 controls and all of the questions sub judice are now moot so the appeal is

Dismissed.

CARLTON, C. J., and ERVIN, ADKINS, BOYD, McCAIN and DEKLE, JJ., concur.

4. Governor's Veto Power

Fla. Const. art. III, § 8

Executive approval and veto. —

(a) Every bill passed by the legislature shall be presented to the governor for approval and shall become a law if the governor approves and signs it, or fails to veto it within seven consecutive days after presentation. If during that period or on the seventh day the legislature adjourns sine die or takes a recess of more than thirty days, the governor shall have fifteen consecutive days from the date of presentation to act on the bill. In all cases except general appropriation bills, the veto shall extend to the entire bill. The governor may veto any specific appropriation in a general appropriation bill, but may not veto any qualification or restriction without also vetoing the appropriation to which it relates.

(b) When a bill or any specific appropriation of a general appropriation bill has been vetoed, the governor shall transmit signed objections thereto to the house in which the bill originated if in session. If that house is not in session, the governor shall file them with the custodian of state records, who shall lay them before that house at its next regular or special session, whichever occurs first, and they shall be entered on its journal. If the originating house votes to re-enact a vetoed measure, whether in a regular or special session, and the other house does not consider or fails to re-enact the vetoed measure, no further consideration by either house at any subsequent session may be taken. If a vetoed measure is presented at a special session and the originating house does not consider it, the measure will be available for consideration at any intervening special session and until the end of the next regular session.

(c) If each house shall, by a two-thirds vote, re-enact the bill or reinstate the vetoed specific appropriation of a general appropriation bill, the vote of each member voting shall be entered on the respective journals, and the bill shall become law or the specific appropriation reinstated, the veto notwithstanding.

Under the Florida Constitution, the governor possesses the authority to veto a bill enacted by the Florida Legislature, but the veto generally must extend to the entire bill. An exception does exist which permits the governor to veto a specific appropriation in a general appropriation bill. However, the governor cannot veto any qualification or restriction in a general appropriation bill without also vetoing the appropriation to which it relates.

Unlike the Federal Constitution, the Florida Constitution does not provide for a "pocket veto." Under the Federal Constitution, when Congress adjourns before the expiration of the period allowed to the President to either sign or veto a bill, the President can disapprove the legislation by simply deciding not to sign the legislation presented to him. Under the Florida Constitution, a bill generally becomes law without the governor's signature if the governor fails to veto it or sign it within seven days after it has been presented to the governor. This seven-day period is expanded to fifteen days if during the original seven-day period the Florida Legislature either adjourns sine die or takes a recess in excess of thirty days. This provision presumably exists because a large number of bills are commonly enacted during the last days of each legislative session, and it is assumed the governor needs more time to evaluate the legislation. The governor also has fifteen days to veto bills presented to him *after* the Florida Legislature adjourns sine die.[36]

The following case is illustrative of the governor's constitutional authority to line-item veto specific appropriations.

International Association of Firefighters
Local S-20 v. State

221 So. 3d 736 (Fla. 1st Dist. Ct. App. 2017)

OSTERHAUS, J.

Local S–20 appeals a decision of the Public Employees Relations Commission dismissing an unfair labor charge against the Governor for vetoing a proviso in the General Appropriations Act (GAA). Had the proviso been approved, it would have given a raise to firefighters who work for the State. We affirm because the Governor has constitutional authority to veto specific appropriations of the GAA, and because the Legislature ultimately resolved the impasse by maintaining the status quo.

I

Article I, § 6 of the Florida Constitution, along with its enabling statute, chapter 447, Florida Statutes, recognizes state employees' right to collectively bargain. *State v. Fla. Police Benevolent Ass'n*, 613 So.2d 415, 418 (Fla. 1992). In the case of state employees, the Governor is considered the public employer in collective bargaining negotiations. § 447.203(2), Fla. Stat. As part of the statute, § 447.403 sets forth the process by which state employees and the Governor must resolve impasses. The Legislature is responsible for resolving impasse issues. § 447.403(2)(b), Fla. Stat. When parties reach an impasse, the Legislature must convene a committee to review impasse issues and recommend a resolution to the Legislature. § 447.403(5)(a), Fla. Stat. Once the Legislature takes action on the resolution, the parties are bound. § 447.403(5)(b), Fla. Stat.

Appellant Local S–20 is the duly authorized bargaining agent for a unit of firefighters employed by the State of Florida. Local S–20 and the Governor bargained over wages, hours, and conditions of employment for fiscal year 2015–2016, and reached an impasse on several issues. Most notably, Appellant sought a $1500 per member raise. Upon reaching impasse, the parties submitted their positions to the Joint Select Committee on Collective Bargaining as required by the statute for resolving impasses. After the Committee completed its work, the Legislature passed the GAA, which included proviso language resolving the impasse by granting a $2000 per member pay raise, an even larger raise than Appellant had sought. The Legislature also passed a catch-all impasse provision in chapter 2015–223, Laws of Florida, providing for the resolution of unaddressed impasses "by maintaining the

---

36. *See Fla. Soc'y of Ophthalmology v. Fla. Optometric Ass'n*, 489 So. 2d 1118 (Fla. 1986).

status quo under the applicable current bargaining agreement." When the GAA was presented to the Governor, he vetoed the $2000 raise-specific proviso. After the Legislature took no subsequent action to override the veto, the impasse was resolved by maintaining the status quo.

When the State presented the bargaining agreement without including the raise, Appellant filed an unfair labor practice charge claiming that the Governor lacked veto authority. But the Public Employees Relations Commission dismissed the charge. It rejected Appellant's claim that the Governor was powerless to veto the raise and approved the State's presentation of a bargaining agreement that maintained wages at the status quo.

II

This case involves the Governor's authority to review and veto public employee, collective bargaining-related matters in the GAA. The Legislature tried to resolve a wage-related impasse in this case by including a $2000 raise in a specific appropriation within the GAA. Because the GAA is not self-executing, however, the act went to the Governor for approval.

The Florida Constitution is clear that the Governor may sign the GAA, veto it, or veto specific appropriations within the act. Article III, § 8, Fla. Const. ("The governor may veto any specific appropriation in a general appropriation bill. . . ."). In this case, if the Governor approved the $2000 raise within the GAA, then the impasse would be resolved. However, if the Governor vetoed either the entire GAA, or the raise-specific proviso within the GAA, then the impasse would remain within the Legislature's purview to resolve by some other means.

The Governor vetoed the specific appropriation here and Appellant takes issue with it. Appellant does not dispute the Legislature's attempt to resolve impasses via the GAA in the first instance, but argues that the Governor was required to approve the raise-specific appropriation in the GAA. See § 447.403(5)(b), Fla. Stat. ("Any actions taken by the Legislature shall bind the parties. . . ."). Based primarily on a statute, Appellant asks us to recognize a limitation on the Governor's constitutional authority to review the GAA, even though the Constitution explicitly allows the Governor to veto the GAA or "any specific appropriation in a general appropriation bill." Article III, § 8, Fla. Const. (emphasis added). We cannot accept Appellant's invitation. The Florida Constitution clearly articulates the Governor's authority to veto the GAA, or specific appropriations therein. *Id.* It authorized him to veto the raise appropriation here. See *Brown v. Firestone*, 382 So.2d 654 (Fla. 1980) (setting forth the exercise of the Governor's veto power). That Appellant's members possess constitutional collective bargaining rights does not alter the Governor's constitutional authority with respect to the GAA. See *Fla. Police Benevolent Ass'n*, 613 So.2d at 418-19 (refusing to elevate the collective bargaining rights of public employees and thus alter "years of strict adherence to the separation of powers doctrine"). The Governor's action in this case comported with his constitutional authority.

Moreover, the Governor's veto did not displace the Legislature's power to resolve the impasse in this case. After the veto, the Legislature retained final authority under § 447.403(5)(b) to resolve the wage impasse, and it did so here. The Legislature knew two things before attempting to resolve the impasse through the GAA: (1) that the Governor could veto specific appropriations, and (2) that it could override any veto. After the Governor exercised his veto authority in this case, nothing stopped the Legislature from exercising its constitutional authority to override his veto. *See* Article III, § 8(c), Fla. Const. A legislative override would have granted state firefighters the $2000 per employee raise they sought. But instead, the Legislature accepted the status quo. In fact, the Legislature enacted a separate act providing a catch-all impasse resolution provision that became law. Chapter 2015–223, § 1, Laws of Florida, provided for unaddressed impasses to be resolved "by otherwise maintaining the status quo under the language of the applicable current bargaining agreement." The Legislature effectively resolved the impasse by choosing not to override the Governor's veto and maintaining the status quo.

Appellant argues that we should follow *Dade County Police Benevolent Association v. Miami — Dade County Board of County Commissioners*, 160 So.3d 482, 483 (Fla. 1st DCA 2015), in which we held that a local executive branch official could not veto the legislative body's resolution of an impasse. But that case presented a different scenario that didn't involve restricting the Governor's constitutional authority to veto appropriations. The mayor in that case did not have constitutional authority to veto the impasse resolution and that veto violated Florida's collective bargaining statute. Here, by contrast, the Governor possessed explicit constitutional authority to veto appropriations within the GAA. See Art. III, § 8(a), Fla. Const. And so, while it is true that public employees possess important, constitutionally protected collective bargaining rights, the Legislature cannot force the Governor's hand to approve and sign the GAA, or specific appropriations therein. *Fla. Police Benevolent Ass'n*, 613 So.2d at 418–19 (warning of separation of powers encroachments). The Legislature here retained and exercised its ultimate authority to resolve the impasse after the Governor's veto, but chose not to override the veto and to maintain the status quo.

III

The decision of the Public Employees Relations Commission is AFFIRMED.

JAY, J., CONCURS; B.L. THOMAS, J., DISSENTS WITH OPINION.

[The dissenting opinion is omitted.]

5. When Laws Take Effect

Fla. Const. art. III, § 9

Effective date of laws. — Each law shall take effect on the sixtieth day after adjournment sine die of the session of the legislature in which enacted or as otherwise provided therein. If the law is passed over the veto of the governor it shall take effect on the sixtieth day after adjournment sine die of the session in which the veto is overridden, on a later date fixed in the law, or on a date fixed by resolution passed by both houses of the legislature.

———————

Generally, the question as to when a recently enacted law becomes effective is resolved by reference to an effective date contained in the newly enacted law or to a joint resolution prescribing an effective date. However, if a law contains no effective date, the Florida Constitution provides that the law will become effective on the sixtieth day after adjournment sine die of the session in which the law was enacted or in which a veto was overridden.

Occasionally, a newly enacted law will contain provisions that are contradictory, ambiguous, or inoperative concerning its effective date.

In re Advisory Opinion to the Governor
Request of June 29, 1979[37]
374 So. 2d 959 (Fla. 1979)

Dear Governor Graham:

We have the honor of acknowledging your communication of June 29, 1979, requesting our advice, pursuant to article IV, section 1(c) of the Florida Constitution and rule 9.500 of the Florida Rules of Appellate Procedure, as to the interpretation of a portion of the constitution affecting your executive power of appointment.

* * *

Questions

[Governor Graham requested the Court's written opinion on the following questions.]

1. Has there been a constitutional creation of judicial vacancies by virtue of CS for SB 268 so as to permit gubernatorial appointments to judicial office and judicial nominating commissions?

2. If so, what is the effective date of the new law?

3. If not, is the law defective in whole or in part?

* * *

It is essential to our response to your inquiry that we recount briefly the sequence of events in 1979 which led to the enactment of CS for SB 268. On March 22 we certified to the legislature, pursuant to article V, section 9 of the Florida Constitution,

———————

37. Unlike the Federal Constitution, the Florida Constitution expressly authorizes the Florida Supreme Court to issue advisory opinions to the Governor on any question affecting the Governor's constitutional powers and duties and to the Attorney General on question regarding the validity of a citizen's petition to amend the state constitution. *See* Fla. Const. art. IV, §§ 1(c) and 10.

our finding that a need exists for ten additional circuit court judgeships and seven additional county court judgeships. [Citation omitted.] On April 2 we certified to the legislature, under the same constitutional provision, our finding that a need exists for ten additional district court of appeal judgeships and for a redefinition of the state's appellate districts. [Citation omitted.] In this latter certification, the court recommended one additional judgeship for the second district, two additional judgeships for the third district, and one additional judgeship for the fourth district. No additional judgeships were recommended for the first district court. We also recommended the creation of a fifth appellate district that would encompass the fifth, seventh, ninth, tenth, and eighteenth judicial circuits, together with a concomitant realignment of the three existing appellate districts affected by the assignment of these judicial circuits to the newly recommended fifth appellate district. Additionally, we recommended that six judgeships be created for the new fifth district.[4]

During its 1979 regular session, the legislature considered the findings and recommendations of the court, and on June 6, the final day of the extended regular session, enacted CS for SB 268 by a two-thirds vote of the membership of both houses. [Footnote omitted.] This bill created the seventeen trial court judgeships recommended by the court in its first certification. It also created eleven new judgeships for the district courts of appeal and established a fifth appellate district, but not in the manner recommended by the court in its second certification. . . .

The act specified an effective date of July 1, 1979. After being enrolled and signed by the required constitutional officers, CS for SB 268 was presented to you on June 20. In your letter of June 29 requesting our advice on these questions, you stated that you would not sign this legislation but that you would allow it to become law without your signature. Accordingly, under article III, section 8(a) of the Florida Constitution, this bill would become law on July 6. We now note that you neither vetoed nor signed CS for SB 268.

Turning now to your request, we consider individually the questions you have posed.

* * *

Part II Effective Date

You indicate that the effective date of CS for SB 268 is in doubt inasmuch as the bill specifies an effective date of July 1 but did not, as we earlier indicated, "become law" until July 6. The constitution provides:

> Each law shall take effect on the sixtieth day after adjournment sine die of the session of the legislature in which enacted or as otherwise provided therein.[13]

---

4. Each district court of appeal is constitutionally required to "consist of at least three judges." Art. V, s 4(a), Fla. Const.

13. Art. III, s 9, Fla. Const.

The possible effective dates created by the events surrounding this bill are July 1 (the "provided" effective date), July 6 (the date on which the bill "became law") and August 5 (the sixtieth day after the session adjourned).

The attorney general has twice opined, once under a similar provision of the 1885 Constitution, and once under the 1968 Constitution, that the appropriate date in these circumstances (and in the absence of an expressed declaration of retroactivity) is the sixtieth day after adjournment.[14] He there reasoned that the effective date provided in the bill is inoperative unless the bill becomes law on or before that date. We see no reason to disagree with the analysis contained in his opinions since it is supported by valid policy reasons related to the administration of the judicial system. Accordingly, we advise you that CS for SB 268 will become effective on August 5, 1979.

Respectfully,

James C. Adkins Joseph A. Boyd, Jr. Ben F. Overton James E. Alderman

[The concurring opinions of Justice Boyd and Justice Overton are omitted.]

[The dissenting opinion of Chief Justice England with whom Justice Hatchett concurred is omitted.]

[The dissenting opinion of Justice Sundberg is omitted.]

---

14. Opin.Fla.Atty.Gen. 067-50 (August 10, 1967); Opin.Fla.Atty.Gen. 071-262 (August 30, 1971).

Chapter 4

The Courts

A. In General

Fla. Const. art. V, §1

Courts. — The judicial power shall be vested in a supreme court, district courts of appeal, circuit courts and county courts. No other courts may be established by the state, any political subdivision or any municipality. The legislature shall, by general law, divide the state into appellate court districts and judicial circuits following county lines. Commissions established by law, or administrative officers or bodies may be granted quasi-judicial power in matters connected with the functions of their offices. The legislature may establish by general law a civil traffic hearing officer system for the purpose of hearing civil traffic infractions. The legislature may, by general law, authorize a military court-martial to be conducted by military judges of the Florida National Guard, with direct appeal of a decision to the District Court of Appeal, First District.

The constitutional provisions concerning the judicial power of the State of Florida have been substantially revised three times in recent years: in 1956, in 1972, and again in 1980. The 1956 revision to the 1885 Florida Constitution changed the appellate court structure by establishing the district courts of appeal as the courts of general appellate jurisdiction and by limiting the jurisdiction of the Florida Supreme Court to a relatively few types of situations. Article V was left as so revised when an otherwise new Florida Constitution was approved by the voters in 1968.

In 1972 another revision of art. V was approved. It left the appellate structure substantially unchanged but rationalized the trial court structure. Prior to the 1972 revision, Florida's trial court structure was a patchwork of courts created over the years to meet different needs in various localities. In addition to circuit courts, county courts and justices of the peace, a county might have a county judges' court, a criminal court of record, a civil court of record, a small claims court, a juvenile court and any number of municipal courts. The 1972 revision of art. V changed all that. There are now two trial courts, circuit and county.[1] The circuit courts are courts of general original jurisdiction (civil and criminal), while the county courts are of

---

1. Municipal courts were phased out by January 3, 1977. *See* Fla. Const. art. V, §20(d)(4).

limited original jurisdiction (civil and criminal). The circuit courts also have writ and limited appellate jurisdiction.

Since the 1956 revision of art. V of the 1885 Florida Constitution, the Florida Supreme Court has been a court of limited jurisdiction, most of which is appellate. However, over the years the limited nature of the Florida Supreme Court's jurisdiction had arguably been subverted by that Court's interpretation of the 1956 revisions. This concern, together with the resultant increased workload, led to the 1980 revision of the Court's jurisdiction.[2] This revision reinforced the intention of the 1956 revision which created the district courts of appeal; with the exception of its death penalty jurisdiction and the possible exception of art. V, § 3(b)(2), the Florida Supreme Court was to be a "law declaring" court while the district courts of appeal (and the circuit courts in their appellate capacity) were to be "error correcting" courts.[3] Thus, under the 1980 amendment to art. V, the district courts of appeal, except in the enumerated cases, are the courts of final appeal as envisioned under the 1956 revision to art. V of the 1885 Florida Constitution.[4] As pointed out in the Committee Notes to Fla. R. App. P. 9.030, "[t]he district courts of appeal will constitute the courts of last resort for the vast majority of litigants under amended Article V."[5] Accordingly, if the Florida Supreme Court has not spoken, decisions of the Florida District Courts of Appeal control.[6]

While the 1968 Florida Constitution, as amended, specifies that the Florida Supreme Court, the district courts of appeal, and the county and circuit courts are to be the only courts,[7] certain quasi-judicial powers of administrative agencies are retained. The Florida Constitution could not realistically do away with these quasi-judicial powers without severely handicapping agencies in carrying out functions the Florida Legislature might wish to give them.[8] The impact, therefore, of art. V, § 1 is that the four enumerated courts are to be the State's only true courts. In addition, the Florida Legislature is authorized to create a civil traffic hearing officer system.

---

2. See the explanation of the 1980 revisions to Fla. Const. art. V, § 3(b) prepared by then-Chief Justice Arthur J. England, Jr., entitled *A Concise Explanation of Proposed Constitutional Amendment Number Two; An Amendment to Modify the Jurisdiction of the Florida Supreme Court*. See also *Jenkins v. State*, 385 So. 2d 1356 (Fla. 1980), which appears later in this chapter; *In re Emergency Amendments to Rules of Appellate Procedure*, 381 So. 2d 1370 (Fla. 1980); and Arthur J. England, Jr., Eleanor Mitchell Hunter & Richard C. Williams, Jr., *Constitutional Jurisdiction of the Supreme Court of Florida: 1980 Reform*, 32 U. Fla. L. Rev. 147 (1980).

3. See *State v. Grawien*, 362 N.W. 2d 428 (Wis. 1985), which uses the terms "law declaring" and "error correcting."

4. Commentary to 1972 Adoption and 1976, 1980, and 1988 Amendments, Fla. Const. art. V, § 3.

5. *Committee Notes*, Fla. R. App. P. 9.030.

6. 921 So. 2d 513 (Fla. 2005).

7. See *Simmons v. Faust*, 358 So. 2d 1358 (Fla. 1978).

8. See Chapter 2.

B. Constitutional Jurisdiction of Florida Courts

1. Supreme Court

Article V, § 3(b) of the Florida Constitution governs the jurisdiction of the Florida Supreme Court. As the Supreme Court explained in *Wells v. State*,[9] "[t]his jurisdiction 'extends only to the narrow class of cases enumerated' in that constitutional provision." Thus, the Florida Supreme Court is "a court of limited jurisdiction,"[10] with authority to hear only those matters specified in Florida's Constitution.[11] As espoused by the court in *State v. Barnum*, the Florida Supreme Court is without power to simply assume jurisdiction in a case to correct what it perceives as error even if the issue is one of importance due to the limitation imposed upon its jurisdiction by the Constitution.[12] Specifically, the Constitution limits the mandatory jurisdiction of the Supreme Court to the following four situations: (1) trial court judgments imposing the death penalty; (2) district court decisions invalidating a state statute or a provision of the state constitution; (3) administrative actions of statewide agencies relating to utility service and rates; and (4) bond validations by trial courts as provided by law.[13] Neither the Florida Supreme Court nor the Florida Legislature has the power to extend the jurisdiction of the Supreme Court beyond the confines of the Constitutional prescription.[14]

a. "Shall hear appeals from final judgments of trial courts imposing the death penalty . . ." Fla. Const. art. V, § 3(b)(1)

Art. V, § 3(b)(1) describes the two instances in which an appeal to the Florida Supreme Court is a matter of right. The first is from the final judgments of trial courts imposing the death penalty. Obviously, because human life is at stake, the Florida Constitution provides for mandatory jurisdiction in the Florida Supreme Court.

---

9. 132 So. 3d 1110 (Fla. 2014).
10. *Baker v. State*, 878 So. 2d 1236, 1245 (Fla. 2004).
11. *Mallet v. State*, 280 So. 3d 1091, 1092 (Fla. 2019).
12. *See* Fla. Const. art V, § 3.
13. Fla. Const. art V, § 3(b).
14. *City of Dunedin v. Bense*, 90 So. 2d 300 (1956).

Robertson v. State

143 So. 3d 907 (Fla. 2014)

PER CURIAM.

This case is before the Court on appellate counsel's amended motion to withdraw from the representation of James Robertson, a prisoner under sentence of death whose direct appeal of his first-degree murder conviction and death sentence is currently pending before this Court under article V, section 3(b)(1), of the Florida Constitution. In the motion, appellate counsel advises this Court that his client, Robertson, wishes to argue in favor of the death sentence. Citing rule 4–1.2(a) of the Rules Regulating The Florida Bar, which requires a lawyer to abide by his or her client's decisions concerning the objectives of representation, appellate counsel seeks an order from this Court permitting him to withdraw from representation to avoid an alleged violation of his ethical responsibility to his client. For the following reasons, we deny the motion to withdraw.

First, article V, section 3(b)(1), of the Florida Constitution states that this Court "[s]hall hear appeals from final judgments of trial courts imposing the death penalty." The Legislature has mandated in section 921.141(4), Florida Statutes (2013), in pertinent part, that "[t]he judgment of conviction and sentence of death shall be subject to automatic review by the Supreme Court of Florida." Thus, our mandatory review of both the validity of the judgment and the propriety of the death sentence is "automatic" and does not depend upon the acquiescence of the death-sentenced defendant.

Our review of each sentence of death is also critical to the maintenance of a constitutional capital sentencing scheme in this state. In 1988, this Court held that "even though [the defendant] expressed a desire to be executed, this Court must, nevertheless, examine the record to be sure that the imposition of the death sentence complies with all the standards set by the Constitution, the Legislature, and the courts." *Goode v. State,* 365 So.2d 381, 384 (Fla.1978). We recognized our obligation to "foster uniformity in death-penalty law" in *Tillman v. State,* 591 So.2d 167, 169 (Fla.1991), and more recently, in *Yacob v. State,* 136 So.3d 539, 549 (Fla.2014), we reemphasized that the death penalty is reserved for only the most aggravated and least mitigated of cases. In that decision, we again noted our obligation to assure that the death penalty is not imposed in an arbitrary or capricious manner in this state and explained that our review is essential to the viability and validity of state law allowing for imposition of the death penalty in Florida. *See id.* at 546–47.

The United States Supreme Court in *Gregg v. Georgia,* 428 U.S. 153, 96 S.Ct. 2909, 49 L.Ed.2d 859 (1976), explained that its earlier decision in *Furman v. Georgia,* 408 U.S. 238, 92 S.Ct. 2726, 33 L.Ed.2d 346 (1972), "mandates that where discretion is afforded a sentencing body on a matter so grave as the determination of whether a human life should be taken or spared, that discretion must be suitably directed and limited so as to minimize the risk of wholly arbitrary and capricious action." *Gregg,* 428 U.S. at 189, 96 S.Ct. 2909. The only way for this Court to ensure that a death sentence is not arbitrarily or capriciously imposed is to provide meaningful appellate review of each death sentence. In fact, the Supreme Court in *Gregg* expressly noted as follows in upholding the Georgia capital sentencing scheme as constitutional:

[T]he Georgia statute has an additional provision designed to assure that the death penalty will not be imposed on a capriciously selected group of convicted defendants. The new sentencing procedures require that the State Supreme Court review *every death sentence* to determine whether it was imposed under the influence of passion, prejudice, or any other arbitrary factor, whether the evidence supports the findings of a statutory aggravating circumstance, and "[w]hether the sentence of death is excessive or disproportionate to the penalty imposed in similar cases, considering both the crime and the defendant." *Id.* at 204, 96 S.Ct. 2909 (emphasis added). The Supreme Court explained that the "provision for appellate review in the Georgia capital-sentencing system serves as a check against the random or arbitrary imposition of the death penalty" and "[i]n particular, the proportionality review substantially eliminates the possibility that a person will be sentenced to die by the action of an aberrant jury." *Id.* at 206, 96 S.Ct. 2909. Florida law similarly requires that this Court shall automatically review every judgment of conviction and sentence of death. § 921.141(4), Fla. Stat.

Our long-established precedent has given life to these constitutional and statutory safeguards against an unconstitutional capital sentencing scheme, even in cases where the defendant expresses a desire to be executed. In *Klokoc v. State*, 589 So.2d 219, 221–22 (Fla.1991), we denied the defendant's request to dismiss the direct appeal, stating that this Court required the benefit of an adversary proceeding to provide a meaningful review of both the judgment and the sentence. In *Ocha v. State*, 826 So.2d 956, 964 (Fla.2002), we explained that "*Klokoc* reiterates this Court's interest in ensuring that every death sentence is tested and has a proper basis in Florida law." The Court in *Ocha* also noted that a death-sentenced defendant may under certain circumstances waive his right to present mitigating evidence at trial, "yet have appellate counsel appointed against his wishes." *Id.*

While appellate counsel urges that we should now recede from *Klokoc* and *Ocha*, which require counsel to provide diligent appellate advocacy addressed to both the judgment and the sentence, a decision to depart from the principles of stare decisis cannot be taken lightly. "The presumption in favor of *stare decisis* is strong," *North Florida Women's Health & Counseling Services, Inc. v. State*, 866 So.2d 612, 637–38 (Fla.2003), although not unwavering. The doctrine is said to bend "where there has been a significant change in circumstances since the adoption of the legal rule or where there has been an error in legal analysis." *Brown v. Nagelhout*, 84 So.3d 304, 309 (Fla.2012) (quoting *Puryear v. State*, 810 So.2d 901, 905 (Fla.2002)). The circumstances of this case meet neither of these requirements.

This Court has also made clear that in order to depart from stare decisis for an error in legal analysis, the "gravity of the error and the impact of departing from precedent must be carefully assessed." *Id.* We have recognized sufficient gravity where the prior decision is "unsound in principle" or "unworkable in practice." *Id.* (quoting *Garcia v. San Antonio Metro. Transit Auth.,* 469 U.S. 528, 547, 105 S.Ct. 1005, 83 L.Ed.2d 1016 (1985)). Again, the circumstances in this case meet neither of these requirements to justify departure from our established precedent, which has served to effectuate the duty of this Court to provide automatic, mandatory review of both judgments of conviction and sentences of death in capital cases.

We conclude that there is simply no reason to depart from our reliable, established, and necessary procedure for requiring current counsel to proceed with diligent appellate advocacy to facilitate our mandatory review in death penalty cases where the defendant, in effect, seeks this Court's assistance in being put to death. By contrast, there are numerous reasons why a decision to recede from *Klokoc* and *Ocha* would be both erroneous and unwise, and would result in a serious threat to the soundness of Florida's capital sentencing scheme — not the least of which is the disruption and delay that would be engendered by granting the motion to withdraw.

In sum, we discern no ethical violation in requiring current counsel to continue to prosecute this appeal fully for the benefit of the Court in meeting its statutory and constitutional duties. Accordingly, the motion to withdraw is hereby denied. Consistent with this Court's prior precedent in analogous situations, and as requested in the motion, Robertson may seek leave to file a pro se supplemental brief setting forth his personal positions and interests with regard to the subject matter of the appeal. *See Klokoc,* 589 So.2d at 222.

It is so ordered.

LABARGA, C.J., and PARIENTE, LEWIS, and PERRY, JJ., concur.

PARIENTE, J., concurs with an opinion in which LABARGA, C.J., and PERRY, J., concur.

QUINCE, J., dissents.

CANADY, J., dissents with an opinion in which POLSTON, J., concurs.

[Concurring and Dissenting Opinions omitted].

———————

The Supreme Court's jurisdiction to hear appeals from final judgments of trial courts imposing the death penalty includes all types of collateral proceedings in death penalty cases.[15] With respect to the Supreme Court's ultimate jurisdiction in post-conviction cases where the death sentence has been imposed, the Court in *State v. Matute-Chirinos*[16] reasserted its jurisdiction:

> [I]n addition to our appellate jurisdiction over sentences of death, we have exclusive jurisdiction to review all types of collateral proceedings in death penalty cases. This includes cases in which this Court has vacated a death

———————

15. *Jimenez v. Bondi,* 259 So. 3d 722 (Fla. 2019).
16. 713 So. 2d 1006 (Fla. 1998).

sentence and remanded for further penalty proceedings. However, our jurisdiction does not include cases in which the death penalty is sought but not yet imposed, *State v. Preston,* 376 So.2d 3 (Fla.1979), or cases in which we have vacated both the conviction and sentence of death and remanded for a new trial.

b. "Shall hear appeals from . . . decisions of district courts of appeal declaring invalid a state statute or a provision of the state constitution." Fla. Const. art. V, § 3(b)(1)

The second instance in which an appeal to the Florida Supreme Court is a matter of right is "from decisions of district courts of appeal declaring invalid a state statute or a provision of the state constitution." This provision is considerably narrower than the one it replaced.[17] Thus, no mandatory jurisdiction exists where a district court of appeal declares a statute valid or construes a provision of the state or federal constitution. This is now part of the courts' art. V, § 3(b)(3) discretionary jurisdiction.

The largest problem under the pre-1980 art. V, § 3(b)(1)[18] was the so-called "inherency doctrine." In a series of cases, the Florida Supreme Court held that the validity of a state statute or a federal statute or treaty could be passed on inherently, that is, without doing so expressly, if the court must have done so in order to reach its final order or decision.[19] After flip-flopping, the Florida Supreme Court finally held that provisions of the state and federal constitutions could not be inherently construed.[20] The status of this doctrine under the amended § 3(b)(1) is uncertain since, unlike art. V, § 3(b)(3), § 3(b)(1) does not contain the limiting word "expressly" which has been held to preclude the application of the inherency doctrine.[21] However, "inherency doctrine" cases involved situations where statutes were "inherently" upheld. It is difficult to see how a court could hold a statute or provision of the state constitution unconstitutional without mentioning it.

What precisely is meant by a "decision of a district court of appeal declaring invalid a state statute or a provision of the state constitution"?[22] This is a difficult

---

17. After providing for Florida Supreme Court jurisdiction in cases where the death penalty was imposed, the pre-1980 art. V, § 3(b)(1) provided Florida Supreme Court review as a matter of right from orders of trial courts (held to be final orders in *Burnsed v. Seaboard Coastline R.R. Co.*, 290 So. 2d 13 (Fla. 1974)) and decisions of district courts of appeal initially or directly passing on the validity of a state statute or a federal statute or treaty, or construing a provision of the state or federal constitution.

18. *Id.*

19. *See Harrell's Candy Kitchen, Inc. v. Sarasota-Manatee Airport Auth.*, 111 So. 2d 439 (Fla. 1959).

20. *Ogle v. Pepin*, 273 So. 2d 391 (Fla. 1973).

21. *See* committee notes on the 1980 amendment in *In re Emergency Amendments to Rules of Appellate Procedure*, 381 So. 2d 1370, 1373 (Fla. 1980).

22. The committee notes on the 1980 amendment are not helpful. *See In re Emergency Amendments to Rules of Appellate Procedure*, 381 So. 2d 1370, 1373 (Fla. 1980).

question because the pre-1980 requirement — that the appeal be from the court that initially made the decision — has been dropped. Therefore, presumably, such a decision could possibly include a district court decision where: (1) the question of statutory or constitutional invalidity was initially considered and decided by the district court;[23] (2) the district court, in a decision accompanied by an opinion,[24] affirmed a trial court final or interlocutory[25] order which had invalidated a state statute or a provision of the state constitution; or (3) the district court, in a decision accompanied by an opinion, reversed the trial court final or interlocutory[26] order that upheld a state statute or provision of the state constitution (at least to the extent that the decision was an outright reversal and not merely a reversal and remand) where the trial court could still find the statute or provision constitutional.

Since the phrase "state statute" is the identical language used in the prior provision, it should have the same meaning in the present provision.[27] Thus, it should not include ordinances of Dade or any other charter county.[28] It should also not include municipal ordinances.[29]

The fact that the district court of appeal should *not* have ruled on the constitutionality of the statute on principles of judicial self-restraint (non-constitutional grounds upon which the case could have been decided) should not deprive the Florida Supreme Court of jurisdiction.[30] The following case illustrates the above principles.

---

23. *See, e.g., Rich v. Ryals*, 212 So. 2d 641 (Fla. 1968), and *Comm'n on Ethics v. Barker*, 677 So. 2d 254 (Fla. 1996).

24. What if the affirmance is per curiam without opinion? It is possible this could also vest jurisdiction in the court. The provision contains none of the limiting language (expressly and directly) found in some of the later discretionary jurisdictional provisions.

25. *See, e.g.*, Fla. R. App. P. 9.130, 9.140.

26. *Id.*

27. *See In re Advisory Op. to Governor*, 112 So. 2d 843 (Fla. 1959).

28. *Delano v. Dade County*, 287 So. 2d 288 (Fla. 1973).

29. *Armstrong v. City of Tampa*, 106 So. 2d 407 (Fla. 1958) (decision quashed on other grounds, 118 So. 2d 195 (Fla. 1960)).

30. *See Williston Highlands Dev. Corp. v. Hogue*, 277 So. 2d 260 (Fla. 1973).

4 · THE COURTS 193

Jackson v. State

926 So. 2d 1262 (Fla. 2006)

PER CURIAM.

Appellants Isiah Jackson and Daly Braxton attempt to invoke this Court's mandatory review jurisdiction by claiming a district court of appeal inherently invalidated a state statute or provision of the state constitution by issuing an unelaborated per curiam decision in each of their cases. *See* art. V, § 3(b)(1), Fla. Const. We consolidate these cases for purposes of this opinion. For the reasons explained below, we hold that article V, section 3(b)(1) of the Florida Constitution does not authorize this Court's jurisdiction over unelaborated per curiam decisions issued by a district court of appeal.

Facts

On March 17, 2004, Isiah Jackson attempted to invoke this Court's jurisdiction by filing a pro se "Notice of Appeal." This notice of appeal was initially treated as a notice to invoke discretionary review and dismissed under *Stallworth v. Moore,* 827 So.2d 974 (Fla.2002). Jackson responded by filing a "Motion to Reclassify Defendant's Case As Filed: Notice of Appeal, Per App. Rule 9.030(a)(1)(A)(ii),"[1] in which he claimed this Court had "unfairly reconfigured" his claim for jurisdiction. This Court vacated its order dismissing Jackson's case, appointed counsel to represent Jackson, and ordered counsel to show cause why this mandatory review proceeding should not be dismissed for lack of jurisdiction. Jackson's appointed counsel filed a "Response to Order to Show Cause Why This Appeal Should Not Be Dismissed" on December 20, 2004, and the State filed a reply on January 24, 2005.

In the motion to reclassify his appeal, Jackson asserted jurisdiction on the grounds that the First District Court of Appeal inherently declared two Florida Statutes, as well as a provision of the Florida Constitution, invalid when it denied Jackson's motion to file a belated appeal following his criminal convictions.[2] Nothing in the district court's decision or the special master's report substantiated Jackson's

---

1. Florida Rule of Appellate Procedure 9.030(a)(1)(A)(ii) mirrors article V, section 3(b)(1) of the Florida Constitution. It states that "[t]he supreme court shall review, by appeal ... decisions of district courts of appeal declaring invalid a state statute or a provision of the state constitution."

2. Jackson claims the district court declared two state statutes, as well as a state constitutional provision, invalid. He was convicted of three counts of sale of cocaine and resisting an officer without violence. He appealed his conviction in the First District Court of Appeal by filing a petition for a belated appeal on the grounds that his attorney ignored his timely request to appeal. The First District relinquished jurisdiction of Jackson's case to the trial court to allow the trial court to appoint a special master and determine whether Jackson was entitled to file a belated appeal. The special master held a hearing and determined that Jackson's right to appeal had not been compromised. The special master recognized that (1) no motion for a new trial was filed in Jackson's case; (2) the judge who sentenced Jackson informed him of his right to appeal; and (3) neither the transcript from the sentencing proceeding nor testimony from Jackson's defense counsel supported Jackson's claim that he had requested the right to appeal. On February 16, 2004, the First District Court of Appeal affirmed the special master's finding by filing an unpublished order stating only:

claim that the trial court invalidated these laws. The First District issued an unpublished order in this case, stating only, "The petition seeking belated appeal is denied on the merits." *See Jackson v. State,* 868 So.2d 527 (Fla. 1st DCA 2004) (table case).

On July 29, 2004, Daly Braxton commenced a similar process by filing a "Notice to Invoke Discretionary Jurisdiction." This notice was treated as a petition for review and dismissed under *Jenkins v. State,* 385 So.2d 1356 (Fla.1980). Braxton responded by filing a "Motion for Clarification," in which he claimed this Court erred in dismissing his original complaint because he had asserted a basis for mandatory review jurisdiction under article V, section 3(b)(1) of the Florida Constitution.[3] On September 3, 2004, this Court vacated its order dismissing Braxton's initial notice to invoke discretionary jurisdiction under *Jenkins* and issued a second order dismissing Braxton's petition for review on the grounds that it did not appear jurisdiction was established under article V, section 3(b)(1) of the Florida Constitution. The September 3 order granted Braxton fifteen days to file a motion for reinstatement, which Braxton did by filing an "Initial Brief of Jurisdiction."[4] In this initial brief and its subsequent amendments, Braxton asserted jurisdiction, in part, on the grounds that the district court invalidated a state statute by affirming a trial court's decision that allegedly invalidated this law.[5] The First District's opinion stated only "Per Curiam Affirmed."

"The petition seeking belated appeal is denied on the merits." *See Jackson v. State,* 868 So.2d 527 (Fla. 1st DCA 2004) (table case). Jackson timely appealed to this Court.

> In this appeal, Jackson claims the district court declared invalid section 924.05, Florida Statutes (2004), which states that "[d]irect appeals provided for in this chapter are a matter of right." He also claims the district court declared invalid section 924.06, Florida Statutes (2004), which describes the type of judgments a criminal defendant may appeal, and article V, section 4(b)(1) of the Florida Constitution, which grants the district courts "jurisdiction to hear appeals, that may be taken as a matter of right, from final judgments or orders of trial courts." Neither the First District's decision nor the special master's report expressly addressed these laws.

3. In his "Notice to Invoke Discretionary Review," Braxton also asserted jurisdiction under article V, section 3(b)(3) of the Florida Constitution. Because the district court's decision in this case was an unelaborated per curiam decision, this Court does not have jurisdiction to review this claim. *Jenkins v. State,* 385 So.2d 1356 (Fla.1980).

4. By order dated October 8, 2004, this Court recognized that Braxton's "'Initial Brief on Jurisdiction' with attachments has been treated as a motion for reinstatement."

5. More specifically, Braxton claims that the trial court invalidated section 775.087, Florida Statutes (1993), by not convicting him under it. On March 23, 1995, a jury found Braxton guilty of one count of burglary with assault, a violation of section 810.02, Florida Statutes (1993), and one count of dealing in stolen property, a violation of section 812.019, Florida Statutes (1993). On April 7, 1995, the trial court held a sentencing hearing, which included a separate proceeding in which Braxton was sentenced as a habitual felony offender. The trial court recognized that Braxton's adult criminal history (i.e., nine arrests, twelve charges, seven felony convictions, two misdemeanor convictions, and multiple violations of community control) reflected a "total inability to comply with any law or authority" and that Braxton's crimes are "escalating in that more and more violence is becoming part of his method." Therefore, the court sentenced Braxton to concurrent sentences of forty years for burglary with assault and fifteen years for dealing in stolen property. Braxton appealed this sentence on the grounds that the facts at trial clearly established that he should have been convicted of burglary with a firearm, a violation of section 775.087, Florida Statutes. In fact, the first

The State filed a response to Braxton's claims on November 12, 2004, and Braxton filed a reply to the State's response on November 22, 2004.

Analysis

This Court has long recognized that it lacks jurisdiction over unelaborated per curiam decisions in the context of discretionary review jurisdiction. Today, we find that the analysis which led us to this determination applies just as readily to the context of mandatory review jurisdiction under article V, section 3(b)(1) of the Florida Constitution. Therefore, we determine that article V, section 3(b)(1) does not authorize this Court to review unelaborated per curiam decisions issued by the district court. By issuing an unelaborated per curiam decision, the district court has not "declared" a statute or constitutional provision invalid, as is required by the language of article V, section 3(b)(1) of the Florida Constitution. In the future, the clerk's office will administratively dismiss notices of appeal and petitions for discretionary review asserting jurisdiction over a district court's unelaborated per curiam decision.

---

information filed in his case charged him with violating both sections 775.087 and 810.02, Florida Statutes. More than a month before trial, the State amended the information by removing all references to the use of the firearm and to a violation of section 775.087. Braxton alleges that it was improper for the trial court to allow the amendment of the information or limit the jury instructions to the crimes charged in the information or both. He claims that if he had been convicted under section 775.087, Florida Statutes, he would have been found guilty of a life felony, instead of a first-degree felony and would, therefore, not have been eligible for status as a habitual felony offender. Braxton appealed this sentence, first, by filing a "Motion to Correct an Illegal Sentence" in the trial court. On March 31, 2004, the trial court issued an order denying this motion. It found that Braxton's sentence as a habitual felony offender was proper, given the fact that he had neither been charged with nor sentenced under section 775.087, Florida Statutes. Braxton appealed this decision to the First District Court of Appeal, which affirmed the trial court's order by stating "Per Curiam Affirmed." Braxton then filed a motion for rehearing in the First District Court asking the court to certify his case as one of great public importance. The First District issued an order denying Braxton's motion on July 30, 2004.

> In addition to his claims of statutory invalidity, Braxton alleges two other bases for jurisdiction, neither of which have merit. He claims the district court violated his constitutional right of access to the courts by rejecting his motion for rehearing in which he requested the First District write an opinion in his case. This argument is without merit. *See Whipple v. State,* 431 So.2d 1011, 1013–14 (Fla. 2d DCA 1983) (rejecting argument that district court's unelaborated per curiam affirmance of the trial court's decision thwarted right of access to the courts because the constitution's guarantee of a right to review does not extend to supreme court review); *see also R.J. Reynolds Tobacco Co. v. Kenyon,* 882 So.2d 986, 989 (Fla.2004) (recognizing that the district court has "inherent discretion" to decide whether to write an opinion, and this Court does not have authority to order a district court to write an opinion). He also claims the trial court erred in allowing the State to amend the information, and he cites a number of this Court's previous cases to support this. The only possible basis for jurisdiction here would be discretionary review jurisdiction, and we have long held that we do not have discretionary jurisdiction over unelaborated "per curiam affirmed" opinions. *Jenkins,* 385 So.2d 1356. These allegations are not sufficient to establish jurisdiction in this Court.

More than twenty-five years have passed since this Court first held that unelaborated per curiam decisions do not constitute a decision of the district court of appeal sufficient to warrant discretionary review jurisdiction. In *Jenkins v. State,* 385 So.2d 1356, 1359 (Fla.1980), this Court held that "the Supreme Court of Florida lacks jurisdiction to review per curiam decisions of the several district courts of appeal . . . rendered without opinion." We based this holding, first, on the language of article V, section 3(b)(3), which limits our jurisdiction to district court opinions that "expressly" conflict with another district court of appeal. In addition, we looked to the history surrounding this constitutional provision and the design of the Florida court system. We noted that "[i]t was never intended that the district courts of appeal should be intermediate courts." *Id.* at 1357 (quoting *Ansin v. Thurston,* 101 So.2d 808, 810 (Fla.1958)). Instead, the district courts were established to preserve the Florida Supreme Court's "function[ ] as a supervisory body in the judicial system for the State, exercising appellate power in certain specified areas essential to the settlement of issues of public importance and the preservation of uniformity of principle and practice." *Id.* at 1357–58. Likewise, when article V, section 3 was amended in 1980, the purpose behind these amendments was to ensure that this Court retained its supervisory role by limiting its jurisdiction and relieving its overburdened caseload. *Id.* at 1359.

In subsequent cases, we applied *Jenkins* to find that we lacked jurisdiction over unelaborated per curiam decisions in virtually all contexts of discretionary review. *See, e.g., Stallworth v. Moore,* 827 So.2d 974, 976–77 (Fla.2002) (finding that this Court's "all-writs" jurisdiction does not authorize it to review a district court's "per curiam denial[ ] of relief issued without opinion or explanation"); *Grate v. State,* 750 So.2d 625, 626 (Fla.1999) (stating that "[r]egardless of how a petition seeking review of a district court decision is styled, this Court does not have jurisdiction to review per curiam decisions rendered without opinion"). In fact, we have even applied *Jenkins* in the context of mandatory review. In *Byrd v. State,* 880 So.2d 616, 617 (Fla.2004), we determined that we lacked jurisdiction over a case in which a concurring opinion declared a statute invalid, because *Jenkins* required that the language warranting jurisdiction be included in the majority opinion.

Applying this same analysis to the cases at hand leads to the conclusion that article V, section 3(b)(1) does not authorize jurisdiction over a district court's unelaborated per curiam decision when the petitioner/appellant asserts jurisdiction on the grounds that a trial court allegedly invalidated a state statute or constitutional provision. While the language of article V, section 3(b)(1) does not require that the district court "expressly" declare a statute invalid, it still requires that the district court of appeal make a declaration. *See* art. V, § 3(b)(1), Fla. Const. (authorizing this Court's jurisdiction over "decisions of district courts of appeal declaring invalid a state statute or a provision of the state constitution").

In conclusion, we hold that article V, section 3(b)(1) of the Florida Constitution does not authorize this Court's jurisdiction over unelaborated per curiam decisions issued by a district court of appeal. As we have long recognized in the context of discretionary review jurisdiction and now apply to mandatory review jurisdiction, per curiam decisions issued without an opinion do not constitute a decision of a district court sufficient to establish jurisdiction under article V, section 3(b)(1) of the Florida Constitution. Therefore, we dismiss the notices of appeal and petitions for discretionary review filed in both *Jackson* and *Braxton*. We also hold that in the future, the clerk's office will dismiss notices of appeal and petitions for discretionary review asserting jurisdiction on similar grounds. No motions for rehearing or clarification will be entertained in these cases or in cases which are dismissed in the future based on the reasoning set forth in this opinion.

It is so ordered.

PARIENTE, C.J., and WELLS, ANSTEAD, QUINCE, CANTERO, and BELL, JJ., concur.

LEWIS, J., concurs in result only.

_____

As held by the Court in the above case, the Florida Supreme Court's mandatory jurisdiction to hear appeals from District Courts of Appeal decisions declaring invalid a state statute or provision of the constitution does not apply to unelaborated per curiam decisions. In its holding, the Court also referred to its decision in *Byrd v. State*,[31] in which it held that the court lacked jurisdiction over the appeal under this section of the Constitution where the opinion from the District Court of Appeal, construing the State Constitution and declaring a State statute unconstitutional, was signed by only one judge from the three-judge panel, with the other two judges concurring in the result, but not joining in the opinion.[32] Further, in *Hanft v. Phelan*,[33] the Supreme Court held that the District Court of Appeal's ruling in the alternative that, under certain circumstances, the statute of repose was unconstitutional, and remanding the case for factual determination below, did not declare state statute invalid as contemplated by the article of the Constitution allowing appeal of District Court decisions declaring state statutes invalid.

Section II(A)(1) of the Florida Supreme Court's *Manual of Internal Operating Procedures* takes into account the holding in *State v. Jackson* and provides in relevant part:[34]

> When a party files a notice seeking appeal, the clerk's office determines whether the case is subject to administrative dismissal based on a lack

_____

31. 880 So. 2d 616 (Fla. 2004).

32. The court in *Byrd* came to its rationale as a result of its decision in *Jenkins v. State*, 385 So. 2d 1356 (Fla. 1980) (holding the language and expressions found in a dissenting or concurring opinion cannot support jurisdiction because they are not the decision of the district court of appeal).

33. 488 So. 2d 531 (Fla. 1986).

34. *The Supreme Court of Florida Manual of Internal Operating Procedures* (rev'd Feb. 18, 2021), https://www.floridasupremecourt.org/content/download/241274/file/02-18-2021-Florida-Supreme -Court-Internal-Operating-Procedures-Manual.pdf.

of jurisdiction. If the clerk's office determines that the case is subject to administrative dismissal, pursuant to guidelines established by the court, the case is docketed and automatically dismissed. In such cases, no rehearing is allowed. The clerk's office will administratively dismiss those cases in which a party seeks appeal from an unelaborated per curiam decision. *See* Jackson v. State, 926 So. 2d 1262 (Fla. 2006).

c. *"When provided by general law, shall hear appeals from final judgments entered in proceedings for the validation of bonds or certificates of indebtedness and shall review action of statewide agencies relating to rates or service of utilities providing electric, gas, or telephone service." Fla. Const. art. V, § 3(b)(2)*

The Florida Constitution permits the Florida Legislature to prescribe mandatory Florida Supreme Court jurisdiction in two other instances. The Florida Legislature has done so.

First, the Florida Legislature has provided for appeal, as a matter of right, to the Florida Supreme Court from "final judgments entered in proceedings for the validation of bonds or certificates of indebtedness."[35] Second, the 1980 amendment added a second provision for review, as a matter of right, of the action of statewide agencies (in present practice the Public Service Commission) relating to rates or service of utilities providing electric, gas, or telephone service. The Florida Legislature has implemented this provision.[36]

GTE Florida, Inc. v. Clark[37] and *Legal Environmental Assistance Foundation, Inc. v. Clark*[38] are examples of the Florida Supreme Court's § 3(b)(2) jurisdiction. The first appears to involve rates and the second service. The standard of review in such cases is explained by the Florida Supreme Court in *Gulf Coast Electric Cooperative, Inc. v. Johnson*:[39]

> We begin our analysis by emphasizing the scope of this Court's review of PSC orders. Although the Florida Constitution vests this Court with mandatory jurisdiction to hear appeals from PSC orders, *see* art. V, § 3(b)(2), Fla. Const., our review function is circumscribed by certain well-established principles:
>
> > Commission orders come to this Court "clothed with the statutory presumption that they have been made within the Commission's jurisdiction

---

35. See Fla. Stat. § 75.08 (1989) and committee notes on the 1980 amendment in *In re Emergency Amendments to Rules of Appellate Procedure*, 381 So. 2d 1370, 1373–1374 (Fla. 1980).

36. *See City of Tallahassee v. Fla. Pub. Serv. Comm'n*, 433 So. 2d 505 (Fla. 1983) and Fla. Stat. § 350.128 (1989).

37. 668 So. 2d 971 (Fla. 1996).

38. 668 So. 2d 982 (Fla. 1996).

39. 727 So. 2d 259, 262 (Fla. 1999).

and powers, and that they are reasonable and just and such as ought to have been made." Moreover, an agency's interpretation of a statute it is charged with enforcing is entitled to great deference. The party challenging an order of the Commission bears the burden of overcoming those presumptions by showing a departure from the essential requirements of law. We will approve the Commission's findings and conclusions if they are based on competent substantial evidence, [footnote omitted] and if they are not clearly erroneous.

AmeriSteel Corp. v. Clark, 691 So.2d 473, 477 (Fla.1997) (citations omitted) (quoting *PW Ventures, Inc. v. Nichols*, 533 So.2d 281, 283 (Fla.1988)). Considering the PSC's specialized knowledge and expertise in this area, this deferential standard of review is appropriate. *See Gulf Oil Co. v. Bevis*, 322 So.2d 30, 32 (Fla.1975), *superseded by statute on other grounds as stated in General Dev. Utils., Inc. v. Hawkins*, 357 So.2d 408, 409 n. 4 (Fla.1978); *see also Public Serv. Comm'n v. Fuller*, 551 So.2d 1210, 1212 (Fla.1989).

d. Discretionary Review

(1) In General

The phrase "by certiorari" has been deleted from the Florida Supreme Court's discretionary jurisdiction. Apparently, disharmony surrounded the "scope" of the previous discretionary review power which before the 1980 amendment to art. V was described as certiorari (constitutional certiorari).[40] "Scope" in this regard had two aspects.

The first dealt with the issues the Court could review. Could the Court consider issues other than the one which gave it jurisdiction? For example, when it granted certiorari to review a question certified by a district court of appeal, could it review the other issues decided by the district court in that case? In *Lawrence v. Florida East Coast Railway Company*,[41] the Court held that it could review "any error in the record once [the Court had] it properly before [it] for [its] review." On the other hand, in *Sunspan Engineering and Construction Company v. Spring-Lock Scaffolding Company*,[42] the Court held that when it granted certiorari to review that part of the interlocutory order of a trial court that passed on the validity of a Florida statute, there was "no basis for certiorari review" to consider other parts of the interlocutory order. The distinction between the two cases may lie in differences between certified questions and interlocutory orders.

---

40. So described to distinguish it from statutory certiorari and common law certiorari, both of which are discussed later in this chapter. *See, e.g., G-W Dev. Corp. v. Village of North Palm Beach Zoning Bd. of Adjustment, infra* at page 320.

41. 346 So. 2d 1012, 1014, n. 2 (Fla. 1977).

42. 310 So. 2d 4, 6 (Fla. 1975).

Arguably, once the Court obtains jurisdiction under its discretionary authority, it can decide all issues, not only the one that was necessary to get it there. "In all proceedings a court shall have such jurisdiction as may be necessary for a complete determination of the cause."[43] As this rule only became effective in 1977, the difference in result between *Sunspan*, a 1975 decision, and *Lawrence*, a 1977 decision, may be attributable to the change. As the committee notes explain:[44]

> [This provision] is derived from [the former rule], which concerned direct appeals to the supreme court. [Which would explain *Rojas v. State*, 288 So. 2d 234 (Fla. 1973).] This provision is intended to guarantee that once the jurisdiction of any court is properly invoked, the court may determine the entire case to the extent permitted by substantive law. The rule does not extend or limit the constitutional or statutory jurisdiction of any court.

The second "scope" aspect is the way in which the Court reviewed whatever it had jurisdiction to review. Was its review limited to the traditional scope of common law certiorari which allowed review of only the lower court's jurisdiction and its adherence to the essential requirements of law?[45] The Court ruled affirmatively in *In re Estate of Kant*,[46] a certified question case. The opinion itself is not a model of clarity. This restriction should not apply in the wake of the 1980 amendment.

(2) "May review any decision of a district court of appeal that expressly declares valid a state statute, or that expressly construes a provision of the state or federal constitution, . . ." Fla. Const. art. V, § 3(b)(3)

This provision makes discretionary two types of review that had previously been mandatory. Furthermore, it adds the word "expressly", which was apparently intended to abolish the inherency doctrine that had applied to rulings on the validity of state statutes.[47]

In *McNamara v. State*,[48] the Florida Supreme Court held:

> Although it is unnecessary to the disposition of this cause to resolve the constitutional question [the lower court had construed a constitutional provision] and, therefore, we will not do so, this does not divest us of jurisdiction to dispose of the other issues involved sub judice. *P. C. Lissenden Co., Inc. v. Board of County Commissioners of Palm Beach County*, 116 So.2d 632 (Fla.1959).

There would appear to be no reason why this rule would not continue to apply after the 1980 change.

---

43. Fla. R. App. P. 9.040(a).

44. *Id*

45. See the discussion of common law certiorari beginning at page 288 of this text.

46. 272 So. 2d 153 (Fla. 1972).

47. See committee notes on the 1980 amendment in *In re Emergency Amendments to the Rules of Appellate Procedure*, 381 So. 2d 1370, 1373 (1980).

48. 357 So. 2d 410, 411 (Fla. 1978).

(3) "May review any decision of a district court of appeal that . . .
expressly affects a class of constitutional or state officers . . ." Fla.
Const. art. V, § 3(b)(3)

Florida State Board of Health v. Lewis

149 So. 2d 41 (Fla. 1963)

THORNAL, Justice.

This matter has been heard on a motion for a stay order pending our consideration of a petition for certiorari to review a decision of the District Court of Appeal, First District.

The matter must be disposed of on jurisdiction grounds.

The State Board of Health promulgated certain regulations governing the commercial spraying of lawns and shrubbery with highly toxic pesticides. Respondent Lewis, alleging the invalidity of the regulations, sought an injunction in the circuit court. The chancellor denied the injunction, holding the regulations valid. The decree was reversed by the District Court of Appeal, First District. That court held the regulations invalid. Lewis v. Florida State Board of Health, Fla.App., 143 So.2d 867. The State Board of Health has petitioned this Court for a writ of certiorari on the jurisdictional ground that the decision of the District Court 'affects a class of constitutional or state officers.' Article V, Section 4(2), Florida Constitution, F.S.A. . . .

* * *

We have stated that the only jurisdictional basis for review by us, which has been asserted by the petitioner, is the claim that the decision 'affects a class of constitutional or state officers.' In this regard it is the position of the petitioner that the State Board of Health consisting of five members constitutes a 'class' of officers which entitles the Board to seek review of the subject decision. The problem which we must resolve is whether a state board, consisting of two or more members comprising a single state entity is a 'class' within the contemplation of the constitutional provision which we have cited.

Admittedly, in common parlance, two or more persons or things possessing common attributes are often considered a 'class.' However, as used in the subject constitutional provision the word 'class' cannot be accorded a definition quite so comprehensive.

The obvious purpose of the provision in question was to permit this Court to review a decision which directly affects one state officer and in so doing similarly affects every other state officer in the same category. For example, in State v. Robinson, Fla., 132 So.2d 156, this Court took jurisdiction of a decision of a District Court of Appeal, 124 So.2d 714, which affected the duties of a particular justice of the peace. In the view of the majority the justification for so doing was that the decision was sufficiently broad in scope that it would, in effect, affect all justices of the peace throughout the state. To this extent the decision affected a 'class' of constitutional officers, to wit: all of the justices of the peace.

In the only other situation where the problem has been considered we have taken the position that an individual member of the State Cabinet, in the exercise of the functions of his particular office, does not constitute a "class." The reason, of course, was that an individual cannot be a class in the sense used in the Constitution. There is only one State Treasurer, not a class of State Treasurers. Larson v. Harrison, Fla., 142 So.2d 727. There is only one Secretary of State, not a class of Secretaries of State. Crown Central Petroleum Corp. v. Standard Oil Co. et al., Fla., 142 So.2d 731.

The obvious purpose of the subject constitutional provision was to authorize this Court to review decisions which, in the ultimate, would affect all constitutional or state officers exercising the same powers, even though only one of such officers might be involved in the particular litigation.

The "class," as the word is employed in Section 4, Article V, supra, means two or more constitutional or state officers who separately and independently exercise identical powers of government. In this sense a group of officers composing a single governmental entity such as a board or commission would not, *as such board or commission*, constitute a class. It is the existence of two or more members of a given class of separate official entities that supplies the jurisdictional foundation for this Court to proceed.

Here, the state entity involved was the Board of Health, as distinguished from the individual members of the Board. The individuals collectively constitute the Board. When, as here, the official action of the Board as an entity of government is brought into question we are confronted by the action of a single state entity rather than a potential class of state entities.

In passing, it is not inappropriate to observe that a decision affecting the powers of one board as an entity of government might well affect the powers of all similar boards and thereby fall within the category of reviewable decisions under the subject provision. For example, a decision defining the duties of a board of county commissioners may affect all other boards of county commissioners and thereby fall within the reviewable category. Admittedly, this is not the situation with which we are currently confronted. We offer the observation merely as illustrative of the constitutional provision in question.

Finding as we do that the subject decision of the District Court affects only the Florida State Board of Health as an entity of state government and, therefore, finding that the decision does not affect "a class of constitutional or state officers," it is incumbent upon us to deny sua sponte the petition for certiorari. It is apparent that this Court is without jurisdiction to review the matter. The motion for a stay order, therefore, becomes moot.

The petition for a writ of certiorari is denied.

It is so ordered.

DREW, O'CONNELL and CALDWELL, JJ., concur.

ROBERTS, C. J., dissents.

Spradley v. State

293 So. 2d 697 (Fla. 1974)

CARLTON, Justice (Retired).

On Petition for Writ of Certiorari, petitioner seeks review of a per curiam affirmance by the District Court of Appeal, First District, of his conviction for murder in the first degree. Spradley v. State, 276 So.2d 511 (1st DCA Fla.1973). After issuance of the writ, and oral argument by the parties, we have concluded, for the reasons outlined below, that we do not have certiorari jurisdiction to review this case; we therefore discharge the writ having been improvidently granted.

[The court here determines that it does not have certiorari jurisdiction under a conflict of decisions theory.]

Petitioner has also argued that this Court has jurisdiction, via certiorari, because the case affects a class of constitutional or state officers. Florida Constitution, Article V, Section 3(b)(3). This is the same basis upon which we reviewed *Richardson*. In *Richardson*, we held:

> The decision below reviewed the failure of the prosecuting attorney of the Criminal Court of Record of Hillsborough County to comply with the discovery requirements of the Rule in question, and the effect of such failure upon the validity of the trial in which the petitioner was convicted. In doing so it also reviewed the exercise of the trial court's discretion in refusing to grant petitioner's motion for mistrial based upon the failure of the prosecuting attorney to disclose the name of a witness who, the petitioner claimed, had knowledge of facts 'relevant to the offense charged' and to the defense of the petitioner, and whose name was required, in the view of the petitioner, to be furnished him by the express provision of the Rule. Thus the decision of the District Court which holds that non-compliance with the discovery requirements of the Rule does not ipso facto constitute ground for reversal of a conviction even though it is made to appear that the Rule has not been strictly complied with, and that such reversal depends upon whether or not the person charged has been prejudiced by non-compliance, affects two classes of constitutional or state officers, viz, prosecuting officers and trial courts in the exercise of their respective powers and duties in the prosecution and trial of criminal cases.

It is true that the decision below was determinative only of the cause reviewed by the appellate court, but the ultimate effect of it affects all prosecuting attorneys and trial judges in the trial of criminal cases. This Court, in Florida State Board of Health v. Lewis, Fla., 149 So.2d 41, speaking of this particular provision of the Constitution, said:

> 'The obvious purpose of the subject constitutional provision was to authorize this Court to review decisions which, in the ultimate, would affect all constitutional or state officers exercising the same powers, even

though only one of such officers might be involved in the particular litigation.'

* * *

A decision which "affects a class of constitutional or state officers" must be one that does more than simply modify or construe or add to the case law which comprises much of the substantive and procedural law of this state. Such cases naturally affect all classes of constitutional or state officers, in that the members of these classes are bound by the law the same as any other citizen. To vest this Court with certiorari jurisdiction, a decision must *directly* and, in some way, *exclusively* affect the duties, powers, validity, formation, termination or regulation of a particular class of constitutional or state officers. This may be a decision in a case in which the class, or some of its members, is directly involved as a party. It may also be in a case in which no member of the class is a party, if the decision generally affects the entire class in some way unrelated to the specific facts of that case.

In the instant case, no member of any class of constitutional or state officers was a party, and any decision as to possible non-compliance with discovery rules by the state attorney did not affect any class of constitutional or state officers in any general way unrelated to the specific facts of this case. The decision affected only the rights of the parties directly involved and the body of our State law as it applies to each and every citizen alike.

* * *

Therefore, having held that this Court does not have jurisdiction, on any basis, to review this case, the writ of certiorari heretofore issued is discharged as having been improvidently granted.

It is so ordered.

ADKINS, C. J., and ROBERTS, BOYD, McCAIN and DEKLE, JJ., concur.

ERVIN, J., concurs in part and dissents in part with opinion. [The opinion of Justice Ervin is omitted.]

The only change in the language of this aspect of Florida Supreme Court jurisdiction in the 1980 amendment was the requirement that the district court decision must "expressly" affect a class of constitutional or state officers. The prior provision did not contain the word "expressly." This word may have been added to forestall any attempt by the Court to hear cases in which it could be argued that the district court inherently made such a decision. The word "expressly" was added to the jurisdictional provision regarding district court decisions declaring valid a state statute or construing a provision of the state or federal constitution for the same reason. The authors have, however, never seen a case where jurisdiction was based on a district court decision that inherently affected a class of constitutional or state officers. It is now clear that "expressly" was also added to preclude Florida Supreme Court review of a decision not containing an opinion, a so-called PCA

(Per Curiam Affirmed).[49] The possibility also exists that the word "expressly" was added to constitutionalize the result of *Spradley v. State*,[50] although the definition of "expressly" would have to be stretched to do so.

(4) "May review any decision of a district court of appeal . . . that expressly and directly conflicts with a decision of another district court of appeal or of the supreme court on the same question of law." Fla. Const. art. V, § 3(b)(3)

The *raison d'etre* for this provision which first appeared in the 1956 revision of the judicial article (which created the district courts of appeal) is well expressed by the Fourth District Court of Appeal in *Miller v. Highlands Insurance Company*:[51]

> . . . We have considered the rationale of *Davis v. Simpson*, . . . and although we respect the opinion of the First District, have reached a contrary conclusion. Our Constitution recognizes that the District Courts of Appeal may from time to time have divergent opinions. A procedure exists by which conflicts may be resolved and the law brought into harmony. Article V, Section 3(b)(3), Florida Constitution.

This conflict provision also insures to the Florida Supreme Court the opportunity to correct a conflict between one of its decisions and a subsequent decision of a district court of appeal.[52] A decision of a district court that conflicts with Florida Supreme Court precedent is a source of concern. The Court has set out the procedures to be followed if a district court thinks an earlier Florida Supreme Court decision is wrong. In *Hoffman v. Jones*,[53] the Fourth District Court of Appeal decided an issue of law contrary to precedent clearly established by the Florida Supreme Court. It then certified that question to the Florida Supreme Court. That Court indicated that the proper procedure would have been to decide the issue of law in accordance with precedent and then certify[54] the question to the Florida Supreme Court. As the Florida Supreme Court observed, it had no jurisdiction, based solely on the district court's certificate, absent a petition by one of the parties asking the Court to take jurisdiction. Given a situation where review could be frustrated by a party not asking for review, it would be better to have the district court decision made in accordance with precedent than against it, thereby avoiding confusion in the law.

---

49. *Sch. Bd. of Pinellas Cty. v. Dist. Court of Appeal*, 467 So. 2d 985 (Fla. 2d Dist. Ct. App. 1985).

50. 293 So. 2d 697 (Fla. 1974).

51. 336 So. 2d 636, 641 (Fla. 4th Dist. Ct. App. 1976) (quashed and remanded on the merits 348 So. 2d 303 (Fla. 1977).

52. The 1972 revision to art. V had allowed conflict to be based on two decisions of the same district court by changing the word "another" to "any." The 1980 revision has changed it back to "another," thus removing that basis for jurisdiction.

53. 280 So. 2d 431 (Fla. 1973).

54. The Supreme Court decision in *Hoffman* was described in *Fitzsimmons v. City of Pensacola*, 297 So. 2d 107 (Fla. 1st Dist. Ct. App. 1974), as an "historic landmark decision."

Conflict review would be analogous because, again, the Court's jurisdiction would not depend simply on conflict, but on a party in the lower court seeking review.

City of Jacksonville v. Florida First National Bank of Jacksonville

339 So. 2d 632 (Fla. 1976)

PER CURIAM.

The Writ of Certiorari having issued and the Court having examined the record and heard argument of counsel, it is now of the opinion that it is without jurisdiction and that the writ was improvidently issued. Therefore, the writ must be and is hereby discharged, and the Petition for Writ of Certiorari is dismissed.

It is so ordered.

OVERTON, C. J. and ROBERTS, ADKINS and SUNDBERG, JJ., concur.

ENGLAND, J., concurs in judgment discharging writ of certiorari with an opinion, with which OVERTON, C. J. and SUNDBERG, J., concur.

BOYD, J., dissents with an opinion.

ENGLAND, Justice (concurring).

The Florida First National Bank of Jacksonville, in its capacity as guardian of Ernest John Dobbert, III and Honore Elizabeth Dobbert, filed separate suits against the City of Jacksonville for damages resulting from the City's alleged negligence in failing to take measures which would have protected the children from abuse at the hands of their father. After the suits were consolidated, the trial court dismissed both for failure to state a cause of action. On appeal the First District Court of Appeal reversed that judgment, concluding that the allegations of the amended complaints state a cause of action, [footnote omitted] after which a petition for a writ of certiorari was filed here.

The issue in the cause is whether the City of Jacksonville may be held liable for the torts of its employees as alleged in the amended complaints of the Bank....

* * *

The decision of the district court is alleged to be in conflict with a number of other Florida appellate decisions dealing with the scope and nature of municipal tort liability, principal among which are *Wong v. City of Miami*, 237 So.2d 132 (Fla. 1970); *Modlin v. City of Miami Beach*, 201 So.2d 70 (Fla. 1967), and *Evett v. City of Inverness*, 224 So.2d 365 (Fla.2d DCA 1969). Were the conflict "direct," of course, we would have jurisdiction.[2] It is not, however, and for that reason we are compelled to discharge the writ we tentatively issued.

---

2. Art. V, § 3(b)(3), Fla. Const.

Years ago this Court identified two basic forms of decisional conflict which properly trigger the exercise of our jurisdiction under what is now Article V, Section 3(b)(3) of the Florida Constitution. In *Nielsen v. City of Sarasota*, 117 So.2d 731, 734 (Fla.1960), the court unanimously held that alleged conflict may exist either (1) where an announced rule of law conflicts with other appellate expressions of law, or (2) where a rule of law is applied to produce a different result in a case which involves "substantially the same controlling facts as a prior case." [footnote omitted] In this case petitioners do not suggest that the district court announced a different rule of law in holding for the respondent-Bank. They suggest, rather, that the appropriate rules governing municipal liability were applied to produce a result different from prior decisions on substantially the same controlling facts.

As the district court's careful opinion shows, however, the facts in this case are so disparate from any other case which has ever considered the scope of municipal liability that the requisite factual similarity is wholly absent. . . .

The absence of a jurisdictional foundation for our review in this case is not a mere technicality. It is a matter of constitutional significance. In this case, the First District Court of Appeal did a thorough and thoughtful job of analyzing Florida case law in order to apply it to the facts of a particular controversy before it. This is precisely what the framers of Article V and the people of Florida expect district court judges to do. A very strong showing of *Nielsen*-type error is required before we find authority to supplant the judgment of those constitutional officers with ours. Whatever the current view of the members of this Court on the scope of municipal liability, we may not arbitrarily jump the jurisdictional requirements of the Constitution in order to decide this case on its merits. We must, therefore, discharge the writ as having been improvidently granted.

OVERTON, C. J., and SUNDBERG, J., concur.

BOYD, Justice (dissenting) [omitted].

Does the following add a third category or does it merely constitute a variety of the second category of conflict?

> The district court mistakenly relied on its earlier decisions in *Le Prince* and *Lane*. On prior occasions, we have said that if a district court of appeal expressly adopts a decision of this Court [footnote omitted] or another district court [footnote omitted] as controlling precedent even though the factual situation under review is materially distinguishable from the case or cases relied on, such reliance constitutes a *misapplication of law* vesting conflict certiorari jurisdiction in this Court.[55]

---

55. *Wale v. Barnes*, 278 So. 2d 601, 604 (Fla. 1973) (emphasis in original).

In the 2011 case of *Florida Insurance Guaranty Association, Inc. v. Devon Neighborhood Association, Inc.*,[56] the Florida Supreme Court affirmed that the misapplication of its precedent does in fact provide a basis for express and direct conflict jurisdiction. See also *Wallace v. Dean*[57] and *Rosen v. Fla. Ins. Guar. Ass'n.*[58]

Niemann v. Niemann

312 So. 2d 733 (Fla. 1975)

HARDING, Circuit Judge:

By petition for writ of certiorari, we have for review a decision of the District Court of Appeal, Fourth District (Niemann v. Niemann, Fla.App., 294 So.2d 415), which allegedly conflicts with a decision of the District Court of Appeal, Third District (Walton v. Walton, Fla.App., 290 So.2d 110), on the same point of law. In the instant case the court below held:

> "The court's authority to effect a change in the title to the property of the parties in a dissolution of marriage is restricted to an award of lump sum alimony, a determination of a special equity, a partition of the property, or a division based upon an agreement of the parties."

In Walton v. Walton, *supra*, the District Court of Appeal in its opinion said:

> "... it appears that today a trial judge is authorized to make a division of real property even if held in an estate by the entireties, if such a division is sought by one of the parties and tried without objection." 290 So.2d at 112.

The court went on to say:

> "In reality, what the appellant is complaining about in the instant appeal is not that the trial court attempted to divide the jointly held property but that he abused his discretion in the manner of the division."

Therefore, it appears that the statement made by the District Court in *Walton*, regarding the authority of a court to effect a division of real property does not constitute the decision of the court.

We have to look at the decision, rather than a conflict in the opinion, to find that we have jurisdiction. Gibson v. Maloney, 231 So.2d 823 (Fla.1970).

After having considered this matter and having heard oral argument, we find no conflict of decisions and, therefore, the writ is discharged and the petition is dismissed.

---

56. 67 So. 3d 187 (Fla. 2011).
57. 3 So. 3d 1035, 1040 (Fla. 2009).
58. 802 So. 2d 291, 292 (Fla. 2001).

ADKINS, C. J. concurs specially with opinion.

McCAIN, J., McCORD, District Judge, and RUDD, Circuit Judge, concur.

As the *Niemann* court said, it is conflict of decisions rather than conflict of opinions that will satisfy the conflict requirements of § 3(b)(3). The Florida Supreme Court must, of course, "look to [the] opinion upon which [the] district court's decision is based to determine [the] probable existence of direct conflict with a decision of the Supreme Court on [the] same point of law."[59] The Court also considered "the record" before determining that no conflict existed.[60]

If a district court of appeal causes the conflict to evaporate by receding from the opinion that created the conflict *after* the Florida Supreme Court accepts jurisdiction, the Florida Supreme Court *may* have discretion to decide the case anyway. This is apparently not the situation if one of the district courts of appeal had receded from the opinion that created the conflict *before* the Florida Supreme Court accepted jurisdiction, but the Florida Supreme Court did not discover that fact until after it had accepted jurisdiction. Consider the following two cases.

Skinner v. State

470 So. 2d 702 (Fla. 1985)

PER CURIAM.

We accepted jurisdiction because of direct and express conflict between the case here, *Skinner v. State*, 450 So.2d 595 (Fla. 5th DCA 1984), and *Golden v. State*, 120 So.2d 651 (Fla. 1st DCA 1960). Since that time the First District Court of Appeal has receded from *Golden* and expressly adopted the reasoning of the case here, *Skinner*, and *Ballard v. State*, 447 So.2d 1040 (Fla. 2d DCA 1984). *See Carter v. State*, 469 So.2d 775 (Fla. 1st DCA 1984), panel decision adopted by court en banc April 25, 1985. The conflict having been resolved while this cause has been pending, *we exercise our discretion* to decline to proceed further and deny review. [Emphasis added.]

It is so ordered.

BOYD, C.J., and ADKINS, OVERTON, ALDERMAN, McDONALD, EHRLICH and SHAW, JJ., concur.

---

59. *Burns v. State*, 676 So. 2d 1366 (Fla. 1996) (citing *Seaboard Air Line R.R. v. Branham*, 104 So. 2d 356 (Fla. 1958)).

60. *Id.*

Bailey v. Hough

441 So. 2d 614 (Fla. 1983)

OVERTON, Judge.

This is a petition to review a decision of the First District Court of Appeal reported as *Hough v. Bailey*, 421 So.2d 708 (Fla. 1st DCA 1982). We accepted jurisdiction in this case because, in its opinion, the First District acknowledged direct conflict with the Second District Court of Appeal's decision in *Kirk v. Bauman*, 336 So.2d 125 (Fla. 2d DCA 1976). After accepting jurisdiction in this case, however, we determined that the Second District, in *Wiggins v. Dojcsan*, 411 So.2d 894 (Fla. 2d DCA 1982), expressly receded from its decision in *Kirk*. In receding from *Kirk*, the Second District in *Wiggins* adopted the view expressed by the Fourth District in *Cacaro v.* *Swan*, 394 So.2d 538 (Fla. 4th DCA), *petition dismissed*, 402 So.2d 608 (Fla.1981), [disapproved in part in *Chiusolo v. Kennedy*, 614 So. 2d 491 (Fla. 1993)] which was also relied on by the First District in its opinion in this case. Consequently, no conflict exists *and there is no basis for this Court to accept jurisdiction in this cause.* The petition for review is denied. [Emphasis added.]

It is so ordered.

ALDERMAN, C.J., and ADKINS, BOYD, McDONALD, EHRLICH and SHAW, JJ., concur.

Many questions have arisen concerning the existence of conflict jurisdiction where one of the decisions allegedly generating the conflict is a decision which is affirmed per curiam without opinion. What constitutes a conflict? Can a conflict exist in this situation after the 1980 amendment? What is the effect of dissenting or concurring opinions? Can they identify conflicts which are not identified because of the lack of a majority opinion? The following cases provide some answers to these questions.

Jenkins v. State

385 So. 2d 1356 (Fla. 1980)

SUNDBERG, Justice.

We here address the question whether this Court currently has jurisdiction to review a decision of a district court of appeal which reads in its entirety "Per Curiam Affirmed" where a dissenting opinion is filed in the case. We answer the question in the negative.

* * *

After ratification by the people of this state at an election held on March 11, 1980, article V, section 3 of the Florida Constitution pertaining to the jurisdiction of the Supreme Court was substantially revised. In particular, section 3(b)(3) underwent a dramatic change. Prior to April 1, 1980 (the effective date of the amendment), the provisions of section 3(b)(3) relating to review of conflicting decisions read as follows:

> May review by certiorari any decision of a district court of appeal . . . that is in direct conflict with a decision of any district court of appeal or of the supreme court on the same question of law. . . .

Post April 1, 1980, that section reads with respect to review of conflicting decisions:

> May review any decision of a district court of appeal . . . that *expressly* and directly conflicts with a decision of another district court of appeal or of the supreme court on the same question of law. . . .

(Emphasis supplied.)

The constitutional amendment must be viewed in light of the historical development of the decisional law extant at the time of its adoption and the intent of the framers and adopters. Our inquiry must begin with the amendment to article V of the Florida Constitution occurring in 1956, whereby the district courts of appeal were created. In grappling with the significance of the revised jurisdiction of this Court, a tone was set early on. In *Ansin v. Thurston*, 101 So.2d 808, 810 (Fla.1958), speaking through Justice Drew, the Court said:

> We have heretofore pointed out that under the constitutional plan the powers of this Court to review decisions of the district courts of appeal are limited and strictly prescribed. *Diamond Berk Insurance Agency, Inc. v. Goldstein*, Fla., 100 So.2d 420; *Sinnamon v. Fowlkes*, Fla., 101 So.2d 375. It was never intended that the district courts of appeal should be intermediate courts. The revision and modernization of the Florida judicial system at the appellate level was prompted by the great volume of cases reaching the Supreme Court and the consequent delay in the administration of justice. The new article embodies throughout its terms the idea of a Supreme Court which functions as a supervisory body in the judicial system for the State, exercising appellate power in certain specified areas essential to the settlement of issues of public importance and the preservation of uniformity of principle and practice, with review by the district courts in most instances being final and absolute.
>
> To fail to recognize that these are courts primarily of final appellate jurisdiction and to allow such courts to become intermediate courts of appeal, would result in a condition far more detrimental to the general welfare and the speedy and efficient administration of justice than that which the system was designed to remedy.

This was followed by *Lake v. Lake*, 103 So.2d 639 (Fla.1958), where Justice Thomas again reviewed the history of and purposes for the 1956 amendment to article V and held that in order to fulfill those purposes, a "per curiam" decision without opinion of a district court of appeal would not be reviewed by this Court upon petition for certiorari based on "direct conflict" jurisdiction except in those rare cases where the "restricted examination required in proceedings in certiorari [revealed] that a conflict had arisen with resulting injustice to the immediate litigant." *Id.* at 643. Some seven years later, however, in an opinion which observed that the rule of *Lake v. Lake* had been eroded *de facto* if not *de jure* by subsequent actions of the Court, a majority of the Court determined that there was jurisdictional power under section 3(b)(3) to review district court decisions rendered "per curiam" without opinion if from the "record proper" conflict with another decision be discerned. *Foley v. Weaver Drugs, Inc.*, 177 So.2d 221 (Fla.1965).

In the interim the Court had already concluded that conflict certiorari jurisdiction could be founded on a dissenting opinion to a per curiam majority decision rendered without opinion. *Huguley v. Hall*, 157 So.2d 417 (Fla.1963). . . .

More recently, the wisdom of the jurisdictional policies expressed in *Foley* and *Huguley* have been brought into question by several members of this Court. *See Florida Greyhound Owners & Breeders Association, Inc. v. West Flagler Associates, Ltd.*, 347 So.2d 408 (Fla.1977) (England, J., concurring; Overton, C. J., concurring specially); *Golden Loaf Bakery, Inc. v. Charles W. Rex Constr. Co.*, 334 So.2d 585, 586 (Fla.1976) (England, J., and Overton C. J., concurring); *AB CTC v. Morejon*, 324 So.2d 625, 628 (Fla.1975) (England and Overton, JJ., dissenting).

It was against this jurisprudential backdrop and in the face of a staggering case load that in November, 1979, this Court urged the legislature, meeting in special session, to enact a proposed amendment to section 3 of article V of the Florida Constitution to limit the jurisdiction of the Supreme Court. . . . The legislature responded through enactment of Senate Joint Resolution No. 20-C, which forms the language of the current section 3 of article V.

* * *

The pertinent language of section 3(b)(3), as amended April 1, 1980, leaves no room for doubt. This Court may only review a decision of a district court of appeal that *expressly* and directly conflicts with a decision of another district court of appeal or the Supreme Court on the same question of law. The dictionary definitions of the term "express" include: "to represent in words"; "to give expression to." "Expressly" is defined: "in an express manner." *Webster's Third New International Dictionary*, (1961 ed. unabr.). The single word "affirmed" comports with none of these definitions. Furthermore, the language and expressions found in a dissenting or concurring opinion cannot support jurisdiction under section 3(b)(3) because they are not the *decision* of the district court of appeal. As stated by Justice Adkins in *Gibson v. Maloney*, 231 So.2d 823, 824 (Fla.1970), "[i]t is conflict of *decisions*, not conflict of *opinions* or *reasons* that supplies jurisdiction for review by certiorari." (Emphasis in original.)

Accordingly, we hold that from and after April 1, 1980, the Supreme Court of Florida lacks jurisdiction to review per curiam decisions of the several district courts of appeal of this state rendered without opinion, regardless of whether they are accompanied by a dissenting or concurring opinion, when the basis for such review is an

4 · THE COURTS

alleged conflict of that decision with a decision of another district court of appeal or of the Supreme Court. The application for review in the instant case having been filed subsequent to March 31, 1980, it is therefore dismissed.

ENGLAND, C. J., and BOYD, OVERTON, ALDERMAN and McDONALD, JJ., concur.

ENGLAND, C. J., concurs specially with an opinion.

ADKINS, J., dissents with an opinion.

[These opinions are omitted.]

Dodi Publishing Co. v. Editorial America, S. A.

385 So. 2d 1369 (Fla. 1980)

OVERTON, Justice.

This is a petition filed April 7, 1980, seeking review of the following per curiam opinion of the Third District Court of Appeal:

PER CURIAM

Affirmed. *See Consolidated Electric Supply, Inc. v. Consolidated Electrical Distributors Southeast, Inc.*, 355 So.2d 853 (Fla. 3d DCA 1978).

The petitioner contends that the cited case, *Consolidated Electric Supply, Inc. v. Consolidated Electrical Distributors Southeast, Inc.*, conflicts with *Williamson v. Answer Phone of Jacksonville*, 118 So.2d 248 (Fla. 1st DCA 1960), and theretofore the instant opinion conflicts with another Florida appellate decision.

The jurisdiction of this Court in this cause in controlled by section 3(b)(3) of article V of the Constitution of the State of Florida, as amended March 11, 1980, effective April 1, 1980, which provides that the Supreme Court: "May review any decision of a district court of appeal . . . that expressly and directly conflicts with a decision of another district court of appeal or of the supreme court on the same question of law." A full discussion of the history and purpose of section 3 of article V, as amended, is contained in *Jenkins v. State*, No. 59,087, 385 So.2d 1356 (Fla. June 26, 1980).

We reject the assertion that we should reexamine a case cited in a per curiam decision to determine if the contents of that cited case now conflict with other appellate decisions. The issue to be decided from a petition for conflict review is whether there is express and direct conflict in the decision of the district court before us for review, not whether there is conflict in a prior written opinion which is now cited for authority.

The petition is dismissed.

SUNDBERG, C. J., and BOYD, ENGLAND, ALDERMAN and McDONALD, JJ., concur.

ADKINS, J., dissents for reasons expressed in *Jenkins*.

In spite of everything said in the two immediately preceding cases, *Jenkins* and *Dodi*, in 1983 the Florida Supreme Court decided the following case.

Stevens v. Jefferson
436 So. 2d 33 (Fla. 1983)

McDONALD, Justice.

We accepted jurisdiction in this cause because the per curiam affirmance* by the district court indicated contrary authority. We have jurisdiction pursuant to article V, section 3(b)(3) of the state constitution.

* * *

ALDERMAN, C.J., and OVERTON and EHRLICH, JJ., concur.

ADKINS, J., concurs in result only.

BOYD, J., dissents with an opinion.

BOYD, Justice, dissenting.

I respectfully dissent to the action of the court in accepting jurisdiction to review the decision of the district court of appeal. The district court's order of affirmance reads in its entirety as follows:

PER CURIAM.

See Orlando Executive Park, Inc. v. P.D.R., 402 So.2d 442 (Fla. 5th DCA 1981); *Fernandez v. Miami Jai-Alai, Inc.*, 386 So.2d 4 (Fla. 3d DCA 1980). *But see Worth v. Stahl*, 388 So.2d 340 (Fla. 4th DCA 1980); *Warner v. Florida Jai Alai*, 221 So.2d 777 (Fla. 4th DCA 1969), *cert. discharged*, 235 So.2d 294 (Fla.1970), which we deem to be in conflict with this decision.

AFFIRMED.

Stevens v. Jefferson, 408 So.2d 634 (Fla. 5th DCA 1981). The order of affirmance is not an opinion in the sense of a discussion, analysis, or statement of the principles of law applied in reaching the decision. Therefore it cannot be, and is not, in express and direct conflict with another decision. Art. V, § 3(b)(3), Fla. Const. Nor does the statement of the district court judges that they "deem" certain decisions "to be in conflict with" their decision in this case suffice as a certification of direct conflict. Art. V, § 3(b)(4), Fla. Const. Therefore, we do not have jurisdiction.

The district court's order merely cites several cases and suggests that some contrary authority exists. It does not contain any statement of law capable of causing confusion or disharmony in the law of the state. Therefore it is not the kind of decision which article V, section 3(b)(3) contemplates as being reviewable by this Court. *See Dodi Publishing Co. v. Editorial America, S.A.*, 385 So.2d 1369 (Fla.1980); *Jenkins v. State*, 385 So.2d 1356 (Fla.1980). The mere suggestion by the district court

---

* *Stevens v. Jefferson*, 408 So.2d 634 (Fla. 5th DCA 1981).

that contrary authority exists, without discussing any points of law, should not be deemed sufficient to create express and direct conflict. *State Farm Mutual Automobile Insurance Co. v. Lawrence*, 401 So.2d 1326 (Fla.1981) (Boyd, J., dissenting).

The majority opinion uses the present case as an opportunity to issue some pronouncements on the law of a tavern keeper's liability even though the district court, in affirming the judgment, did not even find that the case was sufficiently important, complex, or difficult as to require the writing of an opinion. The 1980 amendment to article V was the product of a determination by the legislature and the people that this Court should not be able to review any decision it pleases. This is not the kind of case that calls for the expenditure of our judicial labor when the time and attention of this Court has become such a scarce commodity.

For the foregoing reasons I would discharge the petition for review as improvidently granted. I dissent.

While the authors agree with Justice Boyd, there is apparently precedent for the Florida Supreme Court to hear such a case. "Moreover, there can be no actual conflict discernible in an opinion containing only a citation to other case law . . . unless the citation explicitly notes a contrary holding of another district court or of this Court."[61] The *Florida Star* Court favored the reader with a "[s]ee *Jollie v. State*" for this proposition.[62]

Perhaps even stranger is *Bemis v. State*,[63] which reads in its entirety as follows:

SHAW, Justice.

We have for review *Bemis v. State*, 667 So.2d 779 (Fla. 2d DCA 1995), based on conflict with *Salazar v. State*, 665 So.2d 1066 (Fla. 4th DCA 1995), *quashed*, 679 So.2d 1183 (Fla.1996). We have jurisdiction. Art. V, § 3(b)(3), Fla. Const. We approve the result in *Bemis* based on *Melbourne v. State*, 679 So.2d 759 (Fla.1996).

It is so ordered.

KOGAN, C.J. and OVERTON, GRIMES, HARDING, WELLS and ANSTEAD, J.J., concur.

The district court opinion in *Bemis* does not even rise to the level of a printed PCA.[64] Instead, it is referenced in a table in the *Southern Reporter* captioned "Florida Decisions Without Published Opinions."[65] Whether an opinion was written by the

---

61. *Beaty v. State*, 701 So. 2d 856, 857 (Fla. 1997) (quoting *The Florida Star v. B.J.F.*, 530 So. 2d 286, 288 n. 3 (Fla. 1988)).

62. *Id.*

63. 682 So. 2d 1096 (Fla. 1996).

64. 667 So. 2d 779 (Fla. 2d Dist. Ct. App. 1995).

65. *Id.*

district court and simply not published, or if no opinion was written, where is there precedential value? Admittedly, if an opinion was written and simply not published, it would probably meet the "expressly" requirement of § 3(b)(3), but why should a law-declaring court take the time to consider it?[66]

Ford Motor Co. v. Kikis

401 So. 2d 1341 (Fla. 1981)

ENGLAND, Justice.

This case presents one issue which we have never addressed and another issue which we have never stopped addressing. The first requires clarification of the "expressly" requirement in this Court's constitutional jurisdiction to resolve conflicting appellate decisions. Art. V, § 3(b)(3), Fla. Const. . . .

On Ford's motion, the trial court vacated a jury verdict for Kikis, directed a verdict for Ford, and entered judgment on the verdict. The court alternatively granted Ford's motion for a new trial[1] on the grounds that the verdict was contrary to the manifest weight of the evidence and that the court had erred in refusing to give an instruction requested by Ford. On appeal, the district court reversed the trial court's judgment, directing that the jury verdict be reinstated and judgment entered for Kikis. *Kikis v. Ford Motor Co.*, 386 So.2d 306 (Fla. 5th DCA 1980). Ford asks us to review that decision on the basis of an express and direct conflict with prior appellate decisions.

The first issue — the meaning of the expressly requirement — arises from the fact that the district court below did not identify a direct conflict of its decision with any other Florida appellate decisions. The court's opinion discusses, however, the basis upon which it reversed the trial court's entry of a directed verdict for Ford. This discussion, of the legal principles which the court applied supplies a sufficient basis for a petition for conflict review. It is not necessary that a district court explicitly identify conflicting district court or supreme court decisions in its opinion in order to create an "express" conflict under section 3(b)(3).[2]

* * *

SUNDBERG, C. J., and ADKINS, BOYD, OVERTON and ALDERMAN, JJ., concur.

---

66. One of the authors can recall using the phrase "precedential value" years ago in regard to a PCA. He has since seen the phrase in a reported opinion. He does not know which came first.

1. The order provided that "should the foregoing Final Judgment be reversed by the Appellate Court, the Defendant's Motion for New Trial . . . is . . . granted. . . ."

2. *See* England, Hunter & Williams, *Constitutional Jurisdiction of the Supreme Court of Florida: 1980 Reform*, 32 U. Fla. L. Rev. 147, 188–89 (1980).

Jollie v. State

405 So. 2d 418 (Fla. 1981)

PER CURIAM.

This case involves the legal issue we recently resolved in *Tascano v. State*, 393 So.2d 540 (Fla. 1980), and a procedural issue regarding the jurisdiction of this court which requires clarification in light of the 1980 amendment to article V, section 3, of the Florida Constitution. It is the latter issue which commands our attention here, and for which a recitation of the history of this case and of conflicting decisions on the *Tascano* issue is essential.

On January 2, 1980, the Fifth District Court of Appeal addressed a legal issue concerning requested jury instructions on which disparate views were then held among the district courts of the state. In *Murray v. State*, 378 So.2d 111 (Fla. 5th DCA 1980), a majority of the panel court concluded that this Court's rule on requested instructions was mandatory. A contrary view had been expressed by a panel of judges in the First District Court of Appeal in *Tascano v. State*, 363 So.2d 405 (Fla. 1st DCA 1978). Despite their conclusion on the mandatory nature of the rule, however, the panel majority in *Murray* affirmed his conviction on the ground that the failure to give requested instructions in his situation was harmless error. Judge Orfinger agreed with the *Tascano* judges that the Court's rule was optional, for which reason he concurred in the court's affirmance of Murray's conviction.

Other cases involving this very legal issue were pending in the Fifth District. Shortly after the *Murray* decision was published, the court entered orders summarily disposing of three of them — *Knight v. State*, 379 So.2d 1017 (Fla. 5th DCA 1980), *Allen v. State*, 380 So.2d 541 (Fla. 5th DCA 1980), and *Jollie v. State*, 381 So.2d 351 (Fla. 5th DCA 1980). Each of these dispositions read simply:

"Affirmed. *See Murray v. State* [citation]."

Petitions for certiorari were filed here in *Murray*, *Knight*, and *Allen* before April 1, 1980. A petition for review was filed in *Jollie* after that date. The intervention of the 1980 amendment placed Mr. Jollie in a different position than Messrs. Murray, Knight, or Allen with respect to the possibility of Supreme Court review. That fortuity, it will be seen, has created the procedural problem we now face.

We agreed to review the First District's *Tascano* decision, and we eventually declared that our rule regarding requested jury instructions is indeed mandatory, quashing the district court's contrary decision. *Tascano v. State*, 393 So.2d 540 (Fla. 1980). We accepted jurisdiction in *Murray* on the basis of direct jurisdictional conflict. The *Murray* decision conflicted on its face with the First District's decision in *Tascano* by holding that the rule was mandatory rather than directory and conflicted with the result we reached in *Tascano* because it negated the mandatory effect of the rule by applying the harmless error doctrine. We have consequently this day, by separate opinion in *Murray* on the basis of *Tascano*, concluding that the harmless error rule should not apply. *Murray v. State*, 403 So.2d 417 (Fla. 1981). We have also accepted jurisdiction in *Knight* and *Allen* under the 1972 constitutional provision and granted relief in accordance with decisions in *Tascano* and *Murray. Knight v. State,* 401 So.2d 1333 (Fla. 1981).

Petitioner Jollie's treatment by the Fifth District Court of Appeal was identical to that of Allen and Knight. Jollie, however, became the victim of happenstance, delayed processing through the district court resulting in his case reaching this Court after the effective date of the 1980 constitutional amendment limiting Supreme Court jurisdiction.

Under our interpretation of the 1980 amendment, this Court will not reexamine the case referenced in a "citation PCA" to determine whether the contents of that case now conflict with other appellate decisions. *Dodi Publishing Co. v. Editorial America, S.A.,* 385 So.2d 1369 (Fla. 1980). In a similar light, if the referenced case is a final decision and not pending review in this Court, we will not reexamine the case referenced even when the district court filed that case contemporaneously with the citation PCA. *Robles Del Mar, Inc. v. Town of Indian River Shores*, 385 So.2d 1371 (Fla. 1980). The question which we must now confront is in what posture we should place a citation PCA where the cited case is either pending review in this Court or has previously been reversed by this Court. Restated, we must decide whether Mr. Jollie should be denied relief because he was the recipient of such a decision after the effective date of the 1980 amendment.

The quartet of *Tascano*-related cases from the Fifth District Court of Appeal presents the problem in sharp focus. We here endeavor to deal with this situation in a forthright manner in order to provide clear directions for the avoidance of future difficulties in like situations. This can be done without undermining the intent and purpose of the 1980 reforms.

* * *

Prior to the 1980 amendment, a PCA decision which referenced another district court decision that this Court had reversed or quashed, was prima facie grounds for conflict jurisdiction. This long-standing policy decision was in effect well before the "record proper" doctrine was conceived and adopted in *Foley v. Weaver Drugs*, 177 So.2d 211 (Fla. 1965). The reasoning behind that policy decision continues to have validity. Common sense dictates that this Court must acknowledge its own public record actions in dispensing with cases before it. We thus conclude that a district court of appeal per curiam opinion which cites as controlling authority a decision that is either pending review in or has been reversed by this Court continues to constitute prima facie express conflict and allows this Court to exercise its jurisdiction.

The situation presented in this cause ordinarily applies only to a limited class of cases. The problem arises from the practical situation which faces all appellate courts at one time or another—that is, how to dispose conveniently of multiple cases involving a single legal issue without disparately affecting the various litigants. Traditional practice in dealing with a common legal issue in multiple cases, both in district courts and here, has been to author an opinion for one case and summarily reference that opinion on all others. Being time- [sic] and laborsaving for a court, that practice should not be discouraged.

We believe, however, that there can be improvement in the procedure through which district courts can isolate for possible review in this Court those decisions which merely reference to a lead opinion, as we now have for review, as distinguished from those per curiam opinions which merely cite counsel-advising cases such as in *Dodi Publishing*. There are two prongs to the problem, and we believe each can be treated by the judges of the district courts without undue problems.

First, we suggest the district courts add an additional sentence in each citation PCA which references a controlling contemporaneous or companion case, stating that the mandate will be withheld pending final disposition of the petition for review, if any, filed in the controlling decision. In essence, this will "pair" the citation PCA with the referenced decision in the district court until it is final without review or if review is sought, until that review is denied or otherwise acted upon by this Court. If review of the referenced decision is requested the parties may seek consolidation here. In any event, the district courts' withholding of the mandates will dispose of the need for separate motions to stay mandates in those courts. This simple process, moreover, can be accomplished administratively in the district courts, in the clerks' offices, without significant activity by the judges either before or after the controlling decision is filed with or acted upon by this Court.

A second aspect of the problem calls for a different approach. We recognize that no litigant can guide the district court's selection of the lead case, and that the randomness of the district court's processing would control the party's right of review unless the citation PCA is itself made eligible for review by this Court. To resolve fully this problem we further suggest that the district courts devise one or more methods to distinguish a contemporaneous or companion case — for example, with distinguishing citation signals or by certifying that an identical point is at issue in the cited case* — from cases which offer a mere counsel notification citation. We have no doubt that district court judges can produce one or more methodologies to preserve the review strictures of the 1980 amendment on the one hand, while on the other eliminating the possible injustice inherent in foreclosing review to some of several equally situated litigants.

We reaffirm that mere citation PCA decisions rendered in the traditional form will remain nonreviewable by this Court, for the reasons stated in *Dodi Publishing* and *Robles Del Mar*. The circumstances of those cases are clearly distinguishable from a district court PCA opinion which cites as controlling a case that is pending review in or has been reversed by this Court.

---

  * As an example of the possibilities, see the certification on rehearing in *Griffin v. State*, 389 So.2d 261 (Fla. 4th DCA 1980), pending in this Court (No. 59,964), which states:

    [W]e certify that our affirmance in this case passed upon the same questions we certified . . . in *Lawrence v. State* [388 So.2d 1250 (Fla.App.)]. . . . The decision in this case should abide the decision in *Lawrence*.

We grant review in this proceeding and quash the districts court's decision on the basis of our decisions in *Murray v. State* and *Tascano v. State*.

It is so ordered.

SUNDBERG, C.J., and OVERTON, ENGLAND and McDONALD, JJ., concur.

ADKINS, J., concurs in result only.

BOYD, J., dissents with an opinion.

ALDERMAN, J., dissents.

[The dissenting opinion of Justice Boyd is omitted.]

In Justice Boyd's eloquent dissent, he makes the following comment:[67]

> The majority opinion says that even before *Foley v. Weaver Drugs, Inc.,* [*see Jenkins* for a discussion of *Foley*] a district court decision without opinion but citing a case that had been reversed by the supreme court provided prima facie ground for the exercise of conflict jurisdiction. I have been unable to find any decisional or documentary authority for that statement. The majority cites only "common sense," and refers us to Justice Thomas's formulation of conflict certiorari jurisdiction in *Lake v. Lake*, 103 So.2d 639 (Fla. 1958).

Justice Boyd then establishes, to the authors' satisfaction, that Justice Thomas' comments could only have been an early statement of the "record proper" rule in *Foley*.[68] Justice Boyd then argues, at least by inference, that the 1980 amendment would have outlawed the "pending review or been reversed" rule as set out in *Jollie* no matter what its provenance.[69] The authors agree.

The *Jollie* exception to the "expressly" conflict requirement in § 3(b)(3) has become firmly rooted in Florida jurisprudence. Accordingly, a district court of appeal per curiam opinion which cites as controlling authority a decision that is either pending review in or has been reversed by the Florida Supreme Court continues to constitute prima facie express conflict and allows the Supreme Court to exercise its jurisdiction. The following cases reflect this concept.

---

67. *Jollie v. State*, 405 So. 2d at 423 (Boyd, J., dissenting).
68. *Id.*
69. *Id.* at 423–425.

Harrison v. Hyster Co.

515 So. 2d 1279 (Fla. 1987)

PER CURIAM.

The district court of appeal in *Harrison v. Hyster Co.*, 502 So.2d 100 (Fla. 2d DCA 1987), affirmed the dismissal of petitioners' product liability action upon the authority of *Small v. Niagara Machine & Tool Works*, 502 So.2d 943 (Fla. 2d DCA 1987). The only basis upon which it could be asserted that this Court had jurisdiction to review the *Harrison* decision was the rationale of *Jollie v. State*, 405 So.2d 418 (Fla. 1981), in which we said:

> We thus conclude that a district court of appeal per curiam opinion which cites as controlling authority a decision that is either pending review in or has been reversed by this Court continues to constitute prima facie express conflict and allows this Court to exercise its jurisdiction.

Id. at 420. Since a petition for review of *Small* had been filed in this Court, we accepted jurisdiction on the petition for review filed in the instant case. Subsequently, however, this Court declined to accept jurisdiction in *Small* and denied the petition for review. *Small v. Niagara Machine & Tool Works*, 511 So.2d 999 (Fla. 1987).

The anomaly of reviewing a decision because it was decided upon the authority of another decision which was never reviewed on the merits by this Court has caused us to conclude that we should not have accepted jurisdiction of this case until it was determined to accept jurisdiction in *Small*. *Jollie's* reference to the "controlling authority ... that is ... pending review" refers to a case in which the petition for jurisdictional review has been granted and the case is pending for disposition on the merits. Since *Small* never reached that status, our order accepting jurisdiction in this case was improvidently issued, and we now deny the petition for review.

It is so ordered.

McDONALD, C.J., and OVERTON, EHRLICH, SHAW, BARKETT, GRIMES and KOGAN, JJ., concur.

Wells v. State

132 So. 3d 1110 (Fla. 2014)

PER CURIAM.

Petitioner Arrington R. Wells has filed a notice to invoke this Court's discretionary jurisdiction, pursuant to article V, section 3(b)(3), of the Florida Constitution. Wells seeks review of an unelaborated per curiam decision of the First District Court of Appeal, dismissing his petition to invoke the First District's all writs jurisdiction on the authority of *Baker v. State*, 878 So.2d 1236 (Fla.2004), and *Pettway v. State*, 776 So.2d 930 (Fla.2000). *See Wells v. State*, 114 So.3d 1037, 1038 (Fla. 1st DCA 2013). Wells alleges that the First District's decision expressly and directly conflicts with numerous other district court decisions regarding illegal sentences.

We dismiss Wells' petition for review for lack of jurisdiction. We also take this opportunity to clarify our intention to apply the reasoning of *Gandy v. State*, 846 So.2d 1141 (Fla.2003), to unelaborated dismissals from the district courts of appeal that, like the First District's decision in this case, merely cite to a case not pending review in, or not quashed or reversed by, this Court, or to a statute or rule of procedure, and do not contain any discussion of the facts in the case "such that it could be said that the district court 'expressly addresse[d] a question of law within the four corners of the opinion itself.' "*Id.* at 1144 (quoting *Fla. Star v. B.J.F.*, 530 So.2d 286, 288 (Fla.1988)).

Applying our decisions in *Gandy* and other prior cases holding that this Court lacks discretionary review jurisdiction over unelaborated per curiam affirmances and denials, we conclude that the analysis in those cases is equally valid as to unelaborated per curiam dismissals, such as the First District's decision in this case. Because this Court lacks discretionary review jurisdiction under the Florida Constitution to review this type of case, we authorize the Office of the Clerk to administratively dismiss future petitions for review in similar cases.

Facts

As in all petitions seeking this Court's discretionary jurisdiction pursuant to article V, section 3(b)(3), we are confined to consider only those facts contained within the four corners of the district court's majority opinion. *See Reaves v. State*, 485 So.2d 829, 830 (Fla.1986). In this case, the decision of the First District as to Wells' petition to invoke the district court's all writs jurisdiction reads in its entirety as follows:

PER CURIAM.

DISMISSED. *See Baker v. State*, 878 So.2d 1236 (Fla.2004); *see also Pettway v. State*, 776 So.2d 930 (Fla.2000).

Wells, 114 So.3d at 1038. Wells asserts in his jurisdictional filings in this Court that he is currently serving an illegally enhanced sentence as a Prison Release Reoffender (PRR) because the release date used to qualify Wells as a PRR originated from a temporary detention. He therefore contends that the First District erred in dismissing his all writs petition and that this Court should grant discretionary review to address the merits of his illegal sentence claim, alleging that an express and direct conflict exists between the First District's decision and several decisions of other district courts of appeal relating to the legality of PRR sentences.

Analysis

Article V, section 3(b), of the Florida Constitution governs the jurisdiction of the Florida Supreme Court. As we have explained, this jurisdiction "extends only to the narrow class of cases enumerated" in that constitutional provision. *Gandy*, 846 So.2d at 1143 (quoting *Mystan Marine, Inc. v. Harrington*, 339 So.2d 200, 201 (Fla.1976)).

In a line of cases beginning with *Jenkins v. State*, 385 So.2d 1356 (Fla.1980), this Court addressed the limits of its jurisdiction under article V, section 3(b), to review unelaborated per curiam decisions of the district courts of appeal. In *Jenkins*, 385 So.2d at 1359, this Court held that it lacked jurisdiction to review per curiam decisions of the district courts of appeal "rendered without opinion, regardless of whether they are accompanied by a dissenting or concurring opinion, when the basis for such review is an alleged conflict of that decision with a decision of another district court of appeal or of the Supreme Court." This Court reasoned that the single word "affirmed" in a decision stating in its entirety, "Per Curiam Affirmed," cannot satisfy the constitutional requirement that a decision must "expressly" conflict with a decision of another district court of appeal or of this Court in order to vest this Court with jurisdiction. *Id.*

Subsequently, in *Dodi Publishing Co. v. Editorial America, S.A.*, 385 So.2d 1369 (Fla.1980), and *Jollie v. State*, 405 So.2d 418 (Fla.1981), this Court extended the reasoning of *Jenkins*. When read together, *Dodi Publishing* and *Jollie* "stand for the proposition that this Court does not have jurisdiction to review per curiam decisions of the district courts of appeal that merely affirm with citations to cases not pending review in this Court." *Persaud v. State*, 838 So.2d 529, 531–32 (Fla.2003). This Court has since explained that, "while the holding in *Dodi Publishing* expressly applied only to per curiam decisions from the district courts citing to cases not pending on review in this Court, we had historically applied the decision in *Dodi Publishing* to district court decisions merely citing to a statute, a rule, or a decision of the United States Supreme Court or this Court." *Gandy*, 846 So.2d at 1143 (citing *Persaud*, 838 So.2d at 532).

In *Florida Star*, this Court succinctly summed up its prior decisions in *Dodi Publishing* and *Jollie*, explaining that this Court does not

> have subject-matter jurisdiction over a district court opinion that fails to expressly address a question of law, such as opinions issued without opinion or citation. Thus, a district court decision rendered without opinion or citation constitutes a decision from the highest state court empowered to hear the cause, and appeal may be taken directly to the United States Supreme Court. Moreover, there can be no actual conflict discernible in an opinion containing only a citation to other case law unless one of the cases cited as controlling authority is pending before this Court, or has been reversed on appeal or review, or receded from by this Court, or unless the citation explicitly notes a contrary holding of another district court or of this Court. *See Jollie v. State*, 405 So.2d 418, 420 (Fla.1981).

Fla. Star, 530 So.2d at 288 n. 3.

More recently, in *Stallworth v. Moore*, 827 So.2d 974, 978 (Fla.2002), this Court further extended the reasoning of *Jenkins* and subsequent cases relating to per curiam affirmances without written opinion to unelaborated per curiam *denials* of relief, holding that "this Court does not have discretionary review jurisdiction . . . to review per curiam denials of relief, issued without opinion or explanation, whether they be in opinion form or by way of unpublished order."

Thereafter, in *Gandy,* we further held that this Court does not have discretionary review jurisdiction to review "per curiam unelaborated denials of relief from the district courts of appeal that . . . merely cite to a case not pending on review in this Court, or to a statute or rule of procedure, and do not contain any discussion of the facts in the case such that it could be said that the district court 'expressly addresse[d] a question of law within the four corners of the opinion itself.' "*Gandy,* 846 So.2d at 1144 (quoting *Fla. Star,* 530 So.2d at 288).

Accordingly, based on our case law since *Jenkins,* it is clear that we have explicitly held that this Court lacks discretionary review jurisdiction over the following four types of cases: (1) a per curiam affirmance rendered without written opinion — *see Jenkins,* 385 So.2d at 1359; (2) a per curiam affirmance with a citation to (i) a case not pending review or a case that has not been quashed or reversed by this Court, (ii) a rule of procedure, or (iii) a statute — *see Dodi Publishing,* 385 So.2d at 1369, and *Jollie,* 405 So.2d at 421; (3) a per curiam or other unelaborated denial of relief rendered without written opinion — *see Stallworth,* 827 So.2d at 978; and (4) a per curiam or other unelaborated denial of relief with a citation to (i) a case not pending review or a case that has not been quashed or reversed by this Court, (ii) a rule of procedure, or (iii) a statute — *see Gandy,* 846 So.2d at 1144. None of these four scenarios, however, specifically addresses the situation presented in this case: an unelaborated per curiam *dismissal* with a citation to cases not pending review in, and not quashed or reversed by, this Court.

Applying this Court's decisions in *Jenkins, Dodi Publishing, Stallworth,* and *Gandy* to the notice to invoke this Court's discretionary jurisdiction filed in this case, we conclude that our analysis in those cases as to unelaborated per curiam affirmances and denials is equally valid as to unelaborated per curiam dismissals. We therefore hold that this Court does not have discretionary review jurisdiction over unelaborated per curiam dismissals from the district courts of appeal (1) that are issued without opinion or explanation, whether in opinion form or by way of unpublished order; or (2) that, like the First District's decision in Wells' case, merely cite to a case not pending review in, or not quashed or reversed by, this Court, or to a statute or rule of procedure, and do not contain any discussion of the facts in the case such that it could be said that the district court "expressly addresse[d] a question of law within the four corners of the opinion itself." *Fla. Star,* 530 So.2d at 288.

As we did in *Gandy,* we also take this opportunity to explain that in the future, we will apply the reasoning of this opinion, *Jenkins, Dodi Publishing, Stallworth,* and *Gandy* to similar cases and will dismiss review for lack of jurisdiction. We hereby authorize the Office of the Clerk to administratively dismiss future petitions for review in similar cases.

Conclusion

For the reasons explained above, we hold that this Court lacks discretionary review jurisdiction to review an unelaborated per curiam dismissal from a district court of appeal that is issued without opinion or explanation or that merely cites to a case not pending review in, or reversed or quashed by, this Court, or to a statute or rule of procedure. Accordingly, we dismiss Wells' petition for review.

POLSTON, C.J., and PARIENTE, QUINCE, CANADY, LABARGA, and PERRY, JJ., concur.

LEWIS, J., concurs in result.

Section II(B)(1)(a) of the Florida Supreme Court's *Manual of Internal Operating Procedures* now takes into account the citation PCA where the cited case is either pending review in the Florida Supreme Court or has been reversed by that Court:[70]

> When a party files a notice seeking to invoke discretionary review, the clerk's office determines whether the case is subject to administrative dismissal based on a lack of jurisdiction. If the clerk's office determines that the case is subject to administrative dismissal, the case is docketed and automatically dismissed. In such cases, no rehearing is allowed. The clerk's office will administratively dismiss those cases in which a party seeks discretionary review from:
>
> > (1) a per curiam affirmance (PCA) without written opinion. *See Jenkins v. State*, 385 So. 2d 1356 (Fla. 1980).
> >
> > (2) a per curiam affirmance (PCA) with a citation or citations to a case not pending on review or a case that has not been quashed or reversed by the Court, a rule of procedure, or a statute. *See Dodi Publishing Co. v. Editorial America, S.A.*, 385 So. 2d 1369 (Fla. 1980).
> >
> > (3) a per curiam denial of relief (PCD) without written opinion or other unelaborated denial of relief. *See Stallworth v. Moore*, 827 So. 2d 974 (Fla. 2002).
> >
> > (4) a per curiam denial of relief (PCD), or other unelaborated denial of relief, with a citation or citations to a case not pending on review or a case that has not been quashed or reversed by the Court, a rule of procedure, or a statute. *See Gandy v. State*, 846 So. 2d 1141 (Fla. 2003); or
> >
> > (5) a per curiam dismissal of a case without written opinion or other unelaborated dismissal of a case, see *Wells v. State*, 132 So. 3d 1110 (Fla. 2014).

Two other facets of the PCA problem should be mentioned:

(1) Should a citation PCA which contains a one-sentence parenthetical explanation be considered a case in which an opinion is written?

---

70. *The Supreme Court of Florida Manual of Internal Operating Procedures* (rev'd Feb. 18, 2021), https://www.floridasupremecourt.org/content/download/241274/file/02-18-2021-Florida-Supreme -Court-Internal-Operating-Procedures-Manual.pdf.

Jenkins v. State

634 So. 2d 1143 (Fla. 3d Dist. Ct. App. 1994)

Before SCHWARTZ, C.J., and BASKIN and LEVY, JJ.

PER CURIAM.

Affirmed. *See Massey v. State*, 609 So.2d 598 (Fla.1992) (failure to give notice of habitualization harmless error).

(2) What, if anything, should be done about the following method of reversing the trial court?

Ogden Aviation Services v. Dar

635 So. 2d 50 (Fla. 1st Dist. Ct. App. 1994)

PER CURIAM.

REVERSED. *S.E. Environmental Contractors, Inc. v. Cayasso*, 611 So.2d 7 (Fla. 1st DCA 1992).

BOOTH, LAWRENCE and DAVIS, JJ., concur.

This question apparently has been answered in the following case:

O'Neal v. State

682 So. 2d 1095 (Fla. 1996)

WELLS, Justice.

We have for review the decision of the district court in *State v. O'Neal*, 673 So.2d 881 (Fla. 2d DCA 1996) [PCR], in which the court expressly relied on *Jennings v. State*, 667 So.2d 442 (Fla. 1st DCA 1996). We have jurisdiction. Art. V, § 3(b)(3), Fla. Const.

This Court recently approved the district court's decision in *Jennings. Jennings v. State*, 682 So.2d 144 (Fla.1996). Accordingly, we approve the district court's decision below.

It is so ordered.

KOGAN, C.J., and OVERTON, SHAW, GRIMES, HARDING and ANSTEAD, JJ., concur.

The reader will also note that in *O'Neal*, the "pending review or has been reversed" rule has been apparently expanded to include "recently approved," as well.

Once the Supreme Court accepts jurisdiction to hear an appeal to resolve an alleged conflict of decisions between district courts or between a district court and the Supreme Court on the same issue of law, it may, in its discretion, consider other issues properly raised and argued before the court although the other issues were not the ones on which jurisdiction was based.[71]

(5) "May review any decision of a district court of appeal that passes upon a question certified by it to be of great public importance ..." Fla. Const. art. V, § 3(b)(4)

The 1980 amendment substituted the word "importance" for the word "interest" used in the predecessor provision. This change was explained in the committee notes to the 1980 amendment of the Florida Rules of Appellate Procedure: "The change was to recognize the fact that some legal issues may have 'great public importance,' but may not be sufficiently known by the public to have 'great public interest.'"[72] Although the common practice is now for the district courts of appeal to explicitly set out the question to be certified, the failure to formulate the question does not render the Supreme Court of its jurisdiction to review the case.[73] As the Court explained in *Rupp v. Jackson*,[74] "Presentation of a precise question enhances the probability that we will pass upon the specific question in mind below; furthermore, preciseness may contribute significantly to our decision whether to pass upon the merits of the case at all, a decision which remains solely within our prerogative under the constitution."

This jurisdictional provision obviously exists to "expedite" important societal issues to the Florida Supreme Court. Nonetheless, in our adversarial system the presentation and briefing of issues are left to the actual parties in litigation. Thus, even if an important societal issue is presented in a case, and is certified as such, it can only be effectively presented to the Florida Supreme Court if the actual parties pursue review. As the Court aptly noted in *Taggart Corp. v. Benzing*,[75] "[m]any lawyers do not realize that questions do not automatically proceed upwards to the Supreme Court merely because we certify them. The losing party at our level still has to exercise the initiative and go forward, otherwise the questions die for lack of appropriate presentation."

The following case addresses the issue of whether review is appropriate where a District Court of Appeal certifies an issue as one of great public importance, but the aggrieved party declines to seek Florida Supreme Court review based on the district court's certified question.

---

71. *See Price v. State*, 995 So. 2d 401 (Fla. 2008).

72. *See In re Emergency Amendments to Rules of Appellate Procedure*, 381 So. 2d 1370, 1375 (Fla. 1980).

73. *Frankelstein v. Dep't of Transp.*, 656 So. 2d 921 (Fla. 1995); *see also Rupp v. Jackson*, 238 So. 2d 86 (Fla. 1970).

74. 238 So. 2d 86 (Fla. 1970).

75. 434 So. 2d 964 (Fla. 4th Dist. Ct. App. 1983).

Petrik v. New Hampshire Insurance Co.

400 So. 2d 8 (Fla. 1981)

ALDERMAN, Justice.

John and Claudine Petrik were passengers in their son David's automobile, driven by David, when it collided with a truck owned by Superior Dairies and driven by Irving Charles, Superior's employee. David's car was insured by Automobile Club of Southern California. The policy excluded coverage for "bodily injury to the named insured or a relative." The Petriks sued Superior Dairies and its insurer, New Hampshire Insurance Company, and Irving Charles. These defendants then filed a third-party complaint seeking contribution against David Petrik and his insurer, Automobile Club of Southern California. David's insurer denied coverage based on the family exclusion clause in its policy. The trial court granted summary judgment against David's insurer on the issue of coverage. On appeal, the insurance company sought reversal of the summary judgment, contending that its family exclusion clause was valid and that it was not responsible for the contribution claim against its insured. The district court, Fla.App., 379 So.2d 1287, rejected this contention and, citing its prior decision in *Florida Farm Bureau Insurance Co. v. Government Employees Insurance Co.*, 371 So.2d 166 (Fla. 1st DCA 1979), it held that family exclusion clauses such as this one did not bar recovery of a third-party contribution claim against a joint tortfeasor's insurer. Pursuant to article V, section 3(b)(3), Florida Constitution (1972), it certified the following question as being one of great public interest.

> Does a family exclusion clause in an automobile insurance policy control over the Uniform Contribution Among Joint Tortfeasors Act to prevent one tortfeasor from seeking contribution from another tortfeasor?

Automobile Club of Southern California, the party adversely affected by the district court's resolution of this question, did not seek review of the district court's decision. Therefore, even though the district court has certified this question as being one of great public interest, we do not have jurisdiction because the certified question has not been brought to us for review. As to these parties, the district court's decision on this issue is final and is the law of the case. This is true even though we have subsequently quashed the district court's decision in *Florida Farm Bureau Insurance Co. v. Government Employees Insurance Co.* and answered the certified question contrary to the holding of the district court. *Florida Farm Bureau Insurance Co. v. Government Employees Insurance Co.*, 387 So.2d 932 (Fla.1980).

Pursuant to article V, section 3(b)(3), Florida Constitution (1972), John and Claudine Petrik, in case No. 57,176, and Richard Williams, Superior Dairies, Inc., and New Hampshire Insurance Company, in case No. 57,179, seek to invoke our jurisdiction on the basis of alleged direct conflicts between the district's decision and other decisions of the district courts of appeal and the Supreme Court. Neither petition is based on the certified question. Having considered the jurisdictional briefs, we conclude that the district court's decision on these other issues has not created such direct conflict as would warrant the exercise of our jurisdiction.

Accordingly, the petitions for certiorari are denied.

No motion for rehearing will be entertained by the Court. *See* Fla.R.App.P. 9.330(d).

SUNDBERG, C. J., and BOYD and McDONALD, JJ., concur.

ADKINS, J., dissents [without opinion].

In order for the court to have discretionary jurisdiction based on a certified question, the following three prerequisites must be met: (1) the district court of appeal must pass upon the question certified by it to be of great public importance; (2) there must be a district court "decision" to review; and (3) the question must be in fact "certified" by a majority decision of the district court. The following case addresses a situation in which only six of the twelve judges who participated in an en banc decision concurred in certification.

Floridians for a Level Playing Field v. Floridians Against Expanded Gambling
967 So. 2d 832 (Fla. 2007)

PARIENTE, J.

We have for review the decision in *Floridians Against Expanded Gambling v. Floridians for a Level Playing Field,* 945 So.2d 553 (Fla. 1st DCA 2006), in which the First District Court of Appeal certified a question to be of great public importance. Initially, the Court accepted review pursuant to article V, section 3(b)(4) of the Florida Constitution, which gives us *discretionary* jurisdiction to review "any decision of a district court of appeal that passes upon a question certified by it to be of great public importance." Upon further consideration, we conclude that jurisdiction was improvidently granted and therefore discharge this case for the two reasons explained below.

In order to have discretionary jurisdiction based on a certified question, there are essentially three prerequisites that must be met. First, it is essential that the district court of appeal pass upon the question certified by it to be of great public importance. We have previously discharged jurisdiction where the district court of appeal has not in fact passed upon the question certified.[1] Second, there must be a district court "decision" to review. *See* art. V, § 3(b)(4), Fla. Const. For instance, where a district court is unable to reach a clear majority decision on an issue and elects to certify a question without resolving the merits, we are without jurisdiction to answer such a question under article V, section 3(b)(4) of the Florida Constitution. *See Boler v. State,* 678 So.2d 319, 320 n. 2 (Fla.1996) (stating that if a district court is evenly split on a legal issue and specifically withholds a decision on the merits, there is no "decision" on which to base certified conflict review under article V, section 3(b)(4)).

---

1. *See Pirelli Armstrong Tire Corp. v. Jensen,* 777 So.2d 973 (Fla.2001); *Salgat v. State,* 652 So.2d 815 (Fla.1995); *Gee v. Seidman & Seidman,* 653 So.2d 384 (Fla.1995).

Third, and most important for this case, the question must be in fact "certified" by a majority decision of the district court. For the same reasons that we are without jurisdiction under article V, section 3(b)(4) if there is no majority decision on the merits, we are equally without jurisdiction if there is no clear majority on the decision to certify. Accordingly, we conclude that under article V, section 3(b)(4) of the Florida Constitution, it is required that a majority of those judges participating in the case concur in the decision to certify.

In this case, only six of the twelve judges that participated in the en banc decision concurred in certification.[2] Five judges, although concurring in the majority decision, disagreed with the decision to certify. Importantly, Judge Benton did not fully concur with the majority decision; rather, Judge Benton only concurred in the judgment. This vote indicates Judge Benton's agreement only with the judgment of the majority; that is, its decision to reverse the summary judgment and remand. *See Home Dev. Co. of St. Petersburg v. Bursani,* 168 So.2d 131, 134 (Fla.1964) (distinguishing between the judgment, which is essentially the ultimate decision in the case, and the opinion, which sets "forth the theory and reasoning upon which a decision" is reached); *see also Black's Law Dictionary* 858 (8th ed. 2004) (defining judgment as "[a] court's final determination of the rights and obligations of the parties in a case"). In this sense, "concurring in the judgment" is akin to "concurring in result only," which "expresses agreement with the ultimate decision but not the opinion." *Rowe v. Winn-Dixie Stores, Inc.,* 714 So.2d 1180, 1181 (Fla. 1st DCA 1998), *disapproved on other grounds by Owens v. Publix Supermarkets, Inc.,* 802 So.2d 315 (Fla.2001); *accord* Harry Lee Anstead, Gerald Kogan, Thomas D. Hall & Robert Craig Waters, *The Operation and Jurisdiction of the Supreme Court of Florida,* 29 Nova L.Rev. 431, 460 (2005) ("A concurring in result only opinion indicates agreement only with the decision, that is, the official outcome and result reached, but a refusal to join in the majority's opinion and its reasoning.").

Conversely, certification is separate from the judgment of the court and its reasoning for the judgment as expressed in its opinion. This is evident by comparing the definition of judgment, i.e., "[a] court's final determination of the rights and obligations of the parties in a case," with the definition of a certified question, i.e., "[a] point of law on which a[n] . . . *appellate court seeks guidance*" from a higher court by the procedure of certification. *Black's Law Dictionary* at 858, 241 (emphasis supplied). Moreover, there are separate and specific rules that both permit a party to file a motion seeking certification and authorize the district court to certify the question. *Compare* Fla. R.App. P. 9.030(a)(2)(A)(v) (granting discretionary jurisdiction to

---

2. Three judges, Judges Browning, Webster and Lewis, concurred in the judgment and the certification; Judge Benton concurred in the judgment only; three judges, Judges Kahn, Ervin, and Wolf, dissented as to the reasoning and result reached by the majority but concurred in the certification; and five judges, Judges Padovano, Barfield, Davis, Polston, and Hawkes, joined "the decision and opinion on this issue presented" but dissented from the court's decision to certify. Three judges, Judges Allen, Van Nortwick and Thomas, did not participate in the en banc panel.

the Court if a district court decision certifies a question), *with* Fla. R.App. P. 9.330(a) (authorizing a party to a file motion for certification to the district court); *cf. Floridians,* 945 So.2d at 562 (reversing summary judgment and remanding for a trial, and then certifying two questions to the Court, specifically in accordance with article V, section 3(b)(4) of the Florida Constitution and Florida Rule of Appellate Procedure 9.030(a)(2)(A)(v)). We conclude that by "concurring in the judgment" and failing to indicate his agreement with the decision to certify, Judge Benton's vote cannot be counted as agreeing with the certification. *Cf. Hadden v. State,* 670 So.2d 77, 83 (Fla. 1st DCA 1996) (Benton, J., concurs in result and in certification) (indicating Judge Benton's agreement with the result *and* the decision to certify, but disagreement with the reasoning of the majority opinion).

[6] Even assuming that we had jurisdiction based on either a certification of a question of great public importance or express and direct conflict under article V, section 3(b)(3) of the Florida Constitution, we would nevertheless decline to exercise our jurisdiction. After having reviewed the opinions from this Court that deal with post-election challenges based on various issues regarding the election process, we have determined that it is preferable that the facts of this case be developed regarding the allegations and pervasiveness of the fraud before we articulate a rule of law regarding the election cure doctrine in such circumstances. This is the position advocated by the Secretary of State, Kurt S. Browning, and the Department of State represented by its General Counsel and the Attorney General. As stated in its answer brief:

> The long-standing principle that an election cures irregularities in the process and thereby promotes finality and administrative efficiency is a weighty one; similarly, the ability of citizens to amend the state constitution through the initiative process without fraud is extremely important. This Court should avoid making rulings affecting the application of these principles until the specific allegations of fraud are adjudicated. A fully-developed record with a proven set of facts will allow this Court to carefully consider and balance the competing legal principles; that cannot properly be done based on speculative, unproven factual allegations.

Answer Brief of Respondent Secretary of State at 6.

We believe that the position of the Attorney General is a sound one and conclude, as an alternative basis for discharging jurisdiction, that review in this case is premature.[3] Accordingly, we hereby discharge jurisdiction and dismiss this review proceeding.

It is so ordered.

---

3. Although we agree that review in this case would be premature, we disagree with Judge Padovano to the extent he reasons that certified question jurisdiction was only "meant to apply to a final decision by a district court of appeal." *Floridians,* 945 So.2d at 568 (Padovano, J., concurring in part and dissenting in part).

LEWIS, C.J., and WELLS, ANSTEAD, QUINCE, CANTERO, and BELL, JJ., concur.

(6) "May review any decision of a district court of appeal . . . that is certified by it to be in direct conflict with a decision of another district court of appeal." Fla. Const. art. V, § 3(b)(4)

This source of conflict jurisdiction does not contain the word "expressly." It seems inconceivable, however, that the drafters of the 1980 amendments to the Florida Supreme Court's jurisdiction, having abolished most conflict jurisdiction in § 3(b)(3) when the district court does not write an opinion, would have intended to let a district court decide a case without opinion and then certify that decision as creating conflict.[76] However, it could be argued that the word "expressly" was left out for just that purpose. In any event, it is likely that the relationship between the two conflict provisions is that the latter will allow the district court to add the weight of its certification to the litigant's request for review when it chooses to do so. The committee notes on the changes to the Florida Rules of Appellate Procedure make no comment other than that the jurisdictional statement in the rules tracks the amended constitutional provision.[77]

Davis v. Mandau

410 So. 2d 915 (Fla. 1981)

ALDERMAN, Justice.

The District Court of Appeal, Second District, in *Davis v. Mandau*, 400 So.2d 89 (Fla.2d DCA 1981), affirmed in summary fashion the trial court's entry of summary judgment for respondents but decided that the trial court erred in entering a cost order in favor of respondent Evans to the extent that it taxed the costs of depositions. The district court then certified that the portion of its decision relating to the

---

76. But see *State v. Creighton*, 438 So. 2d 1042 (Fla. 1st Dist. Ct. App. 1983), where the court's opinion in its entirety reads as follows:

> Appeal dismissed. *Whidden v. State*, 159 Fla. 691, 32 So.2d 577 (1947); *State v. Brown*, 330 So.2d 535 (Fla. 1st DCA 1976); *State v. G.P.*, 429 So.2d 786 (Fla. 3d DCA 1983). We certify that the instant decision directly conflicts with *State v. W.A.M.*, 412 So.2d 49 (Fla. 5th DCA), *rev. denied*, 419 So.2d 1201 (Fla.1982).

The Florida Supreme Court accepted jurisdiction based on this certification and the State's petition for review. *State v. Creighton*, 469 So. 2d 735 (Fla. 1985). Note that *Creighton* has been modified. See the discussion in *State v. Allen, infra*, at page 259. Note also *The Supreme Court of Florida Manual of Internal Operating Procedures* (rev'd Feb. 18, 2021), https://www.floridasupremecourt.org/content/download/241274/file/02-18-2021-Florida-Supreme-Court-Internal-Operating-Procedures-Manual.pdf.

77. *In re Emergency Amendments to Rules of Appellate Procedure*, 381 So. 2d 1370, 1375 (Fla. 1980).

award of costs for depositions conflicts with several decisions. Evans, against whom this decision was made, has chosen not to seek review of the district court's decision. Rather, petitioners, who prevailed on this point in the district court, now seek review of the district court's decision on an entirely different basis. They argue that the district court erred in affirming the summary judgments in favor of appellees and attempt to demonstrate conflict of decisions on this point.

In *Petrik v. New Hampshire Insurance Co.*, 400 So.2d 8 (Fla.1981), where the question certified was not brought to us for review, we held that we did not have jurisdiction to review other issues. In the present case, where the conflict certified has not been brought to us for review, we likewise do not have jurisdiction. Furthermore, the district court's decision on the summary judgment issue was effectually an affirmance without opinion with which express and direct conflict cannot be established. *Jenkins v. State*, 385 So.2d 1356 (Fla.1980).

Accordingly, the petition for review is dismissed.

It is so ordered.

BOYD, OVERTON and McDONALD, JJ., concur.

ADKINS, Acting C. J., dissents [without opinion].

What is the result if a district court of appeal *acknowledges* rather than *certifies* that its decision directly conflicts with a decision of another district court of appeal? The following case answers the question.

State v. Vickery

961 So. 2d 309 (Fla. 2007)

CANTERO, J.

We review three cases in which the Fourth and Fifth District Courts of Appeal acknowledged (but did not certify) conflict with the First District Court of Appeal. These are: *Charles v. State*, 890 So.2d 542 (Fla. 4th DCA 2005), *James v. State*, 881 So.2d 85 (Fla. 5th DCA 2004), and *Vickery v. State*, 869 So.2d 623 (Fla. 5th DCA 2004). The issue is whether a claim that alleges ineffective assistance of counsel for failure to request an instruction on a lesser-included offense may be summarily denied. *See Sanders v. State*, 847 So.2d 504 (Fla. 1st DCA 2003) (en banc), *approved*, 946 So.2d 953 (Fla.2006). In acknowledging conflict, the Fifth District in *James* and *Vickery* cited *Sanders*, while the Fourth District in *Charles* cited *Willis v. State*, 840 So.2d 1135 (Fla. 4th DCA 2003) (on motion for rehearing and motion for certification of conflict), *quashed*, 946 So.2d 953 (Fla.2006), in which it had earlier certified conflict with *Sanders*. When the Fourth and Fifth Districts issued their respective decisions in *Charles, James,* and *Vickery*, both *Sanders* and *Willis* were pending review in this Court. We have jurisdiction and consolidate *Charles, James,* and *Vickery* for purposes of this opinion. *See* art. V, § 3(b)(3), Fla Const.; *Jollie v. State*, 405 So.2d 418 (Fla.1981).

Jurisdiction

Before deciding these cases, we address a jurisdictional issue. The district courts in these cases only *acknowledged,* but did not *certify,* their conflict with the First District. For purposes of our jurisdiction, this is an important distinction. While it is a district court's prerogative to acknowledge rather than certify conflict, such an approach does not give us jurisdiction under article V, section 3(b)(4) of the Florida Constitution (establishing this Court's discretionary jurisdiction to review "any decision of a district court of appeal that . . . is *certified* by it to be in direct conflict with a decision of another district court of appeal") (emphasis added).

As already informally recognized, "district court opinions accepted [for review as certified conflict cases under article V, section 3(b)(4) of the Florida Constitution] . . . almost uniformly meet two requirements: they use the word 'certify' or some variation of the root word 'certif.-' in connection with the word 'conflict;' and, they indicate a decision from another district court upon which the conflict is based." Harry Lee Anstead, Gerald Kogan, Thomas D. Hall, & Robert Craig Waters, *The Operation and Jurisdiction of the Supreme Court of Florida,* 29 Nova L.Rev. 431, 529 (2005) (footnote omitted). However, "all of the cases — with few exceptions — in which the district court has merely 'acknowledged' conflict are treated as petitions for [review based on] 'express and direct' conflict [under article V, section (3)(b)(3) of the Florida Constitution], and some are accepted for review on that basis." *Id.* at 530 (footnote omitted).

We thus hold that district court decisions that simply acknowledge, discuss, cite, suggest, or in any other way recognize conflict do not provide a proper basis for a party to seek this Court's review under our "certified conflict" jurisdiction. *See* art. V, § 3(b)(4), Fla. Const. To support such review, conflict must be "certified." Of course, this does not mean that we lose all jurisdiction to review the case. As occurred with the three cases here, jurisdiction may nevertheless exist under our "express and direct conflict" jurisdiction, *see* art. V, § 3(b)(3), Fla. Const. (granting this Court jurisdiction to review district court opinions that "expressly and directly" conflict with the decision of another district court of appeal or with a decision of the Florida Supreme Court), or on some other basis. The difference is that a certification of conflict provides us with jurisdiction per se. On the other hand, when a district court does not certify the conflict, our jurisdiction to review the case depends on whether the decision actually "expressly and directly" conflicts with the decision of another court. We therefore advise district courts that when they intend to certify conflict under article V, section 3(b)(4) of the Florida Constitution, they use the constitutional term of art "certify."

* * *

It is so ordered.

———————

Sometimes the certified conflict does not exist:

Curry v. State

682 So. 2d 1091 (Fla. 1996)

PER CURIAM.

We accepted jurisdiction to review *Curry v. State*, 656 So.2d 521 (Fla. 2d DCA 1995), which certified conflict with *Navarre v. State*, 608 So.2d 525 (Fla. 1st DCA 1992). However, on closer examination, we find that review was improvidently granted.

The cases address different propositions of law which are not in conflict. The district court in *Curry* correctly struck that portion of the defendant's probation order that required him to *pay for* drug evaluation and treatment programs "because this is a special condition not announced orally" in the defendant's presence at sentencing. 656 So.2d at 522.

In contrast, the defendant in *Navarre* objected to a condition of probation requiring him to submit to drug evaluation and screening as not reasonably related to his second-degree murder and battery offenses. 608 So.2d at 526. The First District affirmed the condition of probation, holding that it "is a standard condition of probation that can be imposed on any probationer, irrespective of whether it reasonably relates to the type of offense." *Id.* at 528. The First District was correct because such a requirement was a standard condition of probation provided for in section 948.03(1)(j), Florida Statutes (1988 Supp.). The First District did not address a "special" condition requiring the defendant to pay for his drug evaluation and treatment as did the Second District in *Curry*.

Because no conflict exists between *Curry* and *Navarre*, we accordingly dismiss the petition.

It is so ordered.

KOGAN, C.J., and OVERTON, SHAW, GRIMES, HARDING, WELLS and ANSTEAD, JJ., concur.

NO MOTION FOR REHEARING WILL BE ALLOWED.

(7) **"May review any order or judgment of a trial court certified by the district court of appeal in which an appeal is pending to be of great public importance, or to have a great effect on the proper administration of justice throughout the state, and certified to require immediate resolution by the supreme court."**
Fla. Const. art. V, § 3(b)(5)

This provision is often referred to as the "bypass" provision because it permits an issue to bypass a District Court of Appeal and be resolved by the Florida Supreme Court. There are two important points to note about the provision. First, it covers non-final and final orders of trial courts.[78] Thus, the deletion in 1980 of the Florida

---

78. *See In re Emergency Amendments to Rules of Appellate Procedure*, 381 So. 2d 1370, 1385 (Fla. 1980).

Supreme Court's discretionary jurisdiction to review non-final orders of trial courts, which upon becoming final would be directly appealable to the Florida Supreme Court, was replaced by this provision. However, unlike the earlier provision, this one is tied to certification by the district court. Also unlike the earlier provision, this one is self-executing. Fla. R. App. P. 9.125(b) provides that "the jurisdiction of the Supreme Court is invoked upon rendition of the certificate by the district court of appeal."[79] This is now apparently the only method for review of non-final orders by the Florida Supreme Court.[80]

The following case was among the first cases to reach the Supreme Court under the then-newly approved constitutional bypass provision contained in article V, § 3(b)(5) of the Florida Constitution (1980).

Department of Insurance, State of Florida v. Teachers Insurance Co.

404 So. 2d 735 (Fla. 1981)

Order Accepting Jurisdiction

The District Court of Appeal, First District, has certified, pursuant to article V, Section 3(b)(5) of the Constitution of Florida, that the order of the trial court passes upon a question of great public importance requiring immediate resolution by this Court. We accept jurisdiction.

ADKINS, BOYD, OVERTON and McDONALD, JJ., concur.

ENGLAND, J., dissents with an opinion with which SUNDBERG, C. J., and ALDERMAN, J., concur.

ENGLAND, Justice, dissenting.

I would decline to accept jurisdiction of these cases, which are among the first to reach us under newly-approved article V, section 3(b)(5) of the Florida Constitution (1980). This case does not possess any indicia of immediacy, as did the only case so far accepted and decided under this provision. *See McPherson v. Flynn*, 397 So.2d 665 (Fla. 1981). That case, it will be recalled, brought to us, just days before the 1981 Legislature commenced, a challenge to the seating of one of its members.

The constitution provides in Section 3(b)(5) that the Supreme Court:

> May review any order or judgment of a trial court certified by the district court of appeal in which an appeal is pending to be of great public importance, or to have a great effect on the proper administration of justice throughout the state, and certified to require immediate resolution by the supreme court.

---

79. *Id.* at 1384.

80. *But see Couse v. Canal Auth.*, 209 So. 2d 865 (Fla. 1968) (also discussed later in this chapter).

I do not doubt that these cases are of great public importance, but I suggest they lack the type of immediacy which this provision demands.

On March 19, 1981, a trial judge in the Second Judicial Circuit declared section 627.066, Florida Statutes (1980) to be "unconstitutional in its retroactive application to excessive profits realized during the years 1977, 1978 and 1979." The Insurance Commissioner of Florida, charged with determining the companies' excess profits and directing rebates, appealed the trial court's order to the First District Court of Appeal.

Shortly after the appeal was lodged, both the Commissioner and several (but not all) of the insurance companies filed with the district court suggestions that the appeal be certified to the Supreme Court before decision. The suggestions for certification declared counsel's belief that the issue involved — the retroactive validity of the 1980 excess profits rebate law — was of great public importance and required immediate resolution by the Supreme Court. Various bases for the suggestions of immediacy and importance were expressed. The Commissioner's contentions were:

1. that notices of excess profits indicate that over thirty million dollars in excess profits should be refunded to over one million policyholders in the State of Florida, and should these funds ultimately be ordered refunded as the result of reversal of the trial court's order, any delay in final resolution of the legal issues raised would delay enjoyment of any returned funds, and could result in total deprivation to some policyholders who might decease or become unlocatable during the course of the appellate process; and

2. that prompt final determination is of immediate importance, as application of the excess profits law is an ongoing process in which cumulative calculations from year to year are necessary.

The insurance companies principally suggested:

1. that they would be required to maintain reserves or contingent liabilities so long as the lawsuits were unresolved, thereby causing adverse effects on company earnings estimates;

2. that policyholders would be delayed in receiving excess profit rebates if the statute were ultimately found to be valid;

3. that other auto insurers were affected by the uncertain status of the statute;

4. that future filings required by the law are affected by the retroactive validity of the statute; and

5. that the appeal will affect all people in Florida who pay auto insurance premiums.

One insurance company objected to the suggestions for certification, stating a belief that there is no basis for immediate or emergency consideration by the Court.

At the outset, it is important to note that a district court decision in these cases will not necessarily require our attention or resolution. The case could be truly final after district court action, and the goals of the parties can be met without our intercession. Thus, if the statute were declared valid, review here would be discretionary, and considering that the case involves an issue of arguably limited, precedential significance, it well may not be accepted for review.[1] Moreover, it seems probable that a decision by a three-judge panel of the district court can be reached at least as quickly as by the seven members of this Court. (I assume the parties would request, and I'm sure obtain, expeditious consideration of the issue by that tribunal.) Still, even conceding the possibility of review here and discounting the ease with which we might then review the district court's expository decision,[2] I would still argue against our acceptance of these cases now.

We recently explained the historical development of the constitutional amendment, adopted on March 11, 1980, which gave birth to article V, section 3(b)(5) of the constitution. *Jenkins v. State*, 385 So.2d 1356 (Fla.1980). That explanation, which will not be repeated here, provides a backdrop to an understanding of the evolution of this particular provision.[3]

While I believe the Court's acceptance of this case under the new constitutional bypass provision is improvident, my disagreement does not imply in any way that the district court acted improperly in accepting the various requests for bypass certification. The district courts have had little guidance from this Court, and few of the state's district court judges had intimate acquaintance with the development of this Court's new jurisdictional framework.

All members of this Court did, though. A majority of this Court assumed responsibility for the formulation and adoption of the 1980 jurisdictional amendment. So too, it seems to me, this Court must assume responsibility to establish the standards for bypass certification. We cannot now ask 41 district court judges to guess what we intended, or now intend, to constitute the limited class of exceptions to their primary responsibility to decide direct appeals of cases dealing with statutory validity and constitutional construction.

The assignment of bypass certification to the Court's discretionary jurisdiction in section 3(b)(5) of article V, as contrasted with those cases assigned to the Court for mandatory review in sections 3(b)(1) and 3(b)(2) of article V, leaves no doubt as to the role we must play. Internal control by this Court over its affairs was clearly intended. This is particularly significant when it is recalled that bypass certification demands that we also accelerate the cases on our Court's docket. I start, therefore, from the premise that we must not accept these cases merely because they have been certified by a district court. This provision was specifically designed to guarantee

---

1. England, Hunter and Williams. *Constitutional Jurisdiction of the Supreme Court of Florida: 1980 Reform*, 32 U.Fla.L.Rev. 147, 183–84 (1980).

2. *Id.* at 181, 183 n.210.

3. A more complete history and explanation of the 1980 amendment appears in England, Hunter and Williams, *supra* note 1.

our exercise of discretion, and consistency in its application requires our, not the district courts', decisional control.

The majority's acceptance of these cases for review has started the Court down a path with respect to the immediacy prong of our jurisdiction under section 3(b)(5), which is vastly different in degree from the standard applied in the *Flynn* case. The trial court's order in these cases, plainly and simply, does no more than declare invalid the retroactive application of a state statute. Obviously, that alone cannot meet an "immediacy" standard, for the same constitutional amendment which brought us bypass certification took away the direct appeal of trial court orders just like these.[4] Further, immediacy must relate to something other than the dollar significance of the legal question or the number of persons it affects, although those matters may affect the "importance" of the case.

In my view, the framers of section 3(b)(5) designed this procedure only to deal with disruptions to the system by which justice is administered in the state or to resolve important questions affecting governmental operations. The two examples mentioned frequently during the evolution of the 1980 constitutional amendment,[5] and the *Flynn* case, bear this out. I see none of these problems in the reasons offered for bypass certification here.

In the absence of an articulation by the majority of a reason to accept jurisdiction of these appeals, I can only guess at their view of immediacy. Two possibilities suggest themselves.

First, my silent colleagues may intend to accept for bypass certification all cases involving statutory validity which the district courts choose to certify, in deference to the judgment and discretion of the district courts' judges. That would be unfortunate, not only for the reasons I have already expressed, but also because that deference in effect leaves no way to decline certified cases involving a construction of the federal or state constitution. These matters have had constitutional importance equivalent to validity cases, both before and after the 1980 amendment. The net effect of taking all these matters will be to render futile the struggle which provided the Court with mechanisms to control its own docket.

As a second possibility, my brethren may intend to decline some future cases certified by the district courts based, I suppose, on some subjective assessment of their relative significance. If that is their plan, whether their criteria will be dollar amounts, people affected, or any other feature of the merits of the lawsuits, I fear that my colleagues' ad hoc attempts to apply section 3(b)(5) in its intended form, or develop standards for immediacy, are doomed to failure. The history of this Court's exercise of its discretionary jurisdiction between 1967 and 1980 illustrates with abundant clarity the effects of standardless ad hocracy.[6] The net effect of this

---

4. *Id.* at 164–66.
5. *Id.* at 193–96.
6. *Id.* at 150–53.

approach will not wholly negate the long overdue abolition of direct appeals, but it will reinstate the uncertainty, confusion and waste of resources which formerly attended our exercise of discretionary jurisdiction on the basis of shifting, subjective standards. This, too, will significantly erode the benefits of the 1980 constitutional change.

I would apply these standards to section 3(b)(5) cases:

(1) neither counsel in lawsuits or district court judges should control this Court's decision-making priorities — both groups, being nonhomogeneous and busy, have motives and priorities necessarily different from this Court's;

(2) in order to give effect to the "immediacy" requirement of section 3(b)(5), cases accepted for bypass should be reserved for those rare instances when it is necessary to preserve the integrity of the operation of a governmental system; and

(3) in general, the validity or invalidity of a statute, or a construction of the federal or state constitution, presents no inherent potential for meeting the immediacy prong of section 3(b)(5).

At our urging, the people of Florida reduced our required jurisdiction, expressed their confidence in the ability of the district courts to decide constitutional and statutory issues, and effectively told us to exercise our review role by fairly precise and nonamorphous standards. Before today we made a good start toward those objectives. I see today's decision as a retreat from those principles.

SUNDBERG, C. J., and ALDERMAN, J., concur.

[The opinion of the court on the merits and the dissenting opinion on the merits are omitted.]

(8) **"May review a question of law certified by the Supreme Court of the United States or a United States Court of Appeals which is determinative of the cause and for which there is no controlling precedent of the supreme court of Florida." Fla. Const. art. V, § 3(b)(6)**

This provision merely confers constitutional status on what had theretofore been a provision of the Florida Rules of Appellate Procedure.[81] This procedure has generally been justified on federalism grounds.

> The dissenter on the Court of Appeals urged that the court certify the state-law question to the Florida Supreme Court ... That path is open to this Court and to any court of appeals of the United States. We have, indeed, used it before [footnote omitted] as have courts of appeals. [Footnote omitted.]

> Moreover when state law does not make the certification procedure available, [footnote omitted] a federal court not infrequently will stay its hand,

---

81. *See In re Emergency Amendments to Rules of Appellate Procedure*, 381 So. 2d 1370, 1391 (Fla. 1980).

remitting the parties to the state court to resolve the controlling state law on which the federal rule may turn. Kaiser Steel Corp. v. W. S. Ranch Co., 391 U.S. 593, 88 S.Ct. 1753, 20 L.Ed.2d 835 (1968). Numerous applications of that practice are reviewed in Meredith v. Winter Haven, 320 U.S. 228, 64 S. Ct. 7, 88 L.Ed. 9 (1943), which teaches that the mere difficulty in ascertaining local law is no excuse for remitting the parties to a state tribunal for the start of another lawsuit. We do not suggest that where there is doubt as to local law and where the certification procedure is available, resort to it is obligatory. It does, of course, in the long run save time, energy, and resources and helps build a cooperative judicial federalism. [Footnote omitted.] Its use in a given case rests in the sound discretion of the federal court.[82]

See also *Holden v. N L Industries, Inc.*,[83] which compares this type of certification procedure in a number of states. Note that the Utah Supreme Court's discussion of the Florida rule predates the procedure's inclusion in the Florida Constitution. See *Mosher v. Speedstar Division of AMCA International, Inc.*[84] for an example of a Florida Supreme Court case based upon § 3(b)(6).

It should be noted that under § 3(b)(6), federal district courts do not have authority to certify questions to the Florida Supreme Court.[85] This provision is limited to the United States Supreme Court or a United States Court of Appeal.[86]

In *State of Florida ex rel. Shevin v. Exxon Corp.*,[87] the United States Court of Appeals for the Fifth Circuit elaborated on the factors the Court considers in determining whether to exercise its discretion and decide a matter where there is no controlling precedent under Florida law or whether to certify the question of law to the Florida Supreme Court for consideration. The Court explained as follows:

In determining whether to exercise our discretion in favor of certification, we consider many factors. The most important are the closeness of the question and the existence of sufficient sources of state law — statutes, judicial decisions, attorney general's opinions — to allow a principled rather than conjectural conclusion. But also to be considered is the degree to which considerations of comity are relevant in light of the particular issue and case to be decided. And we must also take into account practical limitations of the certification process: significant delay and possible inability to frame the issue so as to produce a helpful response on the part of the state court.

---

82. *Lehman Bros. v. Schein*, 416 U.S. 386, 389–391 (1974).

83. 629 P.2d 428 (Utah 1981).

84. 675 So. 2d 918 (Fla. 1996).

85. *United States Fire Ins. Co. v. Mikes*, 576 F. Supp. 2d 1303, *aff'd*, 279 Fed. Appx. 879 (M.D. Fla. 2007).

86. Fla. Const. art. V, § 3(b)(6).

87. 526 F.2d 266, 274-275 (5th Cir. 1976).

242   4 · THE COURTS

Although the Florida Supreme Court's review under § 3(b)(6) is discretionary, and it may refuse to answer a question posed to it,[88] in the event the Florida Supreme Court accepts jurisdiction, its answer to question(s) certified to it by the United Supreme Court or United States Court of Appeals is conclusive on the respective courts as to the question(s) of Florida law certified by them to the Florida Supreme Court.[89]

e. Writs

The Florida Supreme Court possesses a limited amount of original jurisdiction. This original jurisdiction is exercised through filing applications with the court for certain discretionary legal writs. These writs are writs of prohibition, mandamus, quo warranto, habeas corpus, and all writs necessary to the complete exercise of its jurisdiction. The Florida Supreme Court has established standards governing the instances in which writ jurisdiction should be exercised. The following cases address these standards.

(1) **"May issue writs of prohibition to courts . . ." Fla. Const.
     art. V, § 3(b)(7)**

Moffitt v. Willis

459 So. 2d 1018 (Fla. 1984)

ADKINS, Justice.

We have before us an original proceeding on suggestion for a writ of prohibition which would quash an order of the circuit court judge wherein he determined the circuit court had the jurisdiction to rule on a complaint against the legislature. We have jurisdiction. Art. V, § 3(b)(7), Fla. Const.

In January 1982, the Miami Herald Publishing Company and twelve other newspaper publishing companies sued the petitioners, H. Lee Moffitt, as Speaker of the House of Representatives and Curtis Peterson, as President of the Senate, for declaratory judgment. The complaint filed in that action alleges that during May and June of 1981, secret meetings of committees of the legislature occurred in violation of legislative rules and the first and fourteenth amendments to the United States Constitution; article II, section 8, Florida Constitution; article III, Florida Constitution; section 11.142, Florida Statutes (1981); and section 286.11 and 286.012, Florida Statutes (1981).

Petitioners filed a motion to dismiss the complaint on the ground that the circuit court lacked jurisdiction over the subject matter under the constitutional doctrine of separation of powers because the complaint relates to the Florida Senate and the Florida House of Representatives. A hearing on the motion was held before the

---

88. *See Green v. Massey*, 384 So. 2d 24 (1980).
89. *See Allen v. Carman's Estate*, 486 F. 2d 490 (5th Cir. 1973).

respondent, the Honorable Ben C. Willis. Judge Willis ordered that the newspaper publishing companies were entitled to a ruling under chapter 86, Florida Statutes (1981), as to the allegations in the complaint relating to the first amendment as to the United States Constitution and the corresponding provision of the Florida Constitution, article I, section 4, Florida Constitution, and also as to section 11.142, Florida Statutes (1981).

The petitioners are now seeking a writ of prohibition to have Judge Willis' order quashed and to have the complaint dismissed. We have permitted the newspaper publishing companies to intervene in this cause.

We agree with the petitioners, grant their petition and direct the dismissal of the civil action pending in the second judicial circuit which is the subject matter of this petition.

One of the issues we are faced with in this case is the jurisdiction of this Court to prohibit proceedings in the circuit court. The intervenors argue that should we determine that our jurisdiction to issue writs of prohibition is now coextensive with that of the district courts of appeal, in respect to circuit court proceedings, forum shopping in the appellate structure and even successive applications to this and other courts may be the result. We disagree.

Before its amendment in 1980, article V, section 3(b)(4), Florida Constitution, provided that this Court might "issue writs of prohibition to courts and commissions in causes within the jurisdiction of the supreme court to review." The 1980 amendments transferred that provision to article V, section 3(b)(7) and eliminated the phrase "and commissions in causes within the jurisdiction of the supreme court to review." This change in article V has been said to have caused some confusion as to whether this Court may issue a writ of prohibition to circuit courts. *See* England and Williams, *Florida Appellate Reform One Year Later*, 9 Fla.St.U.L.Rev. 221 (1981). We do not consider the change to have either expanded or contracted our jurisdiction to issue writs of prohibition to courts. The 1980 amendment of article V was presented to the public as necessary to narrow this Court's jurisdiction in order to reduce our case load selectively. *See, e.g.*, England, Hunter and Williams, *Constitutional Jurisdiction of the Supreme Court of Florida: 1980 Reform*, 32 U.Fla.L.Rev. 147 (1980). We therefore do not consider it reasonable to interpret any changes to have been intended to expand our jurisdiction. However, it is not necessary for us to depend on an expanded version of article V in order to find that we have jurisdiction to issue a writ of prohibition in this instance.

In *State ex rel. Sarasota County v. Boyer*, 360 So.2d 388 (Fla.1978), we fully discussed our jurisdiction to issue writs of prohibition. We stated that, inasmuch as we cannot know with certainty whether we have appellate jurisdiction over the decision until it has been decided and that at that point we could not issue a preventive to undo what has been done, the answer is that it is only necessary to show that on the face of the matter it appears that a lower court is about to act in excess of its jurisdiction in a case which is likely to come within our jurisdiction to review. *Id.* at

392. Although that case involved the district court, the same rationale applies to our jurisdiction to issue the writ to a circuit court. In *Tsavaris v. Scruggs*, 360 So.2d 745 (Fla.1977), we found that this Court had jurisdiction to issue a writ of prohibition to a trial court in a case where the defendant had been indicted for first-degree murder. We could not know whether conviction would result in a sentence of death, but we knew the possibility of a death sentence was real since the crime charged was a capital offense. We have also on many occasions considered an original petition for writ of prohibition asking us to restrain a criminal court of record from proceeding to try a cause. In those instances, the issue presented was the defendant's constitutional right to a speedy trial. *See, e.g., Lowe v. Price*, 437 So.2d 142 (Fla.1983); *Pena v. Schultz*, 245 So.2d 49 (Fla.1971); *Loy v. Grayson*, 99 So.2d 555 (Fla.1957).

We are now presented with a case in which the trial judge has issued an order, in response to a motion to dismiss, which states that the plaintiffs are entitled to a ruling as to the allegations relating to the first amendment of the United States Constitution and article I, section 4 of the Florida Constitution. The defendants, the petitioners here, argue that the trial court lacks jurisdiction because article II, section 3 of the Florida Constitution mandates separation of powers. It is clear to us that if this case were to proceed to trial and then to appeal at the district court, it is most likely that some provision of the state or federal constitution would be construed. The case would then come within our jurisdiction to review. In keeping with our holding in *Sarasota County v. Boyer*, we have jurisdiction to issue a writ of prohibition in this instance.

The fundamental argument raised by the petitioners is that the circuit court does not have jurisdiction to determine and declare the meaning and application of the rules and procedures of the Florida Senate and the Florida House of Representatives. Petitioners maintain that the authority of each house of the legislature, vis-a-vis article III, section 4(a) and article II, section 3 of the Florida Constitution, to determine its own internal procedure is at issue and that neither the constitutionality of any enacted statute, nor any policy commitment of the state of Florida, nor the balancing of compelling interests of the state are at issue. We agree with the petitioners' contentions.

At the outset, we reassert that our duty in this cause is to determine whether the circuit court has the *jurisdiction*. We do not propose to address the merits of the case in the process.

* * *

Just as the legislature may not invade our province of procedural rulemaking for the court system, we may not invade the legislature's province of internal procedural rulemaking. *See, e.g., State v. Garcia*, 229 So.2d 236 (Fla.1969); *State v. Robinson*, 132 So.2d 156 (Fla.1961); *Hay v. Isetts*, 98 Fla. 1026, 125 So. 237 (1929). A member of the legislature can raise a point of order regarding a violation of any of the rules of the house or senate. That is the proper forum for determining the propriety of the activities complained of in the suit below.

Therefore, we find that the circuit court lacks jurisdiction to proceed in this matter. We withhold issuance of a writ of prohibition with the confidence that the respondent will comply with the dictates of this opinion.

It is so ordered.

ALDERMAN, EHRLICH and SHAW, JJ., concur.

BOYD, C.J., concurs in part and dissents in part with an opinion.

MCDONALD, J., concurs in part and dissents in part with an opinion in which BOYD, C.J., and OVERTON, J., concur.

[These opinions are omitted.]

The following was not an original action for prohibition filed in the Florida Supreme Court. Nonetheless, the court's discussion of the elements of a writ of prohibition makes this case one of the leading, if not *the* leading, cases on the subject.

English v. McCrary

348 So. 2d 293 (Fla. 1977)

KARL, Justice.

* * *

Petitioner, Carey English, filed a petition for writ of prohibition with the District Court of Appeal wherein he alleged that he was a reporter for the *Tallahassee Democrat*, that the respondent Honorable Robert McCrary, Jr., refused to permit him to attend a hearing in the dissolution proceedings of Estelle and Harry Morrison, that the respondent failed to give him a good reason for exclusion of the press from the hearing, that the mere desire of litigants to conduct a private hearing is an insufficient predicate upon which the judge may exclude the public and press, that Harry Morrison is the duly elected State Attorney for the Second Judicial Circuit, that the public had a real and genuine interest in any litigation involving this public official and that not to allow the press access was in derogation of the fundamental right of the public and the press to access to all judicial proceedings.

The District Court determined that the suggestion for writ of prohibition did not state a prima facie case for issuance of the writ. The District Court, in reaching this conclusion, expressly stated:

"While the action of the chancellor in the case sub judice in denying the press admittance to the dissolution of marriage hearing may have been an abuse of the trial judge's discretion (though we do not here rule that it was or was not an abuse of discretion) the fundamental initial question is whether or not a chancellor has jurisdiction in a dissolution of marriage proceeding to exercise his discretion to determine whether or not the public and press will be permitted to attend the hearing. If in all instances it is required that such a hearing be open to the public, then the chancellor had no discretion. Otherwise, the chancellor would clearly have the power, authority, and jurisdiction to make the ruling in a particular case. Although the ruling which he makes on the subject might constitute an abuse of discretion in a particular case, the extraordinary Writ of Prohibition would not be available to determine whether or not he correctly exercised his discretion."

The District Court of Appeal, First District, correctly determined, pursuant to all established precedent, that the suggestion for writ of prohibition filed by relator failed to state a prima facie case for issuance of the extraordinary writ of prohibition. None of the requisites essential to issuance of such a writ are present in the record before us. In fact, issuance of the writ under the circumstances presented thwarts the entire concept and purpose of the writ of prohibition. . . .

Prohibition is an extraordinary writ, a prerogative writ, extremely narrow in scope and operation, by which a superior court, having appellate and supervisory jurisdiction over an inferior court or tribunal possessing judicial or quasi-judicial power, may prevent such inferior court or tribunal from exceeding jurisdiction or usurping jurisdiction over matters not within its jurisdiction.

* * *

In Florida, the courts have consistently determined, in accord with the historical understanding and background of the writ of prohibition, that it is meant to be very narrow in scope, to be employed with great caution and utilized only in emergencies. Prohibition may only be granted when it is shown that a lower court is without jurisdiction or attempting to act in excess of jurisdiction. It is preventive and not corrective in that it commands the one to whom it is directed not to do the thing which the supervisory court is informed the lower tribunal is about to do. Its purpose is to prevent the doing of something, not to compel the undoing of something already done. It cannot be used to revoke an order entered. *State ex rel. Harris v. McCauley*, 297 So.2d 825 (Fla. 1974), *State ex. rel. R. C. Motor Lines, Inc. v. Boyd, et al.*, 114 So.2d 169 (Fla. 1959), *State ex rel. Shailer v. Booher*, 241 So.2d 720 (Fla. 4th DCA, 1970). Where proceedings sought to be prohibited have been completed and matters therein disposed of, prohibition may not be used for the sole purpose of establishing principles to govern future cases. . . .

* * *

A clear distinction is drawn between assumption of jurisdiction to which the court has no legal claim and erroneous exercise of jurisdiction with which it is invested. In *State ex rel. Rheinauer v. Malone*, 40 Fla. 129, 23 So. 575, 576 (1898), this Court explicated:

But it does not lie for errors or grievances which may be redressed, in the ordinary course of judicial proceedings, by appeal or writ of error. It is a fundamental principle, and one which will be strictly enforced, that this writ is never allowed to usurp the functions of a writ or error or certiorari, and can never be employed as a process for the correction of errors of inferior tribunals. *The courts will not permit a writ which proceeds upon the ground of an excess or usurpation of jurisdiction to become an instrument itself of usurpation,* or be confounded with a writ of error, which proceeds upon the ground of error in the exercise of a jurisdiction which is conceded. It does not lie to prevent a subordinate court from deciding erroneously, or from enforcing an erroneous judgment, in a case in which it has a right to adjudicate. In the application of the principle, it matters not whether the court below has decided correctly or erroneously; its jurisdiction of the matter in controversy being conceded, *prohibition will not lie to prevent an erroneous exercise of that jurisdiction.* (Emphasis supplied.)

Abuse of discretion by the inferior tribunal acting within its jurisdiction is not a matter to be determined by prohibition. *State v. Hunt,* 70 So.2d 301 (Fla. 1954), *State ex rel. Jacksonville Ice & Cold Storage Co. v. Gray et al.,* 130 Fla. 359, 177 So. 849 (1937). If the existence of jurisdiction depends on controverted facts which the inferior court has the jurisdiction to determine, and the court errs in the exercise thereof, prohibition is not available. *State ex rel. Park v. H. T. Poindexter & Sons Merchandise Co.,* 149 Fla. 765, 7 So.2d 452 (1941), *Burkhart v. Circuit Court of Eleventh Judicial Circuit,* [146 Fla. 457, 1 So.2d 872 (1941)], *State ex rel. Schwarz v. Heffernan,* 142 Fla. 137, 194 So. 313 (1940), *State v. Drumright,* 116 Fla. 496, 156 So. 721 (1934).

The suggestion for writ of prohibition must affirmatively show lack of jurisdiction in the lower court. *Department of Public Safety v. Koonce,* 147 Fla. 616, 3 So.2d 331 (1941), *State v. Rowe,* 104 So.2d 134 (Fla. 1st DCA, 1958).

Relating the aforegoing principles to the case at bar, we conclude that prohibition was not an available remedy under the circumstances presented. The instant case does not involve a situation where the trial court was exceeding its jurisdiction or was without jurisdiction. The most involved here is a possible abuse of discretion.

Accordingly, the decision of the District Court is approved . . . and the writ heretofore issued is discharged.

It is so ordered.

OVERTON, C. J., ADKINS and HATCHETT, JJ., concur.

ENGLAND, J., dissents with an opinion.

SUNDBERG, J., dissents and concurs with ENGLAND, J.

ENGLAND, Justice dissenting.

[The dissenting opinion is omitted.]

As the previous case points out, prohibition is an extraordinary writ designed to keep courts from acting when they have no jurisdiction to act. Frequently, the higher court will not issue the formal writ because of its confidence that the lower court will refrain from acting without jurisdiction once the higher court has determined that such is the case.[90]

(2) "May issue . . . all writs necessary to the complete exercise of its jurisdiction." Fla. Const. art. V, § 3(b)(7)

It has been argued that this provision represents an independent grant of original jurisdiction to the Florida Supreme Court to hear and resolve matters necessary to the complete exercise of its jurisdiction. Alternatively, it has been argued that this provision is simply a mechanism with which the Florida Supreme Court can issue writs to protect its *existing* jurisdiction. As the following cases and commentary reflect, the Court has adopted both of these arguments at different times. This initially left this area of jurisdiction ambiguous and unsettled; however, later rulings of the Supreme Court have brought clarity to it.

Besoner v. Crawford

357 So. 2d 414 (Fla. 1978)

PER CURIAM.

This case was filed with the court as an application for constitutional or other necessary writ pursuant to Florida Appellate Rule 4.5(g) which provides:

> "g. Constitutional writs.
>
> (1) *In Aid of Prescribed Jurisdiction.* Application for constitutional or other writs necessary to the complete exercise of the jurisdiction of the Court will be entertained only after reasonable notice to the adverse party. No such petition will be entertained unless the case is one in which the court may properly acquire jurisdiction and then only when it is made clearly to appear that the writ is in fact necessary in aid of an ultimate power of review and that a supersedeas order entered by the lower court will not completely preserve the Court's jurisdiction, or that the lower court has erroneously refused to enter such an order."

This application is not sought to protect existing jurisdiction of the court. The application seeks to use the constitutional all writs power of the court as an independent basis for jurisdiction.

* * *

Accordingly, this application for constitutional writ is dismissed. The Chief Justice, in the exercise of supervisory power, will communicate with these parties and will take appropriate action with advice of the court.

It is so ordered.

---

90. *See Sas v. Postman*, 687 So. 2d 54, 55 n. 1 (Fla. 3d Dist. Ct. App. 1997).

OVERTON, C. J., and BOYD, HATCHETT and KARL, JJ., concur.

ADKINS, J., dissents [without opinion].

St. Paul Title Insurance Corp. v. Davis
392 So. 2d 1304 (Fla. 1980)

ALDERMAN, Justice.

By way of a petition under the "all writs necessary" provision of article V, section 3(b)(7), Florida Constitution (1980), filed after April 1, 1980, petitioner seeks review of a district court decision affirming per curiam without opinion the trial court's decision. Respondents have moved to dismiss the petition on the basis of lack of jurisdiction. Petitioner's alternate petition for "conflict" review filed under article V, section 3(b)(3) from this same per curiam affirmance was dismissed sua sponte by this Court by order, 385 So.2d 761 (Fla. 1980), because the new section 3(b)(3) does not permit our review of district court decisions which merely read in their entirety: "Per Curiam. Affirmed." *See Jenkins v. State*, 385 So.2d 1356 (Fla. 1980).

We will not allow the "all writs necessary" provision of section 3(b)(7) to be used to circumvent the clear language of section 3(b)(3) and our holding in *Jenkins v. State* that we lack jurisdiction to review per curiam decisions of the several district courts of appeal of this state rendered without opinion when the basis for such review is an alleged conflict of that decision with another. The all writs provision of section 3(b)(7) does not confer added appellate jurisdiction on this Court, and this Court's all writs power cannot be used as an independent basis of jurisdiction as petitioner is hereby seeking to use it. *Besoner v. Crawford*, 357 So.2d 414 (Fla. 1978); *Shevin ex rel. State v. Public Service Commission*, 333 So.2d 9 (Fla. 1976).

We are without jurisdiction in this matter, and, accordingly, we grant respondents' motion and dismiss petition for review under the "all writs necessary" provision of article V, section 3(b)(7), Florida Constitution.

It is so ordered.

SUNDBERG, C.J., and BOYD and OVERTON, JJ., concur.

ADKINS, J., dissents, [without opinion].

Unfortunately, neither *Besoner* nor *St. Paul* appears to completely resolve the confusion caused by *Couse v. Canal Authority*, an earlier case.[91] In *Couse*, the Florida Supreme Court was faced with an order of quick taking in an eminent domain case.[92] The order allowed the canal authority to proceed with its construction while the issue of compensation was being settled and the order of taking thus ultimately

----

91. 209 So. 2d 865 (Fla. 1968).
92. *Id*. at 866.

250   4 · THE COURTS

would become final.[93] The defendants in the lower court had sought to have the complaint dismissed because of a contention that the statute upon which the action was based was unconstitutional.[94] The circuit court found the statute to be constitutional.[95] The defendants asked the Florida Supreme Court to review this non-final order by certiorari.[96] The Court, because it did not believe it had jurisdiction, transferred the case to the appropriate district court of appeal which could, if it wished, hear the matter by common law certiorari.[97] The district court sent the matter back to the Florida Supreme Court.[98]

The problem facing the district court was that because issues decided on interlocutory appeal could not be reviewed again after final judgment,[99] the district court could have foreclosed Florida Supreme Court review of the correctness of the trial court's decision as to the constitutional validity of a statute. However, if the Florida Supreme Court waited for the order to become final, the canal authority would probably have already damaged the land with construction.

The Court, per Justice Drew, found Florida Supreme Court jurisdiction in the "all writs" clause:[100]

> Article V, Sec. 4, by providing for Supreme Court review of interlocutory orders in chancery, which "upon a final decree would be directly appealable" here, does imply that routine review of such orders in law actions shall be deferred until appeal from the final judgment. We think, however, that this implied limitation does not proscribe a limited review by the discretionary writ of certiorari repeatedly held to be available in the absence of other effective appellate process. We recognize, as in previous cases, [footnote omitted] that the jurisdiction of this Court is limited to that prescribed in amended Article V, and that the power to use the writ of certiorari as

---

93. *Id.*

94. *Id.*

95. *Id.*

96. The Florida Supreme Court at the time had no specific authority to review non-final orders in a law proceeding even if the case could be directly appealed to the Florida Supreme Court once the order became final. The jurisdictional provision of the Florida Constitution then, in pertinent part, read: "The Supreme Court may directly review by certiorari interlocutory orders or decrees passing upon chancery [equity] matters which upon final decree would be directly appealable to the supreme court." Fla. Const. art. V, § 4(2) (1885 as revised in 1956). In 1972 this provision was amended to provide this type of review without distinction between law and equity. Fla. Const. art. V, § 3(b)3 (1968 as amended in 1972). Of course, this provision was deleted altogether in the 1980 amendment to the Court's jurisdiction.

97. *Id.* The Florida Rules of Appellate Procedure did not then provide for review of non-final orders in law (as opposed to equity) matters except as to venue and jurisdiction. Fla. R. App. P. 4.2. Compare the present Fla. R. App. P. 9.130.

98. The district court, apparently in order to ensure Supreme Court jurisdiction, certified its decision as one of great public interest. *Cause*, 209 So. 2d at 866. The Supreme Court did not use this as a vehicle for review.

99. *Id.* at 866–867.

100. *Id.* at 867–868.

4 · THE COURTS

an ultimate method of review is now vested in our courts of general appellate jurisdiction, the district courts of appeal. A point not previously considered, however, is that the additional express and unqualified provision in Art. V that the "supreme court may issue all writs necessary or proper to the complete exercise of its jurisdiction" provides ample constitutional authority for use of the writ of certiorari in the situation now presented. The writ, in sum, is essential, even indispensable, to the complete and effective exercise of the prescribed jurisdiction of this Court to decide all appeals from final judgments passing on the validity of a statute.

* * *

The writ remains ancillary in nature, as often stated in previous application of the constitutional writs provision, but our decision here represents a departure from, and effectively overrules, such pronouncements as in *State ex rel. Watson v. Lee*[5] that the "all writs" provision may not be invoked "until jurisdiction is acquired" over the cause by means of independent appellate proceedings. Certainly the writs provision in the context of amended Article V contains no such qualification.

* * *

The opinion of the district court in this cause states a classic case for the exercise of discretionary certiorari jurisdiction to resolve the issue of statutory validity at the time of entry of an order of taking under F.S. Sec. 74.051, F.S.A. Such an order permits irremediable action by the condemning authority which, if petitioner's claims as to unconstitutionality could be substantiated, would authorize relief by certiorari.

Subsequent to *Couse*, the following comment appeared in *Shevin ex rel. State v. Public Service Commission*:[101]

Public counsel has also invoked the all writs clause as a basis for this Court's jurisdiction. That provision confers jurisdiction on the Court to issue "all writs necessary to the complete exercise of its jurisdiction." Fla. Const. Art. V, § 3(b)(4). This language contemplates a situation where the Court has already acquired jurisdiction of a cause on some independent basis, and the complete exercise of that jurisdiction might be defeated if the Court did not issue an appropriate writ or other process; e. g., a stay of related proceedings in another court or their transfer here for consolidation. *Wilson v. Sandstrom*, 317 So.2d 732 (Fla.1975); *State v. Lee*, 8 So.2d 19 (Fla.1942) (the all writs provision "has reference only to ancillary writs ... and does not confer added original or appellate jurisdiction in any case." At 21). In the

---

5. 150 Fla. 496, 8 So. 2d 19 (1942). See also Kilgore v. Bird, 149 Fla. 570, 6 So.2d 541, and State ex rel. Peacock v. Latham, 125 Fla. 788, 170 So. 472.

101. 333 So. 2d 9, 12 (Fla. 1976) (overruled on other grounds in *In re Emergency Amendments to Rules of Appellate Procedure*, 381 So. 2d 1370, 1381–1382 (Fla. 1980)).

present case, we do not have jurisdiction on any independent basis, so there is no occasion for any ancillary writ.

The Court in *Shevin* relied on *State v. Lee,* the very case that *Couse* had overruled. *Besoner,* the most recent of the three case series (*Couse, Shevin,* and *Besoner*), is based in large part on the ambiguous language in former Fla. R. App. P. 4.5(g), "in which the court may properly acquire jurisdiction." Was "may" used in the discretionary sense or the future sense? If in the discretionary sense, that would appear to preclude "all writs" usage in direct appeal cases which, of course, could not be correct. In any event, that language is no longer in the Florida Rules of Appellate Procedure.[102]

St. Paul, of course, relied on *Shevin* and *Besoner.*[103] This still seems to leave largely unanswered the question, does the Florida Supreme Court actually have to have jurisdiction before the all writs provision can be used, or can all writs be used if the Court may obtain jurisdiction of the matter in the future? The latter would seem to be the most likely. Consider *Florida Senate v. Graham,*[104] where the Florida Supreme Court actually cited *Couse* as controlling:

> We find jurisdiction to entertain this matter is vested under article V, section 3(b)(7), which provides in pertinent part that the Supreme Court "[m]ay issue . . . all writs necessary to the complete exercise of its jurisdiction." By the extraordinary provisions of article III, section 16(b), (c) and (f), Florida Constitution (1968), this Court is vested with jurisdiction in the second year following each decennial census to either review a legislative plan of apportionment or actually devise a plan of apportionment depending upon the occurrence or non-occurrence of certain conditions precedent. The mode in which the Court will entertain apportionment is dictated by action or inaction of the legislature in adopting a joint resolution of apportionment, but, irrespective of its action, we will entertain the issue each ten years. Because jurisdiction of the issue of apportionment will vest in this Court with certainty in this year we have the jurisdiction conferred by article V, section 3(b)(7), to issue all writs necessary to the complete exercise and in aid of the ultimate jurisdiction imposed by article III, section 16(b), (c) and (f). *Couse v. Canal Authority,* 209 So.2d 865 (Fla.1968). . . .

There is a good deal more validity to the use of the "all writs" clause in *Florida Senate* because, as the court there pointed out, that jurisdiction did not depend on

---

102. *See* Fla. R. App. P. 9.100.

103. 392 So. 2d 1304 (Fla. 1980).

104. 412 So. 2d 360, 361 (Fla. 1982). See also *State ex rel. Chiles v. Public Employees Relations Commission,* 630 So. 2d 1093, 1095 (Fla. 1994), where *Florida Senate* is cited with approval for the following proposition: the Supreme Court "may issue all writs necessary to aid the Court in exercising its 'ultimate jurisdiction.'"

the decision of one of the litigants in the lower court to seek review after a final judgment or order, as was the case in both *Couse* and *City of Tallahassee v. Mann*.[105]

In *Roberts v. Brown*,[106] the Supreme Court addresses its jurisdiction under the "all writs" provision, and the Court reaffirms its decision in *Besoner*. The court states: "As a preliminary matter, the doctrine of all writs is not an independent basis for this Courts [sic] jurisdiction. *See Besoner v. Crawford*, 357 So. 2d 414, 415 (Fla. 1978). Rather, its use is restricted to preserving jurisdiction that has already been invoked or protecting jurisdiction that likely will be invoked in the future." [107]

In *State v. Jackson*,[108] the most recent case as of the writing of this text, the Supreme Court reaffirms *Roberts*, which reaffirmed *Besoner*, stating:

> This Court "[m]ay issue . . . all writs necessary to the complete exercise of its jurisdiction." Art. V, § 3(b)(7), Fla. Const. "[T]he all writs provision does not constitute a separate source of original or appellate jurisdiction" but instead "operates as an aid to the Court in exercising its 'ultimate jurisdiction,' conferred elsewhere in the constitution." *Williams v. State*, 913 So. 2d 541, 543 (Fla. 2005). The use of the all writs provision "is restricted to preserving jurisdiction that has already been invoked or protecting jurisdiction that likely will be invoked in the future." *Roberts v. Brown*, 43 So. 3d 673, 677 (Fla. 2010)

From the above language of the Court, one can draw the conclusion that use of the all writs provision is not limited to pending cases, but may be used to protect the Court's future exercise of jurisdiction.

(3) "May issue writs of mandamus and quo warranto to state officers and state agencies." Fla. Const. art. V, § 3(b)(8)

The common law limitations on the writ of mandamus are well known. It is well-settled law that mandamus is neither the appropriate vehicle to seek review of an alleged erroneous decision by another court, nor is it the proper vehicle to mandate the doing or undoing of a discretionary act.[109] "[A] writ of mandamus lies to compel a public officer to perform a ministerial duty."[110] "The writ cannot be used to compel a public agency clothed with discretion to exercise that discretion in a given manner."[111] This is only the case if there is not an adequate legal remedy.[112] The writ may not be employed as an appellate remedy to review the quasi-judicial action of

---

105. 411 So. 2d 162 (Fla. 1981).
106. 43 So. 3d 673 (Fla. 2010).
107. *Id*. at 677.
108. 306 So. 3d 936 (Fla. 2020).
109. *Matthew v. Crews*, 132 So. 3d 776 (Fla. 2014)
110. *Sturdivant v. Blanchard*, 422 So. 2d 1028, 1029 (Fla. 1st Dist. Ct. App. 1982).
111. *Graham v. Vann*, 394 So. 2d 180, 182 (Fla. 1st Dist. Ct. App. 1981).
112. *Agency for Health Care Admin. v. Mount Sinai Med. Ctr. of Greater Miami*, 690 So. 2d 689, 692 (Fla. 1st Dist. Ct. App. 1997).

an administrative agency.[113] Further, the writ may not be used to compel a district court of appeal to issue a written opinion instead of a per curiam affirmance without opinion.[114]

Given this definition, consider how the Florida Supreme Court used the writ in *Allen v. Butterworth*:[115]

> This court has previously addressed the constitutionality of legislative acts through its mandamus authority. *See Division of Bond Finance v. Smathers*, 337 So.2d 805 (Fla.1976). Accordingly, we treat all of the petitions filed here as petitions for writs of mandamus. While this Court has entertained mandamus petitions involving constitutional challenges, "[o]rdinarily the initial challenge to the constitutionality of a statute should be made before a trial court." *Id.* at 807. However, mandamus is the appropriate vehicle for addressing claims of unconstitutionality "where the functions of government will be adversely affected without an immediate determination." *Id.*; *see also Dickinson v. State*, 251 So.2d 268, 271 (Fla.1971).

There can be a statutory remedy that supersedes mandamus.[116]

Article V, § 3(b)(8) of the Florida Constitution authorizes the judiciary to issue writs of quo warranto "to state officers and state agencies." "Quo warranto is used 'to determine whether a state officer or agency has improperly *exercised* a power or right derived from the State.'"[117] Petitions for the writ historically have been filed after a public official has acted, and the disputed act had already occurred.[118]

In regard to the writ of quo warranto, the Florida Supreme Court has said that "[t]he rule is well settled in this state that quo warranto does not lie except to test the right of a person to hold an office or franchise or exercise some right or privilege the peculiar powers of which are derived from the state."[119] Although the Florida Supreme Court has original jurisdiction to issue a writ of quo warranto, it seldom does and prefers that these types of issues be first commenced in circuit court.[120] The Court's rationale for preferring that quo warranto actions be taken in the circuit courts is that these courts are better equipped to handle such action. Note the Court's response in the case of *State v. Fernandez*:[121]

---

113. *Anoll v. Pomerance*, 363 So. 2d 329 (Fla. 1978).

114. *Davis v. State*, 982 So. 2d 1246 (Fla. 5th Dist. Ct. App. 2008).

115. 756 So. 2d 52, 54–55 (Fla. 2000).

116. *See Community Health, Inc. v. Dep't of Health & Rehab. Servs.*, 683 So. 2d 643 (Fla. 3d Dist. Ct. App. 1996).

117. *League of Women Voters of Fla. v. Scott*, 232 So. 3d 264, 265 (Fla. 2017) (emphasis in original) (quoting *Fla. House of Representatives v. Crist*, 999 So. 2d 601, 607 (Fla. 2008)).

118. *Id.*

119. *Ex parte Smith*, 118 So. 306, 307 (Fla. 1928). *See also State ex rel. Bruce v. Kiesling*, 632 So. 2d 601 (Fla. 1994).

120. *See Harvard v. Singletary*, 733 So. 2d 1020 (Fla. 1999); *State ex rel. Vance v. Wellman*, 222 So. 2d 449 (Fla. 2d Dist. Ct. App. 1969).

121. 143 So. 638, 641 (Fla. 1932).

While we hold that relator brought the proper action to determine the right of respondent as nominee for constable to the Fifth justice district of Hillsborough county, we think that there are patent reasons why we should not retain jurisdiction of the cause. In the first place, the circuit court has coordinate jurisdiction with this court to grant the writ, the issues are such that testimony will have to be taken, and they may present themselves in such a way as to command a jury. This court has never impaneled a jury, and has no facilities for taking testimony. It was never intended that it perform the function of a nisi prius court; this being peculiarly within the province of the circuit court. If we take original jurisdiction in this contest, other matters of similar character will press us for attention to such an extent that the appellate work will be very much delayed.

This is primarily a court of appeals, and, while it has concurrent jurisdiction with the circuit courts to issue writs of quo warranto, it has consistently declined to do so except in cases where the public interest demanded, and then on an agreed statement of facts. Either party has the right to appeal if aggrieved at the judgment when rendered by the circuit court.

Accordingly, the Florida Supreme Court's quo warranto power has been little used.[122]

(4) "May, or any justice may, issue writs of habeas corpus returnable before the supreme court or any justice, a district court of appeal or any judge thereof, or any circuit judge." Fla. Const. art. V, § 3(b)(9)[123]

The writ of habeas corpus, or the Great Writ as it is commonly known, is deeply rooted in Anglo-American Jurisprudence. The writ of habeas corpus, which literally means "that you have the body," is a writ of inquiry and has traditionally been used to compel the custodian of the prisoner to bring the body of the prisoner into court so that the legality of the detention might be tested.[124]

As the following case indicates, concurrent jurisdiction exists in the circuit courts, district courts of appeal, and the Florida Supreme Court to issue writs of habeas corpus. This confusing jurisdictional structure could be interpreted to permit separate habeas corpus applications at each level. As the following case reflects, the courts have consistently resisted this interpretation.

---

122. *See, e.g., State ex rel. Pettigrew v. Kirk*, 243 So. 2d 147 (Fla. 1970).

123. For a general discussion of habeas corpus in Florida, see Robert Batey, *Habeas Corpus: The Law in Florida* (1980).

124. See *Henry v. Santana*, 62 So. 3d 1122 (Fla. 2011), for a discussion on the history of the writ of habeas corpus.

256   4 · THE COURTS

Florida Parole & Probation Commission v. Baker

346 So. 2d 640 (Fla. 2d Dist. Ct. App. 1977)

HOBSON, Acting Chief Judge.

Appellant appeals an order of the circuit court granting appellee's petition for writ of habeas corpus and ordering his release.

Prior to appellee filing his petition for writ of habeas corpus in the circuit court, he filed a petition for writ of habeas corpus in this court alleging the identical facts as alleged in his petition in the circuit court. This court, on April 20, 1976, denied his petition. On April 21st he filed a petition for rehearing which this court denied on May 13, 1976.

The petition filed in the circuit court was mailed on April 26, 1976 and received on May 5, 1976, both dates being prior to this court's denial of his petition for rehearing.

The circuit, district and supreme courts have concurrent jurisdiction in habeas corpus.[1] It is well established that a petitioner may not have three direct, repetitious applications for habeas corpus available to him upon the same subject matter.[2] The two petitions both involve the same subject matter and, in fact, the petition filed in the circuit court was filed prior to this court's denial of appellee's petition for rehearing.

For the reasons stated above we hold that the defense of *res judicata* is established on this record.

The order appealed granting the writ of habeas corpus and ordering appellee released is hereby reversed and the cause remanded.

McNULTY and OTT, JJ., concur.

In some cases, the writ of habeas corpus has been superseded by Rule 3.850 of the Florida Rules of Criminal Procedure. In *Leichtman v. Singletary*,[125] the court explained:

> The remedy of habeas corpus is not available as a substitute for post-conviction relief under rule 3.850, Florida Rules of Criminal Procedure. *See Finley v. State*, 394 So.2d 215 (Fla. 1st DCA 1981). In *Broom*, the court explained:
>
> > Prior to the adoption of Criminal Procedure Rule No. 1 (now Florida Rule of Criminal Procedure 3.850, hereinafter referred to as "Rule 3"), the proper procedure for collaterally attacking a judgment and sentence in Florida, post-judgment and post-appeal, was by filing a petition for

---

1. Florida Constitution, Art. V, §§ 3, 4, and 5.
2. *State ex rel. Miller v. Kelly*, 88 So. 2d 118 (Fla.1956), and *State ex rel. Scaldeferri v. Sandstrom*, 285 So.2d 409 (Fla.1973).
125. 674 So. 2d 889, 891–892 (Fla. 4th Dist. Ct. App. 1996).

writ of habeas corpus in the county in which the petitioner was incarcerated. However, because of the flood of habeas petitions stemming from the retroactive application of the decision of *Gideon v. Wainwright*, 372 U.S. 335, 83 S.Ct. 792, 9 L.Ed.2d 799 (1963), the Florida Supreme Court adopted Rule 3 effective April 1, 1963. *See Roy v. Wainwright*, 151 So.2d 825 (Fla.1963). The venue for Rule 3 motions, as provided in the rule, is the same court which imposed the judgment or sentence which is being collaterally attacked. Thus, the adoption of Rule 3 tended to relieve the circuit courts where the major prisons were located from this burden. Also, as the opinion in *Roy* indicates, the trial court where petitioner was tried is "best equipped" to adjudicate the rights of that petitioner.

Rule 3 contains the following reference to habeas corpus:

> An application for writ of habeas corpus in behalf of a prisoner who is authorized to apply for relief by motion pursuant to this rule, shall not be entertained if it appears that the applicant has failed to apply for relief, by motion to the court which sentenced him, or that such court has denied him relief, unless it also appears that the remedy by motion is inadequate or ineffective to test the legality of his detention.

523 So.2d at 640.

Accordingly, it has been held that Rule 3 (3.850 motions) completely superseded habeas corpus as the means of collateral attack of a judgment and sentence. *Id.* at 641. As such, the rule is intended to provide a complete and efficacious post-conviction remedy to correct convictions on any grounds which subject them to collateral attack.[1] *Id.*

As stated by the Florida Supreme Court in *Finley*:

> The remedy of habeas corpus is not available as a substitute for post-conviction relief under Rule 3.850, Fla. R.Crim.P. An application for writ of habeas corpus shall not be entertained where the applicant has failed to first apply for post-conviction relief, provided a motion for post-conviction relief is adequate to test the legality of the detention. . . . Therefore, since the issue raised in appellant's petition for habeas corpus may be raised to a motion for post-conviction relief, his failure to exhaust this remedy precludes habeas relief.

394 So.2d at 216 (citations omitted).

---

1. Habeas corpus remains available in the following areas which do not involve a collateral attack of the judgment and sentence and thus are not covered by Rule 3: (1) to attack computations of gain time and other determinations of the parole and probation commission; (2) to test pretrial detention and the denial of pretrial bond or excessive pretrial bond; (3) to determine the right to a delayed appeal; (4) to challenge extradition; and (5) to challenge the effectiveness of appellate counsel in a previous appeal. *State v. Broom*, 523 So.2d 639, 641 (Fla. 2d DCA 1988), *appeal dismissed*, 545 So.2d 1366 (Fla.1989).

2. District Courts of Appeal

Fla. Const. art V, § 4(b)

JURISDICTION. —

(1) District courts of appeal shall have jurisdiction to hear appeals, that may be taken as a matter of right, from final judgments or orders of trial courts, including those entered on review of administrative action, not directly appealable to the supreme court or a circuit court. They may review interlocutory orders in such cases to the extent provided by rules adopted by the supreme court.

(2) District courts of appeal shall have the power of direct review of administrative action, as prescribed by general law.

(3) A district court of appeal or any judge thereof may issue writs of habeas corpus returnable before the court or any judge thereof or before any circuit judge within the territorial jurisdiction of the court. A district court of appeal may issue writs of mandamus, certiorari, prohibition, quo warranto, and other writs necessary to the complete exercise of its jurisdiction. To the extent necessary to dispose of all issues in a cause properly before it, a district court of appeal may exercise any of the appellate jurisdiction of the circuit courts.

----

a. In General

Currently, there are five district courts of appeal which are, in most instances, the final appellate courts in the Florida judiciary. In *Lake v. Lake*,[126] the court enunciated this principle, stating that "[*district courts of appeal*] . . . *were meant to be courts of final, appellate jurisdiction.*" This role is set out in art. V, § 4(b)(1). This means that the one appeal, as a matter of right, from the decision of a trial court shall in most cases be taken directly to the district court of appeal for that appellate district. By now, you should be familiar with the fact that appeals from some trial court decisions go or may go directly to the Florida Supreme Court.[127] The circuit court in most cases hears appeals from county courts.[128]

There are, however, certain aspects of the jurisdiction of the district courts of appeal that must be considered in some detail.

----

126. 103 So. 2d 639, 642 (Fla. 1958).

127. Fla. Const. art. V, §§ 3(b)(1), 3(b)(2), 3(b)(5).

128. Fla. Const. art. V, § 5(b); Fla. Stat. § 26.012 (2012) (providing for the appellate jurisdiction of circuit courts on appeals from county courts).

b. "District courts of appeal shall have jurisdiction to hear appeals, that may be taken as a matter of right, from final judgments or orders of trial courts including those entered on review of administrative action, not directly appealable to the supreme court or a circuit court. . . ." Fla. Const. art. V, § 4(b)(1) (emphasis added)

The above provision establishes the jurisdiction of the district courts of appeal over appeals from final judgments of the circuit courts.

The basis of any right to appeal, especially in a criminal case, to a district court of appeal has been the source of considerable confusion. This confusion has been discussed by the First District Court of Appeal in *State v. Allen*:[129]

> ... [W]e acknowledge that the state's right to appeal depends entirely on the applicability of the statute. The supreme court held in *State v. Creighton*, 469 So.2d 735 (Fla.1985), that the state's right to appeal an order in a criminal case is purely statutory. Although the court receded in part from *Creighton* in the opinion adopting the latest revision of the Florida Rules of Appellate Procedure, *See Amendments to Florida Rules of Appellate Procedure*, 685 So.2d 773 (Fla. 1996)'[130] that opinion does not expand the state's right to appeal. Rejecting dicta in *Creighton* to the contrary, the supreme court said that the right of a citizen to appeal a final order is derived from the Florida Constitution and that it does not depend on the existence of legislation. The court left intact its holding in *Creighton* that the state's right to appeal depends on the existence of a statute. Consequently, the state's right to appeal the order in this case turns on the meaning of the statute purporting to authorize the appeal.

The italicized portion of art. V, § 4(b)(1) is somewhat puzzling. Apparently where the circuit court is to provide initial judicial review of administrative action, there is intended a second review as a matter of right in the district court of appeal. The nature of this proceeding was first considered in *State v. Furen*:[131]

> We turn now to the crucial question in this case, to wit: Was the District Court correct in holding that when the Circuit Court of Pinellas County reviewed and approved the order of the Pinellas County Water and Navigation Authority it sat not as a "trial court" but as an appellate court, so that no *appeal* could be taken to the District Court of Appeal, Second District, under Article V, Section 5(3), Florida Constitution?[132]

---

129. 743 So. 2d 532, 533–534 (Fla. 1st Dist. Ct. App. 1997).

130. Republished as 696 So. 2d 1103 (Fla. 1996).

131. 118 So. 2d 6, 8–9 (Fla. 1960). But see *Board of County Commissioners of Hillsborough County v. Casa Development Ltd.*, 332 So. 2d 651 (Fla. 2d Dist. Ct. App. 1976), concerning the jurisdiction of circuit courts in these kinds of cases.

132. "Jurisdiction. Appeals from trial courts in each appellate district . . . may be taken to the court of appeal of such district as a matter of right, from all final judgments or decrees except those

Appellants contend that when the Circuit Court reviewed the order of the County Authority it was sitting as a trial court and we think this is correct. Chapter 31182, § 8(e), Special Acts of 1955, authorizes anyone who is aggrieved by the Board's ruling to file a petition for rehearing and states that they "shall have the right to have the entire cause reviewed by the Circuit Court of the Sixth Judicial Circuit (Court) of Florida in and for Pinellas county as provided by law for other appeals to the Circuit Court." No other specification for review of the "entire cause" is contained in the Act so we must look to other acts of the legislature and decisions of this court for instructions to review such orders.

This court has repeatedly held that where statutory administrative proceedings are had before administrative officers, boards, commissions or other tribunals, with statutory appeals to the circuit courts, such proceedings do not appear in the judicial department of the state government as a judicial "case" until they are brought to the circuit court by appeal; therefore, the "case" may be fairly regarded as originating in the circuit court through a statutory appeal from the administrative board as much as it would be so originating in the circuit court by injunction, certiorari or other original writ. [Citations omitted.]

These cases consistently support the reasoning that the Circuit Court sat as a trial court when it reviewed the "entire cause" on appeal from the order of the County Authority. Reason and logic also support this conclusion. Such proceedings before boards and commissions are so often conducted with regard to proper decorum or observance of the rules for introduction or consideration of evidence that the work of the circuit court consists largely in preparing an intelligent and orderly "case" for review by the appellate court. Reviewing the "entire cause" connotes consideration of every aspect of it by the circuit court.

The above quote is one explanation of: (1) why this category of "appeal" from the circuit court to the district court of appeal could be construed to be as of right, and (2) why the words "including those entered on review of administrative action" were added to the 1972 revision of what is now art. V, § 4(b)(1). Case law has not, however, borne out this interpretation.

---

from which appeals may be taken direct to the Supreme Court or to a circuit court." Fla. Const. art. V (repealed 1972).

City of Deerfield Beach v. Vaillant
419 So. 2d 624 (Fla. 1982)[133]

ALDERMAN, Chief Justice.

We review the decision of the District Court of Appeal, Fourth District, in *City of Deerfield Beach v. Vaillant*, 399 So.2d 1045 (Fla. 4th DCA 1981), which expressly conflicts with *United Teachers of Dade v. Save Brickell Avenue, Inc.*, 378 So.2d 296 (Fla. 3d DCA 1979). The sole issue before us is whether a final judgment of the circuit court reviewing administrative action is subject to appeal in the district court of appeal or whether this judgment is reviewable only by writ of certiorari. The Fourth District in the present case held that the circuit court's order reversing a decision of the Civil Service Board was reviewable only by writ of certiorari pursuant to Florida Rule of Appellate Procedure 9.030(b)(2)(B). We agree and approve the decision of the Fourth District.

Michael Vaillant was terminated as the superintendent of the Deerfield Beach Wastewater Treatment Plant by the city manager. He appealed to the Civil Service Board of the City of Deerfield Beach which, after hearing, voted to uphold his termination. He then petitioned the circuit court for review of the board's action by certiorari. After examining the entire record "including hundreds of pages of proceedings and testimony taken and given before the Board," the circuit court granted Vaillant's petition, reversed the board's decision, and ordered Vaillant reinstated.

The City of Deerfield Beach appealed to the Fourth District, but the district court, finding its scope of review to be limited when the circuit court has acted in its appellate capacity, treated the appeal as a petition for writ of certiorari and denied it. The district court pointed out that the controversy over which method of review is available in the district court is engendered by the use of the words "certiorari" and "appeal" synonymously with the intention of denoting a seeking out of higher review and that the type of "certiorari" sought in the circuit court here was not a discretionary review but rather was a review to which Vaillant was entitled as a matter of right. It explained that in reviewing the board's action, the circuit court determined whether or not the board provided procedural due process, observed the essential requirements of the law, and supported its findings by substantial competent evidence. Regardless of the nomenclature, the Fourth District determined, the review sought in the circuit court was effectually an "appeal." To establish its appropriate scope of review, the district court relied upon Florida Rule of Appellate Procedure 9.030(b)(2)(B) which provides that the certiorari jurisdiction of the district court may be sought to review final orders of circuit courts acting in their review capacity. Stating that a final judgment of a circuit court acting in its review capacity is not appealable as a matter of right to a district court if it has already been

---

133. The problems raised by the following cases are discussed in Cherie Lee Onkst, *Ignoring the Appeal to Reason in the Appeal of Right: Judicial Review of Administrative Action in Florida After Vaillant*, 14 Stetson L. Rev. 665 (1985).

directly "appealed" to a circuit court, it found inapplicable article V, section 4(b)(1), Florida Constitution, which provides in pertinent part:

> District courts of appeal shall have jurisdiction to hear appeals, that may be taken as a matter of right, from final judgments or orders of trial courts, including those entered on review of administrative action, not directly appealable to . . . a circuit court.

Evaluating the circuit court's judgment in light of its limited standard of review, the district court determined that procedural due process was afforded and that essential requirements of the law were observed.

We agree with the decision and rationale of the Fourth District in the present case [citations omitted]. As a case moves up the appellate ladder, each level of review does not become broader. As Chief Judge Letts, speaking for the court, said:

> [C]ommon sense dictates that no one enjoys three full repetitive reviews to,
>
> 1. a civil service board
>
> 2. a circuit court
>
> 3. a district court of appeal. . . .

City of Deerfield Beach v. Vaillant, 399 So.2d at 1047.

We disapprove *United Teachers of Dade v. Brickell Avenue, Inc.* insofar as it holds that a final judgment of the circuit court acting in its review capacity to review administrative action is appealable as a matter of right to the district court where it has already been directly "appealed" to the circuit court. *Cf. Save Brickell Avenue, Inc. v. City of Miami*, 393 So.2d 1197 (Fla. 3d DCA 1981), wherein the Third District treated as a petition for writ of certiorari an appeal from the circuit court's final judgment entered in a zoning matter brought to the circuit court for review.

We hold that where full review of administrative action is given in the circuit court as a matter of right, one appealing the circuit court's judgment is not entitled to a second full review in the district court. Where a party is entitled as a matter of right to seek review in the circuit court from administrative action, the circuit court must determine whether procedural due process is accorded, whether the essential requirements of the law have been observed, and whether the administrative findings and judgment are supported by competent substantial evidence. The district court, upon review of the circuit court's judgment, then determines whether the circuit court afforded procedural due process and applied the correct law.

Accordingly, we approve the decision of the Fourth District.

It is so ordered.

BOYD, OVERTON, SUNDBERG, McDONALD and EHRLICH, JJ., concur.

ADKINS, J., dissents [without opinion].

4 · THE COURTS

The Florida Supreme Court's decision in *City of Deerfield Beach* was not entirely well received, as the following case illustrates.

Seminole County Board of County Commissioners v. Long

422 So. 2d 938 (Fla. 5th Dist. Ct. App. 1982)

COWART, Judge.

* * *

After this case was briefed and argued and this opinion prepared, the supreme court issued *City of Deerfield Beach v. Vaillant*, 419 So.2d 624 (Fla.1982), holding that a district court of appeal could review a final circuit court order reviewing administrative action only by certiorari, despite the clear language of Article V, section 4(b)(1) of the Florida Constitution.[1] We did not question the district court of appeal's jurisdiction to hear appeals from orders of the circuit court reviewing administrative action where the supreme court did not have such jurisdiction. Heretofore, this court had worked out that problem, giving effect to the plain language of article V, section 4, Florida Constitution, and holding that in such cases our scope of review might be as broad as, but never broader than, the circuit court's scope of review of the administrative action. *McCray v. County of Volusia*, 400 So.2d 511 (Fla. 5th DCA 1981); *Odham v. Petersen*, 398 So.2d 875 (Fla. 5th DCA 1981); *County of Volusia v. Transamerica Business Corp.*, 392 So.2d 585 (Fla. 5th DCA 1980). Our view was based on the belief that the constitutional drafters knew the difference between the words "appeal" and "review" and that the constitutional provision was, not only applicable and binding, but was a well-conceived implementation of long established principles of constitutional magnitude.[2]

---

1. Adopted in 1972, Article V, section 4(b)(1), Florida Constitution, provides in pertinent part: District courts of appeal shall have jurisdiction to hear appeals that may be taken as a matter of right, from final judgments or orders of trial courts, *including those entered on review of administrative action*, not directly appealable to the supreme court or a circuit court. ([E]mphasis added)[.] [Sic.]

2. In the prior constitution, Article V, section 5(c), Florida Constitution (1889), merely allowed "appeals from trial courts" to the district courts of appeal. Even though it did not specifically authorize appeals to district courts of appeal from final orders of the circuit court entered on review of administrative action, the supreme court held that litigants were entitled to such an appeal because the circuit court sitting in review of administrative action is acting as a "trial court."

This court has repeatedly held that where statutory administrative proceedings are had before administrative officers, boards, commissions or other tribunals, with statutory appeals to the circuit courts, such proceedings do not appear in the judicial department of the state government as a judicial "case" until they are brought to the circuit court by appeal; therefore, the "case" may be fairly regarded as originating in the circuit court through a statutory appeal from the administrative board as much as it would be so originating in the circuit court by injunction, certiorari or other original writ. *South Atlantic S. S. Co. of Delaware v. Tutson*, 1939, 139 Fla. 405, 190 So. 675; *Duval Engineering &*

As a constitutional principle for the protection of individual liberty against arbitrary actions of governmental officials, the doctrine of separation of powers of government ranks equal to the guarantees in sections 9 and 10 of article I of the Constitution of the United States, in the first nine amendments thereto and in their state constitutional counterparts. *See* Art. II, § 3, Fla.Const. The fundamental idea of separation of powers is that the judiciary is the operative check on possible arbitrary action by legislative and executive officers. Therein lies the difference between circuit court review of a judgment of a county court, itself a subdivision of the judicial system, and circuit court review of actions of an administrative body, which is a component of another branch of government. The county court judgment is presumed to have been correctly reached in an impartial and detached judicial forum and, on review by appeal, the circuit court is required to defer to the fact findings of the county court, it being the initial judicial tribunal; on certiorari review, the district court should defer to the substantive law applied by the circuit court as appellate court and review the circuit court action only for procedural due process. *See Combs v. State*, 420 So.2d 316 (Fla. 5th DCA 1982).

Under our constitution, the primary purpose of judicial review of executive action is to prevent arbitrary fact-finding and actions by the executive. Upon judicial review of administrative action in the circuit court, by certiorari or otherwise, the administrative action is entitled to none of the deference due initial judicial action. Such judicial "review" partakes more of the nature of an original judicial proceeding (which it is) than of a classic appeal of a lower judicial tribunal. The constitution

---

Contracting Co. v. Johnson, 1944, 154 Fla. 9, 16 So.2d 290; *Alcoma Citrus Cooperative v. Isom*, 1947, 159 Fla. 10, 30 So.2d 528.

These cases consistently support the reasoning that the Circuit Court sat as a trial court when it reviewed the "entire cause" on appeal from the order of the County Authority. Reason and logic also support this conclusion. Such proceedings before boards and commissions are so often conducted without regard to proper decorum or observance of the rules for introduction or consideration of evidence that the work of the circuit court consists largely in preparing an intelligent and orderly "case" for review by the appellate court. Reviewing the "entire cause" connotes consideration of every aspect of it by the circuit court.

* * *

The intent of the Constitution in providing for appeals in "cases" is directed at controversies pending in the judicial system and not controversies pending before an administrative agency of the executive branch of our government; and an order of an administrative agency is not a decision in a "case" within the scope of Section 5 of Article V of the Constitution.

For the purposes of jurisdiction, an "appeal" to the circuit court pursuant to the statute becomes a "case" of original jurisdiction when it enters or is brought into the judicial system, if such an appeal is authorized by statute and the statute is not violative of the Constitution.

State v. Furen, 118 So.2d 5, 8–10 (Fla.1960); *accord, Wexler v. Ring*, 125 So.2d 883 (Fla. 3d DCA 1961). The relevant portion of the constitution was replaced in 1972 by present Article V, section 4(b), Florida Constitution. The inclusion of the words "including those entered on review of administrative action" in the present section was undoubtedly intended to codify *Furen's* holding.

gives litigants the right to one appeal from initial judicial action. A right of direct plenary appeal from a circuit court order reviewing administrative action to the district court of appeal was unquestioned until now. The constitutional provision adopted in 1972 appears to be merely an affirmation and guarantee of prior good law. We prefer this rationale as the basis for appellate review in this case, but if we must justify our review under the *Deerfield* rationale, then we can be deemed to have treated this appeal as a petition for certiorari under Florida Rule of Appellate Procedure 9.040(c) and to have found that the circuit court applied incorrect rules of law relating to the non-technical nature of pleading administrative complaints and as to the breadth of authority and grounds for an employer, even a governmental employer, to discharge an employee under the case law cited above.

The order of the circuit court quashing the board's decision is

REVERSED.

ORFINGER, C.J., and DAUKSCH, J., concur.

The reader should note that the Fifth District Court of Appeal read *Furen* and the 1972 amendment to art. V, § 3(b)(4) the same way as the authors who arrived at their conclusion independent of the district court. The Florida Supreme Court has continued to adhere to its *Deerfield Beach* decision.

Education Development Center, Inc. v. City of West Palm Beach Zoning Board of Appeals

541 So. 2d 106 (Fla. 1989)

BARKETT, Justice.

We have for review *City of West Palm Beach Zoning Board of Appeals v. Education Development Center, Inc.*, 526 So. 2d 775 (Fla. 4th DCA 1988), in which the district court granted certiorari and quashed an order of the circuit court overturning a decision of an administrative agency. Because the district court's opinion conflicts with *City of Deerfield Beach v. Vaillant*, 419 So.2d 624 (Fla.1982), we have jurisdiction.*

The issue here concerns the extent of the district court's certiorari review. We find that the district court exceeded the scope of review and quash the decision below.

The petitioner, Education Development Center, Inc. (Center), owns residential property. The Center appeared at a hearing before the respondent, City of West Palm Beach Zoning Board of Appeals (Board), seeking to convert its property to a private preschool and kindergarten.

---

* Art. V, § 3(b)(3), Fla. Const.

The Board denied the Center's application and the Center appealed to the circuit court. The circuit court reversed the Board, concluding that there was "substantially competent evidence" to support the Center's application as required by the zoning code.

In *City of West Palm Beach Zoning Board of Appeals v. Education Development Center, Inc.*, 504 So.2d 1385 (Fla. 4th DCA 1987), the district court granted the Board's petition for writ of certiorari, concluding that the circuit court had applied an incorrect standard of review. The district court remanded for a redetermination and explained:

> [T]he circuit court departed from the essential requirements of law by applying an incorrect standard of review. The question is not whether, upon review of the evidence in the record, there exists substantial competent evidence to support a position *contrary* to that reached by the agency. Instead, the circuit court should review the factual determination made by the agency and determine whether there is substantial competent evidence to support the agency's conclusion.

Id. at 1386 (emphasis in original).

On remand, the circuit court again reversed, this time finding that "there was no substantial competent evidence to support the City's denial of the petition."

The Board returned a second time to the district court, which in the opinion now before us, *Education Development Center*, 526 So.2d at 775, granted the petition for writ of certiorari and remanded to the circuit court for further proceedings. The basis for the district court's reversal was its disagreement with the trial court's findings that there was no substantial competent evidence to support the Board's decision. In contrast to the circuit court, the district court found:

> There *was* substantial evidence to support the denial of the application to permit the operation of a preschool in this residential area. To find to the contrary, we conclude that the lower tribunal either reinterpreted the inferences which the evidence supported or reweighed the evidence; in either event substituting its judgment for that of the zoning board, which it may not properly do.

Id. at 777 (emphasis supplied).

In *City of Deerfield Beach v. Vaillant*, 419 So.2d 624 (Fla.1982), the Court clearly set forth the standards governing certiorari review. When the circuit court reviews the decision of an administrative agency under Florida Rule of Appellate Procedure 9.030(c)(3), there are *three* discrete components of its certiorari review.

> Where a party is entitled as a matter of right to seek review in the circuit court from administrative action, the circuit court must determine whether procedural due process is accorded, whether the essential requirements of the law have been observed, and whether the administrative findings and judgment are supported by competent substantial evidence.

Vaillant, 419 So.2d at 626. In so doing, the circuit court is not permitted to reweigh the evidence nor to substitute its judgment for that of the agency. *Bell v. City of Sarasota*, 371 So.2d 525 (Fla. 2d DCA 1979).

In turn, the standard of review to guide the district court when it reviews the circuit court's order under Florida Rule of Appellate Procedure 9.030(b)(2)(B) is necessarily narrower. The standard for the district court has only *two* discrete components.

> The district court, upon review of the circuit court's judgment, then determines whether the circuit court afforded procedural due process and applied the correct law.

Vaillant, 419 So.2d at 626. In *Vaillant*, the Court adopted the rationale of the Fourth District Court of Appeal and quoted approvingly from its decision:

> "[C]ommon sense dictates that no one enjoys three full repetitive reviews to,
>
> 1. a civil service board
>
> 2. a circuit court
>
> 3. a district court of appeal. . . ."

Id. (quoting *City of Deerfield Beach v. Vaillant*, 399 So.2d 1045, 1047 (Fla. 4th DCA 1981)).

* * *

We hold that the principles expressed by the Court in *Vaillant* clearly define the standards of review applicable here. There was no contention of a denial of due process and the district court of appeal did not find that the trial judge applied an incorrect principle of law. The district court of appeal simply disagreed with the circuit court's evaluation of the evidence. Accordingly, we reaffirm *Vaillant* and quash the decision of the district court.

It is so ordered.

EHRLICH, C.J., and OVERTON, SHAW, GRIMES and KOGAN, J.J., concur.

McDONALD, J., dissents with an opinion. [This opinion is omitted.]

There is another troubling aspect of the result reached by the Fourth District Court of Appeal in *City of Deerfield Beach*, which was affirmed by the Florida Supreme Court. The District Court apparently based its ruling, at least in part, on the Florida Rules of Appellate Procedure. The operative words from the court's opinion are:[134]

---

134. 399 So. 2d 1045, 1047 (Fla. 4th Dist. Ct. App. 1981).

268 4 · THE COURTS

. . . [B]ut the fact remains we believe that a plenary appeal from this circuit court ruling is not available and that recourse to us must be by certiorari pursuant to Florida Appellate Rule, 9.030(b)(2)(B) which provides:

> "The certiorari jurisdiction of district courts of appeal *may* be sought to review . . . final orders of circuit courts acting in their review capacity." (emphasis supplied)[.] [Sic.]

If it can be assumed that the dispute over whether review by the district court of circuit court review of action of a local government agency is by appeal or common law certiorari is a "dispute concerning any court's jurisdiction," then such use of Rule 9.030(b)(2)(B) appears to be contrary to the committee notes to that rule which state that "[t]his rule is not intended to affect the substantive law governing the jurisdiction of any court and should not be considered as authority for the resolution of disputes concerning any court's jurisdiction. . . ."[135]

The following comment by the First District Court of Appeal in *Irvine v. Duval County Planning Commission*[136] raises yet another concern about *City of Deerfield Beach*:

> By proceeding in this court via petition for certiorari, rather than appeal, petitioner has conformed to the directive of the Florida Supreme Court in *City of Deerfield Beach v. Vaillant*, 419 So.2d 624 (Fla.1982). Appellee, on the other hand, suggests in its response that review should properly be by appeal, citing *County of Volusia v. Transamerica Business Corporation*, 392 So.2d 585 (Fla. 5th DCA 1980). We note that the Fifth District, in view of the *Vaillant* decision, no longer adheres to the position it took in *Transamerica* and other cases indicating that plenary appeal would be the appropriate vehicle for district court review of circuit court decisions in common law certiorari proceedings reviewing quasi-judicial administrative action. *See, Stansberry v. City of Lake Helen*, 425 So.2d 1157 (Fla. 5th DCA 1983), p. 1158, n. 1. *We are of the view that arguments favoring the remedy of appeal might still have validity, since language of the Vaillant opinion seems to limit its application to District Court review of circuit court orders entered in proceedings in which a party is entitled "as a matter of right" to seek review of administrative action in the circuit court.* [Emphasis added.] *Vaillant, supra*, 419 So.2d at 626. *See also, Bennett, Bishop, Herron & Holmes v. Board of County Commissioners of Sarasota County*, 426 So.2d 1260 (Fla. 2d DCA 1983). We conclude, however, that our resolution of this case would not be any different upon review by appeal, since we are of the opinion that the scope of our review by appeal from a denial of common law certiorari would be to determine whether the trial court acted within its jurisdiction,

---

135. Fla. R. App. P. 9.030, Committee Notes to the 1977 Amendment (2006). *See also Cherokee Crushed Stone, Inc. v. City of Miramar*, 421 So. 2d 684 (Fla. 4th Dist. Ct. App. 1982).

136. 466 So. 2d 357, n. 1. (Fla. 1st Dist. Ct. App. 1985) (quashed on other grounds in *Irvine v. Duval County Plan. Comm'n*, 495 So. 2d 167 (Fla. 1986)).

and whether the court departed from the essential requirements of law. Cf., *Odham v. Petersen*, 398 So.2d 875 (Fla. 5th DCA 1981).

Since only a general law could provide for review as a matter of right from an agency to a circuit court, which one provided for review in *City of Deerfield Beach*?[137]

The question whether *City of Deerfield Beach* applied to circuit court review by common law certiorari as well as "appeal" was answered in the following case. It is included here, even though the opinion also discusses matters of concern to circuit court jurisdiction.

Cherokee Crushed Stone, Inc. v. City of Miramar

421 So. 2d 684 (Fla. 4th Dist. Ct. App. 1982)

OPINION ON MOTION TO DISMISS APPEAL

HERSEY, Judge.

Cherokee Crushed Stone, Inc., appellant here, made application to appellee, City of Miramar, for a special exception required to conduct certain mining operations on land zoned agricultural. From an adverse determination by the City Commission appellant sought review in the circuit court by petition for writ of certiorari. The circuit court, after hearing, issued an opinion in the form of an order denying relief. The present appeal concerns this order of the circuit court. Appellee has filed a motion to dismiss the appeal. Appellant's response requests that we address the following issue:

DOES ARTICLE V, SECTION (4)(B)(1) OF THE FLORIDA CONSTITUTION GUARANTEE THE RIGHT TO A PLENARY APPEAL FROM A FINAL ORDER OF A CIRCUIT COURT WHICH HAS EXERCISED ITS CERTIORARI JURISDICTION TO REVIEW ADMINISTRATIVE ACTION?

The action of the City Commission was administrative action; however, neither special nor general law has constituted the City of Miramar an "administrative agency" as contemplated by the Administrative Procedure Act and particularly Section 120.52(1)(c), Florida Statutes (1981). Were it otherwise, appeal from the ruling of

---

137. ". . . [The circuit courts] shall have the power of direct review of administrative action prescribed by general law." Fla. Const. art. V, §5(b). Since as far as the authors can tell, neither the district court nor the supreme court opinion in *City of Deerfield Beach* cites a general law source for the appeal as of right from the agency to the circuit court, such source remains a puzzle. The puzzle is compounded by the comment of the district court that "the 'appeal' to the circuit court under the city provisions now before us was styled 'a review by certiorari.'" *City of Deerfield Beach v. Vaillant*, 399 So. 2d 1045, 1047 (Fla. 4th Dist. Ct. App. 1981). As pointed out by the district court, "the circuit judge treated it as if it were an appeal and reviewed 'the entire record including hundreds of pages of proceedings and testimony.'" *Id.* Thus, "no matter what the magic word, the end product was an appeal to the circuit court." *Id.* "City provisions" regarding review of agency action in the circuit court certainly do not amount to a general law as the constitution requires. Neither would a special law setting out the "city provisions" although, of course, no special law was cited.

the City Commission would be directly to this court (rather than the circuit court) by virtue of Section 120.68, Florida Statutes (1981).

We initially considered the motion to dismiss and prepared this opinion without the benefit of the supreme court's decision in *City of Deerfield Beach v. Vaillant*, 419 So.2d 624 (1982). That opinion appears to resolve the primary issue posed by appellant's question but leaves open an important subsidiary question.

As we have indicated, the municipality involved here has not by special or general law been rendered subject to the Administrative Procedure Act and its administrative action is not subject to direct review by a district court. Further there is no provision of general or special law permitting appeal of this municipality's administrative action to the circuit court. An ordinance of the municipality authorizes the filing of a petition for writ of certiorari with the circuit court to review agency action. While such an ordinance may confer standing on a party to proceed it may not confer jurisdiction on the circuit court where none otherwise exists nor does it determine the scope of review.

There being no review available directly to either the district or the circuit courts, we conclude that review is available only through the trial court's constitutional power to issue its discretionary writ of certiorari.

Resort to the district court from the circuit court in such a case is also limited to a petition for writ of certiorari.

At issue here, then, is the nature and extent of review that should be accorded by the district court to administrative action of an agency *not* subject to the Administrative Procedure Act and initially not "appealable" to the circuit court by virtue of general, special or decisional law. The answer to this question should depend upon the scope of review which has been or should have been afforded by the circuit court.

Section 4(b)(1) of Article V of the Florida Constitution provides that "final judgments or orders of trial courts, including those entered on review of administrative action" are appealable as a matter of right to the district courts unless they are directly appealable to the supreme court or a circuit court. In *City of Deerfield Beach v. Vaillant*, 399 So.2d 1045 (Fla. 4th DCA 1981), this court determined that a final judgment of a circuit court acting in its review capacity is not appealable as a matter of right if it has already been "appealed" (by certiorari) to a circuit court. The difficulty we now perceive in applying that standard is created by the language of the constitutional provision itself. There are only two trial courts, the county court and the circuit court, and only the latter has jurisdiction to review agency or administrative action. If the term "circuit court" is substituted for the term "trial court" in the paraphrased constitutional provision the seeming non sequitur is apparent:

> District courts of appeal shall have jurisdiction to hear *appeals* ... from final judgments of *circuit courts* ... entered on review of administrative action ... not directly appealable to ... a *circuit court*. [Emphasis added.]

Obviously an appeal may not be taken from one circuit court to another circuit court. The only logical interpretation of the literal language of this provision is that an *appeal* to the district court is appropriate from any final judgment or order of a circuit court entered on review of administrative action.

The scope of review in such cases has been subjected to scrutiny by this and other district courts of appeal, and now by the supreme court, and divergent views emerge from the case law. The scope of review afforded has depended in the past upon whether the court takes the position that review is by certiorari in the district court (the pyramid hypothesis of *Campbell v. Vetter* and *City of Deerfield Beach v. Vaillant*) or by appeal. In *Vaillant* this court squarely aligned itself with the view that the circuit court provides an *appeal* of administrative action, reviewable in the district court by petition for writ of *certiorari* despite the fact that the constitution uses the term "appeal." Our reasoning was based upon the proposition that review by the circuit court of administrative action, although referred to as certiorari, is not discretionary and in scope is basically the same as an appeal. *City of Deerfield Beach v. Vaillant, supra; Campbell v. Vetter*, 375 So.2d 4 (Fla. 4th DCA 1979). *See also Campbell v. Vetter*, 392 So.2d 6 (Fla. 4th DCA 1981).

* * *

Several arguments are made against construing Section 4(b)(1) as providing a right of *appeal* from an order of the circuit court entered on review of administrative action. One such argument is that the parties are then afforded, in effect, several appeals, a right not even accorded to criminal defendants. Thus, an administrative order may be "appealed" to the circuit court and the circuit court's decision then reviewed again by the district court. It has been argued that such a chain of review is contrary to traditional concepts of appellate review, may operate to lengthen the process of exhaustion of administrative remedies, and, incongruously, to provide parties in administrative actions greater review rights than are afforded to civil litigants and criminal defendants.

It has also been argued that interpretation of Section 4(b)(1) as not extending the right of appeal to orders entered by the circuit court on review of administrative action is supported by Rule 9.030(b)(1)(A) and (2)(B), Florida Rules of Appellate Procedure. Those portions of the rule provide:

(b) Jurisdiction of District Courts of Appeal.

(2) *Certiorari Jurisdiction.* The certiorari jurisdiction of district courts of appeal may be sought to review.

. . . .

(B) final orders of circuit courts acting in their review capacity.

Although this rule, adopted subsequent to the constitutional revision, "is not intended to affect the substantive law governing the jurisdiction of any court and should not be considered as authority for the resolution of disputes concerning any court's jurisdiction" (committee notes), it has been suggested that the supreme court's action in adopting the rule is an indication (however slight) of its construction of Article V, Section 4(b)(1).

* * *

Summarizing the arguments against permitting an appeal under the circumstances involved in the case on review: (1) a party is thereby afforded more than one appeal from administrative action; (2) one possible interpretation of the appellate rules favors certiorari over appeal; and (3) the scope of review may be variously and therefore confusingly defined depending upon the vehicle the district court permits to be utilized to obtain review. A final argument might well be made (and indeed is made here) that this district is committed by precedent to a contrary view (which now bears the imprimatur of the supreme court).

* * *

[*State v. Furen*, 118 So. 2d 6 (Fla. 1960) (discussed earlier in this chapter)] suggested that when the circuit court sits in review of administrative action it sits as a trial court. This follows from the proposition that administrative action becomes a "judicial case" only when brought to the circuit court, thus the "case" originates in that court. Because proceedings conducted prior to filing of the case with the circuit court "are so often conducted without regard to proper decorum or observance of the rules for introduction or consideration of evidence, the work of the circuit court consists largely in preparing an intelligent and orderly 'case' for review by the appellate court." It follows, held the Supreme Court, that the district court must accord an *appeal* from the judgment of the circuit court rather than review by the more limited (and discretionary) writ of certiorari.

We have now come full circle to the more recent supreme court pronouncement on this issue in *Vaillant*. It seems clear that *Furen*, to the extent that its rationale and holding are inconsistent therewith, has been overruled by *Vaillant*. An issue seemingly unresolved by *Vaillant* is exemplified by the following language in that opinion:

> We hold that *where full review of administrative action is given in the circuit court as a matter of right, one appealing the circuit court's judgment is not entitled to a second full review in the district court.* Where a party is entitled as a matter of right to seek review in the circuit court from administrative action, the circuit court must determine whether procedural due process is accorded, whether the essential requirements of the law have been observed, and whether the administrative findings and judgment are supported by competent substantial evidence. The district court, upon review of the circuit court's judgment, then determines whether the circuit court afforded procedural due process and applied the correct law.

The problem lies in determining whether, in a particular case, "a party is entitled as a matter of right to seek review in the circuit court from administrative action." We have previously adverted to the three possibilities: (1) action by an agency within the penumbra of the Administrative Procedures [sic.] Act which is appealable directly to the district court; (2) action by an agency which the law makes appealable to the circuit court; and (3) action by an agency which is reviewable only by certiorari to the circuit court. It is this latter category into which the present case falls and it is this category which appears, at least on literal terms, to be one in which a party has no entitlement, as a matter of right, to seek review by appeal in the circuit court. In order to resolve this impasse we interpret the supreme court's holding in *Vaillant* as impliedly affirming our underlying premise in *Campbell v. Vetter*, quoted with approval in our version of *Vaillant* (399 So.2d 1045 (Fla. 4th DCA 1981)) that review by certiorari under these circumstances is mandatory, not discretionary, and that the scope of review by the circuit court includes determinations as to whether the administrative agency:

1. Accorded procedural due process;

2. Observed the essential requirements of the law; and

3. Supported its findings by substantial competent evidence.

Under such a rule it becomes clear that "full review of administrative action is given in the circuit court as a matter of right."

We therefore treat the present proceedings as an application for review by certiorari and the parties are requested to proceed accordingly.

The motion to dismiss otherwise is denied.

DELL and WALDEN, JJ., concur.

It seems to the authors that in making common law certiorari an "appeal," the spirit of, if not the letter of, art. V, § 5(b), which provides for direct circuit court review of administrative action only if "provided by general law," was violated.

Although it involves an appeal to the circuit court as a matter of right from a final administrative order of an enforcement board, the following case is presented to highlight the differences between certiorari review and appellate review. [For a detailed discussion of the district court's second-tier review, see *Nader v. Florida Department of Highway Safety and Motor Vehicles*, presented later in this chapter].

Central Florida Investments, Inc. v. Orange County

295 So. 3d 292 (Fla. 5th Dist. Ct. App. 2019)

EDWARDS, J.

Central Florida Investments, Inc., Petitioner ("CFI"), argues that the circuit court, acting in its appellate capacity, departed from the essential requirements of the law by treating CFI's appeal as though it were instead a petition for a writ of certiorari and then dismissing the petition. We agree with CFI that section 162.11, Florida Statutes (2017), provides for a plenary appeal to the circuit court as a matter of right from a final administrative order of an enforcement board. However, the record reveals that CFI requested a more limited review, which the circuit court may have conducted. Because it is unclear whether the circuit court indeed employed the scope of review requested by CFI, we remand for further proceedings.

Our review of the circuit court's appellate decision is by way of second-tier certiorari, which limits our consideration to whether the circuit court: (1) afforded CFI procedural due process and (2) applied the correct law. See Haines City Cmty. Dev. v. Heggs, 658 So. 2d 523, 530 (Fla. 1995); DMB Inv. Tr. v. Islamorada, Vill. of Islands, 225 So. 3d 312, 316 (Fla. 3d DCA 2017).

CFI was cited for a violation of the building code by Orange County Code Enforcement Division with regard to what were deemed to be unsafe conditions in a structure that had been partially demolished during certain activities engaged in by CFI. Because CFI contested the violation and ownership of the building in question, an evidentiary hearing was held before the Orange County Special Magistrate who entered a final administrative order against CFI and in favor of Orange County, Respondent.

CFI took an appeal, ostensibly pursuant to section 162.11, requesting the circuit court to reverse the final order entered by the magistrate. That section provides:

> 162.11 Appeals. An aggrieved party, including the local governing body, may appeal a final administrative order of an enforcement board to the circuit court. Such an appeal shall not be a hearing de novo but shall be limited to appellate review of the record created before the enforcement board. An appeal shall be filed within 30 days of the execution of the order to be appealed.

§ 162.11, Fla. Stat. (2017).

As CFI correctly argues, that statutory section clearly provides for an appeal as a matter of right to the circuit court. See City of Ocala v. Gard, 988 So. 2d 1281, 1282–83 (Fla. 5th DCA 2008). This Court has described the nature of such an appeal as plenary. Id. at 1283. There is nothing in the statute to suggest otherwise. "[W]here the language of a statute is plain and unambiguous there is no occasion for judicial interpretation." DMB Inv. Tr., 225 So. 3d at 317 (quoting Forsythe v. Longboat Key Beach Erosion Control Dist., 604 So. 2d 452, 454 (Fla. 1992)). Accordingly, if CFI had pursued a plenary appeal, the circuit court would have departed from the essential requirements of the law if it provided a more limited review, such as that afforded by first-tier certiorari review.

When CFI appealed the magistrate's order to the circuit court, it did not request a plenary appeal. Instead, CFI specifically requested the circuit court to conduct a first-tier review of the magistrate's order, governed by a three-prong standard of review, to determine whether: (1) procedural due process was afforded; (2) the essential requirements of law were observed; and (3) the magistrate's final order was supported by competent substantial evidence. It is understandable that CFI requested the circuit court to follow that procedure, as there are several Florida Supreme Court cases suggesting that the three-pronged first-tier review is the appropriate scope for a circuit court's appellate review of an agency or board decision; however, none of those cases discuss, concern, or cite section 162.11. See, e.g., Dusseau v. Metro. Dade Cty. Bd. of Cty. Comm'rs, 794 So. 2d 1270, 1273–74 (Fla. 2001); Fla. Power & Light Co. v. City of Dania, 761 So. 2d 1089, 1092 (Fla. 2000); Haines City Cmty. Dev., 658 So. 2d at 530; City of Deerfield Beach v. Vaillant, 419 So. 2d 624, 626 (Fla. 1982). Indeed, section 166.061, Florida Statutes (1980), the predecessor to section 162.11, originally provided that "[a]n aggrieved party may appeal a ruling or order of the enforcement board by certiorari in circuit court." (emphasis added). However, in 1982 the Legislature amended section 166.061 by deleting the word "certiorari." Ch. 82-37, § 10, Laws of Fla. The Legislature then renumbered that section, and in 1985 amended the statute further by using only the unmodified word "appeal" repeatedly. Ch. 85-150, § 3, Laws of Fla. Section 162.11 is the current and controlling grant of appellate review, by appeal and not by certiorari, from an enforcement board to circuit court, as further authorized by the Florida Constitution. See Art. V, § 5(b), Fla. Const.

In the case at hand, the circuit court's initial appellate decision stated: "We treat this appeal as a petition for writ of certiorari, see Orange County v. Lewis, 859 So. 2d 526, 528 n.1 (Fla. 5th DCA 2003), and deny certiorari." Indeed, this Court in Lewis stated that a circuit court's review of an administrative body's decision was by certiorari and was limited to a consideration of the three-prong test mentioned above. 859 So. 2d at 528 n.1. However, as in the above-cited supreme court cases, Lewis does not discuss or cite section 162.11. In a more recent case, this Court noted that "[s]ection 162.11 . . . specifically authorizes appeals of final administrative orders of enforcement boards to the circuit court." City of Palm Bay v. Palm Bay Greens, LLC, 969 So. 2d 1187, 1189 (Fla. 5th DCA 2007).

Review by certiorari is not the same as review by appeal. "The difference between certiorari review and appellate review is important." M.M. v. Dep't of Child. & Fams., 189 So. 3d 134, 138 (Fla. 2016). "[O]n appeal, all errors below may be corrected: jurisdictional, procedural, and substantive." Haines City Cmty. Dev., 658 So. 2d at 526 n.3. "Certiorari review is 'intended to fill the interstices between direct appeal and the other prerogative writs' and allow a court to reach down and halt a miscarriage of justice where no other remedy exists.' " Williams v. Oken, 62 So. 3d 1129, 1133 (Fla. 2011) (quoting Broward Cty. v. G.B.V. Int'l, Ltd., 787 So. 2d 838, 842

(Fla. 2001)). "The writ [of certiorari] never was intended to redress mere legal error." Broward Cty., 787 So. 2d at 842. Certiorari review considers whether the correct law was applied; review by appeal goes further to also consider whether the law was correctly applied. It makes sense that where two levels of appellate review are provided, at least one reviewing court would consider whether the enforcement board correctly applied the law. It has been said that the three-pronged first-tier certiorari review is "akin in many respects to a plenary appeal." Fla. Power & Light Co., 761 So. 2d at 1092. However, section 162.11 provides for an actual appeal, not something similar to an appeal. The Legislature has the power to provide a wider scope of review than is available through certiorari by providing for appeals. Haines City Cmty. Dev., 658 So. 2d at 526 n.3. "Moreover, where the Legislature has directed how a thing shall be done, it is, in effect, a prohibition against it being done in any other way." Op. Att'y Gen. Fla. 81–25 (1981) (citing Alsop v. Pierce, 155 Fla. 185, 19 So. 2d 799, 805–06 (1944)). If a court uses the inappropriate standard of review, that may be considered to be a departure from the essential requirements of the law. City of W. Palm Beach Zoning Bd. of Appeals v. Educ. Dev. Ctr., Inc., 504 So. 2d 1385, 1385–86 (Fla. 4th DCA 1987). Because CFI requested the circuit court, sitting in its appellate capacity, to employ the three-pronged first-tier standard, rather than requesting a plenary appeal, the concept of invited error forecloses CFI's entitlement to relief on that basis. See Pope v. State, 441 So. 2d 1073, 1076 (Fla. 1983).

However, it is not clear whether the circuit court actually employed the three-pronged test as it entertained CFI's appeal. As noted above, the circuit court's initial order clearly said that it treated CFI's appeal as though it were a petition for certiorari, which is not what CFI requested. However, in response to CFI's motion for rehearing, the circuit court noted its agreement with CFI that it was required to determine whether: (1) procedural due process was afforded; (2) the essential requirements of the law were observed; and (3) the administrative body's findings were supported by competent substantial evidence. Rather than confirming that it followed that invited scope of review, when denying CFI's motion for rehearing, the circuit court said only that "there is nothing on the face of the Court's opinion to indicate that the Court did not apply this three part test for first tier review." Nor, we note, is there anything on the face of the circuit court's order to indicate that it did apply the three-pronged test, as invited by CFI, which would be the only permissible reason for treating CFI's section 162.11 appeal as a petition for first-tier certiorari review, and which would otherwise explain what currently appears to be a clear departure from the essential requirement of the law. Accordingly, we remand this matter to the circuit court, sitting in its appellate capacity, with instructions to state whether it applied the three-pronged first-tier scope of review, as invited by CFI, leading it to reject CFI's appeal and affirm the magistrate's final order.

PETITION FOR CERTIORARI GRANTED, REMANDED WITH INSTRUCTIONS.

JACOBUS, B.W., Senior Judge, concurs.

GROSSHANS, J., concurs in result only.

4 · THE COURTS

c. ". . . [District courts of appeal] may review interlocutory orders in such cases to the extent provided by rules adopted by the Supreme Court." Fla. Const. art. V, § 4(b)(1)

The procedures providing for interlocutory orders by district courts of appeal are found in the Florida Rules of Appellate Procedure promulgated by the Florida Supreme Court.

d. "District courts of appeal shall have the power of direct review of administrative action, as prescribed by general law." Fla. Const. art. V, § 4(b)(2)

The principal "general law" in this area is the Florida Administrative Procedure Act, Chapter 120 of the Florida Statutes. The agencies covered by the Administrative Procedure Act are defined by it as follows:[138]

> **Definitions.** — As used in this act:
>
> (1) "Agency" means the following officers or governmental entities if acting pursuant to powers other than those derived from the constitution:
>
> (a) The Governor; each state officer and state department, and each departmental unit described in s. 20.04; the Board of Governors of the State University System; the Commission on Ethics; the Fish and Wildlife Conservation Commission; a regional water supply authority; a regional planning agency; a multicounty special district, but only if a majority of its governing board is comprised of nonelected persons; educational units; and each entity described in chapters 163, 373, 380, and 582 and s. 186.504.
>
> (b) Each officer and governmental entity in the state having statewide jurisdiction or jurisdiction in more than one county.
>
> (c) Each officer and governmental entity in the state having jurisdiction in one county or less than one county, to the extent they are expressly made subject to this chapter by general or special law or existing judicial decisions.
>
> This definition does not include any municipality or legal entity created solely by a municipality; a legal entity or agency created in whole or in part pursuant to part II of chapter 361; a metropolitan planning organization created pursuant to s. 339.175; a separate legal or administrative entity created pursuant to s. 339.175 of which a metropolitan planning organization is a member; an expressway authority pursuant to chapter 348 or any transportation authority under chapter 343 or chapter 349; or a legal or administrative entity created by an interlocal agreement pursuant to s. 163.01(7),

---

138. Fla. Stat. § 120.52 (2021).

unless any party to such agreement is otherwise an agency as defined in this subsection.

* * *

Decker v. University of West Florida

85 So. 3d 571 (Fla. 1st Dist. Ct. App. 2012)

PADOVANO, J.

Daniel Decker, a student at the University of West Florida, seeks judicial review of an administrative order imposing disciplinary sanctions against him for a violation of the university's Academic Misconduct Code. We conclude that the order is not appealable to this court, because the university was not acting as an agency as defined in the Florida Administrative Procedure Act when it rendered the decision. The proper remedy is to seek review by certiorari to the circuit court. Because the notice of appeal was timely and otherwise sufficient to invoke appellate jurisdiction, we transfer the case to the Circuit Court for Escambia County.

A hearing panel assigned by the university found Mr. Decker guilty of cheating and suspended him as a student for two semesters. He appealed the decision to the provost, but the appeal was unsuccessful. On August 2, 2011, the provost wrote to Mr. Decker, explaining the reasons for upholding the decision by the hearing panel. Subsequently, on August 19, 2011, counsel for the university wrote to Mr. Decker, informing him that the provost's decision was final and advising him that he had a right to seek judicial review by filing a petition for writ of certiorari in the circuit court. Mr. Decker appealed to this court in the apparent belief that the decision by the university amounted to final agency action under the Administrative Procedure Act. The notice of appeal was filed on September 19, 2011.

The university moved to dismiss the appeal on the ground that the notice of appeal was untimely. This argument would be well taken if we were to measure the time from the date of the first letter on August 2, 2011, but we are of the view that the second letter dated August 19, 2011, is the one that qualifies as a final administrative order. We base this conclusion on the language of the two letters. When measured from the date of the second letter, the notice of appeal filed on September 19, 2011, a Monday, was timely and therefore effective to invoke appellate jurisdiction.

The university also argued in the motion to dismiss that this court is not the appropriate forum for judicial review. This argument can be summarized in the form of a syllogism. The jurisdiction of the district courts of appeal to hear appeals from administrative orders is limited to decisions by administrative bodies that qualify as "agencies" under the Florida Administrative Procedure Act. The university was not acting as an "agency" with respect to the decision at issue because it was acting under a power created by the Florida Constitution and not by general law. Therefore, the order is not reviewable by appeal to a district court of appeal.

A decision is reviewable by appeal to a district court of appeal under the general provisions of the Administrative Procedure Act only if the person or entity rendering the decision falls within the statutory definition of an agency. *See* § 120.68(1), Fla. Stat.; *Eckert v. Board of Com'rs of North Broward Hosp. Dist.*, 720 So.2d 1151 (Fla. 4th DCA 1998); *Bryant v. Beary*, 665 So.2d 385 (Fla. 5th DCA 1996). The Act limits the definition of an agency to persons or entities "acting pursuant to powers other than those derived from the constitution." § 120.52(1), Fla. Stat. The significance of this limitation is clear: when an officer or agency is exercising power derived from the constitution, the resulting decision is not one that is made by an agency as defined in the Administrative Procedure Act.

The action taken in this case plainly falls within the scope of the power vested in the university by Article IX, section 7 of the Florida Constitution. Section 7(d) provides that the state board of governors shall "operate, regulate, control and be fully responsible for the management of the whole university system," and section 7(c) states that each university within the system shall be operated by a board of trustees under powers granted by the board of governors. *See Graham v. Haridopolos*, 75 So.3d 315 (Fla. 1st DCA 2011); *NAACP, Inc. v. Florida Bd. of Regents*, 876 So.2d 636 (Fla. 1st DCA 2004). The order in question dealt with a matter arising in the course of the operation and management of the university. Hence, the order does not qualify as agency action as defined in the Administrative Procedure Act and it is not appealable to this court.

We recognize that there are a number of cases in which university disciplinary decisions have been reviewed by appeal to a district court of appeal. However, these decisions either predate the adoption of Article IX, Section 7, in November 2002, *see Hardison v. Florida A & M University*, 706 So.2d 111 (Fla. 1st DCA 1998); *Wallace v. Florida A & M University*, 433 So.2d 600 (Fla. 1st DCA 1983); *Morfit v. University of South Florida*, 794 So.2d 655 (Fla. 2d DCA 2001); *Abramson v. Florida Int'l University*, 704 So.2d 720 (Fla. 3d DCA 1998), or rely on precedents predating Article IX, Section 7, *see Matar v. Florida Int'l University*, 944 So.2d 1153 (Fla. 3d DCA 2006); *Heiken v. University of Cent. Florida*, 995 So.2d 1145 (Fla. 5th DCA 2008). Therefore, we do not consider these decisions to be persuasive on the issue presented here.

In the absence of a general law establishing a right to appeal, the order in this case is reviewable by certiorari. Rule 9.190(b)(3) of the Florida Rules of Appellate Procedure provides that "[r]eview of quasi-judicial decisions of any administrative body, agency, board, or commission not subject to the Administrative Procedure Act shall be commenced by filing a petition for certiorari in accordance with rule 9.100(b) and (c) unless review is provided by general law." *See Smull v. Town of Jupiter*, 854 So.2d 780 (Fla. 4th DCA 2003). In this circumstance, appellate review is a matter of right, as it would be in the case of a plenary appeal. *See Broward County v. G.B.V. Int'l, Ltd.*, 787 So.2d 838 (Fla.2001); *City of Deerfield Beach v. Vaillant*, 419 So.2d 624 (Fla.1982).

We know from these authorities that certiorari is the proper remedy. However, the power to issue a writ of certiorari exists in the circuit courts as well as in the district courts of appeal. *See* Fla. Const. Art. V, § 5(b); Art. V, § 4(b)(3). That leaves us to identify the proper appellate forum for filing the petition. In analogous situations, the Florida courts have held that the petition should be filed in the circuit court. For instance, a final administrative decision by a local administrative body is initially reviewable by certiorari to the circuit court. *See Haines City Community Development v. Heggs,* 658 So.2d 523 (Fla.1995). The courts follow the same procedure when a state agency makes a decision that is statutorily excluded from the definition of an agency action. An administrative decision setting a parole release date, for example, is subject to judicial review in the circuit court, even though the parole commission otherwise qualifies as an agency under the Administrative Procedure Act. *See Sheley v. Florida Parole Com'n,* 720 So.2d 216 (Fla.1998). Based on these decisions, we conclude that the petition for writ of certiorari must be filed in the circuit court.

Rule 9.040(c) of the Florida Rules of Appellate Procedure provides that "[i]f a party seeks an improper remedy, the cause shall be treated as if the proper remedy had been sought," and rule 9.040(b)(1) states that "[i]f a proceeding is commenced in an inappropriate court, that court shall transfer the cause to an appropriate court." Applying these two rules, we treat the notice of appeal which was timely filed with the agency clerk, as a petition for writ of certiorari in the circuit court having territorial jurisdiction over the university. *See Johnson v. Citizens State Bank,* 537 So.2d 96 (Fla.1989). In this case, the proper forum is the circuit court for Escambia County.

In summary, we conclude that the notice of appeal was timely and therefore effective to initiate appellate review but that the order in question is not reviewable by appeal to this court. We treat the notice as a petition for writ of certiorari and transfer the case to the circuit court.

LEWIS and WETHERELL, JJ., concur.

Sweetwater Utility Corp. v. Hillsborough County

314 So. 2d 194 (Fla. 2d Dist. Ct. App. 1975)

On Motion to Dismiss

GRIMES, Judge.

Petitioner has filed in this court a petition for writ of certiorari seeking review of certain portions of an ordinance enacted by the Board of County Commissioners of Hillsborough County relating to the determination of appropriate rates of return for franchised sewer utilities in that county. Being uncertain of its remedy, petitioner has simultaneously filed in the Circuit Court of Hillsborough County a complaint for declaratory judgment and other relief directed to the same ordinance. Respondents have now filed a motion to dismiss in this court contending that the Board of County Commissioners of Hillsborough County is not an agency subject to judicial review under the provisions of the new Administrative Procedure Act.

Subsections (1) and (2) of Fla.Stat. §120.68 (1974) call for judicial review of final agency action in the applicable district court of appeal except where review by the Supreme Court is provided by law. The subject matter of this lawsuit does not fall within any area for which judicial review by the Supreme Court is so provided. Accordingly, the issue raised by the motion turns on whether the Board of County Commissioners of Hillsborough County is an agency within the meaning of § 120.52(1)(c) (1974) which reads:

> "(c) Each other unit of government in the state, including counties and municipalities to the extent they are expressly made subject to this act by general or special law or existing judicial decisions."

One might reasonably contend that a board of county commissioners is necessarily a "unit of government *in* the state." Yet, the legislature specifically chose to include counties within this definition only if "expressly made subject to this act by general or special law or existing judicial decisions."

There are several cases arising under the old Administrative Procedure Act in which a county board of public instruction was determined to be a state agency whose actions were reviewable by a petition to the district court of appeal. Board of Public Instruction of Broward County v. State ex rel. Allen, Fla. 1969, 219 So.2d 430; Canney v. Board of Public Instruction of Alachua County, Fla.App.1st 1969, 222 So.2d 803; Adams v. Board of Public Instruction of Okaloosa County, Fla.App.1st, 1969, 225 So.2d 423. However, the rationale underlying these cases was that a county school board is part of the state system of public instruction. On the other hand, a county civil service board was held not to be a state agency within the meaning of the Administrative Procedure Act. More recently, this court in Florida Cities Water Company v. Board of County Com'rs., Fla.App.2d, 1973, 281 So.2d 580, declined to decide as unnecessary to its decision the question of whether the Board of County Commissioners of Sarasota County was a state agency under the old act.

Thus, it appears there is no "existing judicial decision" which would characterize a board of county commissioners as an agency for purposes of judicial review under the new Administrative Procedure Act. Likewise, no general or special law has been called to our attention which would make such boards subject to this act.

This motion is granted, and the petition for certiorari is hereby dismissed.

BOARDMAN, Acting C. J., and SCHEB, J., concur.

The question of when it is proper to abandon the administrative procedure/judicial review provisions of the Florida Administrative Procedure Act and proceed by an original action for declaratory or other relief in the circuit court is a troublesome one. Although it involves the question of district court jurisdiction under art. V, § 4(b)(2) and the Florida Administrative Procedure Act (chapter 120 of the Florida Statutes), the questions raised go far beyond such jurisdiction. *Key Haven Associated Enterprises, Inc. v. Board of Trustees of the Internal Improvement Fund*[139] seems to be the principal, but by no means the only, case in this area of the law. It and the

---

139. 427 So. 2d 153 (Fla. 1982).

general problem are discussed in David L. Dickson, Thomas C. Marks, Jr., & Kathryn A. Vaughan, *Administrative Agencies and Judicial Control: Towards a Florida Abstention Doctrine*, 17 Stetson. L. Rev. 1 (1987). The opinion of Justice Leander Shaw (then-Associate Judge) in the *Sullivan* case should add to your understanding.

State Commission on Ethics v. Sullivan

430 So. 2d 928 (Fla. 1st Dist. Ct. App. 1983)

* * *

SHAW, LEANDER J., Jr., Associate Judge, specially concurring.

Although I concur with the result and much of the reasoning in the majority's opinion, I do not agree that the Commission's motions to dismiss the Sullivans' complaints were apparently meritorious. On this point, for reasons set forth below, the majority's opinion is flawed by reliance on dicta from *Key Haven Associated Enterprises, Inc. v. Board of Trustees of the Internal Improvement Trust Fund*, 427 So.2d 153, (Fla.1982) (hereinafter *Key Haven* (Fla. 1982)). This reliance also fails to take into consideration the fact that the trial court could not have anticipated in 1981 that the traditional exceptions to the doctrine of exhaustion of administrative remedies would thereafter be limited to a single exception: facial unconstitutionality of a statute.[1]

The question of when and under what circumstances a circuit court should intervene into the administrative process is an important one, and, from the viewpoint of the circuit court, no doubt a perplexing one. . . .

* * *

In analyzing the need for judicial intervention into the administrative process, I note and preserve the distinction between judicial intervention by the circuit court and judicial review by the district courts of appeal. The original jurisdiction of the circuit court to intervene by declaratory judgment "does not affect the jurisdiction

---

1. To appreciate *Key Haven*'s (Fla.1982) major constriction in the traditional exceptions to the exhaustion doctrine, contrast it with the discussion of the doctrine and exceptions thereto contained in *Patsy v. Florida International University*, 634 F.2d 900 (5th Cir.1981), reversed on other grounds, ___ U.S. ___, 102 S.Ct. 2557, 73 L.Ed.2d 172 (1982). The Fifth Circuit recognized four exceptions: first, where the remedy is plainly inadequate because no remedy is available, or the remedy is incommensurate with the claim, or the remedy is so untimely as to create a serious risk of irreparable injury; second, where the challenge is to the constitutionality of a statute and the administrative remedy will not obviate the constitutional question; third, where the question of the adequacy of the administrative remedy is pragmatically co-extensive with the merits as when the claim is that the administrative system itself is unlawful or unconstitutional in form or application; and fourth, where exhaustion of administrative remedies would be futile because it is clear the claim will be rejected. In reversing the Fifth Circuit, on other grounds, the Supreme Court added a fifth and pre-eminent exception which is particularly pertinent here: exhaustion is not required when the legislature did not intend that exhaustion be required.

of the district courts of appeal and this Court to *review* agency action pursuant to section 120.68, Florida Statutes (1975)." *Department of Revenue v. Amrep Corp.*, 358 So.2d 1343, 1349 n. 5 (Fla.1978) (my emphasis). There is no question that judicial review of final agency action lies in the district courts of appeal; a suit for declaratory judgment cannot be used to seek such review. *See Rice v. Department of Health and Rehabilitative Services*, 386 So.2d 844 (Fla. 1st DCA 1980), where this Court noted that "the circumstances justifying circuit court intervention do not include the supposed incapacity of a district court of appeal to reach and decide a constitutional issue which has been carried unresolved to that part of the judicial system through the regular processes of Chapter 120. *See Department of Revenue v. Amrep Corp.*, 358 So.2d 1343, 1349 fn. 5 (Fla.1978)." *Rice* at 849.

If chapter 86 and section 120.73 are given their plain meaning, there can be no doubt that the Sullivans, or any other similarly situated persons, have the right to obtain a declaratory judgment under the circumstances here. Section 86.021 provides that "[a]ny person . . . whose rights, status, or other equitable or legal relations are affected by a statute, or any regulation made under statutory authority, . . . may have determined any question of construction or validity arising under such statute, regulation . . . and obtain a declaration of rights, status or other equitable or legal relations thereunder. Further, section 86.111 provides that the "existence of another adequate remedy does not preclude a judgment for declaratory relief." Finally, as noted in *Gulf Pines Memorial Park, Inc. v. Oaklawn Memorial Park, Inc.*, 361 So.2d 695 (Fla.1978), section 120.73 itself provides that nothing in chapter 120 "shall be construed to repeal any provision of the Florida Statutes which grants the right to a proceeding in the circuit court *in lieu of an administrative hearing* or to divest the circuit courts of jurisdiction to render declaratory judgments under the provisions of chapter 86" (my emphasis). On their face, these provisions grant a statutory right to a declaratory judgment on the questions raised by the Sullivans and negate the need to exhaust administrative remedies. Section 120.73, in particular, seems to envisage a procedure whereby the circuit courts through declaratory judgments act as ombudsmen for citizens aggrieved by potential or ongoing agency action. Section 120.73 and chapter 86 can be read as a legislative vote of confidence in the judgment and discretion of the circuit courts, as the courts of general jurisdiction closest to the citizens, to balance the conflicting rights of the citizens against the imperatives of a smoothly functioning administrative process. Admittedly, such a policy may be unwise; it could lead to promiscuous judicial intervention and frustration of the administrative process. However, it is well established that the wisdom of legislation does not furnish grounds for judicial challenge of the legislation, and there is no question that the legislature has the constitutional power to grant such remedies and to assign the concomitant jurisdictional power to the circuit courts. Nevertheless, under the rubrics of primary jurisdiction, deference to the executive branch, and exhaustion of administrative remedies, a judicial policy has evolved which significantly impacts upon these chapter 86 rights. In my view, this judicial policy as it has developed is fundamentally misconceived: it assumes that exhaustion of administrative remedies is a question of judicial policy, based primarily on deference to the executive branch; the courts appear to ignore the fact that administrative agencies and remedies are created by the legislature and, as the United States Supreme Court put it, "the initial question whether exhaustion is required should be answered by reference to the congressional intent; and a court should not defer the exercise of jurisdiction under a federal statute unless it is consistent with that intent.[4]" [footnote omitted] *Patsy v. Board of Regents of the State of Florida,* ___ U.S. ___, ___, 102 S.Ct. 2557, 2561, 73 L.Ed.2d 172 (1982). The court further noted that "policy considerations alone cannot justify judicially imposed exhaustion unless exhaustion is consistent with congressional intent." *Id.* 102 S.Ct. at 2566. I have misgivings about the power of the judiciary to limit statutorily-granted remedies, or the wisdom of doing so, assuming we have the power. Nevertheless, it is this body of controlling case law and the judicial policy underlying it that must be examined.

The basic characteristic of the administrative process which most often justifies judicial intervention short of exhaustion of the administrative process, is the incapacity of the administrative process to address constitutional issues. This administrative infirmity and the constitutional duty of the courts to decide constitutional issues have long been recognized as a justification for judicial intervention without exhaustion of administrative remedies if judicial review of final agency action does not provide an adequate remedy. *See Gulf Pines; Smith v. Willis,* 415 So.2d 1331 (Fla. 1st DCA 1982); *E.T. Legg and Co. v. Franza,* 383 So.2d 962 (Fla. 4th DCA 1980); *Carrollwood State Bank v. Lewis,* 362 So.2d 110 (Fla. 1st DCA 1978); *School Board of Leon County v. Mitchell,* 346 So.2d 562 (Fla. 1st DCA 1977); *State ex rel. Department of General Services v. Willis,* 344 So.2d 580 (Fla. 1st DCA 1977); *Department of Revenue v. Young American Builders,* 330 So.2d 864 (Fla. 1st DCA 1976); and *State Department of Administration, Division of Personnel v. State Department of Administration, Division of Administrative Hearings,* 326 So.2d 187 (Fla. 1st DCA 1976).

Although the presence of a constitutional issue may be the most common occasion for judicial intervention, nothing in sections 120.68 and 120.73 or chapter 86 suggests that judicial intervention is limited to cases presenting constitutional issues. Section 120.68(1) provides for immediate review by the district courts of appeal of preliminary, procedural or intermediate agency action if review of final agency decision would not provide an adequate remedy. *See Communities Financial Corp. v. Florida Department of Environmental Regulation,* 416 So.2d 813 (Fla. 1st DCA 1982), *Mitchell,* and *State ex rel. Department of General Services v. Willis,* which recognize the appropriateness of circuit court intervention when agency action is so egregious or devastating that administrative remedies are too little or too late. Of similar import is the emphasis placed by *Gulf Pines* on the adequacy of the administrative remedy as the test of whether circuit court intervention is appropriate and the recognition that it is pointless to exhaust administrative remedies when only an untimely remedy is afforded.

The Sullivans' complaints posed numerous constitutional issues. Although we obviate these constitutional questions on appeal, the trial judge was presented with a plethora of constitutional issues for which exhaustion of administrative remedies and appeal of final agency action were inadequate. These issues did not arise merely because the Sullivans asserted them; they were bona fide. The Commission maintained then and now that it has direct constitutional authority under article II, section 8 to hear complaints of alleged wrong doings beyond those enumerated in section 8 and chapter 112, part III and that this authority was independent of legislative control. Assuming that the Sullivans were correct in their position that the Commission was proceeding ultra vires and without that jurisdiction, it would not only have been "pointless to require . . . [the Sullivans] to endure the time and expense of full administrative proceedings[,]" as *Gulf Pines* described it at 699; but judicial review of final agency action would not have remedied the possible irreparable injury to their public reputations caused by an exhausted, but ultra vires, administrative proceeding. In this latter respect, this case presents an additional factor warranting circuit court intervention beyond that present in *Gulf Pines*. Thus, in my view, there was no error in initially entertaining the Sullivans' suits in May, 1981; the error was in proceeding to judgment on the very jurisdictional issue decided by this Court in November, 1981.

A recent decision of the Florida Supreme Court, *Key Haven* (Fla.1982), requires examination to ensure there is no conflict with the above. In *Key Haven* (Fla.1982), Key Haven petitioned for a dredge and fill permit from the Department of Environment Regulations (DER). A hearing officer recommended denial of the permit and DER entered an order denying the permit. Although Key Haven had the right under section 253.76, Florida Statutes (1975), to appeal the denial of the permit to the Board of Trustees of the Internal Improvement Fund (IIF) and thence to this Court, it chose to abandon its cause of action for a permit. Instead, Key Haven went to circuit court with a cause of action for inverse condemnation. The circuit court treated the inverse condemnation action as a collateral attack on DER's denial of the dredge and fill permit and dismissed the action for failure to exhaust administrative remedies. This Court adopted the reasoning of the circuit court and affirmed, holding that "Chapter 120 remedies plainly were adequate, and the circuit court correctly declined 'to employ an extraordinary remedy to assist a litigant who has foregone an ordinary one which would have served adequately.'" *Key Haven Associated Enterprises, Inc. v. Board of Trustees*, 400 So.2d 66, 74 (Fla. 1st DCA 1981). On review, the Supreme Court affirmed the dismissal but disagreed, in pertinent part, with the reasoning of this Court. The Supreme Court's analysis was essentially that there were two separate causes of action involved. The first for a dredge and fill permit could only be appealed to the IIF and then by direct review to this Court. The second cause of action for inverse condemnation could have properly been brought in circuit court had Key Haven pursued an appeal to the ultimate state executive authority, the IIF, as it was required to do under section 253.76. In effect, the court's holding was that the second cause of action never accrued and was properly dismissed, because Key Haven failed to obtain the authoritative denial of its permit necessary for an inverse condemnation suit.

There is no suggestion in *Key Haven* (Fla.1982) that the agency action in denying the permit presented any constitutional issues or that the exhaustion of administrative remedies and judicial review would have furnished an inadequate remedy. On the contrary: "Key Haven did not allege in the circuit court that any statute relied upon by DER in denying its dredge-and-fill permit was facially unconstitutional, nor did Key Haven assert that the agency action was improper because of a constitutional violation inherent in the agency's decision making process." *Id.* at 158. Nevertheless, despite the absence of a relevant issue, the court went on to discuss what it saw as the three types of constitutional challenges that could be raised in the context of the administrative decision-making process. If the discussion was intended to establish controlling law, it was contrary to the maxim of judicial review enunciated by Justice Terrell in *State v. Du Bose*, 99 Fla. 812, 128 So. 4, 6 (Fla.1930), that courts "consistently decline to settle questions beyond the necessities of the immediate case. This court [Florida Supreme Court] is committed to the 'method of a gradual approach to the general, by a systematically guarded application and extension of constitutional principles to particular cases as they arise, rather than by out of hand attempts to establish general rules to which future cases must be fitted.'"

Key Haven (Fla.1982) does not appear to be an appropriate case to address, or recede from, a long line of cases which has tested circuit court intervention into the administrative process against the presence of constitutional issues and the adequacy of administrative remedies. Nor does the court state that it is receding from this line of cases. Because this discussion is not essential to the decision in *Key Haven* (Fla.1982), I consider it to be obiter dicta which does not provide controlling judicial precedent. *Myers v. Atlantic Coast Line Railroad Co.*, 112 So.2d 263 (Fla.1959); *State v. Florida State Improvement Commission*, 60 So.2d 747 (Fla.1952); *Pell v. State*, 97 Fla. 650, 122 So. 110 (Fla.1929); *Ex parte Amos*, 112 So. 289 (Fla.1927) (J. Whitfield concurring opinion at 294), and *Ard v. Ard*, 395 So.2d 586 (Fla. 1st DCA 1981). Even so, dicta of the highest court should be given persuasive weight by lower courts unless it is contrary to previous decisions of the highest court. *Horton v. Unigard Insurance Co.*, 355 So.2d 154 (Fla. 4th DCA 1978), *O'Sullivan v. City of Deerfield Beach*, 232 So.2d 33 (Fla. 4th DCA 1970), and *Milligan v. State*, 177 So.2d 75 (Fla. 2d DCA 1965). Accordingly, *Key Haven* (Fla.1982), requires examination to determine if it contradicts previous holdings of the Supreme Court.

Key Haven (Fla.1982) discusses three types of constitutional challenges to the administrative process: (1) Facial Unconstitutionality of a Statute; (2) Facial Unconstitutionality of an Agency Rule; and (3) Unconstitutional Application of a Statute or Agency Rule. Of these, the Court states that an aggrieved party may challenge only the first in circuit court; the latter two may only be challenged after exhaustion of administrative remedies by direct review in the district court of appeal. *Gulf Pines* clearly recognizes the availability of circuit court intervention when a bona fide challenge is presented to the facial unconstitutionality of a statute. However, in stating this proposition, *Key Haven* (Fla.1982), states that "this type of constitutional issue could not, *absent recourse to the circuit courts*, be addressed until the administrative process is concluded and the claim is before a district court of appeal on direct review of the agency action." Id. at 157 (my emphasis). The emphasized statement does not recognize the alternative of an interlocutory appeal to the district courts of appeal under section 120.68(1). *See*, for example, *State Department of Administration, Division of Administrative Hearings*, where this Court intervened to resolve a constitutional challenge to the application of an agency rule. A district court of appeal is well suited to address the issue of the facial unconstitutionality of a statute or rule, since such challenges do not involve fact-finding. This potentially valuable alternative remedy should not be inadvertently abandoned.

Key Haven (Fla.1982) states that a circuit court should not entertain a challenge to the facial unconstitutionality of an agency rule because an adequate remedy remains available in the administrative process. This is contrary to *Gulf Pines* at 699 and other case law which recognize the availability of circuit court intervention to enjoin enforcement of facially unconstitutional agency rules. *See* for example, *Carrollwood State Bank, Mitchell, State ex rel. Department of General Services v. Willis*, and *Young American Builders*, all of which either uphold or recognize the availability of a circuit court challenge to an agency rule. *Gulf Pines* treats the facial constitutionality of rules and statutes interchangeably; logically so, since neither an agency nor a hearing officer can declare either a rule or a statute unconstitutional. Within the administrative process, a rule has the same legal effect as a statute; pragmatically, the facially unconstitutional provisions have the same impact on an aggrieved party whether embodied in a statute or a rule. The *Key Haven* (Fla.1982) court cites *Rice* as an example of a court correctly declining to consider the facial constitutionality of an agency rule until administrative remedies were exhausted. [Footnote omitted.] The reliance on *Rice* for this proposition is factually incorrect: there was no agency rule in *Rice* to challenge; indeed, it was the very absence of an agency rule or order which this Court used as a rationale for refusing review until the agency had interpreted the statute in question. The pertinent proposition of law was that this Court would not consider the constitutional issue until it had been ripened by an agency rule or order.

Key Haven (Fla.1982) also states that a circuit court should not entertain challenges to an agency's application of a facially constitutional statute or rule. No cases are cited for this proposition and research fails to find any so holding. This is also contrary to *Gulf Pines* where the improper retroactive application of a statute was held to justify circuit court intervention. The court held that the improper application of the statute resolved the litigation and obviated the challenge to the facial constitutionality of the statute. It is true that a challenge to the application of a statute or rule will place a greater burden on the petitioner to show that the administrative remedies are inadequate than when the challenge is the facial unconstitutionality of a statute or rule. Thus, intervention by the circuit courts on this type of challenge should be relatively rare. Nevertheless, *Gulf Pines* recognizes the right to challenge such improper application, particularly if the issue is the threshold question of whether the statute or rule is apposite to the proceeding. As the U.S. Supreme Court has put it, "before a man can be punished, the case must be plainly and unmistakably within the statute." *U.S. v. Lacher*, 134 U.S. 624, 628, 10 S.Ct. 625, 626, 33 L.Ed. 1080 (1890). This caveat is particularly pertinent here since the Commission asserts its authority to hear complaints of violations of any Florida Statute which, in the Commission's judgment, constitute a breach of the public trust. In my view, by ruling out entirely such challenges, *Key Haven* (Fla.1982) contradicts *Gulf Pines*. [Footnote omitted.]

I note finally that the three types of constitutional challenges to agency action discussed in *Key Haven* (Fla.1982) are not inclusive in that they omit the type of challenge present here: agency interpretation and application of the constitution itself. The Sullivans' challenges to agency action involved in large part the Commission's interpretation of its own authority under article II, section 8, Florida Constitution. Even if the discussion in *Key Haven* (Fla.1982) is not dicta, it would not preclude the entertainment in circuit court of the issues posed here.

In summary, I believe that the circuit court correctly entertained jurisdiction of the Sullivan's complaints and that this court should forthrightly so hold without relying on a waiver or estoppel theory. Further, that the judicial policy and case law restricting access to the circuit courts under chapter 86 should be revisited and due emphasis placed on the controlling principle: legislative intent.

---

e. "A district court of appeal or any judge thereof may issue writs of habeas corpus returnable before the court or any judge thereof or before any circuit judge within the territorial jurisdiction of the court. . . ." Fla. Const. art. V, § 4(b)(3)

See the discussion of habeas corpus earlier in this chapter.

f. ". . . A district court of appeal may issue writs of mandamus, certiorari, prohibition, quo warranto, and other writs necessary to the complete exercise of its jurisdiction. . . ." Fla. Const. art. V, § 4(b)(3)

Common Law Certiorari

The repositories of the common law writ of certiorari directed to the circuit courts of the State of Florida are the five district courts of appeal. Apparently this is in addition to the "all writs" power. The circuit courts and common law certiorari will be discussed later in this chapter.

Prior to the establishment of the Florida District Courts of Appeal effective July 1, 1957, the authority to issue common law writs of certiorari was vested in the Florida Supreme Court. Subsequent to that date the Supreme Court of Florida was no longer empowered to issue these writs. The power, however, was [allocated] as of that date to the District Courts of Appeal. The extent of their jurisdiction in this respect is governed generally by the precedents previously applicable to the Florida Supreme Court [Citation omitted.][140]

The elements of the writ of certiorari are also explained in *Dresner*:[141]

The type of certiorari which we here discuss is in the nature of the common law writ which issues in the *sound discretion* of a superior court directed to an inferior court *in order to determine from the face of the record whether the lower court has exceeded its jurisdiction or has otherwise deviated from the essential requirements of the law.* It is appropriate in situations where *no other provision is made for the review* of a judgment of a lower court. . . . [Emphasis added.]

The following two cases have not been edited at all for the following reasons: in addition to *Haines City*'s discussion of common law certiorari as a vehicle of review for a district court of appeal to review a decision of a circuit court sitting in its appellate capacity over county courts (it replaces *Combs* which was found in the First Edition of *Florida Constitutional Law*), it harmonizes that review with that of a district court of appeal reviewing a decision of a circuit court sitting in its review capacity over decisions of administrative agencies. *Pettis* presents an excellent discussion of common law certiorari as a vehicle of review for a district court of appeal to review a decision of a circuit court's non-final (interlocutory) orders for which no direct review is provided in the Florida Rules of Appellate Procedure.

Haines City Community Development v. Heggs

658 So. 2d 523 (Fla. 1995)

ANSTEAD, Justice.

We have for review the following question certified to be of great public importance:

AFTER *EDUCATION DEVELOPMENT CENTER, INC. v. CITY OF WEST PALM BEACH*, 541 So.2d 106 (Fla.1989), DOES THE STANDARD OF REVIEW IN *COMBS v. STATE*, 436 So.2d 93 (Fla. 1983), STILL GOVERN A DISTRICT COURT OF APPEAL WHEN IT REVIEWS, PURSUANT TO FLORIDA RULE OF APPELLATE PROCEDURE 9.030(b)(2)(B), AN ORDER OF A CIRCUIT COURT ACTING IN ITS REVIEW CAPACITY OVER A COUNTY COURT?

---

140. *Dresner v. City of Tallahassee*, 164 So. 2d 208, 210 (Fla. 1964).
141. *Id.*

See Haines City Community Dev. V. Heggs, 647 So.2d 855, 857 (Fla. 2d DCA 1994). We have jurisdiction, article V, section 3(b)(4), Florida Constitution, and answer the certified question in the affirmative by holding that the standards of review announced in *Combs* and *Educational Development Center* are the same. We approve the district court decision.

Procedural Facts

This case originates from a final judgment entered in county court in favor of petitioner Haines City Community Development, d/b/a Parkview Village (Parkview), evicting the respondent Leila Heggs for non-payment of rent. Upon appeal, the circuit court reversed the county court's judgment. Parkview then sought common-law certiorari review of the circuit court's order in the Second District Court of Appeal, which denied the petition upon the authority of *Combs v. State*, 436 So.2d 93 (Fla.1983). The district court expressed some concern, however, about the prevailing law defining the standard of review of a district court when reviewing an appellate decision of a circuit court. The court was particularly concerned that we may have recently adopted a different standard for review of administrative proceedings, and it was unclear if the standard was intended to supplant the *Combs* standard.

Law & Analysis

History of Common-Law Writ of Certiorari in Florida

Legal historians have told us that the English common-law writ of certiorari was an original writ issuing out of chancery or the King's Bench, directing that an inferior tribunal return the record of a pending cause so that the higher court could review the proceedings. George E. Harris, *A Treatise on the Law of Certiorari* §1 (1893). The use of the writ was continued in the American courts, both state and federal. A more recent treatise defines certiorari as a discretionary writ issued by an appellate court to a lower court in cases where an appeal or writ of error was unavailable, directing that the record of the lower court be provided for review to determine whether the lower court has exceeded its jurisdiction or not proceeded according to law. 3 Fla.Jur.2d *Appellate Review* §456 (1978).[1]

This Court[2] first recognized its common-law certiorari jurisdiction in *Halliday v. Jacksonville & Alligator Plank Road Co.*, 6 Fla. 304 (1855), and defined its use in rather broad and general terms:

> [A] writ of certiorari will lie from this court to any of the inferior jurisdictions, whenever an appropriate case may be presented, or it shall become necessary for the attainment of justice.

---

1. Our discussion in this opinion will generally be limited to the use of certiorari to review circuit court decisions rendered by that court acting in its review capacity. We will not discuss other possible uses of certiorari such as its use to review interlocutory or non-final orders of a lower court.

2. Interestingly, the present Florida Constitution does not grant the Florida Supreme Court any general power to issue common law writs of certiorari. *See Vetrick v. Hollander*, 464 So.2d 552, 553 (Fla.1985); *Robinson v. State*, 132 So.2d 3, 5 (Fla.1961).

Id. at 305. In 1882, in an opinion which retains its currency and whose clarity remains a hallmark, we defined the writ in more precise terms:

> The question which this *certiorari* brings here is ... whether the Judge exceeded his jurisdiction in hearing the case at all, or adopted any method unknown to the law or essentially irregular in his proceeding under the statute. A decision made according to the form of law and the rules prescribed for rendering it, although it may be erroneous in its conclusion as to what the law is as applied to facts, is not an illegal or irregular act or proceeding remediable by *certiorari.*

Basnet v. City of Jacksonville, 18 Fla. 523, 526–27 (1882); *see also Edgerton v. Mayor of Green Cove Springs,* 18 Fla. 528 (1882).

In *Basnet* and its progeny we refined the nature and scope of certiorari. We described certiorari as appellate in character in the sense that it involves a limited review of the proceedings of an inferior jurisdiction. *Basnet,* 18 Fla. At 527. "It is original in the sense that the subject-matter of the suit or proceeding which it brings before the court are not here reinvestigated, tried and determined upon the merits generally as upon appeal at law or writ of error." *Id.* This explanation, stated another way, importantly emphasizes that certiorari should not be used to grant a second appeal.[3] *Id.; Kennington v. Gillman,* 284 So.2d 405, 406 (Fla. 1st DCA 1973).[4]

---

3. It has been noted that there are at least four distinguishing features between review by common-law certiorari and review by appeal which is provided by law. *G-W Dev. Corp. v. Village of N. Palm Bch. Zoning Bd. of Adjustment,* 317 So.2d 828, 830 (Fla. 4th DCA 1975). First, common-law certiorari is available only "where no direct appellate proceedings are provided by law." *Id.* Second, common-law certiorari is entirely discretionary with the court, as opposed to an appeal which is taken as a matter of right. *Id.* Third, the scope of review by common-law certiorari is traditionally limited and much narrower than the scope of review on appeal. That is, on appeal, all errors below may be corrected: jurisdictional, procedural, and substantive; and judgments below may be modified, reversed, remanded with directions, or affirmed. Fourth, common-law certiorari will only lie to review judicial or quasi-judicial action, never purely legislative action, in contradistinction to review by appeal which is provided by law and by which the legislature can authorize review of a wider scope. *Id.* at 831.

4. The policy behind this rule is simple. The circuit court is the court of final appellate jurisdiction in cases originating in county court. *See* art. V, § 5, Fla. Const. Prior to the establishment of the district courts, we noted that if the role of certiorari was expanded to review the correctness of the circuit court's decision, it would amount to a second appeal. If an appellate court gives what amounts to a second appeal, by means of certiorari, it is not complying with the Constitution, but is taking unto itself the circuit courts' final appellate jurisdiction and depriving litigants of final judgments obtained there. If, in cases originating in courts inferior to the circuit courts, another appeal from the circuit court is afforded in the guise of certiorari, then a litigant will have two appeals from the court of limited jurisdiction, while a litigant would be limited to only one appeal in cases originating in the trial court of general jurisdiction. *Flash Bonded Storage Co. v. Ades,* 152 Fla. 482, 483, 12 So.2d 164, 165 (1943). There are societal interests in ending litigation within a reasonable length of time and eliminating the amount of judicial labors involved in multiple appeals. Further, while obviously important, circuit court opinions are not widely reported and used as precedent. William A Haddad, *The Common Law of Writ of Certiorari in Florida,* 29 U.Fla.L.Rev. 207, 227 (1977).

In *Jacksonville, T. & K.W. Railway Co. v. Boy*, 34 Fla. 389, 393, 16 So. 290, 291 (1894), we reviewed a circuit court decision affirming a county court judgment, and, while repeating certain language from *Basnet*, we also stated that we have the power to review and quash, on common-law certiorari, the proceedings of an inferior tribunal when it proceeds without jurisdiction or when its procedure is illegal, unknown to the law, or essentially irregular. *Id.* at 392, 16 So. 290. Further, in examining the scope of review in other states, we endorsed the practice in Illinois where the superior court determines "whether the inferior court had jurisdiction, or had exceeded its jurisdiction, or had *failed to proceed according to the essential requirements of the law.*" *Id.* at 393, 16 So. 290 (emphasis added). In conclusion, we found that "[t]he judgment of affirmance in the record before the Circuit Court was such an essential irregularity and departure from prescribed rules of procedure in such cases as to require that it be quashed, and a judgment will therefore be entered accordingly." *Id.* at 396, 16 So. 290.

In *Mernaugh v. City of Orlando*, 41 Fla. 433, 27 So. 34 (1899), this Court explicitly incorporated the "essential requirements of law" language into our standard:

> The rule established here is that the Supreme Court has power to review and quash, on the common-law writ of *certiorari*, the proceedings of inferior tribunals when they proceed in a cause without jurisdiction, or when their procedure is essentially irregular and *not according to the essential requirements of law*, and no appeal or direct method of reviewing the proceeding exists.

Id. at 442, 27 So. 34 (emphasis added).

Consistency in Application

It has been correctly noted that despite the announcement of a narrow standard of review, the scope of substantive review by certiorari actually applied was often, for all practical purposes, fully as broad as review by appeal. William H. Rogers & Lewis Rhea Baxter, *Certiorari in Florida*, 4 U.Fla.L.Rev. 477, 498, 500 n. 90 (1951).[5] This tendency was so apparent that the discussion in Florida Jurisprudence noted that in many certiorari cases "it may appear that an error on which the reviewing court questions the lower court's judgment is no more fundamental or in violation of an essential requirement of the law than what otherwise would be reversible error on appeal." Haddad, *supra*, at 221 n. 113.[6] Throughout the years, Florida courts have also used many terms interchangeably to describe a "departure from the essential requirements of law."[7] Beginning in the early 1960s, however, a more consistent prac-

---

5. For a more detailed discussion of this trend see Rogers & Baxter, *supra*, at 498–99.

6. The treatise lists the types of errors held to be departures from the essential requirements of law. Haddad, *supra*, at 221 n. 113; *see* 5 Fla.Jur. *Certiorari* § 31 (1955).

7. For example, in determining whether there was a "departure from the essential requirements of law" reviewing courts have inquired: (1) whether the lower court proceeded "according to justice" or deprived the petitioner of fundamental rights, resulting in serious and material injury or gross injustice; (2) whether the judgment is authorized by law or is invalid, illegal, essentially

tice seemed to emerge of "restricting the scope of review so that the reality of the extent of review on certiorari was to a large degree commensurate with the rhetoric of limited review." Haddad, *supra*, at 221 (footnote omitted).[8]

Despite this "all over the waterfront" picture, some opinions should be noted for their tight and lucid language in capturing the essence of the appropriate use of the writ. In *State v. Smith*, 118 So.2d 792 (Fla. 1st DCA 1960), Judge Wigginton explained:

> Certiorari is a common-law writ which issues in the sound judicial discretion of the court to an inferior court, not to take the place of an appeal, but to cause the entire record of the inferior court to be brought up in order that it may be determined from the face thereof whether the inferior court has exceeded its jurisdiction, or has not proceeded according to the essential requirements of law. Confined to its legitimate scope, the writ may issue within the court's discretion to correct the procedure of courts wherein they have not observed those requirements of the law which are deemed to be essential to the administration of justice. . . . *Failure to observe the essential requirements of law means failure to accord due process of law within the contemplation of the Constitution, or the commission of an error so fundamental in character as to fatally infect the judgment and render it void.* . . .

> It seems to be the settled law of this state that the duty of a court to apply to admitted facts a correct principle of law is such a fundamental and essential element of the judicial process that a litigant cannot be said to have had the remedy by due course of law [guaranteed by the Florida Constitution], if the judge fails or refuses to perform that duty.

Id. at 795 (footnote omitted) (emphasis added).

In 1985, Chief Justice Boyd also captured the essence of the standard:

> The required "departure from the essential requirements of law" means something far beyond legal error. It means an inherent illegality or irregularity, an abuse of judicial power, an act of judicial tyranny perpetrated with disregard of procedural requirements, resulting in a gross miscarriage of

---

irregular, or prejudicial; (3) whether the court rendering judgment lacked jurisdiction; (4) whether the circuit court's appellate judgment violates established principles of law; (5) whether the judgment results in a substantial injury to the legal rights of the petitioner; (6) whether the judgment constitutes a palpable miscarriage of justice; or (7) whether the lower court applied the wrong rule of law to the evidence. 5 Fla.Jur. *Certiorari* §§ 25, 30, 31 (1955).

8. Mr. Haddad attributes this trend to the greater caseload in the appellate courts and further noted that typical of cases granting certiorari were those in which the reviewing court quashed affirmances of criminal convictions where virtually no evidence was found on a material element of the crime; those in which the circuit court reversed a lower court on the basis of a patently erroneous statement of law; and those in which the circuit court dismissed an appeal because the record was late and the fault was apparently that of the lower court clerk rather than of the appellant or his attorney. *Id.*

justice. The writ of certiorari properly issues to correct essential illegality but not legal error.

Jones v. State, 477 So.2d 566, 569 (Fla.1985) (Boyd, C.J., concurring specially).

Combs

In *Combs v. State*, 436 So.2d 93 (Fla.1983), this Court held that the district court had applied too narrow a certiorari standard of review. Melvin Combs was convicted in county court of driving while intoxicated. At trial, Combs claimed that certain statements he made at the accident scene were privileged. The county court rejected the claim, and, on appeal after conviction, the circuit court affirmed. In denying certiorari, the district court stated that its review was limited to: "violations which effectively deny appellate review such as a circuit judge rendering a decision without allowing briefs to be filed and considered, a circuit judge making a decision without a record to support the decision or the circuit court dismissing an appeal improperly." *Combs v. State*, 420 So.2d 316, 317 (Fla. 5th DCA 1982) (citation omitted). In rejecting this scope of review as too narrow, we acknowledged that application of the phrase "departure from the essential requirements of law" had generated much confusion. *Combs*, 436 So.2d at 95. We attributed the confusion mainly to the difficulty encountered by the courts in maintaining the distinction between certiorari review and the standard used in reviewing legal error on appeal.[9]

In an effort to clarify the certiorari standard, we elaborated on the meaning and boundaries of "departure from the essential requirements of law":

> [T]he phrase "departure from the essential requirements of law" should not be narrowly construed so as to apply only to violations that effectively deny appellate review or that pertain to the regularity of procedure. *In granting writs of common-law certiorari, the district courts of appeal should not be as concerned with the mere existence of legal error as much as with the seriousness of the error.* Since it is impossible to list all possible legal errors serious enough to constitute a departure from the essential requirements of law, the district courts must be allowed a large degree of discretion so that they may judge each case individually. The district courts should exercise this discretion only when there has been *a violation of clearly established principle of law resulting in a miscarriage of justice.*

> It is this discretion, which is the essential distinction between review by appeal and review by common-law certiorari. A district court may refuse to grant a petition for common-law certiorari, even though there may have been a departure from the essential requirements of law. The district

---

9. *See, e.g., In re Camm*, 294 So.2d 318 (Fla.), *cert. denied*, 419 U.S. 866, 95 S.Ct. 121, 42 L.Ed.2d 103 (1974); *Westerman v. Shell's City, Inc.*, 265 So.2d 43 (Fla.1972); *Goodkind v. Wolkowsky*, 151 Fla. 62, 9 So.2d 553 (1942); *Biscayne Beach Theatre, Inc. v. Hill*, 151 Fla. 1, 9 So.2d 109 (1942).

courts should use this discretion cautiously so as to avert the possibility of common-law certiorari being used as a vehicle to obtain a second appeal.

Combs, 436 So.2d at 95–96 (emphasis added) (citations omitted). We concluded in *Combs* that the district court reached a correct result, albeit for the wrong reason, in denying certiorari, despite its use of an erroneous standard of review. *Id.* at 96.[10]

Educational Development Center

The case of *Education Development Center v. City of West Palm Beach*, 541 So.2d 106 (Fla.1989), unlike *Combs*, began in an administrative agency — a zoning board of appeals. Further, in contrast to *Combs*, we held that the district court had applied too broad a standard of review.

In *Education Development Center* [hereinafter *EDC*], the petitioner sought permission from the Zoning Board of Appeal (Board) to convert its residential property to a private preschool and kindergarten. The Board denied EDC's application and EDC appealed to the circuit court. The circuit court reversed, and concluded there was "substantially competent evidence" to support EDC's application as required by the zoning code. Subsequently, the district court granted the Board's petition for certiorari, and found that the circuit court had applied an incorrect standard of review.[11] *EDC*, 541 So.2d at 107.

On remand and reconsideration, the circuit court again reversed the zoning board decision, this time finding that "there was no substantial competent evidence

---

10. We applied *Combs* in *State v. Pettis*, 520 So.2d 250 (Fla.1988), to further clarify the distinction between "essential illegality" and mere "legal error." The state made a pretrial motion to prevent Pettis from questioning a police officer at trial about five departmental reprimands the officer had received. Upon the denial of the motion in limine, the state filed a petition for writ of certiorari, which was granted by the Fourth District Court of Appeal. Accordingly, the Fourth District quashed the order denying the state's motion in limine. In its opinion, the district court held that Pettis could not use evidence of the officer's prior reprimands to impeach his character for truthfulness because the officer's character trait was not an essential element of the charge or defense. *Id.* at 251.

While we agreed that the trial judge erred in permitting the police officer to be questioned concerning unrelated reprimands, we did not believe it rose to the level of being a departure from the essential requirements of law:

[W]e cannot say that the ruling was a departure from the essential requirements of law. While some pretrial evidentiary rulings may qualify for certiorari, it must be remembered that the extraordinary writ is reserved for those situations where "there has been a violation of a clearly established principle of law resulting in a miscarriage of justice." *Combs v. State*, 436 So.2d 93, 96 (Fla.1983).

Id. at 254 (footnote omitted).

11. The district court explained:

[T]he circuit court departed from the essential requirements of law by applying an incorrect standard of review. The question is not whether, upon review of the evidence in the record, there exists substantial competent evidence to support a position *contrary* to that reached by the agency. Instead, the circuit court should review the factual determination made by the agency and determine whether there is substantial competent evidence to support the agency's conclusion.

City of West Palm Beach v. Education Dev. Ctr., 504 So.2d 1385, 1386 (Fla. 4th DCA 1987).

296   4 · THE COURTS

to support the City's denial of the petition." *Id.* at 108. Upon a second review in the district court, the circuit court's decision was again quashed, based upon the district court's disagreement with the trial court as to the existence of substantial competent evidence to support the Board's decision.[12] *City of W. Palm Beach v. Education Dev. Ctr.*, 536 So.2d 775, 777 (Fla. 4th DCA 1988).

In our review of *EDC*, we relied on *City of Deerfield Beach v. Vaillant*, 419 So.2d 624, 626 (Fla.1982), to define the district court's standard of review, and stated:

> [T]he principles expressed by the Court in *Vaillant* clearly define the standards of review applicable here. There was no contention of a denial of due process and the district court of appeal did not find that the trial judge applied an incorrect principle of law. The district court of appeal simply disagreed with the circuit court's evaluation of the evidence. Accordingly, we reaffirm *Vaillant* and quash the decision of the district court.

541 So.2d at 108–09.

Combs and EDC

To some extent *Combs* and *EDC* may be viewed as the bookends of appellate certiorari review, one pointing out an overly strict standard, while the other quashes the use of an overly broad standard. However, both decisions mandate a narrow standard of review and emphasize that certiorari should not be utilized to provide "a second appeal."

In *Combs* we held that a district court's review of an appellate circuit court decision should determine whether there was a "departure from the essential requirements of law." We emphasized that there must be "a violation of a clearly established principle of law resulting in a miscarriage of justice." On the other hand, *EDC* held that a district court's review of an appellate circuit court's decision which reviewed an administrative agency decision should consider whether the "circuit court afforded procedural due process and applied the correct law." Accordingly, the question becomes whether these two standards are different, and, if so, whether a difference is justified.[13]

---

12. 2 In contrast to the circuit court, the district court found:
   There was substantial evidence to support the denial of the application to permit the operation of a preschool in this residential area. To find to the contrary, we conclude that the lower tribunal either reinterpreted the inferences which the evidence supported or reweighed that evidence; in either event substituting its judgment for that of the zoning board, which it may not properly do.

13. Post-*EDC* and post-*Combs* cases have consistently applied the standards of review espoused in each case. *See, e.g.,* post-*EDC* cases: *Branch v. Charlotte County*, 627 So.2d 577 (Fla. 2d DCA 1993); *Manatee County v. Kuehnel*, 542 So.2d 1356 (Fla. 2d DCA 1989), *review denied*, 548 So.2d 663 (Fla.1989); post-*Combs* cases: *State v. Frazee*, 617 So.2d 350 (Fla. 4th DCA 1993); *Horatio Enterprises, Inv. v. Rabin*, 614 So.2d 555 (Fla. 3d DCA 1993); *Slater v. State*, 543 So.2d 869 (Fla. 2d DCA 1989).

Vaillant illustrates the relationship of these standards. In *Vaillant*, we agreed with the decision and rationale of the Fourth District which reviewed the case before it came to us. 419 So.2d at 626. The district court had determined that *procedural due process was afforded and that essential requirements of the law were observed. We actually held*, however, that a district court, upon review of a circuit court's judgment, determines whether the circuit court "*afforded procedural due process and applied the correct law.*" *Id.* (emphasis added). When the above two standards are juxtaposed, we conclude that "applied the correct law" is synonymous with "observing the essential requirements of law." *See, e.g., Manatee County v. Kuehnel*, 542 So.2d 1356, 1358 (Fla. 2d DCA) (holding that when district court reviews decision of circuit appellate court standard of review is whether court afforded procedural due process and observed essential requirements of law), *review denied*, 548 So.2d 663 (Fla.1989). Therefore, when the *Combs* and *EDC* standards are reduced to their core, they appear to be the same. Moreover, we can see no justifiable reason for adopting different standards for district court review in such cases.

Common-law certiorari has been made available to review quasi-judicial orders of local agencies and boards not made subject to the Administrative Procedure Act when no other method of review is provided. *See De Groot v. Sheffield*, 95 So.2d 912 (Fla. 1957). If the administrative action was initially reviewable by certiorari to the circuit court, the district court then has jurisdiction to review the circuit court's decision by a second petition for writ of certiorari. Phillip J. Padovano, *Florida Appellate Practice* § 3.7 (1988) (citing *Tomeu v. Palm Beach County*, 430 So.2d 601 (Fla. 4th DCA 1983)). However, certiorari in circuit court to review local administrative action under Florida Rule of Appellate Procedure 9.030(c)(3) is not truly discretionary common-law certiorari, because the review is of right. *Vaillant*, 419 So.2d at 625–26; *see also EDC*, 541 So.2d at 108. In other words, in such review the circuit court functions as an appellate court, and among other things, is not entitled to reweigh the evidence or substitute its judgment for that of the agency. *See EDC*, 541 So.2d at 108.

As a case travels up the judicial ladder, review should consistently become narrower, not broader. We have held that circuit court review of an administrative agency decision, under Florida Rule of Appellate Procedure 9.030(c)(3), is governed by a three-part standard of review: (1) whether the procedural due process is accorded; (2) whether the essential requirements of law have been observed; and (3) whether the administrative findings and judgment are supported by competent substantial evidence. *Vaillant*, 419 So.2d at 626. The standard of review for certiorari in the district court effectively eliminates the substantial competent evidence component. The inquiry is limited to whether the circuit court afforded procedural due process and whether the circuit court applied the correct law. As explained above, these two components are merely expressions of ways in which the circuit court decision may have departed from the essential requirements of the law. In short, we have the same standard of review as a case which begins in the county court. *See* William A. Haddad, "Writ of Certiorari in Florida," *in* The Florida Bar, *Florida Appellate Practice* § 18.3 (3d ed. 1993).

This standard, while narrow, also contains a degree of flexibility and discretion.[14] For example, a reviewing court is drawing new lines and setting judicial policy as it individually determines those errors sufficiently egregious or fundamental to merit the extra review and safeguard provided by certiorari. This may not always be easy since the errors in question must be viewed in the context of the individual case. It may also be true that review of administrative decisions may be more difficult, since care must be exercised to determine the nature of the administrative proceeding under review, and to distinguish between quasi-judicial proceedings and those legislative in nature. There is no complete catalog that the court can turn to in resolving a particular case.

Conclusion

The district court's opinion in this case is an excellent example of the correct application of the limited standard of review available to litigants after they have had the benefit of an appeal in the circuit court. The district court opinion noted:

> In this case, even if we were to conclude that the circuit court's order departed from the essential requirements of the law, we cannot say that such a departure was serious enough to result in a miscarriage of justice. The order did nothing more than reverse a county court's eviction judgment based on a peculiar set of facts. It did not deprive the petitioner of its day in court, nor has it foreclosed the petitioner from seeking eviction of the respondent because of future non-payment of rent. *See State v. Roess*, 451 So.2d 879 (Fla. 2d DCA 1984). Thus, we are unable to conclude that this is one of "those few extreme cases where the appellate court's decision is so erroneous that justice requires that it be corrected." *Combs*, 436 So.2d at 95.

Heggs, 647 So.2d at 856. This analysis captures the essence of our holdings in *Combs* and *EDC*.

We answer the certified question in the affirmative and hold that the standards of review announced in *Combs* and *Educational Development Center* are the same. We approve the decision below.

It is so ordered.

---

14. One critic has noted:
    Some errors are so fundamental as to clearly fall within the term; others clearly do not fall within any reasonable interpretation. The vagueness of the phrase, however, means that there is a large grey area. Properly conceived, the discretion often mentioned in relation to common law certiorari should be exercised in this grey area. This should not be an unprincipled or arbitrary discretion but should depend on the court's assessment of the gravity of the error and the adequacy of other relief. A judicious assessment by the appellate court will not usurp the authority of the trial judge or the role of any other appellate remedy, but will preserve the function of this great writ of review as a "backstop" to correct grievous errors that, for a variety of reasons, are not otherwise effectively subject to review.

Haddad, *supra*, at 228.

GRIMES, C.J., and OVERTON, SHAW, KOGAN, HARDING and WELLS, JJ., concur.

State v. Pettis

520 So. 2d 250 (Fla. 1988)

GRIMES, Justice.

We review *State v. Pettis*, 488 So.2d 877 (Fla. 4th DCA 1986), because of direct and express conflict with *State v. Wilson*, 483 So.2d 23 (Fla. 2d DCA 1985). Art. V, § 3(b)(3), Fla. Const.

Pettis was charged with a drug offense. The state made a pretrial motion to prevent Pettis from questioning a police officer at the trial about five departmental reprimands he had received. The reprimands had occurred during the officer's former employment with another police force, and the most recent of them had taken place about three years earlier. None of the reprimands involved Pettis or anyone connected with him. Upon the denial of the motion in limine, the state filed a petition for writ of certiorari. The Fourth District Court of Appeal granted certiorari and quashed the order denying the state's motion in limine. In its opinion, the district court held that Pettis could not use evidence of the officer's prior reprimands to impeach his character for truthfulness because the officer's character trait was not an essential element of the charge or defense. § 90.405(2), Fla.Stat. (1983). The court pointed out that Pettis had not defended on ground that the officer had an interest, bias or motive to lie as did the defendants in *Mendez v. State*, 412 So.2d 965 (Fla. 2d DCA 1982), and *D.C. v. State*, 400 So.2d 825 (Fla. 3d DCA 1981).

Pettis filed a motion for rehearing, asserting that because the state could not appeal the order denying the motion in limine, it had no authority to seek review of the order by petition for common law certiorari. As a consequence, the district court of appeal on rehearing withdrew its prior opinion and stated:

> The petition for writ of certiorari is denied upon authority of *Jones v. State*, 477 So.2d 566 (Fla.1985). *See also R.L.B. v. State*, 486 So.2d 588 (Fla.1986).

488 So.2d at 877.

In *Jones v. State*, 477 So.2d 566 (Fla. 1985), this Court considered the question of whether the district court of appeal could entertain a petition for certiorari from an order challenging the dismissal of probation violation charges. We reasoned that since there was no statutory right of appeal from the dismissal of probation violation charges, the district court could not review the dismissal by way of certiorari.

Subsequent to *Jones*, the Second District Court of Appeal entertained a petition for certiorari to review an order denying the state's motion to exclude certain evidence from the defendant's criminal trial. Just as in *Pettis*, the district court was faced with the question of whether it had authority to grant certiorari to review the denial of the state's pretrial motion in limine. Concluding that it had such authority the district court reasoned:

Since the time the state filed its petition, and respondents responded, the supreme court issued its decisions in *Jones v. State*, 477 So.2d 566 (Fla.1985); *State v. G.P.*, 476 So.2d 1272 (Fla.1985); and *State v. C.C.*, 476 So.2d 144 (Fla.1985), which appear to hold that the state may not seek certiorari review of any interlocutory or final order for which a statutory right to appeal has not been granted. We, however, read the decisions to mean that the state may not use the petition for writ of common law certiorari to obtain appellate review of an order that is only reviewable, if at all, by direct appeal. If there is no statutory right to appeal, then certiorari cannot be used to supply the right. On the other hand, we do not believe the above decisions preclude the state from seeking common law certiorari review, as opposed to statutory appellate review, of an interlocutory order (such as the denial of its motion in limine in this case) which departs from the essential requirements of law and for which the state would have no other avenue of review.

State v. Wilson, 483 So.2d at 24–25. We agree with this analysis.

The right of appeal from a final judgment is prescribed by statute. *State v. Creighton*, 469 So.2d 735 (Fla.1985). [See the discussion of this case beginning at page 304 of this text.] The cases of *State v. C.C.*, 476 So.2d 144 (Fla. 1985), *State v. G.P.*, 476 So.2d 1272 (Fla. 1985), and *Jones v. State*, 477 So.2d 566 (Fla.1985), were each concerned with the review of final orders of dismissal from which there was no statutory right of appeal. Those decisions were bottomed on the premise that the state should not be permitted to circumvent the absence of a statutory right of appeal through the vehicle of a petition for certiorari.

The orders involved in *Pettis* and *Wilson* were nonfinal orders. The review of nonfinal orders is controlled by court rule. *State v. Smith*, 260 So.2d 489 (Fla.1972). State appeals from certain nonfinal orders are authorized by Florida Rule of Appellate Procedure 9.140(c)(1)(B). With respect to common law certiorari,[1] Florida Rule of Appellate Procedure 9.030(b)(2) provides in part:

(2) *Certiorari Jurisdiction.* The certiorari jurisdiction of district courts of appeal may be sought to review:

(A) non-final orders of lower tribunals other than as prescribed by Rule 9.130;

The reference to rule 9.130 is not inadvertent because the orders covered by that rule are ones from which an interlocutory appeal may be taken as contrasted to a petition for certiorari. Subsection (a)(2) of rule 9.130 excludes nonfinal orders in criminal cases. The committee note under rule 9.130 states:

1977 Revision. This rule replaces former Rule 4.2 and substantially alters current practice. This rule applies to review of all non-final orders, except

---

1. The authority of the district courts of appeal to issue writs of certiorari is derived from article V, section 4(b)(3) of the Florida Constitution.

those entered in criminal cases, and those specifically governed by Rules 9.100 and 9.110.

The Advisory Committee was aware that the common law writ of certiorari is available at any time and did not intend to abolish that writ. However, since that writ provides a remedy only where the petitioner meets the heavy burden of showing that a clear departure from the essential requirements of law has resulted in otherwise irreparable harm, it is extremely rare that erroneous interlocutory rulings can be corrected by resort to common law certiorari. It is anticipated that since the most urgent interlocutory orders are appealable under this rule, there will be very few cases where common law certiorari will provide relief. *See Taylor v. Board of Public Instruction of Duval County*, 131 So.2d 504 (Fla. 1st DCA 1961).

The right of district courts of appeal to review nonfinal orders in criminal cases by certiorari was recognized in dictum by this Court in *State v. Harris*, 136 So.2d 633 (Fla.1962). Several years later in *State v. Smith* the question was directly presented. In that case, the Court upheld the district court's reasoning that the state could not appeal a pretrial order requiring an eyewitness to a murder to be examined for visual acuity. However, the district court had treated the interlocutory appeal as a petition for writ of common law certiorari, and this Court reversed the denial of that petition on the premise that the trial judge's order had departed from the essential requirements of law.

In *State v. Steinbrecher*, 409 So.2d 510 (Fla. 3d DCA 1982), the Third District Court of Appeal specifically addressed this question in the following manner:

> Respondent argues that there is no authority for certiorari review of a pretrial ruling excluding evidence. We disagree. Rule 9.140(c) of the Florida Rules of Appellate Procedure does limit matters which may be appealed by the state before trial as of right. However, this limitation as to appeals is not a bar to this court's power of discretionary review. . . .
>
> We believe, therefore, that the correct interpretation of Florida law is that if the requirements permitting certiorari jurisdiction otherwise exist, a pretrial order excluding evidence which has the effect of substantially impairing the ability of the state to prosecute its case is subject to certiorari review.

409 So.2d at 511.

In many other cases the district courts of appeal have granted common law certiorari to quash nonappealable interlocutory orders in criminal cases which departed from the essential requirements of law. *E.g., State v. Edwards*, 490 So.2d 235 (Fla. 5th DCA 1986); *State v. Maisto*, 427 So.2d 1120 (Fla. 3d DCA 1983); *State v. Busciglio*, 426 So.2d 1233 (Fla. 2d DCA 1983); *State v. Joseph*, 419 So.2d 391 (Fla. 3d DCA 1982); *State v. Horvatch*, 413 So.2d 469 (Fla. 4th DCA 1982); *State v. Love*, 393 So.2d 66 (Fla. 3d DCA 1981); *State v. Dumas*, 363 So.2d 568 (Fla. 3d DCA 1978), *cert. denied*, 372 So.2d 471 (Fla.1979); *State v. Latimore*, 284 So.2d 423 (Fla. 3d DCA 1973), *cert. denied*, 291 So.2d 7 (Fla. 1974); *State v. Gillespie*, 227 So.2d 550 (Fla. 2d DCA

1969); *State v. Williams*, 227 So.2d 253 (Fla. 2d DCA 1969), *cert. denied*, 237 So.2d 180 (Fla.1970).

The ability of the district courts of appeal to entertain state petitions for certiorari to review pretrial orders in criminal cases is important to the fair administration of criminal justice in this state. Otherwise, there will be some circumstances in which the state is totally deprived of the right of appellate review of orders which effectively negate its ability to prosecute. If a nonfinal order does not involve one of the subjects enumerated in Florida Rule of Appellate Procedure 9.140(c)(1), the state would not be able to correct an erroneous and highly prejudicial ruling. Under such circumstances, the state could only proceed to trial with its ability to present the case significantly impaired. Should the defendant be acquitted, the principles of double jeopardy prevent the state from seeking review; thus, the prejudice resulting from the earlier order would be irreparable.[2] The filing of a petition for certiorari is an apt remedy under these circumstances. Only those are granted in which the error is serious. Very little delay is involved because the petitions are usually denied on their face as not demonstrating a departure from the essential requirements of law. In fact, it would be counterproductive for the state to have a full right of interlocutory appeal from all pretrial orders because this would mean the district court of appeal would have to entertain the appeal on its merits which would often result in unnecessary delay.[3]

Our statements in *State v. C.C.*, *State v. G.P.*, and *Jones v. State* that no right of review by certiorari exists in criminal cases if no right of appeal exists are limited to orders of final dismissal.[4] These cases shall not be construed to prohibit district courts of appeal from entertaining state petitions for certiorari from pretrial orders in criminal cases.

We agree that the trial judge below erred in permitting the police officer to be questioned concerning unrelated reprimands. *See A. Mcd. v. State*, 422 So.2d 336 (Fla. 3d DCA 1982); *Morrell v. State*, 297 So.2d 579 (Fla. 1st DCA 1974). However, we cannot say that the ruling was a departure from the essential requirements of law.[5] While some pretrial evidentiary rulings may qualify for certiorari, it must

---

2. The defendant does not suffer the same prejudice because he always has the right of appeal from a conviction in which he can attack any erroneous interlocutory orders.

3. From a practical standpoint, the state's ability to seek review of pretrial rulings by petition for certiorari may also inure to the benefit of some defendants. If the rule were otherwise, a trial judge, aware of the precariousness of the state's position, might decide to resolve all doubts in favor of the prosecution on the premise that the defendant can always have the action reviewed while the state cannot. Of course, the judge's order would ultimately come to the appellate court with a presumption of correctness. Therefore, the defendant could be prejudiced because the judge was bending over backward to keep from foreclosing the state's remedies.

4. Of course, the district courts of appeal also have jurisdiction to review by certiorari final orders of circuit courts acting in their review capacity. Fla.R.App.P. 9.030(b)(2)(B).

5. In view of the nature of certain of the police officer's reprimands which Pettis proposed to introduce, we do not agree with Justice Shaw that the trial judge's ruling was in direct conflict with an existing appellate decision.

be remembered that the extraordinary writ is reserved for those situations where "there has been a violation of a clearly established principle of law resulting in a miscarriage of justice." *Combs v. State*, 436 So.2d 93, 96 (Fla.1983). Therefore, we approve the denial of the petition for certiorari but not upon the reasoning implicit in its rehearing order.

It is so ordered.

EHRLICH, BARKETT and KOGAN, JJ., concur.

OVERTON, J., concurs in result only with an opinion.

McDONALD, C.J., concurs in result only.

SHAW, J., dissents with an opinion.

OVERTON, Justice, concurring in result only.

I concur in result only. Initially, I should make clear that I would support an amendment to our appellate rules to allow the state a greater opportunity for a review of non-final trial court actions in criminal cases. However, I disagree with broadening certiorari jurisdiction to allow the state to seek review of a trial court's non-final order. In my view, the majority opinion represents a departure from historically established common law principles governing certiorari.

I am deeply concerned that the decision could have major ramifications on the appellate process. In my opinion, the decision could (1) cause common law certiorari to be substantially extended beyond the intended purpose of the writ, and, (2) as a result, restrict our control of interlocutory appeals.

Common law certiorari is an extremely limited remedy which is not to be used as a substitute for an appeal. The scope of the inquiry of a petition for certiorari is supposed to be limited to issues of jurisdiction and procedural regularity. *See generally* Rogers and Baxter, *Certiorari in Florida*, 4 U.Fla.L.Rev. 477 (1951), and Haddad, *The Common Law Writ of Certiorari in Florida*, 29 U.Fla.L.Rev. 207 (1977). This Court specifically addressed the scope of a writ of certiorari in *Basnet v. City of Jacksonville*, 18 Fla. 523 (1882), where we stated:

> The question which the certiorari brings here is... whether the Judge *exceeded his jurisdiction* in hearing the case at all, or *adopted any method unknown to the law* or essentially irregular in his proceeding. ... *A decision made according to the form of law and the rules prescribed for rendering it, although it may be erroneous in its conclusion as to what the law is as applied to facts, is not an illegal or irregular act or proceeding remediable by certiorari.*

Id. at 526–27 (emphasis added).

Granting a petition for certiorari on these grounds is justified because the actions constituted a departure from the essential requirements of law. As we expressed in *Basnet*, that means something more than just legal error. We further refined the scope of certiorari jurisdiction in our recent decision in *Combs v. State*, 436 So.2d

93, 95–6 (Fla.1983), when we stated that, in granting writs of certiorari, appellate courts should not be "as concerned with the mere existence of legal error as much as with the seriousness of the error," and that the error must be such that it is "a violation of a clearly established principle of law resulting in a miscarriage of justice." Clearly, as held by the majority, the circumstances of this case do not meet this test.

I believe we are sending very confusing signals to the district courts of appeal of this state on the use of common law certiorari for review of criminal actions, including juvenile proceedings. The confusion becomes readily apparent after a review of our recent decisions on this subject. *See, e.g., State v. Creighton*, 469 So.2d 735 (Fla. 1985); *State v. C.C.*, 476 So.2d 144 (Fla. 1985); *State v. G.P.*, 476 So.2d 1272 (Fla. 1985); *Jones v. State*, 477 So.2d 566 (Fla. 1985).

In *Creighton*, the jury had returned a verdict of not guilty on count one, but guilty on count two. After the verdict, the defendant renewed a motion for judgment of acquittal of count two made at the end of the state's case and the trial judge granted that motion for acquittal. The issue was whether the state was entitled to a review of the trial court's order granting the judgment of acquittal. We reviewed the history of the authority of the state to seek review of trial court criminal decisions, stating that at common law a writ of error would lie for the defendant but not for the state. *State v. Burns*, 18 Fla. 185 (1881). We recognized that the issue was solely a question of law and that double jeopardy was not applicable. We held, however, "that the state's right of appeal in criminal cases depends on statutory authorization and is governed strictly by the statute" and that nowhere in the statutes "is provision made for appeal by the state from an order granting a judgment of acquittal." 469 So.2d at 740–41.

In *State v. C.C.*, the Court was considering consolidated appeals by the state concerning five separate juvenile cases. As applied to the juvenile C.C., the state was appealing the trial court's suppression of certain statements he made to the police; with regard to E.V., the trial court dismissed charges on double jeopardy grounds resulting from a prior mistrial where the trial judge had excused himself; concerning C.A.Q., the trial court suppressed physical evidence on the ground it was obtained by an illegal search; and, for A.M.E. and S.E., the trial court dismissed the delinquency petitions on the ground that the facts proffered, even if shown by the evidence, would not constitute a violation of the statutory offense. We held the statutory sections providing a right to review in criminal cases apply only to adult criminal matters, not to juvenile cases and found no interlocutory review was permitted.

In *State v. G.P.*, the trial court had dismissed a petition for delinquency because of the juvenile's constitutional right to a speedy trial had been violated. We held that the state had no right to appeal under the statute, nor did it have a right to have this type of juvenile order reviewed by petition for writ of certiorari. 476 So.2d at 1273.

In *State v. Jones*, the trial court had dismissed probation violation charges on the basis of Jones' claim of double jeopardy, res judicata, and collateral estoppel. The state sought review of that decision by petition for writ of certiorari. The district court of appeal accepted review and granted the writ. We quashed the district court decision, finding certiorari was not the proper remedy and held that

> article V, section 4(b)(1) of the state constitution permits interlocutory review only in cases in which an appeal may be taken as a matter of right. Moreover, we approved *State v. G.P.* and held that no right of review by certiorari exists if no right of appeal exists. *State v. G.P.*, 476 So.2d 1272 (Fla.1985). The district court erred in the instant case, therefore, in reviewing by certiorari a case it could not review by appeal.

Id. at 566. That decision, in my view, should clearly control the instant case.

I disagree with the statement by the majority that our decision in *State v. Smith*, 260 So.2d 489 (Fla.1972), expressly allows certiorari review of this type of matter. The real issue in *Smith* was whether the legislature, by legislative act, could authorize appeals by the state from pretrial orders. The district court of appeal held the statute unconstitutional on the basis that interlocutory appeals could be granted only by rule of this Court. We agreed with the district court, finding the statute was "ineffective unless a rule of this Court breathes life into the legislative act." *Id.* at 490. The district court, however, had considered the issue on the merits believing it had proper authority under common law certiorari and denied relief. We considered its decision on the merits and directed the district court to grant the writ of certiorari. The question of whether the state was entitled to an appellate court ruling on the merits by petition for certiorari was not addressed, argued, or ruled upon by either the district court of appeal or this Court. This Court's order with instructions to grant the writ of certiorari was clearly not a resolution of the question.

Interestingly, we emphatically stated in *Smith* that *this Court has the sole authority to establish by rule the methods of interlocutory review. Id.* at 489. We should accept that responsibility, bite the bullet, and provide the state a broader but controlled means of discretionary review of non-final orders rather than attempt to utilize common law certiorari jurisdiction in a manner that may compromise the basic principles for which that review process was created.

SHAW, Justice, dissenting.

I agree with the portion of the opinion concluding that the right to petition for certiorari review is not contingent on having a right of appeal, but I believe the majority adopts an overly restrictive view of this right to petition for certiorari. Moreover, I do not agree that the trial judge's error was not a departure from the essential requirements of law and would quash the district court decision below.

In *Jones v. State*, 477 So.2d 566 (Fla. 1985), and *State v. G.P.*, 476 So.2d 1272 (Fla.1985), we erroneously relied on *State v. C.C.*, 476 So.2d 144 (Fla.1985), for a proposition which was not addressed in *C.C.* In *C.C.* the issue was whether the state had the right to appeal trial court orders in juvenile cases to the district courts of appeal under either article V, section 4(b)(1) of the Florida Constitution or sections 924.07 and 924.071, Florida Statutes (1981). A divided court held that it did not. However, there was no issue raised concerning the right of the state to seek review by writ of certiorari under article V, section 4(b)(3) of the Florida Constitution. In *G.P.* the primary issue was whether the state had the right to appeal in a juvenile case under article V, section 4(b)(1). This issue as on point and controlled by *C.C.* However, the second issue in *G.P.*, whether the state had the right to seek a writ of certiorari in such cases, was not addressed by *C.C.* Nevertheless, without explanation, we took a quantum leap by announcing that the state has no greater right by certiorari than it does by appeal. In *Jones*, again without explanation and relying on *C.C.* and *G.P.*, we expanded this proposition.

The difficulty with *G.P.* and *Jones*, as Chief Justice Boyd in his special concurrence to *Jones* recognized, is that they directly conflict with decades of well-established case law. In *State v. Harris*, 136 So.2d 633 (Fla.1962), we addressed the controlling issue here of whether Section 924.07, limiting the right of the state to take appeals from adverse decisions in criminal proceedings to those enumerated, also limited the right of the state to obtain review by certiorari of nonappealable orders. With unmistakable clarity, we held:

> The statute [section 924.07] deals only with direct appeals in criminal proceedings and clearly does not and was not intended to proscribe the authority of the state to seek either common law certiorari now exercised by the district courts or constitutional certiorari of the variety now exercised by this Court.

Harris, 136 So.2d at 634. *See also State v. Smith*, 260 So.2d 489 (Fla.1972), (district court erred in denying certiorari review to state of nonappealable order); *State v. Steinbrecher*, 409 So.2d 510 (Fla. 3d DCA 1982) (Florida Rule of Appellate Procedure 9.140(c) limiting matters which may be appealed as of right by state does not bar certiorari review, also expressly recedes from contrary ruling in *State v. Steinbrecher*, 393 So.2d 66 (Fla. 3d DCA 1981)); *State v. Love*, 393 So.2d 66 (Fla. 3d DCA 1981) (grants common law certiorari review of interlocutory order in criminal proceeding); *State v. Dumas*, 363 So.2d 568 (Fla. 3d DCA 1978), *cert. denied*, 372 So.2d 471 (1979) (grants common law certiorari review of interlocutory order in criminal proceeding); *State v. Gibson*, 353 So.2d 670 (Fla. 2d DCA 1978) (treating state appeal of nonappealable order under section 924.07 as petition for certiorari and granting review); *State v. Wilcox*, 351 So.2d 89 (Fla. 2d DCA 1977) (treating state appeal of nonappealable order under section 924.07 as petition for certiorari and granting review); *State v. Caivano*, 304 So.2d 139 (Fla. 2d DCA 1974), *cert. denied*, 314 So.2d 774 (1975) (treating state appeal of nonappealable order under section 924.07 as petition for certiorari and granting review); *State v. Gillespie*, 227 So.2d 550 (Fla. 2d DCA 1969) (granting state certiorari review of nonappealable discovery order); *State v. Williams*, 227 So.2d 253 (Fla. 2d DCA 1969), *cert. denied*, 237 So.2d 180 (1970) (granting certiorari review of nonappealable discovery orders and citing *Harris* as authority for proposition that sections 924.07 and 924.071 do not limit state's right to seek certiorari review of interlocutory orders); *State v. Staley*, 97 So.2d 147 (Fla. 2d DCA 1957) (granting certiorari review of order from circuit court acting in its appellate capacity); *State v. Atwell*, 97 So.2d 125 (Fla. 2d DCA 1957) (holding that section 924.07 does not limit state's right to seek certiorari review and granting review of order from circuit court acting in its appellate capacity). See also cases cited by Chief Justice Boyd in his special concurrence to *Jones*, 477 So.2d at 567–68.

Historically, the common law writ of certiorari was only available to seek review of final judgments from which there was no right of appeal, for example, the nonappealable final judgments of a circuit court acting in its appellate capacity. However, this restriction of the writ to final judgments worked an obvious injustice when the adverse order was interlocutory and the party against whom the order was rendered had no adequate remedy either by appeal of the final judgment or by petition for writ of certiorari. Accordingly, exceptions were developed which permitted petitions for writs of certiorari to seek review of interlocutory orders of, e.g., circuit courts acting in either their appellate or trial capacity. The tests for certiorari review of interlocutory orders were stated in *Huie v. State*, 92 So.2d 264, 269 (Fla.1957):

> Our consistent position has been that it is only in a case where it clearly appears that there has been a departure from the essential requirements of the law *and in addition* thereto that there is no full, adequate and complete remedy by appeal after final judgment available to the petitioner in certiorari that we will ever consider granting a writ of certiorari to review an interlocutory order in a law action. (Emphasis in original.)

The standard of review in writs of certiorari differed significantly from that of appeals. In appeals, any error could be raised and corrected; in certiorari, only those which departed from the essential requirements of law were reviewable. This standard of review, however, presented major problems. It was imprecise and lent itself to uneven application from case to case and court to court. If applied stringently, it required the appellate court to turn a blind eye to errors which were in some instances dispositive and unjust. If applied liberally, it tended to blur or eliminate the distinctions between discretionary review by certiorari and review by right of appeal. If applied unevenly, it created conflicts of law between the circuits and districts, and denied equal protection of the law.[1]

The ideal remedy to the problems of certiorari review of interlocutory orders in criminal cases is to create an all-inclusive list of interlocutory orders which under all circumstances require review prior to trial and to establish a right of appeal for such orders. This would permit the appellate court to fully examine the purported error on the merits and would negate the right, or need, to seek certiorari review. This ideal remedy is difficult, if not impossible, to devise, however, because of the difficulty of devising a list which is neither underinclusive nor overinclusive. If the list is underinclusive, there is no adequate remedy for unlisted errors; if it is overinclusive, the appellate courts will be unnecessarily intruding, thereby delaying the

---

1. This paragraph draws heavily on two law review articles examining Florida's experience with certiorari review. Rogers & Baxter, *Certiorari in Florida*, 4 U.Fla.L.Rev. 477 (1951); Haddad, *The Common Law Writ of Certiorari in Florida*, 29 U.Fla.L.Rev. 207 (1977).

trial process. Thus, short of omniscience, it is necessary to devise a solution which retains a degree of discretionary, i.e., certiorari, review. Sections 924.07 and 924.071, Florida Statutes (1985) and Florida Rules of Appellate Procedure 9.130 and 9.140, in pertinent part, identify the most common interlocutory orders for which appeal by right is always appropriate and for which appellate intrusion into the trial process is justified. This list is by design underinclusive in order to prevent unnecessary intrusion.[2] Therefore, as we held in *Harris*, it is necessary to permit certiorari review of interlocutory orders which are nonappealable and for which appeal on final judgment will be inadequate.

The *Harris* rule is embodied in both the Florida Constitution and Florida Rules of Appellate Procedure. Article V, section 4(b)(3), Florida Constitution, grants the district courts of appeal the power to issue writs of certiorari. Certiorari review, which is discretionary and independent of the right to appeal, is also governed by Florida Rule of Appellate Procedure 9.030(b)(2):

> (2) *Certiorari Jurisdiction.* The certiorari jurisdiction of district courts of appeal may be sought to review:
>
>> (A) non-final orders of lower tribunals other than as prescribed by Rule 9.130.
>
>> (B) final orders or circuit courts acting in their review capacity.

(Footnote omitted.) Subsection (b)(2)(A) is controlling here. By its terms, it authorizes discretionary review by the district courts of appeal of non-final orders of lower tribunals *in addition* to those non-final orders specified in rule 9.130 which are subject to an appeal by right. Rule 9.030(b)(2) implements the common law certiorari jurisdiction of the district courts of appeal and codifies the *Harris* holding. The committee notes to the 1977 revision recognized this relationship "[t]he items stating the certiorari jurisdiction of the ... district courts of appeal refer to the ... 'common law certiorari' jurisdiction of the district courts of appeal." Fla.R.App.P. 9.030.

It is important to recognize that in criminal cases the adequacy of an appeal of a final judgment is significantly different depending on whether the order adversely affects the state or the defendant. The state cannot appeal an acquittal whereas a defendant may appeal a conviction. Consequently, without an ameliorating rule, the state has no remedy, adequate or otherwise, for the erroneous suppression of evidence when an acquittal occurs. Rule 9.140(c)(1)(B) and section 924.071(1) provide a remedy for the state even though a reciprocal interlocutory right of appeal is not provided to the defendant for an erroneous refusal to suppress evidence. This remedy, however, is not applicable to other evidentiary rulings which may be

---

2. This does not mean that we and the legislature should not continue to review and amend sections 924.07 and 924.071 and rules 9.130 and 9.140 in order to identify additional rulings from which the right of appeal is appropriate. For example, rule 9.140(c)(1)(B) permits appeals of orders suppressing evidence only if the evidence is obtained by search or seizure. This unnecessary restriction may result in irremediable harm. *See, e.g., McPhadder v. State*, 475 So.2d 1215 (Fla.1985).

equally devastating to the state. The case at hand illustrates this point. The trial court declined to grant a motion in limine which could be ruinous to the state's case in chief and for which the state has no adequate remedy if an acquittal occurs. This would also frustrate the district court's exercise of jurisdiction. By contrast, had the motion in limine been granted and a conviction obtained, the defendant would have an adequate remedy on appeal of the final judgment.

One of the tests for granting a writ of certiorari is that the lower court order be a departure from the essential requirements of law. *Huie.* The commentators,[3] and case law, show that this imprecise formulation of law has historically been unevenly applied to the detriment of equal protection and consistency of decisional law. Consequently, there is a need to provide specificity. Departure from the essential requirements of law is best understood if read in pari materia with the constitutional evolution of this Court's discretionary authority to review lower court decisions. Prior to the creation of the district courts of appeal in 1957 and the concomitant amendment of article V of the Florida Constitution, this Court had the unrestricted authority to review circuit court orders by a common law writ of certiorari. Thereafter, this unrestricted authority was constitutionally assigned to the district courts of appeal[4] and this Court's certiorari authority was limited to specific instances, one of which was a decision by a district court of appeal which was in direct conflict with a decision of another district court of appeal or of the Supreme Court on the same point of law.[5] This strongly suggests that direct and express conflict of decisions is a specific example of a departure from the essential requirements of law. One reaches the same conclusion if direct and express conflict is analyzed from an equal protection of the laws perspective. Applying this insight, it logically follows that a decision of a circuit court which conflicts with a decision of an appellate court is a departure from the essential requirements of law as it denies equal protection of the law and introduces confusion and inconsistency into the law. These conclusions are supported by an overall view of Florida's constitutional court system. The overall role of this Court is to supervise the district courts to ensure they are consistently applying settled law. The district courts' supervisory authority over circuit courts' essentially parallels this Court's authority over district courts.[6] Our constitutional

---

3. *See* supra n. 1 at 257.

4. *Robinson v. State*, 132 So.2d 3 (Fla.1961). The extent of district court certiorari jurisdiction is governed generally by precedences previously applicable to this Court. *Dresner v. City of Tallahassee*, 164 So.2d 208 (Fla.1964).

5. In 1980, our certiorari review authority was deleted entirely from the constitution by substituting the more accurate description of discretionary authority. However, because the common law writ of certiorari was a part of the common law of England which was incorporated by statute into this state's law, this Court's certiorari power exists independently of the constitutional grant of jurisdiction. *Kilgore v. Bird*, 149 Fla. 570, 6 So.2d 541 (1942). *See also* 3 Fla.Jur.2d, *Appellate Review, Part Two, Certiorari,* § 461 and cases cited therein.

6. In this connection, note also that the origin of the common law writ of certiorari is the supervisory authority of a higher court over a lower court. *Harrison v. Frink*, 75 Fla. 22, 77 So. 663 (1918).

court system cannot function effectively unless decisional conflicts at all levels are treated as departures from the essential requirements of law.

In the case at hand, the majority concludes that the trial judge erred in ruling that the police officer could be questioned concerning unrelated reprimands and that this ruling conflicts with *A. McD. v. State*, 422 So.2d 336 (Fla. 3d DCA 1982), and *Morrell v. State*, 297 So.2d 579 (Fla. 1st DCA 1974). I agree. The majority goes on to hold, however, that this erroneous ruling and conflict of decisions is not a departure from the essential requirements of law. I dissent from this holding. This narrow view of common law certiorari, departures from the essential requirements of law, and the power of supervisory courts will not only produce unjust results in individual cases, it will also create a judicial system where uncorrected conflicts of law routinely occur from district to district, circuit to circuit, and trial court to trial court. We should not truncate this valuable tool of appellate oversight which has evolved over centuries of common law jurisprudence and which is critical to the complete exercise of appellate jurisdiction. Art. V, §§ 3(b)(7), 4(b)(3), and 5(b), Fla. Const.

I dissent for the above reasons and would quash the decision below.

––––––––––

As the various opinions in *Pettis* indicate, in the nonappealable interlocutory order setting, common law certiorari standards are not always easy to apply. The same is true in the two other venues of common law certiorari: review of circuit courts sitting as (1) appellate courts for the county courts, and (2) review courts for agencies.

When a circuit court sits in its appellate capacity, the only method for a party to obtain district court review of the circuit court's ruling is by petition for writ of common law certiorari, which is commonly referred to as "second-tier" certiorari review.[142] As the Florida Supreme Court pronounced in the *City of Deerfield v. Valliant*,[143] the second-tier certiorari review cannot be used as a means of granting a second appeal, and it cannot be used simply because the district court disagrees with the outcome of the circuit court's decision. Instead, the Florida Supreme Court has held that the district courts should only act when the error is one that is a departure from the essential elements of law resulting in a miscarriage of justice.[144] As recognized by the Florida Supreme Court in *Haines City Community Development v. Heggs,* when the district court exercises its discretion in performing a second-tier certiorari review, a balance must be struck between respecting the finality of appellate review provided by the circuit court's appellate decision and the necessity of having the availability of certiorari to use in a narrow group of cases, which "merit

––––––––––

142. *Dep't of Highway Safety and Motor Vehicles v. Nader*, 4 So. 3d 705 (Fla. 2d Dist. Ct. App. 2009).

143. 419 So. 2d 624 (Fla. 1892).

144. *Haines City Cmty. Dev. v. Heggs*, 658 So. 2d 523 (Fla. 1995).

extra review and safeguard provided by certiorari."[145] The following case provides a detailed analysis and discussion of the district court's second-tier review function.

Nader v. Florida Department of Highway Safety & Motor Vehicles

87 So. 3d 712 (Fla. 2012)

PARIENTE, J.

In this case before us, *Department of Highway Safety and Motor Vehicles v. Nader,* 4 So.3d 705 (Fla. 2d DCA 2009), the Second District Court of Appeal determined two distinct but related issues: the first involving the administrative suspension of a driver's license for refusal to submit to a breath test, and the second involving the scope of certiorari review by an appellate court of the circuit court's decision concerning the administrative suspension. In its decision in *Nader,* the Second District passed upon the two questions involving these issues, which it certified to be of great public importance:

> 1. DOES A LAW ENFORCEMENT OFFICER'S REQUEST THAT A DRIVER SUBMIT TO A BREATH, BLOOD, OR URINE TEST, UNDER CIRCUMSTANCES IN WHICH THE BREATH-ALCOHOL TEST IS THE ONLY REQUIRED TEST, VIOLATE THE IMPLIED CONSENT PROVISIONS OF SECTION 316.1932(1)(A)(1)(a) SUCH THAT THE DEPARTMENT MAY NOT SUSPEND THE DRIVER'S LICENSE FOR REFUSING TO TAKE ANY TEST?

> 2. MAY A DISTRICT COURT GRANT COMMON LAW CERTIORARI RELIEF FROM A CIRCUIT COURT'S OPINION REVIEWING AN ADMINISTRATIVE ORDER WHEN THE CIRCUIT COURT APPLIED PRECEDENT FROM ANOTHER DISTRICT COURT BUT THE REVIEWING DISTRICT COURT CONCLUDES THAT THE PRECEDENT MISINTERPRETS CLEARLY ESTABLISHED STATUTORY LAW?

Id. at 711. As more fully discussed below, we answer the first question in the negative and answer the second question in the affirmative.[1]

Facts

The facts in this case arise from an arrest after the driver, Susan Nader, failed a roadside sobriety test and then had her license suspended based on a refusal to submit to a breath test:

> On August 26, 2007, at approximately 1:30 a.m., Susan Nader was stopped by a Tampa police officer because she was driving with only her parking lights on and had stayed at an intersection through more than one cycle of the traffic lights. After she failed a roadside sobriety test, she was arrested and

---

145. *Id.* at 531.

1. Based on these certified questions, we have jurisdiction. *See* art. V, § 3(b)(4), Fla. Const.

transported to a breath test center operated by the Hillsborough County Sheriff's Office.[2]

Nader, 4 So.3d at 706. The record reflects that she refused to take a breath test and thus her license was suspended.

Nader requested an administrative hearing, during which she argued that the implied consent warning given was improper because she was requested to submit to a "breath, blood, or urine" test when the law requires only a breath test. After the hearing officer upheld the license suspension, Nader appealed the decision to the circuit court pursuant to a statutory provision that provides for the method of review by a circuit court.

* * *

Accordingly, we answer the first certified question in the negative. We now address the second certified question, which presents the issue of whether the Second District's decision to grant the Department's petition for certiorari exceeded the limited scope of its second-tier certiorari review.

Second Certified Question

Common-Law Certiorari Proceedings

A petition for writ of certiorari is a method for a litigant to obtain review of a circuit court order that is distinctly different from appellate review. A district court's certiorari review of a circuit court's decision may occur in two discrete situations: (1) certiorari review of a nonfinal order entered by the circuit court; and (2) second-tier certiorari, which is certiorari review of an order of the circuit court sitting in its appellate capacity to review a ruling from either the county court or an administrative or other governmental entity.

In the first situation, involving nonfinal orders entered by the circuit court in the course of ongoing proceedings, a party seeking review through a petition for writ of certiorari must demonstrate: (1) a material injury in the proceedings that cannot be corrected on appeal (sometimes referred to as irreparable harm); and (2) a "depart[ure] from the essential requirements of the law." *Belair v. Drew,* 770 So.2d 1164, 1166 (Fla.2000). As stated in *Martin-Johnson, Inc. v. Savage,* 509 So.2d 1097, 1099 (Fla.1987):

A non-final order for which no appeal is provided by Rule 9.130 is reviewable by petition for certiorari only in limited circumstances. The order must depart from the essential requirements of law and thus cause material

---

2. The arrest report stated the officer observed Nader's car "with only parking lights on sitting at an intersection. The vehicle [sat through] a couple of light cycles. The driver of the [vehicle] had the distinct odor of an alcoholic beverage on her breath as she spoke. Her eyes were bloodshot and watery. Her speech was at times slurred [and] thick-tongued. She was unsteady on her feet. She was unsure of her location. She performed SFSTs [standardized field sobriety tests] which showed clues of impairment."

injury to the petitioner throughout the remainder of the proceedings below, effectively leaving no adequate remedy on appeal.

Because Florida Rule of Appellate Procedure 9.130 limits the types of appealable nonfinal orders and because appellate review of the final order is available, the case law is very specific that when a litigant petitions the appellate court for a writ of certiorari as to a nonfinal order, both the requirements of irreparable harm and a departure from the essential requirements of law must be met. Further, the law is clear that certiorari relief is intended to be available only in very limited circumstances and should not be a means of circumventing rule 9.130 or interfering with ongoing proceedings in the trial court.

Separate from the limited review available to nonfinal orders, the second situation involves second-tier certiorari, which likewise can be divided into two subcategories of cases: those involving circuit court review of county court orders and those involving circuit court review of administrative decisions. Review of these final orders are also different from full appellate review, but the reasoning for the narrow review is based primarily on the principle that a litigant is not entitled to a second appeal.

The first subcategory of second-tier certiorari cases involves final decisions, judgments, or orders rendered by the county court after a full hearing or trial. Those final decisions are appealed to the circuit court sitting in its appellate capacity, and in those circumstances, appellate review by the circuit court is similar to appellate review by district courts of appeal. Because the assumption is that the litigant has already received full appellate review by the circuit court (either sitting in three-judge panels or by one judge alone), the district court's discretion to grant certiorari review is restricted to those errors that "depart from the essential requirements of law." As stated in the oft-cited opinion of *Combs v. State,* 436 So.2d 93 (Fla.1983), which addressed the scope of this certiorari review:

> [T]he phrase "departure from the essential requirements of law" should not be narrowly construed so as to apply only to violations which effectively deny appellate review or which pertain to the regularity of procedure. *In granting writs of common-law certiorari, the district courts of appeal should not be as concerned with the mere existence of legal error as much as with the seriousness of the error. Since it is impossible to list all possible legal errors serious enough to constitute a departure from the essential requirements of law, the district courts must be allowed a large degree of discretion so that they may judge each case individually.* The district courts should exercise this discretion only when there has been a *violation of a clearly established principle of law resulting in a miscarriage of justice.*
>
> *It is this discretion which is the essential distinction between review by appeal and review by common-law certiorari.*

Id. at 95–96 (emphasis added).

The second subcategory of second-tier certiorari cases comprises those that involve review of decisions rendered by administrative or other governmental agencies — the type of second-tier certiorari that is involved in this case. In *Haines City Community Development v. Heggs,* 658 So.2d 523 (Fla.1995), the Court observed:

> As a case travels up the judicial ladder, review should consistently become narrower, not broader. We have held that circuit court review of an administrative agency decision, under Florida Rule of Appellate Procedure 9.030(c)(3), is governed by a three-part standard of review: (1) whether procedural due process is accorded; (2) whether the essential requirements of law have been observed; and (3) whether the administrative findings and judgment are supported by competent substantial evidence. [*City of Deerfield Beach v.*] *Vaillant,* 419 So. 2d [624,] 626 [(Fla. 1982)]. The standard of review for certiorari in the district court effectively eliminates the substantial competent evidence component. The inquiry is limited to whether the circuit court afforded procedural due process and *whether the circuit court applied the correct law.* As explained above, these two components are merely expressions of ways in which the circuit court decision may have departed from the essential requirements of the law. In short, we have the same standard of review as a case which begins in the county court. *See* William A. Haddad, "Writ of Certiorari in Florida," *in* The Florida Bar, *Florida Appellate Practice* § 18.3 (3d ed.1993).
>
> *This standard, while narrow, also contains a degree of flexibility and discretion. For example, a reviewing court is drawing new lines and setting judicial policy as it individually determines those errors sufficiently egregious or fundamental to merit the extra review and safeguard provided by certiorari. This may not always be easy since the errors in question must be viewed in the context of the individual case.*

Id. at 530–31 (emphasis added) (footnote omitted).

However, appellate courts must exercise caution not to expand certiorari jurisdiction to review the correctness of the circuit court's decision. This would deprive litigants of the finality of judgments reviewed by the circuit court and ignore "societal interests in ending litigation within a reasonable length of time and eliminating the amount of judicial labors involved in multiple appeals." *Id.* at 526 n. 4. "A more expansive review would also afford a litigant two appeals from a court of limited jurisdiction, while limiting a litigant to only one appeal in cases originating in a trial court of general jurisdiction." *Custer Med. Ctr. v. United Auto. Ins. Co.,* 62 So.3d 1086, 1093 (Fla.2010).

Moreover, certiorari jurisdiction cannot be used to *create* new law where the decision below recognizes the correct general law and applies the correct law to a new set of facts to which it has not been previously applied. In such a situation, the law at issue is not a clearly established principle of law. *See Ivey v. Allstate Ins. Co.,* 774 So.2d 679, 682–83 (Fla.2000). This does not mean, however, that clearly established law consists only of prior judicial precedent. In *Kaklamanos,* 843 So.2d at 890, we explicitly held that "'clearly established law' can derive from a *variety of legal sources,* including recent controlling case law, rules of court, statutes, and constitutional law." (Emphasis added.) Accordingly, a district court may grant a writ of certiorari after determining that the decision is in conflict with the relevant statute, so long as the legal error is also "sufficiently egregious or fundamental to fall within the limited scope" of certiorari jurisdiction. *Id.*

* * *

To the extent that the Second District advocates a rule allowing second-tier certiorari review when an appellate court merely disagrees with precedent from another court, we reject this as overly broad. First, we note that there is presently an important difference between the review of administrative proceedings, which proceed directly to the circuit court, and the review of county court proceedings, which can be either appealed to the circuit court or heard by the district court through certified question. In the latter situation, the appellate rules expressly provide for a means by which the county court can certify a question to be of great public importance to the district court, thus providing a method by which the county court can receive a ruling on whether precedent from another district controls. *See* Fla. R.App. P. 9.030(b)(4)(A); Fla. R.App. P. 9.160. In that circumstance, the circuit court appellate review is essentially bypassed and, if the appeal is accepted, the district court engages in plenary appellate review over the legal issue raised by the county court decision. *See, e.g., Geico Indem. Co. v. Physicians Grp.,* 47 So.3d 354 (Fla. 2d DCA 2010). The option of certification of a question to the district court is not presently available, either by rule or statute, for a circuit court hearing an appeal of an administrative decision.

However, even with that procedural difference, we emphasize that the district court should not grant relief merely because it disagrees with the precedent from another district court; rather, the district court must determine whether the decision of the circuit court, even though it followed an opinion from another district court, is a departure from the essential requirements of law resulting in a miscarriage of justice. Here, the Second District, in granting second-tier certiorari after reviewing the provisions of the implied consent law in detail, concluded that while the circuit court attempted to obey controlling precedent, its decision (and the decision in *Clark*) was in fact contrary to clearly established statutory law. *Nader,* 4 So.3d at 707–10.

Further, the Second District noted the "dramatic" ramifications of the situation in this case, where if the district court was unable to act, circuit courts would be required to overturn every driver's license suspension based on a refusal to submit to a breath test in which a similar form was used. *See id.* at 710. The Second District stressed that its second-tier certiorari jurisdiction could not be used merely to grant a second appeal but was reserved for those situations where there was a violation of clearly established principles of law resulting in a miscarriage of justice. *Id.* at 710–11. The district court concluded that this standard was met in this case, and thus it was authorized to grant certiorari relief and quash a circuit court decision where the court below obeyed the controlling precedent, but in doing so, disobeyed the plain language of the statute. *Id.* at 711.

We agree that the Second District did not exceed the scope of its authority to grant certiorari relief and uphold the license suspension in this case. Throughout this Court's pronouncements concerning the proper application of second-tier certiorari review, this Court has repeatedly emphasized that certiorari review cannot be used as a means of granting a second appeal and cannot be used simply because the district court disagrees with the outcome of the circuit court's decision. Instead, we have held that district courts should act only where the error is one that is a departure from the essential requirements of law. Because it would be impossible to create an exhaustive list of such situations, this Court has repeatedly emphasized that district courts must be "allowed a large degree of discretion so that they may judge each case individually." *Combs,* 436 So.2d at 96.

Here, the Second District properly used second-tier certiorari. In reviewing whether it should grant certiorari in this case, the Second District focused entirely on whether the circuit court had applied the correct law, and when it determined that the incorrect law had been applied, it looked to the seriousness of the error. The Second District did not reanalyze the application of the law to the facts. Moreover, in *Kaklamanos,* we recognized that statutory provisions constitute "clearly established law." Thus, the Second District correctly based its certiorari analysis on those factors that we have stressed. This result is not changed simply because the circuit court followed binding precedent from another district that was clearly contrary to the plain language of the statute itself. To hold otherwise would prevent a district court from using its second-tier certiorari review to correct "a violation of clearly established principle of law that resulted in a miscarriage of justice," simply because a prior decision of another district court of appeal analyzed the controlling statute. Such a result would treat case law interpreting a statute as more authoritative than the statute itself—a proposition that is not supported by our precedent. Further, as pointed out by the Second District, the failure to apply the correct law would have dramatic and wide-reaching ramifications for license suspensions since the standard form affidavit was used by the Department throughout the State.[5]

The dissent contends that our decision "eviscerates over one hundred years" of well-established jurisprudence in order to permit a circuit court to bring an issue to the district court through second-tier certiorari. To the contrary, our decision has expressly rejected such a proposition. We have neither created new law with regard to second-tier certiorari, nor expanded second-tier certiorari to create any exception for "matters of great public importance." The test that has always applied to second-tier certiorari governs this case: it should be granted only when there is a

---

5. The Third District most recently granted certiorari relief to rectify exactly the same error as in Nader, relying on Nader and adopting the Second District's reasoning that the propriety of the request and warning to submit to testing involves "clearly established law" and the contrary interpretation in Clark "disobeyed the plain language of the statute." State Dep't of Highway Safety & Motor Vehicles v. Freeman, 63 So.3d 23, 27 (Fla. 3d DCA 2011).

departure from the essential requirements of law resulting in a miscarriage of justice. *See Heggs,* 658 So.2d at 530.

District courts of appeal must be able to correct serious errors resulting in a miscarriage of justice. As recognized by *Heggs,* the certiorari standard must contain "a degree of flexibility and discretion." *Id.* The determination must be made by the district court of appeal in a cautious manner to ensure that the error is "sufficiently egregious or fundamental to merit the extra review and safeguard provided by certiorari." *Id.* at 531. It is this last admonition that bears emphasis; a balance must be struck between respecting the finality of appellate review provided by the circuit court's appellate decision and the necessity of having the availability of certiorari to use in a narrow group of cases, which "merit the extra review and safeguard provided by certiorari." *Id.* By our decision, we reaffirm our holding in *Kaklamanos* — that statutes also constitute "clearly established law," meaning that a district court can use second-tier certiorari to correct a circuit court decision that departed from the essential requirements of statutory law. *See Kaklamanos,* 843 So.2d at 890 ("'[C]learly established law' can derive from a variety of legal sources, including recent controlling case law, rules of court, *statutes,* and constitutional law" (emphasis added)).

Conclusion

In conclusion, we answer the first certified question in the negative. The Second District properly found that there was no violation of the implied consent law under the circumstances of this case. Accordingly, we approve of the Second District's decision and disapprove the Fourth District's opinion in *Clark* to the extent that it concluded to the contrary. We answer the second question in the affirmative and hold that a district court may exercise its discretion to grant certiorari review of a circuit court decision reviewing an administrative order, so long as the decision under review violates a clearly established principle of law resulting in a miscarriage of justice, even if the circuit court decision was based on precedent from another district.

We further refer the issue to the Florida Bar Appellate Court Rules Committee to consider whether a circuit court should be able to certify a question of great public importance to the district court in circumstances where it is reviewing a decision of an administrative agency, similar to a county court's authority by rule to certify final orders to the district.

It is so ordered.

CANADY, C.J., and QUINCE, POLSTON, LABARGA, and PERRY, JJ., concur.

LEWIS, J., dissents with an opinion.

LEWIS, J., dissenting. [Dissenting opinion omitted.]

3. Circuit Courts and County Courts

Fla. Const. art. V, § 5(b)

Jurisdiction. — The circuit courts shall have original jurisdiction not vested in the county courts, and jurisdiction of appeals when provided by general law. They shall have the power to issue writs of mandamus, quo warranto, certiorari, prohibition and habeas corpus, and all writs necessary or proper to the complete exercise of their jurisdiction. Jurisdiction of the circuit court shall be uniform throughout the state. They shall have the power of direct review of administrative action prescribed by general law.

Fla. Const. art. V, § 6(b)

Jurisdiction. — The county courts shall exercise the jurisdiction prescribed by general law. Such jurisdiction shall be uniform throughout the state.

The circuit courts are the general trial courts in Florida and have original jurisdiction not vested in the county courts. They are "tribunals of plenary jurisdiction and have authority over any matter not expressly denied them by the constitution or applicable statutes."[146] "Circuit courts shall have jurisdiction of appeals from final administrative orders of local government code enforcement boards and appeals as otherwise expressly provided by law."[147] Once the circuit court renders an opinion in an appeal from a county court, the matter may not be appealed to the district court of appeal, but it may be reviewed by a common law writ of certiorari. "It is well established that certiorari should not be used as a vehicle for a second appeal in a typical case tried in county court."[148] "In considering a petition for second-tier certiorari review from a circuit court appellate division, this court exercises its discretion to grant review only when the circuit court has not afforded procedural due process or has violated a clearly established principle of law resulting in a miscarriage of justice."[149]

---

146. *Allstate Ins. Co. v. Kaklamanos*, 843 So. 2d 885 (Fla. 2003).

147. Fla. Stat. § 26.012(1) (2021).

148. *Ivey v. Allstate Ins. Co.*, 774 So.2d 679, 682 (Fla. 2000). *See also Custer Med. Ctr. v. United Auto Ins. Co.*, 62 So. 3d 1086, 1093 (Fla. 2010) ("The policy behind prohibiting certiorari to function as a second appeal is that the circuit court possesses final appellate jurisdiction in cases originating in the county court.").

149. *I Creatives, Inc., v. Premier Printing Solutions, Inc.*, 163 So. 3d 606 (3d Dist. Ct. App. 2015) (citing *Ivey v. Allstate Ins. Co.*, 774 So.2d 679, 680 (Fla. 2000)).

Most original trial court jurisdiction is vested in the circuit courts. However, by statute the county courts have original jurisdictions over certain matters.[150]

---

150. Fla. Stat. § 34.01 (2021) provides:

(1) County courts shall have original jurisdiction:

(a) In all misdemeanor cases not cognizable by the circuit courts.

(b) Of all violations of municipal and county ordinances.

(c) Of all actions at law, except those within the exclusive jurisdiction of the circuit courts, in which the matter in controversy does not exceed, exclusive of interest, costs, and attorney fees:

1. If filed on or before December 31, 2019, the sum of $15,000.

2. If filed on or after January 1, 2020, the sum of $30,000.

3. If filed on or after January 1, 2023, the sum of $50,000.

Effective July 1, 2030, and every 10 years thereafter, the $50,000 jurisdictional limit in subparagraph 3. must be adjusted and increased by the percentage change in the Consumer Price Index for All Urban Consumers, U.S. City Average, All Items, 1982-1984 = 100, or successor reports, for the preceding 10 calendar years as initially reported by the United States Department of Labor, Bureau of Labor Statistics. The adjusted jurisdictional limit must be rounded to the nearest $5,000. However, the jurisdictional limit may not be lower than $50,000. The Office of Economic and Demographic Research must calculate the adjusted jurisdictional limit and certify the adjusted jurisdictional limit to the Chief Justice of the Supreme Court beginning January 31, 2030, and every 10 years thereafter. The Office of Economic and Demographic Research and the Office of the State Courts Administrator must publish the adjusted jurisdictional limit on their websites.

(d) Of disputes occurring in the homeowners' associations as described in s. 720.311(2)(a), which shall be concurrent with jurisdiction of the circuit courts.

(2) The county courts shall have jurisdiction previously exercised by county judges' courts other than that vested in the circuit court by s. 26.012, except that county court judges may hear matters involving dissolution of marriage under the simplified dissolution procedure pursuant to the Florida Family Law Rules of Procedure or may issue a final order for dissolution in cases where the matter is uncontested, and the jurisdiction previously exercised by county courts, the claims court, small claims courts, small claims magistrates courts, magistrates courts, justice of the peace courts, municipal courts, and courts of chartered counties, including but not limited to the counties referred to in ss. 9, 10, 11, and 24, Art. VIII of the State Constitution of 1885, as preserved by s. (6)(e), Art. VIII of the State Constitution of 1968.

(3) Judges of county courts shall also be committing trial court judges. Judges of county courts shall be coroners unless otherwise provided by law or by rule of the Supreme Court.

(4) Judges of county courts may hear all matters in equity involved in any case within the jurisdictional amount of the county court, except as otherwise restricted by the State Constitution or the laws of Florida.

(5) A county court is a trial court.

a. Common Law Certiorari

G-W Development Corp. v.
Village of North Palm Beach Zoning Board of Adjustment

317 So. 2d 828 (Fla. 4th Dist. Ct. App. 1975)

OWEN, Judge.

Absent statutory authority, does the circuit court have jurisdiction to review a quasi-judicial decision of a municipal zoning board? We answer this question in the affirmative.

* * *

The jurisdiction of the circuit courts derives from Art. V, § 5(b) of the Florida Constitution (1972) which provides as follows:

> Jurisdiction. The circuit courts shall have original jurisdiction not vested in the county courts, and jurisdiction of appeals when provided by general law. *They shall have the power to issue writs of* mandamus, quo warranto, *certiorari,* prohibition and habeas corpus, and all writs necessary or proper to the complete exercise of their jurisdiction. Jurisdiction of the circuit court shall be uniform throughout the state. *They shall have the power of direct review of administrative action prescribed by general law.* (e. s.)

This constitutional provision confers upon the circuit courts two independent jurisdictional bases for reviewing administrative action: the first is by common law certiorari; the second is as may be prescribed by general law, otherwise commonly referred to as statutory certiorari.

Courts and other legal authorities have always recognized a distinction between review by common law certiorari and review by appeal which is provided by law. *Arvida Corporation v. City of Sarasota,* 213 So.2d 756, 761 (2nd DCA Fla. 1968); Rogers & Baxter, "Certiorari in Florida," 4 U. of Fla. Law Review 477, at 493 et seq. (1951); 5 Fla.Jur., Certiorari, § 5 (1955). There are at least four distinguishing features.

First, and perhaps most significantly, common law certiorari is generally available only "where no direct appellate proceedings are provided by law." *Board of Public Instruction of Duval County v. Sack,* 212 So.2d 819, 821 (1st DCA Fla. 1968); 5 Fla.Jur., Certiorari, § 8, at 491, and § 24, at 515; 14 Am.Jur.2d, Certiorari, § 11 (1964). The writ is available to obtain review where no other method of appeal is available. *De Groot v. Sheffield,* 95 So.2d 912, 916 (Fla.1957); *Codomo v. Shaw,* 99 So.2d 849, 852 (Fla.1958). Thus, review by common law certiorari and that by appeal are ordinarily mutually exclusive.[1]

---

1. See generally, 5 Fla. Jur., Certiorari, § 9, for the exceptions to this rule which are not relevant here.

Second, common law certiorari is entirely discretionary with the court, as opposed to an appeal which is taken as a matter of right. *Arvida Corporation v. City of Sarasota*, supra; 5 Fla.Jur., Certiorari, § 10; 14 Am.Jur.2d, Certiorari, § 4.

Third, the scope of review by common law certiorari is traditionally limited and much narrower than the scope of review on appeal. As stated in 5 Fla.Jur., Certiorari, § 24, at 514–16:

> As a general rule, it has been stated, certiorari goes only to jurisdiction and legality or regularity in procedure. More broadly, it is said that common-law certiorari lies to determine whether the lower court exceeded its jurisdiction or did not proceed according to the essential requirements of the law in cases where no direct appellate proceedings are provided by law. Or, as it has been so often even more fully expressed, certiorari is a common-law writ that issues in the sound judicial discretion of a superior court to an inferior court, not to take the place of an appeal, but to cause the entire record of the inferior court to be brought up by certified copy for inspection, in order that the superior court may determine from the face of the record whether the inferior court has exceeded its jurisdiction or has not proceeded according to the essential requirements of the law in cases where no direct appellate proceedings are provided by law. As so conceived, review on certiorari is said to be limited as compared with review on appeal. [footnotes omitted]

See also, Arvida Corporation v. City of Sarasota, supra; Rogers & Baxter, supra, at 493–502 and cases cited therein; 1 Fla. Jur., Administrative Law, § 181 (1955). In the case of appellate review of administrative decisions by statutory certiorari, the "review" is sometimes even broader and may be, as was the case with Chapter 176, "in the nature of a trial de novo." *Dade County v. Carmichael*, 165 So.2d 227, 229 (3rd DCA Fla.1964).

Finally, common law certiorari will only lie to review judicial or quasi-judicial action, *Kilgore v. Bird*, 149 Fla. 570, 6 So. 2d 541, 544 (1942); 2 Yokley, Zoning Law and Practice, § 18-8, at 378 (1965), never purely legislative action, id. § 18-9, at 394, in contradistinction to review by appeal which is provided by law and by which the legislature can authorize review of a wider scope. An example of this is provided by Chapter 176 itself which authorized review of "*any decision* of the board of adjustment," § 176.16, F.S. (e. s.), which has been interpreted to include review of such purely legislative action as adopting zoning ordinances. *See, Dade County v. Carmichael*, supra.

Considering Art. V § 5, in the light of this traditional and well defined distinction between statutory and common law certiorari, it becomes obvious that the drafters of this provision intended to provide for both methods of review; the second sentence granting the circuit courts the power to issue writs of certiorari obviously refers to common law certiorari; the last sentence conferring "the power of *direct review* of administrative action prescribed by general law," just as obviously refers to statutory certiorari. They cannot, as appellees in the case at bar argue, possibly refer to one and the same power, because, by definition, certiorari review is not direct appellate review and is not provided for by law, but, entirely to the contrary, is only available, at the discretion of the court, when there is no other right to review provided by law.

Once it is determined that the Constitution confers two separate types of certiorari jurisdiction upon the circuit court, there is no problem in concluding that where the legislature fails to provide for statutory review, or statutory certiorari as it is called, common law certiorari is still available. This principle has been recognized rather uniformly by cases and legal writers alike: *see, Codomo v. Shaw*, supra, at 852; *Board of Public Instruction of Duval County v. Sack*, supra; *State v. Simmons*, 104 Fla. 487, 140 So. 187, 190 (1932); 2 Yokley, Zoning Law and Practice, §18-9, at 389–90; Rogers & Baxter, supra.

In short, the Florida Constitution has always vested common law certiorari jurisdiction in the circuit courts. Wherever the legislature has seen fit to vest the circuit court with statutory certiorari jurisdiction, such jurisdiction is independent and cumulative, so that where the statutory remedy for some reason fails, or is simply rescinded, as here, common law certiorari is still available to review, at least to the limited extent that review is permitted under the writ, the quasi-judicial action of inferior tribunals. Chapter 176, F.S., having been repealed, leaving the circuit court with no statutory certiorari jurisdiction to review the orders of the North Palm Beach Municipal Zoning Board, the court still had jurisdiction to review by petition for common law certiorari.

* * *

Reversed and remanded.

WALDEN, C. J., and MORIARITY, HERBERT, W., Associate Judge, concur.

b. Legislative or Quasi-Judicial?

Article V, §5 grants circuit courts the power of direct review of administrative action prescribed by general law and the power to issue writs of certiorari; however, whether a court could properly review a county board's action by way of certiorari depends upon whether the action of the board was quasi-judicial or quasi-legislative in nature. The next case illustrates this point.

Board of County Commissioners of Hillsborough County v. Casa Development, Ltd.

332 So. 2d 651 (Fla. 2d Dist. Ct. App. 1976)

GRIMES, Judge.

This is an appeal from an order overturning the Hillsborough Board of County Commissioners' denial of an application for issuance of a water and sewer franchise.

In 1973, appellees obtained an appropriate zoning classification for the construction of a residential development on 820 acres in northwest Hillsborough County. In 1975, appellees filed an application for water and sewer franchises under the provisions of Chapter 59-1352, Laws of Florida, Special Acts of 1959, whereby Hillsborough County is authorized to issue water and sewer franchises to parties in the unincorporated areas of the county desiring to render public water and sewer service. At its regular meeting of February 5, 1975, the Board denied the application.

Appellees first filed a notice of appeal in the circuit court. They later filed a petition for writ of certiorari in the same action, characterizing it as an amendment to their appeal. The action thereafter proceeded as if it were certiorari, except that the court permitted a limited supplementation of the record with respect to matters that were directly brought to the commissioners' attention at the time of the meeting in which the application was denied. The court ultimately rejected the Board's action in denying the application and ordered the Board to issue water and sewer franchises to the appellees for periods of twenty-five years.

There is immediately apparent a serious question concerning the nature and scope of judicial review which was available to attack the action of the Board in denying the application. The Administrative Procedure Act does not pertain because the Board of County Commissioners is not an agency covered by the Act. *Sweetwater Utility Corp. v. Hillsborough County*, Fla. App.2d 1975, 314 So.2d 194. However, the Special Act which authorized Hillsborough County to issue water and sewer franchises contains a provision of its own relating to review of board action under the law. Thus, Section 7 of the Special Act states:

> Section 7. Within fifteen (15) days from the effective date of any action, rule or regulation adopted or promulgated by said board of county commissioners, any person, firm or corporation aggrieved thereby may appeal such action of said board to the circuit court of said county, and it shall be the duty of said board to cause to be prepared and certified at the cost of appellant a transcript of all proceedings taken and had before said board, and said court shall hear and determine the cause on such record. In the event the action of said board is not sustained, the court shall tax the cost of preparing the transcript against said board.

Relying upon this provision, the court concluded that he had the authority to "hear and determine" the cause pursuant to appellees' notice of appeal.

Despite its clear language, we hold that the Special Act was ineffective to confer jurisdiction on the circuit court to hear an appeal from the commission order. *Cf. Codomo v. Shaw*, Fla.1958, 99 So.2d 849. The jurisdiction of the circuit court is specifically set forth in Article V, Section 5 of the 1968 Constitution of Florida as follows:

§ 5. *Circuit courts*

(a) *Organization.* There shall be a circuit court serving each judicial circuit.

(b) *Jurisdiction.* The circuit courts shall have original jurisdiction not vested in the county courts, and jurisdiction of appeals when provided by general law. They shall have the power to issue writs of mandamus, quo warranto, certiorari, prohibition and habeas corpus, and all writs necessary or proper to the complete exercise of their jurisdiction. Jurisdiction of the circuit court shall be uniform throughout the state. They shall have the power of direct review of administrative action prescribed by general law.

Consistent with the spirit of Article V to provide a uniform court system throughout the state, circuit courts have jurisdiction of appeals and the power of direct review of administrative action only when provided by "general law." Obviously, the Special Act in question does not qualify as a "general law."

Since Article V, Section 5 does grant circuit courts the power to issue writs of certiorari, the next question to be considered is whether the court could properly review the county board's action by way of certiorari. The answer to this question turns upon whether the action of the Board was quasi-judicial or quasi-legislative in nature.

Traditionally, the review of the actions of commissions and boards acting in a quasi-judicial capacity has been by certiorari in which the reviewing court examines the record to determine whether the action taken below was in accord with essential requirements of law and supported by competent substantial evidence. *Harris v. Goff*, Fla.App.1st, 1963, 151 So. 2d 642. Where agencies and boards have acted in a quasi-executive or quasi-legislative capacity, the proper method of attack is a suit in circuit court for declaratory or injunctive relief on grounds that the action taken is arbitrary, capricious, confiscatory or violative of constitutional guarantees. *Harris v. Goff, supra.*

When determining whether certain action was quasi-judicial in nature as contrasted to quasi-legislative, the district court of appeal stated in *Bloomfield v. Mayo,* Fla.App.1st, 1960, 119 So.2d 417:

It seems clear from the decision of the Supreme Court that the test of a quasi-judicial function turns on whether or not the statutory tribunal had exercised a statutory power given it to make a decision having a judicial character or attribute, and consequent upon some notice or hearing to be had before it as a condition for the rendition of the particular decision made. . . .

Before an administrative proceeding can be quasi-judicial in character, there must be a requirement for a hearing to be held upon notice at which the affected parties are given a fair opportunity to be heard in accord with the basic requirements of due process, including the right to present evidence and to cross-examine adverse witnesses, and the judgment of the agency or board should be contingent upon the showing made at the hearing. *De Groot v. Sheffield*, Fla.1957, 95 So.2d 912; *Harris v. Goff, supra.*

Measured by this test, the action of the Board of County Commissioners of Hillsborough County was clearly quasi-legislative in character. The Special Act contained no criteria which required the issuance of a franchise under specified circumstances. While there was a public hearing upon notice, a quasi-judicial type of hearing was neither contemplated nor conducted. About all that happened was that appellees' representative made some unsworn statements in support of the application and the county attorney responded with opinions of his own. It was obvious from the discussion that the appellees had been negotiating with the county for some time concerning the issuance of a franchise upon certain conditions. Appellees were unwilling to meet these conditions, so the Board voted to deny the application. Therefore, a review by certiorari was an inappropriate remedy. *Town of Belleair v. Moran*, Fla.App.2d, 1971, 244 So.2d 532.

The appellees' reliance upon *State v. Furen*, Fla.1960, 118 So.2d 6, as authority for the procedure followed below is misplaced. First, that case was decided before the adoption of the new Constitution, and the constitutional jurisdiction of the circuit court at that time was substantially different. Moreover, the board action taken in that case was ultimately considered to be quasi-judicial in nature. The net effect of the *Furen* cases was that in the review of quasi-judicial board action, the circuit court acts as a court of original jurisdiction for purposes of the right to appeal its ruling to the district court of appeal. *See Alliance for Conservation of Nat. Resources v. Furen*, Fla. App.2d, 1960, 122 So.2d 51.

The confusion generated by the posture of the case below was manifested by the decision to admit some but not all of the testimony proffered with respect to the Board's recent change of policy on the issuance of water and sewer franchises in view of ecological demands and the development of its own regional waste treatment facility. In essence, the proceeding was neither "fish nor fowl." The record of the hearing before the County Commission was inadequate in the sense that it was not the record of a quasi-judicial hearing. Therefore, the court allowed the record to be supplemented in a limited manner but severely curtailed the Board's effort to present testimony tending to show that its action was not arbitrary, capricious, confiscatory or violative of constitutional guarantees.

While it appears that the appellees improvidently sought a review of the denial of their application for a franchise by way of appeal and/or certiorari, we are loath to dismiss their action when they have not yet had their day in court. This is particularly true in view of the fact that they followed a procedure specifically set forth in the Special Act which authorized the issuance of the franchises. Therefore, we hereby reverse the judgment and remand the case with directions for the pleadings to be recast and the case to be tried as if the appellees had filed an original suit in circuit court for declaratory or injunctive relief. This will also permit a full-blown consideration in the proper forum of the appellees' contention that the County Board was estopped to refuse to issue the requested franchises. We believe our determination to remand is consistent with the constitutional mandate that no cause should be dismissed because an improper remedy has been sought. Fla.Const. art. V, §2 (1968). *See State v. Johnson*, Fla.1974, 306 So.2d 102.

HOBSON, Acting C. J., and BOARDMAN, J., concur.

It would be helpful at this point to review what the Fourth District Court of Appeal had to say about circuit court review of agency action in *Cherokee Crushed Stone, Inc. v. City of Mirimar*,[151] excerpted earlier in this chapter.

However clear or unclear one finds the definition of quasi-judicial in *Casa Development*, it becomes more complex in land use cases. These issues are discussed in some detail in the following case.

The following two cases focus on what is meant by "quasi-judicial" in the sense that a writ of common law certiorari can only be issued to a lower court or tribunal, including an administrative agency engaged in an exercise of quasi-judicial power.

Martin County v. Yusem

690 So. 2d 1288 (Fla. 1997)

WELLS, Justice.

We have for review a decision addressing the following question certified to be of great public importance:

> CAN A REZONING DECISION WHICH HAS LIMITED IMPACT UNDER *SNYDER*, BUT DOES REQUIRE AN AMENDMENT OF THE COMPREHENSIVE LAND USE PLAN, STILL BE A QUASI-JUDICIAL DECISION SUBJECT TO STRICT SCRUTINY REVIEW?

Martin County v. Yusem, 664 So.2d 976, 982 (Fla. 4th DCA 1995) (on motions for rehearing and certification). We have jurisdiction. Art. V, §3(b)(4), Fla. Const. We answer the certified question in the negative and hold that amendments to a comprehensive land use plan which was adopted pursuant to chapter 163, Florida Statutes, are legislative decisions subject to the "fairly debatable" standard of review. Accordingly, we quash in part the decision of the district court to the extent that it is inconsistent with the following analysis. In reaching our conclusion, we have been greatly aided by Judge Pariente's well-reasoned dissenting opinion. We approve in part the district court's decision to the extent that it permitted Yusem to file a new

---

151. 421 So. 2d 684 (Fla. 4th Dist. Ct. App. 1982).

application for amendment without prejudice and remand to the trial court for consideration of claims which have not been considered.

Melvyn Yusem owns fifty-four acres of land in Martin County. In 1982, Martin County (County) adopted by ordinance a comprehensive plan for land use planning in the county. Subsequently, in 1990, the County replaced its earlier plan by adopting a comprehensive land use plan (Plan) pursuant to the 1985 Local Government Comprehensive Planning Act. *See generally* § 163.3184, Fla. Stat. (1985). Under the Plan, Yusem's fifty-four acres are part of a 900-acre tract which was included within the Plan's Primary Urban Service District (PUSD). Although up to two units per acre were allowed in the PUSD under the Plan, the future land use map, a component of the Plan, restricted this 900-acre tract to only one residential unit per two acres. *See* § 163.3177(6)(a), Fla. Stat. (1989).

Yusem requested an amendment to the future land use map for his property from "Rural Density," which allows development of .5 units per acre, to "Estate Density," which allows development of up to two units per acre. In conjunction with this amendment, Yusem requested a rezoning of his property from "A-1" (agricultural) to "Planned Unit Development" (residential).[1]

Yusem advocated adoption of the proposal at a hearing before the Martin County Board of County Commissioners (Board). After considering the different arguments on the proposal, a majority of the Board, by a vote of three to two, voted to begin the amendment-adoption process by transmitting a copy of the complete proposed amendment to the Department of Community Affairs (Department). *See* § 163.3184, Fla. Stat. (1989).[2] The Department analyzed the data and analysis received and recommended that the County either abandon the amendment or revise the data and analysis to demonstrate that the proposed amendment is a logical extension of a more intensive land use in the nearby area.

Thereafter, the Board held another hearing on the proposed amendment. Other than the Department's report, no new evidence was presented. Rather than resubmitting the proposal with data and analysis supporting it, the Board voted three to two to deny Yusem's proposal.

Yusem then sought relief in the circuit court. Yusem first filed a petition for certiorari but voluntarily dismissed it, choosing instead to file a complaint for declaratory and injunctive relief. In finding in Yusem's favor, the trial court relied upon *Snyder v. Board of County Commissioners*, 595 So.2d 65 (Fla. 5th DCA 1991) (*Snyder I*), quashed, 627 So.2d 469 (Fla.1993). The trial court noted that *Snyder I* involved a rezoning question; however, it found the basic rationale of that case to apply in the

---

1. Neither party argues that this requested zoning change did not require an amendment to the Plan.

2. Chapter 163, part II, Florida Statutes (Local Government Comprehensive Planning and Land Development Regulation Act), provides for a two-stage amendment-adoption process: transmittal and adoption. § 163.3184(3),(7), Fla. Stat. (1989).

plan-amendment context. The trial court then found that when a planning decision has an impact on a limited number of persons or property or identifiable parties and is contingent on a fact or facts, the action is quasi-judicial. Consequently, the trial court framed the issue in the case as follows: "whether or not the requested land use amendment is consistent with the Martin County Comprehensive Plan and whether or not the requested land use amendment is a logical and consistent extension of present uses in the general area of Plaintiff's land." Since resolution of the issue was contingent upon facts, the court applied the strict-scrutiny standard of review and concluded that the County improperly denied Yusem's requested amendment.

On appeal, the Fourth District reversed the trial court's ruling based upon a determination that the court was without jurisdiction to decide the merits of the action. However, in its opinion, the panel divided, with the majority agreeing that the County's decision was subject to a strict-scrutiny standard of review. *Martin County v. Yusem*, 664 So.2d 976 (Fla. 4th DCA 1995). The district court relied upon our decision in *Board of County Commissioners v. Snyder*, 627 So.2d 469 (Fla.1993) (*Snyder II*), in which this Court held that rezoning actions that have a limited impact on the public and that can be seen as policy applications, rather than policy setting, are quasi-judicial decisions. The district court, similar to the trial court, concluded that the County's action was essentially a quasi-judicial rezoning decision because to increase the density on Yusem's fifty-four acres would have a limited impact on the public.

The district court distinguished this case from *Section 28 Partnership, Ltd. v. Martin County*, 642 So.2d 609, 612 (Fla. 4th DCA 1994), *review denied*, 654 So.2d 920 (Fla.1995). In *Section 28 Partnership*, the district court found the denial of a comprehensive plan amendment involving the development of a 638-acre tract was legislative. In contrast to Yusem's requested amendment, the tract that was the subject of the proposed amendment in *Section 28 Partnership* was surrounded by pristine land (it was situated at the headwaters of the Loxahatchee River and was bordered on two sides by the Jonathan Dickinson State Park), and the amendment would have created a new category of property under the Plan. *Yusem*, 664 So.2d at 977.

Further, the district court found support for its decision in *City of Melbourne v. Puma*, 630 So.2d 1097 (Fla.1994). In *Puma*, we accepted jurisdiction over the Fifth District's decision involving a rezoning from a low-density residential to a commercial classification. *See Yusem*, 664 So.2d at 977–78. We remanded *Puma* for further consideration in light of our opinion in *Snyder II. Puma*, 630 So.2d at 1097. Neither our opinion nor the Fifth District's opinion in *Puma* set forth the fact that the rezoning in that case required an amendment to the comprehensive land use plan.[3] However, because the rezoning in *Puma* did require an amendment to the comprehensive plan, the district court in *Yusem* found that this Court's resolution of *Puma*

---

3. The district court noted that the rezoning request required an amendment to the comprehensive plan in its opinion following remand from this Court. *See City of Melbourne v. Puma*, 635 So.2d 159 (Fla. 5th DCA 1994).

was consistent with its conclusion that amendments to comprehensive plans are not necessarily legislative. *Yusem*, 664 So.2d at 978.[4] The district court's majority found support for its logic in respect to the meaning of our *Puma* decision in an article by Thomas G. Pelham. *See* Thomas G. Pelham, *Quasi-Judicial Rezonings: A Commentary on the Snyder Decision and the Consistency Requirement*, 9 J. Land Use & Envtl. L. 243 (1994).

Judge Pariente dissented, writing that the adoption of a comprehensive land use plan, which required the county to determine whether it should alter its overall plan for managed growth, local services, and capital expenditures as embodied in the future land use map, was a legislative act; therefore, decisions concerning the amendment of a comprehensive plan should similarly be treated as legislative acts. 664 So.2d at 979. Further, Judge Pariente distinguished this case from our decision in *Snyder*, in which we found the denial of a request to rezone a particular parcel of land to a designation which was consistent with the policies of the plan was a quasi-judicial decision, because the rezoning request in this case was inconsistent with the plan and required a plan amendment. Judge Pariente noted that a bright-line rule finding that all plan amendments were legislative acts would provide clarity to the procedures involved in this otherwise confusing area of the law. *Id.* at 982. Therefore, Judge Pariente would have found that the trial court should have reviewed the county's action in a trial de novo under the deferential "fairly debatable" standard of review. *Id.*

On motion for rehearing and clarification, the court certified the foregoing question, asking us to clarify whether a rezoning decision which has a limited impact under *Snyder II* but requires an amendment to the comprehensive plan is still a quasi-judicial decision subject to strict-scrutiny review. *Yusem*, 664 So.2d at 982 (on motions for rehearing and certification).

To resolve this question, the County advocates that we adopt the dissent's view and find that amendments to a comprehensive plan are legislative decisions subject to a fairly debatable standard of review. The County notes that this proceeding was

---

4. Additionally, the district court relied upon *Battaglia Properties, Ltd. v. Florida Land & Water Adjudicatory Commission*, 629 So.2d 161 (Fla. 5th DCA 1993). The majority in *Yusem* found that two members of the three-judge panel in *Battaglia* concluded that an amendment to a comprehensive plan was not a legislative decision under *Snyder I*. *Yusem*, 664 So.2d at 978. However, *Battaglia* is distinguishable from the case at bar. In *Battaglia*, the developer sought and received an amendment to the comprehensive plan necessary for the development of the property, but the amendment contained new zoning conditions on the property. The issue in that case was the propriety of new zoning conditions in conjunction with an amendment to the comprehensive plan. *Battaglia*, 629 So.2d at 165. Judge Sharp found that the zoning changes at issue in *Battaglia* were legislative decisions. *Id.* Judge Goshorn would have found that the conditional rezoning changes were quasi-judicial decisions but agreed with the result reached by Judge Sharp. *See id.* at 169 (Goshorn, J., concurring specially). Judge Cowart concluded that the rezoning decisions were quasi-judicial and dissented from the majority's conclusion. *Id.* (Cowart, Senior Judge, dissenting). *Battaglia* is thus distinguishable from the case at bar, which confronts purely the question of the proper standard of review of amendments to a comprehensive plan.

clearly a legislative proceeding because Yusem's request was to change, rather than apply, the existing plan. It is on this basis that the County distinguishes the case involving a request for a plan amendment from *Snyder II* involving a request for rezoning.

Yusem responds by arguing that the hearing before the Board was clearly quasi-judicial because during the hearing, he presented detailed evidence in support of his request; the hearing was directed at one specific property owner and one 54-acre parcel of land; and the County reviewed the facts and applied the standards contained in the plan. Yusem argues that there is no logical or factual reason to distinguish this case from *Snyder II*, and the trial court should strictly scrutinize this plan-amendment proceeding, which also involved a rezoning request. Several other parties have submitted amicus briefs in support of their positions.

Chapter 163, part II, Florida Statutes (1989) (Local Government Comprehensive Planning and Land Development Regulation Act) (the Act), was intended to enhance present advantages and encourage appropriate uses of land and resources. *See* § 163.3161(3), Fla. Stat. (1989). In furtherance of these goals, the Act requires each local government to adopt a comprehensive plan to prescribe the "principles, guidelines, and standards for the orderly and balanced future economic, social, physical, environmental, and fiscal development of the area." § 163.3177(1), Fla. Stat. (1989); *see Snyder II*, at 475 (stating that a comprehensive plan is intended to provide for the future use of land, which contemplates a gradual and ordered growth). A comprehensive plan includes several elements including a future land use element. *See* § 163.3177, Fla. Stat. (1989). With reference to this element, we have noted:

> [T]he future land use plan element of the local plan must contain both a future land use map and goals, policies, and measurable objectives to guide future land use decisions. This plan element must designate the "proposed future general distribution, location, and extent of the uses of land" for various purposes. *Id.*, § 163.3177(6)(a). It must include standards to be utilized in the control and distribution of densities and intensities of development. In addition, the future land use plan must be based on adequate data and analysis concerning the local jurisdiction, including the projected population, the amount of land needed to accommodate the estimated population, the availability of public services and facilities, and the character of undeveloped land. *Id.*, § 163.3177(6)(a).

Snyder II, at 473.

In *Snyder II*, in the rezoning context, we distinguished legislative actions which result in the formulation of a general rule of policy and quasi-judicial actions which result in the application of a general rule of policy. *Id.* at 474. We recognized that comprehensive rezonings which affect a large portion of the public are legislative determinations; however, we also recognized that rezonings which impact a limited number of persons and in which the decision is contingent upon evidence presented at a hearing are quasi-judicial proceedings properly reviewable by petition for certiorari. *Id.* at 474–75. In reaching this decision, we stressed that in a quasi-judicial rezoning proceeding, the landowner has the burden of proving that the proposal is *consistent with the comprehensive plan* and complies with all procedural requirements of the zoning ordinance before the burden shifts to the government to demonstrate that maintaining the existing zoning classification accomplishes a legitimate public purpose. *Id.* at 476.[5] In *Snyder II*, we plainly did not deal with the issue of the appropriate standard of review for amendments to a comprehensive land use plan.

Thereafter, we issued our brief opinion in *Puma*. As discussed above, in *Puma*, we accepted jurisdiction over the Fifth District's decision concerning a rezoning from a low density residential to a commercial classification. Although the rezoning in *Puma* required an amendment to the comprehensive land use plan, the amendment to the plan was not the focus of our decision in *Puma*. We recognize that our remand in *Puma* for further consideration in light of our opinion in *Snyder II* could logically be read as did the majority in *Yusem* since the underlying fact that the rezoning required an amendment to the comprehensive land use plan was not discussed in the opinion.

We also recognize that subsequent to *Snyder* and *Puma*, several district courts have employed a functional analysis in determining whether a plan amendment is either quasi-judicial or legislative. In some cases, the district courts have concluded that amendments to comprehensive plans are legislative decisions subject to the fairly debatable rule. *See, e.g., City Envtl. Servs. Landfill, Inc. v. Holmes County*, 677 So.2d 1327 (Fla. 1st DCA 1996) (county's decision to deny amendment creating new land use classification based on environmental risks, traffic, and road repair was legislative); *Martin County v. Section 28 Partnership, Ltd.*, 676 So.2d 532 (Fla. 4th DCA), *review denied*, 686 So.2d 581 (Fla.1996); *Board of County Comm'rs v. Karp*, 662 So.2d 718 (Fla. 2d DCA 1995) (finding amendment to comprehensive plan for 5.5-mile corridor affecting 179 acres and 48 parcels was legislative); *Section 28 Partnership, Ltd. v. Martin County*, 642 So.2d 609 (Fla. 4th DCA 1994) (finding plan amendment requiring creation of new classification of property allowing development of land near headwaters of Loxahatchee River and state park was legislative), *review denied*, 654 So.2d 920 (Fla.1995). Whereas in this case, the trial court and the district court used a functional analysis to reach the opposite conclusion: that an amendment to the comprehensive plan was a quasi-judicial decision subject to strict-scrutiny review. The district court concluded that the decision by the County should be functionally viewed as having limited impact on the public since the

---

5. We additionally noted that even in a situation in which the denial of a zoning application would be inconsistent with the plan, the local government should have the discretion to decide that the maximum development density should not be allowed provided the government approves some development that is consistent with the plan and the decision is supported by competent, substantial evidence. *Snyder II*, 627 So.2d at 475.

Board hearing addressed the change in land use designation for a particular piece of property.

While we continue to adhere to our analysis in *Snyder* with respect to the type of rezonings at issue in that case, we do not extend that analysis or endorse a functional, fact-intensive approach to determining whether amendments to local comprehensive land use plans are legislative decisions. Rather, we expressly conclude that amendments to comprehensive land use plans are legislative decisions. This conclusion is not affected by the fact that the amendments to comprehensive land use plans are being sought as part of a rezoning application in respect to only one piece of property.[6]

As this Court noted in *Snyder II*, a comprehensive land use plan must be based upon adequate data and analysis in providing for gradual and ordered growth in the future use of land. *Snyder II*, 627 So.2d at 475; *see also Machado v. Musgrove*, 519 So.2d 629 (Fla. 3d DCA 1987) (finding that a local land use plan is like a constitution for all future development within the governmental boundary). Consequently, we agree with Judge Pariente's dissent below that *Snyder's* functional analysis in rezoning cases is not applicable in comprehensive plan amendment cases:

> [I]n contrast to the rezonings at issue in *Snyder*, the review of the proposed amendment here required the County to engage in policy reformulation of its comprehensive plan and to determine whether it now desired to retreat from the policies embodied in its future land use map for the orderly development of the County's future growth. The county was required to evaluate the likely impact such amendment would have on the county's provision of local services, capital expenditures, and its overall plan for growth and future development of the surrounding area. The decision whether to allow the proposed amendment to the land use plan to proceed to the DCA for its review and then whether to adopt the amendment, involved considerations well beyond the landowner's 54 acres.

Yusem, at 981 (Pariente, J., dissenting). We also agree with Judge Stone's concurring opinion in *Section 28 Partnership* that there is no reason to treat a county's decision rejecting a proposed modification of a previously adopted land use plan as any less legislative in nature than the decision initially adopting the plan. *See Section 28 Partnership*, 642 So.2d at 613 (Stone, J., concurring).

Our conclusion that amendments to comprehensive plans are legislative decisions is further supported by the procedures for effecting such amendments under the Act. Amendments to comprehensive plans are evaluated on several levels of

---

6. We do note that in 1995, the legislature amended section 163.3187(1)(c), Florida Statutes, which provides special treatment for comprehensive plan amendments directly related to proposed small-scale development activities. Ch. 95-396, § 5, Laws of Fla. We do not make any findings concerning the appropriate standard of review for these small-scale development activities.

government to ensure consistency with the Act and to provide ordered development. *See* § 163.3184(8), Fla. Stat.

The Act provides for a two-stage process for amending a comprehensive plan: transmittal and adoption. In the first stage, the local government determines whether to transmit the proposed amendment to the Department for further review. *See* § 163.3184(3) Fla. Stat. If the local government transmits the proposed amendment, the process moves into the second stage. The Department, after receiving the amendment, provides the local government with its objections, recommendations for modifications, and comments of any other regional agencies. *See* § 163.3184(4), Fla. Stat. At this point, the local government has three options: (1) adopt the amendment; (2) adopt the amendment with changes; or (3) not adopt the amendment. *See* § 163.3184(7), Fla. Stat. (1989).[7]

Upon adoption of the amendment by the local government, the Department again reviews the amendment. *See* § 163.3184(8), Fla. Stat. (1989). After this review and an administrative hearing, if an amendment is determined not to be in compliance with the Act, the State Comprehensive Plan, and the Department's minimum criteria rule, *see* § 163.3184(1)(b), Fla. Stat., then the matter is referred to the Administration Commission. *See* § 163.3184(9)(b), (10)(b), Fla. Stat. The Administration Commission, composed of the Governor and the Cabinet, *see* § 163.3164(1), Fla. Stat., is then empowered to levy sanctions against a local government, including directing state agencies not to provide the local government with funding for future projects. *See* § 163.3184(11)(a), Fla. Stat. (1989).

This integrated review process ensures that the policies and goals of the Act are followed. The strict oversight on the several levels of government to further the goals of the Act is evidence that when a local government is amending its comprehensive plan, it is engaging in a policy decision. This is in contrast to a rezoning proceeding, which is only evaluated on the local level. *See Snyder.*

Moreover, our conclusion today that amendments to a comprehensive plan are legislative decisions subject to the fairly debatable rule is consistent with section 163.3184, Florida Statutes (1989). As noted above, once a local government decides to adopt an amendment, the Department issues a notice of intent to find whether an amendment is in compliance with state law, *see* § 163.3184(9)(a), Fla. Stat., or is not [in] compliance with state law, *see* § 163.3184(10)(a), Fla. Stat. In this proceeding, the determination of compliance is made using the fairly debatable rule. *Id.* By our decision today, we make clear that this standard applies at any stage in such proceedings.

---

7. In 1993, the legislature amended section 163.3184, Florida Statutes, to require the Department to review a plan amendment if it determines that this review is necessary or if it is requested to do so by a regional planning council, affected person, or local government transmitting the plan. *See* ch. 93-206, § 10, Laws of Fla. For a discussion of the changes made by the legislature in 1993, *see* David L. Powell, *Managing Florida's Growth: The Next Generation*, 21 Fla. St. L.Rev. 223 (1993).

Additionally, our decision today will further the proper administration of justice in Florida. Currently in Florida, there is much confusion surrounding the proper procedural vehicle for challenging a local government's decision concerning an amendment to a comprehensive plan. *See, e.g., Yusem; Martin County v. Section 28 Partnership, Ltd.*, 676 So.2d 532 (Fla. 4th DCA 1996) (original action); *Section 28 Partnership, Ltd. v. Martin County*, 642 So.2d 609 (Fla. 4th DCA 1994) (petition for certiorari). By our holding that all amendments to comprehensive plans are legislative activities subject to the fairly debatable standard, parties will know to file such challenges as original actions in the circuit court. *See Hirt v. Polk County Board of County Comm'rs*, 578 So.2d 415, 416 (Fla. 2d DCA 1991).

One of the amicus briefs suggests that the trial court did not properly have subject-matter jurisdiction in the case, arguing that section 163.3184(13), Florida Statutes (1989) ("Exclusive Proceedings"), provides that proceedings under that section are the sole method for determining whether a plan amendment is in compliance with the Act. Accordingly, it is argued that Yusem should have pursued the administrative procedures outlined in section 163.3184, Florida Statutes, prior to initiating court review. *See City of Jacksonville v. Wynn*, 650 So.2d 182 (Fla. 1st DCA 1995). However, we note that section 163.3184 only expressly prescribes administrative proceedings to review decisions of the Department. *See* § 163.3184(9)(a), (10)(a), Fla. Stat. (1989). The Department is an agency as defined in section 120.52, Florida Statutes (1995), and its actions as an agency are subject to the Administrative Procedure Act. However, a county's actions are only subject to the Administrative Procedure Act to the extent the county is expressly made subject to the Act. *See* § 120.52(1)(c), Fla. Stat. Since section 163.3184 does not expressly subject a county's decision to deny a requested amendment to the comprehensive plan as "agency action," Yusem was not required to exhaust any additional administrative remedies prior to the filing of an action in the circuit court. It is on this basis that we distinguish *Wynn*, because in that case the parties were seeking review of the decision of the Department to find Jacksonville's comprehensive plan in compliance with the Growth Management Act.

Last, we note the following. The fairly debatable standard of review is a highly deferential standard requiring approval of a planning action if reasonable persons could differ as to its propriety. *See B & H Travel Corp. v. State Dep't of Community Affairs*, 602 So.2d 1362 (Fla. 1st DCA 1992). In other words, "[a]n ordinance may be said to be fairly debatable when for any reason it is open to dispute or controversy on grounds that make sense or point to a logical deduction that in no way involves its constitutional validity." *City of Miami Beach v. Lachman*, 71 So.2d 148, 152 (Fla.1953). The procedural requirements inuring to a quasi-judicial proceeding are distinct from those inuring to a legislative proceeding. *See generally City Envtl. Servs. Landfill, Inc. v. Holmes County*, 677 So.2d 1327 (Fla. 1st DCA 1996). However, we do point out that even with the deferential review of legislative action afforded by the fairly debatable rule, local government action still must be in accord with the procedures required by chapter 163, part II, Florida Statutes, and local ordinances. *Cf. David v.*

City of Dunedin, 473 So.2d 304 (Fla. 2d DCA 1985) (finding null and void an ordinance enacted in violation of the notice provisions of the relevant statutes).

Accordingly, we hold that all comprehensive plan amendments are legislative decisions subject to the fairly debatable standard of review. We find that amendments to a comprehensive plan, like the adoption of the plan itself, result in the formulation of policy. We approve in part the district court's decision to the extent that it permitted Yusem to file a new application for amendment without prejudice, and we remand to the trial court for consideration of claims which have not been considered. We agree with the district court that in light of the manner in which this area of law was evolving at the time of his filing the action, justice would best be served by allowing the landowner to start anew. *Yusem*, 664 So.2d at 978.

It is so ordered.[8]

KOGAN, C.J., and OVERTON, SHAW, GRIMES and HARDING, JJ., concur.

ANSTEAD, J., recused.

See Bernard R. Appleman, *Why Classifying a Small-scale Land Use Amendment as a Legislative Decision Is Not Justified*, 80 Fla. Bar J. 53 (April 2006).

The "fairly debatable" test discussed in *Yusem* is in contrast to the "strict scrutiny" test used in land use decisions that are quasi-judicial. This test is discussed in the *Snyder* case and mentioned frequently in *Yusem*.

The following case, *Grace v. Town of Palm Beach*, raises the issue of the availability of declaratory and other relief under chapter 86 of the Florida Statutes in lieu of the common law certiorari remedy. Building on *Snyder* and *Yusem*, it seems that if the agency is acting in a quasi-judicial capacity, the *only* remedy is to seek review in the circuit court by common law certiorari. The authors can find no explanation for this, with the possible exception of *Yusem*, *supra* page 326, which discusses the impact of chapter 86.111.[152] The authors have also found no explanation for why the apparent existence of the declaratory judgment remedy would not actually preclude the use of common law certiorari since the writ will only lie in the absence of an adequate legal remedy. Perhaps declaratory relief is considered equitable in nature for this purpose, or perhaps it's not considered adequate. The dichotomy of remedy established (quasi-judicial common law certiorari and presumably legislative-declaratory relief) appears to be quite workable; however, a judicial explanation of the apparent inconsistencies discussed above would be appreciated.

---

8. We do not address any of the other issues raised by the parties.

152. "The existence of another adequate remedy does not preclude a judgment for declaratory relief. . . ." Fla. Stat. § 86.111 (2021).

Grace v. Town of Palm Beach

656 So. 2d 945 (Fla. 4th Dist. Ct. App. 1995)

STONE, Judge.

We affirm a final order of dismissal.

The trial court was correct in determining that it lacked jurisdiction to review de novo the action of the town commission granting a special exception to change the use of a well-known estate from residential to a private club. The commission's decision was reviewable only by a petition for writ of certiorari filed within 30 days of the action, as the special exception was approved in a quasi-judicial proceeding. *See Board of County Comm'rs of Brevard County v. Snyder*, 627 So.2d 469, 474 (Fla.1993); *Hirt v. Polk County Bd. of County Comm'rs*, 578 So.2d 415, 417 (Fla. 2d DCA 1991). *See also Sun Ray Homes, Inc. v. County of Dade*, 166 So.2d 827, 829 (Fla. 3d DCA 1964); *City of St. Petersburg v. Cardinal Indus. Dev. Corp.*, 493 So.2d 535, 537 (Fla. 2d DCA 1986); *City of Fort Pierce v. Dickerson*, 588 So.2d 1080, 1082 (Fla. 4th DCA 1991); *Battaglia Fruit Co. v. City of Maitland*, 530 So.2d 940, 943 (Fla. 5th DCA), *dismissed*, 537 So.2d 568 (Fla.1988); § 10.50, Palm Beach Town Code.

Appellants, neighboring property owners, do not dispute that the special exception proceedings were quasi-judicial, and would have been subject to review by petition for writ of certiorari within 30 days. Here, however, after 30 days had passed, they sought de novo review by declaratory judgment, primarily on the grounds that an approved incidental use allows guest suites at the club to be occupied by member-guests for limited periods of time. According to Appellants, this permitted occupancy contravenes a separate town ordinance that does not permit living quarters in private clubs in residential neighborhoods. Appellants assert that the effect of approving the special exception was to amend the distinct code provision prohibiting club living quarters — a *legislative* action, therefore subject to de novo review.

The holding of *Snyder* was, inter alia, that zoning decisions, including those approving or disapproving a request for a variance or a special exception, resulting from a proceeding in which zoning provisions are applied to a specific property affecting a limited number of people, are quasi-judicial in nature. But here Appellants allege that the town's approval created a new policy which amounted to a modification of the code and, therefore, legislative action. *See Josephson v. Autrey*, 96 So.2d 784 (Fla.1957).

We conclude that the commission hearing was quasi-judicial and that Appellants' remedy was by petition for certiorari within 30 days after the date the decision was rendered. We also note that section 10.50 of the town code provides for this method of review, stating that any person wishing to appeal such a decision "may" petition for writ of certiorari within 30 days. Appellees correctly point out that by allowing persons to characterize any portion of zoning action believed to be erroneous as "legislative" would render meaningless the *Snyder* analysis, as well as the 30 day time limit for filing certiorari petitions under rule 9.100, Florida Rules of Appellate

4 · THE COURTS

Procedure, and the town code. We cannot conclude that, by allowing very limited use of member guest suites, the town in fact was amending its other ordinance.

Appellants rely on *Hirt* to support their contention that the town's action was legislative, but that case actually supports the trial court's dismissal. The appellant in *Hirt* was seeking relief similar to that sought here. The *Hirt* court determined that certiorari was the proper remedy for the appellant, a landowner whose property was adjacent to the property being developed as a PUD. The developer's proposal was approved by the county, despite the contention that the proposal was contrary to provisions in other county ordinances. The challenge, like the instant one, was not to the validity of the underlying ordinance; instead, the argument was that by not requiring compliance with other provisions of the ordinances, the county was not enforcing those ordinances. The court determined the challenge was analogous to that in *Sun Ray Homes*, which led to its conclusion that the board's action was quasi-judicial.

In *Sun Ray Homes*, the Board of County Commissioners upheld the granting of a permit to erect a sign on the property of the appellee Electro Neon Sign Co., adjoining the appellant Sun Ray Homes' property. The appellant contended the permit was issued contrary to provisions of the code. The court determined that the action of the board "was clearly quasi-judicial because it was a review of an interpretation and application of an ordinance." 166 So.2d at 829.

In *Cardinal Industries*, the property owner challenged the denial of an application for special exception both by petition for certiorari and complaint for declaratory judgment, but then dismissed the petition for certiorari. The appellate court concluded that the proper method to attack the sufficiency of the evidence for denial of the application was by way of petition for certiorari, while a declaratory judgment suit would be the way to test the validity of the city code.

We have considered *Josephson* and deem it inapposite. In *Josephson*, a neighboring landowner utilized a remedy provided by a then existing statute to contest a zoning appeals board decision to grant a variance. At that time, sections 176.16–.17, Florida Statutes (1957), provided a remedy for any person aggrieved by a decision of a zoning board. Under that statute, the aggrieved party could file a verified petition setting forth the alleged decision of the board, specifying the grounds of illegality. Chapter 176 of the Florida Statutes was repealed in 1973 by chapter 73-129, § 5, at 247–48, Laws of Florida. Today, the supreme court's *Snyder* decision sets forth the standard for determining the nature of the proceeding and the appropriate method of review. *Josephson* does not support Appellants' argument that a party aggrieved by the decision of a local government argued to be, in part, unauthorized under the zoning ordinances, can disregard the *Snyder* analysis and instead seek a declaratory judgment rather than filing a timely petition for certiorari.

We find no error as to Appellants' other issue. Therefore, the final order is affirmed.

PARIENTE and SHAHOOD, JJ., concur.

The Florida constitution provides that circuit courts shall have jurisdiction of appeals when provided by *general law*.[153] In the case of *Pleasures II Adult Video, Inc. v. City of Sarasota*,[154] the Second District Court of Appeals held that a city ordinance cannot confer certiorari jurisdiction on a circuit court to review executive decisions.

C. Other Limitations on the Exercise of Judicial Power

The Florida courts, like their federal counterparts, have adopted a number of doctrines that limit the instances in which the courts will exercise jurisdiction. These doctrines include separation of powers used as a near alter-ego of the doctrine of case or controversy in the United States Constitution; political or other nonjusticiable questions; and the avoidance, where possible, of the exercise of judicial review. In addition, there are jurisdictional restrictions which apply simply because of the structural relationship of the Florida judiciary. Finally, a body of case law has developed in Florida prescribing the respect that must be afforded to lower federal court decisions. The following sections present case illustrations of how the Florida courts have interpreted and applied each of these restrictions.

1. Case or Controversy and Separation of Powers

Unlike the federal Constitution, the Florida Constitution does not contain a specific nexus between the exercise of judicial power and the concept of case or controversy.[155] Nevertheless, Florida courts have *more or less* adhered to the requirement that what amounts to a case or controversy must exist as a prerequisite to the exercise of judicial power. In addition, the Florida courts have rather generally adopted the federal doctrines of mootness, ripeness, taxpayer standing, and citizen standing, even though the Florida Constitution would not compel such a result. The following cases represent Florida's interpretation of these doctrines.

a. In General

The following statement by Justice Kogan (for the Court) in *Department of Revenue v. Kuhnlein*[156] seems to sum up the issue of the Florida case or controversy rule very well:

> ... [E]xcept as otherwise required by the constitution, Florida recognizes a general standing requirement in the sense that every case must involve a real controversy as to the issue or issues presented. *See Interlachen Lakes*

---

153. Fla. Const. art. V, § (5)(b).
154. 833 So. 2d 185 (Fla. 2d Dist. Ct. App. 2002).
155. *Compare* U.S. Const. art. III, §§ 1, 2, *with* Fla. Const. art. V, § 1.
156. 646 So. 2d 717, 720–721 (Fla. 1994).

4 · THE COURTS

Estates, Inc. v. Brooks, 341 So.2d 993 (Fla.1976). Put another way, the parties must not be requesting an advisory opinion, *id.*, except in those rare instances in which advisory opinions are authorized by the Constitution. *E.g.*, art. IV, § 1(c), Fla. Const. (advisory opinions to Governor).

b. Mootness

Southeastern Utilities Service Co. v. Redding

131 So. 2d 1 (Fla. 1961)

DREW, Justice.

This compensation case presents the very narrow issue of whether, under the provisions of Section 440.30, Florida Statutes (1959), F.S.A., construed in pari materia with Rule 1.21 of the 1954 Florida Rules of Civil Procedure, 30 F.S.A., an employer or carrier voluntarily paying compensation to an injured employee may take the employee's deposition prior to the filing of a formal claim by such employee.

As a prelude to the discussion of the question involved, however, it is pertinent to point out the fact that as to the parties to this litigation this question has become moot because Redding, the employee, subsequent to the order of the full commission holding such deposition may not be taken prior to the filing of a formal claim by the employee, filed a formal claim against the petitioner, thereby voluntarily subjecting himself to the provisions of the aforesaid statute and rule. Although the question, by virtue of the events above related, has become moot so far as the immediate parties to this proceeding are conserved, we have determined to retain jurisdiction of the matter and determine this unsettled question because of our view that it is one of wide public interest involving the duties and responsibilities and authority of the Florida Industrial Commission and affects the future administration of the beneficent provisions of the Workmen's Compensation Law of this State.[1]

[The court then rules on the substantive question presented.]

Certiorari is granted and the questioned order of the full commission is quashed with directions to reinstate the order of the deputy commissioner.

---

1. Barrs v. Peacock, 1913, 65 Fla. 12, 61 So. 118; State ex rel. Railroad Com'rs v. Southern Tel. & Const. Co., 1913, 65 Fla. 67, 61 So. 119; Joughin v. Parks, 1932, 107 Fla. 833, 143 So. 145, 306, 147 So. 273; Pitt v. Belote, 1933, 108 Fla. 292, 146 So. 380; Tau Alpha Holding Corp. v. Board of Adjustments, 1937, 126 Fla. 858, 171 So. 819; Pace v. King, Fla. 1949, 38 So.2d 823; Bowden v. Carter, Fla.1953, 65 So.2d 871.

The holdings in the above cases on this point may be summarized by the following quotation from Tau Alpha Holding Corp. v. Board of Adjustments, supra:

"* * * although questions raised in a litigated case may before their adjudication in due course become moot in so far as they affect that case, the court is warranted in adjudicating them if they are of great public import and the real merits of the controversy are unsettled." [126 Fla. 858, 171 So. 820.]

THOMAS, C. J., and TERRELL, HOBSON, ROBERTS, THORNAL and O'CONNELL, JJ., concur.

To the same effect, see *Valdez v. Chief Judge of the Eleventh Judicial Circuit of Florida*,[157] where even though moot as to *Valdez* and the others, the future questionable use of a particular Florida Rule of Judicial Administration caused the Court to elect to consider and "determine the question presented because of the potential harm emanating from future enforcement of the order"[158] [which was predicated upon the Rule of Judicial Administration]. Judicial economy appears to be a key consideration in a Florida court's willingness to hear a moot case. Not only must the question be an important one (*Southeastern Utilities*), but it also must be likely to keep happening. Consider the following comment by the Third District Court of Appeal sitting *en banc* in *Sunbeam Television Corporation v. State*:[159]

> On the court's own motion, the court grants rehearing en banc, *see* Fla. R. App. P. 9.331(d)(1), and adopts the dissent of Judge Cope to the panel opinion of this court. Although in the meantime the underlying criminal trial has ended, we decline to treat the case as moot because the issue presented is likely to recur. *See Godwin v. State*, 593 So.2d 211, 212 (Fla.1992); *Holly v. Auld*, 450 So.2d 217, 218 n. 1 (Fla. 1984).

In *Godwin, supra*, the Florida Supreme Court identified three instances in which cases should not be dismissed for mootness. The Court articulated that where an appeal raises questions of great "pubic importance," or "[is] likely to recur," or has "collateral legal consequences that affect the rights of a party," the case should not be dismissed as moot.

In general, mootness indicates that whatever legally cognizable injury had existed has been cured by the mere passage of time. Ripeness, on the other hand, means that the situation forming the basis of a complaint is so remote that no injury presently exists.

The next case is treated by the First District Court of Appeal as being moot as to Montgomery. The question the reader should ponder is whether this case was ever ripe as to Montgomery.

---

157. 640 So. 2d 1164 (Fla. 3d Dist. Ct. App. 1994).
158. *Id.* at 1165.
159. 723 So. 2d 275, 280 (Fla. 3d Dist. Ct. App. 1998) (en banc).

Montgomery v. Department of Health and Rehabilitative Services

468 So. 2d 1014 (Fla. 1st Dist. Ct. App. 1985)

PER CURIAM.

Appellants, who are recipients of food stamps, appeal a final order of the Division of Administrative Hearings dismissing, for lack of standing, their challenge to proposed Rule 10C-3.60, Florida Administrative Code, which establishes the terms under which food stamp recipients may be required to participate in a workfare program.[1] Although by its terms, Rule 10C-3.60 purports to be effective throughout the state, the rule will be utilized in only two counties at present, since the legislature has appropriated only enough funds to continue to establish workfare projects in two counties, rather than statewide.[2] Further implementation will take place only when and if specifically authorized by legislative action. Orange County, appellants' residence, is not one of the two counties in which a workfare program will be instituted. On these facts we conclude, contrary to the decision of the hearing officer, that appellants have standing to challenge the proposed rule. Nevertheless, we affirm the dismissal of appellants' rule challenge on the grounds of mootness for the reasons set forth below.

Appellants are heads of households and would likely be affected by the implementation of workfare in Orange County. They timely filed their petition challenging the validity of proposed Rule 10C-3.60 on August 10, 1984.[3] At the time they filed their petition, it was still uncertain which counties would be participating in workfare. Counties interested in participating were required to express their interest in writing to the Department of Health and Rehabilitative Services (HRS) on or before September 1, 1984. Orange County did not express an interest in writing by that date, thus eliminating any immediate concern that appellants may be subjected to workfare.

In Florida, the courts have adopted the federal "injury-in-fact" test governing standing, *Department of Offender Rehabilitation v. Jerry*, 353 So.2d 1230 (Fla. 1st DCA 1978), and the federal "zone of interest" test where applicable. *Florida Medical Association, Inc. v. Department of Professional Regulation*, 426 So.2d 1112 (Fla.

---

1. "Workfare is a component of the joint federal-state Food Stamp Program requiring food stamp recipients to perform labor at government work sites equivalent to the value of their food stamp allotments. State implementation of workfare is not mandatory but, if elected, must be conducted consistent with federal regulations." *Perkins v. Department of Health and Rehabilitative Services,* 452 So.2d 1007, 1008 (Fla. 1st DCA 1984).

2. Line Item 764, 1984 General Appropriations Act, Ch. 84-220, Laws of Fla.

3. Appellants' petition alleges the proposed rule is an invalid exercise of delegated legislative authority because it imposes workfare without legislative authorization, unconstitutionally delegates authority to the federal government, improperly incorporates nonexistent materials by reference, violates the Workfare Policy Act, Section 409.028, Florida Statutes (1983), and implements provision of the 1984 General Appropriations Act which is unconstitutional.

1st DCA 1983).[4] In this case, we are only concerned with whether appellants have met the injury-in-fact test.

To have standing, appellants were required to show an injury which is both real and immediate, not conjectural or hypothetical. *Jerry, supra*, at 1235. When appellants filed their rule challenge petition, they were heads of households who would likely be subjected to the terms of workfare under proposed Rule 10C-3.60. Under the circumstances as outlined in their petition, the injury they would suffer if Rule 10C-3.60 was promulgated was real and immediate, not conjectural. Since it appeared that HRS was about to devise the terms under which workfare would be implemented statewide in Florida, persons subjected to workfare under those terms would have standing to challenge the proposed regulation. *See, Professional Firefighters of Florida, Inc. v. Department of Health and Rehabilitative Services*, 396 So.2d 1194 (Fla. 1st DCA 1981) (firefighters, performing paramedic duties which were not previously subject to statewide regulation or licensing, held to have standing to challenge agency's proposed new licensing or certification requirement).

However, notwithstanding the fact that the proposed rule purports to be slated for statewide application, we are not required to close our eyes to the fact that in actual effect, only a pilot program has been implemented by legislative appropriation of start-up funds, and that food stamp recipients in Orange County where appellants reside will not be subject to the pilot program. Accordingly, even though we find that appellants have standing to challenge the proposed rule, the fact that workfare will not be implemented in Orange County raises the issue of mootness. *State Department of Health and Rehabilitative Services v. Alice P.*, 367 So.2d 1045, 1053 (Fla. 1st DCA 1979).

Mootness has been defined as "the doctrine of standing set in a time frame: The requisite personal interest that must exist at the commencement of the litigation (standing) must continue throughout its existence (mootness)." Monaghan, *Constitutional Adjudication: The Who and When*, 82 Yale L.J. 1363, 1384 (1973), quoted with approval in *United States Parole Commission v. Geraghty*, 445 U.S. 388, 397, 100 S.Ct. 1202, 1209, 63 L.Ed.2d 479, 491 (1980). Mootness occurs in two basic situations: "[W]hen the issues presented are no longer 'live' or [when] the parties lack a legally cognizable interest in the outcome." *Powell v. McCormack*, 395 U.S. 486, 496, 89 S.Ct. 1944, 1951, 23 L.Ed.2d 491, 502 (1969).

A case becomes moot, for purposes of appeal, where, by a change of circumstances prior to the appellate decision, an intervening event makes it impossible for the court to grant a party any effectual relief. 3 Fla.Jur.2d, *Appellate Review*, § 287, p. 337. Mootness can be raised by the appellate court on its own motion. *DeHoff v. Imeson*, 153 Fla. 553, 15 So.2d 258 (1943); *Barrs v. Peacock*, 65 Fla. 12, 61 So. 118 (1913).

---

4. The federal law of standing is complex, inconsistent, and unreliable. 4 Davis, *Administrative Law Treatise*, § 24:1 (Second Edition, 1983). The Florida law of standing borrows much of its underpinnings from the federal law and thus arguably may be said to be subject to the same vagaries.

The rule discouraging review of moot cases is derived from the requirement of the United States Constitution, Article III, under which the existence of judicial power depends upon the existence of a case or controversy. *Liner v. Jafco, Inc.*, 375 U.S. 301, 84 S.Ct. 391, 11 L.Ed.2d 347 (1964). It is the function of a judicial tribunal to decide actual controversies by a judgment which can be carried into effect, and not to give opinions on moot questions, or to declare principles or rules of law which cannot affect the matter in issue. 2 Am.Jur.2d, *Administrative Law*, § 572, p. 389.

If this court were to remand this case to the hearing officer for a determination of the validity of proposed Rule 10C-3.60, any eventual determination would have no present effect on appellants. Thus, our opinion follows the general principle of current ripeness law: that a regulation "is ripe for challenge when an affected person has to choose between disadvantageous compliance and risking sanctions." 4 Davis, *Administrative Law Treatise*, Section 25:13 (2d Ed.1983). The two appellants in the case at bar are not confronted with that choice and, therefore, they cannot receive effectual relief. For appellants to be subjected to Rule 10C-3.60's terms, additional funding must be appropriated beyond that available for the two counties envisioned by the General Appropriations Act, Orange County must opt for participation in the workfare program, appellants must be residing in Orange County when the first two events occur, and appellants must still have the status of heads of households subject to the terms of the rule.[5]

Appellants argue that this court may still grant them some effectual relief by returning this case to the hearing officer because should the hearing officer hold that proposed Rule 10C-3.60 is invalid, that will mean appellants will not be subject to the rule when and if workfare is implemented in Orange County. We decline to accept appellants' invitation given the uncertainty that the above enumerated events will occur in such a sequence so as to subject appellants to workfare. Should workfare be eventually initiated in appellants' county and appellants be subject to the terms of the rule at that time, appellants may initiate a rule challenge pursuant to Section 120.56, Florida Statutes.

Finally, we recognize that in the case at bar, the substantive issues regarding the validity of proposed Rule 10C-3.60 are still "live" ones between HRS and those individuals who would be "substantially affected" in the two counties where workfare will be implemented. Here, of course, appellants filed their rule challenge only on their own behalf; and even had they attempted to assert the interests of others, the fact that the issues raised are moot as to appellants requires dismissal. *See Sosna v. Iowa*, 419 U.S. 393, 95 S.Ct. 553, 42 L.Ed.2d 532 (1975). The only relevant exception

---

5. We have not overlooked the distinctions that may be made between rule-making under Section 120.54, and a rule challenge under Section 120.56. However, in the context of the present controversy, in which petitioners did not avail themselves of the opportunities for pre-adoption input by way of evidence of argument, or by participation at a public hearing on the proposed rule, we conclude that petitioners' claims of invalidity of the proposed rule (see footnote 3) can be as fully vindicated in a rule challenge proceeding as in the rules' formative stage.

to the general rule of mootness can be found in *Sosna* and its progeny, wherein the Supreme Court has held that a federal class action suit does not ordinarily become moot merely because the controversy has become moot *as to some, but not all, of the plaintiffs*, provided that the requirements of class suits, as stated in Federal Rule of Civil Procedure 23 have been met. *Sosna*, 419 U.S. at 399–403, 95 S.Ct. at 557–559; *Geraghty*, 445 U.S. at 396–399, 100 S.Ct. at 1208–1210. Those cases allow the requisite "controversy" to exist, at the time of appellate review, "between a named defendant and a member of the class represented by the named plaintiff, even though the claim of the named plaintiff has become moot." *Sosna*, 419 U.S. at 402, 95 S.Ct. at 559. *See also Craig v. Boren*, 429 U.S. 190, 192, 97 S.Ct. 451, 454, 50 L.Ed.2d 397, 403 (1976). Although the substantive issues remain in the case at bar as to substantially affected individuals in the two counties where workfare will be implemented, and those individuals could supply the requisite controversy, "a proposed rule challenge is not, under Florida law, a proper proceeding for the maintenance of a class action." *State, Department of Health and Rehabilitative Services v. Alice P.*, 367 So.2d 1045, 1050 (Fla. 1st DCA 1979). *Cf. Medley Investors, Ltd. v. Lewis*, 465 So.2d 1305 (Fla. 1st DCA 1985).

In that appellants cannot fall under the class action suit exception of the mootness doctrine, the survival of the substantive claims as to others does not save this case from dismissal as to appellants on the ground of mootness.

AFFIRMED.

ERVIN, C.J., and SMITH and NIMMONS, JJ., concur.

c. Ripeness

Bryant v. Gray

70 So. 2d 581 (Fla. 1954)

MATHEWS, Justice.

This is a suit seeking a declaratory judgment filed in the Circuit Court of Leon County.

In the case of State ex rel. Ayres v. Gray, Fla., 69 So.2d 187, we held that it was necessary to hold an election at the General Election in November, 1954, to elect a Governor to serve for the balance of the unexpired term of the late Dan T. McCarty, beginning on the first Tuesday after the first Monday in January, 1955.

The petitioner seeks a final decree construing Sections 2 and 19 of Article IV of the State Constitution, F.S.A.

As a basis for a declaratory decree the petitioner alleges that he is legally eligible to become a candidate for the office of Governor of Florida and for nomination by a recognized political party and "is prepared to comply with the provisions of Chapter 99 of Florida Statutes 1953 [F.S.A.], relating to qualification of candidates for nomination and election to the office of Governor of the State of Florida". Petitioner also alleges that he is "desirous of seeking election in the general election of 1956 for a full term as Governor of the State of Florida" but that he is in doubt as to whether, if he seeks election in 1954 and is elected Governor of Florida for the unexpired term, he may thereafter seek re-election in the General Election of 1956. Petitioner is "prepared" to become and "desirous" of becoming a candidate, but at no place does he allege specifically that he *will* become a candidate for the unexpired term or for the full term. He alleges that he is in doubt as to whether or not he could seek re-election to the office of Governor at the General Election in 1956 in the event he should seek, and be elected to the office of Governor for the unexpired term in the General Election to be held in 1954.

R. A. Gray, Secretary of State, Brailey Odham and LeRoy Collins who are candidates for nomination for the office of Governor in the Primary Election to be held in 1954 for the unexpired term of the late Dan T. McCarty, are made defendants, or respondents.

In the answer filed by the Honorable R. A. Gray, Secretary of State it is stated:

* * * However, this defendant avers that said question does not presently involve his official duties under Section 199.13, F.S. [F.S.A.], and related statutes, concerning political party candidates who may desire to qualify in the 1954 primaries for nomination for the office of Governor for said residue of term and concerning party nominees and others who may desire to run in the 1954 general election for the office of Governor for said residue of term; hence, said question involves no immediate official duties of this defendant. * * *

In the answer filed by the Honorable LeRoy Collins, it is stated:

* * * That he is not now personally concerned with nor interested in, his own eligibility to be a candidate in any other election, or for any term other than the one for which he is now a candidate; That the program which he will present to the people of Florida in the forthcoming election will be directed to the said unexpired portion of the term for which Dan McCarty was elected, and no other term.

In the answer filed by the Honorable Brailey Odham, it is stated:

* * * that he has qualified with the defendant Secretary of State as a candidate for nomination and election to said office for the residue of the term of the late Governor Dan McCarty, and has presented and will present his candidacy to the people of the State of Florida without regard to the question of whether or not this defendant will be eligible for re-election to the office of Governor of Florida in the general election to be held in the year 1956.

Further answering said Petition, this defendant says that in furtherance of his candidacy he has and will present to the people of the State of Florida his program for operation of the affairs of the State of Florida for and during the residue of the term of the late Governor Dan McCarty, and that no controversy exists between him and the petitioner herein as to whether or not this defendant, if elected to the office of Governor of Florida in the general election of 1954, will be eligible for re-election to said office in that general election to be held in the year of 1956, and that the question presented in said Petition does not and will not affect this defendant in offering of his candidacy to the people of the State of Florida for the residue of the term aforesaid.

It, therefore, appears that there is no immediate or present controversy between the appellant, Bryant, on the one hand, and the Honorable R. A. Gray, as Secretary of State, Honorable Brailey Odham or Honorable LeRoy Collins, on the other hand.

The appellant, Bryant, says that he is desirous of being a candidate for a full term in the election of 1956 and *might* be a candidate for the unexpired term in 1954. He is not sure. In order that he might be assisted in making up his mind in coming to a decision, the petition for declaratory decree was filed, praying for a decree concerning matters which may, or may not, materialize. If he decides to run for Governor in the 1954 primaries for the Democratic nomination for the unexpired term of the late Dan T. McCarty, and if he is nominated and elected in November, 1954, and if he lives until January, 1955, and becomes Governor and if he serves out the unexpired term, and if in the meantime there has been no constitutional amendment affecting the questions proposed, and if he decides to become a candidate for the Democratic nomination in the primaries of 1956, and if he should be nominated and then lives to be elected, may he succeed himself and serve for a full four-year term?

It appears from the record that petitioner obtained the answer he sought in a final decree entered by the Circuit Court in and for Leon County and is now appealing from that decree without an adverse party. No present right is involved. His question is hypothetical and is too remote as to time and too uncertain as to contingencies. He does not allege that he will be nominated or elected to either the unexpired term or a full term. There is no certainty that he will be. There is no certainty that the Constitution will be the same in 1956 as it is today. The Legislature meets in 1955 and under the provisions of Section 3, Article XVII of the State Constitution, a constitutional amendment could be proposed and voted upon by the people which could change the entire picture prior to the primaries and general election to be held in 1956. We have held that the moving party should show a doubt as to the existence or nonexistence of some right, status, immunity, power or privilege. Caldwell v. North, 157 Fla. 52, 24 So.2d 806; Ready v. Safeway Rock Co., 157 Fla. 27, 24 So.2d 808.

In the case of May v. Holley, Fla., 59 So.2d 636, 639, we held that "Before any proceeding for declaratory relief should be entertained it should be clearly made to appear that there is a bona fide, actual, present practical need for the declaration; that the declaration should deal with a present, ascertained or ascertainable state of facts or present controversy as to a state of facts". We also held that there must some person or persons who have, or reasonably may have an actual, present, adverse and antagonistic interest in the subject matter. The relief sought should not merely be legal advice by the courts or to give an answer to satisfy curiosity.

4 · THE COURTS

In the case of Local No. 234, etc., v. Henley & Beckwith, Inc., Fla., 66 So. 2d 818, we held that there must be a bona fide dispute between the contending parties as to a present justiciable question.

In Ervin v. Taylor, Fla., 66 So.2d 816, we held that the Court was without jurisdiction where there was no actual adversaries as to a present, actual dispute or controversy. In City of Hollywood v. Broward County, Fla., 54 So.2d 205, we held a suit prematurely brought where the county's application for a funding program had not been acted upon by the Improvement Commission and the Board of Administration had not passed on the legal and fiscal sufficiency of the proposed program.

In the case of Ervin v. City of North Miami Beach, Fla., 66 So.2d 235, this Court dismissed the appeal of its own motion because there was no actual existing controversy as to the violation of certain ordinances; and in the case of Ervin v. Taylor, supra, the appeal was reversed, with directions to dismiss the petition for declaratory decree because there were no actual, bona fide, adverse parties to the action and no actual existing controversy.

The Circuit Court in and for Leon County, Florida, was without jurisdiction to enter a declaratory decree for the reasons herein stated and the petition for a declaratory decree should have been dismissed without prejudice, on the Court's own motion.

Reversed, with directions to set aside the decree appealed from and to dismiss the petition for declaratory decree, without prejudice.

THOMAS, SEBRING, HOBSON and DREW, JJ., concur.

ROBERTS, C. J., and TERRELL, J., dissent.

TERRELL, Justice (dissenting).

If the question presented was nothing more than one between individuals, I might go along with the majority opinion, but the applicable constitutional provisions are susceptible of more than one interpretation and then I think the time and circumstances under which the appeal is brought present an important public question. I think the candidates and the electorate are entitled to have this question answered, the atmosphere clarified and the doubts and uncertainties removed before they vote in the November election. Such was the theory that impelled us to answer the question presented in State ex rel. Ayres v. Gray, Fla., 69 So.2d 187.

I therefore dissent.

ROBERTS, C. J., concurs.

ROBERTS, Chief Justice (dissenting).

I concur in the view of Mr. Justice TERRELL that this court should take jurisdiction of the question here presented, for the reasons stated in his dissenting opinion, and would hold that where a person becomes Governor by election of the people, either for a two-year term or a four-year term, the provisions of Section 2 of Article IV of the Constitution of the State of Florida would be a bar to his succeeding himself in such office. There are abundant reasons for so holding, but no useful purpose would be served in here detailing them in view of the opinion of the majority of the court that the cause should be dismissed.

Compare this case to *Holley v. Adams*,[160] where the following discussion appears:

The appellees maintain that Holley only seeks advice as to his future action and is not entitled to relief under the decision in Bryant v. Gray, 70 So.2d 581 (Fla. 1954). The *Bryant* case, a suit for declaratory decree, sought a construction of the constitutional provision declaring the Governor ineligible for re-election for the next succeeding term. It was alleged that plaintiff *Bryant desired* to be a candidate and *might be* a candidate for the next succeeding term. He was not sure. The question was therefore hypothetical and too remote as to time and too uncertain as to contingencies to warrant declaratory relief.

In the case *sub judice*, Holley alleges that he *intends* to be a candidate and has *publicly announced his intention* to be a candidate. He has filed with the Secretary of State a declaration of such intention, designation of campaign treasurer and campaign fund and depository collection, deposit and disbursement of campaign funds. These circumstances call into play the principle announced in James v. Golson, 92 So.2d 180 (Fla.1957), which held that under the provisions of § 86.011(2) (formerly § 87.01(2), Fla.Stat., F.S.A.[)] [sic.] the Court may render a declaratory judgment,

Of any fact upon which the existence or nonexistence of such immunity, power, privilege or right does or may depend, whether such immunity, power, privilege or right now exists or will arise in the future. Any person seeking a declaratory judgment may also demand additional, alternative, coercive, subsequent or supplemental relief in the same action.

the fact that a controversy had not matured is not always essential.

The action for declaratory judgment was appropriate and the Circuit Court had jurisdiction.

The distinction between *Bryant* and *Holley* is discussed as follows in *Olive v. Maas*:[161]

Particularly instructive on the issues of jurisdiction and standing, given the facts in this case, is our previous decision in *Holley v. Adams*, 238 So.2d 401 (Fla.1970). In that case, Holley, a circuit court judge, intended to become a candidate for nomination and election to the office of Justice of the Supreme Court of Florida. Having declared his intention to run, he was faced with the "resign to run" provision of the Florida Statutes. Wishing to

---

160. 238 So. 2d 401, 404 (Fla. 1970).
161. 811 So. 2d 644, 648–649 (Fla. 2002).

not resign from his position as a circuit court judge unless he was successful in his quest to become a justice of this Court, he sought a declaration, pursuant to chapter 86, that the "resign to run" provision was unconstitutional. The trial court exercised its jurisdiction and declared the provision constitutional.

On appeal, the secretary of state maintained that the declaratory judgment should have never been entered in the first place because Holley was simply seeking an advisory opinion. The secretary of state suggested that Holley was not entitled to relief pursuant to the Court's prior decision in *Bryant v. Gray*, 70 So.2d 581 (Fla.1954). In *Bryant*, the petitioner had filed a complaint seeking a declaratory judgment as to the constitutionality of a provision declaring the governor ineligible for re-election for the next succeeding term. The complaint alleged that Bryant, who "desired" to serve the balance of the unexpired term of deceased Governor McCarty, also "desired" to become a candidate for the next succeeding term. Bryant sought the declaration because he reasoned that if he ran for the unexpired term and then found himself precluded from running for the succeeding full term, he might not want to run for the unexpired term. Bryant never alleged that he would become a candidate for the unexpired term or full term. The Court concluded that the trial court was without jurisdiction because the question which Bryant presented was "hypothetical and too remote as to time and too uncertain as to contingencies" to warrant declaratory relief. *Id.* at 584.

The *Holley* Court found *Bryant* distinguishable and the secretary of state's argument unpersuasive. Particularly, the Court noted that Holley had publicly announced his intention to become a candidate, that he had filed with the Secretary of State a declaration of such intention, and that he had designated a campaign treasurer as well as a depository for campaign funds. The Court concluded that Holley's request for a declaratory judgment was not too hypothetical or remote, and that "the fact that a controversy had not matured is not always essential." *Holley*, 238 So.2d at 404 (citing *James v. Golson*, 92 So.2d 180 (Fla.1957)). Ultimately, the Court determined that the circuit court appropriately exercised its declaratory judgment jurisdiction.

d. *Taxpayer Standing*

North Broward Hospital District v. Fornes

476 So. 2d 154 (Fla. 1985)

ALDERMAN, Justice.

We review the decision of the Fourth District Court of Appeal in *Fornes v. North Broward Hospital District*, 455 So.2d 584 (Fla. 4th DCA 1984), which certified the following question to be of great public importance:

> Does a taxpayer who alleges that the taxing authority is acting illegally in expending public funds, which will increase his tax burden, have standing to sue to prevent such expenditure, or is it necessary that he suffer some other special injury distinct from other taxpayers (as opposed to other inhabitants) or launch a constitutional attack upon the taxing authority's action in order to have standing?

Id. at 586. We quash the district court's holding that a taxpayer has standing to challenge the expenditure of public funds by simply alleging that such expenditure will increase her tax burden. Rather, we continue to adhere to precedent and hold that absent a constitutional challenge, a taxpayer must allege a special injury distinct from other taxpayers in the taxing district to bring suit.

Petitioner North Broward Hospital District, a special taxing district, operates certain hospitals in Broward County. To finance the expansion, operation, and maintenance of these hospitals, the appointed commissioners levy taxes against property owners residing in the district. Fornes owns property within the district and pays taxes to the district.

The District decided to expand North Broward Hospital. To comply with its charter requiring that competitive bids from at least three different sources be sought for all construction contracts in excess of five thousand dollars, the District developed specifications of the expansion project and invited bids from the public. Fornes sued the District, alleging that the portion of the specifications relating to the structural precast concrete set forth criteria which effectively limited the number of qualified suppliers and permitted favoritism in the bidding. In her amended complaint, Fornes alleged that the contract was awarded, but, because the specifications eliminated competition and permitted favoritism, the contract award was not the result of lawful competitive bidding procedures and prevented the project from being completed at the lowest possible cost to the taxpayers. Fornes requested a temporary and permanent injunction restraining the District from carrying out the terms of the contract and asked for a rebidding.

The District moved to dismiss on the basis that Fornes did not have standing to sue because she had failed to allege either a special injury distinct from other taxpayers or a constitutional challenge to the taxing statutes at issue. The trial court granted the District's motion to dismiss, citing *Godheim v. City of Tampa*, 426 So.2d 1084 (Fla. 2d DCA 1983). The Fourth District Court of Appeal reversed and held that

Fornes as a taxpayer within the District had standing to sue to prevent the illegal expenditure of public funds by alleging that the expenditure will increase her tax burden but certified the question to this Court.

The District argues that the law in Florida is well-established that in order to challenge government expenditures, a taxpayer must allege and prove a special injury distinct from other taxpayers in the taxing unit and that the only exception to this requirement is where the taxpayer constitutionally challenges the exercise of governmental taxing and spending powers. Fornes responds that the injury she will sustain because of increased taxes is sufficient to confer standing. She contends that this Court has consistently upheld the standing of taxpayers to sue to enjoin the unauthorized or unlawful expenditure of public funds which result in an increased tax burden. Fornes emphasizes that this is an action for violation of competitive bidding laws which were passed to protect taxpayers against collusion between public officials and bidders and urges that the present decision of the district court is in harmony with past taxpayer standing cases.

We disagree with Fornes. Since this Court's decision in *Henry L. Doherty & Co. v. Joachim*, 146 Fla. 50, 200 So. 238 (1941), we have consistently held that a mere increase in taxes does not confer standing upon a taxpayer to challenge a governmental expenditure. In that case, we stated:

> Both parties seem to recognize the rule announced in *Rickman v. White-hurst, et al.*, 73 Fla. 152, 74 So. 205, that in the event an official threatens an unlawful act, the public by its representatives must institute the proceedings to prevent it, unless a private person can show a damage peculiar to his individual interests in which case equity will grant him succor.

200 So. at 239. An exception to this special injury requirement was established in *Department of Administration v. Horne*, 269 So.2d 659 (Fla.1972). In that case, plaintiffs brought suit as taxpayers, alleging the unconstitutionality of certain sections of an appropriations act as violative of constitutional provisions. We stated: "Thus we find that where there is an attack upon *constitutional* grounds based directly upon the Legislature's *taxing and spending* power, there is standing to sue without the *Rickman* requirement of special injury, which will still obtain in other cases." 269 So.2d at 663. More recently in *Department of Revenue v. Markham*, 396 So.2d 1120 (Fla.1981), this Court reiterated the standing requirements in this state and held that "[i]t has long been the rule in Florida that, in the absence of a constitutional challenge, a taxpayer may bring suit only upon a showing of special injury which is distinct from that suffered by other taxpayers in the taxing district." *Id.* at 1121. This Court has refused to depart from the special injury rule or expand our exception established in *Horne. See United States Steel Corp. v. Save Sand Key, Inc.*, 303 So.2d 9 (Fla.1974).

Fornes has made several policy arguments why a taxpayer should be permitted to attack the legality of a governmental action which increases his tax burden, but these same reasons have been previously rejected by this Court. We find no reason to modify our rule. We agree with the Third District Court of Appeal's language in *Paul v. Blake*, 376 So.2d 256 (Fla. 3d DCA 1979), which stated:

> We recognize that all these standing rules are based on highly debatable policy choices, but they represent, in our view, a reasonable effort to guarantee that the state and counties lawfully exercise their taxing and spending authority without unduly hampering the normal operations of a representative democratic government. We adhere to these rules today because they are based on long-established precedent and seem both reasonable and fair.

376 So.2d at 259–60. In the present case, Fornes does not allege any special injury to her, and consequently, she has no standing to sue to enjoin the District's planned expansion.

Accordingly, we quash the decision of the district court and remand this case for further proceedings consistent with this opinion.

It is so ordered.

BOYD, C.J., and ADKINS, OVERTON and McDONALD, JJ., concur.

EHRLICH, J., dissents with an opinion, in which SHAW, J., concurs.

EHRLICH, Justice, dissenting.

The majority's decision here will only serve to insulate those government officials who ignore or violate the law from accountability to the citizens whose trust they violate. In order to shelter those who breach their oaths of office, the Court recedes from more than a century of case law which recognized taxpayer standing. I agree that the *Rickman* rule requires a special injury. In 1882, this Court recognized that a taxpayer who will have to provide the funds for government's illegal expenditures has been specially injured.

> The complainants, simply as tax-payers, in their own behalf and in behalf of other tax-payers, have a standing which entitles them to a remedy against a threatened wrongful proceeding which might involve them and the whole people of the county in great expense and confusion, and jeopardize the titles to property.

Lanier v. Padgett, 18 Fla. 842, 846 (1882). Nor has the Court heretofore deviated from that position in cases relating to tax-payer standing to protest illegal expenditures.

> Resident tax-payers have the right to invoke the interposition of a Court of Equity to prevent an illegal disposition of the moneys of a municipal corporation, or the creation of a debt which they, in common with other property holders, may otherwise be compelled to pay.

Peck v. Spencer, 26 Fla. 23, 29, 7 So. 642, 644 (1890).

> Courts of equity have jurisdiction to restrain municipal corporations and their officers from making unauthorized appropriations, or otherwise illegally and wrongfully disposing of the corporate funds to the injury of property holders and tax-payers in the corporation, and a bill for this purpose is

properly brought by an individual tax-payer on behalf of himself and other tax-payers in the municipality.

Chamberlain v. City of Tampa, 40 Fla. 74, 81, 23 So. 572, 574 (1898). "A resident taxpayer has the right to enjoin the illegal creation of a debt which he, in common with other property holders and taxpayers, may otherwise be compelled to pay." *Crawford v. Gilchrist*, 64 Fla. 41, 52–53, 59 So. 963, 967 (1912).

In *Rickman*, the Court began its reasoning from the proposition "the right of a citizen and taxpayer to maintain a suit to prevent the unlawful expenditure by public officials of public moneys, unless otherwise provided by legislative enactment, is generally recognized." 73 Fla. at 157, 74 So. at 207. The Court then went on to hold that the illegal action complained of by the taxpayer in that case gave rise to a cause of action if the taxpayer was able to allege special injury or an increase of taxes, but not if his only complaint was that it would "shame his sense of pride in the faithful observance by public officials of the obligations of their public duties." *Id.* The Court denied *Rickman* standing because his complaint neither attacked the validity of the bonds issued nor alleged waste or misappropriation of funds.

> There is no allegation of special injury to the complainant, nor that the cost of constructing the roads and bridges by the method proposed will entail a greater cost than the method prescribed by the general act, *nor that the money is being wasted or improvidently expended.* What, then, gives the complainant his standing in equity? Is it the mere abstract conception that an act done by the county officials not in strict conformity of law ipso facto operates to injur[e] [sic.] a citizen of the county? If *so*, then any citizen of the county, *whether taxpayer or not*, whether he resides in the special road district or beyond its limits, may maintain the action.

73 Fla. at 157–58, 74 So. at 207 (emphasis supplied).

Uncontrovertably, the *Rickman* rule recognized improper or improvident expenditure of public funds as a special injury which gives a taxpayer standing to bring suit.

Henry L. Doherty & Co., upon which the majority relies, does not address a taxpayer suit to enjoin illegal expenditures. *Doherty* involved a land-use decision which converted a pathway used by pedestrians and cyclists to private ownership. The petitioner alleged that the ordinance vacating the pathway was improperly enacted without notice and that he was inconvenienced by the loss of easy access from his property to the beach. The Court held that petitioner's injury was no different in kind from that suffered by others who would no longer be able to use the walkway, thus he lacked standing to protest the ordinance. This case did *not* involve illegal expenditures of tax revenues and therefore is not controlling — or even applicable — to the case now before the Court.

The only case cited by petitioner in its brief which may be read as directly addressing the issue before the Court is *Department of Revenue v. Markham*. There, in what is indisputable dicta, this Court, blithely ignoring the body of cases which do address taxpayer standing to protest illegal expenditure of public funds, grafted onto the special injury requirement the condition that it be "distinct from that suffered by other taxpayers in the taxing district." *Horne*, which establishes standing to protest constitutional issues, and *Rickman*, which stands for the opposite proposition, were cited as authority. In reality, rather than having "long been the rule in Florida," as the author asserts, this statement was newborn, springing fully formed from the author's mind, entirely without legal parentage.

The majority buttresses its action by claiming it to be a matter of public policy. There is a certain irony in that argument. The legislature, that body responsible for the determination of public policy, has given the citizens of the state the broadest possible rights of access to government through the Sunshine Act and the Public Records Act. Thus, while the legislature mandates the citizen's right to know just how and to what extent the public trust (and the public coffers) are being violated, this Court holds that public policy requires that we deny them the power to do anything about it.

I would approve the opinion of the district court.

SHAW, J., concurs.

The question of the correctness of the taxpayer standing rule as described by the Florida Supreme Court in *Fornes* seemingly will not go away. Consider the following from the Fifth District Court of Appeal in *Clayton v. School Board of Volusia County*:[162]

> Our first inquiry is whether *Fornes* precludes standing since Clayton admittedly is not economically impacted differently from any other taxpayer. This restriction truly creates a standing rule that is an anomaly: if everyone is injured, no one can sue. In announcing this rule as it applies to taxpayer actions, the majority in *Fornes* stated:
>
>> Since this court's decision in *Henry L. Doherty & Co. v. Joachim*, 146 Fla. 50, 200 So. 238 (1941), we have consistently held that a mere increase in taxes does not confer standing upon a taxpayer to challenge a governmental expenditure. In that case we stated:
>>
>>> Both parties seem to recognize the rule announced in *Rickman v. Whitehurst, et al.*, 73 Fla. 152, 74 So. 205, that in the event an official threatens an unlawful act, the public by its representatives must institute the proceedings to prevent it, unless a private person can show a damage peculiar to his individual interests in which case equity will grant him succor.

---

162. 667 So. 2d 942, 943 (Fla. 5th Dist. Ct. App. 1996) (quashed by *School Bd. of Volusia County v. Clayton*, 691 So. 2d 1066 (Fla. 1997)).

In a strong dissent, Justice Ehrlich asserted that the *Fornes'* majority simply misread the precedent when it held that an illegal public action that raises the taxpayer obligation or wastes public money cannot constitute the necessary "injury" which authorizes a taxpayer suit. A careful reading of *Chamberlain v. City of Tampa*, 40 Fla. 74, 23 So. 572 (1898), *Rickman* and *Joachim* lends support to Justice Ehrlich's contention, and we respectfully request that the present court reconsider the *Fornes* decision.[1]

The Florida Supreme Court was not inclined to change its mind.

School Board of Volusia County v. Clayton
691 So. 2d 1066 (Fla. 1997)

HARDING, Justice.

We have for review *Clayton v. School Board of Volusia County*, 667 So.2d 942 (Fla. 5th DCA 1996), which certified the following questions to be of great public importance:

DOES THE "UNIQUENESS OF THE PARTICULAR CASE" STANDARD PERMIT A TAXPAYER CHALLENGE TO THE ACTION OF A PUBLIC BOARD WHICH IS ALLEGED TO BE ACTING IN EXCESS OF ITS STATUTORY AUTHORITY AND WHICH ACTION EITHER INCREASES THE TAX BURDEN OR WASTES PUBLIC MONEY?

The court also expressed the question in the alternative:

DOES THE ACTION OF A PUBLIC BOARD WHICH EITHER INCREASES TAXES OR WASTES PUBLIC MONEY RISE TO THE LEVEL OF A CONSTITUTIONAL ISSUE WHEN IT IS ASSERTED THAT THE PUBLIC BOARD EXCEEDED ITS AUTHORITY GRANTED BY THE LEGISLATURE?

Clayton, 667 So.2d at 946. We have jurisdiction. Art. V, § 3(b)(4), Fla. Const.

We answer the first certified question in the negative, and decline to reach the alternative question.

Volusia County School Board sought to acquire property in DeBary, Florida, and filed a petition for eminent domain. *Clayton*, 667 So.2d at 943. After the petition was filed, the Board changed the description of the property it sought to acquire. *Id.* The value of the property was set under a negotiated agreement between the Board and the then-owner of the property; the valuation was not submitted to a jury. *Id.*

---

1. Our analysis is not criticism of the 1985 supreme court. We recognize the authority of the supreme court and our obligation to apply the law as directed by its decisions. We do not believe it inappropriate, however, after a reasonable period of time and after observing the effect of a particular decision on the litigants that come before us, to request that the supreme court review a decision that is so often challenged before our court. It is up to the supreme court to determine whether the request deserves consideration.

The purchase price was over $500,000, which was more than twice the amount of the appraisals in the record. *Id.* The Board approved the purchase by a bare majority vote. *Id.*

Clayton filed a petition for writ of mandamus in circuit court alleging that the Board's purchase did not comply with the requirements of section 235.054(1)(b), Florida Statutes (1995). That Section states, in relevant part:

> Prior to acquisition of the property, . . . [f]or each purchase in an amount in excess of $500,000, the board shall obtain at least two appraisals by appraisers approved pursuant to s. 253.025(6)(b). If the agreed purchase price exceeds the average appraised value, the board is required to approve the purchase by an extraordinary vote.

§ 235.054(1)(b), Fla. Stat. (1995). Clayton alleged that the Board was required to, but did not, obtain an extraordinary vote to approve the purchase because of this section.

Before addressing the merits of the issue, the circuit court found that Clayton did not have standing to bring the action because he did not allege a constitutional challenge or a special injury, as required by this Court's decision in *North Broward Hospital District v. Fornes*, 476 So.2d 154 (Fla.1985). Accordingly, the circuit court dismissed the petition.

On appeal, the Fifth District Court of Appeal recognized that *Fornes* precluded a taxpayer from bringing suit solely because the tax burden suffered by all taxpayers increased. *Clayton v. School Board of Volusia County*, 667 So.2d at 945. In *Fornes*, the taxpayer had alleged that the taxing authority illegally levied taxes against her property. She argued that the illegal levy would increase her tax burden. We stated that there were two means to achieve standing in a taxpayer case, holding "absent a constitutional challenge, a taxpayer must allege a special injury distinct from other taxpayers in the taxing district to bring suit." *Fornes*, 476 So.2d at 154. We explained that a constitutional challenge meant "an attack upon *constitutional* grounds based directly upon the Legislature's *taxing and spending* power." *Id.* at 155 (quoting *Department of Administration v. Horne*, 269 So.2d 659 (Fla.1972)). Because we found that an illegal public action which raises taxpayers' obligations or wastes public money did not constitute a "special injury" which distinguished Fornes from other taxpayers, and there was no allegation of a constitutional challenge, we held that she did not have standing to bring the suit. *Id.* at 155–56. Accordingly, Clayton would not have standing under *Fornes*.

The district court in *Clayton* suggested that this Court reconsider *Fornes*, but held that, in the alternative, Clayton did have standing under an exception to the *Fornes* requirement that a taxpayer allege special injury. *Clayton*, 667 So.2d at 945. The court held that the contested school board action not only had "constitutional implications," but also came within the "unique circumstances" exception announced in another *Clayton* case, *State ex rel. Clayton v. Board of Regents*, 635 So.2d 937 (Fla.1994). Accordingly, the court held that Clayton had standing to seek the writ. *Clayton v. School Board of Volusia County*, 667 So.2d at 947. However, the court certified the questions here.

We reaffirm our opinion in *Fornes*, and, consistent with that opinion, we hold that Clayton does not have standing to bring the action. The requirement that a taxpayer seeking standing allege a "special injury" or a "constitutional challenge" is consistent with long established precedent. *See, e.g., Rickman v. Whitehurst*, 73 Fla. 152, 74 So. 205 (1917) (requiring that taxpayer suffer special injury before standing is conveyed); *Henry L. Doherty & Co. v. Joachim*, 146 Fla. 50, 200 So. 238 (1941) (stating that a mere increase in taxes does not confer standing on a taxpayer seeking to challenge a government expenditure).

The first certified question—whether the "unique circumstances" of the case are enough to grant standing—is based on our *State ex rel. Clayton v. Board of Regents*, 635 So.2d 937 (Fla.1994), decision. In that case, Clayton[1] filed a petition for writ of mandamus arguing that the Board of Regents violated the common law in appointing a member of the Board to the position of president of the University of South Florida. *Board of Regents*, 635 So.2d at 938. We found that Clayton did have standing to bring the petition because of the *unique* circumstances present there. *Id.* Accordingly, we will not extend that decision beyond the unique circumstances present in that case. Further, we make it clear that our finding that unique circumstances existed in that case should not be interpreted as having created an exception to *Fornes*.

We find that Clayton must satisfy the *Fornes* requirement of alleging either a constitutional violation or a special injury. Because he has not done so, we hold that he does not have standing to bring the writ.

We quash the decision below. We answer the first certified question in the negative, as explained above. Because Clayton has not alleged a constitutional violation, we decline to reach the second question. At his request, we do grant leave to file an amended complaint where he can assert a constitutional violation. We remand for proceedings consistent with this opinion.

It is so ordered.

KOGAN, C.J., and OVERTON, GRIMES, WELLS and ANSTEAD, JJ., concur.

SHAW, J., dissents.

---

1. Clayton, petitioner in the instant case, was the respondent in *Board of Regents*.

Clayton v. School Board of Volusia County

696 So. 2d 1215 (Fla. 5th Dist. Ct. App. 1997)

On Remand from the Supreme Court

HARRIS, Judge.

Because the supreme court has reaffirmed its holding in Fornes[1] that a citizen taxpayer has no standing, individually or as a representative of a class, to challenge even the "illegal" acts of elected or appointed officials unless such illegality rises to constitutional proportions, and because Clayton's current complaint alleges only that the School Board members violated a state statute, we affirm the trial court's dismissal of the complaint but remand with instructions that Clayton be permitted, if he can, to allege a constitutional[2] basis for his challenge.

We recognize, as does Clayton, that absent a constitutional basis for a challenge, the *Fornes* standing rule, applied to cases of this type, creates a rare situation in which there is a wrong without a remedy. That is because even though the citizen taxpayer, who is also a voter, may "throw the rascals out" at the next election, even if such action exacts a measure of retribution it will not restore the looted treasury nor undo the illegally increased tax obligation. It is in this regard that our expansive limitation rule on taxpayer actions is unique. *See Texfi Industries, Inc. v. City of Fayetteville*, 44 N.C.App. 268, 261 S.E.2d 21, 23 (1979), *rev. denied*, 299 N.C. 741, 267 S.E.2d 671 (1980) ("Rule that a taxpayer has no standing to challenge question of general public interest that affects all taxpayers equally does not apply where taxpayer shows that tax levied upon him is for unconstitutional, illegal or unauthorized purpose"); *William Penn Parking Garage, Inc. v. City of Pittsburgh*, 464 Pa. 168, 346 A.2d 269, n. 21 (1975) ("[f]irst, a taxpayer is permitted to sue in order to prevent waste or illegal expenditure of public funds"); *Byrd v. Independent School District No. 194*, 495 N.W.2d 226, 231 (Minn.App.1993) ("ISD 194 asserts appellants Byrd and Hoiness lack standing because they are motivated more by private gain than public good. We disagree. As the trial court noted, both Byrd and Hoiness are taxpayers of ISD 194. Taxpayers have a real and definite interest in preventing an illegal expenditure of tax money"); *Nebraska School District No. 148 v. Lincoln Airport Authority et. al.*, 220 Neb. 504, 371 N.W.2d 258, 261 (1985) ("[a]nother established principle, which is conceded by the defendant, is that a resident taxpayer may invoke the interposition of a court of equity to prevent the illegal disposition of money of a municipal

---

1. *North Broward Hospital District v. Fornes*, 476 So.2d 154 (Fla.1985).

2. While we are not convinced that it is the type of "constitutional challenge" contemplated by the supreme court, we note that Clayton's complaint at least has a constitutional connection. Article II, section 8 of the Florida Constitution provides that: "A public office is a public trust. The people shall have the right to secure and sustain that trust against abuse." Article II, section 5 requires the public officer to take an oath to "faithfully perform the duties" of his office, a duty that presumably includes the obligation to obey the statutory laws of this state. If such public officer, or group of public officers, refuse to follow statutory directions, they have violated an obligation created by the constitution.

corporation or the illegal creation of a debt which he, in common with other property holders, may otherwise be compelled to pay"); *County of Sonoma et. al. v. State Board of Equalization*, 195 Cal.App.3d 982, 241 Cal.Rptr. 215, 219 (1st Dist.1987) ("Plaintiff Whorton is a taxpayer, although not a taxpayer who is challenging an assessment of taxes against himself. His assertion of standing is premised on the theory that defendants are without authority to create a *de facto* exemption from Sonoma County's sales tax and have illegally expended funds by administering the sales tax law while recognizing such an improper exemption . . . [P]laintiff Whorton is not challenging the exercise of the Board's legitimate discretion, but rather the extent of the Board's authority under section 6353. In the circumstances of the case, we hold that Whorton has standing to challenge the Board's interpretation and application of section 6353"); *Beshear v. Ripling*, 292 Ark. 79, 728 S.W.2d 170, 171 (1987) ("[h]e clearly had standing as a taxpayer to pursue the relief authorized by Ark. Const. art. 6, sec. 13, which provides: '[a]ny citizen of any county, city or town may institute suit on behalf of himself and all others interested, to protect the inhabitants thereof against the enforcement of any illegal exaction whatever.' It is self-executing, and it permits taxpayers to challenge the legality of expenditures of public funds"); *Champ v. Poelker*, 755 S.W.2d 383, 387 (Mo.App.E.D. 1988) ("[w]here no general revenue is involved in the issuance of bonds, 'a taxpayer has no legitimate interest in connection with such bonds' [Citation omitted.] A loss of revenue from IDA coffers cannot increase the burden of public debt or taxation, and therefore, appellants have not suffered 'a direct, pecuniary injury in the form of an increased tax burden'").[3]

---

3. *Rickman v. Whitehurst*, 73 Fla. 152, 155, 74 So. 205, 206 (Fla.1917), although cited by the supreme court as authority for reaffirming the *Fornes* rule, lends at least some support to the proposition that standing is appropriate if the public body acts without authority in disposing of public assets or in increasing a taxpayer's burden. *Rickman* holds: "In the first place the complainant has the right to maintain the bill if the acts complained of were unauthorized and not within the powers of the board of county commissioners, and tended to produce a resultant injury to the complainant by increasing the burden of his taxes. The right of a citizen and taxpayer to maintain a suit to prevent the unlawful expenditure by public officials of public moneys, unless otherwise provided by legislative enactment, is generally recognized. The nature of the powers exercised by county commissioners who are vested by law with the power of levying taxes for county purposes and the expenditure of county funds, the danger of the abuse of such powers which are delegated to them by legislative enactment and the necessity for prompt action to prevent their flagrant abuse and irremedial injuries flowing therefrom would seem to fully justify courts of equity in interfering upon the application of a county taxpayer and citizen . . . The principle on which the right rests is that the taxpayer is necessarily affected and his burden of taxation increased by any unlawful act of the county commissioners which may increase the burden to be borne by the taxpayers of the county, and no relief from such injury is obtainable elsewhere than in a court of equity . . . [standing was denied in this case because] [t]here is no allegation of special injury to the complainant, nor that the cost of constructing the roads and bridges by the method proposed will entail a greater cost than the method prescribed by the general act, nor that the money is being wasted or improvidently expended. What, then, gives the complainant his standing in equity? Is it the mere abstract conception that an act done by the county officials not in strict conformity of law *ipso facto*

360   4 · THE COURTS

Taxpayers such as Clayton, if they desire to prevent or reverse an illegal disposition of public funds, the illegal creation of a public debt or the illegal assessment of taxes, may wish to consider again amending their constitution in order to specifically include injuries caused by the misfeasance or malfeasance of public officials within the "any injury" provision presently appearing in Article I, section 21 of their constitution: "[t]he courts shall be open to every person for redress of any injury." Or they may prevail upon the Legislature to create such cause of action under its authority granted by the "Taxpayers' Bill of Rights" (Article I, section 25) which provides:

> By general law the legislature shall prescribe and adopt a Taxpayers' Bill of Rights that, in clear and concise language, sets forth taxpayers' rights and responsibilities and government's responsibilities to deal fairly with taxpayers under the laws of this state.

DISMISSAL AFFIRMED but REMANDED for further action consistent with *School Board of Volusia County v. Clayton*, 691 So.2d 1066 (Fla.1997).

COBB, J., concurs.

ANTOON, J., concurs in result only.

On Motion for Clarification

HARRIS, *Judge*.

The School Board moves for clarification of our opinion on remand. It urges that, because the lower court did not adjudicate the merits of the cause, there has been no determination that an illegal action took place. That is, of course, true. But, the School Board suggests that by using the term "illegal action" in our opinion we may have indicated that we believe that the law was violated in the purchase of the property in the present case. We have not, and cannot, make that determination from the record before us.

We did hold in our initial opinion that the School Board cannot avoid the extraordinary vote requirement by merely commencing the acquisition through eminent domain and then converting to negotiation for the ultimate purchase. We did not determine that Clayton's allegations that the School Board actually paid an amount sufficient to invoke the requirement of the extraordinary vote were proved, only that the allegations before the trial court were sufficient to require the court to consider the issue. Since we were reversed by the supreme court on the standing issue, our original opinion in this regard becomes meaningless in any event.

Our reference to "illegal action" was unrelated to the specific facts of this case, but instead was in connection with our discussion about the supreme court's limitation of standing only as to unconstitutional, as opposed to illegal, actions of governmental officials and the resulting limited options of citizens confronted with officials

---

operates to injure a citizen of the county? If so, then any citizen of the county, whether taxpayer or not, whether he resides in the special road district or beyond its limits, may maintain the action."

who will not follow the law. Obviously, whether the School Board acted improperly in this case has not been determined and, quite possibly, will never be determined because of the standing limitation.

CLARIFICATION granted as set out above.

COBB and ANTOON, J.J., concur.

In its opinion on remand from the Florida Supreme Court, the Fifth District opined:[163]

> We recognize, as does Clayton, that absent a constitutional basis for a challenge, the *Fornes* standing rule, applied to cases of this type, creates a rare situation in which there is a wrong without a remedy. That is because even though the citizen taxpayer, who is also a voter, may "throw the rascals out" at the next election, even if such action exacts a measure of retribution it will not restore the looted treasury nor undo the illegally increased tax obligation. . . .

Compare the comment of the Second District in *City of Sarasota v. Windom*:[164]

> . . . In closing, we recognize that the standing rules are founded upon public policy choices that are debatable. *See Paul v. Blake*, 376 So.2d 256 (Fla. 3d DCA 1979). But where litigants who bring an action challenging governmental injury are unable to distinguish their situation from others similarly situated, the result is an unwarranted consumption of limited judicial resources. *See United States v. Richardson*, 418 U.S. 166, 180, 94 S.Ct. 2940, 41 L.Ed.2d 678 (1974) (Powell, J., concurring). If a majority of the citizenry concurs with the plaintiffs' position, the remedy is only as far away as the next election.

See Richard D. Connor, Jr., *Taxpayer Standing in Florida: Is Everybody Nobody?*, 14 Stetson L. Rev. 687, (1985) for a critical analysis of the existing Florida standing requirements. See also Thomas C. Marks, Jr., *Adhere Resolutely to a Mistake: The Florida Taxpayer-Standing Cases*, 33 Stetson L. Rev. 401 (2004).

---

163. *Clayton v. Sch. Bd. of Volusia Cty.*, 696 So. 2d 1215, 1216 (Fla. 5th Dist. Ct. App. 1997).
164. 736 So. 2d 741, 743–744 (Fla. 2d Dist. Ct. App. 1999).

e. Citizen Standing

United States Steel Corp. v. Save Sand Key, Inc.

303 So. 2d 9 (Fla. 1974)

ROBERTS, Justice.

This cause is before us on certiorari granted to review the decision of the District Court of Appeal, Second District, reported at 281 So.2d 572 (Fla.App.1973), which directly conflicts with this Court's decision in Sarasota County Anglers Club, Inc. v. Kirk, 200 So.2d 178 (Fla.1967), thus vesting jurisdiction in this Court. Article V, Section 3(b)(3), Florida Constitution, 1973, F.S.A.

The Attorney General of this State and respondent, Save Sand Key, a non-profit Florida corporation organized for the specific purpose of securing for the public use as much as possible of Sand Key, a gulf-front island in Pinellas County owned by petitioner, United States Steel Corporation, filed a complaint for declaratory and injunctive relief against petitioner. In its action, Save Sand Key sought to enjoin United States Steel from interfering with certain alleged rights of the public generally, including individual members of the plaintiff corporation, to use a portion of the soft sand beach area of Sand Key. Such rights to the public use of United States Steel's lands were alleged to have been acquired by the public by prescription, implied dedication and/or general and local custom. Inter alia, respondent alleged that petitioner recently commenced construction of rental and high-rise condominium apartment buildings based upon its development plan for Sand Key, that petitioner has fenced portions of Sand Key around its present construction sites which alleged effectively and substantially prohibits and interferes with the rights of the public to the full use and enjoyment of the tract. Respondent by its complaint sought injunctive relief from any future acts which interfere with, impair or impede the exercise of the public's rights and from an alleged public nuisance in the form of a purpresture blocking enjoyment of those rights.

United States Steel moved to dismiss the complaint as filed by Save Sand Key, Inc. alleging, inter alia, that Save Sand Key had no standing to sue because it did not allege a special injury differing in kind from injury to the general public and because the respondent (plaintiff below) corporation was not itself claiming any right or title to the United States Steel's lands and was therefore not a real party in interest.

* * *

Sarasota County Anglers Club, Inc. v. Burns, 193 So.2d 691 (Fla.App.1967), 200 So.2d 178 (Fla.1967), a suit strikingly similar in nature to the instant cause involved a declaratory judgment action by the Anglers Club, a private non-profit corporation identical in type to respondent corporation acting in behalf of its members, and a private citizen against the Trustees of the Internal Improvement Fund, a landowner and the town of Longboat Key, seeking to enjoin fill operations at Longboat Key to the detriment of the club and others interested in fishing, bathing, and boating in the area, seeking that the land in question be impressed with a public easement for boating, bathing, navigation and other public uses, and praying for a decree declaring the dredge-fill permit to be illegal and void. Finding that the plaintiffs were not in a position to maintain this action, the trial court dismissed the complaint. Upon appeal the District Court of Appeal affirmed the order of dismissal by the trial court and succinctly stated,

> Suffice it to say that we agree with the chancellor in his finding and holding that the plaintiffs are not in a position to maintain this action. [O'Dell v. Walsh, 81 So.2d 554 (Fla.1955)]. Plaintiffs claim as authority to bring this action as authorized by Section 64.11, Florida Statutes, F.S.A., is untenable as to the facts in the case sub judice, and its application limited to those cases referred to in 823.05, Florida Statutes, F.S.A. Further, we must agree with the chancellor that the plaintiffs have failed to show in what manner they have been damaged as private citizens differing in kind from the general public, and, therefore, have no right to sue. [Deering v. Martin, 95 Fla. 224, 116 So. 54 (1928)].

Upon certification of the decision to this Court, we held:

> The history, factual background, questions presented and disposition are clearly set out in the opinion of the District Court. Argument having been heard and the court having considered the records and briefs, it is our opinion that the ruling of the District Court is correct and it is adopted as the opinion of this court. Sarasota County Anglers Club v. Kirk, Fla., 200 So.2d 178.

Sub judice, as in Sarasota County Anglers Club, Inc. v. Burns, supra, there is no statutory authority for this cause of action wherein respondents, inter alia, seek to assert property rights in real estate owned by petitioner and no special injury differing in kind from that suffered by the public generally was alleged.

* * *

Our decision in Department of Administration v. Horne, 269 So.2d 659 (Fla.1972), relative to the question of standing arose from facts clearly distinguishable from the instant cause, and cannot serve as precedent for the District Court of Appeal's departure from the special injury rule in the case sub judice. Further, our holding therein affirming the trial court's finding of standing allowed only a very limited exception to the special injury rule. In *Horne*, supra, taxpayers contested the validity of provisions of the General Appropriations Act on constitutional grounds which related solely to the taxing and spending power. Therein, this Court, speaking through Justice Dekle, in a very narrow holding stated:

> All of these are valid reasons for allowing the exception which we hereby approve, *limited to constitutional challenges on taxing and spending as earlier indicated.*

* * *

> Essentially, the 'Rickman Rule' requires a showing of special injury. We find, however, that the *instant case presents a valid exception* to the so-called

'Rickman Rule.' Appellees have alleged the *unconstitutionality* of certain sections of an appropriations act. These sections are said to be violative of constitutional provisions which place limitations upon enacting legislation regarding state funds. We hold that such allegation *in this narrow area* satisfied the requirement for 'standing' to attack an appropriations act. (e. s.)

The narrowness of this holding is exemplified by the following excerpt from that decision,

Applying this rationale, the U. S. Supreme Court said Mrs. Flast had standing to challenge the constitutionality of the 1965 Education Act because the establishment clause imposes a specific limitation upon the federal taxing and spending power. Thus we find that where there is an attack upon *constitutional* grounds based directly upon the Legislature's *taxing and spending* power, there is standing to sue without the *Rickman* requirement of special injury, *which will still obtain in other cases.* (e. s.)

Clearly, by its decision in Department of Administration v. Horne, supra, this Court did not intend to abrogate in any way the special injury rule in cases as those sub judice, but, in fact, recognized that it would still obtain in other cases. The District Court erred in finding that the special injury concept as a basis for standing no longer serves a valid purpose and that it should no longer be a viable expedient to the disposition of these cases. The standing test adopted by the Second District Court of Appeal constitutes a significant change in the law with which we cannot agree.

We adhere resolutely to our holding in Sarasota County Anglers Club, Inc. v. Kirk, supra, and other decisions of this Court relative to the concept of special injury in determining standing. *See,* inter alia, Henry L. Doherty & Co. v. Joachin, 146 Fla. 50, 200 So. 238 (1941), Town of Flagler Beach v. Green, 83 So.2d 598 (Fla.1955).

Accordingly, the decision of the District Court is quashed and this cause is remanded with directions to reinstate the order of the trial court.

It is so ordered.

ADKINS, C. J., DEKLE, J., and HENDRY, District Court Judge, concur.

ERVIN, J., dissents with opinion. [The dissenting opinion is omitted.]

As the Supreme Court in *Save Sand Key* makes clear, the *Horne* exception to the special injury requirement of taxpayer standing is *loosely* patterned after *Flast v. Cohen*.[165] What is not immediately clear from the *Save Sand Key* opinion is whether it also applies to create an exception to the special injury requirement of citizen standing. The better guess is that yes, the *Horne* exception applies also to citizen

---

165. *United States Steel Corp. v. Save Sand Key, Inc.,* 303 So. 2d 9, 13 (Fla. 1974).

standing. This is at odds with federal constitutional law where the *Flast* exception *does not* apply to citizen standing.[166]

Compare *Save Sand Key* to the following three cases.

In *Putnam County Environmental Council, Inc. v. Board of County Commissioners of Putnam County*,[167] it was held that the requisite "special injury" did exist where a group involved "in the original acquisition of land for use as a state forest and its continued, active connection with that state forest further demonstrate[d] an interest greater than that which all persons share in the community good." Thus, the Council had standing to challenge an environmental threat to the forest.

In *Friends of the Everglades, Inc. v. Board of Trustees of the Internal Improvement Trust Fund*,[168] the district court held that the "special injury" rule did not apply to cases where review was sought under the Florida Administrative Procedure Act. The court opined, "In [cases including *Save Sand Key*], the test for standing which was established by common law is 'special injury.' Standing under chapter 120, Florida Statutes (1989), is established by statute. [Citation omitted.] One of the major purposes of the APA is '[E]xpansion of public access to the activities of governmental agencies."[169] Here the court cited *Florida Home Builders Association v. Department of Labor and Employment Security*.[170] It then "decline[d] to apply the 'special injury' analysis to determinations regarding standing under the APA."[171] The court in the *Putnam County* case, above, cautioned that "[t]o the extent that *Friends of the Everglades, Inc.* can be read to hold that a group successful in having land acquired by the state for environmental protection purposes does not possess standing to challenge an environmental threat to that land, we disagree therewith."[172] In the authors' opinion it is doubtful that anything said in *Putnam County* could be read that way. And, even if it could, it would clearly be obiter dicta.[173]

In *Upper Keys Citizens Association, Inc. v. Wedel*,[174] the district court held that "the 'special injury' requirement has no application where a person affected seeks to challenge a zoning action on the ground that said action was illegally enacted, or conducted contrary to the provisions of a [municipal] charter." *Save Sand Key* was distinguished as a case where "non-profit corporations attempted to enjoin what [was] alleged to be [a] public nuisance[]."[175]

---

166. *Flast v. Cohen*, 392 U.S. 83 (1968).

167. 757 So. 2d 590, 594 (Fla. 5th Dist. Ct. App. 2000).

168. 595 So. 2d 186 (Fla. 1st Dist. Ct. App. 1992).

169. *Id.* at 189.

170. 412 So. 2d 351, 352–353 (Fla. 1982).

171. *Friends of the Everglades*, 595 So. 2d 186, 189 (Fla. 1st Dist. Ct. App. 1992).

172. 757 So. 2d 590, 591 (Fla. 5th Dist. Ct. App. 2000).

173. As defined by *Black's Law Dictionary* 1100 (7th ed. 1999), "something said in passing."

174. 341 So. 2d 1062, 1064 (Fla. 3d Dist. Ct. App. 1977).

175. *Id.* at 1063.

f. Associational Standing

In regard to so-called associational standing, consider the following from *Hillsborough County v. Florida Restaurant Association*:[176]

Standing

The Association, which has 2,766 members statewide, 154 of which operate in Hillsborough County, brought the suit on behalf of the thirty-seven of that number who serve alcoholic beverages on the premises of their public food establishments and who, accordingly, were affected by the ordinance.

We agree with the trial court on this threshold issue and find that the Association has standing to contest the validity of the ordinance. That is so because the Association has met the three-prong test which confers standing to an association to sue for the benefit of its members who are more directly affected by the governmental action than the association itself. Further, we find that the three-prong test[1] for association standing in the context of administrative proceedings, *Florida Home Builders Ass'n v. Dep't of Labor & Employment Sec.*, 412 So.2d 351 (Fla.1982), is equally applicable to the case before us. *See also Hunt v. Washington State Apple Advertising Comm'n*, 432 U.S. 333, 97 S.Ct. 2434, 53 L.Ed.2d 383 (1977); *Warth v. Seldin*, 422 U.S. 490, 95 S.Ct. 2197, 45 L.Ed.2d 343 (1975); *City of Lynn Haven v. Bay County Council of Registered Architects, Inc.*, 528 So.2d 1244 (Fla. 1st DCA1988); *Florida Ass'n of Counties, Inc. v. Dep't of Admin., Div. of Retirement*, 580 So.2d 641 (Fla. 1st DCA 1991), *aff'd*, 595 So.2d 42 (Fla.1992). Although the County argues that only thirty-seven out of the total 2,766 members of the Association are directly affected by the ordinance, it neglects to note that these thirty-seven represent forty-one percent of the total Hillsborough County membership in the Association. We do not find that a specific number or percentage is required in order to meet the standing requirement of *Florida Home Builders* but only that a substantial number of the Association's members have been affected in the instant case. Looking at the remaining

---

176. 603 So. 2d 587, 589 (Fla. 2d Dist. Ct. App. 1992).

1. The three-prong test of *Florida Home Builders* is:

1. A substantial number of the Association's members, although not necessarily a majority, are substantially affected by the challenged rule;
2. The subject matter of the rule is within the association's general scope of interest and activity; and
3. The relief requested is the type appropriate for a trade association to receive on behalf of its members.

See also Warth v. Seldin, 422 U.S. 490, 95 S.Ct. 2197, 2211–12, 45 L.Ed.2d 343 (1975), which provides that the association must allege that its members or any one of them are suffering immediate or threatened injury of the kind comprising a justiciable issue had the members themselves brought suit and that the nature of the issue does not make the individual participation of each association member indispensable to a proper resolution of the case.

two prongs of the test for association standing, it is clear the Association has satisfied those requirements as well.

g. Standing to Challenge Administrative Action

The requirement for such a challenge is clearly set out by the Florida Supreme Court in *Legal Environmental Assistance Foundation, Inc. v. Clark*:[177]

> *Section 120.68(1) sets forth the standard for judicial review of administrative action and states that "[a] party who is adversely affected by final agency action is entitled to judicial review." Thus, there are four requirements for standing to seek such review: (1) the action is final; (2) the agency is subject to provisions of the act; (3) the person seeking review was a party to the action; and (4) the party was adversely affected by the action.* See Daniels v. Florida Parole & Probation Comm'n, 401 So.2d 1351 (Fla. 1st DCA 1981), aff'd sub nom. Roberson v. Florida Parole & Probation Comm'n, 444 So.2d 917 (Fla.1983).

As noted by the First District Court of Appeal in *Abbott Laboratories v. Mylan Pharmaceuticals, Inc.*,[178] "[t]he test for determining whether a party has standing in appellate proceedings, governed by the quoted language in section 120.68(1), is different from the standing test required to participate in an administrative hearing. To have standing to challenge the validity of an administrative rule in a rule challenge proceeding before an ALJ, a person must be 'substantially affected'." "An intervenor must similarly be 'substantially affected' to participate in the rule challenge proceedings. §120.56(1)(e), Fla. Stat."[179] Standing at the appellate level is governed by section 120.68(1). Under this statute, a person has standing if four conditions are satisfied: "(1) the action is final; (2) the agency is subject to the provisions of the [Administrative Procedure] Act; (3) [the person seeking review] was a party to the action which he seeks to appeal; and (4) [the party] was adversely affected by the action.' *Daniels v. Florida Parole and Probation Comm'n*, 401 So.2d 1351, 1353 (Fla. 1st DCA 1981)."[180]

h. Third Party Standing

Pesci v. Maistrellis[181] made the following point about third party standing:

> Furthermore, we do not perceive that the issue of standing acts as an impediment to prevent a civil litigant such as the petitioner from asserting the privacy interests of jurors who are to be the subjects of a court-ordered jury interview. We find persuasive, in that regard, *Edmonson v. Leesville*

---

177. 668 So. 2d 982, 986 (Fla. 1996).
178. 15 So. 3d 642, 651 (Fla. 1st Dist. Ct. App. 2009).
179. *Id.*
180. *Id.* at 652.
181. 672 So. 2d 583, 586 (Fla. 2d Dist. Ct. App. 1996).

Concrete Co., 500 U.S. 614, 111 S.Ct. 2077, 114 L.Ed.2d 660 (1991), in which the Supreme Court held that a civil litigant has standing to raise equal protection claims of jurors excluded by the opposing party because of their race. In our view, a civil litigant's interest in preserving the legally protected sanctity of jury deliberations giving rise to a favorable verdict is no less compelling than the litigant's interest in ensuring that a jury be fairly selected without regard to considerations of race.

We conclude, therefore, that the petitioner has standing to assert the privacy interests of the jurors in this case and has established that the effect of the trial court's order would create "material harm irreparable by post-judgment appeal." *Parkway Bank*, 658 So.2d 646, 649. Accordingly, we have jurisdiction to determine whether the order departs from the essential requirements of the law. *Id.*

Chapter 5

Local Government

A. In General

Local governments in Florida consist of charter and non-charter counties, municipal corporations, and school and other districts. The only one of these described in the Florida Constitution as a political subdivision of the State is the county.[1] However, other units of local government have been described elsewhere as political subdivisions of the State.

In *City of Miami v. Lewis*,[2] the Third District Court of Appeal held that a municipal corporation is a "political subdivision" within a statutory definition of the term so that it did not have to "post bond to supersede a judgment on appeal." However, counties are the only local government units described as "political subdivisions" by the Florida Constitution.

B. Counties

1. In General

Fla. Const. art. VIII, § 1(a)

POLITICAL SUBDIVISIONS. This state shall be divided by law into political subdivisions called counties. Counties may be created, abolished or changed by law, with provision for payment or apportionment of the public debt.

———

There are two principal types of counties described in the Florida Constitution. These are charter and non-charter counties. In addition, special constitutional provisions exist which provide special status to identified counties. For example, Dade County operates under a unique metropolitan form of government.[3] Duval County

---

1. Fla. Const. art. VIII, § 1(a).
2. 104 So. 2d 70 (Fla. 3d Dist. Ct. App. 1958).
3. *See* Fla. Const. art. VIII, § 6(e) & (f).

370   5 · LOCAL GOVERNMENT

is operated as a consolidated county of sorts. However, generally, Florida's counties are characterized as being either charter or non-charter.[4]

Fla. Const. art. VIII, § 1(f)

NON-CHARTER GOVERNMENT. Counties not operating under county charters shall have such power of self-government as is provided by general or special law. The board of county commissioners of a county not operating under a charter may enact, in a manner prescribed by general law, county ordinances not inconsistent with general or special law, but an ordinance in conflict with a municipal ordinance shall not be effective within the municipality to the extent of such conflict.

Fla. Const. art. VIII, § 1(g)

CHARTER GOVERNMENT. Counties operating under county charters shall have all powers of local self-government not inconsistent with general law, or with special law approved by vote of the electors. The governing body of a county operating under a charter may enact county ordinances not inconsistent with general law. The charter shall provide which shall prevail in the event of conflict between county and municipal ordinances.

The 1968 revision of the Florida Constitution introduced the concept of "home rule" for counties and municipalities. The term "home rule" refers to the ability of a county or municipality to govern itself from within and not have to seek legislative authorization whenever it desired to act. As indicated by the language of the above provisions, the 1968 Constitution specifically authorized charter and non-charter counties to exercise self-governance. This was not so under the 1885 Constitution. The 1885 Florida Constitution contained no substantive provisions relating to the general power of counties comparable to art. VIII, §§ 1(f) and (g).[5] Instead, it merely provided that "[t]he State shall be divided into political divisions to be called counties."[6] Under the 1885 Constitution, counties were without inherent powers and as a result, all county power had to be derived "wholly from the state" through legislative action expressly granting counties the power to perform or exercise certain governmental actions contemplated by the county.[7] However, the 1968 revision of the Constitution affords counties the ability to exercise broad home rule powers. The Florida Legislature, by statute, has granted both charter and non-charter counties

----

4. As of the writing of this text, twenty of Florida's sixty-seven counties have adopted the charter form of government. The procedures for adoption of county charter status are found in Fla. Stat. § 125.60 (2021).

5. Nabors, Giblin & Nickerson, P.A., *Primer on Home Rule & Local Government Revenue Sources*, at 2 (April 2010).

6. *Id.*

7. *See Amos v. Matthews*, 126 So. 308 (Fla. 1930).

the broad exercise of home rule powers as authorized by the Constitution.[8] However, a county's exercise of home rule powers is not unchecked in that it cannot circumvent the limitations imposed by the Constitution. The following cases are illustrative of the constitutional limitations on a county's exercise of home rule powers.

2. Non-Charter Counties

Non-charter counties are counties whose source of governmental power emanates from legislative authorization. As such, the Florida Legislature has a relatively "free hand" to control these political subdivisions. As the following case suggests, the current statutory provisions regulating non-charter counties broadly empower such counties to exercise all necessary power to carry on county government. See also the discussion in *Hillsborough County v. Florida Restaurant Association, infra* page 427, of the power of the two types of counties.

a. ". . . [S]hall have such power of self-government as is provided by general or special law." Fla. Const. art. VIII, §1(f)

Speer v. Olson
367 So. 2d 207 (Fla. 1978)

ADKINS, Justice.

This is an appeal from a Final Judgment of the Circuit Court of Pasco County validating general obligation bonds issued by a Pasco County Municipal Service Taxing Unit for acquisition of sewer and water systems. We have jurisdiction. Article V, Section 3(b)(2), Florida Constitution.

The Board of County Commissioners of Pasco County enacted an ordinance creating a Municipal Service Taxing Unit to be known as West Pasco Water and Sewer Unit (hereinafter referred to as the "Unit"). The Unit was composed of the entire unincorporated area of the county. The commissioners called a special election by the residents of the Unit for the purpose of securing their approval for the issuance of $41.5 million general obligation bonds by the Unit. The proposed bond issue passed by a majority of 79 percent.

The appellants (taxpayers) initiated suit in circuit court to contest the legality of the election and its results. Immediately thereafter, Pasco County filed a complaint seeking validation of the bonds. The appellants intervened in the latter suit and sought dismissal contending, as in their earlier action, that the commissioners' use of their emergency powers to establish the Unit was invalid and that the issuance of general obligation bonds for the expansion of sewer and water systems was improper. The actions were consolidated.

---

8. *See* Fla. Stat. §125.01 (2021).

The circuit court held the election was valid and validated the bonds. The appellants (taxpayers) have appealed to this Court.

The first question is whether Chapter 125, Florida Statutes, could be utilized by the county to authorize general obligation bonds for the acquisition of sewer and water systems. The pertinent portions of Chapter 125 read as follows:

125.01 Powers and duties. —

(1) The legislative and governing body of a county shall have the power to carry on county government. To the extent not inconsistent with general or special law, this power shall include, but shall not be restricted to, the power to:

* * *

(k) Provide and regulate waste and sewage collection and disposal, water supply, and conservation programs.

* * *

(q) Establish, and subsequently merge or abolish those created hereunder, municipal service taxing or benefit units for any part or all of the unincorporated area of the county, within which may be provided fire protection, law enforcement, beach erosion control, recreation service and facilities, water, streets, sidewalks, street lighting, garbage and trash collection and disposal, waste and sewage collection and disposal, drainage, transportation, and other essential facilities and municipal services from funds derived from service charges, special assessments, or taxes within such unit only. It is hereby declared to be the intent of the Legislature that this paragraph is the authorization for all counties to levy additional taxes, within the limits fixed for municipal purposes, within such municipal service taxing units under the authority of the second sentence of Article VII, Section 9(b) of the State Constitution.

* * *

(r) Levy and collect taxes, both for county purposes and for the providing of municipal services within any municipal service taxing unit, and special assessments, borrow and expend money, and issue bonds, revenue certificates, and other obligations of indebtedness, which power shall be exercised in such manner, and subject to such limitations, as may be provided by general law. There shall be no referendum required for the levy by a county of ad valorem taxes, both for county purposes and for the providing of municipal services within any municipal service taxing unit.

* * *

Chapter 125, Florida Statutes, implements the provisions of Art. VIII, Section 1(f), Florida Constitution (1968), which gives counties *not operating under county charters*, such as Pasco County, such powers of self-government as are provided by general or special law. [Emphasis added.] This provision of the Florida Constitution also authorizes the board of county commissioners of such a county to enact ordinances in the manner prescribed by Chapter 125, Florida Statutes, which are not inconsistent with general law.

The intent of the Legislature in enacting the recent amendments to Chapter 125, Florida Statutes, was to enlarge the powers of counties through home rule to govern themselves.

The first sentence of Section 125.01(1), Florida Statutes, (1975), grants to the governing body of a county the full power to carry on county government. Unless the Legislature has pre-empted a particular subject relating to county government by either general or special law, the county governing body, by reason of this sentence, has full authority to act through the exercise of home rule power. There is no statute, general or special, which either specifically authorizes or restricts Pasco County with respect to the issuance of general obligation bonds to acquire sewage and water systems and to pledge for their payment the net revenues to be derived from the operation of such facilities and ad valorem taxes levied within the area of the Unit. The first sentence of Section 125.01(1), Florida Statutes (1975), therefore, empowers the county board to proceed under its home rule power to accomplish this purpose. This was done by the enactment of the ordinance and the adoption of the bond resolution after the bond election.

The precise approach used in authorizing the proposed bonds by Pasco County was previously employed in the case of *State v. Orange County*, 281 So.2d 310 (Fla.1973). . . . This Court noted that the intent of the Legislature in enacting Chapter 125 was to obviate the necessity of going to the Legislature to get a special act passed authorizing bonds of the type proposed:

> Instead of going to the Legislature to get a special bill passed authorizing such building fund revenue bonds, the Orange County Commissioners under the authority of the 1968 Constitution and enabling statutes now may pass an ordinance for such purpose, as they did in this case, because there is nothing inconsistent thereto in general or special law. On the contrary, there is ample delegated authority for such purpose. The object of Article VIII of the 1968 Constitution was to do away with the local bill evil to this extent.

As a result of this decision, a great many county capital projects have been financed throughout the state by using the device of a home rule ordinance.

Furthermore, in the case of *Tucker v. Underdown*, 356 So.2d 251 (Fla.1978), the Board of County Commissioners of Brevard County, Florida, established six municipal service taxing units pursuant to Section 125.01(1)(q), Florida Statutes (1975), and county home rule ordinances, in the unincorporated area of the county. Appellants in that case questioned the constitutionality of Sections 125.011(1)(q) and 125.01(1)(r), Florida Statutes (1975), and contended that the levy of ad valorem taxes for the purposes of raising tax revenues to be devoted to solid waste disposal, and its *interrelated but optional reduction of user charges imposed to meet debt service and operating costs under the prior bond issue*, constituted an impermissible financing scheme to meet solid waste disposal needs. This Court disagreed with the contentions of the appellants and held that the previous sections of Chapter 125 were constitutional and that such a financing scheme was entirely appropriate, thereby affirming the final judgment of the lower court.

[The Court then affirms the circuit court as to its rulings on the method used in the bond validation proceedings.]

The final judgment of the trial court validating the proposed issue of bonds is affirmed.

BOYD, OVERTON, SUNDBERG and HATCHETT, JJ., concur.

ALDERMAN, J., concurs in result only.

ENGLAND, C. J., dissents [without opinion].

Even though, unlike a charter county ordinance, the ordinance of a non-charter county will not have effect within a municipality if it conflicts with a municipal ordinance, no conflict occurs if the ordinances are considered to "coexist."

b. ". . . [M]ay enact county ordinances not inconsistent with general or special law, but an ordinance in conflict with a municipal ordinance shall not be effective within the municipality to the extent of such conflict." Fla. Const. art. VIII, § 1(f)

Misty's Cafe, Inc. v. Leon County

640 So. 2d 170 (Fla. 1st Dist. Ct. App. 1994)

PER CURIAM.

Misty's Cafe, Inc., the appellant, challenges the entry of an injunction prohibiting operation of its commercial establishment within Leon County. We affirm.

In October of 1993, appellant began operation of a restaurant in Leon County which featured "bottomless" dancers. That is, the dancers were wearing shirts or other articles of clothing over the top half of the torso, but were otherwise nude.

Article VII of the Leon County Code contains the following provision:

> It shall be unlawful for any person to engage in nude or semi-nude entertainment in any commercial establishment at which alcoholic beverages are, or are available to be, sold, dispensed, consumed, possessed or offered for sale or consumption on the premises. . . .

The City of Tallahassee has an ordinance which provides:

> It is unlawful for any female person to appear or be in a place where food or alcoholic beverages are offered for sale or consumption on the premises,

so costumed or dressed that one or both breasts are wholly or substantially exposed to public view.

Chapter 15, § 15-22, Tallahassee Municipal Code.

Appellant's commercial establishment operates within [Tallahassee] an incorporated area of Leon County. Shortly after opening, Leon County sought an injunction prohibiting operation of appellant's establishment in violation of Chapter 11 of the Code of Leon County.

In its memorandum of law filed in opposition to the motion for injunctive relief, appellant argued that the city and county ordinances cited above were in conflict, and therefore the ordinance of Leon County, which is a non-chartered county, is subordinate to the ordinance passed by a municipality. *See*, Article VIII, § 1(f), Florida Constitution. Accordingly, appellant was obliged only to comply with the city ordinance. Because the city ordinance by its terms prohibits only topless dancing, there was no basis to enjoin the appellant from violations of the law. . . .

On appeal, appellant again argues that the Leon County ordinance is inapplicable to it because of the conflict with the city ordinance noted above. . . .

Leon County argues in response that the two ordinances are not in conflict but are supplemental. . . .

As suggested by appellant, Article VIII, § 1(f) of the Florida Constitution provides that an ordinance of a non-chartered county shall be ineffective in the incorporated areas of the county when the county ordinance is "in conflict" with a municipal ordinance. The term conflict is not defined in the constitution. In *Florida Board of County Commissioners of Dade County v. Wilson*, 386 So.2d 556, 560 (Fla.1980), the supreme court, *citing State ex rel. Dade County v. Brautigam*, 224 So.2d 688 (Fla.1969) referred to an ordinance as being "in conflict" with general law when the ordinance was not able to "coexist" with a legislative provision. The term "coexist" is not defined in *Florida County Commissioners* or in *Brautigam*.

Obviously, the county ordinance in question is much broader in scope than the city ordinance. While they are not identical, the ordinances are not mutually exclusive. We cannot agree that the county ordinance is ineffective within the incorporated areas of the city simply because it is not identical in its scope to a city ordinance. If appellant's argument is correct — that a county ordinance must yield in the incorporated areas of the county when it is not identical in scope to a city ordinance — then a county is only able to enact ordinances that mirror city ordinances already in existence. In other words, a county would be able to criminalize only what the city has already criminalized. We cannot agree that such a result was intended by Article VIII, § 1(f). In sum, we find that the statutes do coexist, and provide by their mutual operation that nude dancing, without regard to "bottomless" or "topless" distinctions, is not permitted within the incorporated areas and unincorporated areas of the county.

* * *

Accordingly, the order under review is AFFIRMED.

SMITH, LAWRENCE and BENTON, JJ., concur.

In an attempt to remove themselves from underneath a county regulatory scheme, some municipalities have attempted to adopt "opt-out" ordinances with the sole intent and purpose of opting the city out of the non-charter county's ordinance by creating a conflict and relying upon the fact that a non-charter county ordinance would not be effective with the municipality to the extent of such conflict. The Florida courts have generally held such municipal ordinances invalid due to the absence of their having a legitimate "municipal purpose."[9]

3. Charter Counties

a. In General

Charter counties possess more autonomy than non-charter counties. The source of the governmental power of such counties is the county charter, authorized by the Florida Constitution, which in many ways acts as a type of constitution for the charter county.

This autonomy is expressed in a number of ways in the provisions of Fla. Const. art. VIII, §1. First, *non*-charter counties possess only that power of self-government that is consistent with general or special law. Thus, the Florida Legislature may affect the powers of non-charter counties by general or special law. However, the Florida Legislature can only impact on the powers of self-government of a charter county through a general law, or a special law that is approved by a vote of the electors in the affected county.

Second, a non-charter county may enact only those ordinances that are consistent with both general and special law. However, a charter county may enact all ordinances that are consistent with general law. Hence, the Florida Legislature may not affect the ordinance-making authority of a charter county by special law.

Third, if a conflict exists between a non-charter county ordinance and an ordinance of a municipality located within that non-charter county, the Florida Constitution provides that the municipal ordinance will supersede the non-charter county ordinance within the municipality. However, in a charter county, the charter itself may provide that the charter county ordinance will prevail in the event of a conflict.

---

9. *See City of Ormond Beach v. Cnty. of Volusia*, 535 So. 2d 302 (Fla. 5th Dist. Ct. App. 1989).

b. ". . . [S]hall have all powers of local self-government not inconsistent with general law, or with special law approved by vote of the electors." Fla. Const. art. VIII, §1(g)

Hollywood, Inc. v. Broward County

431 So. 2d 606 (Fla. 4th Dist. Ct. App. 1983)

HURLEY, Judge.

This appeal concerns the validity of a Broward County ordinance that requires a developer/subdivider, as a condition of plat approval, to dedicate land or pay a fee to be used in expanding a county level park system sufficiently to accommodate the new residents of the platted development. The appellant has asserted that Broward County lacks legal authority to adopt this type of ordinance. We do not agree and, thus, we affirm the trial court's conclusion that the ordinance is valid.

The appellant is a real estate development corporation that paid a fee under the ordinance and later commenced this action seeking declaratory and injunctive relief as well as a refund of the fee. The appellant has challenged the part of the ordinance that requires, as a condition of plat approval, the dedication of land or the payment of a fee for use by the county in acquiring and developing county level parks. [Footnote omitted.]

The ordinance has three alternate provisions: (1) the developer can dedicate three acres for every one thousand residents of the proposed subdivision, (2) the developer can pay an amount of money equal to the value of land that would have been dedicated, or (3) the developer can pay an impact fee according to a schedule in the ordinance. The developer in this case chose option two and paid an amount equal to the value of the land that would have been dedicated. At trial, the county introduced evidence that the ordinance seeks to impose fees only for those capital acquisition costs that the county will incur because of the new subdivision residents and that the money collected will be used for the substantial benefit of those residents. The trial court concluded that the ordinance is a valid and constitutional exercise of the county's legislative powers.

We discern two principal thrusts in appellant's overall attack on the ordinance: (1) the appellant asserts that the Broward County Commission lacks authority under the Broward County Charter to enact this type of ordinance and (2) the appellant asserts that no Florida court has countenanced the imposition of land or fee requirements for use by a county in expanding its county level parks. Included in these attacks are allegations that the ordinance violates fundamental constitutional rights including due process and equal protection and allegations that the ordinance constitutes an unconstitutional taking without just compensation and is, in fact, an illegal tax. In response, the appellee contends that the ordinance does not exceed the broad home rule powers of the Broward County Charter and that the ordinance merely exacts reasonable and valid regulatory fees.

I
The Charter

At the outset, we note that counties, as political subdivisions of the state, derive their sovereign powers exclusively from the state. Florida charter counties, such as Broward County, derive their sovereign powers from the state through Article VIII, Section 1(g) of the Florida Constitution which provides in pertinent part:

> Counties operating under county charters shall have all powers of local self-government not inconsistent with general law, or with special law approved by the vote of the electors. The governing body of a county operating under a charter may enact county ordinances not inconsistent with general law.

Through this provision, the people of Florida have vested broad home rule powers in charter counties such as Broward County.

The people have said that charter county governments shall have all the powers of local government unless the state government takes affirmative steps to preempt local legislation.[2] Of course, the power of charter county governments is limited by certain provisions of the Florida Constitution such as the Declaration of Rights in Article I and the limitations on taxing power found in Article VII. In addition, the counties' power is limited, just as is the state's power, by the provisions of the United States Constitution and any federal legislation that binds the states.

In the absence of preemptive federal or state statutory or constitutional law, the paramount law of a charter county is its charter. *Cf. City of Miami Beach v. Fleetwood Hotel, Inc.*, 261 So.2d 801 (Fla.1972) (city charter). In essence, the charter acts as the county's constitution and, thus, ordinances must be in accordance with the charter.

The people of Broward County have empowered their county government with very broad powers by incorporating the following provisions into their charter:

> Section 1.03. GENERAL POWERS OF THE COUNTY.

> A. Unless provided to the contrary in this Charter, Broward County "shall have all powers of local self-government not inconsistent with general law or with special law approved by vote of the electors."

> Section 1.08. CONSTRUCTION.

> The powers granted by this Charter shall be construed liberally in favor of the county government. The specified powers in this Charter shall not be construed as limiting, in any way, the general or specific power of the government, as stated in this Article.

Pursuant to these provisions, the people of Broward County have conferred all the powers a Florida charter county can have, subject only to other contrary provisions in the charter.

---

2. In the present case, the appellant has not asserted that the Broward County ordinance violates a statute.

The appellant relies on another provision in the charter as establishing by inference that the county government violated the charter in enacting the ordinance under review. That provision provides:

Section 6.12. PLAT ORDINANCE.

The legislative body of each municipality within Broward County and the County Commission for the unincorporated area shall, within six (6) months after the effective date of this Charter, create a mandatory plat ordinance.

No plat of lands lying within Broward County, either in the incorporated or unincorporated areas, may be recorded in the Official Records prior to approval by the County Commission. The County Commission shall enact an ordinance establishing standards, procedures and minimum requirements to regulate and control the platting of lands within the incorporated and unincorporated areas of Broward County. The governing body of each municipality may enact an ordinance establishing additional standards, procedures and requirements as may be necessary to regulate and control the platting of lands within its boundaries.

We can find nothing in this provision which suggests that the people of Broward County intended to prohibit their county government from enacting an ordinance requiring dedications or fees for expanding parks as a condition of plat approval. Thus, we find appellant's first attack to be ineffective. [Footnote omitted.]

[The Court then upholds the ordinance under the theory of *Contractors & Builders Association of Pinellas County v. City of Dunedin*, 329 So. 2d 314 (Fla. 1976). This case is located in Chapter 6 of this book.]

V

Summary

To summarize, we hold (1) that the ordinance does not violate the provisions of the Broward County Charter and (2) that subdivision exactions for county level parks are permissible so long as (a) the exactions are shown to offset, but not exceed, reasonable needs sufficiently attributable to the new subdivision residents and (b) the funds collected are adequately earmarked for the acquisition of capital assets that will sufficiently benefit those new residents. Accordingly, the judgment of the trial court is AFFIRMED.

DOWNEY and BERANEK, JJ., concur.

380   5 · LOCAL GOVERNMENT

c. ". . . [M]ay enact county ordinances not inconsistent with general law." Fla. Const. art. VIII, §1(g)

McLeod v. Orange County

645 So. 2d 411 (Fla. 1994)

PER CURIAM.

By notice of appeal, we have for review *Orange County v. State*, No. 93-1371 (Fla. 9th Cir. Ct. June 8, 1993), in which the circuit court validated a proposed bond issue by Orange County. We have jurisdiction. Art. V, §3(b)(2), Fla. Const.; §75.08, Fla. Stat. (1993).

In August of 1991, Orange County, a charter county, adopted Orange County Ordinance 91-17 (August 6, 1991) pursuant to section 166.231, Florida Statutes (1991), and the Orange County Charter. The ordinance levied a public service tax on the purchase of electricity, metered or bottled gas, water service, fuel oil, and telecommunication services within the unincorporated area of Orange County. In November of 1992, the county adopted Orange County Ordinance 92-35 (November 10, 1992), Orange County Ordinance 92-B-10 (November 10, 1992), and Orange County Ordinance 92-B-11 (November 10, 1992), which supplemented Ordinance 92-B-10. Ordinance 92-35 authorized the financing of Orange County capital projects through public service tax revenue bonds, payable from a public service tax. In its final judgment, the circuit court found that Ordinances 92-B-10 and 92-B-11 authorized the issuance of Orange County Public Service Tax Revenue Bonds, Series 1992:

> (a) to pay all or a part of the "Cost" of any "Project" or "Projects" (as such terms are defined in the Bond Resolution), including all appurtenant facilities, without limitation as to the location of such Project or Projects within the County, and with the first Project to be the acquisition of various parcels of environmentally-sensitive land (the "Initial Project"), . . . , (b) to capitalize interest on the Bonds, (c) to fund a debt service reserve account, if necessary, and (d) to pay costs associated with the issuance of the Bonds.

The circuit court validated the bonds and confirmed the three ordinances.

McLeod, a resident of and property owner in the unincorporated section of the county, challenges the public service tax and asserts that absent a general law empowering it to do so, Orange County as a charter county is without the power or authority to enact a public service tax pursuant to section 166.231, Florida Statutes (1991).[1] We disagree. Article VII, section 9(a), and article VIII, section 1(g) of the

---

1. The statute reads, in part:
   (1)(a) A municipality may levy a tax on the purchase of electricity, metered or bottled gas (natural liquefied petroleum gas or manufactured), and water service. . . .
   . . . .
   (2) . . . [F]uel oil shall be taxed at a rate not to exceed 4 cents per gallon. . . .
   (9) A municipality may levy a tax on the purchase of telecommunications services

Florida Constitution give a charter county the right to impose a public service tax if the imposition is not inconsistent with general or special laws.

We find the logic employed in *State ex rel. Volusia County v. Dickinson*, 269 So.2d 9 (Fla.1972), apropos to the resolution of this case.[2] The crux of the *Volusia* holding is that "unless precluded by general or special law, a charter county may without more under authority of existing general law impose by ordinance any tax in the area of its tax jurisdiction a municipality may impose." 269 So.2d at 11. This conclusion was dictated by our reading of articles VII and VIII of the Florida Constitution. Article VII, section 9(a) provides that:

> (a) Counties, school districts, and municipalities shall . . . be authorized by law to levy ad valorem taxes and may be authorized by general law to levy other taxes, for their respective purposes, except ad valorem taxes on intangible personal property and taxes prohibited by this constitution.

Article VIII, section 1(g) provides that:

> (g) CHARTER GOVERNMENT. Counties operating under county charters shall have all powers of local self-government not inconsistent with general law, or with special law approved by vote of the electors. The governing body of a county operating under a charter may enact county ordinances not inconsistent with general law.

Read together, the articles give charter counties the authority to levy any tax that a municipality may impose, if it is within the county's taxing jurisdiction. 269 So.2d at 11. This would include a public service tax pursuant to section 166.231.

* * *

Appellant also asserts that Orange County should have enacted Ordinance 91-17 pursuant to procedures established in section 166.041, Florida Statutes (1991), and not pursuant to section 125.66(1), Florida Statutes (1991). We disagree. Section 166.041 enumerates the procedures a municipality must follow when enacting an ordinance. Section 125.66(1) enumerates the procedures a county must follow when enacting an ordinance. Section 125.66(1) specifically states that "in exercising the ordinance-making powers conferred by s. 1, Art. VIII of the State Constitution, counties shall adhere to the procedures prescribed herein." We find that the County properly enacted the ordinance pursuant to procedures established in section 125.66(1).

* * *

We affirm the final judgment validating the proposed bond issue.

It is so ordered.

GRIMES, C.J., OVERTON, SHAW, KOGAN and HARDING, JJ., and McDONALD, Senior Justice, concur.

---

2. In *Volusia*, we held that charter counties may levy an excise tax on the sale of cigarettes in unincorporated areas of the county.

In the following excerpt from *Lowe v. Broward County*,[10] the Fourth District Court of Appeal set forth the analysis to be used to determine whether a local government ordinance is inconsistent with general law:

> There are "two separate and distinct ways that a local government ordinance may be found to be inconsistent with state law[.]" *Tallahassee Mem'l Reg'l Med. Ctr., Inc. v. Tallahassee Med. Ctr., Inc.*, 681 So.2d 826, 831 (Fla. 1st DCA 1996). First, the local government ordinance must not specifically conflict with a state statute. *See id.; City of Casselberry v. Orange County Police Benevolent Ass'n*, 482 So.2d 336, 340 (Fla.1986). The supreme court has written that the test of such a conflict is whether one must violate one provision in order to comply with the other. *Jordan Chapel Freewill Baptist Church v. Dade County*, 334 So.2d 661 (Fla. 3d DCA 1976). Putting it another way, a conflict exists when two legislative enactments "cannot coexist." *E.B. Elliott Advertising Co. v. Metropolitan Dade County*, 425 F.2d 1141 (5th Cir.1970), *pet. dismissed*, 400 U.S. 805, 91 S.Ct. 12, 27 L.Ed.2d 12 (1970); *Metropolitan Dade County v. Santos*, 430 So.2d 506 (Fla. 3d DCA 1983), *pet. for review denied*, 438 So.2d 834 (Fla.1983).
>
> *Laborers' Int'l Union of N. Am., Local 478 v. Burroughs*, 541 So.2d 1160, 1161 (Fla.1989) (quoting *Laborers' Int'l Union of N. Am., Local 478 v. Burroughs*, 522 So.2d 852, 856 (Fla. 3d DCA 1987)).
>
> The second way an ordinance may be inconsistent with state law is if the Legislature "has preempted a particular subject area." *Tallahassee Mem'l*, 681 So.2d at 831 (citation omitted). Florida law recognizes two types of preemption: express or implied. *See Santa Rosa County v. Gulf Power Co.*, 635 So.2d 96, 101 (Fla. 1st DCA 1994). For the Legislature to expressly preempt an area, the preemption language of the statute must be specific; "express preemption cannot be implied or inferred." *Hillsborough County v. Florida Restaurant Ass'n*, 603 So.2d 587, 590 (Fla. 2d DCA 1992). Writing for the first district, Judge Wolf has observed that implied preemption
>
>> is a more difficult concept. The courts should be careful in imputing an intent on behalf of the Legislature to preclude a local elected governing body from exercising its home rule powers. Implied preemption should be found to exist only in cases where the legislative scheme is so pervasive as to evidence an intent to preempt the particular area, and where strong public policy reasons exist for finding such an area to be preempted by the Legislature. The scope of the preemption should also be limited to the specific area where the Legislature has expressed their will to be the sole regulator.
>
> *Tallahassee Mem'l*, 681 So.2d at 831 (citations omitted).

---

10. 766 So. 2d 1199 (Fla. 4th Dist. Ct. App. 2000).

5 · LOCAL GOVERNMENT

d. "... The charter shall provide which shall prevail in the event of conflict between county and municipal ordinances." Fla. Const. art. VIII, § 1(g)

As enumerated in the following case, Fla. Const. art. VIII, § 1(g) was intended to specifically provide charter counties the authority to preempt conflicting municipal ordinances. However, this preemptive right is limited to regulatory powers; when the preemption goes beyond regulation and intrudes upon a municipality's provision of services, it triggers the dual referendum requirement of Fla. Const. art. VIII, § 4. The tension between Fla. Const. art. VIII, § 4, Transfer of Powers and the preemption power of charter counties will be discussed later in this chapter.

Broward County v. City of Fort Lauderdale

480 So. 2d 631 (Fla. 1985)

EHRLICH, Justice.

This case is before us to answer a question certified by a district court to be of great public importance. We have jurisdiction. Art. V, § 3(b)(4), Fla. Const.

The Broward County Commission sought to regulate certain aspects of the sale of handguns in the county. In pursuing this goal, the commission held a county-wide referendum to amend the county charter. Pursuant to article VIII, section 1(g) of the Florida Constitution,[1] the charter provided that, with two exceptions, municipal ordinances would prevail when conflict arose with county ordinances. The amendments added a third exception providing that county ordinances relating to handgun control would prevail.[2] The amendments were approved, and the commission enacted a handgun ordinance.

---

1. (g) CHARTER GOVERNMENT. Counties operating under county charters shall have all powers of local self-government not inconsistent with general law, or with special law approved by vote of the electors. The governing body of a county operating under a charter may enact county ordinances not inconsistent with general law. The charter shall provide which shall prevail in the event of conflict between county and municipal ordinances.

2. The language sought to be added to the county charter consisted of the following underscored provisions:

> Section 8.04 CONFLICT OF COUNTY ORDINANCES WITH MUNICIPAL ORDINANCES.
>
> Notwithstanding any other provisions of this Charter, any county ordinance in conflict with a municipal ordinance shall not be effective within the municipality to the extent of such conflict regardless of whether such municipal ordinance was adopted or enacted before or after the County ordinance, provided that the county ordinance shall prevail over municipal ordinances whenever the County shall set minimum standards protecting the environment by prohibiting or regulating air or water pollution, or the destruction of the resources of the County belonging to the general public within the parameters set forth in Section 8.17 of this Charter. As set forth in this Charter, a county ordinance shall also prevail over a municipal ordinance in the area of land use planning. *A County ordinance shall also prevail over a municipal ordinance in matters relating to Handgun Management within the parameters set forth in Section 8.19 of this Charter.* In the event a

The city unsuccessfully sought an injunction to stop the referendum. It argued that article VIII, section 4 of the Florida Constitution[3] required a city-wide as well as county-wide referendum. Section 4 requires dual referenda whenever there is a transfer of any function or power from one governmental entity to another. The district court agreed with the city, reversed the trial court, and certified the following question:

> WHETHER, IN A CHARTER COUNTY, A TRANSFER OF POWER OCCURS, THEREBY INVOKING THE PROVISIONS OF ARTICLE VIII, SECTION 4 OF THE CONSTITUTION OF THE STATE OF FLORIDA, WHERE, PURSUANT TO CHARTER AMENDMENT, A COUNTY ORDINANCE RELATING TO HANDGUN MANAGEMENT PREVAILS OVER A MUNICIPAL ORDINANCE RELATING TO THE SAME SUBJECT MATTER TO THE EXTENT OF ANY CONFLICT.

City of Fort Lauderdale v. Broward County, 458 So.2d 783, 786 (Fla. 4th DCA 1984). We answer the question in the negative and quash the decision below.

The problem arises because of the seemingly conflicting provisions of sections 1(g) and 4. If we construe "any function or power" in section 4 to give full effect to the all-encompassing adjective "any," then, assuming that virtually all ordinances constitute exercise of governmental power, all county preemptions pursuant to section 1(g) will be "transfers of power."

The circumstances of this case are the obverse of those in *Sarasota County v. Town of Longboat Key,* 355 So.2d 1197 (Fla.1978), wherein we rejected the county's attempt to completely preempt five essential municipal functions under section 1(g) without the dual referenda required by section 4. We held that section 1(g) did not exempt a charter county from application of section 4: "We are . . . reluctant to elevate the general provisions of Article VIII, Section 1(g) to a dominant position over the specific provisions of Article VIII, Section 4." *Id.* at 1201. In the case sub judice,

---

county ordinance and a municipal ordinance shall cover the same subject matter without conflict, both the municipal ordinance and the county ordinance shall be effective, each being deemed supplemental, one to the other.
Section 8.19 HANDGUN MANAGEMENT.
The County Commission may adopt a countywide ordinance relating to Handgun Management which may provide for law enforcement authorities to make criminal history checks for handgun purchasers prior to the delivery of a handgun not to exceed ten (10) days, exclusive of Saturdays, Sundays, and Holidays, and to provide standards for transfers of handguns and licensing of handgun dealers.
458 So.2d at 784, n. 3.
3. The section states:
Transfer of powers. — By law or by resolution of the governing bodies of each of the governments affected, any function or power of a county, municipality or special district may be transferred to or contracted to be performed by another county, municipality or special district, after approval by vote of the electors of the transferor and approval by vote of the electors of the transferee, or as otherwise provided by law.
Art. VIII, § 4, Fla. Const.

to construe section 4 as having the breadth seemingly dictated by the troublesome adjective "any" would eviscerate section 1(g) and elevate section 4 to a dominant position. This we must not do.

It is a fundamental rule of construction of our constitution that a construction of the constitution which renders superfluous, meaningless or inoperative any of its provisions should not be adopted by the courts. Where a constitutional provision will bear two constructions, one of which is consistent and the other which is inconsistent with another section of the constitution, the former must be adopted so that both provisions may stand and have effect. Construction of the constitution is favored which gives effect to every clause and every part thereof. Unless a different interest is clearly manifested, constitutional provisions are to be interpreted in reference to their relation to each other, that is in pari materia, since every provision was inserted with a definite purpose. *Burnsed v. Seaboard Coastline Railroad,* 290 So.2d 13, 16 (Fla.1974) (citations deleted).

Our task herein, then, must be to glean the intent of the framers and strike the balance necessary to give both provisions the effect intended.

Dean D'Alemberte's commentaries on the sections at issue offer an indication of intent. As to section 1(g):

> This entirely new subsection provides for the broadest extent of county self-government or "home rule" as it is commonly described. It was taken with only editorial changes from the Revision Commission recommendation.

> Under subsection (c) of this section [Art. VIII, §1], charter governments may be established, amended or repealed only by general or special act which is approved by a vote of the electors of the county at a special election called for that purpose.

> As a result of the provisions of subsections [sic] (f) of this section (non-charter government), the power which may be granted to county governments under a charter is the power to have county ordinances take precedence over municipal ordinances. Also, where the non-charter government may be empowered by the legislature to adopt ordinances as long as they are not inconsistent with general or special law, the charter counties may adopt ordinances as long as they are not inconsistent with general law.

Commentary to Art. VIII, §1, Fla.Const., 26A Fla.Stat.Ann. (West 1970). As to section 4:

> This section was taken from the Revision Commission recommendation. It is an entirely new section which gives to the legislature and to the various local governing units, special districts included, the authority to transfer powers. Such transfers under the 1885 Constitution, when not provided by the general power of the legislature over municipalities and counties, was accomplished by special constitutional amendment (*see* Article VIII, Section 10(a), Sections 12–21, and Article XX, Section 1). All of these specific provisions related to the assessment and collection of municipal taxes. In

1954, the 1885 Constitution was amended by a general provision (Article VIII, Section 22, House Joint Resolution 851, 1953, adopted in 1954) providing that the tax assessor and the county tax collector may by special or general act, with the approval of the electors of a municipality, be authorized to assess and collect municipal taxes.

Commentary to Art. VIII, § 4, Fla. Const., 26A Fla.Stat.Ann. (West 1970).

Section 1(g), as we conclude both from the commentary and an understanding of the constitutional scheme vis-a-vis charter counties, was intended to specifically give charter counties two powers unavailable to non-charter counties: the power to preempt conflicting municipal ordinances, and the power to avoid intervention of the legislature by special laws. The power to preempt is the power to exercise county power to the exclusion of municipal power. Preemption is a transfer of power, from exclusive municipal authority or concurrent authority, to exclusive county authority. It is clear from reading the transcripts of the Florida Constitution Revision Commission's discussion of preliminary versions of what would become section 1(g), that the preemption power was specifically included to eliminate the necessity of most if not all special laws when a charter county sought to preempt city ordinances in such areas as speed limits and other regulatory matters. Transcripts of Florida Constitution Revision Committee, Vol. 50 (1966) (available in Florida Supreme Court library). Section 4, on the other hand, was intended to provide for a more convenient procedure whereby local governments could transfer functions and powers without the cumbersome procedure of seeking a special law or constitutional amendment.

Thus, on the one hand the constitution has a provision intended to expand the power of charter counties, while on the other hand it includes a provision to expand the shared power of governmental units to transfer powers and functions. Both were intended to reduce the need for special laws and constitutional amendments. The conflict arises when the expansive power of a charter county collides with the requirements of section 4. But section 4 did not contemplate giving municipalities veto power over a charter county's preemptive power. Rather, section 4 contemplated situations where a law authorizes dual referenda or where the city and county mutually desire to shift a function or power of the type which required special law or constitutional amendment under the 1885 constitution.

A line must be drawn between these overlapping provisions. We hold that section 1(g) permits *regulatory* preemption by counties, while section 4 requires dual referenda to transfer functions or powers relating to *services*. A charter county may preempt a municipal regulatory power in such areas as handgun sales when countywide uniformity will best further the ends of government. § 125.86(7), Fla. Stat. (1983). Dual referenda are necessary when the preemption goes beyond regulation and intrudes upon a municipality's provision of services.

The case law on point reflects the underlying principle we now adopt. In *Sarasota County,* the county sought to preempt municipal control of air and water pollution control services and functions, parks and recreation, roads and bridges, planning and zoning, and police. The opinion includes the language from only one of the proposed charter amendments, relating to air and water pollution. It is clear from the language of that amendment that the county sought to consolidate all pollution control and enforcement under county authority. Presumably, the remaining amendments also sought to preempt broad control and enforcement powers. The wholesale assumption of the burden of providing what had been municipal services, going far beyond regulatory preemption, required dual referenda under section 4.

In *City of Palm Beach Gardens v. Barnes,* 390 So.2d 1188 (Fla.1980), the issue of preemption under section 1(g) was not raised. However, the question of whether dual referenda were required under section 4 was at issue. The city in that case contracted with the county sheriff to provide police services to the city. This Court held that contracting for services, without divesting ultimate authority to supervise and control, did not constitute a transfer of powers vis-a-vis section 4. Thus, provision of services may be transferred without section 4 implications if the ultimate responsibility for supervising those services is not transferred.

In *Miami Dolphins, Ltd. v. Metropolitan Dade County,* 394 So.2d 981 (Fla.1981), opponents to a tourist development tax plan challenged a provision that would allocate some of the funds raised by the county to renovation of the city-owned Orange Bowl stadium. This Court rejected the argument that the plan was an unconstitutional transfer of powers since jurisdiction over the stadium would not be transferred. Instead, the county merely planned to make funds available to the city for the renovation. Again, control over municipal services was not transferred.

In *City of Coconut Creek v. Broward County Board of County Commissioners,* 430 So.2d 959 (Fla. 4th DCA 1983), the district court approved a county ordinance permitting county veto of municipally approved plats. While section 4 was not an issue in the decision, the district court found support in section 1(g) and direct statutory authority for this narrow exercise of county regulatory preemption.

We believe the distinction between regulatory preemption, and transfer of functions and powers relating to services, achieves the balance between sections 1(g) and 4 intended by the framers of the 1968 constitution.

Accordingly, the decision of the district court is quashed. We remand for action consistent with this opinion.

It is so ordered.

BOYD, C.J., and ADKINS, OVERTON, McDONALD and SHAW, JJ., concur.

C. Municipal Corporations

Fla. Const. art. VIII, § 2

Municipalities. —

(a) ESTABLISHMENT. Municipalities may be established or abolished and their charters amended pursuant to general or special law. When any municipality is abolished, provision shall be made for the protection of its creditors.

(b) POWERS. Municipalities shall have governmental, corporate and proprietary powers to enable them to conduct municipal government, perform municipal functions and render municipal services, and may exercise any power for municipal purposes except as otherwise provided by law. Each municipal legislative body shall be elective.

(c) ANNEXATION. Municipal annexation of unincorporated territory, merger of municipalities, and exercise of extra-territorial powers by municipalities shall be as provided by general or special law.

1. In General

Municipalities are nothing more than creatures of the Legislature, and as such, they may be established or abolished at the will of the Legislature.[11] This plenary power that the Legislature has over municipalities is limited only by the Constitution.[12] The Legislature has, through general law, provided the procedures for the incorporation[13] and dissolution[14] of municipalities.

State ex rel. Lee v. City of Cape Coral

272 So. 2d 481 (Fla. 1973)

[Since this is a per curiam affirmance, it is Justice Ervin's opinion dissenting in part and concurring in part that must be read to find out what the majority opinion means.]

PER CURIAM:

Affirmed.

CARLTON, C. J., ROBERTS, McCAIN and DEKLE, JJ., and LEE, Circuit Judge, concur.

ERVIN, J., dissents in part and concurs in part with opinion.

BOYD, J., dissents in part and concurs in part and concurs with ERVIN, J.

ERVIN, Justice (dissenting in part, concurring in part).

In the 1960s, Gulf American Corporation developed a massive tract of closely knit subdivisions in a previously undeveloped area of Lee County. The development was known as Cape Coral. In 1970, the Legislature passed a Special Act, Ch. 70-623,

---

11. Fla. Const. art. VIII, § 2(a).
12. *Town of Palm Beach v. Vlahos*, 15 So. 2d 839 (Fla. 1943).
13. Fla. Stat. § 165.041 (2021).
14. Fla. Stat. § 165.051 (2021).

tentatively establishing and organizing the "City of Cape Coral." Actual implementation of the Act was dependent upon approval through referendum of the people residing within the proposed City limits. The referendum passed successfully.

Although the subdivision area comprised 30 square miles in area, the boundaries set up by Special Act encompassed an area of 100 square miles. The additional 70 square miles are very sparsely inhabited, and City services to this area are severely limited at the present time. Various people living in these outlying no-service areas petitioned the Lee County Circuit Court for a writ of Quo Warranto directed against the City, contesting the City's right to jurisdiction over them.

The trial court ultimately declared the act organizing and establishing the City of Cape Coral constitutional and concluded,

> "By virtue of the facts set forth above and the extensive viewing of the premises, which constituted 46 miles of riding in the area in question, the Court reaches the conclusion that the Defendant has established a need for the city and the benefits to be derived for most of the properties lying south of State Road 78 and Pondella Road. That the Defendant has established benefits to two of the Parcels here involved, though same may be delayed into the future a reasonable time. The rest of the lands the Court finds are too remote from the populated area and too remote from any city benefits.

> "The Court further finds that to order an ouster of some of the lands would create an hiatus, leaving certain acreage completely surrounded by other lands not ousted. The case of the City of Coral Gables, et al. v. State ex rel. Landis, Atty., et al. [122 Fla. 17], 164 So. 535 indicates that this problem should not affect the rights of the Plaintiffs herein where it is so obviously an infringement upon the property rights of an individual, and this Court finds that to allow these lands to remain in the corporate limits would amount to an unlawful taking of the property rights of certain Defendants, it is therefore,

> "ORDERED, ADJUDGED AND DECREED, that the property of the Plaintiffs Stuckey, Jackson, Morris, Nelson, Jeffcott and Maxwell, as described in Paragraph 5 C, D, E, F, G and H of Plaintiffs' Complaint are hereby ousted and declared not to be within the corporate limits of the City of Cape Coral, it is further,

> "ORDERED ADJUDGED AND DECREED that the Lee property described in Paragraph 5 A and B of Plaintiffs' Complaint is ordered included in the corporate limits of the City of Cape Coral; however, said City is ousted from the right and jurisdiction to tax said properties until such time as roads, sewer and water have been made available to said lands, which is hereby determined to mean road frontage on a completely graded road and the utilities mentioned within fifty feet of the closest property line."

I concur with the trial court's determination that the legislature's special act establishing the City of Cape Coral is constitutional. Article VIII, Section II(a) of the Florida Constitution (1968) grants to the Legislature of the State of Florida the power to establish and abolish municipalities by either special or general law. This authority is not unlimited but must be exercised within the framework of other provisions of the Constitution having to do with due process and equal protection. *See* State v. City of Avon Park, 108 Fla. 641, 149 So. 409 (1933); State ex rel. Davis v. Town of Lake Placid, 109 Fla. 419, 147 So. 468 (1933); State ex rel. Davis v. City of Stuart, 97 Fla. 69, 120 So. 335 (1929). I recognize the principles espoused in these aforecited cases but find also that these cases are inapposite to the situation at bar.

I feel we should reverse the judgment of the trial court in ousting any of the properties involved in this suit. Cape Coral, pursuant to the recognition accorded it by a legislative charter is accepted as a growing community with the potential to become an important residential area of some 275,000 lots in the development. More than 240,000 lots have been sold indicating sufficient interest to believe the municipality will grow in population. Florida is in a period of growth, not in the depression period of the 1930s. The trial court has misapplied the aforecited 1930 cases to the instant circumstances pertaining to Cape Coral.

Since most of the lands located within the City of Cape Coral are part of a comprehensive development program, all such lands should be included in one governmental operation.

In City of Fort Lauderdale v. Town of Hacienda Village, Inc., 172 So.2d 451, 452, this court opined:

> "Short of invading private property rights, the Legislature has plenary power to fix municipal boundaries and to establish municipal jurisdiction over any part of the State. It is for the Legislature to determine when and to what extent a particular area of the State shall be incorporated. There is no purely private right to have any particular area invested with the powers of municipal government. The ultimate decision in such matters is purely a legislative function which the people have granted to the State Legislature by the Constitution itself. Article VIII, Section 8, Florida Constitution, F.S.A. Incidentally, we are not here dealing with the possible impact of Article VIII, Section 11, Florida Constitution, which affects only Dade County.

> "In performing these functions the Legislature is empowered to fix boundaries to accommodate both the present needs and future growth of a municipality. The urbanization of the State is evidenced by the extensive development of metropolitan areas in the environs of large cities. This condition not only justifies but, in many instances, actually requires a long range legislative perspective in planning the orderly development of these metropolitan areas. Gillete v. Tampa, Fla., 57 So.2d 27."

The above principle enunciated in *Town of Hacienda*, supra, is particularly applicable to the instant case. The whole area of the City of Cape Coral is in the process of being developed and the need for long range planning for orderly development is a necessary ingredient.

At the present time the record indicates there is sufficient municipal need and potential to justify a municipal government for Cape Coral rather than to dump many of the residential planned subdivision lots on Lee County a non-charter county. The average annual local ad valorem city taxes seem minuscule — $8.00 per lot.

Although factually the case of Gillete v. City of Tampa, 57 So.2d 27 (Fla.1952) is dissimilar, therein this court did set out certain principles which I believe are properly applicable to the case sub judice. Therein this court quoted with approval the following language found in Henrico County v. City of Richmond, 177 Va. 754, 15 S.E.2d 309:

> "Moreover, it is no answer to an annexation proceeding to assert that individual residents of the county do not need or desire the governmental services rendered by the city. A county resident may be willing to take a chance on police, fire and health protection, and even tolerate the inadequacy of sewerage, water and garbage service. As long as he lives in an isolated situation his desire for lesser services and cheaper government may be acquiesced in with complacency, but when the movement of population has made him a part of a compact urban community, his individual preferences can no longer be permitted to prevail. It is not so much that he needs the city government, as it is that the area in which he lives needs it."

This important case needs careful examination because of its tremendous impact on other developing planned Florida cities — not a precipitous ouster washout. Advance planning to meet the area's potential urban needs, including transit, zoning, ecological, health, police, fire, sewage, water, garbage and other needs, is highly essential.

I make note of the fact that county charter governments are now sanctioned by the 1968 Constitution in order to meet metropolitan needs of community urbanization either existing or reasonably anticipated, even though outlying rural areas are embraced. I see little reason why the Legislature cannot now embrace for municipal purposes large areas of outlying lands in a developing community area similarly as if they were included in a county charter metro government. It appears to me ouster of outlying, remote lands which have a clear potential of community urbanization is no longer the appropriate remedy. Instead, temporary tax relief only should be granted where it is obvious there is no present correlation between municipal services and taxes assessed therefor.

The problems of population growth and urbanization cannot be solved by ignoring them — by nostalgically believing that Florida's developing areas are still frontiers and wildernesses impervious to residential settlement. County charters and municipal governments are accepted as modern methods of coping with local population growth and urbanization in Florida communities. We should not reject or emasculate them until it is clear beyond reasonable doubt that there is no present or potential need for their utilization. The record herein is devoid of any such conclusive showing.

BOYD, J., concurs.

Just as the Legislature has the power to create a municipality, it likewise has the power to abolish a municipality. In the case of *State ex rel. Gibbs v. Couch*,[15] the Florida Legislature demonstrated such power when it simultaneously abolished the existing municipality of the City of Daytona Beach and created in its place a new municipality covering the same territory, all by special act. The plenary power that the Legislature has over municipalities not only allowed it to abolish the municipality, but it also allowed it to abolish the then-existing municipal government consisting of various elected officials and authorized the Governor to appoint the members of the new City Commission. Florida Statutes § 165.051 provides the exclusive manner in which a municipality may be dissolved, i.e., by either a special act of the Legislature or by an ordinance of the governing body of the municipality, approved by vote of the qualified voters.

2. Municipal Home Rule Power

The home rule power of municipal corporations has had a checkered history that is accurately reflected in the following case. Under the 1885 Constitution, all municipal powers were dependent upon a specific delegation of authority by the Legislature in a general or special act.[16] Powers not granted a municipality by the Legislature were deemed to be reserved to the Legislature. This reservation of authority was known as "Dillon's Rule," named after famed American jurist John F. Dillon, who authored one of the earliest treatises on the subject of municipal corporations.[17] With the 1968 revision of the Florida Constitution, municipalities were granted broad home rule powers under art. VIII, § 2(b), and Dillon's Rule was effectively abolished. In 1973, the Florida Legislature enacted the Municipal Home Rule Powers Act to "secure for municipalities the broad exercise of home rule powers granted by the constitution."[18]

---

15. 190 So. 723 (Fla. 1939).
16. *City of Boca Raton v. State*, 595 So. 2d 25 (Fla. 1992).
17. *Id.*
18. Fla. Stat. § 166.021(4) (2021).

City of Boca Raton v. State

595 So. 2d 25 (Fla. 1992)

GRIMES, Justice.

This is an appeal from a final judgment which declined to validate special assessment improvement bonds proposed to be issued by the City of Boca Raton. We have jurisdiction under article V, section 3(b)(2) of the Florida Constitution, and chapter 75, Florida Statutes (1989).

In an effort to revitalize its downtown area, the City of Boca Raton (the City) determined to construct a wide range of specifically enumerated improvements in the infrastructure. The estimated cost of the improvements was $44,000,000. The City determined to obtain a portion of the money to pay the cost from the issuance of bonds in an amount not to exceed $21,000,000. The bonds were to be repaid from special assessments levied over a period of years against the downtown property to be benefitted by the improvements. The City's effort to validate the bonds was opposed by the State pursuant to chapter 75, Florida Statutes (1989), as well as by several property owners. At the trial, the issues devolved into (1) whether the City had the authority to levy special assessments to pay the bonds, and (2) even if such authority existed, whether this proposal met the legal requirements of a proper special assessment.

Following the presentation of testimony, the trial judge held that the City did not have the authority to impose special assessments to fund the bonds. In this respect, the final judgment stated in pertinent part:

> 12. Boca Raton lacks the power to specially assess without a specific grant of authority from the legislature. Article VII, Section 1(a) has preempted all forms of taxation other than ad valorem taxes to the State. Article VIII, Section 2(b) of the Florida Constitution does not supersede Article VII, Section 1(a) of said Constitution. Chapter 166 of the Florida Statutes does not supersede Article VII, Section 1(a) of the Florida Constitution. Only the State holds the power to impose assessments. By passing Chapter 166 the State did not grant specific statutory authority to municipalities to levy special assessments. Municipalities have only been able to pass such assessments when the State which holds this power has specifically authorized municipalities to pass special assessments. No such authorization exists in today's case.

* * *

In deciding whether the City has authority to impose special assessments to pay off the bonds, it is necessary to recount the history of municipal powers in Florida. Under the constitution of 1885, all municipal powers were dependent upon a specific delegation of authority by the legislature in a general or special act. Article VIII, section 8 of the 1885 constitution provided in pertinent part:

> The Legislature shall have power to establish, and to abolish, municipalities to provide for their government, to prescribe their jurisdiction and powers, and to alter or amend the same at any time.

Powers not granted a municipality by the legislature were deemed to be reserved to the legislature. This reservation of authority was known as "Dillon's Rule" as expressed in John F. Dillon, *The Law of Municipal Corporations* § 55 (1st ed. 1872). Under the 1885 constitution, the Florida courts consistently followed Dillon's Rule. *See, e.g., Williams v. Town of Dunnellon,* 125 Fla. 114, 169 So. 631 (1936); *Heriot v. City of Pensacola,* 108 Fla. 480, 146 So. 654 (1933); *Amos v. Mathews,* 99 Fla. 1, 126 So. 308 (1930); *Malone v. City of Quincy,* 66 Fla. 52, 62 So. 922 (1913).

As Florida's population began to boom after World War II, the legislature was flooded with local bills and population acts designed to permit municipalities to provide solutions to local problems. Thus, when our constitution was amended in 1968, municipalities were granted broad home rule powers under article VIII, section 2(b), which provides in pertinent part:

(b) POWERS. Municipalities shall have governmental, corporate and proprietary powers to enable them to conduct municipal government, perform municipal functions and render municipal services, and may exercise any power for municipal purposes except as otherwise provided by law.

Talbot D'Alemberte, the reporter for the Constitutional Revision Commission, described the difference between the above-quoted provisions of the 1968 and the 1885 constitutions as follows:

The apparent difference is that under the new language, all municipalities have governmental, corporate and proprietary powers unless provided otherwise by law, whereas under the 1885 Constitution, municipalities had only those powers expressly granted by law.

26A Fla.Stat.Ann. 292 (1970) (Commentary by Talbot "Sandy" D'Alemberte).

In the first litigated case involving the scope of municipal powers decided after the adoption of the 1968 constitution, this Court held that the City of Miami Beach had no power to enact a rent-control ordinance in the absence of a legislative enactment authorizing the exercise of such a power. *City of Miami Beach v. Fleetwood Hotel, Inc.,* 261 So.2d 801 (Fla.1972). Prompted by this decision, the legislature in 1973 enacted the Municipal Home Rule Powers Act,[1] now codified in chapter 166, Florida Statutes (1989). Thereafter, this Court upheld a subsequent rent-control ordinance enacted by the City of Miami Beach on the premise that section 166.021(1) now authorized municipalities to exercise any power for municipal purposes except when expressly prohibited by law. *City of Miami Beach v. Forte Towers, Inc.,* 305

---

1. Ch. 73-129, § 1, Laws of Fla.

Article VIII, Section 2, Florida Constitution, expressly grants to every municipality in this state authority to conduct municipal government, perform municipal functions, and render municipal services. The only limitation on that power is that it must be exercised for a valid "municipal purpose." It would follow that municipalities are not dependent upon the Legislature for further authorization. Legislative statutes are relevant only to determine limitations of authority.

So.2d 764 (Fla.1974). Thereafter, we acknowledged the vast breadth of municipal home rule power when we said:

> Article VIII, Section 2, Florida Constitution, expressly grants to every municipality in this state authority to conduct municipal government, perform municipal functions, and render municipal services. The only limitation on that power is that it must be exercised for a valid "municipal purpose." It would follow that municipalities are not dependent upon the Legislature for further authorization. Legislative statutes are relevant only to determine limitations of authority.

State v. City of Sunrise, 354 So.2d 1206, 1209 (Fla.1978).

Section 166.021 provides in pertinent part:

(1) As provided in s. 2(b), Art. VIII of the State Constitution, municipalities shall have the governmental, corporate, and proprietary powers to enable them to conduct municipal government, perform municipal functions, and render municipal services, and may exercise any power for municipal purposes, except when expressly prohibited by law.

(2) "Municipal purpose" means any activity or power which may be exercised by the state or its political subdivisions.

(3) The Legislature recognizes that pursuant to the grant of power set forth in s. 2(b), Art. VIII of the State Constitution, the legislative body of each municipality has the power to enact legislation concerning any subject matter upon which the state Legislature may act, except:

(a) The subjects of annexation, merger, and exercise of extraterritorial power, which require general or special law pursuant to s. 2(c), Art. VIII of the State Constitution;

(b) Any subject expressly prohibited by the constitution;

(c) Any subject expressly preempted to state or county government by the constitution or by general law; and

(d) Any subject preempted to a county pursuant to a county charter adopted under the authority of ss. 1(g), 3, and 6(e), Art. VIII of the State Constitution.

(4) The provisions of this section shall be so construed as to secure for municipalities the broad exercise of home rule powers granted by the constitution. It is the further intent of the Legislature to extend to municipalities the exercise of powers for municipal governmental, corporate, or proprietary purposes not expressly prohibited by the constitution, general or special law, or county charter and to remove any limitations, judicially imposed or otherwise, on the exercise of home rule powers other than those so expressly prohibited.

Thus, a municipality may now exercise any governmental, corporate, or proprietary power for a municipal purpose except when expressly prohibited by law, and a municipality may legislate on any subject matter on which the legislature may act, except those subjects described in paragraphs (a), (b), (c), and (d) of section 166.021(3). The provisions of section 166.021(3)(a) and (d) are irrelevant to the instant case. Therefore, it would appear that the City of Boca Raton can levy its special assessment unless it is expressly prohibited by law-section 166.021(1), expressly prohibited by the constitution-section 166.021(3)(b), or expressly preempted to the state or county government by the constitution or by general law-section 166.021(3)(c).

* * *

As their second argument, the State and the property owners contend that by virtue of the enactment of chapter 170, Florida Statutes (1989), which authorizes municipalities to impose special assessments upon certain conditions, the legislature has preempted the authority of municipalities to impose special assessments under any other circumstances. It is conceded that the City of Boca Raton did not follow the requirements of chapter 170 in its attempt to impose special assessments in this case. This argument cannot prevail because it is evident that chapter 170 is not the only method by which municipalities may levy a special assessment. Thus, section 170.19, Florida Statutes (1989), states that "[t]his chapter . . . shall be construed as an additional and alternative method for the financing of the improvements referred to herein." Further, section 170.21, Florida Statutes (1989), states that "[t]his chapter shall not repeal any other law relating to the subject matter hereof, but shall be deemed to provide a supplemental, additional, and alternative method of procedure for the benefit of all cities, towns, and municipal corporations of the state. . . ."[3]

This Court has recently construed a provision similar to sections 170.19 and 170.21 to find that counties had sufficient home rule power to issue bonds irrespective of the existence of a statute which authorized counties to issue bonds. In *Taylor v. Lee County,* 498 So.2d 424 (Fla.1986), the county sought to issue bonds to finance a new bridge pursuant to its home rule authority. Taylor argued that since chapter 159, Florida Statutes (1985), specifically authorized the county to issue bonds, the county ordinance must rely on and conform to that chapter. The Court noted that section 159.14, Florida Statutes, by its express terms, provided supplemental and additional authority to that conferred by other laws. The Court concluded that chapter 125, Florida Statutes (1985) (the county home rule statute) gave the county ample authority to issue the bonds and held that in areas in which a noncharter county has authority to act, it may choose between adopting an ordinance pursuant to its home rule power or adopting it pursuant to another statutory authority.

In addition, the premise that chapter 170 is not considered the exclusive means of making special assessments was reaffirmed last year when the legislature amended section 197.3631, Florida Statutes (1989), to read in part: "Section 197.3632 is additional authority for local governments to impose and collect non-ad valorem

---

3. The title assigned to chapter 170 also reflects this intent. The title reads "Supplemental and Alternative Method of Making Local Municipal Improvements."

assessments supplemental to the home rule powers pursuant to ss. 125.01 and 166.021 and chapter 170, or any other law." Ch. 90-343, §7, Laws of Fla.

We note that chapter 170 was enacted in 1923, fifty years before the Municipal Home Rule Powers Act. Therefore, no legislative intent that it would be the sole method of passing special assessments can be inferred from its presence. The fact that it was not one of the many statutes repealed by the Municipal Home Rule Powers Act does not evince a similar legislative intent in the absence of language indicating that it is intended to be exclusive. Thus, we hold that the City of Boca Raton had the authority to impose a special assessment under its home rule power.

* * *

It is so ordered.

OVERTON, BARKETT, KOGAN and HARDING, JJ., concur.

McDONALD, J., concurs in part and dissents in part with an opinion, in which SHAW, C.J., concurs.

McDONALD, Justice, concurring in part and dissenting in part.

SHAW, C.J., concurs.

[Concurring and dissenting opinions omitted.]

Basic Energy Corp. v. Hamilton County

652 So. 2d 1237 (Fla. 1st Dist. Ct. App. 1995)

PER CURIAM.

In these consolidated appeals from non-final orders pursuant to Florida Rule of Appellate Procedure 9.130(a)(3)(B) and 9.130(A)(3)(C)(ii), pertaining to the exercise of eminent domain powers by the city of Jasper, the parties raise the following issue: whether the city's authority to construct jails provides a basis for the exercise of its eminent domain power when the city intends to donate the property condemned to the State of Florida for the construction of a state prison facility.[1]

The city of Jasper and Hamilton County joined together to form a Prison task Force for the purpose of attracting additional prison industry to their area. Pursuant to that purpose, the city initiated eminent domain proceedings directed to appellant's property. It is clear from the record that the city intended to acquire the property and donate it to the state for construction of a state prison facility. At hearing, the Jasper city manager indicated the plan was to donate the property to the state, that a state facility was contemplated, and the city would not be involved in its operation or management. Asked if the facility contemplated was a city or county jail, he replied it would be a state correctional facility. He said the prison expansion

---

1. The temporary injunction allowed the city and county to conduct tests on the property, and those tests have already been carried out; thus as to the temporary injunction, this issue appears to be moot.

would provide 1100 additional prison beds and 300 jobs for local citizens, and add 20% to the city's utility revenues, and that the plan was consistent with the city's economic development strategy.

The trial court found the city was authorized to acquire the property in question "by eminent domain for the public purpose of jail or correctional purposes," that "construction of a jail, prison or correctional institution and the operation and maintenance of the same is a proper public purpose" for which the city could exercise its eminent domain power, and that "the property sought to be acquired by petitioner herein is necessary for the public purpose of constructing a jail."

On appeal, appellant contends the city's purpose in exercising its eminent domain power in this case is not a valid municipal purpose. Appellee relies on its authority to construct jails pursuant to section 180.06, Florida Statutes, as the valid municipal purpose to be served. However, since it is quite clear the city does not intend to build or operate a jail,[2] section 180.06 is not determinative. Further, the question is not whether a particular statute specifically permits the exercise of authority; rather, as the following excerpts demonstrate, the question is whether the exercise of authority is for a valid municipal purpose, and if so, whether there is any constitutional or statutory limitation on the exercise of that authority.

"Article VIII, section 2, Florida Constitution, expressly grants to every municipality the authority to conduct municipal government, perform municipal functions, and render municipal services. The only constitutional limitation placed on the municipalities' authority is that such powers be exercised for valid 'municipal purposes.'" *City of Ocala v. Nye*, 608 So.2d 15 (Fla.1992). Municipalities may exercise

---

2. Section 180.06 authorizes municipalities to construct and operate jails. The terms "jail" and "prison" have different legal significance. According to *Black's Law Dictionary* (6th ed. 1991), the definition of "jail" includes:

> A place of confinement that is more than a police station lockup and less than a prison. It is usually used to hold persons either convicted of misdemeanors . . . or persons awaiting trial or as a lockup for intoxicated and disorderly persons.

The definition of "prison" includes:

> A state or federal correctional institution for incarceration of felony offenders for terms of one year or more. The words "prison" and "penitentiary" are used synonymously to designate institutions for the imprisonment of persons convicted of the more serious crimes as distinguished from reformatories and county or city jails.

In addition, it is clear from the way the terms are used in the Florida Statutes that jails and prisons are not considered to be one and the same. For example, there are separate chapters in the Florida Statutes dealing with "Jails and Jailers" (chapter 950) and the "State Correctional System" (chapter 944). The state correctional system includes all prisons and state correctional institutions. Section 944.02(1), Florida Statutes (1993). "The words 'penitentiary,' 'state prison,' or 'state prison farm,' whenever the same are used in any of the laws of this state, as a place of confinement or punishment for a crime, shall be construed to mean and refer to the custody of the Department of Corrections within the state correctional system. . . ." Section 944.08, Florida Statutes (1993). The legislation concerning the sentencing guidelines distinguishes between state prison sentences and time spent in county jail. *See, e.g.*, section 921.161, Florida Statutes (1993). Section 922.051, Florida Statutes (1993) also recognizes the distinction between state prisons and county jails.

any power for valid municipal purposes unless expressly prohibited by law. *Id.*[3] Thus, "whenever a municipality exercises its powers, a two-tiered question is presented. First, was the action taken for a municipal purpose? If so, was that action *expressly* prohibited by the constitution, general or special law, or county charter." *City of Winter Park v. Montesi*, 448 So.2d 1242, 1244 (Fla. 5th DCA 1984), *review denied*, 456 So.2d 1182 (Fla.1984).

"A municipality exists in order to provide services to its inhabitants." *State v. City of Orlando*, 576 So.2d 1315 (Fla.1991). A valid municipal purpose must relate "to the conduct of municipal government, exercise of a municipal function, or provision of a municipal service." *See Ormond Beach v. County of Volusia*, 535 So.2d 302, 304 (Fla. 5th DCA 1988). Generally, a municipal purpose is one that is related to the health, morals, safety, protection or welfare of the municipality. *Id. See also, City of Winter Park v. Montesi*, 448 So.2d at 1244, *citing State v. City of Jacksonville*, 50 So.2d 532 (Fla.1951).

The purpose asserted by appellee and considered by the trial court involves the provision of state correctional facilities. The donation of land for the construction of a state prison may incidentally relate to the protection of municipal inhabitants; however, this purpose is no more particular to residents of the city of Jasper than to any other inhabitants of the state. Thus, we conclude no *municipal* purpose has been asserted. While we do not hold that no valid municipal purpose could exist for the exercise of eminent domain authority in this case, we conclude the purpose asserted by appellee does not support the exercise.[4]

REVERSED and REMANDED for further proceedings consistent with this opinion.

ERVIN, JOANOS and MINER, JJ., concur.

The broad view of "municipal purpose" appears, however, to have been set back and the apparently discredited *Fleetwood* case given new life in *State v. City of Orlando*, beginning at page 660 of this book.

---

3. Section 166.401, Florida Statutes, provides that municipalities may exercise the power of eminent domain "for the uses or purposes authorized pursuant to this part." Section 166.411(1), Florida Statutes, provides that municipalities may exercise the power of eminent domain for "good reason connected in anywise with the public welfare or the interests of the municipality and the people thereof." Since the use of eminent domain is "one of the most harsh proceedings known to the law, . . . when the sovereign delegates the power to a political unit or agency a strict construction will be given against the agency asserting the power." *Peavy-Wilson Lumber Co. v. Brevard County*, 159 Fla. 311, 31 So.2d 483, 485 (1947).

4. The record suggests an alternative municipal purpose might be one of economic development or economic welfare; however, that purpose was not asserted by appellee in this court or before the trial court, thus it has not been developed in the record or in the arguments before us.

3. Creation and Merger of Municipal Corporations and Annexation by Municipal Corporations

Sullivan v. Volusia County Canvassing Board

679 So. 2d 1206 (Fla. 5th Dist. Ct. App. 1996)

THOMPSON, Judge.

We affirm the final judgment holding valid the election process that created the City of Deltona and dissolved the Deltona Fire District and the Deltona Municipal Services District.

Donald M. Sullivan, Clarence Salyers, Bruce Crane, and Eugene Harralson, the plaintiffs below, contend that the election process was defective because of various alleged notice and ballot irregularities. We affirm because, while this appeal was pending, the legislature passed Senate Bill 532 which provides:

Senate Bill No. 532
A bill to be entitled

An act relating to Volusia County; declaring the referendum election held pursuant to chapter 95-498, Laws of Florida, establishing the City of Deltona to be legal and valid; providing an effective date.

Be it enacted by the Legislature of the State of Florida:

Section 1. Notwithstanding any provision of general or special law to the contrary, the referendum election held in Volusia County on September 5, 1995, to establish the city of Deltona as authorized by chapter 95-498, Laws of Florida, and all acts and proceedings held in connection with said referendum, are hereby declared legal and valid.

Section 2. This act shall take effect upon becoming a law.

The legislature has the power to create and dissolve municipalities. *See* Art. VIII, § 2, Fla. Const. And, what the legislature could have authorized, it can ratify. *Charlotte Harbor & N. Ry. Co. v. Welles*, 260 U.S. 8, 11, 43 S.Ct. 3, 4, 67 L.Ed. 100 (1922). In other words:

If the thing wanting, or which failed to be done, and which constitutes the defects in the proceeding, is something the necessity for which the legislature might have dispensed with by prior statute, then it is not beyond the power of the legislature to dispense with it by subsequent statute. And if the irregularity consists in doing some act, or in the mode or manner of doing some act, which the legislature might have made immaterial by prior law, it is equally competent to make the same immaterial by subsequent law.

Middleton v. City of St. Augustine, 42 Fla. 287, 29 So. 421, 431 (Fla.1900) (quoting Judge Cooley, Constitutional Limitations). *See also, State v. Haines City*, 137 Fla. 616, 188 So. 831 (Fla.1939); *County of Orange v. Webster*, 546 So.2d 1033 (Fla.1989); *County of Palm Beach v. State*, 342 So.2d 56 (Fla.1976); *Givens v. Hillsborough County*, 46 Fla.

502, 35 So. 88 (Fla.1903). After-the-fact validating legislation is perfectly proper to cure procedural defects. *County of Palm Beach*, 342 So.2d at 58.

Further, the special act incorporating the city subject to a referendum was sufficient to place interested voters on inquiry notice. *See State ex rel. Watson v. City of Miami*, 153 Fla. 653, 15 So.2d 481 (Fla.1943); *North Ridge General Hospital, Inc. v. City of Oakland Park*, 374 So.2d 461 (Fla.1979), *appeal dismissed*, 444 U.S. 1062, 100 S.Ct. 1001, 62 L.Ed.2d 744 (1980).

Finally, the curative act is limited to the proceedings in connection with the City of Deltona referendum election and therefore does not suffer the defects found in the acts described in *Certain Lots Upon Which Taxes Are Delinquent v. Town of Monticello*, 159 Fla. 134, 31 So.2d 905 (Fla.1947).

AFFIRMED.

W. SHARP and GRIFFIN, JJ., concur.

a. ". . . *Merger of municipalities, and exercise of extra-territorial powers by municipalities shall be as provided by general or special law." Fla. Const. art. VIII, § 2(c)*

City of Long Beach Resort v. Collins

261 So. 2d 498 (Fla. 1972)

PER CURIAM.

This is a direct appeal from the 14th Judicial Circuit Court which inherently passed upon the constitutionality of a state statute by its order of dismissal for failure to state a cause of action; we accordingly have jurisdiction under Fla. Const. art. V, § 4, F.S.A. and Evans v. Carroll, 104 So.2d 375 (Fla.1958); Harrell's Candy Kitchen, Inc. v. Sarasota-Manatee Airport Authority, 111 So.2d 439 (Fla. 1959); and Milliken v. State, 131 So.2d 889 (Fla.1961).

The statute in question is House Bill No. 5288, which was passed by the Legislature in 1970. It provides for merging the several cities along the western Gulf resort area of Panama City, Florida. (Petitioner suggests that the real attempt is at "consolidation" rather than at "merger," citing Fla.Const. art. VIII, § 3 (1968).) Among the grounds recited for unconstitutionality of the act are that it constitutes:

(a) A denial of equal protection under the Federal and State Constitutions in not allowing residents within these municipalities to vote on the proposed merger or consolidation, whereas the residents of the surrounding unincorporated areas were permitted to vote on the issue (it passed by such vote of only the unincorporated area residents).

(b) A deprivation of property rights without due process under both constitutions.

(c) Denial of franchise or referendum to the residents in the city.

402 5 · LOCAL GOVERNMENT

(d) An unconstitutional delegation of power to the new municipality sought to be created.

(e) It constitutes class legislation favoring the residents of unincorporated areas over those dwelling within the city limits.

Intervenor-petitioner City of Long Beach Resort, Florida, a municipality, urges additionally that:

(a) Intervenor City which holds a franchise for the sale and distribution of water within its city and also to existing Panama City Beach, has issued water revenue bonds which have an outstanding balance plus accrued interest; and that to abolish Intervenor City and said City of Panama City Beach would jeopardize said bonds and properties in that no provision is made by the new act for the protection of the bond holders.

(b) Intervenor would be deprived of its property without due process of law contrary to the U. S. and Florida Constitutions.

(c) That the act's provision for payment of debts from revenues collected ONLY within respective former municipalities would deny intervenor city-water supplier that portion of its income from water distribution into Panama City Beach and thus lose income therefrom to pay said bonds.

Petitioners brought proceedings both in quo warranto and for declaratory decree as to said House Bill No. 5288. The entire complaints in both causes were dismissed by the trial judge.

During appellate proceedings there has been a tender as reflected by motions filed before this Court to pay the Long Beach Resort bonds in full with interest pursuant to a call of said bonds by the City of Panama City Beach, in accordance with their terms. The tender has been refused on the ground that "information regarding the source of funds used to make the tender of payment of bonds" has not been furnished and that appellees "refuse to allow a certified public accountant employed by appellant access to the books and records of the City of Panama City Beach pertaining to the Long Beach Resort Water System, thereby preventing evaluation that the tender of funds for payment of the bonds was made from 'net revenues derived from the operation of the water system of the City of Long Beach Resort,' as required by bond provisions."

Such a call of the bonds and tender, supported by affidavit before this court, render moot the above additional questions raised by intervenor. Accordingly, the motion to dismiss intervenor's appeal is granted and is remanded to the trial court for disposition as may be indicated solely on the two objections raised regarding, (1) the providing of information as to the source of funds for tender of payment, and (2) access to the records of the old City of Panama City Beach, so as to afford evaluation, if necessary, that the tender meets requirements of the bond issue.

We revert now to the basic question here regarding the constitutionality of House Bill No. 5288, particularly in regard to the denial of the vote to city residents while granting it to adjoining unincorporated area residents in voting on the consolidation of the several municipalities along the famous "Miracle Strip" and its adjoining areas West of the resort City of Panama City, Florida.

The Legislature, by various special acts, created the Town of Edgewater Gulf Beach (1953), the City of West Panama City Beach (1967), the City of Long Beach Resort (1953) and the City of Panama City Beach (1953), all located along the glittering white sand beaches west of Panama City, Florida. Then, in 1970, the Legislature passed a sequence of bills which would have the effect of consolidating the four municipalities, together with five adjoining unincorporated areas, into a single governmental entity.

The first five of these special acts[1] designated unincorporated areas contiguous to the several existing municipalities and granted the residents of each of these unincorporated areas the right of referendum to determine whether or not they would be joined with the consolidated, new City of Panama City Beach created by the final one of this series of Acts, House Bill 5288 (Ch. 70-874). None of the residents and citizens of the former municipalities was granted the right of referendum on the issue of consolidation ("merger"). (It is into the corporate entity of existing City of *West* Panama City Beach that all are to be "merged." That city is then to become a new City of Panama City Beach.)

This was the prerogative of the Legislature which has life and death powers over municipalities which are created, modified and can be abolished by the Legislature. Saunders v. City of Jacksonville, 157 Fla. 240, 25 So.2d 648 (Fla.1946); State ex rel. Landis v. Town of Lake Placid, 117 Fla. 874, 158 So. 497 (1935); State v. Town of Boynton Beach, 140 Fla. 327, 156 So. 539 (1934); Smith v. Treadwell, 161 So.2d 49 (1st DCA Fla. 1964).

There is no doubt of the Legislature's power to annex territory to an existing municipality. MacGuyer v. City of Tampa, 89 Fla. 138, 103 So. 418 (1925).

Town of San Mateo City v. State, 117 Fla. 546, 158 So. 112 (1935), upheld a statute which submitted a referendum vote to freeholders only. The Legislature may make its acts effective upon the happening of a contingency, which includes the approval of the affected citizens or a class of the affected citizens. *San Mateo, supra,* and State ex rel. Cheyney v. Sammons, 62 Fla. 303, 57 So. 196 (1911).

No constitutional infirmity having been demonstrated, the trial court's orders dismissing the amended petitions, and the final judgments entered for appellees, are accordingly

Affirmed.

The cause is remanded as set forth earlier in this opinion, however, solely on Intervenor's challenge on the bonds, for disposition by the trial court on (1) the providing

---

1. House Bills 5283 through 5287, all to become law on June 17, 1970 (as was the contested House Bill 5288); also known as Chapters 70,869 through 70,874, Laws of Florida.

of information to Intervenor by appellees as to the source of funds for tender of payment and (2) access to records of the original City of Panama City Beach to afford evaluation that the tender of payment of the bonds meets bond issue requirements.

It is so ordered.

ROBERT, C. J., ERVIN, CARLTON, ADKINS and BOYD, JJ., and SPECTOR, Circuit Judge, concur.

DEKLE, J., dissents with Opinion.

[The dissenting opinion of Justice Dekle is omitted.]

Annexation is the process of bringing contiguous unincorporated land into the corporal limits of a municipality. There are three ways in which annexation is accomplished: (1) by general law;[19] (2) by special law; or (3) voluntarily. In a voluntary annexation, the owners of the unincorporated land file a petition for the municipality to annex their contiguous land into the corporal limits of the municipality. Depending upon the type of annexation, referendum may or may not be required.

(1) Annexation Under the Provisions of General Law

SCA Services of Florida, Inc. v. City of Tallahassee

418 So. 2d 1148 (Fla. 1st Dist. Ct. App. 1982)

ERVIN, Judge.

After the Florida Attorney General refused appellant SCA Services of Florida's request to bring an action in quo warranto challenging various municipal annexations,[1] the appellant brought this action seeking invalidation of the annexation ordinances. The lower court dismissed the appellant's petition for writ of quo warranto with prejudice, relying on this court's opinion in a challenge to a different annexation attempt in *SCA Services of Florida, Inc. v. City of Tallahassee*, 393 So.2d 35 (Fla. 1st DCA 1981), *rev. denied*, 402 So.2d 612 (Fla. 1981). We affirm the lower court's determination but for a different reason.

Annexation is a power reposing exclusively in the legislature. The vehicle utilized by the legislature to accomplish a municipal annexation is by special act. However, the legislature has determined to share the power to annex with municipal corporations by enacting Chapter 171, Florida Statutes, the "Municipal Annexation or Contraction Act." *North Ridge General Hospital, Inc. v. City of Oakland Park*, 374 So.2d 461, 464 (Fla. 1979), *appeal dismissed*, 444 U.S. 1062, 100 S.Ct. 1001, 62 L.Ed.2d 744

---

19. See the Municipal Annexation or Contraction Act, which can be found in Chapter 171 of the Florida Statutes.

1. The City of Tallahassee enacted ordinances annexing the Tallahassee and Governor's Square Malls and the Goosepond area of Leon County.

(1980). That act provides that annexation by a municipality is accomplished by passage of a municipal ordinance utilizing the procedures set forth in Chapter 171.

Because the challenged annexations at bar were accomplished by several ordinances, any assault upon those ordinances focuses upon Chapter 171. By its own terms, "The purposes of this act [Chapter 171] are to set forth procedures for adjusting the boundaries of municipalities . . . and to set forth criteria for determining when annexations . . . may take place. . . ." § 171.021, Fla. Stat. (Supp. 1974). Reading the purposes of the act *in pari materia* with the legislative mandate in Section 171.022,[2] preempting all other means by which a municipality may accomplish an annexation on its own, it is apparent that the legislature intended to provide a clearly defined and exclusive method by which an annexation could be accomplished.

The legislature has also set forth in Section 171.081[3] the method by which judicial review of any annexation by ordinance may be sought. Again, reading Section 171.081 *in pari materia* with the foregoing sections on preemption and the purposes of the act, it is apparent that the legislature has manifested its intent that there be a sole and exclusive procedure for challenging a municipal government's failure to comply with Chapter 171, Florida Statutes.[4] This procedure requires that the complainant:

---

2. Section 171.022, Florida Statutes, states:

Preemption; effect on special laws. —

(1) It is further the purpose of this act to provide viable and usable general law standards and procedures for adjusting the boundaries of municipalities in this state.

(2) The provisions of any special act or municipal charter relating to the adjusting of municipal boundaries in effect on October 1, 1974, are repealed except as otherwise provided herein.

3. Section 171.081, Florida Statutes, states:

Appeal on annexation or contraction. —

No later than 30 days following the passage of any annexation or contraction ordinance, any party affected who believes that he will suffer material injury by reason of the failure of the municipal governing body to comply with the procedures set forth in this chapter for annexation or contraction or to meet the requirements established for annexation or contraction as they apply to his property may file a petition in the circuit court for the county in which the municipality or municipalities are located seeking review by certiorari. In any action instituted pursuant to this section, the complainant, should he prevail, shall be entitled to reasonable costs and attorney's fees.

4. Appellant has relied on *Orange County v. City of Orlando*, 327 So.2d 7 (Fla. 1976) for its authority to seek review by a means other than as provided for in Chapter 171. In that case the Florida Supreme Court stated that upon the Attorney General's refusal to challenge a municipal annexation by means of quo warranto, a party could seek relief by injunctive and declaratory relief. *Id.* at 8. We find that case inapplicable for two reasons: First, the case involved a challenge to three annexation ordinances passed pursuant to the requirements of a special act. *See City of Orlando v. Orange County*, 309 So.2d 16 at 16 (Fla. 4th DCA 1975). Second, the facts suggest that the case involved annexations occurring prior to the October 1, 1974 effective date of the "Municipal Annexation or Contraction Act." Chapter 171, Florida Statutes. *See* Ch. 74-190, § 3, Laws of Fla. Although we now hold that Chapter 171 provides the exclusive means by which citizens may attack a municipal annexation accomplished by ordinance, it is unclear whether the legislature also sought to preempt the Attorney General's right to proceed in quo warranto to challenge an annexation by ordinance. Because that question is not before us, we decline to address it.

(1) be a "party affected"; (2) allege "that he will suffer material injury by reason of the failure of the municipal governing body to comply with the procedures set forth in" Chapter 171 "or to meet the requirements established for annexation . . . as they apply to his property"; (3) file his complaint seeking judicial review within thirty days following passage of the annexation ordinance, and (4) seek review by certiorari in circuit court.

SCA asserted that its constitutional right of access to courts is barred since it is not a "party affected." Art. I, § 21, Fla. Const. Section 171.031(5), Florida Statutes, defines "parties affected" as "any . . . firms owning property in, or residing in, either a municipality proposing annexation . . . *or owning property that is proposed for annexation. . . .*" (e.s.) SCA has alleged that it has the exclusive franchise for hauling garbage in the unincorporated area of Leon County. Certainly, an exclusive franchise right is a property right, *see* 36 Am. Jur. 2d *Franchises* § 5 (1968), and this right exists in the unincorporated area. Thus, appellant is a "party affected" and meets the first criterion under section 171.081.

The appellant has alleged and argued that certain prerequisites for annexation under Chapter 171 were not satisfied by the City, including the failure to plan for garbage services in the areas to be annexed, and that its exclusive franchise rights may be harmed by the annexation. This satisfies the second criterion, but appellant's efforts falter as to the third and fourth requirements of Section 171.081. Appellant sought a writ of quo warranto but should have sought certiorari. More significant is the fact that appellant filed this action more than thirty days after passage of the annexation ordinances.

Thus, appellant's action, having been untimely filed, was properly dismissed.

AFFIRMED.

McCORD and BOOTH, JJ., concur.

(2) Annexation by Special Law

North Ridge General Hospital, Inc. v.
City of Oakland Park

374 So. 2d 461 (Fla. 1979)

SUNDBERG, Justice.

[The part of this opinion dealing with legislative title and notice requirements of article III is reproduced in Chapter 3 of this book.]

Appellants' contention that chapter 75-452 denies them equal protection of the law is equally without merit. The power to annex an unincorporated area to a municipality reposes in the legislature.[4] The legislature has chosen to share this power with municipal corporations[5] and chapter 171, Florida Statutes (1975), delineates the procedures to be followed when annexation is effected at the municipal level rather than in the legislative forum. When a municipality initiates annexation, subsections (1) and (2) of section 171.0413 provide for a referendum to enable the electors of the annexing municipality and of the area proposed to be annexed to vote on the annexation issue. Further, section 171.081 provides for limited judicial review of the annexation process. In contrast, chapter 75-452, the vehicle employed by the legislature to annex appellants' property, fails to provide either of these procedures. Thus, the right to a referendum and judicial review is predicated upon whether the municipality initiates annexation pursuant to the statutory authority of chapter 171 or whether the legislature chooses to effect the annexation by special act. Although appellants concede that the legislature possesses the power to enact both general and special laws concerning municipal annexation, they posit that this latter power has been exercised so as to deny equal protection to those whose property is annexed by special act. For the following reason we find that chapter 75-452, Laws of Florida, withstands constitutional scrutiny.

The legislature has wide discretion in creating statutory classifications. There is a presumption in favor of the validity of a statute which treats some persons or things differently from others.

> [If] any state of facts can reasonably be conceived that will sustain the classification attempted by the Legislature, the existence of that state of facts at the time the law was enacted will be presumed by the courts. The deference due to the legislative judgment in the matter will be observed in all cases where the court cannot say on its judicial knowledge that the Legislature could not have had any reasonable ground for believing that there were public considerations justifying the particular classification and distinction made.

---

4. Art. VIII, § 2(c), Fla.Const.; *City of Long Beach Resort v. Collins*, 261 So.2d 498 (Fla. 1972); *City of Auburndale v. Adams Packing Ass'n*, 171 So.2d 161 (Fla.1965); *MacGuyer v. City of Tampa*, 89 Fla. 138, 103 So. 418 (1925).

5. *Smith v. Ayers*, 174 So.2d 727 (Fla.1965); *City of Sebring v. Harder Hall, Inc.*, 150 Fla. 824, 9 So.2d 350 (1942); *Klich v. Miami Land & Dev. Co.*, 139 Fla. 794, 191 So. 41 (1939).

Lewis v. Mathis, 345 So.2d 1066, 1068 (Fla. 1977); *accord, Yoo Kun Wha v. Kelly*, 154 So.2d 161 (Fla.1963); *Anderson v. Board of Public Instruction for Hillsborough County*, 102 Fla. 695, 136 So. 334 (1931). Further, one who assails the classification has the burden of showing that it is arbitrary and unreasonable. *State v. City of Miami Beach*, 234 So.2d 103 (Fla.1970); *Shelton v. Reeder*, 121 So.2d 145 (Fla.1960); *State ex rel. Bennett v. Lee*, 123 Fla. 252, 166 So. 565 (1936).

It is well-settled that the legislature is entitled to annex an area with or without an affirmative vote of the affected property owners.[6] As noted by appellants, however, subsections (1) and (2) of section 171.0413 require a referendum when annexation is initiated by the municipality. The reasoning behind this distinction is readily apparent. The legislators are the elected representatives of those residing within the annexing municipality as well as of the residents of the area proposed to be annexed. Consequently, these officials are obliged to consider the interest of both sets of constituents in debating the annexation issue. When a municipality seeks to annex a neighboring area, however, there is a danger that the interests of those persons in the area proposed to be annexed will not be fully aired, because the elected officials of the municipality are not also the elected representatives of the neighboring area. In order to ensure proper representation of the interests of all persons to be affected by the municipally-initiated annexation, chapter 171 provides for a referendum on the annexation question and other procedural safeguards.

An examination of section 171.044, Florida Statutes (1975) demonstrates the legislative intent underlying the method of annexation employed in the case before us. Under section 171.044, property owners may *voluntarily* petition a municipality for annexation. A referendum is not required in order to complete annexation pursuant to this provision. The legislature apparently concluded that when the property owners themselves seek annexation, a referendum is unnecessary to protect their interests; these persons would not voluntarily petition for annexation had they not concluded that it would be to their benefit. It is evident that similar reasoning underlies the absence of a referendum when members of the legislature effect annexation by special act. Hence, we conclude that this is a reasonable basis for the differing procedural requirements governing municipally-initiated annexation and annexation by the legislature pursuant to special act. Accordingly, the order of the Circuit Court for Broward County upholding chapter 75-452, Laws of Florida, is affirmed.

It is so ordered.

ENGLAND, C. J., and ADKINS, BOYD, OVERTON, HATCHETT and ALDERMAN, JJ., concur.

---

6. *State ex rel. Davis v. City of Clearwater*, 106 Fla. 761, 139 So. 377 (1932); *State v. City of Miami*, 103 Fla. 54, 137 So. 261 (1930); *Nabb v. Andreu*, 89 Fla. 414, 104 So. 591 (1925).

5 · LOCAL GOVERNMENT

(3) Voluntary Annexation

City of Center Hill v. McBryde et al.

952 So. 2d 599 (Fla. 5th Dist. Ct. App. 2007)

ORFINGER, J.

Petitioners, City of Center Hill ("City") and Sumter Cement Company, LLC ("SCC"), seek certiorari review of an order of the circuit court, sitting in its appellate capacity, which quashed an ordinance passed by the City annexing a parcel of SCC's real property into the City. [Footnote omitted.] For the reasons explained hereafter, we deny the petition.

SCC owns 1,235 acres of land in unincorporated Sumter County. SCC petitioned the City to annex the property and to rezone it to permit the operation of a cement plant and lime rock quarry. Not surprisingly, Clyde McBryde and William Sander, the owners of nearby properties in unincorporated Sumter County, were not enthusiastic about SCC's proposal and actively opposed it, citing noise, pollution and traffic concerns. Nonetheless, the City, after proper notice and a public hearing, approved the annexation ordinance and the rezoning request.

McBryde and Sander, unhappy with the City's decision, sought certiorari review in the circuit court, arguing that the annexed property was not reasonably compact as required by statute, as it created a 100-acre "pocket" of unincorporated territory ("the parcel") surrounded by hundreds of acres of municipal property. In response, the City and SCC argued that the annexed property was reasonably compact, as required by section 171.044, Florida Statutes (2005). After due consideration, the trial court granted certiorari and quashed the annexation ordinance, finding:

> 4. . . . [I]t is clear from the proposed annexation map that the annexation results in creation of an impermissible pocket of unincorporated property surrounded by hundreds of acres of municipal property. Whether "small" or "big," the City's voluntary annexation departs from the essential requirements of law because the annexed property creates a pocket. Furthermore, the [City's and SCC's] argument that the annexation does not create a pocket is not supported by competent substantial evidence because [their] own expert did not know what a pocket was for the purposes of annexation.

The City and SCC seek certiorari review of this determination.

* * *

Property annexed by municipalities must be contiguous, reasonably compact, and not create enclaves. *See City of Sunrise v. Broward County,* 473 So.2d 1387, 1389 (Fla. 4th DCA 1985). Specifically, section 171.044(1), Florida Statutes (2005), provides that "[t]he owner or owners of real property in an unincorporated area of a county which is contiguous to a municipality and reasonably compact may petition the governing body of said municipality that said property be annexed to the municipality." "Any annexation proceeding in any county in the state shall be designed in such a manner as to ensure that the area will be reasonably compact." § 171.031(12), Fla. Stat. (2005). "Compactness" means the "concentration of a piece of property in a single area and precludes any action which would create enclaves, pockets, or finger areas in serpentine patterns."[2] *Id.* However, section 171.013 does not define the terms "pockets" or "finger areas in serpentine patterns." Instead, the only definition of the term "pockets," in the context of annexation compactness, was provided by this Court in *City of Sanford v. Seminole County,* 538 So.2d 113 (Fla. 5th DCA 1989). In that case, the circuit court determined that an annexation was impermissible because the proposed annexation "tend[ed] to create pockets of unincorporated property. . . ." *Id.* at 114. On review, this Court recognized that the annexation statute did not define the term "pockets." Using the rules of statutory construction, this Court concluded that a pocket is "a small isolated area or group." *Id.* at 115.

The City and SCC argue that the circuit court "vetoed" the City's annexation ordinance based on an erroneous interpretation of the term "pockets." They contend that the circuit court failed to follow the definition of the term adopted in *City of Sanford,* the single case defining that term. Specifically, the City and SCC argue that the circuit court applied a strained interpretation of the term "pockets" to the parcel, a 100-acre parcel that is neither "small" nor "isolated."

In its order, the circuit court, while acknowledging the *City of Sanford* decision, determined that whether "big" or "small," the City's proposed annexation of SCC's property improperly created a pocket. The City and SCC argue that the circuit court misapplied the law in reaching this conclusion. They contend that because the parcel, totaling almost one hundred acres, is "big," it is not, by definition, a pocket as defined in *City of Sanford,* which must be "small" and "isolated." We disagree.

The issue of whether a parcel of property is "small" and "isolated" is relative to, and necessarily dependent upon, the size and configuration of the parcel and the surrounding municipal property. Size, be it small or large, is a relative term that can only be determined in relation to something else. Although we said in *City*

---

2. In *City of Sunrise v. Broward County,* 473 So.2d 1387, 1388 (Fla. 4th DCA 1985), the court explained the purpose of the compactness requirement:

> In order to understand the concepts of compactness and the prohibition against the creation of enclaves in the context of annexation proceedings, it is helpful to consider the general purpose and goals of a municipal corporation as described by the attorney general in his opinion at 077-18, quoting from 56 Am.Jur.2d *Municipal Corporations, Etc.* § 69:
>
> > The legal as well as the popular idea of a municipal corporation in this country, both by name and use, is that of oneness, community, locality, vicinity; a collective body, not several bodies, a collective body of inhabitants — that is, a body of people collected or gathered together *in one mass, not separated into distinct masses,* and having a community of interest because residents of the same place, not different places. So, as to territorial extent, the idea of a city is one of *unity, not of plurality;* of compactness or contiguity, not separation or segregation.
>
> 1977 Op. Att'y. Gen. Fla. 077-18, (February 18, 1977) at p. 38.

(Emphasis in original.)

of Sanford that a pocket is "a small isolated area or group," we did so recognizing that whether a parcel is small and isolated must be determined in relationship to the overall scope and configuration of the parcel in question and the surrounding municipal property. The statutory requirement that pockets not be created by annexations was intended to insure that no vestiges of unincorporated property be left "in a sea of incorporated property." Alison Yurko, *A Practical Perspective About Annexation in Florida-Making Sense of Florida Statutes Chapters 164 and 171 in 2003 and Beyond,* 32 Stetson L.Rev. 517, 533 (2003). Given the configuration of the City, SCC's property, and the parcel, that is precisely what would occur here.[3]

Should the annexation proceed, an impermissible pocket, albeit one of approximately one hundred acres, would be created. Given the scope of the overall annexation and the configuration of the properties, the parcel is, relatively speaking, small and isolated.[4] Although in absolute terms the 100-acre parcel is not insignificant, relative to the 1,235 acre annexation, a pocket is created.[5] We conclude that the circuit court's order properly applied the statutory requirement that annexations be compact.

CERTIORARI DENIED.

D. Special Districts

Special Districts are units of local government that are created by general law, special act, local ordinance, or by rule of the Governor and Cabinet to perform specialized governmental functions and services,[20] such as fire control, hospitals, and water management districts. Special Districts are a legitimate alternative method available for use by the private and public sectors, as authorized by state law, to manage, own, operate, construct, and finance basic capital infrastructure and facilities. They also are used to provide specialized services.[21] There are two main types of

---

3. McBryde and Sander aptly describe the unincorporated parcel as looking like a balloon on a string, should the annexation proceed.

4. "It isn't the size that counts so much as the way things are arranged." E.M. Forster, *Howard's End* 88 (Barnes & Noble Classics ed., New York 1993) (1910).

5. We find no merit in the remaining issue argued by the City and SCC.

20. Fla. Stat. §189.403(1). The term "special district" does not include a school district, a community college district, a special improvement district created pursuant to Fla. Stat. §285.17, a municipal service taxing or benefit unit as specified in Fla. Stat. §125.01, or a board which provides electrical service and which is a political subdivision of a municipality or is part of a municipality.

21. Fla. Stat. §189.402.

Special Districts: Dependent[22] and Independent[23] Special Districts. Generally, Special Districts do not have inherent home rule power, having instead only those powers that are expressly conferred upon them by the Legislature (in their charter) or that are necessary by implication to carry out their object and purpose under the laws in which they operate. The following case is illustrative of the above principles.

Halifax Hospital Medical Center v. State

278 So. 3d 545 (Fla. 2019)

Halifax Hospital Medical Center, a special tax district, appeals a circuit court judgment denying validation of revenue bonds. We have jurisdiction, *see* art. V, § 3(b)(2), Fla. Const., and affirm, holding that Halifax is not authorized to carry out the project for which it sought to issue the bonds.

Background

Halifax was created by a special act of the Legislature in 1925. Ch. 11272, Laws of Fla. (1925); ch. 79-577, § 2, Laws of Fla. Since that time, Halifax's enabling act has undergone many revisions and amendments. Ch. 79-577, 79-578, 84-539, 89-409, 91-352, 2003-374, Laws of Fla. Halifax's current enabling act is chapter 2003-374, Laws of Florida, and section 3 of this act constitutes Halifax's charter. Halifax's charter provides geographic boundaries for Halifax within Volusia County, grants Halifax certain authority to "establish, construct, operate, and maintain . . . hospitals, medical facilities, and other health care facilities and services," and authorizes Halifax to issue bonds "for the purposes set forth in this act." Ch. 2003-374, § 3(1), (5), (8).

In the proceedings below, Halifax sought validation of bonds that it intended to issue for the purpose of financing the construction of a hospital outside the geographic boundaries established in the special act. The proposed hospital would have been located in Deltona, Florida, and operated by Halifax with the expectation that

---

22. Fla. Stat. § 189.403(2) defines a Dependent special district as follows: "Dependent special district" means a special district that meets at least one of the following criteria:

(a) The membership of its governing body is identical to that of the governing body of a single county or a single municipality.

(b) All members of its governing body are appointed by the governing body of a single county or a single municipality.

(c) During their unexpired terms, members of the special district's governing body are subject to removal at will by the governing body of a single county or a single municipality.

(d) The district has a budget that requires approval through an affirmative vote or can be vetoed by the governing body of a single county or a single municipality.

This subsection is for purposes of definition only. Nothing in this subsection confers additional authority upon local governments not otherwise authorized by the provisions of the special acts or general acts of local application creating each special district, as amended.

23. Fla. Stat. § 189.403(3) defines an Independent special district as follows: "Independent special district" means a special district that is not a dependent special district as defined in subsection (2). A district that includes more than one county is an independent special district unless the district lies wholly within the boundaries of a single municipality.

Deltona residents would constitute the majority of the hospital's patients. Before filing the complaint for bond validation, Halifax agreed to undertake this project by entering into an interlocal agreement with the City of Deltona pursuant to section 163.01, Florida Statutes (2017), the Interlocal Act.[1] An intervenor challenged Halifax's complaint for bond validation, arguing that Halifax lacks the authority to operate a facility in Deltona because Deltona is outside Halifax's geographical boundaries. The circuit court agreed and denied the complaint for bond validation. Halifax appealed that ruling to this Court, invoking our mandatory jurisdiction to review final orders entered in proceedings for the validation of bonds. *See* art. V, § 3(b)(2), Fla. Const.; § 75.08, Fla. Stat. (2017). Consistent with its arguments below, Halifax and its amici argue that Halifax possesses authority to operate a hospital anywhere it desires outside its boundaries so long as there is a demonstrated need for the facility and so long as Halifax demonstrates that it can do so profitably, thereby increasing revenue available to serve the needs of the district. In the alternative, Halifax contends that the interlocal agreement it entered with City of Deltona pursuant to the Interlocal Act serves as a sufficient grant of authority to build and operate the hospital.

Analysis

As a "special tax district," ch. 2003-374, §§ 1, 3(1), 3(16), Halifax has only the powers granted to it by legislative enactment, either expressly or by necessary implication. *See Bd. of Comm'rs of Jupiter Inlet Dist. v. Thibadeau*, 956 So.2d 529, 532 (Fla. 4th DCA 2007) ("[I]ndependent special districts are created by the legislature, and, like agencies, their powers are limited to those granted them." (citations omitted)); *State, Dep't of Envtl. Regulation v. Falls Chase Special Taxing Dist.*, 424 So.2d 787, 793 (Fla. 1st DCA 1982) ("An agency has only such power as expressly or by necessary implication is granted by legislative enactment."); *see also City of Cape Coral v. GAC Utils., Inc. of Fla.*, 281 So.2d 493, 496 (Fla. 1973). Because the scope of Halifax's authority is a matter of statutory construction, we review the issue de novo. *City of Parker v. State*, 992 So.2d 171, 175-76 (Fla. 2008).[2]

---

1. The full title of section 163.01 is the Florida Interlocal Cooperation Act of 1969.

2. Halifax urges us to defer to its interpretation of chapter 2003-374 under the principle that an agency is entitled to deference concerning its interpretation of any statute it is charged with administering. We decline to afford that deference. Halifax's position implicates a recent amendment to article V, section 21 of the Florida Constitution, providing that courts of this state shall not defer to an agency's statutory interpretation. The parties disagree over the applicability of that amendment to this case. However, we need not resolve that dispute for the purposes of this case because the statute at issue is unambiguous. Even before this new constitutional provision we did not apply the deference principle to unambiguous statutes. *See, e.g., GTC, Inc. v. Edgar*, 967 So.2d 781, 785 (Fla. 2007) ("[It is only] when a statutory term is subject to varying interpretations and ... has been interpreted by the executive agency charged with enforcing the statute [that] this Court [would have] follow[ed] a deferential principle of statutory construction. ...").

Statutory Analysis

A court's determination of the meaning of a statute begins with the language of the statute. *Lopez v. Hall*, 233 So.3d 451, 453 (Fla. 2018) (citing *Holly v. Auld*, 450 So.2d 217, 219 (Fla. 1984)). If that language is clear, the statute is given its plain meaning, and the court does not "look behind the statute's plain language for legislative intent or resort to rules of statutory construction." *City of Parker*, 992 So.2d at 176 (quoting *Daniels v. Fla. Dep't of Health*, 898 So.2d 61, 64 (Fla. 2005)).

The General and Special Laws Defining the Scope of Halifax's Authority

Our analysis necessarily begins with chapter 189, Florida Statutes, the general law authorizing special districts. In addition to serving as the common authority for special districts in general, chapter 189 is expressly cited as the foundation for Halifax's creation in the special law creating Halifax. Ch. 2003-374, § 1, Laws of Fla.

Chapter 189 "provide[s] general provisions for the definition, creation, and operation of special districts." § 189.011(1), Fla. Stat. (2017). According to chapter 189, a special district is "a unit of local government created for a special purpose, as opposed to a general purpose, *which has jurisdiction to operate within a limited geographic boundary* and is created by general law, special act, local ordinance, or by rule of the Governor and Cabinet." *Id.* § 189.012(6) (emphasis added). Because the very essence of a chapter 189 "special district" is statutorily prescribed as operation within "a limited geographic boundary," § 189.012(6), that inescapably becomes the default authority for all special districts. In other words, although the Legislature certainly can grant a special district authority to operate outside of its defined geographic boundary, that extraordinary grant of authority would need to be express and unambiguous — clear enough to demonstrate that the Legislature has created a special district that will operate with a power not generally contemplated for chapter 189 special districts.

Chapter 2003-374 does not contain an express grant of authority for Halifax to operate hospitals outside the geographic boundaries established for the district and, when the relevant language is considered as a whole, only authorizes Halifax to operate within the district. Chapter 2003-374 provides in relevant part:

> The district may establish, construct, operate, and maintain such hospitals, medical facilities, and other health care facilities and services as are necessary. The hospitals, medical facilities, and other health care facilities and services shall be established, constructed, operated, and maintained by the district for the preservation of the public health, for the public good, *and for the use of the public of the district*. Maintenance of such hospitals, medical facilities, and other health care facilities and services *in the district* is hereby found and declared to be a public purpose and necessary for the general welfare of the residents of the district.

Ch. 2003-374, § 3(5) (emphasis added).

Halifax seeks to isolate the first sentence of this provision, arguing that because the first sentence does not expressly *limit* its authority to "construct, operate, and maintain" medical facilities to the district's geographic boundaries, it acts as a grant of authority to do so outside of its boundaries.[3] As already discussed, that reading would be contrary to chapter 189, and clearly insufficient to overcome the general rule stated in that chapter — which is that special districts are created to operate within their defined geographic boundaries.

In addition, it would be inappropriate to isolate the first sentence from the rest of the paragraph. *Trafalgar Woods Homeowners Ass'n, Inc. v. City of Cape Coral*, 248 So.3d 282, 284 (Fla. 2d DCA 2018) ("[U]nder a longstanding fundamental principle applicable to statutes and ordinances, 'words, phrases, clauses, sentences and paragraphs of a statute may not be construed in isolation[.]' Rather, the sentence must be read in the context of the entire provision." (citation omitted)). Specifically, the second sentence references the "hospitals, medical facilities, and other health care facilities" authorized for construction, operation, and maintenance (in the first sentence), and explains that these facilities are being authorized "for the use of the public of the district." More importantly, the first sentence itself only authorizes Halifax to construct, operate, and maintain facilities "as are necessary." Necessary to what? Read in context, these words can only reasonably be understood to mean necessary to fulfillment of the public purpose for which the district is being created, which the third and last sentence explains as follows: "Maintenance of such hospitals, medical facilities, and other health care facilities and services *in the district* is hereby found and declared to be a public purpose and *necessary for the general welfare of the residents of the district*." (Emphasis added.) Read together, this language is plain: it grants Halifax the authority to construct, operate, and maintain health care facilities within its district, which is defined according to the geographic boundaries in section 1 of Halifax's charter. Ch. 2003-374, § 3(1).[4]

---

3. Halifax attempts to bolster this argument using a backwards approach to statutory construction. Before acknowledging the language currently in effect, Halifax quotes its 1925 enabling act and then traces the history of legislative revisions in an effort to dictate how the 2003 act should be read. We reject Halifax's approach. *Nat. Auto Serv. Ctrs., Inc. v. F/R 550, LLC*, 192 So.3d 498, 504 (Fla. 2d DCA 2016) ("The interpretation of a statute begins 'with the plain meaning of the actual language' the statute employs." (quoting *Diamond Aircraft Indus., Inc. v. Horowitch*, 107 So.3d 362, 367 (Fla. 2013))); *see also Rollins v. Pizzarelli*, 761 So.2d 294, 299 (Fla. 2000) ("[W]hen the statutory language is clear, legislative history cannot be used to alter the plain meaning of the statute.").

4. In addition to attempting to infer the authority to operate extraterritorially from various provisions beyond section 5, Halifax contends that its enabling act incorporates chapter 617, Florida Statutes, by reference and that this reference, combined with the power granted in the enabling act for Halifax to establish corporations, ch. 2003-374, § 3(3), gives Halifax the authority to establish and operate a hospital in Deltona. Halifax gleans this conclusion from sections 617.0301 and 617.0303(8)-(9), Florida Statutes (2018), which authorize the creation of corporations for any lawful purpose and grants a nonprofit corporation the authority to operate anywhere in the United States and to acquire property anywhere. Halifax's reliance on these provisions is misplaced. Not only must Halifax's activities serve its stated purpose, *see, e.g.*, § 189.012(6), but also, the bounds of Halifax's authority to create and establish a corporation is not what is at issue, as the bonds were not sought for the purpose of creating a corporation, but for the purpose of financing a hospital outside its geographic boundaries.

For these reasons, we agree with the trial court that the Legislature has not authorized Halifax to establish, construct, operate, or maintain the out-of-district Deltona hospital for which it sought to issue revenue bonds. We now turn to Halifax's argument that any lack of authority is cured though the Interlocal Act and its interlocal agreement with the City of Deltona.

The Interlocal Act

Under the Interlocal Act, "[a] public agency," including a special district, "may exercise jointly with any other public agency of the state, of any other state, or of the United States Government any power, privilege, or authority which such agencies share in common and which each might exercise separately." § 163.01(3)(b), (4), Fla. Stat. (2017). The purpose of the Interlocal Act is "to permit local governmental units to make the most efficient use of their powers by enabling them to cooperate with other localities on a basis of mutual advantage and thereby to provide services and facilities in a manner and pursuant to forms of governmental organization that will accord best with geographic, economic, population, and other factors influencing the needs and development of local communities." § 163.01(2). It is "intended to authorize the entry into contracts for the performance of service functions of public agencies." § 163.01(14).

By its terms, the Interlocal Act requires that any "power, privilege, or authority" that an agency commits to perform be one that it "might exercise separately" in the absence of an interlocal agreement. *See* § 163.01(4). Because Halifax does not have the independent authority to establish and operate a hospital in Deltona, it does not gain this authority under the Interlocal Act.

Halifax contends that failing to recognize that the Interlocal Act grants it the authority to act outside its geographic boundaries will strip the Interlocal Act of meaning. However, the Interlocal Act expressly states its effect: "to authorize the entry into contracts for the performance of service functions of public agencies." § 163.01(14). Our decision does not deny this effect, and we cannot give the Interlocal Act a greater effect than its provisions establish. *See Holly*, 450 So.2d at 219 (explaining that this state's courts are "without power to construe an unambiguous statute in a way which would extend . . . its express terms or its reasonable and obvious implications" (quoting *Am. Bankers Life Assurance Co. of Fla. V. Williams*, 212 So.2d 777, 778 (Fla. 1st DCA 1968) (emphasis omitted). Additionally, Halifax's primary argument ignores the reality that the federal government, Florida's state government, as well as the primary local governmental subdivision of the State — counties — do have overlapping geographic boundaries with all special districts, and that many other local governmental entities have overlapping geographic boundaries as well. Given these realities, it is hardly true that the Interlocal Act will be stripped of all meaning unless we construe it as authorizing all special districts to operate outside of their geographic boundaries, as they deem appropriate, by interlocal agreement.

Halifax further argues that section 163.01(9)(a) shows that the Legislature contemplated that the Interlocal Act would lift geographic restrictions on agency action, as this subsection references extraterritorial activity. Specifically, section 163.01(9)(a) provides as follows:

> All of the privileges and immunities from liability; exemptions from laws, ordinances, and rules; and pensions and relief, disability, workers' compensation, and other benefits which apply to the activity of officers, agents, or employees of any public agents or employees of any public agency when performing their respective functions within the territorial limits for their respective agencies shall apply to the same degree and extent to the performance of such functions and duties of such officers, agents, or employees extraterritorially under the provisions of any such interlocal agreement.

This language, standing alone, does not confer the authority that Halifax seeks. The Interlocal Act applies broadly to any public agency, "including, but not limited to, [a] state government, county, city, school district, single and multipurpose special district, single and multipurpose public authority," and others. § 163.01(3)(b). Some of these public agencies have broader powers than a special district, which is confined only to the powers granted expressly or by necessary implication in a legislative enactment, *Falls Chase Special Taxing Dist.*, 424 So.2d at 793. Even a special district can have the power to operate outside its geographic boundaries when that power is provided by the special district's enabling act. Also, while a municipality generally cannot exercise extraterritorial powers, it can do so when authorized by law. Art. VIII, § 2(c), Fla. Const.; Op. Att'y Gen. Fla. 2008-01 (2008); Op. Att'y Gen. Fla. 2003-03 (2003). Therefore, the fact that the Interlocal Act contemplates that some functions under interlocal agreements will be performed extraterritorially does not mean that the Legislature granted all public agencies the right to act extraterritorially.

In fact, interpreting the Interlocal Act to have such an effect would render other statutes superfluous. Most notably, section 166.0495, Florida Statutes (2018), authorizes "[a] municipality [to] enter into an interlocal agreement pursuant to s. 163.01 with an adjoining municipality or municipalities within the same county to provide law enforcement services within the territorial boundaries of the other adjoining municipality or municipalities." *See also* § 288.9604(1), Fla. Stat. (2018) (authorizing the Florida Development Finance Corporation "to function within the corporate limits of any public agency with which it has entered into an interlocal agreement for any of the purposes of this act"). When drafting section 166.0495, the Legislature was clearly aware of the Interlocal Act, and yet, it perceived the need to create section 166.0495 to authorize extraterritorial operation of ordinary municipal functions under an interlocal agreement. Even if the language of Halifax's enabling act and the Interlocal Act were ambiguous, we would avoid any construction of them that would render other statutes superfluous. *See Hawkins v. Ford Motor Co.*, 748 So.2d 993, 1000 (Fla. 1999).

Conclusion

Because neither Halifax's enabling act nor the Interlocal Act gives Halifax the authority to operate outside its geographic boundaries, the circuit court properly denied the bond validation. In reaching this decision, we have not overlooked the concerns that Halifax and its amici raise about the effect of a determination that Halifax cannot operate extraterritorially. However, this Court is not the proper forum for a policy decision as to whether Halifax or any other special district should be allowed to operate extraterritorially. *See Holly*, 450 So.2d at 219. In any event, we note that this decision is based on the specific language of Halifax's enabling act, which we are not authorized to rewrite or construe contrary to its plain meaning. *See Westphal v. City of St. Petersburg*, 194 So.3d 311, 313-14 (Fla. 2016). For these reasons, we affirm the circuit court's order denying bond validation.

It is so ordered.

CANADY, C.J., and POLSTON, LABARGA, LAGOA, LUCK, and MUÑIZ, JJ., concur.

It should be noted that the only way for Halifax Health Medical Center to operate the hospital outside of its taxing district would be to seek a legislative change to its charter. The Florida Legislature subsequently passed HB 523,[24] which changed Halifax Health Medical Center's enabling legislation [charter] and gave it the right to build the new hospital outside of its taxing district boundary.[25] This bill was signed into law by Florida's Governor on May 10, 2019.

E. Other Units of Local Government

The Florida Constitution references a number of governmental entities other than counties and municipalities. They include *inter alia* special taxing units and municipal service taxing units. The legal standing of such entities is often left to the courts for resolution.

---

24. Chapter 2019-172, Laws of Florida.

25. According to the Final Bill Analysis, the bill amended the charter of the Halifax Hospital Medical Center by providing express authority for certain operations and services outside the district boundaries in Brevard, Flagler, Lake, and Volusia Counties. This authority includes all facilities and services in which the district was engaged as of January 1, 2019. The bill expressly prohibits using revenues derived from ad valorem taxes or non-ad valorem assessments levied within the district for any purpose outside the district. The bill also authorizes the district to own, operate facilities, and provide Hospice services throughout Florida. According to the Economic Impact Statement, the bill will facilitate the timely completion and opening of a hospital in the City of Deltona and beginning in fiscal year 2021-2022, it projects annual revenues will exceed annual expenditures for the hospital. The district projects that by its sixth year of operation the hospital will have created 519 jobs and have an annual economic impact of $107 million. Further, it projects this extension of services and facilities will continue to reduce the district's reliance on ad valorem tax collections to help fund its operations. The bill was approved by the Governor on May 10, 2019, ch. 2019-172, L.O.F., and became effective on that date.

5 · LOCAL GOVERNMENT

Lederer v. Orlando Utilities Commission

981 So. 2d 521 (Fla. 5th Dist. Ct. App. 2008)

ORFINGER, J.

Deborah Lederer appeals a final summary judgment entered in favor of the Orlando Utilities Commission ("the OUC") in a negligence action that Ms. Lederer filed against the OUC after she fell on a damaged water meter cover. After the accident, Ms. Lederer notified the OUC of her injuries and communicated with the OUC's risk management director. However, she did not notify the Florida Department of Financial Services ("the Department") of the claim until more than four years after the accident. Her failure to do so was the basis for the trial court's summary judgment against her. We affirm.

Ms. Lederer brought a negligence action against the OUC, alleging that an OUC employee failed to properly replace the lid over the water meter in her yard, causing her to fall and injure herself. She pled that all "conditions precedent and notice requirements [had] been complied with or otherwise waived." In response to the complaint, the OUC filed a motion to dismiss, arguing that Ms. Lederer had failed to provide the requisite presuit notice under section 768.28(6), Florida Statutes (2001), to the Department. The motion to dismiss was denied. The OUC then answered the complaint and moved for summary judgment, arguing that Ms. Lederer had failed to comply with the presuit requirements of section 768.28(6). The OUC asserted that since it is not a "municipality" within the meaning of section 768.28(6), Ms. Lederer was required to notify the Department of her claim within the three-year statutory period. The trial court granted the OUC's motion, concluding that while Ms. Lederer had properly notified the OUC of her claim, she had failed to comply with section 768.28(6), by not providing timely presuit written notice of her claim to the Department. The court determined that the OUC is not a "municipality" so as to exempt Ms. Lederer's claim from that notification requirement. The court subsequently entered a final summary judgment in favor of the OUC, and this appeal followed.

* * *

Section 768.28(6), Florida Statutes, is part of a statutory waiver of sovereign immunity. As a result, strict compliance is required. *See Levine v. Dade County Sch. Bd.*, 442 So.2d 210, 212 (Fla.1983). The statute requires that before a tort claim may be filed against a county or other state agency, the claimant must give written notice of the claim to the agency and to the Department within three years after the claim accrues. However, presuit notice to the Department is not required if the claim is brought against a municipality.

In *McSwain v. Dussia*, 499 So.2d 868 (Fla. 1st DCA 1986), the court rejected the plaintiff's argument that notice to the Department of Insurance (now the

Department of Financial Services) was not required for a claim against an agency of a county or municipality. Specifically, the court explained:

> [W]e conclude that whether the hospital authority is an agency of the city of Jacksonville, rather than an agency of Duval County, makes no difference. The record shows that the Authority is not a municipality, as distinguished from an agency of a municipality; and only if the claim is against a "municipality" itself is notice on the Department of Insurance excused. Although it might appear reasonable, in deciding this issue, to inquire whether the Department of Insurance has any interest or will play any part in assisting the municipal agency to dispose of the claim, the supreme court has held that such questions are not relevant to the notice requirement and that the statute must be given literal effect.

Id. at 870 (internal citation omitted). *McSwain* holds that only when a claim is against a municipality itself, as opposed to a municipal agency, is notice to the Department excused. Ms. Lederer tries to distinguish *McSwain* by arguing that the OUC is an integral component of the City of Orlando ("the City"), much like its police or fire department. Hence, the dispositive issue is whether the OUC is a municipal or quasi-municipal agency, in which case notice to the Department was required, or simply a component part of the City, such as its police or fire department, wherein notice was not required.

The OUC was created in 1923 by a special act passed by the Legislature, chapter 9861, Laws of Florida (1923), and took effect after the affirmative vote of a majority of the freeholders of the City. *See* ch. 9861, §13, Laws of Fla. (1923); *Gaines v. City of Orlando,* 450 So.2d 1174, 1181 (Fla. 5th DCA 1984); *see also Orlando Utils. Comm'n v. State,* 478 So.2d 341, 342 (Fla.1985); *City of Orlando v. Evans,* 132 Fla. 609, 182 So. 264, 265 (1938); *Northcutt v. Orlando Utils. Comm'n,* 614 So.2d 612, 615 (Fla. 5th DCA 1993), *approved sub nom, Ford v. Orlando Utils. Comm'n,* 629 So.2d 845 (Fla.1994). The special act established the OUC as a "part of the government of the City of Orlando," but provided that the OUC would have substantial autonomy to operate independent of the City government. *Gaines,* 450 So.2d at 1180.

For instance, the City Council selects the OUC's board members. *See* ch. 9861, §4, Laws of Fla. (1923); ch. 31092, §1, Laws of Fla. (1955); ch. 86–421, §§2, 3, Laws of Fla. While the OUC has its own president and its own board separate from the Orlando City Council, the Mayor of the City sits on the OUC's board. *See* ch. 86–421, §§2, 3, Laws of Fla. Further, the OUC is required to submit monthly accounting statements along with detailed annual reports to the City Council. *See* ch. 9861, §8, Laws of Fla. (1923); ch. 10968, §3, Laws of Fla. (1925). In addition, only the City is authorized to exercise the right of eminent domain to appropriate property for its water supply. *See* ch. 13198, §1, Laws of Fla. (1927). Still, both the City and the OUC are "authorized to do all things necessary or required to carry into effect the provisions of this act." *See* ch. 61–2589, §1, Laws of Fla.; ch. 97–334, §1, Laws of Fla.

At the same time, the OUC acts independently and beyond the control of the City with respect to the powers it has under the special act. The OUC has the authority to furnish electric power, energy services, and water to users in any part of Orange County. *See* ch. 9861, §9, Laws of Fla. (1923). It also has "full authority" over "the management and control of the electric light and water works plant of the City of Orlando," *see* ch. 31092, §1, Laws of Fla. (1955); *see also* ch. 9861, §6, Laws of Fla. (1923); and to "prescribe rates, rules and regulations governing the sale and use of electricity, power and water wherever furnished by said Commission and to change the same at its pleasure," *see* ch. 31077, §1, Laws of Fla. (1955); *see also* ch. 9861, §11, Laws of Fla. (1923). Subsequent special acts have expanded this authority, giving the OUC, for example, the authority to "acquire, establish, construct, maintain and/or operate" electric generating plants within Brevard County and parts of Osceola County. *See* ch. 9861, §9, Laws of Fla. (1923); ch. 61–2589, §1, Laws of Fla.; ch. 97–334, §1, Laws of Fla. The OUC has also been given authority to borrow money, incur debt, and issue notes, *see* ch. 82–343, §1, Laws of Fla.; ch. 82–415, §2, Laws of Fla.; issue revenue bonds and make agreements with the City and "holders of any revenue bonds or other obligations issued to finance," *see* ch. 24758, §3, Laws of Fla. (1947); ch. 86–421, §2, Laws of Fla.; bill for sewer service, *see* ch. 24758, §1, Laws of Fla. (1947); and discontinue service (with the City's consent) due to nonpayment, *see* ch. 24758, §2, Laws of Fla. (1947).

As this Court recognized in *Gaines*, the interconnected relationship between the City and the OUC is both unique and strange. 450 So.2d at 1181. While the OUC is a part of the City for some purposes, it is independent and beyond the control of the City as to the powers granted to it under the special act. *See Gaines*, 450 So.2d at 1181; *see also* ch. 9861, §1, Laws of Fla. (1923); *State*, 478 So.2d 341; *Evans*, 182 So. at 265. "The City and its electors have no control over the OUC; but neither does the OUC have control over the City." *Gaines*, 450 So.2d at 1182.

In *City of Tampa v. Easton*, 145 Fla. 188, 198 So. 753, 754 (1940), the Florida Supreme Court explained that a municipality "is a legal entity consisting of population and defined area, with such governmental functions and also corporate public improvement authority as may be conferred by law in a charter or other legislative enactment under the [Florida] Constitution." The elements essential to the existence of "municipality" are a community of people, and a territory occupied by them. *State v. Town of Lake Placid*, 109 Fla. 419, 147 So. 468, 471 (1933); *see City of Winter Haven v. A.M. Klemm & Son*, 132 Fla. 334, 181 So. 153 (1938) (explaining that to "establish" municipality, community of people and territory must exist, occupying sufficient area to require organized agency for management of local affairs of quasi-public nature); Black's Law Dictionary 1018 (6th ed. 1990) (defining municipality as "legally incorporated or duly authorized association of inhabitants of limited area for local governmental or other public purposes; . . . [a] city, borough, town, township, or village"); *see also* 62 C.J.S. *Municipal Corporations* §2 (2002) (explaining that word "municipal" means of or pertaining to city or town or its corporate government, and defining municipality as a legally incorporated or duly authorized association of inhabitants or particularly designated place or limited territorial area, established for prescribed local governmental and public utility or other public purposes). Clearly, as Ms. Lederer concedes, the OUC is not a municipality. The OUC does not have citizens or a geographically-defined area and is not a general purpose unit of government.

Further, the OUC does not share an identity with the City. The OUC is purely a creation of the Florida Legislature. When the Legislature created the OUC, it was made "part of the government of the City of Orlando," *see* ch. 9861, §1, Laws of Fla. (1923), but endowed with "substantial autonomy to operate independently from the city government," *see Gaines,* 450 So.2d at 1180. Thus, while the OUC may be a public utility designated as part of the City's government, it remains a distinct legal entity that operates mostly independently of the City.

For these reasons, we conclude that the OUC is not a city department, as argued by Ms. Lederer. *See Cobo v. O'Bryant,* 116 So.2d 233, 237 (Fla.1959) (holding that Legislature had absolute discretion to grant powers to operate and manage city utility to independent utility commission outside city's control, and in doing so, Legislature merely created "a municipal agency to operate the publicly owned property for the benefit of the public"). We premise that conclusion on the OUC's status as a legislatively created body with substantial autonomy to operate independently of the City. *See* 1 McQuillin, *The Law of Municipal Corporations,* § 2.30 (3d ed. 2008) (explaining that department created by state is generally considered separate entity while department created by city is not entity separate form municipality even though distinct city department); *see also Fla. City Police Dep't v. Corcoran,* 661 So.2d 409, 410 (Fla. 3d DCA 1995) (explaining that although city police department is integral part of city government, it is not entity subject to suit because it is merely "vehicle through which the city government fulfills its policing functions . . ."); *N. Miami Beach Water Bd. v. Gollin,* 171 So.2d 584 (Fla. 3d DCA 1965) (finding city water board was not autonomous body, separate and apart from city).

We recognize that the distinction between a municipal department and a municipal or quasi-municipal agency is not always clear. Generally, a municipal department is not a separate legal entity and does not have the capacity to sue or be sued. Examples of such subordinate entities comprising an integral part of a municipality would generally include a police or fire department, planning department or city attorney's office. 56 Am.Jur.2d *Municipal Corporations* § 787 (2008). Conversely, districts and authorities created by the Legislature for particular purposes are generally classified as "special purpose" units, "special districts," or municipal or quasi-municipal agencies to distinguish them from local government units that are more self-governing, or "general purpose" units of local government. 1 McQuillin, *The Law of Municipal Corporations,* § 2.28 (3d ed. 2008). Such special purpose units or quasi-municipal bodies may be municipal agencies, but not municipal departments. They are bodies that possess a limited number of specific powers and have only those powers that have been expressly granted to them by the Legislature or that are necessary for them to discharge their duties and carry out their objects and purposes. 1 McQuillin, *The Law of Municipal Corporations,* § 2.13 (3d ed. 2008).

Our conclusion that the OUC is not a municipality or a municipal department resolves the issue before us. As a result, we need not determine precisely what the OUC is. We simply need to determine that it is not a municipality or municipal department. Consequently, we agree with *McSwain,* and hold that Ms. Lederer was required to provide notice of her claim to the Department within three years after the accident occurred. Since she failed to do so, the trial court properly granted summary judgment in the OUC's favor. *See Motor v. Citrus County Sch. Bd.,* 856 So.2d 1054, 1055 (Fla. 5th DCA 2003) (finding that summary judgment is appropriate when plaintiff failed to provide required notice within three-year deadline as notice to Department is essential condition precedent to maintaining cause of action); *Wall v. Palm Beach County,* 743 So.2d 44 (Fla. 4th DCA 1999) (affirming summary judgment in favor of county on grounds that claimant failed to give notice of intent to sue Department pursuant to section 768.28(6)).

AFFIRMED.

LAWSON, J., concurs. [Dissenting opinion omitted.]

Eldred v. North Broward Hospital District
498 So. 2d 911 (Fla. 1986)

OVERTON, Justice.

This is a petition to review *North Broward Hospital District v. Eldred*, 466 So.2d 1210 (Fla. 4th DCA 1985), in which the district court held that North Broward Hospital District, as a special taxing district, was within the sovereign immunity provisions of section 768.28, Florida Statutes (1975), and certified the following question:

> Is North Broward Hospital District, by its operation of the hospitals within said district, a corporation primarily acting as an instrumentality or agency of the state?

466 So.2d at 1211. We have jurisdiction. Art. V, § 3(b)(4), Fla. Const. We approve the decision of the district court with the qualification that a special taxing district is an "independent establishment of the state" under the provisions of section 768.28(2).

The relevant facts reflect that the petitioners' minor son received a judgment for damages against North Broward Hospital District in the amount of $900,000. The respondent district moved to limit its liability to $50,000 on the grounds that it was a governmental entity entitled to the benefits of section 768.28, Florida Statutes (1975). The trial court denied the motion, but the district court reversed, concluding that the hospital was a state agency or subdivision within the definition of the phrase as set forth in section 768.28(2).

The issue is whether the provisions of section 768.28 waiving sovereign immunity and limiting liability for governmental entities were intended to apply to special taxing districts. The applicable portion of section 768.28 effectively waives immunity for governmental entities within operational level functions. The statute does place a cap, however, on the amount of governmental liability. The applicable portion of section 768.28(2) reads as follows:

> As used in this act, "state agencies or subdivisions" include the executive departments, the legislature, the judicial branch, and the independent establishments of the state; counties and municipalities; and corporations primarily acting as instrumentalities or agencies of the state, counties, or municipalities.

Petitioners argue that the definition excludes special taxing districts for hospitals. According to petitioners, North Broward Hospital District is primarily a private hospital because it is required to charge all patients who are able to pay, and may treat without charge only indigent patients. Correspondingly, petitioners contend that the hospital's public attributes, including the power to levy ad valorem taxes, are incidental and exist only to cancel deficits incurred for indigent care. Petitioners rely on our 1952 decision in *Suwannee County Hospital Corp. v. Golden*, 56 So.2d 911 (Fla.1952), which held that a legislatively-created special taxing district for a hospital in Suwannee County was not entitled to sovereign immunity because its established activities "fall more clearly in the category of 'proprietary' functions [rather] than 'governmental' functions." *Id.* at 913.

We reject these contentions and find that *Golden* no longer applies. Since *Golden*, three significant events occurred. First, Florida adopted a new constitution in 1968 that expressly recognized special taxing districts as separate local governmental entities; second, in 1973 the Florida Legislature enacted section 768.28, effectively waiving sovereign immunity for all governmental entities; and, third, in *Commercial Carrier Corp. v. Indian River County*, 371 So.2d 1010 (Fla.1979), this Court found that the governmental proprietary analysis had no continuing validity after the enactment of section 768.28.

With regard to the first point, the 1968 Constitution identified special taxing districts as one of four local governmental entities, authorizing each to levy ad valorem taxes. Art. VII, § 9, Fla. Const. Special taxing districts are also considered local governmental entities for the transfer of powers and functions with counties or municipalities. Art. VIII, § 4, Fla. Const. Additionally, special taxing districts, along with other local governmental entities, are authorized to issue bonds, article VII, section 12, and to establish civil service systems, article III, section 14. Numerous court decisions of this state recognize the governmental status of special taxing districts. *See Michel v. Douglas*, 464 So.2d 545 (Fla.1985) (hospital employee records subject

5 · LOCAL GOVERNMENT

to Florida Public Records Act); *North Broward Hospital District v. Mizell*, 148 So.2d 1 (Fla.1962) (conduct of medical staff overseeing public hospital governed by principles applicable to other public officers); *National Union v. Southeast Volusia Hospital District*, 436 So.2d 294 (Fla. 1st DCA 1983) (hospital district subject to Public Employees Relations Act), *Southeast Volusia Hospital District v. National Union*, 429 So.2d 1232 (Fla. 5th DCA 1983) (hospital district subject to Public Employees Relations Act); *review dismissed*, 452 So.2d 568 (Fla.1984); *NewsPress Publishing Co. v. Carlson*, 410 So.2d 546 (Fla. 2d DCA 1982) (public hospital subject to Government in the Sunshine Law); *Jess Parrish Memorial Hospital v. Laborers' International Union*, 397 So.2d 989 (Fla. 1st DCA) (public hospital subject to Public Employees Relations Act), *review denied*, 411 So.2d 383 (Fla.1981); *North Brevard County Hospital District, Inc. v. Florida Public Employees Relations Commission*, 392 So.2d 556 (Fla. 1st DCA 1980) (hospital district subject to Public Employees Relations Act); *Hitt v. North Broward Hospital District*, 387 So.2d 482 (Fla. 4th DCA 1980) (public hospital could not summarily deprive employee of state-created status).

In 1973, the legislature enacted section 768.28 waiving sovereign immunity for all its agencies and subdivisions "to the extent specified in this act." In *Cauley v. City of Jacksonville*, 403 So.2d 379 (Fla. 1981), this Court found that one of the purposes of section 768.28 was to establish uniform liability for various governmental entities, thereby eliminating the inconsistent application of governmental liability reflected in the case law. If we accept petitioners' argument, however, a county or municipal hospital, supported by ad valorem taxation, would be covered by 768.28, while a special taxing district hospital, also supported by ad valorem taxation, would not. This would result in an inconsistent application of governmental liability which is contrary to the intent of the statute. For the reasons expressed in *Commercial Carrier*, the theory of our *Golden* decision, rendered in 1951, is no longer applicable to this type of governmental liability.

In conclusion, we find this special taxing district is a constitutionally established local governmental entity charged with the responsibility to provide for the "public health . . . and good" of the citizens within the district. The provisions of the 1968 Constitution leave no doubt that special taxing districts are included as one of four types of local governmental entities, along with counties, school districts, and municipalities. In our view, the legislature clearly intended the provisions of section 768.28(2) to include special taxing districts within the phrase "independent establishments of the state."

Although we hold that section 768.28 applies to special hospital taxing districts, and limits the judgment in this case in accordance with its provisions, we note that the legislature may direct the North Broward Hospital District to pay the balance of this judgment. *See Hess v. Metropolitan Dade County*, 467 So.2d 297 (Fla.1985).

For the reasons expressed, we approve the decision of the district court of appeal, as modified.

It is so ordered.

McDONALD, C.J., and BOYD, EHRLICH and BARKETT, JJ., concur.

SHAW, J., concurs specially with an opinion.

ADKINS, J., dissents [without opinion].

SHAW, Justice, specially concurring.

I concur but note that the courts below and the parties before this Court did not have the benefit of *Avallone v. Board of County Commissioners*, 493 So.2d 1002 (Fla.1986), which held that government units are liable to the limits of insurance purchased.

See the separate opinion of Justice McDonald in *Hillsborough County Hospital and Welfare Board v. Taylor.*[26]

The sovereign immunity limit of liability was $50,000 at the time the action accrued in the preceding case. As of the writing of this text, the limit has been raised to $200,000.[27]

F. State-Local Relationships

It frequently becomes necessary for the courts to mediate power disputes between various levels of government. These disputes can involve the issue of whether the state has preempted the power of subordinate governmental entities to act in a given area, as well as conflicts between political subdivisions.

The following cases are illustrative of the types of governmental disputes that the courts have been called upon to resolve.

---

26. 546 So. 2d 1055 (Fla. 1989).
27. Fla. Stat. § 768.28(5) (2021).

1. Preemption by the State

Hillsborough County v. Florida Restaurant Association, Inc.

603 So. 2d 587 (Fla. 2d Dist. Ct. App. 1992)

DANAHY, Acting Chief Judge.

The Florida Restaurant Association [the Association] sued Hillsborough County, a chartered County [the County], seeking declaratory and injunctive relief after the County enacted an ordinance requiring that a health warning sign be posed in certain establishments that serve alcohol. After both parties moved for summary judgment, the trial court entered final summary judgment in favor of the Association. In its judgment, the trial court declared the ordinance unconstitutional and permanently enjoined its enforcement. The County appeals; we reverse.

The ordinance at issue is No. 91-11 enacted by the County's governing body, the Board of County Commissioners, on February 2, 1991, and titled "Hillsborough County Alcoholic Beverage Public Awareness Ordinance." The ordinance requires that all vendors of alcoholic beverages in the county post a sign, in a size not less than 8 1/2 × 11 inches, conspicuously on their premises. The following words are required to be on the sign:

"HEALTH WARNING"

ALCOHOL IN BEER, WINE SPIRITS AND LIQUOR, ALONE OR
IN COMBINATION WITH OTHER NON-ALCOHOLIC
INGREDIENTS CAN CAUSE

BIRTH DEFECTS
ADDICTION
INTOXICATION

REDUCE YOUR RISKS:

DO NOT DRINK DURING PREGNANCY.

DO NOT DRINK BEFORE DRIVING OR OPERATING MACHINERY.

DO NOT MIX ALCOHOL WITH OTHER DRUGS, BOTH PRESCRIPTION
AND NON-PRESCRIPTION. IT CAN BE FATAL.

Failure to post the sign could result in criminal prosecution.

In the trial court the Association did not dispute that consumption of alcohol carries with it the risks of which the sign warns but argued merely that the County acted *ultra vires* in enacting the ordinance given the state's pervasive regulatory scheme in the preparation, service, or sale of alcoholic beverages contained in chapters 561 and 562 as well as the regulation of food service establishments in chapter 381. Even though the Association recognized that the County acted pursuant to its police power to protect the public health, safety, welfare, or morals of the community, it successfully argued that the field had been either expressly or impliedly preempted to the state by this pervasive regulatory scheme. Finally, the Association successfully contended that the County acted contrary to the local government article of our constitution when it enacted an ordinance which is inconsistent with general law.

In this appeal the County raises three issues: (1) that the Association lacks standing to seek relief, (2) that there has been no implied or express preemption to the state, and (3) that the ordinance is not inconsistent with general law. The County contends that the subject matter of the ordinance is public health information. Therefore, the subject matter of the ordinance has not been preempted by the state's regulatory scheme for the manufacture, packaging, distribution, and sale of alcohol; and, further, the ordinance is not inconsistent with any general law; thus it is constitutional.

[The Court's discussion of "association standing in the context of administrative proceedings" is omitted.]

Express Preemption

Turning to the substantive issue of preemption to the state of any regulation touching on the sale of alcohol within food service establishments, we agree with the County that the state regulatory scheme is not so pervasive that the County has no room to act under its police powers. There is express preemption language in section 381.061(9), Florida Statutes (1989),[2] but this subsection merely enables the Department of Health and Rehabilitative Services to adopt rules for the training of managers in food safety protection standards when they are responsible for the storage, preparation, display, and serving of foods to the public. To find a subject matter expressly preempted to the state, the express preemption language must be a specific statement; express preemption cannot be implied or inferred. *Board of Trustees v. Dulje*, 453 So.2d 177 (Fla. 2d DCA1984).

The preemption language of section 381.061(9) provides:

> The regulation of food safety protection standards for any required training and testing of food service establishment personnel is hereby preempted to the state. The ranking of food service establishments is also preempted to the state, provided, however, that any local ordinances establishing a ranking system in existence prior to October 1, 1988, shall remain in effect. *The regulation and inspection of food service establishments licensed by chapter 509* and regulation of food safety protection standards for required training and testing of food service establishment personnel *are preempted to the state.*

---

2. Section 381.061, Florida Statutes (1989), has been repealed. Ch. 91-297, §58, Laws of Fla. Its substantive provisions were transferred to new section 381.0072 titled "Food protection" in a general reorganization of this chapter and the duties of the Department of Health and Rehabilitative Services relating to the public health.

(Emphasis added.) The Association would have us focus on the broad language, italicized above, of "regulation and inspection" in this statute which is in addition to the remaining narrower preemption language of "standards for . . . training," "ranking" under certain circumstances, and "testing of . . . personnel." According to the Association, the broad language of "regulation and inspection" is indeed the express preemption which prohibits the County from imposing the sign requirement. We cannot agree. First, such generalized language does not *expressly* refer to signage requirements as it must for us to find an express preemption. *Board of Trustees v. Dulje.* Second, using the well-established doctrine of *noscitur a sociis,* which finds words of general import colored by the more particular words accompanying them, *Shadow West Apartments, Ltd. v. State, Dep't of Transp.,* 498 So.2d 589 (Fla. 2d DCA 1986), we cannot construe the italicized language so broadly as the Association would wish; to do so would give the general words a meaning wholly unrelated to the more specific terms in this subsection. *See id.* The broad-brush interpretation the Association wishes us to adopt would render the other narrower express preemption language, respecting standards for training, testing, and ranking, redundant and useless. We must assume that the legislature did not enact a pointless provision. *Johnson v. Feder,* 485 So.2d 409 (Fla.1986); *City of North Miami v. Miami Herald Publishing Co.,* 468 So.2d 218 (Fla.1985). Thus, we cannot agree with the trial court that a health warning sign requirement treads on ground *expressly* reversed by the state to itself in chapter 381.061(9). Although the legislature deals with health concerns in the food handling context in chapter 381, there is no ground to equate those concerns with the County's regarding alcohol consumption as set forth in the ordinance absent a definite express preemption provision pertaining to consumer warning signs.

Implied Preemption

We also agree with the County that since the subject matter of the ordinance is founded on a public health concern about alcohol consumption in certain circumstances, it has not been impliedly preempted by the state's interest in the conduct, management and operation of the manufacturing, packaging, distributing and selling aspects of alcohol. Absent an express preemption provision about the posting of health warning signs on premises licensed under chapters 561 and 562, only if there is a danger of conflict with the pervasive regulatory scheme of the senior legislative body will the actions of the junior legislative body be held to be impliedly preempted. *Tribune Co. v. Cannella,* 458 So.2d 1075, 1077 (Fla.1984) (construing the statutory scheme of chapter 119, the Public Records Act).

Under the standard for determining implied preemption in *Tribune Co. v. Cannella,* the legislative scheme must be so pervasive that it completely occupies the field, thereby requiring a finding that an ordinance which attempts to intrude upon that field is null and void. The Association alleges that Florida's scheme regulating alcohol manufacture, packaging, distributing and selling meets this requirement. The Association fails to recognize, however, that this scheme itself reserves spheres of regulation to junior legislative bodies. *See, e.g.,* § 561.14 (hours of operation in absence of county or municipal ordinance); § 562.45(2)(a) (local regulation of hours and location of operation, sanitary regulations); § 562.45(2)(b) (type of entertainment or conduct permitted in licensed premises); and, not least of all, Art. VIII, § 5, Fla. Const. (local option whether to allow sale of alcohol in the county at all). Before the legislature in 1987 specifically reserved to counties the right to regulate entertainment and conduct in licensed premises, this court had already held that local government acts are not specifically limited to those referenced by the Beverage Law. *Board of County Comm'rs v. Dexterhouse*, 348 So.2d 916 (Fla. 2d DCA 1977), *aff'd sub nom. Martin v. Board of County Comm'rs*, 364 So.2d 449 (Fla.1978), *appeal dismissed*, 441 U.S. 918, 99 S.Ct. 2024, 60 L.Ed.2d 392 (1979).

In *Dexterhouse*, we held that an ordinance prohibiting any female from displaying her breasts in a certain manner in a licensed establishment did not interfere or conflict with the state's regulation of alcohol and that the ordinance there was a valid exercise of the county's police power. The instant ordinance does not even rise to the level of prohibiting certain conduct as did the ordinance in *Dexterhouse*. Although the County admits that its aim is to influence conduct, the sign mainly functions as an educational tool so that patrons who consume alcohol do so with full information as to the possible consequences in the enumerated circumstances. The patron is obviously free to ignore the warning. In sum, we find that the legislative scheme is not so pervasive that it has completely occupied the field thereby impliedly preempting the ordinance.

[Note: the remainder of the opinion is included because it deals with what could be considered another type of preemption issue.]

Inconsistent with General Law

Having thus far found that the ordinance has been neither expressly nor impliedly preempted by state law, our final task is to determine whether, under article VIII, section 1(g), Florida Constitution (1968), the County, pursuant to its charter, has enacted an ordinance which is inconsistent with general law.[3] *Board of Trustees v. Dulje*. If it has enacted such an inconsistent ordinance, the ordinance must be declared null and void.

An ordinance is inconsistent with general law where it is "contradictory in the sense of legislative provisions which cannot coexist." *State ex rel. Dade County v.*

---

3. Article VIII, section 1(g), of the Florida Constitution provides:
   (g) CHARTER GOVERNMENT. Counties operating under county charters shall have all powers of local self-government not inconsistent with general law, or with special law approved by vote of the electors. The governing body of a county operating under a charter may enact county ordinances not inconsistent with general law. The charter shall provide which shall prevail in the event of conflict between county and municipal ordinances.

This section, which first appeared in the new Florida Constitution of 1968, "provides for the broadest extent of county self-government or 'home rule' as it is commonly described." Art. VIII, § 1(g), Fla. Const. D'Alemberte commentary, *reprinted* in 26A Fla.Stat.Ann. 266, 271 (West 1970).

Brautigam, 224 So.2d 688 (Fla.1969) (construing an ordinance concerning cigarette taxes). The Association has cited no law to us, nor have we found any, which can be construed as incapable of coexisting with the ordinance we review, and therefore inconsistent. If anything, the requirement of a health warning sign shows a vendor's concern for the health and well-being of the clientele. *Compare* §§ 561.701–706, Fla. Stat. (1989) (the Responsible Vendor's Act). The Responsible Vendor's Act provides for a voluntary program which does have a sign requirement as a precondition to certification, but the sign required there merely warns that underage patrons who attempt to buy alcohol and those who use controlled substances illegally on the premises may be subject to ejectment. The Association warns that in the future the legislature could impose a different sign-posting requirement (or a requirement that no signs be posted at all) within its pervasive regulatory scheme which would result in a conflict with the ordinance before us. That argument is unpersuasive because it suggests that we speculate on future legislation. We decline to do so. We find that the ordinance is not inconsistent with general law. Thus, the ordinance is valid as a proper exercise of the County's broad, residual power of self-government granted it by article VIII, section 1(g) of the state constitution.

Although not necessary to our holding, we take note of section 125.01, Florida Statutes (1991), the general law granting certain powers of self-government to counties which do not operate under a charter. This statute, implementing article VIII, section 1(f) of the Florida constitution (non-charter government), describes the more limited powers of self-government enjoyed by such counties. *Speer v. Olson*, 367 So.2d 207 (Fla.1978). *See generally* Wolff, *Home Rule in Florida: A Critical Appraisal*, XIX Stetson L.Rev. 853, 881 (1990); Sparkman, *The History and Status of Local Government Powers in Florida*, XXV U.Fla.L.Rev. 271 (1973); Note, *Charter County Government in Florida: Past Litigation and Future Proposals*, XXXIII U.Fla.L.Rev. 505 (1981). Under this more limited "home rule" power, subsection (1)(o) provides that a non-chartered county may "establish and enforce regulations for the sale of alcoholic beverages in the unincorporated areas of the county pursuant to general law," and, subsection (1)(w) allows the non-chartered county to "exercise all powers and privileges not specifically prohibited by law." It is clear, then, that even if we were reviewing this ordinance in a case where it had been enacted by a non-chartered county, we would reach the same result. This would be so because there is nothing in section 125.01, or elsewhere in our statutes, prohibiting a non-chartered county from enacting such a health warning ordinance under the powers of self-government granted to it by the legislature. It would not be reasonable to hold that the ordinance would be valid under article VIII, section 1(f) (non-charter government) and its implementing statute, section 125.01, but not valid under the broader power of self-government pursuant to article VIII, section 1(g) (charter government). This analysis of article VIII, section 1(f) and Florida statute section 125.01 only serves to underscore the conclusion reached under the analysis presented earlier in this opinion.

In sum, we find no constitutional or legislative obstacle to this ordinance. Accordingly, we reverse the final summary judgment entered in favor of the Association

432   5 · LOCAL GOVERNMENT

and remand with instructions to enter a final summary judgment in favor of the County.

FRANK and PARKER, JJ., concur.

———

Preemption can also have an impact on municipal corporations, as the following language from *Zorc v. City of Vero Beach*[28] emphasizes:

> ... Clearly, any conflict between the City Charter and section 286.011(8) is negated under Article VIII, Section 2(b) of the Florida Constitution which provides that municipalities may exercise any power for municipal purposes *except as provided by law* (emphasis supplied). Municipal ordinances are inferior to laws of the state and must not conflict with any controlling provision of a statute. *See Thomas v. State*, 614 So.2d 468, 470 (Fla.1993). A municipality cannot forbid what the legislature has expressly licensed, authorized or required, nor may it authorize what the legislature has expressly forbidden. *See Thomas v. State*, 583 So.2d 336, 340 (Fla. 5th DCA 1991), *approved*, 614 So.2d 468 (Fla.1993).

The same rule should generally apply to other units of local government. There are, however, exceptions. Consider the following case.

2. Non-Preemption Type Conflict Between State and Local Government

City of Temple Terrace v. Hillsborough Association for Retarded Citizens, Inc.
322 So. 2d 571 (Fla. 2d Dist. Ct. App. 1975)

GRIMES, Judge.

This is an appeal from a judgment declaring that the defendants' operation of a home for the mentally retarded was not amenable to a city zoning ordinance because their activities partook of the sovereign immunity of the State of Florida.

On May 29, 1974, the Hillsborough Association for Retarded Citizens, Inc. (Association) entered into a contract with the Division of Retardation, Department of Health and Rehabilitative Services of the State of Florida, to provide respite care facilities and services to mentally retarded citizens. On June 13, 1974, the defendant Cook, who was a member of the Board of Directors of the Association, purchased a five bedroom house in a residential area of the City of Temple Terrace which was zoned "single family residential." The following month, the Association took possession of the house with Mr. Cook's permission and began operating its respite care center on the premises.

* * *

———

28. 722 So. 2d 891, 898 (Fla. 4th Dist. Ct. App. 1998).

The City of Temple Terrace, joined by several persons who live near the center, filed suit to enjoin the operation on grounds that it was a nuisance and was in violation of the zoning ordinances of the city. After the taking of testimony, the court entered a judgment in which it found that even though the use of the premises was contrary to the city's single family residential zoning ordinance, the ordinance could not be enforced against the operation of the facility. The court reasoned that when it was performing respite care services for the retarded, the Association stood in the shoes of the State of Florida and, as such, was not subject to municipal zoning ordinances. The court further found that the plaintiffs failed to support their claim that the defendants' use of the premises constituted a nuisance.

The appellants present essentially three questions: (1) whether a state agency (the Division of Retardation of the Department of Health and Rehabilitative Services) is subject to municipal zoning; (2) whether the Association is entitled to whatever immunity the Division may have; and (3) whether the operation of the respite care center constituted a nuisance. Since the ease by which these questions may be answered is opposite to the order in which the questions are presented, we shall dispose of them in inverse order.

* * *

The broad issue remaining in the case concerns the extent, if any, to which the use of land by a governmental unit is subject to applicable zoning regulations. In deciding this type of case, the courts have used varying tests. One approach utilized by a number of courts is to rule in favor of the superior sovereign. Thus, where immunity from a local zoning ordinance is claimed by an agency occupying a superior position in the governmental hierarchy, it is presumed that immunity was intended in the absence of express statutory language to the contrary. *E.g., Aviation Services, Inc. v. Board of Adjustment*, 1956, 20 N.J. 275, 119 A.2d 761. A second test frequently employed is to determine whether the institutional use proposed for the land is "governmental" or "proprietary" in nature. If the political unit is found to be performing a governmental function, it is immune from the conflicting zoning ordinance. *E.g., City of Scottsdale v. Municipal Court*, 1962, 90 Ariz. 393, 368 P.2d 637. On the other hand, when the use is considered proprietary, the zoning ordinance prevails. *E.g., Taber v. City of Benton Harbor*, 1937, 280 Mich. 522, 274 N.W. 324. Where the power of eminent domain has been granted to the governmental unit seeking immunity from local zoning, some courts have concluded that this conclusively demonstrates the unit's superiority where its proposed use conflicts with zoning regulations. *E.g., Mayor of Savannah v. Collins*, 1954, 211 Ga. 191, 84 S.E.2d 454. Other cases are controlled by explicit statutory provisions dealing with the question of whether the operation of a particular governmental unit is subject to local zoning. *E.g., Mogilner v. Metropolitan Plan Commission*, 1957, 236 Ind. 298, 140 N.E.2d 220.

When the governmental unit which seeks to circumvent a zoning ordinance is an arm of the state, the application of any of the foregoing tests has generally resulted in a judgment permitting the proposed use. This has accounted for statements of hornbook law to the effect that a state agency authorized to carry out a function of the state is not bound by local zoning regulations. 2 Anderson, American Law of Zoning § 9.06 (1968); 8 McQuillin, Municipal Corporations § 25.15 (1965).

Recently, however, several courts have advanced a new test for the resolution of the question of whether one governmental unit is subject to the zoning regulations of another. In *Rutgers, State University v. Piluso*, 1972, 60 N.J. 142, 286 A.2d 697, the court rejected the criteria often used to resolve the conflicts between governmental units and municipal ordinances as being too simplistic. Even though the dispute involved an attempt on the part of a township to impose its zoning upon an instrumentality of the state, the court adopted what it termed a "balancing of interests" test to decide the case. Thus, the court stated:

> The rationale which runs through our cases and which we are convinced should furnish the true test of immunity in the first instance, albeit a somewhat nebulous one, is the legislative intent in this regard with respect to the particular agency or function involved. That intent, rarely specifically expressed, is to be divined from a consideration of many factors, with a value judgment reached on an overall evaluation. All possible factors cannot be abstractly catalogued. The most obvious and common ones include the nature and scope of the instrumentality seeking immunity, the kind of function or land use involved, the extent of the public interest to be served thereby, the effect local land use regulation would have upon the enterprise concerned and the impact upon legitimate local interests. . . . In some instances one factor will be more influential than another or may be so significant as to completely overshadow all others. No one, such as the granting or withholding of the power of eminent domain, is to be thought of as ritualistically required or controlling. And there will undoubtedly be cases, as there have been in the past, where the broader public interest is so important that immunity must be granted even though the local interests may be great. The point is that there is no precise formula or set of criteria which will determine every case mechanically and automatically.

See also City of Newark v. University of Delaware, Del.Ch.1973, 304 A.2d 347; *Long Branch Division of United Civic and Taxpayers Organization v. Cowan*, 1972, 119 N.J.Super. 306, 291 A.2d 381; *Town of Oronoco v. City of Rochester*, 1972, 293 Minn. 468, 197 N.W.2d 426. A comprehensive note in 84 Harv.L.Rev. 869 (1971) persuasively argues for the use of the balancing of interests principle.

Before attempting to decide which test should be applied to reach a decision in the instant case, it is necessary to consider the Florida law on the subject. The court below and all parties recognize that no appellate court in Florida has squarely passed on this question. The earliest Florida decision involving a conflict between governmental units over the application of a zoning ordinance is *State ex rel. Helseth v. DuBose*, 1930, 99 Fla. 812, 128 So. 4. There, the City of Vero Beach refused to issue a building permit to Indian River County for the purpose of constructing a jail in violation of the provisions of the city's zoning ordinance. The Supreme Court ruled for the county, finding the application of the ordinance in this particular instance to be unreasonable and arbitrary in light of the location of the property and the proposed use. The court drew no distinction between public and private property owners in the application of zoning ordinances to their land and stated that the vestiture of title in the country was immaterial. Since counties are said to partake of the sovereign immunity of the state[1] this case could be cited for the proposition that state agencies are subject to municipal zoning in the same manner as private property owners.

On the other hand, the Supreme Court seemed to suggest the application of a governmental-proprietary test in *Nichols Engineering & Research Corp. v. State ex rel. Knight*, Fla.1952, 59 So.2d 874. This case held that the construction of an incinerator by the City of Miami, which had been authorized and designated a governmental function by statute, was not objectionable on the ground that the property on which it was to be situated had not been "adequately zoned" for the purpose. The court in *A1A Mobile Home Park, Inc. v. Brevard County*, Fla.App.4th, 1971, 246 So.2d 126, also appeared to adopt a governmental-proprietary test in passing upon whether the land use activity of a county was subject to its own zoning restrictions.

In *City of Treasure Island v. Decker*, Fla.App.2d, 1965, 174 So.2d 756, this court held that the City of St. Petersburg could impose its zoning regulations upon the City of Treasure Island with respect to a toll collection facility located on a portion of causeway within the city limits of St. Petersburg. The opinion emphasized that the legislative grant of authority to Treasure Island to construct and operate the toll facility did not specifically exempt it from the legislatively delegated zoning authority of St. Petersburg. This case, of course, dealt with two governmental units of equal stature in the governmental hierarchy.

A more recent case on intergovernmental conflict over zoning is *Orange County v. City of Apopka*, Fla.App.4th, 1974, 299 So.2d 652. Here, three municipalities sought to construct an airport in an unincorporated area of Orange County. Under the zoning regulations, airports were only allowed in the subject area by special exception. The zoning authority declined to grant an exception. The municipalities brought suit for a declaration that they were not subject to the zoning regulations of Orange County. After noting that the established law of Florida seemed to be that a governmental unit is not bound by its *own* zoning regulations when acting in a governmental capacity, the court declined to extend the application of the governmental-proprietary function test for resolving zoning conflicts to those cases in which one governmental unit proposed to use property in the jurisdiction of *another* governmental unit contrary to existing zoning regulations. The court said:

> Rather than become limited by the governmental-proprietary distinction which could lead to situations which cry for relief, we feel the better rule, the rule allowing for the greatest flexibility and fairness, is one which requires that one governmental unit be bound by the zoning regulations

---

1. *Kaulakis v. Boyd*, Fla.1962, 138 So. 2d 505.

of another governmental unit in the use of its extraterritorial property, purchased or condemned, in the absence of specific legislative authority to the contrary. In the absence of express legislative immunity from zoning, the intruding governmental unit should apply to the host governmental unit's zoning authority for a special exception or for a change in zoning, whichever is appropriate. The zoning authority is then in a position to consider and weigh the applicant's need for the use in question and its effect upon the host unit's zoning plan, neighboring property, environmental impact, and the myriad other relevant factors. If the applicant is dissatisfied with the decision of the zoning authority, it is entitled, pursuant to Section 163.250, F.S.1971, F. S.A.,[2] to a judicial determination *de novo* wherein the circuit court can balance the competing public and private interests essential to an equitable resolution of the conflict. The court can consider, inter alia, the type of function involved, the applicant's legislative grant of authority, the public need therefor, the existing land use scheme, alternative locations for the facility in less restrictive zoning areas, alternative methods for providing the needed improvement, and the detriment to the adjoining landowners. If after weighing all pertinent factors the court finds the host government is acting unreasonably, the zoning ordinance should be held inapplicable to the proposed improvement, just as was done in *State ex rel. Helseth v. DuBose*, 99 Fla. 812, 128 So. 4 (1930).

The District Court of Appeal construed *State ex rel. Helseth v. DuBose, supra*, as having utilized a "balancing-of-public-interest test" and decided to adopt that criterion. That same court more recently reaffirmed its position in *Palm Beach County v. Town of Palm Beach*, Fla.App.4th, 1975, 310 So.2d 384, by directing the application of a "balancing-of-competing interest test" to determine whether Palm Beach County would be entitled to use certain property in the Town of Palm Beach as an ocean front beach and recreational facility in violation of the zoning regulations of Palm Beach.

With no sure precedent to go by, we will now examine the merits of the several tests which have been used to decide this type of case.

Superior Sovereign Test

The argument in favor of this view is that since a municipality is a creature of the state legislature, it should not be permitted to use its zoning to thwart a state function. The premise upon which this contention is made seems to have been weakened by the adoption of Florida's new Constitution. Article VIII, Section 2(b) of the Florida Constitution provides:

(b) POWERS. Municipalities shall have governmental, corporate and proprietary powers to enable them to conduct municipal government, perform

---

2. On rehearing, the court receded from its reference to §163.250 but otherwise adhered to its opinion.

municipal functions and render municipal services, and may exercise any power for municipal purposes except as otherwise provided by law. . . .

Thus, even though municipalities may be created by statute, their powers are derived from the Constitution.

However, in *City of Miami Beach v. Fleetwood Hotel, Inc.*, Fla.1972, 261 So.2d 801, the Supreme Court cast doubt on the broad scope of municipal home rule which many had thought was provided in the 1968 Constitution. Specifically, the court held that the City of Miami Beach could not adopt a rent control ordinance absent a legislative enactment authorizing the exercise of such power.

Thereafter, in 1973, the legislature passed the Municipal Home Rule Powers Act. Included in this act was Fla.Stat. § 166.021(4) (1973) which stated:

> The provisions of this section shall be so construed as to secure for munici-palities the broad exercise of home rule powers granted by the constitution. It is the further intent of the legislature to extend to municipalities the exer-cise of powers for municipal governmental, corporate, or proprietary pur-poses not expressly prohibited by the constitution, general or special law, or county charter and to remove any limitations, judicially imposed or other-wise, on the exercise of home rule powers other than those so expressly prohibited. . . .

In the passage of Fla.Stat. § 166.042 (1973), the legislature repealed the legislative grant of zoning power (what had been Chapter 176) in recognition that the zoning power of municipalities now comes directly from the Constitution. The Municipal Home Rule Powers Act placed two pertinent exceptions upon the constitutionally-based legislative powers of municipalities. First, Fla.Stat. § 166.021(3)(b) (1973) pro-vides that municipalities may not enact legislation concerning any subject expressly prohibited by the Constitution. Second, Fla.Stat. § 166.021(3)(c) (1973) states that municipalities may not enact legislation concerning any subject expressly pre-empted to state or county government by the Constitution or by general law. The Constitution does not expressly prohibit zoning legislation by municipalities. Nei-ther does the Constitution nor general law expressly preempt zoning power to state or county government.

The Supreme Court considered the validity of a new rent control ordinance pro-mulgated by the City of Miami Beach following the passage of the Home Rule Pow-ers Act in *City of Miami Beach v. Forte Towers, Inc.*, Fla.1974, 305 So.2d 764. The court held that the enactment of a rent control ordinance was not "expressly prohib-ited by law" and came within the grant of power contained in Fla.Stat. § 166.021(1).

All of this leads us to believe that the instant case should not be decided solely upon the theory that since the state stands higher than a municipality upon the lad-der of governmental hierarchy, the decisions of its administrators should necessarily preempt the zoning authority of those charged with governing a municipality. With this in mind, we shall consider the validity of the other recognized tests for deciding this type of case.

Governmental-Proprietary Test

The wisdom of the governmental-proprietary test is subject to question. *E. g.,* *Township of Washington v. Village of Ridgewood*, 1958, 26 N.J. 578, 141 A.2d 308; 2 Anderson, American Law of Zoning § 9.05 (1968). Its applicability in Florida now seems limited to situations where a governmental unit seeks to violate its own zoning ordinance. *See Orange County v. City of Apopka, supra.* Presumably, if a governmental agency is authorized to perform a function, it should not make any difference whether this function is governmental or proprietary in nature for the purpose of complying with local zoning. Some of the fallacies of applying such a test may be seen by comparing the case of *County of Westchester v. Village of Mamaroneck*, 1964, 22 A.D.2d 143, 255 N.Y.S. 2d 290, with that of *Jefferson County v. City of Birmingham*, 1951, 256 Ala. 436, 55 So.2d 196. The decision first cited above held that the operation of a sewage disposal plant was governmental in nature, whereas the second held it was proprietary. In the case *sub judice*, the services provided by the Association for the Division of Retardation appear to be governmental in nature, but we are not inclined to decide the case based upon this characterization.

Power of Eminent Domain Test

Cases which have applied this test generally take the position that where a political unit is authorized to condemn, it is automatically immune from local zoning regulations when it acts in furtherance of its designated public function. Yet, the power to condemn simply provides a method whereby property can be acquired. Such power has nothing to do with the use of the property. The leading case favoring the adoption of this test is *State ex rel. Askew v. Kopp*, Mo.1960, 330 S.W.2d 882. However, the Supreme Court of Missouri two years after its decision in *Askew* modified the doctrine of absolute immunity which had been established in that case. Thus, in *St. Louis County v. City of Manchester*, Mo.1962, 360 S.W.2d 638, the court held that a city's power of eminent domain did not necessarily conflict with a county's authority to regulate land uses through its zoning ordinances. The court held that while the city had the right to acquire the property by eminent domain, it had not been specifically authorized by statute to select the exact location of a sewage plant in disregard of the county's zoning ordinance. In the instant case, the Association is not asserting that it has the right to disregard the city's zoning on the basis of any kind of right of eminent domain which might be available to the Division of Retardation. Even if it were, we would not consider this power as controlling our decision in the case.

Statutory Guidance Test

If the legislature had specifically provided that the Division of Retardation could place respite centers in any location it wished without regard to local zoning, such a legislative declaration would control. Likewise, if there was a law which required the Division of Retardation to respect municipal zoning in its selection of sites for respite centers, this too, would be decisive. As it turns out, there is no legislative guidance either way. Obviously, the Association argues that since the legislature has not restricted the Division's authority, it must be presumed that the legislature intended for the Division to have the right to disregard municipal zoning. On the other hand, the city contends that since the legislature didn't specifically authorize the Division to ignore municipal zoning, it must be presumed that the legislature intended the Division to respect municipal zoning ordinances. It is more likely that the legislature didn't express itself on the subject because it wasn't thinking about the problem. We hesitate to suggest that there is a presumption running in either direction. While we acknowledge that a specific legislative statement on the subject would control, in the absence of such a statement we must look to other criteria in order to reach a decision.

Balancing of Interests Test

Thus, we arrive at the balancing of interests test, which is sometimes referred to as the balancing of competing interests test or the balancing of public interests test. For the reasons previously given in discussing this test, we believe that it presents the fairest method by which this type of case can be decided. It permits a case by case determination which takes into consideration all of the factors which may properly influence the result.

The old tests were adopted at a time when state government was much smaller. The myriad of agencies now conducting the functions of the state have necessarily resulted in a diminution of centralized control. The decision of a person administering an outlying function of a state agency with respect to the site where this function should be performed is not necessarily any better than the decision of the local authorities on the subject of land use. The adoption of the balancing of interests test will compel governmental agencies to make more responsible land-use decisions by forcing them to consider the feasibility of other sites for the facility as well as alternative methods of making the use of the proposed site less detrimental to the local zoning scheme.

Our burgeoning population and the rapidly diminishing available land make it all the more important that the use of land be intelligently controlled. This can only be done by a cooperative effort between interested parties who approach their differences with an open mind and with respect for the objectives of the other. When the state legislature is silent on the subject, the governmental unit seeking to use land contrary to applicable zoning regulations should have the burden of proving that the public interests favoring the proposed use outweigh those mitigating against a use not sanctioned by the zoning regulations of the host government.

There may be cases in which a state agency may be so convinced of the overriding public need for a particular land use that it may choose to go forward without resort to local authorities. Yet, under normal circumstances one would expect the agency to first approach the appropriate governing body with a view toward seeking a change in the applicable zoning or otherwise obtaining the proper approvals necessary to permit the proposed use.

As was the District Court of Appeal in *Orange County v. City of Apopka, supra,* we are reluctant to reverse the decision of the court below. Like the judgment entered in that case, the judgment below was well considered and there is ample authority for the conclusions which were reached. Nevertheless, we adopt the rationale of our sister court in determining to use the balancing of interests test to decide the consequences resulting from the exercise of a governmental function by one governmental unit within the geographic limits of a different governmental unit, and we do so without regard to the fact that one of those governmental units is the state.

The court below rendered its decision on the basis of the superior sovereign test. Therefore, the judgment is reversed, and the case is remanded with directions to conduct further proceedings directed toward the decision of the case through the application of the balancing of interests test.

Reversed and remanded.

HOBSON, A. C. J., and SCHEB, J., concur.

On Petition for Rehearing

GRIMES, Judge.

In addition to the usual petitions for rehearing, there have now been filed in this cause motions by the Department of Health and Rehabilitative Services and the Attorney General for permission to file amicus curiae briefs. The Department of Health and Rehabilitative Services points out that it was not a party in the case and says it was first informed of our opinion on the date the motion was filed. The Attorney General says that our opinion conflicts with the previous uniform practice of all state agencies.

The very filing of these motions serves to illustrate the need to employ a balancing of interests test to decide these cases. The sovereign immunity approach presupposes that the sovereign, in its wisdom, has already carefully weighed the needs of the public against the hardships likely to be inflicted on nearby property owners in deciding to locate a governmental facility in an area where the proposed activity is prohibited by local zoning laws. To the contrary, it appears that many times, as in this case, the decision of whether to conduct a governmental activity at a location precluded by zoning laws is not being consciously made by persons charged with the responsibility of considering the effect of this activity upon the persons who live nearby.

The motions for permission to file amicus curiae briefs come too late and are hereby denied. The petitions for rehearing are also denied.

Recognizing that our opinion would and believing that it should require state agencies affirmatively to take into consideration the effect that their activities may have on local zoning laws and the people sought to be protected by these laws, we hereby certify this case to the Supreme Court as involving a question of great public interest in order that the rules which should be followed may be definitely established on a statewide basis.

HOBSON, A. C. J., and SCHEB, J., concur.

The Florida Supreme Court adopted "as [its] own" the preceding opinion of the Second District Court of Appeal.[29]

G. Local-Local Relationships

Fla. Const. art. VIII, § 3

Consolidation. — The government of a county and the government of one or more municipalities located therein may be consolidated into a single government which may exercise any and all powers of the county and the several municipalities. The consolidation plan may be proposed only by special law, which shall become effective if approved by vote of the electors of the county, or of the county and municipalities affected, as may be provided in the plan. Consolidation shall not extend the territorial scope of taxation for the payment of pre-existing debt except to areas whose residents receive a benefit from the facility or service for which the indebtedness was incurred.

Fla. Const. art. VIII, § 4

Transfer of powers. — By law or by resolution of the governing bodies of each of the governments affected, any function or power of a county, municipality or special district may be transferred to or contracted to be performed by another county, municipality or special district, after approval by vote of the electors of the transferor and approval by vote of the electors of the transferee, or as otherwise provided by law.

The following opinions discuss the concepts of consolidation and the less formal transfer of powers. They also discuss the constitutional prerequisites for consolidating governmental entities or transferring governmental power.

---

29. *Hillsborough Ass'n for Retarded Citizens, Inc. v. City of Temple Terrace*, 332 So. 2d 610, 612 (Fla. 1976).

1. Consolidation

Albury v. City of Jacksonville Beach

295 So. 2d 297 (Fla. 1974)

[The consolidation in this case occurred under the provisions of the 1885 Constitution. It should be noted that this part of the 1885 Constitution was retained under the schedule to Article VIII of the 1968 Constitution. Although accomplished under a *specific* provision of the 1885 Constitution, it is illustrative of the sort of problem that may plague consolidation attempts under the new general consolidation provision of the 1968 Constitution.]

BOYD, Justice.

This is an appeal from an opinion and order of the District Court of Appeal, First District, (Case No. S-448, opinion filed November 8, 1973, not yet reported). We have jurisdiction by virtue of Article V, Section 3(b)(1).

Plaintiffs, Beaches and Baldwin, in their amended complaint, sought a declaration as to their legal status and relationship to the Defendant-City under the new charter adopted in 1967. Further, Beaches and Baldwin sought to determine whether they might levy municipal occupational license taxes on persons engaging in occupations in their jurisdictions, as well as whether they have a right to receive directly from the state and federal agencies revenues designated under general law to be distributed to municipalities. In the Consolidated Government's counterclaim, it and its Tax Collector sought different declarations as to many of the same points, plus further judicial clarification of its authority to enact ordinances pre-empting ordinances of the Beaches and Baldwin. The trial court granted substantially the relief sought by the Consolidated Government, holding the Beaches and Baldwin to subordinate urban services districts and no longer entitled to levy occupational license taxes or to otherwise assert legal standing as incorporated municipalities. On appeal, the District Court of Appeal, First District, reversed on the authority of this Court's opinion in Jackson v. Consolidated Government of the City of Jacksonville, 225 So.2d 497 (Fla.1969); it held that the Beaches and Baldwin continue to exist as quasi-municipal corporations; that, as such, they are empowered to exercise all municipal functions which they were permitted to perform under their original municipal charters and the general laws of the State immediately prior to the consolidation; and, that they are corporate entities having the same rights as duly constituted municipal corporations to share in, receive, and expend revenues allocable to municipal corporations by both the federal and state governments. We agree.

An examination of pertinent legislative history shows that, prior to 1967, the Plaintiffs were created by special acts of the Legislature in accordance with the existing constitution. In 1967, pursuant to the constitutional authority vested in the Legislature by Article VIII, Sections 8 and 9, the Legislature adopted Chapter 67-1320, Laws of Florida, 1967, by which the present City of Jacksonville was created. Four days later another statute (Chapter 67-1535, Laws of Florida, 1967) was introduced which altered materially the original charter act; this amendatory act was passed by the Legislature. Thereafter, there was passed Chapter 67-1547, Laws of Florida, 1967, also amending the basic act. All three acts, which together comprise the present charter of the consolidated City of Jacksonville, were subject to a referendum held in Duval County and were approved.

According to the original act, Chapter 67-1320, a single government was created (Section 1.01) which had any and all powers of the cities, county, or any former government (Section 3.01) including the power to levy occupational license tax (Section 3.02). By the terms of Chapter 67-1320, the corporate municipal structures of the Beaches and Baldwin were effectively abolished, becoming a part of urban services districts whose sole function was to act in accordance with such power and authority as might be delegated to them by the Consolidated Government for convenience in administering municipal functions. Under Chapter 67-1320, the Consolidated Government was empowered to levy both an occupational license tax against all businesses and professions in the county in the exercise of its county function, and to levy a second occupational license tax against all businesses and professions operating within the urban services districts of the City in the exercise of its municipal function. Since there is no authority in Chapter 67-1320 for the urban services districts to levy or collect occupational license taxes, if there had been no amendments to that chapter, it would be clear that only the Consolidated Government would be entitled to levy occupational license taxes against businesses and professions operating in the county at large and in the urban services districts.

We note, however, that Chapter 67-1535 was enacted within days after the original charter act. This act effectively restored to the Beaches and Baldwin the powers which the first act took away. Since it was adopted by the Legislature subsequent to the prior act divesting them of authority, and since the last expression of the Legislature will prevail in cases of conflicting statutes,[1] and since all three were approved by referendum, the modifications became effective simultaneously with the original act. Therefore, we must conclude that the intent of the Legislature and the people was to preserve the powers formerly granted to the municipal governments of the Beaches and Baldwin including the power to tax and authority to receive federal and state grants.

This Court has held in Jackson, supra, that the legislative intent was to preserve the smaller governmental entities of the Beaches and Baldwin as quasi-municipalities. If that is not what the people and the Legislature intended or presently desire, appropriate changes should be made by them and not by this Court.

Concerning the authority of the consolidated government to collect occupational license taxes in the quasi-municipalities, we observe that the opinion of the District Court of Appeal herein reviewed correctly finds each quasi-municipality to be authorized to collect such a tax. No challenge is made against payment of a

---

1. DeConingh v. City of Daytona Beach, 103 So.2d 233 (Fla.App.1958).

county-wide occupational tax to what was formerly Duval County. The record and admissions of counsel show that business and professional persons in other parts of old Duval County are now required by ordinance to pay two license taxes, one being a municipal tax paid to the Consolidated Government and the other being to the same entity of government in place of the old Duval County occupational license.

A careful examination of the Constitution and Statutes of Florida leads us to the conclusion that whenever any one of the small quasi-municipalities is collecting occupational license taxes, the consolidated government can collect only that tax which would have been payable to old Duval County had consolidation never occurred.

To require business and professional persons in the small quasi-municipalities to pay three such license taxes (one to the quasi-municipality and two to the Consolidated Government — one "county" and one "municipal"), while their neighbors would pay only the latter two, would be unconstitutionally discriminatory and a denial of due process of law unless it should be clearly shown that a higher quality of governmental services was being furnished them than in other parts of the Consolidated Government. No such justification is shown by this record.

Accordingly, we affirm the decision of the District Court of Appeal, and since the case is disposed of as an appeal, the petition for certiorari is denied.

It is so ordered.

ADKINS, C. J., and ERVIN, McCAIN, DEKLE and OVERTON, JJ., concur.

ROBERTS, J., specially concurring with opinion.

ROBERTS, Justice (specially concurring).

The history, factual background, questions presented and disposition are clearly set out in the opinion of the District Court. Argument having been heard and the court having considered the records and briefs, it is my opinion that the ruling of the District Court is correct and should be adopted as the opinion of this Court.

Accordingly, I would agree to the judgment only of this Court affirming the decision of the District Court.

Town of Baldwin v. Consolidated City of Jacksonville

610 So. 2d 95 (Fla. 1st Dist. Ct. App. 1992)

SHRIVERS, Judge.

This appeal is from a final order granting summary judgment and declaring annexation ordinances passed by the Town of Baldwin unconstitutional. We affirm.

Fred Miller and A.G. Ambrose each own land in Duval County. The two parcels total approximately 57 acres and adjoin the Town of Baldwin, which is also in Duval County. In April and September 1990, at the petition of Miller and Ambrose, Baldwin's town council passed ordinances annexing the two parcels into its incorporated area.

In October 1990 Jacksonville filed an amended complaint seeking declaratory and injunctive relief. The complaint alleges that the annexed land "is located entirely within the boundary of the corporate limits of the Consolidated City of Jacksonville." The complaint also alleges that the boundary of the corporate limits of Jacksonville is coextensive with the territorial boundary of Duval County; with the exceptions of Baldwin and three beach cities, "there have been no unincorporated areas located within the territorial boundaries of Duval County." Accordingly, Jacksonville sought an adjudication that Baldwin's annexation ordinances are unconstitutional.

Baldwin answered the complaint and denied that (1) the annexed property is located within the boundary of the corporate limits of the Consolidated City of Jacksonville, and (2) there have been no unincorporated areas located within the territorial boundaries of Duval County.

Both parties moved for summary judgment. As background, Baldwin quotes from *City of Jacksonville Beach v. Albury*, 291 So.2d 82 (Fla. 1st DCA 1973), *aff'd*, 295 So.2d 297 (Fla.1974).

> [The Beach Cities' and Baldwin's] freedom to function as independent corporate entities is restricted only by the right of the consolidated government of the City of Jacksonville to adopt ordinances in the exercise of its county governmental functions binding on the territory and inhabitants of those urban service districts comprising the Beaches and Baldwin only to the extent as would have been permitted by Duval County prior to consolidation.
>
> . . . .
>
> [The Beach Cities and Baldwin] are empowered to exercise all municipal functions, powers, duties, and authority normally possessed and exercised by other duly chartered municipal corporations in this state.

Id. at 89–90. Baldwin argued that it thus has the same power to annex as any municipality.

Jacksonville also moved for summary judgment. It argued that Chapter 78-536, Laws of Florida, states that the consolidated governments of the City of Jacksonville and Duval County "shall . . . extend territorially throughout Duval County . . . and shall have jurisdiction as a municipality throughout Duval County except in . . . the Town of Baldwin." All lands are incorporated as either the municipal corporation of Jacksonville or several 'quasi municipal' corporations, such as Baldwin. Therefore, there are no unincorporated lands within the boundaries of Duval County. Section 171.043, Florida Statutes, prohibits annexation of an area "included within the boundary of another incorporated municipality." Further, pursuant to section 2.06 of Jacksonville's Charter, only the legislature can expand the territory of Baldwin unless the Charter itself provides otherwise; the Charter does not provide otherwise.

The trial court entered a final order granting Jacksonville's motion for summary judgment, denying Baldwin's motion for summary judgment, and declaring Baldwin's annexation ordinances unconstitutional and void ab initio. The order states, "Within the boundaries of Duval County there is no unincorporated land."

We affirm the trial court's order. Article VIII, section 9, of the 1885 Florida Constitution, as preserved by Article VIII, section 6(e), of the 1968 constitution, empowered the legislature to establish

> a Municipal corporation to be known as the City of Jacksonville extending throughout the present limits of Duval County, in the place of any or all county . . . and local governments. . . . Such municipality may exercise all the powers of a municipal corporation . . . which would accrue to it if it were a county. All property of Duval County and of the municipalities in said county shall vest in such municipal corporation when established. . . .

The legislature divided the City of Jacksonville into a general services district (Duval County) and five urban services districts: #1) the former city limits of Jacksonville, #2) Jacksonville Beach, #3) Atlantic Beach, #4) Neptune Beach, and #5) the Town of Baldwin. The first Charter of the City of Jacksonville states that all the governments in Duval County

> are hereby consolidated into a single body politic and corporate. . . . The consolidated government shall . . . succeed to and possess all the properties . . . of the former governments. . . . The consolidated government shall have jurisdiction, and extend territorially throughout the present limits of Duval County.

Ch. 67-1320, §§ 1.01 and 1.02, Laws of Fla. (1967). In 1978 the Charter was amended to clarify that Jacksonville's municipal powers extended throughout the county, except for the Beach Cities and Baldwin.

The conflict in this case is between (1) Baldwin's right as a quasi-municipal corporation to exercise municipal functions (such as annexation of unincorporated land) just as any other municipal corporation in Florida pursuant to *Albury*, and (2) the right of any incorporated municipality (such as the City of Jacksonville) to be protected from annexation of land within its boundaries by another municipality pursuant to section 171.043(1). Appellee correctly states, "The essence of the issue in this case is whether the area in Jacksonville designated as 'general services district' is part of the [incorporated] City of Jacksonville."

Chapter 67-1320, Laws of Florida (1967), consolidated all of Duval County into "a single body politic and corporate." The consolidation was initiated "pursuant to the power granted by section 9 of article VIII of the [Florida] Constitution." Section 9 states, "The Legislature shall have power to establish, alter or abolish, a *Municipal corporation* to be known as the City of Jacksonville, extending territorially throughout the present limits of Duval County. . . ." (emphasis added). Therefore, according to the Florida Constitution, the Consolidated City of Jacksonville is a municipal corporation extending throughout Duval County; there is no unincorporated land in Duval County.

The 1967 legislature amended Chapter 1320 in Chapter 1535, the intent of which was to "preserve for the people residing in the (second through fourth) urban districts the same local governmental structure . . . and laws which existed in those areas prior to the effective date of this charter." Ch. 67-1535, § 2A.01, Laws of Fla. The second through fourth urban districts also (1) retained use of its property and the entitlement to "own, acquire, encumber and transfer property in its own name," and (2) remained subject to all special and general laws which applied to their former governments "as if the municipal charters of those former governments were still in full force and effect." Ch. 67-1535, §§ 2A.05 and 2A.06, Laws of Fla. Accordingly, the supreme court held in *Jackson v. Consolidated Government of the City of Jacksonville*, 225 So.2d 497 (Fla.1969), that the consolidated city "will extend throughout the territory, but that one or more municipal or local governments in the territory may continue in existence [as] quasi municipal corporations." *Id.* at 503.

Baldwin argues that because *Albury* classifies it as a "duly constituted municipal corporation," which is empowered to exercise all municipal functions that they were permitted to perform under state law prior to consolidation, they can annex as freely as any municipality.

However, "[m]unicipal annexation of unincorporated territory, merger of municipalities, and exercise of extraterritorial powers by municipalities shall be as provided by general or special law." Art. VIII, § 2(c), Fla. Const. Regardless of whether Baldwin is relying on section 171.04(1), Florida Statutes (1965), or section 171.043(1), Florida Statutes (1989), general law provides that no municipality can annex land "within the boundary of another incorporated municipality."

Because (1) according to the Florida Constitution there is no unincorporated land in Duval County, (2) the land annexed by Baldwin is in Duval County, and (3) no municipality can unilaterally annex incorporated land, the trial court correctly ruled that Baldwin's attempted annexation of land within Duval County is unconstitutional.

AFFIRMED.

SMITH and KAHN, JJ., concur.

2. The Tension Between Fla. Const. art. VIII, § 4, Transfer of Powers and the Preemption Power of Charter Counties

City of New Smyrna Beach v. County of Volusia

518 So. 2d 1379 (Fla. 5th Dist. Ct. App. 1988)

ORFINGER, Judge.

The pivotal issue in this case is the facial constitutionality of an amendment to the Volusia County Charter which establishes a Beach Trust Commission, and which authorizes the County Council, with the advice of the Commission, to adopt a Unified Beach Code "comprehensively regulating public health, safety and welfare on and pertaining to the [Atlantic Ocean] beach" within the county. The trial court implicitly found the charter amendment to be facially constitutional. We affirm.

This action commenced when four municipalities located in Volusia County challenged the proposed Charter Amendment 4, requesting an injunction to prohibit a county-wide election for approval of the amendment, and a declaratory judgment to determine the constitutionality of the amendment. The trial court denied the request for injunctive relief but reserved ruling on the request for declaratory judgment.

Subsequently, the election was held and Amendment 4 was adopted by a majority of those voting in the election. Three of the four cities then entered voluntary dismissals, leaving the City of New Smyrna Beach (City) as the sole plaintiff. The City amended its complaint alleging that the amendment failed to pass by majority vote within the municipal limits of the City. After the County filed its answer, a non-jury trial was held based on stipulated facts and on the testimony of certain witnesses.

The municipal boundaries of the City include all beaches and oceanfront property within the city limits. Since 1943, the City has performed various governmental activities and operations relating to its beaches. The County, by agreement with the City, provides life guard services and has maintained traffic signals on thoroughfares leading to the beach. The County also has partially provided ambulance services exclusively allocated to the beach and provides coordinated civil defense for the City's beaches.

In the early 1980s, because of the conflicting policies of the various municipalities within the county with regard to beach access and regulation, a Chamber of Commerce committee recommended that a single entity be established to regulate and manage the beaches. In 1983 the Volusia Interlocal Beach Commission (VIBC) was created by agreement between the cities of Daytona Beach Shores, Ormond Beach, Ponce Inlet, and Volusia County to study problems relating to beach management.[1]

---

1. The City of New Smyrna Beach declined to participate in the VIBC. It was the City's position that it did not share the same problems faced by those beach communities north of Ponce Inlet.

The VIBC issued a final report, recommending a uniform regulatory plan applicable to all Volusia County beaches.

In 1985, a Charter Review Commission was formed to study beach management. In August of 1986, the Commission issued its final report in which it expressed its concern for the political inequities resulting from the control of the beaches by municipalities. The Commission also determined that there "is a definite need to protect the traditional rights of public access and enjoyment of Volusia beaches." The report further stated that vehicular access to the beach had been dramatically reduced by the policies of beachfront cities. The Commission found that without a county-wide uniform access fee, "public rights of beach access are in great jeopardy," that off-beach parking was needed to protect public access and that a county-wide beach agency was the most effective method of providing such facilities.

To address the concerns and issues which had been identified during its study, the Commission recommended the adoption of a Charter Amendment[2] to create a

---

2. The pertinent portions of the Charter Amendment provide:
Section 205 — Unified Countywide Beach Regulations
Section 205.1. THE BEACH: PUBLIC RIGHT OF ACCESS AND USE.
The public has a right of access to the beaches and a right to use the beaches for recreation and other customary purposes. This right of access and use is a public trust, which the Council shall by ordinance define, protect, and enforce. Because prohibiting motor vehicle access to the beaches would deny beach use to many, the Council shall authorize, as permitted by law, vehicular access to any part of the beach not reasonably accessible from public parking facilities on or adjacent to the beach.
Section 205.2. BEACH TRUST COMMISSION
The BEACH TRUST COMMISSION is created to consist of residents of municipalities and unincorporated areas in the coastal area appointed by their governing bodies with representation apportioned on the basis of population, as provided by ordinance. The Council shall assign administrative duties under this article to the Commission and a County department.
Section 205.3. UNIFIED BEACH CODE
With the advice of the Commission, the Council shall have the power and it shall be its duty, on or before January 1, 1988, to enact an ordinance, to be known as the Unified Beach Code ("Code"), comprehensively regulating public health, safety, and welfare on and pertaining to the beach, including, but not limited to, regulation of: individual conduct; pedestrian safety; vehicular access and fees; operation and parking of vehicles on beaches and approaches; and vendors, concessionaires, and special events.
Section 205.4. VEHICULAR ACCESS FEES
The Council shall have the exclusive power to impose a uniform, reasonable vehicular beach access fee, but no other fee shall be charged for individual beach access or use. Revenues derived from vehicular access fees and all other revenues derived from the beach shall be expended solely for direct beach purposes permitted by law. Directly and by grants to municipalities, the Council shall expend such revenues to maintain a uniform level of services responsive to use and demand.
Section 205.5. DELIVERY OF SERVICES ON THE BEACH
No function or power relating to services is transferred from any municipality to the County. The municipalities may continue to deliver any services on their beaches, which shall not be duplicated by the County. However, if authorized by a municipality, the County shall assume, at the County's expense, any municipal beach service.

Beach Trust Commission for the purpose of unifying beach regulations. As previously indicated, the proposed charter amendment was submitted to the electorate and was approved by a majority vote. The tabulated results indicated that a majority of those voting within each of the affected cities approved the amendment, except for those precincts within New Smyrna Beach, where the majority disapproved it.

At the heart of this controversy is the tension between two apparently conflicting provisions of the Florida Constitution. The first provision provides for the exercise of powers by a chartered county government:

> Counties operating under county charters shall have all powers of local self-government not inconsistent with general law, or with special law approved by vote of the electors. The governing body of a county operating under a charter may enact county ordinances not inconsistent with general law. The charter shall provide which shall prevail in the event of conflict between county and municipal ordinances.

Art. VIII, § 1(g), Fla. Const. The second provision provides for the transfer of powers between county and municipal governments:

> By law or by resolution of the governing bodies of each of the governments affected, any function or power of a county, municipality or special district may be transferred to or contracted to be performed by another county, municipality or special district, after approval by vote of the electors of the transferor and approval by vote of the electors of the transferee, or as otherwise provided by law.

Art. VIII, § 4, Fla. Const. The city argues that the provisions of Amendment 4 constitute a transfer of the City's powers relating to the beaches and beach services, and are thus invalid absent approval by the dual referenda specified in Article VIII, section 4.

The City relies on *Sarasota County v. Town of Longboat Key*, 355 So.2d 1197 (Fla.1978), where the county commission adopted an ordinance proposing five amendments to the county charter which would transfer the responsibilities for performing five distinct governmental functions from four Sarasota County cities to the county. These functions were: (1) air and water pollution control; (2) parks and recreation; (3) roads and bridges; (4) planning and zoning; and (5) police. The trial court issued an injunction prohibiting the referendum and the county appealed. On appeal, there was no serious dispute that the proposed charter amendment involved

---

Section 205.6. EFFECT OF UNIFIED BEACH CODE

The County shall have jurisdiction over the coastal beaches and approaches as well as exclusive authority to regulate the beaches and public beach access and use. To the extent sovereign immunity has been waived, the County shall assume any governmental liability arising after the Code takes effect for claims in areas controlled by the County under this article, including claims alleging failure to warn of dangers, but unless otherwise agreed, the County will not be liable for any act of a municipality. Any ordinance enacted pursuant to this article shall prevail in the event of conflict with a municipal ordinance.

a transfer of functions between different units of government. Rather, the county argued that under section 1(g) of Article VIII, charter counties were excluded from the dual referendum requirement. The court rejected this argument and expressed its reluctance to "elevate the general provisions of Article VIII, Section 1(g) to a dominant position over the specific provision of Article VIII, Section 4." In rejecting this argument, the court held that a transfer of governmental powers requires the distinctive features prescribed in Article VIII, section 4, i.e., a law or resolution of the governing bodies of each of the governments affected. It concluded that the five proposed amendments constituted attempts to transfer powers and functions from the cities to the county which were invalid because the requirements of Article VIII, section 4 had not been complied with.

Subsequent decisions of the supreme court have distinguished, and in fact, have clarified the holding of *Sarasota County*. In *City of Palm Beach Gardens v. Barnes*, 390 So.2d 1188 (Fla.1980) the court held that a contract between the city and the county sheriff to perform law enforcement services within the city did not fall within the ambit of Article VIII, section 4. In *Miami Dolphins v. Metropolitan Dade County*, 394 So.2d 981 (Fla.1981), a group of Dade County citizens, joined by the intervenor Miami Dolphins, challenged a plan by the county to use revenues of a tourist room tax to modernize and improve the Orange Bowl Football Stadium. The contestants argued that the plan improperly attempted to transfer a function from the city (as owner of the stadium) to the county, thus requiring compliance with the procedure specified in Article VIII, section 4. The court rejected this contention, distinguished *Sarasota County*, and held that the ordinance in question did not seek to transfer jurisdiction over the Orange Bowl from the city to the county, but simply allocated certain tax revenues for the renovation of the stadium, which the city was asked to accept.

The most recent resolution of this issue by the supreme court, and the one on which the County relies heavily, is *Broward County v. City of Fort Lauderdale*, 480 So.2d 631 (Fla.1985). There, the city sought to enjoin a county-wide referendum to amend the county charter to provide that county ordinances relating to the regulation of handguns would prevail over conflicting municipal ordinances. The trial court denied the request and the city appealed. The Fourth District read *Sarasota County* broadly, and when it determined that the purpose of the amendment was to restrict the city's power over handgun management, concluded that the proposal was for a transfer of power from the city to the county, which could not be accomplished without compliance with Article VIII, section 4. 458 So. 2d at 785.

In quashing the decision of the district court of appeal, the supreme court reviewed the respective functions of section 1(g) and section 4 of Article VIII, and distinguished them thusly:

> We hold that section 1(g) permits *regulatory* preemption by counties, while section 4 requires dual referenda to transfer functions or powers relating to *services*. A charter county may preempt a municipal regulatory power in such areas as handgun sales when county-wide uniformity will best further

the ends of government. § 125.86(7), Fla.Stat. (1983). Dual referenda are necessary when the preemption goes beyond regulation and intrudes upon a municipality's provision of services.

* * *

We believe the distinction between regulatory preemption, and transfer of functions and powers relating to services, achieves the balance between sections 1(g) and 4 intended by the framers of the 1968 constitution. [Emphasis in original.]

480 So.2d at 635. The court again revisited *Sarasota County*, and observed that in that case, the "wholesale assumption of the burden of providing what had been municipal services [went] far beyond regulatory preemption. . . ." *Id.*

The City argues that the operative provisions of Amendment 4 impermissibly shift the responsibility of control of beach services from the City to the County. However, the amendment reveals that it is carefully drafted to pertain only to regulatory matters. The expressed intent of the amendment is to guarantee beach access to the public. To effectuate this purpose, section 205.1 mandates the County Council to authorize "as permitted by law"[3] vehicular access in areas of the beach not reasonably accessible from public parking facilities. Section 205.4 gives to the Council exclusive power to impose reasonable vehicular beach access fee and prohibits municipalities from charging any additional fees. Section 205.3 authorizes a comprehensive unified beach code regulating all aspects of the public health, safety, and welfare on and pertaining to the beach. Finally, section 205.6 grants to the County exclusive *regulatory* jurisdiction over the beaches and approaches. On their face, none of these provisions relate to the provision of services. Rather, they pertain exclusively to the Court's regulatory powers over the beaches, an area which the Beach Trust Commission found to be "conducive to uniform countywide enforcement." § 125.86(7), Fla.Stat. (1985). Moreover, section 205.5 expressly disclaims any intent to assume control over services provided by municipalities and prohibits the County from duplicating any services already provided by the City. The City argues

---

3. Section 161.58(2), Florida Statutes provides the procedure whereby local governments may authorize vehicular traffic on beaches:

(2) Vehicular traffic, except that which is necessary for cleanup, repair, or public safety, or for the purpose of maintaining existing authorized public access ways, is prohibited on coastal beaches. Notwithstanding the provisions of this subsection, the local government with jurisdiction over a coastal beach or part of a coastal beach, by a three-fifths vote of its governing body, may authorize vehicular traffic on all or portions of the beaches under its jurisdiction. Any such local government shall be authorized by a three-fifths vote of its governing body to charge a reasonable fee for vehicular traffic access. The revenues from any such fees shall be used only for beach maintenance purposes. Except where authorized by the local government, any person driving any vehicle on, over, or across the beach shall be guilty of a misdemeanor of the second degree, punishable as provided in s. 775.082, s. 775.083, or s. 775.084. [Footnote omitted.]

§ 161.58(2), Fla. Stat. (1985). See also *City of Daytona Beach Shores v. State*, 483 So.2d 405 (Fla.1985).

that Amendment 4 divests it of functions and powers relating to the beach that it has previously exercised. However, the control to be exercised by the county, i.e., access fees, regulation of traffic, rules pertaining to individual conduct, operation and parking of vehicles on the beach, etc., clearly relates to regulation of those members of the public making use of the beach. These matters, like regulation of firearms, are areas which section 1(g) authorizes the county to regulate on a county-wide basis, preempting local governments. *Broward County*; §125.86(7), Fla. Stat. (1985).

We reject the City's contention that the amendment does not address a county-wide concern. The Charter Review Commission determined from its study that the regulation of the beach has county-wide economic, political and recreational implications. Certainly use of the beaches is not confined to only those residents of the municipalities which directly abut the beach. We conclude that there is a logical basis shown by this record for the finding that uniform regulation of the beach is required in the public interest. We find nothing in the amendment which attempts to usurp the powers of the municipalities to provide services to the beaches as they do to other areas within their respective limits. By its express language, "[n]o function or power relating to services is transferred from any municipality to the County." §205.5. The amendment contemplates distribution of beach access revenues to the cities for the continued provision of services. We therefore conclude that the amendment does not facially conflict with Article VIII, section 4.

We also affirm the trial court's conclusion that it is premature to determine the constitutionality of the amendment as it applies to the City. The amendment is not self-executing, but requires the adoption of a Unified Beach Code. The effect of any such code was not before the trial court and is not before us here. We have carefully considered the remaining arguments raised by the City but find them to be without merit.

AFFIRMED.

DAUKSCH and COWART, JJ., concur.

Chapter 6

Taxation and Finance

A. Taxation

1. What Is a Tax?

The Florida Supreme Court has defined a tax as "an enforced burden or contribution imposed by sovereign right for the support of the government, the administration of the law, and to execute the various functions the sovereign is called on to perform."[1] In *State ex rel. Gulfstream Park Racing Association v. Florida State Racing Commission*,[2] the Florida Supreme Court defined it thusly:

> In common parlance, a tax is a forced charge or imposition, it operates whether we like it or not and in no sense depends on the will or contract of the one on whom it is imposed.

Governmental entities in Florida obtain the necessary revenue to fund their operations from primarily four revenue sources: (1) taxes; (2) fees and charges; (3) special assessments; and (4) debt financing. Certain constitutional restrictions apply to the imposition, administration, and collection of taxes that are not applicable to other fees and charges imposed by government. These non-tax charges run the gamut from impact fees to special assessments and have their own special rules for validity under Florida case law. In the absence of statutory authorization, a fee or special assessment that does not meet these rules will be deemed an "illegal tax" because the Florida Constitution authorizes units of local government to impose only ad valorem taxes and no other taxes "except as provided by general law."[3]

To the extent possible, governmental entities will often attempt to characterize a charge as a fee rather than as a tax to avoid the sometimes onerous constitutional and statutory requirements regulating the imposition of taxes. It therefore becomes necessary for the courts to delineate the boundaries between taxes and other governmental fees and charges. The following cases represent the Florida Supreme Court's attempt to make this distinction regarding taxes, impact fees, user fees, and other charges and special assessments.

---

1. *Klemm v. Davenport*, 129 So. 904, 907 (Fla. 1930).
2. 70 So. 2d 375, 379 (Fla. 1953).
3. Fla. Const. art. VII, § 1(a).

a. Impact Fees and User Service Charges

Fees charged by local governmental entities generally fall into two categories: (1) regulatory fees; and (2) user charges or fees. Regulatory fees are imposed under the police power of the local government entity in the exercise of its sovereign function and cannot exceed the cost of, and must be used solely to pay the cost of, the regulatory activity for which they are imposed.[4] Impact fees are a form of regulatory fees and are charged by local governmental entities to finance additional infrastructure required to serve new growth and development. Their use has become an accepted method of paying for public improvements that must be constructed to serve new growth.[5] To be valid, impact fees cannot exceed the pro rata share of the cost of expanding the facilities or infrastructure for which they are charged and must be "earmarked" or used solely for the purpose of meeting the cost of expanding the facility or infrastructure for which they are charged. Stated another way, the fees must be used for the benefit of those paying the fee. The Florida courts have adopted what is known as the "dual rational nexus test" to determine the validity of impact fees.

User fees, on the other hand, are imposed under the proprietary power of the local government entity and are charged in exchange for a particular governmental service which benefits the party paying the fee in a manner not shared by other members of society. User fees are paid by choice, in that the party paying the fee has the option of not utilizing the governmental service and thereby avoiding the charge.[6] In determining the validity of user fees, the courts look to whether the fees are spent for the benefit of those who paid the fees and whether the fees are reasonable. The following case illustrates the above principles.

Contractors & Builders Association of Pinellas County v. City of Dunedin

329 So. 2d 314 (Fla. 1976)

HATCHETT, Justice.

In an action for declaratory judgment, brought against the City of Dunedin in Circuit Court, provisions of certain ordinances [footnote omitted] were adjudged defective, as being an *ultra vires* attempt by the city to impose taxes; and the city was enjoined from collecting fees the ordinances required as a precondition for municipal water and sewerage service. In addition, the Circuit Court ordered the City to refund the fees, but only to persons who had paid under protest. On appeal to the District Court of Appeal, Second District, that court reversed the circuit court judgment, *City of Dunedin, Florida v. Contractors and Builders Association of Pinellas*

---

4. Nabors, Giblin & Nickerson, P.A., *Primer on Home Rule and Local Government Revenue Sources*, at 28 (April 2010).

5. *St. Johns Cnty. v. Northeast Fla. Builders Ass'n, Inc.*, 583 So. 2d 635 (Fla. 1991).

6. *State v. City of Port Orange*, 650 So. 2d 1, 3 (Fla. 1994).

County, etc. et al., 312 So.2d 763; and, on June 10, 1975, certified that its decision passed upon a question of great public interest. As is customary in cases where such certificates have been entered, we exercise our discretion to review on its merits the decision below. . . .

Plaintiffs in the trial court, petitioners here, are building contractors, an incorporated association of contractors, and owners of land situated within the city limits of Dunedin. [Footnote omitted.] They do not complain of all the fees Dunedin requires to be collected upon issuance of building permits, [footnote omitted] but contend that monies which the city collects and earmarks for "capital improvements to the [water and sewerage] system as a whole" (R. 725) constitute taxes, which a municipality is forbidden to impose, in the absence of enabling legislation. It is agreed on all sides that "a municipality cannot impose a tax, other than ad valorem taxes, unless authorized by general law." 312 So.2d at 766, and that no general law gives such authorization here. Respondent contends that these fees are not taxes, but user charges analogous to fees collected by privately owned utilities for services rendered. For the reasons stated in Judge Grimes' scholarly opinion, we accept this analogy, but we decline to uphold a revenue generating ordinance that omits provisions we deem crucial to its validity. We are unpersuaded, moreover, that the limitations, which the city has in fact placed on fees collected pursuant to Dunedin, Fla., Code §§ 25-31, 25-71(c) and (d), can suffice to make those fees "just and equitable," within the meaning of Fla.Stat. § 180.13(2) (1973). In principle, however, we see nothing wrong with transferring to the new user of a municipally owned water or sewer system a fair share of the costs new use of the system involves.

* * *

The avowed purpose of the ordinance in the present case is to raise money in order to expand the water and sewerage systems, so as to meet the increased demand which additional connections to the system create. *The municipality seeks to shift to the user expenses incurred on his account.* A private utility in the same circumstances would presumably do the same thing, in which event surely even petitioners would not suggest that the private corporation was attempting to levy a tax on its customers. [Footnote omitted.]

Under the constitution, Dunedin, as the corporate proprietor of its water and sewer systems, can exercise the powers of any other such proprietor (except as Fla. Stat. §§ 180.01 *et seq.,* or statutes enacted hereafter, may otherwise provide.)[6] Municipal corporations have "governmental, corporate and proprietary powers" and "may exercise any power for municipal purposes, except as otherwise provided by law." Fla.Const. art. VIII, § 2(b); *City of Miami Beach v. Fleetwood Hotel, Inc.,* 261 So.2d

---

6. Chapter 180 was enacted before the 1968 Constitution was adopted, and some language in the chapter is anachronistic. The statutes refer to "powers granted by this chapter," Fla.Stat. §§ 180.03(1), .21 (1973), whereas, under the 1968 Constitution, the provisions of Chapter 180 are restrictions on the exercise of power the constitution itself confers, rather than the grant of powers these statutory provisions formerly constituted.

801 (Fla.1972).[7] "Implicit in the power to provide municipal services is the power to construct, maintain and operate the necessary facilities." *Cooksey v. Utilities Commission*, 261 So.2d 129, 130 (Fla.1972). There are no provisions in Chapter 180, Florida Statutes, expressly governing capital acquisition other than through deficit financing,[8] but it is provided that the "legislative body of the municipality ... may establish just and equitable rates or charges" for water and sewerage. Fla.Stat. § 180.13(2) (1973). *See* generally Annot., 61 A.L.R.3d 1236, 1248–1259 (1975).

* * *

Water and sewer rates and charges do not, therefore, cease to be "just and equitable" merely because they are set high enough to meet the system's capital requirements, as well as defray operating expenses. . . .

. . . . Dunedin distinguishes between residential and commercial users, on one hand, and industrial users, on the other . . . and petitioners do not question this distinction. Here the issue is whether differential connection charges are "just and equitable", when they vary depending on the time at which the connection to the utility system is made.

Raising expansion capital by setting connection charges, which do not exceed a *pro rata* share of reasonably anticipated costs of expansion, is permissible where expansion is reasonably required, *if use of the money collected is limited to meeting the costs of expansion.*[10] Users "who benefit especially [sic], not from the maintenance of the system, but by the extension of the system . . . should bear the cost of that extension." *Hartman v. Aurora Sanitary District, supra*, 177 N.E.2d at 218. On the other hand, it is not "just and equitable" for a municipally owned utility to impose the entire burden of capital expenditures, including replacement of existing plant, on persons connecting to a water and sewer system after an arbitrarily chosen time certain.

The cost of new facilities should be borne by new users to the extent new use requires new facilities, but only to that extent. When new facilities must be built in any event, looking only to new users for necessary capital gives old users a windfall at the expense of the new users.

* * *

---

7. But a municipality's power to tax is subject to the restrictions enumerated in Fla.Const. art. VII § 9 including the restriction discussed above. *City of Tampa v. Birdsong Motors, Inc.*, 261 So.2d 1 (Fla.1972).

8. Special assessments are another common means of financing sewer construction. Fla.Stat. § 170.01 (1973). The fees in controversy here are not special assessments. They are charges for use of water and sewer facilities; the property owner who does not use the facilities does not pay the fee. Under no circumstances would the fees constitute a lien on realty.

10. The "costs of expansion" may sometimes be difficult to identify precisely when certain kinds of capital expenditures are made; in this matter, too, "perfection is not the standard of municipal duty." *Rutherford v. City of Omaha, supra* 160 N.W.2d at 228.

6 · TAXATION AND FINANCE

. . . . If the ordinance in the present case had so restricted use of the fees which it required to be collected, there would be little question as to its validity. We conclude that the ordinance in the present case cannot stand as it is written.

* * *

The failure to include necessary restrictions on the use of the fund is bound to result in confusion, at best. City personnel may come and go before the fund is exhausted, yet there is nothing in writing to guide their use of these moneys, although certain uses, even within the water and sewer systems, would undercut the legal basis for the fund's existence. There is no justification for such casual handling of public moneys, and we therefore hold that the ordinance is defective for failure to spell out necessary restrictions on the use of fees it authorizes to be collected. [Footnote omitted.] Nothing we decide, however, prevents Dunedin from adopting another sewer connection charge ordinance, incorporating appropriate restrictions on use of the revenues it produces. Dunedin is at liberty, moreover, to adopt an ordinance restricting the use of moneys already collected. . . .

The decision of the District Court of Appeal is quashed and this case is remanded to the District Court with directions that the District Court dispose of the question of costs; and that the District Court thereafter remand for further proceedings in the trial court not inconsistent with this opinion. In the trial court's consideration *de novo* of the question of refunds the chancellor is at liberty to take into account all pertinent developments since entry of his original decree.

It is so ordered.

ADKINS, C. J., and ROBERTS, OVERTON and ENGLAND, JJ., concur.

While *City of Dunedin*[7] remains the seminal case with regard to the legal requirements for the imposition of impact fees, a two-pronged dual rational nexus test has emerged under Florida case law in the years following the decision. This test was first articulated by the Third District Court of Appeal in *Wald Corporation v. Metropolitan Dade County*,[8] which was decided in the same year as *City of Dunedin*.[9] The Third District in *Wald* surveyed constitutional tests used by courts in other states to evaluate subdivision exactions. The Third District enunciated a "rational nexus" or "reasonable connection" test and held that dedication or impact fee ordinances are valid when there is a reasonable connection between the required dedication or fee and the anticipated needs of the community because of the new development.[10]

---

7. 329 So. 2d 314 (Fla. 1976).

8. 338 So. 2d 863 (Fla. 3d Dist. Ct. App. 1976).

9. *See* J. Michael Marshall & Mark A. Rothenberg, *An Analysis of Affordable/Work-force Housing Initiatives and Their Legality in the State of Florida, Part II*, Fla. Bar J., Vol. 82, No. 7, July/Aug. 2008, at 53–54, https://www.floridabar.org/the-florida-bar-journal/an-analysis-of-affordable-work-force-housing-initiatives-and-their-legality-in-the-state-of-florida-part-ii/.

10. *Id.*

In 1983, the Fourth District Court of Appeal in *Hollywood, Inc., v. Broward County,*[11] based upon the decisions in *City of Dunedin, Wald,* and its prior holding in *Admiral Development Corp. v. City of Maitland,*[12] expounded upon the aforesaid test and articulated what has become known as the "dual rational nexus" test. In rendering its decision, the Court in the Fourth District stated:

> [f]rom City of Dunedin, Wald, and Admiral Development, we discern the general legal principle that reasonable dedication or impact fee requirements are permissible so long as they offset needs sufficiently attributable to the subdivision and so long as the funds collected are sufficiently earmarked for the substantial benefit of the subdivision residents. [Footnote omitted.] In order to satisfy these requirements, the local government must demonstrate a reasonable connection, or rational nexus, between the need for additional capital facilities and the growth in population generated by the subdivision. In addition, the government must show a reasonable connection, or rational nexus, between the expenditures of the funds collected and the benefits accruing to the subdivision. In order to satisfy this latter requirement, the ordinance must specifically earmark the funds collected for use in acquiring capital facilities to benefit the new residents.

This "dual rational nexus" test was ultimately adopted by the Florida Supreme Court in 1991 in *St. Johns County v. Northeast Florida Builders Association, Inc.,*[13] and remains substantially unchanged. In addition to the rules established under case law for the imposition of impact fees to pay for new development, in 2006 the Florida legislature enacted the "Florida Impact Fee Act,"[14] which imposes additional statutory requirements with regard to levying impact fees.

b. Special Assessments

A special assessment is a common method used by counties, municipalities, and special districts to pay for services, such as fire and rescue services, and the cost of construction of infrastructure and capital improvements, such as sewer and street improvements, within certain areas of their respective boundaries. A special assessment is similar to a tax in that it is a forced contribution from the property owner; however, the two are distinguishable in that while both are mandatory, a special assessment must confer a special benefit on the land burdened by the assessment. There is no such requirement for a tax, which may be levied throughout a particular taxing unit for the general benefit of the residents.[15] A legally imposed special assessment will not be deemed a tax; however, if not validly imposed, the courts will deem it to be an "illegal tax." There are two requirements for the imposition of

---

11. 431 So. 2d 606 (Fla. 4th Dist. Ct. App. 1983).
12. 267 So. 2d 860 (Fla. 4th Dist. Ct. App. 1972).
13. 583 So. 2d 635 (Fla. 1991).
14. Fla. Stat. § 163.31801 (2021).
15. *City of Boca Raton v. State*, 595 So.2d 25 (Fla. 1992).

a valid special assessment. First, the property assessed must derive a special benefit from the service provided.[16] Second, the assessment must be fairly and reasonably apportioned among the properties that receive the special benefit.[17] Thus, a special assessment is distinguished from a tax because of its special benefit and fair apportionment requirements. In *City of Cooper v. Joliff*,[18] the Fourth District Court of Appeal stated, "[f]or almost a century, our supreme court has called upon local governments to ensure the limitations on taxation set forth in our constitution are not avoided by blurring the line between taxes and special assessments." The following cases depict how the Supreme Court applies the above requirements to determine the validity of a special assessment.

(1) Special Benefit Requirement

Lake County v. Water Oak Management Corp.

695 So. 2d 667 (Fla. 1997)

OVERTON, Justice.

We have for review *Water Oak Management Corp. v. Lake County*, 673 So.2d 135 (Fla. 5th DCA 1996), in which the district court certified the following question to be of great public importance:

> IS LAKE COUNTY'S FUNDING BY SPECIAL ASSESSMENT OF SOLID WASTE DISPOSAL AND/OR FIRE PROTECTION SERVICES VALID UNDER THE FLORIDA CONSTITUTION?

We have jurisdiction. Art. V, §3(b)(4), Fla. Const. We reword the certified question as follows:

> DO LAKE COUNTY'S SOLID WASTE DISPOSAL AND FIRE PROTECTION SERVICES FUNDED BY SPECIAL ASSESSMENT PROVIDE A SPECIAL BENEFIT TO THE ASSESSED PROPERTIES?

For the reasons expressed, we answer the reworded question in the affirmative.

Water Oak Management Corporation and other property owners in Lake County filed suit seeking to invalidate Lake County's special assessments for fire protection and solid waste disposal services. The trial court granted summary judgment in favor of Lake County, finding the assessments to be valid. On appeal, the Fifth District Court of Appeal affirmed, without discussion, the summary judgment as to the solid waste disposal assessment based on this Court's recent decision in *Sarasota County v. Sarasota Church of Christ, Inc.*, 667 So.2d 180 (Fla.1995). The district court found, however, that the special assessment for fire protection services was invalid because the services funded by the assessment provided no special benefit to the assessed properties. The district court determined that a special benefit is one that

---

16. *Atl. Coast Line R.R. v. City of Gainesville*, 83 Fla. 275, 91 So. 118 (1922).

17. *South Trail Fire Control Dist. v. State*, 273 So.2d 380 (Fla.1973).

18. 227 So. 3d 633 (Fla. 4th Dist. Ct. App. 2017).

is "different in type or degree from benefits provided the community as a whole."[1] Because everyone in the county has access to "basic garden variety Lake County fire protection services," the district court found the assessment to be invalid. In so holding, the district court certified the aforementioned question.

First, based on our opinion in *Harris v. Wilson*, 693 So.2d 945 (Fla.1997), we agree with the district court's summary conclusion that the solid waste disposal special assessment at issue in this case is valid. In *Harris*, we recently approved a very similar assessment. *See also Sarasota County.* We disagree, however, with the district court's conclusion that the fire protection services funded by the special assessment in this case do not provide a special benefit to the assessed properties and thus is invalid. The relevant facts regarding these services were set forth by the district court as follows:

> In 1980, Lake County created various fire control districts within the county to facilitate the provision of fire protection services in the unincorporated area. Lake County funded these districts through a special ad valorem tax levy. In 1984, the voters of Lake County and the voters within each fire control district approved the imposition of a special assessment for fire protection. Consequently, in 1985 Lake County changed its fire control program to impose a special assessment against property for fire protection. Lake County also established the maximum amount of the assessment for various land uses. Lake County provided and funded fire control services in this manner until 1990.

> On December 11, 1990, Lake County adopted Ordinance 1990-24 which created a single MSTU[1] consisting of the entire unincorporated area of Lake County, the city of Minneola, and the town of Lady Lake. This ordinance had the effect of consolidating all the county's previously created fire control districts into a single unit and authorized the collection of special assessments pursuant to section 197.3632, Florida Statutes (1993). Lake County's affidavit filed in support of the motion for summary judgment recites that the properties assessed are "benefited" because they receive fire protection.[2]

> Lake County's fire protection budget is based on the fire department's overall costs of operation. The budget provides funding for fire stations, fire fighter salaries, equipment, training, and other general operating expenses. The fire protection special assessment is determined by setting

---

1. The district court obtained this language from section 170.01(2), Florida Statutes (1995), which governs the authority for municipalities to levy special assessments.

1. Municipal Service Taxing Unit. It is acknowledged by Lake County that this is incorrect nomenclature for such an assessment.

2. Lake County further argues that if no fire protection services were present in Lake County, the entire county would be rated a ten on the Insurance Services Office ["ISO"] schedule for insurance premiums, but, due to the proximity to hydrants, most Lake County properties are at some level less than ten.

the county fire protection budget, then deducting revenues received from other sources. The assessment covers approximately sixty-eight percent of the budget and eliminates the use of the county's general funds for this purpose. Lake County provides a number of services under the umbrella of "fire protection services" such as fire suppression activities, first-response medical aid, educational programs and inspections. The medical response teams stabilize patients and provide them with initial medical care. The fire department responds to automobile and other accident scenes and is involved in civil defense. Fire services are provided to all individuals and property involved in such incidents.

Water Oak, 673 So.2d at 136–37.

In reviewing a special assessment, a two-prong test must be addressed: (1) whether the services at issue provide a special benefit to the assessed property; and (2) whether the assessment for the services is properly apportioned. *Sarasota County*, 667 So.2d at 183; *City of Boca Raton v. State*, 595 So.2d 25, 30 (Fla.1992). As reflected by the district court's decision and the reworded certified question, the case before us deals with the first prong, special benefit.

The property owners urge us to approve the district court's decision. They argue that the special assessment for fire protection services is unconstitutional because those services do not provide a "unique" benefit to the assessed properties and are not "different in type or degree from benefits provided the community as a whole." They assert that in *St. Lucie County-Fort Pierce Fire Prevention & Control District v. Higgs*, 141 So.2d 744 (Fla.1962), this Court correctly rejected assessments for fire protection because those services were of a general nature and did not provide a unique benefit to the assessed properties. We reject this contention and find that the property owners have misconstrued our decision in *Higgs*. In fact, this Court has previously determined that fire protection services do provide a special benefit to real property. *South Trail Fire Control Dist. v. State*, 273 So.2d 380 (Fla.1973); *Fire Dist. No. 1 v. Jenkins*, 221 So.2d 740 (Fla.1969).

In evaluating whether a special benefit is conferred to property by the services for which the assessment is imposed, the test is not whether the services confer a "unique" benefit or are different in type or degree from the benefit provided to the community as a whole;[2] rather, the test is whether there is a "logical relationship" between the services provided and the benefit to real property. *Whisnant v. Stringfellow*, 50 So.2d 885 (Fla.1951); *Crowder v. Phillips*, 146 Fla. 440, 1 So.2d 629 (1941) (on rehearing). Although fire protection services are generally available to the community as a whole, the greatest benefit of those services is to owners of real property.

---

2. The district court erred in comparing the special assessment to section 170.01(2), the statute governing municipal powers, and in stating that the services funded through a special assessment must be "different in type or degree from benefits provided the community as a whole." There is no such limitation in the constitution or statute governing county governments.

As we stated in *Jenkins*:

> On the question of to what extent property may be said to be specially benefited by the creation and operation of a Fire District, much may be said. Fire protection and the availability of fire equipment afford many benefits.

> Fire Insurance premiums are decreased; public safety is protected; the value of business property is enhanced by the creation of the Fire District; a trailer park with fire protection offers a better service to tenants, which would reflect in the rental charge of the spaces. It is not necessary that the benefits be direct or immediate, but they must be substantial, certain, and capable of being realized within a reasonable time.

221 So.2d at 741. As we concluded in *Jenkins*, fire protection services do, at a minimum, specially benefit real property by providing for lower insurance premiums and enhancing the value of the property. Thus, there is a "logical relationship" between the services provided and the benefit to real property. However, to be valid, the assessment for fire protection services must still meet the apportionment test; that is, the assessment must be properly apportioned as to the special benefit received by the assessed property. This was the reason we disapproved the fire protection services assessment in *Higgs*. In that case, the assessment was levied on "'taxable property, including homesteads, *to the extent that taxes may be lawfully levied upon homesteads.*'" 141 So.2d at 745–46 (quoting ch. 59-1806, Laws of Fla.) (alteration in original). We concluded that the fees assessed in that case constituted a tax rather than a special assessment because "no parcel of land was *specially* or peculiarly benefited *in proportion to its value.*" *Id.* at 746 (second emphasis added). Specifically, the assessment in that case was actually a tax because it had been wrongfully apportioned based on the assessed value of the properties rather than on the special benefits provided to the properties. In sum, we disapproved the assessment in *Higgs* based on the assessment's failure to meet the apportionment prong rather than the special benefit prong. Thus, the contention of the property owners that *Higgs* controls the issue of whether fire services provide a special benefit to the assessed properties is without merit. Rather, *Higgs* addresses the question of apportionment, which is not before us in this review.

Contrary to the assertions of the opponents to the assessment here, we do not believe that today's decision will result in a never-ending flood of assessments. Clearly, services such as general law enforcement activities, the provision of courts, and indigent health care are, like fire protection services, functions required for an organized society. However, unlike fire protection services, those services provide no direct, special benefit to real property. *Whisnant*. Thus, such services cannot be the subject of a special assessment because there is no logical relationship between the services provided and the benefit to real property.

Accordingly, we find that Lake County's solid waste disposal and fire protection services funded by special assessment provide a special benefit to the assessed properties; we answer the certified question, as reworded, in the affirmative; and we quash that portion of the district court's decision that rules the fire protection services special assessment invalid.

It is so ordered.

KOGAN, C.J., and SHAW and ANSTEAD, JJ., concur.

WELLS, J., dissents with an opinion, in which GRIMES and HARDING, JJ., concur.

WELLS, Justice, dissenting.

I dissent. Consistent with my separate dissenting opinions first in *Sarasota County v. Sarasota Church of Christ*, 667 So.2d 180 (Fla.1995), and then in *Harris v. Wilson*, 693 So.2d 945 (Fla.1997), and *State v. Sarasota County*, 693 So.2d 546 (Fla.1997), I cannot concur with the majority's conversion of this state's local-government tax base to a general-assessment tax base, thereby demolishing constitutional provisions for ad valorem tax caps, homestead exemptions, and bonding referendums. The majority's path of demolition began in *Sarasota Church of Christ*, when it eliminated "special" from "special assessment." Today, the Court broadens the path further. Most alarmingly the majority changes the test for determining what is a special assessment. I would approve the decision of the district court in this case which held that the fire protection services in this case did not provide a *special* benefit to the real property in the service district.

This Court has previously addressed questions concerning special assessments for fire prevention districts. *See South Trail Fire Control Dist. v. State*, 273 So.2d 380 (Fla.1973); *Fire District No. 1 v. Jenkins*, 221 So.2d 740 (Fla.1969); *St. Lucie County-Fort Pierce Fire Prevention & Control Dist. v. Higgs*, 141 So.2d 744 (Fla.1962). However, the results in these cases may not have appeared consistent. Compare *South Trail Fire Control Dist.* (finding proper the apportionment of a special assessment for fire protection which required commercial property owners to pay on an area basis and other property owners to pay on a flat-rate basis) *and Jenkins* (finding valid special assessments for fire protection against each parcel of real estate, including mobile home rental spaces, in the fire district), *with Higgs* (finding invalid a special assessment for fire protection to each parcel of land in a fire district with boundaries coinciding with the county). In reconciling these cases, I do not agree with the majority that this Court reached its decision in *Higgs* (finding the assessment was invalid) on the basis that the assessment failed the "apportionment" prong rather than the "special benefit" prong. *See* majority op. at 669–670. The reason for my disagreement is simply that the word "apportionment" is not in the *Higgs* opinion. Rather, that opinion is succinctly and accurately characterized by the district court in this case:

> In *St. Lucie County-Fort Pierce Fire Prevention and Control Dist. v. Higgs*, 141 So.2d 744 (Fla.1962), however, the high court held that a special act creating a county-wide fire prevention district was invalid because no parcel of land was specially or peculiarly benefited in proportion to its value; rather,

the assessment was a general one on all property in the county-wide district for the benefit of all. 141 So.2d at 746.

Water Oak Management Corp. v. Lake County, 673 So.2d 135, 137 (Fla. 5th DCA 1996); *see also Murphy v. City of Port St. Lucie*, 666 So.2d 879, 881 (Fla.1995) (stating that the special assessment in *Higgs* was invalid because the county attempted to assess *all* properties in order to provide fire protection to the entire county). In fact, *Higgs* is founded upon Justice Thornal's succinct and lucid opinion in *Fisher v. Board of County Commissioners*, 84 So.2d 572 (Fla.1956). *Fisher* is a case which I have relied upon in my dissents on this issue and which the majority ignores as if it did not exist.

I do not believe that this Court should in this case rewrite our decisional law. Rather, I conclude that we can reconcile our conflicting decisions on this issue as the district court did below. *See Water Oak Management Corp.*, 673 So.2d at 137–38. The court there found that the divergence of these cases suggests that the question of a "special benefit" is a decision based primarily on the facts of each case. *Id.* As an example, the district court stated that the creation of a fire district within a limited area of the county, which brought fire services which were formerly distant into close proximity with the property, would seem to offer a special benefit of the kind envisioned in *Jenkins. Water Oak Management Corp.*, 673 So.2d at 137–38. However, I completely agree with the district court that a county's determination to specially assess all property in a county for the same historically provided county-wide fire protection services on the basis that these services now provide a special benefit is not proper. *Id.*

Furthermore, I take particular issue with the majority's test for the determination of a special benefit. The majority states:

> In evaluating whether a special benefit is conferred to property by the services for which the assessment is imposed, the test is not whether the services confer a "unique" benefit or are different in type or degree from the benefit provided to the community as a whole; rather, the test is whether there is a "logical relationship" between the services provided and the benefit to real property. *Whisnant v. Stringfellow*, 50 So.2d 885 (Fla.1951); *Crowder v. Phillips*, 146 Fla. 440, 1 So.2d 629 (1941) (on rehearing).

Majority op. at 669 (footnote omitted). By making this statement, the majority subtly revises history and definitely erases the distinction between a special assessment and a tax for several reasons. First, in both *Whisnant* and *Crowder*, this Court struck the levy as being a tax rather than a special assessment. *See Whisnant* (finding a levy for a county health unit a tax rather than a special assessment on the basis that this unit provided no special or peculiar benefit to the real property located in the district); *Crowder* (finding a levy for the construction of a hospital in a district coextensive with Leon County a tax on the basis that the hospital provided a benefit to the entire community and not just landowners).

Additionally, while both *Whisnant* and *Crowder* mention the need for a "logical relationship" for a special assessment to be valid, the majority takes this statement out of context. For in each of these cases this Court recognized that a logical relationship alone is not enough; the special assessment must also provide a special or peculiar benefit to the real property located in the district. *Whisnant*, 50 So.2d at 885–886; *Crowder*, 146 Fla. at 441–43, 1 So.2d at 631. To hold otherwise spurns the historical test for determining whether a levy is a special assessment announced in *City of Boca Raton v. State*, 595 So.2d 25 (Fla.1992).

In *City of Boca Raton*, this Court expressly relied upon and, in the eyes of any objective reader, revalidated this Court's statement in *Klemm v. Davenport*, 100 Fla. 627, 631, 129 So. 904, 907 (1930):

> A tax is an enforced burden of contribution imposed by sovereign right for the support of the government, the administration of the law, and to execute the various functions the sovereign is called on to perform. A special assessment is like a tax in that it is an enforced contribution from the property owner, it may possess other points of similarity to a tax, but it is inherently different and governed by entirely different principles. It is imposed upon the theory that that portion of the community which is required to bear it receives some special or peculiar benefit in the enhancement of value of the property against which it is imposed as a result of the improvement made with the proceeds of the special assessment.

There is simply no way to reconcile the majority's new "logical relationship" test with the "peculiar benefit" analysis first stated in *Klemm* and later cited in *City of Boca Raton*. I can only conclude that the majority has receded from *City of Boca Raton*, though it states elsewhere in the opinion that it relies upon it. *See* majority op. at 669.

In sum, I would affirm the district court's conclusion that Lake County's special assessment for fire protection fails the special-benefit test. *See Water Oak Management Corp.* I would not rephrase the adequate question certified by the district court[3] and would answer the certified question in respect to fire protection in the negative.

GRIMES and HARDING, JJ., concur.

For purposes of a special assessment for the provision of municipal services to unincorporated areas of the county, the county may, but apparently is not required to, create one or more Municipal Service Benefit Units.[19]

In determining whether a special assessment confers a special benefit to burdened property, the courts look to whether there is a "logical relationship" between the services provided and the benefit to real property. In holdings subsequent to its

---

3. In its rephrased question, the majority answers the issue of the propriety of the solid waste special assessment, even though this issue is not discussed in the district court's opinion, and I would not address it here.

19. *See Sockol v. Kimmins Recycling Corp.*, 729 So. 2d 998 (Fla. 4th Dist. Ct. App. 1999).

decision in *Water Oak Management Corporation*, the Florida Supreme Court has sometimes appeared to recede from the "logical relationship" test and return to the "unique benefit" test, but the Supreme Court in *City of North Lauderdale v. SMM Properties, Inc.*[20] reiterated that the "logical relationship" remains the standard by which the court judges whether a special assessment confers a special benefit to burdened property. The Florida courts have held that there is no logical relationship between services such as emergency medical services, general law enforcement, the provision of the courts, and indigent healthcare, and the benefit to real property. Thus, the aforesaid services cannot be the subject of a special assessment.[21]

(2) Fair and Reasonable Apportionment Requirement

City of Boca Raton v. State

595 So. 2d 25 (Fla. 1992)

GRIMES, Justice.

[The facts of this case are reproduced in Chapter 5 of this book.]

* * *

... [T]hose opposing the bond issue make two arguments. First, they contend that the special assessment is really a tax, which the City may not impose because of the language of article VII, section 1(a) of the Florida Constitution, which provides:

> (a) No tax shall be levied except in pursuance of law. No state ad valorem taxes shall be levied upon real estate or tangible personal property. All other forms of taxation shall be preempted to the state except as provided by general law.

However, a legally imposed special assessment is not a tax. Taxes and special assessments are distinguishable in that, while both are mandatory, there is no requirement that taxes provide any specific benefit to the property; instead, they may be levied throughout the particular taxing unit for the general benefit of residents and property. On the other hand, special assessments must confer a specific benefit upon the land burdened by the assessment. *City of Naples v. Moon*, 269 So.2d 355 (Fla.1972). As explained in *Klemm v. Davenport*, 100 Fla. 627, 631–34, 129 So. 904, 907–08 (1930):

> A tax is an enforced burden of contribution imposed by sovereign right for the support of the government, the administration of the law, and to execute the various functions the sovereign is called on to perform. A special assessment is like a tax in that it is an enforced contribution from the property owner, it may possess other points of similarity to a tax but it is inherently different and governed by entirely different principles. It is imposed upon the theory that that portion of the community which is required to bear it receives some special or peculiar benefit in the

---

20. 825 So. 2d 343 (Fla. 2002).
21. *See Collier Cnty. v. State*, 733 So. 2d 1012 (Fla. 1999).

enhancement of value of the property against which it is imposed as a result of the improvement made with the proceeds of the special assessment. It is limited to the property benefited, is not governed by uniformity and may be determined legislatively or judicially.

. . . .

. . . [I]t seems settled law in this country that an ad valorem tax and special assessment though cognate in immaterial respects are inherently different in their controlling aspects. . . .

There are two requirements for the imposition of a valid special assessment. First, the property assessed must derive a special benefit from the service provided. *Atlantic Coast Line R.R. v. City of Gainesville,* 83 Fla. 275, 91 So. 118 (1922). Second, the assessment must be fairly and reasonably apportioned among the properties that receive the special benefit. *South Trail Fire Control Dist. v. State,* 273 So.2d 380 (Fla.1973). Thus, a special assessment is distinguished from a tax because of its special benefit and fair apportionment. We do not believe that the special assessment proposed by the City constitutes a tax which would be prohibited by article VII, section 1(a) of the Florida Constitution.[2]

* * *

We now turn to the legality of the special assessment which underlies the bond issue proposed by the City of Boca Raton. The opponents' primary contention is that the special assessments are not directly proportional to and less than the special benefits to be provided each parcel. They also argue that certain properties are improperly excluded from the assessments. At the outset, we note that the City made specific findings that the improvements would constitute a special benefit to the subject property, that the benefits would exceed the amount of the assessments, and that the benefits would be in proportion to the assessments. The apportionment of benefits is a legislative function, and if reasonable persons may differ as to whether the land assessed was benefitted by the local improvement, the findings of the city officials must be sustained. *Rosche v. City of Hollywood,* 55 So.2d 909 (Fla.1952).

To better understand the opponents' position, it is necessary to discuss the manner in which the proposed assessments will be made. The City's ordinance permits and its resolution provides that the special assessments are to be apportioned among the benefitted properties in relation to the property values of the various tracts as determined by the latest available real property assessment roll prepared by the county tax appraiser. Robert J. Harmon, the City's urban economic consultant, testified that his analysis showed that the subject properties "would at least on a cumulative basis receive $7 of benefit for every $1 that they were paying in assessments." He expressed the opinion that the use of ad valorem values in making

---

2. We also note that the trial judge held that the proposed levy was a special assessment and not a tax. If it is not a tax, it is not preempted to the State under article VII, section 1(a) of the Florida Constitution.

special assessments, which has been nationally recognized for at least twenty years, was the most equitable method that could be employed for the City's project. He gave an example of what he called the self-correcting mechanism of the ad valorem method when he stated:

If a property, for example, initially represented one percent of the entire tax base of downtown Boca Raton, they would pay one percent of the assessment. If over ten years the assessed value of that particular property, if it did not benefit to the same degree as the rest of downtown, their percentage of the total assessment would go down proportionally.

And the reverse would be also true. If a property benefitted more in its total percentage of the total assessed value of downtown increased, as will be the case with particularly the large developments, their percentage of the total assessment increases.

He added that if in any given year a property owner felt that his benefit was inequitable there was an appeal process in place by which he could seek to have his assessment adjusted. When asked how an improved property could receive the same proportional benefit as a vacant lot, he explained that while improved property would initially pay a higher assessment, over a period of time the cumulative payments would tend to equalize because the vacant properties as they were developed would ultimately carry higher assessments due to increased construction costs.

Mr. Harmon also testified that the small number of residential properties in the downtown area as well as churches had been excluded from the assessment because they would receive much less benefit from the project than business properties. However, he pointed out that should those properties be changed to a business use, they would then be subject to the assessment.

The trial court found against the bond opponents on these issues. From our review of the record, we conclude there is competent substantial evidence to support these findings. The City was not required to specifically itemize a dollar amount of benefit to be received by each parcel. *See Cape Dev. Co. v. City of Cocoa Beach,* 192 So.2d 766 (Fla.1966). Moreover, we reject the contention that the assessment cannot be sustained because it will be applied on an ad valorem basis. In fact, in an early case this Court upheld a special assessment for local improvements which was imposed upon an ad valorem basis. *Richardson v. Hardee,* 85 Fla. 510, 96 So. 290 (1923); *see also City of Naples v. Moon,* 269 So.2d 355 (Fla.1972) (approving special assessment based in part upon assessed values). As we explained in *Meyer v. City of Oakland Park,* 219 So.2d 417, 419–20 (Fla.1969):

Many elements enter into the question of determining and prorating benefits in a case of this kind. They are physical condition, nearness to or remoteness from residential and business districts, desirability for residential or commercial purposes, and many other peculiar to the locality where the lands improved are located. As stated by the Court in *City of Ft. Myers v. State of Florida and Langford,* 95 Fla. 704, 117 So. 97, 104:

No system of appraising benefits or assessing costs has yet been devised that is not open to some criticism. None have attained the ideal position of exact equality, but, if assessing boards would bear in mind that benefits actually accruing to the property improved in addition to those received by the community at large must control both as to benefits prorated and the limit of assessments for cost of improvement, the system employed would be as near the ideal as it is humanly possible to make it.

While front foot or square foot methodologies for apportioning costs of special improvement projects are more traditional, other methods are permissible. As we stated in *South Trail Fire Control District v. State*, 273 So.2d 380, 384 (Fla.1973):

The manner of the assessment is immaterial and may vary within the district, as long as the amount of the assessment for each tract is not in excess of the proportional benefits as compared to other assessments on other tracts.

We do not believe that *Fisher v. Board of County Commissioners*, 84 So.2d 572 (Fla.1956), mandates a contrary result. In that case, there was no credible evidence that the amount of the benefit was related to the property valuation.

We reverse the final judgment and remand with directions that the bond issue be approved.[4]

It is so ordered.

OVERTON, BARKETT, KOGAN and HARDING, JJ., concur.

McDONALD, J., concurs in part and dissents in part with an opinion, in which SHAW, C.J., concurs.

McDONALD, Justice, concurring in part and dissenting in part.

I concur with the holding that Florida municipalities possess the constitutional and statutory power to impose special assessments by ordinance and that the City of Boca Raton could lawfully impose a valid special assessment. I part company with the majority and the trial judge where they conclude that the proposal under scrutiny is a valid special assessment. Reviewing the evidence in the light most favorable to the City, I fail to find any special benefits to the assessed properties or its owners. There is a general benefit to all the citizens of the City. Hence, I believe that the project can only be paid by taxes, which requires a referendum and assessment against all taxpayers. I would therefore disapprove the bonds.

SHAW, C.J., concurs.

In an apparent matter of first impression, the Supreme Court in *Morris v. Cape Coral*[22] held that a two-tier methodology for assessing developed and undeveloped

---

4. As in other bond validation cases, we do not pass upon the economic desirability of these bonds but only upon whether they may be legally issued.

22. 163 So. 3d 1174 (Fla. 2015).

property was a reasonable method of apportioning costs associated with providing fire protection services.

2. Constitutional Limitations: Who Is Allowed to Tax?

Fla. Const. art. VII, § 1

Taxation; appropriations; state expenses; state revenue limitation. —

(a) No tax shall be levied except in pursuance of law. No state ad valorem taxes shall be levied upon real estate or tangible personal property. All other forms of taxation shall be preempted to the state except as provided by general law.

Fla. Const. art. VII, § 9

Local taxes. —

(a) Counties, school districts, and municipalities shall, and special districts may, be authorized by law to levy ad valorem taxes and may be authorized by general law to levy other taxes, for their respective purposes, except ad valorem taxes on intangible personal property and taxes prohibited by this constitution.

The Florida Constitution provides special rules for the imposition of taxes by governmental entities. In *Miller v. Higgs*,[23] the Florida Supreme Court described the power to tax in these terms:

> Subject only to constitutional restrictions and the will of the people expressed through elections, the legislature's power and discretion in regard to taxation are broad, plenary, unlimited and supreme. Fla.Jur.2d, *Taxation*, section 5:4. All questions as to mode, form, character, or extent of taxation, exemption or nonexemption, apportionment, means of assessment and collection, and all other incidents of the taxing power, are for the legislature to decide. *Id.* As long as the legislature does not violate constitutional restrictions, the courts have no concern with the wisdom or policy of the tax, the political or other motives behind it, or the amounts to be raised, since such matters are exclusively for the lawmaking body to decide. However, where the legislature transcends its power and violates a limitation placed on the taxing power by the constitution, the judiciary has the right and duty to declare the tax invalid. *Id.* at section 5:10.

---

23. 468 So. 2d 371, 375 (Fla. 1st Dist. Ct. App. 1985), *overruled on other grounds by Capital City Country Club v. Tucker*, 613 So. 2d 448 (Fla. 1993).

6 · TAXATION AND FINANCE

This view was expounded before in *Eastern Air Lines, Inc. v. Department of Revenue*,[24] where the Florida Supreme Court outlined the standard of review to be used in determining the constitutionality of tax legislation:

> When the state legislature, acting within the scope of its authority, undertakes to exert the taxing power, every presumption in favor of the validity of its action is indulged. Only clear and demonstrated usurpation of power will authorize judicial interference with legislative action. [Citation omitted.] In the field of taxation particularly, the legislature possesses great freedom in classification. The burden is on the one attacking the legislative enactment to negate every conceivable basis which might support it. [Citations omitted.] The state must, of course, proceed upon a rational basis and may not resort to a classification that is palpably arbitrary. [Citation omitted.] A statute that discriminates in favor of a certain class is not arbitrary if the discrimination is founded upon a reasonable distinction or difference in state policy. [Citation omitted.]

The authors have been unable to harmonize the view expressed above with the apparently contrary view found in the following excerpts from two more recent cases:

> In addition, it is a fundamental rule of construction that the authority to tax must be strictly construed against the taxing authority and in favor of the taxpayer and all ambiguities or doubts must be resolved in favor of the taxpayer. *Maas Bros. v. Dickinson*, 195 So.2d 193 (Fla.1967); *Florida Dep't of Revenue v. Quotron Sys., Inc.*, 615 So.2d 774 (Fla. 3d DCA 1993); *Florida Hi-Lift v. Department of Revenue*, 571 So.2d 1364 (Fla. 1st DCA 1990); *Florida S & L Servs., Inc. v. Department of Revenue*, 443 So.2d 120 (Fla. 1st DCA 1983). As eloquently stated by *Maas Brothers*, "This salutary principle is found in the reason that the duty to pay taxes, while necessary to the business of the sovereign, is still a duty of pure statutory creation and taxes may be collected only within the clear definite boundaries recited by statute." *Id.*; . . . [25]

> We agree with the trial judge and conclude that the authority to tax must be strictly construed and that any ambiguities or doubts must be resolved in favor of the taxpayer. *See Mikos v. Ringling Bros. Barnum & Bailey Combined Shows, Inc.*, 475 So.2d 292 (Fla. 2d DCA 1985).[26]

The following cases represent applications of the principle that with the exception of ad valorem taxes on real property and tangible personal property at the local governmental level, a tax must be authorized by general law.

---

24. 455 So. 2d 311, 314 (Fla. 1984).

25. *Warning Safety Lights of Georgia, Inc. v. State Dep't of Revenue*, 678 So. 2d 1377, 1379 (Fla. 4th Dist. Ct. App. 1996).

26. *Department of Revenue v. GTE Mobilnet of Tampa, Inc.*, 727 So. 2d 1125, 1128 (Fla. 2d Dist. Ct. App. 1999).

474   6 · TAXATION AND FINANCE

Alachua County v. Adams
702 So. 2d 1253 (Fla. 1997)

GRIMES, Senior Justice.

This is an appeal from a decision of the First District Court of Appeal holding chapter 94-487, Laws of Florida, to be an unconstitutional special act. *Alachua County v. Adams*, 677 So.2d 396 (Fla. 1st DCA 1996). We have jurisdiction under article V, section 3(b)(1) of the Florida Constitution.

There are two provisions of the Florida Constitution relevant to the determination of this case.

SECTION 1. Taxation; appropriations; state expenses; state revenue limitation. —

(a) No tax shall be levied except in pursuance of law. No state ad valorem taxes shall be levied upon real estate or tangible personal property. *All other forms of taxation shall be preempted to the state except as provided by general law.*

Art. VII, § 1(a), Fla. Const. (emphasis added).

SECTION 9. Local taxes. —

(a) *Counties*, school districts, and municipalities shall, and special districts may, be authorized by law to levy ad valorem taxes and *may be authorized by general law to levy other taxes, for their respective purposes*, except ad valorem taxes on intangible personal property and taxes prohibited by this constitution.

Art. VII, § 9(a), Fla. Const. (emphasis added).

As authorized by these constitutional provisions, the legislature has enacted the following general law:

212.055 Discretionary sales surtaxes; legislative intent; authorization and use of proceeds. —

. . . .

(2) LOCAL GOVERNMENT INFRASTRUCTURE SURTAX. —

(a)1. The governing authority in each county may levy a discretionary sales surtax of 0.5 percent or 1 percent. . . .

. . . .

(d)1. The proceeds of the surtax authorized by this subsection [sic.] . . . shall be expended . . . to finance, plan, and construct infrastructure. . . . *Neither the proceeds nor any interest accrued thereto shall be used for operational expenses of any infrastructure. . . .*

2. For the purposes of this paragraph, "infrastructure" means:

a. Any fixed capital expenditure or fixed capital outlay associated with the construction, reconstruction, or improvement of public facilities which have a life expectancy of 5 or more years and any land acquisition, land improvement, design, and engineering costs related thereto.

§ 212.055, Fla. Stat. (1995) (emphasis added).

However, in 1994 the legislature enacted chapter 94-487, Laws of Florida. This special law, applicable only to Alachua County, stated in pertinent part:

Section 1. *In addition to the uses authorized by s. 212.055(2),* Florida Statutes, the board of county commissioners of Alachua County and the municipalities of Alachua County may use local government infrastructure surtax revenues for *operation and maintenance of parks and recreation programs and facilities established with the proceeds of the surtax.*

Ch. 94-487, Laws of Fla. (emphasis added).

Thereafter, Alachua County and all of the municipalities within the county entered into an interlocal agreement specifying that the surtax proceeds be used to operate and maintain a county-wide recreational program. Dwight Adams, a citizen and taxpayer of the county, disputed the constitutionality of chapter 94-487 and threatened legal action to enjoin the pending referendum on the surtax. Consequently, Alachua County and the City of Gainesville filed a declaratory judgment action, seeking a declaration of the legality of the surtax and the interlocal agreement. The trial judge held that chapter 94-487, Laws of Florida, was an unlawful special act which purported to amend the county's power to levy the local government infrastructure surtax in violation of article VII, section 1(a) of the Florida Constitution. This judgment was affirmed by the First District Court of Appeal. *Adams,* 677 So.2d 396.

Appellants point out that article VII, section 1(a), by its express language, relates only to the "forms of taxation." They suggest that the "form" of the tax authorized by section 212.055 is a sales tax, whereas the special act relates only to the purposes for which the revenues may be spent. Thus, they posit that while the county's authorization to impose a surtax must be based on general law, the uses for which the proceeds may be expended can be changed by special law.

To this argument, the court below stated:

Appellants' distinction between taxing and spending in this case is unpersuasive and largely semantic. As the Florida Supreme Court recently held in a different context, "the power of a municipality to tax should not be broadened by semantics. . . ." *State v. City of Port Orange,* 650 So.2d 1, 3 (Fla.1994).

Adams, 677 So.2d at 398. We agree.

The "form of taxation" rationale misconstrues article VII, section (1)(a). The overriding purpose of this article is to make a constitutional division of tax revenues between those available for state uses and those reserved for local government. The phrase "all other forms of taxation" obviously refers to any tax other than those previously designated ad valorem taxes on real property and tangible personal property. This provision is designed to prevent the legislature from undermining non-ad valorem tax sources needed to support state government by the enactment of special laws authorizing local governments to impose non-ad valorem taxes for local purposes.

Moreover, appellants ignore article VII, section (9)(a), which does not contain the phrase "all other forms of taxation." This provision permits the legislature to authorize counties to levy non-ad valorem taxes, of whatever form or description, but only by general law. A determination that a special law may allow a county to redirect the tax proceeds in a manner explicitly contrary to the general law which authorized the tax in the first place would clearly undercut the purpose of article VII, section 9(a).

Appellants' reliance upon *Rowe v. Pinellas Sports Authority*, 461 So.2d 72 (Fla.1984), is misplaced. Significantly, neither section (1)(a) nor section (9)(a) of article VII of the constitution was ever mentioned in that opinion. Further, there was no argument that the tax revenues could not be pledged to pay off the bonds which would raise the money to be used to build a stadium. Rather, the point discussed was whether a special act could properly authorize these bonds to be issued by the Pinellas County Sports Authority rather than the county itself. The special act simply changed the manner in which the money would be borrowed. The tax authorized by the general law was not altered because the tax revenues were still to be used for the purpose of allowing the stadium to be built. The cases of *Wilson v. Hillsborough County Aviation Authority*, 138 So.2d 65 (Fla.1962), and *Kirkland v. Phillips*, 106 So.2d 909 (Fla.1958), do not bear on the issue before us because they were decided prior to 1968 when the pertinent constitutional provisions were different from those in our present constitution.

Section 212.055(2) is a general law that authorizes counties to levy an infrastructure tax under precisely defined conditions. These conditions prescribe the rates of taxes, the uses for the revenue raised by the taxes, and the procedure to be followed for approving the taxes. To permit chapter 94-487 to stand would convert subsection 212.055(2) into a general grant of sales tax authority to counties, subject only to the enactment of special law. If Alachua County can be authorized to levy the sales tax surcharge to fund operations and maintenance of facilities, then some other county can be authorized by special law to fund general governmental operations. This is the exact consequence that sections (1)(a) and (9)(a) of article VII of the Florida Constitution were intended to prevent.

Chapter 94-487, which is a special act relating only to Alachua County, purports to amend section 212.055(2), a general taxing statute, to levy the surtax for uses that are not only not permitted to any other county but are also positively prohibited to all counties. In the face of the unambiguous restrictions imposed by article VII, section 1(a) and article VII, section 9(a) of the Florida Constitution, we declare chapter 94-487 to be unconstitutional.

6 · TAXATION AND FINANCE

We affirm the decision of the court below.

It is so ordered.

KOGAN, C.J., and SHAW, HARDING and WELLS, JJ., concur.

OVERTON, J., dissents with an opinion, in which ANSTEAD, J., concurs.

OVERTON, Justice, dissenting.

The majority, through its construction of our constitution, has restricted the ability of citizens of local governmental entities to vote to impose an authorized tax upon themselves and to use the tax revenue for purposes specifically identified by special law. The majority opinion not only restricts the power of the people to provide wanted services for themselves, but also restricts the power of the legislature to provide the people with a means to have the desired local governmental services. This majority opinion is directly contrary to prior decisions of this Court that allowed special laws to be used in the manner desired by Alachua County in this instance. The majority summarily dismisses those cases by saying they were decided before the 1968 constitution was adopted. Interestingly, the majority's interpretation of the 1968 constitution makes its provisions more restrictive of local governments' authority than the 1885 constitution when, in fact, the philosophy of the 1968 constitution was to "broaden" local governments' control of the tax structure.

The issue in this case is whether our present constitution prohibits the legislature from expanding or contracting by special law the class of permitted uses for the proceeds of a discretionary sales surtax set out by general law. Article VII, section 1(a), of the Florida Constitution plainly states that only the "form of taxation" must be authorized by general law. Article VII, section 9, states that counties may be authorized by general law to levy various forms of taxes. Pursuant to these provisions, the legislature enacted section 212.055(2), Florida Statutes (1995), *authorizing* the levy of a sales surtax. The statute also sets forth how the tax revenue must be used. The special law in issue set forth in chapter 94-487, Laws of Florida, simply expanded the permitted *uses* of the sales surtax revenues in Alachua County. Consistent with our prior decisions, this special law does not violate the Florida Constitution. In my view, the decision of the majority is contrary to the mandate of this Court to "interpret statutes in such a manner as to uphold their constitutionality." *Capital City Country Club, Inc. v. Tucker,* 613 So.2d 448, 452 (Fla.1993).

The majority has ignored another constitutional provision that is directly applicable in this case. It deals directly with prohibited special laws. Article III, section 11(a)(2) provides:

SECTION 11. Prohibited special laws —

(a) There shall be no special law or general law of local application pertaining to:

. . . .

(2) assessment or collection of taxes for state or county purposes, including extension of time therefor, relief of tax officers from due performance of their duties, and relief of their sureties from liability.

Our prior decisions interpreting the predecessor of this provision made it clear that a permitted use of tax revenues was different from the authorization to impose the tax.[1] In *Wilson v. Hillsborough County Aviation Authority*, 138 So.2d 65, 67 (Fla.1962), we said that there was a distinction between the "form of taxation" and the purpose to which the revenue could be used and allocated. We wrote:

The provision of Section 20, Article III, Florida Constitution, proscribing local laws for the "assessment and collection of taxes" for county purposes was designed merely to provide uniformity in the assessment and collection process. It has never been construed to prohibit local laws which authorize a particular tax for a particular local county purpose.

Similarly, in *Kirkland v. Phillips*, 106 So.2d 909, 913 (Fla.1958), we stated:

It is true that by Section 550.16, Florida Statutes, the Legislature has by general law made provision for the distribution of the so-called additional race track tax monies. *The fact that the Legislature has made this provision by general law would offer no constitutional impediment to a legislative provision by special or local law allocating the use of these funds for a special county purpose in a particular county.*

(Emphasis added.)

The majority states that these cases are inapplicable to the issue presented because they were decided prior to the 1968 revision of the Florida Constitution. However, I can find nothing under article VII or article III, section 11, of the 1968 constitution that alters the legislature's ability to enact special laws expanding or contracting the class of permitted uses for which the proceeds of properly authorized local taxes

---

1. The predecessor to article III, section 11(a), is article III, section 20, Florida Constitution of 1885. The drafters of the 1968 constitution chose not to change the language or substance of article III, section 20. That section read:

Section 20 *The Legislature shall not pass special or local laws in any of the following enumerated cases:* that is to say, regulating the jurisdiction and duties of any class of officers, except municipal officers, or for the punishment of crime or misdemeanor; regulating the practice of courts of justice, except municipal courts; providing for changing venue of civil and criminal cases; granting divorces; changing the names of persons; vacating roads; summoning and empaneling grand and petit juries, and providing for their compensation; *for assessment and collection of taxes for State* [sic.] *and county purposes*; for opening and conducting elections for State and county officers, and for designating the places of voting; for the sale of real estate belonging to minors, estates of decedents, and of persons laboring under legal disabilities; regulating the fees of officers of the State and county; giving effect to informal or invalid deeds or wills; legitimizing children; providing for the adoption of children; relieving minors from legal disabilities; and for the establishment of ferries.

(Emphasis added.)

may be utilized. The authors of the 1968 constitution knew of this Court's interpretation regarding this particular use of special laws and chose not to alter it by constitutional amendment. Only the construction by judicial fiat that the majority now places on the language of article VII alters this particular use of special laws by the legislature.

We also decided a case under the 1968 constitution in which we found valid a special law that expanded the means of funding local government projects. In *Rowe v. Pinellas Sports Authority*, 461 So.2d 72, 74 (Fla.1984), we confronted the following factual circumstances:

> In 1977 the Florida legislature enacted what is now section 125.0104, Florida Statutes (1983), the "Local Option Tourist Development Act." This statute authorizes Florida's counties, after referendum to levy a tourist development tax, to be used for certain enumerated purposes.
>
> Pursuant to its statutory authorization, in 1978 Pinellas County, after a referendum, adopted ordinance 78-20. Section 2 of that ordinance set forth the "tourist development plan" whereby all receipts from the tax were to be placed in a trust fund "to be used exclusively for tourist advertising and promotion for Pinellas County and its committees." Section 3 of the ordinance, not a part of the tourist development plan, provided that all or any portion of the tax revenues might be pledged by the Board of County Commissioners to secure revenue bonds issued for certain projects, including "convention centers, sports arenas, sports stadiums, coliseums, or auditoriums."
>
> In 1982 ordinance 82-19 was enacted which amended ordinance 78-20. The amended ordinance expanded the tourist development plan (section 2) of the first ordinance to include purposes other than "tourist advertising and promotion," specifically, the construction of sports stadiums.
>
> In November 1983 the Board of County Commissioners adopted a resolution authorizing the Pinellas Sports Authority to proceed with development of a bond issue to finance the stadium.

The general law authorizing the imposition of the tourist development tax restricted the use of the revenue in the following way:

(5) AUTHORIZED USES OF REVENUE.

. . . .

(b) In any county in which the electors of the county or the electors of the sub-county special tax district have approved by referendum the ordinance levying and imposing the tourist development tax, the revenues to be derived from the tourist development tax may be pledged to secure and liquidate revenue bonds *issued by the county* for the purposes set forth in sub-paragraph (a)1.

§ 125.0104, Fla. Stat. (1983) (emphasis added). The general law in that case did not authorize the pledging of tourist tax revenues to secure bonds issued by a sports authority. Instead, that general law only allowed the revenues derived from the tourist development tax to be pledged to secure bonds issued by the county. The charter of the Pinellas Sports Authority, however, was enacted as a special law. Ch. 77-635, § 8(c), Laws of Fla. The charter of the sports authority allowed the county to pledge tourist tax revenues to secure sports authority bonds. Therefore, the special law enlarged the class of permitted uses of tourist tax revenues beyond that authorized by general law. In upholding that special law against constitutional attack, we stated:

> Appellants also contend that Pinellas County's tourist development tax revenues may not be pledged to pay off bonds that have been issued by another governmental entity, in this case, the [Pinellas Sports Authority].

However, section 8(c) of the [Pinellas Sports Authority] charter, chapter 77-635, Laws of Florida, provides that the county is authorized

> to enter into cooperative agreements with the authority non ad valorem moneys of county ... to the payment of ... debt service costs ... or any part thereof of the authority while bonds issued by the authority.

> The [Pinellas Sports Authority] charter empowers the county to pledge non ad valorem moneys of the county, including tourist development tax revenues, to the payment of obligations issued by the Pinellas Sports Authority.

> When a special act (such as the [Pinellas Sports Authority] charter) and a general law conflict, the special act will prevail. *State ex rel. Johnson v. Vizzini*, 227 So.2d 205 (Fla.1969). Because section 8(c) of the [Pinellas Sports Authority] charter was enacted by subsequent special act, the authority for the pledging of tourist development tax revenues by the county to secure obligations issued by the [Pinellas Sports Authority] controls over any limitation imposed upon such a pledge by section 125.0104(5), Florida Statutes (1983).

Rowe, 461 So.2d at 77. In my view, it is clear by the *Rowe* decision that this Court has not read the article VII limitations in the 1968 constitution to preclude the type of special law that expanded the means of allocating and using revenue from a tax authorized by general law.

The majority's interpretation of the 1968 constitution makes its provisions more restrictive of local governmental control of the tax structure than the provisions under the 1885 constitution. In fact, the philosophy of the 1968 constitution was to give local governments more control, not less. For example, an analysis by the Legislative Reference Bureau of the 1968 constitutional revisions explains that article VII, section 9, governing local taxes, was intentionally "broadened" from its form under the 1885 constitution.

In conclusion, the majority finds that the provisions of article VII now require that both the tax itself and the use of the tax revenues be authorized by general law.

6 · TAXATION AND FINANCE

As explained above, this is contrary to prior decisions of this Court that separate the form of taxation from the allocation of the revenue. To be intellectually correct, the majority should merely state that it is overruling these prior decisions.

The people in local governmental entities lose by this decision, and the Constitution Revision Commission should develop a means for the people in a particular geographical area to enact a tax upon themselves for specific uses applicable to their community.

ANSTEAD, J., concurs.

McGrath v. City of Miami

789 So. 2d 1168 (Fla. 3d Dist. Ct. App. 2001)

PER CURIAM.

Appellant, Patrick McGrath III, and intervenors/appellants, Miami Dade County and Laureen Varga, appeal from a final declaratory judgment which granted summary judgment in favor of the appellee, City of Miami ("City"), finding an ordinance to be validly enacted and upholding the constitutionality of a parking tax statute. We reverse.

In 1999, the Florida Legislature enacted Section 218.503(5), Florida Statutes (2000) ("statute"), which provides for a parking tax and states in pertinent part that:

> The governing authority of any municipality with a resident population of 300,000 or more on April 1, 1999, and which has been declared in a state of financial emergency pursuant to this section within the previous two fiscal years may impose a discretionary per vehicle surcharge of up to 20 percent on the gross revenues of the sale, lease, or rental of space at parking facilities within the municipality that are open for use to the general public.

The statute was implemented by the City in July of 1999 when it passed and adopted ordinance No. 11813 ("ordinance"). Thereafter, the appellants/taxpayers challenged the constitutionality of the statute.

Under the Florida Constitution, a municipality may not impose any non-ad valorem tax, such as the parking tax at issue here, except as authorized by general law. *See* Art. VII, §§ 1(a) and 9(a), Fla. Const. Thus, in order to be constitutional, the statute must be a general law as opposed to a special law. *See City of Tampa v. Birdsong*, 261 So.2d 1 (Fla.1972). A general law is one that operates uniformly among a class of entities while a special law relates to particular entities. *See Dept. of Business Regulation v. Classic Mile, Inc.*, 541 So.2d 1155 (Fla.1989).

The statute here constitutes a special law because by anchoring the 300,000 population classification to the specific date of April 1, 1999, it does not operate uniformly among all cities that reach the 300,000 population threshold as is required of a general law. Cities that reach the population threshold after April 1, 1999 are forever excluded from the class. As worded, the statute is no different than if it had identified by name the three particular cities to which it relates. *See Fort v. Dekle*, 138 Fla.

871, 190 So. 542 (1939); *Walker v. Pendarvis*, 132 So.2d 186 (Fla.1961); *Ocala Breeders' Sales Company, Inc. v. Florida Gaming Centers, Inc.*, 731 So.2d 21 (Fla. 1st DCA 1999).

Since a statute which constitutes a special law cannot impose a non-ad valorem tax, the statute is unconstitutional. *See Alachua County v. Adams*, 702 So.2d 1253 (Fla.1997). Accordingly, the trial court erred in finding the ordinance was validly enacted and in granting summary judgment for the City. Therefore, the case must be reversed and the cause remanded to grant summary judgment in favor of the appellants/taxpayers.

Reversed.

Gallant v. Stephens

358 So. 2d 536 (Fla. 1978)

ENGLAND, Justice.

By direct appeal we are asked to review an order of the Pinellas County Circuit Court upholding the constitutionality of Sections 125.01(1)(q) and (1)(r), Florida Statutes (1975), which together authorize counties to create "municipal service taxing units" having the power to impose ad valorem taxes without voter approval. We have jurisdiction under Article V, Section 3(b)(1) of the Florida Constitution.

Following a series of legislative attempts to deal with this subject,[1] Sections 125.01(1) (q) and (1)(r) were amended in 1975 to read:

> (1) The legislative and governing body of a county shall have the power to carry on county government. To the extent not inconsistent with general or special law, this power shall include . . . the power to: . . .

> (q) Establish . . . municipal service taxing or benefit units for any part or all of the unincorporated area of the county within which may be provided . . . essential facilities and municipal services from funds derived from . . . taxes within such unit only. It is hereby declared to be the intent of the Legislature that this paragraph is the authorization for all counties to levy additional taxes, within the limits fixed for municipal purposes, within such municipal service taxing units under the authority of the second sentence of Art. VII, Section 9(b) of the state constitution.

---

1. As originally enacted in 1971, this legislation provided authority for counties to create "special purpose districts," without indicating whether referenda would be required. Ch. 71-14, §1, Laws of Florida. The Attorney General later opined that Art. VII, §9(b) of the Florida Constitution required a referendum. Ops. Att'y Gen.Fla. 072-162 and 073-178. In 1974 the Legislature amended these provisions by substituting "municipal service taxing or benefit units" for "special purpose districts." Ch. 74-191, §1 Laws of Florida. Despite an expression of intent in the legislation to the effect that §125.01(1)(q) was enacted to extend taxing power under the second sentence of Art. VII, §9(b), the Attorney General later advised that these units must be evaluated on the basis of their functions, not title, and that referenda were nonetheless required in the absence of a statutory directive to the contrary. Op.Att'y Gen.Fla. 075-24. In 1975 the Legislature added the last sentence of present §125.01(1)(r) to provide specifically that referenda were not required. Ch. 75-63, §1, Laws of Florida.

6 · TAXATION AND FINANCE

(r) Levy and collect taxes, both for county purposes and for the providing of municipal services within any municipal service taxing unit . . . There shall be no referendum required for the levy by a county of ad valorem taxes both for county purposes and for the providing of municipal services within any municipal service taxing unit.

Purportedly acting pursuant to this legislative authorization, the Board of County Commissioners of Pinellas County adopted a resolution creating a municipal service taxing unit, for a variety of services, coextensive with the entire unincorporated area of the county.[2] The Board designated itself the governing body of the taxing unit. Appellant, a taxpayer and property owner in the unincorporated area of Pinellas County, challenges the constitutionality of the resolution and enabling legislation.[3] His principal challenge is grounded in Article VII, Section 9 of the Florida Constitution (1975), which provides in relevant part:

(a) Counties, school districts, and municipalities shall, and special districts may, be authorized by law to levy ad valorem taxes and may be authorized by general law to levy other taxes, for their respective purposes. . . .

(b) Ad valorem taxes . . . shall not be levied in excess of the following millages upon the assessed value of real estate and tangible personal property: for all county purposes, ten mills; for all municipal purposes, ten mills; for all school purposes, ten mills; and for special districts a millage authorized by law approved by vote of the electors who are owners of freeholds therein not wholly exempt from taxation. A county furnishing municipal services may, to the extent authorized by law, levy additional taxes within the limits fixed for municipal purposes.[4]

The principal issue before us is whether the Legislature has the power to authorize a county to furnish municipal-type services funded by ad valorem taxes, solely in its unincorporated area, without referendum, by creating a taxing unit comprising that geographical area. Other issues presented by the parties neither aid in the resolution of this important question, nor obviate the need to resolve it.[5]

---

2. Services embraced within the taxing unit include road repair, fire protection, law enforcement, recreation, garbage collection and disposal, and sewage collection. Each of these services is specifically identified in § 125.01(1)(q) as a type of "municipal service".

3. Opposing appellant's challenge are various Pinellas County officials, the Department of Revenue, the City of St. Petersburg, and the Florida League of Cities, Inc. Amicus briefs have also been filed by the parties in *Tucker v. Underdown*, 356 So.2d 251 (Fla.1978), involving common issues.

4. Although not relevant to this proceeding, we note that subsection 9(b) was amended in 1976 to authorize taxing powers for certain water management purposes. S.J.Res. 1061, Journal of the Senate (1975), approved by the voters of Florida on November 2, 1976.

5. The only other issue which warrants discussion is appellant's contention that, under Art. VIII, § 1(f), Fla.Const., Pinellas County lacked the authority to create the municipal service taxing unit by "resolution" rather than by ordinance. This argument ignores § 125.01(1)(t), Fla.Stat. (1975), which implements Art. VIII, § 1(f) by authorizing a county to "[a]dopt ordinances and resolutions necessary for the exercise of its powers".

The overall scheme of Article VII, Section 9 provides the starting point for our analysis. Entitled "Local Taxes," that section provides certain local governmental units — counties, municipalities and school districts — with the authority to levy ad valorem taxes on real and tangible personal property[6] for county, municipal and school purposes up to a maximum of ten mills for each. It also authorizes "special districts" to tax for their districts to the extent of millage limits prescribed by the Legislature, with the approval of voters within the district. In addition, the last sentence of Section 9(b) expressly provides that a "county furnishing municipal services may, to the extent authorized by law, levy additional taxes within the limits fixed for municipal purposes."

Against this pattern of millage and referenda strictures on local ad valorem taxation, the parties urge diametrically opposite positions. Appellant argues that the characteristics of a constitutionally authorized "special district" are indistinguishable from Pinellas County's proposed municipal service taxing unit, but for the absence of voter approval, and that the resolution and its enabling legislation are in reality designed both to avoid the legislative necessity of setting a millage limitation and to circumvent the referendum requirement for special districts. Appellees argue that the two entities are fundamentally different, in that special districts are separate units of local government while municipal taxing units are, by virtue of the last sentence of Article VII, Section 9(b), mere methods by which counties can tax not only for the county services they provide, but also for identifiable municipal services they offer. To support their point, appellees suggest that if municipal service taxing units are equated with special districts then the last sentence of Section 9(b) is meaningless.

Disposition of these conflicting positions, and the resolution of this case, requires that we resolve three questions. The major one is whether the last sentence of Section 9(b) enables a county, without referendum, to levy a municipal service tax in addition to other county taxes on county residents in unincorporated areas, or whether it restricts additional county levies for services furnished only to municipalities.

In construing provisions of the Florida Constitution, we are obliged to ascertain and effectuate the intent of the framers and the people. *State ex rel. Dade County v. Dickinson*, 230 So.2d 130 (Fla.1969); *Gray v. Bryant*, 125 So.2d 846 (Fla.1960). Where possible, we are guided by circumstances leading to the adoption of a provision. In this case we have attempted to discern the rationale which led to the adoption of the last sentence in Article VII, Section 9(b). Its history in the 1966 Constitution Revision Commission and in the Florida Legislature supports appellee's view of its import.

---

6. The power to tax intangible personal property, which is not involved here, is available only to the state. Art. VII, §§ 1(a), 2 and 9(a), Fla.Const.

It is reasonably clear from the minutes and notes of the Commission, and from the reports of the Legislature, that the focus of the last sentence of Section 9(b) was the delivery of municipal-type services by counties to all county residents, rather than the more narrow delivery of services solely to residents of intra-county municipalities. In fact, a proposal to restrict the last sentence of Section 9(b) so that it would authorize additional taxation only to the extent a county furnished municipal services "in unincorporated areas" was defeated in the Legislature on the ground that it would prevent counties from offering municipal services as well within municipal boundaries.[7] No historical material contradictory to these indicators has been called to our attention.

Consistent with this apparent rationale for the last sentence of Section 9(b), the Legislature has fashioned Sections 125.01(1)(q) and (1)(r).[8] In matters of constitutional interpretation, the Legislature's view of its authority is highly persuasive.

> [W]here a constitutional provision may well have either of several meanings, it is a fundamental rule of constitutional construction that, if the Legislature has by statute adopted one, its action in this respect is well-nigh, if not completely, controlling.[9]

Both the historical and legislative interpretations are also consistent with our decision in *State ex rel. Dade County v. Dickinson*, 230 So.2d 130 (Fla.1969), where we construed Section 9(b) to authorize a county-wide tax up to 20 mills for the combined municipal and county services offered by Dade County.[10]   Indeed,   our   comments in that case may have precipitated passage of one feature of Section 125.01(1)(q). We there noted that the distinction between county and municipal purposes is an uncertain one, requiring immediate legislative attention. Section 125.01(q), as enacted in 1971, expressly identified a non-exhaustive list of services which may be provided by municipal service taxing and benefit units.

For these reasons we conclude that the last sentence of Section 9(b) provides express authority for Sections 125.01(1)(q) and (1)(r), sanctioning taxing units as a method by which counties may tax to provide municipal services, within the 10 mill limit for "municipal purposes", without voter approval. Wholly independent of this county taxing power is the authority provided for "special districts" to meet the need for special purpose services in any geographical area which may (but need not) be within one county, under legislatively-set and voter-approved millage limitations.[11]

---

7. These materials are found in the files of the Florida Supreme Court Library, entitled "Chronological Development of 1968 Constitution. Art. VII, § 9 — Local Taxes."

8. See also § 200.071(3), Fla. Stat. (1975).

9. *Greater Loretta Improvement Ass'n v. State ex rel. Boone*, 234 So.2d 665, 669 (Fla.1969).

10. Of course, the Court limited to an aggregate of 10 mills the revenues to be derived from the delivery of municipal services by both the county and any municipalities within county boundaries.

11. Statutes have defined special districts as local units of special government (excluding school districts) created by authority of general or special law for the purpose of performing specialized functions within limited boundaries. §§ 165.031(5) and 218.31(5), Fla. Stat. (1975).

The second question to be answered in this litigation is whether the services offered by Pinellas County are in fact "municipal services." The trial court specifically found that the services proposed in the Pinellas County resolution do constitute municipal services, and that finding has not been challenged in this appeal.[12]

Finally, we need to inquire whether the county may offer these services solely in its unincorporated area. Section 125.01(1)(r) expressly so provides. The answer to this question, however, also calls into play another constitutional provision — Article VII, Section 2 — which requires ad valorem taxes to be imposed "at a uniform rate within each taxing unit". Appellant notes that Pinellas County has designated itself as the governing body of the taxing unit, and that its proposal for a tax solely within its unincorporated areas obviously would not be "uniform" within county boundaries since it would not fall on the residents of intra-county municipalities. Appellees counter this contention by viewing the uniformity clause as applying to the objects of taxation — the subjects within the unit actually being taxed — rather than to the taxing authority itself. They suggest that a tax for Pinellas County's municipal taxing service unit is uniform within the "taxing unit" — that is, the unincorporated area — and they support this view by reference to Article VII, Section 1(h) of the Constitution and our decision in *Alsdorf v. Broward County*, 333 So.2d 457 (Fla.1976). Together these authorities require a lower county-imposed tax rate in municipalities which receive no substantial benefit from the services provided by the tax revenue, thereby destroying uniformity within the county notwithstanding that the tax is "county" imposed.

Appellees' position is undoubtedly correct. Their view of the uniformity requirement in Article VII, Section 2 represents the only interpretation consistent with the whole Constitution. *See Burnsed v. Seaboard Coastline Railroad*, 290 So.2d 13 (Fla.1974).

We hold, therefore, that Sections 125.01(1)(q) and (1)(r), Florida Statutes (1975), are constitutional, and that the Pinellas County Commission's resolution establishing a municipal service taxing unit in the unincorporated area of the county without voter approval is valid. The order of the Pinellas County Circuit Court is affirmed.

It is so ordered.

OVERTON, C. J., and ADKINS, BOYD, SUNDBERG, HATCHETT and KARL, JJ., concur.

———————

Almost contemporaneously with the *Gallant* decision, the Florida Supreme Court concluded that the Florida Legislature possessed authorization to allow a county to create multiple municipal service taxing units (MSTUs) within the unincorporated

———————

12. See note 2 above.

6 · TAXATION AND FINANCE

area of a county, even if the MSTU only encompassed a small part of the unincorporated area of the country.[27]

State v. City of Daytona Beach

484 So. 2d 1214 (Fla. 1986)

OVERTON, Justice.

This is a direct appeal from a final judgment validating revenue bonds for redevelopment in the downtown area of the City of Daytona Beach. We have jurisdiction. Art. V, § 3(b)(2), Fla. Const. For the reasons expressed, we affirm the bond validation.

The City of Daytona Beach sought validation of improvement revenue bonds not exceeding $20 million to finance the acquisition and construction of a marina, streets, sidewalks, lighting, and other improvements in the downtown area. In 1981, the city adopted resolution No. 81-415, which declared certain property referred to as the "downtown area" to be a slum or blighted area, and established the Community Redevelopment Agency, vesting in the city commission the power to issue bonds. In accordance with that resolution, in August, 1982, the city enacted two ordinances which established a community redevelopment plan for the downtown area and created a redevelopment trust fund. In January, 1985, the city enacted ordinance No. 85-1, which provided for the issuance of the redevelopment improvement revenue bonds that are the subject of this appeal. These bonds are revenue obligations pursuant to article VII, section 11(c), Florida Constitution, and a referendum was not required. The city prescribed three sources of payment for the bonds: (1) operating revenue of the marina; (2) utilities service tax; and (3) downtown area tax increment revenue, to be derived in part from special taxing districts. The controversy in this case centers around the third source of payment.

In opposing the validation of these bonds, the state attorney contended that requiring contribution of tax increment revenue funds from special taxing districts other than the Downtown Redevelopment Authority is unconstitutional as a violation of article VII, section 9(a), of the Florida Constitution, which provides:

> Counties school districts, and municipalities shall, and special districts may, be authorized by law to levy ad valorem taxes and may be authorized by general law to levy other taxes, for their respective purposes, except ad valorem taxes on intangible personal property and taxes prohibited by this constitution.

The state attorney asserts that special tax district funds, including ad valorem taxes, may be utilized only to further the "respective purposes of the district," and argues that the redevelopment project has no relevant or purposeful connection with the Ponce de Leon Port Authority, East Volusia Mosquito Control District, East Volusia

---

27. *See Tucker v. Underdown*, 356 So. 2d 251 (Fla. 1978).

Transportation Authority, or Halifax Hospital Medical Center, each of which is a taxing authority that contributes to the redevelopment trust fund. He relies on the First District Court of Appeal's decision in *State ex rel. City of Gainesville v. St. Johns River Water Management District*, 408 So.2d 1067 (Fla. 1st DCA 1982), in which the court held that the water management district, "as a special taxing district created for water management purposes, is prohibited by article VII, section 9(a), Florida Constitution, from levying taxes for, or making appropriations to, the redevelopment trust fund." 408 So.2d at 1068.

After the *St. Johns* decision was rendered, the legislature enacted three laws that pertain to this case. Chapter 84-539, Laws of Florida, provides Halifax Hospital Medical Center with the power to foster community redevelopment within the district through financial contribution of tax increment funds to the redevelopment trust fund. Section 163.353, Florida Statutes (Supp.1984), which provides general authority to taxing districts to appropriate funds to redevelopment trust funds, reads as follows:

> Power of taxing authority to tax or appropriate funds to a redevelopment trust fund in order to preserve and enhance the tax base of the authority. — Notwithstanding any other provision of general or special law, the purposes for which a taxing authority may levy taxes or appropriate funds to a redevelopment trust fund include the preservation and enhancement of the tax base of such taxing authority and the furthering of the purposes of such taxing authority as provided by law.

Section 163.387, Florida Statutes (Supp.1984), provides that no taxing authority is exempt from contributing to a redevelopment trust fund.

We disagree with the state attorney's contention that these statutes are unconstitutional in that they violate the intent of article VII, section 9(a) by allowing the use of ad valorem tax increment revenue of special taxing districts for purposes unrelated to the special taxing districts. Tax increment financing is a method for financing a redevelopment project and is based on the premise that a portion of the increased ad valorem taxes generated as a result of the property improvement should be available to pay for the redevelopment. This Court upheld tax increment financing in *State v. Miami Beach Redevelopment Agency*, 392 So.2d 875 (Fla.1981). In that decision, we define "ad valorem tax increment" as follows:

> It is the difference between the amount of ad valorem taxes levied by those local governments each year and the amount that would have been produced by the same levy on the assessed value of taxable property in the redevelopment area before the implementation of the plan. Thus the tax increment revenues are measured by the increase in proceeds brought about by the increased value of the property, to be achieved by the improvements made under the redevelopment plan.

Id. at 893–94. We note that the ad valorem tax base of a special taxing district is not reduced because the redevelopment creates an increase in tax revenues for those districts, and the amount of their contribution will never exceed the amount of the increment.

We find that it is within the legislature's power to make community redevelopment one of the "respective purposes" of special taxing districts and to broaden the purpose of a special taxing district if it determines there is a need to do so.

We find no constitutional infirmity and, accordingly, affirm the final judgment validating the bonds.

It is so ordered.

ADKINS, EHRLICH and BARKETT, JJ., concur.

SHAW, J., dissents with an opinion, in which BOYD, C.J., and McDONALD, J., concur.

SHAW, Justice, dissenting.

Pledging ad valorem taxes as payment for local bonds requires a referendum vote by the electors. Art. VII, §12(a), Fla. Const. Coining a new label "ad valorem tax increment" does not change the substance of the ad valorem taxes. They are still ad valorem taxes and a referendum is required before they are pledged to finance or refinance capital projects. The violence the majority does to the plain meaning of article VII, section 12(a) is compounded by reading out of the Constitution the limiting language in article VII, section 9(a) that special districts are only authorized to levy taxes *for their respective purposes. State ex rel. City of Gainesville v. St. Johns Water Management District*, 408 So.2d 1067 (Fla. 1st DCA 1982). The Ponce de Leon Port Authority, East Volusia Mosquito Control District, East Volusia Transportation Authority and Halifax Hospital Medical Center were not created for the purpose of developing downtown Daytona Beach and cannot constitutionally levy what amounts to ad valorem taxes for that purpose. Further, assuming for the sake of argument that they could levy such taxes to pay bonds on capital projects, they could not do so without conducting a referendum of the electors within each special district.

BOYD, C.J., and McDONALD, J., concur.

3. Constitutional Limitations on How Those Taxing May Tax

a. Ad Valorem Taxation

(1) Rate

Fla. Const. art. VII, § 2

Taxes; rate. — All ad valorem taxation shall be at a uniform rate within each taxing unit, except the taxes on intangible personal property may be at different rates but shall never exceed two mills on the dollar of assessed value; provided, as to any obligations secured by mortgage, deed of trust, or other lien on real estate wherever located, an intangible tax of not more than two mills on the dollar may be levied by law to be in lieu of all other intangible assessments on such obligations.

The requirement of "a uniform rate within each taxing unit"[28] is limited to non-state taxes. Fla. Const. art. VII, §1(a) precludes a state ad valorem tax on real property or tangible personal property, while art. VII, §2 allows different rates on intangible personal property. Intangible personal property is the only type of property upon which the state can levy an ad valorem tax.

This provision apparently means that while the law authorizing a particular type of taxing unit to levy an ad valorem tax on real or tangible personal property must be uniform, rates may vary between different taxing units. As Harold L. Sebring, former dean of Stetson University College of Law, puts it in his work on state and local taxation:[29]

> ... [T]he rule is that the tax burden must fall equally and impartially on all taxable property subject to it, so that no higher rate will be imposed on one parcel of taxable property than on other similarly situated which are taxed for the same public purpose. However, this provision does not preclude the proper classification of different types of property for the purpose of taxation.

Hayes v. Walker

44 So. 747 (Fla. 1907)

WHITFIELD, J. This writ of error was taken to a judgment of the circuit court for Hillsborough County sustaining a demurrer to the petition and remanding the petitioner in a habeas corpus proceeding. The errors assigned are: (1) Remanding the petitioner; (2) sustaining the demurrer to the petition; (3) quashing the writ of habeas corpus; (4) sustaining the constitutionality of chapters 5857 and 5859, pp. 700, 704, Laws Florida approved May 17, 1907.

All questions as to whether or not the matters here presented can properly be determined in this proceeding have been expressly waived, and the court will consider as properly presented all points shown by the record to be material to the right of the plaintiff in error to be discharged from custody by habeas corpus.

The contention briefly stated is that the plaintiff in error is illegally deprived of his liberty by the chief of police of the city of Tampa, Fla., under a commitment from the municipal court of the city of Tampa, for the alleged reason that the offense for which he was sentenced to custody was not committed within the territory of the

---

28. Fla. Const. art. VII, §2.

29. Harold L. Sebring, 3 *An Introduction to the Law of State and Local Taxation: With Special Emphasis on Florida Law* 731 (1966).

city of Tampa, and consequently the judgment and commitment of the municipal court of the city of Tampa under which the plaintiff in error is deprived of his liberty are illegal and do not authorize the detention of the plaintiff in error in the custody of the chief of police of the city of Tampa. The territory within which the offense was committed was placed within the corporate limits and authority of the city of Tampa by two statutes (chapters 5857 and 5859, pp. 700–704, Laws Florida), both of which were approved and became effective on May 17, 1907.

* * *

One of the statutes mentioned (chapter 5857, p. 700, approved May 17, 1907) is entitled "An act to extend the corporate limits of the city of Tampa." The first section of this act provides: "That the corporate limits of the city of Tampa be, and the same are hereby extended so as to include the following adjacent territory, not now included within the corporate limits of the city of Tampa, to wit: [then follows a description of the territory which includes that involved here.]" The second section provides that: "All public property, rights and franchises theretofore belonging to the territory described in the preceding section as a part of Fort Brooke, shall hereafter belong to the city of Tampa, which shall also assume and be liable for all of the debts and obligations of the said town of Fort Brooke, provided, however, that the real estate or other property within the territory above described shall not be liable for nor taxed to pay any existing bonded indebtedness of the city of Tampa."

* * *

It is insisted that the proviso, contained in the second section of the act, that the territory and property placed within the limits and jurisdiction of the city of Tampa by the first section of the act shall not be liable for nor taxed to pay any existing bonded indebtedness of the city of Tampa, violates sections 1 and 5 of article 9 of the Constitution. These sections provide as follows:

> Section 1. The Legislature shall provide for a uniform and equal rate of taxation, and shall prescribe such regulations as shall secure a just valuation of all property, both real and personal, excepting such property as may be exempted by law for municipal, educational, literary, scientific, religious or charitable purposes.

> Sec. 5. The Legislature shall authorize the several counties and incorporated cities or towns in the state to assess and impose taxes for county and municipal purposes, and for no other purposes, and all property shall be taxed upon the principles established for State taxation. But the cities and incorporated towns shall make their own assessments for municipal purposes upon the property within their limits.

If this contention is well founded, and the proviso contained in the second section of the act is unconstitutional for the reason stated, it is clearly of such import that the provisions of section 1 of the act, without the proviso of section 2, would cause results not contemplated or desired by the Legislature, and the entire act must be held inoperative.

By the proviso in the second section of the act the Legislature has expressly provided that certain conditions shall attach to the incorporation of the territory and property mentioned in the first section within the limits and jurisdiction of the city of Tampa. If the proviso in the second section is inoperative because unconstitutional, and the first section is held to be operative, it would cause an unconditional annexation of the territory, when the Legislature has plainly expressed its purpose to attach stated conditions to the annexation.

The constitutional provisions quoted above, that require the Legislature to provide for a uniform and equal rate of taxation and a just valuation of all property, and require that the Legislature shall authorize incorporated cities or towns to assess and impose taxes for municipal purposes, and for no other purposes, and that all property shall be taxed for municipal purposes upon the principles established for state taxation, do not prohibit the Legislature from making proper and reasonable classifications of property for purposes of municipal taxation, so long as such classifications are not arbitrary, unreasonable, and unjustly discriminating, and apply similarly to all under like conditions, and do not deprive persons of property without just compensation or without due process of law, or do not deny to any person the equal protection of the laws, or do not violate any other provision of the organic law. *See* 27 Am. & Eng. Ency. Law (2d Ed.) 601; Levy v. Smith, 4 Fla. 154; Edgerton v. Mayor, etc., Green Cove Springs, 19 Fla. 140. *See*, also, Bloxham v. Florida, Cent. & P. R. Co., 35 Fla. 625, text 734, 17 South. 902; Florida Cent. & P. R. Co. v. Reynolds, 183 U.S. 471, 22 Sup. Ct. Rep. 176, 46 L. Ed. 283.

Classifications for purposes of legislation may be made with reference to similarity of situation, circumstances, requirements, and convenience to best subserve the public interest. The test as to the validity of classifications for purposes of legislation is good faith, not wisdom. 7 Cyc. 185.

Under section 8 of the Constitution of Florida, "the Legislature shall have power to establish and to abolish municipalities, to provide for their government, to prescribe their jurisdiction and powers, and to alter or amend the same at any time. When any municipality shall be abolished, provision shall be made for the protection of its creditors." This provision secures to the Legislature broad and comprehensive authority over municipalities and over their jurisdiction and powers.

The provisions contained in the second section of chapter 5857, p. 701, Laws Florida approved May 17, 1907, make a classification of the property incorporated by section 1 of the act into the city of Tampa, and it cannot be said that such classification is on its face unreasonable, unjustly discriminating, or arbitrary, or that it does not apply similarly to all under like conditions, or that such classification violates any organic law. The reasons for such a classification as are indicated from a consideration of the act and of the facts as to the indebtedness of the city of Tampa stated in the petition and admitted by the demurrer appear to be founded upon equitable principles, within the bounds of which the Legislature should be accorded a wide discretion in the interest of the public welfare.

A careful consideration of the provisions of the second section of chapter 5857, p. 701, Acts 1907, does not lead to a positive conclusion that the section is obnoxious to the taxation sections of the Constitution. If they do not appear beyond reasonable doubt to be unconstitutional, they should, in deference to the legislative department of the government, be held to be operative, and they are held to be operative.

The other statute (chapter 5859) is entitled "An act to amend sections two * * * of chapter 5363 of the Laws of Florida approved June 8th, A. D. 1903, entitled 'an act to amend chapter 4883 of the Laws of Florida, approved May 29th, 1889, being the city charter of the city of Tampa, and providing for its government, jurisdiction, powers and duties, and relating to the same, and to confirm and continue grants, and to make valid and binding upon the city of Tampa grants made by the county commissioners of Hillsborough county and the town of Fort Brooke, as to territory described in this act and as to territory that may hereafter be acquired by the city of Tampa, and to abolish the municipal government of the town of Fort Brooke and to define the corporate limits of the city of Tampa."

Section 2 of chapter 5363, p. 559, Acts 1903, fixes the corporate limits of the city of Tampa. Section 1 of chapter 5859, p. 704, Acts 1907, amends section 2 of chapter 5363 by abolishing the municipal government of the town of Ft. Brooke and by placing within the territorial limits of the city of Tampa the territory involved here. The section also contains the following: "All public property, rights and franchises belonging to the territory described above and which has heretofore been a part of the town of Fort Brooke shall hereafter belong to the city of Tampa, which city shall also assume and be liable for all of the debts and obligations of the town of Fort Brooke, provided, however, that the real estate or other property within the territory above described which has heretofore been a part of the town of Fort Brooke, shall not be liable for nor taxed to pay any existing bonded indebtedness of the city of Tampa."

As chapter 5857 places the territory where the offense is alleged to have been committed within the limits of the city of Tampa, thereby displacing any other municipal authority, it may not be necessary to consider chapter 5859 on the same subject. But the principles above announced apply as well in the construction of one as of the other.

* * *

Even if chapter 5859 be not considered, the provision of chapter 5857, placing the territory upon which the offense is alleged to have been committed within the corporate limits and jurisdiction of the city of Tampa, is not unconstitutional on the grounds assigned, and is effectual for the purpose intended, consequently the plaintiff in error is not entitled to be discharged from custody on habeas corpus as here presented. The judgment of the circuit court should therefore be affirmed, and it is so ordered.

SHACKLEFORD, C. J., and COCKRELL, J., concur.

TAYLOR, J., concurs in the opinion.

HOCKER and PARKHILL, JJ., concur in the conclusion.

[These concurring opinions are omitted.]

—————

Article VII, § 2 of the Florida Constitution provides that all ad valorem taxation shall be at a uniform rate within each taxing unit. The above case construed art. IX, § 1 of the 1885 Constitution, the predecessor to art. VII, § 2. The 1885 Constitution required a "uniform and equal rate of taxation." The words "and equal" in the 1885 Constitution have been displaced in our current Constitution with the phrase "within each taxing unit." Such revision was simply for the sake of clarity.[30]

(2) Assessments of Value for Purposes of Ad Valorem Taxation

Fla. Const. art. VII, § 4

Taxation; assessments. — By general law regulations shall be prescribed which shall secure a just valuation of all property for ad valorem taxation, provided:

(a) Agricultural land, land producing high water recharge to Florida's aquifers, or land used exclusively for noncommercial recreational purposes may be classified by general law and assessed solely on the basis of character or use.

(b) As provided by general law and subject to conditions, limitations, and reasonable definitions specified therein, land used for conservation purposes shall be classified by general law and assessed solely on the basis of character or use.

(c) Pursuant to general law tangible personal property held for sale as stock in trade and livestock may be valued for taxation at a specified percentage of its value, may be classified for tax purposes, or may be exempted from taxation.

(d) All persons entitled to a homestead exemption under Section 6 of this Article shall have their homestead assessed at just value as of January 1 of the year following the effective date of this amendment. This assessment shall change only as provided in this subsection.

(1) Assessments subject to this subsection shall be changed annually on January 1st of each year; but those changes in assessments shall not exceed the lower of the following:

a. Three percent (3%) of the assessment for the prior year.

b. The percent change in the Consumer Price Index for all urban consumers, U.S. City Average, all items 1967 = 100, or successor reports for the

—————

30. *Williams v. Jones*, 326 So. 2d 425 (Fla. 1975).

preceding calendar year as initially reported by the United States Department of Labor, Bureau of Labor Statistics.

(2) No assessment shall exceed just value.

(3) After any change of ownership, as provided by general law, homestead property shall be assessed at just value as of January 1 of the following year, unless the provisions of paragraph (8) apply. Thereafter, the homestead shall be assessed as provided in this subsection.

(4) New homestead property shall be assessed at just value as of January 1st of the year following the establishment of the homestead, unless the provisions of paragraph (8) apply. That assessment shall only change as provided in this subsection.

(5) Changes, additions, reductions, or improvements to homestead property shall be assessed as provided for by general law; provided, however, after the adjustment for any change, addition, reduction, or improvement, the property shall be assessed as provided in this subsection.

(6) In the event of a termination of homestead status, the property shall be assessed as provided by general law.

(7) The provisions of this amendment are severable. If any of the provisions of this amendment shall be held unconstitutional by any court of competent jurisdiction, the decision of such court shall not affect or impair any remaining provisions of this amendment.

(8)a. A person who establishes a new homestead as of January 1 and who has received a homestead exemption pursuant to Section 6 of this Article as of January 1 of any of the three years immediately preceding the establishment of the new homestead is entitled to have the new homestead assessed at less than just value. The assessed value of the newly established homestead shall be determined as follows:

1. If the just value of the new homestead is greater than or equal to the just value of the prior homestead as of January 1 of the year in which the prior homestead was abandoned, the assessed value of the new homestead shall be the just value of the new homestead minus an amount equal to the lesser of $500,000 or the difference between the just value and the assessed value of the prior homestead as of January 1 of the year in which the prior homestead was abandoned. Thereafter, the homestead shall be assessed as provided in this subsection.

2. If the just value of the new homestead is less than the just value of the prior homestead as of January 1 of the year in which the prior homestead was abandoned, the assessed value of the new homestead shall be equal to the just value of the new homestead divided by the just value of the prior homestead and multiplied by the assessed value of the prior homestead. However, if the difference between the just value of the new homestead and

the assessed value of the new homestead calculated pursuant to this sub-subparagraph is greater than $500,000, the assessed value of the new homestead shall be increased so that the difference between the just value and the assessed value equals $500,000. Thereafter, the homestead shall be assessed as provided in this subsection.

b. By general law and subject to conditions specified therein, the legislature shall provide for application of this paragraph to property owned by more than one person.

(e) The legislature may, by general law, for assessment purposes and subject to the provisions of this subsection, allow counties and municipalities to authorize by ordinance that historic property may be assessed solely on the basis of character or use. Such character or use assessment shall apply only to the jurisdiction adopting the ordinance. The requirements for eligible properties must be specified by general law.

(f) A county may, in the manner prescribed by general law, provide for a reduction in the assessed value of homestead property to the extent of any increase in the assessed value of that property which results from the construction or reconstruction of the property for the purpose of providing living quarters for one or more natural or adoptive grandparents or parents of the owner of the property or of the owner's spouse if at least one of the grandparents or parents for whom the living quarters are provided is 62 years of age or older. Such a reduction may not exceed the lesser of the following:

(1) The increase in assessed value resulting from construction or reconstruction of the property.

(2) Twenty percent of the total assessed value of the property as improved.

(g) For all levies other than school district levies, assessments of residential real property, as defined by general law, which contains nine units or fewer and which is not subject to the assessment limitations set forth in subsections (a) through (d) shall change only as provided in this subsection.

(1) Assessments subject to this subsection shall be changed annually on the date of assessment provided by law; but those changes in assessments shall not exceed ten percent (10%) of the assessment for the prior year.

(2) No assessment shall exceed just value.

(3) After a change of ownership or control, as defined by general law, including any change of ownership of a legal entity that owns the property, such property shall be assessed at just value as of the next assessment date. Thereafter, such property shall be assessed as provided in this subsection.

(4) Changes, additions, reductions, or improvements to such property shall be assessed as provided for by general law; however, after the adjustment for any change, addition, reduction, or improvement, the property shall be assessed as provided in this subsection.

(h) For all levies other than school district levies, assessments of real property that is not subject to the assessment limitations set forth in subsections (a) through (d) and (g) shall change only as provided in this subsection.

(1) Assessments subject to this subsection shall be changed annually on the date of assessment provided by law; but those changes in assessments shall not exceed ten percent (10%) of the assessment for the prior year.

(2) No assessment shall exceed just value.

(3) The legislature must provide that such property shall be assessed at just value as of the next assessment date after a qualifying improvement, as defined by general law, is made to such property. Thereafter, such property shall be assessed as provided in this subsection.

(4) The legislature may provide that such property shall be assessed at just value as of the next assessment date after a change of ownership or control, as defined by general law, including any change of ownership of the legal entity that owns the property. Thereafter, such property shall be assessed as provided in this subsection.

(5) Changes, additions, reductions, or improvements to such property shall be assessed as provided for by general law; however, after the adjustment for any change, addition, reduction, or improvement, the property shall be assessed as provided in this subsection.

(i) The legislature, by general law and subject to conditions specified therein, may prohibit the consideration of the following in the determination of the assessed value of real property:

(1) Any change or improvement to real property used for residential purposes made to improve the property's resistance to wind damage.

(2) The installation of a solar or renewable energy source device.

(j)(1) The assessment of the following working waterfront properties shall be based upon the current use of the property:

a. Land used predominantly for commercial fishing purposes.

b. Land that is accessible to the public and used for vessel launches into waters that are navigable.

c. Marinas and drystacks that are open to the public.

d. Water-dependent marine manufacturing facilities, commercial fishing facilities, and marine vessel construction and repair facilities and their support activities.

(2) The assessment benefit provided by this subsection is subject to conditions and limitations and reasonable definitions as specified by the legislature by general law.

The Florida Constitution requires that property be valued for ad valorem tax purposes at its "just valuation." This term has been statutorily defined to be "an annual determination of the just or fair market value" of the appraised property.[31] The statutes provide a list of eight factors that county appraisers are required to consider in determining the just valuation of property:[32]

> **Factors to consider in deriving just valuation.** — In arriving at just valuation as required under s. 4, Art. VII of the State Constitution, the property appraiser shall take into consideration the following factors:
>
> (1) The present cash value of the property, which is the amount a willing purchaser would pay a willing seller, exclusive of reasonable fees and costs of purchase, in cash or the immediate equivalent thereof in a transaction at arm's length;
>
> (2) The highest and best use to which the property can be expected to be put in the immediate future and the present use of the property, taking into consideration the legally permissible use of the property, including any applicable judicial limitation, local or state land use regulation, or historic preservation ordinance, and any zoning changes, concurrency requirements, and permits necessary to achieve the highest and best use, and considering any moratorium imposed by executive order, law, ordinance, regulation, resolution, or proclamation adopted by any governmental body or agency or the Governor when the moratorium or judicial limitation prohibits or restricts the development or improvement of property as otherwise authorized by applicable law. The applicable governmental body or agency or the Governor shall notify the property appraiser in writing of any executive order, ordinance, regulation, resolution, or proclamation it adopts imposing any such limitation, regulation, or moratorium;
>
> (3) The location of said property;
>
> (4) The quantity or size of said property;
>
> (5) The cost of said property and the present replacement value of any improvements thereon;
>
> (6) The condition of said property;
>
> (7) The income from said property; and
>
> (8) The net proceeds of the sale of the property, as received by the seller, after deduction of all of the usual and reasonable fees and costs of the sale, including the costs and expenses of financing, and allowance for unconventional or atypical terms of financing arrangements. When the net proceeds of the sale of any property are utilized, directly or indirectly, in the determination of just valuation of realty of the sold parcel or any other parcel under the

---

31. Fla. Stat. § 192.001(2) (2021) (amended several times since 1970).
32. Fla. Stat. § 193.011 (2021).

provisions of this section, the property appraiser, for the purposes of such determination, shall exclude any portion of such net proceeds attributable to payments for household furnishings or other items of personal property.

The following cases represent illustrative applications of these rules and factors.

Miami Atlantic Development Corp. v. Blake

334 So. 2d 29 (Fla. 3d Dist. Ct. App. 1975)

PER CURIAM.

Plaintiff appeals a summary final judgment finding that the defendant tax assessor properly assessed its property as individual condominium units for the 1973 tax year.

Plaintiff, Miami Atlantic Development Corporation, is the owner of the Crystal House, a luxury residential high rise located on Collins Avenue, Miami Beach, Florida. Having decided to change the status of the building from an apartment house to a condominium, plaintiff on December 29, 1972, executed and recorded a declaration of condominium in the public records of Dade County. The tax assessor, for the 1973 tax year beginning January 1, assessed the Crystal House as a condominium. Plaintiff corporation on behalf of itself and all other similarly situated instituted this action contesting the 1973 ad valorem tax assessment on the grounds that the Crystal House was an apartment building on January 1, 1973 and, therefore, the tax assessor incorrectly assessed the building as a condominium. Following pretrial discovery, both parties moved for summary judgment. Final summary judgment upholding the validity of the tax assessment was entered and plaintiff corporation appeals therefrom. We affirm.

Upon plaintiff's execution and recordation of the declaration of condominium on December 29, 1972, the Crystal House Condominium was created as of that date. *See* § 711.08, Fla.Stat., F.S.A. and McCaughan, *The Florida Condominium Act Applied*, 17 U.Fla.L.Rev. 1, 27 (1964–65).

One of the factors to be considered in arriving at a just valuation is "the highest and best use to which the property can be expected to be put in the immediate future and the present use of the property." § 193.011(2), Fla.Stat., F.S.A. The courts have held that the assessment must be made on the basis of the actual use or any immediate expected use to which the property is designed to be put during the expected tax year. *Lanier v. Overstreet*, Fla. 1965, 175 So.2d 521; *McKinney v. Hunt*, Fla.App. 1971, 251 So.2d 6. There is no question that the Crystal House in the very immediate future was expected to be used as a condominium and, in fact, by March of 1973 the sale of the first condominium unit had been consummated. We conclude that plaintiff has failed to demonstrate that the tax assessor wrongfully assessed the Crystal House as a condominium.

* * *

500   6 · TAXATION AND FINANCE

Affirmed.

———————

In the case of *Gilreath v. Westgate Daytona, Ltd.*,[33] the Fifth District Court of Appeal held that a county property appraiser could not assess a condominium for purposes of ad valorem taxes as a timeshare prior to becoming a timeshare under applicable Florida statutes. The court in *Gilreath* distinguished its decision from that of the Third District Court of Appeal in the previous case, *Atlantic Development Corp. v. Blake*, in which a sale, closing, and transfer of title to an individual condominium unit had taken place. In *Gilreath*, the buyers entered into voidable contracts subject to the approval of the point of sale authorizing the conversion of the property from condominium property to timeshare estates; no closing or transfer of title had taken place, nor could have taken place, unless the point of sale was approved, thereby creating the timeshare estate.[34]

Schultz v. TM Florida-Ohio Realty Ltd. Partnership

577 So. 2d 573 (Fla. 1991)

PER CURIAM.

We have for review *Schultz v. TM Florida-Ohio Realty Ltd. Partnership*, 553 So.2d 1203 (Fla. 2d DCA 1989), in which the Second District Court of Appeal certified the following question as being of great public importance:

> WHAT IS THE PROPER METHOD OF ASSESSING FOR AD VALOREM PURPOSES INCOME-PRODUCING PROPERTY WHICH IS ENCUMBERED BY A LONG-TERM LEASE WHICH DOES NOT RETURN TO THE OWNER RENT CONSISTENT WITH THE CURRENT RENTAL VALUE FOR SIMILAR PROPERTY?

553 So.2d at 1225. We have jurisdiction pursuant to article V, section 3(b)(4), Florida Constitution.

The property that is the subject of the assessment at issue is approximately an 11-acre tract of land improved with a large department store-type building occupied by two tenants, a K-Mart and a waterbed store. The property is owned by the respondent, TM Florida-Ohio Realty Ltd. Partnership (taxpayer), and is encumbered by a 22-year lease agreement with K-Mart Department Stores that commenced in 1970 and that contains four five-year options to renew.

The respondent filed an action in circuit court contesting the 1986 assessment of the property by the property appraiser of Pinellas County in the amount of $3,981,400. After a trial at which experts for both parties testified, the trial court entered a final judgment declaring null and void the portion of the assessment

———————

33. 871 So. 2d 961 (Fla. 5th Dist. Ct. App. 2004).
34. *Id.* at 969.

which exceeds $2,950,000, the amount found to be the fair market value of the property by the taxpayer's expert. Although the trial court found "no problem in the methodology by which [the taxing authority] appraised the property in 1986," the court could not "judicially countenance an 89.1 percent increase in the appraisal evaluation in the space of one year" because the taxpayer could not have anticipated such an increase.

The trial court's reduced assessment was affirmed on appeal. The district court rejected the property appraiser's contention that the assessment must be upheld because: 1) section 193.011, Florida Statutes (1985),[1] merely requires a property appraiser to consider the various factors affecting the value of property; and 2) the evidence established that the appraiser considered each of those factors, including the "submarket"[2] rental income under the long-term lease. In the district court's view "submarket rental income from a long-term lease on real property should be *weighed* in arriving at a proper valuation of the property for ad valorem tax purposes." 553 So.2d at 1208 (emphasis added). Reasoning that the property appraiser's failure to accord any weight to the actual submarket rental income from the property resulted in an assessment that exceeded the fair market value of the property, the district court concluded that the appraiser did not give "proper consideration to the income factor specified in section 193.011, as did in effect the trial court in arriving at its reduced assessment." 553 So.2d at 1205. Although the property appraiser's alternative motions for rehearing and rehearing en banc were denied by the district court, the question as set forth above was certified to this court as being of great public importance. *Id.* at 1225.

We find our decision in *Valencia Center v. Bystrom*, 543 So.2d 214 (Fla.1989), controlling and agree with the dissenting opinion below that the decision under review

---

1. Section 193.011, Florida Statutes (1985), provides in pertinent part:
   Factors to consider in deriving just valuation. — In arriving at just valuation as required under s. 4, Art. VII of the State Constitution, the property appraiser shall take into consideration the following factors:
   (1) The present cash value of the property . . . ;
   (2) The highest and best use to which the property can be expected to be put in the immediate future and the present use of the property . . . ;
   (3) The location of said property;
   (4) The quantity of size of said property;
   (5) The cost of said property and the present replacement value of any improvements thereon;
   (6) The condition of said property;
   (7) The income from said property; and
   (8) The net proceeds of the sale of the property. . . .
   2. The rental income under the subject lease is considered "submarket" because it is below the current rental rate for similar property.

conflicts with *Valencia Center* and this Court's decision in *Oyster Pointe Resort Condominium Association v. Nolte*, 524 So.2d 415 (Fla.1988). *See Schultz*, 553 So.2d at 1225 (Parker, J. dissenting). As we noted in *Valencia Center,*

> This Court has found that the just valuation at which property must be assessed under the constitution and Section 193.011 is synonymous with fair market value. . . . In arriving at fair market value, the assessor *must consider, but not necessarily use,* each of the factors set out in section 193.011. *Oyster Pointe Resort Condominium Ass'n v. Nolte*, 524 So.2d 415 (Fla.1988). The particular method of valuation, and the weight to be given each factor, is left to the discretion of the assessor, and his determination will not be distributed on review as long as each factor has been lawfully considered and the assessed value is within the range of reasonable appraisals. *Blake v. Xerox Corp.*, 447 So.2d 1348 (Fla.1984).

543 So.2d at 216–17 (emphasis added). In *Valencia Center*, we went on to specifically reject the taxpayer's argument that an assessment should be decreased where the property is encumbered by a long-term below-market lease. *Id.* at 217. In rejecting that argument we noted that

> this issue too has already been addressed by this Court. In *Department of Revenue v. Morganwoods Greentree, Inc.*, 341 So.2d 756, 758 (Fla.1977), we stated:
>
> > We reaffirm the general rule that in the levy of property tax the assessed value of the land *must represent all the interests in the land. This means that despite the mortgage, lease, or sublease of the property, the landowner will still be taxed as though he possessed the property in fee simple.* The general property tax ignores fragmenting of ownership and seeks payment from only one "owner."
>
> (Citations omitted.) Here, the overall interest consists of two parts: the interest remaining in the hands of the owner-lessor, Valencia, and the interest held by the lessee, Publix. The amount a willing buyer would pay for the "fee simple" equals the value of both the lessor's and lessee's interests. The owner in this case, Valencia, has simply transferred a large part of the property's value to the lessee. Failing to consider the transferred interest would result in an assessment below fair market value.

543 So.2d at 217 (emphasis added).

In accord with our opinion in *Valencia Center*, we answer the certified question as follows: When determining the fair market value of income-producing property which is encumbered by a long-term submarket lease, the assessor must consider but not necessarily use each of the factors set out in section 193.011. The ultimate method of valuation employed and the weight, if any, to be given each factor considered is within the discretion of the assessor. However, the resulting valuation must represent the value of all interests in the property — in other words, the fair market value of the unencumbered fee.

The taxpayer in this case has failed to meet its burden to show that the challenged valuation was not arrived at lawfully and is not supported by any reasonable hypothesis of legality. *See Oyster Pointe*, 524 So.2d at 417. As noted above, the trial court specifically found that the methodology by which the property was appraised was not "erroneous or improper." This finding is supported by the record.

It is clear from the extensive testimony of the property appraiser's expert that each of the eight criteria outlined in section 193.011 was considered in reaching the final valuation. The expert detailed the consideration given the income factor and specifically testified that the tax appraiser's office was aware of the lease which encumbered the property and of the income it generated. Based on his testimony, after making calculations according to an accepted income formula, it was concluded that the rent received was "submarket," that is, leases negotiated during 1986 for similar property would return a higher rental rate than that received for the subject property. Therefore, in order to arrive at a valuation of the unencumbered interest in the property, the income factor was afforded no weight and the cost factor served as the primary basis for the assessment. The taxpayer's expert agreed that the income received from the property was submarket and that if the challenged assessment must reflect the fair market value of the unencumbered fee interest in the property it would not be excessive.

Accordingly, because the taxpayer failed to show that the property appraiser did not follow the requirements of law or that the assessed value is not within the range of reasonable appraisals, the decision below is quashed and the cause is remanded for reinstatement of the assessment of the property appraiser.

It is so ordered.

SHAW, C.J., and McDONALD, BARKETT, GRIMES and KOGAN, JJ., concur.

OVERTON, J., dissents [without opinion].

––––––––––

As pointed out in *Schultz, supra*, the property appraiser must consider the criteria set forth in Fla. Stat. §193.011 when determining the just valuation of property. The property appraiser's assessment is presumed to be correct. As the Florida Supreme Court pointed out in *Shultz*, a taxpayer can overcome the property appraiser's presumptively correct assessment by providing proof that the assessment "is not within the range of reasonable appraisals" but that under this standard, the trial court would be correct in upholding the assessment as long as the assessment was "supported by any reasonable hypothesis of legality."[35] It should be noted that in 1997, the Florida Legislature enacted §194.301 expressly abrogating the "every-reasonable hypothesis standard" and providing that "in any . . . action in which a taxpayer challenges an ad valorem tax assessment of value, the property appraiser's assessment is presumed correct if the appraiser proves by a preponderance of the

––––––––––

35. *Shultz v. TM Fla.-Ohio Realty Ltd. P'ship*, 577 So.2d 573, 575-76 (Fla. 1991).

504	6 · TAXATION AND FINANCE

evidence that the assessment was arrived at by complying with s. 193.011, any other applicable statutory requirements relating to classified use values or assessment caps, and professionally accepted practices, including mass appraisal standards, if appropriate."[36] This statute provided that if presumption of correctness were lost, the taxpayer had the burden to prove by a preponderance of the evidence that the challenged assessment was in excess of just value. Despite the legislative mandate, the "any reasonable hypothesis" standard continued to be applied in cases reviewing decisions on post-1997 ad valorem tax challenges.[37] In 2009, the Florida Legislature enacted Fla. Stat. § 194.3015[38] to redress the courts' continued application of the "any reasonable hypothesis" standard in reviewing challenges to the property appraiser's assessment."[39]

Appleby v. Nolte

682 So. 2d 1140 (Fla. 4th Dist. Ct. App. 1996)

PER CURIAM.

We reverse the final judgment entered in favor of the Indian River County Property Appraiser and remand with direction to enter final judgment consistent herewith.

Appellants are contesting the assessed value of their homes for ad valorem tax purposes. They are all residents of John's Island, equity members of the John's Island Club (Club), a Florida corporation which operates a country club associated with the residential development. Appellants all had equity memberships that entitled them to full golf privileges and, like all other equity members with lesser use privileges, upon dissolution of the Club, they would receive their proportionate share of all of the property and assets, after payment of its debts. The Club limits its membership to a total of 1382: 1125 golf memberships and 257 non-golf memberships called Sport Specials. The full golf memberships are scarce.

Appellee/property appraiser took into consideration appellants' membership status in the Club when appraising the value of their property. Homes or condominiums owned by people who were members with full golf privileges were assessed at

---

36. Fla. Stat. § 193.011 (1997).

37. *CVS EGL Fruitville Sarasota, FL, LLC v. Todora*, 124 So. 3d 289, 291 (Fla. 2nd Dist. Ct. App. 2013).

38. Section 194.3015, Florida Statutes (2009) provides in relevant part:

(1) It is the express intent of the Legislature that a taxpayer shall never have the burden of proving that the property appraiser's assessment is not supported by any reasonable hypothesis of a legal assessment. All cases establishing the every-reasonable hypothesis standard were expressly rejected by the Legislature on the adoption of chapter 97-85, Laws of Florida. It is the further intent of the Legislature that any cases published since 1997 citing the every-reasonable-hypothesis standard are rejected to the extent they are interpretative of legislative intent.

(2) This section is intended to clarify existing law and apply retroactively.

39. *Id.*

values approximately forty percent higher than homes owned by persons with the sport special memberships, or by persons who were not members at all. The property appraiser began this practice when it became evident that when homes were sold in John's Island, homeowners with full golf memberships who were willing to relinquish their membership to make room for the buyer were able to sell their homes much more quickly and at substantially higher prices than homeowners who had the Sport Special or no membership to relinquish. Appellants argue that increasing the assessed value on their homes based on their personal golf memberships is an inappropriate ad valorem tax on intangible personal property. The trial court disagreed, concluding that "[t]he right associated with each of these six properties to be considered for a golf membership in The John's Island Club is part of the value of the real property owned by plaintiffs," and reasoning, "[t]he fact that a particular piece of property has associated with it the ability to be considered for golf membership in The John's Island Club adds value to that property which is reflected in the sales price of that property."

The Club's official name is "John's Island Club, Inc.," a non-profit Florida corporation; therefore, it is composed of "members" in place of shareholders.

Persons who close on the purchase of a residential unit in John's Island will have an opportunity to acquire an equity membership in the Club, if an equity membership is then available. Equity membership requires an equity contribution, $85,000 in 1994, and approval by the Board of Directors. An "approved" candidate receives a Membership Certificate, which is not transferable unless the member dies or divorces, and then only if the successor to the certificate is approved by the board.

The Club will be obligated to repurchase an Equity Membership only if an individual, who is acceptable to the Club, is willing to acquire the retiring member's membership. Owner-members may arrange through the Club for the reissue of a membership certificate to the buyer of the member's residential unit or lot in John's Island, if the buyer has been approved for membership in the Club. The ability to designate which applicant shall be given priority for the resigned membership, combined with the demand for full golf memberships is what led to higher sales prices for properties owned by golf members willing to resign. The standard contract for sale used in sales of properties in John's Island frequently includes the following clause:

> This Contract for Sale and Purchase is contingent upon Buyers becoming a Member of the John's Island Club and acquiring a *GOLF* Membership in the John's Island Club and same being made available at closing. Neither the price of such Membership nor dues or assessments relating to it, nor prorations thereof, are included in the purchase price of the property and Buyer's obligation for such amounts shall be made subject to separate settlement at time of closing.

This clause assures that the buyer will not have to purchase in the absence of approval for membership in the Club. Similarly, the seller will not have to sell without getting back the equity share in the Club.

The record indicates that golf memberships were owned by both residents and non-residents of John's Island. Resident owners could, and did, sell their properties in John's Island, while retaining their golf memberships. Members could retire their membership without selling their property in John's Island. Persons buying residential units in John's Island from owners who did not have golf memberships could nevertheless acquire a golf membership if one was available and they were approved.

The parties agree that when two similar homes in John's Island are listed for sale, and the owners of one home are golf members of the Club, willing to resign their membership, and the owners of the second home are not golf members, the sale price on the home owned by members will be substantially higher.

The Florida Constitution prohibits counties from levying ad valorem taxes on intangible personal property. Art. VII, §9(a), Fla. Const. Counties may levy ad valorem taxes on real property and tangible personal property. Tangible personal property consists of goods, chattels, and other articles of value capable of manual possession and whose chief value is intrinsic to the article itself. §192.001(11)(d), Fla. Stat. (1993). Neither party argues that appellant's "ability to resign their membership coupled with the right to arrange for a buyer of their property to purchase it" is tangible personal property. Appellants argue that their interest is intangible personal property, not subject to ad valorem taxation. Appellee argues that appellants' interest is real property that is subject to ad valorem taxation.

Section 192.001(11), Florida Statutes (1993), states:

> "Personal property," for the purposes of ad valorem taxation, shall be divided into four categories as follows:
>
> . . . .
>
> (b) "Intangible personal property" means money, all evidences of debt owed to the taxpayer, **all evidences of ownership in a corporation** or other business organization having multiple owners, and all other forms of property where value is based upon that which the property represents rather than its own intrinsic value.

(Emphasis added.) The "Membership Certificates" fit the above definition in deciding whether the constitutional proscription applies.

Appellee bases his assessments on a list that indicates which owners in John's Island hold membership certificates entitling them to full golf privileges, and which do not. Properties owned by golf members were being assessed approximately forty percent higher than those owned by non-golf members. Appellee has based his assessment partially on the value of the real property, and partially on evidence of ownership in a corporation, contrary to article 7, section 9 of the Florida Constitution, which prohibits counties from levying an ad valorem tax on intangible personal property. Accordingly, an ad valorem tax may not be based on appellant's ownership interest in John's Island Club, Inc.

Furthermore, appellee's assessments are based on who owns the property. If a golf member owns a residential unit, the assessment is one amount. If a non-golf member owns the same residential unit, the assessment is a lower amount. The Florida Supreme Court has held that ownership in one party or another is not a valid criterion for valuing property. *Interlachen Lakes Estates, Inc. v. Snyder*, 304 So.2d 433 (Fla. 1973).

GLICKSTEIN and STEVENSON, JJ., and BROWN, LUCY C., Associate Judge, concur.

> [T]he constitutional rights of a taxpayer are infringed if his property is assessed at a percentage of value substantially higher than the percentage at which all other property in the county is generally assessed. . . . [40]

Because of the uniqueness of certain property, the Florida Legislature has enacted special valuation rules for certain types of property. An illustration of this approach is timeshare property.

To facilitate the valuation and taxation of fee timeshare real property, the managing entity responsible for operating and maintaining the fee timeshare real property is considered the agent of the timeshare period titleholder.[41] Under these rules the property is valued in its entirety (by combining the value of the individual timeshare periods or estates), and then this value is allocated among the timeshare period titleholders.[42]

The following case represents the Florida Supreme Court's most recent interpretation of these special rules.

Oyster Pointe Resort Condominium Association, Inc. v. Nolte

524 So. 2d 415 (Fla. 1988)

KOGAN, Justice.

This consolidated appeal is from decisions of the Fourth District Court of Appeal, 497 So.2d 740 and 1306 (1986), declaring section 192.037, Florida Statutes (1983), valid upon the authority of *Spanish River Resort Corp. v. Walker*, 497 So.2d 1299 (Fla. 4th DCA 1986). We have jurisdiction. Art. V, § 3(b)(1), Fla. Const.

The properties in this consolidated appeal are four condominium developments consisting of fee time-share estates known as Oyster Pointe Resort, Oyster Bay II, Driftwood Vacation Villas, and Driftwood Ocean Villas. The fee time-share units here are sold as a term of years followed by a tenancy in common in the real property. The units are then transferred by warranty deed to each time-share owner,

---

40. *Southern Bell Telephone & Telegraph Co. v. Broward Cnty.*, 665 So. 2d 272, 274 (Fla. 4th Dist. Ct. App. 1995) (quoting *Southern Bell Telephone & Telegraph Company v. Markham*, 632 So. 2d 272, 275 (Fla. 4th Dist. Ct. App. 1994), and *Deltona Corp. v. Bailey*, 336 So. 2d 1163, 1168 (Fla. 1976)).

41. Fla. Stat. § 192.037(1).

42. Fla. Stat. § 192.037(2)-(3).

giving each owner an undivided interest in the subject property. For the year 1983, the property appraiser valued each time-share unit based on a market approach to value, utilizing comparable sales data of the other individual fee time-share estates. The assessment of the time-share units resulted in a valuation that was increased more than tenfold over the prior year and over identical adjoining units, the ownership of which had not been fragmented. The property appraiser based his actions on his interpretation of section 192.037(2), Florida Statues (1982), effective January 1, 1983. He read the statute as requiring him to appraise each individual time-share week and then to combine them into a single listing on the tax roll. The tax bills for the individual time-share units were sent to the managing entity as agent for the time-share unit owners.

The uncontroverted testimony at trial was that the sales price of the time-share units included not only the costs attributable to real property and tangible personal property, but many other cost components typical of and peculiar to time-share estates (i.e., marketing costs and other intangible values such as the right to participate in an exchange network of resorts and a reservation and front-desk system, together with other services and amenities ordinarily associated with a hotel).

All three cases were consolidated for trial. The trial court by amended final judgment approved the assessment process followed by the property appraiser. The district court affirmed the trial court and, on the authority of *Spanish River*, expressly found section 192.037(2) constitutional.

Three of the issues posed by each case are identical: (1) whether section 192.037 is constitutional on due process and equal protection grounds; (2) whether the property appraiser correctly assessed the time-share units under section 192.037(2) by assessing each individual time-share week; and (3) whether the property appraiser, when assessing time-share units under the market value approach, must net from the sales price all elements of the purchase price other than its real property component. The fourth issue raised, pertinent only to the *Oyster Pointe Resort* case, is whether all fifty-two units of the Oyster Pointe Resort should be assessed for 1983 ad valorem tax purposes pursuant to the provisions of section 192.037.

In our recent opinion of *Day v. High Point Condominium Resorts, Ltd.*, 521 So.2d 1064 (Fla.1988), we addressed the first issue presented to us in this appeal. We found section 192.037 constitutional on both due process and equal protection grounds. We see no need to engage in any further discussion on this issue, and for the reasons expressed in *Day* we uphold the validity of section 192.037.

The second issue before us questions whether the property appraiser correctly assessed the time-share units under section 192.037(2) by assessing each individual time-share week. Section 192.037(2) states:

> Fee time-share real property shall be listed on the assessment rolls as a single entry for each time-share development. The assessed value of each time-share development shall be the value of the combined individual time-share periods or time share estates contained therein.

The time-share unit owners argue that the language of subsection (2) directs the property appraiser to assess the time-share development as a whole (i.e., the land, buildings and improvements thereon) unaffected by its subdivision into time-share weeks. To support their interpretation the petitioners make two points. In the first sentence of section 192.037(2), the unit to be assessed is referred to as "fee time-share real property," defined in section 192.011(14), Florida Statutes (1982), as "the land and buildings and other improvements to land that are subject to time-share interests which are sold as a fee interest in real property." In the second sentence of section 192.037(2), the word "value" is used in the singular. Thus, the petitioners contend, it is obvious the legislature intended the valuation of the time-share development as a single unit with an allocation of the total value among the time-share ownership interests therein, rather than a valuation of each individual time-share unit with the resulting individual values combined to derive the value of the time-share development as a whole.

This argument was expressly rejected by the Fourth District Court of Appeal in *Spanish River*. We are also unpersuaded by this argument and quote with approval the district court's analysis of the pertinent provisions of section 192.037:

> Section 192.037(2) must be read in pari materia with all of the other subsections in section 192.037, particularly the preceding subsection (1). Subsection (1) provides that the managing entity shall be considered the agent for *all* the time-share unit holders, so that, as subsection (2) contemplates, only a single entry for each development need appear on the assessment rolls. However, Subsection (2) quite clearly goes on to provide that that single assessment entry shall be the value of the combined *individual* time-share periods. While we are not very impressed with this statutory choice of words, we are confident that the language employed contemplates that the single assessment entry is to reflect the sum of the individual assessments of each time-share unit. Our conclusion is bolstered by all the other statutory enactments or amendments which took place during this same period. For example, there are now at least thirteen separate occasions on which the term "fee" has been engrafted into the applicable statutes. In addition, section 721.03(5), Florida Statutes (1983), now clearly specifies that "the treatment of time-share estates for ad valorem purposes and special assessments shall be as prescribed in Chapters 192 through 200." This quoted language, appearing contemporaneously with the enactment of section 192.037, is an unmistakable expression of the legislature's intent to bring individual time-share units or "weeks" within the ambit of ad valorem taxation. . . . In this context, the use of the word "fee" on so many occasions cannot be ignored.

497 So.2d at 1302 (emphasis in the original). In light of the foregoing analysis, we conclude the property appraiser is authorized to assess the time-share units under section 192.037(2) by assessing each individual time-share week.

The third issue presented requires us to discuss whether the property appraiser must net from the sales price all elements of the purchase price other than the real property component when valuing time-share units under a market value approach. The method of valuation utilized is within the administrative discretion of the property appraiser, and the valuation is presumed correct so long as the determination was arrived at lawfully. *Blake v. Xerox Corp.*, 447 So.2d 1348 (Fla.1984). The burden is on the taxpayer to show the property appraiser departed from the essential requirements of the law and the appraisal is not supported by any reasonable hypothesis of legality. 447 So.2d at 1350. Section 193.011, Florida Statutes (1983),* sets forth the eight criteria a property appraiser must consider when determining the fair market value of real property for tax assessment purposes. When sales of comparable properties are used to determine fair market value, as was done here, the property appraiser performs a standard appraisal. In so doing, he considers all and uses some of the factors set forth in section 193.011. *Bystrom v. Valencia Center, Inc.*, 432 So.2d 108 (Fla. 3d DCA 1983), *pet. for review denied*, 444 So.2d 418 (Fla.1984).

Petitioners claim the determination of the fair market value of the time-share units is invalid because the property appraiser failed to properly consider Section 193.011(8), which directs the property appraiser to take into account the "usual and reasonable fees and costs" associated with the sale of the property. They argue that only the real property component of the sales price (i.e. the land, buildings and improvements thereon) should be used to determine the fair market value or "just valuation" of the property for tax assessment purposes. Petitioners urge the

---

* Section 193.011 provides as follows:

In arriving at just valuation as required under s. 4, Art. VII of the State Constitution, the property appraiser shall take into consideration the following factors:

(1) The present cash value of the property, which is the amount a willing purchaser would pay a willing seller, exclusive of reasonable fees and costs of purchase, in cash or the immediate equivalent thereof in a transaction at arm's length;

(2) The highest and best use to which the property can be expected to be put in the immediate future and the present use of the property, taking into consideration any applicable local or state land use regulation and considering any moratorium imposed by executive order, law, ordinance, regulation, resolution, or proclamation adopted by any governmental body or agency or the Governor when the moratorium prohibits or restricts the development or improvement of property as otherwise authorized by applicable law;

(3) The location of said property;

(4) The quantity or size of said property;

(5) The cost of said property and the present replacement value of any improvements thereon;

(6) The condition of said property;

(7) The income from said property; and

(8) The net proceeds of the sale of the property, as received by the seller, after deduction of all of the usual and reasonable fees and costs of the sale, including the costs and expenses of financing, and allowance for unconventional or atypical terms of financing arrangements. When the net proceeds of the sale of any property are utilized, directly or indirectly, in the determination of just valuation of realty of the sold parcel or any other parcel under the provisions of this section, the property appraiser, for the purposes of such determination, shall exclude any portion of such net proceeds attributable to payments for household furnishings or other items of personal property.

excessive marketing costs, the atypical financing costs, and the other extraordinary costs associated with fee time-share estates are part of the "reasonable fees and costs of sale" contemplated under section 193.011(8). Thus these costs should be deducted from the sales price in arriving at the net proceeds of the sale, the figure upon which the tax assessment is calculated under the market value approach.

The excessive costs of sale cited by petitioners comprise approximately 75–80% of the purchase price of the fee time-share units. However, as we read section 193.011(8), these costs are not among the "reasonable fees and costs of sale" contemplated by the legislature to be excluded from the ad valorem appraisal process. Subsection (8) must be read in pari materia with subsection (1) "which limits the consideration of sales costs to 'reasonable fees and costs of purchase.'" *Spanish River*, 497 So.2d at 1304 (emphasis omitted). Our conclusion is the legislature intended the phrase "reasonable fees and costs of sale" to include only those fees and costs typically associated with the closing of the sale of real property such as reasonable attorney's fees, broker's commissions, appraisal fees, documentary stamp costs, survey costs and title insurance costs. *See* Note, *Ad Valorem Taxation of Time-Share Properties: Should Time-Share Estates Be Separately Assessed and Taxed?*, 37 U.Fla.L.Rev. 421 (1985). Until the legislature modifies section 193.011(8), the costs cited by the petitioners cannot be deducted from the purchase price of the time-share units as "reasonable fees and costs of sale." Thus, the property appraiser correctly applied the eighth criterion of section 193.011 by not deducting from the sales price of the time-share units the marketing costs and other costs cited by the petitioners. It was within the property appraiser's administrative discretion to determine the value of the time-share units under a market approach to value, and the petitioners have failed to show the property appraiser did not follow the requirements of law in determining the assessment of the time-share units.

We note that in using the market approach to value, the property appraiser relied solely upon comparable sales of similar properties to arrive at the fair market value of the time-share units. We are mindful of the petitioners' point that an appraisal based on the original purchase price of the units includes the unusually high marketing costs necessary to attract potential buyers for the time-share units, costs they allege will never be recouped upon resale. Because there have been very few, if any, resales of these time-share units, no assessments have been based on resale prices. As the Fourth District Court of Appeal aptly notes in *Spanish River*, if a pattern of lower resale prices emerges, then the property appraiser will have to adjust his appraisals accordingly and reassess the time-share units. 497 So.2d at 1303.

Finally, the petitioners in the *Oyster Pointe Resort* case take issue with the property appraiser's determination that all fifty-two dwelling units in the Oyster Pointe Resort development should be assessed for 1983 ad valorem tax purposes pursuant to the provisions of section 192.037, Florida Statutes (1983). They allege that on January 1, 1983, six units in the Oyster Pointe development were whole ownership condominium units in which no time-share interests had been created and therefore should not have been assessed as time-share units. A careful reading of the record in this case reveals no evidence this issue was ever raised in the trial court or on appeal to the district court. The proper method for challenging the validity of a tax assessment is through the circuit court. §194.171, Fla. Stat. (1983). We decline to address this evidentiary issue raised for the first time on appeal.

For the reasons expressed in this opinion, we approve the decision of the Fourth District Court of Appeal holding section 192.037, Florida Statutes (1983), constitutional. We also hold the property appraiser correctly applied the eighth criterion of section 193.011, Florida Statutes (1983), and properly assessed the time-share units under section 192.037 by assessing each individual time-share week using the market approach to value.

It is so ordered.

McDONALD, C.J., and OVERTON, EHRLICH, SHAW and BARKETT, JJ., concur.

———————

As of 1989, Fla. Stat. §192.037 has included the following additional language:

(11) If there is an inadequate number of resales to provide a basis for arriving at value conclusions, then the property appraiser shall deduct from the original purchase price "usual and reasonable fees and costs of the sale." For purposes of this subsection, "usual and reasonable fees and costs of the sale" for timeshare real property shall include all marketing costs, atypical financing costs, and those costs attributable to the right of a timeshare unit owner or user to participate in an exchange network of resorts. For time-share real property, such "usual and reasonable fees and costs of the sale" shall be presumed to be 50 percent of the original purchase price; provided, however, such presumption shall be rebuttable.

(12) Subsections (10) and (11) apply to fee and non-fee timeshare real property.

Should this change the result in *Oyster Pointe*?

The ad valorem tax system is primarily a county-administered tax. Generally, the counties, school districts, municipalities, and special districts establish their millage rates, but property is valued and tax collected at the county level. Although the State Department of Revenue has actual supervisory responsibilities[43] for the ad valorem system, the valuation of property and collection of ad valorem revenues is conducted at the county level.

The following case raises the issue of discrepancies between counties. In the absence of major discrepancies which violate due process or equal protection guarantees, minor discrepancies are constitutionally tolerated.

———————

43. Fla. Stat. §195.002 (2021).

Straughn v. GAC Properties, Inc.

360 So. 2d 385 (Fla. 1978)

ENGLAND, Justice.

We granted certiorari to review the decision of the Fourth District Court of Appeal in *GAC Properties, Inc. v. Lanier*, 345 So.2d 812 (Fla. 4th DCA 1977), on the basis of an asserted conflict with *Spooner v. Askew*, 345 So.2d 1055 (Fla.1976), and *Armstrong v. State ex rel. Beaty*, 69 So.2d 319 (Fla.1954).[1] The general proposition of law addressed in all these decisions is whether real property in one county of the state may be valued and assessed for ad valorem tax purposes by reference to the valuation of real property in another county. The narrow question presented in this case is whether a cause of action lies against the Department of Revenue to compel equalization of ad valorem tax valuations where real property situated in one county is assessed on the basis of a higher value than that assigned to allegedly identical property located in another county.

* * *

The *Spooner* and *Armstrong* decisions quite clearly state that inter-county assessment uniformity is not required by the Constitution, and that variations even between adjacent counties are not a basis for lowering tax assessments which are neither greater than 100% of fair market value nor unequally or improperly determined in relation to other properties within the same county.[2] These principles flow from the constitutional directive that Florida's counties each have their own tax appraiser.[3] We recognized in *Spooner*, of course, that the legislature has in recent years endeavored to equalize real property tax assessments among the counties by developing statewide valuation standards, and by superimposing the department as a monitoring force in an effort to achieve uniformity in procedures and equalization of results. We carefully noted the limits on the department's authority, however, and observed that in the last analysis the ability of the legislature to harmonize tax assessments throughout the state

> must remain conditioned by the Constitution's directive that a class of county officers are [sic] assigned the primary responsibility to perform assessment functions. At best the legislative goal can be achieved only incrementally through cooperative efforts of the assessors and the Department,

---

1. Art. V, § 3(b)(3), Fla. Const.

2. Count II of GAC Properties' complaint does not contend that the assessment in Osceola County exceeds 100% of fair market value. It does assert that the valuation is unequal in relation to other properties in Osceola County, but that challenge to the assessment is properly directed only to the tax appraiser for Osceola County, and not to the department. GAC Properties will have its day in court on that issue under allegations set out in paragraph 10(d) of Count I of its complaint. But see *Deltona Corp. v. Bailey*, 336 So.2d 1163 (Fla.1976), regarding limitations on any claim of intra-county disparities in tax assessments.

3. Art VIII, § 1(d), Fla. Const.

and by the development of procedures which will accommodate the responsibilities of both.[4]

We decline to hold, merely on the basis of an allegation that different values have been assigned to adjacent properties of like character in different counties, that a taxpayer can claim a violation of the "just valuation" requirement or that the department can be compelled to equalize the values. The trial court properly dismissed that count of the complaint which sought relief from the department.

The decision of the court below is quashed, and the case is remanded for the district court to reinstate the trial court's order of dismissal.

OVERTON, C. J., and BOYD, SUNDBERG and HATCHETT, JJ., concur.

While most property is valued for ad valorem tax purposes at fair market value, special valuations exist for agricultural land, non-commercial recreational land, and land producing high water recharge to Florida's aquifers.[44] Under these special rules, such property is valued on the basis of its current character or use, rather than its highest and best use. This results in such property being valued at lower levels than the Florida Constitution would otherwise require.

In addition, the Florida Constitution authorizes the Florida Legislature to value tangible personal property held for sale as stock in trade, and livestock, at a specified percentage of its value, or to totally exempt such property from taxation.[45] Pursuant to this authorization, the Florida Legislature has exempted inventory from taxation.[46]

---

4. 345 So.2d at 1059–60. In also noting that the relatively new procedures for improving statewide uniformity had not seasoned in 1973 to the point of "flawless harmony" (*Id.* at 1060), we did not intend to imply that they would ever eradicate all inter-county variations. Infinite variations in the subjects of tax assessment, as well as the nature of the assessment process, preclude any serious prospect of ever achieving an assessment of each parcel of property within the state that is in complete and harmonious uniformity with every other parcel. All possible efforts toward the goal of uniformity should be pursued vigorously, but reasonable efforts short of the goal must always be tolerated.

44. Fla. Const. art VII, § 4(a).

45. Fla. Const. art VII, § 4(b).

46. Fla. Stat. § 196.185 (2021).

6 · TAXATION AND FINANCE

Straughn v. K & K Land Management, Inc.

326 So. 2d 421 (Fla. 1976)

SUNDBERG, Justice.

This is an appeal from the Circuit Court of the Tenth Judicial Circuit, in and for Polk County, which entered a final judgment declaring Section 193.461(4)(c), Florida Statutes to be unconstitutional. This Court has jurisdiction pursuant to Article V, Section 3(b)(1), Florida Constitution.

Appellant Straughn is Executive Director of the Department of Revenue, State of Florida. Appellant Rhoden is Tax Assessor for Polk County, Florida. Rhoden reclassified land owned by appellee as non-agricultural by denying appellee's application for an agricultural assessment for the year 1973. This determination by the Tax Assessor resulted in a reassessment of the subject property and a substantial increase in appellee's tax liability.

Section 193.461(4)(c), Florida Statutes, reads as follows:

> Sale of land for a purchase price which is three or more times the agricultural assessment placed on the land shall create a presumption that such land is not used primarily for bona fide agricultural purposes. Upon a showing of special circumstances by the landowner demonstrating that the land is to be continued in bona fide agriculture, this presumption may be rebutted.

It was upon the authority of this rebuttable statutory presumption that the Tax Assessor based his action. "Purchase price paid" is set forth by Section 193.461(3)(b), Florida Statutes,[1] as one of seven criteria to be considered by tax assessors in making their determination as to whether property qualifies as agricultural for purposes of the lower tax assessment. Presumably evidence tending to confirm the agricultural

---

1. "Subject to the restrictions set out in this section, only lands which are used primarily for bona fide agricultural purposes shall be classified agricultural. 'Bona fide agricultural purposes' means good faith commercial agricultural use of the land. In determining whether the use of the land for agricultural purposes is bona fide, the following facts may be taken into consideration:

"1. The length of time the land has been so utilized;

"2. Whether the use has been continuous;

"3. The purchase price paid;

"4. Size, as it relates to specific agricultural use;

"5. Whether an indicated effort has been made to care sufficiently and adequately for the land in accordance with accepted commercial agricultural practices, including, without limitation, fertilizing, liming, tilling, mowing, reforesting, and other accepted agricultural practices;

"6. Whether such land is under lease and, if so, the effective length, terms, and conditions of the lease; and

"7. Such other factors as may from time to time become applicable."

nature of assessable land, i.e. "special circumstances", should conform to the other six statutory considerations if the presumption established by Section 193.461(4)(c), Florida Statutes, is to be overcome.

In the instant case, the circuit court found Section 193.461(4)(c), Florida Statutes, to be unconstitutional as (1) an unlawful delegation of legislative authority without adequate standards and guidelines and (2) a contravention of the constitutional requirement that assessment be made solely on the "basis of character or use". The court also concluded that the land in question was on January 1, 1973 — the relevant date for purposes of classification according to use — being used for bona fide agricultural purposes as defined by Section 193.461(3)(b), Florida Statutes, and therefore it qualified for the lower agricultural tax rate. Appellant Rhoden was ordered to make his assessment reflect this determination.

We are not persuaded that Section 193.461(4)(c), Florida Statutes, constitutes an unconstitutional effort to delegate legislative authority without proper guidelines. The phrase "special circumstances", indicating what must be shown in order to overcome the statutory presumption at issue, should be read *in pari materia* with Section 193.461(3)(b), Florida Statutes, and the seven criteria for determination of taxable status enumerated therein. These considerations, which must be weighed by local tax assessors, limit the discretion of such officials to a degree sufficient to escape constitutional infirmity. *See Schechter Poultry Corp. v. United States*, 295 U.S. 495, 55 S.Ct. 837, 79 L.Ed. 1570 (1935); *Conner v. Joe Hatton, Inc.*, 216 So.2d 209 (Fla.1968); and *Husband v. Cassel*, 130 So.2d 69 (Fla.1961), for discussion of the constitutional requirements in this regard. Further, we believe that the phrase "to be continued" as used in the challenged statute is neither ambiguous nor otherwise likely to lead to invidious classification. It simply requires the landowner who rebuts the presumption to demonstrate that he has not abandoned a bona fide agricultural use, as at January 1 of the year in question.

Nor are we persuaded that the challenged statute is unconstitutional under Article VII, Section 4(a), Florida Constitution, which provides that "agricultural land or land used exclusively for non-commercial recreational purposes may be classified by general law and assessed solely on the basis of character or use." It is alleged that the statutory presumption impinges upon the nature of the assessment authorized by the Constitution. We conclude, however, that the challenged statutory language affects only the *classification* of purportedly agricultural property, not its assessment. Further, the constitutional provision quoted above is permissive, not mandatory; that is, the Legislature could constitutionally remove the favored treatment of agricultural property, which constitutes an exception to the general constitutional mandate of full valuation for tax purposes. As we said in *Rainey v. Nelson*, 257 So.2d 538, 539 (Fla.1972), "[T]here is no deprivation of a property right in denying special tax treatment to this property owner since there is no 'right' to the special treatment in the first instance." In *Rainey*, this Court went on to uphold as a valid exercise of the State's police power Section 193.461(4)(b), Florida Statutes, which authorized county agricultural boards to reclassify lands as non-agricultural when such property is bounded by urban or metropolitan development on two or more sides and when such boards find that continued use of such property for agricultural purposes will deter orderly expansion of the community.

The test for the constitutionality of statutory presumption is twofold. First, there must be a rational connection between the fact proved and the ultimate fact presumed. *Tot v. United States*, 319 U.S. 463, 466, 63 S.Ct. 1241, 87 L.Ed. 1519 (1943); *United States v. Gainey*, 380 U.S. 63, 66, 85 S.Ct. 754, 13 L.Ed.2d 658 (1965). Second, there must be a right to rebut in a fair manner. *Goldstein v. Maloney*, 62 Fla. 198, 57 So. 342 (1911); *Black v. State*, 77 Fla. 289, 81 So. 411 (1919).

We find that the instant statute meets both tests. The reduced taxation for farmland is based on a legislative determination that agriculture cannot reasonably be expected to withstand the tax burden of the highest and best use to which such land might be put. The agricultural assessed value is the amount that could be invested with a reasonable expectation of an annual return to the owner similar to what he would gain from other commercial enterprises with similar risks, liquidity, degree and level of management, etc. The rational presumption imposed by the Legislature is that land purchased for three or more times its assessed agricultural value is not intended to be put to "good faith commercial agricultural use" per Section 193.461(3)(b), Florida Statutes, *supra*. Property not put to such use is not entitled to the legislatively-created exception to taxation at full value represented by the agricultural use tax status. But a property owner may yet overcome the presumption that land purchased at three times its agricultural value falls into the non-agricultural category. Tax assessors, and courts which review their work, can scrutinize the then status of property laid before them for evidence of "special circumstances" suggesting that the agricultural use will continue. In this effort, the six other statutory considerations set forth in Section 193.461(3)(b), Florida Statutes will be most significant. In short, a sale for a purchase price which is three or more times the agricultural assessment placed on the land creates a red flag for the assessor to re-evaluate the classification of such land as agricultural and places the burden upon the taxpayer to come forward with evidence of "special circumstances" within the framework of Section 193.461(3)(b), Florida Statutes, to establish that the land continues to be used for "bona fide agricultural purposes."

This statutory presumption is no exception to the general rule that presumptions are

> ... decisive only in the absence of contrary evidence and must give way when in conflict with distinct and convincing proof.... [W]hen substantial evidence contrary to a presumption is introduced, the underlying facts that originally raised the presumption may or may not retain some degree of probative force as evidence, but they no longer have any artificial or technical force. In other words, the presumption falls out of the case, and cannot acquire the attribute of evidence in the claimant's favor....

13 Fla.Jur., Evidence, § 76, 83–84.

518   6 · TAXATION AND FINANCE

Del Vecchio v. Bowers, 296 U.S. 280, 286, 56 S.Ct. 190, 193, 80 L.Ed. 229, 233 (1935); *Harlem Taxicab Ass'n v. Nemesh*, 89 U.S.App.D.C. 123 191 F.2d 459, 461 (1951); *Mercury Cab Owners' Ass'n v. Jones*, 79 So.2d 782, 784 (Fla.1955).

We make no determination on whether the presumption has been overcome by the testimony and evidence in this cause. We leave that determination to the trial judge who may, if he deems it necessary, allow the parties to present additional testimony on that issue.

Accordingly, the judgment is reversed, and the cause is remanded to the trial court for further proceedings not inconsistent herewith.

ADKINS, C. J., ROBERTS, BOYD, OVERTON and ENGLAND, JJ., and FERRIS, Circuit Judge, concur.

Similar to the 3% cap that was placed on the increase in annual assessments for homestead property as part of the "Save Our Homes" amendment in 1992 (which took effect in 1995), the constitution was amended in 2008 to provide a 10% cap on the amount in which the annual assessment of "non-homestead" residential real property[47] and other (non-residential) real property[48] could increase. Once property changes from homestead to non-homestead, it must then be reassessed at its fair market value for ad valorem tax purposes before it can receive the benefit of the 10% limitation in future tax years. The following case is illustrative of this point.

Orange County Property Appraiser v. Sommers

84 So. 3d 1277 (Fla. 5th Dist. Ct. App. 2012)

MONACO, J.

This case of first impression compels us to consider what the innocent looking phrase, "placed on the tax roll," means with respect to the ten per cent cap on increases in the assessment of continuously owned non-homestead residential real property that previously enjoyed the status of homestead property. The phrase is found in section 193.1554(3), Florida Statutes (2010). The trial court concluded that the phrase meant that the homestead value of continuously owned residential property remained in place even after the property no longer bore a homestead classification, and that the assessment on the property could not be increased by more than the ten per cent limit found in section 193.1554(3). The appellants, Orange County Property Appraiser and Orange County Tax Collector, appeal the final judgment finding that the 2009 assessed value of the residential property owned by the appellees, Bernard D. Sommers and Arlene P. Sommers, was incorrect. We conclude that the trial court misinterpreted the statute and reverse.

---

47. Art. VII, § 4(g).
48. Art. VII, § 4(h).

The facts are neither complicated, nor contested. Mr. and Mrs. Sommers owned a home in Maitland, Florida, from 1960 to 2010. They continuously resided in that house from the date of purchase until they moved to a different residence in November 2008. Although they were not living in the home, they still owned it until January 2010, at which time they sold it. It is uncontested that the house was not homestead from the day Mr. and Mrs. Sommers moved out in 2008, to the day it was sold in 2010.

In 2008, the property enjoyed the homestead exemption because it was the Sommers' residence on January 1st of that year. The Property Appraiser assessed the home in 2008 in compliance with the "Save Our Homes" assessment cap contained in Article VII, Subsection 4(d) of the Florida Constitution, and implemented in section 193.155(1), Florida Statutes (2010). The assessment cap on the Sommers' property, assessed as homestead, was three per cent. After applying the homestead exemption with the Save Our Homes cap, the Property Appraiser assessed the taxable value of the Sommers' home for that year at $134,060.

In 2009, because Mr. and Mrs. Sommers no longer lived in the home, the property became a "nonhomestead residential" property for ad valorem tax purposes. The Property Appraiser assessed the Sommers' home as of January 1, 2009, using the just value or fair market value standard, at $279,955. Compared to the taxable value of the homestead in 2008 of $134,060, the assessment in 2009, was an increase in the taxable value of the home of $145,895, or 108.1%.

Mr. and Mrs. Sommers disputed the 2009 assessment and filed a petition with the Orange County Value Adjustment Board ("VAB"), seeking relief. They paid their taxes in full, but under protest. At the VAB hearing before a special magistrate, the Sommers argued that because the Property Appraiser had increased the assessment of their now non-homestead residential property by an amount in excess of ten per cent of the previous-year assessment, the Appraiser had violated the ten per cent cap imposed on assessment increases for that classification of property under newly adopted Subsection 4(g) of Article VII of the Florida Constitution and section 193.1554, Florida Statutes. The Property Appraiser countered that he properly assessed the Sommers' nonhomestead residential property at its just value for 2009 and that only in 2010 would the Sommers' property be subject to the ten per cent cap on assessment increases pursuant to section 193.1554.

The special magistrate recommended that the Sommers' petition be denied and that the 2009 assessment be upheld. The VAB thereafter approved the recommendation. Mr. and Mrs. Sommers commenced the underlying action in the circuit court to appeal the decision of the VAB. Eventually, however, the trial court granted the motion of the Sommerses for summary judgment, holding that the ten per cent cap on an increase of an assessment of nonhomestead residential property set forth in subsection 4 of Article VII of the state constitution and section 193.1554(3), Florida Statutes, applied to the Sommers' property for 2009. This timely appeal followed.

The section of the Florida Constitution governing the valuation of real property for ad valorem tax purposes and a number of statutes concerning the same matter must be spread upon the table in order to understand the arguments of the parties. We begin with the constitution.

The Florida Constitution mandates the just valuation of all property for ad valorem tax purposes. Art. VII, § 4, Fla. Const.; *Bystrom v. Whitman*, 488 So.2d 520, 521 (Fla.1986). General law provides, concomitantly, that all real property shall be assessed according to its just value on January 1 of each year. *See* § 192.042(1), Fla. Stat. Homestead property is treated somewhat differently in that it is benefitted by a number of tax breaks after it is justly valued. *See, e.g.,* § 196.031, Fla. Stat. (2010). In the event of a termination of homestead status, however, real property must be assessed as provided by general law. Art. VII, § 4(d)((6).

Article VII, Section 4(g), of the Florida Constitution considers the subject of non-homestead residential property. It provides:

> (g) For all levies other than school district levies, assessments of residential real property, as defined by general law, which contains nine units or fewer and **which is not subject to the assessment limitations set forth in subsections (a) through (d) [including the homestead exemption]** shall change only as provided in this subsection.
>
> (1) Assessments subject to this subsection shall be changed annually on the date of assessment provided by law; **but those changes in assessments shall not exceed ten percent (10%) of the assessment for the prior year.**

We have added emphasis to certain provisions of this passage because it is informative with regard to the codification by the legislature of its requirements. Section 4(g) essentially defines nonhomestead residential property as being residential real property of less than nine units which is not accorded homestead treatment for real property tax purposes. That is to say, in order to be classified as nonhomestead residential property and to receive the benefit of the ten per cent tax increase limitation, a parcel of real estate cannot at the same time be subject to the homestead exemption.

Section 193.1554, Florida Statutes, which implements these constitutional requirements, provides in pertinent part:

> (1) As used in this section, the term "nonhomestead residential property" means residential real property that contains nine or fewer dwelling units, including vacant property zoned and platted for residential use, **and that does not receive the exemption under s. 196.031** (the homestead exemption).
>
> (2) For all levies other than school district levies, nonhomestead residential property shall be assessed at just value as of January 1, 2008. Property placed on the tax roll after January 1, 2008, shall be assessed at just value as of January 1 of the year in which the property is placed on the tax roll.

(3) Beginning in 2009, or **the year following the year the property is placed on the tax roll,** whichever is later, the property shall be reassessed annually on January 1. **Any change resulting from such reassessment may not exceed 10 percent of the assessed value of the property for the prior year.**

(4) If the assessed value of the property as calculated under subsection (3) exceeds the just value, the assessed value of the property shall be lowered to the just value of the property.

(Emphasis added.)

In accordance with the constitution, the statute also underscores that nonhomestead residential real property is a parcel that has nine or fewer units and which does not already enjoy a homestead exemption. Thus, if a property is homestead property, it cannot by definition also enjoy the ten per cent limitation for nonhomestead property. The conflict in the present case, however, stems from the words "placed on the tax roll" found in subsection (3). It says that nonhomestead residential property is subject to the ten per cent increase limitation beginning in the "year following the year the property is placed on the tax roll."

More specifically, the issue before us is whether the ten per cent cap applies to residential property that changes its classification from homestead to nonhomestead, but does not change ownership. Orange County argues that Mr. and Mrs. Sommers cannot enjoy the Save Our Homes cap on their property once it was no longer their homestead. Thus, according to Orange County, once the house became a nonhomestead property, the assessor was required to assess the house at its just or fair market value. Only in subsequent years would it be the beneficiary of the ten per cent cap. Otherwise, the property which is currently not entitled to the Save Our Homes discount, would inherently benefit from that discount if the 2008 homestead value of the house was utilized as the base value, so long as it continued to be owned by Mr. and Mrs. Sommers.

The Sommerses argue to the contrary that section 193.1554(3), Florida Statutes, which governs non-homestead residential property, does not allow an assessment that exceeds ten per cent of the assessed value for the property for the prior year. They insist that their house has been on the tax roll since 1960, albeit as a homestead property, and that the simple change in the classification of the property does not put it on the tax roll anew. That is, the Sommers say their property was "placed on the tax roll" in 1960, not in 2008.

While we certainly understand the position adopted by Mr. and Mrs. Sommers, we conclude that the legislature did not intend a single piece of residential property to be entitled to both the homestead exemption and tax cap and the ten per cent non-homestead tax cap at the same time. Article VII, Section 4(g) and section 193.1554(2) simply do not contemplate a single parcel receiving the benefit of both exemptions at the same time. The appellants are, therefore, correct that once the property changes classification from homestead to nonhomestead, it must then be revalued at its fair market value for ad valorem tax purposes before it can receive the benefit of the ten percent limitation in future tax years.

The architecture of the ad valorem tax structure within Florida confirms this conclusion. When real property first becomes classified as homestead, it is "assessed at just value as of January 1st of the year following the establishment of the homestead..." *See* Art. VII, §4(d)(4), Fla. Const. Analogously, when lands classified as agricultural are diverted to nonagricultural use, or are no longer used for agriculture, or are rezoned to a nonagricultural use at the request of the owner, those lands must also be reclassified and reassessed at just value accordingly. *See* §193.461(4)(a), Fla. Stat. (2010). In similar fashion, nonhomestead residential property is also required to be assessed at just value on January 1st of the year following a change of ownership or control. *See* §193.1554(5), Fla. Stat. (2010). The pattern is clear.

Finally, we note that the 2012 Florida Legislature adopted legislation intended, in part, to clarify the current issue. CS/HB 7097 would amend section 193.1553(2) to read as follows:

> (2) For all levies other than school district levies, nonresidential real property and residential real property that is not assessed under s. 193.155 or s. 193.1554 shall be assessed at just value as of January 1 of the year that the property becomes eligible for assessment pursuant to this section.

The House of Representatives Final Bill Analysis for CA/HB 7097 contains the following passage:

> The bill also... clarifies that certain nonhomestead property is to be assessed at just value when it is subject to a new assessment limitation.

Later, after discussing the unfortunate use of the term "placed on the tax roll," the analysis repeats that:

> The bill amends ss. 193.1554, F.S., and 193.1555, F.S., to clarify that property is to be assessed at just valuation when it is subject to a new limitation.

We accept this statutory modification and bill analysis as persuasive in assessing the intention of the legislature in its adoption of the subject statutes. It appears to confirm our independent analysis of the meaning of the terms and the intention of the legislature.

Accordingly, the judgment is reversed and remanded for action consistent with this opinion.

REVERSED and REMANDED.

LAWSON and EVANDER, JJ., concur.

4. Constitutional Limitations: Exemptions and Who Cannot Be Taxed or Taxed Beyond a Certain Point

a. Ad Valorem Tax Exemption

Fla. Const. art. VII, § 3

Taxes; exemptions. —

(a) All property owned by a municipality and used exclusively by it for municipal or public purposes shall be exempt from taxation. A municipality, owning property outside the municipality, may be required by general law to make payment to the taxing unit in which the property is located. Such portions of property as are used predominantly for educational, literary, scientific, religious or charitable purposes may be exempted by general law from taxation.

(b) There shall be exempt from taxation, cumulatively, to every head of a family residing in this state, household goods and personal effects to the value fixed by general law, not less than one thousand dollars, and to every widow or widower or person who is blind or totally and permanently disabled, property to the value fixed by general law not less than five hundred dollars.

(c) Any county or municipality may, for the purpose of its respective tax levy and subject to the provisions of this subsection and general law, grant community and economic development ad valorem tax exemptions to new businesses and expansions of existing businesses, as defined by general law. Such an exemption may be granted only by ordinance of the county or municipality, and only after the electors of the county or municipality voting on such question in a referendum authorize the county or municipality to adopt such ordinances. An exemption so granted shall apply to improvements to real property made by or for the use of a new business and improvements to real property related to the expansion of an existing business and shall also apply to tangible personal property of such new business and tangible personal property related to the expansion of an existing business. The amount or limits of the amount of such exemption shall be specified by general law. The period of time for which such exemption may be granted to a new business or expansion of an existing business shall be determined by general law. The authority to grant such exemption shall expire ten years from the date of approval by the electors of the county or municipality, and may be renewable by referendum as provided by general law.

(d) Any county or municipality may, for the purpose of its respective tax levy and subject to the provisions of this subsection and general law, grant historic preservation ad valorem tax exemptions to owners of historic properties. This exemption may be granted only by ordinance of the county or municipality. The amount or limits of the amount of this exemption and the requirements for eligible properties must be specified by general law. The period of time for which this exemption may be granted to a property owner shall be determined by general law.

(e) By general law and subject to conditions specified therein:

(1) Twenty-five thousand dollars of the assessed value of property subject to tangible personal property tax shall be exempt from ad valorem taxation.

(2) The assessed value of solar devices or renewable energy source devices subject to tangible personal property tax may be exempt from ad valorem taxation, subject to limitations provided by general law.

(f) There shall be granted an ad valorem tax exemption for real property dedicated in perpetuity for conservation purposes, including real property encumbered by perpetual conservation easements or by other perpetual conservation protections, as defined by general law.

(g) By general law and subject to the conditions specified therein, each person who receives a homestead exemption as provided in section 6 of this article; who was a member of the United States military or military reserves, the United States Coast Guard or its reserves, or the Florida National Guard; and who was deployed during the preceding calendar year on active duty outside the continental United States, Alaska, or Hawaii in support of military operations designated by the legislature shall receive an additional exemption equal to a percentage of the taxable value of his or her homestead property. The applicable percentage shall be calculated as the number of days during the preceding calendar year the person was deployed on active duty outside the continental United States, Alaska, or Hawaii in support of military operations designated by the legislature divided by the number of days in that year.

It is well-settled law in Florida that all property, with the exception of state and county-owned property, is subject to taxation unless expressly exempted by the Legislature. State and county-owned property is immune from taxation, and thus can never be taxed.[49] Municipal property, on the other hand, is exempt as long as the property is owned and used by the municipality for municipal or public purposes.

The Florida Constitution establishes a number of exemptions from ad valorem taxation. Generally, it creates the right to the exemption, and the Florida Legislature defines the extent of that right by statute. The Legislature, however, is without authority to grant an exemption from taxes where the exemption does not have a constitutional basis.[50] The statutory provisions concerning exemptions are codified at Chapter 196 of the Florida Statutes.

---

49. *See Dickinson v. City of Tallahassee*, 325 So. 2d 1 (1975).
50. *See Archer v. Marshall*, 355 So. 2d 781 (Fla. 1978).

6 · TAXATION AND FINANCE

The following cases do not provide an exhaustive discussion of all ad valorem tax exemptions. Rather, they are illustrative of the types of exemptions authorized by the Florida Constitution and the manner in which these exemptions have been construed by the Florida courts.

Canaveral Port Authority v. Department of Revenue

690 So. 2d 1226 (Fla. 1996)

Revised Opinion

WELLS, Justice.

We have for review *Florida Department of Revenue v. Canaveral Port Authority*, 642 So.2d 1097 (Fla. 5th DCA 1994), which expressly and directly conflicts with the opinion in *Sarasota-Manatee Airport Authority v. Mikos*, 605 So.2d 132 (Fla. 2d DCA 1992), *review denied*, 617 So.2d 320 (Fla.1993). We have jurisdiction. Art. V, § 3(b)(3), Fla. Const.

Canaveral Port Authority (CPA) filed suit challenging Brevard County's authority to assess ad valorem taxes pursuant to section 196.199(4), Florida Statutes (1991), on the fee interest of real property owned by CPA and leased to private entities engaged in nongovernmental activities.[1] Specifically, the leased properties were being used as warehouses, gas stations, deli restaurants, fish markets, charter boat sites, and docks. CPA alleged that it was immune from taxation because it was a political subdivision, or in the alternative, it was exempt from taxation pursuant to section 315.11, Florida Statutes (1991). After a nonjury trial, the trial court found in accord with *Sarasota-Manatee* that CPA was a political subdivision of the state and thus was immune from ad valorem taxation.

The Fifth District reversed. The court declined to address whether the legislature can create political subdivisions because, unlike the port authority at issue in *Sarasota-Manatee*, the legislature had not designated CPA a political subdivision. *Canaveral*, 642 So.2d at 1100. Instead, the court looked to case law and found that CPA was not a political subdivision because it did not act as a branch of general administration of the policy of the state. *Id.* at 1100–01. The district court further held that the CPA property at issue was not exempt from taxation because it was not used in direct connection with port business. *Id.* at 1102.

We approve the Fifth District's decision holding that CPA's fee-simple interest in property is not immune from ad valorem taxation. We do so based upon our conclusion that immunity from ad valorem taxation, which this Court has recognized as necessary to the proper functioning of state government,[2] must be kept within

---

1. As the district court noted, the lessees had been required to pay ad valorem taxes on buildings and improvements they had constructed on the property leased from CPA, but CPA had not been assessed ad valorem taxes on the land.

2. *See Dickinson v. City of Tallahassee*, 325 So.2d 1 (Fla.1975); *State ex rel. Charlotte County v. Alford*, 107 So.2d 27 (Fla.1958); *Park-N-Shop, Inc. v. Sparkman*, 99 So.2d 571 (Fla.1957).

narrow bounds. In *Dickinson v. City of Tallahassee*, 325 So.2d 1 (Fla.1975), this Court acknowledged that the State's immunity was necessitated by the compelling policy reasons of fiscal management and constitutional homogenization. *Id.* at 4. We further stated:

> [I]t is inconsistent with sound governmental principles to suggest that a State which cannot finance itself on a deficit basis would indirectly authorize an indeterminate amount of revenue to be taken from all its citizens for the benefit of some of its municipal governments.

Id. (footnote omitted). The compelling policy reasons specified in *Dickinson* continue to exist with regard to the State. However, the reasons become less than compelling when what comprises "the state" is expanded beyond the entities collectively referred to as "the State" in *Dickinson*.[3]

Accordingly, we find that only the State and those entities which are expressly recognized in the Florida Constitution as performing a function of the state comprise "the state" for purposes of immunity from ad valorem taxation. What comprises "the state" is thus limited to counties,[4] entities providing the public system of education,[5] and agencies, departments, or branches of state government that perform the administration of the state government.[6] CPA is not such an entity and therefore is not immune from ad valorem taxation. *See Hillsborough County Aviation Authority v. Walden*, 210 So.2d 193, 194–95 (Fla.1968).

We reject the Second District's holding in *Sarasota-Manatee* that classification as a political subdivision and, consequently, immunity from ad valorem taxation is dependent upon whether an entity is more like a county than a municipality. We recognize the confusion on this issue may have arisen because of cases that have stated that "[t]he state and its political subdivisions, *like a county*, are immune from taxation since there is no power to tax them." *Dickinson*, 325 So.2d at 3 (emphasis added) (*quoting Orlando Utilities Comm'n v. Milligan*, 229 So.2d 262, 264 (Fla. 4th DCA 1969), *cert. denied*, 237 So.2d 539 (Fla.1970)); *see also Hillsborough County*, 210 So.2d at 194–95; *Orange County Fla. v. Florida Dep't of Revenue*, 605 So.2d 1333, 1334 (Fla. 5th DCA 1992), *approved*, 620 So.2d 991 (Fla.1993). We herein clarify that immunity does not flow from a judicial determination that an entity is "like a county."

---

3. In *Dickinson*, the Court referred collectively to the State of Florida, its agencies and departments, Leon County, and the Leon County School Board as the state. 325 So.2d at 2.

4. *See* Art. VIII, § 1, Fla. Const.

5. *See* Art. IX, § 4, Fla. Const.

6. We note that our holding differs from that of the Fifth District in that we find that what comprises the state for purposes of ad valorem tax immunity must have a basis in the Florida Constitution. The Fifth District's opinion holds only that what makes an entity a political subdivision entitled to immunity from taxation is its role as a branch of the general administration of the policy of the state. *Canaveral*, 642 So.2d at 1100–01. We quash the Fifth District's decision to the extent that it finds an entity may be a part of the state without any constitutional basis.

6 · TAXATION AND FINANCE

We also reject the Second District's analysis in *Sarasota-Manatee* recognizing the Sarasota-Manatee Airport Authority as a "political subdivision" in part because the legislature designated it as such. 605 So.2d at 133. The Florida Constitution does not empower the legislature to designate what entities are immune from ad valorem taxation. *See Orange County*, 605 So.2d at 1334.

Because CPA is not immune from ad valorem taxation, we address CPA's alternative argument that it is exempt from ad valorem taxation pursuant to section 315.11, Florida Statutes (1991).[7] Section 315.11, which was passed in 1959, provides a statutory exemption from various state and local taxes for port authorities including port authority property.[8] This section has never made the exemption it provides dependent on the use of port authority property.

Respondent contends that sections 196.001 and 196.199, Florida Statutes (1991), supersede section 315.11 and make CPA's leased property taxable to the extent the property is leased to nongovernmental entities for nongovernmental uses. Section 196.001 provides that all property is subject to taxation unless expressly exempted.[9] Section 196.199 establishes the exemptions that apply to property owned by CPA and leased to nongovernmental entities. These statutes were adopted by the legislature in 1971. Ch. 71-133, Laws of Fla. In the same act, the legislature repealed an exemption in CPA's enabling legislation which was similar to the exemption provided by section 315.11.[10] Although the legislature did not expressly repeal the exemption

---

7. Immunity and exemption differ in that immunity connotes an absence of the power to tax while exemption presupposes the existence of that power. *Dickinson*, 325 So.2d at 3; *Orlando Utilities*, 229 So.2d at 264.

8. Section 315.11, Florida Statutes (1991), specifically provides:

As adequate port facilities are essential to the welfare of the inhabitants and the industrial and commercial development of the area within or served by the unit, and as the exercise of the powers conferred by this law to effect such purposes constitutes the performance of proper public and governmental functions, and as such port facilities constitute public property and are used for public purposes, the unit shall not be required to pay any state, county, municipal or other taxes or assessments thereon, whether located within or without the territorial boundaries of the unit, or upon the income therefrom, and any bonds issued under the provisions of this law, their transfer and the income therefrom (including any profit made on the sale thereof) shall at all times be free from taxation within the state. The exemption granted by this section shall not be applicable to any tax imposed by chapter 220 on interest, income, or profits on debt obligations owned by corporations.

9. Subdivision (1) provides for the taxation of all real and personal property. § 196.001, Fla.Stat. (1991). Subdivision (2) provides for the taxation of all leasehold interests in property owned by the United States, the state, or any political subdivision, municipality, agency, authority, or other public body corporate of the state. § 196.001 Fla.Stat. (1991).

10. Chapter 28922, article XII, section 1, Laws of Florida (1953), the special act creating CPA, provides:

All property, real and personal, tangible and intangible, now owned or hereafter acquired and held by the Canaveral Port Authority, the governing authority of the Canaveral Port District, shall be exempt from all taxation levied and assessed pursuant to the Constitution and Laws of the State of Florida by any taxing unit.

In chapter 71-133, section 14, Laws of Florida, the legislature provided in part:

provided by section 315.11, we find that by passing chapter 71-133, it imposed a limitation on that exemption. In view of the express language used in sections 196.001, 196.199(2), and 196.199(4), particularly the term "authorities," we conclude that the legislature intended to provide only a limited exemption for fee interests in port authority property. Together, sections 196.001, 196.199(2), and 196.199(4) require ad valorem taxation of fee interests in property owned by an authority and subject to a lease by a nongovernmental lessee unless the lessee is serving a governmental, municipal, or public purpose or function as defined in section 196.012(6) or uses the property exclusively for a literary, scientific, religious, or charitable purpose. We therefore construe section 315.11 in conjunction with sections 196.001, 196.199(2), and 196.199(4), and hold that section 315.11 provides an exemption only when port authority property is being used for a purpose which is specifically set forth in section 196.199(2) and (4). If the property is being used for some purpose other than that provided for in section 196.199(2) and (4), then the fee interest will be subject to taxation.

Our construction of these statutes is consistent with this Court's earlier analysis of sections 196.001(2) and 196.199, Florida Statutes, in *Williams v. Jones*, 326 So.2d 425 (Fla.1975). There we stated:

> The practical effect of Sections 196.001(2) and 196.199, Florida Statutes, is to withdraw exemption from certain users of property and to impose an ad valorem real property tax upon them consistent with the tax imposed upon persons who make similar uses of property.

Id. at 432. Furthermore, this construction gives effect to the policy consideration enunciated in *Williams*:

> The operation of the commercial establishments represented by appellants' cases is purely proprietary and for profit. They are not governmental functions. If such a commercial establishment operated for profit in Panama City Beach, Miami Beach, Daytona Beach, or St. Petersburg Beach is not exempt from tax, then why should such an establishment operated for profit on Santa Rosa Island Beach be exempt? No rational basis exists for such a distinction.

Id. at 433. Similarly, no rational basis exists for exempting from ad valorem taxation a commercial establishment operated for profit on CPA property while a similar establishment located near, but not on, CPA property is not exempt.

Accordingly, we conclude that the fee interest in the property at issue is not exempt from ad valorem taxation because the property is leased to a nongovernmental entity

---

> All special and local acts or general acts of local application granting specific exemption from property taxation are hereby repealed to the extent that such exemption is granted. . . .

Consequently, the exemption granted CPA in its enabling legislation was repealed. *See Straughn v. Camp*, 293 So.2d 689 (Fla.1974).

6 · TAXATION AND FINANCE

for a nongovernmental use.[11] We approve the Fifth District's decision on both the immunity and exemption issues to the extent they are consistent with our opinion. We disapprove the Second District's decision in *Sarasota-Manatee* finding immune from ad valorem taxation the authority at issue in that case.

We do specifically and expressly point out that irrespective of the leases, the County cannot tax the property in excess of its total appraised value.

It is so ordered.

KOGAN, C.J., and GRIMES and HARDING, JJ., concur.

OVERTON, J., dissents with an opinion, in which SHAW and ANSTEAD, JJ., concur.

OVERTON, Justice, dissenting.

I dissent.

The critical issue in this case is clear. We must decide whether there is constitutional authority for counties and school districts, as constitutional governmental entities, to directly tax special districts, also constitutional governmental entities, for property that the special districts own and lease for private purposes. We must remain cognizant that while the lessees might use the special district properties for nongovernmental purposes, the lease revenues are used by the special districts for public purposes. In simple terms, this type of taxation results in no net gain to the public. Instead, it simply transfers funds from the pockets of one set of taxpayers (those in special districts) to the pockets of another set of taxpayers (those in counties, school districts, and municipalities). As stated, the real issue is clear. We cannot, however, simply state the answer without tracing the constitutional underpinnings of local governmental taxation in Florida.

First, it must be completely understood that the Florida Constitution contemplates, and this Court has unanimously confirmed, that the State, its counties, and its school districts are immune from ad valorem taxation. Second, the constitution contemplates, and this Court has never disagreed, that special districts should be treated as co-equals with school districts and counties. Third, we need to avoid the temptation to analogize municipalities and special districts. There can be no doubt that the constitution expressly distinguishes municipalities from counties, school districts, and special districts. Fourth, we must develop a full awareness of the significant role played by special districts in the governance of this State. Finally, we must acknowledge that, if allowed, the type of intergovernmental taxation proposed here will, at best, have detrimental effects on special districts and, more probably, will write special districts out of our constitution. I find that, after reviewing these

11. The parties agree that the uses of the property in this case were nongovernmental. If a dispute had arisen on this issue, the trial court would be required to resolve it as held by *State Department of Revenue v. Port of Palm Beach District*, 650 So.2d 700 (Fla. 4th DCA 1995), *review granted*, 659 So.2d 1088 (Fla.1995). The determination should be made in accord with our decision in *Sebring Airport Authority v. McIntyre*, 642 So.2d 1072 (Fla.1994); *see also Williams*, 326 So.2d at 432–33.

five historical and policy considerations, there can be no doubt that special districts are immune from ad valorem taxation.

I digress briefly, though, to emphasize one issue not raised by this case. We are not asked to alter any of our prior decisions relating to leasehold interests. There is no dispute that private lessees that use government property for nongovernmental purposes are subject to taxation on their leasehold interests. We must not confuse such taxation of leasehold interests with the direct taxation of special districts at issue here. In this case, the special district was directly assessed a tax on its property. This direct taxation is unprecedented. As the Fifth District Court of Appeal wrote in this case:

> This appears to be the first time the property appraiser had attempted to assess such taxes. Prior to this time, the lessees had been required to pay ad valorem taxes on buildings and improvements they had constructed on the property, but the CPA had not been assessed ad valorem taxes on the land.

Florida Dep't of Revenue v. Canaveral Port Auth., 642 So.2d 1097, 1098 n. 3 (Fla. 5th DCA 1994). Florida has 922 special districts. These include fire districts, hospital districts, water districts, port authorities, and airport authorities. Accordingly, I think that the broad and substantial ramifications that will ensue from changing the status quo are unjustified.

Governmental Immunity from Taxation

In *Dickinson v. City of Tallahassee*, 325 So.2d 1 (Fla.1975), this Court addressed the concept of intergovernmental taxation. The City of Tallahassee attempted to impose a utility tax upon "the State of Florida and its agencies and departments, on Leon County, and on the Leon County School Board." *Id.* at 2. We rejected such an effort. We stated that "[p]recedent and logic both dictate that the sovereign's general freedom from taxation derives from an 'immunity', not from an 'exemption'." *Id.* at 3. We then quoted with approval the observation that "[t]he state and its political subdivisions, like a county, are immune from taxation since there is no power to tax them." *Id.* The core policy rationale underlying this decision was that "broad grounds of fundamentals in government" dictate against governmental entities taxing each other when, instead, those entities should be cooperating to further the public interest. *Id.* We therefore found that the State, counties, and school districts were expressly immune from taxation. No special district was a party in the *Dickinson* case. The Department of Revenue and Brevard County now suggest, twenty-one years later, that the reasoning of *Dickinson* does not extend to special districts. They argue that special districts are not "like a county" and, therefore, do not represent a political subdivision of the State immune from taxation. Our constitution refutes this assertion.

Constitutional Similarity Between Counties, Special Districts and School Districts

It is significant that only four governmental entities have ad valorem taxing authority under our constitution. Those four entities are counties, special districts, school districts, and municipalities. The authority is contained in article VII, section 9(a), of the Florida Constitution, which reads as follows:

> *Counties, school districts, and municipalities shall, and special districts may, be authorized by law to levy ad valorem taxes* and may be authorized by general law to levy other taxes, for their respective purposes, except ad valorem taxes on intangible personal property and taxes prohibited by this constitution.

(Emphasis added.) The constitution gives no indication that special districts should be treated differently than counties and school districts. In addition to the similar treatment accorded to these governmental entities in the section quoted above, the constitution expressly mentions special districts seventeen other times. Indeed, counties and special districts are mentioned in the very same sentence fourteen times. It is clear that the constitution envisions counties and school districts receiving equal treatment under the law. County lands, under *Dickinson*, cannot be taxed when they are leased for nongovernmental purposes. Special district properties should be treated the same. Some may suggest, however, that the constitution also mentions municipalities in the same sentence with counties and school districts multiple times. They then conclude that special districts could be treated in a manner similar to municipalities. This approach, though, fails to acknowledge that our constitution expressly sets municipalities apart from counties, school districts, and special districts.

Municipalities are Different

The relationship between municipalities and the other three governmental taxing entities (counties, school boards, and special districts) is different because the constitution grants municipalities an express exemption from taxation in article VII, section 3(a), which reads as follows:

> *All property owned by a municipality and used exclusively by it for municipal or public purposes shall be exempt from taxation.* A municipality, owning property outside the municipality, may be required by general law to make payment to the taxing unit in which the property is located. Such portions of property as are used predominantly for educational, literary, scientific, religious or charitable purposes may be exempted by general law from taxation.

(Emphasis added.) Municipalities are not immune from taxation. Therefore, the framers of the 1968 Florida Constitution had to expressly provide an exemption for municipal property used for municipal or public purposes. In fact, the constitution goes one step further. It provides that municipalities owning property outside their municipal limits may be forced, by general law, to make "payment" to the taxing unit in which the property is located. A "payment" is different from an ad valorem tax. In fact, this provision limits intergovernmental taxation by requiring the legislature to establish the method of payment.

Recently, we addressed the municipal exemption in the unique factual situation presented by *Capital City Country Club, Inc. v. Tucker*, 613 So.2d 448 (Fla.1993). In that case, Capital City Country Club leased 192 acres of land owned by the City of Tallahassee. The term of the lease was ninety-nine years. Rent of one dollar per year was paid to the City of Tallahassee. The lease contained a provision that required the club to be responsible for all ad valorem taxes levied against the property. The club conceded that the golf course was not being used for municipal or public purposes. We held that the golf course property was subject to real estate taxation and, by reason of its agreement with the city, the club was obligated to pay those taxes. We further rejected the club's contention that the imposition of real estate taxes on the land and the imposition of intangible taxes on the leasehold interest constituted double taxation. The *Capital City* case is inapposite here. Specifically, we limited *Capital City* by noting that "it is a municipality which owns the property *rather than some other governmental entity." Id.* at 450 (emphasis added).

In addition, I note that the City of Tallahassee was not a party in *Capital City* and the issue of taking city revenues to pay these taxes was not before the Court.

More importantly, though, the constitution does in fact treat municipalities differently. There is, however, no separate provision for special districts. In the absence of a separate provision, special districts should be viewed similarly to those governmental entities (counties and school districts) with which they repeatedly appear in the constitution. To do otherwise is to create an "ugly duckling" governmental taxing entity. Counties and school districts are immune. Municipalities are constitutionally exempt. Special districts would fall into a third category. Such a third category would be judicially created by this Court and would find no basis in the constitution. Special districts, governmental entities with important public responsibilities, should not be treated as "ugly ducklings."

The Important Public Functions Served by Special Districts

I reject the argument that special districts provide only a limited governmental function. I also reject the suggestion that *Dickinson* should apply only to counties, entities providing the public system of education, and agencies, departments, or branches of state government that perform the administration of state government. Such an approach has no constitutional support.

Special districts have been given very substantial governmental responsibilities. It is special districts that manage the State's water supply. Further, special districts are involved in transportation, health care, and public safety matters. The constitution recognizes the importance of special districts by granting them the following rights and responsibilities. Special districts may have ad valorem taxing authority. Art. VII, §9, Fla. Const.[12] Special districts are considered to be local governmental entities in matters concerning the transfer of powers and functions among such entities. Art. VII, §4, Fla. Const. Special districts may issue revenue bonds to finance port facilities that are payable "solely from the revenue derived from the

---

12. The special district in this case, Canaveral Port Authority, actually does have such ad valorem taxing authority.

sale, operation, or leasing of the projects." Art. VII, § 10, Fla. Const. Special districts may issue bonds payable from ad valorem taxation. Art. VII, § 12, Fla. Const. Special districts are authorized to establish civil service systems. Art. III, § 14, Fla. Const. Finally, special districts must comply with the dictates of the public records and meetings provisions. Art. I, § 24, Fla.Const.

Not only does the constitution give special districts important rights and responsibilities; but, indeed, this Court has also found that special districts are important governmental entities. For instance, special districts are entitled to sovereign immunity under the provisions of section 768.28, Florida Statutes (1995). *Eldred v. North Broward Hosp. Dist.*, 498 So.2d 911 (Fla.1986) (special districts called "independent establishments of the state"). The employee records of special districts are subject to the Florida Public Records Act. *Michel v. Douglas*, 464 So.2d 545 (Fla.1985). Special districts are subject to the Public Employees Relations Act. *See National Union v. Southeast Volusia Hosp. Dist.*, 436 So.2d 294 (Fla. 1st DCA 1983); *Southeast Volusia Hosp. Dist. v. National Union of Hosp. & Health Care Employees*, 429 So.2d 1232 (Fla. 5th DCA 1983), *review dismissed*, 452 So.2d 568 (Fla.1984); *Hitt v. North Broward Hosp. Dist.*, 387 So.2d 482 (Fla. 4th DCA 1980). Finally, special districts are subject to the government-in-the-sunshine law. *News-Press Publishing Co. v. Carlson*, 410 So.2d 546 (Fla. 2d DCA 1982).

In light of the crucial duties and responsibilities held by special districts, it makes no sense to unduly burden the taxpayers in these districts by judicially stripping the districts of their immunity. The public policy ramifications of such a stripping would undoubtedly be significant.

Public Policy Ramifications

If we allow counties, school districts, and municipalities to tax special districts, four negative public policy ramifications will ensue. First, the taxpayers of special districts will be denied the benefits of their bargain. A special district with ad valorem taxing authority must have its millage rate authorized by law and then have that tax approved by a vote of those electors who are holders of freeholds within the special district not wholly exempt from taxation. Art. VII, § 9(b), Fla. Const. The creation of a special district, therefore, is similar to the creation of a contract. The voters approve a certain millage rate with the expectation that a certain level of services will be provided through the tax revenues generated. The special district's budget is constructed based upon projected revenues. If the unprecedented tax at issue in this case is approved, special districts will undoubtedly experience a budget shortfall. Special district taxpayers will then receive either a reduced level of services or a request for increased taxes. Neither is fair.

Further, the type of taxation at issue deprives many special district taxpayers of input as to the expenditure of their taxes. Indeed, many of those taxpayers will receive no benefits from their taxes. This is because, in the case of multi-county special districts, the taxes will be largely paid by special district residents living outside the borders of the taxing entity.

Second, the Department of Revenue and Brevard County are concerned that the lessees in this case are using governmental property for nonpublic purposes. I reiterate that this view ignores the fact that the lease revenues are being used for the public purposes of the special district. It also ignores the fact that the constitution foresees and authorizes the use of leases by port authorities. Article VII, section 10, of the Florida Constitution reads, in relevant part, as follows:

> Neither the state nor any county, school district, municipality, special district, or agency of any of them, shall become a joint owner with, or stockholder of, or give, lend or use its taxing power or credit to aid any corporation, association, partnership, or person; but this shall not prohibit laws authorizing:
>
> . . . .
>
> (c) the issuance and sale by any county, municipality, *special district* or other local governmental body of (1) *revenue bonds to finance or refinance the cost of capital projects for* airports or *port facilities,* or (2) revenue bonds to finance or refinance the cost of capital projects for industrial or manufacturing plants to the extent that the interest thereon is exempt from income taxes under the then existing laws of the United States, when in either case, the *revenue bonds are payable solely from revenue derived from the* sale, operation, or *leasing of the projects.*

(Emphasis added.) There is no justification for taxing CPA simply because it has entered leases that are expressly authorized by the constitution.

Third, drawing a line of distinction between special districts and counties or school districts creates a constitutional caste system. Governmental entities treated the same in the text of the constitution should not, by whim, be given varying degrees of importance. Such an outcome is analogous to a judicial decision declaring that the executive branch of government has less importance than the judicial or legislative branches. There is no more constitutional support for a finding of inequality among governmental entities at issue in this proceeding than there would be for a determination of inequality among the three branches of government.

Fourth, the taxation at issue in this case, if allowed, will severely limit the use of special districts in Florida. This is not simply a prediction that "the sky is falling." Instead, it is well supported by the absurd scenario presented by the Broward County amicus brief. Broward County is a successor in interest to the Port Everglades Authority. It takes the position that the authority should be immune from taxation and thereby relieved of all liability for taxes that Broward County itself assessed for the years 1990 through 1994. This situation highlights the incongruous results that would be expected if special districts are stripped of their immunity. Indeed, Broward County makes the point that it is only concerned with those taxes assessed on property leased for nongovernmental purposes between 1990 and 1994. That same property, presumptively still leased for nongovernmental purposes, is now immune because it is owned by the county. This reinforces the view that special districts will become the "ugly ducklings" of governmental entities if stripped of their immunity. Many will likely transfer their powers to immune entities. It makes no sense whatsoever to create a system in which the Canaveral Port Authority is liable for taxes at its port for using property in the same way that Broward County uses its port property with immunity. Needless to say, the framers of the constitution certainly did not envision such an outcome.

Conclusion

Accordingly, for the reasons expressed, I dissent. This Court has no authority to destroy the constitutional concept of special districts in order that counties, school districts, and municipalities might divide the spoils derived solely by this judicial fiat. I would find that the taxpayers of the Canaveral Port Authority and other special districts are immune from this unjustified and inequitable intergovernmental taxation. Such taxation violates the core policy rationale upon which governmental immunity is based; that is, "broad grounds of fundamentals in government" dictate that governmental entities should not tax each other, but rather, they should cooperate to further the public interest. *Dickinson*, 325 So.2d at 3.

SHAW and ANSTEAD, JJ., concur.

Markham v. Broward County

825 So. 2d 472 (Fla. 4th Dist. Ct. App. 2002)

KLEIN, J.

In 1994 Port Everglades Authority, which had been an independent special district created by special act of the legislature, was dissolved by the legislature, and Broward County became the owner of its real property. Much of that property is leased to private for-profit businesses. The Broward County Property Appraiser contends that county property, leased for non-governmental purposes, is subject to ad valorem taxation. We disagree and affirm.

In *Canaveral Port Authority v. Department of Revenue*, 690 So.2d 1226, 1228 (Fla.1996), our supreme court held that the Canaveral Port Authority, an independent special district, was not immune from ad valorem taxation on property leased to lessees who were not performing governmental functions. The court clarified which governmental entities are immune from taxation:

> [O]nly the State and those entities which are expressly recognized in the Florida Constitution as performing a function of the state comprise "the state" for purposes of immunity from ad valorem taxation. What comprises "the state" is thus limited to counties, entities providing the public system of education, and agencies, departments, or branches of state government that perform the administration of the state government [footnotes omitted].

Although *Canaveral* holds that counties are immune from taxation, the appraiser argues that the legislature, in chapter 196, Florida Statutes, waived this immunity where property is leased for non-governmental purposes. He relies on section 196.001, Florida Statutes (1993), which provides:

> Unless expressly exempted from taxation, the following property shall be subject to taxation in the manner provided by law:
>
> (1) All real and personal property in this state and all personal property belonging to persons residing in this state.

The appraiser argues that "all real and personal property" means exactly what it says, and that this constitutes a waiver of immunity.[1] This argument ignores the distinction between immunity from taxation and exemption from taxation. "Exemption presupposes the existence of a power to tax whereas immunity connotes the absence of that power." *Orlando Util. Comm'n v. Milligan,* 229 So.2d 262, 264 (Fla. 4th DCA 1969); *Dickinson v. City of Tallahassee,* 325 So.2d 1, 3 (Fla.1975); *Canaveral,* 690 So.2d at 1226 n. 7.

In order to waive immunity, a statute must be clear and unambiguous. *Manatee County v. Town of Longboat Key,* 365 So.2d 143 (Fla.1978). The legislature did not use the term "immunity" in chapter 196, but has used that term in regard to ad valorem taxation in other statutes. *See* §192.032(2). It has also used the term "immunity" when waiving sovereign immunity for torts. §768.28. The exemptions in chapter 196 apply only to property which does not have immunity. County property is immune. *Canaveral.*

The appraiser also argues that counties which are charter counties, such as Broward County, are not immune, notwithstanding *Canaveral,* because "charter counties and municipalities are placed in the same category for all practical purposes." *State ex rel. Volusia County v. Dickinson,* 269 So.2d 9, 10 (Fla.1972). The appraiser relies on this dicta and the fact that cities are not immune from taxation, *Dickinson v. City of Tallahassee,* 325 So.2d 1 (Fla.1975), to conclude that charter counties are not immune. We cannot agree. All counties are political subdivisions of the state, Art. VIII, §1, Fla. Const., and under *Canaveral* are immune.

We have considered the other arguments raised by the appraiser and find them to be without merit. Affirmed.

GUNTHER, J., and HAWLEY, ROBERT A., Associate Judge, concur.

---

1. State and county property being used for governmental purposes would be exempt from taxation because of exemptions provided in section 196.199.

City of Sarasota v. Mikos

374 So. 2d 458 (Fla. 1979)

OVERTON, Justice.

This is an appeal from a final judgment of a circuit court construing article VII, section 3(a), Florida Constitution, and holding that vacant property owned by the City of Sarasota was not exempt from county ad valorem taxation. We have jurisdiction[1] and reverse.

If the holding of the trial court were allowed to stand and were implemented statewide, it would have a substantial effect on the taxing structure of both city and county governments and would destroy the balance and equality of treatment established in the 1968 constitution for local governmental units.

The record reflects that at the time of the suit, the appellant City of Sarasota owned certain vacant real property within its municipal boundaries. The city held this property either as open space or in reserve to meet future public needs. Prior to 1977 the property had been totally exempt from ad valorem taxation. In 1977 appellee Mikos, the property appraiser for Sarasota County, denied the exemption on these properties on the ground that they were vacant and, therefore, not in use for a municipal or public purpose as required by chapter 196, Florida Statutes (1977), and article VII, section 3(a), Florida Constitution.

The city exhausted its administrative remedies and filed this action to cancel the assessment and to enjoin the collection of the taxes. The property appraiser filed a motion to dismiss the complaint on the ground that the city had not alleged any "actual present use of the property as being used exclusively for municipal, public, or governmental purposes." The circuit court granted the motion, construing article VII, section 3(a), Florida Constitution, "to require activity upon or an active use of lands owned by a Florida municipal corporation on January 1 of each year in order for those lands to be exempt from ad valorem taxation."

The city argues that our construction of the constitutional section involved should be neither technical nor liberal, but should attempt to give effect to the section's purpose as indicated by a fair interpretation of the language. It asserts that the obvious purpose of the section is to grant municipalities a tax exemption and that an interpretation of article VII, section 3(a), which limits the discretion of municipalities to hold vacant land in the public interest, would conflict with the home-rule powers given to municipalities in article VIII, section 2(b), Florida Constitution.

The city further argues that requiring an active use of land is not a prerequisite for an exemption. It contends that the constitution requires only that property be used exclusively for municipal or public purposes and that holding unimproved land for future use or open space is a use of land for a public purpose.

---

1. Art. V, § 3(b)(1), Fla. Const.

In response to the city's arguments, the property appraiser contends that an actual active public use of property as of January 1 each year is necessary for municipal property to be exempt from ad valorem taxes. He bases this contention on his interpretation of the "actual use" doctrine previously adopted by this court. *E.g., Dade County Taxing Authority v. Cedars of Lebanon Hospital*, 355 So.2d 1202 (Fla.1978); *Lake Worth Towers, Inc. v. Gerstung*, 262 So.2d 1 (Fla.1972).

The property appraiser also asserts that the legislature intended to allow the municipal tax exemption only for property that is in active use and not for property intended for public use at a future date. The basis for this assertion is that former section 196.191(2), Florida Statutes (1969), allowed an exemption for property that was "intended for public purposes." This section was repealed in 1971, and its replacement, section 196.199(1)(c), Florida Statutes (1977), does not expressly allow an exemption for property intended for public use. It is the appraiser's view that this change shows legislative intent to eliminate the exemption for municipal property which did not have an active public use as of January 1. The property appraiser further asserts that the city need not hold vacant land for future public needs because condemnation and zoning are available for those purposes, and that the municipality must designate, request, and prove the public purpose of vacant land.

We reject the contentions of the property appraiser. Article VII, section 3(a), Florida Constitution, provides:

> *All property owned by a municipality and used exclusively by it for municipal or public purposes shall be exempt from taxation.* A municipality owning property outside the municipality may be required by general law to make payment to the taxing unit in which the property is located. Such portions of property as are used predominantly for educational, literary, scientific, religious or charitable purposes may be exempted by general law from taxation. [Emphasis added.]

The proper resolution of the question before the court depends upon the meaning of the phrase "used exclusively by it for municipal or public purposes." Although we agree that the actual use rather than the intended future use of the property on the assessment date controls, the issue is whether the vacant property in question owned by the City of Sarasota was actually "used" for the required "public purposes."

A reading of section 3(a) of article VII clearly establishes that it is a self-executing provision and therefore does not require statutory implementation. The change in the language of chapter 196 is irrelevant because although a statute may grant additional exemptions, it may not repeal the exemptions granted municipalities by the constitution. In our view, the city's holding of vacant land to meet the future needs of the public and to preserve natural open spaces is not a private use. We do not believe municipalities are required to dedicate land for a particular purpose, construct buildings, or otherwise be active on their land in order to maintain the tax exempt status or the property. Neither the constitution nor common sense requires there be an active use of such property. We hold that vacant land held by a municipality is presumed to be in use for a public purpose if it is not actually in use for a private purpose on tax assessment day. This holding eliminates the need for a city to designate a use and prove a public purpose for all vacant land each year, as demanded by the property appraiser. In this case, our holding requires a finding that the vacant land set aside by the City of Sarasota for parks and open spaces or held in reserve for public needs met the use test for public or municipal purposes on January 1, 1977, as required by the constitution.

We recognize that property owned by a municipality is not exempt from taxation if it is used for a private purpose. *See Panama City v. Pledger*, 140 Fla. 629, 192 So. 470 (1939) (land leased to a private corporation is not in use for a public purpose); *City of Bartow v. Roden*, 286 So.2d 228 (Fla.2d DCA 1973) (land leased to a private enterprise for nonaeronautical activities is not in use for public purpose); *Illinois Grain Corp. v. Schleman*, 144 So.2d 329 (Fla. 2d DCA 1962) (land leased to a private corporation is not in use for a public purpose). None of these cases even imply that unimproved vacant land owned by a municipality falls within the category of land held for a private purpose.

If the contentions of the property appraiser were adopted, the tax burden of county residents would be reduced at the expense of city taxpayers. This result is contrary to the purpose of our present constitution which provides that each local governmental entity shall have the same basic taxing authority, shall pay its own way, and shall not receive benefits at the expense of another local governmental unit. This philosophy is illustrated by article VII, section 9(b), which specifies that counties, school boards, and municipalities may tax up to a maximum of ten mills each; by article VIII, section 1(h), which prohibits the taxation of residents of municipalities for services rendered by the county exclusively for the benefit of residents in unincorporated areas; and by article VII, section 3(a), which provides that the legislature may require a municipality owning property outside the municipality to make payment to the taxing unit in which the property is located. Each of these provisions is designed to assure a fair tax structure for the taxpayers residing in each local government's jurisdiction and to prevent one local government from being unjustly benefited at the expense of another.

For the foregoing reasons, the judgment of the circuit court is reversed, and the cause is remanded for proceedings consistent with this opinion.

It is so ordered.

ENGLAND, C. J., and ADKINS, SUNDBERG, HATCHETT and ALDERMAN, JJ., concur.

Capital City Country Club, Inc., v. Tucker

613 So. 2d 448 (Fla. 1993)

GRIMES, Justice.

We review *Capital City Country Club, Inc. v. Tucker*, 580 So.2d 789 (Fla. 1st DCA 1991), in which the court certified a question as one of great public importance. We have jurisdiction under article V, section 3(b)(4) of the Florida Constitution.

Capital City Country Club, a nonprofit corporation, leases 192 acres for use as a private golf course in the City of Tallahassee for a rental of $1 per year. The lease was executed in 1956 for a period of ninety-nine years and requires the club to be responsible for all ad valorem taxes levied against the property.

The club filed suits, which were later consolidated, challenging the assessment of ad valorem real estate taxes on the property for the tax years of 1988 and 1989. The club asserted that the property was exempt from real estate taxes because the club had paid intangible taxes on its leasehold interest in the property. Alternatively, the club contended that even if the property was subject to real estate taxes, the value of the club's leasehold interest subject to intangible taxes should have been deducted from the fair market value of the property for the purpose of determining the real estate taxes. The trial court held that real estate taxes were properly imposed against the property based upon its fair market value without deduction of the leasehold interest.

The district court of appeal affirmed this judgment.

The question as certified appears to have been inadvertently misworded. Therefore, we have chosen to present the issues in two separate questions which are reworded as follows:

I.

IS LAND OWNED BY A MUNICIPALITY EXEMPT FROM REAL ESTATE TAXATION IF IT WAS LEASED TO A PRIVATE PARTY PRIOR TO APRIL 15, 1976, AND IS USED FOR NONGOVERNMENTAL PURPOSES?

II.

IF THE LAND IS SUBJECT TO REAL ESTATE TAXATION, SHOULD THE VALUE OF THE LEASEHOLD INTEREST BE EXCLUDED FROM THE APPRAISAL IN ORDER TO ARRIVE AT A LEGAL ASSESSMENT?

In answering these questions, we find it is unnecessary to recount the erratic path which the taxing of interests created when government-owned real property is leased for nonpublic purposes has taken in Florida.[1] We wish to emphasize, however, that in this case it is the real property that is being taxed rather than the leasehold

---

1. See Robert S. Goldman, II *Florida State and Local Taxes,* 206–217 (The Fla.Bar 1984).

interest in that property. Furthermore, it is a municipality which owns the property rather than some other governmental entity.

Article VII, section 4 of the Florida Constitution requires that there be a just valuation of all property for ad valorem taxation. However, article VII, section 3 of the Florida Constitution provides in part:

(a) All property owned by a municipality and used exclusively by it for municipal or public purposes shall be exempt from taxation.

While the club concedes that the golf course is not being used for municipal or public purposes, it points out that intangible taxes have been imposed upon its leasehold interest. The club contends that the property is exempt from an additional real estate tax by section 196.199(4), Florida Statutes (1991), which reads as follows:

Property owned by any municipality, agency, authority, or other public body corporate of the state which becomes subject to a leasehold interest or other possessory interest of a nongovernmental lessee other than that described in paragraph (2)(a), after April 14, 1976, shall be subject to ad valorem taxation unless the lessee is an organization which uses the property exclusively for literary, scientific, religious, or charitable purposes.

The club asserts that when this section was passed as part of chapter 80-368, Laws of Florida, the legislature intended to exempt from real estate taxation leases entered into before April 15, 1976. While it may well be that this is what the legislature intended, the question arises as to whether it had authority to do so.

In *Lykes Bros., Inc. v. City of Plant City,* 354 So.2d 878 (Fla.1978), the city leased land to a meat packing company in 1964 with the promise never to impose municipal taxes on the company's property in order to induce it to relocate its plant. However, after the land was annexed into the city limits, the city, in 1975, began to impose ad valorem taxes on the company's leasehold[2] and tangible personal property. We first held that in the absence of statutory authority, the city's agreement to withhold the imposition of taxes on the property was ultra vires and void. *Id.* at 880. However, Lykes contended that the city's promise was subsequently ratified by section 196.199(3), Florida Statutes (1973), which authorized municipalities to covenant to withhold taxes on leasehold estates created before December 31, 1971. We agreed with the trial judge's conclusion that the constitution required taxation of private leaseholds in government-owned property used for nonpublic purposes. *Id.* at 881. However, we found it unnecessary to reach the question of the constitutionality of section 196.199(3) if it were construed to pertain to pre-1972 governmental leases for nonpublic purposes. *Id.* Instead, we stated:

Lykes' contention with respect to the application and validity of Section 196.199(3) — that an ultra vires municipal contract can be legislatively

---

2. At that time leasehold interests in governmental property being used for nonpublic purposes were subject to real property taxation. *Williams v. Jones,* 326 So.2d 425 (Fla.1975), *appeal dismissed,* 429 U.S. 803, 97 S.Ct. 34, 50 L.Ed.2d 63 (1976).

ratified if it could have been authorized initially — is generally correct, but it neglects an additional requirement. The legislative attempt at ratification must itself be consistent with the Constitution. At the time Section 196.199(3) was enacted, the Legislature no longer possessed the constitutional power to authorize tax exoneration of property owned by a municipality and used by a private lessee predominantly for non-public purposes. Moreover, we do not read into the language of Section 196.199(3) a legislative attempt to exceed this constitutional limitation by giving legal effect to otherwise invalid pre-1972 contracts, and thereby creating a new category of tax exemption.

354 So.2d at 881 (footnotes omitted).

The Fifth District Court of Appeal passed directly upon the issue before us in *City of Orlando v. Hausman,* 534 So.2d 1183 (Fla. 5th DCA 1988), *review denied,* 544 So.2d 199 (Fla.1989). In that case, a number of private tenants leased property from the City of Orlando for nonmunicipal or nonpublic purposes. They contended that the properties were exempt from real estate taxation because their leasehold interests were subject only to intangible taxes. *Id.* Relying on the prior decision in *Orlando Utilities Commission v. Milligan,* 229 So.2d 262 (Fla. 4th DCA 1969), *cert. denied,* 237 So.2d 539 (Fla.1970), the court held that because the property was being used for private purposes, there was no exemption from real property taxation. *But see Miller v. Higgs,* 468 So.2d 371 (Fla. 1st DCA), *review denied,* 479 So.2d 117 (Fla.1985). In response to the argument that the leasehold interests were subject only to intangible taxation, the court pointed out that there was no evidence that the property appraiser had included the leasehold interests of the tenants in his assessment. *Hausman,* 534 So.2d at 1185.

The legislature is without authority to grant an exemption from taxes where the exemption does not have a constitutional basis. *Archer v. Marshall,* 355 So.2d 781 (Fla.1978). Thus, we conclude that the legislature could not constitutionally exempt from real estate taxation municipally owned property under lease which is not being used for municipal or public purposes. We cannot accept the contention that by imposing a state intangible tax which cannot exceed two mills, art. VII, § 2, Fla .Const., on nonpublic leaseholds of municipal land, the legislature can exempt the land from the higher level of local taxation permitted by article VII, section 9 of our constitution. However, we do not believe it is necessary to hold any portion of section 196.199 unconstitutional.

If it is reasonably possible to do so, we are obligated to interpret statutes in such a manner as to uphold their constitutionality. *State v. Gale Distributors, Inc.,* 349 So.2d 150 (Fla.1977). Further, it is well settled that all property is subject to taxation unless expressly exempt, and exemptions are strictly construed against the party claiming them. *State ex rel. Szabo Food Servs., Inc. v. Dickinson,* 286 So.2d 529 (Fla.1973). Section 196.199(4) does not specifically exempt from real estate taxes land which is subject to a lease entered into before April 15, 1976; it does so only by inference. Therefore, in order to sustain its constitutionality, we do not interpret section 196.199(4) as exempting from real estate taxes land leased from a municipality for nongovernmental purposes before April 15, 1976. Consequently, we hold that the golf course property is subject to real estate taxation. By reason of its agreement in the lease, the club is obligated to pay these taxes.

The answer to the second certified question is controlled by our recent decisions in *Valencia Center, Inc. v. Bystrom*, 543 So.2d 214 (Fla.1989), and *Schultz v. TM Florida-Ohio Realty Ltd.*, 577 So.2d 573 (Fla.1991). In *Valencia*, the property owner had entered into a pre-1965 long-term lease which was highly favorable to the lessee and which precluded the property from being used for its highest and best use. 543 So.2d at 215. The legislature had enacted a statute which directed the property appraiser to assess the property on the highest and best use permitted by the lease rather than on the basis of a use not permitted by the lease or of income which could be derived from a use not permitted by the lease. *Id.* at 215–16. We held that the statute was invalid because it purported to provide favored tax treatment in violation of article VII, section 4 of the Florida Constitution. *Id.* at 216. As a consequence of our decision, the property was taxed as though the landowner possessed the property in fee simple. *Schultz* was another submarket lease case in which we held that the appraisal for real estate taxes "must represent the value of all interests in the property — in other words, the fair market value of the unencumbered fee." 577 So.2d at 575.

We reject the club's contention that the imposition of real estate taxes on the fair market value of the land and the imposition of intangible taxes on the leasehold interest constitutes double taxation of the property. Intangible personal property is property which is not itself intrinsically valuable, but which derives its chief value from that which it represents. §§ 199.023(1), 192.001(11)(b), Fla.Stat. (1991). The intangible tax is being imposed on the rights afforded to the club under the lease. The real estate taxes, on the other hand, are being imposed on the land itself. In Florida, real estate taxes are collected by the county, while the intangible tax on leasehold interests is collected by the state. In this case, the club, as the holder of a leasehold interest, is legally responsible for the intangible tax. The club's responsibility for the real estate taxes, however, is contractual. It stems from the pass-through provision in the lease wherein the club agreed to pay the real estate taxes assessed against the land. Absent this provision, the city, as owner of the property, would be responsible for the real estate tax because the land is not being used for a municipal or public purpose. It is clear that the club's leasehold and the city's real property are completely separate interests. There is no unconstitutional double taxation where there are two taxpayers and two separate taxable transactions or privileges. *In re Advisory Opinion to the Governor*, 509 So.2d 292 (Fla.1987).

While not a perfect analogy, assume the existence of land worth $100,000 encumbered by a mortgage securing the payment of a $125,000 promissory note. The promissory note would be subject to the intangible tax based on the $125,000 face value of the note even though the value of the property securing the note was only $100,000. Under the club's theory, the real property value for ad valorem purposes would necessarily have a value of negative $25,000. The point is that the value of a person's leasehold interest has nothing to do with the value of the underlying real property for ad valorem tax purposes. In the case of a lease, the lessee's interest may or may not have value, depending on whether or not the contract rent is greater or lesser than the market or economic rent. The value of the real property for ad valorem taxation is its fair market value without regard to any leases or encumbrances on the property.

Accordingly, we answer both certified questions in the negative. We disapprove *Miller v. Higgs* to the extent that it conflicts with this opinion.

We approve the decision of the court below.

It is so ordered.

BARKETT, C.J., and OVERTON, SHAW, KOGAN and HARDING, JJ., concur.

McDONALD, J., recused.

From the above cases, it should be noted that property owned by a governmental entity may be immune or exempt from ad valorem property taxes; however, if such property is leased to a private entity that uses the property for non-governmental or proprietary purposes, the leasehold interest could be subject to an intangible tax based on the value of the leasehold interest. Leasehold interest in property owned by the United States, the state, counties, municipalities, agencies, authorities, and other public bodies corporate of the state shall be exempt from ad valorem and intangible tax only when the lessee serves or performs a governmental, municipal, or public purpose or function. In all such cases, all other interests in the leased property shall be exempt from ad valorem taxation.[51]

Colding v. Herzog

467 So. 2d 980 (Fla. 1985)

OVERTON, Justice.

This is a petition to review a decision of the Second District Court of Appeal reported as *Herzog v. Colding*, 437 So.2d 226 (Fla. 2d DCA 1983), holding that household goods and personal effects in Florida are not subject to ad valorem taxation, and approving, in its entirety, the First District Court of Appeal's opinion in *Department of Revenue v. Markham*, 381 So.2d 1101 (Fla. 1st DCA 1979). The district court certified the following question to be of great public importance:

WHETHER HOUSEHOLD GOODS AND PERSONAL EFFECTS ARE SUBJECT TO AD VALOREM TAXATION UNDER THE STATUTES AND CONSTITUTION OF THE STATE OF FLORIDA.

437 So.2d at 227. We have jurisdiction, article V, section 3(b)(4), Florida Constitution. We answer the question in the negative and approve both the decision of the

---

51. Fla. Stat. § 196.199(2)(a) (2021).

district court in the instant case and the reasoning expressed on the identical issue by the district court in *Markham*.

The respondents in this case are Missouri residents who own a house in Collier County, Florida, which they use as a part-time dwelling. Neither the house nor the household goods and personal property contained in the house are used for commercial purposes. The respondents contested an ad valorem tax on the household goods and personal effects contained in their Florida house assessed by the Collier County tax appraiser pursuant to rule 12D-7.02 of the Florida Administrative Code. That rule, which was enacted by the Department of Revenue, provides, in part, that household goods and personal effects belonging to persons not making their permanent home in Florida are not exempt from ad valorem taxation. No such tax is assessed against Florida residents. The trial court approved the tax, entering summary judgment for the petitioners. The district court reversed. Adopting this historical review and analysis of the identical statutory provisions contained in the First District Court of Appeal's decision in *Markham*, the district court held that household goods and personal effects in Florida are not subject to ad valorem taxation irrespective of whether the goods are owned by residents or non-residents.

The property appraiser and the Department of Revenue challenge the district court's decision, arguing that the Florida Constitution prohibits the legislature from excluding or exempting household goods and personal effects from ad valorem taxation, and that this Court should both quash the district court's decision in the instant case and disapprove the reasoning expressed by the First District Court of Appeal in *Markham*. Initially, the petitioners assert that this Court should refuse to consider the analysis and reasoning in the *Markham* decision because we quashed that decision on the ground that "the lawsuit was improperly commenced by one who lacked legal standing and should never have been entertained." *Department of Revenue v. Markham*, 396 So.2d 1120, 1121 (Fla.1981). We disagree. Because of its disposition on a standing issue, this Court neither rejected nor disapproved the legal analysis in the district court's *Markham* decision. The district court's opinion is not precedent, but its analysis may nevertheless be considered by this Court in resolving the instant case.

In *Markham*, the district court exhaustively analyzed the history of the taxation of household goods in this state. The court concluded that when section 200.01, Florida Statutes (1965), was amended by the legislature in 1967[1] to exclude household goods

---

1. As amended by chapter 67-377, Laws of Florida, section 200.01, Florida Statutes (1967) reads: Definition of Tangible Personal Property. — (1) "Tangible personal property" shall include all goods, chattels, vehicles (except motor vehicles and household furnishings, wearing apparel, effects of the person actually employed in the use of serving the creature comforts of the owner and not held for commercial purposes), animals and other articles of value capable of manual possession and whose chief value shall consist of the thing itself and not what it represents. The words "personal property," as used in this chapter, shall be synonymous with tangible personal property.

546   6 · TAXATION AND FINANCE

and personal effects used for the comfort of the owner and for non-commercial purposes from the definition of "tangible personal property," such goods and effects were "effectively eliminated from the operation of the taxing statutes, regardless of residency of the owner." 381 So.2d at 1105 (footnote omitted). The statutory definition was reorganized in a 1970 "revisor's bill" which separated "personal property" into "household goods," "intangible personal property," "inventory," and "tangible personal property."[2] The *Markham* district court found that the legislature did not intend to create "a separate taxable category of 'household goods' . . . when such goods are used for the comfort of the owner and his family, and not held for commercial purposes or resale." *Id.* at 1108. The court further concluded that "the elimination of the useless expenditure of manpower and resources not justified by adequate return to the public treasury" provided a legitimate public purpose for excluding such property from taxation. *Id.* at 1111.

The petitioners argue that the Florida Legislature does not have the power to exempt household goods and personal property from ad valorem taxation because article VII, section 4, of the Florida Constitution requires the legislature to provide the means to tax "all property."[3] They assert that we should sustain rule 12D-7.02 because the "plain-language" of article VII, section 3(b), limits the household goods and personal effects exemption to Florida residents.[4] According to the petitioners, no other constitutional provision either expressly or implicitly establishes a basis for the legislature to exempt household goods and personal effects from ad valorem taxation.

We agree with the petitioners that all property is subject to ad valorem taxation unless it is constitutionally exempted. This principle does not, however, prohibit the legislature from classifying property or from excluding certain property from taxation when the expense of assessment and collection would exceed the revenue generated from the tax. Were the legislature not permitted such authority, Florida taxpayers would be forced to subsidize tax collection costs. Such a result would be illogical and was never intended by the authors of the constitution. Further, if we were to accept petitioners' interpretation of article VII, section 3(b), we would be required to find that the household goods and personal effects belonging to all Florida residents without "head of a family" status are also subject to taxation. We reject that position and agree with the district court's conclusion in *Markham* that,

---

Prior to the 1967 amendment, section 200.01 excluded only "motor vehicles" from the definition of "tangible personal property."

2. See chapter 70-243, Laws of Florida, creating section 192.001, Florida Statutes. Section 192.001(11)(d), which defines "tangible personal property," excludes "household goods" from the definition.

3. Article VII, section 4, provides: "By general law regulations shall be prescribed which shall secure a just valuation of all property for ad valorem taxation."

4. Article VII, section 3(b) provides, in part: "There shall be exempt from taxation, cumulatively, to every head of a family residing in this state, household goods and personal effects to the value fixed by general law, not less than one thousand dollars. . . ."

through its power to classify property for taxation purposes, the legislature has properly excluded household goods and personal effects without reference to the residency of the property owners.

Because they concluded the legislature did not intend to tax household goods belonging to *either* residents or non-residents, neither the district court in the decision under review nor the *Markham* court addressed whether an ad valorem household goods tax imposed exclusively on non-residents would violate the privileges and immunities clause contained in article IV, section 2, of the United States Constitution. We also believe it is unnecessary to consider that question.

Our decision in this case is prospective only for the taxable year commencing January 1, 1985, except for those nonresident taxpayers who have timely judicially challenged the ad valorem tax on household goods and personal effects. Because the tax has been assessed in good faith reliance pursuant to a presumptively valid rule, we find that the taxpayers against whom the tax was assessed, other than those who challenged the tax, are not entitled to a refund. *See Osterndorf v. Turner*, 426 So.2d 539 (Fla.1982), *Gulesian v. Dade County School Board*, 281 So.2d 325 (Fla.1973).

For the reasons expressed, we approve the decision of the district court of appeal.

It is so ordered.

BOYD, C.J., and ADKINS, ALDERMAN, McDONALD, EHRLICH and SHAW, JJ., concur.

The Florida Constitution provides that portions of property used predominantly for philanthropic purposes, i.e., educational, literary, scientific, religious or charitable purposes, may be exempt from taxation by general law.[52] Generally, in order to qualify for the exemption, the philanthropic organization must own and use the property for philanthropic (exempt) purposes. Where the property is being used for both profit-making and philanthropic purposes, the Florida courts have held that the portion used for profit making purposes is taxable and the portion used for philanthropic purposes is exempt from ad valorem taxation. Further, where philanthropic organizations permit their property to be used by groups that do not use the property for exempt purposes, they may be given a prorated exemption from ad valorem taxes based on the ratio that the predominate use for exempt purposes bears to the non-exempt use. The following cases are illustrative of the above rules.

---

52. *See* Fla. Const. Art. VII, § 3(a).

Saint Andrew's School of Boca Raton, Inc. v. Walker

540 So. 2d 207 (Fla. 4th Dist. Ct. App. 1989)

LETTS, Judge.

The trial court ruled that certain on-campus faculty housing at a not-for-profit, co-educational, church-related school, was not exempt from ad valorem taxes. The school appeals and we reverse.

Until 1986, *all* the faculty housing was granted total exemption by the property appraiser under section 196.198, Florida Statutes (1987). Commencing in 1986, twenty-three out of forty-one of the faculty residences were declared to be taxable. (The land on which the twenty-three residences stand continues to be exempt.)

Simply stated, the assessor maintains that in order to qualify for exemption, the statute requires that the property in question be "*used exclusively* for educational purposes" (emphasis supplied) and that the chapter defines "exclusive use of property" as "used one hundred percent for exempt purposes." *See* §196.012(2), Fla.Stat. However, we note that the 1988 supplement to the statute, effective June 16, 1988, has changed the language of the definition from "used one hundred percent" to "use of property *solely* for exempt purposes." (emphasis added). Nobody disputes the fact that the twenty-three faculty members and their families lead some semblance of private lives behind their on-campus residential doors which the appraiser claims results in a failure to satisfy the one hundred percent requirement. However, the school cites three cases out of the Second District which interpret the language of the statute in a "broader sense."

In *Walden v. Berkeley Preparatory School, Inc.,* 337 So.2d 1029 (Fla. 2d DCA 1976), *cert. denied,* 344 So.2d 327 (Fla.1977), the Second District found that a headmaster's residence *some distance from the campus,* nevertheless, came within the provision of chapter 196 in a "broader sense." *See also Walden v. University of Tampa, Inc.,* 304 So.2d 134 (Fla. 2d DCA 1974), *cert. denied,* 315 So.2d 476 (Fla.1975); *Walden v. University of South Florida Foundation,* 328 So.2d 460 (Fla. 2d DCA), *cert. denied,* 336 So.2d 605 (Fla.1976).

In *Berkeley,* the court noted:

> The property was purchased by the school for use as a headmaster's residence, and the headmaster is required to live there. But, the property is also used for cookouts and picnics for student groups, teas for students and parents, faculty entertainment, individual counseling of students and parents, entertainment and housing of school guests, and like matters. And, while the premises are not used continually for such purposes, they are available at all times for such uses.

> The record indicates a belief on the part of school authorities that such activities foster a personal relationship which is an important factor in its educational process. The educational need to use the residence for this purpose is not controverted in the record.

Id. at 1030.

Similarly, the record, sub judice, reveals that all of the faculty on-campus homes are used for the same purposes as detailed above. Moreover, in addition to the facts enunciated in *Berkeley,* some twenty percent of the students, in the case before us, board at the school and are in need of twenty-four hour supervision. The school literature stresses the desirability of the faculty residing on-campus for security reasons, emotional needs associated with homesickness and other general welfare items. Classes are regularly taught in these homes. The school derives no income from them and only members of the faculty can live there. Indeed, many of the faculty employment contracts require them to live there. Furthermore, unlike *Berkeley,* where the home in question was off-campus, the homes in the instant case are *all* on campus. Finally, the presence of faculty housing on this campus is one of the factors which supports the school's continued accreditation as a boarding facility.

At oral argument our attention was drawn to the fact that university, fraternity and sorority houses are exempt from taxation, citing *Gamma Phi Chapter of Sigma Chi Building Fund Corporation v. Dade County,* 199 So.2d 717 (Fla.1967). As we read it, that is not the actual holding of *Sigma Chi,* but in the opinion, the court makes it clear that fraternities at universities are exempt.

The *Sigma Chi* case raises another distinction. In 1967, when it was written, Florida had a statute that specifically exempted university and college fraternities "used solely as their clubhouse or home." *See* § 192.06(8) Fla.Stat. That same statute became section 196.191 in 1969, was repealed in 1971 and replaced by section 196.198 which exempted fraternities and sororities "as being essential to the educational process." This 1971 version was already enacted at the time *Berkeley's* "broader sense" opinion was issued in 1976. Furthermore, at the time of *Berkeley,* the one hundred percent use requirement in section 196.012(2) was already in place by reason of the 1971 amendment.

In the case at bar, the appraiser concedes the viability of the "broader sense" doctrine as it pertains to the headmaster's house, but rejects it as to the assistant headmaster's house. Yet, the record is clear that the assistant headmaster's school-related use, associated with his residence, parallels or exceeds the school-related use of the headmaster's house. Since the "use" is critical, we fail to appreciate the appraiser's distinction except for command status. Command status should not be the criterion and, indeed, the appraiser's office appears to agree because it has even exempted the maintenance man's residence.

There does not appear to be any other Florida case directly on point, but there are some out-of-state cases, of which we approve, which exempt faculty living-quarters and hold that they are exclusively used for educational purposes. *See, e.g., Order of St. Benedict v. Gordon,* 417 A.2d 881 (R.I.1980); *St. Paul's School v. City of Concord,* 117 N.H. 243, 372 A.2d 269 (1977).

In sum, from the facts sub judice, we conclude that the primary purpose of having faculty members live on this campus is so that they can "participate effectively in the educational scheme of the school and not merely to have a place of residence."

St. Paul's, 372 A.2d at 275. As to the appraiser's argument that the nonexempted residences are not used one hundred percent for educational purposes, that is severely weakened by the fact that the appraiser has, in fact, exempted thirteen other faculty residences. This exempted baker's dozen is explained away as being "integrated into the student housing." However, at least two residences exempted are *not* so integrated, and in any event, all thirteen inescapably have the same residential quality, where private family life goes on within, contemporaneously with school activities. If one hundred percent is supposed to be the magic, all-or-nothing-at-all, then by the appraiser's same logic, *none* of the faculty on-campus residences would qualify. In contrast, by our logic they *all* do.

Finally, as to legislative intent, we are not given an explanation for the recent statutory substitution of the word "solely" in place of "one hundred percent", enacted after the briefs were filed. *See* Ch. 88–102 §1, Laws of Fla. (1988). However, we are unanimous in our conclusion that "solely" connotes something less rigid and more susceptible to compromise, than the one hundred percent rule, quite apart from the "broader sense" doctrine adopted by the case law and admitted to by the appraiser. It is true that the 1988 legislative substitution was not in existence at the time the instant controversy was before the trial court. However, the 1988 subsection is in the nature of a clarification and, therefore, pertinent. We also note the legislative's somewhat confusing employment of the following language in subsection (1) of section 196.012:

> Exempt use of property, or use of property for exempt purpose means *predominant* or exclusive use. . . . [emphasis supplied]

> Elsewhere, in subsection (3), predominant is defined as use in "excess of fifty percent." Certainly this housing is used predominantly for exempt purposes.

We also find it significant that fraternity and sorority houses have been exempted by the legislature "as being essential to the educational process." *See* §196.198, Fla.Stat. With the utmost of respect to these noble Greek letter institutions, it is unlikely that they are any more essential to the educational process than on-campus faculty housing at a nonprofit, co-educational, church-affiliated, boarding high school and we cannot believe the legislature thinks otherwise. Our comparison of fraternities vis-a-vis faculty housing is not inapt because the supreme court made a similar one in *Presbyterian Homes of Synod of Florida v. Wood,* 297 So.2d 556, 559 (Fla.1974).

We conclude, under the facts of the case now before us, that such faculty housing is used exclusively for educational purposes and is exempt from ad valorem taxation under chapter 196 of the Florida Statutes.

REVERSED AND REMANDED.

GLICKSTEIN, J., and POLEN, MARK E., Associate Judge, concur.

6 · TAXATION AND FINANCE

Underhill v. Edwards

400 So. 2d 129 (Fla. 5th Dist. Ct. App. 1981)

ORFINGER, Judge.

Appellants (trustees of a private, not-for-profit hospital,) question the correctness of the trial court's conclusion that a portion of the otherwise exempt hospital building could be properly assessed and placed on the tax rolls. By cross appeal, the property appraiser questions the propriety of the trial court's conclusion that a back assessment of the property in question was void because in the tax year to which the back-assessment related, the property in question was assessed as "exempt." We affirm.

The findings and conclusions of the trial court are set out the final judgment which followed a non-jury trial and which we recite in full:

> In this action, plaintiffs contest the ad valorem assessment and taxation of the first floor of the new wing of Fish Memorial Hospital in DeLand, Florida, for the years 1976, 1977 and 1978. Plaintiffs are the trustee-owners of the hospital. For the three tax years in dispute, plaintiffs applied for exemption of the entire hospital property, including the new wing, on the basis of alleged charitable use. In 1976, the defendant Property Appraiser granted the exemption application for the entire property, including the first floor of the new wing. In 1977, however, the Property Appraiser denied the application with respect to the first floor of the new wing because of his determination that that portion of the property was not actually used for a charitable purpose. In addition, the Property Appraiser determined that that portion of the property had been exempted erroneously in 1976 and he therefore back-assessed it for 1976 taxes on the 1977 tax roll pursuant to section 193.092, Florida Statutes. The application for exemption was also denied in 1978. Plaintiffs paid the taxes for 1976, 1977 and 1978 under protest and in this action they seek a refund of the taxes paid. The action was tried before the Court sitting without a jury. The Court has carefully considered the testimony and other evidence adduced at the trial and the arguments of counsel. Being fully advised in the premises, the Court finds, determines and declares as follows:
>
> The real property involved in this action is the first floor of the new wing of Fish Memorial Hospital in DeLand, Florida, more particularly described on the 1977 and 1978 ad valorem real property tax rolls of Volusia County as Parcel No. 7009 01 06 0010. Said parcel, consisting of the first floor of the new wing only, will be referred to sometimes in this judgment as the subject property.
>
> As of the first days of January, 1977 and 1978, and at all other times during each of those years, the subject property was held and used for a private

purpose and not for a charitable or other exempt purpose within the meaning of the Constitution and laws of the State of Florida. The subject property was held by the plaintiffs for the purpose of renting it to private medical doctors who, as lessees, used and occupied it as office space for the conduct of their private medical practices for professional compensation and profit. Such a use of real property is not a charitable use or purpose within the meaning of Article 7, Section 3(a), Florida Constitution of 1968, nor is it a charitable purpose as defined in Section 196.012(6), Florida Statutes. The evidence demonstrates without dispute that the lessee-doctors do not conduct their medical practices on a charitable basis, but, instead, conduct their practices in an ordinary manner for professional compensation and profit.

The lessee physicians are members of the medical staff of plaintiffs' hospital and, as such, they render incidental services to the hospital in the same manner as other medical staff members who conduct their medical practices in offices not located on or adjacent to the hospital premises. However, the benefits which the hospital derives from its arrangement of leasing the first floor of the new wing to private medical doctors does not qualify the subject property for exemption from ad valorem taxation. Such benefits are clearly incidental and they do not change the actual private use of the subject property. Under the Constitution and laws of Florida, *only those portions* of property which are used predominantly for charitable purposes are entitled to charitable tax exemption. Article 7, Section 3(a), Florida Constitution of 1968; Section 196.196(2), Florida Statutes. Those portions of real property in Florida which are used predominantly for private, non-exempt purposes are not entitled to exemption. Such property is subject to taxation. Section 196.001, Florida Statutes. It must bear its fair share of the tax burden along with other private properties and property interests which are subject to taxation. *See Williams v. Jones*, 326 So.2d 425 (Fla. 1976); *Volusia County v. Daytona Beach Racing and Recreational Facilities District*, 341 So.2d 498 (Fla. 1976).

The fact that the subject doctors' offices are adjacent to a charitable hospital facility does not alter the result. The actual charitable use of the hospital qualifies the *hospital* for exemption; it does not qualify the subject *doctors' offices* for exemption. That portion of the property must stand on its own use, not the use of the adjacent hospital facility. The evidence clearly demonstrates that the subject private doctors' offices exist and function independently from the hospital and that the subject property is not a part of the hospital as such, although it happens to be a part of the building in which the hospital is located.

The evidence supports the Property Appraiser's decision to assess and tax the entire first floor of the new wing, including the corridors and other common areas, as well as the doctors' offices themselves. The corridors and other common areas in the first floor of the new wing exist and function predominantly to serve the private doctors' offices, just as the common areas in the hospital exist predominantly to serve the hospital. The Court finds, upon consideration of the evidence, that the entire first floor of the new wing, including the common areas, is predominantly used for private, non-charitable purposes.

The Court finds that the subject property was subject to taxation and was not entitled to exemption in 1977 and 1978 and that the disputed assessments and taxes levied on the subject property for those years were correct and lawful in all respects.

The back-assessment for the year 1976 involved the circumstance of a difference in judgment by successive tax assessors, and is precluded by applicable Florida law. *Korash v. Mills*, 263 So.2d 579 (Fla. 1972); *Markham v. Friedland*, 245 So.2d 645 (Fla. 4th DCA 1971). The 1976 taxes were paid under protest by the plaintiffs and should be refunded.

The Court finds that the plaintiffs are not estopped to challenge the 1976 tax assessment on the basis that they failed to exhaust administrative remedies, and that this Court has jurisdiction of the issue of the 1976 tax payment. *Lake Worth Towers, Inc. v. Gerstung*, 262 So.2d 1 (Fla. 1972).

The plaintiffs seek interest on the refund of taxes paid since the date of May 31, 1978. The Court has concluded that such interest cannot be awarded in an action of this nature where no money judgment against the state or the taxing authority is involved. *State ex rel. Four-Fifty-Two-Thirty Corp. v. Dickinson*, 322 So.2d 525 (Fla. 1975); *Mailman v. Green*, 111 So.2d 267 (Fla. 1959); *Hansen v. Port Everglades Steel Corporation*, 155 So.2d 387 (Fla. 2d DCA 1963).

It is therefore ORDERED and ADJUDGED that final judgment is hereby entered in this action against the plaintiffs and in favor of the defendants for the tax years 1977 and 1978; as to those assessments and collections, plaintiffs take nothing by this action and the defendants go hence without day. It is further adjudged that the defendants herein shall refund to the plaintiffs the tax payment (without interest) for the year 1976 paid under protest by the plaintiffs . . .

Appellants' only issue on appeal is that they are entitled to an exemption of the first floor of the new wing of the hospital because that portion represents only a very small percentage of the otherwise exempt property and this incidental use of this small portion does not destroy the predominant charitable use of the property. The trial court completely and correctly addressed this problem. There was no attempt by the property appraiser to remove the exemption from the hospital itself, but only from that *portion* of the building used for private purposes. This is authorized under Article 7, section 3(a) of the Florida Constitution (1968) and by sections 196.192 and 196.196, Florida Statutes.

The trial court also correctly determined that the first floor of the new wing which had been assessed as "exempt" on the 1976 tax roll could not be back assessed,[1] because the property had not "escaped taxation" for that year. It had not been missed, overlooked or forgotten. *Okeelanta Sugar Refinery, Inc. v. Maxwell*, Fla.App. 1966, 183 So.2d 567. Once the tax roll has been certified for a given tax year and the tax levied thereon is paid for a particular described property, that property cannot be taxed again for that particular year. *Okeelanta; Markham v. Friedland*, 245 So.2d 645 (Fla. 4th DCA 1971). In the 1976 tax year it was the "judgment" of the property appraiser that the entire hospital property was exempt (which included the questioned first floor) and the property was so assessed on the tax roll. In *Korash v. Mills*, 263 So.2d 579 (Fla. 1972), relied on by appellee here, the total improvement consisting of an oceanfront motel was omitted from the assessment by error. Thus, it was held that a back assessment under the subject statute was proper, because the improvements had been totally overlooked; they had in fact "escaped taxation." The court emphasized that it was not the judgment of the property appraiser that was involved; if a change in valuation had been attempted, it would have been stricken down. After certification of the tax roll a change "reevaluating" the amount of the valuation will not be allowed. *Korash, supra.* The determination that a parcel of property is exempt is as much a part of the assessment process as is the determination of its taxable value, and the judgment of the assessor must be applied in reaching that conclusion. We hold, therefore, that a determination in 1977 that the property should not have been exempted in 1976 is a change in judgment and is prohibited under the cited cases.

This leaves the property appraiser's contention that the trial court had no jurisdiction to consider the back assessment because appellants did not exhaust their administrative remedies or file their action within sixty days of the contested assessment as required by section 194.171(2), Florida Statutes (1977), citing *Coe v. ITT Development Corporation*, 362 So.2d 8 (Fla. 1978). The same statute [formerly numbered as section 192.21(2), Florida Statutes] was construed in *Lake Worth Towers Inc. v. Gerstung*, 262 So.2d 1 (Fla. 1972) wherein it was held that the statute would not bar a late challenge to an assessment charged to be unauthorized or void, "which may be enjoined or relieved against at any time." *Id.* at 4. The court then defined a "void" assessment as one not authorized by law or where the property is not subject to the tax assessed, or where the tax roll is illegal due to some

---

1. Section 193.092, Florida Statutes (1977) provides:

(1) When it shall appear that any ad valorem tax might have been lawfully assessed or collected upon any property in the state, but that such tax was not lawfully assessed or levied, and has not been collected for any year within a period of three years preceding the year in which it is ascertained that such tax has not been assessed or levied or collected, the officers authorized shall make the assessment of taxes upon such property in addition to the assessment of such property for the current year, and shall assess the same separately for such property as may have escaped taxation at and upon the basis evaluation applied to such property for the year or years in which it escaped taxation. . . .

affirmative wrongdoing by the taxing official. A "voidable" assessment is defined as one which is made in good faith, but is irregular or unfair. We deem this assessment void because there was no statutory authority for the property appraiser to change his judgment after the year for which the tax roll had been certified. Thus the sixty day statute does not apply.

The judgment appealed from is AFFIRMED.

SHARP and COWART, JJ., concur.

———————

While the Florida Constitution provides that portions of property used predominately for philanthropic purposes may be exempt from ad valorem taxation, questions frequently arise as to whether the property in question, in fact, meets the definition of the respective philanthropic purpose in order to be entitled to the exemption. Unless the specific philanthropic exemption is defined in the Constitution, the Courts often have to resort to the definition contained in the statute implementing the constitutional provision. As the following case illustrates, where the Legislature has defined a term and such definition is clear and unambiguous, it is not subject to judicial construction and must be given its plain and obvious meaning.

Crapo v. Gainesville Area Chamber of Commerce, Inc.

274 So. 3d 453 (Fla. 1st Dist. Ct. App. 2019)

BILBREY, J.

The Property Appraiser and Tax Collector for Alachua County (hereafter, Alachua County) challenge a final summary judgment holding real property owned by the Gainesville Area Chamber of Commerce to be exempt from ad valorem taxation. We affirm.

Prior to 2014, the Gainesville Area Chamber of Commerce was granted an exemption from ad valorem taxation. However, in 2014, the Chamber was denied that exemption. It challenged that denial before the Value Adjustment Board, but the Board denied relief. The Chamber then sought relief in the circuit court. Finding the activities of the Chamber to serve a "charitable purpose," the circuit court held the Chamber was entitled to an exemption. Alachua County now challenges that holding.

Unless expressly exempted, all real property in the state is subject to taxation. *See* §196.001(1), Fla. Stat. (2014). However, Article VII, section 3(a), of the Florida Constitution provides:

> Such portions of property as are used predominantly for educational, literary, scientific, religious or **charitable purposes** may be exempted by general law from taxation.

(Emphasis added).

The term "charitable purposes" is not defined in the Constitution. But the term is defined in section 196.012(7), Florida Statutes (2014), as providing a function or service which is of such a community service that its discontinuance could legally result in the allocation of public funds for the continuance of the function or service. It is not necessary that public funds be allocated for such function or service but only that any such allocation would be legal.

This statute is clear and unambiguous, and therefore, we do not engage in any statutory construction. *See State v. Jett*, 626 So.2d 691, 693 (Fla. 1993) ("It is a settled rule of statutory construction that unambiguous language is not subject to judicial construction, however wise it may seem to alter the plain language."). The question presented in this appeal is therefore a simple one: do the activities of the Gainesville Chamber of Commerce qualify as "charitable purposes" as the Florida Legislature has defined that term in section 196.012(7)?

Alachua County has not challenged the findings of fact made by the circuit court that

> [t]he Chamber is the delegated local provider of economic development and related functions and services which grow the tax base, create jobs and promote the prosperity and general welfare of the Gainesville-Alachua County are. It was established in Alachua County for the express purpose of improving the quality of life in Alachua County through the creation of jobs, increased capital investment, increased local competitiveness for business development, and general economic activity.

(Internal quotation marks omitted).

The trial court also found that the "Chamber does not use its property for a profit-making purpose. All income generated by the Chamber is used for charitable purpose."

Given these activities, the Chamber performs a community service such that a discontinuance of such service "could legally result in the allocation of public funds for the continuance of the function or service." § 196.012(7). As the trial court further found, "there is no doubt that economic development serves a public purpose for which public funds can be allocated." The Department of Economic Opportunity, created by section 20.60, Florida Statutes, is but one example of such a public service. The purpose of this publically-funded department is to "create, expand, and retain business in this state, to recruit business from around the world, and to facilitate other job-creating efforts." § 20.60(4)(a).

While not challenging the constitutionality of section 196.012(7), Alachua County argues that despite its unambiguous language, a tax exemption for "charitable purposes" should be limited to "benevolent" purposes, such as providing material assistance to the needy. As the promotion of business and economic development is not traditionally understood as a charitable activity, property used for business and economic development should not be entitled to a tax exemption under the charitable purposes provision of the state constitution, Alachua County argues.

The dissent agrees with Alachua County, but in its analysis, undertakes judicial construction of an unambiguous statute. *See Mendenhall v. State*, 48 So.3d 740 (Fla. 2010) (holding courts should not construct an unambiguous statute). Further, the dissent has overlooked the plain meaning of section 196.012(7) to impose what it believes should be the meaning of "charitable purposes" under the statute: to provide relief to the needy. While relief to the needy is a laudable charitable purpose, the statute is not so limited. Creating an ambiguity where one did not previously exist would exceed our authority. As the Florida Supreme Court explained in *Velez v. Miami-Dade County Police Department*, 934 So.2d 1162, 1164-65 (Fla. 2006):

> [W]e are without power to construe an unambiguous statute in a way which would extend, modify, or limit, its express terms or its reasonable and obvious implications. To do so would be an abrogation of legislative power.

(Quotation marks and citations omitted).

The dissent relies on the Florida Constitution explaining that the "plain meaning of the word 'charitable' as used in the Florida Constitution is controlling, and the statute must be construed as limited to that meaning." (Dissent at pp. 460–61). As noted, Article VII, section 3(a) of the Florida Constitution does indeed provide that the Legislature is to enact laws exempting from taxation property used "predominantly for education, literary, scientific, religious or charitable purposes. . . ." However, as also noted, the Constitution does not define the term "charitable." Therefore, the "plain meaning" on which the dissent relies is not actually provided by our Constitution. Instead, the dissent tries to invoke a well-established canon of construction to reach its conclusion.

The dissent asserts that the Chamber, which argues for affirmance of the lower court's ruling under review, improperly equates "charitable purposes" with "public purposes." But this ignores the fact that it was the Legislature which first equated charitable purpose, for determining tax exemption, with public purpose. The Legislature plainly stated in section 196.012(7) that a charitable purpose is an activity for which "public funds" could be legally allocated.

In conclusion, the function of the Chamber mirrors some of the functions already undertaken by the State, and thus, the Chamber performs a function the discontinuance of which could result in the legal allocation of public funds. Therefore, the Chamber is entitled to an exemption from ad valorem taxation pursuant to the application of the unambiguous terms of section 196.012(7). The trial court's judgment granting such an exemption is AFFIRMED.

ROBERTS, J., concurs; KELSEY, J., dissents with opinion.

[Dissenting opinion omitted.]

b. Restrictions on Estate, Inheritance, and Income Taxes

Fla. Const. art. VII, § 5

Estate, inheritance and income taxes. —

(a) NATURAL PERSONS. No tax upon estates or inheritances or upon the income of natural persons who are residents or citizens of the state shall be levied by the state, or under its authority, in excess of the aggregate of amounts which may be allowed to be credited upon or deducted from any similar tax levied by the United States or any state.

(b) OTHERS. No tax upon the income of residents and citizens other than natural persons shall be levied by the state, or under its authority, in excess of 5% of net income, as defined by law, or at such greater rate as is authorized by a three-fifths (3/5) vote of the membership of each house of the legislature or as will provide for the state the maximum amount which may be allowed to be credited against income taxes levied by the United States and other states. There shall be exempt from taxation not less than five thousand dollars ($5,000) of the excess of net income subject to tax over the maximum amount allowed to be credited against income taxes levied by the United States and other states.

(c) EFFECTIVE DATE. This section shall become effective immediately upon approval by the electors of Florida.

The above provision is the source of the oft-made statement that the Florida Constitution prohibits the imposition of a state income, inheritance, or estate tax. This statement is partially accurate, but too simplistic.

First, the provision explicitly authorizes the imposition of a limited income tax on artificial entities such as corporations. Second, the provision prohibiting the imposition of an estate, inheritance, or income tax upon natural persons expressly authorizes the state to impose such taxes to the extent of any credit or deduction allowed for any similar tax levied by the United States or any state. This provision primarily exists under the theory that if the tax is going to be imposed, whether or not Florida imposes it, Florida should impose the tax and collect the tax revenue that otherwise would either go to the federal government or another state government. As the following case reflects, this provision does not permit the imposition of such a tax by Florida if it would result in an increase in the overall tax burden on the natural person or estate.

Prior to January 1, 2005, Florida employed a "pick up" tax system for purposes of taxing estates. Under this system, Florida "picked up" all, or a portion, of the credit for state death taxes allowed for federal estate tax purposes. Accordingly, Florida imposed estate or inheritance taxes up to the amount of the allowable federal credit. Due to a change in federal law, the credit was eliminated after December 31, 2004. Since Florida's estate tax was based solely on the federal credit, when the credit was eliminated, so were estate taxes in Florida.[53] The *Golder* case is left in the Sixth Edition to show the view that Florida has taken in case the federal credit is ever restored. See § 2058 of the Internal Revenue Code.

Department of Revenue v. Golder

326 So. 2d 409 (Fla. 1976)

ROBERTS, Justice.

This cause is before us on direct appeal from a final judgment of the Circuit Court in and for Dade County directly passing upon the constitutionality of Section 198.02, Florida Statutes. We have jurisdiction pursuant to Article V, Section 3(b)(1), Constitution of Florida.

On December 29, 1971, Max Lavin died a resident of Dade County, Florida. Appellee, petitioner-below, Harriet Golder, is the duly qualified and acting executrix of the estate of Max Lavin. At the time of his death, Max Lavin owned certain properties (realty) situated in the State of Pennsylvania and other property (realty) situated in the State of New Jersey, in addition to the bulk of his estate with a situs in Florida. As finally determined for federal estate tax purposes, the gross estate was valued at $1,016,173.97, with the Pennsylvania and New Jersey properties being valued at $200,000.00 and $7,500.00 respectively. Petitioner paid an inheritance tax to the State of Pennsylvania in the amount of $9,088.15, paid an inheritance tax to the State of New Jersey in the amount of $527.60, and paid Florida Estate Taxes in the total amount of $10,301.08. The total federal credit allowable to this estate for death taxes actually paid to the several states is $19,692.20. The total of the state taxation of this estate by Pennsylvania, New Jersey, and Florida exceeds the credit allowable upon the federal taxes by $206.43. By letter to the Department of Revenue, appellee requested a refund of this amount, pursuant to Section 198.29, Florida Statutes. By return letter, the Department of Revenue denied that any refund was due and asserted that further tax was due in the amount of $5,370.03, together with interest at the rate of 6% per annum from September 29, 1972, until date of payment.

* * *

In essence, Section 198.02, Florida Statutes, provides that the estates of resident decedents shall be taxed in the amount equal to the greater of (1) the total federal credit less the amounts paid to the other states or (2) a proportionate part of the federal credit determined by the ratio of the estate's property with a taxable situs in Florida to the total gross estate for federal tax purposes.

The appellant, Department of Revenue, contended that the total tax is the proportionate part of the federal credit. Appellee, however, urged that the maximum

---

53. *Estate Tax*, Fla. Dep't of Revenue, https://floridarevenue.com/taxes/taxesfees/pages/estate_tax.aspx (visited April 23, 2022).

tax that can be levied under the constitution is the amount of the federal credit less the amounts paid to the other states.

Confronted with the question of whether or not the Florida Estate Tax Law can result in the levying upon an estate of a resident decedent of a tax which will make the tax burden upon that estate greater than it would otherwise be, the trial court held that under Section 5, Article VII, Florida Constitution, the Legislature is without power to levy or authorize the levy of an estate tax which has the effect of increasing the tax burden upon the estate of a resident of Florida, and held that *to the extent that Section 198.02, Florida Statutes, purports to do so, it is illegal, invalid and unenforceable.*

Specifically, the trial court opined:

> The Court's task in reaching this determination has been alleviated to a great degree by the prior decision of the Florida Supreme Court on substantially the same issue. *Green v. State ex rel Phipps*, [Fla.] 166 So.2d 585 (1964). The decision in the *Green* case involved whether the Legislature had authorized such a levy under Section 198.02, *Florida Statutes*, as then in effect and whether, under the provisions of Section 11, Article IX of the 1885 Constitution of Florida, it could. The Supreme Court held that the Legislature had not and could not levy such a tax, in a decision that traced the history of the constitutional proscription and implementing legislation from its inception.

> Since the *Green* case, the Constitution of Florida was amended in 1968 with the subject matter of the previous Section 11, Article IX now being contained in Section 5, Article VII of the Florida Constitution. Thereafter, the Legislature in 1971 amended Section 198.02, *Florida Statutes*, to provide for a tax which could have the effect of increasing the tax burden on the estate of a resident of Florida. Defendants concede that this is exactly what the Supreme Court in the *Green* case held was unauthorized under the prior provisions of the Constitution of Florida.

> The precise question for this Court's determination is therefore whether the proscription of the prior constitutional provision was carried forward in the new provision in 1968.[2] Having reviewed the available contemporaneous commentary on the provision and in view of the Supreme Court's subsequent actions and decisions, the Court is of the opinion that the substance of the prior prohibition was carried forward unchanged. *See* e. g. 'Commentary' by Talbot D'Alemberte, Florida Statutes Annotated; *Dickenson [Dickinson] v. Maurer*, 229 So.2d 917 [247] (Fla.1969); *In re Advisory Opinion to Governor*, 243 So.2d 573 (Fla.1971).

---

2. The subsequent amendment of Section 5, Article VII in 1971 to authorize corporate income taxes did not alter the pertinent language of the estate tax prohibition other than to alter its reference to 'natural persons who are residents or citizens of this State' and therefore the Court finds has no bearing on the issue here involved.

The case sub judice is controlled by this Court's earlier decision in *Green v. State ex rel. Phipps*, supra, and, therefore, the learned trial judge was correct in his judgment awarding a peremptory writ of mandamus.

As applied to the particular facts of this case, Section 198.02 would have the effect of increasing the tax burden upon the estate of a resident of Florida, and accordingly, we find that Section 198.02, Florida Statutes, as applied to the specific facts of this case produces an unconstitutional result. Therefore, it is not necessary to pass on the constitutionality vel non of the statute.

The other matters and things presented have been considered and found to be without harmful error, and so the judgment of the trial court is affirmed.

It is so ordered.

ADKINS, C. J., and BOYD, OVERTON, SUNDBERG and HATCHETT, JJ., concur.

When the corporate income tax authorized by Fla. Const. art. VII, §5 was first enacted, an issue arose as to whether the tax could be imposed upon appreciation that occurred during the time that the Florida Constitution prohibited such an income tax. Borrowing heavily from federal income tax law, the Florida Supreme Court adopted the principle of "realization" as the guiding principle for determining when taxation was appropriate.

Department of Revenue v. Leadership Housing, Inc.

343 So. 2d 611 (Fla. 1977)

OVERTON, Chief Justice.

This cause is before this Court on direct appeal from a circuit court judgment which declared unconstitutional provisions of Chapter 220, Florida Statutes (1975). We have jurisdiction. [Footnote omitted.]

The issue concerns the validity of the state corporate income tax upon increases in the value of capital assets which occurred prior to November 2, 1971, but were not realized by the sale or transfer of the capital assets until after the effective date of the corporate income tax constitutional amendment and the enactment of the Florida Income Tax Code. We reverse, holding that appreciation in value of a capital asset is not income until it is realized from a sale, exchange or other disposition of the asset, and that the present Florida corporate income tax on such capital gain is constitutional and proper.

The voters of Florida adopted in 1924 a constitutional provision prohibiting any state income tax. [Footnote omitted.] That provision remained effectively unchanged until November 2, 1971, when the Florida Constitution was amended to permit imposition of a tax on the income of other than natural persons. [Footnote omitted.] Following the amendment, the Florida Legislature enacted the Florida

Income Tax Code, Chapter 220, Florida Statutes (1975), which imposed an income tax commencing January 1, 1972, on other than natural persons.

The corporate appellees commenced this action as a suit for declaratory and injunctive relief, seeking a declaration that their capital gains from appreciation of real estate accruing prior to the 1971 constitutional amendment and the enactment of the taxing legislation were constitutionally protected from taxation.

* * *

The appellees' first contention of unconstitutionality is based on their assertion that the constitutional income tax prohibition in effect from 1924 to 1971 was intended to apply to all income in the broadest sense of the term. They argue appreciation in the value of property is such income, and that the authors and adopters of the constitutional prohibition intended that anything that partook of the nature of income would be protected from taxation. The appellees admit that the effect of their construction and the trial court's order would allow the Legislature to tax as income unrealized accretions in value to capital assets occurring after November 2, 1971, but they assume that the Florida Legislature would decline to tax it.

We realize some authorities suggest appreciation constitutionally may be taxed as it accrues. *See* 1 Surrey & Warren, Federal Income Taxation, 816–18 and 822–32 (1972); Lowndes, Current Conceptions of Taxable Income, 25 Ohio St.L.J. 151 (1964). Nevertheless, we decline to hold that appreciation as it occurs is income. Such a holding might well be a tax benefit for the appellees, but it could be a tax liability for many others. The appellees' theory would also radically alter the cost bases of many capital assets, requiring such to be changed to the fair market value of the assets on the date of the removal of the constitutional prohibition, or the date of the statutory enactment of the Code. Unlike Section 1053 of the Internal Revenue Code, 26 U.S.C. §1053, and its predecessors, which awarded cost bases in such assets equal to the greater of either the actual cost of the asset or its fair market value as of the effective date of the first taxing statute, a judicial decision here would not automatically incorporate the option afforded by Congress in selecting the greater of the two bases. The practical effect of the judicial decision asked for by the appellees could require a downward valuation of assets which had depreciated, imposing greater tax liability on some taxpayers.

The entire issue in this case turns on the meaning of income with respect to capital appreciation. Economists and legal scholars are unable to agree whether appreciation in value of a capital asset is income to the asset holder as it accrues or later when it is realized by separation from capital. *Compare, e. g.*, Lowndes, Current Conceptions of Taxable Income, *supra*, H. Simons, Personal Income Taxation 88 (1938), *with* Mullock, The Constitutional Aspects of Realization, 31 *U.Pitt.L.Rev.* 615 (1970), and Seligman, 9 Am.Econ.Development 517 (1919).

The appellant contends that appreciation in value of capital assets is not income until it is realized at the time of disposition, adopting the definition of income in *Eisner v. Macomber*, 252 U.S. 189, 40 S.Ct. 189, 64 L.Ed. 521 (1920).

We agree and find the proper interpretation is that capital appreciation is not true income until it has been separated from its capital. The separation from capital referred to as the doctrine of "realization" may occur on the receipt of money, other property or rights, or when some other economic benefit is enjoyed by the asset holder. This construction and interpretation follow some economists' theory of the relation of capital to income, specifically that the former is likened to the tree or the land and the latter the fruit or the crop. We approve of the appellant's reliance on *Eisner v. Macomber, supra,* and its concept of when capital appreciation becomes income. The definition contained therein is as follows:

> ... 'Income may be defined as the gain derived from capital, from labor, or from both combined,' provided it be understood to include profit gained through a sale or conversion of capital assets. . . .

> ... [It is] *not* a gain *accruing to* capital, not a *growth* or *increment* of value *in* the investment; but a gain, a profit, something of exchangeable value *proceeding from* the property, *severed from* the capital however invested or employed, and *coming in,* being '*derived*,' that is *received* or *drawn by* the recipient (the taxpayer) for his *separate* use, benefit and disposal; — *that* is income derived from property. Nothing else answers the description." 252 U.S. at 207, 40 S.Ct. at 193.

We recognize that the *Eisner* doctrine and definition has been developed to include as realized income such things as (1) the value of a lessee-erected improvement on realty upon reversion of the realty to the lessor, *Helvering v. Bruun,* 309 U.S. 461, 60 S.Ct. 631, 84 L.Ed. 864 (1940); (2) interest coupons detached from bonds and given as a gift, *Helvering v. Horst,* 311 U.S. 112, 61 S.Ct. 144, 85 L.Ed. 75 (1940); (3) property transferred by a husband to his wife in a property settlement connected with divorce, *United States v. Davis,* 370 U.S. 65, 82 S.Ct. 1190, 8 L.Ed.2d 335 (1962). All the aforementioned circumstances constituted events upon which economic gains were enjoyed at the time of the events. No assertion is made in these cases that appreciation in and of itself is taxable. We reject appellees' arguments that the appreciation became immunized from income taxation as it accrued by the Florida constitutional prohibition. We hold that bare appreciation is not income subject to income taxation. The citation by the United States Supreme Court to *Eisner v. Macomber* and its concept of realization recently in *Ivan Allen Company v. United States,* 422 U.S. 617, 633, 95 S.Ct. 2501, 45 L.Ed.2d 435 (1975), further convinces us of the correctness of this position. We believe the realization doctrine is the fairest for all taxpayers.

* * *

In summary, we hold that appreciation becomes income only upon the sale, exchange, or other disposition of the capital asset together with the accretions thereto, and that such realized gain is income in the year of disposition regardless of when it accrued.

We reverse the trial court, uphold the constitutionality of Chapter 220 as it pertains to the taxation of capital gains accruing prior to November 2, 1971, and dissolve the injunctive order issued by the trial court in this cause.

It is so ordered.

SUNDBERG and HATCHETT, JJ., and MILLS, District Court Judge, concur.

BOYD, J., concurs specially with an opinion.

ROBERTS (Retired), J., dissents with an opinion, with which ADKINS, J., concurs.

[The concurring opinion of Justice Boyd and the dissenting opinion of Justice Roberts are omitted.]

c. Homestead Exemption from the Ad Valorem Tax

Fla. Const. art. VII, § 6

Homestead exemptions. —

(a) Every person who has the legal or equitable title to real estate and maintains thereon the permanent residence of the owner, or another legally or naturally dependent upon the owner, shall be exempt from taxation thereon, except assessments for special benefits, up to the assessed valuation of twenty-five thousand dollars and, for all levies other than school district levies, on the assessed valuation greater than fifty thousand dollars and up to seventy-five thousand dollars, upon establishment of right thereto in the manner prescribed by law. The real estate may be held by legal or equitable title, by the entireties, jointly, in common, as a condominium, or indirectly by stock ownership or membership representing the owner's or member's proprietary interest in a corporation owning a fee or a leasehold initially in excess of ninety-eight years. The exemption shall not apply with respect to any assessment roll until such roll is first determined to be in compliance with the provisions of section 4 by a state agency designated by general law. This exemption is repealed on the effective date of any amendment to this Article which provides for the assessment of homestead property at less than just value.

(b) Not more than one exemption shall be allowed any individual or family unit or with respect to any residential unit. No exemption shall exceed the value of the real estate assessable to the owner or, in case of ownership through stock or membership in a corporation, the value of the proportion which the interest in the corporation bears to the assessed value of the property.

(c) By general law and subject to conditions specified therein, the Legislature may provide to renters, who are permanent residents, ad valorem tax relief on all ad valorem tax levies. Such ad valorem tax relief shall be in the form and amount established by general law.

(d) The legislature may, by general law, allow counties or municipalities, for the purpose of their respective tax levies and subject to the provisions of general law, to grant either or both of the following additional homestead tax exemptions:

(1) An exemption not exceeding fifty thousand dollars to a person who has the legal or equitable title to real estate and maintains thereon the permanent residence of the owner, who has attained age sixty-five, and whose household income, as defined by general law, does not exceed twenty thousand dollars; or

(2) An exemption equal to the assessed value of the property to a person who has the legal or equitable title to real estate with a just value less than two hundred and fifty thousand dollars, as determined in the first tax year that the owner applies and is eligible for the exemption, and who has maintained thereon the permanent residence of the owner for not less than twenty-five years, who has attained age sixty-five, and whose household income does not exceed the income limitation prescribed in paragraph (1).

The general law must allow counties and municipalities to grant these additional exemptions, within the limits prescribed in this subsection, by ordinance adopted in the manner prescribed by general law, and must provide for the periodic adjustment of the income limitation prescribed in this subsection for changes in the cost of living.

(e)(1) Each veteran who is age 65 or older who is partially or totally permanently disabled shall receive a discount from the amount of the ad valorem tax otherwise owed on homestead property the veteran owns and resides in if the disability was combat related and the veteran was honorably discharged upon separation from military service. The discount shall be in a percentage equal to the percentage of the veteran's permanent, service-connected disability as determined by the United States Department of Veterans Affairs. To qualify for the discount granted by this paragraph, an applicant must submit to the county property appraiser, by March 1, an official letter from the United States Department of Veterans Affairs stating the percentage of the veteran's service-connected disability and such evidence that reasonably identifies the disability as combat related and a copy of the veteran's honorable discharge. If the property appraiser denies the request for a discount, the appraiser must notify the applicant in writing of the reasons for the denial, and the veteran may reapply. The Legislature may, by general law, waive the annual application requirement in subsequent years.

(2) If a veteran who receives the discount described in paragraph (1) predeceases his or her spouse, and if, upon the death of the veteran, the surviving spouse holds the legal or beneficial title to the homestead property

and permanently resides thereon, the discount carries over to the surviving spouse until he or she remarries or sells or otherwise disposes of the homestead property. If the surviving spouse sells or otherwise disposes of the property, a discount not to exceed the dollar amount granted from the most recent ad valorem tax roll may be transferred to the surviving spouse's new homestead property, if used as his or her permanent residence and he or she has not remarried.

(3) This subsection is self-executing and does not require implementing legislation.

(f) By general law and subject to conditions and limitations specified therein, the Legislature may provide ad valorem tax relief equal to the total amount or a portion of the ad valorem tax otherwise owed on homestead property to:

(1) The surviving spouse of a veteran who died from service-connected causes while on active duty as a member of the United States Armed Forces.

(2) The surviving spouse of a first responder who died in the line of duty.

(3) A first responder who is totally and permanently disabled as a result of an injury or injuries sustained in the line of duty. Causal connection between a disability and service in the line of duty shall not be presumed but must be determined as provided by general law. For purposes of this paragraph, the term "disability" does not include a chronic condition or chronic disease, unless the injury sustained in the line of duty was the sole cause of the chronic condition or chronic disease.

As used in this subsection and as further defined by general law, the term "first responder" means a law enforcement officer, a correctional officer, a firefighter, an emergency medical technician, or a paramedic, and the term "in the line of duty" means arising out of and in the actual performance of duty required by employment as a first responder.

The Florida Constitution recognizes two separate homestead exemptions. The homestead exemption from forced sale is discussed in Chapter 8. The homestead exemption from ad valorem taxation is discussed in this chapter. These provisions are found in two different articles of the Florida Constitution and are separate and distinct concepts; the principles relating to one do not necessarily govern the other.[54]

---

54. *Estate Tax*, Fla. Dep't of Revenue, https://floridarevenue.com/taxes/taxesfees/pages/estate_tax.aspx (visited April 23, 2022).

6 · TAXATION AND FINANCE

(1) "Every person who has the legal or equitable title to real estate and maintains thereon the permanent residence of the owner . . . shall be exempt from taxation thereon . . ." Fla. Const. art. VII, § (6)(a)

Robbins v. Welbaum

664 So. 2d 1 (Fla. 3d Dist. Ct. App. 1995)

GERSTEN, Judge.

Appellant Joel W. Robbins, Dade County Property Appraiser, ("Property Appraiser") appeals a summary judgment in favor of appellees R. Earl Welbaum and Joan Welbaum ("the Welbaums"), which allows the Welbaums to claim a homestead exemption on their residence held in a qualified personal residence trust ("QPRT"). Recognizing this as a case of first impression in Florida, we affirm.

On December 1, 1992, the Welbaums executed a QPRT, transferring their residence to an irrevocable inter vivos trust. A QPRT is part of the federal income tax code which allows homeowners to transfer property to their children while avoiding future estate taxes. *See* I.R.C. § 2702; Peter A. Borrok, *Four Estate Planning Devices to Get Excited About*, N.Y.St.B.J., Jan. 1995, at 32; David C. Humphreys, Jr., *Qualified Personal Residence Trusts: "Have Your Grits and Eat Them, Too!"*, S.C.Law., Nov.–Dec. 1994, at 45.

Under the language of the QPRT, the Welbaums relinquished "absolutely and forever all of his or her possession or enjoyment of or right to the principal and income from the trust estate." Both of the Welbaums have a present possessory right to live on the residential property until the earlier of either ten years[1] from the QPRT's creation date or his or her spouse's death.

As trustees of the QPRT, the Welbaums applied for a homestead exemption from ad valorem taxes for 1993. The Property Appraiser denied the application because the Welbaums did not hold a life estate in the property. The Welbaums petitioned the Dade County Value Adjustment Board, contesting the Property Appraiser's decision, and the board granted the exemption. The Property Appraiser then filed a circuit court action challenging the board's decision. The Welbaums moved for summary judgment, which the trial court granted.

The Property Appraiser contends that the Welbaums do not qualify for homestead exemption because their use of the residence is limited by the QPRT. According to the Property Appraiser, the house cannot constitute the Welbaum's permanent residence, as the Welbaums have the present intent of moving within ten year's time. The Welbaums assert they are entitled to homestead exemption because they indisputably hold equitable title in the home, which is their permanent residence.

---

1. According to the trust agreement, Joan Welbaum has a fifteen-year present possessory right in the home, while her husband has a ten-year present possessory right. For the purposes of this opinion, however, the time frame during which both parties may reside in the home will be referenced by the more limited ten-year provision.

Section 196.031, Florida Statutes (Supp. 1994), allows individuals to claim a home exempt from ad valorem taxation if they hold legal or beneficial title to that home and, in good faith, make it their permanent residence. For homestead exemption purposes only, individuals holding beneficial title includes residents whose stay on the property is limited by jointure or settlement. §196.041, Fla.Stat. (1993).

Here, both parties agree the QPRT is valid under I.R.C. §2702 and creates a jointure or settlement under the meaning of §196.041 of the Florida Statutes. As such, the Welbaums hold beneficial title to their residence for homestead purposes, and because they have, in good faith, made it their permanent residence, they are entitled to homestead exemption.

The Property Appraiser argues that there should be a minimum time period during which a claimant must hold an interest in property before being deemed to hold beneficial title to the property for homestead exemption purposes. Neither the statute nor the constitution places such a time limit on beneficial title, and we decline to do so as well. It is enough that the Welbaums held beneficial title, under the definition of §196.041, during the year in which they claim the exemption.

Accordingly, we hold that in circumstances such as these, individuals placing their permanent residence in a QPRT are entitled to homestead exemption.

Affirmed.

(2) "**Every person who has he legal or equitable title to real estate and maintains thereon the permanent residence of the owner, or another legally or naturally dependent upon the owner, shall be exempt from taxation thereon . . ." Fla. Const. art. VII, §(6)(a)**

Garcia v. Andonie

101 So. 3d 339 (Fla. 2012)

LABARGA, J.

This case is before the Court on the Miami-Dade Property Appraiser's (Property Appraiser) appeal of the Third District Court of Appeal's decision in *De La Mora v. Andonie,* 51 So.3d 517 (Fla. 3d DCA 2010). [Footnote omitted.] In *Andonie,* the Third District affirmed a circuit court's grant of an ad valorem homestead tax exemption to David and Ana Andonie (the Taxpayers), and declared a portion of section 196.031(1), Florida Statutes (2006), invalid and unenforceable because the statutory provision limits the class of property owners otherwise eligible for ad valorem tax relief under article VII, section 6(a), of the Florida Constitution. This Court has jurisdiction of the appeal under article V, section 3(b)(1) of the Florida Constitution.

Overview

In this appeal, the Property Appraiser argues that the Third District erred by concluding that a portion of section 196.031(1) is invalid and unenforceable. The

Property Appraiser also argues that the record evidence in this case is insufficient to establish the Taxpayers' entitlement to the ad valorem tax exemption provided for in article VII, section 6(a), of the Florida Constitution. Accordingly, the Property Appraiser argues that the Third District erred in affirming the circuit court's judgment that grants the Taxpayers the ad valorem tax exemption provided for in article VII, section 6(a), of the Florida Constitution. In this opinion, we discuss two separate issues relating to a property owner's entitlement to the ad valorem tax exemption provided for in article VII, section 6(a), of the Florida Constitution. [Footnote omitted.]

First, we address the legal elements that must be proven to establish entitlement to this constitutional tax exemption. Relative to this issue of law, we hold that the express language of the Florida Constitution, as amended in 1968, creates the right for every person who owns Florida real property to receive a prescribed reduction in the taxable value of that property [Footnote omitted.] where the owner maintains on the property *either* (1) the permanent residence of the owner *or* (2) the permanent residence of another legally or naturally dependent on the owner — provided the individual for whom the permanent residence is maintained has no legal impediment to residing on the property on a permanent basis. Based on this conclusion, we hold consistent with the Third District's decision in *Andonie* that section 196.031(1), Florida Statutes (2006), is invalid and unenforceable to the extent that it imposes a substantive requirement for entitlement not contained in the Constitution and thereby materially limits the class of taxpayers entitled to ad valorem tax relief under the Florida Constitution.

The second issue we address relates to the facts and procedural posture of this particular case. The Property Appraiser concedes that the taxpayers here would be entitled to the ad valorem tax exemption had they introduced sufficient evidence establishing that they were, in fact, maintaining the permanent residence of their minor children on their Florida property. The Property Appraiser argues, however, that the evidence introduced by the Taxpayers — an affidavit establishing that the Florida property is being used as the permanent residence of the Taxpayers' minor children — was "self-serving" and, thus, insufficient. We conclude that the Property Appraiser's argument regarding the sufficiency of the evidence was not preserved below and is thus waived. Further, we conclude that the Property Appraiser's factual arguments predicated on the insufficiency of the evidence are flawed because the Property Appraiser had the burden of proof in the circuit court proceeding that gave rise to this appeal. Moreover, we conclude that the uncontroverted evidence of record establishes that the Taxpayers' minor children live on the property and have the legal right to live on the property permanently in accordance with their parents' intent. Based on the foregoing, we affirm the Third District's decision that, in turn, affirms the circuit court's grant of the exemption to the Taxpayers.

We first examine the legal elements of entitlement that must be established by an owner of Florida property to obtain the ad valorem tax relief that is guaranteed to owners of Florida property as a matter of constitutional right.

The Legal Elements of Entitlement for the Constitutional Homestead Tax Exemption

The determination of a statute's constitutionality and the interpretation of a constitutional provision are both questions of law reviewed de novo. *See Zingale v. Powell*, 885 So.2d 277, 280 (Fla.2004) ("Although we take into consideration the district court's analysis on the issue, constitutional interpretation, like statutory interpretation, is performed *de novo*."). If the language in the constitution is clear, there is no need to resort to other tools of construction. *Lawnwood Med. Ctr., Inc. v. Seeger*, 990 So.2d 503, 510 (Fla.2008). Unless the text of the constitution suggests that a technical meaning of a word is intended, "words used in the constitution should be given their usual and ordinary meaning." *See id.* at 512 (internal citations omitted). Accordingly, where the text of a constitutional provision does not suggest that a technical meaning was intended, the Court is not at liberty to add words so as to impose a technical meaning. *See id.* Constitutional analysis must begin with examination of explicit language of provisions in question and, where the language is unambiguous and addresses the matter at issue, the provision should be enforced as written. *See Ford v. Browning*, 992 So.2d 132, 136 (Fla.2008) (citing *Fla. Soc'y of Ophthalmology v. Fla. Optometric Ass'n*, 489 So.2d 1118, 1119 (Fla.1986)). Based on the foregoing authority, we first examine the plain language of the constitutional provision that creates the right to an ad valorem tax exemption for owners of Florida property.

The Florida Constitution provides *every* owner of Florida real property the right to apply for [Footnote omitted.] and receive a reduction in the assessed value of real property for ad valorem tax purposes, under specified circumstances. *See* art. VII, § 6(a), Fla. Const. Before the Florida Constitution was amended by the people of Florida in 1968, an owner of real property seeking to establish entitlement to a homestead tax exemption was required to both "reside" on the property in question *and* make the property either (1) his or her permanent home or (2) the permanent home of others legally or naturally dependent upon the owner. [Footnote omitted.] When the Florida Constitution was amended in 1968, the homestead tax exemption provision was renumbered and the requirement that the property owner reside on the property was removed. *See* art. VII, § 6(a), Fla. Const. Article VII, Section 6(a), of the Florida Constitution, as amended in 1968, states in relevant part:

> *Every person who has* the legal or equitable *title to real estate and maintains thereon the permanent residence of* the owner, or *another legally or naturally dependent upon the owner, shall be exempt from taxation* thereon ... upon establishment of right thereto in the manner prescribed by law. Art. VII, § 6(a), Fla. Const. (emphasis added).

> Thus, the plain language of the Florida Constitution, as amended in 1968, requires that the property owner maintain on the property either (1) the permanent residence of the owner; *or* (2) the permanent residence of another legally or naturally dependent upon the owner. Accordingly, under the Florida Constitution there are two separate and independent means by which a property owner's entitlement to the homestead tax exemption

may be accomplished. [Footnote omitted.] And, where a property owner claims a homestead tax exemption based on the owner's act of maintaining the permanent residence of his or her dependents on the property, the owner need not also prove that he or she is residing on the property, permanently or otherwise, because the two textual means by which entitlement to the exemption may be established under the constitution are stated independently and as alternatives to one another. *See* art. VII, § 6(a), Fla. Const.; *see also* § 196.031(6), Fla. Stat. (2006) (explaining permanent resident of state other than Florida who is receiving tax exemption in that state is not precluded from also obtaining homestead tax exemption in Florida where owner maintains the permanent residence of dependents on Florida property); *see generally Matter of Cooke,* 412 So.2d 340, 341 (Fla.1982) (interpreting the 1968 constitutional revisions to the forced-sale homestead exemption provided for in the Florida Constitution and stating, "[W]e hold that although it is not necessary that the head of the family reside in the state or intend to make the property in question his permanent residence, he must establish that he intended to make this property his family's permanent residence.").

Notwithstanding the specific elements of entitlement to the ad valorem tax exemption contained in article VII, section 6(a), of the Florida Constitution (1968), section 196.031(1), a legislative enactment intended to implement the constitutional tax exemption contains a substantive element of entitlement that is no longer required by the Constitution:

> Every person who, on January 1, has the legal title or beneficial title in equity to real property in this state and *who resides thereon* and in good faith makes the same his or her permanent residence, or the permanent residence of another or others legally or naturally dependent upon such person, is entitled to an exemption . . . as defined in s. 6, Art. VII of the State Constitution.

§ 196.031(1), Fla. Stat. (2006) (emphasis added). Under the requirements of section 196.031(1), every property owner seeking the constitutional ad valorem tax exemption must establish that he is residing on the Florida property, regardless of whether the tax exemption is being claimed because the property is being maintained as the permanent residence of the property owner or as the permanent residence of the owner's dependents. *See* § 196.031(1), Fla. Stat. (2006). Accordingly, the "and who resides thereon" element of entitlement set forth in section 196.031(1) — although accurately reflecting the requirements contained in the Florida Constitution as it existed before the 1968 revisions — is inconsistent with the requirements of the constitution as amended in 1968.

We have held that although the Legislature is permitted to enact laws regulating "the manner" of establishing the right to the constitutional homestead tax exemption, it cannot substantively alter or materially limit the class of individuals entitled to the exemption under the plain language of the constitution. *See Sparkman v.*

State, 58 So.2d 431, 432 (Fla.1952) (declaring invalid statute that imposed one-year residence requirement for entitlement to homestead tax exemption, even though constitutional provision in question authorized Legislature to "prescribe appropriate and reasonable laws regulating the manner of establishing the right to [the] exemption"). Because the plain language of article VII, section 6(a), of the Florida Constitution permits an owner of Florida property to obtain the exemption based on the act of maintaining the permanent residence of his or her natural or legal dependents on the property—irrespective of the owner's citizenship or place of residence, requirements that were removed from the Constitution—the additional "and who resides thereon" requirement imposed by section 196.031(1) substantively limits and narrows the class of property owners and taxpayers eligible for the ad valorem tax exemption under the plain language of the Florida Constitution. [Footnote omitted.] Accordingly, we hold, consistent with the result reached by the Third District in *Andonie,* that the "and who resides thereon" criterion contained in section 196.031(1) is invalid and unenforceable as a legal element of entitlement [Footnote omitted.] for the ad valorem tax exemption as provided for under the plain language of article VII, section 6. [Footnote omitted.]

We note that the Department of Revenue, the agency with statewide control over the administration of ad valorem taxation, [Footnote omitted.] is a respondent before this Court. The Department argues that the Third District's decision in *Andonie* is consistent with the Florida Constitution, Florida statutes, and the public policy that governs homestead tax exemption. Further, in its brief, the Department maintains that the plain language of article VII, section 6(a), and the record before us permits the taxpayers here to establish entitlement to the ad valorem tax exemption. Accordingly, the Department of Revenue, the agency with the legal duty of prescribing rules and regulations for the collection of taxes, properly acknowledges the supremacy of the constitution over any administrative rule or statute that might limit the class of individuals eligible for the exemption under the plain language of the constitution. *See* § 195.027(1), Fla. Stat. (2006) (providing Department of Revenue shall prescribe rules for assessing and collecting taxes that are in compliance with the constitution). Thus, the Department, through its arguments to this Court, properly recognizes that although it has the authority to prescribe procedural rules for the collection and assessment of taxes, it is without the authority to impose substantive rules or elements of entitlement that limit the class of property owners and taxpayers otherwise eligible to receive the tax exemption under the Constitution.[11]

---

11. In *Andonie,* the Third District concluded that *Florida Administrative Code Rule 12D-7.014(2)* is unenforceable because the rule is based on the authority of *Beekman v. Beekman, 53 Fla. 858, 43 So. 923 (1907),* a matrimonial case that the Third District concluded was not applicable to the "interpretive issue" in this case. *See Andonie, 51 So.3d at 522. Beekman* stands for the general proposition that under Florida common law an unemancipated minor cannot make his own choice of domicile. *43 So. at 924.* Here, however, we are not presented with a circumstance where a minor child is attempting to establish a home away from that of his parents. Rather, in this case it is the adult parents who have made a choice as to where their children will live. Further, unlike the facts

6 · TAXATION AND FINANCE

See generally, Dep't of Prof'l Regulation v. Florida Soc'y of Prof'l Land Surveyors, 475 So.2d 939, 942 (Fla. 1st DCA 1985) (explaining all rulemaking authority is limited by statute that confers such power); *see also Sparkman,* 58 So.2d at 432 (stating, "Express or implied provisions of the Constitution cannot be altered, contracted or enlarged by legislative enactments.") (quoting *State ex rel. West v. Butler,* 70 Fla. 102, 69 So. 771, 777 (1915)). Based on the foregoing, we conclude that the legal elements of entitlement to the constitutional homestead exemption require a property owner to establish that the owner is maintaining on Florida real property *either* (1) the permanent residence of the owner *or* (2) the permanent residence of another legally or naturally dependent on the owner. And the additional element of entitlement contained in section 196.031(1) requiring all property owners to demonstrate that they reside on the property is therefore invalid and unenforceable to the extent it limits the class of individuals eligible for the constitutional tax exemption.

We next turn to the appropriate legal standards to be used to determine whether a piece of property is being used as the "permanent residence" of either a property owner or the property owner's dependents. Section 196.012(18), Florida Statutes (2006), defines "permanent residence" for ad valorem taxation purposes and states that the inquiry to be made in determining whether one's property qualifies as a "permanent residence" is whether the property in question is being used as the "true" permanent home of the individual:

> Permanent residence" means that place where a person has his or her true, fixed, and permanent home and principal establishment to which, whenever absent, he or she has the intention of returning. . . .

§ 196.012(18), Fla. Stat. (2006). Accordingly, because the legislative definition of "permanent residence," consistent with the constitutional context from which it emerges, requires a determination as to whether the property is being used as the true permanent home or residence of the owner or his dependents, most determinations regarding whether a permanent residence is being maintained on Florida property will involve some level of factual inquiry regarding the actual use of the residential property in question. [Footnote omitted.] Indeed, section 196.015 states that "[i]ntention to establish a permanent residence in this state is a factual determination," *see* § 196.015, Fla. Stat. (2006), not an issue of law. Although section 196.015 contains a number of relevant discretionary factors that "may" be considered to make the factual determination as to whether the applicant for the tax exemption has the requisite intent to

---

presented in *Beekman,* here, the Taxpayers as parents have actually maintained the permanent residence of their minor children in Florida, and the Property Appraiser concedes that the parents have the legal right to insist that their children remain permanently on the Florida property. Moreover, regardless of the applicability of *Beekman* to issues of domiciliary law, the issue here is not one of domicile, but rather, one involving the meaning of "permanent residence" as used in article VII, section 6(a), and *section 196.012(18), Florida Statutes (2006).* Accordingly, we agree with the Third District and the Department of Revenue that neither *Florida Administrative Code Ann. r. 12D-7.014(2) (1976)* nor this Court's decision in *Beekman* upon which the rule is based, are controlling authority relative to the issue of constitutional interpretation before us.

establish a permanent residence on his or her Florida property, this provision also cautions that no one factor is "conclusive" on this issue of fact. *Id.*

Thus, in most instances, an individual's intent to establish a permanent residence on a piece of Florida real property will present an issue of fact. We have held, however, that some individuals — those who do not possess the legal right to permanently reside in Florida — cannot, as a matter of law, establish that their permanent residence is being maintained on Florida real property. *See Juarrero v. McNayr,* 157 So.2d 79, 81 (Fla.1963) (holding non-citizen in the United States under temporary visa "cannot 'legally,' 'rightfully,' or in 'good faith' make or declare" a "permanent home" of this state for purposes of establishing entitlement to homestead tax exemption).

In *Juarrero* we concluded that citizenship is not a prerequisite for eligibility to the constitutional ad valorem tax exemption. *Id.* at 81. Nevertheless, we also held in *Juarrero* that where a non-citizen possesses only a temporary visa, he cannot legally form the intent to reside on Florida property permanently because he has no assurance that he can continue to reside in good faith for any fixed period of time in this country. *Id.* Hence, the rationale of *Juarrero* instructs that those without limitations or legal impediments on their right to live permanently on Florida property are included in the class of individuals for whom a permanent residence may be maintained on Florida property. And conversely, those who do not possess the legal right to reside permanently in Florida cannot be included in the class of individuals for whom a permanent residence may be maintained on Florida property. Thus, in a given case, the question of whether a property owner has maintained a permanent residence on Florida property — whether for the owner or another dependent upon the owner — will present a mixed question of fact and law. The question of fact centers upon whether the Florida property is being used and maintained as the "true" and actual permanent home of either the owner or the owner's dependents, to be governed by the definition of permanent residence contained in section 196.012(18) and the factors set forth in section 196.015. And the legal question presented is whether the individual for whom the permanent residence is being maintained has a legal impediment to or restriction from living permanently on the Florida property. Accordingly, we affirm the decision of the Third District in *Andonie,* which reaches a consistent result.

Having defined the legal elements of entitlement that must be met for an owner of Florida property to establish entitlement to the constitutional tax exemption provided for in article VII, section 6(a), we now turn to the facts and the procedural history of this case.

This Case

The Taxpayers are a husband and wife, both citizens of Honduras, who are residing lawfully in the United States under a temporary (E-2) [Footnote omitted.] visa issued by the United States Department of Homeland Security. The Taxpayers have three minor children — ages seven, twelve, and fourteen — who, unlike their parents, are citizens of the United States and the State of Florida. The Taxpayers own a residential condominium in Key Biscayne, Florida, and live on the property with their three minor children. [Footnote omitted.] The record before this Court contains no evidence that suggests that the Taxpayers' children have ever lived outside of Florida, nor is there an indication that the children have a legal impediment to residing in Florida on a permanent basis. For the 2006 tax year, the Taxpayers submitted to the Property Appraiser a timely application for a reduction in the assessed taxable value of their Florida property as provided for in article VII, section 6(a), of the Florida Constitution. On the sworn application form generated by the Property Appraiser, the Taxpayers averred that their Florida property was being maintained as the permanent residence of their minor children, each of whom is a citizen of the United States and naturally and legally dependent on the Taxpayers. The Taxpayers did not seek to establish that the property was being used as their own permanent residence.

The Property Appraiser administratively denied the Taxpayers' application for the ad valorem tax exemption for the stated reason that the Taxpayers are not permanent residents of Florida. The Taxpayers, as permitted by section 194.011(3), Florida Statutes (2006), petitioned the Miami-Dade County Value Adjustment Board to challenge the Property Appraiser's denial.

After conducting a hearing on the Taxpayers' petition, the Miami-Dade Value Adjustment Board granted the Taxpayers' ad valorem tax exemption and, in so doing, overturned the Property Appraiser's administrative denial of the exemption. The Property Appraiser then appealed the decision of the Value Adjustment Board to the circuit court. *See* § 194.036(1), Fla. Stat. (2006) (stating that appeals of the decisions of the Value Adjustment Board are made to the circuit court); *see also* § 194.036(3), Fla. Stat. (2006) (stating "the circuit court proceeding shall be de novo, and the burden of proof shall be upon the party initiating the action"). The Property Appraiser alleged in the circuit court that the Taxpayers were not entitled to the ad valorem tax exemption provided for in article VII, section 6(a), because the Taxpayers could not establish that the Florida property was being used as the Taxpayers' permanent residence. The Property Appraiser also alleged that the exemption granted to the Taxpayers by the Value Adjustment Board violated the Florida Constitution and, for this reason, the Department of Revenue became a party plaintiff to the circuit court action as permitted by section 194.181(5), Fla. Stat. (2007).

In the circuit court, the Property Appraiser moved for summary judgment and alleged that because the Taxpayers were residing in the United States on a temporary visa, they were legally prohibited from obtaining the constitutional tax exemption at issue. Significantly, the Property Appraiser — the party that bore the burden of proof in the circuit court proceeding — did not introduce any evidence so as to establish that the Taxpayers' minor children were not living on the property or that the children had a legal or factual impediment to living permanently on the Florida property — nor did the Property Appraiser prove to any degree that the Taxpayers' children are legally permitted to live anywhere other than the United States. To the contrary, the Property Appraiser introduced evidence establishing that each of the Taxpayers' three children was a citizen of the United States and was residing on the Taxpayers' property, and at the hearing on the Property Appraiser's motion for summary judgment, counsel for the Property Appraiser informed the circuit court that "this has nothing to do with whether the children are allowed to reside in the United States or reside in the residence they want."

In response to the Property Appraiser's motion for summary judgment, the Taxpayers submitted a sworn affidavit that affirmatively avers that the Taxpayers' residential property is, in fact, being used as the permanent residence of the three minor children, and that the children have a legal right to live in Florida, the United States, and on the property, permanently. Further, the Taxpayers' affidavit established that it was the Taxpayers' intent as parents that their children remain permanently in the United States, a place where the children had the right to live. In the circuit court proceeding, the Property Appraiser raised no objection and made no challenge to the Taxpayers' affidavit or the averments of facts contained therein. Based on the arguments made by the Property Appraiser in the circuit court, the Taxpayers filed a cross motion for summary judgment on the basis that the uncontroverted facts established that the Florida property was being used as the permanent residence of their minor children who were legally and naturally dependent on the Taxpayers and had the legal right to live on the property permanently consistent with their parents' intent.

In accordance with the respective positions taken by the parties, the circuit court entered an order granting the Taxpayers an ad valorem tax exemption for the 2006 tax year on the bases that there was no dispute in the facts and that the Taxpayers, by maintaining the permanent residence of their legally dependent children on the property, established entitlement to the exemption under the plain language of article VII, section 6(a), of the Florida Constitution. The Property Appraiser then appealed the circuit court's order granting the tax exemption to the Third District Court of Appeal. This appeal was the foundation of the Third District's opinion in *Andonie.*

In *Andonie,* the Third District affirmed the circuit court's order granting the Taxpayers' motion for summary judgment. In its opinion, the Third District referred to the definition of "permanent residence" contained in section 196.012(18) and concluded that the Taxpayers' affidavit, which established that the true and actual permanent residence of the minor children was on the Florida property, went uncontested and sufficiently established that the Taxpayers' property was used as the children's permanent residence. The Third District also concluded in *Andonie* that the "and who resides thereon" criterion contained in section 196.031(1) is unenforceable; based on this ruling, the Property Appraiser appealed the Third District's decision to this Court under the authority of article V, section 3(b)(1), of the Florida Constitution.

In this Court, the Property Appraiser argues that the evidence introduced by the Taxpayers in the circuit court is "self-serving" and insufficient to establish that the

Taxpayers' Florida property is in fact being used as the minor children's permanent residence. The Property Appraiser's arguments regarding the sufficiency of the evidence are unavailing for several reasons.

* * *

Conclusion

The plain language of article VII, section 6(a), permits every owner of Florida real property to apply for and receive ad valorem tax relief where it is sufficiently demonstrated that the owner has maintained on that property the permanent residence of another legally or naturally dependent on the owner. We therefore affirm the decision of the Third District in *Andonie* that holds as much. We conclude that here the Property Appraiser failed to sufficiently preserve for appellate review any argument regarding the sufficiency of the evidence introduced in the circuit court below, and the record here sufficiently demonstrates that the Taxpayers maintained on their Florida property the permanent residence of their minor children, each of whom is legally and naturally dependent on the Taxpayers. We emphasize that the result we reach in this case is dependent on the fact that it was demonstrated that the property is being used as the permanent residence of the owners' dependent, minor children, and the evidence establishes that the minor children for whom the permanent residence was maintained have no impediment, legal or otherwise, to residing permanently on the property in accordance with their parents' intent. We therefore affirm the decision of the Third District in *Andonie* to the extent it is consistent with our holding here today.

It is so ordered.

POLSTON, C.J., and PARIENTE, LEWIS, QUINCE, CANADY, LABARGA, and PERRY, JJ., concur.

(3) "Not more than one exemption shall be allowed any individual or family unit or with respect to any residential unit." Fla. Const. art. VII, § (6)(b)

Wells v. Haldeos

48 So. 3d 85 (Fla. 2d Dist. Ct. App. 2010)

WHATLEY, Judge.

Mike Wells, as the Property Appraiser of Pasco County, appeals a final judgment finding that James Haldeos was entitled to receive a homestead tax exemption on his property. Mr. Haldeos has owned and permanently resided on property located in Pasco County since 2005. Mr. Haldeos's wife, Rosa Accomando, with whom he has been separated since 2003, owns and permanently resides on property in the state of New York, and she receives a residency-based property tax exemption in New York. Because his wife receives this property tax exemption in New York, the Property Appraiser denied Mr. Haldeos a homestead exemption based on his position that a married couple cannot receive more than one homestead exemption.

Florida's homestead exemption derives from Article VII, Section 6(a) of the Florida Constitution, which provides that a homestead exemption extends to "[e]very person who has the legal or equitable title to real estate and maintains thereon the permanent residence of the owner, or another legally or naturally dependent upon the owner." However, section 6(b) directs that "[n]ot more than one exemption shall be allowed any individual or family unit or with respect to any residential unit." Art. VII, § 6(b), Fla. Const. (emphasis added). The Property Appraiser contends that a married couple is a "family unit" and is therefore entitled to only one exemption. As noted by the trial court, there is no constitutional or statutory definition of "family unit," and there is no case law interpreting the term.

In the final judgment, the trial court noted that all of the material facts were stipulated to by the parties and were not in dispute. [Footnote omitted.] Mr. Haldeos and his wife have established two separate permanent residences in good faith. Mr. Haldeos has no financial connection with his wife and they do not provide benefits, income, or support to each other. He has a Florida driver's license and his vehicle is registered in Pasco County. At the hearing, the attorney for the Property Appraiser stated that

> we agree in this case that if there isn't an absolute [prohibition on married couples from receiving two homestead exemptions], this case would be the outlier that would surely be entitled to a homestead. We're not trying to say that they're trying to disprove factually a family unit, that there's any financial aspects involved, or that there is any relationship on-going because we have nothing to surmise that or nothing has been developed.

The trial court found that it would defy logic for two people "who have no contact with one another, who don't have any connections of a financial, emotional or any other way to call them a family unit." Based on this reasoning, the trial court ruled that Mr. Haldeos and his wife constitute separate "family units" and may obtain two separate homestead exemptions.

The Property Appraiser argues on appeal that this interpretation of the term "family unit" is contrary to the intent of section 196.031(5), Florida Statutes (2009), which provides as follows:

> A person who is receiving or claiming the benefit of an ad valorem tax exemption or a tax credit in another state where permanent residency is required as a basis for the granting of that ad valorem tax exemption or tax credit is not entitled to the homestead exemption provided by this section.

We do not agree that the trial court's ruling is at odds with section 196.031(5), as the statute clearly prohibits an individual from receiving two residency-based tax credits. If the legislature had intended, as the Property Appraiser suggests, to prohibit a married couple from receiving two such tax exemptions, it could have included married couples in the above language.

The Property Appraiser further argues that the statute must be strictly construed against the taxpayer where "the homestead exemption provides relief from an ad valorem tax." *DeQuervain v. Desguin,* 927 So.2d 232, 236 (Fla. 2d DCA 2006). While we agree with this premise, we note that "[w]here the statute's language is clear or unambiguous, courts need not employ principles of statutory construction to determine and effectuate legislative intent." *See Fla. Dep't of Children & Family Servs. v. P.E.,* 14 So.3d 228, 234 (Fla.2009). Section 196.031(5) clearly and unambiguously refers to a "person" and not a married couple or family unit.

Although there is no constitutional or statutory guidance on the issue at bar, the Florida Department of Revenue has enacted a rule instructing property appraisers that married couples may be considered separate "family units" in certain circumstances. Florida Administrative Code Rule 12D-7.007(7), provides as follows:

> If it is determined by the property appraiser that separate permanent residences and separate "family units" have been established by the husband and wife, and they are otherwise qualified, each may be granted homestead exemption from ad valorem taxation under Article VII, Section 6, 1968 State Constitution. The fact that both residences may be owned by both husband and wife as tenants by the entireties will not defeat the grant of homestead ad valorem tax exemption to the permanent residence of each.

In determining whether Mr. Haldeos was entitled to a homestead exemption, the Property Appraiser was required to follow rule 12D-7.007(7): "The Department of Revenue shall prescribe reasonable rules and regulations for the assessing and collecting of taxes, and such rules and regulations shall be followed by the property appraisers, tax collectors, clerks of the circuit court, and value adjustment boards." § 195.027(1), Fla. Stat. (2009).

In a case involving the protection of a homestead from a judgment, the Fourth District held that when a married couple is separated, the husband can claim a homestead exemption for a residence in which he resides and owns, even though he still owns a home with his estranged wife for which they claim a homestead tax exemption. *Law v. Law,* 738 So.2d 522, 524 (Fla. 4th DCA 1999). In that case, the argument was made that the husband's home could not be homestead because the home he owned with his wife was, as a matter of law, his homestead, and a person cannot have two homesteads. *Id.* The Fourth District held:

> We see nothing inconsistent with our public policy if we extend a homestead exemption to each of two people who are married, but legitimately live apart in separate residences, if they otherwise meet the requirements of the exemption. When we say "legitimately" we mean that there is no "fraudulent or otherwise egregious act" by the beneficiary of the homestead exemption.

Id. at 525.

The court agreed that the husband could not have two homesteads and that a husband and wife in an intact marriage could not have two homesteads. However, the court held that the husband's homestead could be different from the wife's homestead "where their separation was bonafide," and it was the intent of the husband to live in his separate home. *Id.; see generally Judd v. Schooley,* 158 So.2d 514, 517 (Fla.1963) (holding that the wife could claim a permanent home in Florida and receive a homestead exemption even though her husband was legally domiciled in another state).

Although opinions of the Florida Attorney General are not binding on this court, we note that they have favored the granting of two separate homestead exemptions to a husband and wife where they establish separate permanent residences. 75 Op. Att'y Gen. 146 (1975); 05 Op. Att'y Gen. 60 (2005).

The Property Appraiser urges that if married couples can be considered separate "family units" in these circumstances, such a result would make his job in reviewing homestead exemptions virtually administratively unworkable, because no property appraiser will have the staff and available resources to verify whether a married couple is, in fact, maintaining two separate permanent residences. While we recognize that property appraisers will be required to review the financial information of separated couples in these unique circumstances, we note that the person claiming the homestead exemption has the burden of proving that he or she qualifies for such. *Schooley v. Judd,* 149 So.2d 587, 590 (Fla. 2d DCA 1963), *reversed on other grounds,* 158 So.2d 514 (Fla.1963).

Accordingly, we conclude that in the unique circumstances presented in this case, where the husband and wife have established two separate permanent residences in good faith and have no financial connection with and do not provide benefits, income, or support to each other, each may be granted a homestead exemption if they otherwise qualify.

Affirmed.

SILBERMAN, J., Concurs.

KELLY, J., Concurs in result only.

(4) "By general law and subject to conditions and limitations specified therein, the Legislature may provide ad valorem tax relief equal to the total amount or a portion of the ad valorem tax otherwise owed on homestead property to: (1) The surviving spouse of a veteran who died from service-connected causes while on active duty as a member of the United States Armed Forces. . . ." Fla. Const. art. VII, § (6)(f)

Department of Revenue v. Bell

290 So. 3d 1060 (Fla. 2d Dist. Ct. App. 2020)

CASANUEVA, Judge.

This appeal presents the issue of whether section 196.081(4), Florida Statutes (2013), enacted to implement article VII, section 6(f)(1), of the Florida Constitution, is constitutional. The trial court granted final summary judgment in favor of the plaintiff, Teri Ann Bell, concluding that the permanent residency requirement set forth in section 196.081(4) is invalid and unenforceable because that "substantive requirement" materially limited the class of persons eligible for the benefit provided by the Florida Constitution. We agree and therefore affirm the final summary judgment.

I. Facts

The parties agree upon the material facts. Ms. Bell is an un-remarried widow who owns and resides on real property located in Hillsborough County, Florida. She was married to a member of the United States Army who was killed in action in Iraq in March of 2007.

In 2013, Ms. Bell filed her application to receive the ad valorem tax relief provided for in article VII, section 6(f)(1), of the Florida Constitution and implemented by section 196.081(4). Her application for the tax exemption was denied by the Hillsborough County Property Appraiser solely on the basis that Ms. Bell's husband was not a Florida resident as of January 1, 2007, the year he was killed in action, as required by the language of the implementing statute. After administrative appeals provided no relief, Ms. Bell commenced the instant action.

Relevant Provisions

The focus of this appeal is the interplay between a constitutional provision, article VII, section 6(f)(1), and a legislative enactment intended to implement the constitutional provision, section 196.081(4). First, in 2012, the citizens of this State voted to add a provision to the Florida Constitution, article VII, section 6(f)(1), which provides:

(f) By general law and subject to conditions and limitations specified therein, the Legislature may provide ad valorem tax relief equal to the total amount or a portion of the ad valorem tax otherwise owed on homestead property to:

(1) The surviving spouse of a veteran who died from service-connected causes while on active duty as a member of the United States Armed Forces.

The Florida Legislature then amended section 196.081 in an effort to implement the new constitutional provision. *See* ch. 2012-54, Laws of Fla. Section 196.081 provides, in pertinent part:

(4) Any real estate that is owned and used as a homestead by the surviving spouse of a veteran who died from service-connected causes while on active duty as a member of the United States Armed Forces and for whom a letter from the United States Government or United States Department of Veterans Affairs or its predecessor has been issued certifying that the veteran who died from service-connected causes while on active duty is exempt from taxation if the veteran was a permanent resident of this state on January 1 of the year in which the veteran died.

1In this case, we consider whether section 196.081(4) violates "the express pronouncements of [the supreme] court that '[e]xpress or implied provisions of the Constitution cannot be altered, contracted or enlarged by legislative enactments.'" *Sparkman v. State*, 58 So. 2d 431, 432 (Fla. 1952) (*quoting State v. Butler*, 69 So. 771, 777 (Fla. 1915)).

II. Discussion

Because the issue before this court is one of constitutional interpretation and application, our review of the circuit court's constitutional determination is de novo. *See Zingale v. Powell*, 885 So. 2d 277, 280 (Fla. 2004). "[T]he polestar of constitutional construction is voter intent. 'We are obligated to give effect to [the] language [of a Constitutional amendment] according to its meaning and what the people must have understood it to mean when they approved it.'" *Benjamin v. Tandem Healthcare, Inc.*, 998 So. 2d 566, 570 (Fla. 2008) (second and third alterations in original) (citation omitted) (quoting *City of St. Petersburg v. Briley, Wild & Assocs., Inc.*, 239 So. 2d 817, 822 (Fla. 1970)). And "[w]here the language of the Constitution 'is clear, unambiguous, and addresses the matter in issue, then it must be enforced as written,' as the 'constitutional language must be allowed to "speak for itself."'" *Israel v. Desantis*, 269 So. 3d 491, 495 (Fla. 2019) (quoting *Fla. Soc'y of Ophthalmology v. Fla. Optometric Ass'n*, 489 So. 2d 1118, 1119 (Fla. 1986)); *see also Pleus v. Crist*, 14 So. 3d 941, 944 (Fla. 2009) ("If that language is clear, unambiguous, and addresses the matter in issue, then it must be enforced as written." (quoting *Lawnwood Med. Ctr., Inc. v. Seeger*, 990 So. 2d 503, 511 (Fla. 2008))). Thus, we begin our analysis with the plain language of the applicable constitutional provision, article VII, section 6(f)(1), of the Florida Constitution. *See Israel*, 269 So. 3d at 495; *see also Benjamin*, 998 So. 2d at 570 ("In interpreting a constitutional amendment, we begin with the amendment's plain language"); *Oliva v. Fla. Wildlife Fed'n, Inc.*, 281 So. 3d 531, 537 (Fla. 1st DCA 2019).

Article VII, Section 6(f)(1)

The plain language of article VII, section 6(f), grants the legislature the authority and power pursuant to "general law and subject to conditions and limitations specified therein" to "provide ad valorem tax relief equal to the total amount or a portion of the ad valorem tax otherwise owed on homestead property." Subsection (1) of article VII, section 6(f), identifies the class of individuals who may receive the tax relief as follows: "The surviving spouse of a veteran who died from service-connected causes while on active duty as a member of the United States Armed Forces."

We conclude and hold that the plain text of the constitutional provision is clear and that it unambiguously identifies the relevant class of beneficiaries. The language of article VII, section 6(f)(1), speaks for itself and provides that, to receive the benefit, the following must be established:

1. the applicant is a surviving spouse;

2. the applicant's deceased spouse was a member of the United States Armed Forces; and

3. the decedent spouse died from service-connected causes while on active duty as a member of the United States Armed Forces.

The provision's plain text grants the legislature the authority to enact legislation to address the matter of the amount of ad valorem tax relief to be afforded the surviving spouse, and the legislature is also "permitted to enact laws regulating 'the manner' of establishing the right to the" tax relief. *Garcia v. Andonie*, 101 So. 3d 339, 345 (Fla. 2012); *see also Sparkman*, 58 So. 2d at 432.

In light of this unambiguous language, we have no need to employ the canons of construction. *See Endsley v. Broward County*, 189 So. 3d 938, 941 (Fla. 4th DCA 2016). We simply consider whether the legislative enactment intended to implement this constitutional provision is within the authority granted to the legislature, or whether the statute impermissibly alters, contracts, or enlarges the constitutional provision. *See Sparkman*, 58 So. 2d at 432.

Section 196.081(4)

For the narrow issue presented in this appeal, the pertinent statutory language is the permanent residency requirement. Specifically, the critical statutory language contains the following requirements:

1. the deceased veteran was a permanent resident of the State of Florida; and

2. the veteran's residency status existed on January 1 of the year of the veteran's death.

See § 196.081(4). To resolve the dispute at issue in this case, the statute's residency requirements must be measured against the constitutional provision.

Measurement

The class of beneficiaries established by the plain text of article VII, section 6(f)(1), is the surviving spouse of a veteran who died from service-connected causes while on active duty. The text of the constitutional provision does not limit this benefit to surviving spouses whose spouse was a Florida resident on January 1 of the year of death. Clearly, however, the statutory language of section 196.081(4) does contain such a limit. The practical operation and effect of the statutory provision is to substantively limit and narrow the class of individuals eligible for the tax relief under the plain language of the constitutional provision.

Our supreme court confronted a similar provision in *Garcia*, 101 So. 3d at 344-45. There, the court held that the statutory provision limiting the constitutional class eligible to receive a benefit was invalid and unenforceable. *Id.* at 345. The court noted: "We have held that although the Legislature is permitted to enact laws regulating 'the manner' of establishing the right to the constitutional homestead tax exemption, it cannot substantively alter or materially limit the class of individuals entitled to the exemption under the plain language of the constitution." *Id.*

Here, we conclude that the transgression is the same. While the language of article VII, section (6)(f), grants the legislature authority to enact legislation to implement the manner of establishing the right to, and the amount of, the tax relief, the legislature cannot substantively alter or materially limit the class of individuals eligible for the exemption under the plain language of the constitution. *See Garcia*, 101 So. 3d at 345. ("Because the plain language of article VII, section 6(a), of the Florida Constitution permits an owner of Florida property to obtain the exemption based on the act of maintaining the permanent residence of his or her natural or legal dependents on the property — irrespective of the owner's citizenship or place of residence, requirements that were removed from the Constitution — the additional 'and who resides thereon' requirement imposed by section 196.031(1) substantively limits and narrows the class of property owners and taxpayers eligible for the ad valorem tax exemption under the plain language of the Florida Constitution."). The class of persons eligible under the statute is in conflict with the class eligible under the plain language of the constitutional provision, and thus the statutory provision is invalid and unenforceable.

The people of this state said that, to be eligible for this benefit, the recipient must be the surviving spouse of a veteran who died from service-connected causes while on active duty as a member of the United States Armed Forces. It is undisputed that Ms. Bell meets the requirements set forth in the constitutional provision, and the legislature was without authority to divest her of that benefit by narrowing the class of individuals eligible for the tax relief.

III. Conclusion

Having determined that section 196.081(4) has substantively and materially limited the class of individuals eligible for tax relief as set forth in article VII, section(6)(f)(1), we hold that the statutory provision is invalid and unenforceable, and we affirm the final summary judgment.

Affirmed.

NORTHCUTT and BADALAMENTI, JJ., Concur.

Fla. Const. art. VII, § 4

Taxation; assessments. —

* * *

(d) All persons entitled to a homestead exemption under Section 6 of this Article shall have their homestead assessed at just value as of January 1 of the year following the effective date of this amendment. This assessment shall change only as provided in this subsection.

(1) Assessments subject to this subsection shall be changed annually on January 1st of each year; but those changes in assessments shall not exceed the lower of the following:

a. Three percent (3%) of the assessment for the prior year.

b. The percent change in the Consumer Price Index for all urban consumers, U.S. City Average, all items 1967 = 100, or successor reports for the preceding calendar year as initially reported by the United States Department of Labor, Bureau of Labor Statistics.

(2) No assessment shall exceed just value.

(3) After any change of ownership, as provided by general law, homestead property shall be assessed at just value as of January 1 of the following year, unless the provisions of paragraph (8) apply. Thereafter, the homestead shall be assessed as provided in this subsection.

(4) New homestead property shall be assessed at just value as of January 1st of the year following the establishment of the homestead, unless the provisions of paragraph (8) apply. That assessment shall only change as provided in this subsection.

(5) Changes, additions, reductions, or improvements to homestead property shall be assessed as provided for by general law; provided, however, after the adjustment for any change, addition, reduction, or improvement, the property shall be assessed as provided in this subsection.

(6) In the event of a termination of homestead status, the property shall be assessed as provided by general law.

(7) The provisions of this amendment are severable. If any of the provisions of this amendment shall be held unconstitutional by any court of competent jurisdiction, the decision of such court shall not affect or impair any remaining provisions of this amendment.

* * *

Article VII, § 4 of the Florida Constitution sets forth the guidelines for the taxation of homesteads. One of the polestar provisions in art. VII, § 4 is the "Save Our Homes" tax cap, which limits the amount of the tax assessor's annual assessments to no more than 3% of the previous year's assessment. The primary purpose of this amendment is to prevent homeowners who are on a fixed income from losing their homes due to the rising value of property.[55]

Smith v. Krosschell

937 So. 2d 658 (Fla. 2006)

LEWIS, C.J.

We have for review the decision in *Smith v. Krosschell,* 892 So.2d 1145 (Fla. 2d DCA 2005), in which the Second District Court of Appeal has certified conflict with the decision of the Third District Court of Appeal in *Robbins v. Kornfield,* 834 So.2d 955 (Fla. 3d DCA 2003). We have jurisdiction. *See* art. V, § 3(b)(4), Fla. Const. For the reasons expressed below, we quash the decision in *Krosschell* and remand for further proceedings consistent with this opinion.

Facts And Proceedings Below

In 2000, Krosschell received homestead exemption status for the real property which has generated this litigation. During March of that year, a field inspection of the real property was conducted to verify the information in the records of the property appraiser (Smith). The property appraisal records were subsequently updated to reflect the inspection, but at that time a data entry error occurred. Although Krosschell's home on the real property encompassed 3,746 square feet of base living area, when the data was entered to update the records, the square foot base living area of the home was entered as zero (0). In effect, this data entry error effectively deleted Krosschell's entire dwelling from the property records as though the property was raw land without any improvements. Thus, due to this data error, Krosschell's property was undervalued by $100,100, and this valuation produced by the erroneous data was certified on the 2000 tax roll.

After the error was discovered, Smith issued a certificate of correction in an attempt to correct the error, but the statutory time requirements for notice to Krosschell to afford time for a challenge to the assessed value before the Value Adjustment Board (Board) could not be satisfied for the year 2000. The Board had already conducted proceedings for 2000, and Krosschell would have been unable to challenge the correct assessment until the Board convened again in 2001. Therefore, the original assessed value of $188,700 (i.e., the assessed value which did not include Krosschell's house) was reinstated for the year 2000.

---

55. *See Smith v. Welton,* 729 So. 2d 371 (Fla. 1999).

In August 2001, Krosschell received a 2001 notice of proposed property taxes based on the correct data, which included the correct assessed value of $288,800 for the year 2000 (i.e., the assessment of Krosschell's property that included the previously eliminated improvement), and an assessed value of $297,400 for 2001. Krosschell appealed these values, but the Board concluded that Smith had acted properly in correcting the data and assessing the value of the property.

Krosschell proceeded to file a complaint in the circuit court. In a motion for summary judgment, he claimed that there had been a fifty-eight percent increase in the 2001 assessment over the 2000 assessment which violated the "Save Our Homes" tax cap in the Florida Constitution, a provision which permits increases of annual assessments of homesteaded property to be no more than three percent of the previous year's assessment. He asserted this position even though the initial 2000 assessment of his property was based on an error which excluded the existing structure. Krosschell further contended that section 197.122(1) of the Florida Statutes (2000), which authorized a property appraiser to correct "acts of omission or commission" at any time, was inapplicable in the instant proceeding, and the statute that did apply, section 193.155 of the Florida Statutes (2000), did not allow for correction of the data entry error that occurred here.

Smith also filed a motion for summary judgment in which he argued that the erroneous assessment of Krosschell's property was a mistake of fact resulting from the data entry error that could be corrected. The circuit court granted summary judgment in favor of Krosschell, denied Smith's motion, and entered judgment which required Smith to appraise Krosschell's property at $188,700 for the year 2000 (i.e., the assessment value based on the data error without the existing home), concluding that this amount, even though based on a data entry error, established the base year just valuation for the property.

The Second District affirmed the summary judgment and concluded that Smith had no statutory authority on these facts to make a retroactive change in the base year assessment of Krosschell's homestead. *See Krosschell*, 892 So.2d at 1146. In support of its holding, the district court relied on *Smith v. Welton*, 729 So.2d 371 (Fla.1999), in which this Court held that on the facts presented there section 193.155(8)(a) of the Florida Statutes did not provide property appraisers the authority to make a retroactive change in the base year assessment of homesteaded property. *See Krosschell*, 892 So.2d at 1146. The Second District recognized that this statutory section had been amended in 2001 to allow property appraisers to make such a change; however, the court determined that the amendment applied only prospectively because there was no indication of legislative intent that it be applied retroactively. *See id.* at 1146–47. Concluding that all ambiguities in tax statutes are to be resolved in favor of the taxpayer, the Second District held that the 2000 version of the statute applied in the present case, and, therefore, Smith could not change the original assessed value of Krosschell's property. *See id.* at 1147.

The Second District certified direct conflict with *Robbins v. Kornfield*, 834 So.2d 955 (Fla. 3d DCA 2003), in which the Third District held that the same 2001 amendment to section 193.155 authorized property appraisers to retroactively correct errors in the calculation of the base year just value assessment of a property. *See Kornfield*, 834 So.2d at 957. This Court received oral argument in this case and subsequently ordered supplemental briefing from the parties to specifically address section 197.122 of the Florida Statutes, the statute that Krosschell claimed in his motion for summary judgment to be inapplicable in the present controversy.

Analysis

After receiving supplemental briefing from the parties, we conclude that it is unnecessary in the instant case to resolve the issue of whether the 2001 amendment to section 193.155 applies retroactively. This conclusion is based on our determination that the decisions in *Krosschell* and *Kornfield* involve consideration of errors that are fundamentally different, and section 193.155(8)(a) of the Florida Statutes does not apply to the data entry error that occurred in the instant case.

A review of the conflict case, *Kornfield,* and the decision of this Court in *Smith v. Welton,* each of which interprets and applies section 193.155(8)(a), demonstrates that in each of these cases, a property appraiser underassessed some aspect of a homesteaded property. In *Kornfield,* the appraiser failed to consider a 1,610 square foot addition that had been made to the homesteaded property, and this addition escaped taxation for nine years. *See* 834 So.2d at 956. In *Smith,* a property appraiser mistakenly underassessed 15,000 square feet of improvements to a 19,000 square foot building that served as a homestead. *See* 729 So.2d at 371–72. Thus, in each of these cases, the appraiser made an error in judgment when evaluating the property. On the other hand, in the instant case there has been no allegation that Smith made an error in judgment when he evaluated Krosschell's property; instead, a purely clerical data entry error occurred, and the square footage of Krosschell's base living area was accidentally eliminated and entered as zero.

Neither this Court nor any district court has utilized section 193.155(1) to address the correction of an administrative or clerical mistake such as a data entry error which totally eliminates the improvements on real property which are in place and previously in the records. Rather, the correction of mathematical, administrative, or clerical error such as this has been addressed under section 197.122(1) of the Florida Statutes or one of its statutory predecessors. This statutory provision provides, in pertinent part:

> No act of omission or commission on the part of any property appraiser . . . shall operate to defeat the payment of taxes; but *any acts of omission or commission may be corrected at any time by the officer or party responsible for them* in like manner as provided by law for performing acts in the first place, and when so corrected they shall be construed as valid ab initio and

shall in no way affect any process by law for the enforcement of the collection of any tax.

§ 197.122(1), Fla. Stat. (2005) (emphasis supplied). In the decision most similar to the instant case, a key-punch operator incorrectly entered the assessed value of a property as $260,000 rather than the correctly assessed value of $775,000. *See Robbins v. First Nat'l Bank of South Miami*, 651 So.2d 184, 184–85 (Fla. 3d DCA 1995). The Third District concluded that this error was correctable pursuant to section 197.122(1). *See id.* at 185.

In 1978, the First District concluded that a computer error that omitted a zero in the property owner's tax bill was correctable under a statutory predecessor to section 197.122(1). *See Straughn v. Thompson*, 354 So.2d 948, 949 (Fla. 1st DCA 1978); *see also Allen v. Dickinson*, 223 So.2d 310, 310 (Fla.1969) (holding that acts of omission or commission of "the purely ministerial or administrative type" are correctable under a statutory predecessor to section 197.122(1)); *McNeil Barcelona Assocs., Ltd. v. Daniel*, 486 So.2d 628, 629 (Fla. 2d DCA 1986) (multiplication of square footage by improper factor to obtain assessment value was correctable under a statutory predecessor to section 197.122(1)). We conclude that the computer data entry error that occurred in the instant case is more comparable to the clerical and mathematical errors that occurred in *Robbins, Straughn,* and *McNeil Barcelona* than the under-assessments resulting from the errors in evaluation or judgment that occurred in *Kornfield* and *Welton.* Accordingly, we conclude that section 197.122(1), not 193.155(8)(a), applies to the error that occurred in the instant case, and pursuant to this statute, this error "may be corrected at any time." § 197.122(1), Fla. Stat. (2005).

To the extent Krosschell claims that permitting the correction of Smith's clerical error pursuant to section 197.122(1) violates the "Save Our Homes" cap of the Florida Constitution, the argument is without merit. Article VII, section 6, of the Florida Constitution affords a homestead tax exemption to individuals who maintain a permanent residence on real estate to which they hold legal or equitable title. *See* art. VII, § 6, Fla. Const. In fact, elimination of the entire residence as occurred here in error may even impact the homestead classification status of the property if correct. In 1992, Florida voters approved a constitutional amendment to limit the amount that the assessed value of a homesteaded property may be increased in any given year. The "Save Our Homes" amendment provides, in pertinent part:

(c) All persons entitled to a homestead exemption under Section 6 of this Article shall have their homestead assessed at just value as of January 1 of the year following the effective date of this amendment. This assessment shall change only as provided herein.

(1) Assessments subject to this provision shall be changed annually on January 1st of each year; but those changes in assessments shall not exceed the lower of the following:

a. Three percent (3%) of the assessment for the prior year.

590   6 · TAXATION AND FINANCE

b. The percent change in the Consumer Price Index for all urban consumers, U.S. City Average, all items 1967 = 100, or successor reports for the preceding calendar year as initially reported by the United States Department of Labor, Bureau of Labor Statistics.

Art. VII, § 4(c), Fla. Const. The purpose of this amendment "is to encourage the preservation of homestead property in the face of ever increasing opportunities for real estate development, and rising property values and assessments." *Zingale v. Powell,* 885 So.2d 277, 281 (Fla.2004).

We have previously held that "fair market value and just valuation should be declared legally synonymous," and that fair market value "is the amount a purchaser willing but not obliged to buy, would pay to one willing but not obliged to sell." *Walter v. Schuler,* 176 So.2d 81, 85–86 (Fla.1965) (internal quotation marks omitted). Thus, under our precedent, an initial value assessment based on a clear and admitted data entry error which eliminates all improvements on the property not only would generate issues of homestead classification status but is not a "just value" assessment and it does not reflect the "fair market value" of the property. The "Save Our Homes" cap on annual assessments applies to homestead property that has been assessed at just value, and the cap is not implicated where there has been a data entry error which has eliminated all improvements from the records. Therefore, a clerical mistake such as the computer data entry error that occurred here produces a base year assessment that does not under these circumstances represent a "fair market value" of the homesteaded property, and the Save Our Homes cap does not forever "lock in" the erroneous data and resulting assessment, thereby allowing property owners to forever pay artificially reduced taxes as long as they own the property. Instead, we conclude that section 197.122(1) applies to correct this error, thereby allowing the appraiser to correct the erroneous data previously entered and erroneously changed to establish forever a "true just value" upon which the cap can be applied to tax increases in future years.

Were we to hold otherwise, manifestly unfair results would occur. Under Krosschell's argument, if the value of a $3 million homestead was, due to a data entry error of removing all improvements from the records, wrongly assessed at $1.00 in its base year, the next year the homestead could be assessed at no more that [*sic*] $1.03, then $1.06 the following year, and so on in perpetuity. Under such an interpretation, some homeowners would obtain an erroneous permanent windfall on their homestead property taxes, even if admittedly based on obvious data entry errors, while other homeowners would bear a comparatively disproportionate share of the tax burden solely because their homesteads had been assessed based on correct data. The "Save Our Homes" Amendment was never designed or intended to allow a homestead owner to perpetuate an admitted data error and subvert the payment of property taxes forever. The law cannot encourage and advance consequences based on an admitted and clear computer entry error. As we once stated in an earlier case, "[j]ustice may be 'blind' but it is not stupid," *see Korash v. Mills,* 263 So.2d 579, 582 (Fla.1972), and we cannot adopt a statutory interpretation that would produce such an absurd and unfair result. *See Warner v. City of Boca Raton,* 887 So.2d 1023, 1033 n. 9 (Fla.2004) (noting that statutory provisions should not be construed in a manner that would lead to an absurd result). Our interpretation of section 197.122(1) comports with the basic purpose of taxation: "That all taxpayers share in proportion to their assessments, the support of their government and the protection and services afforded to their property and to themselves, and that none bears an added or unfair burden by reason of other taxpayers not paying their just share." *Korash,* 263 So.2d at 582.

In conclusion, we hold that section 197.122(1), rather than section 193.155(8)(a), applies to correct the computer data entry error which occurred in the instant case and, pursuant to that subsection, Smith possesses the statutory authority to correct the erroneous data and result on the assessment of Krosschell's property "at any time." § 197.122(1), Fla. Stat. (2005). Accordingly, we quash *Krosschell* and remand this case to the district court for further consideration consistent with this opinion.

It is so ordered.

WELLS, ANSTEAD, PARIENTE, QUINCE, CANTERO, and BELL, JJ., concur.

Zingale v. Powell

885 So. 2d 277 (Fla. 2004)

PARIENTE, C.J.

In this case, we construe article VII, section 4(c) of the Florida Constitution, known as the "Save Our Homes" amendment, which limits the annual change in property tax assessments on homestead exempt property to three percent of the previous assessment or the change in the Consumer Price Index, whichever is less. We must decide whether a homeowner qualifies for the provision's limit on increases in property tax assessments immediately upon meeting the ownership and residency requirements for a homestead exemption, or instead only upon being granted the homestead exemption. We conclude that the cap is tied to the grant of a homestead exemption, and therefore quash the decision below, in which the Fourth District Court of Appeal reached a contrary conclusion. *See Powell v. Markham,* 847 So.2d 1105, 1106 (Fla. 4th DCA 2003).[1]

I. Facts and Procedural History

Robert and Ann Powell purchased a home in Fort Lauderdale in 1990. They have continuously used the home as their primary residence since its purchase, but did not apply for a homestead exemption until September 2001, after the Broward County Property Appraiser notified them of an increase of almost $40,000 in their ad valorem property taxes. The steep rise in the Powells' property taxes resulted from a correspondingly large increase in the assessed value of their home, from

---

1. We have jurisdiction to review any decision in which a district court expressly construes a provision of the state or federal constitution. *See* art. V, § 3(b)(3), Fla. Const.

$2.3 million to almost $3.9 million. In addition to filing for a homestead exemption in 2001, the Powells also sought to have the Save Our Homes cap applied to limit the increase in their assessment from 2000 to 2001. Their homestead exemption application was approved for 2001, but the property appraiser did not reduce the 2001 assessment to the limits of the Save Our Homes cap for that year. The Powells subsequently filed suit to challenge Broward County's refusal to apply the Save Our Homes cap to the increase in the assessed value of their home from 2000 to 2001.[2] The trial court granted judgment on the pleadings in favor of the defendants. The trial court concluded that "[b]ecause the Powells' property did not 'receive' the Homestead Exemption until 2001, that is their base year, one year after which commences their entitlement to the assessment limitations of the Constitution." The Powells appealed.

The Fourth District reversed the trial court order, concluding that the cap applied to homeowners who qualified for the exemption, not just to those who applied for it. Therefore, the Fourth District held that the cap applied to the increase in the assessed value of the Powells' home from 2000 to 2001. *See Powell*, 847 So.2d at 1106–07. In dissent, Judge Stone concluded that because the Powells had not timely applied for a homestead exemption for 2000, they were not entitled to application of the cap on increases in value based on an assessment for 2000. *See id.* at 1107 (Stone, J., dissenting). Zingale, Executive Director of the State Department of Revenue, seeks review of the Fourth District's decision.

II. Analysis

Like the Fourth District before us, we must determine the meaning of the language in article VII, section 4(c) of the Florida Constitution. This provision took its place in the Florida Constitution after the voters of this State approved a citizens' initiative on November 3, 1992.[3] Although we take into consideration the district court's analysis on the issue, constitutional interpretation, like statutory interpretation, is performed *de novo. Cf. BellSouth Telecomm., Inc. v. Meeks*, 863 So.2d 287, 289 (Fla.2003) ("Statutory interpretation is a question of law subject to *de novo* review.")

Article VII, section 4(c) provides:

(c) All persons entitled to a homestead exemption under Section 6 of this Article shall have their homestead assessed at just value as of January 1 of

---

2. Pursuant to the requirements for parties in a tax suit under section 194.181, Florida Statutes (2001), the Powells named as defendants William Markham, the Broward County Property Appraiser, Judith M. Fink, Director of the Broward County Revenue Collection Division, and James A. Zingale, Executive Director of the Florida Department of Revenue.

3. The initiative was placed on the ballot pursuant to the provisions of article XI, section 3, Florida Constitution, for constitutional amendments. The organization that drafted, circulated, and promoted the petition was named "Save Our Homes, Inc." *See Florida League of Cities v. Smith*, 607 So.2d 397, 400 n. 6 (Fla.1992); *In re Advisory Opinion to Attorney General-Homestead Valuation Limitation*, 581 So.2d 586, 587 (Fla.1991).

the year following the effective date of this amendment. This assessment shall change only as provided herein.

(1) Assessments subject to this provision shall be changed annually on January 1st of each year; but those changes in assessments shall not exceed the lower of the following:

a. Three percent (3%) of the assessment for the prior year.

b. The percent change in the Consumer Price Index for all urban consumers, U.S. City Average, all items 1967 = 100, or successor reports for the preceding calendar year as initially reported by the United States Department of Labor, Bureau of Labor Statistics.

(2) No assessment shall exceed just value.

(3) After any change of ownership, as provided by general law, homestead property shall be assessed at just value as of January 1 of the following year. Thereafter, the homestead shall be assessed as provided herein.

(4) New homestead property shall be assessed at just value as of January 1st of the year following the establishment of the homestead. That assessment shall only change as provided herein.

(5) Changes, additions, reductions, or improvements to homestead property shall be assessed as provided for by general law; provided, however, after the adjustment for any change, addition, reduction, or improvement, the property shall be assessed as provided herein.

(6) In the event of a termination of homestead status, the property shall be assessed as provided by general law.

(7) The provisions of this amendment are severable. If any of the provisions of this amendment shall be held unconstitutional by any court of competent jurisdiction, the decision of such court shall not affect or impair any remaining provisions of this amendment.

Article VII, section 6, which is referred to in subsection 4(c), provides in pertinent part:

(a) Every person who has the legal or equitable title to real estate and maintains thereon the permanent residence of the owner, or another legally or naturally dependent upon the owner, shall be exempt from taxation thereon, except assessments for special benefits, up to the assessed valuation of five thousand dollars, upon establishment of right thereto in the manner prescribed by law.[4]

---

4. Article VII, subsection 6(d) authorizes an increase of the homestead exemption to $25,000 for 1982 and subsequent years.

Both constitutional provisions reduce the tax burden on homestead property. The First District Court of Appeal has succinctly stated:

> The purpose of the amendment is to encourage the preservation of homestead property in the face of ever increasing opportunities for real estate development, and rising property values and assessments. The amendment supports the public policy of this state favoring preservation of homesteads. Similar policy considerations are the basis for the constitutional provisions relating to homestead tax exemption (Article VII, Section 6, Florida Constitution), exemption from forced sale (Article X, Section 4(a), Florida Constitution), and the inheritance and alienation of homestead (Article X, Section 4(c), Florida Constitution).

Smith v. Welton, 710 So.2d 135, 137 (Fla. 1st DCA 1998) (footnote omitted); *see also* Op. Att'y Gen. Fla. 02–28 (2002).

Zingale and the county property appraisers appearing as amici in this case assert that a homeowner's entitlement to the benefits of the cap in article VII, section 4(c) is dependent upon establishing the right to a homestead exemption under article VII, section 6 "in the manner prescribed by law," i.e., by timely application for a homestead exemption. In *Horne v. Markham,* 288 So.2d 196, 199 (Fla.1973), this Court held that article VII, section 6 does not create an absolute right to a homestead exemption but instead requires that taxpayers establish the right thereto by following the procedures required by law. As stated in *Horne* and still the case today, these procedures include a timely application under chapter 196, Florida Statutes. Zingale and his amici claim that without a requirement that a homeowner obtain a homestead exemption to qualify for the cap, the property appraiser cannot ascertain whether property is in fact homestead property and thus eligible for the limit on the increase in the assessed value of the homestead property.

The Powells contend that a homeowner becomes entitled to the benefits of the cap upon meeting the ownership and eligibility requirements for homestead status, and that article VII, section 4(c) does not require that the property be granted a homestead exemption in order to trigger the cap's protection. They maintain that the requirements in article VII, section 6 for establishing a homestead exemption do not apply to obtaining the benefit of the cap in article VII, section 4(c). They also assert that subsection 4(c)(4) supports this construction because it requires an assessment of new homestead property at just value for the "year following the establishment of the homestead," rather than the year following the establishment of the homestead *exemption.* Thus, according to the Powells, they are entitled to the benefits of the cap based upon demonstrating their eligibility to receive the homestead exemption rather than upon demonstrating that they have received the homestead exemption. However, Zingale asserts that "establishment of the homestead" in subsection 4(c)(4) in fact means successfully applying for the homestead exemption.

Our task in this case of constitutional interpretation follows principles parallel to those of statutory interpretation. *See Coastal Fla. Police Benev. Ass'n v. Williams,*

838 So.2d 543, 548 (Fla.2003) ("The rules which govern the construction of statutes are generally applicable to the construction of constitutional provisions."). In a recent case concerning construction of another constitutional provision enacted by referendum on a ballot initiative, we explained the principles to be applied when interpreting constitutional provisions:

> We agree with the petitioners that "[a]ny inquiry into the proper interpretation of a constitutional provision must begin with an examination of that provision's explicit language." *Florida Society of Ophthalmology v. Florida Optometric Assn.,* 489 So.2d 1118, 1119 (Fla.1986). Likewise, this Court endeavors to construe a constitutional provision consistent with the intent of the framers and the voters. In *Gray v. Bryant,* 125 So.2d 846, 852 (Fla.1960), this Court stated:

> The fundamental object to be sought in construing a constitutional provision is to *ascertain the intent of the framers* and the provision must be construed or interpreted in such manner as to *fulfill the intent of the people,* never to defeat it. Such a provision must never be construed in such manner as to make it possible for the will of the people to be frustrated or denied. (Emphasis added.)

> Moreover, in construing multiple constitutional provisions addressing a similar subject, the provisions "must be read in pari materia to ensure a consistent and logical meaning that gives effect to each provision." *Advisory Opinion to the Governor-1996 Amendment 5 (Everglades),* 706 So.2d 278, 281 (Fla.1997).

Caribbean Conservation Corp. v. Florida Fish & Wildlife Conservation Comm'n, 838 So.2d 492, 501 (Fla.2003) (footnote omitted).

We thus begin with the actual language used. The first paragraph of subsection 4(c) provides that "[a]ll persons *entitled* to a *homestead exemption . . .* shall have their homestead assessed at just value as of January 1 of the year following the effective date of this amendment." (Emphasis supplied.) In its decision below, the Fourth District, focusing on the word "entitled," concluded that persons who owned property eligible for a homestead exemption should receive the benefit of the cap. *See Powell,* 847 So.2d at 1106–07. The majority rejected Judge Stone's dissenting view that a timely application for a homestead exemption was necessary to establish entitlement to the benefits of the cap, concluding that the Powells were seeking the assessment cap, rather than a homestead exemption, for the year 2000. *See id.* at 1107.

We conclude that the Fourth District's focus on the word "entitled" in the first paragraph of subsection 4(c) is misplaced. Under the plain language of this provision, the entitlement to a baseline just value assessment applies solely to the initial assessment required by the provision. We have already determined that the initial year for the baseline assessment was January 1, 1994. *See Fuchs v. Wilkinson,* 630 So.2d 1044, 1045–46 (Fla.1994) ("[F]rom the plain reading of the amendment, January 1, 1994 (the year following the effective date of the amendment), is the date homestead property is to be 'assessed at just value.'"). Thus, the provision that the Powells and the Fourth District rely on is not applicable to them because they did not seek to invoke the baseline assessment of January 1, 1994. In fact, the Powells do not contend that January 1, 1994 is the date for the baseline assessment but rather claim that date as January 1, 2000, more than a year before they applied for a homestead exemption.

The Fourth District's resolution of the issue is also contrary to the implementing legislation for article VII, section 4(c). Section 193.155, Florida Statutes (2001), provides:

> Homestead property shall be assessed at just value as of January 1, 1994. Property receiving the homestead exemption after January 1, 1994, shall be assessed at just value as of January 1 of the year in which the property receives the exemption.

Section 193.155(6) specifies that "[o]nly property that receives a homestead exemption is subject to this section." Therefore, under the implementing statute, the initial baseline assessment would be in 2001, the year in which the Powells obtained the homestead exemption. Because the first paragraph of article VII, section 4(c) applies only to the initial, January 1, 1994, assessment, we reject the Powells' suggestion that the reference in section 193.155 to property that receives the homestead exemption after January 1, 1994, places the statute in conflict with the constitutional provision.

In fact, section 193.155 is consistent with another provision of the cap, article VII, section 4(c)(4), which provides that "new homestead property shall be assessed at just value as of January 1st of the year following the establishment of the homestead."[5] There is no definition in article VII, section 4(c) of "new homestead property"; however, since subsection 4(c)(3) deals with assessments following changes in ownership, it is logical to construe "new homestead property" as property newly receiving the homestead exemption, and "establishment of the homestead" as a successful application for the exemption independent of any ownership change. This construction would then allow homeowners who had not received a homestead exemption entitling them to the January 1, 1994, baseline assessment, or whose property did not previously qualify for an exemption, to obtain the baseline assessment upon receiving a homestead exemption.

This construction of the first paragraph of subsection 4(c), when considered in conjunction with the other provisions of article VII, section 4(c), allows every homeowner who receives a homestead exemption to receive the benefit of the cap with the only variation being when the baseline year is established. For those homeowners

---

5. Section 193.155(1) requires the baseline assessment as of January 1 of the year in which the property receives the exemption, while article IV, section 4(c)(4) requires the baseline assessment "as of January 1st of the year following the establishment of the homestead." In this case, Zingale acknowledges that the baseline assessment was on January 1, 2001, consistent with the statute, rather than January 1, 2002, the year following the grant of the homestead exemption. Therefore, we need not address the different baseline assessments in the constitutional provision and the statute.

whose property had already received a homestead exemption under article VII, section 6 as of the effective date of the amendment, the baseline year pursuant to the first paragraph of subsection 4(c) would be January 1, 1994. For property in which ownership has changed, subsection 4(c)(3) provides that homestead property would be assessed at a baseline the year following the change of ownership. Lastly, subsection 4(c)(4) allows any homeowner who obtains a homestead exemption to have a baseline assessment in the year following the "establishment" of the homestead.

Conversely, if article VII, section 4(c)(4) is construed to mean that "new homestead property" is established when the ownership and residency requirements are met without regard to a successful homestead application, there is no identifiable starting point for the cap in the case of a homeowner who had not obtained a homestead exemption before January 1, 1994. The Powells assert that the January 1, 2000, assessment is their baseline, but their position appears to rest solely on the fact that they are challenging the increased assessment for 2001 rather than on the inherent operation of subsection 4(c). Their interpretation thus relies more on the timing of their assertion of the right to the cap than on the starting point for their legal entitlement thereto.

Construing the reference in subsection 4(c)(4) to "new homestead property" as property newly obtaining a homestead exemption is also consistent with article VII, section 6, which conditions the exemption "upon establishment of the right thereto in the manner prescribed by law." *Horne*, 288 So.2d at 199 (quoting art. VII, §6, Fla. Const.). As Judge Stone observed below, section 196.011(1)(a), which implements the homestead exemption, requires a timely application, by March 1, to obtain the exemption for that year. The provision further specifies that failure to timely file results in waiver for that year. *See Powell*, 847 So.2d at 1107 (Stone, J., dissenting).

Although subsection 4(c) establishes a constitutional right to receive the benefit of the cap on increases in valuation, and section 6 establishes a constitutional right to an exemption of part of a property's value from taxation, both provisions are parts of a coordinated constitutional scheme relating to taxation and have as their underlying purpose the protection and preservation of homestead property.[6] Therefore, we conclude that subsection 4(c) and section 6 should be read *in pari materia* so that only those homeowners who have applied for and received the homestead exemption are entitled to the benefits of either constitutional provision. Under an *in pari materia* construction, a successful application for a homestead application is necessary both to obtain the exemption and to qualify for the cap.

---

6. The link between article VII, sections 4 and 6 is demonstrated not only by the reference to section 6 in subsection 4(c), but also by subsection 6(d), which provides that the increase in the homestead exemption "shall stand repealed on the effective date of any amendment to section 4 which provides for the assessment of homestead property at a specified percentage of its just value." Before the adoption of subsection 4(c), this Court held that the provision would not trigger the repealer in subsection 6(d). *See Florida League of Cities*, 607 So.2d at 401.

Additionally, this construction facilitates a logical, orderly scheme that is entirely consistent with the purpose of the amendment. Although taxpayers have a right to the constitutional cap, the right is not self-executing. Requiring a timely filing for a homestead exemption imposes only a slight burden on the taxpayer in comparison to the tax benefit received. At the same time, this requirement prevents substantial uncertainty in taxing authorities' annual taxing and budgeting process. By allowing only homeowners who have received a homestead exemption to qualify for the cap, property appraisers will be able to ascertain who is eligible for the benefits of the cap simply by checking the tax roll. [Footnote omitted.] Without this requirement, there would be no reliable way to determine which taxpayers might qualify for the cap. In this orderly scheme, taxing authorities drawing up annual budgets will also be able to rely on the list of properties for which there is a homestead exemption in determining the limits on tax revenue imposed by the cap, rather than having to ascertain which properties *might* be eligible *if* the property owner applied for the cap.

III. Conclusion

Applied to the facts of this case, our conclusion that the grant of a homestead exemption is necessary for a homeowner to obtain the baseline assessment for the Save Our Homes cap in article VII, subsection 4(c) precludes the Powell's from benefiting from the cap for the increase in their property taxes from 2000 to 2001. Under subsection 4(c)(4), the Powells' successful application for the exemption in 2001 constituted an "establishment of the homestead," which triggered the baseline assessment for the Save Our Homes cap. Under section 193.155, their baseline year is 2001, and thereafter they will receive the benefits of the cap. Any change in their assessment from 2001 to 2002 and for every year thereafter should be limited to the lesser of 3 percent or the change in the Consumer Price Index.

Accordingly, we quash the decision of the Fourth District and remand for proceedings consistent with this opinion.

It is so ordered.

WELLS, ANSTEAD, LEWIS, QUINCE, CANTERO and BELL, JJ., concur.

d. *Limitation on Which Property Can Be Taxed to Provide Services in Unincorporated Areas*

Fla. Const. art. VIII, §1(h)

TAXES; LIMITATION. Property situate within municipalities shall not be subject to taxation for services rendered by the county exclusively for the benefit of the property or residents in unincorporated areas.

———

Although somewhat ambiguous, this provision was enacted to prevent taxpayers from being subjected to ad valorem tax to fund municipal services which did not benefit the taxed property. The following cases are an interpretation and application of this constitutional provision.

City of St. Petersburg v. Briley, Wild & Associates, Inc.

239 So. 2d 817 (Fla. 1970)

MASON, Circuit Judge.

[The ultimate issue in this case was the authority of Pinellas County to use county ad valorem taxes to pay for the expansion of the sanitary sewage facilities in Pinellas County. St. Petersburg had its own sewage treatment resources and did not use the County's, but the ad valorem taxes to be used would include those collected from property within the city limits of St. Petersburg.[56]]

* * *

The critical question in this case is whether the expenditure of county-wide levied tax monies is authorized for the proposed project. Article VIII, Section 1(h), proscribes the use of tax monies received from taxes levied upon property situate within municipalities "for services rendered by the County, exclusively for the benefit of the property or residents in unincorporated areas." The record discloses that Pinellas County is composed of unincorporated areas, plus approximately twenty-three cities and towns. It is conceded by the appellees that the fund from which it is proposed to pay the plaintiff's bill and to construct the proposed sewer expansion was created by the receipts from ad valorem taxes levied by the County upon property situate within the municipalities of the County, as well as upon property lying within the unincorporated areas of the County. Therefore, if the services proposed to be rendered by the County and to be paid from such fund are services "exclusively for the benefit of property and residents in the unincorporated areas" the County may not use such county-wide levied tax monies for such purpose. We are called upon to decide first what is proscribed by the language "exclusively for the benefit of property and residents in the unincorporated areas" as used in Article VIII, Section 1(h) of the 1968 Florida Constitution, and second, whether or not the record herein supports the findings of the trial judge that the proposed project is not for such proscribed services, but will benefit the property and residents of the municipalities as well as those of the unincorporated areas.

This is a case of first impression in Florida since the constitutional provision construed by the trial court is new in the 1968 Constitution, neither it nor a similar one being incorporated in the Constitution of 1885. In reviewing his construction of the provision we are called upon to decide what is meant by the language which says that "property situate within municipalities shall not be subject to taxation for services rendered by the County *"exclusively for the benefit of the property or residents in unincorporated areas."* (Emphasis supplied.) The key phrase to be interpreted is the phrase "exclusively for the benefit of the property or residents in unincorporated

---

56. This substantive issue concerning the use of county ad valorem tax revenues (collected in part from city residents) to pay for projects that may only benefit residents of unincorporated sections of the county is a very important one and will be considered later in this chapter. This case appears here solely for the issue of constitutional interpretation.

areas," for the proscription here is against the taxation of municipally-situated property to pay for services rendered exclusively for the benefit of the unincorporated areas of the County. It is evident from this language of proscription that the cost of services rendered by the County which are not rendered "exclusively for the benefit of the property or residents in unincorporated areas", but which benefit property situate in incorporated areas may be taxed against municipally-situate property as well as that outside of cities. We must determine what is meant by the term "exclusively for the benefit of" as here used by the framers of this provision, and as understood by the people at the time they adopted it in the General Election of 1968. We are obligated to give effect to this language according to its meaning and what the people must have understood it to mean when they approved it. Advisory Opinion to the Governor, 156 Fla. 48, 22 So.2d 398 (1945); In Re Advisory Opinion to the Governor, Fla., 223 So.2d 35 (1969). If the language is clear and not entirely unreasonable or illogical in its operation we have no power to go outside the bounds of the constitutional provision in search of excuses to give a different meaning to words used therein. Vocelle v. Knight Bros. Paper Co., Fla.App., 118 So.2d 664; Cassady v. Consolidated Naval Stores Co., Fla., 119 So.2d 35. The term "exclusive", which is the adjective from which the adverb "exclusively" is derived, is defined in Webster's New International Dictionary as "single", "sole"; "as an exclusive agent"; also "singly devoted", "undivided"; "limiting or limited to possession, control, or use by a single individual, organization, etc.," "as the exclusive privileges of the citizens of a country." If we give the phrase this literal interpretation it would be to hold that if the service proposed to be rendered by the County would be of the slightest benefit to property located in a particular municipality, however minute in quantity or quality, such service could not be said to be "exclusively for the benefit" of the unincorporated areas of the County, and it would, therefore, subject such municipal property to county taxation for such service. But, there is another and cardinal rule of statutory construction applicable to the construction of constitutional provisions and that is that the fundamental object is to ascertain and give effect to the intent of the framers and adopters thereof, and constitutional provisions must be interpreted in such a manner as to fulfill this intention, rather than to defeat it. 6 Fla.Jur. 281. Furthermore, constitutional interpretation is actuated by the rule of reason, and unreasonable or absurd consequences should, if possible, be avoided. Florida Dry Cleaning & Laundry Board v. Everglades Laundry, 137 Fla. 290, 188 So. 380. A literal interpretation should not be accorded if it leads to an unreasonable conclusion or to a result not intended by the lawmakers. Lanier v. Tyson, Fla.App. (1962), 147 So.2d 365 [quashed in *Tyson v. Lanier*, 156 So. 2d 833 (Fla. 1963)].

To prevent an interpretation of this language which would lead to an unreasonable conclusion, or to one such as was not intended by the framers, we are privileged to look to the historical background of this particular provision. In Re Advisory Opinion to the Governor, Fla., 223 So.2d 35 (1969). When this particular proposal was before the Revisory Commission which framed the 1968 Constitution, there was considerable debate as to its meaning and purpose, as reflected by the minutes of such Revisory Commission. Also, when this proposal was considered by the Committee of the Whole of the House of Representatives, further debate reflected the purpose and intent of the proposal. An examination of the minutes of both bodies leads us to conclude that the purpose of the Revisory Commission in drafting this provision, and the House of Representatives in accepting it as so drafted, is to prevent double taxation of municipally-situated property for a single benefit. That the framers of the provision, and the people in adopting it, intended to prevent future taxation by counties of city-located property for services from which the owners of said property received no real or substantial benefit. To interpret the language used in this provision to mean that the County could tax city-located property for minute benefits rendered to such property would do violence to the intent and purpose of the framers and of the people in adopting the 1968 Constitution. It is evident from such historical background that the evil sought to be remedied was the taxation of municipally-located property for services rendered by the County which result in no real or substantial benefit to such property. We, therefore, hold that Article VIII, Section 1(h) of the 1968 Constitution of Florida prohibits the taxation of municipally-situate property by the County for any services rendered by the County where no real or substantial benefit accrues to city property from such services. Conversely, this provision permits such taxation where such service is found to be of real and substantial benefit to such property.

* * *

. . . We hold that the proper interpretation of the language of this section of the Constitution does not require a direct and primary use benefit from a particular service to city-located property in order to remove the same from the proscription of the constitutional provision. It is sufficient to authorize county taxation of such property if the benefits accruing to the municipal areas are found to be real and substantial and not merely illusory, ephemeral and inconsequential. That it was not the intent of the framers of this provision of the Constitution to require a direct benefit to city-located property in order to avoid the proscription is evidenced by the fact that attempts to amend the provision to substitute the words "directly" and "primarily" for the word "exclusively" were defeated before the proposition was submitted to the people for approval.

* * *

It is impossible to separate as between the various areas of the country the deleterious effect upon the public health of contamination and pollution occurring in a particular area. It is unrealistic to say that the elimination of pollution and contamination of the soils, waters and streams of the unincorporated areas of Pinellas County will not be of substantial benefit, health-wise and recreation-wise, to the incorporated areas.

We can conceive of services sought to be rendered by a county within a particular unincorporated area which would have no consequential benefits to the municipalities of the county such as, for instance, a library set up in an unincorporated area for the use and benefit of the area residents or, perhaps, a park or recreation facility for the residents of such area. Even the establishment of fire-fighting facilities in a particular unincorporated area may not reasonably be said to be of consequential benefit to the incorporated areas. But, in the field of public health a different situation may readily exist. We believe that the record before the trial judge amply substantiates his conclusion that the proposed project would be of beneficial use to and in the best interest of the present and future welfare and well-being of the residents of all areas of Pinellas County, and that, therefore, the proscription of Article VIII, Section 1(h) is not applicable to the particular project involved in this suit.

We conclude that the judgment below is without error and should be affirmed:

It is so ordered.

ERVIN, C. J., and DREW, CARLTON and BOYD, JJ., concur.

Alsdorf v. Broward County

333 So. 2d 457 (Fla. 1976)

ENGLAND, Justice.

This matter was brought to us by direct appeal from a final judgment rendered by the Broward County Circuit Court, construing Article VIII, Section 1 (h) of the 1968 Florida Constitution as being inherently too vague to be self-executing. We have jurisdiction to review that judgment under Article V, Section 3 (b) (1) of the Florida Constitution.

This lawsuit began as a class action by twenty-four mayors of Florida municipalities, in their governmental capacities and as citizen-taxpayers, seeking declaratory and other forms of relief against Broward County in connection with the County's 1973–74 budget. [Footnote omitted.] The mayors' lawsuit challenges Broward County's expenditure of various sums raised by property tax levies from residents within municipal boundaries, in the light of Article VIII, Section 1 (h) of the Florida Constitution, which provides:

> (h) Taxes; limitation. Property situate within municipalities shall not be subject to taxation for services rendered by the county exclusively for the benefit of the property or residents in unincorporated areas.

Following a four day non-jury trial, the trial court entered final judgment against the mayors and dismissed their lawsuit, finding

> ... that Article VIII, Sec. 1 (h) of the Florida Constitution (1968), is too vague by itself to be workable. There are no standards, no guidelines by which to aide the municipalities and counties in their attempt to work within the Constitutional provision. This Court feels that it is the legislature's duty to supply the necessary standards so as to make the provision workable.

The mayors attack that judgment here. [Footnote omitted.]

We previously construed the language of this constitutional provision in *City of St. Petersburg v. Briley, Wild & Assocs., Inc.*, 239 So.2d 817 (Fla.1970). In that case we held that the term "exclusively" could not be read literally, and that county taxation of municipal properties is barred only when county services bring to municipal property owners no "real or substantial benefit". We there held, on the facts of that case, that tax-supported expenditures for a county sewage treatment plant benefited the residents of intra-county municipalities by preserving their health, even though no lines, mains, pumping stations or other physical facilities were constructed within city boundaries.[3]

Other Florida appellate decisions have upheld the use of city-derived property tax revenues for a county fire department,[4] for county sewer facilities,[5] and for county roads, canals and related improvements.[6]

Unlike previous litigants who have challenged individual county expenditures, the mayors in this lawsuit challenge an array of county expenditures, asserting that each provides no "real and substantial benefit" to city dwellers within the county.[7] The trial court analyzed these assertions and found from the evidence adduced at trial that, while "some of the items listed in the plaintiffs' lawsuit clearly benefit all citizens of the County . . . numerous other items benefit only the residents of the unincorporated areas and, therefore, must necessarily come within the purview of this lawsuit." Nonetheless, the court dismissed the mayors' lawsuit on the ground that legislative guidelines were needed to make the constitutional provision work. We disagree.

Both appellant and appellee support their positions here with our decision in *Gray v. Bryant*, 125 So.2d 846 (Fla.1960). Appellant cites several portions of that decision for support and points out that the constitutional provision at issue there was held to require no legislative implementation for its effectiveness. Appellee finds support for its position in the Court's language on page 851, to the effect that:

> The basic guide, or test, in determining whether a constitutional provision should be construed to be self-executing, or not self-executing, is whether or not the provision lays down a sufficient rule by means of which the right

---

3. The Court also suggested, although it was not germane to the controversy, that county parks, libraries, and perhaps even fire-fighting equipment, might be services for which the county could not tax municipal properties.

4. *Dressel v. Dade County*, 219 So.2d 716 (3d DCA Fla.1969) (decided without reference to Article VIII, Section 1 (h) of the Constitution).

5. *City of Waldo v. Alachua County*, 249 So.2d 419 (Fla.1971) (decided without reference to Article VIII, Section 1 (h) of the Constitution).

6. *Burke v. Charlotte County*, 286 So.2d 199 (Fla.1973).

7. Plaintiffs' complaint has challenged 34 separate county activities, constituting over one-third of the county's budgeted activities. These include funding of the county commission, the county attorney, the county auditor, the county comptroller, and the county's data processing, personnel, purchasing, planning, development, engineering, mosquito control and water management departments. After trial, the primary county activity at issue was the county sheriff's road patrol.

or purpose which it gives or is intended to accomplish may be determined, enjoyed, or protected without the aid of legislative enactment.

From this appellee argues that the complexity of financing, budgeting and conducting a variety of necessary governmental activities in a county which contains multiple municipalities, coupled with the ever present factual uncertainty of what is and is not of "real and substantial benefit" to particular municipal residents, requires an affirmation of the trial court's conclusion.

We recognize the logic of appellee's argument. We concede, in fact, that the practical consequences of holding for the mayors may pose such horrendous fiscal problems for the administration of 67 counties that their governmental operations may be virtually incapacitated by uncertainty and lawsuits. If there were any practical way to avoid that result consistent with the Constitution, we would readily adopt it. But neither party here has offered such a solution, and we can conceive of none.[8] We simply cannot abdicate our responsibility to follow the will of the people as expressed in the Constitution, on the grounds of administrative complexity.

The mandate against city taxation for exclusive county activities is absolute and unequivocal. The people appear to have directed this consequence despite the fact that extensive judicial labor is required to separate the permissible from the impermissible. Indeed, we fail to see any way in which legislative intervention would lessen that labor.[9]

Our view of the self-executing nature of this constitutional position has three bases.

(1) The language of the Constitution is reasonably straight forward and unambiguous. The intent of this tax limitation provision is both obvious and understandable.[10] Practical considerations aside, there is no reason that the words cannot be applied to mean precisely what they say (with the gloss previously given the term "exclusively" in *Briley*).

(2) The format of the particular provision is not unique to our Constitution. The identical mandatory negative "shall not" or its equivalent appears in numerous other provisions as a direct check on governmental and nongovernmental acts,

---

8. It has been suggested that we recede from *Briley* by adopting a literal view of "exclusively", and by so doing leave the area for adoption of this provision so narrow as to be inconsequential and unenforceable. Tempting as this appears, this solution merely offers an absurd result in place of an impractical one. 239 So.2d at 822.

9. If the Legislature attempted to enumerate county services within or without the constitutional ban (it doesn't matter which), we would still be obliged to entertain and ultimately rule on challenges to individual service items.

10. A fair portrayal of the history of the concerns which led to the adoption of this provision, and the related governmental attempts to deal with those concerns which have evolved after it became effective, is set forth in January 1976 issue of the Florida Municipal Record, an official publication of the Florida League of Cities.

6 · TAXATION AND FINANCE

some of which also bar ad valorem taxation on various subjects.[11] We are not willing to lessen the negative directive in this provision in light of the implications which that action could have in other areas.

(3) The trial court found as a fact that several of the county expenditures enumerated in the mayors' complaint are of no real or substantial benefit to municipal residents.[12] Neither party has challenged the trial court's findings as being without factual support in the record. This appears to prove appellants' point that the Constitution can operate without legislative clarification.

We conclude, therefore, that Article VIII, Section 1 (h) of the Florida Constitution is self-executing, and that with or without legislative interpretation the courts will be required to draw the lines between acceptable and prohibited municipal taxation.[13] We must, therefore, reverse the trial court's decision and remand this proceeding for further action by the trial court in light of our opinion.

We recognize, however, that the fiscal effect of our decision may significantly affect Broward County and that neither it nor the Legislature has provided revenue for this eventuality. Under these circumstances, we direct the trial court to exercise

---

11. See, for example, Article I, Sections 3 ("There shall be no law respecting the establishment of religion. . . .", 4 ("No law shall be passed to restrain or abridge the liberty of speech or of the press."), 6 ("The right of employees . . . to bargain collectively shall not be denied or abridged.") and 10 ("No bill of attainder, ex post facto law or law impairing the obligation of contracts shall be passed."); Article VII, Section 1 (b) ("Motor vehicles, boats [etc] . . . shall not be subject to ad valorem taxes.") and 9 (b) ("Ad valorem taxes . . . shall not be levied in excess of the following millages. . . ."); Article VIII, Section 3 ("Consolidation shall not extend the territorial scope of taxation for the payment of pre-existing debt. . . ."); Article X, Sections 1 ("The legislature shall not take action on any proposed amendment to the constitution of the United States unless a majority of the members thereof have been elected after the proposed amendment has been submitted for ratification."), 4 (c) ("The homestead shall not be subject to devise if the owner is survived by spouse or minor child. . . ."), and 9 ("Repeal of amendment of a criminal statute shall not affect prosecution or punishment for any crime previously committed."). *Cf., Dade County Classroom Teachers Ass'n, Inc. v. Florida Legislature*, 269 So.2d 684 (Fla.1972).

12. The trial court identified four categories of services and facilities in Broward County, listing some items believed to be within each category. One category involves items from which all cities receive benefits all of the time, such as the county commission. Another involves items from which all cities receive benefits some of the time, such as the sheriff's office and the personnel office. Items in these categories were found to be properly taxable to city residents. As to the necessary extent of real and substantial benefit, see *Dressel v. Dade County*, 219 So.2d 716 (3d DCA Fla.1969). Another category involves items from which some but not all municipalities benefit, such as emergency medical services available only in West Broward County and the county library. Items in this category would require an identification and allocation of revenues and expenditures. The last category involves items from which no city benefits, such as the building and zoning department.

13. Appellee suggests that the likely result of holding as we do will be (1) consolidation of cities and counties, (2) abolition of cities, (3) proliferation of special tax districts, or (4) expanded user fees. That assertion may be correct. See *Gallant v. Stephens*, Case No. 75-8681, Sixth Jud.Cir. Court (12/ 19/ 75), holding that a county commission may constitute all unincorporated areas as a special tax unit for ad valorem taxes without a referendum.

its inherent equitable powers to fashion a suitable remedy for the resolution of this controversy.

> In a changing world marked by the ebb and flow of social and economic shifts, new conditions constantly arise which make it necessary, that no right be without a remedy, to extend the old and tried remedies. It is the function of courts to do this. It may be done by working old fields, but, when it becomes necessary, they should not hesitate to 'break new ground' to do so.[14]

The parties may be able to agree among themselves on an arrangement which recognizes the rights of municipal taxpayers and the obligations incurred by county government. If such a settlement is now possible, the courts should not intervene. Otherwise, the plaintiffs are entitled to remedial orders which take into account the equities on both sides.

The decision of the circuit court is reversed and this case is remanded for further action consistent with this opinion.

OVERTON, C. J., and ADKINS, SUNDBERG and HATCHETT, JJ., concur.

BOYD, J., dissents with an opinion.

ROBERTS, J., dissents and concurs with BOYD, J.

BOYD, Justice (dissenting).

I respectfully dissent to the majority opinion.

This Court should be fully aware that Broward is one of Florida's largest and perhaps the fastest growing counties in the Nation. It has many municipalities and unincorporated areas which appear to be the same with no major differences in public services offered in such areas. To require the County to separate tax dollars expended based upon municipal boundaries imposes an unrealistic and impossible task.

As we stated in *City of St. Petersburg v. Briley, Wild and Associates*, 239 So.2d 817 (Fla.1970), and *Burke v. Charlotte Co.*, 286 So.2d 199 (Fla.1973), there is no requirement that funds expended by counties outside of municipalities be "direct and primary," but "real and substantial" to the benefit of municipal residents. It is hard to imagine any expenditure which could be made in populous Broward County which could benefit only persons in the unincorporated areas without real and substantial benefits to at least some of those residents of incorporated areas.

Such a division stated in the constitutional provision construed by the majority opinion could only be accomplished in those rural areas of the state having small municipalities wherein the services furnished in the towns or cities can be clearly identified as separate in nature from rural benefits provided for agricultural and similar purposes.

---

14. *State ex rel. Watkins v. Fernandez*, 106 Fla. 779, 143 So. 638, 641 (1932).

I would adopt the trial court's judgment except that I would hold that under *Gray v. Bryant*, 125 So.2d 846 (Fla.1960), the constitutional provision is self-executing in rural or semi-rural areas in which municipal limits clearly distinguish between city and rural areas. The separation of tax dollars as stated in the Constitution cannot be accomplished in the vast metropolitan complex of Broward County.

ROBERTS, J., concurs.

Alsdorf v. Broward County

373 So. 2d 695 (Fla. 4th Dist. Ct. App. 1979)

BERANEK, Judge.

Plaintiff appeals a judgment entered May 18, 1977, by the Circuit Court in Broward County. The controversy below relates to the validity of certain county taxes as levied against incorporated and unincorporated areas of the county. The parties now involved are the plaintiffs — mayor and residents of certain municipalities; the defendant — Broward County; and the intervenors — taxpayers who are residents and owners of land in the unincorporated areas of the county. The case, in an earlier form, was considered by the Florida Supreme Court in *Alsdorf v. Broward County*, 333 So.2d 457 (Fla.1976). This opinion sets forth the background from a factual and legal point of view. Suit was initially brought by numerous municipal mayors in their official capacities and as individual taxpayers. Basically the mayors challenged county property taxes levied on real estate within municipal boundaries in light of Article VIII, Section 1(h) of the Florida Constitution which provides: "Taxes; Limitation. Property situate within municipalities shall not be subject to taxation for services rendered by the county exclusively for the benefit of the property or residents in unincorporated areas." The plaintiffs contended numerous county expenditures for various services were of no "real and substantial benefit" to the residents of the municipalities and that taxing of the land within the municipalities was, therefore, improper under the aforementioned constitutional provision. The trial court initially dismissed the action on the ground that the constitutional provision was too vague without further legislative guidelines. The Supreme Court reversed and held the constitutional provision to be self-executing. The case was remanded to the trial court with directions, "that with or without legislative interpretation the courts will be required to draw the lines between acceptable and prohibited municipal taxation." The Supreme Court directed the trial court to exercise its "inherent equitable powers to fashion a suitable remedy for the resolution of this controversy." In short, the trial court was ordered to decide the very difficult question of which county services were of real and substantial benefit to municipal dwellers. [Footnote omitted.] The Supreme Court also encouraged the parties to agree among themselves to a settlement of the controversy.

After remand a settlement did not occur although substantial efforts were made in that regard. The defendant/county and the plaintiffs entered into a stipulation which disposed of many of the matters in controversy and which further isolated the issues to be tried before the court. Basically, the stipulation of the county and the plaintiffs was that three issues remained to be tried. These issues were the county programs relating to (1) libraries, (2) emergency medical services, and (3) parks and recreation. In addition the county and plaintiffs stipulated that the Sheriff's road patrol was of no benefit to the incorporated areas and that the municipalities would not be taxed for this service. The Sheriff's road patrol had been a major dispute in the previous trial. At that time the county took a completely contrary position and asserted the road patrol to be of benefit to city residents.

Before the stipulation was filed and before the second trial began, certain taxpayers who were residents of the unincorporated areas of the county petitioned to intervene. Over objection of the plaintiffs, intervention was allowed. Basically, the intervenors sought to litigate the issue of the Sheriff's road patrol and to overturn the stipulation of the plaintiffs and the county which removed it as an issue to be litigated. Intervenors' position was that the road patrol was of benefit to municipal residents and that, therefore, the tax burden for this service should be spread county-wide on municipal and unincorporated lands alike rather than placing the entire tax burden on the unincorporated area.

An extended non-jury trial resulted in the judgment in question. The trial court made numerous factual findings in its attempt to carry out the mandate of the Supreme Court of determining exactly which services were of real and substantial benefit to municipal residents. The essential provisions of the final judgment are five in number.[2]

The judgment was not a clear-cut victory for any party. The mayors, as plaintiffs below, now occupy the position of appellants. Broward County and the intervenors are the appellees. Although some of the trial court's rulings were adverse to the positions or the stipulations of the county in the trial court, the county does not seek reversal of these findings on appeal.

Initially, the trial court determined as a matter of fact that the county library program was of real and substantial benefit to municipal residents and that the taxation of the municipalities in this respect was proper. Appellants urge error in this ruling.

In regard to the county-wide emergency medical service program, the court found that taxation of certain municipalities was improper. This finding was based on the fact that the county was not truly providing services to the municipal residents but was instead offering to municipal governments the option of co-operating in the county-wide program. The trial court ruled that the county taxes were improper in those situations where the individual city was providing its own emergency medical service. Therefore, the ruling was that an allocable portion of the overall expense of the emergency medical service constituted an improper tax on the municipalities

---

2. It should be noted that this appeal presents no question as to the procedures of Chapter 125, Florida Statutes (1973), as was involved in *Manatee County v. Town of Longboat Key*, 352 So.2d 869 (Fla. 2d DCA 1977).

but only as to those cities who were providing their own programs. This ruling is not questioned on appeal.

In regard to parks and recreation, the trial court considered the entire county program and determined that the greatest portion of the program was properly taxable against both municipal and unincorporated lands. However, the court isolated certain "neighborhood parks" which were located solely in unincorporated areas and concluded that a tax on municipal properties for the expense of neighborhood parks was improper. This ruling is also not questioned on appeal.

As to the Sheriff's road patrol, the court refused to accept the stipulation of the county and the plaintiffs to the effect that this service was of no benefit to municipal residents. The court, at the insistence of the intervenors, found that the Sheriff's road patrol was of real and substantial benefit to municipal residents and that the tax burden for this service should thus be spread throughout the entire county and not merely limited to unincorporated lands. Appellants/plaintiffs alone assert this to be error. The last ruling was in regard to a request for refunds of alleged improperly collected taxes. All requested funds were denied. Again, only appellants/plaintiffs urge error in this regard.

In addition to the above points on libraries, the road patrol and refunds, appellants also assert error regarding the intervention and the rejection of the stipulation between plaintiffs and the county. Appellants divide their attack into five separate issues which will be dealt with herein.

I. Libraries

The trial court found as a matter of fact that the municipal residents gained real and substantial benefit from the county-wide library system. This finding is in accordance with the criterion established in *City of St. Petersburg v. Briley, Wild & Associates, Inc.*, 239 So.2d 817 (Fla.1970). The benefit to the city need not be direct and primary. It is only necessary that the benefit not be illusory or inconsequential. A good deal of conflicting evidence was presented by the plaintiffs mostly concerning their dissatisfaction with the county-wide library program. Substantial conflicting evidence was presented by the county and the trial court basically reached a factual determination on conflicting evidence. The findings of the trial court will not be disturbed on appeal if supported by competent substantial evidence. *LaCroix v. Higgins*, 289 So.2d 743 (Fla. 4th DCA 1974). Appellants' argument is basically one of dissatisfaction with the existing library system. The fact that appellants might prefer a different system as a matter of policy does not mean that the municipal residents themselves do not receive real and substantial benefit. The trial court is, therefore, affirmed in this regard.

II. Intervention

* * *

III. Rejection of Stipulation

* * *

IV. Sheriff's Road Patrol

Having allowed intervention and having rejected the stipulation, the trial court proceeded with trial on the factual question of whether the Sheriff's road patrol resulted in real and substantial benefit to the municipalities of the county. Once again, this was a factual question to be determined in accordance with the criterion established in *City of St. Petersburg v. Briley, Wild & Associates, Inc., supra.* As with the question of libraries, substantial evidence was presented on this issue. The final judgment recites the evidence and appellants do not actually take issue with these factual determinations. It is merely appellants' position that the trial court should never have considered the matter in view of the stipulation. Among many other things, it was shown that the Sheriff's road patrol generally enforced the law in the entire county. The Sheriff served as the chief officer of both the county and circuit courts. In doing so, the road patrol assisted civil deputies in service of process and was involved in service of and enforcement of any court order, whether it related to a municipal resident or a resident living in an unincorporated area. In addition, all of the Sheriff's vehicles were intentionally driven and maintained in such a fashion so as to increase the visibility of the police presence in the municipalities. It was shown and is uncontested on appeal that the Sheriff's road patrol assisted the city police forces when called upon to do so. Further, by limiting crime in the unincorporated areas adjoining the municipalities the road patrol was of substantial assistance to the municipal police and residents in the contiguous cities. We conclude that the trial court's factual finding of benefit of a real and substantial nature is supported by competent substantial evidence and same is hereby affirmed.

V. Refunds

The trial court denied all requests for refunds of improperly collected taxes. Only plaintiffs/appellants contest this finding on appeal. We affirm. The only taxes actually improperly collected here were in the area of emergency medical services and neighborhood parks. Taxes attributable to the emergency medical services program were only improperly collected in those towns which had rejected the county-wide program and were providing their own emergency medical programs. The taxes attributable to an unknown number of neighborhood parks were the only county-wide taxes in question.

In denying the request for refunds herein, we believe the trial court properly exercised its inherent equitable powers. One of the major considerations in such a determination is whether the taxing authority acted in good faith. In this regard, the Supreme Court decision in *Gulesian v. Dade County School Board*, 281 So.2d 325 (Fla.1973), is persuasive. *See also, Coe v. Broward County*, 358 So.2d 214 (Fla. 4th DCA 1978). In the instant situation the evidence is clear that the county exercised good faith and there is no assertion to the contrary. Further, there was total failure of proof as to the amounts of taxes in question or as to identification of those who should receive refunds.

We would conclude by stressing the continued existence of the provision in the Florida Constitution which prohibits the taxation of municipal property for services rendered exclusively for the benefit of unincorporated areas. With this provision we cannot, and do not, disagree. Accordingly, this decision is limited to the facts, taxable years and circumstances of this particular case and should not be hailed as a precedent, providing "carte blanche" approval of any tax levied on municipal property. The relationship between individual cities and counties and the services provided by county agencies to municipal residents will continue to change based upon development and expansion of areas and programs. What has been proper for any given tax period is subject to appropriate change and re-evaluation.

Having considered all matters presented by appellants, we conclude the other of the trial court is in accordance with law and is hereby affirmed.

AFFIRMED.

DOWNEY, C. J., and LETTS, J., concur.

B. Finance

Governmental units in Florida use a variety of financing mechanisms to borrow the enormous sums of money necessary to finance the acquisition or construction of infrastructure and capital projects such as roads, sewer and drainage systems, schools, jails, sports stadiums, convention centers, and other public buildings and projects. The financing vehicles available to the various governmental units run the gamut, from those designed to cover short-term financing needs such as commercial paper, certificates of indebtedness, and tax and bond anticipation notes, to those designed to provide long-term financing needs, such as bonds. The latter, bonds, will be the predominant focus of this section in the text.

In very simplistic terms, a bond is nothing more than a debt security instrument, in which the bondholders (the individuals who purchase the bonds) agree to lend money to a governmental unit in exchange for a predetermined interest rate for a prescribed period of time, e.g., twenty or thirty years. The bond issuer (government entity), usually, through a resolution adopted by its governing body, pledges particular types of revenue sources as collateral to the bondholders to guarantee the repayment of the bonds.[57] The bondholders are given a security interest in or a lien on the particular revenue source(s) that is pledged, much like a bank or other financial institution is given a security interest in the property (collateral) which the loan proceeds are used to finance. Since under Florida law there can be no mortgage on public property (absent voter approval), the only security that bondholders have to guarantee repayment is the security interest in or lien on the specific revenue source

---

57. Nabors, Giblin & Nickerson, P.A., *Primer on Home Rule & Local Government Revenue Sources*, at 37 (April 2010).

that is pledged.[58] In the event the governmental entity issuing the bond defaults, i.e., fails to meet the debt service (principal and interest payments), the bondholder's recourse is to levy the pledged revenue source(s) or compel taxation if the taxing power of the government unit was pledged.

Depending upon the type of revenue source(s) pledged, bonds are generally classified into one of two primary categories: (1) revenue bonds or (2) general obligation bonds. A revenue bond is one in which the governmental entity issuing the bond pledges the revenues that are generated from the project for which the bond is issued as security to the bondholder. If the revenues are not sufficient to pay the debt service, a bondholder has no recourse against the issuing governmental entity and cannot compel taxation to make up the shortfall to cover the debt service. Revenue bonds may be issued without voter approval (referendum). Revenue bonds issued by governmental entities in Florida can be classified into six general categories:[59] (1) Typical Revenue Bonds;[60] (2) Certificates of Participation;[61] (3) Equipment Leases;[62] (4) Industrial Development or Private Activity Bonds;[63] (5) Tax Increment Bonds;[64] and (6) Special Assessment Bonds.[65]

A general obligation bond, on the other hand, is one in which the governmental entity issuing the bond pledges its "full faith and credit" or "taxing power." Generally, voter approval (referendum) is required for the issuance of general obligation bonds. If the entity issuing the bonds is a unit of local government, a bond will not be considered a general obligation bond unless the ad valorem (property) taxing power of the unit of local government is actually pledged. Units of local government may be authorized by general law to impose other non-ad valorem taxes, such

---

58. *Id.*

59. Grace E. Dunlap & Alexandra M. MacLennan, *Public Finance* 1.4–1.6, The Florida Bar, City, County, &Local Gov't Law Certification Review Course (2010).

60. Typical Revenue Bonds include those payable from utility revenues, such as water and sewer revenues, and excise tax revenues, such as sales and gas tax.

61. Certificates of Participation are typically used by school districts to fund the construction of buildings. In these transactions the governmental entity enters into a lease transaction and an investor purchases a share of the lease revenues. Each certificate represents an undivided interest in lease payments from the governmental unit.

62. Equipment Leases are very much like certificates of participation and are typically used for computer, vehicle and other equipment financing.

63. This is a type of "conduit" financing in which a governmental entity, such as a local industrial development authority, borrows money (through the issuance of bonds) on behalf of private entities to finance private industrial projects. The responsibility for repayment of the bonds is passed through to the private entity. These bonds are a form of incentive for private companies to construct, expand or renovate their facilities since they will enjoy the benefit of lower financing costs.

64. Tax Increment Bonds are issued for purposes of community redevelopment and are payable from the increased or additional tax revenues generated as a result of the increase in assessed value of the property after the redevelopment project. The "tax increment" is the difference between the tax generated before the redevelopment and the tax generated after the redevelopment.

65. Special Assessment Bonds are payable from the special assessments levied against the property benefitted by the improvements being financed. Since validly imposed special assessments are not considered a tax, special assessment bonds are considered to be revenue bonds.

as municipal utilities or gasoline taxes. If only these non-ad valorem tax revenues are pledged, the bonds will not be deemed to be general obligation bonds and no referendum will be required, unless there is a provision in the charter of the unit of government requiring otherwise.[66]

The authority for governmental entities in Florida to issue bonds and other instruments of indebtedness is found in statutory law.[67] The statutes which authorize the issuance of bonds contain various restrictions, such as limiting the amount of interest that can be paid to bondholders, and must be strictly adhered to by the issuing governmental unit. In addition to the statutory restrictions, the Florida Constitution imposes a number of additional restrictions on the issuance of bonds, such as requiring projects financed by bonds to constitute a public purpose and prohibiting the pledging of the "credit" or "taxing power" of the government entity to aid private entities.

To determine whether a proposed bond issuance meets the statutory and constitutional requirements, the Florida Legislature grants any governmental entity authorized to issue bonds the option of obtaining a judicial determination (validation) of the bonds by filing a complaint in the circuit court of the county where the proceeds of the bond issue are to be expended, or where the seat of state government is situated.[68] During the bond validation proceeding, the circuit court determines whether the governmental entity has the authority to incur bonded debt or issue certificates of debt and the legality of all proceedings in connection therewith, including the taxes, assessments, or revenues to be pledged as security for the bond issuance.[69]

Although voluntary under Florida law, some governmental units opt to have their bonds validated in circuit court. This provides an added level of protection to the issuing government unit that does so in that if no appeal is taken within the time prescribed, or if taken and the judgment is affirmed, such judgment is forever conclusive as to all matters adjudicated and can never be called into question in any court by any person or party.[70]

A bond validation judgment is appealed to the Florida Supreme Court under its mandatory jurisdiction.[71] In its review of bond validation cases, the Supreme Court is limited to the following issues: (1) whether the public body has the authority to issue bonds; (2) whether the purpose of the obligation is legal; and (3) whether the bond issuance complies with the requirements of law.[72] In the following cases, we

---

66. *See State v. Sarasota*, 549 So. 2d 659 (Fla. 1989).

67. See Fla. Stat. chs. 125, 130, 132, 154, 157, 159, 163, 166, 215, and 218 for the authority for the issuance of bonds by various governmental entities in Florida.

68. Fla. Stat. § 75.02 (2021).

69. *Id.*

70. *Id.*

71. Art. V, § 3(b)(2).

72. *State v. Osceola County*, 752 So. 2d 530 (Fla. 1999).

will examine the limitations imposed by the Florida Constitution on the issuance of bonds.

1. Limitations on State and Local Aid to the Private Sector

Fla. Const. art. VII, § 10

Pledging credit. — Neither the state nor any county, school district, municipality, special district, or agency or any of them, shall become a joint owner with, or stockholder of, or give, lend or use its taxing power or credit to aid any corporation, association, partnership, or person; but this shall not prohibit laws authorizing:

(a) the investment of public trust funds;

(b) the investment of other public funds in obligations of, or insured by, the United States or any of its instrumentalities;

(c) the issuance and sale by any county, municipality, special district or other local governmental body of (1) revenue bonds to finance or refinance the cost of capital projects for airports or port facilities, or (2) revenue bonds to finance or refinance the cost of capital projects for industrial or manufacturing plants to the extent that the interest thereon is exempt from income taxes under the then existing laws of the United States, when, in either case, the revenue bonds are payable solely from revenue derived from the sale, operation or leasing of the projects. If any project so financed, or any part thereof, is occupied or operated by any private corporation, association, partnership or person pursuant to contract or lease with the issuing body, the property interest created by such contract or lease shall be subject to taxation to the same extent as other privately owned property.

(d) a municipality, county, special district, or agency of any of them, being a joint owner of, giving, or lending or using its taxing power or credit for the joint ownership, construction and operation of electrical energy generating or transmission facilities with any corporation, association, partnership or person.[73]

The status and impact of state and local governmental aid to the private sector under the 1885 Florida Constitution was described by the Florida Supreme Court in *Linscott v. Orange County Industrial Development Authority:*[74]

The Constitution of 1885, article IX, section 10, prohibited government bodies from obtaining money for, or pledging the public credit to, any

---

73. For a discussion of subsection (d), see *Schultz v. Crystal River Three Participants*, 686 So. 2d 1391 (Fla. 5th Dist. Ct. App. 1997).

74. 443 So. 2d 97, 99–100 (Fla. 1983).

private entity. Under case law, revenue bonds payable solely from capital project revenues (non-recourse bonds) were held to be pledges of the public credit and were prohibited unless it could be shown that the capital project served a predominantly or paramount public purpose. Contrast *State v. Town of North Miami*, 59 So.2d 779 (Fla.1952), where non-recourse revenue bonds were held to be invalid because they served a predominantly private purpose with only incidental public benefit and *State v. Board of Control*, 66 So.2d 209 (Fla.1953), where the bonds were validated because they served a predominantly public purpose with only incidental private benefit. In *Town of North Miami*, the trial court ruled that the non-recourse bonds for the construction of a private plant were valid because they did not involve a pledge of the public credit. Implicit in our decision overruling the circuit court was a determination that the bonds involved either obtaining money for, or pledging the public credit to, a private entity.

Town of North Miami, and its progeny, began to have a significant effect on Florida's economic development in the 1960s because of a ruling by the Internal Revenue Service, later codified, which made the interest on industrial revenue bonds exempt from federal income tax. As a result of this ruling, Florida was placed at a competitive disadvantage with other states which could offer tax exempt, non-recourse revenue bonds to private entities for capital projects. [Footnote omitted.] *See*, for example, *State v. Jacksonville Port Authority*, 204 So.2d 881 (Fla.1967), where non-recourse bonds for a major port expansion were held to be invalid. . . .

The Florida Supreme Court, in *Linscott* found that this situation caused a change in policy in the 1968 Florida Constitution:[75]

. . . Significantly, *Jacksonville Port Authority* was decided in July, 1967, when the Florida Legislature was considering revisions to the Constitution of 1885. The legislative interest in the economic impact of *Jacksonville Port Authority* was evidenced by the immediate passage of legislation attempting to nullify the court ruling. *See* 204 So.2d at 892. Concurrently, in August, 1967, each house adopted joint resolutions proposing revisions to the constitutional provisions prohibiting the pledge of public credit to private entities. In pertinent part, the thrust of the Senate version was to overturn *Jacksonville Port Authority*; that of the House version to overturn *Town of North Miami*. [Footnote omitted.] These differing versions, subsections 10(c)(1) and (2) respectively, became House Joint Resolution No. 1-2X 559-60, Laws of Florida (1968), which was submitted to, and approved by, the voters of Florida in November, 1968. [Footnote omitted.]

The prohibition against the lending of public credit was materially changed by the 1968 Constitution. This is a very muddled and confusing area of law. The following

---

75. *Id*. at 100.

Nohrr v. Brevard County Educational Facilities Authority

247 So. 2d 304 (Fla. 1971)

ADKINS, Justice.

This is a direct appeal from the final judgment of the Circuit Court of Brevard County, Florida, validating certain revenue bonds. Fla.Const., art. V, § 4(2), F.S.A.; F.A.R., Rule 2.1(a), (5) (a), 32 F.S.A.; Fla.Stat. § 75.08, F.S.A.

The revenue bonds were authorized under the provisions of Ch. 69-345, Laws of Florida, Fla.Stat. (1969) § 243.18 et seq., F.S.A., known as the "Higher Educational Facilities Authorities Law," (hereinafter referred to as the Educational Facilities Law). When this law was enacted the Legislature made a finding that there was an urgent need existing among institutions of higher education in Florida to obtain financing for expansion and improvement of higher educational facilities in order to meet the growing public demand. Fla.Stat. § 243.19, F.S.A. The Educational Facilities Law permitted the various Florida counties, wherever and whenever a need and public purpose was declared, to create a "County Educational Facilities Authority" which would assist institutions of higher education to obtain the necessary financing to develop and expand their educational facilities.

On December 31, 1969, the Board of County Commissioners of Brevard County, Florida, found that public need existed in the county and that the public interest would be served if a "County Educational Facilities Authority" (hereinafter referred to as the Authority) was created. The Board then adopted the resolution creating the Authority.

Subsequently, Florida Institute of Technology, a private higher educational institution in Brevard County (hereinafter referred to as F.I.T.) applied to the Authority for assistance in financing the construction at F.I.T. of a dormitory-cafeteria, together with necessary equipment and other facilities. After discussion and negotiation, the Authority adopted a resolution authorizing the issuance of $880,000 in revenue bonds at not more than seven and one-half per cent per annum, the proceeds of which would be used to construct the dormitory-cafeteria at F.I.T. and to pay for all expenses and costs incurred in connection therewith. The rents and other revenues received from the project, as well as the project, are to be assigned, pledged and mortgaged as security for the payment of the principal and interest on the revenue bonds.

A complaint seeking the validation of the revenue bonds was filed by the Authority and the State of Florida filed its answer denying generally the validity of the bonds.

At the final hearing, an intervenor, Philip F. Nohrr (hereinafter referred to as Defendant) was permitted to file an answer in which he attacked the validity of the proposed revenue bonds.

6 · TAXATION AND FINANCE

Final judgment was rendered validating the bonds and Defendant Nohrr appealed. The State of Florida did not appeal.

* * *

The next question is whether the Educational Facilities Law violates Fla.Const., art. VII, §10, by granting the credit of the state or county, or an agency of either, to the revenue bonds issued.

Fla.Stat. Ch. 243, F.S.A., authorizes a board of county commissioners to establish a county educational facilities authority to issue revenue bonds for financing the construction of facilities for private higher educational institutions in the county. Such an authority cannot be created without a declaration of the board of county commissioners that it is needed. Fla.Stat. §243.31, F.S.A., Fla.Stat. §§243.24 and 243.25, F.S.A., authorize the county educational facilities authority to take title, by purchase or gift, of lands, structures, property, etc., in its name or in the name of the private educational institution as its agent; however, after the revenue bonds financing any acquisition or construction of such a project are liquidated the authority must convey the structures or other facilities to the educational institution free and clear of all liens. Fla.Stat. Ch. 243, F.S.A., was enacted after the adoption of the 1968 Constitution.

Fla.Stat. §243.29, F.S.A. (Educational Facilities Law), provides as follows:

> Revenue bonds issued under the provisions of this part shall not be deemed to constitute a debt or liability of the state or of the county or a pledge of the faith and credit of the state or of any such county, but *shall be payable solely from the funds herein provided therefor from revenues. All such revenue bonds shall contain on the face thereof a statement of the effect that neither the State of Florida nor the authority shall be obligated to pay the same or the interest thereon except from revenues of the project* or the portion thereof for which they are issued and that neither the faith and credit nor the taxing power of the State of Florida or of any political subdivision thereof is pledged to the payment of the principal of or the interest on such bonds. The issuance of revenue bonds under the provisions of this part shall not directly or indirectly or contingently obligate the state or any political subdivision thereof to levy or to pledge any form of taxation whatever therefor or to make any appropriation for their payment. (Emphasis supplied.)

Fla.Const., art. VII, §10 (1968), provides:

> *Pledging credit. —*
>
> Neither the state nor any county, school district, municipality, special district, or agency of any of them, shall become a joint owner with, or stockholder of, or give, lend or use its taxing power or credit to aid any corporation, association, partnership or person; but this shall not prohibit laws authorizing:
>
> (a) the investment of public trust funds;

(b) the investment of other public funds in obligations of, or insured by, the United States or any of its instrumentalities;

(c) the issuance and sale by any county, municipality, special district or other local governmental body of (1) revenue bonds to finance or refinance the cost of capital projects for *airports or port facilities*, or (2) revenue bonds to finance or refinance the cost of capital projects for *industrial or manufacturing plants* to the extent that the interest thereon is exempt from income taxes under the then existing laws of the United States, when, *in either case*, the revenue bonds are payable solely from revenue derived from the sale, operation of leasing of the projects. If any project so financed, or any part thereof, is occupied or operated by any private corporation, association, partnership or person pursuant to contract or lease with the issuing body, the property interest created by such contract or lease shall be subject to taxation to the same extent as other privately owned property. (Emphasis supplied.)

It appears that the framers of Fla. Const., art. VII, § 10(c) (1968), provided that public revenue bond financing of airport or port facilities and industrial or manufacturing plants by the means and within the limits prescribed in said section ipso facto did not involve the lending or use of a public unit's taxing power or credit to aid any corporation, association, partnership, or person. In other words, it was provided that the public revenue bond financing of these projects (airports, ports or industrial or manufacturing plants) alone, in contrast to the financing of any other projects, was recognized by the Constitution itself as not constituting the lending or use of public credit. Moreover, the naming of these particular projects was not intended to be exclusive, denying ab initio public revenue bond financing of all other types of projects. The language employed is not that no public revenue bonds shall be issued to finance any projects except those described in Section 10(c), but that the prohibition against lending a public unit's credit does not apply to the projects described in Section 10(c). This language may or may not apply to other projects, depending upon the particular circumstances in each instance.

All other proposed public revenue bond projects not falling into the exempted class described in Section 10(c) of Article VII would, of course, have to run the gauntlet of prior case decisions to test whether the lending or use of public credit for any of them was contemplated. *See*, for example, the case of State v. Jacksonville Port Authority, 204 So.2d 881 (Fla.1967), which presents a good index to decisions of this Court on both sides of the subject. It will be noted that under similar language in the 1885 Constitution (Section 10, Article IX) to that appearing in the first paragraph of Section 10 of Article VII of the 1968 Constitution the cases hold that the validity of each proposed public revenue bond financing project depends upon the circumstances, e. g., whether the purpose of the project serves a paramount public purpose, although there might be an incidental private benefit, and other criteria.

Under the foregoing construction of Section 10(c), Article VII, the dormitory-cafeteria projects involved here are not revenue projects that contemplate the lending or use of the credit of the county or its commissioners. The word "credit," as used in Fla.Const., art. VII, § 10 (1968), implies the imposition of some new financial liability upon the State or a political subdivision which in effect results in the creation of a State or political subdivision debt for the benefit of private enterprises.

In order to have a gift, loan or use of public credit, the public must be either directly or contingently liable to pay something to somebody. Neither the full faith and credit nor the taxing power of the State of Florida or of any political subdivision thereof is pledged to the payment of the principal of, or the interest on, these revenue bonds. The purchasers of the revenue bonds may not look to any legal or moral obligation on the part of the state, county, or authority to pay any portion of the bonds. This contention of Defendant is without merit. State v. Inter-American Central Authority, 84 So.2d 9 (Fla.1955); State v. Florida Development Commission, 84 So.2d 707 (Fla.1956).

* * *

Defendant next contends that the lower court erred in holding that the proposed revenue bonds were for a public purpose. Fla.Stat. § 243.19, F.S.A., contains a finding by the Legislature that projects financed under the Educational Facilities Law are, in effect, for a public purpose. The Board of County Commissioners of Brevard County, in activating the Authority, made a finding that there was a need for the Authority to function, as required by Fla.Stat. § 243.21, F.S.A.

Certainly, the financing of college dormitories and dining facilities as an aid in providing for the education of the youth of this State is a public purpose. It matters not whether the education is furnished by a state institution or by a private institution. The finding of the Legislature is determinative, and Defendant has failed to show that such determination was so clearly wrong as to be beyond the power of the Legislature. Similar laws have been upheld by other courts. Clayton v. Kervick, 52 N.J. 138, 244 A.2d 281 (1968); Vermont Educational Buildings Financing Agency v. Mann, 127 Vt. 262, 247 A.2d 68, appeal dismissed, 396 U.S. 801, 90 S.Ct. 9, 24 L. Ed.2d 58 (1968); Opinion of the Justices, 354 Mass. 779, 236 N.E.2d 523 (1968); In re Opinion of the Justices, 99 N.H. 536, 114 A.2d 801 (1955).

* * *

ERVIN, CARLTON, McCAIN and DEKLE, J.J. concur.

ROBERTS, C. J., dissents.

BOYD, J., dissents with opinion.

BOYD, Justice (dissenting):

I must dissent to the majority opinion. The 1968 Constitution does not include this type of bond issue among those specifically authorized under subsection (c), Section 10, Article VII.

As the Supreme Court pointed out in *Nohrr*, "the lending of credit means the assumption by the public body of some degree of direct or indirect obligation to pay a debt of the third party. Where there is no direct or indirect undertaking by the public body to pay the obligation from public funds, and no public property is placed in jeopardy by a default of the third party, there is no lending of public credit."

It should be further noted that in *Nohrr* the Florida Supreme Court found that "public revenue bond financing of airport or port facilities and industrial or manufacturing plants . . . ipso facto did not involve the lending or use of a public unit's taxing power or credit to aid any corporation, association, partnership or person."[76] Thus, if a project could be brought under this umbrella, or Fla. Const. art. VII, §§ 10 (a), (b), and (d), it would not be prohibited by Fla. Const. art. VII, § 10.

State v. Jacksonville Port Authority

305 So. 2d 166 (Fla. 1974)

OVERTON, Justice.

These consolidated appeals are from separate judgments of the Duval County Circuit Court entered in proceedings for the validation of bonds. In each instance, the question before us is whether a specified capital project constitutes an industrial plant within the meaning of Article VII, Section 10(c), Florida Constitution, and Ch. 159, Part II, F.S.A. We have jurisdiction pursuant to Article V, Section 3(b)(2), Florida Constitution, and Section 75.08, F.S.A. (1973).

In separate resolutions of the Jacksonville Port Authority, each of these projects was approved for the issuance of $1 million (principal amount) in industrial Development Revenue Bonds pursuant to Ch. 159, Part II, Florida Statutes. Separate bond validation proceedings were duly conducted before the Circuit Court of Duval County.

The first proposed capital project is for a food distribution center under construction by Publix Super Markets, Inc., in Jacksonville, Florida. It is to be located in a structure containing approximately 250,000 square feet on a land area of approximately fifty acres. When completed, the facility will be part of a food distribution system for some 180 retail outlets in the state. The circuit court validated the bond issuance for the food distribution center, specifically finding, inter alia, that the project would make a significant contribution to the economic growth of the City of Jacksonville. The court also stated, ". . . [t]he project will constitute an industrial plant within the meaning of the [Florida Industrial Development Financing] Act and Section 10(c), Article VII of the Constitution of Florida."

---

76. 247 So. 2d 304, 308 (Fla. 1971).

The second proposed capital project is a laundry facility in Jacksonville, to be occupied by Dixie Uniform Supply, a division of Neway Uniform and Towel Supply of Florida, Inc., hereinafter referred to as "Neway." The proposed plant will have a working area of 28,000 square feet. The work to be performed in the new facility will include the laundering, servicing, and renovating of industrial working garments. Special cleaning agents, not used in normal commercial laundries, will be needed to remove the petroleum-based soils in the fabrics laundered. Customers will be limited to specified industries and will not include the general public. The present Neway facility employs sixty people and has a current dollar volume business in excess of $1 million. This laundry facility project was disapproved by the trial court, which cited the evidence and record presented as well as the reasoning of the Supreme Court of Missouri in State ex rel. Keystone Laundry and Dry Cleaners, Inc. v. McDonnell, 426 S.W.2d 11, 18 (Mo.1968). Construing the word "industry" within a state constitutional provision similar to Florida's, the Missouri court said:

A laundry is purely a service institution. Neither the size nor the cost of the building and equipment nor the number of employees is controlling.

The State has appealed to urge reversal of the trial court's validation of bonds for the Publix food distribution center, while Neway seeks to overturn the trial court's decision refusing to validate the issuance of bonds for the Neway laundry facility project.

The constitutional language governing these cases is contained in Section 10(c) of Article VII, Florida Constitution. It provides that neither the state nor any other governmental unit shall give, lend or use its taxing power or credit to aid any corporation, association, partnership, or person. It further provides that the restriction shall not prohibit laws authorizing "... revenue bonds to finance or refinance the cost of capital projects for industrial or manufacturing plants...."

To implement this constitutional language, the legislature enacted Chapter 159, Part II, §§ 159.25 through 159.43, F.S.A. [Footnote omitted.] The term "project" is defined by § 159.27(5), F.S.A., in these words:

'Project' means any capital project comprising an *industrial or manufacturing plant*, including one or more buildings and other structures, whether or not on the same site or sites; ... [Emphasis supplied.]

The phrase "industrial plant" is not specifically defined within the bond financing provisions of the Florida Constitution or the above-cited implementing provisions of Chapter 159, F.S.A. Yet it seems clear from a reading of Section 159.27(5), F.S.A., that the legislature intended the phrase to be liberally construed. Previous decisions of this Court support this view, as illustrated in State v. Jacksonville Port Authority, 266 So.2d 1 (Fla.1972), where we approved the trial court's validation and confirmation of a bond issue for the acquisition and construction of a plant to bottle, store, and distribute domestic and foreign wines as well as other spirituous liquors. In State v. County of Dade, 250 So.2d 875 (Fla.1971), we approved a $3.85 million bond issue to finance the acquisition of a meat processing plant. Our holdings in these earlier cases are entirely consistent with the broad definition of "industry" in common usage. For example, in Webster's New International Dictionary, Unabridged (1961) the word "industry" is defined as:

> 3b. A department or branch of a craft, art, business, or manufacture: a division of productive or profit-making labor, esp. one that employs a large personnel and capital, esp. in manufacturing. c. a group of productive or profit-making enterprises or organizations that have a similar technological structure of production and that produce or supply technically substitutable goods, services, or sources of income, [as] poultry industry. . . .

If a beverage bottling plant and a meat processing facility are eligible for funding by means of Industrial Development Revenue Bonds, we see no reason why the food distribution centers should not also qualify. The proposed laundry facility we approve somewhat less readily, for it will be involved primarily in the rendering of services as opposed to the processing or distribution of products. It should be noted, however, that this particular facility is not designed to serve the consuming public generally, as would, for example, an ordinary commercial laundry; it will not even maintain a cash register. In conjunction with its other cleaning services, Neway proposes to operate the facility to meet the specialized laundering needs of a variety of industries in the Jacksonville area. While the clientele and the nature of the cleaning services are not alone determinative of whether the proposed project qualifies as an "industrial plant," there are certainly proper factors for consideration along with the size of the plant, the number of employees, etc. In this regard, we disagree with the holding of the Missouri Supreme Court in Keystone Laundry and Dry Cleaners v. McDonnell, supra. Viewing the Neway project as a comprehensive whole, we feel it qualifies.

We hold, therefore, that the above-described food distribution plant and laundry facility are "industrial plants" as contemplated by Article VII, Section 10(c), Florida Constitution, and Ch. 159, Part II, Florida Statutes. Since the projects will contribute to the prosperity of the state [footnote omitted] and since they meet the other requirements of the Act and the Constitution, they qualify for the issuance of Industrial Development Revenue Bonds by the Jacksonville Port Authority.

The judgment of the trial court in Case No. 44,820 is affirmed; the judgment in Case No. 45,392 is reversed.

ADKINS, C. J., ERVIN, J., and SIEGENDORF, Circuit Judge, concur.

ROBERTS and McCAIN, JJ., dissent.

———

In *Nohrr*, the court stated, "[a]ll other proposed public revenue bond projects not falling into the exempted class described in Section 10(c) of Article VII would, of course, have to run the gauntlet of prior case decisions to test whether the lending

6 · TAXATION AND FINANCE

or use of the public credit for any of them was contemplated."[77] The Florida Supreme Court was referring to cases decided under the 1885 Florida Constitution and directed the reader to *State v. Jacksonville Port Authority*,[78] "which presents a good index to decisions of this Court on both sides of the subject."[79] What was apparently initially ignored was that while the limitation on the pledging of credit in the 1885 Florida Constitution included a prohibition on "obtaining money for" the private sector, this particular prohibition was not carried over to the 1968 Florida Constitution. If a revenue bond is truly a non-recourse bond, then the change should make a difference. That difference was apparently not recognized in the first of the two following cases, but apparently was in the second, although not specifically mentioned.

Orange County Industrial Development Authority v. State
427 So. 2d 174 (Fla. 1983)

EHRLICH, Justice.

This cause is before the Court on direct appeal from a judgment of the circuit court denying validation of industrial development revenue bonds, the proceeds of which are for the construction of a television station. We have jurisdiction. Art. V, § 3(b)(2), Fla. Const. We find that the proposed project does not qualify as an industrial or manufacturing plant under Chapter 159, Florida Statutes (1981), nor does the project serve a paramount public purpose and we thus affirm the order of the trial court.

Appellant, the Orange County Industrial Development Authority, sought validation of $9,000,000 of industrial development revenue bonds requested by the Outlet Company and WCPX-TV, Outlet's television station in Orlando. The money would be spent to buy land and build a new 45,000 square feet facility to accommodate two broadcast studios and related offices, as well as to acquire and install machinery, equipment and other appurtenances. The station would not be a completely new project in the Orlando area but rather an expansion of an existing business, since WCPX-TV (formerly WDBO) has for many years been in operation as a commercial television station and the CBS network affiliate in the Orlando area. Executives of WCPX anticipated that a minimum of twenty-five jobs would be created by this project, increasing employment at the station from 110 to 135 persons. A major rationale for the bond money request was the station presently turning away profitable commercial production business due to the size of the present physical facility. It was also claimed that the new facilities would allow the station to increase its local news services as well as the projection of public service announcements.

The trial court, in a brief order, found that the proposed project did not qualify as an industrial or manufacturing plant. In addition, that court further found that the

---

77. *Id.* at 308–309. Of course, §§ 10(a), (b), and (d) also take the requisite bonds out of the prohibition in Fla. Const. art. VII, § 10.
78. 204 So. 2d 881 (Fla. 1967).
79. *Nohrr*, 247 So. 2d 304, 309. (Fla. 1971).

project did not serve a paramount public purpose. The trial court then denied the petition for validation.

* * *

This Court has recognized that the listing of particular authorized projects in article VII, section 10(c) of the Florida Constitution was not intended to deny public revenue bond financing of other types of projects. In *Nohrr v. Brevard County Educational Facilities Authority*, 247 So.2d 304 (Fla.1971), we said that "the naming of these particular projects was not intended to be exclusive." 247 So.2d at 308. This Court then went on to establish a two-prong test for determining whether revenue bonds for other projects would be validly authorized pursuant to the constitution. The two criteria are (1) whether the revenue bonds contemplate a pledge of the credit of the state or political subdivision and (2) whether the funded project serves a paramount public purpose, although there might be an incidental private benefit. 247 So.2d at 309. This test was reaffirmed in subsequent decisions. *See State v. Orange County Industrial Development Authority*, 417 So.2d 959 (Fla.1982); *State v. Leon County*, 400 So.2d 949 (Fla.1981); *State v. City of Miami*, 379 So.2d 651 (Fla.1980); *Wald v. Sarasota County Health Facilities Authority*, 360 So.2d 763 (Fla.1978).

As far as the first prong is concerned, there is no disagreement that the instant bonds will be payable solely from the sale, operation or leasing of the project and will not constitute a debt, liability or obligation of the appellant, the state, or any other subdivision thereof. The first criterion is thus clearly and easily met. The second, however, is not.

Running throughout this Court's decisions on paramount public purpose is a consistent theme. It is that there is required a paramount public purpose with only an incidental private benefit. If there is only an incidental benefit to a private party, then the bonds will be validated since the private benefits "are not so substantial as to tarnish the public character" of the project. *State v. City of Miami*, 379 So.2d 651, 653 (Fla.1980). *See also Panama City v. State*, 93 So.2d 608 (Fla.1957); *State v. Daytona Beach Racing & Recreational Facilities District*, 89 So.2d 34 (Fla.1956); *Gate City Garage, Inc. v. City of Jacksonville*, 66 So.2d 653 (Fla.1953). If, however, the benefits to a private party are themselves the paramount purpose of a project, then the bonds will not be validated even if the public gains something therefrom. "Every new business, manufacturing plant, or industrial plant which may be established in a municipality will be of some benefit to the municipality." *State v. Town of North Miami*, 59 So.2d 779, 784 (Fla.1952). "Incidental benefits accruing to the public from the establishment of some private enterprise is [sic] not sufficient to make the establishment of such enterprise a public purpose." *Adams v. Housing Authority of Daytona Beach*, 60 So.2d 663, 669 (Fla.1952), *overruled on other grounds, Baycol, Inc. v. Downtown Development Authority*, 315 So.2d 451 (Fla.1975). *Contra, State v. Housing Finance Authority of Polk County*, 376 So.2d 1158 (Fla.1979).

In the instant case, we find that the proposed project would not serve a paramount public purpose but rather a paramount private purpose. The Outlet Company would save around $300,000 per year for the life of the bonds. There will be no benefit to the public other than the improved local news coverage which might produce a more informed citizenry in the central Florida area, a minimal increase in employment, limited economic prosperity to the community, and an alleged advancement of the general welfare of the people. A broad, general public purpose, though, will not constitutionally sustain a project that in terms of direct, actual use, is purely a private enterprise. *State v. Manatee County Port Authority*, 193 So.2d 162 (Fla.1966); *State v. Town of North Miami*, 59 So.2d 779 (Fla.1952).

Appellant's reliance upon *State v. City of Jacksonville*, 50 So.2d 532 (Fla.1951), is misplaced. While there we allowed the issuance of municipal revenue certificates to finance the addition of television equipment for a radio station, that station was owned not by a private party but by the City of Jacksonville. The presence of municipal ownership was significant in our finding a public purpose in the project. Municipal ownership is absent in the project *sub judice*. We hold, then, that the proposed television station does not serve a paramount public purpose and hence is proscribed by our constitution.

Our discussion leads to this conclusion: the commercial television station at issue is not an industrial or manufacturing plant and does not serve a paramount public purpose. The project thus is not a proper one for which the Orange County Industrial Development Authority may authorize bonds. Hence, we affirm the trial court's invalidation of these bonds.

It is so ordered.

BOYD, OVERTON and McDONALD, JJ., concur.

ALDERMAN, C.J., dissents with an opinion, with which ADKINS, J., concurs.

[The dissenting opinion is omitted.]

Linscott v. Orange County Industrial Development Authority

443 So. 2d 97 (Fla. 1983)

SHAW, Justice.

This is a direct appeal from a judgment of the circuit court validating the issuance of industrial development revenue bonds for the construction of a regional headquarters office of a multi-state insurance company. We have jurisdiction under article V, section 3(b)(2), Florida Constitution. We find that the bonds do not involve a pledge of the public credit and that the project serves a public purpose as determined under chapter 159, part II, Florida Statutes (1981).

The Orange County Industrial Development Authority (Authority) adopted a resolution authorizing the issuance of tax exempt revenue bonds in a principal amount not to exceed $4,500,000 to finance the construction of a regional headquarters facility (project) in Orange County for American States Insurance Company. The resolution specified that the bonds would be payable solely from the revenue and proceeds derived from the sale, operation, or leasing of the project and would not constitute a debt, liability, or obligation of the Authority or the state or any political subdivision thereof; that the Authority would not be obligated to pay either the bonds or service charges thereon except from revenues and proceeds pledged therefor; and that neither the faith and credit nor the taxing power of the Authority or the state or any political subdivision thereof would be pledged to the payment of the bond service charges.

* * *

With the adoption of the Constitution of 1968, the "*paramount* public purpose" test developed by case law under the Constitution of 1885 lost much of its viability. The test is still applicable when a pledge of public credit is involved, but where such pledge is not involved, as here, it is enough to show only that a public purpose is served. We recognized this change in the equation in *Housing Finance Authority of Polk County*:

> Under the constitution of 1968, it is immaterial that the primary beneficiary of a project be a private party, if the public interest, even though indirect, is present and sufficiently strong. *State v. Putnam County Development Authority*, 249 So.2d 6 (Fla.1971). Of course, public bodies cannot appropriate public funds indiscriminately, or for the benefit of private parties, where there is not a reasonable and adequate public interest. An indirect public benefit may be adequate to support the public participation in a project which imposes no obligation on the public, and the qualification of the direct beneficiary complies with the principles of due process and equal protection.

376 So. 2d at 1160.

Chapter 159, part II, Florida Statutes (1981), contains a legislative determination that private economic development serves a public purpose and that it is in the public interest to facilitate the financing of capital projects such as a headquarters facility by the issuance of non-recourse revenue bonds. This legislative determination is entitled to great weight, particularly since it is consistent with the implicit recognition in section 10(c) that the public interest is served by facilitating private economic development. *State v. Orange County Industrial Development Authority*, 417 So.2d 959, 962 (Fla.1982). Further, section 159.33 specifically provides that bonds issued under the provisions of part II shall not constitute a pledge of public credit but shall be payable solely from the revenues of the capital project.

Appellant has failed to show that the bonds in question constitute a pledge of public credit or that the legislative determination of public purpose was so clearly wrong as to be beyond the power of the legislature.

Accordingly, we affirm the trial court's judgment validating the bonds and the power of the Orange County Industrial Development Authority to issue said bonds.

It is so ordered.

ALDERMAN, C.J., and ADKINS and McDONALD, JJ., concur.

OVERTON and EHRLICH, JJ., concur in result only.

BOYD, J., dissents with an opinion.

[The dissenting opinion of Justice Boyd is omitted.]

Although the outcome in *Linscott* is not surprising based on earlier decisions under the 1968 Florida Constitution, the shift in method of analysis is. The concurrence of Justices Overton and Ehrlich in the *Linscott* result, but not the *Linscott* opinion probably evidences this. Assuming that the bifurcated *Linscott* approach remains the law in interpreting art. VII, §10 of the 1968 Florida Constitution, two points must be noted.

First, rather than being a separate consideration, as cases such as *Nohrr* had suggested, the pledge of public credit will now apparently only enhance the requisite depth of the public nature of the project. This outcome had already been suggested in *State v. City of Miami*,[80] where the Supreme Court had little difficulty in finding a paramount public purpose in a convention center and parking garage even though it would also benefit the developer and the University of Miami, a private university. The bonds involved were not non-recourse bonds, but rather pledged "the net revenues derived by the City from or in connection with the convention center-garage *and other revenues of the City exclusive of ad valorem tax revenues.*"[81]

Second, great emphasis is placed on the legislative view of public purpose:

> ... What constitutes a public purpose is, in the first instance, a question for the legislature to determine, and its opinion should be given great weight. *Jackson Lumber Co. v. Walton County*, 95 Fla. 632, 116 So. 771 (1928). A legislative declaration of public purpose is presumed to be valid, and should be deemed correct unless so clearly erroneous as to be beyond the power of the legislature. *Wald v. Sarasota County Health Facilities Authority*, 360 So.2d 763 (Fla.1978); *Nohrr v. Brevard County Educational Facilities Authority*, 247 So.2d 304 (Fla.1971); *Price v. City of St. Petersburg*, 158 Fla. 705, 29 So.2d 753 (1947); *State v. Monroe County*, 148 Fla. 111, 3 So.2d 754 (Fla.1941).[82]

There are a number of statutes that authorize various types of revenue bond financing beneficial to the private sector. The one in *Housing Finance Authority of Polk County*[83] was Fla. Stat. §159.601 (1978), the Florida Housing Finance Authority Law. Another is the Florida Industrial Development Financing Act, Fla. Stat. §§159.25–159.431 (1987). After the Florida Supreme Court decided in January 1983 that revenue bond financing of an expansion of a commercial television station

---

80. 379 So. 2d 651 (Fla. 1980).

81. *Id.* at 652 (emphasis supplied). *See also Poe v. Hillsborough Cnty.*, 695 So. 2d 672 (Fla. 1997).

82. *State v. Hous. Fin. Auth. of Polk Cnty.*, 376 So. 2d 1158 (Fla. 1979).

83. *Id.* at 1160.

628 6 · TAXATION AND FINANCE

violated art. VII, § 10(c) of the Florida Constitution,[84] the 1983 Session of the Florida Legislature added "a motion picture production facility," defined as including property useful to, among other things, "television productions."[85] Whether this will change the result in *Orange County* remains to be seen.

As the following case appears to indicate, while the reasoning of *Linscott* may have been accepted, disputes can still arise as to whether or not projects rise even to the level of being a public purpose.

Northern Palm Beach County Water Control District v. State

604 So. 2d 440 (Fla. 1992)

CORRECTED OPINION

PER CURIAM.

This is an appeal from a final judgment which declined to validate water control and improvement bonds proposed to be issued by the Northern Palm Beach Water Control District (District). We have jurisdiction pursuant to article V, section 3(b)(2) of the Florida Constitution, and chapter 75, Florida Statutes (1989).

The District is a drainage district organized and existing under chapter 59-994, Laws of Florida, as amended and supplemented by chapter 89-462, Laws of Florida, and the applicable provisions of chapter 298, Florida Statutes (1989). The District sought validation of water control and improvement bonds to finance on-site road improvements in Unit of Development No. 31 (Unit 31), a unit of the District created for the purpose of draining and reclaiming the land located within the unit. The Unit 31 site, also known as Ballen Isles of the JDM Country Club, is being developed by Hansen-Florida II, Inc., and will include single family residences, multi-family housing, park areas, and three golf courses.

The Circuit Court of the Fifteenth Judicial Circuit appointed three commissioners to prepare a report regarding the District's water management plan for Unit 31. The commissioners' report determined that the estimated cost of the improvements would be less than the benefits assessed against the lands in Unit 31. The report distinguished between two separate components of the planned improvements. The first component improvements, consisting of the water management system, the water and sewer facilities, and exterior road improvements, are not at issue here. The Program Two improvements, which are the subject of this appeal, include interior or on-site road improvements such as paving, stripping, signs, landscaping, irrigation, bridges, an overpass, culverts, street lighting, security gatehouses, and a secondary drainage system consisting of storm drain pipes, inlets, manholes and surface drainage. The commissioners' report assessed the benefits of the Program

---

84. *Orange Cnty. Indus. Dev. Auth. v. State*, 427 So. 2d 174 (Fla. 1983).

85. 1983 Fla. Laws ch. 83-271, now codified as parts of Fla. Stat. § 159.27 (1987) (amended several times since codification).

Two improvements to be $18,125,000. The circuit court entered an order approving and confirming the report.

In December 1989, the Board of Supervisors of the District adopted a general bond resolution which authorized the issuance of Water Control and Improvement Bonds, Unit of Development No. 31, Program Two, in a principal amount not to exceed $16,312,500. The bond resolution provided that the bonds "shall not be general obligations or indebtedness" of the District, but instead are "special obligations payable solely" from, and secured by, a first lien and pledge of the proceeds of the drainage tax levied on the lands in Unit 31. In March 1990, the Board of Supervisors adopted a resolution levying a $42,625,000 drainage tax on the lands in Unit 31 in proportion to the benefits to be derived from the construction of the Program Two improvements. The amount levied consisted of an initial assessment of $18,125,000, plus the $24,500,000 interest estimated to accrue on the bonds.

After the bond validation hearing, the circuit court entered a final judgment which declined to validate the bonds because "[t]he intended use of the proceeds of this bond issue serves no valid public purpose." The final judgment also stated that the District failed to comply with its enabling legislation because it "did not meet the requirements of the *Safe Neighborhoods Act*, as enumerated in Sections 163.501– 163.522, Florida Statutes."

The scope of judicial inquiry in bond validation proceedings is limited to the following issues: 1) determining if the public body has the authority to issue the bonds; 2) determining if the purpose of the obligation is legal; and 3) ensuring that the bond issuance complies with the requirements of law. *Taylor v. Lee County*, 498 So.2d 424 (Fla.1986). Only two questions are presented for our consideration here: 1) whether the revenue bond proceeds will be used for a valid public purpose, and 2) whether the District has complied with the requirements of its enabling legislation in issuing the bonds.

As to the first issue, the State contends that these bonds violate article VII, section 10 of the Florida Constitution, which prohibits the District from using its taxing power or pledging public credit to aid private enterprise, and that no valid public purpose can be served by financing the construction of roadways within a private development where public access will be limited by security gatehouses. The District asserts that in enacting chapters 59-994 and 89-462 the legislature found a public purpose in designating roads for the exclusive use and benefit of a unit of development and its residents.

Article VII, section 10[1] of the Florida Constitution prohibits the state and its subdivisions, including special districts such as this water control district, from using

---

1. Article VII, section 10 of the Florida Constitution provides in pertinent part:
   Neither the state nor any county, school district, municipality, special district, or agency of any of them, shall become a joint owner with, or stockholder of, or give, lend or use its taxing power or credit to aid any corporation, association, partnership or person. . . .

its taxing power or pledging public credit to aid any private person or entity. However, if the project falls within one of the four subsections of article VII, section 10, then no constitutional prohibition is involved. *See Linscott v. Orange County Indus. Dev. Auth.*, 443 So.2d 97 (Fla.1983). The on-site road improvements planned for Unit 31 do not fall within these four subsections. Thus, in order to determine if the bonds run afoul of the constitution, we must first determine whether the District's taxing power or pledge of credit is involved. If either is involved, then the improvements must serve a paramount public purpose. *See Orange County Indus. Dev. Auth. v. State*, 427 So.2d 174 (Fla.1983). However, if we conclude that neither is involved, then the paramount public purpose test is not applicable and "it is enough to show only that a public purpose is served." *Linscott*, 443 So.2d at 101.

Section 298.36(1), Florida Statutes (1989), authorizes the board of supervisors of a water control district to "levy a tax" in proportion to the benefits to be derived from the works and improvements of the district. The District's resolution also refers to the assessment as a "drainage tax." However, we find that a special assessment rather than a tax is at issue in this case. *See Lake Howell Water & Reclamation Dist. v. State*, 268 So.2d 897 (Fla.1972). As this Court explained in *City of Boca Raton v. State*, 595 So.2d 25, 29 (Fla.1992), "there is no requirement that taxes provide any specific benefit to the property.... [But] special assessments must confer a specific benefit upon the land burdened by the assessment." We also noted that special assessments must be "reasonably apportioned among the properties that receive the special benefit." *Id.* Because this is a special assessment, rather than a tax, no use of the District's taxing power is involved. Moreover, the general bond resolution provides that the District cannot be compelled to exercise its taxing power in order to pay the bonds.

The resolution further provides that the bonds "shall be special obligations payable solely" from the drainage assessments to the landowners for the Program Two improvements, and that the bonds "shall not constitute a lien upon any of the facilities or properties" of the District. "Where there is no direct or indirect undertaking by the public body to pay the obligation from public funds, and no public property is placed in jeopardy by a default of the third party, there is no lending of public credit." *State v. Housing Fin. Auth.*, 376 So.2d 1158, 1160 (Fla.1979); *see also Nohrr v. Brevard County Educ. Facilities Auth.*, 247 So.2d 304 (Fla.1971). Thus, the bonds do not contemplate a pledge of the District's credit. Because neither the District's taxing power nor a pledge of its credit is involved here, the bonds need only serve a public purpose rather than a paramount public purpose. *See Linscott*, 443 So. 2d 97.

Chapter 59-994 created the District and imbued it with a number of powers, including the authority to "issue negotiable or other bonds" and "to construct, improve, pave and maintain roadways and roads" needed to access and develop those areas which are made suitable for settlement and development as a result of the operations of the District. Ch 59-994, §3, Laws of Fla. Chapter 89-462 empowered the District to construct roads "for the exclusive use and benefit of a unit of development and its landowners, [and] residents," to "finance and maintain said roads and their associated elements as part of a water management plan," and to

6 · TAXATION AND FINANCE

"construct and maintain security structures to control the use of said roads." Ch. 89-462, §6, Laws of Fla. Chapter 298, Florida Statutes (1989), also authorizes water control districts to issue bonds to pay for the costs of proposed improvements. *See, e.g.,* §§298.36(2), 298.47, Fla.Stat. (1989). This enabling legislation evidences a clear legislative expression that the on-site controlled access roads at issue in this case serve a valid public purpose. In addition, the District's Board of Supervisors adopted a resolution stating that the designation of roads for the exclusive use and benefit of Unit 31 is a public purpose "in the best interest of the health, safety, and general welfare of these areas and their inhabitants, visitors, property owners and workers." This Court has stated that a legislative declaration of public purpose is presumed to be valid, and should be deemed correct unless so clearly erroneous as to be beyond the power of the legislature. *Nohrr,* 247 So.2d 304. Although these legislative expressions of public purpose are not controlling, they are "entitled to great weight." *State v. Leon County,* 400 So.2d 949, 951 (Fla.1981).

As to the public purposes actually served by these bonds, we note that the roadway improvements at issue will provide access to the water management facilities and aid in the development of the reclaimed lands. However, the fact that public access to the roads will be limited raises a question of whether the stated public purposes are only incidental to a primary private purpose, the development of Unit 31 by Hansen-Florida II, Inc. "A broad, general public purpose . . . will not constitutionally sustain a project that in terms of direct, actual use, is purely a private enterprise." *Orange County,* 427 So.2d at 179. In *Orange County,* the Court found that the expansion of a television station's broadcast facilities did not serve a paramount public purpose even though the public would receive a number of benefits from the proposed expansion. However, the Court also noted that the presence of public ownership would be a significant factor in a finding of public purpose. *Id.*

In this case, the District will retain ownership of the roadways in question. This public ownership coupled with the legislative declaration of public purpose contained in the District's enabling legislation leads us to the conclusion that the on-site road improvements serve a public purpose. Thus, the proposed water control and improvement bonds are not prohibited by article VII, section 10 of the Florida Constitution.

As to the second issue, the State contends that the District failed to comply with its enabling legislation by not meeting the requirements of the Safe Neighborhoods Act, sections 163.501–163.522, Florida Statutes (1989).[2] Thus, the State contends that the District did not have the authority to issue the bonds. The District argues that

---

2. The District's enabling legislation provides in pertinent part:
   It is to the benefit of the land in the district and its ultimate users and residents to include provision in a water management plan *pursuant to and in furtherance of the Safe Neighborhoods Act, ss. 163.501–163.522, Florida Statutes,* for roads for the exclusive use and benefit of a unit of development and its residents.
Ch. 89-462, §6, Laws of Fla. (emphasis added).

compliance with chapter 163 is a collateral issue outside the scope of the bond validation hearing.

In light of the legislature's 1991 amendment of the District's enabling legislation, we need not address these arguments. Chapter 91-408, section 2, Laws of Florida, declares the inclusion of "provision in a water management plan for roads for the exclusive use and benefit of a unit of development and its residents" to be a "public purpose" and deletes reference to the Safe Neighborhoods Act.

Accordingly, we reverse the final judgment and remand with directions that the bond issue be approved.[3]

It is so ordered.

OVERTON, BARKETT, GRIMES and HARDING, JJ., concur.

SHAW, C.J., dissents with an opinion, in which KOGAN, J., concurs.

McDONALD, J., dissents [without opinion].

SHAW, C.J., dissenting.

The majority opinion trips lightly over the matter of how public financing of the construction and beautification of a private country club roadway serves a valid public purpose within the purview of article VII, section 10, Florida Constitution. I would affirm the trial court's judgment invalidating the bonds.

I. Facts

A. Private Country Club

The Northern Palm Beach Water Control District ("District"), a public drainage district of the State of Florida, proposes to issue $16,312,500 in government revenue bonds to pay for the construction and maintenance of approximately 24,000 feet of roadway within Unit of Development No. 31, otherwise known as the JDM Country Club ("Club"), a planned 1,313-acre private golf and tennis club. The District's Board of Supervisors ("Board") adopted a formal Water Management Plan ("Plan") for the Club, which provides in part:

> The Unit 31 site, known as JDM Country Club, is being developed as a Planned Community District under the procedures and requirements of the City of Palm Beach Gardens Code of Ordinances. The development will include [2,384 single family dwelling units], park areas and three golf courses.

The homes within the Club will occupy prime residential sites abutting, or lying in close proximity to, the fairways and greens of the three golf courses and, according to Paul Urschalitz, the District's security expert, will vary in price from a quarter-million to over a million dollars apiece:

---

3. We do not pass upon the economic desirability of these bonds, but only upon whether they may be legally issued. *See, e.g., State v. City of Sunrise*, 354 So.2d 1206 (Fla.1978).

6 · TAXATION AND FINANCE

Q. Would you anticipate looking at the type homes — did you have a chance to get an idea of what type of homes they're going to put in there?

A. Yes.

Q. What type of price range homes did you look at?

A. I think they're listed in this document, two hundred and fifty thousand to over a million. . . .

In addition to the roadway itself, the District will pay for extensive roadway improvements within the Club. Tracy Bennett, the District's engineer, testified:

> The onsite roadway improvements include paving of the roadways, the stripping, the signage, landscaping with the roadways, irrigation to maintain the landscaping and sodding, bridges, an overpass, culverts, street lighting, security gatehouses, and secondary drainage system consisting of storm drainage pipes, inlets, manholes and surface drainage.

B. "Caribbean Island" Motif

The District's Plan calls for extensive roadside landscaping paid for by the District to enhance the private Club's "Caribbean Island" theme.

> Extensive landscaping within the onsite roadway rights-of-way system is planned. . . . The overall theme of the development is to provide a Caribbean Island effect. Strong emphasis in the roadway planting will be on various palm species 20 to 30 feet high with a full-canopied backdrop, accented with dwarf palms and a wide variety of blooming groundcover plants. The remaining open areas will be sodded. The most intensive landscaping treatment is the median, followed by right-of-way adjacent to a development parcel, then right-of-way adjacent to lake open areas. . . .

According to the Plan,[4] the initial cost to the District of this garden-like landscaping is vast. The Plan states:

Estimated Costs of Improvements for Unit of Development No. 31

. . . .

III. Roadway Improvements

| A. Onsite [Roads] | $5,705,000 |
| B. Landscaping Onsite Roads | $5,803,000 |

Thus, the District, a public entity, will pay nearly six million dollars in initial roadside landscaping costs — more than the cost of the entire roadway itself — to promote the private Club's "Caribbean Island" motif. This amounts to almost *one and one-half million dollars of landscaping per mile of proposed roadway* for the private Club.

---

4. Two-page Exhibit No. 12 of the Plan, which detailed "Roadway Plantings," was omitted from the appendix to the District's brief.

C. Security Gatehouses

In addition to the "Caribbean Island" landscaping and other improvements noted above, the District will also pay for the construction and maintenance of three gatehouses to be staffed by security personnel to block all public access to the private Club. The District's official Plan provides:

> In addition, the Board of Supervisors has the power to provide, control ingress and egress, and maintain roads for the exclusive use and benefit of a Unit of Development and its landowners, residents and invitees.
>
> . . . .
>
> The onsite roadway system [is] planned for the exclusive use and benefit of [the Club] and its landowners, residents, and invitees. . . .

Peter Pimental, executive director of the District testified as follows:

> A. Want me to explain? What we proposed to do is construct these gatehouses as Mr. Bennett testified and with those gatehouses would be the security people who would control the ingress and egress to the project and those people or persons who have reason to be inside would be allowed inside the project. Those that have no purpose or no reason to be there, will not be permitted to just wander through the project.
>
> Q. How would you define reason to be there?
>
> A. There would be service directed, service oriented persons, residents, invitees, guests, police, fire, emergency service, all of those would have access to the project.
>
> Q. So if I was out on a Sunday afternoon driving around, just wanted to ride through the District, I would be restricted under your rules?
>
> A. Yes.
>
> Q. So it is not open to the public at all?
>
> A. Perhaps not. . . .

Thus, all on-site improvements within the Club — including the landscaping and roadway itself — that are paid for by the public District will be closed to the general public.

D. Financing

To pay for the District's proposed on-site improvements within the Club, the Board adopted a general bond resolution that authorizes issuance of Water Control and Improvement Bonds in a principal amount not to exceed $16,312,500. The resolution provides that the bonds shall not be general obligations or indebtedness of the District, but shall instead be special obligations payable solely from, and secured by, a first lien and pledge of the proceeds of a drainage tax levied on the lands of the Club. The Board subsequently adopted a resolution levying a $42,625,000 drainage tax on the lands of the Club in proportion to the benefits to be derived from the construction of the improvements. The tax, which consists of an initial assessment of $18,125,000 plus $24,500,000 interest expected to accrue on the bonds, will be paid solely by the landowners within the Club. The landowners will thus ultimately foot the bill for the District's proposed roadway improvements within the Club.

The bonds will be issued in the denomination of $5,000, or multiples thereof, will mature within 30 years, and significantly, will pay interest periodically (twice a year) from the District to bondholders at a rate to be determined later. In paying this interest, the Board covenants that it will comply with specific requirements of the federal tax code concerning the tax status of certain government bonds. These provisions, which are designed to stimulate funding for public projects, specify that interest payments by state and local governments to their investors may be tax-exempt for the investors. The Board's bond resolution states:

> Section 4.08. *Compliance with Tax Requirements.* The Issuer hereby covenants and agrees, for the benefit of the Owners from time to time of the Bonds, to comply with the requirements applicable to it contained in Section 103 and Part IV of Subchapter B of Chapter 1 of the Code and to the extent necessary to preserve the exclusion of interest on the Bonds from gross income for federal income tax purposes.

Because the District's interest payments to bondholders will be tax-exempt for the holders, the bonds will be readily marketable even though the District may offer the bonds at an interest rate substantially below that of privately-issued, taxable securities. This reduced interest rate will minimize the District's financial obligations to bondholders and the resulting tax obligations of the Club's landowners.

II. The Applicable Law

In *Taylor v. Lee County*, 498 So.2d 424, 425 (Fla.1986), Justice McDonald explained the nature of this Court's inquiry in bond validation proceedings:

> The scope of judicial inquiry in bond validation proceedings is limited. Specifically, courts should: 1) determine if a public body has the authority to issue the subject bonds; 2) determine if the purpose of the obligation is legal; and 3) ensure that the authorization of the obligations complies with the requirements of law.

In the present case, we are concerned primarily with whether the purpose of the District's bonds is legal.

Article VII, section 10, Florida Constitution, bars governments within Florida from using their taxing power or credit to aid private corporations or persons:

> SECTION 10. Pledging credit. — Neither the state nor any county, school district, municipality, special district, or agency of any of them, shall become a joint owner with, or stockholder of, or give, lend or use its taxing power or credit to aid any corporation, association, partnership or person. . . .

The purpose of section 10 is to prevent state government from using its vast resources to monopolize,[5] or otherwise "destroy,"[6] a segment of private enterprise, and also "to protect public funds and resources from being exploited in assisting or promoting private ventures when the public would be at most only incidentally benefited." *Bannon v. Port of Palm Beach Dist.*, 246 So.2d 737, 741 (Fla.1971). To pass constitution muster, a government bond issue must serve a truly public purpose, i.e., it must bestow a benefit on society that which is normally attendant to any successful business venture.[7]

During the pendency of the present case and immediately prior to oral argument before this Court, the legislature amended chapter 89-462, section 6, Laws of Florida, which concerns the Northern Palm Beach County Water Control District, to provide that restricted roadways serve a public purpose.

> Section 6. Roads for exclusive use and benefit of a unit of development and its residents. — It is hereby found and declared that among the many causes of deterioration in residential neighborhoods are the proliferation of crime, excessive automobile flow, and excessive noise levels from automobile traffic. It is to the benefit of the land in the district and its ultimate users and residents and it is hereby declared to be a public purpose to include provision in a water management plan for roads for the exclusive use and benefit of a unit of development and its residents. Therefore . . . the district has the power to adopt by resolution, a water management plan for a unit of development, that will permit the district to exercise the following powers:
>
> (1) To provide roads for the exclusive use and benefit of a unit of development and its landowners, residents and invitees to control ingress and egress.
>
> . . . .

(3) To construct and maintain security structures to control the use of said roads.

Ch. 91-408, § 2, Laws of Florida (emphasis and strike-through omitted).

---

5. *See Adams v. Housing Auth.*, 60 So.2d 663, 669 (Fla.1952).

6. *See State v. Town of North Miami*, 59 So.2d 779, 785 (Fla.1952).

7. This Court has used a myriad of terms in assessing the sufficiency of public purpose in revenue bond proceedings. *See, e.g., State v. City of Orlando*, 576 So.2d 1315, 1317 (Fla.1991) ("a paramount public purpose," and "a valid [public] purpose"); *State v. City of Panama City Beach*, 529 So.2d 250, 256 (Fla.1988) ("valid [public] purposes"), *receded from on other grounds*, 576 So.2d 1315 (Fla.1991); *Linscott v. Orange County Indus. Dev. Auth.*, 443 So.2d 97, 101 (Fla.1983) ("a public purpose"); *Orange County Indus. Dev. Auth. v. State*, 427 So.2d 174, 179 (Fla.1983) ("paramount public purpose"); *State v. Miami Beach Redevelopment Agency*, 392 So.2d 875, 886 (Fla.1980 ("some substantial benefit to the public"); *State v. Housing Fin. Auth.*, 376 So.2d 1158, 1160 (Fla.1979) ("if the public interest, even though indirect, is present and sufficiently strong," and "a reasonable and adequate public interest"); *Nohrr v. Brevard County Educ. Facilities Auth.*, 247 So.2d 304, 309 (Fla.1971) ("a public purpose").

III. Conclusion

Simply designating a project "public" by legislative fiat does not necessarily make it so, especially where uncontroverted facts attest otherwise. A quote from Lewis Carroll makes the point:

"I don't know what you mean by 'glory,'" Alice said.

Humpty Dumpty smiled contemptuously. "Of course you don't — till I tell you. I meant 'there's a nice knock-down argument for you!'"

"But 'glory' doesn't mean 'a nice knock-down argument,'" Alice objected.

"When I use a word," Humpty Dumpty said, in rather a scornful tone, "it means just what I choose it to mean — neither more nor less."

"The question is," said Alice, "whether you can make words mean so many different things."

"The question is," said Humpty Dumpty, "which is to be master — that's all."

Lewis Carroll, *Through the Looking Glass* 113 (Dial Books for Young Readers, NAL Penguin, Inc. 1988) (1872). Under our constitutional system of government in Florida, courts, not legislators or water control districts, are the ultimate "masters" of the constitutional meaning of such terms as "public purpose" in judicial proceedings.

While a restricted roadway may serve a valid public purpose under certain circumstances, I conclude that no reasonable and sufficient public purpose is served by issuance of government bonds to finance the construction and landscaping of roadways within the private JDM Country Club. The extraordinary expensive roadside landscaping to enhance the "Caribbean Island" motif of the private residences and golf courses within the Club would serve virtually no reasonable public purpose even if the Club were to be open to the general public. The fact that security gatehouses will be erected for the sole purpose of barring the public from the premises renders any alleged benefit to the public from the landscaping or roadway moot.[8]

It is perfectly clear to me that the District's bond project serves a simple, very private, purpose. It allows the owners of the proposed 2,384 residences within the Club to capitalize on a massive tax-break, intended for public projects, in financing the construction of a luxurious environment for their own private use. The undertaking smacks of state-sponsored, economic apartheid. I can conceive of few more private projects.

Rather than relying on an eleventh hour legislative declaration of public purpose and this Court's own examination of a cold record, I would place great weight on

---

8. I disagree with the majority's conclusion that because the District will retain ownership of the proposed roadway this demonstrates the existence of sufficient public purpose. To my mind, public ownership of the roads is meaningless if the roads are reserved for the exclusive use of the private country club residents and guests. The fact that the roads will provide some service access to water management facilities within the Club evinces no reasonable public purpose when those facilities exist for the sole benefit of private Club residents.

the reasoned judgment of the respected trial judge, for he alone had the opportunity to personally observe — on both direct and cross-examination — the demeanor of many of the Club's main functionaries, and he is far more familiar with the local circumstances surrounding this issue. Sufficient competent evidence supports his ruling.

I would affirm the trial court's judgment invalidating the bonds.

---

2. Controls on the Pledging of the Credit of the State

Fla. Const. art. VII, § 11

State bonds; revenue bonds. —

(a) State bonds pledging the full faith and credit of the state may be issued only to finance or refinance the cost of state fixed capital outlay projects authorized by law, and purposes incidental thereto, upon approval by a vote of the electors; provided state bonds issued pursuant to this subsection may be funded without a vote of the electors at a lower net average interest cost rate. The total outstanding principal of state bonds issued pursuant to this subsection shall never exceed fifty percent of the total tax revenues of the state for the two preceding fiscal years, excluding any tax revenues held in trust under the provisions of this constitution.

(b) Moneys sufficient to pay debt service on state bonds as the same becomes due shall be appropriated by law.

(c) Any state bonds pledging the full faith and credit of the state issued under this section or any other section of this constitution may be combined for purposes of sale.

(d) Revenue bonds may be issued by state or its agencies without a vote of the electors to finance or refinance the cost of state fixed capital outlay projects authorized by law, and purposes incidental thereto, and shall be payable solely from funds derived directly from sources other than state tax revenues.

(e) Bonds pledging all or part of a dedicated state tax revenue may be issued by the state in the manner provided by general law to finance or refinance the acquisition and improvement of land, water areas, and related property interests and resources for the purpose of conservation, outdoor recreation, water resource development, restoration of natural systems, and historic preservation.

(f) Each project, building, or facility to be financed or refinanced with revenue bonds issued under this section shall first be approved by the Legislature by an act relating to appropriations or by general law.

Bonds pledging the full faith credit and credit of the state may generally only be issued upon approval by a vote of the electors. Three primary exemptions exist to this rule.

First, state bonds authorized by statute to finance the construction of air and water pollution abatement facilities and solid waste disposal facilities may be issued without approval of the electorate.[86] Second, state bonds authorized by statute to finance or refinance the acquisition of real property or the rights to real property, or state bridge construction, which pledge the full faith and credit of the state, may be issued without the approval of the electorate.[87] Third, state bonds pledging the full faith and credit of the state for the construction of educational buildings, may, in certain instances, be issued without an election.[88]

The following cases discuss the requirements necessary for state bonds to be issued.

State v. Division of Bond Finance of Department of General Services

246 So. 2d 102 (Fla. 1971)

BOYD, Judge.

This cause is before us on appeal from the final judgment of the Circuit Court of the Second Judicial Circuit, validating certain proposed State of Florida, Escambia County, bridge bonds, dated November 1, 1970, in the aggregate principal amount of $4,900,000.00 to be issued by the Division of Bond Finance of the Department of General Services of the State of Florida. The project to be financed by these bonds is the construction of a new four-lane toll bridge and causeway across Santa Rosa Sound to replace the existing two-lane Pensacola Beach Bridge and Causeway. The nature of the project is not at issue in this appeal.

The proposed plan of financing calls for the bonds to be secured by and payable from (1) net tolls collected on the project, (2) eighty per cent (80%) gasoline tax funds accruing to the Department of Transportation and allocated to Escambia County,[1] and (3) the full faith and credit of the State of Florida; all allegedly pursuant to the provisions of Article XII, Section 9(c), of the revised Florida Constitution and other applicable provisions of law.

The question before us is whether the proceedings taken by the Division of Bond Finance and the other State agencies in connection with the proposed financing

---

86. Fla. Const. art. VII, § 14.

87. Fla. Const. art. VII, § 17.

88. Fla. Const. art. XII, § 9(d).

1. This bond issue does not pledge the entire amount of gas tax funds, but only the portion thereof not "used * * * for the payment of obligations pledging revenues allocated pursuant to Article IX, Section 16, of the Constitution of 1885, as amended." Article XII, Section 9(c) (5), Florida Constitution, F.S.A.

program, purporting to pledge the full faith and credit of the State of Florida, comply with the requirements of the Florida Constitution as contained in Article XII, Section 9(c), and in Article VII, Section 11 for the issuance of bonds to be secured by such a pledge.

This is the first case dealing with such subject matter to be brought before the courts, since the revision of the Florida Constitution permitting the State's credit to be pledged for highway bond issues under the conditions specified therein.

The learned trial judge held:

> The Bonds shall be 'State Bonds' within the meaning of said Section 9(c), Article XII, of the Constitution of the State of Florida and will be secured by a valid pledge of the full faith and credit of the State of Florida in the manner provided by such Resolution and Lease-Purchase Agreement.

> The issuance of the Bonds is not required, by any of the provisions of the Constitution or laws of the State of Florida, to be approved by the qualified electors who are freeholders, or by the qualified electors, residing in the State of Florida, Escambia County, or any other political subdivision of the State of Florida, and the Bonds are not subject to the limitations and conditions provided by Subsections (a) and (c) of Section 11 of Article VII of the Florida Constitution.

We agree with the court below that in adopting Article XII, Section 9(c), the people intended to provide an alternative method of financing state bonds without a referendum in certain particular instances. Article XII, Section 9(c), provides in part as follows:

> When authorized by law, state bonds pledging the full faith and credit of the state may be issued without any election: (i) to refund obligations secured by any portion of the 'second gas tax' allocated to a county under Article IX, Section 16, of the Constitution of 1885, as amended; (ii) to finance the acquisition and construction of roads in a county when approved by the governing body of the county and the state agency supervising the state road system; and (iii) to refund obligations secured by any portion of the 'second gas tax' allocated under paragraph 9(c) (4).

The issuance of bonds pledging the full faith and credit of the State has been "authorized by law", as required by the above-quoted provision of the Constitution, by Florida Statutes § 215.60 F.S.A., which provides, in part, as follows:

> The issuance of state bonds to finance the acquisition and construction of roads, primarily payable from the revenues provided for by Article XII, Section 9(c), of the state constitution and pledging the full faith and credit of the State, is hereby authorized, pursuant to the provisions of said section of the Constitution and this Act.

The bond issue before us has met the requirements of the 1968 Constitution and the Statutes of Florida and, although it pledges the full faith and credit of the State without a referendum, the issue is for a specifically exempted purpose and is valid.

6 · TAXATION AND FINANCE

Accordingly, the judgment below is affirmed.

It is so ordered.

ERVIN, ADKINS, McCAIN and DEKLE, JJ., concur.

ROBERTS, C. J., dissents with opinion.

ROBERTS, C. J. (dissenting).

I respectfully dissent because I do not believe that it was ever the intention of the Constitutional Revision Commission, or the Legislature, or the people of Florida to deal so lightly with the pledging of the general credit of this state which involves the overall taxing power of the state.

Florida had long cherished the proposition that it was free of state bonds and a general pledge of credit except when authorized by a statewide vote of the people. It is, therefore, difficult for me to accept the proposition that they have disposed of their credit in such a simple manner or assigned it to a board or bureau not answerable to the electorate at large.

Division of Bond Finance v. Smathers

337 So. 2d 805 (Fla. 1976)

BOYD, Justice.

We have before us an original proceeding in mandamus brought by the Division of Bond Finance of the Department of General Services, the Governor, as the Chairman of the Governing Board of the Division of Bond Finance and the State Treasurer, as Treasurer of the Governing Board of the Division of Bond Finance, against the Secretary of State, the Executive Director of the Department of Natural Resources, and the Department of Natural Resources, questioning the constitutional validity of the following proviso which appears after Item 853 in Section 1 of the General Appropriations Act, Chapter 76-285, Laws of Florida:

> Provided that any future sales of general obligation bonds for environmentally endangered lands shall have as the first priority the repayment of monies expended for debt service from the Land Acquisition Trust Fund.

* * *

... We need to look no farther than the first of these six sections to resolve the matter. Article VII, Section 11(a) of the Florida Constitution provides:

> §11. *State bonds — revenue bonds* (a) State bonds pledging the full faith and credit of the state may be issued only to finance or refinance the cost of state capital projects upon approval by a vote of the electors; provided state bonds issued pursuant to this subsection (a) may be refunded without a vote of the electors at a lower net average interest cost rate. The total outstanding principal of state bonds issued pursuant to this subsection (a) shall never exceed fifty per cent of the total tax revenues of the state for the two preceding fiscal years.

The proviso requires that the proceeds of general obligation bonds for environmentally endangered lands be expended for purposes other than the financing or refinancing of the cost of State capital projects. It is violative of Article VII, Section 11(a) on its face.

Accordingly, a peremptory writ of mandamus shall issue commanding the Secretary of State to expunge from Section 1, Chapter 76-285, Laws of Florida, the following language:

> Provided that any future sales of general obligation bonds for environmentally endangered lands shall have as the first priority the repayment of monies expended for debt service from the Land Acquisition Trust Fund.

and further commanding the Department of Natural Resources and its Director to take no action inconsistent with this opinion.

It is so ordered.

OVERTON, C. J., and ENGLAND, SUNDBERG and HATCHETT, JJ., concur.

3. Local Bonds

Fla. Const. art. VII, § 12

Local bonds. — Counties, school districts, municipalities, special districts and local governmental bodies with taxing powers may issue bonds, certificates of indebtedness or any form of tax anticipation certificates, payable from ad valorem taxation and maturing more than twelve months after issuance only:

(a) to finance or refinance capital projects authorized by law and only when approved by vote of the electors who are owners of freeholds therein not wholly exempt from taxation; or

(b) to refund outstanding bonds and interest and redemption premium thereon at a lower net average interest cost rate.

The same general restrictions which are applicable to state bonds are also applicable to local bonds. Generally, any local bond which pledges the ad valorem tax revenues of the issuing entity and matures more than 12 months after issuance can only be issued after it has been approved by the electorate of the affected entity.

However, if the ad valorem revenues of the issuing entity are not at risk, no election is required.[89] As the following case suggests, at some point the ad valorem taxes of a governmental entity may be at risk, even if not specifically pledged.

---

89. *See State v. Miami Beach Redevelopment Agency*, 392 So. 2d 875 (Fla. 1980). *See also Miccosukee Tribe of Indians of Fla. v. S. Fla. Water Mgmt. Dist.*, 48 So.3d 811 (Fla. 2010).

County of Volusia v. State
417 So. 2d 968 (Fla. 1982)

BOYD, Justice.

This cause is before the Court on appeal from a judgment of the circuit court denying the complaint of the County of Volusia for validation of capital improvement bonds in the amount of $40,000,000. We have jurisdiction. Art. V, § 3(b)(2), Fla .Const.

The County seeks to issue the bonds to finance construction of a jail to be located on Indian Lake Road eleven miles from DeLand, the county seat. The payment of the bonds is to be secured by the county's pledge of all legally available, unencumbered sources of county revenue including all money derived from regulatory fees and user charges assessed by the county. The county also covenants to do all things necessary to continue receiving the various revenues pledged.

. . . The [trial] court determined that most of the various revenues from regulatory fees and user charges could not be pledged to the payment of the bonds because such county revenues may not be diverted from their lawful purposes, which are to defray the costs incurred by the county in providing the services to which the various fees and charges relate. Second, the court found that the pledge of all legally available revenues other than ad valorem taxation would have the effect of requiring the levy of increased ad valorem taxation so that, under article VII, section 12, Florida Constitution,[1] the bonds may not be issued without approval of the eligible voters by referendum. . . .

. . . We affirm the trial court's judgment denying validation. We hold that the pledge of all the legally available, unencumbered revenues of the county other than ad valorem taxation, along with a covenant to do all things necessary to continue receiving the revenues, as security for the bonds, will have the effect of requiring increased ad valorem taxation so that a referendum is required. Our disposition of the case on this ground makes it unnecessary to reach and settle the questions of whether the various non-ad valorem revenues may be pledged to the financing of a jail facility. . . .

* * *

We discuss now the dispositive issue and hold that the pledge of *all* legally available, unencumbered revenues — *i.e.*, all revenues, other than ad valorem taxation, which the governing body has the authority to spend or pledge at its discretion — calls

---

1. Article VII, section 12, provides:

   Counties, school districts, municipalities, special districts and local governmental bodies with taxing powers may issue bonds, certificates of indebtedness or any form of tax anticipation certificates, payable from ad valorem taxation and maturing more than twelve months after issuance only: (a) to finance or refinance capital projects authorized by law and only when approved by vote of the electors who are owners of freeholds therein not wholly exempt from taxation. . . .

into play the referendum requirement of article VII, section 12 because it in effect constitutes a promise to levy ad valorem taxes. The county correctly states that this Court has approved pledges of various local government revenue sources without referendum even though the encumbrance of the funds would have an incidental effect on the exercise of the ad valorem taxing power. *State v. Alachua County*, 335 So.2d 554 (Fla.1976); *Town of Medley v. State*, 162 So.2d 257 (Fla.1964). In *Town of Medley v. State*, 162 So.2d 257 (Fla.1964), a municipality proposed to construct a water supply system and building together with storm sewers and streets and to finance these improvements by the sale of revenue bonds. As security for the payment of the bonds, the town pledged to their retirement the revenues to be earned by the water system, together with revenues from the following four specific sources: the proceeds from cigarette taxes, a municipal utility franchise tax, utilities taxes, and occupational license taxes. The bond issue was challenged on the ground that diverting these revenues from the town's general operating fund would require increased ad valorem taxes in order to replace those funds, and that such a result required approval by referendum. This Court responded:

> Only bonds or certificates of indebtedness which directly obligate the ad valorem taxing power are encompassed by [the constitutional referendum requirement]. The incidental effect on use of the ad valorem taxing power occasioned by the pledging of other sources of revenue does not subject such bonds or certificates to that constitutional requirement.

162 So.2d at 258. The Court said that to hold otherwise would prevent a local government from pledging non-ad valorem funds previously used for general operating expenses without a referendum, a result not required in light of the purpose of the constitutional requirement.

In *State v. Alachua County*, 335 So.2d 554 (Fla.1976), we held that the county's pledge of its annual revenue sharing funds and its annual share of state race track funds to the repayment of bonds issued to finance various capital projects and public improvements without referendum did not violate article VII, section 12. Citing *Town of Medley v. State* as authority, we again held that only a direct pledge of, and not indirect impact on, the ad valorem taxing power required referendum approval.

The present case differs from both *Town of Medley v. State* and *State v. Alachua County*. One point of distinction is that here the county has attempted to pledge all legally available revenue sources other than ad valorem taxation, rather than several specific sources. Secondly, here the county has further promised to fully maintain the programs and services which generate the service fees and user charges. To maintain all of the programs that produce the revenues, while devoting the revenues themselves to the retirement of the bonds, will inevitably require that ad valorem taxes be increased so that the county will have sufficient operating revenue to maintain the programs and services that generate the pledged revenues.

In *State v. Halifax Hospital District*, 159 So.2d 231 (Fla.1963), a special district with ad valorem taxing power attempted to pledge as security for bonds all of its available revenues. The district also covenanted to fully maintain its operations in order to ensure that it continued to receive the pledged revenues. The general operations of the district were funded through ad valorem taxation. This Court held that the district's pledge of all available non-ad valorem revenues, together with the promise to maintain all operations during the life of the bonds, would have more than mere incidental effect on the ad valorem taxing power. The Court held that therefore the bonds could not be validated without the approval of the voters.

That which may not be done directly may not be done indirectly. *See, e.g., State v. Halifax Hospital District*, 159 So.2d 231 (Fla.1963). While the county has not directly pledged ad valorem taxes to the payment of the bonds, its pledge of all other available revenues, together with its promise to do all things necessary to continue to receive the various revenues, will inevitably lead to higher ad valorem taxes during the life of the bonds, which amounts to the same thing. We find in this case that the pledge of all available revenues, together with a promise to maintain the programs entitling the county to receive the various revenues, will have a substantial impact on the future exercise of ad valorem taxing power and brings this case within the rule of *Halifax Hospital District*. The taxpayers of Volusia County must have an opportunity to vote on the bond issue.

* * *

Accordingly, the order denying validation is affirmed.

It is so ordered.

SUNDBERG, C. J., and McDONALD and EHRLICH, JJ., concur.

ALDERMAN, J., dissents with an opinion, in which ADKINS and OVERTON, JJ., concur.

ALDERMAN, Justice, dissenting.

I would reverse the trial court and remand with directions that these bonds be validated.

* * *

I disagree, . . . with the majority's conclusion that these bonds require referendum approval under article VII, section 12, Florida Constitution. This Court has repeatedly upheld the validity of pledges of local non-ad valorem revenue sources without referendum approval. In *State v. Tampa Sports Authority*, 188 So.2d 795 (Fla.1966), we affirmed the trial court's validation of bonds to be issued for the development and maintenance of a sports facility where the city and county agreed that repayment of the bonds should be from available moneys derived from sources other than the proceeds of ad valorem taxation. Citing *State v. City of Jacksonville*, 53 So.2d 306 (Fla.1951), we said:

> We have repeatedly held that when certificates of indebtedness are for an authorized public purpose and are payable solely from revenues derived from utilities service, excise taxes, licenses or some other source than ad

valorem taxes, they may be issued without an approving vote of the free-holders as required by Section 6, Article IX of the Constitution.

188 So. 2d at 797. *See also State v. Monroe County*, 81 So.2d 522 (Fla.1955).

We have upheld such pledges by local governments even though ad valorem taxes probably would be affected. In *Town of Medley v. State*, 162 So.2d 257 (Fla.1964), the trial court denied validation of public improvement revenue bonds which were to be repaid with revenues from a proposed water system, proceeds of the cigarette tax, franchise taxes on electric power, utility taxes, and occupational license taxes. Although no ad valorem taxes were pledged and the ordinance authorizing the bond issue specifically provided that the town would not be obligated to levy ad valorem taxes for repayment of the bonds, the trial court concluded that validation of the bonds would result in an increase in real property taxes without vote of the freeholders. In reversing the order denying validation, this Court held:

> In any instance in which a municipality has been using funds from special non-ad valorem sources of revenue to meet its operating costs and then diverts those funds by pledging them to payment of a specific indebtedness as done here, the result will probably be that ad valorem taxes will have to be increased to make up the deficiency in funds available for operating expenses.
>
> Nevertheless, this result does not make the revenue bonds or certificates subject to the provisions of Section 6, Article IX, of our State Constitution, F.S.A. A contrary holding would mean that any pledging of non-ad valorem revenues previously used for the general operating expenses of a municipality would require approval by vote of the freeholders and such was never the purpose of the cited constitutional provision.
>
> Only bonds or certificates of indebtedness which directly obligate the ad valorem taxing power are encompassed by Section 6, Article IX, Fla.Const. The incidental effect on use of the ad valorem taxing power occasioned by the pledging of other sources of revenue does not subject such bonds or certificates to that constitutional requirement.

162 So.2d at 258. More recently, we reaffirmed this position in *State v. Alachua County*, 335 So.2d 554 (Fla.1976).

This issue is not governed by *State v. Halifax Hospital District*, 159 So.2d 231 (Fla.1963), wherein we declined to affirm validation of hospital improvement bonds to be repaid from gross revenues of the hospital. In that case, we held that the hospital's pledge of all gross revenues *coupled with its pledge not to reduce during the life of the bonds the currently assessed ad valorem tax levy for maintenance and operation of the hospital* required referendum approval. We found that the hospital's pledge of ad valorem taxes was as much an obligation of the bond resolution as was the pledge of the gross revenues. Volusia County, unlike the Halifax Hospital District, has not expressly pledged ad valorem taxes to continue the operation of those governmental functions needed to generate the revenues to repay the bonds.

In the present case, as in *Town of Medley* and *Alachua County*, the authorizing documents specifically state that the ad valorem taxing power is not directly pledged to repayment of the bonds and such repayment cannot be compelled by the bondholders. The pledge of non-ad valorem funds results in a diversion of funds from the county's general revenue and probably will require ad valorem taxes to be increased to make up the deficiency in funds available for operating expenses, but I would hold, as we did in *Town of Medley* and *Alachua County*, that such an incidental effect on Volusia County's ad valorem taxing power does not require referendum approval pursuant to article VII, section 12 of the Florida Constitution.

* * *

Accordingly, I would reverse the trial court's order and remand with directions that these bonds be validated.

ADKINS and OVERTON, JJ., concur.

————

The dichotomy between a direct pledge of ad valorem tax revenues and an indirect pledge of those revenues continues.

Murphy v. City of Port St. Lucie

666 So. 2d 879 (Fla. 1995)

PER CURIAM.

We have for review a final judgment validating the City of Port St. Lucie's (City) 1994A Bonds and 1994A Assessments. We have jurisdiction. Art. V, § 3(b)(2), Fla. Const. We affirm the trial court's final judgment validating the bonds and assessments.

Material Facts

Appellee sought validation of special assessment bonds in an amount not to exceed $17,600,000 to finance the expansion of water and sewer utility lines into areas of the City designated as Special Assessment District No. 1 (also referred to as Special Assessment Area No. 1), Phase I (SAD 1, Phase I). At this time, the City also enacted an ordinance (Assessment Ordinance) providing an alternative source of authority to Chapter 170, Florida Statutes (1993), for the levy and collection of special assessments. Additionally, the City Council adopted a resolution to provide for the levy and collection of special assessments against the properties within SAD 1, Phase I, which would be specially benefited by the provision of central water and/or sewer service.

Subsequently, the City filed a complaint in the circuit court for validation of the Special Assessment Bonds, Series 1994A. After a hearing, the trial court found that

648   6 · TAXATION AND FINANCE

all the requirements of law with respect to the issuance of the 1994A Bonds and the levy and collection of the 1994A Assessments had been satisfied. Consequently, it validated the 1994A Bonds and the 1994A Assessments. This appeal followed.[1]

Law and Analysis

* * *

Next, appellant argues that the covenant to budget and appropriate in the Master Bond Ordinance violates article VII, section 12, of the Florida Constitution. The gist of appellant's argument is that this ordinance provision obligates all of the City's non-ad valorem funds, and, in effect, promises to levy ad valorem taxes without a referendum. Appellant relies on *County of Volusia v. State*, 417 So.2d 968 (Fla.1982), where the county attempted to pledge all legally available revenue sources (other than ad valorem taxes), including regulatory fees and user charges, as security for bonds used to construct a jail. We find *Volusia County* distinguishable from this case. First, the Master Bond Ordinance states:

> [T]he City may covenant, for the benefit of the Owners of the Bonds of such Series, to budget and appropriate in any Bond Year or Fiscal Year, solely from Non Ad Valorem Revenues, such funds as may be necessary to *supplement* the Pledged Revenues to the extent necessary to pay the Debt Service Requirement on the Bonds of such Series.

Port St. Lucie, Fla., Ordinance No. 94-35 § 3.04(E) (1994) (emphasis added). As this section clearly states, the non-ad-valorem revenues are being considered only as a *supplemental* source of revenue in the event the pledged revenues are insufficient to pay for the debt service. In contrast, in *Volusia County*, the non-ad-valorem revenue was being used as the sole source of income. Second, unlike *Volusia*, there is no provision in this resolution for the City to continue services for the purpose of generating income to pay the bonds. Thus, because any potential impact on ad valorem taxation is incidental, section 3.01 does not violate article VII, section 12, of the Florida Constitution.

* * *

Conclusion

In sum, because we find that the City acted within its authority and complied with all the requirements of the law in issuing the instant bonds, we affirm the trial court's final judgment validating the bonds and the assessments.

It is so ordered.

GRIMES, C.J., and OVERTON, SHAW, KOGAN, HARDING, WELLS and ANSTEAD, J.J., concur.

---

1. A group of City residents, including Murphy, were opposed to the expansion project and filed petitions with the city clerk to have the City's ordinances reconsidered.

The following year, the Florida Supreme Court further explained its role in the bond validation proceedings:

> This Court has consistently held that "[t]he sole purpose of a validation proceeding is to determine whether the issuing body had the authority to act under the constitution and laws of the state and to ensure that it exercised that authority in accordance with the spirit and intent of the law." *McCoy Restaurants, Inc. v. City of Orlando*, 392 So.2d 252, 253 (Fla.1980). The legislature never intended for bond validation proceedings to be used to decide collateral issues or issues that did not directly address the power to issue bonds and the validity of the proceedings. *State v. City of Miami*, 103 So.2d 185, 188 (Fla.1958). The scope of this Court's inquiry in bond validation proceedings is thus limited to the following considerations: "1) determining if the public body has the authority to issue the bonds; 2) determining if the purpose of the obligation is legal; and 3) ensuring that the bond issuance complies with the requirements of law." *Rowe v. St. Johns County*, 668 So.2d 196, 198 (Fla.1996).[90]

Wilson v. Palm Beach County Housing Authority
503 So. 2d 893 (Fla. 1987)

OVERTON, Justice.

This is a direct appeal from a final judgment validating revenue bonds of the Palm Beach County Housing Authority. We have jurisdiction, article V, section 3(b)(2), Florida Constitution, and we affirm the final judgment validating the bonds.

The Palm Beach County Housing Authority was created pursuant to section 421.27, Florida Statutes (1985), and seeks to validate revenue bonds for financing the acquisition and construction of low income housing. The proposed bonds are payable solely from the housing projects' revenues and the bond proceeds investment earnings. Pledges of these revenues and earnings and of mortgages on the projects secure the proposed bonds.

The only issue before this Court is whether the housing authority's grant of a mortgage security interest mandates an election for bond approval. The trial court rejected the argument that the bonds would be valid only with electorate approval.

Appellants contend that this Court's decisions in *Boykin v. Town of River Junction*, 121 Fla. 902, 164 So. 558 (1935), and *Nohrr v. Brevard County Educational Facilities Authority*, 247 So.2d 304 (Fla. 1971) [the *Nohrr* opinion is found herein, *supra* page 469], require an election to approve bonds secured by a mortgage on physical property. In *Boykin*, the local governmental entity issuing the bonds had ad valorem taxing authority. We deleted the mortgage provision from the bonds in *Nohrr*,

---

90. *See State v. Miami Beach Redevelopment Agency*, 392 So. 2d 875 (Fla. 1980). *See also Miccosukee Tribe of Indians of Fla. v. S. Florida Water Mgmt. Dist.*, 48 So. 3d 811 (Fla. 2010).

noting that, although there would be no coercion to impose a tax for those particular bonds issued to benefit a private educational institution, there easily could be coercion if the bonds were for a public institution. In *Nohrr*, although the issuing authority did not have taxing power, we stated that the relationship with the county or the legislature could be such that those entities "would feel morally compelled to levy taxes or to appropriate funds to prevent the loss of those properties [public schools] through the process of foreclosure." 247 So.2d at 311.

In the instant case, it is clear the Palm Beach County Housing Authority has no ad valorem taxing authority and, in issuing these bonds, there is no direct or indirect pledge of taxing power. We reject the applicability of *Boykin* and *Nohrr*, and conclude that under these circumstances the mortgage provisions do not constitute a debt, liability, or obligation of Palm Beach County, the state of Florida, or any political subdivision, nor do they pledge the full faith and credit of Palm Beach County, the state of Florida, or any political subdivision. Further, we reject the argument that those entities would experience coercion to levy a tax to prevent the foreclosure of the project. We recede from *Nohrr* to the extent it conflicts with this opinion.

Accordingly, we affirm the trial court's validation of the revenue bonds.

It is so ordered.

McDONALD, C.J., and EHRLICH, SHAW, BARKETT, GRIMES and KOGAN, JJ., concur.

---

4. Tax Increment Financing (TIF) Bonds

The issue of tax increment financing was briefly discussed in *State v. City of Daytona Beach*,[91] reproduced earlier in this chapter. Tax increment financing is a method of financing used ostensibly in community redevelopment projects and is based on the premise that a portion of the increased ad valorem tax revenues generated as a result of the enhanced value of the property after the improvements should be available to pay for the redevelopment. The "tax increment" is the difference between the amount of ad valorem tax revenue collected prior to the redevelopment of the blighted area and the amount of ad valorem tax revenue collected after the blighted area has been redeveloped. This "increment" is what is pledged as security for bonds that are issued to fund the redevelopment project. The controversy surrounding this method of financing stems from whether the pledge of the "tax increment" is deemed a pledge of ad valorem tax revenues, which requires a referendum be held prior to issuance of the bonds pursuant to Fla. Const. art. VII, §12.

---

91. 484 So. 2d 1214 (Fla. 1986).

The Florida Supreme Court first upheld the constitutionality of the issuance of tax increment financing bonds without a referendum in the case of *State v. Miami Beach Redevelopment Agency*.[92] However, on September 6, 2007, in its decision in *Strand v. Escambia County*,[93] the Supreme Court receded from its opinion in *Miami Beach* and overturned nearly twenty-seven years of case law that held that a referendum was not required before tax increment funding bonds could be issued. On September 17, 2008, the Supreme Court reversed itself citing the doctrine of *stare decisis*, and Justice Wells, writing for the court, reasoned as follows:

> [F]or the past twenty-seven years there has been widespread reliance upon the *Miami Beach* decision in the issuance of bond financing by local government authorities, including school boards, enabling the financing of many public works that have enhanced the quality of life in our State. Tax increment financing and the undergirding principles of our *Miami Beach* decision have been inextricably woven into the financial fabric of our State. We conclude that receding from the precedent of *Miami Beach* would cause serious disruption to the governmental authorities that have relied upon that precedent for planning public works that are in various stages of development and approval.

Strand v. Escambia County

992 So. 2d 150 (Fla. 2008)

WELLS, J.

We have before us an appeal from a final judgment validating a proposed bond issue from the Circuit Court of the First Judicial Circuit, in and for Escambia County, Florida. We have jurisdiction. *See* art. V, §3(b)(2), Fla. Const. Upon consideration of appellee Escambia County's motion for rehearing, we withdraw our revised opinion, filed on September 28, 2007, and substitute the following opinion. We affirm the circuit court's final judgment.

I. Factual and Procedural Background

On May 4, 2006, Escambia County (County) adopted Ordinance 2006-38 (Ordinance). The Ordinance establishes the Southwest Escambia Improvement District (District) in the southwest portion of the County, running to the peninsula known as Perdido Key. The Ordinance also establishes the Southwest Escambia Improvement Trust Fund (Trust Fund), which will be used to finance or refinance infrastructure improvements in the District, and authorizes the use of tax increment financing to fund the Trust Fund. In conjunction with the adoption of the Ordinance, the County adopted Resolution R2006-96 (Resolution) on May 4, 2006, authorizing the County to issue bonds not exceeding $135,000,000 for the District. The stated purpose of these bonds is to finance a four-lane road-widening project in

---

92. 392 So. 2d 875 (Fla. 1980).
93. 32 Fla. L. Weekly S587 (Fla. 2007).

the District to improve economic development within that area and alleviate traffic congestion. The bonds are to reach maturity no later than the thirty-fifth year after revenues are first deposited into the Trust Fund.

The Ordinance provides that the bonds are to be "payable out of revenues pledged to and received by the County and deposited to its Southwest Escambia Improvement Trust Fund." Ordinance § 4(4). The Ordinance requires the County to appropriate to the Trust Fund by February 1 of each year an amount equal to the "Tax Increment"[1] so long as any applicable indebtedness is outstanding. *Id.* § 4(1)-(3). The funds equaling the Tax Increment that are placed into the trust are known as "Tax Increment Revenues." *Id.* § 2.

The Resolution employs the term "Trust Fund Revenues," which are the moneys other than "Supplemental Revenues"[2] deposited in the Trust Fund pursuant to the provisions of the Ordinance. Resolution art. I, § 101 (May 4, 2006). The Resolution provides that the bonds shall be repaid from "Pledged Funds,"[3] which are the funds deposited in the Trust Fund including the Trust Fund Revenues and the Supplemental Revenues. *Id.* art. III, § 301. The Resolution does require that if necessary, the County shall appropriate in its annual budget non-ad valorem revenues if available as Supplemental Revenues sufficient to secure the indebtedness in each fiscal year. However, the Resolution expressly states that the County does not covenant to maintain any services or programs now provided which generate non-ad valorem tax revenues. *Id.* § 304(m).

The Ordinance and the Resolution dictate that the bonds do not pledge the full faith and credit or taxing power of the County, the State, or any political divisions thereof. Section 4 of the Ordinance states as follows:

> (4) The revenue Bonds and notes of every issue under this part are payable out of revenues pledged to and received by the County and deposited to

---

1. The Ordinance defines "Tax Increment" as:
   [T]he amount equal to the lesser of (a) the amount by which (i) the tax revenues that would have been generated at the millage rate in effect for the current Fiscal Year at the current Assessed Valuation exceeds (ii) the tax revenues that would have been generated at the millage rate in effect for the current Fiscal Year at the Base Assessed Valuation and (b) an amount equal to the sum of (i) 110% of the debt service of any outstanding indebtedness secured by the Tax Increment Revenues coming due in such Fiscal Year and (ii) an amount sufficient to restore any deficiencies in payment of debt service for such indebtedness for prior periods and to fund any planned expenditures described in Section 4(6) hereof.

2. "Supplemental Revenues" are County revenues derived from a source other than ad valorem taxation on real and personal property that are appropriated and deposited into the Trust Fund in the event that the Trust Fund Revenues are not sufficient to pay the debt service on the bonds. Resolution art. I, § 101; art. III, § 304.

3. "Pledged Funds" are "collectively, (i) the Trust Fund Revenues; (ii) the Supplemental Revenues, . . . and (iii) except for moneys, securities and instruments in the Rebate Account, all moneys, securities and instruments held in the Funds and Accounts established by this Resolution." Resolution art. I, § 101.

6 · TAXATION AND FINANCE

its Southwest Escambia Improvement Trust Fund. The lien created by such bonds, notes or other forms of indebtedness shall not attach until the revenues referred to herein are deposited in the Southwest Escambia Improvement Trust Fund at the times, and to the extent that, such Tax Increment Revenues accrue. The holders of such bonds, notes or other forms of indebtedness have no right to require the imposition of any tax or the establishment of any rate of taxation in order to obtain the amounts necessary to pay and retire such bonds, notes or other forms of indebtedness.

(5) Revenue Bonds issued under the provisions of this part shall not be deemed to constitute . . . a pledge of the faith and credit of the County or the state or any political subdivision thereof, but shall be payable solely from the revenues provided therefor.

Ordinance § 4(4)-(5). Section 103(i) of the Resolution reiterates that the bonds are payable solely from the Pledged Funds and "shall not constitute an indebtedness, liability, general or moral obligation, or a pledge of the faith, credit or taxing power of the Issuer, the State, or any political subdivision thereof." Section 301 adds that no bondholder shall ever have the right to compel the exercise of the ad valorem taxing power of the Issuer, the State or any political subdivision thereof, or taxation in any form of any real or personal property therein, or the application of any funds of the Issuer, the State or any political subdivision thereof . . . other than the Pledged Funds as provided in this Resolution.

Section 302 explains that the bonds "shall not constitute a lien upon any property owned by or situated within the corporate territory of the Issuer, but shall constitute a lien only on the Pledged Funds." Accordingly, no lien created by the bonds shall attach until the revenues are deposited in the Trust Fund. Finally, the Resolution includes a finding that "[t]he estimated Pledged Funds will be sufficient to pay all principal of and interest on the [bonds]." Resolution art. I, § 103(h).

On May 16, 2006, the County filed a complaint for validation in the Escambia County Circuit Court, seeking validation of the bond issuance. The state attorney promptly filed his answer, and Dr. Gregory Strand intervened pursuant to section 75.07, Florida Statutes (2006). Dr. Strand argued that the bond issuance was distinguishable from the bond issuance approved by this Court in *State v. Miami Beach Redevelopment Agency*, 392 So.2d 875 (Fla.1980), and therefore required a referendum pursuant to the requirement of article VII, section 12 of the Florida Constitution.[4]

---

4. Article VII, section 12 of the Florida Constitution states:
   Local Bonds. — Counties, school districts, municipalities, special districts and local governmental bodies with taxing powers may issue bonds, certificates of indebtedness or any form of tax anticipation certificates, payable from ad valorem taxation and maturing more than twelve months after issuance only:

654   6 · TAXATION AND FINANCE

On August 18, 2006, the circuit court entered the final judgment validating the bond issuance. The circuit court concluded that the County had the authority to issue the bonds and that the bonds were not subject to referendum pursuant to article VII, section 12. The circuit court cited to our decisions in *Miami Beach* and *Penn v. Florida Defense Finance & Accounting Service Center Authority*, 623 So.2d 459 (Fla.1993). Dr. Strand, the intervenor, appeals that final judgment.

II. Standard of Review

In *City of Gainesville v. State*, 863 So.2d 138, 143 (Fla.2003), this Court explained the scope of a bond validation proceeding as follows:

We have previously explained the scope of a bond validation proceeding: "[C]ourts should: (1) determine if a public body has the authority to issue the subject bonds; (2) determine if the purpose of the obligation is legal; and (3) ensure that the authorization of the obligation complies with the requirements of law." *State v. City of Port Orange*, 650 So.2d 1, 2 (Fla.1994).

This Court reviews the "trial court's findings of fact for substantial competent evidence and its conclusions of law de novo." *Id.* (citing *Panama City Beach Cmty. Redev. Agency v. State*, 831 So.2d 662, 665 (Fla.2002); *City of Boca Raton v. State*, 595 So.2d 25, 31 (Fla.1992)). The final judgment of validation comes to this Court clothed with a presumption of correctness. *Wohl v. State*, 480 So.2d 639, 641 (Fla.1985).

III. Analysis

Dr. Strand raises three issues in his appeal: (A) whether the circuit court abused its discretion in denying his motion for continuance; (B) whether the circuit court's final judgment is supported by competent, substantial evidence; and (C) whether the bonds required a referendum pursuant to the requirement of article VII, section 12 of the Florida Constitution.

* * *

[The court found that the circuit court did not abuse its discretion in denying Dr. Strand's motion and the circuit court's final judgment was supported by competent, substantial evidence.]

C. Legal Authority to Issue Bonds Without a Referendum

The circuit court determined that the bonds could be validated without the referendum required by article VII, section 12, Florida Constitution, because the bonds to be issued under the Ordinance and the Resolution do not constitute an indebtedness, liability, or pledge of the faith, credit, or taxing power of the County. On appeal, Dr. Strand argues that the bonds should not have been validated because the

---

(a) to finance or refinance capital projects authorized by law and only when approved by vote of the electors who are owners of freeholds therein not wholly exempt from taxation; or

(b) to refund outstanding bonds and interest and redemption premium thereon at a lower net average interest cost rate.

County did not comply with the Community Redevelopment Act, chapter 163, Florida Statutes. The County responds that chapter 163 does not apply to the County's issuance of the bonds. Rather, the County intends to issue the bonds based upon the powers granted to the County by section 125.01, Florida Statutes (2006).[5] We agree with the County. We find that this issue is controlled by our decision in *Penn,* in which we previously affirmed the Escambia County Circuit Court's validation of bonds issued under a similar tax ordinance and resolution and issuance structure.[6]

Dr. Strand further argues, as the appellant in *Penn* contended, that this financing mechanism violates article VII, section 12 of the Florida Constitution, which requires a referendum for bonds payable from ad valorem taxation and maturing more than twelve months after issuance. We rejected this argument in *Penn* because we found the financing mechanism in that case indistinguishable from the financing mechanism that we approved in *Miami Beach.* Likewise, we find that the financing mechanism in the instant case is not distinguishable from that which we approved in the *Miami Beach* case. Thus, we reject Dr. Strand's argument that the bonds in this case require a referendum.

On rehearing, Dr. Strand argues, and the dissenters to our present opinion agree, that we should recede from our decision in *Miami Beach.* In *Miami Beach,* we reviewed a judgment of the Circuit Court for Dade County which validated bonds issued pursuant to sections 163.385 and 163.387, Florida Statutes (1977), which authorized the issuance of bonds utilizing tax increment financing to finance redevelopment projects.

---

5. Section 125.01, Florida Statutes (2006), states:

Powers and duties. —

(1) The legislative and governing body of a county shall have the power to carry on county government. To the extent not inconsistent with general or special law, this power includes, but is not restricted to, the power to:

(m) Provide and regulate arterial, toll, and other roads, bridges, tunnels, and related facilities

. . . .

(r) Levy and collect taxes, both for county purposes and for the providing of municipal services within any municipal service taxing unit, and special assessments; borrow and expend money; and issue bonds, revenue certificates, and other obligations of indebtedness. . . .

(w) Perform any other acts not inconsistent with law, which acts are in the common interest of the people of the county, and exercise all powers and privileges not specifically prohibited by law.

6. In *Penn* we stated:

Under the ordinances, the bonds will be secured by lease payments from the city and county, which in turn are secured by tax increment revenues measured in part by future increases in ad valorem tax receipts. Any shortfall will be made whole by non-ad valorem revenues, but the bondholders' lien attaches only to monies actually deposited in the trust funds.

623 So.2d at 461.

In *Miami Beach,* the opponents of the bond issuance contended that the bonds were payable from ad valorem taxation and therefore required a referendum. The opponents maintained that the bonds were payable from ad valorem taxation because the required contributions of Dade County and the City of Miami Beach to the repayment fund were to be derived from taxes levied on the real property in the redevelopment area. In response, the Miami Beach Redevelopment Agency (Agency) argued that the bonds did not come within the referendum requirement because there was no pledge of the ad valorem taxing power of the county and city. *Miami Beach,* 392 So.2d at 893–94. In its brief, the Agency maintained that "[t]he crux of the matter is that there is no pledge of the ad valorem taxing power to which bondholders may look, and which they may legally enforce, as a source of funds to pay the bonds." Answer Brief to Initial Brief of Appellant at 32, *State v. Miami Beach Redev. Agency,* 392 So.2d 875 (Fla.1980) (No. 57997).

In our *Miami Beach* opinion, we decided the issue in favor of the Agency stating:

> The Agency contends in effect that where there is no direct pledge of ad valorem tax revenues, but merely a requirement of an annual appropriation from any available funds, the referendum provision of article VII, section 12 is not involved. We agree with this view....

392 So.2d at 894. We thereafter delineated the history of judicial precedents which led to our conclusion and held:

The bonds in the instant case are payable from a trust fund, and the fund will receive revenue from two sources. One source is the money the Agency receives from sales, leases, and charges for the use of, redeveloped property. This source is analogous to revenues generated by a utility or facility. The other source is the money to be contributed each year by the county and city, measured by the tax increment. The source of this revenue is not limited to any specific governmental revenue. That the statutory duty to make the annual contributions would become a contractual duty, part of the obligation of the bonds, does not mean, however, that these bonds are payable from ad valorem taxation, in the constitutional sense of the term.

The Agency notes that even though the money the county and city will use to make the contributions may come from ad valorem tax revenues, we have indicated this does not bring the bonds within the referendum requirement. *Tucker v. Underdown,* 356 So.2d 251 (Fla.1978). In that case, county bonds previously issued without referendum to finance a solid waste disposal system had been validated as payable from user charges, giving bondholders no power to compel the levy of ad valorem taxes for operating expenses or debt service. The subsequent lawsuit concerned whether the county had violated the covenants of the earlier bond issue by levying and spending ad valorem taxes for these purposes. The Court held that it had not.

Tucker v. Underdown supports the argument that there is nothing in the constitution to prevent a county or city from using ad valorem tax revenues where they are required to compute and set aside a prescribed amount, when available, for a discreet [sic] purpose. The purpose of the constitutional limitation is unaffected by the legal commitment; the taxing power of the governmental units is unimpaired. *What is critical to the constitutionality of the bonds is that, after the sale of bonds, a bondholder would have no right, if the redevelopment trust fund were insufficient to meet the bond obligations and the available resources of the county or city were insufficient to allow for the promised contributions, to compel by judicial action the levy of ad valorem taxation.* Under the statute authorizing this bond financing the governing bodies are not obliged nor can they be compelled to levy any ad valorem taxes in any year. The only obligation is to appropriate a sum equal to any tax increment generated in a particular year from the ordinary, general levy of ad valorem taxes otherwise made in the city and county that year. Issuance of these bonds without approval of the voters of Dade County and the City of Miami Beach, consequently, does not transgress article VII, section 12.

Miami Beach, 392 So.2d at 898–99 (emphasis added). Two members of the Court dissented from this conclusion. In his concurring in part and dissenting in part opinion, Justice Boyd specifically expressed the view that the promised annual contributions to the trust fund based on the tax increment revenues constituted a pledge by the county and the city of their general revenue and made the bonds general obligation bonds, which were payable from ad valorem taxation. *Id.* at 900 (Boyd, J., concurring in part and dissenting in part). Thus, the arguments advocated here by Dr. Strand and the present dissenters were previously advanced in *Miami Beach* and rejected by this Court.

In 1990, we reinforced our holding in *Miami Beach* in our decision in *State v. School Board of Sarasota County*, 561 So.2d 549 (Fla.1990). We stated:

> Regarding the bonds' validity, the issue presented is whether a referendum is required by article VII, section 12 of the Florida Constitution (1968). We conclude that because these obligations are not supported by the pledge of ad valorem taxation, they are not "payable from ad valorem taxation" within the meaning of article VII, section 12, and referendum approval is not required.

In *State v. Miami Beach Redevelopment Agency*, 392 So.2d 875 (Fla.1980), we interpreted the words "payable from ad valorem taxation" in article VII, section 12 and held that a referendum is not required when there is no direct pledge of the ad valorem taxing power. We noted that although contributions may come from ad valorem tax revenues: "What is critical to the constitutionality of the bonds is that, after the sale of the bonds, a bondholder would have no right, if [funds] were insufficient to meet the bond obligations . . . to compel by judicial action the levy of ad valorem taxation. . . . [T]he governing bodies are not obliged nor can they be compelled to levy any ad valorem taxes in any year." *Id.* at 898–99. The agreements here, as in *Miami Beach*, although supported in part by ad valorem revenues, expressly provide that neither the bondholders nor anyone else can compel use of the ad valorem taxing power to service the bonds.

Id. at 552 (footnote omitted) (alterations in original). Again, the majority's decision was met by a dissent, which maintained that the financing mechanism employed in those cases were equivalent to issuing bonds and pledging ad valorem taxation to support them. Again, the dissenters' view was rejected by the Court.

As referenced earlier, we affirmed the validation of a bond issuance in Escambia County in *Penn* on the basis of our decision in *Miami Beach*. We also relied on *Miami Beach* in affirming a bond validation in *State v. Inland Protection Financing Corp.*, 699 So.2d 1352 (Fla.1997).

We have stated that we are committed to the doctrine of stare decisis. *N. Fla. Women's Health & Counseling Services, Inc. v. State*, 866 So.2d 612, 637 (Fla.2003). In that case, we pointed out that the "doctrine of *stare decisis*, or the obligation of a court to abide by its own precedent, is grounded on the need for stability in the law and has been a fundamental tenet of Anglo-American jurisprudence for centuries." *Id.* We observed that the doctrine was memorialized by this Court a century and a half ago in *Tyson v. Mattair*, 8 Fla. 107 (1858). We then set forth the questions to be considered when asked to recede from precedent, expressly stating that the presumption in favor of precedent is strong. The questions to be asked are:

> (1) Has the prior decision proved unworkable due to reliance on an impractical legal "fiction"? (2) Can the rule of law announced in the decision be reversed without serious injustice to those who have relied on it and without serious disruption in the stability of the law? And (3) have the factual premises underlying the decision changed so drastically as to leave the decision's central holding utterly without legal justification?

N. Fla. Women's Health, 866 So.2d at 637. In the instant case, we do not find that the answers to these questions overcome the presumption in favor of stare decisis.

In answer to the first question, we have not been presented with evidence showing that the *Miami Beach* decision has proven unworkable due to reliance on a legal fiction. Rather, we find that the holding of the majority in *Miami Beach* was scrutinized and tested by the dissenters in *Miami Beach* and later in the *School Board of Sarasota County* decision, and determined by the Court's majority to be developed from seasoned historic precedent.

In answer to several questions, we conclude that for the past twenty-seven years there has been widespread reliance upon the *Miami Beach* decision in the issuance of bond financing by local government authorities, including school boards, enabling the financing of many public works that have enhanced the quality of life in our State. Tax increment financing and the undergirding principles of our *Miami Beach* decision have been inextricably woven into the financial fabric of our State. We conclude that receding from the precedent of *Miami Beach* would cause serious disruption to the governmental authorities that have relied upon that precedent for planning public works that are in various stages of development and approval.

Finally, we do not find that any changes have occurred since the *Miami Beach* decision that affect that decision. There have in fact been no changes which would affect our construction of the applicability of article VII, section 12, to bond issues using the tax increment financing structure determined to be valid in *Miami Beach* — article VII, section 12 of the Florida Constitution has not been amended. The Constitutional Revision Commission which met in 1997 and 1998 proposed nine revisions to other sections of the Florida Constitution but did not propose any revision to the constitution that would change the holding of *Miami Beach. See* Fla. Constitution Revision Comm'n, Nine Proposed Revisions for the 1998 Ballot, http://www.law.fsu.edu/crc /ballot.html; *Fla. Dep't of Revenue v. City of Gainesville,* 918 So.2d 250, 264 (Fla.2005) ("This determination [relating to the term 'municipal or public purpose'] is consistent with the principle that the Legislature 'is presumed to have adopted prior judicial constructions of a law unless a contrary intention is expressed,' *Florida Dep't of Children Families v. F.L.,* 880 So.2d 602, 609 (Fla.2004), which is equally applicable on the constitutional level. *See generally Coastal Fla. Police Benev. Ass'n v. Williams,* 838 So.2d 543, 548 (Fla.2003) (stating that rules governing statutory construction are generally applicable to construction of constitutional provisions).").

Alternatively, Dr. Stand contends that if we do not recede from *Miami Beach* and its progeny, we should find that it does not control the decision in this case. Dr. Strand argues that, instead, this case should be controlled by this Court's decision in *County of Volusia v. State,* 417 So.2d 968 (Fla.1982). In that case, we affirmed the Volusia County Circuit Court's denial of validation of a bond issue in part because the circuit court found that Volusia County's pledge of all legally available revenues other than ad valorem taxes would have the effect of requiring the levy of increased ad valorem taxation so that, under article VII, section 12, the bonds could not be issued without a referendum. In *County of Volusia,* we specifically affirmed the circuit court, holding:

> That which may not be done directly may not be done indirectly. *See, e.g., State v. Halifax Hospital District,* 159 So.2d 231 (Fla.1963). While the county has not directly pledged ad valorem taxes to the payment of the bonds, its pledge of all other available revenues, together with its promise to do all things necessary to continue to receive the various revenues, will inevitably lead to higher ad valorem taxes during the life of the bonds, which amounts to the same thing. We find in this case that the pledge of all available revenues, together with a promise to maintain the programs entitling the county to receive the various revenues, will have a substantial impact on the future exercise of ad valorem taxing power and brings this case within the rule of *Halifax Hospital District.* The taxpayers of Volusia County must have an opportunity to vote on the bond issue.

417 So.2d at 972. In the present case, the County argues that *County of Volusia* is distinguishable because section 304(m)(1) of the Resolution expressly does not covenant to maintain any services or programs now provided or maintained by the County which generate non-ad valorem revenues. The County further points out that we approved a similar financing mechanism in *Murphy v. City of Port St. Lucie,* 666 So.2d 879 (Fla.1995).

We agree that as in *City of Port St. Lucie,* the instant Ordinance and Resolution differ from those in *County of Volusia* in that non-ad valorem revenues here are to be used only as a supplemental source of funding in the event that the Trust Fund revenues are insufficient for debt service and in that the County expressly does not covenant to maintain services or programs for the purpose of generating income to repay the bonds. *See City of Port St. Lucie,* 666 So.2d at 881.[7]

IV. Conclusion

For the reasons stated above, we affirm the final judgment of validation of the Escambia County Circuit Court.

It is so ordered.

ANSTEAD and PARIENTE, JJ., and CANTERO, Senior Justice, concur.

QUINCE, C.J., concurs in part and dissents in part.

LEWIS, J., dissents with an opinion, in which QUINCE, C.J., concurs.

BELL, J., recused.

[Dissenting and concurring opinions omitted.]

---

5. Arbitrage Bonds

Is it a valid public purpose to issue bonds and reinvest the proceeds to make a profit? The next case answers this question.

State v. City of Orlando

576 So. 2d 1315 (Fla. 1991)

GRIMES, Justice.

This is an appeal from a judgment validating certain bonds that the City of Orlando proposes to issue. We have jurisdiction under article V, section 3(b)(2) of the Florida Constitution.

The City of Orlando adopted resolutions providing for the issuance of revenue bonds in an amount not to exceed $500,000,000. The bonds, which may be issued either as tax-exempt or taxable obligations, are to be used to finance qualifying projects of local agencies either through the execution of Local Agency Loan Agreements or through the purchase of local agency securities. Local agencies are defined

---

7. Likewise, we find that our decision in *Frankenmuth Mutual Insurance Co. v. Magaha,* 769 So.2d 1012, 1025 (Fla.2000), is distinguishable because in that case, we found that the size of the lease payments together with the consequences of the nonsubstitution clause in the lease-purchase agreements which were the subject of that action would eventually force the county to spend ad valorem taxes to make the lease payments. The present Ordinance and Resolution do not contain a clause similar to the nonsubstitution clause in *Frankenmuth.*

as governmental units in the State of Florida. Thus, the city will issue the bonds and use the proceeds to buy debt instruments of, or make loans to, such governmental units. As ultimately approved by the trial court, the qualifying projects of the local agencies may include the purchase of liability coverage contracts and the funding of self-insurance reserves as well as such projects as the building of roads, water systems, jails, utility facilities, and sports facilities.

The resolutions specifically provide that the bonds shall not be deemed to constitute a debt liability or obligation of the state or any political subdivision or municipality, except that the local agencies may be liable to the extent of their respective obligations under the loan agreements. Thus, the bonds would be payable only from the funds derived from repayment of the loans by the local agencies. The local agencies could pledge ad valorem taxes to repay the loans, but only after complying with the constitutional requirements for making such pledges. The funds would be handled pursuant to trust indentures with financial institutions, and the city, itself, could borrow some of the money pursuant to a local agency loan agreement. The final judgment states that it shall not estop any person from challenging in a collateral proceeding the validity of any specific project that is financed by a local agency or the validity of any local agency proceeding designed to authorize such financing.

The state contends that the proposed bond issue is illegal because it does not identify any specific projects to be financed, the local agencies who will receive the financing, and the revenue sources that the local agencies would use for repayment to the city. The city responds that, pursuant to the authority of section 166.111, Florida Statutes (1989), the city is authorized to issue these bonds either for the purpose of investing the proceeds at a profit or for the purpose of establishing a pool of funds to make loans to cities and counties and to invest in their debt obligations. In testimony taken at the hearing, it was represented that the city, together with the local agencies, will be able to benefit from economies associated with large-scale financing and will be able to generate income for itself that would be used for valid municipal purposes.

Our determination of this case requires us to analyze this Court's decision in *State v. City of Panama City Beach*, 529 So.2d 250 (Fla.1988). In that opinion, we discussed the checkered history of municipal bond financing in Florida. We also explained that most of the bond validation cases this Court had considered in the past involved the borrowing of money to finance some kind of capital project. The legal issue usually presented in these cases was whether the use of bond proceeds for a particular project constituted a paramount public purpose. *See, e.g., Orange County Indus. Dev. Auth. v. State*, 427 So.2d 174 (Fla.1983).

The case of *State v. City of Panama City Beach* presented a new issue. In that case, the city proposed to issue $300,000,000 in revenue bonds, with the proceeds to be invested with an insurance company under a contract that would provide a guaranteed rate of return in excess of the interest rate on the city's bonds. The estimated $1.5 million profit was to be used for park and recreational facilities, self-insurance reserves, or other municipal purposes. We recognized that this was the first time the legality of the issue of this type of bond, known as an arbitrage bond, had come before the Court. Because we concluded that the profit from the financing scheme would be used for valid municipal purposes, we upheld the bond issue.

The bond issue now before us builds upon the rationale of *State v. City of Panama City Beach*. The City of Orlando proposes to lend the bond proceeds to other governmental entities throughout the state. However, neither the governmental entities to whom the bond proceeds will be lent nor the revenues from which these entities will repay their loans are identified. While the final judgment places some limitation on how the governmental entities may spend the borrowed monies, no specific projects or uses for the money are identified. The amount of profits which the City of Orlando might expect cannot be estimated. Such profits as may be earned by the city will be placed in general revenue for later use as the city commissioners may determine. While ultimately approving the bond issue, the trial judge observed in a memorandum accompanying his ruling,

> The chief financial officer of the city testified that the employment of this bond issue required such sophistication it could not be understood by counsel for the state and taxpayer defendant, which makes one wonder whether it might be beyond one or more individual city councilpersons, and "municipal purpose" might become something demonstrated by using mirrors.

The proposed bond issue could be invalidated because of its failure to provide enough details by which its legality can be measured. Clearly, we are unable to say whether the profits the city hopes to obtain will be used for a paramount public purpose. By allowing the city council to later decide how to spend the profits, the city has deprived this Court of the ability to determine whether the expenditures will meet a paramount public purpose.

The lack of specificity mentioned above could probably be corrected by amending the documents that control the issuance of the bonds. However, in the course of our consideration of this case, we have become concerned with a deeper problem. In *State v. City of Panama City Beach*, we limited our focus to how the profits from the issuance of the arbitrage bonds were to be used. In bond validation proceedings, we now believe that the overall purpose of the bond issue should be examined. When viewed in this light, it is obvious that the primary purpose of the current bond issue is to obtain proceeds that will be used to invest for a profit.

Article VIII, section 2(b) of the Florida Constitution provides:

> (b) POWERS. Municipalities shall have governmental, corporate and proprietary powers to enable them to conduct municipal government, perform municipal functions and render municipal services, and may exercise any power for municipal purposes except as otherwise provided by law. Each municipal legislative body shall be elective.

We now conclude that borrowing money for the primary purpose of reinvestment is not a valid municipal purpose as contemplated by article VIII, section 2(b). A municipality exists in order to provide services to its inhabitants. As noted in then-Chief Justice McDonald's dissenting opinion in *State v. City of Panama City Beach*, we "see no valid public purpose in investing for investing's sake. Making a profit on an investment is an aspect of commerce more properly left to commercial banking and business entities." 529 So.2d at 257 (McDonald, C.J., dissenting).

We have not overlooked the fact that the city may derive an incidental benefit from the economies of large-scale financing by borrowing some of the money under a local agency agreement to use for legitimate municipal purposes. This was a primary motivation for the enactment of section 163.01 et seq., Florida Statutes (1989), known as the Florida Interlocal Cooperation Act of 1969. The act is not applicable to this case because the City of Orlando has not entered into an interlocal agreement with another public agency for the issuance of these bonds. Here, the city, acting alone, proposes to issue bonds and lend the proceeds with the intention of making a profit.

Accordingly, we recede from *State v. City of Panama City Beach* to the extent that it conflicts with this opinion. Our ruling shall be prospective only and shall have no effect on any bonds that may have been previously issued or approved. It does not prohibit the investment of bond proceeds pending later expenditures on the project contemplated by the bond issue. Further, our opinion should not be construed to place limitations upon either the ability of municipalities to invest for a profit any funds it may have on hand or the right to issue bonds to repay previously borrowed funds used for valid municipal projects. §§ 166.101(8), 166.111, 166.261, Fla.Stat. (1989); *State v. City of Sunrise*, 354 So.2d 1206 (Fla.1978). We hold the proposed bond issue of the City of Orlando to be invalid and reverse the final judgment entered below.

It is so ordered.

SHAW, C.J., and OVERTON, McDONALD, BARKETT and KOGAN, JJ., concur.

Chapter 7

The Declaration of Rights and the Taking of Property

A. Introduction

In reviewing the Declaration of Rights in the Florida Constitution, the reader finds many provisions which are similar, and in some instances identical, to provisions in the Bill of Rights in the Federal Constitution. This leads one to wonder whether the Florida Declaration of Rights has any independent significance, or whether it simply restates what the Federal Bill of Rights already requires. In fact, the Declaration of Rights has served three primary purposes.

First, prior to the enactment of the Fourteenth Amendment to the United States Constitution and the judicial doctrine of selective incorporation, which applied many of the guarantees of the Bill of Rights to the states, the protection of individual civil rights was primarily left to the state constitutions. As a result, the state declarations of rights possessed a historical importance. While the significance of a state's Declaration of Rights has diminished in the wake of the recent predominance of the Federal Bill of Rights, it has not been eliminated.

Second, a state Declaration of Rights can afford greater individual protection than the similar incorporated Bill of Rights provision. In *Oregon v. Hass*,[1] the United States Supreme Court enunciated this distinction:

> . . . *Hass* suggests that "when state law is more restrictive against the prosecution than federal law," this Court has no power "to compel a state to conform to federal law." [Citation omitted.] This, apparently, is proffered as a reference to our expressions that a State is free *as a matter of its own law* to impose greater restrictions on police activity than those this court holds to be necessary upon federal constitutional standards. . . . But, of course, a State may not impose such greater restrictions as a matter of *federal constitutional law* when this Court specifically refrains from imposing them. [Footnote omitted and emphasis in original.] . . .

Third, a state Declaration of Rights may protect a right that is simply not protected under the Federal Bill of Rights. For example, Fla. Const. art. 1, § 23 recognizes and protects a right of privacy. Although certain provisions of the Federal

---

1. 420 U.S. 714, 719 (1975).

665

666   7 · THE DECLARATION OF RIGHTS AND THE TAKING OF PROPERTY

Constitution implicate privacy interests, there is no *explicit* provision in the Federal Bill of Rights recognizing a right to privacy. This is an illustration of a state constitution providing more protection of individual rights than the Federal Constitution requires.

Traylor v. State[2]
596 So. 2d 957 (Fla. 1992)

SHAW, Chief Justice.

* * *

I. Facts

* * *

II. Federalism

The courts of at least eleven states have chosen to interpret the self-incrimination provisions of their own state constitutions in a manner independent of the federal Court's Fifth Amendment jurisprudence.[2] Under our federalist system of government, states may place more rigorous restraints on government intrusion than the federal charter imposes; they may not, however, place more restrictions on the fundamental rights of their citizens than the federal Constitution permits. *PruneYard Shopping Ctr. v. Robins*, 447 U.S. 74, 100 S.Ct. 2035, 64 L. Ed.2d 741 (1980).[3] Federalist principles recognize that although some government intrusion into the life of the individual is inevitable, such intrusion is to be minimized. Government encroachment is thus restricted by both the federal and state constitution.

The federal Constitution secures a common degree of protection for the citizens of all fifty states, but the federal Court has wisely exercised restraint in construing the extent of this protection for several reasons. First, under our federalist system,

---

2. While the decision in this case regarding a Florida citizen's right against self-incrimination has been called into question by *Rigterink v. State*, 66 So. 3d 866 (Fla. 2011), the principle that state courts are free to interpret state constitutional provisions to grant greater protections than similar provisions under the Federal Constitution remains intact.

2. As of 1986, courts in the following states had construed the self-incrimination provisions of their state constitutions independently of the federal Court's Fifth Amendment holdings: Alaska, California, Georgia, Hawaii, Louisiana, Massachusetts, Michigan, New Hampshire, Pennsylvania, Vermont, and Wyoming. *See Scott v. State*, 519 P.2d 774 (Alaska 1974); *In re Misener*, 38 Cal.3d 543, 213 Cal.Rptr. 569, 698 P.2d 637 (1985); *State v. Armstead*, 152 Ga.App. 56, 262 S.E.2d 233 (1979); *State v. Miyasaki*, 62 Haw. 269, 61 P.2d 915 (1980); *State in re Dino*, 359 So.2d 586 (La.), *cert. denied*, 439 U.S. 1047, 99 S.Ct. 722, 58 L.Ed.2d 706 (1978); *Attorney Gen. v. Colleton*, 387 Mass. 790, 444 N.E.2d 915 (1982); *People v. Conte*, 421 Mich. 704, 365 N.W.2d 648 (1984); *State v. Benoit*, 126 N.H. 6, 490 A.2d 295 (1985); *Commonwealth v. Bussey*, 486 Pa. 221, 404 A.2d 1309 (1979); *State v. Badger*, 141 Vt. 430, 450 A.2d 336 (1982); *Westmark v. State*, 693 P.2d 220 (Wyo.1984). Mary A. Crossley, Note, *Miranda and the State Constitution: State Courts Take a Stand*, 39 Vand. L. Rev. 1693, 1717–18 n. 181 (1986).

3. *See also Oregon v. Hass*, 420 U.S. 714, 95 S.Ct. 1215, 43 L.Ed.2d 570 (1975); *Cooper v. California*, 386 U.S. 58, 87 S.Ct. 788, 17 L.Ed.2d 730 (1967). *See generally, State v. Hunt*, 91 N.J. 338, 450 A.2d 952 (1982).

7 · THE DECLARATION OF RIGHTS AND THE TAKING OF PROPERTY   667

many important decisions concerning basic freedoms have traditionally inhered in the states. Second, the federal Court's precedent is binding on all jurisdictions within the union; once it settles a matter, further experimentation with potentially rewarding alternative approaches in other jurisdictions is foreclosed. Third, federal precedent applies equally throughout fifty diverse and independent states; a ruling that may be suitable in one may be inappropriate in others. And fourth, the federal union embraces a multitude of localities; the Court oftentimes is simply unfamiliar with local problems, conditions and traditions. *See generally San Antonio Indep. Sch. Dist. v. Rodriguez*, 411 U.S. 1, 93 S.Ct. 1278, 35 L.Ed.2d 16 (1973).

State courts do not suffer these prudential concerns to the same degree as the federal Court. First, unlike their federal counterparts, state courts and constitutions have traditionally served as the prime protectors of their citizens' basic freedoms. State constitutions were the initial and prime charters of individual rights throughout most of our nation's existence:

> By 1776 most American citizens enjoyed guarantees against encroachment on their liberties by state governments because most of the original thirteen colonies had adopted constitutions with provisions protecting individual rights. The framers of the federal Bill of Rights, which the states adopted in 1791, naturally relied on these state provisions as sources for their document. The federal document sought to provide citizens with protections against interference by the federal government analogous to existing state constitutional protections against interference by state governments.
>
> For the first one hundred and fifty years of our nation's existence, the origins of state constitutional provisions were of little importance for federal constitutional jurisprudence. During this period the federal constitution and state constitutions operated independently in regulating the interaction between government and citizen. The federal Bill of Rights protected citizens only from actions of the federal government, while state constitutions limited only intrusive action by the states. Because state governments affected individuals far more frequently during this period than did the federal government, state constitutions were the primary documents protecting the liberties of the people from governmental interference.

Mary A. Crossley, Note, *Miranda and the State Constitution: State Courts Take a Stand*, 39 Van.L.Rev. 1693, 1696 (1986) (footnotes omitted). State courts function daily as the prime arbiters of personal rights.[4] An assertive state court thus impinges on no traditional federal prerogative where basic rights are concerned.

---

4. *See* William J. Brennan, *Introduction: Chief Justice Hughes and Justice Mountain*, 10 Seton Hall L.Rev. xii (1979) ("[I]t is the state courts at all levels, not the federal courts, that finally determine the overwhelming number of the vital issues of life, liberty and property that trouble countless human beings of this Nation every year.").

Second, unlike the federal Court, a state court's decision construing its own constitution is controlling only as to courts within that state; the ruling will not stifle the development of alternative methods of constitutional analysis in other jurisdictions.

> To stay experimentation ... is a grave responsibility. Denial of the right to experiment may be fraught with serious consequences to the nation. It is one of the happy incidents of the federal system that a single courageous state may, if its citizens choose, serve as a laboratory; and try novel ... experiments without risk to the rest of the country.

New State Ice Co. v. Liebmann, 285 U.S. 262, 311, 52 S.Ct. 371, 386–87, 76 L.Ed. 747 (1932) (Brandeis, J., dissenting). And finally, no court is more sensitive or responsive to the needs of the diverse localities within a state, or the state as a whole, than that state's own high court. In any given state, the federal Constitution thus represents the floor for basic freedoms; the state constitution, the ceiling. *See* Stewart G. Pollock, *State Constitutions as Separate Sources of Fundamental Rights*, 35 Rutgers L. Rev. 707, 709 (1983).

Federal and state bills of rights thus serve distinct but complementary purposes. The federal Bill of Rights facilitates political and philosophical homogeneity among the basically heterogeneous states by securing, as a uniform minimum, the highest common denominator of freedom that can prudently be administered throughout all fifty states. The state bills of rights, on the other hand, express the ultimate breadth of the common yearnings for freedom of each insular state population within our nation. Accordingly, when called upon to construe their bills of rights, state courts should focus primarily on factors that inhere in their own unique state experience, such as the express language of the constitutional provision, its formative history, both preexisting and developing state law, evolving customs, traditions and attitudes within the state, the state's own general history, and finally any external influences that may have shaped state law.

When called upon to decide matters of fundamental rights, Florida's state courts are bound under federalist principles to give primacy to our state Constitution and to give independent legal import to every phrase and clause contained therein.[5] We are similarly bound under our Declaration of Rights to construe each provision freely in order to achieve the primary goal of individual freedom and autonomy.

---

5. Under the federalist principles expressed above, where a proposed constitutional revision results in the loss or restriction of an independent fundamental state right, this loss must be made known to each participating voter at the time of the general election. *Cf. People Against Tax Revenue Mismanagement v. County of Leon*, 583 So.2d 1373, 1376 (Fla.1991) ("This is especially true if the ballot language gives the appearance of creating new rights or protections, when the actual effect is to reduce or eliminate rights or predictions already in existence.").

III. Florida Declaration Of Rights

The text of our Florida Constitution begins with a Declaration of Rights — a series of rights so basic that the framers of our Constitution accorded them a place of special privilege. These rights embrace a broad spectrum of enumerated and implied liberties that conjoin to form a single overarching freedom: They protect each individual within our borders from the unjust encroachment of state authority — from whatever official source — into his or her life. Each right is, in fact, a distinct freedom guaranteed to each Floridian against government intrusion. Each right operates in favor of the individual, against government. This Court over half a century ago addressed the fundamental principle of robust individualism that underlies our system of constitutional government in Florida:

> It is significant that our Constitution thus commences by specifying those things which the state government must not do, before specifying certain things that it may do. These Declarations of Rights . . . have cost much, and breathe the spirit of that sturdy and self-reliant philosophy of individualism which underlies and supports our entire system of government. No race of hothouse plants could ever have produced and compelled the recognition of such a stalwart set of basic principles, and no such race can preserve them. They say to arbitrary and autocratic power, from whatever official quarter it may advance to invade these vital rights of personal liberty and private property, "Thus far shalt thou come, but no farther."

State ex rel. Davis v. City of Stuart, 97 Fla. 69, 102–03, 120 So. 335, 347 (1929). No other broad formulation of legal principles, whether state or federal, provides more protection from government overreaching or a richer environment for self-reliance and individualism than does this "stalwart set of basic principles."

Under our Declaration of Rights, each basic liberty and each individual citizen has long been held on equal footing with every other:

> Every particular section of the Declaration of Rights stands on an equal footing with every other section. They recognize no distinction between citizens. Under them every citizen, the good and the bad, the just and the unjust, the rich and the poor, the saint and the sinner, the believer and the infidel, have equal rights before the law.

Boynton v. State, 64 So.2d 536, 552–53 (Fla.1953). Each right and each citizen, regardless of position, is protected with identical vigor from government overreaching, no matter what the source. *Id.* at 552.

Special vigilance is required where the fundamental rights of Florida citizens suspected of wrongdoing are concerned, for here society has a strong natural inclination to relinquish incrementally the hard-won and stoutly defended freedoms enumerated in our Declaration in its effort to preserve public order. Each law-abiding member of society is inclined to strike out at crime reflexively by constricting the constitutional rights of all citizens in order to limit those of the suspect — each is inclined to give up a degree of his or her own protection from government intrusion in order to permit greater intrusion into the life of the suspect. The framers of our Constitution, however, deliberately rejected the short-term solution in favor of a fairer, more structured system of criminal justice:

> These rights [enumerated in the Declaration of Rights] curtail and restrain the power of the State. It is more important to preserve them, even though at times a guilty man may go free, than it is to obtain a conviction by ignoring or violating them. The end does not justify the means. Might is not always right. Under our system of constitutional government, the State should not set the example of violating fundamental rights guaranteed by the Constitution to all citizens in order to obtain a conviction.

Bizzell v. State, 71 So.2d 735, 738 (Fla. 1954). Thus, even here — especially here — where the rights of those suspected of wrongdoing are concerned, the framers drew a bright line and said to government, "Thus far shalt thou come, but no farther."

IV. Privilege Against Self-Incrimination

A. Florida Section 9

* * *

V. Right To Choose Representation

A. Florida Section 16

* * *

B. Florida Section 2

* * *

VI. Application To Present Case

* * *

OVERTON, McDONALD, and GRIMES, JJ., concur.

BARKETT, J. concurs in part and dissents in part with an opinion [omitted], in which KOGAN, J., concurs.

KOGAN, J., concurs in part and dissents in part with an opinion [omitted], in which BARKETT, J., concurs.

———————

The issue of whether a state constitutional provision can extend greater protection than the Federal Constitution, where the lower court has cited both federal and state precedent, is often resolved as a matter of federal appellate law. The following case is the most important recent pronouncement by the United States Supreme Court in this area.

Florida v. Powell

559 U.S. 50 (2010)

Justice GINSBURG delivered the opinion of the Court.

* * *

I

* * *

II

We first address Powell's contention that this Court lacks jurisdiction to hear this case because the Florida Supreme Court, by relying not only on Miranda but also on the Florida Constitution, rested its decision on an adequate and independent state ground. *See Coleman v. Thompson*, 501 U.S. 722, 729, 111 S.Ct. 2546, 115 L.Ed.2d 640 (1991) ("This Court will not review a question of federal law decided by a state court if the decision . . . rests on a state law ground that is independent of the federal question and adequate to support the judgment."). "It is fundamental," we have observed, "that state courts be left free and unfettered by us in interpreting their state constitutions." *Minnesota v. National Tea Co.*, 309 U.S. 551, 557, 60 S.Ct. 676, 84 L.Ed. 920 (1940). "But it is equally important that ambiguous or obscure adjudications by state courts do not stand as barriers to a determination by this Court of the validity under the federal constitution of state action." *Ibid.*

To that end, we announced, in *Michigan v. Long*, 463 U.S. 1032, 1040–1041, 103 S. Ct. 3469, 77 L.Ed.2d 1201 (1983), the following presumption:

> "[W]hen . . . a state court decision fairly appears to rest primarily on federal law, or to be interwoven with the federal law, and when the adequacy and independence of any possible state law ground is not clear from the face of the opinion, we will accept as the most reasonable explanation that the state court decided the case the way it did because it believed that federal law required it to do so."

At the same time, we adopted a plain-statement rule to avoid the presumption: "If the state court decision indicates clearly and expressly that it is alternatively based on bona fide separate, adequate, and independent grounds, we, of course, will not undertake to review the decision." *Id.*, at 1041, 103 S.Ct. 3469.[2]

---

2. Dissenting in *Michigan v. Long*, 463 U.S. 1032, 103 S.Ct. 3469, 77 L.Ed.2d 1201 (1983), Justice STEVENS did not urge, as he now does, inspection of state-court decisions to count the number of citations to state and federal provisions and opinions, or heroic efforts to fathom what the state court really meant. See *post*, at 1207–1210 (dissenting opinion). Instead, his preferred approach was as clear as the Court's. In lieu of "presuming that adequate state grounds are *not* independent unless it clearly appears otherwise," he would have "presum[ed] that adequate state grounds are independent unless it clearly appears otherwise." *Long*, 463 U.S., at 1066, 103 S.Ct. 3469; see *post*, at 1207, n. 1. Either presumption would avoid arduous efforts to detect, case by case, whether a state ground of decision is truly "independent of the [state court's] understanding of federal law." *Long*,

672   7 · THE DECLARATION OF RIGHTS AND THE TAKING OF PROPERTY

Under the Long presumption, we have jurisdiction to entertain this case. Although invoking Florida's Constitution and precedent in addition to this Court's decisions, the Florida Supreme Court treated state and federal law as interchangeable and interwoven; the court at no point expressly asserted that state-law sources gave Powell rights distinct from, or broader than, those delineated in Miranda. *See Long*, 463 U.S., at 1044, 103 S.Ct. 3469.

Beginning with the certified question—whether the advice the Tampa police gave to Powell "vitiate[d] Miranda," 998 So.2d, at 532 (some capitalization omitted)—and continuing throughout its opinion, the Florida Supreme Court trained on what Miranda demands, rather than on what Florida law independently requires. See, e.g., 998 So.2d, at 533 ("The issue before this Court is whether the failure to provide express advice of the right to the presence of counsel during custodial interrogation violates the principles espoused in *Miranda v. Arizona*, 384 U.S. 436, 86 S. Ct. 1602, 16 L.Ed.2d 694."); *id.*, at 538 ("[T]he issue of [what] Miranda requires ... has been addressed by several of the Florida district courts of appeal."); *id.*, at 542 (Powell received a "narrower and less functional warning than that required by Miranda."). [Footnote omitted.] We therefore cannot identify, "from the face of the opinion," a clear statement that the decision rested on a state ground separate from Miranda. *See Long*, 463 U.S., at 1041, 103 S.Ct. 3469 (the state court "need only make clear by a plain statement in its judgment or opinion that the federal cases are being used only for the purpose of guidance, and do not themselves compel the result that the court has reached").[4] "To avoid misunderstanding, the [Florida] Supreme Court must itself speak with the clarity it sought to require of its State's police officers." *Ohio v. Robinette*, 519 U.S. 33, 45, 117 S.Ct. 417, 136 L.Ed.2d 347 (1996) (GINSBURG, J., concurring in judgment).

Powell notes that "'state courts are absolutely free to interpret state constitutional provisions to accord greater protection to individual rights than do similar provisions of the United States Constitution.'" Brief for Respondent 19–20 (quoting *Arizona v. Evans*, 514 U.S. 1, 8, 115 S.Ct. 1185, 131 L.Ed.2d 34 (1995)). *See also, e.g., Oregon v. Hass*, 420 U.S. 714, 719, 95 S.Ct. 1215, 43 L.Ed.2d 570 (1975); *Cooper*

---

463 U.S., at 1066, 103 S.Ct. 3469. Today, however, the dissent would require this Court to engage in just that sort of inquiry.

4. Justice STEVENS agrees that the Florida Supreme Court's decision is interwoven with federal law, *post*, at 1209–1210, and lacks the plain statement contemplated by *Long, post*, at 1207. Nevertheless, he finds it possible to discern an independent state-law basis for the decision. As *Long* makes clear, however, "when ... [the] state court decision fairly appears to ... be interwoven with ... federal law," the only way to avoid the jurisdictional presumption is to provide a plain statement expressing independent reliance on state law. 463 U.S., at 1040, 103 S.Ct. 3469. It is this plain statement that makes "the adequacy and independence of any possible state law ground ... clear from the face of the opinion." *Id.*, at 1040–1041, 103 S.Ct. 3469. See also *Ohio v. Robinette*, 519 U.S. 33, 44, 117 S.Ct. 417, 136 L.Ed.2d 347 (1996) (GINSBURG, J., concurring in judgment) ("*Long* governs even when, all things considered, the more plausible reading of the state court's decision may be that the state court did not regard the Federal Constitution alone as a sufficient basis for its ruling.").

v. California, 386 U.S. 58, 62, 87 S.Ct. 788, 17 L.Ed.2d 730 (1967). Powell is right in this regard. Nothing in our decision today, we emphasize, trenches on the Florida Supreme Court's authority to impose, based on the State's Constitution, any additional protections against coerced confessions it deems appropriate. But because the Florida Supreme Court's decision does not "indicat[e] clearly and expressly that it is alternatively based on bona fide separate, adequate, and independent [state] grounds," *Long*, 463 U.S., at 1041, 103 S.Ct. 3469, we have jurisdiction to decide this case.

[The Court then reaches the merits.]

For the reasons stated, the judgment of the Supreme Court of Florida is reversed, and the case is remanded for further proceedings not inconsistent with this opinion.

It is so ordered.

Justice STEVENS, with whom Justice BREYER joins as to Part II, dissenting.

Today, the Court decides a case in which the Florida Supreme Court held a local police practice violated the Florida Constitution. The Court's power to review that decision is doubtful at best; moreover, the Florida Supreme Court has the better view on the merits.

I

In this case, the Florida Supreme Court concluded that "[b]oth *Miranda* and article I, section 9 of the Florida Constitution require that a suspect be clearly informed of the right to have a lawyer present during questioning," and that the warnings given to Powell did not satisfy either the State or the Federal Constitution. 998 So.2d 531, 542 (2008). In my view, the Florida Supreme Court held on an adequate and independent state-law ground that the warnings provided to Powell did not sufficiently inform him of the "'right to a lawyer's help'" under the Florida Constitution, *id.*, at 535. This Court therefore lacks jurisdiction to review the judgment below, notwithstanding the failure of that court to include some express sentence that would satisfy this Court's "plain-statement rule," *ante*, at 1202.

* * *

As the majority's decision today demonstrates, reasonable judges may well differ over the question whether the deficiency is serious enough to violate the Federal Constitution. That difference of opinion, in my judgment, falls short of providing a justification for reviewing this case when the judges of the highest court of the State have decided the warning is insufficiently protective of the rights of the State's citizens. In my view, respect for the independence of state courts, and their authority to set the rules by which their citizens are protected, should result in a dismissal of this petition.

I respectfully dissent.

B. Basic Rights

Fla. Const. art. I, § 2

Basic rights. — All natural persons, female and male alike, are equal before the law and have inalienable rights, among which are the right to enjoy and defend life and liberty, to pursue happiness, to be rewarded for industry, and to acquire, possess and protect property. No person shall be deprived of any right because of race, religion, national origin or physical disability.

---

1. Introduction

This provision, stating that all natural persons are equal before the law, has been identified by the Florida judiciary as the source of the state's equal protection clause. Technically, artificial entities, like corporations, are not entitled to protection under this provision. However, these entities may have been extended comparable protection under substantive due process. Although the Florida Constitution prohibits discrimination on the basis of race, religion, national origin, or physical disability, it does not specifically prohibit gender-based discrimination.

2. "To Acquire, Possess and Protect Property"

The overlap with substantive due process is fairly obvious. This appears to be illustrated by the following quotation from *Gulf Power Company v. Bevis:*[3]

> A regulated public utility is, of course, entitled to an opportunity to earn a fair rate of return on its invested capital. City of Miami v. Florida Public Service Commission, 208 So.2d 249 (Fla.1968). Failure to allow the utility the opportunity to earn a fair rate of return would violate the rights to due process, to just compensation for taking of property and the right to possess and protect property. Fla.Const., Art. I, §§ 2, 9; Art. X, § 6, F.S.A., U.S .Const. Amends. V and XIV.

Despite the overlap with due process, recent cases dealing with constitutional limits on the exercise of police power affecting private property rights[4] have cited art. I, § 2, rather than due process. Consider the following case and determine whether it could not have been resolved under the due process clause of the Declaration of Rights.

---

3. 289 So. 2d 401, 403, n. 1 (Fla. 1974).

4. See *Corn v. State*, 332 So. 2d 4 (Fla. 1976), for the view that this constitutional provision imposes a "duty to protect rights of property and the business community" from individuals.

Shriners Hospitals for Crippled Children v. Zrillic

563 So. 2d 64 (Fla. 1990)

BARKETT, Justice.

We have consolidated for review two cases that arose out of *Zrillic v. Estate of Romans*, 535 So.2d 294 (Fla. 5th DCA 1988). One presents an issue concerning the district court's express declaration of validity of section 732.803 of the Florida Statutes (1985), which pertains to charitable devises.[1] The other alleges an express and direct conflict with *Hooper v. Stokes*, 107 Fla. 607, 145 So. 855 (1933); *Milam v. Davis*, 97 Fla. 916, 123 So. 668, *cert. denied*, 280 U.S. 601, 50 S.Ct. 82, 74 L.Ed. 646 (1929), and *In re Estate of Herman*, 427 So.2d 195 (Fla. 4th DCA 1982).[2]

I.

Lorraine E. Romans, a resident of Seminole County, Florida, executed her Last Will and Testament on May 5, 1986. After suffering from a lingering illness, she died on July 19, 1986, survived by her daughter, Lorraine E. Zrillic. The testator's will, admitted to probate on December 19, 1986, included the following provisions:

> EIGHTH: I give and bequeath several sealed boxes of family antique dishes and figurines specifically designated, to my daughter, LORRAINE E. ZRIL-LIC, 16531 Blatt Blvd., No. 204, Ft. Lauderdale, Florida. I have intentionally limited her inheritance since I have contributed substantially during my life for her education and subsequent monies I have been required to expend primarily due to her promiscuous type of life. My daughter, LORRAINE E. ZRILLIC, has not shown or indicated the slightest affection or gratitude to me for at least five years preceeding [sic] the date of this Will. My executor will know the appraised value of these antiques for estate tax purposes. . . .
>
> . . . .
>
> ELEVENTH: All the rest residue and remainder of my estate, of whatever nature and wherever situated of which I may be siezed [sic] or possessed or to which I may be entitled at the time of my death, including lapsed legacies and any property over which I have a power of appointment I give, devise and bequeath as a charitable donation to the SHRINERS HOSPITAL[S] for CRIPPLED CHILDREN. . . .

Pursuant to section 732.803,[3] Zrillic timely requested the circuit court to issue an order avoiding the charitable devise. Timely responses were filed by: Shriners

---

1. This section is commonly known as Florida's mortmain statute.
2. We have jurisdiction pursuant to article V, section 3(b)(3) of the Florida Constitution.
3. Section 732.803 of the Florida Statutes (1985), provides:
   (1) If a testator dies leaving lineal descendants or a spouse and his will devises part or all of the testator's estate:
   (a) To a benevolent, charitable, educational, literary, scientific, religious, or missionary institution, corporation, association, or purpose,

Hospitals for Crippled Children (petitioner in No. 73,639); and James G. Lloyd, James C. Erdman, and Betty C. Merrick, as copersonal representatives of the Estate of Lorraine E. Romans (petitioners in No. 73,640). Copetitioners filed the same two affirmative defenses in the circuit court, alleging that: (1) Zrillic lacked standing to avoid the charitable devise because she was expressly disinherited; and (2) section 732.803 violated the equal protection provisions of the constitutions of the United States and the state of Florida.

The circuit court ruled that Zrillic did have standing, but that section 732.803 was unconstitutional. Zrillic appealed the circuit court's decision as to the constitutionality of the statute, and the copersonal representatives of the Estate of Romans cross-appealed on the issue of standing.

The Fifth District Court of Appeal affirmed in part and reversed in part, finding that Zrillic had standing, but that section 732.803 did not violate either constitution. 535 So.2d 294. Both Shriners Hospitals and the copersonal representatives of the Estate of Romans petitioned this Court to review that decision.

We are presented with two issues. The threshold question is whether a lineal descendant, whose legacy was expressly limited by the decedent's will, had standing to set aside a charitable devise in that will. The second question concerns the constitutionality of section 732.803.

II.

[The Florida Supreme Court here finds that Zrillic has standing.]

Now we move on to discuss the constitutionality of section 732.803. First, we address whether the section imposes an unreasonable restriction on a property owner's right to dispose of property by will. Then we analyze the equal protection claim.

(b) To this state, any other state or country, or a county, city, or town in this or any other state or country, or

(c) To a person in trust for any such purpose or beneficiary, whether or not the trust appears on the face of the instrument making the devise, the devise shall be avoided in its entirety if one or more of the lineal descendants or a spouse who would receive any interest in the devise, if avoided, files written notice to this effect in the administration proceeding within 4 months after the date letters are issued, unless:

(d) The will was duly executed at least 6 months before the testator's death, or

(e) The testator made a valid charitable devise in substantially the same amount for the same purpose or to the same beneficiary, or to a person in trust for the same purpose or beneficiary, as was made in the last will or by a will or a series of wills duly executed immediately next to the last will, one of which was executed more than 6 months before the testator's death.

(2) The testator's making of a codicil that does not substantially change a charitable devise as herein defined within the 6-month period before the testator's death shall not render the charitable gift voidable under this section.

III.

Property rights are protected by article I, section 2 of the Florida Constitution:

> SECTION 2. Basic rights.—All natural persons are equal before the law and have inalienable rights, among which are the right to enjoy and defend life and liberty, to pursue happiness, to be rewarded for industry, and *to acquire, possess and protect property; except that the ownership, inheritance, disposition and possession of real property by aliens ineligible for citizenship may be regulated or prohibited by law.* No person shall be deprived of any right because of race, religion or physical handicap.

(Emphasis added.) These property rights are woven into the fabric of Florida history. *See* Declaration of Rights, §§ 1, 18, Fla. Const. (1885) (as amended prior to the 1968 revision); Declaration of Rights, §§ 1, 17, Fla. Const. (1868); art. I, § 1, Fla. Const. (1865); art. I, § 1, Fla. Const. (1861); Art. I, § 1, Fla. Const. (1838).

To interpret the extent of property rights under the constitution, we must make a common sense reading of the plain and ordinary meaning of the language to carry out the intent of the framers as applied to the context of our times. *See In re Advisory Opinion to the Governor Request of June 29, 1979*, 374 So.2d 959, 964 (Fla.1979). It is commonly understood that acquire means to gain, obtain, receive, or to come into possession or ownership of property, *see, e.g.,* I *The Oxford English Dictionary* 115 (2d ed. 1989), and it *"[i]ncludes taking by devise." Black's Law Dictionary* 23 (5th ed. 1979) (emphasis supplied). Possess commonly means to have, hold, own, or control "anything which may be the subject of property, for one's own use and enjoyment, either as owner or as the proprietor of a qualified right in it." *Id.* at 1046–47; *see also, e.g.,* XII *The Oxford English Dictionary* 171–72 (2d ed. 1989). Protect generally means to guard, preserve and keep safe from harm, encroachment, injury, alteration, damage, or loss. *See, e.g.,* XII *The Oxford English Dictionary* 677–78 (2d ed. 1989); *American Heritage Dictionary* 995 (2d College ed. 1985). Thus, the phrase "acquire, possess and protect property" in article I, section 2, includes the incidents of property ownership: the "[c]ollection of rights to use and enjoy property, *including [the] right to transmit it to others." Black's Law Dictionary* 997 (5th ed. 1979) (emphasis supplied).[4]

This common sense reading of the language in article I, section 2, leads to the conclusion that the right to devise property is a property right protected by the Florida Constitution. Our conclusion is supported by the provision's express exception for aliens ineligible for citizenship. There would be no need to carve out an exception for "ownership, *inheritance, disposition* and possession of real property" unless those property rights already were subsumed in the clause modified by the

---

4. These same principles of property also are embodied in the takings clauses of the constitutions of the United States and the state of Florida, which require that property owners be compensated when the government substantially interferes with an owner's use of property. *E.g., First English Evangelical Lutheran Church v. County of Los Angeles*, 482 U.S. 304, 107 S.Ct. 2378, 96 L. Ed.2d 250 (1987); *Palm Beach County v. Tessler*, 538 So.2d 846 (Fla.1989).

exception. Furthermore, by narrowly limiting the class of persons whose rights may be restricted by the legislature, i.e., aliens ineligible for citizenship, it is clear that the framers intended all other people, including testators, be free from unreasonable legislative restraint.

We are aware that some decisions in Florida and elsewhere vary from this conclusion, relying upon an old legal distinction between "property" rights and "testamentary" rights. *See generally* 1 W. Bowe & D. Parker, *Page on the Law of Wills* chs. 1–3 (rev. ed. 1960). The distinction those courts have drawn is that property rights are inalienable rights grounded in natural law, whereas freedom of testation is purely a creation of statute that did not exist at common law. The genesis of that distinction lies in long-abandoned feudal notions of property. In feudal England, only the king owned real property, which represented the bulk of wealth, and only the king could decide who could exercise real property rights when a person died. During the decline of feudalism, Parliament enacted the Statute of Wills to grant citizens the lawful right to devise real property, qualified by regulations necessary to preserve order. Hence, devising property came to be regarded as a right created by statute, not a "property" right inherent in the common law of England. *See generally* 1 W. Bowe & D. Parker, *Page on the Law of Wills* chs. 1–3 (rev. ed. 1960). 1 D. Redfearn, *Wills and Administration in Florida* chs. 1, 15 (L. Jeffries 6th ed. 1986); A. Reppy & L. Tompkins, *Historical and Statutory Background of the Law of Wills* ch. 1 (1928).

That analysis is inapplicable in our society where feudalism never existed and where property rights rest on an express constitutional foundation that is distinguishable from the common law roots of feudal England. Yet all too often courts have failed to thoroughly analyze the distinction, instead giving unquestioning allegiance to an antiquated way of thinking. *See Taylor v. Payne*, 154 Fla. 359, 362–63, 17 So.2d 615, 617, *appeal dismissed*, 323 U.S. 666, 65 S.Ct. 49, 89 L.Ed. 541 (1944); *see also In re Estate of Greenberg*, 390 So.2d 40, 43 (Fla.1980) (following *Taylor*), *appeal dismissed*, 450 U.S. 961, 101 S.Ct. 1475, 67 L.Ed.2d 610 (1981); *In re Estate of Blankenship*, 122 So.2d 466, 469 (Fla.1960) (following *Taylor*), *Arthritis Foundation v. Beisse*, 456 So.2d 954 (Fla. 4th DCA 1984) (following *Taylor*), *review denied*, 467 So.2d 999 (Fla.1985). The plain meaning of the language of the Florida Constitution compels us to conclude that the people chose not to blindly adhere to the old English distinction, and instead came to regard testamentary disposition of property as a specifically express constitutional property right. *Accord In re Estate of Beale*, 15 Wis.2d 546, 552, 113 N.W.2d 380, 383 (1962) (the right to make a will is a constitutional right); *Nunnemacher v. State*, 129 Wis. 190, 196, 108 N.W. 627, 628 (1906) (the right to pass property by will or inheritance is a natural right under the state constitution and cannot be wholly taken away or substantially impaired by the legislature).

Of course, even constitutionally protected property rights are not absolute, and "are held subject to the fair exercise of the power inherent in the State to promote the general welfare of the people through regulations that are reasonably necessary to secure the health, safety, good order, [and] general welfare." *Golden v. McCarty,*

337 So.2d 388, 390 (Fla.1976); *see also Palm Beach Mobile Homes, Inc. v. Strong*, 300 So.2d 881, 884 (1974) (the degree of a constitutionally protected property right "must be determined in the light of social and economic conditions which prevail at a given time"); *cf. Department of Agric. & Consumer Servs. v. Mid-Florida Growers, Inc.*, 521 So.2d 101, 103 (Fla.) (a property regulation may be reasonable but still may require the state to compensate a landowner), *cert. denied*, 488 U.S. 870, 109 S.Ct. 180, 102 L.Ed.2d 149 (1988).

The question we must resolve is whether section 732.803 is reasonably necessary to limit the property rights guaranteed by article I, section 2 of the Florida Constitution. We find that it is not. Statutes that restrict charitable gifts originated in feudal England as part of the struggle for power and wealth between the king and the organized church. *See generally, e.g.,* 1 D. Redfearn, *Wills and Administration in Florida* chs. 1, 15 (L. Jeffries 6th ed. 1986); 79 Am.Jur.2d Wills § 176 (1975). The church acquired wealth through exercising its ecclesiastical jurisdiction over personal property, which was subject to much abuse, and its acquisition of real property by subinfeudation, which deprived the king and lords of some benefits and control over property disposition. *See generally* J. Dukeminer & J. Krier, *Property* 152–53 (2d ed. 1988); 1 D. Redfearn, *Wills and Administration in Florida* ch. 1 (L. Jeffries 6th ed. 1986); II F. Pollock & F. Maitland, *The History of English Law* ch. VI § 3 (2d ed. 1968). Mortmain statutes were promulgated primarily to restrict the church's ability to acquire property. However, mortmain statutes became less and less effective as feudalism declined. *See generally* J. Dukeminer & J. Krier, *Property* 152–53 (2d ed. 1988).

Over time, society's attitude has changed to the point where charitable gifts, devises and trusts now are favored and will be held valid whenever possible. 79 Am.Jur.2d Wills § 176 (1975). *See also* 4A *Powell on Real Property* para. 577 (1986). As society's attitude changed, so did the rationale employed to support the few mortmain-type statutes that survived.[5] Today, they are justified by their supporters as a means of protecting a testator's family from disinheritance. The expressed concern is that charitable organizations either exert undue influence, or that testators who may be laboring under the apprehension of impending death are peculiarly susceptible to influence. *E.g., Taylor v. Payne*, 154 Fla. 359, 364, 17 So.2d 615, 618, *appeal dismissed*, 323 U.S. 666, 65 S.Ct. 49, 89 L.Ed. 541 (1944); 1 W. Bowe & D. Parker, *Page on the Law of Wills* § 3.15 (rev. ed. 1960).

Although it may be reasonable for the legislature to protect family members who are dependent or in financial need, it is unreasonable to presume, as the statute seems to do, that all lineal descendants are dependents, in need, or are not otherwise provided for. Florida law is replete with protections for surviving family members who may have been dependent on the testator. For example, the Florida Constitution expressly provides protection in the form of homestead exemptions

---

5. The parties agree that only Florida, Georgia, Idaho and Mississippi have mortmain-type statutes still in effect. *Accord Shriners' Hospital for Crippled Children v. Hester*, 23 Ohio St.3d 198, 203 n. 5, 492 N.E.2d 153, 157 n. 5 (1986).

for real and personal property, art. X, § 4, Fla. Const.; *see also* §§ 732.401–.4015, Fla. Stat. (1985), and a coverture restriction, art. X, § 5, Fla. Const.; *see also* § 732.111, Fla. Stat. (1985). The Probate Code provides for an elective share, §§ 732.201–.215, Fla. Stat. (1985), personal property exemptions, § 732.402, Fla.Stat. (1985), and a family allowance, § 732.403, Fla.Stat. (1985). The Probate Code also protects against fraud, duress, mistake, and undue influence. § 732.5165, Fla.Stat. (1985).

No similar protections are assured by section 732.803. To the contrary, the charitable devise restriction fails to protect against windfalls for lineal descendants who have had no contact with the decedent or who have been neglectful or abusive to the decedent but who may benefit from the avoidance of a charitable devise. It also fails to protect against windfalls for lineal descendants whose legacy was specifically limited by the decedent. Another significant flaw is that artful will drafting easily defeats the effect of the statute: If the testator names anybody other than a spouse or lineal descendent to take the charitable devise in the event the charitable devise fails, nobody would have standing to petition to avoid the charitable devise. *See In re Estate of Shameia*, 257 So.2d 77, 78–79 (Fla. 2d DCA 1972).

Neither the ancient purpose nor the modern justification underlying the restriction on charitable devises is well served by section 732.803. The statute is not reasonably necessary to accomplish the asserted state goals at the cost of offending property interests protected by the Florida Constitution.

IV.

* * *

... We find that section 732.803 is unconstitutional for the reasons expressed above. This cause is remanded for further proceedings in accordance herewith.

It is so ordered.

EHRLICH, C.J., and SHAW and KOGAN., JJ., concur.

GRIMES, J., concurs in result with an opinion.

McDONALD, J., concurs in result and dissents in part with an opinion, in which OVERTON, J., concurs.

[The concurring opinion of Justice Grimes and concurring and dissenting in part opinion of Justice McDonald are omitted.]

The *Zrillic* decision was subsequently determined to be retroactively applicable to cases pending in the trial court when the Florida Supreme Court's opinion was announced. *See Florida Elks Children's Hospital v. Stanley.*[5]

Judicial references to the state constitutional right "to acquire, possess and protect property" appear more frequently now than in the past. For example, in *Ricketts*

---

5. 610 So. 2d 538 (Fla. 5th Dist. Ct. App. 1992).

7 · THE DECLARATION OF RIGHTS AND THE TAKING OF PROPERTY 681

v. Village of Miami Shores, the court held that an ordinance banning front-yard vegetable gardens did not violate the right to acquire, possess, and protect property.[6] Additionally, in *Snyder v. Board of County Commissioners of Brevard County,*[7] a case concerning land use, the Fifth District Court of Appeal identified the right of majority ownership as "one of the most fundamental and cherished rights" and "the cornerstone that anchors the capitalistic form of government guaranteed by the federal and state constitutions."

In apparent reliance on this provision, the Fourth District Court of Appeal has held that the Florida Constitution requires greater protection from governmental seizure of property than that which is required under federal constitutional law.[8]

3. "No Person Shall be Deprived of Any Right Because of Race, Religion, National Origin, or Physical Disability"

This provision overlaps with the federal and state equal protection clauses. It was amended in 1974 to add the physical disability limitation. This provision does not literally impose a governmental action requirement for its applicability. The Florida Supreme Court, however, has found such a requirement.

Schreiner v. McKenzie Tank Lines, Inc.
432 So. 2d 567 (Fla. 1983)

OVERTON, Justice.

This is a petition to review a decision of the First District Court of Appeal reported as *Schreiner v. McKenzie Tank Lines, Inc.*, 408 So.2d 711 (Fla. 1st DCA 1982). This case requires a construction of the basic rights provision, article I, section 2, of the Florida Constitution. The critical issue is whether the deprivation clause portion of article I, section 2, applies only to protect individuals from government action, or whether the deprivation clause was also intended to protect against private party conduct where no government action is involved. The district court held that article I, section 2, should not apply to private action and should receive no broader construction than that given the fourteenth amendment to the United States Constitution. The district court then certified the following question to be one of great public importance:

> Is there a requirement of state action, similar to that of the fourteenth amendment to the U.S. Constitution, that must be found to exist prior to

---

6. 232 So. 3d 1095 (Fla. 3d DCA App. 2017); *see also Nelson P. v. Goss*, 279 So. 3d 212 (Fla. 2d DCA App. 2019).

7. 595 So. 2d 65, 70 (Fla. 5th Dist. Ct. App. 1991) (quashed by *Board of County Commissioners of Brevard County*, 627 So. 2d 469 (Fla. 1993).

8. *See Cochran v. Harris*, 654 So. 2d 969 (Fla. 4th Dist. Ct. App. 1995).

invoking one's right to seek relief under the Florida Constitution of 1968, article I, section 2?

408 So.2d at 721. We have jurisdiction. Art. V, §3(b)(4), Fla. Const. In summary, we answer the certified question in the affirmative and approve the decision of the district court. We agree that state action must be present for relief to be granted under article I, section 2, because we find that the framers of this constitutional provision did not intend that article I, section 2, have a broader application than the related provision of the fourteenth amendment to the United States Constitution.

The uncontroverted facts reflect the following. Petitioner, James Schreiner, was employed as a repairman by the respondent McKenzie Tank Lines, Inc. During the course of his employment, Schreiner operated motor vehicles on the highway. While working, Schreiner suffered epileptic seizures on three different occasions. After the first seizure, his driver's license was revoked by the State of Florida. Following the second seizure, Schreiner's doctor told him that he would have to limit his work to activities which did not require him to be off the surface of the ground. Then, when Schreiner suffered a third seizure while working, his employment was terminated. He initiated this action, which was dismissed by the trial court. On appeal, the only issue considered by the district court was whether Schreiner was unconstitutionally deprived of his employment due to a physical handicap in violation of article I, section 2, of the Florida Constitution, which reads as follows:

> *Basic rights.* — All natural persons are equal before the law and have inalienable rights, among which are the right to enjoy and defend life and liberty, to pursue happiness, to be rewarded for industry, and to acquire, possess and protect property; except that the ownership, inheritance, disposition and possession of real property by aliens ineligible for citizenship may be regulated or prohibited by law. No person shall be deprived of any right because of race, religion or physical handicap.

In its thorough opinion, the district court addressed three issues. First, the district court considered whether the deprivation clause portion of article I, section 2, is self-executing and found that it is. Second, the district court considered whether this provision of the Florida Constitution, like the equal protection clause of the fourteenth amendment to the United States Constitution, requires state action and found that it does. Third, the district court, based on its finding that state action is required, considered whether state action was present in this case and found it was not. We agree with the district court's answers as set out in its opinion and find that it is only necessary for us to discuss the state action requirement of article I, section 2.

At the outset, two points must be noted. First, the United States Supreme Court has held that the equal protection clause of the fourteenth amendment protects against discrimination by "states," and "erects no shield against merely private conduct, however discriminatory or wrongful." *Shelley v. Kraemer,* 334 U.S. 1, 13, 68 S.Ct. 836, 842, 92 L.Ed. 1161 (1948) (footnote omitted). "Individual invasion of individual rights is not the subject-matter of the amendment." *The Civil Rights Cases*, 109 U.S. 3, 11, 3 S.Ct. 18, 21, 27 L.Ed. 835 (1883). *See Burton v. Wilmington Parking Authority*, 365 U.S. 715, 81 S.Ct. 856, 6 L.Ed.2d 45 (1961). The critical question is whether article I, section 2, of the Florida Constitution was drafted and adopted with the intent to broaden the application of the deprivation clause to protect against the "individual invasion of individual rights" as well as to protect against state action.

Second, following the termination of Schreiner's employment by respondent, the legislature enacted section 23.161–167, Florida Statutes (1977). These provisions make it unlawful for private persons employing fifteen or more employees to discharge an employee because of race, color, religion, sex, national origin, age, handicap, or marital status.

The basic rights provision of article I, section 2, of the Florida Constitution, has three parts. The first is the equal protection clause, which provides that, "[a]ll natural persons are equal before the law. . . ." Petitioner concedes that the Florida equal protection clause protects only against improper state action, and does not apply to purely private action. The second part identifies the inalienable rights of Florida's citizens, "which are the right to enjoy and defend life and liberty, to pursue happiness, to be rewarded for industry, and to acquire, possess and protect property. . . ." This inalienable rights clause does contain the exception "that the ownership, inheritance, disposition and possession of real property by aliens ineligible for citizenship may be regulated or prohibited by law." The third part of article I, section 2, is the deprivation clause, which provides that "[n]o person shall be deprived of any right because of race, religion or physical handicap."

Petitioner, while agreeing that the equal protection clause of article I, section 2, is limited to state action, contends that the inalienable rights and deprivation clauses apply not only to state action but also to private action. This contention is based on the petitioner's observation that although the equal protection clause refers to "law" and "or under law," such reference is absent from the inalienable rights and due process clauses. Petitioner also asserts that both the Michigan and New York constitutions have similar provisions which have been interpreted as allowing claims for private actions. We reject these contentions.

We agree with the district court that although the United States Supreme Court's construction of the fourteenth amendment is not controlling, it does give us persuasive advice as to how to construe article I, section 2 of the Florida Constitution. As noted by the district court in its opinion, in the majority of states with constitutional provisions similar to Florida's, state action is required. We do not find the constructions of the Michigan and New York constitutions to be persuasive. The Michigan provision is not similar to, but is broader than Florida's constitutional provision. Further, the Connecticut provision, which is almost identical to the Michigan provision, has been construed to require state action. *See Lockwood v. Killian*, 172 Conn. 496, 375 A.2d 998 (1977). In addition, the assertion that the New York Constitution protects against purely private action is erroneous. In *Sharrock v. Dell Buick-Cadillac, Inc.*, 45 N.Y.2d 152, 379 N.E.2d 1169, 408 N.Y.S.2d 39 (1978), the New York

Court of Appeals concluded that, although there was no specific requirement of state action in the New York Constitution, "state involvement" was required.

Although we conclude, as have the United States Supreme Court and the majority of jurisdictions which have addressed this question, that state action is required in the context of this case, our decision is primarily based on the intent of the drafters of article I, section 2, of the Florida Constitution. After reviewing all of the transcripts available from meetings of the Constitutional Revision Commission, we conclude, as did the district court, that there was no intent by the framers to expand article I, section 2, to protect against private conduct as well as government conduct. Neither the Commission's background information nor the Commission's explanation of the provisions to the public support the assertion that an expansion of the protection provided by article I, section 2, was contemplated. That would have been a major policy change and reason dictates that such a change would have produced discussion, explanation, and debate. There is no indication that this type of major change was contemplated in the published explanation to the people. [Footnote omitted.] We do not agree that the comments of Commissioner Ervin are sufficient to support such a change, particularly when the actions of the Commission and its chairman are considered. [Footnote omitted.] When this provision was adopted, the law was clear that the constitution did not provide protection against the individual invasion of individual rights.

The petitioner's contention that the legislature, by enacting section 23.161-167, has impliedly interpreted article I, section 2, as applying to private acts, is without merit. In section 23.161-167, the legislature created a right of action for employment discrimination against a private person employing fifteen or more persons. The legislature's enactment of this provision suggests no broad interpretation of article I, section 2. If the petitioner's position were correct, there would be no need for this statutory provision and, rather than implementing the constitutional provision, it would have constituted a limitation on its application. We conclude that the legislature, in adopting section 23.161-167, was creating new *statutory* rights against private employment discrimination by businesses that employ more than fifteen persons and was not implementing or interpreting article I, section 2.

We agree with the district court and hold that article I, section 2, deals with the relationship between the people and the state and that, consistent with the construction of the fourteenth amendment, individual invasion of individual rights were never intended to be the subject matter of this provision.

For the reasons expressed, we approve the decision of the district court and adopt it as the opinion of this Court.

It is so ordered.

ALDERMAN, C.J., and BOYD, McDONALD and EHRLICH, JJ., concur.

ADKINS, J., concurs in result only.

The Florida Supreme Court has also recognized the necessity of governmental action for the privacy provisions of art. 1, § 23 of the Florida Constitution to apply.[9]

4. "All Natural Persons, Female and Male Alike, Are Equal Before the Law"

The Florida courts have generally adopted the federal equal protection analysis in construing the state equal protection clause. However, this does not mean that the state provision must always be interpreted to reach the same result as the federal analysis.[10]

In the following *heavily edited* case, both the majority and the dissent discuss the levels of scrutiny in equal protection analysis. Much of what is written could also apply to substantive due process, a subject discussed later in this chapter. To repeat, the case is heavily edited. It is not here for the reader to learn about the constitutionality of curfews.

State v. J.P.

907 So. 2d 1101 (Fla. 2004)

QUINCE, J.

We have for review two decisions of the Second District Court of Appeal in which the district court certified questions of great public importance regarding the constitutionality of juvenile curfew ordinances enacted by the city councils of Tampa and Pinellas Park. *See J.P. v. State*, 832 So.2d 110 (Fla. 2d DCA 2002) (finding Tampa curfew ordinance unconstitutional); *State v. T.M.*, 832 So.2d 118 (Fla. 2d DCA 2002) (finding Pinellas Park curfew ordinance unconstitutional). We have jurisdiction. *See* art. V, § 3(b)(4), Fla. Const.

History of the Cases

These cases are before this Court for the second time. The City of Tampa and the City of Pinellas Park enacted similar juvenile curfew ordinances. J.P. was cited for violation of the Tampa ordinance; T.M., A.N., and D.N. were cited for violation of the Pinellas Park ordinance. The State Attorney's Office filed petitions for delinquency against these juveniles. Prior to trial, the juveniles moved to dismiss their cases, arguing that the ordinances are unconstitutional because the ordinances infringe on their fundamental rights of free speech, association, and assembly, are vague and overbroad, and are inconsistent with state law. In the case of J.P., the trial court denied the motion, and J.P. pled no contest but reserved the right to appeal the denial of his motion. In the case of T.M., A.N., and D.N., the trial court granted the juveniles' motions to dismiss. The trial court reasoned that the juveniles' parents

---

9. *See* the discussion of Fla. Const. art. I, § 23, appearing later in this chapter.

10. *State v. Barquet*, 262 So. 2d 431 (Fla. 1972).

have a fundamental right to raise their children without governmental intrusion. In assessing the constitutionality of the Pinellas Park ordinance, the trial court applied the strict scrutiny test. The trial court determined that while Pinellas Park has a compelling interest in reducing juvenile crime and victimization, the ordinance is not narrowly tailored in the least restrictive manner to achieve that interest.

In both cases, the losing party appealed to the Second District Court of Appeal. In reviewing the ordinances, the Second District applied intermediate or heightened scrutiny, rather than strict scrutiny. Under this standard, the district court ruled that both ordinances were constitutional. *State v. T.M.*, 761 So.2d 1140, 1143 (Fla. 2d DCA 2000), *quashed*, 784 So.2d 442 (Fla.2001); *J.P. v. State*, 775 So.2d 324, 324 (Fla. 2d DCA 2000), *quashed*, 788 So.2d 953 (Fla.2001).

In reviewing the decisions in both *T.M.* and *J.P.*, this Court held that strict scrutiny should be applied when reviewing a juvenile curfew ordinance. *T.M. v. State*, 784 So.2d 442, 444 (Fla.2001); *J.P. v. State*, 788 So.2d 953, 953 (Fla.2001).

On remand, the Second District applied the strict scrutiny standard and concluded that both the Tampa and Pinellas Park juvenile curfew ordinances are unconstitutional. *J.P.*, 832 So.2d at 114; *T.M.*, 832 So.2d at 121.

* * *

The Ordinances

* * *

Standard of Review

* * *

[An] approach, which was taken by this Court in *T.M.* and *J.P.*, assumes that once a constitutional right has been recognized, its exercise by minors should be protected by strict scrutiny, just as it is for adults. . . . "Rather than using children's status to divest them of rights or to weaken the formal protections of those rights, courts taking this . . . approach factor in the unique attributes of minors in determining whether the government has a compelling interest justifying restrictions on minors' freedoms." . . .

* * *

When a statute or ordinance operates to the disadvantage of a suspect class or impairs the exercise of a fundamental right, then the law must pass strict scrutiny. . . . Although the juvenile curfew ordinances target a certain age group, the United States Supreme Court has ruled that age is not a suspect classification under the Equal Protection Clause. *See Gregory v. Ashcroft*, 501 U.S. 452, 470, 111 S.Ct. 2395, 115 L.Ed.2d 410 (1991). Thus, strict scrutiny is applicable here because fundamental rights are implicated by the juvenile curfew ordinances. A fundamental right is one which has its source in and is explicitly guaranteed by the federal or Florida Constitution. . . . The fundamental rights to privacy and freedom of movement are implicated by these ordinances. It is settled law that each of the personal liberties enumerated in the Declaration of Rights of the Florida Constitution is a fundamental right. *See generally Traylor v. State*, 596 So.2d 957 (Fla.1992). . . .

Fundamental Rights

The juvenile respondents claim that the curfew ordinances implicate their fundamental rights to privacy, free speech, assembly, and free movement. They also claim that a parent's right to raise his or her children, sometimes referred to as family privacy, is also implicated by the ordinances.

* * *

Because the juveniles' fundamental rights to privacy and freedom of movement are burdened by the curfew ordinances, the cities must have a compelling governmental interest in regulating the activities of minors during the hours of the curfew and the ordinances must be narrowly tailored to accomplish their goals by the least intrusive means available. We address each part of this strict scrutiny test in turn below.

Compelling Governmental Interest

The cities assert that the ordinances serve several compelling interests, including reducing juvenile crime, protecting juveniles from victimization, protecting all citizens, residents, and visitors from juvenile crime, and promoting parental control over juveniles. . . .

* * *

. . . We . . . conclude that the findings stated in the ordinances satisfy the compelling interest prong of the strict scrutiny test. Thus, the real issue presented by these ordinances is whether they are narrowly tailored to meet those goals.

Narrowly Tailored

In order for an ordinance to be narrowly tailored, "there must be a sufficient nexus between the stated government interest and the classification created by the ordinance." [Citation omitted.] Thus, in regard to the ordinances' impact on juveniles' fundamental rights, the constitutionality of the ordinances will hinge upon the nexus between the asserted interests and the means chosen, and whether this is the least restrictive alternative to achieve the goals.

In determining whether an ordinance is narrowly tailored, courts have looked to the scope of the curfew, including what hours the curfew is in effect and what age group is covered. In several federal cases, the courts have found the scope to be "limited" and not restrictive because the curfew restrictions did not begin until relatively late at night, ended early in the morning, or only applied to minors under seventeen or eighteen years of age. *See, e.g., Schleifer*, 159 F.3d at 852. However, some of the ordinances that courts have struck as unconstitutional have covered the identical age groups and the same hours as those upheld by other courts. *See, e.g., Waters v. Barry*, 711 F.Supp. 1125, 1141 (D.D.C.1989) (concluding that District of Columbia's juvenile curfew applicable to persons under eighteen years between 11:00 p.m. and

6:00 a.m. violated the minors' associational rights and liberty interests). Thus, the scope of the curfew may not be the best assessment of whether an ordinance is narrowly tailored for purposes of passing strict scrutiny.

The scope of the exceptions to the curfew is of more significance in assessing whether an ordinance is narrowly tailored.... Where a curfew sweeps too broadly and includes within its ambit "a number of innocent activities which are constitutionally protected," it does not satisfy the narrowly tailored aspect of strict scrutiny....

In *J.P.*, the Second District concluded that the Tampa ordinance was not narrowly drawn to serve the stated purposes of reducing juvenile crime and victimization. [Citation omitted.] The district court cited three separate problems with the Tampa ordinance: (1) the ordinance imposes criminal sanctions rather than a civil infraction fine; (2) the applicability of the curfew to all persons under the age of seventeen unless one of the exceptions applies "necessarily includes minors involved in legal, wholesome activities who have the permission of their parents"; and (3) "the coverage includes the entire city without any finding that there is a city-wide emergency or problem." [Citation omitted.] In *T.M.*, the Second District "follow[ed] the reasoning expressed in *J.P.*," and concluded that "the Pinellas Park ordinance, which is even broader in its application, must necessarily fail the strict scrutiny test." [Citation omitted.] The district court noted that the Pinellas Park ordinance is more inclusive because it applies to seventeen-year-olds and only provides an exception involving parental permission for *emergency* errands. [Citation omitted.]

We agree with the Second District that the ordinances are not "narrowly tailored" because the broad coverage of both curfews includes otherwise innocent and legal conduct by minors even where they have the permission of their parents and the ordinances impose criminal penalties for curfew violations....

1. Broad Coverage

* * *

2. Imposition of Criminal Sanctions

* * *

Conclusion

In light of the problems discussed above, we conclude that the Tampa and Pinellas Park juvenile curfew ordinances are not narrowly tailored and thus fail to survive strict scrutiny.[9] Accordingly, we answer the certified questions in the negative and approve the decisions of the Second District Court of Appeal in *J.P.* and *T.M.* to the extent that they are consistent with this opinion.

---

9. The juveniles also contend that the ordinances violate their Fourth Amendment right to be free from unreasonable searches and seizures and their Fifth Amendment right to remain silent. In light of our conclusion that the ordinances do not pass strict scrutiny, we need not reach these Fourth and Fifth Amendment challenges to the ordinances.

It is so ordered.

PARIENTE, C.J., and ANSTEAD and LEWIS, JJ., concur.

WELLS, J., dissents with an opinion, in which CANTERO, J., concurs.

CANTERO, J., dissents with an opinion, in which WELLS and BELL, JJ., concur.

WELLS, J., dissenting.

I join in Justice Cantero's dissent.

* * *

CANTERO, J. concurs.

CANTERO, J., dissenting.

Today the majority holds that a minor has a right of privacy to remain on *public* streets literally in the middle of the night. I cannot agree with such an expansive reading of the right to privacy. In my opinion, the ordinances at issue do not even implicate — much less infringe upon — the minors' constitutional rights to privacy or any purported right to "freedom of movement." I believe the rational basis standard should apply to review of these ordinances. Even applying the standard most federal circuit courts have employed, however — a heightened review — the ordinances still survive attack, as the Second District Court of Appeal originally held in this case four years ago. Finally, as other courts have found, the ordinances survive even strict scrutiny analysis, as they are narrowly tailored to serve the compelling interest that even the majority concedes exists.

I. Which Standard Applies?

The first issue in every case considering the constitutionality of a statute or ordinance is which standard applies. Not only is the applicable standard the threshold determination in any constitutional analysis; it is often the most crucial. In this case, it has made all the difference. The district court originally reviewed these ordinances under a heightened scrutiny, and upheld them. *See State v. T.M.*, 761 So.2d 1140, 1146, 1150 (Fla. 2d DCA 2000) (*T.M.I*). On remand from this Court, it applied strict scrutiny, and invalidated them. *See J.P. v. State*, 832 So.2d 110, 112 (Fla. 2d DCA 2002) (*J.P.III*). Therefore, we should thoughtfully analyze the applicable standard.

* * *

Courts use three different standards for determining a law's constitutionality: rational basis review, intermediate (or heightened) scrutiny, and strict scrutiny. These three standards act like lenses of different strength, from simple eyeglasses, to a magnifying glass, to a microscope. At each level, the court more closely examines the government's purpose in enacting the law and the means used to attain it.

The most common, and least intrusive, standard is the rational basis test. It is used when the law at issue does not involve a suspect classification (such as a racial one) or infringe on a fundamental right. . . . Under that test, a statute or ordinance must be rationally related to a legitimate governmental interest. [Citation omitted.]

Where fundamental rights of minors are involved, courts sometimes invoke "intermediate" or "heightened" scrutiny. . . . To withstand such heightened review, the ordinance must be substantially related to the achievement of important government interests. . . . Finally, when a statute or ordinance infringes on the fundamental rights of adults, the law must pass the most exacting standard of review, called strict scrutiny. . . . For an ordinance to withstand strict scrutiny, it must be necessary to promote a compelling governmental interest and must be narrowly tailored to advance that interest. . . .

The majority concludes that strict scrutiny review applies "because fundamental rights are implicated by the juvenile curfew ordinances." [Citation omitted.] The majority acknowledges that the ordinances do not implicate the minors' freedom of speech and of assembly. [Citation omitted.] Nevertheless, it holds that the ordinances implicate the rights to privacy and freedom of movement. [Citation omitted.] I will address these in turn.

A. Minors' Rights to Privacy

Regarding the minors' asserted right to privacy, the majority states that "the cities' asserted compelling interest of preventing victimization of minors could outweigh the minors' privacy rights during the curfew hours, if the ordinances were narrowly tailored to achieve that goal as required by strict scrutiny." [Citation omitted.] But the majority never answers whether the juvenile curfew ordinances implicate the minors' privacy rights in the first place. If they do not, then the ordinances need not be considered under a strict scrutiny analysis. I do not see how an ordinance prohibiting minors from remaining in public unsupervised during late night hours violates their right to *privacy*.

In cases involving fundamental rights, the judicial analysis must begin with a careful description of the asserted fundamental liberty interest. . . .

With this principle in mind, the issue is not whether minors have a "right to privacy." The real question is whether the scope of that right includes a right to remain in public unsupervised at any hour of day or night. Only if minors have a fundamental right to such activity may we then ask whether the State has an important (intermediate scrutiny) or compelling (strict scrutiny) interest in curtailing that right, and whether the law is substantially related (intermediate scrutiny) or narrowly tailored (strict scrutiny) toward that interest. The majority never answers this question. It simply assumes that any fundamental right to privacy that minors possess necessarily includes the right to remain unsupervised in public late at night. Because of the many factors that distinguish minors from adults, I do not believe that minors have such a right at all, and much less that any such right is so fundamental that it cannot be circumscribed.

* * *

The majority . . . concludes that the Florida Constitution's privacy provision "affords Florida citizens greater protection in the area of privacy than does the federal Constitution." [Citation omitted.] That Florida's right of privacy may be more expansive than the federal right, however, does not make it all-encompassing. The right to privacy is not a wild card that, when played, suddenly renders any ordinance unconstitutional. We have recognized that article I, section 23 "was not intended to provide an absolute guarantee against all governmental intrusion into the private life of an individual." . . .

The majority essentially holds that minors have a fundamental right to roam in public unsupervised during any time of the day or night. This would protect a minor's right to be on the street in the middle of the night, regardless of the costs to the community in the form of higher crime rates, law enforcement costs and other negative consequences. Neither the record in this case nor common sense suggests that the purported independence of juveniles to be out in the public during the late night and early morning hours constitutes such a fundamental right. As one court has emphasized, "[f]orbidding preventive measures such as curfews propels localities to the harshest of alternatives — waiting for juveniles actually to commit criminal offenses and then apprehending, prosecuting, and punishing them." *Schleifer,* 159 F.3d at 855. Neither the State nor its citizens — whether children or adults — benefit from relegating the State to such a strictly remedial role.

B. Minors' Right to Freedom of Movement

The majority also holds that the ordinances implicate the minors' "constitutional right of freedom of movement." [Citation omitted.] I do not find any such right in either the Constitution or the cases interpreting it. . . .

* * *

C. Parents' Right to Raise their Children

* * *

II. Application of the Different Standards

As I have noted, because I believe that the ordinances do not implicate fundamental rights, the correct standard is the rational basis test. Most federal circuit courts and state supreme courts considering this particular issue have held that the proper analysis is either rational basis review or intermediate scrutiny. . . .

In my opinion, under *any* standard, the ordinances survive. Below I apply (A) rational basis review; (B) intermediate scrutiny; and finally (C) strict scrutiny.

A. Rational Basis Review

Under the rational basis test, review is limited to determining whether the ordinance in question is rationally related to legitimate governmental interests. . . .

* * *

B. Intermediate Scrutiny

Even if, as the majority holds, the ordinances implicate the fundamental rights of minors, they should be subjected only to intermediate scrutiny. This standard asks whether the ordinance is substantially related to important governmental interests.

See, e.g., United States v. Virginia, 518 U.S. 515, 533, 116 S.Ct. 2264, 135 L.Ed.2d 735 (1996).

* * *

C. Strict Scrutiny

... Under this standard, the ordinance must promote a compelling (rather than a "legitimate" or "important") governmental interest *and* must be narrowly tailored to advance that interest....

* * *

A. The Scope of the Ordinances

* * *

B. The Relevance and Severability of Criminal Penalties

* * *

III. Conclusion

For the reasons stated, I would hold that the Tampa and Pinellas Park curfew ordinances are constitutional. Juveniles do not have a fundamental right to be out in public places during the late night hours without adult supervision. Even if they did, the state may limit a minor's fundamental rights to a greater extent than an adult's. Finally, even if the ordinances infringe on fundamental rights, they promote a compelling governmental interest and are narrowly tailored to achieve their purposes.

For all these reasons, I respectfully dissent.

WELLS and BELL, JJ., concur.

When construing the state equal protection clause, the Florida Supreme Court in *Duncan v. Moore* held:[11]

> Equal protection is not violated merely because some persons are treated differently than other persons. It only requires that persons similarly situated be treated similarly. In the absence of a fundamental right or a protected class, equal protection demands only that a distinction which results in unequal treatment bear some rational relationship to a legitimate state purpose.

------

11. 754 So. 2d 708, 712 (Fla. 2000).

Jackson v. State

191 So. 3d 423 (Fla. 2016)

QUINCE, J.

This case is before the Court for review of the decision of the Fourth District Court of Appeal in *Jackson v. State,* 137 So.3d 470 (Fla. 4th DCA 2014). Because the district court expressly declared a state statute valid, this Court has jurisdiction to review the decision. *See* art. V, § 3(b)(3), Fla. Const.

Appellant, Jermaine Jackson, was convicted of one count of robbery with a firearm while wearing a mask and sentenced to the statutory maximum of life in prison. *Jackson,* 137 So.3d at 472. Jackson was 20 years old when he committed the crime, but 21 years old when he was tried and sentenced. If he had been sentenced under the youthful offender statute, he faced a six-year cap as to his sentence....

Before this Court, Jackson raises a facial challenge to the constitutionality of section 958.04(1)(b). Jackson argues that section 958.04(1)(b) violates equal protection because the age-at-sentencing classification creates arbitrary and irrational distinctions between otherwise eligible defendants. He claims that no other Florida statute distinguishes between defendants based solely on their age at sentencing and therefore this classification triggers strict scrutiny.... For the reasons that follow, we hold that section 958.04(1)(b) is constitutional as amended and does not violate equal protection or due process.

In 2008, the Legislature changed the requirements for youthful offender sentencing from someone who *committed a crime* before their twenty-first birthday, to someone who is younger than 21 *at the time of sentencing.* The statute, in relevant part, states that

> The court may sentence as a youthful offender any person ... [w]ho is found guilty of or who has tendered, and the court has accepted, a plea of nolo contendere or guilty to a crime that is, under the laws of this state, a felony if the offender is younger than 21 years of age at the time sentence is imposed.

§ 958.04(1)(b), Fla. Stat. (2008).

Constitutional challenges to statutes are pure questions of law, subject to de novo review. *Crist v. Ervin,* 56 So.3d 745, 747 (Fla.2010). Generally, statutes are presumed constitutional, and the challenging party has the burden to establish the statute's invalidity beyond a reasonable doubt. *See State v. Lick,* 390 So.2d 52, 53 (Fla.1980). It is the Court's duty to "construe challenged legislation to effect a constitutional outcome whenever possible." *Fla. Dep't of Revenue v. Howard,* 916 So.2d 640, 642 (Fla.2005).

A statutory classification will be deemed to violate equal protection only if it causes "different treatments so disparate as relates to the difference in classification so as to be wholly arbitrary." *In re Estate of Greenberg,* 390 So.2d 40, 42 (Fla.1980),

694   7 · THE DECLARATION OF RIGHTS AND THE TAKING OF PROPERTY

abrogated by Shriners Hospitals for Crippled Children v. Zrillic, 563 So.2d 64 (Fla.1990). Where no suspect classification is involved, "the statute need only bear a reasonable relationship to a legitimate state interest." *Id.* Some inequality or imprecision will not "render a statute invalid." *Acton v. Fort Lauderdale Hosp.,* 440 So.2d 1282, 1284 (Fla.1983).

In analyzing whether or not section 958.04(1)(b) violates equal protection, the first question is whether or not the statute affects a fundamental right or a suspect class. Neither this Court nor any other Florida court has determined whether youthful offender status is a fundamental right. However, courts in other states have held that youthful offender status is not a fundamental right for eligible defendants. *See People v. Robert Z.,* 134 Misc.2d 555, 511 N.Y.S.2d 473 (N.Y.Co.Ct.1986) ("There is no constitutional right to youthful offender treatment. Such treatment is entirely a gratuitous creature of the Legislature, subject to such conditions as the Legislature may impose without violating constitutional guarantees." (citations and emphasis omitted)); *State v. Johnson,* 276 S.C. 444, 279 S.E.2d 606, 607 (1981) ("The statutory right to youthful offender treatment is simply not a fundamental right."); *Hilber v. State,* 89 Wis.2d 49, 277 N.W.2d 839, 842 (1979) ("Hilber and Mayes argue that the statutory right to youthful offender treatment is 'fundamental,' but their arguments are not convincing and are not supported by any authority. Indeed, differences in the treatment of criminal defendants have been viewed as being subject to the rational basis test." (citations omitted)). We agree with our sister courts.

The discretionary nature of youthful offender sentencing provides further support that it is not a fundamental right for defendants. A "lower court is under no obligation to sentence [a defendant] under the Youthful Offender Act unless the lower court believes such a sentence would be appropriate." *Holmes v. State,* 638 So.2d 986, 987 (Fla. 1st DCA 1994); *see also Ellis v. State,* 475 So.2d 1021, 1023 (Fla. 2d DCA 1985) ("[A]pplication of the Youthful Offender Act to any particular defendant is discretionary with the trial judge who is in the best position to determine whether sentencing under the act is the most desirable treatment for that defendant.").

Moreover, the youthful offender statute does not involve a suspect class. Under a constitutional analysis, a suspect class is one where strict scrutiny is required when questions of equal protection arise. Generally, classifications such as race, national origin, or alienage have been held to be suspect classifications. *San Antonio Indep. Sch. Dist. v. Rodriguez,* 411 U.S. 1, 61, 93 S.Ct. 1278, 36 L.Ed.2d 16 (1973). Youth, however, is not a suspect classification. *See* art. I, §2, Fla. Const. (defining the protected classes as "race, religion, national origin, or physical disability"); *see also Gregory v. Ashcroft,* 501 U.S. 452, 470, 111 S.Ct. 2395, 115 L.Ed.2d 410 (1991) (holding that age is not a suspect classification under the Equal Protection Clause).

Because section 958.04(1)(b) does not affect a fundamental right or suspect class, the rational basis test applies. *Miller v. State,* 971 So.2d 951, 952 (Fla. 5th DCA 2007). Under rational basis analysis, a statute must be upheld if the classification bears a rational relationship to a legitimate government objective. *Id.* The statute must be upheld if there is any conceivable state of facts or plausible reason to justify it, regardless of whether the Legislature actually relied on such facts or reason. *McElrath v. Burley*, 707 So.2d 836, 839 (Fla. 1st DCA 1998).

The Legislature did not provide guidance when it amended section 958.04(1)(b). However, as the Fourth District noted, an examination of the statute's legislative intent gives possible insight into the amendment. The legislative intent of Chapter 958 states, in relevant part,

> The purpose of this chapter is to improve the chances of correction and successful return to the community of youthful offenders sentenced to imprisonment by providing them with enhanced vocational, educational, counseling, or public service opportunities *and by preventing their association with older and more experienced criminals during the terms of their confinement.*

§ 958.021, Fla. Stat. (2008) (emphasis added).

Section 958.04(1)(b) bears a rational relationship to the legitimate government objective of preventing the association between young offenders and older criminals. By requiring that a defendant be sentenced before the age of 21 in order to be eligible for youthful offender sentencing, section 958.04(1)(b) ensures that defendants entering the program are truly youthful. It also ensures that defendants eligible for the program will complete their sentence without being exposed to more experienced and sophisticated criminals during their incarceration. Because the statute bears a rational relationship to this legitimate government objective, it does not violate equal protection.

* * *

Jackson has failed to demonstrate that section 958.04(1)(b), as amended, violates equal protection or due process. Accordingly, we affirm the Fourth District.

It is so ordered.

LABARGA, C.J., and LEWIS, CANADY, POLSTON, and PERRY, JJ., concur.

PARIENTE, J., dissents with an opinion.

[The dissenting opinion of Justice Pariente is omitted.]

C. Florida Rational Basis Test

Estate of McCall v. United States

134 So. 3d 894 (Fla. 2014)

LEWIS, J.

This case is before the Court to answer four questions of Florida law certified by the United States Court of Appeals for the Eleventh Circuit that are determinative of a cause pending in that court and for which there appears to be no controlling precedent. We have jurisdiction. Art. V, § 3(b)(6), Fla. Const. . . .

As explained below, we answer the first rephrased certified question in the affirmative and hold that the cap on wrongful death noneconomic damages provided in section 766.118, Florida Statutes, violates the Equal Protection Clause of the Florida Constitution. We find it unnecessary to answer the remaining certified questions because Florida's Wrongful Death Act is of statutory origin, and the present case is under the Federal Tort Claims Act and its procedures.

* * *

The Petitioners filed an action against the United States under the Federal Tort Claims Act (FTCA) [for the wrongful death of Michelle McCall who, after delivering a healthy baby boy, loss severe blood and, as a result, went into shock and cardiac arrest never to regain consciousness while under the care of Air Force family practice doctors], 28 U.S.C. §§ 1346(b), 2671–80. *Id.* at 947. In addition to finding the United States liable under the FTCA, the United States District Court for the Northern District of Florida determined that the Petitioners' economic damages, or financial losses, amounted to $980,462.40. *Id.* The district court concluded that the Petitioners' noneconomic damages, or nonfinancial losses, totaled $2 million, including $500,000 for Ms. McCall's son and $750,000 for each of her parents. *Id.*

However, the district court limited the Petitioners' recovery of wrongful death noneconomic damages to $1 million upon application of section 766.118(2), Florida Statutes (2005), Florida's statutory cap on wrongful death noneconomic damages based on medical malpractice claims. *Id.*[1] . . .

On appeal to the Eleventh Circuit, the Petitioners challenged the district court's rulings with regard to both the application and the constitutionality of the cap mandated by Florida law on wrongful death noneconomic damages for medical malpractice claims. *Id.* at 948. The Petitioners contended that the statutory cap violates . . . the right to equal protection under article I, section 2 . . . . *Id.*

---

1. Under the FTCA, damages are "determined by the law of the State where the tortious act was committed, 28 U.S.C. § 1346(b), . . . subject to the limitations that the United States shall not be liable for 'interest prior to judgment or for punitive damages.'" *Hatahley v. United States,* 351 U.S. 173, 182, 76 S.Ct. 745, 100 L.Ed. 1065 (1956) (quoting 28 U.S.C. § 2674).

7 · THE DECLARATION OF RIGHTS AND THE TAKING OF PROPERTY

The Eleventh Circuit . . . granted a motion filed by the Petitioners to certify four questions to this Court regarding the . . . challenges to the statutory cap under the Florida Constitution. *Id.*

Statutory Provision

At issue is Florida's statutory cap on wrongful death[2] noneconomic damages in medical negligence actions as articulated in section 766.118. Section 766.118(2) states:

(2) Limitation on noneconomic damages for negligence of practitioners.

(a) With respect to a cause of action for personal injury or wrongful death arising from medical negligence of practitioners, regardless of the number of such practitioner defendants, noneconomic damages shall not exceed $500,000 per claimant. No practitioner shall be liable for more than $500,000 in noneconomic damages, regardless of the number of claimants.

(b) Notwithstanding paragraph (a), if the negligence resulted in a permanent vegetative state or death, the total noneconomic damages recoverable from all practitioners, regardless of the number of claimants, under this paragraph shall not exceed $1 million. In cases that do not involve death or permanent vegetative state, the patient injured by medical negligence may recover noneconomic damages not to exceed $1 million if:

> 1. The trial court determines that a manifest injustice would occur unless increased noneconomic damages are awarded, based on a finding that because of the special circumstances of the case, the noneconomic harm sustained by the injured patient was particularly severe; and

> 2. The trier of fact determines that the defendant's negligence caused a catastrophic injury to the patient.

(c) The total noneconomic damages recoverable by all claimants from all practitioner defendants under this subsection shall not exceed $1 million in the aggregate.

§ 766.118(2), Fla. Stat.[3] Noneconomic damages refer to "nonfinancial losses . . . including pain and suffering, inconvenience, physical impairment, mental anguish . . . loss of capacity for enjoyment of life, and other nonfinancial losses to the extent

---

2. The legal analyses for personal injury damages and wrongful death damages are not the same. The present case is exclusively related to wrongful death, and our analysis is limited accordingly.

3. Section 766.118 separates the cap on noneconomic damages into two categories, providing different limitations on damages for practitioners and nonpractitioners. *See* § 766.118(2), (3), Fla. Stat. Section 766.118(3), Florida Statutes, limits noneconomic damages for the negligence of nonpractitioner defendants. The Petitioners asserted that they were entitled to recover under this subsection as well; however, the federal district court noted that "no evidence at trial singled out a specific nonpractitioner for negligent conduct." *McCall,* 642 F.3d at 948–49 (quoting *Estate of McCall v. United States,* 663 F.Supp.2d 1276, 1295 (N.D.Fla.2009)). The federal district court concluded that the Petitioners had failed to establish that Ms. McCall's death resulted from the negligence of a nonpractitioner, and the Eleventh Circuit affirmed this determination. *Id.* at 949.

the claimant is entitled to recover such damages under general law, including the Wrongful Death Act." §766.202(8), Fla. Stat. (2005) (incorporated in §766.118(1)(b), Fla. Stat. (2005)).

Equal Protection

We have rephrased the first question certified to this Court by the Eleventh Circuit which addresses whether the cap on wrongful death noneconomic damages under section 766.118 violates the right to equal protection guaranteed by the Florida Constitution. The Florida Constitution provides, in pertinent part:

> All natural persons, female and male alike, are equal before the law. Art. I, §2, Fla. Const. This Court has stated "[t]he constitutional right of equal protection of the laws means that everyone is entitled to stand before the law on equal terms with, to enjoy the same rights as belong to, and to bear the same burden as are imposed upon others in a like situation." *Caldwell v. Mann,* 157 Fla. 633, 26 So.2d 788, 790 (1946).

Unless a suspect class or fundamental right protected by the Florida Constitution is implicated by the challenged provision, the rational basis test will apply to evaluate an equal protection challenge. *See Amerisure Ins. Co. v. State Farm Mut. Auto. Ins. Co.,* 897 So.2d 1287, 1291 n. 2 (Fla.2005). To satisfy the rational basis test, a statute must bear a rational and reasonable relationship to a legitimate state objective, and it cannot be arbitrary or capriciously imposed. *Dep't of Corr. v. Fla. Nurses Ass'n,* 508 So.2d 317, 319 (Fla.1987). Stated another way, the test for consideration of equal protection is whether individuals have been classified separately based on a difference which has a reasonable relationship to the applicable statute, and the classification can never be made arbitrarily without a reasonable and rational basis.

Having carefully considered the arguments of both parties and the amici, we conclude that section 766.118 violates the Equal Protection Clause of the Florida Constitution under the rational basis test. The statutory cap on wrongful death noneconomic damages fails because it imposes unfair and illogical burdens on injured parties when an act of medical negligence gives rise to multiple claimants. In such circumstances, medical malpractice claimants do not receive the same rights to full compensation because of arbitrarily diminished compensation for legally cognizable claims. Further, the statutory cap on wrongful death noneconomic damages does not bear a rational relationship to the stated purpose that the cap is purported to address, the alleged medical malpractice insurance crisis in Florida.

Arbitrary Distinctions

* * *

... The plain language of this statutory plan irrationally impacts circumstances which have multiple claimants/survivors differently and far less favorably than circumstances in which there is a single claimant/survivor and also exacts an irrational and unreasonable cost and impact when, as here, the victim of medical negligence has a large family, all of whom have been adversely impacted and affected by the death. Three separate noneconomic damage determinations were assessed by the federal district court based on the evidence presented. The damages suffered by Ms. McCall's parents were determined to be $750,000 each, and Ms. McCall's surviving son sustained damages determined to be $500,000. Applying the cap, the federal court then reduced the amounts of damages so each claimant would receive only half of his or her respective damages. Yet, if Ms. McCall had been survived only by her son, *he would have recovered the full amount of his noneconomic damages: $500,000.* Here, the cap delineated in section 766.118 limited the recovery of a surviving child (and surviving parents) simply because others also suffered losses. In a larger context, under section 766.118, the greater the number of survivors and the more devastating their losses are, the less likely they are to be fully compensated for those losses.

* * *

Section 766.118, Florida Statutes, has the effect of saving a modest amount for many by imposing devastating costs on a few — those who are most grievously injured, those who sustain the greatest damage and loss, and multiple claimants for whom judicially determined noneconomic damages are subject to division and reduction simply based upon the existence of the cap. Under the Equal Protection Clause of the Florida Constitution, and guided by our decision in *Phillipe,* we hold that to reduce damages in this fashion is not only arbitrary, but irrational, and we conclude that it "offends the fundamental notion of equal justice under the law." *Phillipe,* 769 So.2d at 972; *see also id.* at 971 ("Differentiating between a single claimant and multiple claimants bears no rational relationship to the Legislature's stated goal of alleviating the financial crisis in the medical liability insurance industry.").

* * *

The Alleged Medical Malpractice Crisis

In addition to arbitrary and invidious discrimination between medical malpractice claimants, the cap on noneconomic damages also violates the Equal Protection Clause of the Florida Constitution because it bears no rational relationship to a legitimate state objective, thereby failing the rational basis test. *See Fla. Nurses Ass'n,* 508 So.2d at 319. . . . Our precedent expressly states that a proper equal protection analysis under the rational basis test "requires this Court to determine: (1) whether the challenged statute serves a legitimate governmental purpose, *and* (2) whether it was reasonable for the Legislature to believe that the challenged classification would promote that purpose." *Warren v. State Farm Mut. Auto. Ins. Co.,* 899 So.2d 1090, 1095 (Fla.2005) (emphasis supplied); *see also Zapo v. Gilreath,* 779 So.2d 651, 655 (Fla. 5th DCA 2001); *Fla. Dept. of Ins. v. Keys Title & Abstract Co.,* 741 So.2d 599, 602 (Fla. 1st DCA 1999). Thus, under *Warren,* and contrary to the view of the concurring in result opinion, both prongs of the rational basis test must be evaluated to determine the constitutionality of a statute.

. . .

The Florida Legislature attempted to justify the cap on noneconomic damages by claiming that "Florida is in the midst of a medical malpractice insurance crisis of unprecedented magnitude." Ch.2003–416, §1, Laws of Fla., at 4035. The Legislature asserted that the increase in medical malpractice liability insurance premiums has resulted in physicians leaving Florida, retiring early from the practice of medicine, or refusing to perform high-risk procedures, thereby limiting the availability of health care. *Id.*

In enacting the statutory cap on noneconomic damages, the Legislature relied heavily on a report prepared by the Governor's Select Task Force on Healthcare Professional Liability Insurance (Task Force), which concluded that "actual and potential jury awards of noneconomic damages (such as pain and suffering) are a key factor (perhaps the most important factor) behind the unavailability and un-affordability of medical malpractice insurance in Florida." Report of Governor's Select Task Force on Healthcare Professional Liability Insurance (Task Force Report) (Jan. 29, 2003), at xvii.

To evaluate the constitutionality of the cap on noneconomic damages imposed by section 766.118, we are not required to accept the findings of the Legislature or the Task Force at face value. Instead:

> While courts may defer to legislative statements of policy and fact, courts may do so only when those statements are based on actual findings of fact, and *even then courts must conduct their own inquiry:*

> The general rule is that findings of fact made by the legislature are presumptively correct. However, it is well-recognized that the findings of fact made by the legislature must actually be findings of *fact*. They are not entitled to the presumption of correctness if they are nothing more than recitations amounting only to conclusions and *they are always subject to judicial inquiry.*

N. Fla. Women's Health & Counseling Serv., Inc. v. State, 866 So.2d 612, 627 (Fla.2003) (quoting *Moore v. Thompson*, 126 So.2d 543, 549 (Fla.1960)) (some emphasis supplied).

Our consideration of the factors and circumstances involved demonstrates that the conclusions reached by the Florida Legislature as to the existence of a medical malpractice crisis are not fully supported by available data. Instead, the alleged interest of health care being unavailable is completely undermined by authoritative government reports. Those government reports have indicated that the numbers of physicians in both metropolitan and non-metropolitan areas have increased.... Thus, during this purported crisis, the numbers of physicians in Florida were actually increasing, not decreasing.

Additionally, an analysis of claim activity certainly does not provide a rational basis for the clear discrimination presented by the legislation. Although assertions of a malpractice insurance crisis are often accompanied by images of runaway juries entering verdicts in exorbitant amounts of noneconomic damages, *see, e.g.,* Task Force Report at xvii, one study revealed that in Florida cases which resulted in payments of $1 million or more over a fourteen-year period, *only 7.5 percent involved a jury trial verdict. See* Neil Vidmar, Kara MacKillop & Paul Lee, *Million Dollar Medical Malpractice Cases in Florida: Post–Verdict and Pre–Suit Settlements,* 59 Vand. L.Rev. 1343, 1345–46 (2006).[5] Moreover, 10.1 percent of settlements that involved payments of $1 million or more were resolved *without a legal action ever being filed. Id.* at 1360. Such statistics led the authors of the study to conclude that jury trials constitute only a very small portion of medical malpractice payments. *Id.* at 1345. The authors also concluded that "tort reform efforts focused on jury verdicts are misdirected, at least with respect to $1 million verdicts in Florida. Not only do jury trials constitute only a small portion of $1 million payments, [but] the settlements following verdicts *tend to be substantially less than the jury awards." Id.* at 1381 (emphasis supplied).[6] Thus, available data indicates the Task Force's finding that noneconomic damage awards by juries are a primary cause of the purported medical malpractice crisis in Florida is most questionable.

* * *

Based upon these statements and reports, although medical malpractice premiums in Florida were undoubtably high in 2003, we conclude the Legislature's determination that "the increase in medical malpractice liability insurance rates is forcing physicians to practice medicine without professional liability insurance, to leave Florida, to not perform high-risk procedures, or to retire early from the practice of medicine" is unsupported. Ch.2003–416, §1, Laws of Fla., at 4035. Thus, the finding by the Legislature and the Task Force that Florida was in the midst of a bona fide medical malpractice crisis, threatening the access of Floridians to health care, is dubious and questionable at the very best.

The Impact of Damage Caps on the Alleged Crisis

Even if these conclusions by the Legislature are assumed to be true, and Florida was facing a dangerous risk of physician shortage due to malpractice premiums, we conclude that section 766.118 still violates Florida's Equal Protection Clause because the available evidence fails to establish a rational relationship between a cap on noneconomic damages and alleviation of the purported crisis. *See generally Fla. Nurses Ass'n,* 508 So.2d at 319 (stating that for legislation to be constitutional under the rational basis standard, it must bear a rational and reasonable relationship to a legitimate state objective).

---

5. Further, a national study reflects that from 1991 until 2003, judgments at trial accounted for *only 4 percent of all malpractice payments.* Amitabh Chandra, Shantanu Nundy, & Seth A. Seabury, *The Growth of Physician Medical Malpractice Payments: Evidence From The National Practitioner Data Bank,* Health Affairs at W5–240, W5–243 (May 31, 2005), available at http://content .healthaffairs.org/content/early/2005/05/31/hlthaff.w5.240.full.pdf+html.

6. According to the authors, with one exception, cases with verdicts in excess of $4 million settled for, on average, 37 percent less than the verdict. *Million Dollar Medical Malpractice Cases in Florida,* 59 Vand. L. Rev. at 1380.

Reports have failed to establish a direct correlation between damages caps and reduced malpractice premiums. Weiss Ratings, which evaluates the performance of the malpractice insurance industry, has detailed two particularly salient findings. First, based upon data acquired from 1991 until 2002, the median medical malpractice premiums paid by physicians in three high-risk specialties — internal medicine, general surgery, and obstetrics/gynecology — rose by 48.2 percent in states that have damages caps, but in states *without* caps, the median annual premium increased at a *slower* rate — by 35.9 percent. Martin D. Weiss, Melissa Gannon & Stephanie Eakins, *Medical Malpractice Caps: The Impact of Non–Economic Damage Caps on Physician Premiums, Claims Payout Levels, and Availability of Coverage,* at 7–8 (rev. ed. June 3, 2003), available at http://www.weissratings.com/pdf/ malpractice.pdf. Second, the study noted that among states *with* caps on damages, only 10.5 percent (two of nineteen states with caps) experienced static or declining medical malpractice premium rates following the imposition of caps. In contrast, among states *without* damages caps, 18.7 percent (six of thirty-two states[7] without caps) experienced static or declining medical malpractice premiums. *Id.* at 8.

Additionally, Robert White, the President of First Professionals Insurance Company (FPIC), testified during a Senate Judiciary Committee meeting that a $500,000 cap on noneconomic damages would achieve "virtually nothing" with regard to stabilizing medical malpractice insurance rates. Testimony of Robert White, Senate Judiciary Committee Meeting, July 14, 2003, at 48, 50–51. Earlier in 2003, Mr. White informed a group of Palm Beach physicians: "No responsible insurer can cut its rates after a bill [that caps noneconomic damages at $250,000] passes." Phil Galewitz, "Underwriter Gives Doctors Dose of Reality," *Palm Beach Post,* Jan. 29, 2003, at 1A. Mr. White advised that "[e]ven if a cap is approved by the legislature and survives the likely legal challenge . . . *it would yield on average only a 16 percent premium cut.*" *Id.* (emphasis supplied). Interestingly, during his testimony before the Senate Judiciary Committee, Mr. White acknowledged that in 2002, the experience of FPIC was more positive in Florida than in Missouri, *a state which at that time had implemented caps on damages.* Testimony of Robert White, Senate Judiciary Committee Meeting, at 59.

* * *

Although at first glance this statutory subsection may appear to compel medical malpractice insurance companies to reduce their rates in response to the 2003 legislation, FLOIR nonetheless advised that "[e]ven after application of the presumed factor, we anticipate insurers will file for rate increases." Press Release, Florida Office of Insurance Regulation, *Office of Insurance Regulation Releases Presumed Factor* (Nov. 10, 2003), available at http://www. floir.com/PressReleases/viewmediarelease .aspx?id=1316. Moreover, despite any intended moderation of medical malpractice

---

7. The study states that "the District of Columbia is being referred to as a 'state' since it effectively operates as such with regard to insurance regulation." *Medical Malpractice Caps,* at 7 n. 4.

premiums based upon the calculation of the presumed factor, the 2013 Annual Report on Medical Malpractice Financial Information, Closed Claim Database and Rate Filings, prepared by FLOIR compared the premiums of Florida doctors in four specialties (family practice, obstetrics, emergency, and orthopedics) with other sampled states and concluded that "Florida is either the highest (of nine states) or the second highest state as far as premiums go in all but one of the scenarios." 2013 FLOIR Annual Report (Oct. 1, 2013) at 57–58, available at http://www.floir.com/Office/DataReports.aspx#rec (CY2012). Therefore, despite assertions that the presumed factor created in section 627.062(8)(a) caused massive rate reductions by medical malpractice insurers to pass savings onto their customers, the data suggests otherwise. Subdivision (8) was even repealed from section 627.062 in 2011, having been designated "obsolete" by the Legislature. Ch.2011–39, §12, Laws of Fla., at 514, 536–37.

. . .

We conclude that the record and available data fail to establish a legitimate relationship between the cap on wrongful death noneconomic damages and the lowering of medical malpractice insurance premiums. Accordingly, we hold that section 766.118 fails the rational basis test and violates the Equal Protection Clause of the Florida Constitution. *See generally Fla. Nurses Ass'n,* 508 So.2d at 319.

The Current Status of Medical Malpractice in Florida

* * *

. . . [E]ven if there had been a medical malpractice crisis in Florida at the turn of the century, the current data reflects that it has subsided. No rational basis currently exists (if it ever existed) between the cap imposed by section 766.118 and any legitimate state purpose. *See generally Fla. Nurses Ass'n,* 508 So.2d at 319. At the present time, the cap on noneconomic damages serves no purpose other than to arbitrarily punish the most grievously injured or their surviving family members. Moreover, it has never been demonstrated that there was a proper predicate for imposing the burden of supporting the Florida legislative scheme upon the shoulders of the persons and families who have been most severely injured and died as a result of medical negligence. Health care policy that relies upon discrimination against Florida families is not rational or reasonable when it attempts to utilize aggregate caps to create unreasonable classifications. Accordingly, and for each of these reasons, the cap on wrongful death noneconomic damages in medical malpractice actions does not pass constitutional muster.

* * *

Conclusion

Based on the foregoing, we answer the first rephrased certified question in the affirmative and hold that the cap on wrongful death noneconomic damages in section 766.118, Florida Statutes, violates the Equal Protection Clause of the Florida Constitution. We defer answering the remaining certified questions. We return this case to the Eleventh Circuit Court of Appeals.

It is so ordered.

LABARGA, J., concurs.

PARIENTE, J., concurs in result with an opinion, in which QUINCE and PERRY, JJ.,

concur. [The concurring opinion of Justice Pariente is omitted.]

POLSTON, C.J., dissents with an opinion, in which CANADY, J., concurs.

[The dissenting opinion of Chief Justice Polston is omitted.]

The reader will note that the Court in *Estate v. McCall* seems to use a "reasonableness" approach when describing the rational basis test. If the Court had applied a true rational basis test, would the law have been upheld?

Shriners Hospital for Crippled Children v. Zrillic

563 So. 2d 64 (Fla. 1990)

BARKETT, Justice.

[For the facts of this case, see page 675 of this text.]

IV.

We also find that section 732.803 violates the equal protection guarantees of article I, section 2 of the Florida Constitution, and the fourteenth amendment of the United States Constitution.

> It is well settled under federal and Florida law that all similarly situated persons are equal before the law. *McLaughlin v. Florida*, 379 U.S. 184, 85 S.Ct. 283, 13 L.Ed.2d 222 (1964); *Haber v. State*, 396 So.2d 707 (Fla.1981); *Soverino v. State*, 356 So.2d 269 (Fla.1978). Moreover, without exception, all statutory classifications that treat one person or group differently than others must appear to be based at a minimum on a rational distinction having a just and reasonable relation to a legitimate state objective. *In re Greenberg's Estate*, 390 So.2d 40 (Fla. 1980), *appeal dismissed sub nom. Pincus v. Estate of Greenberg*, 450 U.S. 961, 101 S.Ct. 1475, 67 L.Ed.2d 610 (1981); *Graham v. Ramani*, 383 So.2d 634 (Fla. 1980); *Department of Health & Rehabilitative Services v. Heffler*, 382 So.2d 301 (Fla.1980).

Palm Harbor Special Fire Control Dist. v. Kelly, 516 So.2d 249, 251 (Fla.1987). Equal protection analysis requires that classifications be neither too narrow nor too broad to achieve the desired end. Such underinclusive or overinclusive classifications fail to meet even the minimal standards of the rational basis test quoted above.[6]

---

6. We have previously applied the rational basis test in the context of a probate dispute where neither a suspect class nor a fundamental right was implicated. *See In re Estate of Greenberg*, 390 So.2d 40 (Fla.1980), *appeal dismissed*, 450 U.S. 961, 101 S.Ct. 1475, 67 L.Ed.2d 610 (1981) (a testator has no fundamental right to appoint a personal representative). Although the express constitutional

Section 732.803 creates a class consisting of only those testators who die within six months after executing a will that devised property to a "benevolent, charitable, educational, literary, scientific, religious, or missionary institution, corporation, association, or purpose," a governmental body, or a trustee thereof. This classification is underinclusive because "it does not affect many charitable gifts made without proper deliberation, nor does it void legacies to persons who are in an equal position with religious persons to influence a testator." *Estate of French*, 365 A.2d 621, 624 (D.C. 1976), *appeal dismissed*, 434 U.S. 59, 98 S.Ct. 280, 54 L.Ed.2d 238 (1977). The statute does not protect against overreaching by unscrupulous lawyers, doctors, nurses, housekeepers, companions, or others with a greater opportunity to influence a testator. There is no reason to believe that testators need more protection against charities than against unscrupulous and greedy relatives, friends, or acquaintances.[7]

The classification also is overinclusive because "it voids many intentional bequests by testators who were not impermissibly influenced or who do not have immediate family members in need of protection." *Estate of French*, 365 A.2d at 624. *Accord In re Estate of Cavill*, 459 Pa. 411, 416, 329 A.2d 503, 506 (1974). As our sister court in Ohio said of its analogous statute:

> Unfortunately, a large number of cases falling within the scope of R.C. 2107.06 involve the estates of testators who did *not* execute their last will under the belief that their death was near. Furthermore, out of the remaining cases impacted by the statute in which the testator did believe that he was near death, it is reasonable to assume that few involved bequests that were based upon unsound judgment or the result of undue influence by a governmental, benevolent, religious, educational or charitable beneficiary.

Shriners' Hosp. for Crippled Children v. Hester, 23 Ohio St.3d 198, 201, 492 N.E.2d 153, 156 (1986) (emphasis in original).

There is no rational distinction to automatically void a devise upon request when the testator survives the execution of the will by five months and twenty-eight days, but not when the testator survives a few days longer. *Accord In re Estate of Cavill*, 459 Pa. at 414–18, 329 A.2d at 505–06. Nor is it rational to apply the statute in cases where the testator dies suddenly due to an accident during the six-month period after making the charitable bequest.

The effect of section 732.803 is to defeat the testator's express intent without any reasonable relation to the evil sought to be cured. We agree with the analogous

---

property right at issue in the instant case may well qualify for application of a more stringent test, we need not address that issue because the charitable devise restriction in section 732.803 fails to satisfy even the rational basis test.

7. "Modern policies ... do not seem to suggest that testators need more protection against charities than against greedy relatives." ABA Real Property, Probate and Trust Law Section, Committee on Succession, *Restrictions on Charitable Testamentary Gifts*, 5 Real Prop., Prob. and Trust J. 290, 298 (1970) (quoted in Note, *Pennsylvania's Mortmain Statute Declared Unconstitutional*, 80 Dick.L.Rev. 152, 153 (1975) (emphasis omitted)).

decisions of our sister courts in *Hester, Estate of French*, and *In re Estate of Cavill*. The classification established in section 732.803 does not draw a rational distinction, and it is neither just nor reasonably related to a legitimate governmental purpose.[8]

For the aforementioned reasons, we overrule *Taylor*, approve the decision of the court below as to standing, but quash the decision as to its discussion of the constitutionality of section 732.803. We find that section 732.803 is unconstitutional for the reasons expressed above. This cause is remanded for further proceedings in accordance herewith.

It is so ordered.

EHRLICH, C.J., and SHAW and KOGAN, JJ., concur.

GRIMES, J., concurs in result with an opinion.

McDONALD, J., concurs in result and dissents in part with an opinion, in which OVERTON, J., concurs.

[The concurring opinion of Justice Grimes and concurring and dissenting in part opinion of Justice McDonald are omitted.]

———

Compare the *Zrillic* view of the equal protection rational basis test with that at the federal level as annunciated in *McGowan v. Maryland*:[12] "A statutory discrimination will not be set aside if any state of facts reasonably may be conceived to justify it."

Does the following part of Justice McDonald's opinion in *Zrillic*,[13] which concurs in result and dissents in part, support the idea that the majority opinion is in error, especially if the *McGowan* explanation of the rational basis test is the correct one?

> I confess that the facts of this case are not attractive for application of the statute, but could well be present in another series of events. Surely one would have to say that, had the testator, in her last few days, succumbed to a television evangelist's call to be with the Lord by delivering her property to his church and thus leave unprotected a physically handicapped child, a rational basis for the statute would exist. The legislature has the right to put conditions on devises of property. It may be that in today's society the legislature *should* not effect legislation like section 782.803, but that is for it to decide. Our role is to decide whether the legislature *could* do so and, contrary to the majority's views, I believe it can.

It should thus be, by now, obvious to the reader that for what is called the rational basis test (the lowest level of judicial scrutiny), the Florida Courts appear to use the

---

8. Certainly the statute would fail to pass constitutional muster under a heightened scrutiny analysis as well. *See supra* n. 6.

12. 366 U.S. 420, 426 (1961).

13. 563 So. 2d 64, 72. (McDonald, J., concurring in result and dissenting in part, in which Overton, J., concurs) (emphasis in original).

word "reasonable" almost interchangeably with the word "rational." And while some might disagree, an argument can be made that "reasonable" implicates a somewhat greater degree of scrutiny than "rational," and the cases seem to prove this point. It is eye-opening to ask if the outcomes in the rational basis test cases assembled here (and also in the earlier section on the right to acquire, possess, and protect property, as well as the later section on substantive due process) would have been the same under a correctly used[14] federal rational basis test.

D. Right to Assemble

Fla. Const. art. I, § 5

Right to assemble. — The people shall have the right peaceably to assemble, to instruct their representatives, and to petition for redress of grievances.

Under current state interpretations, the right to assemble has been largely subsumed under the First Amendment to the United States Constitution, and has received little interpretation at the state level. However, in *Krivanek v. Take Back Tampa Political Committee*,[15] the Florida Supreme Court recognized the constitutional significance of the right to petition governments:

> Given its constitutional underpinnings, the right to petition is inherent and absolute. This does not mean, however, that such a right is not subject to reasonable regulation. Quite the contrary, reasonable regulations on the right to vote and on the petition process are necessary to ensure ballot integrity and a valid election process. . . .

E. The Right to Work and the Right to Bargain Collectively

Fla. Const. art. I, § 6

Right to work. — The right of persons to work shall not be denied or abridged on account of membership or non-membership in a labor union or labor organization. The right of employees, by and through a labor organization, to bargain collectively shall not be denied or abridged. Public employees shall not have the right to strike.

---

14. *See City of Cleburne, Texas v. Cleburne Living Center, Inc.*, 473 U.S. 432 (1985), where an incorrectly-used rational basis test produced a result similar to the those reached under Florida's rational/reasonable approach.

15. 625 So. 2d 840, 843 (Fla. 1993).

708   7 · THE DECLARATION OF RIGHTS AND THE TAKING OF PROPERTY

While recognizing the right of workers to bargain collectively, the Florida Constitution prohibits public employees from striking under the above provision. The courts and the attorney general have concluded that closed shops, union shops, and agency shops are all prohibited under this provision. Although not subject to extensive litigation, the so-called "right to work" provision has been addressed in court opinions.[16]

Headley v. City of Miami
215 So. 3d 1 (Fla. 2017)

QUINCE, J.

* * *

Facts

This case involves a certified bargaining agreement ("CBA") between Miami Lodge No. 20, Fraternal Order of Police (the Union), which represents officers employed by the City of Miami's police department, and the City of Miami ("the City"). The agreement covered the period of October 1, 2007, through September 30, 2010. *Headley*, 118 So.3d at 888. On July 28, 2010, the City declared a "financial urgency" and invoked the process set forth in section 447.4095, Florida Statutes (2010). *Id.* It notified the Union that it intended to implement changes regarding wages, pension benefits, and other economic terms of employment. *Id. . . .*

On August 31, 2010, the City's legislative body voted to unilaterally alter the terms of the CBA in order to address the financial urgency, and adopted changes that:

> [I]mposed a tiered reduction of wages, elimination of education pay supplements, conversion of supplemental pay, a freeze in step and longevity pay, modification of the normal retirement date, modification of the pension benefit formula, a cap on the average final compensation for pension benefit calculations, alteration of the normal retirement form, and modification of average final compensation.

Id. The Union then filed an unfair labor practice ("ULP") charge with PERC on September 21, 2010, arguing that the City improperly invoked section 447.4095 and unilaterally changed the CBA before completing the impasse resolution process provided for in section 447.4095. *Id.* at 889.

The hearing officer . . . issued an order recommending dismissal of the Union's ULP charge. *Id.* The hearing officer found that the statute had been properly invoked by the City and the parties were not required to proceed through the impasse procedures before implementing the changes. *Id.*

---

16. *See Cannery, Citrus, Drivers, Warehousemen & Allied Emps. of Local 444 v. Winter Haven Hosp., Inc.*, 279 So. 2d 23 (Fla. 1973).

The First District affirmed PERC's final order, finding that it did not err in interpreting or applying section 447.4095. *Id.* at 896. Petitioner now seeks review, arguing that an employer must demonstrate that funds are available from no other possible reasonable source before unilaterally modifying a CBA and that modification can only be made after completing the impasse resolution process.

Analysis

Petitioner first argues that before unilaterally modifying a CBA pursuant to the financial urgency statute, an employer must demonstrate that funds are available from no other possible reasonable source. Deciding this issue will require the interpretation of section 447.4095, Florida Statutes (2010). Issues of statutory interpretation are subject to de novo review. *See, e.g. Fla. Dep't of Envtl. Prot. v. Contract Point Fla. Parks, LLC*, 986 So.2d 1260, 1264 (Fla. 2008). . . .

. . .

. . . Petitioner argues that PERC's interpretation of the financial urgency statute violates the Union's right to collectively bargain under article 1, section 6 and its right to contract under article 1, section 10 because the statute impermissibly allows for unilateral changes to CBAs. Generally, an agreement regarding wages, hours, or terms and conditions of employment reached through the collective bargaining process cannot be unilaterally modified during the term of the agreement absent a compelling state interest. *Headley*, 118 So.3d at 890.

The statute at issue in this case, section 447.4095, provides:

> Financial urgency—In the event of a financial urgency requiring modification of an agreement, the chief executive officer or his or her representative and the bargaining agent or its representative shall meet as soon as possible to negotiate the impact of the financial urgency. If after a reasonable period of negotiation which shall not exceed 14 days, a dispute exists between the public employer and the bargaining agent, an impasse shall be deemed to have occurred, and one of the parties shall so declare in writing to the other party and to the commission. The parties shall then proceed pursuant to the provisions of s. 447.403. An unfair labor practice charge shall not be filed during the 14 days during which negotiations are occurring pursuant to this section.

The statute does not define "financial urgency," and the term is not defined elsewhere in chapter 447. *Headley*, 118 So.3d at 891. Moreover, the legislative history does not provide any guidance related to the meaning of the term. *Id.* The staff analysis merely notes, "The term is undefined in the bill or in chapter 447 and that its interpretation is left to practice." *Id.* (citing Fla. S. Comm. on Govt. Ops., CS for SB 888 (1995) Staff Analysis (March 27, 1995) (on file with comm.)). Because there are other statutes that apply where the government is facing a financial emergency or bankruptcy, we adopt PERC's definition that a financial urgency is a dire financial condition requiring immediate attention and demanding prompt and decisive action, but not necessarily a financial emergency or bankruptcy.

We have long held that a "statute must be given its plain and obvious meaning." *Holly v. Auld*, 450 So.2d 217, 219 (Fla. 1984) (quoting *A.R. Douglass, Inc. v. McRainey*, 102 Fla. 1141, 137 So. 157, 159 (1931)). If the language of the statute is "clear and unambiguous and conveys a clear and definite meaning" there is no need to resort to statutory construction. *Id.*; accord *Forsythe v. Longboat Key Beach Erosion Control Dist.*, 604 So.2d 452, 454 (Fla. 1992). Because a government entity acting under section 447.4095 has the potential to impair two fundamental rights afforded to public employees, the statute must be given a strict construction. *State v. J.P.*, 907 So.2d 1101, 1109 (Fla. 2004). Based on the plain language of the statute, a financial urgency may only be invoked where modification of the agreement is required. If there are other means of addressing the financial condition, then modification is not "required."

We have previously set forth the standard that must be followed where a government entity attempts to change a bargaining agreement to address a revenue shortfall. In *Chiles v. United Faculty of Florida*, 615 So.2d 671 (Fla. 1993), the Legislature eliminated raises that had been authorized following an impasse between the State and various public employee unions. *Id.* There, we held that the raise was a fully enforceable contract and once it had been funded by the Legislature, "the state and all its organs are bound by that agreement under the principles of contract law." *Id.* at 672–73. While we recognized that the Legislature must have leeway to respond to emergencies, we stated that the right to contract severely limits the Legislature's ability to alter a contract. *Id.* at 673. Therefore, we held that "the legislature has authority to reduce previously approved appropriations to pay public workers' salaries made pursuant to a collective bargaining agreement, but only where it can demonstrate a compelling state interest." *Id.* at 673. Before doing so, "the legislature must demonstrate no other reasonable alternative means of preserving its contract with public workers, either in whole or in part." *Id.* Further, "the legislature must demonstrate that the funds are available from no other possible reasonable source." Finding that the Legislature did not satisfy the requirements of this test, we ordered the reinstatement of the pay raises. *Id.*

Section 447.4095 is the codification of the strict scrutiny standard we outlined in *Chiles*. The term "financial urgency" represents the first prong of strict scrutiny. As previously stated, a financial urgency is "a dire financial condition requiring immediate attention and demanding prompt and decisive action, but not necessarily a financial emergency or bankruptcy." *Headley*, 118 So.3d at 892; *see also Hollywood Fire Fighters*, 133 So.3d at 1045 (quoting *Headley*). In showing that its current financial condition is dire and requires immediate attention, the local government establishes a compelling state interest and satisfies the first prong of strict scrutiny.

The phrase "requiring modification of an agreement" represents the second prong of strict scrutiny. While a local government may be able to show that its financial condition requires immediate attention and demands prompt and decisive action, this may not necessarily require modification of the agreement. As we stated in *Chiles*, "the mere fact that it is politically more expedient to eliminate all or part of the contracted funds is not in itself a compelling reason." *Chiles*, 615 So.2d at 673.

Thus, the term "requiring modification" forces the local government to demonstrate that the only way of addressing its dire financial condition is through modification of the CBA. To do this, the local government must demonstrate that the funds are available from no other reasonable source. This satisfies the second requirement of strict scrutiny, that the law be narrowly tailored to achieve a compelling state interest.

. . .

We have long recognized the right to bargain collectively and the right to contract free of impairment. *See Hillsborough Cty. Govtl. Emps. Ass'n v. Hillsborough Cty. Aviation Auth.*, 522 So.2d 358, 362 (Fla. 1988) ("The right to bargain collectively is, as part of the state's constitution's declaration of rights, a fundamental right. As such, it is subject to official abridgment only upon a showing of a compelling state interest."); *Yamaha Parts Distribs., Inc. v. Ehrman*, 316 So.2d 557, 559 (Fla. 1975) ("Virtually no degree of contract impairment has been tolerated in this state."). Thus, our conclusions as to this issue "are compelled by the Florida Constitution." *Chiles*, 615 So.2d at 673. . . .

Petitioner also argues that the First District erred in construing the statute to allow an employer to unilaterally modify the CBA without first proceeding through the impasse resolution process set forth in section 447.403, Florida Statutes (2010). This issue centers on the procedure to be followed once a local government has declared a financial urgency requiring modification of an agreement.

As the First District explained:

> Section 447.4095 provides for an expedited period of negotiation, not to exceed 14 days, upon declaration of a financial urgency by a local government and requires the parties to meet as soon as possible after the declaration to "negotiate the impact" of the financial urgency. The statute further provides that, if a dispute remains between the parties after the expiration of the expedited negotiation period, an impasse shall be deemed to have occurred and "[t]he parties shall then proceed pursuant to the provisions of s. 447.403." § 447.4095, Fla. Stat.

> The impasse resolution process in section 447.403 begins with the appointment of a special magistrate who is charged with conducting a hearing and making a recommendation to the local government's legislative body as to the resolution of any disputed issues. See § 447.403(3), Fla. Stat. The statute does not establish a deadline for the hearing, but it does provide for at least 45 days of post-hearing procedures. See § 447.403(3) — (4), Fla. Stat. (providing 15 days for the special magistrate to submit his or her recommended decision to the parties, 20 days for the parties to reject the special magistrate's recommendations, and then 10 days for the local government's chief executive officer to submit his or her recommendations to the legislative body). The legislative body is not required to accept the special magistrate's recommendations and, thus, the end-result of the impasse resolution

process may be the local government unilaterally imposing changes to the agreement. See § 447.403(4), Fla. Stat.

Headley, 118 So.3d at 894. Petitioner argues that by requiring the parties to proceed through the impasse resolution process under section 447.403, the statute mandates that no changes may be made to the agreement until after the conclusion of that process. Petitioner argues that because the public employer seeks to change a mandatory term[3] of the agreement, collective bargaining[4] is required. Respondent argues that the Legislature specifically used the term "impact" in reference to "impact bargaining," which is a type of bargaining applicable to managerial decisions that impact terms and conditions of employment within the bargaining unit. Impact bargaining requires only notice and an opportunity to negotiate before the proposed changes are implemented. In essence, the parties dispute the modification may be made.

Employing the rules of statutory interpretation is appropriate here, as both parties provide reasonable interpretations of the statute and the statute is ambiguous as to when a modification may be made. "Impact" is a term of art in public sector labor law. *See Sch. Dist. of Indian River Cty. v. Fla. Pub. Emps. Relations Comm'n*, 64 So.3d 723, 729 (Fla. 4th DCA 2011). Under the concept of impact bargaining, if the modification of a subject classified as a management right[5] would have an effect on the employees' terms and conditions of employment, then the public employer is required to give those employees' bargaining agent an opportunity to bargain the impact of that modification. *See Jacksonville Supervisors Ass'n v. City of Jacksonville*, 26 F.P.E.R. 31140 (2000). The statutory language that Respondent relies on as an indicator that the Legislature intended to allow for impact bargaining is "negotiate the impact of the financial urgency." § 447.4095, Fla. Stat. (2013).

It is true that when the words in a statute are technical in nature and have a fixed legal meaning, it is presumed that the Legislature intended that the words be given their technical meaning. *See* 48A Fla. Jur. 2d Statutes § 135 (2014). However, under the principle of expressio unius, est exclusion alterius, meaning "the mention of one thing implies the exclusion of another," legislative direction as to how a thing shall be done is, in effect, a prohibition against it being done any other way. *See Sun Coast*

---

3. Chapter 447 does not provide a list of subjects to be treated as mandatory in terms of bargaining. Accordingly, PERC is tasked to make that decision on a case-by-case basis. Public Employees Relations Commission, Scope of Bargaining 2 (2d ed. 2005).

4. Collective bargaining means a process of mutual obligations in which a public employer and a bargaining agent have to meet at reasonable times, negotiate in good faith, and effect a written contract encompassing agreements reached concerning the wages, hours, terms and conditions of employment. § 447.309(1), Fla. Stat. (2013).

5. The Florida Legislature defines public employers' rights as:

[T]he right of the public employer to determine unilaterally the purpose of each of its constituent agencies, set standards of services to be offered to the public, and exercise control and discretion over its organization and operations. It is also the right of the public employer to direct its employees, take disciplinary action for proper cause, and relieve its employees from duty because of lack of work or for other legitimate reasons. § 447.209, Fla. Stat. (2013).

Int'l, Inc. v. Dep't of Bus. Reg., 596 So.2d 1118, 1121 (Fla. 1st DCA 1992). Therefore, section 447.4095 permits the unilateral implementation of changes to the CBA only after parties have completed the impasse resolution proceedings and failed to ratify the agreement. If the Legislature had intended the changes to take effect earlier or under any other circumstances, it would have stated as much. This is especially true considering that the changes here are unlike the changes that are usually the result of impact bargaining. As noted by Petitioner, impact bargaining results from management making decisions outside of the scope of an agreement which affect the agreement in some way. Bargaining under the financial urgency statute, on the other hand, seeks to alter the terms of the agreement itself. Impact bargaining requires a threshold determination as to whether the employer's decision affects employees' wages, hours, or working conditions. Bargaining under financial urgency inherently seeks to change wages, hours, or working conditions. Moreover, altering the agreement effectively alters the "status quo" between the parties that will remain in place until they are changed through bargaining.

The interpretation set forth by PERC and the First District would allow a local government, once it has declared a financial urgency, the ability to exercise a management right to unilaterally alter the terms and conditions of a contract before completing the procedures set forth by the Legislature in section 447.4095. This interpretation does not comport with our acknowledgment of and respect for the constitutional right of collective bargaining and prohibition of the impairment to contract. Therefore, we also quash the decision of the First District and remand the case for proceedings that are consistent with this decision.

It is so ordered.

LABARGA, C.J., and PARIENTE, and LEWIS, JJ., concur.

POLSTON, J., concurs in result with an opinion. [The concurring opinion of Justice Polston is omitted.]

CANADY, J., dissents. [The dissenting opinion of Justice Canady is omitted.]

LAWSON, J., did not participate.

In *Headley,* the Florida Supreme Court held that a local government, like the Legislature, can modify the salaries of public workers made pursuant to a collective bargaining agreement only when it can demonstrate a compelling state interest and no other way of addressing its dire financial condition. Should a governor's right to veto the Legislature's decision to resolve a collective bargaining impasse between the governor and public workers be controlled by this same logic and precedent?

In *International Association of Firefighters Local S-20 v. State,*[17] the Florida Supreme Court had the opportunity to consider this issue but ultimately dismissed

---

17. 257 So. 3d 364 (Fla. 2018).

714   7 · THE DECLARATION OF RIGHTS AND THE TAKING OF PROPERTY

its review of the case upon deciding that "jurisdiction was improvidently" granted. Consider the words of Justice Lewis in his dissent from the majority's decision to discharge jurisdiction of the case:

> I dissent from the majority's decision to discharge jurisdiction in this case. The right to bargain collectively is a fundamental right. *See* art. I, §6, Fla. Const.; *Hillsborough Cty. Governmental Emps. Ass'n v. Hillsborough Cty. Aviation Auth. (Hillsborough)*, 522 So.2d 358, 362 (Fla. 1988). The government of Florida belongs to the people. *See Traylor v. State* , 596 So.2d 957, 963 (Fla. 1992) (explaining that "[e]ach right" in the Declaration of Rights is "a distinct freedom guaranteed to each Floridian against government intrusion" and "operates in favor of the individual, against [the] government"). The people of Florida have voted and voiced their desire with regard to how they want their government operated.
>
> . . .
>
> After the 1968 constitutional revision, the Legislature had an obligation to effectuate the fundamental right to collectively bargain. In *Dade County Classroom Teachers' Ass'n v. Ryan*, 225 So.2d 903, 906 (Fla. 1969), the Court held that it is essential that the Legislature "enact appropriate legislation setting out standards and guidelines and otherwise regulate the subject within the limits of said Section 6." This Court has also held that if the Legislature failed to implement the rights in question the "Court [would], in an appropriate case, have no choice but to fashion such guidelines by judicial decree in such manner as may seem to the Court best adapted to meet the requirements of the constitution." *Dade Cty. Classroom Teachers Ass'n v. Legislature of Fla.*, 269 So.2d 684, 688 (Fla. 1972).
>
> There can be no doubt that when any party, including a Governor, is involved in a direct dispute and at the same time maintains the power to act as final arbiter of the dispute through the power of veto — the impasse resolution process is subverted. *See In re Murchison*, 349 U.S. 133, 136, 75 S.Ct. 623, 99 L.Ed. 942 (1955) ("A fair trial in a fair tribunal is a basic requirement of due process."). The old maxim remains true: "[N]o man is allowed to be a judge in his own cause; because his interest would certainly bias his judgment, and, not improbably, corrupt his integrity." *Caperton v. A.T. Massey Coal Co.*, 556 U.S. 868, 876, 129 S.Ct. 2252, 173 L.Ed.2d 1208 (2009) (quoting The Federalist No. 10, at 59 (J. Madison) (J. Cooke ed. 1961)). In this context, the use of veto authority, after the impasse has been resolved by the Legislature, allows the Governor to act as a judge in his own cause, thereby obstructing due process. *See id.* (recognizing that no individual should be allowed to judge his or her own case given the inherent risk of bias in doing so). With the Governor holding the power to veto the Legislature's decision resolving the impasse, the fundamental right of public employees to collectively bargain is rendered hollow. *See Int'l Ass'n of Firefighters Local S-20 v. State (Local S-20)*, 221 So.3d 736, 740 (Fla. 1st DCA 2017) (Thomas,

J., dissenting). In acting as the third-party decision maker, the Legislature's decision should be implemented in a process that does not include executive branch veto.

The Legislature has an obligation to the people of Florida to create a system that shields fundamental rights against due process violations. The Legislature cannot dodge the issue of a flawed system as merely "subject to politics." Fundamental rights must be balanced to exist and be protected within a constitutional framework. It is the responsibility of the Legislature to create a constitutional structure that would not leave any party that was a participant in the dispute as the final decider. This may not be an easy task; however, it is a necessary task nonetheless to protect fundamental rights as presently contemplated.

Within these narrow circumstances the Legislature may consider a number of alternatives including the implementation of a state compelling interest test in which the Governor would be required to demonstrate a compelling state interest to sustain a veto of a legislative resolution of an impasse. *See Local S-20*, 221 So.3d at 740-41 (Thomas, J., dissenting) ("[O]nce the Legislature has ruled in the public employees' favor and against the Governor, it cannot be reconciled with Article I, section 6 of the Florida Constitution to allow the Governor to render the Legislature's decision a nullity through the veto authority."). In recognizing that public employees have the right to collectively bargain as a fundamental right, the Legislature may decide that this fundamental right should be subject to official abridgment only upon a showing of a compelling state interest. *Hillsborough*, 522 So.2d 358. Nevertheless, members of the Legislature cannot throw up their hands and simply say "oh well." Democracy can be dangerous and full of complexities; and, while the overall structure remains in concept, the moving parts move as directed by the people.

F. Prohibited Laws

Fla. Const. art. I, § 10

Prohibited Laws. — No bill of attainder, ex post facto law or law impairing the obligation of contracts shall be passed.

———————

1. Obligation of Contract

Pomponio v. Claridge of Pompano Condominium, Inc.

378 So. 2d 774 (Fla. 1979)

ENGLAND, Chief Justice.

The present cause is before us to determine the constitutionality of section 718.401(4), Florida Statutes (1977), which provides for the deposit of rents into the registry of the court during litigation involving obligations under a condominium lease. [Footnote omitted.] We have jurisdiction pursuant to article V, section 3(b) (1) of the Florida Constitution. The question of whether this statute impermissibly impairs the obligation of contracts in violation of article I, section 10 of the Florida and federal constitutions — an issue expressly reserved in an earlier case concerning the statute's operation [Footnote omitted.] — is now squarely presented.

The Claridge of Pompano Condominium, Inc. ("the Association"), and several individual unit owners who are members of the Association brought suit against the developer of the condominium and the lessors of a ninety-nine year recreational lease associated with the condominium. [Footnote omitted.] The Association, as a representative of the unit owners, is the named lessee under the recreational lease. As required by section 718.401(4), the trial court granted the Association and unit owners' motion to permit payment of rents into the registry of the court, despite the developer and lessors' contention that the provision is unconstitutional. By this appeal, the developer and lessors seek to have the ruling reversed. We hold that the statute is unconstitutional.

The parties argue, respectively, that the rent deposit statute either permissibly modifies a contractual remedy or impermissibly impairs substantial contract rights and obligations. Yet a proper analysis of this issue cannot hinge exclusively on any supposed distinction between "remedies" and "obligations." The United States Supreme Court has discarded this distinction as "an outdated formalism,"[4] and we choose to do likewise. To formulate a more logical approach to the question of impairment, it is necessary at the outset to examine the interpretive development of the contract clause in the decisions of the United States Supreme Court.

While the intent of the framers with respect to the contract clause has generated considerable speculation, its origins remain too obscure to be of any assistance in its construction.[5] It is nonetheless clear that in the early decisions of the United States

---

4. *United States Trust Co. v. New Jersey*, 431 U.S. 1, 19 n.17, 97 S.Ct. 1505, 52 L.Ed.2d 92 (1977).

5. "In the construction of the contract clause, the debates in the Constitutional Convention are of little aid." *Home Bldg. & Loan Ass'n v. Blaisdell*, 290 U.S. 398, 427, 54 S.Ct. 231, 235–36, 78 L. Ed. 413 (1934). *See also Allied Structural Steel Co. v. Spannaus*, 438 U.S. 234, 257, 98 S.Ct. 2716, 57 L.Ed.2d 727 (1978) (Brennan, J., dissenting). The most unkind of observers has concluded that the provision was "apparently motivated by the economic self-interest of the framers," Comment, *Revival of the Contract Clause*, 39 Ohio St.L.J. 195, 196 (1978), but a variety of other, more noble, purposes have also been suggested. *See* Comment, *The Contract Clause and the Constitutionality of*

7 · THE DECLARATION OF RIGHTS AND THE TAKING OF PROPERTY

Supreme Court the clause was interpreted literally as a strict prohibition.[6] As with other seemingly absolute constitutional provisions, however, it soon became evident that some degree of flexibility would have to be read into the clause to ameliorate the harshness of such rigid application.[7] In order to accommodate necessary legislation without deviating from the principle that all laws impairing the obligations of contract are constitutionally prohibited, the Court developed two basic analytical devices — the "obligation-remedy" distinction and the "reserved powers" doctrine[8] — both of which dominated contract clause interpretation for the next century.

The "Obligation-Remedy" Test

Home Building & Loan Association v. Blaisdell, 290 U.S. 398, 54 S.Ct. 231 (1934), is the most important case in the history of contract clause interpretation.[9] In *Blaisdell*, the Court upheld a mortgage moratorium statute that Minnesota had enacted to provide relief for homeowners threatened with foreclosure. The statute enabled a court to extend the time for redemption beyond that provided for in the mortgage contract. Though the statute directly affected lenders' foreclosure rights, the Court ruled that it did not violate the contract clause, reasoning that "the State . . . continues to possess authority to safeguard the vital interests of its people."[10]

In its decision, the *Blaisdell* majority traced the judicial history of the obligation-remedy distinction[11] and the reserved powers doctrine[12] to contract clause analysis. It then concluded:

> It is manifest from this review of our decisions that there has been a growing appreciation of public needs and of the necessity of finding ground for a rational compromise between individual rights and public welfare. . . .

Retroactive Application of Exemption Statutes: A Reconsideration, 9 Pac.L.J. 889, 892–93 (1978), and sources cited therein.

6. *See, e.g., Trustees of Dartmouth College v. Woodward*, 17 U.S. (4 Wheat.) 518, 4 L.Ed. 629 (1819). Until the late nineteenth century, the contract clause was the subject of the Court's attention more frequently than any other provision except the commerce clause, B. Wright, The Contract Clause of the Constitution 91–92 (1938), and as the Court itself recently observed, "it was perhaps the strongest single constitutional check on state legislation during our early years as a Nation. . . ." *Allied Structural Steel Co. v. Spannaus*, 438 U.S. 234, 241, 98 S.Ct. 2716, 2721, 57 L.Ed.2d 727 (1978).

7. *See generally* Comment, *The Contract Clause Reemerges: A New Attitude Toward Judicial Scrutiny of Economic Legislation*, 1978 S.Ill.U. L.J. 258, 260.

8. For a brief discussion and comparison of these two approaches, *see, e. g.,* Comment, *Revival of the Contract Clause*, 39 Ohio St.L.J. 195, 196–98 (1978); Comment, *supra* note 4, at 260–62.

9. The United States Supreme Court has itself stated that "[t]he *Blaisdell* opinion . . . amounted to a comprehensive restatement of the principles underlying the application of the Contract Clause," *City of El Paso v. Simmons*, 379 U.S. 497, 508, 85 S.Ct. 577, 583–84, 13 L.Ed.2d 446 (1965), and "is regarded as the leading case in the modern era of Contract Clause interpretation." *United States Trust Co. v. New Jersey*, 431 U.S. 1, 15, 97 S.Ct. 1505, 1514, 52 L.Ed.2d 92 (1977).

10. 290 U.S. at 434, 54 S.Ct. at 238–39.

11. *Id.* at 429–34, 54 S.Ct. 231.

12. *Id.* at 434–38, 54 S.Ct. 231.

It is no answer to say that this public need was not apprehended a century ago, or to insist that what the provision of the Constitution meant to the vision of that day it must mean to the vision of our time. . . ."The case before us must be considered in the light of our whole experience and not merely in that of what was said a hundred years ago."[13]

Having jettisoned the analytical framework which governed prior contract clause cases, the Court formulated a new test against which legislation would be measured:

The question is not whether the legislative action affects contracts incidentally, or directly or indirectly, but whether the legislation is addressed to a legitimate end and the measures taken are reasonable and appropriate to that end.[14]

Thus, beginning with *Blaisdell*, the Court began to permit certain "reasonable" impairments of contractual obligations.[15] This new and more flexible approach to contract clause analysis later was refined and developed by the Court in three major cases.[16]

The Evolving "Reasonableness" Test

In *City of El Paso v. Simmons*, 379 U.S. 497, 85 S.Ct. 577 (1965), the Court stated that it would not even "pause to consider . . . again the dividing line under federal law between 'remedy' and 'obligation'. . . ."[17] Instead, the majority noted that "decisions dating from [*Blaisdell*] have not placed critical reliance on the distinction between obligation and remedy," and proceeded to demonstrate that its post-Depression rulings had been made "without any regard to whether the measure was substantive or remedial."[18] Recognizing that "'[t]he Constitution is "intended to preserve practical and substantial rights, not to maintain theories,"'"[19] the Court in *Simmons* clearly refuted the notion that statutes could be properly measured by any criteria other than reasonableness:

---

13. *Id.* at 442–43, 54 S.Ct. at 241–42 (quoting from *Missouri v. Holland*, 252 U.S. 416, 433, 40 S. Ct. 382, 64 L.Ed. 641 (1920)).

14. 290 U.S. at 438, 54 S.Ct. at 240. In our opinion, however, there is considerable merit to the argument that, without regard to the particular approach which it claimed to be applying, the Court both before and after *Blaisdell* actually proceeded to work practical solutions based on the facts and circumstances of each case. See Comment, *The Role of the Contract Clause in Municipalities' Relations with Creditors*, 1976 Duke L.J. 1321, 1327. If this theory is correct, then the "new test" unveiled in *Blaisdell* was really no more than an attempt to restate what the Court had actually been doing all along, with an implicit admission that the traditional obligation-remedy distinction had been used merely for the purpose of post-analytical labelling and categorization.

15. Comment, *supra* note 5, at 198.

16. *See* notes 17–31 and accompanying text *infra*.

17. 379 U.S. at 506, 85 S.Ct. at 582.

18. *Id.* at 506–07 n.9, 85 S.Ct. at 582–83 n.9.

19. *Id.* at 515, 85 S.Ct. at 587 (quoting from *Faitnote Iron & Steel Co. v. City of Asbury Park*, 316 U.S. 502, 514 (1942)).

7 · THE DECLARATION OF RIGHTS AND THE TAKING OF PROPERTY   719

This Court's decisions have never given a law which imposes unforeseen advantages or burdens on a contracting party constitutional immunity against change. . . . Laws which restrict a party to those gains reasonably to be expected from the contract are not subject to attack under the Contract Clause, notwithstanding that they technically alter an obligation of a contract.[20]

In resolving the controversy before it, the *Simmons* majority applied what Justice Black decried in dissent as a "balancing" test,[21] giving due consideration for the "buyer's undertaking," whether "the buyer was substantially induced to enter into these contracts" because of the promise, and the significance of the "State's vital interest,"[22] and concluded that the Texas statute at issue was constitutionally permissible because "[t]he measure taken . . . was a mild one indeed, hardly burdensome to the purchaser . . . , but nonetheless an important one to the State's interest."[23]

The next major decision in the interpretive development of the contract clause was *United States Trust Co. v. New Jersey*, 431 U.S. 1, 97 S.Ct. 1505 (1977).[24] The Court's analysis in *United States Trust* both expanded upon the "balancing" test of *Simmons* and refined the "reasonableness" standard of *Blaisdell*:

[a] finding that there has been a technical impairment is merely a preliminary step in resolving the more difficult question whether that impairment is permitted under the Constitution.

. . . [T]he Contract Clause limits otherwise legitimate exercises of state legislative authority, and the existence of an important public interest is not always sufficient to overcome that limitation. . . . Moreover, the scope of the State's reserved power depends on the nature of the contractual relationship with which the challenged law conflicts.

*   *   *

. . . The Court in *Blaisdell* recognized that laws intended to regulate existing contractual relationships must serve a legitimate public purpose. . . . Legislation adjusting the rights and responsibilities of contracting parties must

---

20. 379 U.S. at 515, 85 S.Ct. at 587.

21. *Id.* at 517, 528–33, 85 S.Ct. 577 (Black, J., dissenting).

22. *Id.* at 514–15, 85 S.Ct. at 587.

23. *Id.* at 516–17, 85 S.Ct. at 588.

24. In *United States Trust*, the Court had this to say about the obligation-remedy distinction:
    [I]t was . . . recognized very clearly that the distinction between remedies and obligations was not absolute. . . . More recent decisions have not relied on the remedy/ obligation distinction, primarily because it is now recognized that obligations as well as remedies may be modified without necessarily violating the Contract Clause.
    Although now largely an outdated formalism, the remedy/ obligation distinction may be viewed as approximating the result of a more particularized inquiry into the legitimate expectations of the contracting parties.
431 U.S. at 19 n.17, 97 S.Ct. at 1517 n.17 (citations omitted and emphasis added).

be upon reasonable conditions and of a character appropriate to the public purpose justifying its adoption.[25]

The Court concluded that the correct standard to be employed in assessing the validity of legislation affecting a state's own contracts is that:

[a]s with laws impairing the obligations of private contracts, *an impairment may be constitutional if it is reasonable and necessary to serve an important public purpose.*[26]

In finding that the challenged statute did not satisfy this test, the Court emphasized that while "[t]he extent of impairment is certainly a relevant factor in determining its reasonableness," an enactment cannot be considered "necessary" if the legislature "without modifying the covenant at all, ... could have adopted alternative means of achieving their ... goals," because "a State is not free to impose a drastic impairment when an evident and more moderate course would serve its purposes equally well."[27]

In its most recent pronouncement on the subject, *Allied Structural Steel Co. v. Spannaus*, 438 U.S. 234, 98 S.Ct. 2716 (1978), the Court invalidated a Minnesota law which retroactively imposed upon certain private companies with voluntary pension plans additional obligations as to employees who would not have been entitled to such benefits under the original terms of the plan. Without any mention of the obligation-remedy distinction, the majority reviewed the underpinnings of the Court's post *Blaisdell* decisions and formulated its statement of the proper approach to contract clause challenges thusly:

In applying these principles to the present case, the first inquiry must be whether the state law has, in fact, operated as a substantial impairment of a contractual relationship. *The severity of the impairment measures the height of the hurdle the state legislation must clear. Minimal alteration of contractual obligations may end the inquiry at its first stage. Severe impairment, on*

---

25. *Id.* at 21–22, 97 S.Ct. at 1517–18. The majority put to rest any notion that a "reasonableness" standard was utilized in *Blaisdell* solely because of the emergency conditions which prompted the Minnesota legislation at issue in that case:

Blaisdell suggested further limitations that have since been subsumed in the overall determination of reasonableness. ... Undoubtedly the existence of an emergency and the limited duration of a relief measure are factors to be assessed in determining the reasonableness of an impairment, but they cannot be regarded as essential in every case.

Id. at 22–23 n.19, 97 S.Ct. at 1518 n.19. Although the Court in a more recent decision appeared to make more of the "broad and desperate emergency economic conditions" of which judicial notice was taken in *Blaisdell*, it was careful to point out that the reference "is not to suggest that only an emergency of great magnitude can constitutionally justify a state law impairing the obligations of contracts." *Allied Structural Steel Co. v. Spannaus*, 438 U.S. 234, 249 & n.24, 98 S.Ct. 2716, 2725, & n.24 (1978).

26. 431 U.S. at 25, 97 S.Ct. at 1519 (emphasis added).

27. *Id.* at 27–31, 97 S.Ct. at 1520–22.

the other hand, will push the inquiry to a careful examination of the nature and purpose of the state legislation.[28]

Several factors to be considered in this balancing test were identified in *Spannaus*:

(a) Was the law enacted to deal with a broad, generalized economic or social problem?[29]

(b) Does the law operate in an area which was already subject to state regulation at the time the parties' contractual obligations were originally undertaken, or does it invade an area never before subject to regulation by the state?[30]

(c) Does the law effect a temporary alteration of the contractual relationships of those within its coverage, or does it work a severe, permanent, and immediate change in those relationships — irrevocably and retroactively?[31]

Analysis and Conclusion

We recognize that this Court, when construing a provision of the Florida Constitution, is not bound to accept as controlling the United States Supreme Court's interpretation of a parallel provision of the federal Constitution. Yet such rulings have long been considered helpful and persuasive, and are obviously entitled to great weight.[32] With this in mind, we now choose to adopt an approach to contract clause analysis similar to that of the United States Supreme Court. That Court's decisions[33] in this area of law convince us that such an approach is the one most likely to yield results consonant with the basic purpose of the constitutional prohibition.

In our view, any realistic analysis of the impairment issue in Florida must logically begin both with *Yamaha Parts Distributors Inc. v. Ehrman*,[34] which applied the well-accepted principle that virtually no degree of contract impairment is tolerable in this state, and with the notion enunciated in *Louisiana ex rel. Ranger v. New Orleans*,[35] that "he who pays too late, pays less."[36] These concepts direct our inquiry

---

28. 438 U.S. at 244–45, 98 S.Ct. at 2723 (footnotes omitted and emphasis added). Reasoning that the effect of the statute on the employer's contractual obligation was severe and that the law "simply does not possess the attributes of those state laws that in the past have survived challenge under the Contract Clause of the Constitution," *see* notes 29–31 and accompanying text *infra*, the Court concluded that "if the Contract Clause means anything at all, it means that Minnesota could not constitutionally do what it tried to do to the company in this case." *Id.* at 250–51, 98 S.Ct. at 2726.

29. *Id.* at 250 (citing *Home Bldg. & Loan Ass'n v. Blaisdell*, 290 U.S. 398, 445, 54 S.Ct. 231 (1934)).

30. *Id.* (citing *Veix v. Sixth Ward Bldg. & Loan Ass'n*, 310 U.S. 32, 38, 60 S.Ct. 792, 84 L.Ed. 1061 (1940)).

31. *Id.* (citing *United States Trust Co. v. New Jersey*, 431 U.S. 1, 22, 97 S.Ct. 1505 (1977)).

32. *See, e. g., Dudley v. Harrison, McCready & Co.*, 127 Fla. 687, 699, 173 So. 820, 825 (1937); *State v. Hetland*, 366 So.2d 831, 836 (Fla. 2d DCA 1979); *Leveson v. State*, 138 So.2d 361, 364 (Fla. 3d DCA 1962); *Houston v. State*, 113 So.2d 582, 584–85 (Fla. 1st DCA 1959).

33. *See* notes 9–31 and accompanying text *supra*.

34. 316 So.2d 557 (Fla.1975).

35. 102 U.S. 203, 26 L.Ed.132 (1880).

36. *Id.* at 207. As applied to this rent deposit statute, the rubric should be rephrased to read that "he who receives payment too late, receives less."

to the actual effect of the rent deposit statute on the lessor's contractual right to receive its bargained-for rent. That effect, when fully analyzed, persuades us that in the absence of contractual consent [footnote omitted] significant contract rights are unreasonably impaired by the statute's operation.[38]

Preliminarily, it should be noted that the deposit into court of moneys which one or another contract litigant may withdraw only after incurring some legal cost or a modest delay is constitutionally permissible.[39] Our conclusion in *Yamaha* that "virtually" no impairment is tolerable necessarily implies that some impairment is tolerable, although perhaps not so much as would be acceptable under traditional federal contract clause analysis.

To determine how much impairment is tolerable, we must weigh the degree to which a party's contract rights are statutorily impaired against both the source of authority under which the state purports to alter the contractual relationship and the evil which it seeks to remedy. Obviously, this becomes a balancing process to determine whether the nature and extent of the impairment is constitutionally tolerable in light of the importance of the state's objective, or whether it unreasonably intrudes into the parties' bargain to a degree greater than is necessary to achieve that objective.

Section 718.401(4), of course, does more than provide a procedure for the deposit of rents subject to disbursement upon compliance with some procedural showing or its equivalent. [Footnote omitted.] This statute potentially allows the retention in court of at least some portion of the deposited rent during the entire term of litigation. Barring the current use of court-retained rent moneys is an economic deprivation for which a landlord obviously has not bargained, producing potential erosion of value (at least in our persistently inflationary economy) which goes beyond mere inconvenience. To this extent at least, the statute "impairs" the landlord's contract.[41]

---

38. We recognize the difficulty of narrowing the focus of attention on the issue of impairment so as to synthesize in subjective consideration the wisdom or necessity of this legislation. The judicial mind is required to do so, however, despite the difficulty. We must remind ourselves that the very real economic problems of condominium unit owners, as magnified by the alleged imbalance in bargaining power between unit owners and landlords, and the pervasive influence of the condominium industry on Florida's economy and citizens, are not alone determinative of the impairment question. These considerations are relevant, of course, in this context as well as others. *See Avila South Condominium Ass'n v. Kappa Corp.*, 347 So.2d 599 (Fla.1977).

39. The deposit procedure of Florida Rule of Civil Procedure 1.600, for example, does not "impair" contract rights in the constitutional sense. Unlike the statutory rent deposit provision at issue in this case, our rule does not direct that disputed moneys are required to be deposited in court, but permits such a procedure to be invoked "by leave of the court." Thus, the decision as to whether or not a temporary deprivation is justified and whether withdrawal should be allowed in whole or in part, will be vested in the sound discretion of the trial judge, who can assess from the circumstances in each case the relative merit or frivolity of the claim asserted and the legitimate needs of the parties.

41. In *State ex rel. Women's Benefit Ass'n v. Port of Palm Beach Dist.*, 121 Fla. 746, 759, 164 So. 851, 856 (1935), we said:

To "impair" has been defined as meaning to make worse; to diminish in quantity, value, excellency or strength; to lessen in power, to weaken. Whatever legislation lessens the

The degree of impairment created by section 718.401(4) is confined to amounts deemed by the legislature not to be essential to the maintenance of the property in dispute. Withdrawals are authorized for amounts "necessary for payment of taxes, mortgage payments, maintenance and operating expenses, and other necessary expenses incident to maintaining and equipping the leased facilities."[42] This formulation precludes a uniform level of impairment in each case, inasmuch as the impairment in any particular situation will depend directly on the disparity between the contract amount of rent and the landlord's property maintenance obligations — that is, the lessor's built-in profit.[43] In this formulation, of course, all other needs or desires of the lessor for its promised rents are wholly ignored.[44]

On the other side of the ledger is the state's interest in requiring a unit owner's deposit of leasehold rents into court during the course of litigation. This provision rests on the state's exercise of its police power to promote the health, safety, and welfare of its citizens. While the specific objectives for section 718.401(4) are neither expressly articulated nor plainly evident from a reading of the statute,[45] the litigants have suggested that the legislature's concern was the protection of unit owners from the lessor's foreclosure for non-payment of rent during the pendency of the litigation. To this assertion we have two answers. There is to our knowledge neither a documented threat of massive condominium foreclosures in Florida nor any documentation of the underlying premise that unit owners would withhold rents from landlords pending litigation with them.

---

efficacy of the means of enforcement of the obligation is an impairment. Also if it tends to *postpone* or *retard* the enforcement of the contract, it is an impairment. (Emphasis in the original.)

42. It is unclear whether funds may be withdrawn from the deposited rents in order to improve the leased premises. One incidental effect of the uncertainty could well be that lessees' prospects for promised additional (or improved) facilities, such as tennis courts, swimming pools, or meeting halls, may be thwarted by a suit instituted by some unit owners which requires significant rent deposits.

43. As a practical matter, the amount of "spread" will also vary from month to month depending upon such factors as seasonal maintenance needs and due dates for tax or mortgage payments. Thus, in some months the landlord may be able to withdraw virtually all, and in others none, of the rent deposits.

44. *See* note 48 *infra*. The present lessors, in fact, would seem to be effectively barred from any disbursement under the statute in its present form. Section 718.401(4) provides that the "unit owner or association shall pay [rents] into the registry of the court." The provision permits disbursement of these rents, however, only "[w]hen the unit owner has deposited the required funds." As the Court stated in *Century Village*, the terms "unit owner" and "association" are not interchangeable. 361 So.2d at 133–34. Were the present statute read as it seemingly was intended, rents deposited by the Association would be totally inaccessible to the lessor. The precise terms of the present statute need not be interrelated, however, since it impermissibly impairs the obligation of contracts even if the restricted withdrawal privilege were available.

45. By contrast, the legislative intent in *Blaisdell* was spelled out in the statute, 290 U.S. at 416, 54 S.Ct. 231, and in the *Women's Benefit Ass'n* case, there were reports of the emergency conditions to document the legislative history and intended effect of the constitutional amendment at issue. 121 Fla. at 765–66, 164 So. at 858 (Buford, J., dissenting).

We believe that the balance between the state's probable objectives and its method of implementation, on the one hand, and the degree of contract impairment inflicted in furtherance of its policy, on the other, favors preservation of the contract over this exercise of the police power. Bearing on our view is the fact that the manner in which the police power has been wielded here is not the least restrictive means possible. *See City of El Paso v. Simmons*, 379 U.S. 497, 516–17, 85 S.Ct. 577 (1965). Contrast, for example, Florida's Residential Landlord and Tenant Act, which similarly requires the payment of rent into the court's registry during the pendency of a lawsuit between parties to the lease,[46] but which authorizes the court to disburse to a landlord all or any portion of the funds on deposit upon a showing of "actual danger of loss of the premises or *other personal hardship resulting from the loss of rental income from the premises.*"[47] In that statute the legislature has acknowledged that the consequences of rent detention may extend to a deprivation of sums needed for purposes other than the preservation of the controverted property. The severity of impairment wreaked by section 718.401(4) would have been mitigated by a "personal hardship" provision like that in the landlord-tenant act, but none is present.[48]

Therefore, in the face of an express constitutional prohibition against any law "impairing the obligation of contracts,"[49] the state's justification for an exercise of the police power to impair the lessor's contractual bargain does not, in our opinion, provide sufficient countervailing considerations. As applied retroactively, absent a lessor's express consent to its incorporation into the terms of the contract, the statute is invalid. Accordingly, the trial court's order authorizing payment of rents into the registry of the court is hereby vacated.

It is so ordered.

BOYD, OVERTON and SUNDBERG, JJ., concur.

Although *Pomponio* involved a private contract, it also discussed the rule applied to impairment of public contracts. As to public contracts, also consider the following from *Coastal Petroleum Company v. Chiles*:[18]

> ... [U]nder the contracts clause of our state constitution, little tolerance has been shown for the state's attempts to alter its own contracts. For example,

---

46. §83.60(2), Fla. Stat. (1977).

47. §83.61, Fla. Stat. (1977) (emphasis supplied).

48. As the United States Supreme Court has observed:

The severity of an impairment of contractual obligations can be measured by the factors that reflect the high value the Framers placed on the protection of private contracts. Contracts enable individuals to order their personal and business affairs according to their particular needs and interests. Once arranged, those rights and obligations are binding under the law, and the parties are entitled to rely on them.

Allied Structural Steel Co. v. Spannaus, 438 U.S. 234, 245, 98 S.Ct. 2716, 2723 (1978).

49. U.S. Const. art. I, §10, cl. 1; art. I, §10, Fla. Const.

18. 672 So. 2d 571, 573–574 (Fla. 1st Dist. Ct. App. 1996).

7 · THE DECLARATION OF RIGHTS AND THE TAKING OF PROPERTY

in *Chiles v. United Faculty of Florida*, 615 So.2d 671 (Fla.1993), an agreement for pay raises for state workers was reached and initially funded by the legislature. When a shortfall in projected revenue required legislative action to balance the budget, the legislature attempted to postpone the raise. The supreme court held this action violated article 1, section 10, explaining:

> The right to contract is one of the most sacrosanct rights guaranteed by our fundamental law. It is expressly guaranteed by article 1, section 10 of the Florida Constitution.... The legislature has only a very severely limited authority to change the law to eliminate a contractual obligation it has itself created.

Id. at 673. While recognizing that the legislature has authority to reduce previously approved appropriations where it can demonstrate a compelling state interest, the court emphasized:

> Before that authority can be exercised, however, the legislature must demonstrate no other reasonable alternative means of preserving its contract with public workers, either in whole or in part.

Id. The court concluded that the state had not met that burden where it had not demonstrated that the funds were unavailable from other possible reasonable sources.

> Similarly, the trustees here have failed to demonstrate that imposing the bond at issue is the only means available to protect the state lands, particularly in light of the existing surety requirements of section 377.2425, Florida Statutes, and Coastal's agreement in the lease contract to assume "responsibility for all damages caused by [its] operations." Accordingly, we must conclude that the $1.9 billion bond requirement would substantially impair the obligation of the lease contract in violation of article I, section 10.

The United States Court of Appeals for the Eleventh Circuit characterized the difference between the federal and Florida contract clauses in *Geary Distributing Company, Inc. v. All Brand Importers, Inc.*:[19]

> ... [T]he Supreme Court of Florida adopted an approach to the Florida contract clause that the court termed "similar" to that of the United States Supreme Court's approach to the federal contract clause. [Citation omitted.] Although the approach is similar, Florida courts interpreting the Florida contract clause appear to tolerate less impairment than the federal courts interpreting the federal contract clause....

In *Chiles v. United Faculty of Florida*,[20] the Florida Supreme Court concluded that "[t]he legislature has only a very severely limited authority to change the law to eliminate a contractual obligation it has itself created."

---

19. 931 F.2d 1431, 1434 n. 4 (11th Cir. 1991).
20. 615 So. 2d 671, 673 (Fla. 1993).

Searcy, Denney, Scarola, Barnhart & Shipley, Etc. v. State

209 So. 3d 1181 (Fla. 2017)

PER CURIAM.

This case is before the Court for review of the decision of the Fourth District Court of Appeal in *Searcy Denney Scarola Barnhart & Shipley, P.A. v. State*, 194 So.3d 349 (Fla. 4th DCA 2015). In a separate decision, the district court certified the following question to be of great public importance:

> AFTER THE ENACTMENT OF SECTION 768.28, FLORIDA STATUTES, AND THE ADOPTION OF FLORIDA SENATE RULE 4.81(6), IS IT CONSTITUTIONALLY PERMISSIBLE FOR THE FLORIDA LEGISLATURE TO LIMIT THE AMOUNT OF ATTORNEYS' FEES PAID FROM A GUARDIANSHIP TRUST ESTABLISHED BY A LEGISLATIVE CLAIMS BILL?

Searcy Denney Scarola Barnhart & Shipley, P.A. v. State, 190 So.3d 120 (Fla. 4th DCA 2015). Accordingly, we have jurisdiction. See art. V, § 3(b)(4), Fla. Const. . . .

Facts and Procedural Background

This case arose after the birth of Aaron Edwards, during which he sustained a catastrophic brain injury as a result of the negligence of employees at Lee Memorial Health System (Lee Memorial) in 1997. The law firm of Searcy Denney Scarola Barnhart & Shipley, P.A. (Searcy Denney) was retained by the family to seek compensation under a standard contingency fee agreement providing for a payment of 40 percent of any recovery if a lawsuit was filed, plus costs. The agreement also stated that "[i]n the event that one of the parties to pay my claim for damages is a governmental agency, I understand that Federal and Florida Law may limit the amount of attorney fees charged by [Searcy Denney], and in that event, I understand that the fees owed to [Searcy Denney] shall be the amount provided by law."

The case proceeded to a five-week jury trial in 2007, at which the jury found Lee Memorial Health System's employees negligent, and that the negligence resulted in damages to the child in the amount of $28.3 million. The jury also awarded the mother $1.34 million and the father $1 million. Because the hospital was an independent special district of the State of Florida, the trial court enforced the sovereign immunity damage limitations in section 768.28(5), Florida Statutes (2007), and entered a judgment against the hospital for $200,000. This ruling was affirmed per curiam in *Lee Memorial Health System v. Edwards*, 22 So.3d 81 (Fla. 2d DCA 2009), and is not at issue in this case.

Searcy Denney and various other firms were involved in litigation of the medical malpractice suit, the first appeal, and a subsequent two-year lobbying effort to secure a claims bill from the Legislature on behalf of the injured child and his parents.[1]

---

1. In addition to Searcy Denney, the case involves William S. Frates, P.A., Edna L. Caruso, P.A., Vaka Law Group, P.L., and Grossman Roth, P.A.

Because the waiver of sovereign immunity in section 768.28 limited the family's recovery to only $200,000 of the $28.3 million judgment, a claims bill for the excess judgment amount was filed in the Florida Legislature in 2011, but was not passed during that legislative session. However, in 2012 the Legislature passed a claims bill, chapter 2012–249, Laws of Florida, directing Lee Memorial to pay $10 million, with an additional $5 million to be paid in annual installments of $1 million each to "the Guardianship of Aaron Edwards, to be placed in a special needs trust created for the exclusive use and benefit of Aaron Edwards, a minor." Ch. 2012–249, § 2, Laws of Fla. The claims bill further stated that payment of fees and costs from funds awarded in the claims bill shall not exceed $100,000. . . .

Searcy Denney, with the full support of the family, then petitioned the guardianship court to approve a closing statement allowing $2.5 million for attorneys' fees and costs. This requested amount was based on the contract that existed with the Edwards family, as limited by the provisions of section 768.28(8), Florida Statutes. Section 768.28(8), a provision of the limited waiver of sovereign immunity statute, states in pertinent part, "No attorney may charge, demand, receive, or collect, for services rendered, fees in excess of 25 percent of any judgment or settlement."

Because the petition to approve the closing statement also contended that the limit on fees contained in the claims bill was unconstitutional, the State of Florida intervened to defend the constitutionality of the claims bill enactment. And because of competing claims for a portion of the proceeds of the claims bill, the guardianship court appointed a guardian ad litem for the injured child. The evidence presented to the guardianship court revealed that the firms seeking fees and costs spent more than 7000 hours representing the family at trial, on appeal, and during the claims bill process. The evidence also demonstrated that costs of more than $500,000 were expended during the representation. As to the law firm's request for fees and costs of $2.5 million from funds provided by the claims bill, the guardianship court, relying on precedent from this Court and the Fourth District,[2] denied the request for fees in that amount, concluding that the court lacked judicial authority to contravene the fee and cost limitation the Legislature placed in the claims bill. The guardianship court also denied the request to find the fee limitation invalid and sever it from the remainder of the claims bill. Searcy Denney and the other firms appealed the order of the guardianship court denying the $2.5 million in fees and costs, contending that the $100,000 fee and cost limitation in the claims bill was an unconstitutional impairment of their contract with the Edwards family, and that the provision should be severed from the claims bill. Alternatively, the firms argued in the district court that the guardianship court had inherent jurisdiction to depart from the

---

2. The decisions relied upon were *Gamble v. Wells*, 450 So.2d 850 (Fla. 1984), and *Noel v. Sheldon J. Schlesinger, P.A.*, 984 So.2d 1265 (Fla. 4th DCA 2008).

legislative limitation because section 768.28(8), Florida Statutes, would allow a fee up to 25 percent of the award.[3]

The Fourth District rejected these contentions, stating that "[a]lthough sympathetic to Appellants' situation, we must disagree with their legal arguments based on separation of powers principles, supported by reasoning set forth from the Florida Supreme Court." Searcy Denney, 194 So.3d at 349....

. . .

Based on the precedent discussed above [*Gamble v. Wells*, 450 So.2d 850 (Fla. 1984), the majority of the district court panel held that the guardianship court was correct in recognizing the Legislature's prerogative to limit the payment of fees and costs to $100,000....

. . .

Thus, the certified question presented in this case turns on the validity of the additional provision in the claims bill that states: "The total amount paid for attorney's fees, lobbying fees, costs, and other similar expenses relating to this claim may not exceed $100,000." Ch. 2012–249, § 3, Laws of Fla.

* * *

Impairment of Contract

Article I, section 10, of the United States Constitution prohibits any law that impairs the obligation of contracts. See art. I, § 10, U.S. Const. In Florida, article I, section 10, of the Florida Constitution mandates that "[n]o ... law impairing the obligation of contracts shall be passed." "As part of the Florida Constitution's Declaration of Rights, this right belongs to the people ... as against the government." *Citrus County Hosp. Bd. v. Citrus Mem'l Health Found., Inc.*, 150 So.3d 1102, 1106 (Fla. 2014) (quoting *Traylor v. State*, 596 So.2d 957, 963 (Fla. 1992) (explaining that "each right" in the Declaration of Rights is "a distinct freedom guaranteed to each Floridian against government intrusion" and "operates in favor of the individual, against [the] government")). To impair a preexisting contract, a law must "have the effect of rewriting antecedent contracts" in a manner that "chang[es] the substantive rights of the parties to existing contracts." *Manning v. Travelers Ins. Co.*, 250 So.2d 872, 874 (Fla. 1971).

The Searcy Denney "Contract for Services" executed January 19, 1999, provides for a contingency fee of up to 40 percent of the recovery if suit is filed, plus 5 percent if an appeal is filed or if, "[f]ollowing a judgment entered either as a result of Court or arbitration proceedings, additional proceedings (such as garnishment, attachment, or supplementary proceedings) are brought by or at the direction of SEARCY DENNEY SCAROLA BARNHART & SHIPLEY, P.A. in an effort to collect on any judgment." The contract also provides that

---

3. The fee allowed by the claims bill is less than 1 percent of the $15 million provided by the Legislature.

7 · THE DECLARATION OF RIGHTS AND THE TAKING OF PROPERTY 729

[i]n the event that one of the parties responsible to pay my claim for damages is a governmental agency, I understand that Federal and Florida law may limit the amount of attorney fees charged by SEARCY DENNEY SCAROLA BARNHART & SHIPLEY, P.A. In that event, I understand that the attorney fees owed to SEARCY DENNEY SCAROLA BARNHART & SHIPLEY, P.A. shall be the amount provided by law.

Searcy Denney's services under the contract resulted in a $28.3 million judgment. Because the limited waiver of sovereign immunity in section 768.28 limited payment under that $28.3 million judgment to $200,000 in the judicial proceeding, Searcy Denney and the other firms assisting the family followed the express provisions of section 768.28(5), which allows the excess judgment, in whole or in part, to be paid by the Legislature in a discretionary claims bill. Thus, the firms' efforts at seeking such a claims bill from the Legislature were anticipated by the provisions of section 768.28(5). The provisions of the limited waiver of sovereign immunity statute that recognized the fee limit embodied in section 768.28(8) were also anticipated at the time of the execution of the contract.

As noted earlier, the law firms' services were in accord with Senate Rule 4.81(6), which provides that a claims bill may not be considered by the Senate until all available administrative and judicial remedies have been exhausted. We are constrained to conclude that in entering into this contract with the Edwards family, and in pursuing this case through trial, appeal, and the legislative claims bill process, Searcy Denney and the other firms assisting the family were acting in good faith and with the expectation that, pursuant to contract, fees may be recovered in an amount up to 25 percent of any portion of the judgment recovered — regardless of the method or vehicle of recovery.

State regulations that restrict a party to gains it reasonably expected from the contract do not constitute substantial impairment. *U.S. Fidelity & Guar. Co. v. Dep't of Ins.*, 453 So.2d 1355, 1360 (Fla. 1984) (quoting *Energy Reserves Group, Inc. v. Kansas Power & Light Co.*, 459 U.S. 400, 411, 103 S.Ct. 697, 74 L.Ed.2d 569 (1983)). In this case, the contract at issue called for a fee of 40 percent of the recovery, which is a standard contingency provision.[4] However, section 768.28 limited that fee to 25 percent, and the contract clearly recognized the validity of such a limitation, as do we. Searcy Denney and the Edwards family reasonably expected that fees would be paid based on that limitation set forth in the waiver of sovereign immunity statute if a governmental entity was responsible for payment. Thus, the $100,000 fee

---

4. We note that rule 4–1.5(f)(4)(B)(i)b. of the Rules of Professional Conduct governing attorneys' fees for legal services provides that in contingency fee agreements for personal injury and other similar litigation, under certain conditions pertinent here, fees are limited to 40 percent of recovery up to $1 million, 30 percent of recovery between $1 million and $2 million, and 20 percent of any portion of the recovery exceeding $2 million. The fee sought by Searcy Denney does not exceed these amounts.

provision contained in the claims bill significantly limited the gains reasonably expected from the contract.

We reiterated in *Pomponio v. Claridge of Pompano Condominium, Inc.*, 378 So.2d 774 (Fla. 1979), as we earlier held in *Yamaha Parts Distributors Inc. v. Ehrman*, 316 So.2d 557 (Fla. 1975), that "virtually no degree of contract impairment is tolerable." *Pomponio*, 378 So.2d at 780; *see also Fla. Ins. Guar. Ass'n, Inc. v. Devon Neighborhood Ass'n, Inc.*, 67 So.3d 187, 193 n.6 (Fla. 2011). However, we also recognized that the holding that "virtually" no impairment is tolerable "necessarily implies that some impairment is tolerable." *Pomponio*, 378 So.2d at 780. The question thus becomes how much impairment is tolerable and how to determine that amount. To answer that question, in *Pomponio* we proposed a balancing test that "allow [ed] the court to consider the actual effect of the provision on the contract and to balance a party's interest in not having the contract impaired against the State's source of authority and the evil sought to be remedied." Scott v. Williams, 107 So.3d 379, 385 (Fla. 2013) (quoting *Fla. Ins. Guar. Ass'n*, 67 So.3d at 193 n.6). "[T]his becomes a balancing process to determine whether the nature and extent of the impairment is constitutionally tolerable in light of the importance of the State's objective, or whether it unreasonably intrudes into the parties' bargain to a degree greater than is necessary to achieve that objective." *Pomponio*, 378 So.2d at 780.

An impairment may be constitutional if it is reasonable and necessary to serve an important public purpose. *Id.* at 778–79 (quoting *U.S. Trust Co. v. New Jersey*, 431 U.S. 1, 25, 97 S.Ct. 1505, 52 L.Ed.2d 92 (1977)). However, where the impairment is severe, "[t]he severity of the impairment is said to increase the level of scrutiny to which the legislation will be subjected." *U.S. Fidelity*, 453 So.2d at 1360 (quoting *Energy Reserves*, 459 U.S. at 411, 103 S.Ct. 697). There must be a "significant and legitimate public purpose behind the regulation." *Energy Reserves*, 459 U.S. at 411, 103 S.Ct. 697.

Where a legislatively imposed fee limitation substantially impairs a party's preexisting contract for representation and payment of agreed-upon attorneys' fees, especially when those fees meet the measure that the Legislature has found reasonable under section 768.28(8), we can discern no apparent benefit to the injured party attempting to obtain redress for injury pursuant to the contract. In this case, in order to obtain representation, the Edwards family agreed to pay fees in accord with the limits of sovereign immunity; and the family supports the claim for fees by Searcy Denney pursuant to that contract and the statute.

Nor do we see any significant or legitimate public purpose to be achieved by the limitation. Because up to 25 percent of the monies recovered by judgment in circuit court are legislatively approved as a fee under section 768.28(8), we can discern no legitimate public purpose or justification to disapprove that same percentage fee when a further portion of the judgment is paid by legislative enactment expressly anticipated in section 768.28. This is especially true when the legislative action substantially impairs the preexisting contract, as it does in this case. We do, however, see harm arising from such an enactment. As Chief Judge Ciklin aptly stated, the claims bill's attorneys' fee limitation and the district court's affirmance of it have "now invaded and will continue to wreak a chilling effect upon the sacrosanct and fundamental constitutional right to access to our courts—particularly for those suffering damages at the hands of government." Searcy Denney, 194 So.3d at 367 (Ciklin, C.J., dissenting). We also agree with Chief Judge Ciklin that "the state has not shown that its draconian limitation on attorney's fees and costs was necessary to accomplish some type of 'important public purpose.'" *Id.* at 361 (Ciklin, C.J., dissenting).

The right to contract for legal services in order to petition for redress is a right that is related to the First Amendment, and any impairment of that right not only adversely affects the right of the lawyer to receive his fee but the right of the party to obtain, by contract, competent legal representation to ensure meaningful access to courts to petition for redress. The United States Supreme Court has stated, "We hold that the freedom of speech, assembly, and petition guaranteed by the First and Fourteenth Amendments gives petitioner the right to hire attorneys on a salary basis to assist its members in the assertion of their legal rights." *United Mine Workers of America, Dist. 12 v. Illinois State Bar Ass'n*, 389 U.S. 217, 221–22, 88 S.Ct. 353, 19 L. Ed.2d 426 (1967) (vacating judgment enjoining union from hiring salaried attorney to assist members in assertion of legal rights with respect to workers' compensation claims). This same constitutional right extends to a party's right and practical ability to retain an attorney by contingency fee contract in order to have meaningful access to courts. The "draconian limitation" on the fees in this case, in contravention of the preexisting contract and the provisions of section 768.28, sets an unfortunate precedent that, if allowed to stand, would effectively chill the right of future litigants to obtain effective counsel to make their case for compensation due for injuries caused by the State or its agencies and subdivisions.

The First Amendment to the United States Constitution guarantees, in pertinent part, the right of the people to "petition the Government for a redress of grievances."[5] Such a petition may be filed in the courts, and Florida guarantees access to courts in article I, section 21, of the Declaration of Rights in Florida's constitution. However, the right to petition for redress is not confined to the courts. *See Cal. Motor Transp. Co. v. Trucking Unlimited*, 404 U.S. 508, 510, 92 S.Ct. 609, 30 L.Ed.2d 642 (1972) ("Certainly the right to petition extends to all departments of the Government."). Therefore, the legislative fee limitation in contravention of the contract and the statute chills, and effectively impairs, the rights of parties to obtain effective counsel to seek redress for them in both the courts and from the Legislature.

For all these reasons, we conclude that the $100,000 fee limitation contained in the claims bill impermissibly impairs the preexisting contract between Searcy Denney and the Edwards family, and that nothing has been presented to justify this

---

5. This First Amendment right to petition for redress has been made applicable to the States by the Fourteenth Amendment to the United States Constitution. See DeJonge v. Oregon, 299 U.S. 353, 364, 57 S.Ct. 255, 81 L.Ed. 278 (1937).

violation of the family's constitutional right to contract with legal counsel to seek full redress of injury, as well as Searcy Denney's contract right to receive the agreed-upon fees. This is especially true where, as here, the services producing the judgment and claims bill, and the fee amount sought under the contract, are in accord with sections 768.28(5) and (8). The Legislature has expressly provided for both the claims bill mechanism and for fees payable from the judgments obtained under the limited waiver of sovereign immunity statute. We conclude the permissible fees based upon recovery of those funds include funds recovered pursuant to the claims bill process.

* * *

Conclusion

Based on the foregoing, we answer the certified question in the negative and hold that the fee limitation in the claims bill, chapter 2012–249, Laws of Florida, is unconstitutional and may not stand when such a limitation impairs a preexisting contract. We further hold that the valid portion of the act may be severed from the invalid portion and still accomplish the beneficial purpose of the act in providing compensation due to the injured child in this case. Accordingly, we quash the decision of the Fourth District in *Searcy Denney Scarola Barnhart & Shipley, P.A. v. State of Florida*, 194 So.3d 349 (Fla. 4th DCA 2015), and remand to the district court for proceedings consistent with this decision.

It is so ordered.

PARIENTE, LEWIS, and QUINCE, JJ., and PERRY, Senior Justice, concur.

CANADY, J., dissents with an opinion. [The dissenting opinion of Justice Canady is omitted.]

POLSTON, J., dissents with an opinion, in which LABARGA, C.J., concurs.

POLSTON, J., dissenting.

I would answer the certified question in the affirmative. The Florida law limiting the amount of attorneys' fees does not unconstitutionally impair a pre-existing contract that expressly contemplates and accepts that Florida law may limit the amount of attorneys' fees.

As acknowledged by the majority, it is well-settled law that the Florida Legislature has complete discretion in its decision to grant a legislative claims bill, which is an act of grace. *See Gamble v. Wells*, 450 So.2d 850 (Fla. 1984). The Legislature could indisputably have chosen to make no award to the injured person and pay no attorneys' fees. But the Legislature awarded $15,000,000 to the Guardianship of Aaron Edwards. Ch. 2012–249, Laws of Florida. It also provided $100,000 for attorneys' fees and other costs:

> Section 3. The amount paid by Lee Memorial Health System pursuant to s. 768.28, Florida Statutes, and the amount awarded under this act are intended to provide the sole compensation for all present and future claims

arising out of the factual situation described in this act which resulted in the injuries suffered by Aaron Edwards. *The total amount paid for attorney's fees, lobbying fees, costs, and other similar expenses relating to this claim may not exceed $100,000.*

Id. (emphasis added).

The majority holds that this award of attorneys' fees unconstitutionally impairs the fee agreement between the Searcy Denney firm and its clients. However, the fee agreement specifically provides that "[i]n the event that one of the parties to pay my claim for damages is a governmental agency, I understand that Federal and Florida Law may limit the amount of attorney fees charged by [Searcy Denney], and in that event, I understand that the fees owed to [Searcy Denney] shall be the amount provided by law." (Emphasis added.) Lee Memorial Health System of Lee County is a governmental agency, and the Florida law enacted by the Legislature limited the amount of attorneys' fees to $100,000. Accordingly, because the fee agreement explicitly anticipates and agrees to an award of fees as limited by Florida law and in the amount provided by law, there is no impairment of contract. For there to be an unconstitutional impairment of the contract as the majority concludes, the fee agreement would have to be written differently.

* * *

2. Ex Post Facto Laws

Shenfeld v. State

44 So. 3d 96 (Fla. 2010)

CANADY, C.J.

In this case, we consider whether a statutory amendment relating to the circumstances in which a probationary period is tolled pending consideration of an alleged probation violation may constitutionally be applied to a probationer who was placed on probation before the amendment became effective. We have for review the decision of the Fourth District Court of Appeal in *Shenfeld v. State*, 14 So.3d 1021 (Fla. 4th DCA 2009), in which the Fourth District certified that its decision is in direct conflict with the decisions of the First District Court of Appeal in *Harris v. State*, 893 So.2d 669 (Fla. 1st DCA 2005), and *Frye v. State*, 885 So.2d 419 (Fla. 1st DCA 2004). We have jurisdiction. *See* art. V, § 3(b)(4), Fla. Const. For the reasons that follow, we agree with the Fourth District that the application of the statutory amendment to a probationer who was placed on probation before the amendment became effective did not violate the constitutional prohibition of ex post facto laws.

Background

In July 2002, Jason Shenfeld pleaded guilty to a robbery committed earlier that year. In September 2002, the trial court adjudicated Shenfeld guilty, sentenced him to five years' incarceration, suspended the sentence, and ordered him to serve five years of drug offender probation. In 2004, Shenfeld filed a motion to terminate his probation. The trial court declined to terminate probation, but it modified Shenfeld's probation to administrative probation. On July 23, 2007, before Shenfeld's probation expired, an affidavit of violation of probation was filed, alleging that Shenfeld had committed several violations by committing new crimes. Shenfeld had been arrested without a warrant for allegedly committing first-degree murder, sexual battery, and false imprisonment on July 21, 2007. On October 1, 2007, after Shenfeld's probation would have expired absent tolling, an amended affidavit was filed. The amended affidavit changed the dates of Shenfeld's alleged violations. *Shenfeld*, 14 So.3d at 1023.

When Shenfeld was placed on probation, section 948.06(1), Florida Statutes (2001), provided that "[u]pon the filing of an affidavit alleging a violation of probation or community control and following issuance of a warrant under s. 901.02, the probationary period is tolled until the court enters a ruling on the violation." Florida district courts of appeal held that under the 2001 version of section 948.06(1), "[b]oth the filing of an affidavit of violation and the issuance of an arrest warrant are required to toll the probationary period, and the mere filing of the affidavit is insufficient." *Jones v. State*, 964 So.2d 167, 170 (Fla. 5th DCA 2007) (citing *Sepulveda v. State*, 909 So.2d 568, 570 (Fla. 2d DCA 2005)). In 2007, the Legislature amended section 948.06(1) to allow for tolling of the probationary period "[u]pon the filing of an affidavit alleging a violation of probation or community control and following issuance of a warrant under s. 901.02, a warrantless arrest under this section, or a notice to appear under this section." §948.06(1)(d), Fla. Stat. (2007). This amendment became effective June 20, 2007. Ch. 2007-210, §7, at 1938, Laws of Fla. The amended statute thus was in effect when Shenfeld violated his probation.

Relying on the 2001 version of section 948.06(1), Shenfeld moved to dismiss the affidavits of violation of probation. Shenfeld contended that because he was arrested without a warrant and no arrest warrant for the violations was issued during his probationary period, his probation was never tolled and the trial court lacked jurisdiction to revoke his probation once the probationary period expired. Shenfeld further asserted that application of the 2007 version of section 948.06(1) to him was an ex post facto violation.

The trial court denied Shenfeld's motion to dismiss, explaining that its denial was on the basis that the original affidavit of violation was timely and the amended affidavit did not allege new charges.

Shenfeld appealed his sentence and the trial court's ruling on his motion to dismiss to the Fourth District Court of Appeal.

... Shenfeld argued that the trial court violated the prohibition on ex post facto laws by retroactively applying section 948.06(1), Florida Statutes (2007), in his case. Shenfeld continued to assert his argument that had the trial court applied the probation tolling statute that was in effect when he was originally placed on probation, the trial court would not have had jurisdiction to consider the alleged violations of

7 · THE DECLARATION OF RIGHTS AND THE TAKING OF PROPERTY

probation. The Fourth District concluded that the application of section 948.06(1), Florida Statutes (2007), to Shenfeld's revocation of probation proceeding was not an ex post facto violation because it determined that the 2007 amendment to section 948.06(1) was procedural in effect. The Fourth District reasoned that the revision was procedural in nature because the purpose and effect of the amendment was to toll the probationary period in order to allow the alleged violations of probation to be heard.

Analysis

On appeal, Shenfeld contends that the 2007 version of section 948.06(1) could not constitutionally be applied to him and that the trial court therefore erred in denying his motion to dismiss. Specifically, Shenfeld asserts that the ex post facto clauses of the United States Constitution and the Florida Constitution prohibit retroactive application of section 948.06(1), Florida Statutes (2007), in his revocation of probation proceeding. The State contends that section 948.06(1), Florida Statutes (2007), was not applied retroactively in this case and, alternatively, that if the statute was applied retroactively, the application was constitutional.

The United States Constitution provides that "[n]o State shall ... pass any ... ex post facto Law." U.S. Const. art. I. § 10, cl. 1. The Florida Constitution similarly states that "[n]o ... ex post facto law ... shall be passed." Art. I, § 10, Fla. Const.

The constitutional prohibition of ex post facto laws forbids the enactment of "laws with certain retroactive effects." *Stogner v. California,* 539 U.S. 607, 610, 123 S. Ct. 2446, 156 L.Ed.2d 544 (2003). The four categories "of *ex post facto* laws set forth by Justice Chase more than 200 years ago in *Calder v. Bull*[, 3 U.S. (3 Dall.) 386, 1 L. Ed. 648 (1798),]" have been "recognized as providing an authoritative account of the scope of the *Ex Post Facto* Clause." *Stogner,* 539 U.S. at 611, 123 S.Ct. 2446. These are the four categories set forth by Justice Chase:

> 1st. Every law that makes an action done before the passing of the law, and which was innocent when done, criminal; and punishes such action. 2d. Every law that aggravates a crime, or makes it greater than it was, when committed. 3d. Every law that changes the punishment, and inflicts a greater punishment, than the law annexed to the crime, when committed. 4th. Every law that alters the legal rules of evidence, and receives less, or different, testimony, than the law required at the time of the commission of the offense, in order to convict the offender.

Id. at 612, 123 S.Ct. 2446 (quoting *Calder,* 3 U.S. (3 Dall.) at 390–91) (emphasis removed). All ex post facto claims must be evaluated in the light of these four categories. In determining whether an ex post facto violation has occurred, it is "a mistake to stray beyond *Calder's* four categories." *Carmell v. Texas,* 529 U.S. 513, 539, 120 S.Ct. 1620, 146 L.Ed.2d 577 (2000) (emphasis removed).

It is evident that the four *Calder* categories do not encompass every law effective after the commission of an offense and applied in the proceedings regarding the offense. The prohibition of ex post facto laws thus "does not give a criminal a right to be tried, in all respects, by the law in force when the crime charged was committed." *Dobbert v. Florida,* 432 U.S. 282, 293, 97 S.Ct. 2290, 53 L.Ed.2d 344 (1977) (quoting *Gibson v. Mississippi,* 162 U.S. 565, 590, 16 S.Ct. 904, 40 L.Ed. 1075 (1896)). And the mere fact that a statutory change "[alters] the situation of a party to his disadvantage" is not sufficient to bring that change within the scope of the ex post facto clause. *Collins v. Youngblood,* 497 U.S. 37, 50, 110 S.Ct. 2715, 111 L.Ed.2d 30 (1990) (quoting from and overruling *Kring v. Missouri,* 107 U.S. 221, 235, 2 S.Ct. 443, 27 L. Ed. 506 (1883)). Detriment to the defendant is necessary but not sufficient to establish an ex post facto violation. "[E]ven if a law operates to the defendant's detriment, the *ex post facto* prohibition does not restrict 'legislative control of remedies and modes of procedure which do not affect matters of substance.'" *Miller v. Florida,* 482 U.S. 423, 433, 107 S.Ct. 2446, 96 L.Ed.2d 351 (1987) (quoting *Dobbert,* 432 U.S. at 293, 97 S.Ct. 2290); *see also Beazell v. Ohio,* 269 U.S. 167, 171, 46 S.Ct. 68, 70 L.Ed. 216 (1925). Such matters of substance are implicated only when the law falls within one of the four *Calder* categories.

The 2007 revision to section 948.06(1) at issue here is a matter of procedure that does not fall within any of those categories. The statutory provision expanding the circumstances under which a probationary term could be tolled "neither made criminal a theretofore innocent act [first category], nor aggravated a crime previously committed [second category], nor provided greater punishment [third category], nor changed the proof necessary to convict [fourth category]." *Dobbert,* 432 U.S. at 293, 97 S.Ct. 2290. Instead, the statutory change simply altered the "modes of procedure" governing the adjudication of probation violations by permitting the tolling of a probationary term without the issuance of an arrest warrant.

Shenfeld's reliance on *State v. Williams,* 397 So.2d 663 (Fla.1981), is unavailing. In *Williams,* this Court held that a statute — enacted after the commission of the charged offense — which allowed the trial court to retain jurisdiction over the first third of the defendant's statutory maximum sentence could not be constitutionally applied retroactively. The trial court's retention of jurisdiction gave it the authority to bar the defendant's parole or gain-time release. This Court explained that retroactive application of the statute would attach "the legal consequences of the trial court's parole veto and no gain-time release to those who committed crimes before the provision's effective date" and that as a consequence "the prisoners' sentences are enhanced." *Id.* at 665. The statutory change at issue in *Williams* thus fell squarely within *Calder's* third category — that is, laws inflicting "a greater punishment" than was applicable to the offense at the time it was committed. The statutory revision at issue in this case, in contrast, did nothing to increase the punishment applicable to Shenfeld.

The statutory change challenged by Shenfeld is akin to a statutory extension of a statute of limitations which becomes effective before the statute has run. Such a statutory change-unlike a statute reviving a previously time-barred prosecution — does not fall within the scope of any of the four *Calder* categories. *See Stogner,* 539 U.S. at 613, 632–33, 123 S.Ct. 2446 (stating that "[a]fter (but not before) the original statute of limitations had expired, a party such as Stogner was not 'liable to any punishment'" and concluding "that a law enacted after expiration of a previously applicable limitations period violates the *Ex Post Facto* Clause when it is applied to revive a previously time-barred prosecution"); *Reino v. State,* 352 So.2d 853, 861 (Fla.1977) (recognizing that "the legislature could have amended [the statute of limitations] retroactively" with respect to crimes for which "[p]rosecution was not yet barred"). The probation statute amendment here became effective before Shenfeld's probationary term had expired. If the time for bringing criminal charges may constitutionally be extended before the prosecution has been time-barred, it follows that a provision for tolling may be applied to a probationary term that has not yet expired.

Conclusion

We approve the decision of the Fourth District. The 2007 revision to section 948.06(1), Florida Statutes (2007), was procedural in nature. Its application in Shenfeld's revocation of probation proceeding did not violate the prohibition on ex post facto laws.

It is so ordered.

PARIENTE, LEWIS, QUINCE, POLSTON, LABARGA, and PERRY, JJ., concur.

G. Substantive Due Process

Fla. Const. art. I, § 9

Due process. — No person shall be deprived of life, liberty or property without due process of law, . . .

----

1. In General

The following case, while rather old, represents a venerable treatment of this doctrine.

L. Maxcy, Inc. v. Mayo

139 So. 121 (Fla. 1931)

* * *

On Rehearing.

PER CURIAM.

* * *

We have therefore granted the Attorney General's petition for rehearing, in order to give consideration to and decide the constitutional validity of arsenical spraying of citrus trees, which is in terms forbidden by section 1 of the act under attack. We have done so at this time, because prior to the filing of the petition for a rehearing, whatever statutory exemption might have existed with reference to the consequences of arsenical spraying, necessarily expired on December 6, 1931, thereby leaving only the constitutional point to be decided.

Section 1 of chapter 11844, Acts of 1927, as amended by chapter 14485, Acts of 1929, Ex. Sess., provides that it shall be a criminal offense for any person, partnership, association, or corporation, owning, managing, tending, or cultivating citrus groves, or trees, to use arsenic or any of its derivatives, or any combination, compound, or preparation containing arsenic, as a spray or fertilizer on bearing citrus trees, except when authorized by the federal government or state plant board, for the purpose of destroying the Mediterranean fruit fly.

* * *

Complainants are grove owners having citrus trees, and assert in their bill of complaint that they have a constitutional right to use such sprays for the protection of their property. They aver in substance that such use constitutes and is a part of their inherent right of enjoyment of such property itself. They further say that the statute in terms recognizes that arsenic may be legitimately employed as a protective means to destroy pests which habitually attack and destroy citrus trees and fruit. They contend that a legislative fiat which undertakes not merely to regulate, but to entirely prohibit, the use of arsenic in sprays, however small in amount it may be, is purely arbitrary and unreasonable, beyond the constitutional limits of the state's police power, and is in violation of both the federal and state Constitutions as being in effect a deprivation of property without due process of law, and a denial of the equal protection of the laws. Weaver v. Palmer Bros. Co., 270 U.S. 402, 46 S. Ct. 320, 70 L. Ed. 654.[1]

* * *

---

1. In this case a law of Pennsylvania forbidding the use of shoddy in comfortables, even when sterilized, was declared so far arbitrary and unreasonable as to violate the due process clause of the Fourteenth Amendment to the United States Constitution.

It is established by the record that arsenical sprays, when applied to bearing citrus trees by dusting or spraying on the limbs and foliage, has an inevitable tendency to injuriously affect and injure the quality of the fruit produced. This is done by the action of the arsenic after it is absorbed into the tree. The result is invariably observed that fruit picked from citrus trees which have been subjected to frequent arsenical spraying appears in every respect like other citrus fruit of normal characteristics, but is in fact always inferior in taste and quality. It is demonstrated that this inferiority, so occasioned in the fruit, cannot be detected from its appearance when offered in the market. Here the consumer is easily deceived and defrauded by the fruit's appearance as good, when it is intrinsically bad.

On the other hand, it is equally well established that arsenical sprays can be, and regularly have been for many years past, used in protecting citrus trees from insect pests which attack them, and that such use is regarded as perfectly proper and legitimate under ordinary conditions. But notwithstanding the use of arsenical sprays as a destroyer of citrus enemies, it is likewise well established that by their use ostensibly to guard against pests, citrus growers in the past have been enabled to produce and put on the market an immature and inferior grade of citrus fruit which is capable of passing all the ordinary maturity tests prescribed by the laws of Florida designed to prevent the shipment and sale of green or immature oranges. Chapter 10103, Acts of 1925, as amended by chapter 11875, Acts of 1927; sections 3220–3524, Comp. Gen. Laws 1927.

Therefore, it stands on the record as an undisputed fact that while arsenical spraying of citrus trees may be legitimately employed for a proper purpose, it may be just as easily employed by unscrupulous citrus growers for an illegitimate purpose; that by their use such growers are habitually deceiving and defrauding their customers, by presenting to them fruit which to all outward appearances is of high grade and quality, when as a matter of fact it is of inferior grade — insipid, unpalatable, and unfit for human consumption — although passing the maturity tests.

Just what exact amount of arsenic must be used to produce such deficient fruit as will amount to a fraud on the customer is not shown by the record. Neither was it known at the time the statute was enacted. Just what percentage of arsenic in a spray used on bearing citrus trees would have that effect is shrouded in doubt. But it is reasonably certain that a comparatively small quantity will have that effect. And it is also certain that when sprayed on citrus trees under favorable circumstances, arsenic and its derivatives has a peculiar affinity for assimilation with the sugars and acids of the fruit, so that it is transformed into the substances of the fruit itself in more or less definitely ascertainable quantities. Thus, the inherent nature and tendency of all spraying of arsenic on citrus trees is for the trees to absorb and take in the drug through its foliage and transit it to the substance of the fruit, notwithstanding the fact that small and infrequent applications can be made which will not materially affect the fruit as to quality.

But, because of the fact that the statute does not simply regulate the use of arsenic, so as to avoid the evils of its improper use, but undertakes to entirely prohibit such use altogether for any purpose, complainants contend that the statute is unreasonable and arbitrary, and must be struck down as an unconstitutional interference with the fundamental right of complainants to protect their rights of property in the citrus trees owned by them. The evil which exists, if any, complainants say, is in the excessive, not normal, use of arsenic as a dust or spray. Therefore there should be a statutory degree of permitted tolerance in its use, such as is asserted to have been recognized by the federal authorities with reference to citrus fruits shipped in interstate commerce — not an absolute prohibition of all use.

* * *

This court takes judicial notice of the fact that the citrus industry of Florida is one of its greatest assets. Its promotion and protection is of the greatest value to the state, and its advancement redounds greatly to the general welfare of the commonwealth. For this reason the Legislature necessarily has a wide field of police power within which to pass laws to foster, promote, and protect the citrus fruit industry of Florida from injurious practices which may tend to injure or destroy either the reputation or value of Florida citrus products in the world's markets. Sligh v. Kirkwood, 65 Fla. 123, 61 So. 185; Id., 237 U. S. 52, 35 S. Ct. 501, 59 L. Ed. 835.

Under the police power, the Legislature has the right to adopt suitable statutory regulations for the protection of health, the prevention of fraud, and the preservation of the prevailing public morals. This power which the Legislature has to promote the general welfare of a state is very great, and the discretion which the legislative department of the government has, in the employment of means to that end, is very large. Powell v. Pennsylvania, 127 U. S. 678, 8 S. Ct. 992, 1257, 32 L. Ed. 253.

Legislative determinations that certain practices are evil, and that they should be entirely forbidden, are entitled to great weight. But it is always open to interested parties to show that the Legislature has transgressed the limits of its authority, even in the field of police regulations enacted under guise of the police power. Invalidity of legislative action may be shown by things that are judicially noticed, or by facts established by allegations and proof, the burden being always on the attacking party to establish the invalidating facts claimed to exist. Pennsylvania Coal Co. v. Mahon, 260 U. S. 393, 43 S. Ct. 158, 67 L. Ed. 322, 28 A. L. R. 1321; Quong Wing v. Kirkendall, 223 U. S. 59, 32 S. Ct. 192, 56 L. Ed. 350.

It has long since become an established rule of constitutional law in these United States that power and discretion, however exerted, and by whomsoever exercised, must be used in such manner as not to infringe upon or impair the fundamental rights of life, liberty, property, and the pursuit of happiness. The very idea (as one opinion delivered by the Supreme Court of the United States puts it) that one man may be compelled to hold his life, business, property, means of living, or any material thing essential to his enjoyment of life, at the mere will of another, is intolerable in any country where freedom prevails, and is the very essence of slavery itself. Yick Wo v. Hopkins, 118 U. S. 356, 6 S. Ct. 1064, 30 L. Ed. 220.

* * *

7 · THE DECLARATION OF RIGHTS AND THE TAKING OF PROPERTY 741

State laws prohibiting apparently well-established uses and practices in connection with the handling, disposition, and marketing of commodities of trade and commerce, when enacted under guise of the state's police power, and therefore entitled to every reasonable presumption in their favor to sustain them, may nevertheless, when attacked in a judicial forum, be made to appear so arbitrary and unreasonable in their application to a particular state of facts, that the courts will not hesitate to declare them inoperative and void, as violative of the due process clause of the Fourteenth Amendment to the Constitution of the United States. Weaver v. Palmer Bros., 270 U. S. 402, 46 S. Ct. 320, 70 L. Ed. 654.

In the case at bar, it is conceded that the use of arsenical sprays can be, and frequently is, made to serve the unrighteous purpose of producing a condition in citrus fruit which deceives and defrauds — that tends for a certainty to destroy the reputation of Florida citrus products in the market.

Just what amount of such use might be safely permitted without producing this unhappy result was unknown to informed authority at the time the Legislature passed the statute here considered. And, indeed, to judge from the testimony now before the court coming from experts supposed to be familiar with this subject, the question now of how much arsenical spraying can be permitted as a safe and harmless practice is far from settled. Therefore, it seems that the Legislature in 1927 in order to make the evil aimed at impossible of accomplishment, not only undertook to regulate the use of arsenic, but made it a criminal offense to employ it in any quantity whatsoever, as a spray or dust to be actually applied to the bearing trees.

*　*　*

Acts innocent and innocuous in themselves may accordingly be prohibited, if this is practically made necessary to be done, in order to secure efficient enforcement of valid police regulations covering the same general field. Purity Extract & Tonic Co. v. Lynch, 226 U. S. 192, 33 S. Ct. 44, 57 L. Ed. 184; Id., 100 Miss. 650, 56 So. 316; Hebe Co. v. Shaw, 248 U. S. 297, 39 S. Ct. 125, 63 L. Ed. 255; Pierce Oil Corp. v. Hope, 248 U. S. 498, 39 S. Ct. 172, 63 L. Ed. 381; Id., 127 Ark. 38, 191 S. W. 405, Ann. Cas. 1918E, 143; Village of Euclid v. Ambler Realty Co., 272 U. S. 365, 47 S. Ct. 114, 71 L. Ed. 303, 54 A. L. R. 1016; Everard's Breweries v. Day, 265 U. S. 545, 44 S. Ct. 628, 68 L. Ed. 1174.

But the doctrine justifying the inclusion of what may be termed innocent acts can be applied only as a necessary means to a legitimate end. Such inclusion must be reasonably required for the accomplishment of the legislative intent with respect to the ultimate object. It cannot be relied on to sustain a measure of prohibition so loosely or broadly drawn as to bring within its scope matters which are not properly subject to police regulations or prohibitions. Tyson & Bro.-United Ticket Offices v. Banton, 273 U. S. 418, 47 S. Ct. 426, 432, 71 L. Ed. 718, 58 A. L. R. 1236; Adams v. Tanner, 244 U. S. 590, 37 S. Ct. 662, 664, 61 L. Ed. 1336, L. R. A. 1917F, 1163, Ann. Cas. 1917D, 973, reversing Wiseman v. Tanner (D. C.), 221 F. 694; Weaver v. Palmer

Bros. Co., supra. "It is not permissible to enact a law which, in effect, spreads an all-inclusive net for the feet of everybody upon the chance that, while the innocent will surely be entangled in its meshes, some wrongdoers also may be caught." Tyson & Bro. v. Banton, supra. "* * * There is no profession, possibly no business, which does not offer peculiar opportunities for reprehensible practices; and as to every one of them, no doubt, some can be found quite ready earnestly to maintain that its suppression would be in the public interest. Skillfully directed agitation might also bring about apparent condemnation of any one of them by the public. Happily for all, the fundamental guaranties of the Constitution cannot be freely submerged if and whenever some ostensible justification is advanced and the police power invoked." Adams v. Tanner, supra.

Bearing these stated principles in mind, is the present statute valid when it undertakes to prohibit using as a spray on bearing citrus trees, any arsenic or its derivatives whatsoever, when the real purpose of the Legislature is to guard against the harmful effects to citrus fruit caused by an improper and injudicious use of arsenical sprays on the trees?

The harmful effects designed to be avoided are six in number and have been summarized in the record as follows: (1) Change in taste of fruit caused by interference with sugar content; (2) formation of citric acid retarded; (3) total amount of sugars reduced; (4) vitamin C content lessened or destroyed; (5) juice contents reduced in volume, and interior of fruit rendered dry and ricy; (6) keeping qualities adversely affected, both as to fresh and canned fruit. That such harmful effects are commonly experienced almost solely as the result of indiscriminate and promiscuous use of arsenic as a spray on bearing citrus trees, is beyond dispute.

But, so appellants contend, it is only the unwise and improper use of excessive quantities of arsenic which result that way — the Legislature has no right to spread a net to catch all users of legitimate sprays, merely because some users accomplish evil designs by their own particular use of them. In this connection appellants emphasize that even this statute itself, in its provisos, authorizes the use of arsenic as an insect pest destroyer, and that its use for protection of citrus trees has been long established as a regular and proper practice by responsible citrus growers, who for many years in the past have experienced no harmful results therefrom when properly employed.

But for the Legislature by statute to attempt a mere regulation of the use of arsenical sprays on thousands of citrus trees scattered about the state as they are, and subject to being sprayed by the growers at varying times throughout the year, would require the state to provide an army of enforcement officers to execute such a law. That would result in such grave difficulties in the way of results from attempted enforcement, as to suggest the likelihood that the legislative measure would prove wholly ineffective for the particular purpose designed to be accomplished.

Hence the Legislature has adopted an absolute prohibition of all use of arsenic as a spray, evidently on the theory that balancing the good against evil in the practice, the evil far outweighs the good. It therefore appears that in order to render the statute reasonably certain of benefit, it is necessary that all use whatsoever of arsenic sprays be prohibited, in order to preserve the general welfare of Florida's citrus industry, and the thousands of people who depend upon it for their livelihood and well being.

* * *

When put to the choice by the practical necessities of the case, the Legislature may exercise its power to suppress an evil by prohibiting entirely a stated practice out of which that evil largely grows, even though by so doing, innocent acts may be forbidden and long-established customs of the people henceforth made unlawful. The application of that rule supports the validity of the statutory provision involved here, making it contrary to law to use arsenical sprays on bearing citrus trees, even though a limited use thereof would occasion no harm if it could be properly supervised.

We therefore hold that section 1 of chapter 11844, Acts of 1927, as amended by chapter 14485, Acts of 1929, Ex. Sess., making it a criminal offense to use arsenical sprays on bearing citrus trees, is a valid exercise of the police power of this state, and is constitutional. . . .

* * *

BUFORD, C. J., and WHITFIELD, TERRELL, BROWN, and DAVIS, JJ., concur.

ELLIS, J. (dissenting) [omitted].

———————

While applying a substantive due process analysis, the Florida courts appear to have attempted to determine whether or not the state has a valid purpose for the action which it contemplates. If a valid governmental purpose has been established, the second part of the analysis involves determining whether or not the means selected by the state to achieve its valid purpose is a reasonable one.

This a subjective test, which leaves the court open to the criticism that it is merely second-guessing the wisdom of legislative decisions. The following cases are illustrations of the Florida Supreme Court applying substantive due process.

State v. Saiez

489 So. 2d 1125 (Fla. 1986)

BARKETT, Justice.

We have before us *State v. Saiez*, 469 So.2d 927 (Fla. 3d DCA 1985). This appeal concerns the constitutionality of a statute. We have jurisdiction pursuant to article V, section 3(b)(1) of the Florida Constitution.

On February 24, 1984, Salvadore Saiez was charged with three violations of section 817.63, Florida Statutes (1983). Under counts 1 and 3 Saiez was charged with the unlawful possession of embossing machines. Under count 2 Saiez was charged with possession of incomplete credit cards. Section 817.63 provided in relevant part:

> Possession of machinery, plates or other contrivance or incomplete credit cards. — ... *a person possessing with knowledge of its character any machinery, plates or any other contrivance designed to reproduce instruments purporting to be the credit cards of an issuer who has not consented to the preparation of such credit cards, violates this subsection* and is subject to the penalties set forth in s. 817.67(2). . . . (Emphasis added.)

Saiez filed a motion to dismiss counts 1 and 3, alleging that the portion of the statute prohibiting the possession of the machinery designed to reproduce instruments purporting to be credit cards was unconstitutional because it prohibited the mere possession of embossing machines regardless of whether they were being used legitimately. The trial court agreed and dismissed counts 1 and 3. The Third District Court of Appeal affirmed the dismissal. For reasons other than those expressed by the Third District, we affirm its decision.

* * *

Although Saiez's overbreadth and vagueness challenges fail, section 817.63 is nevertheless unconstitutional. It violates substantive due process under the fourteenth amendment to the United States Constitution and article I, section 9 of the Florida Constitution. The due process clauses of our federal and state constitutions establish a "sphere of personal liberty" for every individual subject only to reasonable intrusion by the state in furtherance of legitimate state interests. *See Del Percio*, 476 So.2d at 202 (quoting from *Richards v. Thurston*, 424 F.2d 1281, 1284 (1st Cir. 1970)).

The legislature enacts penal statutes, such as section 817.63, under the state's "police power" which derives from the state's sovereign right to enact laws for the protection of its citizens. *See Carroll v. State*, 361 So.2d 144, 146 (Fla.1978). Such power, however, is not boundless and is confined to those acts which may be reasonably construed as expedient for protection of the public health, safety, welfare, or morals. *Hamilton v. State*, 366 So.2d 8, 10 (Fla.1978); *Newman v. Carson*, 280 So.2d 426, 428 (Fla.1973). The due process clauses of our federal and state constitutions do not prevent the legitimate interference with individual rights under the police power, but do place limits on such interference. *State v. Leone*, 118 So.2d 781, 784

7 · THE DECLARATION OF RIGHTS AND THE TAKING OF PROPERTY   745

(Fla.1960). *See also Coca-Cola Co., Food Division v. State, Department of Citrus,* 406 So.2d 1079, 1084–85 (Fla.1981), *appeal dismissed sub nom. Kraft, Inc. v. Florida Department of Citrus,* 456 U.S. 1002, 102 S.Ct. 2288, 73 L.Ed.2d 1297 (1982); *State ex rel. Walters v. Blackburn,* 104 So.2d 19 (Fla.1958); *Conner v. Sullivan,* 160 So.2d 120, 122 (Fla. 1st DCA 1963), *cert. denied,* 165 So.2d 176 (Fla.1964). *See generally* W. LaFave and A. Scott, Handbook on Criminal Law § 20, at 136–137 (1972).

Moreover, in addition to the requirement that a statute's purpose be for the general welfare, the guarantee of due process requires that the means selected shall have a reasonable and substantial relation to the object sought to be attained and shall not be unreasonable, arbitrary, or capricious. *See Nebbia v. New York,* 291 U.S. 502, 525, 54 S.Ct. 505, 510, 78 L.Ed. 940 (1934); *Lasky v. State Farm Insurance Co.,* 296 So.2d 9, 15 (Fla.1974); *L. Maxcy, Inc. v. Mayo,* 103 Fla. 552, 139 So. 121, 129 (1931).

Section 817.63 was obviously an attempt by the legislature to curtail credit card fraud. There is no question that the curtailment of credit card fraud is a legitimate goal within the scope of the state's police power. Having established that the legislative purpose is proper, we must now determine whether the means chosen by the legislature bears a rational relationship to the concededly proper goal. We determine that it does not.

In *Delmonico v. State,* 155 So.2d 368 (Fla.1963), this Court declared a statute that prohibited the possession of spearfishing equipment in an area of Monroe County to be unconstitutional. The Court explained:

> Fundamental to much of appellants' argument is the contention that the particular section of the statute here involved . . . is improper because it fails to require proof of the intent essential to any crime such as a showing that the equipment was possessed with an intent to put it to unlawful use. Instead the law penalizes the mere possession of equipment which in itself is wholly innocent and virtually indispensable to the enjoyment of the presently lawful and unrestricted right of appellants in common with the public at large to engage in spearfishing in waters on all sides of the area covered by the statute. . . .

> In order to meet constitutional limitations on police regulation, this prohibition, i.e. against possession of objects having a common and widespread lawful use, must under our previous decisions be reasonably "required as incidental to the accomplishment of the primary purpose of the Act." There is little doubt that the penalty against possession of such equipment will simplify the problem of enforcing the primary prohibition against spearfishing in the area covered by the statute. Expediency, however, is not the test, and we conclude that convenience of enforcement does not warrant the broad restriction imposed by Sec. 370.172(3).

Id. at 369–70 (footnotes omitted). *See also Foster v. State,* 286 So.2d 549, 551 (Fla. 1973) ("[i]t would be an unconstitutional act — in excess of the State's police power — to criminalize the simple possession of a screwdriver").

The same rationale was employed by this Court in *Robinson v. State*, 393 So.2d 1076 (Fla.1980). In that case, a statute that prohibited the wearing of any mask or covering "whereby any portion of the face is so hidden, concealed, or covered as to conceal the identity of the wearer" was deemed unconstitutional. The Court explained that the statute violated due process in that it was "susceptible of application to entirely innocent activities" and created "prohibitions that completely lack any rational basis." *Id.* at 1077. Compare *State v. Yu*, 400 So.2d 762, 765 (Fla.1981) (court found the challenged legislation bore a reasonable relationship to legitimate state objectives and did not violate due process), *appeal dismissed sub nom. Wall v. Florida*, 454 U.S. 1134, 102 S.Ct. 988, 71 L.Ed.2d 286 (1982).

* * *

In the instant case, as in *Delmonico*, *Robinson*, and *Walker*, the legislature has chosen a means which is not reasonably related to achieving its legitimate legislative purpose. It is unreasonable to criminalize the mere possession of embossing machines when such a prohibition clearly interferes with the legitimate personal and property rights of a number of individuals who use embossing machines in their businesses and for other non-criminal activities. As Judge Grimes phrased it in *Walker*, "without evidence of criminal behavior, the prohibition of this conduct lacks any rational relation to the legislative purpose" and "criminalizes activity that is otherwise inherently innocent." 444 So.2d at 1140. Such an exercise of the police power is unwarranted under the circumstances[3] and violates the due process clauses of our federal and state constitutions.

Accordingly, we find the portion of section 817.63 that prohibits the mere possession of embossing machines to be unconstitutional. The trial court was correct in dismissing the charges against Saiez based on that portion of the statute. We therefore affirm the district court's decision upholding the trial court's order dismissing those charges.

It is so ordered.

BOYD, C.J., and ADKINS, OVERTON, EHRLICH and SHAW, JJ., concur.

McDONALD, J., concurs in result only.

---

3. We note there are instances where the public interest may require the regulation or prohibition of innocent acts in order to reach or secure enforcement of law against evil acts. *See State v. Leone*, 118 So.2d at 784. The instant case is simply not one of those instances. This is evident from the subsequent legislative history of section 817.63. In the 1985 legislative session, section 817.63 was repealed and replaced with section 817.631, Florida Statutes (1985), which provides:

> Possession and transfer of credit-card-making equipment. — A person who receives, possesses, transfers, buys, sells, controls, or has custody of any credit-card-making equipment with intent that such equipment be used in the production of counterfeit credit cards violates this section and is subject to the penalties set forth in s. 817.67(2).

State v. Adkins

96 So. 3d 412 (Fla. 2012)

CANADY, J.

In this case we consider the constitutionality of the provisions of chapter 893, Florida Statutes (2011), the Florida Comprehensive Drug Abuse Prevention and Control Act, that provide that knowledge of the illicit nature of a controlled substance is not an element of any offenses under the chapter but that the lack of such knowledge is an affirmative defense.

Based on its conclusion that section 893.13, Florida Statutes (2011) — which creates offenses related to the sale, manufacture, delivery, and possession of controlled substances — is facially unconstitutional under the Due Process Clauses of the Florida and the United States Constitutions, the circuit court for the Twelfth Judicial Circuit issued an order granting motions to dismiss charges filed under section 893.13 in forty-six criminal cases. The circuit court reasoned that the requirements of due process precluded the Legislature from eliminating knowledge of the illicit nature of the substance as an element of the offenses under section 893.13. On appeal, the Second District Court of Appeal certified to this Court that the circuit court's judgment presents issues that require immediate resolution by this Court because the issues are of great public importance and will have a great effect on the proper administration of justice throughout the State. We have jurisdiction. *See* art. V, § 3(b)(5), Fla. Const.

For the reasons explained below, we conclude that the circuit court erred in determining the statute to be unconstitutional. Accordingly, we reverse the circuit court's order granting the motions to dismiss.

I. Background

Section 893.13, part of the Florida Comprehensive Drug Abuse Prevention and Control Act, provides in part that except as otherwise authorized "it is unlawful for any person to sell, manufacture, or deliver, or possess with intent to sell, manufacture, or deliver, a controlled substance" or "to be in actual or constructive possession of a controlled substance." § 893.13(1)(a), (6)(a), Fla. Stat. (2011). Depending on the controlled substance involved and the circumstances of the offense, a violation of section 893.13 can be punished as a misdemeanor, a third-degree felony, a second-degree felony, or a first-degree felony. *See, e.g.*, § 893.13(1)(a)(1), (1)(a)(2), (1)(a)(3), (1)(b), Fla. Stat. (2011).

Section 893.13 itself does not specify what mental state a defendant must possess in order to be convicted for selling, manufacturing, delivering, or possessing a controlled substance. In *Chicone v. State*, 684 So.2d 736 (Fla.1996), this Court addressed whether section 893.13 should be interpreted to include a mens rea — that is, a "guilty mind" — element. In reviewing a conviction for possession of cocaine, this Court determined that "guilty knowledge" was one of the elements of the crime of possession of a controlled substance and that the State was required to prove that

Chicone knew he possessed the substance and knew of the illicit nature of the substance in his possession. *Id.* at 738–41. This Court reasoned that the common law typically required "scienter or mens rea [as] a necessary element in the indictment and proof of every crime" and that the penalties facing defendants convicted under chapter 893, Florida Statutes, were much harsher than the usual penalties for crimes where a knowledge element is not required. *Chicone*, 684 So.2d at 741. This Court further reasoned that the Legislature "would have spoken more clearly" if it had intended to not require proof of guilty knowledge to convict under section 893.13. *Chicone*, 684 So.2d at 743.

More recently, in *Scott v. State*, 808 So.2d 166 (Fla.2002), this Court clarified that the "guilty knowledge" element of the crime of possession of a controlled substance contains two aspects: knowledge of the presence of the substance and knowledge of the illicit nature of the substance. 808 So.2d at 169. In addition, this Court clarified that the presumption of knowledge set out in *State v. Medlin*, 273 So.2d 394 (Fla.1973), and reiterated in *Chicone*—that a defendant's knowledge of the illicit nature of a controlled substance can be presumed from evidence that the defendant had possession of the controlled substance—can be employed only in cases in which the State proves actual, personal possession of the controlled substance. *Scott*, 808 So.2d at 171–72.

In response to this Court's decisions, the Legislature enacted a statute now codified in section 893.101, Florida Statutes (2011). Section 893.101 provides in full:

(1) The Legislature finds that the cases of *Scott v. State*, Slip opinion No. SC94701 [808 So.2d 166] (Fla.2002)[,] and *Chicone v. State*, 684 So.2d 736 (Fla.1996), holding that the state must prove that the defendant knew of the illicit nature of a controlled substance found in his or her actual or constructive possession, were contrary to legislative intent.

(2) The Legislature finds that *knowledge of the illicit nature of a controlled substance is not an element* of any offense under this chapter. *Lack of knowledge of the illicit nature of a controlled substance is an affirmative defense* to the offenses of this chapter.

(3) In those instances in which a defendant asserts the affirmative defense described in this section, the possession of a controlled substance, whether actual or constructive, shall give rise to a permissive presumption that the possessor knew of the illicit nature of the substance. It is the intent of the Legislature that, in those cases where such an affirmative defense is raised, the jury shall be instructed on the permissive presumption provided in this subsection.

(Emphasis added.) The statute thus expressly eliminates knowledge of the illicit nature of the controlled substance as an element of controlled substance offenses and expressly creates an affirmative defense of lack of knowledge of the illicit nature of the substance. The statute does not eliminate the element of knowledge of the presence of the substance, which we acknowledged in *Chicone*, 684 So.2d at 739–40 and *Scott*, 808 So.2d at 169.

* * *

The United States District Court for the Middle District of Florida recently concluded, however, that section 893.13 is unconstitutional because it does not require sufficient mens rea on the part of the defendant to sustain a conviction. *See Shelton v. Sec'y, Dep't of Corr.,* 802 F.Supp.2d 1289 (M.D.Fla.2011). First, the Middle District reasoned that to withstand constitutional scrutiny, section 893.13 should have provided lighter penalties, "such as fines or short jail sentences, not imprisonment in the state penitentiary." *Shelton,* 802 F.Supp.2d at 1301 (quoting *Staples v. United States,* 511 U.S. 600, 616, 114 S.Ct. 1793, 128 L.Ed.2d 608 (1994)). Second, the Middle District reasoned that because of the substantial social stigma associated with a felony conviction, a conviction under section 893.13 should require a guilty mind. *Shelton,* 802 F.Supp.2d at 1302. And third, assuming that a defendant could be convicted under section 893.13 for delivering or transferring a container without being aware of its contents, the Middle District concluded that section 893.13 violates due process by regulating potentially innocent conduct. *Shelton,* 802 F. Supp.2d at 1305.

Citing *Shelton* as persuasive — not binding — authority, the circuit court in this case concluded that section 893.13 is facially unconstitutional because it violates the Due Process Clauses of article I, section 9 of the Florida Constitution and the Fourteenth Amendment to the United States Constitution. The circuit court reasoned that the Legislature did not have authority to dispense with a mens rea element for a serious felony crime.

The State now appeals the circuit court's decision in this Court. The State asserts that section 893.13, as modified by section 893.101, is facially constitutional and that the circuit court therefore erred in granting the motions to dismiss.

II. Analysis

* * *

"The constitutionality of a statute is a question of law subject to de novo review." *Crist v. Ervin,* 56 So.3d 745, 747 (Fla.2011). In considering a challenge to the constitutionality of a statute, this Court is "obligated to accord legislative acts a presumption of constitutionality and to construe challenged legislation to effect a constitutional outcome whenever possible." *Fla. Dep't of Revenue v. City of Gainesville,* 918 So.2d 250, 256 (Fla.2005) (quoting *Fla. Dep't of Revenue v. Howard,* 916 So.2d 640, 642 (Fla.2005)). "[A] determination that a statute is facially unconstitutional means that no set of circumstances exists under which the statute would be valid." *Id.*

"Enacting laws — and especially criminal laws — is quintessentially a legislative function." *Fla. House of Representatives v. Crist,* 999 So.2d 601, 615 (Fla. 2008). "[T]he Legislature generally has broad authority to determine any requirement for intent or knowledge in the definition of a crime." *State v. Giorgetti,* 868 So.2d 512, 515 (Fla.2004). We thus have recognized that generally "[i]t is within the power of the Legislature to declare an act a crime regardless of the intent or knowledge of the violation thereof." *Coleman v. State ex rel. Jackson,* 140 Fla. 772, 193 So. 84, 86 (1939). "The doing of the act inhibited by the statute makes the crime[,] and moral turpitude or purity of motive and the knowledge or ignorance of its criminal character are immaterial circumstances on the question of guilt." *Id.*

Given the broad authority of the legislative branch to define the elements of crimes, the requirements of due process ordinarily do not preclude the creation of offenses which lack a guilty knowledge element.

* * *

... [B]oth the Supreme Court and this Court have repeatedly recognized that the legislative branch has broad discretion to omit a mens rea element from a criminal offense.

* * *

It is within the power of the legislature to declare conduct criminal without requiring specific criminal intent to achieve a certain result; that is, the legislature may punish conduct without regard to the mental attitude of the offender, so that the general intent of the accused to do the act is deemed to give rise to a presumption of intent to achieve the criminal result. The legislature may also dispense with a requirement that the actor be aware of the facts making his conduct criminal. A recent decision from the district court of appeal has recognized these principles. *State v. Oxx*, 417 So.2d 287 (Fla. 5th DCA 1982).

The question of whether conviction of a crime should require proof of a specific, as opposed to a general, criminal intent is a matter for the legislature to determine in defining the crime. The elements of a crime are derived from the statutory definition. There are some authorities to the effect that infamous crimes, crimes mala in se, or common-law crimes may not be defined by the legislature in such a way as to dispense with the element of specific intent, but these authorities are suspect.

Gray, 435 So.2d at 819–20 (some citations omitted).

In a limited category of circumstances, the omission of a mens rea element from the definition of a criminal offense has been held to violate due process.

* * *

In *Schmitt v. State*, 590 So.2d 404, 413 (Fla.1991), we concluded that "a due process violation occurs if a criminal statute's means is not rationally related to its purposes and, as a result, it criminalizes innocuous conduct." Specifically, we considered a statute prohibiting the possession of a depiction involving "actual physical contact with a [minor] person's clothed or unclothed genitals, pubic area, buttocks, or if such person is a female, breast." *Id.* at 408 (quoting § 827.071(1)(g), Fla. Stat. (1987)). We held that the statute violated due process because it criminalized family photographs of innocent caretaker-child conduct, such as bathing the child or changing a diaper. While Florida's civil child abuse statute expressly excluded from the definition of sexual child abuse physical contact that "may reasonably be construed to be a normal caretaker responsibility," the criminal statute declared depictions of such acts to be a felony. *Id.* at 413 (quoting § 415.503(17)(d), Fla. Stat. (1987)).

... [T]his Court determined that statutes criminalizing the possession of embossing machines, lawfully obtained drugs not in their original packaging, and spearfishing equipment — without requiring proof of intent to use the items illegally — were not reasonably related to achieving a legitimate legislative purpose and interfered with the property rights of individuals who used those items for non-criminal purposes. *See State v. Saiez,* 489 So.2d 1125 (Fla.1986); S, *State v. Walker,* 444 So.2d 1137 (Fla. 2d DCA), *aff'd,* 461 So.2d 108 (Fla.1984) (adopting district court of appeal's opinion); *Delmonico v. State,* 155 So.2d 368 (Fla.1963).

* * *

[S]ections 893.13 and 893.101 — unlike the provisions we invalidated in *Schmitt, 1969 Piper Navajo, Saiez, Walker,* and *Delmonico* — are rationally related to the Legislature's goal of controlling substances that have a high potential for abuse, and the statutes do not interfere with any constitutionally protected rights. The Legislature tailored section 893.13 to permit legitimate, medical uses of controlled substances but to prohibit non-medically necessary uses of those substances. Section 893.13 expressly excludes from criminal liability individuals who possess a controlled substance that "was lawfully obtained from a practitioner or pursuant to a valid prescription," § 893.13(6)(a), Fla. Stat. (2011), and the following persons and entities who handle medically necessary controlled substances as part of their profession: pharmacists, medical practitioners, hospital employees, government officials working in their official capacity, common carriers, pharmaceutical companies, and the employees and agents of the above, § 893.13(9), Fla. Stat. (2011).

Because there is no legally recognized use for controlled substances outside the circumstances identified by the statute, prohibiting the sale, manufacture, delivery, or possession of those substances without requiring proof of knowledge of the illicit nature of the substances does not criminalize innocuous conduct or "impinge[ ] on the exercise of some constitutionally protected freedom." *Gray,* 435 So.2d at 819. Because the statutory provisions at issue here do not have the potential to curtail constitutionally protected speech, they are materially distinguishable from statutes that implicate the possession of materials protected by the First Amendment, such as those at issue in *Smith* and *X-Citement Video.* There is no constitutional right to possess contraband. "[A]ny interest in possessing contraband cannot be deemed 'legitimate.'" *Illinois v. Caballes,* 543 U.S. 405, 408, 125 S.Ct. 834, 160 L.Ed.2d 842 (2005) (quoting *United States v. Jacobsen,* 466 U.S. 109, 123, 104 S.Ct. 1652, 80 L.Ed.2d 85 (1984)).

Nor is there a protected right to be ignorant of the nature of the property in one's possession. *See Turner v. United States,* 396 U.S. 398, 417, 90 S.Ct. 642, 24 L.Ed.2d 610 (1970) ("'Common' sense tells us that those who traffic in heroin will inevitably become aware that the product they deal in is smuggled, *unless they practice a studied ignorance to which they are not entitled.*") (emphasis added) (citation and footnotes omitted); *Balint,* 258 U.S. at 254, 42 S.Ct. 301 (upholding as constitutional a statute that "require[d] every person dealing in drugs to ascertain at his peril whether that which he sells comes within the inhibition of the statute"). Just as "common sense and experience" dictate that a person in possession of Treasury checks addressed to another person should be "aware of the high probability that the checks were stolen," a person in possession of a controlled substance should be aware of the nature of the substance as an illegal drug. *Barnes v. United States,* 412 U.S. 837, 845, 93 S.Ct. 2357, 37 L.Ed.2d 380 (1973). Because controlled substances are valuable, common sense indicates that they are generally handled with care. As a result, possession without awareness of the illicit nature of the substance is highly unusual. *[Citation omitted.]*

Any concern that entirely innocent conduct will be punished with a criminal sanction under chapter 893 is obviated by the statutory provision that allows a defendant to raise the affirmative defense of an absence of knowledge of the illicit nature of the controlled substance. In the unusual circumstance where an individual has actual or constructive possession of a controlled substance but has no knowledge that the substance is illicit, the defendant may present such a defense to the jury.

Because we conclude that the Legislature did not exceed its constitutional authority in redefining section 893.13 to not require proof that the defendant knew of the illicit nature of the controlled substance, we likewise conclude that the Legislature did not violate due process by defining lack of such knowledge as an affirmative defense to the offenses set out in chapter 893. The Legislature's decision to treat lack of such knowledge as an affirmative defense does not unconstitutionally shift the burden of proof of a criminal offense to the defendant.

* * *

Here, the Legislature's decision to make the absence of knowledge of the illicit nature of the controlled substance an affirmative defense is constitutional. Under section 893.13, as modified by section 893.101, the State is not required to prove that the defendant had knowledge of the illicit nature of the controlled substance in order to convict the defendant of one of the defined offenses. The conduct the Legislature seeks to curtail is the sale, manufacture, delivery, or possession of a controlled substance, regardless of the defendant's subjective intent. As a result, the defendant can concede all elements of the offense but still coherently raise the "separate issue," *Patterson,* 432 U.S. at 207, 97 S.Ct. 2319, of whether the defendant lacked knowledge of the illicit nature of the controlled substance. The affirmative defense does not ask the defendant to disprove something that the State must prove in order to convict, but instead provides a defendant with an opportunity to explain why his or her admittedly illegal conduct should not be punished. "It is plain enough that if [the sale, manufacture, delivery, or possession of a controlled substance] is shown, the State intends to deal with the defendant as a [criminal] unless he demonstrates the mitigating circumstances." *Patterson,* 432 U.S. at 206, 97 S.Ct. 2319. Thus, the affirmative defense does not improperly shift the burden of proof to the defendant.

III. Conclusion

In enacting section 893.101, the Legislature eliminated from the definitions of the offenses in chapter 893 the element that the defendant has knowledge of the illicit nature of the controlled substance and created the affirmative defense of lack of such knowledge. The statutory provisions do not violate any requirement of due process articulated by this Court or the Supreme Court. In the unusual circumstance where a person possesses a controlled substance inadvertently, establishing the affirmative defense available under section 893.101 will preclude the conviction of the defendant. Based on the foregoing, we conclude that the circuit court erred in granting the motions to dismiss and we reverse the circuit court's order.

It is so ordered.

POLSTON, C.J., and LABARGA, J., concur.

PARIENTE, J., concurs in result with an opinion. [This opinion is omitted.]

LEWIS, J., concurs in result.

QUINCE, J., dissents.

PERRY, J., dissents with an opinion.

PERRY, J., dissenting.

I respectfully dissent. I cannot overstate my opposition to the majority's opinion. In my view, it shatters bedrock constitutional principles and builds on a foundation of flawed "common sense."

Innocent Possession

The majority pronounces that "common sense and experience" dictate that "a person in possession of a controlled substance should be aware of the nature of the substance as an illegal drug" and further that, "[b]ecause controlled substances are valuable, common sense indicates that they are generally handled with care. As a result, possession without awareness of the illicit nature of the substance is highly unusual." Majority op. at 421–22.

But common sense to me dictates that the potential for innocent possession is not so "highly unusual" as the majority makes it out to be.

> [T]he simple acts of possession and delivery are part of daily life. Each of us engages in actual possession of all that we have on our person and in our hands, and in constructive possession of all that we own, wherever it may be located. Each of us engages in delivery when we hand a colleague a pen, a friend a cup of coffee, a stranger the parcel she just dropped.

State v. Washington, 18 Fla. L. Weekly Supp. 1129, 1133 (Fla. 11th Cir.Ct. Aug. 17, 2011) (footnote omitted), *rev'd,* ___ So.3d ___ (Fla. 3d DCA 2012). "[C]arrying luggage on and off of public transportation; carrying bags in and out of stores and buildings; carrying book bags and purses in schools and places of business and work; transporting boxes via commercial transportation—the list extends *ad infinitum.*" *Shelton v. Sec'y, Dep't of Corr.,* 802 F.Supp.2d 1289, 1305 (M.D.Fla.2011).

754   7 · THE DECLARATION OF RIGHTS AND THE TAKING OF PROPERTY

Given this reality, "[i]t requires little imagination to visualize a situation in which a third party hands [a] controlled substance to an unknowing individual who then can be charged with and subsequently convicted . . . without ever being aware of the nature of the substance he was given." *State v. Brown,* 389 So.2d 48, 51 (La.1980) (finding that such a situation offends the conscience and concluding that "the 'unknowing' possession of a dangerous drug cannot be made criminal"). For example,

> [c]onsider the student in whose book bag a classmate hastily stashes his drugs to avoid imminent detection. The bag is then given to another for safekeeping. Caught in the act, the hapless victim is guilty based upon the only two elements of the statute: delivery (actual, constructive, or attempted) and the illicit nature of the substance. *See* FLA. STAT. §§ 893.02(6), 893.13(1) (a). The victim would be faced with the Hobson's choice of pleading guilty or going to trial where he is presumed guilty because he is in fact guilty of the two elements. He must then prove his innocence for lack of knowledge against the permissive presumption the statute imposes that he does in fact have guilty knowledge. Such an outcome is not countenanced under applicable constitutional proscriptions.

Shelton, 802 F.Supp.2d at 1308. The trial court order presently under review provides even more examples of innocent possession: a letter carrier who delivers a package containing unprescribed Adderall; a roommate who is unaware that the person who shares his apartment has hidden illegal drugs in the common areas of the home; a mother who carries a prescription pill bottle in her purse, unaware that the pills have been substituted for illegally obtained drugs by her teenage daughter, who placed them in the bottle to avoid detection. *State v. Adkins,* Nos. 2011 CF 002001, et al., slip op. at 14 (Fla. 12th Cir.Ct. Sept. 14, 2011).

> As the examples illustrate, even people who are normally diligent in inspecting and organizing their possessions may find themselves unexpectedly in violation of this law, and without the notice necessary to defend their rights. The illegal drugs subject to the statute include tablets which can also be and are commonly and legally prescribed. A medicine which is legally available, can be difficult for innocent parties to recognize as illegal, even if they think they know the contents. For example, the mother of the teenage daughter carries the pill bottle, taking it at face value as a bottle for the pills it ought to contain, even during the traffic stop at which she consents to [a] search of her belongings, confident in her own innocence. These examples represent incidents of innocence which should be protected by the requirement of [a] *mens rea* element, particularly given the serious penalties for the crime of drug possession required under Florida law.

Id. at 14–15. Other examples of innocent possession spring easily and immediately to mind: a driver who rents a car in which a past passenger accidentally dropped a baggie of marijuana under the seat; a traveler who mistakenly retrieves from a luggage carousel a bag identical to her own containing Oxycodone; a helpful college student who drives a carload of a friend's possessions to the friend's new apartment, unaware that a stash of heroin is tucked within those possessions; an ex-wife who is framed by an ex-husband who planted cocaine in her home in an effort to get the upper hand in a bitter custody dispute. The list is endless.

The majority nevertheless states that there is not "a protected right to be ignorant of the nature of the property in one's possession," elaborating that "'[c]ommon' sense tells us that those who traffic in heroin will inevitably become aware that the product they deal in is smuggled, *unless they practice a studied ignorance to which they are not entitled.*" Majority op. at 421 (quoting *Turner v. United States,* 396 U.S. 398, 417, 90 S.Ct. 642, 24 L.Ed.2d 610 (1970)). But the above examples, and surely countless others, do not involve such a "studied ignorance." Rather, they involve genuinely innocent citizens who will be snared in the overly broad net of section 893.13. And therein lies the point:

> Section 893.13 does not punish the drug dealer who possesses or delivers controlled substances. It punishes *anyone* who possesses or delivers controlled substances — however inadvertently, however accidentally, however unintentionally. . . . What distinguishes innocent possession and innocent delivery from guilty possession and guilty delivery is not merely what we possess, not merely what we deliver, *but what we intend.* As to that — as to the state of mind that distinguishes non-culpable from culpable possession or delivery — § 893.13 refuses to make a distinction. The speckled flock and the clean are, for its purposes, all one.

Washington, 18 Fla. L. Weekly Supp. at 1133.

Presumption of Innocence and Burden of Proof

The majority rather cavalierly offers that, "[i]n the unusual circumstance where a person possesses a controlled substance inadvertently, establishing the affirmative defense available under section 893.101 will preclude the conviction of the defendant." Majority op. at 423. As discussed at length above, I do not agree that innocent possession is such an "unusual circumstance." Moreover, the majority's passing reference to simply "establishing the affirmative defense" implies that it is an inconsequential and easy thing to do. The majority further minimizes the enormity of the task, making it seem even friendly, in stating that "[t]he affirmative defense does not ask the defendant to disprove something that the State must prove in order to convict, but instead provides a defendant with an opportunity to explain why his or her admittedly illegal conduct should not be punished." *Id.* at 423.

But the affirmative defense at issue is hardly a friendly opportunity; rather, it is an onerous burden that strips defendants — including genuinely innocent defendants — of their constitutional presumption of innocence. "The principle that there is a presumption of innocence in favor of the accused is the undoubted law, axiomatic and elementary, and its enforcement lies at the foundation of the administration of our criminal law." [Citation omitted.] "What will become of the innocent?" The answer to that question in the present context is as inevitable as it is disturbing. Under the majority's decision and the above examples, the innocent will from the start be presumed guilty. The innocent will be deprived of their right to simply deny the charges and hold the State to its burden of proving them guilty beyond a reasonable doubt. The innocent will instead be forced to assert an affirmative defense, whereupon "the possession of a controlled substance, whether actual or constructive, shall give rise to a permissive presumption that the possessor knew of the illicit nature of the substance." § 893.101(3), Fla. Stat. (2011).

The innocent will then have no realistic choice but to shoulder the burden of proof and present evidence to overcome that presumption. *See generally Stimus v. State,* 995 So.2d 1149, 1151 (Fla. 5th DCA 2008) (recognizing that a defendant who raised an affirmative defense "had the burden to establish the defense and present evidence" regarding same). The innocent will thus have to bear the considerable time and expense involved in conducting discovery, calling witnesses, and otherwise crafting a case for their innocence — all while the State, with its vastly superior resources, should be bearing the burden of proving their guilt.

The innocent will then hear their jury instructed on the permissive presumption that they knew of the illicit nature of the substance in question. § 893.101(3), Fla. Stat. (2011). Finally, the innocent — in I fear far too many cases — may be found guilty, convicted, and sentenced to up to life in prison. *See Shelton,* 802 F.Supp.2d at 1302 ("Sentences of fifteen years, thirty years, and life imprisonment [possible under section 893.13] are not by any measure 'relatively small.' ").

Such convictions and sentences will be a disgrace when, on a profoundly foundational level, "the law holds that it is better that ten guilty persons escape than that one innocent suffer." *Coffin,* 156 U.S. at 456, 15 S.Ct. 394 (quoting 2 William Blackstone, Commentaries *357). The majority opinion breaks that sacred law and, as discussed below, threatens bedrock principles of the presumption of innocence and burden of proof in contexts well beyond the one at hand.

* * *

Conclusion

"Brave" indeed, in the most foreboding sense of that word. The majority opinion sets alarming precedent, both in the context of section 893.13 and beyond. It makes neither legal nor common sense to me, offends all notions of due process, and threatens core principles of the presumption of innocence and burden of proof. I would find section 893.13 facially unconstitutional and affirm the trial court order under review.

Jackson v. State

191 So. 3d 423 (Fla. 2016)

QUINCE, J.

[For the facts of this case, see page 693 of this text.]

Substantive due process protects fundamental rights that are so "implicit in the concept of ordered liberty" that "neither liberty nor justice would exist if they were sacrificed." *Palko v. Conn.*, 302 U.S. 319, 325–26, 58 S.Ct. 149, 82 L.Ed. 288 (1937). Analyzing a substantive due process claim begins with a "careful description of the asserted right." *Reno v. Flores,* 507 U.S. 292, 302, 113 S.Ct. 1439, 123 L. Ed.2d 1 (1993). As discussed above, eligibility for youthful offender sentencing is not a fundamental right; instead, eligibility is at the discretion of the trial court. Therefore, section 958.04(1)(b) need only satisfy the rational basis test. Under substantive due process, the test "is whether the statute bears a rational relation to a permissible legislative objective that is not discriminatory, arbitrary, capricious, or oppressive." *Lasky v. State Farm Ins. Co.,* 296 So.2d 9, 15 (Fla.1974). Courts will not be concerned with whether the particular legislation in question is the most prudent choice, or is a perfect panacea, to cure the ill or achieve the interest intended. If there is a legitimate state interest that the legislation aims to effect, and if the legislation is a reasonably related means to achieve the intended end, it will be upheld. *State v. Walker,* 444 So.2d 1137, 1138–39 (Fla. 2d DCA), *aff'd,* 461 So.2d 108 (Fla.1984).

The Youthful Offender statutes are the means to achieve the State's goal of providing rehabilitation to young offenders and preventing association between young offenders and older criminals. Section 958.04(1)(b) as amended serves a legitimate state interest by ensuring that only those who are truly youthful are eligible for youthful offender sentencing. By restricting eligibility to those who are younger than 21 at the time of sentencing, the legislation guarantees that young offenders will not associate with older, more experienced offenders. For this reason, section 958.04(1)(b) does not violate due process.

Jackson has failed to demonstrate that section 958.04(1)(b), as amended, violates equal protection or due process. Accordingly, we affirm the Fourth District.

It is so ordered.

LABARGA, C.J., and LEWIS, CANADY, POLSTON, and PERRY, JJ., concur.

PARIENTE, J., dissents with an opinion.

[The dissenting opinion of Justice Pariente is omitted.]

2. A Higher Level of Scrutiny

Not all substantive due process claims are measured by the rational/reasonable basis test. Consider the following comment from *Mizrahi v. North Miami Medical*

Center, Ltd.[21] Note also how the court correctly equates the rational/reasonable basis test in equal protection and substantive due process. It might also have included the right to acquire, possess, and protect property.[22]

> As appellants did not raise a substantive due process challenge to section 768.21(8), either at the trial level or on appeal, we need not address the statute's constitutionality with regard to substantive due process. Notwithstanding this, we do not find that substantive due process is at all implicated here. The constitutional guarantee of substantive due process protects *fundamental* rights from encroachment by the government, and fundamental rights are those rights flowing from either the federal or Florida constitution. *See De Ayala v. Florida Farm Bureau Cas. Ins. Co.,* 543 So.2d 204, 206 (Fla.1989). Certainly there is no such constitutional right to wrongful death damages; wrongful death actions did not exist at common law and were created by the legislature. *See White v. Clayton,* 323 So.2d 573, 575 (Fla.1975). Thus, no fundamental right is implicated here. Further, where no fundamental right is at stake, the standard for evaluating substantive due process challenges is virtually identical to the rational basis test for evaluating equal protection challenges. *See* 10 Fla. Jur.2d, *Constitutional Law* § 427 (1998), citing *Wood v. United States,* 866 F.2d 1367, 1371 (11th Cir. 1989). Therefore, the rational basis analysis we apply to appellants' claim would likewise apply to a substantive due process claim.[23]

3. Due Process and Conclusive Presumptions

Castellanos v. Next Door Co.

192 So. 3d 431 (Fla. 2016)

PARIENTE, J.

This case asks us to evaluate the constitutionality of the mandatory fee schedule in section 440.34, Florida Statutes (2009), which eliminates the requirement of a reasonable attorney's fee to the successful claimant. Considering that the right of a claimant to obtain a reasonable attorney's fee has been a critical feature of the workers' compensation law, we conclude that the mandatory fee schedule in section 440.34, which creates an irrebuttable presumption that precludes any consideration of whether the fee award is reasonable to compensate the attorney, is unconstitutional under both the Florida and United States Constitutions as a violation of due process. *See* art. I, § 9, Fla. Const.; U.S. Const. amend. XIV, § 1.[1] . . .

---

21. 712 So. 2d 826 (Fla. 3d Dist. Ct. App. 1998).

22. *See supra* page 517.

23. 712 So. 2d 826, 828 n. 3.

1. Castellanos challenges the constitutionality of the statute on numerous grounds, arguing that it violates the right of access to courts under article I, section 21, of the Florida Constitution; the separation of powers doctrine; due process; equal protection; the right to contract and speak

The Petitioner, Marvin Castellanos, was injured during the course of his employment with the Respondent, Next Door Company. Through the assistance of an attorney, Castellanos prevailed in his workers' compensation claim, after the attorney successfully refuted numerous defenses raised by the employer and its insurance carrier. However, because section 440.34 limits a claimant's ability to recover attorney's fees to a sliding scale based on the amount of workers' compensation benefits obtained, the fee awarded to Castellanos' attorney amounted to only $1.53 per hour for 107.2 hours of work determined by the Judge of Compensation Claims (JCC) to be "reasonable and necessary" in litigating this complex case.

Castellanos had no ability to challenge the reasonableness of the $1.53 hourly rate, and both the JCC and the First District were precluded by section 440.34 from assessing whether the fee award — calculated in strict compliance with the statutory fee schedule — was reasonable. Instead, the statute presumes that the ultimate fee will always be reasonable to compensate the attorney, without providing any mechanism for refutation.

The right of a claimant to obtain a reasonable attorney's fee when successful in securing benefits has been considered a critical feature of the workers' compensation law since 1941. *See Murray v. Mariner Health*, 994 So.2d 1051, 1057–58 (Fla.2008). From its outset, the workers' compensation law was designed to assure, as the current legislative statement of purpose provides, "the quick and efficient delivery of disability and medical benefits to an injured worker." § 440.015, Fla. Stat. (2009).

Yet, while the Legislature has continued to enunciate this purpose, in reality, the workers' compensation system has become increasingly complex to the detriment of the claimant, who depends on the assistance of a competent attorney to navigate the thicket.[3] Indeed, as this Court long ago observed, allowing a claimant to "engage competent legal assistance" actually "discourages the carrier from unnecessarily resisting claims" and encourages attorneys to undertake representation in non-frivolous claims, "realizing that a reasonable fee will be paid for [their] labor." *Ohio Cas. Grp. v. Parrish*, 350 So.2d 466, 470 (Fla.1977).

---

freely; the right to be rewarded for industry; and constitutes an unconstitutional taking of property. We decide the constitutional issue in this case on the basis of the constitutional rights of the claimant under due process and do not address the other grounds raised.

3. To name just a few of the ways in which the workers' compensation system has become increasingly complex and difficult, if not impossible, for an injured worker to successfully navigate without the assistance of an attorney: (1) the elimination of the provision that the workers' compensation law be liberally construed in favor of the injured worker, § 440.015, Fla. Stat.; (2) reductions in the duration of temporary benefits, § 440.15(2) (a), Fla. Stat.; (3) an extensive fraud and penalty provision, § 440.105, Fla. Stat.; (4) a heightened standard of "major contributing cause" that applies in a majority of cases rather than the less stringent "proximate cause" standard in civil cases, § 440.09(1), Fla. Stat.; (5) a heightened burden of proof of "clear and convincing evidence" in some types of cases, §§ 440.02(1), 440.09(1), Fla. Stat.; (6) the elimination of the "opt out" provision, §§ 440.015, 440.03, Fla. Stat.; and (7) the addition of an offer of settlement provision that allows only the employer, and not the claimant, to make an offer to settle, § 440.34(2), Fla. Stat.

We reject the assertion of Justice Polston's dissenting opinion that our holding "turns this Court's well-established precedent regarding facial challenges on its head." Dissenting op. at 455 (Polston, J.). It is immaterial to our holding whether, as Justice Polston points out, the statutory fee schedule could, in some cases, result in a constitutionally adequate fee. It certainly could.

But the facial constitutional due process issue, based on our well-established precedent regarding conclusive irrebuttable presumptions, is that the statute precludes *every* injured worker from challenging the reasonableness of the fee award. *See Recchi Am. Inc. v. Hall,* 692 So.2d 153, 154 (Fla.1997) (clarifying that its holding "invalidates the irrebuttable presumption altogether," including as applied to certain situations). It is the irrebuttable statutory presumption — not the ultimate statutory fee awarded in a given case — that we hold unconstitutional.

* * *

B. Violation of Due Process

Section 440.34 provides a fee schedule that must be followed in every case by the JCC in calculating and awarding attorney's fees, based on the amount of benefits recovered by the claimant. The statute does not allow for any consideration of whether the fee is reasonable or any way for the JCC or the judiciary on review to alter the fee, even if the resulting fee is grossly inadequate — or grossly excessive — in comparison to the amount of time reasonably and necessarily expended to obtain the benefits.

Stated another way, the statute establishes a conclusive irrebuttable presumption that the formula will produce an adequate fee in every case. This is clearly not true, and the inability of any injured worker to challenge the reasonableness of the fee award in his or her individual case is a facial constitutional due process issue.

In considering the constitutionality of the statute, we do not view the absolute limitation from the point of view of the attorney's rights, because the attorney always has the option to refuse representation, especially in complex low-value claims. Rather, we view the conclusive irrebuttable presumption in the context of the complete frustration of the entire workers' compensation scheme designed to provide workers with "full medical care and wage-loss payments for total or partial disability regardless of fault and without the delay and uncertainty of tort litigation." *Martinez v. Scanlan,* 582 So.2d 1167, 1172 (Fla.1991). We accordingly reject the argument that Castellanos, as the claimant rather than the attorney, lacks standing to raise the constitutional violation.

As the First District has explained, the injured worker, rather than the attorney, is the "true party in interest." *Pilon,* 574 So.2d at 1201. A "barrier to review a decision to award a fee," the First District stated in *Pilon,* "could ultimately result in a net loss of attorneys willing to represent workers' compensation claimants." *Id.* This in turn would result "in a chilling effect on claimants' ability to challenge employer/carrier decisions to deny claims for benefits and disrupt the equilibrium of the parties' rights intended by the legislature in enacting section 440.34." *Id.*

Because Castellanos has standing to challenge the constitutionality of the statute, we turn to the merits of his argument. This Court has set forth the following three-part test for determining the constitutionality of a conclusive statutory presumption, such as the fee schedule provided in section 440.34: (1) whether the concern of the Legislature was "reasonably aroused by the possibility of an abuse which it legitimately desired to avoid"; (2) whether there was a "reasonable basis for a conclusion that the statute would protect against its occurrence"; and (3) whether "the expense and other difficulties of individual determinations justify the inherent imprecision of a conclusive presumption." *Recchi*, 692 So.2d at 154 (citing *Markham v. Fogg*, 458 So.2d 1122, 1125 (Fla.1984)).

In *Recchi*, this Court fully adopted the reasoning of the First District, which concluded that a statute violated the constitutional right to due process where it provided no opportunity for an employee working in a drug-free workplace program to rebut the presumption that the intoxication or influence of drugs contributed to his or her injury. *Id.* "According to the district court of appeal, the irrebuttable presumption failed the three-pronged test because the expense and other difficulties of individual determinations did not justify the inherent imprecision of the conclusive presumption." *Id.* (citing *Hall v. Recchi Am. Inc.*, 671 So.2d 197, 201 (Fla. 1st DCA 1996)).

The same, and more, can be said of the conclusive presumption in section 440.34. We address each prong of the due process test to explain why.

1. Whether the Concern of the Legislature was Reasonably Aroused by the Possibility of an Abuse Which it Legitimately Desired to Avoid

As to the first prong, one of the Legislature's asserted justifications for the fee schedule is to standardize fees. *See Alderman v. Fla. Plastering*, 805 So.2d 1097, 1100 (Fla. 1st DCA 2002) ("Section 440.34(1), Florida Statutes [,] reflects a legislative intent to standardize attorney's fee awards in workers' compensation cases."). The conclusive presumption certainly does that, although it does so in a manner that lacks any relationship to the amount of time and effort actually expended by the attorney. As the First District has recognized, a fee schedule has typically been considered merely a starting point in determining an appropriate fee award. *See, e.g., Fumigation Dep't v. Pearson*, 559 So.2d 587, 590 (Fla. 1st DCA 1989) ("For purposes of determining an attorney's fee award under section 440.34(1), Florida Statutes, a starting point in the analysis is the amount of benefits obtained for the claimant by his attorney."); *Martin Marietta Corp. v. Glumb*, 523 So.2d 1190, 1195 (Fla. 1st DCA 1988) ("Although the amount of benefits obtained is a significant factor, it is not determinative of the maximum amount that can be awarded as a fee.").

To the extent the Legislature was also concerned about the excessiveness of attorney's fee awards, however, this is not a reasonable basis for the unyielding formulaic fee schedule. Other factors, such as Rule Regulating The Florida Bar 4–1.5, already prevent against excessive fees. That Rule provides a number of factors to be considered as a guide to determining a reasonable fee, including, among many others, "the time and labor required, the novelty, complexity, and difficulty of the questions involved, and the skill requisite to perform the legal service properly." R. Reg. Fla. Bar 4–1.5(b)(1)(A). In fact, since *Lee Engineering*, this Court has made clear that it does not condone excessive fee awards.

The effect of the limitation on the fee amounts paid to claimants' attorneys is revealed in the mandatory annual reporting of all attorney's fees to the Office of the Judges of Compensation Claims, as required by section 440.345, Florida Statutes. The report demonstrates the one-sided nature of the fees paid, with claimants' attorneys consistently receiving a lower percentage of the total fees than defense attorneys and the gap only increasing over the past decade. . . . Further, claimants' attorneys are prohibited by statute from negotiating a different fee with the claimant, and the JCC is precluded from approving a different fee — even if the negotiated rate would actually produce a more reasonable fee than the statutory fee schedule. *See* § 440.34(1), Fla. Stat. ("The judge of compensation claims shall not approve a compensation order, a joint stipulation for lump- sum settlement, a stipulation or agreement between a claimant and his or her attorney, or any other agreement related to benefits under this chapter which provides for an attorney's fee in excess of the amount permitted by this section."). In fact, it is a *crime* for an attorney to accept any fee not approved by the JCC, which is of course constrained to award a fee only pursuant to the statutory fee schedule. *See* § 440.105(3)(c), Fla. Stat. ("It is unlawful for any attorney or other person, in his or her individual capacity or in his or her capacity as a public or private employee, or for any firm, corporation, partnership, or association to receive any fee or other consideration or any gratuity from a person on account of services rendered for a person in connection with any proceedings arising under this chapter, unless such fee, consideration, or gratuity is approved by a judge of compensation claims or by the Deputy Chief Judge of Compensation Claims.").[4]

2. Whether There was a Reasonable Basis for a Conclusion That the Statute Would Protect Against its Occurrence

Even assuming, however, that the first prong of the due process test is satisfied because the Legislature desired to avoid excessive fees, there is no reasonable basis to assume that the conclusive fee schedule actually serves this function — as required by the second prong of the test. Excessive fees can still result under the fee schedule, just as inadequate ones can — for instance, in a simple and straightforward case where the claimant obtains a substantial amount of benefits. *See Murray*, 994 So.2d

---

4. We note that the First District Court of Appeal recently concluded in an as-applied constitutional challenge to sections 440.105 and 440.34 that the restrictions in those sections are unconstitutional violations of a claimant's right to free speech, free association, petition, and right to form contracts, and held "that the criminal penalties of section 440.105(3)(c), Florida Statutes, are unenforceable against an attorney representing a workers' compensation client seeking to obtain benefits under chapter 440, as limited by other provisions." *Miles v. City of Edgewater Police Dep't*, 190 So.3d 171, 184 (Fla. 1st DCA 2016). The issue of the constitutionality of that provision is not before us.

at 1057. The fee schedule does nothing to adjust fees downward when the recovery is high, even if the time required to obtain significant benefits was relatively minor and the resulting fee is actually excessive.

As this Court stated in *Murray:*

> In some cases such as the present case, the amount of benefits is small, but the legal issues are complex and time consuming, and require skill, knowledge, and experience to recover the small but payable benefits. In other cases, the amount of benefits is substantial, but the legal issues are simple and direct, and do not require exceptional skill, knowledge, and experience. In the former case, a mandatory, rigid application of the formula results in an inadequate fee; in the latter, such application of the formula results in an excessive fee.

Id. at 1057 n. 4.

The First District has also observed that a customary fee based on an hourly rate is likely to be more significant in a case in which the value of the attorney's services greatly exceeds the financial benefit obtained on behalf of the client. *See Alderman,* 805 So.2d at 1100. For example, the work necessary to establish a connection between chemical exposure and respiratory illness might not bear a reasonable relationship to the benefit obtained, and to apply the statutory formula in such a case might result in a fee that is inadequate and unfair. *See Glumb,* 523 So.2d at 1195. In other words, the elimination of any authority for the JCC or the judiciary on review to alter the fee award completely frustrates the purpose of the workers' compensation scheme.

3. Whether the Expense and Other Difficulties of Individual Determinations Justify the Inherent Imprecision of a Conclusive Presumption

But even if none of that were true, the third prong of the test for evaluating a conclusive presumption — that the feasibility of individual assessments of what constitutes a reasonable fee in a given case must justify the inherent imprecision of the conclusive presumption — certainly weighs heavily against the constitutionality of the fee schedule. Indeed, the JCC in this case actually made these individual determinations, but the inherent imprecision of the conclusive presumption prevented both the JCC and the First District from doing anything about the unreasonableness of the resulting fee.

Courts have, in fact, long operated under the view that the fee schedule was merely a starting point, and judges of compensation claims have determined, awarded, and approved attorney's fees without undue expense or difficulty to avoid unfairness and arbitrariness since the reasonable attorney's fee provision was adopted in 1941. Under prior versions of the statutory scheme, the JCC considered legislatively enumerated factors, and, after the deletion of these factors, continued to consider whether the fee was reasonable and not excessive. *See, e.g., S. Bell Tel. & Tel. Co. v. Rollins,* 390 So.2d 93, 95 (Fla. 1st DCA 1980); *E. Coast Tire Co. v. Denmark,* 381 So.2d

336, 339–40 (Fla. 1st DCA 1980). This type of review to control abuse, limit excessive fees, and award reasonable fees provides no basis for concern about abuse.

The cases cited in opposition are readily distinguishable. Although the United States Supreme Court held that the unreasonably low fee provisions at issue in those cases passed constitutional muster despite the existence of a fee schedule, the judiciary still had discretionary authority to raise or lower the final fee according to articulated standards — unlike the conclusive presumption established by section 440.34.

For example, the Longshore and Harbor Workers' Compensation Act (LHWCA), the federal statutory workers' compensation scheme, which provides benefits to maritime workers, prohibits an attorney from receiving a fee unless approved by the appropriate agency or court. This provision has been upheld by the United States Supreme Court. *See U.S. Dep't of Labor v. Triplett,* 494 U.S. 715, 721–26, 110 S.Ct. 1428, 108 L.Ed.2d 701 (1990) (upholding the LHWCA provision, as incorporated into the Black Lung Benefits Act of 1972, against Fifth Amendment Due Process challenge).

Unlike the conclusive fee schedule in section 440.34, however, the Code of Federal Regulations creates factors to guide the adjudicator in awarding a fee "reasonably commensurate with the necessary work done." *Triplett,* 494 U.S. at 718, 110 S.Ct. 1428. In other words, the fee provision in the LHWCA does not establish a conclusive irrebuttable presumption without consideration of whether the fee is "reasonable," but actually allows for the award of a "reasonable attorney's fee" — the precise constitutional problem with section 440.34.

In addition, in the federal cases cited in *Triplett,* the fees were intentionally set low due to the simple and non-adversarial nature of the services required — a far cry from the complex nature of Florida's current workers' compensation system. Indeed, Florida's workers' compensation law has become increasingly complex over the years. As a result of the complexity of the statutory scheme, the JCC specifically concluded in this case that it was "highly unlikely that [Castellanos] could have succeeded and obtained the favorable results he did without the assistance of capable counsel."

The stated goal of the workers' compensation system remains to this date the "quick and efficient delivery of disability and medical benefits to an injured worker" so as "to facilitate the worker's return to gainful reemployment at a reasonable cost to the employer." § 440.015, Fla. Stat. This case, and many others like it, demonstrate that despite the stated goal, oftentimes the worker experiences delay and resistance either by the employer or the carrier.[5] Without the likelihood of an adequate attorney's

---

5. Several related cases arising out of the First District, which are currently pending in this Court, illustrate that this is not an isolated case. In each of these cases, there was either an outright denial of benefits or multiple defenses raised by the E/C, and in each case, the attorney for the E/C expended a number of hours equal to or exceeding the hours expended by the claimant's attorney.

For example, in *Diaz v. Palmetto General Hospital,* 191 So.3d 882 (Fla.2016), the statutory fee award was $13.28 per hour for 120 hours of work deemed to be necessarily and reasonably expended

fee award, there is little disincentive for a carrier to deny benefits or to raise multiple defenses, as was done here. This is the exact opposite of the original goal of the attorney's fee provision, as this Court recognized long ago. *See Ohio Cas. Grp.,* 350 So.2d at 470 ("[I]n adding attorney's fees to the injured worker's compensation award, Section 440.34, Florida Statutes (1975), discourages the carrier from unnecessarily resisting claims in an attempt to force a settlement upon an injured worker.").

While the E/C's attorney is adequately compensated for the hours reasonably expended to unsuccessfully defend the claim, as here, the claimant's attorney's fee may be reduced to an absurdly low amount, such as the $1.53 hourly rate awarded to the attorney for Castellanos. In effect, the elimination of any requirement that the fee be "reasonable" completely eviscerates the purpose of the attorney's fee provision and fails to provide any penalty to the E/C for wrongfully denying or delaying benefits in contravention to the stated purpose of the statutory scheme.

And although there is a "mutual renunciation of common-law rights and defenses by employers and employees alike," § 440.015, Fla. Stat., the employer under the workers' compensation law has the prerogative to raise a whole host of defenses to denying benefits, while the employee is at the mercy of the E/C in being required to see the doctors that are chosen by the E/C. As this case shows, to navigate the current workers' compensation system, after a denial by the E/C of benefits, would be an impossibility without the assistance of an attorney. The JCC explicitly found as much in this case.

Virtually since its inception, the right of a claimant to obtain a reasonable prevailing party attorney's fee has been central to the workers' compensation law. While the incentive for an attorney to represent a claimant in a relatively high-value case is readily apparent, the exact opposite is true in a low-value complex case, such as this one.

But the conclusive fee schedule prevents all injured workers — whether they have small-value or high-value claims — from presenting evidence to prove that the fee is inadequate in any given case. Without the ability of the attorney to present, and the JCC to determine, the reasonableness of the fee award and to deviate where necessary, the risk is too great that the fee award will be entirely arbitrary, unjust, and grossly inadequate. We therefore conclude that the statute violates the state and federal constitutional guarantees of due process.[6]

* * *

---

by the attorney for the claimant. The E/C's attorney spent 175 hours litigating the case, which was found to be a reasonable amount of time given its complex nature. Just as in this case, the JCC in *Diaz* found that the injured worker would not have recovered benefits without the aid and assistance of an attorney.

6. Although Castellanos has also raised a strong argument based on the state constitutional right of access to courts in article I, section 21, of the Florida Constitution, because we conclude that the due process challenge is dispositive, we do not address the many other constitutional challenges to the statute.

III. Conclusion

The right of an injured worker to recover a reasonable prevailing party attorney's fee has been a key feature of the state's workers' compensation law since 1941. Through the 2009 enactment of a mandatory fee schedule, however, the Legislature has created an irrebuttable presumption that every fee calculated in accordance with the fee schedule will be reasonable to compensate the attorney for his or her services. The $1.53 hourly rate in this case clearly demonstrates that not to be true. We conclude that the mandatory fee schedule is unconstitutional as a violation of due process under both the Florida and United States Constitutions. Accordingly, we answer the rephrased certified question in the affirmative, quash the First District's decision upholding the patently unreasonable fee award, and direct that this case be remanded to the JCC for entry of a reasonable attorney's fee.

It is so ordered.

LABARGA, C.J., and QUINCE, and PERRY, JJ., concur.

LEWIS, J., concurs with an opinion.

CANADY, J., dissents with an opinion, in which POLSTON, J., concurs.

[The concurring opinion of Justice Lewis and the dissenting opinion of Justice Polston are omitted.]

4. Distinguishing Substantive from Procedural Due Process

Consider the following explanation by Justice Barkett in *Department of Law Enforcement v. Real Property*:[24]

II. THE DUE PROCESS REQUIREMENT

The basic due process guarantee of the Florida Constitution provides that "[n]o person shall be deprived of life, liberty or property without due process of law." Art. I, § 9, Fla. Const. Substantive due process under the Florida Constitution protects the full panoply of individual rights from unwarranted encroachment by the government. To ascertain whether the encroachment can be justified, courts have considered the propriety of the state's purpose; the nature of the party being subjected to state action; the substance of that individual's right being infringed upon; the nexus between the means chosen by the state and the goal it intended to achieve; whether less restrictive alternatives were available; and whether individuals are ultimately being treated in a fundamentally unfair manner in derogation of their substantive rights. Substantive due process may implicate, among other things, the definition of an offense, *see State v. Bussey*, 463 So.2d 1141

---

24. 588 So. 2d 957, 960 (Fla 1991). Please note that some of the cases cited by Justice Barkett may no longer be good law.

(Fla.1985); *Baker v. State*, 377 So.2d 17 (Fla.1979); the burden and standard of proof of elements and defenses, *see, e.g., State v. Cohen*, 568 So.2d 49, 51 (Fla.1990); the presumption of innocence, *see State v. Rodriguez*, 575 So.2d 1262 (Fla.1991); *State v. Harris*, 356 So.2d 315, 317 (1978); vagueness, *see, e.g., Perkins v. State*, 576 So.2d 1310 (Fla.1991); *Bussey; State v. Barquet*, 262 So.2d 431, 436 (Fla.1972); the conduct of law enforcement officials, *see Haliburton v. State*, 514 So.2d 1088 (Fla.1987); *State v. Glosson*, 462 So.2d 1082 (Fla.1985); the right to a fair trial, *see Kritzman v. State*, 520 So.2d 568 (Fla.1988); and the availability or harshness of remedies, *see In re Forfeiture of 1976 Kenworth Tractor Trailer Truck*, 576 So.2d 261 (Fla.1990); *Roush v. State*, 413 So.2d 15 (Fla.1982). [Footnote omitted.]

Procedural due process serves as a vehicle to ensure fair treatment through the proper administration of justice where substantive rights are at issue. Procedural due process under the Florida Constitution

> guarantees to every citizen the right to have that course of legal procedure which has been established in our judicial system for the protection and enforcement of private rights. It contemplates that the defendant shall be given fair notice[ ] and afforded a real opportunity to be heard and defend[ ] in an orderly procedure, before judgment is rendered against him.

State ex rel. Gore v. Chillingworth, 126 Fla. 645, 657–58, 171 So. 649, 654 (1936) (citations omitted); *accord, e.g., Fuentes v. Shevin*, 407 U.S. 67, 80, 92 S.Ct. 1983, 1994, 32 L.Ed.2d 556 (1972) (procedural due process under the fourteenth amendment of the United States Constitution guarantees notice and an opportunity to be heard at a meaningful time and in a meaningful manner). The manner in which due process protections apply vary with the character of the interests and the nature of the process involved. *Hadley v. Department of Admin.*, 411 So.2d 184, 187 (Fla.1982); *accord Mathews v. Eldridge*, 424 U.S. 319, 334, 96 S.Ct. 893, 902, 47 L.Ed.2d 18 (1976). There is no single, inflexible test by which courts determine whether the requirements of procedural due process have been met. *Hadley*, 411 So.2d at 187.

While the doctrines of substantive and procedural due process play distinct roles in the judicial process, they frequently overlap. Hence, many cases do not expressly state the distinction between procedural and substantive due process. *See, e.g., State v. Rodriguez*, 575 So.2d 1262 (Fla.1991) (in criminal cases the state must provide notice of each essential element and proof beyond a reasonable doubt); *accord, e.g., In re Winship*, 397 U.S. 358, 90 S.Ct. 1068, 25 L.Ed.2d 368 (1970).[25]

---

25. This is not intended to be a complete catalog of substantive due process. Rather, our discussion merely focuses on substantive due process as relevant to the issue at hand.

H. Imprisonment for Debt

Fla. Const. art. I, § 11

Imprisonment for debt. — No person shall be imprisoned for debt, except in cases of fraud.

While this is a fairly common provision found in many state constitutions, it does possess certain subtleties. As the following case suggests, in some instances, individuals may be imprisoned for failure to pay restitution.[26]

Del Valle v. State

80 So. 3d 999 (Fla. 2011)

PER CURIAM.

Carlos Del Valle seeks review of the decision of the Third District Court of Appeal in *Del Valle v. State*, 994 So.2d 425 (Fla. 3d DCA 2008), on the basis that it expressly and directly conflicts with decisions of the Second, Fourth, and Fifth District Courts of Appeal in *Blackwelder v. State*, 902 So.2d 905 (Fla. 2d DCA 2005), *Shepard v. State*, 939 So.2d 311 (Fla. 4th DCA 2006), and *Osta v. State*, 880 So.2d 804 (Fla. 5th DCA 2004). We have jurisdiction. *See* art. V, § 3(b)(3), Fla. Const.

These cases present two separate questions of law regarding probation revocation for failure to pay restitution: (1) whether a trial court, before finding a violation of probation for failure to pay restitution, must inquire into the probationer's ability to pay and determine whether the failure to pay was willful; and (2) whether the burden-shifting scheme of section 948.06(5), Florida Statutes (2011),[1] which places the burden on the probationer to prove his or her inability to pay by clear and convincing evidence, is constitutional. Regarding the first issue, the underlying constitutional principle is that an indigent probationer should not be imprisoned based solely on inability to pay a monetary obligation. Based on our fidelity to this principle, we approve the holdings of all the district courts of appeal, except the Third District, that before a trial court may properly revoke probation and incarcerate a probationer for failure to pay, it must inquire into the probationer's ability to pay and determine whether the probationer had the ability to pay but willfully refused to do so. Under Florida law, the trial court must make its finding regarding whether the probationer willfully violated probation by the greater weight of the evidence.

* * *

---

26. Individuals also may be imprisoned for failure to pay familial support obligations. *See Bowen v. Bowen*, 471 So. 2d 1274 (Fla. 1985).

1. The 2008 version of section 948.06(5) at issue in this case is identical to the current 2011 version of the statute.

Facts

Del Valle was charged with possession of cocaine and an unrelated, subsequent charge of third-degree grand theft. Del Valle was declared indigent, appointed a public defender, and ultimately entered a plea in each case, which resulted in his placement on probation for two years. As a condition of probation, Del Valle was responsible for paying $1,809.90 in restitution (at the rate of $80 per month) and an additional $25 per month toward the cost of supervision.

On February 14, 2008, an affidavit of violation of probation was filed, which alleged that Del Valle failed to make the required monthly payments and was $375 in arrears with respect to the cost of supervision and $1,040.92 in arrears with respect to the payment of restitution. The violation report attached to the affidavit of violation classified Del Valle as unemployed and indicated that he was provided with a job referral and job search log. Further, one section of the probation report read: "Subject stated that he is attending Miami-Dade College for his Associate Degree but has failed to bring in documentation that he is attending the college."

Following the filing of the affidavit of violation of probation, the State offered to reinstate Del Valle to probation. However, during a July 17, 2008, hearing, the trial court rejected probation alone and required any offer by the State to include boot camp as a condition of probation. The State was not ready to proceed, so the case was continued and Del Valle was released on his own recognizance.

On August 7, 2008, another probation violation hearing was held. At the hearing, the State offered the testimony of two of Del Valle's probation officers. One officer testified that he informed Del Valle of the terms of his probation, including both the restitution payment and the obligation to pay a monthly cost of supervision. The second officer then testified that Del Valle was in arrears for both restitution and cost of supervision. After the testimony of both officers, the defense presented no witnesses, and after a brief recess the court found that "the state has sustained its burden of proof in proving both affidavits of violation of probation." The court further modified the probation to include "the special condition that he enter into and complete the Miami-Dade County Boot Camp Program, including the after care."[2] The court then also extended the probation for two years with early termination upon successful completion of the boot camp program. . . .

* * *

Del Valle appealed the decision of the trial court to the Third District Court of Appeal. The Third District affirmed the trial court, stating in full:

---

2. A boot camp program is a form of incarceration. The Miami-Dade County Boot Camp Program, which Del Valle was required to complete in this case, is a program run by the Miami-Dade County Corrections and Rehabilitation Department as "a cost effective, population reducing, realistic reform program which serves the offender, and ultimately the community." Miami-Dade County Corrections and Rehabilitation Department, Boot Camp, http:// www.miamidade.gov/ corrections/ boot_camp.asp (last visited November 4, 2011).

Affirmed. *See Gonzales v. State,* 909 So.2d 960, 960 (Fla. 3d DCA 2005) ("If the probationer's defense is inability to pay, 'it is incumbent upon the probationer or offender to prove by clear and convincing evidence that he or she does not have the present resources available to pay restitution or the cost of supervision despite sufficient bona fide efforts legally to acquire the resources to do so.' § 948.06(5), Fla. Stat. (2004)").

Del Valle v. State, 994 So.2d 425, 425 (Fla. 3d DCA 2008).

* * *

Analysis

* * *

Constitutional Principles

The Equal Protection and Due Process Clauses of the United States Constitution ensure that an indigent probationer is not incarcerated based solely upon inability to pay a monetary obligation. *See Bearden v. Georgia,* 461 U.S. 660, 664, 103 S.Ct. 2064, 76 L.Ed.2d 221 (1983); U.S. Const. amends. V, XIV. Further, the Florida Constitution contains its own due process clause that parallels the language of the Fourteenth Amendment and states that "[n]o person shall be deprived of life, liberty or property without due process of law." Art. I, § 9, Fla. Const. The Florida Constitution contains a separate and specific provision that ensures that "[n]o person shall be imprisoned for debt, except in cases of fraud." Art. I § 11 Fla. Const.

In *Bearden,* although under different factual conditions, the United States Supreme Court explained the circumstances under which the State is justified in using imprisonment as a sanction to enforce collection:

> If the probationer has willfully refused to pay the fine or restitution when he has the means to pay, the State is perfectly justified in using imprisonment as a sanction to enforce collection. ... *But if the probationer has made all reasonable efforts to pay the fine or restitution, and yet cannot do so through no fault of his own, it is fundamentally unfair to revoke probation automatically without considering whether adequate alternative methods of punishing the defendant are available.*

461 U.S. at 668–69, 103 S.Ct. 2064 (emphasis added) (footnote omitted) (citation omitted). Thus, the United States Supreme Court clearly established the following principle:

> [I]n revocation proceedings for failure to pay a fine or restitution, *a sentencing court must inquire into the reasons for the failure to pay.* If the probationer willfully refused to pay or failed to make sufficient bona fide efforts legally to acquire the resources to pay, the court may revoke probation and sentence the defendant to imprisonment within the authorized range of its sentencing authority. If the probationer could not pay despite sufficient bona fide efforts to acquire the resources to do so, the court must consider alternate measures of punishment other than imprisonment. Only if alternate

7 · THE DECLARATION OF RIGHTS AND THE TAKING OF PROPERTY 771

measures are not adequate to meet the State's interests in punishment and deterrence may the court imprison a probationer who has made sufficient bona fide efforts to pay. To do otherwise would deprive the probationer of his conditional freedom simply because, through no fault of his own, he cannot pay the fine. *Such a deprivation would be contrary to the fundamental fairness required by the Fourteenth Amendment.*

Id. at 672–73, 103 S.Ct. 2064 (emphasis added).

This Court analyzed and applied *Bearden* in *Stephens v. State,* 630 So.2d 1090, 1091 (Fla.1994), articulating a clear rule: "We agree and hold that, before a person on probation can be imprisoned for failing to make restitution, there must be a determination that that person has, or has had, the ability to pay but has willfully refused to do so."

* * *

Determination of Willfulness

We next turn to the requirement that the trial court make a determination of willfulness and whether a failure to make such a determination can be considered harmless error, as the Third District has held, or constitutes fundamental error, as the First District has held. . . .

The First District has held that although the burden of proving inability to pay shifts to the probationer after the State establishes nonpayment, the trial court must make an inquiry and determination with regard to the probationer's ability to pay. *See Martin v. State,* 937 So.2d 714, 715–16 (Fla. 1st DCA 2006). In fact, the First District has held that the failure of the trial court to make a finding of willfulness is reversible error:

Section 948.06(5) does not relieve the trial court of its duty to determine that the violation was willful by proving the probationer's ability to pay. *Martin,* 937 So.2d at 716; *Blackwelder v. State,* 902 So.2d 905, 907 n. 1 (Fla. 2d DCA 2005). Because ability to pay is an essential element for a finding that a probationer willfully violated probation for failure to pay supervisory costs, the revocation of Appellant's probation based on the alleged violation of Condition (2) constitutes fundamental error. *Hobson [v. State],* 908 So.2d [1162,] 1164 [(Fla. 1st DCA 2005)]. In *Friddle v. State,* 989 So.2d 1254, 1255 (Fla. 1st DCA 2008), we held that revoking the defendant's probation based on his failure to pay restitution, without a specific finding that he had the ability to pay, compelled reversal. For the same reason, the finding that Appellant willfully violated Condition (2) must be stricken from the probation revocation order.

Odom v. State, 15 So.3d 672, 678 (Fla. 1st DCA 2009).

Conversely, the Third District, while acknowledging the necessity of a determination of ability to pay, has concluded that the failure of a trial court to make this determination is harmless, thus eroding the underlying constitutional principle expressed in *Bearden* that a probationer may not be deprived of his conditional freedom simply because, through no fault of his own, he cannot pay a monetary obligation. [*Guardado*, 562 So. 2d at 696–97.]

The Third District's holding that the failure of a trial court to make a specific finding of ability to pay is harmless directly contradicts the clear rule established by this Court in *Stephens* and the rationale upon which the principle of law announced by the United States Supreme Court's decision in *Bearden* is based. The specific question addressed in *Bearden* was "whether a sentencing court can revoke a defendant's probation for failure to pay the imposed fine and restitution, *absent evidence and findings that the defendant was somehow responsible for the failure* or that alternative forms of punishment were inadequate." *Bearden*, 461 U.S. at 665, 103 S.Ct. 2064 (emphasis added). In answering that question in the negative, the Supreme Court clearly articulated its belief that a specific inquiry with regard to ability to pay is required to pass constitutional scrutiny:

> We hold, therefore, that in revocation proceedings for failure to pay a fine or restitution, a sentencing court must inquire into the reasons for the failure to pay. . . . To do otherwise would deprive the probationer of his conditional freedom simply because, through no fault of his own, he cannot pay the fine. Such a deprivation would be contrary to the fundamental fairness required by the Fourteenth Amendment.

Bearden, 461 U.S. at 672–73, 103 S.Ct. 2064.

[T]his Court in *Stephens*, 630 So.2d at 1091, recognized that in *Bearden*, "the [United States Supreme] Court held that a court *must investigate* the reasons for failing to pay a fine or restitution in probation revocation proceedings." (Emphasis added.) This Court did not simply "[r]ecogniz[e] the illegality of . . . an unconditional plea agreement waiver by a probationer," dissenting op. at 1017, in *Stephens*, but instead unmistakably held that "before a person on probation can be imprisoned for failing to make restitution, there must be a determination that that person has, or has had, the ability to pay but has willfully refused to do so." 630 So.2d at 1091.

Regardless of whether the State or the probationer has the burden of proof with regard to ability, or inability, to pay, both this Court and the United States Supreme Court have made it abundantly clear that there must be both an inquiry into a probationer's ability to pay *and* a determination of willfulness. This flows from both state and federal constitutional requirements. The Third District's holding in *Guardado* ignores the inquiry required by *Bearden*, which, according to that opinion, is necessary "[w]hether analyzed in terms of equal protection or due process." *Bearden*, 461 U.S. at 666, 103 S.Ct. 2064. Further, *Guardado* is inconsistent with this Court's requirement expressed in *Stephens* regarding a specific finding of willfulness. A probationer cannot have his probation constitutionally revoked absent an inquiry into ability to pay *and* a specific finding of willfulness, and a trial court's failure to conduct such an inquiry *or* make such a finding cannot be deemed harmless. Although *Guardado* was decided prior to this Court's decision in *Stephens,* it has been improperly extended and relied on in decisions rendered after *Stephens,* including *Gonzales,* upon which the Third District relied in *Del Valle. See, e.g., Del Valle,* 994 So.2d at 425 (citing *Gonzales,* 909 So.2d at 960); *Gonzales,* 909 So.2d at 960 (citing *Guardado,* 562 So.2d at 696–97).

The absence of a specific finding of willfulness in a probation revocation proceeding cannot be considered harmless error. An automatic revocation of probation without such a finding would be unconstitutional. To comply with the rules set forth in *Bearden* and *Stephens,* trial courts must inquire into a probationer's ability to pay *and* make an explicit finding of willfulness based on the greater weight of the evidence. The failure to comport with these requirements constitutes fundamental error.

We emphasize that the probationer's ability to pay is an element of willfulness in the context of determining whether there is a willful violation for failure to pay a monetary obligation as a condition of probation. *See Odom,* 15 So.3d at 678–79 ("[A]bility to pay is an essential element for a finding that a probationer willfully violated probation for failure to pay. . . ."). As stated by this Court in *Stephens,* 630 So.2d at 1091, there must be a determination that the probationer has, or has had, the ability to pay but has willfully refused to do so. Thus, the trial court must inquire into a probationer's ability to pay before determining willfulness.

Constitutionality of Section 948.06(5)

* * *

This Case

In this case, the trial court found a violation of probation based on Del Valle's failure to pay restitution and costs, but did not inquire into Del Valle's ability to pay or his financial resources before finding a violation of probation and ordering that Del Valle attend boot camp. The only evidence presented as to the violation was that Del Valle had been informed of the terms of his probation and that he was in arrears of both the restitution amount and the costs of supervision. Although the trial court failed to make an inquiry into ability to pay or a finding of willfulness before modifying Del Valle's probation, the Third District, relying on its prior opinion in *Guardado,* affirmed the trial court's order, apparently finding the trial court's failure to conduct an inquiry or make a finding of willfulness to be harmless.

* * *

In short, Del Valle's probation violation and the trial court's order requiring Del Valle to complete the boot camp program were based on nothing more than his failure to pay restitution, without regard as to whether he had the ability to pay but had willfully refused to do so. This is contrary to the constitutional principles espoused in *Bearden* and *Stephens* and contrary to the Florida Constitution's protection against imprisonment for debt.

Conclusion

In accordance with our analysis above, we conclude that, as held by this Court in *Stephens* and the United States Supreme Court in *Bearden,* before a probationer can be imprisoned for failure to pay a monetary obligation such as restitution, the trial court must inquire into a probationer's ability to pay and make an explicit finding of willfulness based on the greater weight of the evidence. Further, in all probation revocation proceedings in which the violation alleged is a failure to pay a monetary obligation as a condition of the probation, we hold that the State must present sufficient evidence of the probationer's willfulness, which includes evidence on ability to pay, to support the trial court's finding of willfulness. After evidence of willfulness is introduced by the State, the burden may then be properly shifted to the probationer to assert and prove inability to pay. However, we hold that it is unconstitutional to require the probationer to prove inability to pay by clear and convincing evidence — a higher burden than the burden required of the State to prove the violation.

Accordingly, we quash the decision of the Third District below and further disapprove *Gonzales v. State,* 909 So.2d 960 (Fla. 3d DCA 2005), and *Guardado v. State,* 562 So.2d 696 (Fla. 3d DCA 1990), to the extent that they allow a probationer to have his or her probation revoked absent an inquiry by the trial court into ability to pay and a specific finding of willfulness. . . .

It is so ordered.

PARIENTE, QUINCE, LABARGA, and PERRY, JJ., concur.

CANADY, C.J., dissents with an opinion.

LEWIS, J., dissents with an opinion, in which POLSTON, J., concurs.

[The dissenting opinions of Justices Canady and Lewis are omitted.]

I. Search and Seizure

Fla. Const. art. I, § 12

Searches and seizures. — The right of the people to be secure in their persons, houses, papers and effects against unreasonable searches and seizures, and against the unreasonable interception of private communications by any means, shall not be violated. No warrant shall be issued except upon probable cause, supported by affidavit, particularly describing the place or places to be searched, the person or persons, thing or things to be seized, the communication to be intercepted, and the nature of evidence to be obtained. *This right shall be construed in conformity with the 4th Amendment to the United States Constitution, as interpreted by the United States Supreme Court.* [Emphasis added.] Articles or information obtained in violation of this right shall not be admissible in evidence *if such articles* *or information would be inadmissible under decisions of the United States Supreme Court construing the 4th Amendment to the United States Constitution.* [Emphasis added.]

In 1982, the search and seizure provision of the Florida Constitution was amended to require conformity between it and the Fourth Amendment of the United States Constitution as interpreted by the United States Supreme Court. This amendment was prompted by decisions of the Florida Supreme Court construing the search and seizure provision of the state constitution as affording greater protection of individual rights than the analogous provision in the Federal Constitution.[27] Since the passing of the amendment, questions have arisen concerning the overlap and interrelationship between traditional search and seizure privacy protections and the fundamental right of privacy expressed in Fla. Const. art. I, § 23. The interplay between the Fourth Amendment of the United States Constitution and Fla. Const. art. I, § 23 was discussed by the Fifth District Court of Appeal in *State v. Geiss.*[28] The context was the drawing of an individual's blood by search warrant.

> The trial court erred in concluding that the search warrant violated Geiss's state constitutional right to privacy as expressed in article I, section 23 of the Florida Constitution. In pertinent part, article 1, section 23 provides that: "Every natural person has the right to be let alone and free from governmental intrusion into his private life *except as otherwise provided herein.*" (Emphasis added.) In other words, this provision cannot be interpreted without reference to other provisions in the Florida Constitution addressing governmental intrusion into one's private life.
>
> Significantly, article 1, section 12 of the Florida Constitution requires that the state constitutional right against unreasonable searches and seizures "shall be construed in conformity with the 4th Amendment to the United States Constitution, as interpreted by the United States Supreme Court." Because article 1, section 12 expressly authorizes governmental searches and seizures to the extent found to be reasonable under the Fourth Amendment by the United States Supreme Court, the "except as otherwise provided herein" language of article 1, section 23 must be read as authorizing governmental intrusion into one's private life to the same measure. *See L.S. v. State,* 805 So.2d 1004, 1008 (Fla. 1st DCA 2001) ("Article I, section 23, does not modify the applicability of Article I, section 12, so as to provide more protection than that provided under the Fourth Amendment. . . .") (citing *State v. Hume,* 512 So.2d 185, 188 (Fla.1987)). Thus, if the search warrant

---

27. *See State v. Sarmiento,* 397 So. 2d 643 (Fla. 1981).

28. 70 So. 3d 642 (Fla. 5th Dist. Ct. App. 2011), *review granted, State v. Geiss,* 70 So. 3d 587 (Fla. 2011), *review dismissed, State v. Geiss,* 88 So. 3d 111 (Fla. 2012).

was valid under the Fourth Amendment, it cannot be barred by article I, section 23.[29]

Recent decisions of the Florida Supreme Court appear to limit privacy rights in search and seizure contexts to the Fourth Amendment of the United States Constitution with no mention of the fundamental right of privacy under the state constitution.[30] While Florida courts are required to "conform" to federal law where there is controlling precedent by the United States Supreme Court, Florida courts can make their own interpretation of the law where no such controlling precedent exists. However, any such decisions are subject to review by the United States Supreme Court.

Jardines v. State[31]

73 So. 3d 34 (Fla. 2011)

PERRY, J.

We have for review *State v. Jardines,* 9 So.3d 1 (Fla. 3d DCA 2008), in which the district court certified conflict with *State v. Rabb,* 920 So.2d 1175 (Fla. 4th DCA 2006). We have jurisdiction. *See* art. V, §3(b)(4), Fla. Const. We quash the decision in *Jardines* and approve the result in *Rabb.*

Police conducted a warrantless "sniff test" by a drug detection dog at Jardines' home and discovered live marijuana plants inside. The trial court granted Jardines' motion to suppress the evidence, and the State appealed. The district court reversed, and Jardines sought review in this Court. Jardines claims that the warrantless "sniff test" violated his right against unreasonable searches under the Fourth Amendment. The issue presented here is twofold: (i) whether a "sniff test" by a drug detection dog conducted at the front door of a private residence is a "search" under the Fourth Amendment and, if so, (ii) whether the evidentiary showing of wrongdoing that the government must make prior to conducting such a search is probable cause or reasonable suspicion.

* * *

I. Background

On November 3, 2006, Detective Pedraja of the Miami-Dade Police Department received an unverified "crime stoppers" tip that the home of Joelis Jardines was being used to grow marijuana. One month later, on December 6, 2006, Detective Pedraja and Detective Bartlet and his drug detection dog, Franky, approached the

---

29. *Id.* at 645–646.

30. *See McGraw v. State*, 289 So. 3d 836 (Fla. 2019); *State v. Markus*, 211 So. 3d 894 (Fla. 2017).

31. The United States Supreme Court upheld this decision in *Florida v. Jardines*, 133 S. Ct. 1409 (2013).

residence. The underlying facts, which are discussed more fully below, are summarized briefly in the separate opinion of a district court judge in *Jardines:*

> The Miami-Dade County Police Department received a Crime Stoppers tip that marijuana was being grown at the home of defendant-appellee Joelis Jardines. One month later the detective went to the home at 7 a.m. He watched the home for fifteen minutes. There were no vehicles in the driveway, the blinds were closed, and there was no observable activity.
>
> After fifteen minutes, the dog handler arrived with the drug detection dog. The handler placed the dog on a leash and accompanied the dog up to the front door of the home. The dog alerted to the scent of contraband.
>
> The handler told the detective that the dog had a positive alert for the odor of narcotics. The detective went up to the front door for the first time, and smelled marijuana. The detective also observed that the air conditioning unit had been running constantly for fifteen minutes or so, without ever switching off. [N. 8. According to the detective, in a hydroponics lab for growing marijuana, high intensity light bulbs are used which create heat. This causes the air conditioning unit to run continuously without cycling off.]
>
> The detective prepared an affidavit [footnote omitted] and applied for a search warrant, which was issued. A search was conducted, which confirmed that marijuana was being grown inside the home. The defendant was arrested.
>
> The defendant moved to suppress the evidence seized at his home. The trial court conducted an evidentiary hearing at which the detective and the dog handler testified. The trial court suppressed the evidence on authority of *State v. Rabb.*

Jardines, 9 So.3d at 10–11 (Cope, J., concurring in part and dissenting in part) (footnote omitted).

The State appealed the suppression ruling, and the district court reversed based on the following reasoning:

> In sum, we reverse the order suppressing the evidence at issue. We conclude that no illegal search occurred. The officer had the right to go up to defendant's front door. Contrary to the holding in *Rabb,* a warrant was not necessary for the drug dog sniff, and the officer's sniff at the exterior door of defendant's home should not have been viewed as "fruit of the poisonous tree." The trial judge should have concluded substantial evidence supported the magistrate's determination that probable cause existed. Moreover, the evidence at issue should not have been suppressed because its discovery was inevitable. To the extent our analysis conflicts with *Rabb,* we certify direct conflict.

778   7 · THE DECLARATION OF RIGHTS AND THE TAKING OF PROPERTY

Jardines, 9 So.3d at 10 (footnote omitted). Jardines sought review in this Court based on certified conflict with *State v. Rabb,* 920 So.2d 1175 (Fla. 4th DCA 2006),[2] which we granted.[3]

II. The Applicable Law

The Fourth Amendment to the United States Constitution contains both the Search and Seizure Clause and the Warrant Clause and provides as follows in full:

> The right of the people to be secure in their persons, houses, papers, and effects, against unreasonable searches and seizures, shall not be violated, and no warrants shall issue, but upon probable cause, supported by oath or affirmation, and particularly describing the place to be searched, and the persons or things to be seized.

U.S. Const. amend. IV.[4] With respect to the meaning of the amendment, the courts have come to accept the formulation set forth by Justice Harlan in *Katz:*[5]

---

2. The Fourth District Court of Appeal in *State v. Rabb,* 920 So.2d 1175 (Fla. 4th DCA 2006), affirmed the trial court's suppression of illicit drugs (marijuana found growing in Rabb's house) following a warrantless "sniff test" by a drug detection dog at the front door of Rabb's home. The district court based its ruling on *Kyllo v. United States,* 533 U.S. 27, 121 S.Ct. 2038, 150 L.Ed.2d 94 (2001), reasoning as follows:

> [Our logic here] is no different than that expressed in *Kyllo,* one of the recent pronouncements by the United States Supreme Court on law enforcement searches of houses. The use of the dog, like the use of a thermal imager, allowed law enforcement to use sense-enhancing technology to intrude into the constitutionally-protected area of Rabb's house, which is reasonably considered a search violative of Rabb's expectation of privacy in his retreat. Likewise, it is of no importance that a dog sniff provides limited information regarding only the presence or absence of contraband, because as in *Kyllo,* the quality or quantity of information obtained through the search is not the feared injury. Rather, it is the fact that law enforcement endeavored to obtain the information from inside the house at all, or in this case, the fact that a dog's sense of smell crossed the "firm line" of Fourth Amendment protection at the door of Rabb's house. Because the smell of marijuana had its source in Rabb's house, it was an "intimate detail" of that house, no less so than the ambient temperature inside Kyllo's house. Until the United States Supreme Court indicates otherwise, therefore, we are bound to conclude that the use of a dog sniff to detect contraband inside a house does not pass constitutional muster. The dog sniff at the house in this case constitutes an illegal search.

Rabb, 920 So.2d at 1184.

3. We note that the First District Court of Appeal in *Stabler v. State,* 990 So.2d 1258 (Fla. 1st DCA 2008), also certified conflict with *Rabb.* In *Stabler,* the district court held that a dog "sniff test" conducted at an apartment door that opens onto a common area accessible to the general public does not constitute a "search" for Fourth Amendment purposes. As noted herein, *Stabler* is distinguishable from *Rabb* in that *Stabler* involved a "sniff test" conducted at an apartment or other temporary dwelling, not a "sniff test" conducted at a private residence. *See infra* note 10.

4. The comparable provision of the Florida Constitution is contained in article I, section 12, which further provides: "This right shall be construed in conformity with the 4th Amendment to the United States Constitution, as interpreted by the United States Supreme Court." Art. I, § 12, Fla. Const.

5. *Katz v. United States,* 389 U.S. 347, 88 S.Ct. 507, 19 L.Ed.2d 576 (1967) (addressing the issue of whether police, without a warrant, can listen to and record one end of a telephone conversation in a

As the Court's opinion states, "the Fourth Amendment protects people, not places." The question, however, is what protection it affords to those people. Generally, as here, the answer to that question requires reference to a "place." *My understanding of the rule that has emerged from prior decisions is that there is a twofold requirement, first that a person have exhibited an actual (subjective) expectation of privacy and, second, that the expectation be one that society is prepared to recognize as "reasonable."* Thus a man's home is, for most purposes, a place where he expects privacy, but objects, activities, or statements that he exposes to the "plain view" of outsiders are not "protected" because no intention to keep them to himself has been exhibited. On the other hand, conversations in the open would not be protected against being overheard, for the expectation of privacy under the circumstances would be unreasonable.

Katz, 389 U.S. at 361, 88 S.Ct. 507 (emphasis added) (Harlan, J., concurring); *see California v. Ciraolo,* 476 U.S. 207, 211, 106 S.Ct. 1809, 90 L.Ed.2d 210 (1986) ("*Katz* posits a two-part inquiry: first, has the individual manifested a subjective expectation of privacy in the object of the challenged search? Second, is society willing to recognize that expectation as reasonable?"). In sum, "wherever an individual may harbor a 'reasonable expectation of privacy' he is entitled to be free from unreasonable governmental intrusion." *Terry v. Ohio,* 392 U.S. 1, 9, 88 S.Ct. 1868, 20 L.Ed.2d 889 (1968) (quoting *Katz,* 389 U.S. at 361, 88 S.Ct. 507 (Harlan, J., concurring)).

A. Federal "Dog Sniff" Cases

The United States Supreme Court has addressed the issue of "sniff tests" by drug detection dogs in three cases. First, in *United States v. Place,* 462 U.S. 696, 103 S.Ct. 2637, 77 L.Ed.2d 110 (1983), that Court addressed the issue of whether police, based on reasonable suspicion, could temporarily seize a piece of luggage at an airport and then subject the luggage to a "sniff test" by a drug detection dog. After Place's behavior at an airport aroused suspicion, police seized his luggage and subjected it to a "sniff test" by a drug detection dog at another airport and ultimately discovered cocaine inside. The federal district court denied Place's motion to suppress, and the court of appeals reversed. The United States Supreme Court affirmed, concluding that the seizure, which lasted ninety minutes, was an impermissibly long Terry[6] stop, but the Court ruled as follows with respect to the dog "sniff test":

The Fourth Amendment "protects people from unreasonable government intrusions into their legitimate expectations of privacy." We have affirmed that a person possesses a privacy interest in the contents of personal luggage that is protected by the Fourth Amendment. A "canine

---

public phone booth via an electronic listening and recording device attached to the outside surface of the booth).

6. *Terry v. Ohio,* 392 U.S. 1, 88 S.Ct. 1868, 20 L.Ed.2d 889 (1968) (addressing the issue of whether police, based on an evidentiary showing of less than probable cause, can temporarily seize and search a person).

sniff" by a well-trained narcotics detection dog, however, does not require opening the luggage. It does not expose noncontraband items that otherwise would remain hidden from public view, as does, for example, an officer's rummaging through the contents of the luggage. Thus, the manner in which information is obtained through this investigative technique is much less intrusive than a typical search. Moreover, the sniff discloses only the presence or absence of narcotics, a contraband item. Thus, despite the fact that the sniff tells the authorities something about the contents of the luggage, the information obtained is limited. This limited disclosure also ensures that the owner of the property is not subjected to the embarrassment and inconvenience entailed in less discriminate and more intrusive investigative methods.

In these respects, the canine sniff is *sui generis.* We are aware of no other investigative procedure that is so limited both in the manner in which the information is obtained and in the content of the information revealed by the procedure. Therefore, we conclude that the particular course of investigation that the agents intended to pursue here — exposure of respondent's luggage, which was located in a public place, to a trained canine — did not constitute a "search" within the meaning of the Fourth Amendment.

Place, 462 U.S. at 706–07, 103 S.Ct. 2637 (quoting *United States v. Chadwick,* 433 U.S. 1, 7, 97 S.Ct. 2476, 53 L.Ed.2d 538 (1977)).

Second, in *City of Indianapolis v. Edmond,* 531 U.S. 32, 121 S.Ct. 447, 148 L.Ed.2d 333 (2000), the United States Supreme Court addressed the issue of whether police could stop a vehicle at a drug interdiction checkpoint and subject the exterior of the vehicle to a "sniff test" by a drug detection dog. Police stopped Edmond and other motorists at a dragnet-style drug interdiction checkpoint, and a drug detection dog was walked around the exterior of each vehicle. Later, Edmond filed a class action lawsuit against the city, claiming that the checkpoints violated his Fourth Amendment rights, and he sought a preliminary injunction barring the practice. The federal district court denied the injunction, and the court of appeals reversed. The United States Supreme Court affirmed, explaining that "[w]e have never approved a checkpoint program whose primary purpose was to detect evidence of ordinary criminal wrongdoing." *Edmond,* 531 U.S. at 41, 121 S.Ct. 447. With respect to the dog "sniff test," the Court stated as follows:

It is well established that a vehicle stop at a highway checkpoint effectuates a seizure within the meaning of the Fourth Amendment. The fact that officers walk a narcotics-detection dog around the exterior of each car at the Indianapolis checkpoints does not transform the seizure into a search. *See United States v. Place,* 462 U.S. 696 [103 S.Ct. 2637, 77 L.Ed.2d 110] (1983). Just as in *Place,* an exterior sniff of an automobile does not require entry into the car and is not designed to disclose any information other than the presence or absence of narcotics. *See ibid.* Like the dog sniff in *Place,* a sniff by a dog that simply walks around a car is "much less intrusive than a typical search." *Ibid.*

Edmond, 531 U.S. at 40, 121 S.Ct. 447 (citation omitted) (quoting *Place,* 462 U.S. at 707, 103 S.Ct. 2637).

And third, in *Illinois v. Caballes,* 543 U.S. 405, 125 S.Ct. 834, 160 L.Ed.2d 842 (2005), the United States Supreme Court addressed the issue of whether police, during the course of a lawful traffic stop, could subject the exterior of a vehicle to a "sniff test" by a drug detection dog. After Caballes was stopped for speeding and while the officer was writing the citation, a second officer arrived at the scene and subjected the exterior of the vehicle to a dog "sniff test." The dog alerted at the trunk and the officers searched the trunk and found marijuana. The state trial court denied Caballes' motion to suppress, and the Illinois Supreme Court reversed. The United States Supreme Court reversed, ruling as follows:

> Official conduct that does not "compromise any legitimate interest in privacy" is not a search subject to the Fourth Amendment. *Jacobsen,* 466 U.S., at 123 [104 S.Ct. 1652]. We have held that any interest in possessing contraband cannot be deemed "legitimate," and thus, governmental conduct that only reveals the possession of contraband "compromises no legitimate privacy interest." *Ibid.* This is because the expectation "that certain facts will not come to the attention of the authorities" is not the same as an interest in "privacy that society is prepared to consider reasonable." *Id.,* at 122 [104 S.Ct. 1652] (punctuation omitted). In *United States v. Place,* 462 U.S. 696 [103 S.Ct. 2637, 77 L.Ed.2d 110] (1983), we treated a canine sniff by a well-trained narcotics-detection dog as "*sui generis*" because it "discloses only the presence or absence of narcotics, a contraband item." *Id.,* at 707 [103 S. Ct. 2637]; *see* also *Indianapolis v. Edmond,* 531 U.S. 32, 40 [121 S.Ct. 447, 148 L.Ed.2d 333] (2000). . . .

> Accordingly, the use of a well-trained narcotics-detection dog—one that "does not expose noncontraband items that otherwise would remain hidden from public view," *Place,* 462 U.S., at 707 [103 S.Ct. 2637]—during a lawful traffic stop generally does not implicate legitimate privacy interests. In this case, the dog sniff was performed on the exterior of respondent's car while he was lawfully seized for a traffic violation. Any intrusion on respondent's privacy expectations does not rise to the level of a constitutionally cognizable infringement.

Caballes, 543 U.S. at 408–09, 125 S.Ct. 834 (citation omitted).

Further, the Court in *Caballes* distinguished its ruling in *Kyllo v. United States,* 533 U.S. 27, 121 S.Ct. 2038, 150 L.Ed.2d 94 (2001), as follows:

> This conclusion is entirely consistent with our recent decision that the use of a thermal-imaging device to detect the growth of marijuana in a home constituted an unlawful search. *Kyllo v. United States,* 533 U.S. 27 [121 S. Ct. 2038, 150 L.Ed.2d 94] (2001). Critical to that decision was the fact that

the device was capable of detecting lawful activity — in that case, intimate details in a home, such as "at what hour each night the lady of the house takes her daily sauna and bath." *Id.,* at 38 [121 S.Ct. 2038]. The legitimate expectation that information about perfectly lawful activity will remain private is categorically distinguishable from respondent's hopes or expectations concerning the nondetection of contraband in the trunk of his car. A dog sniff conducted during a concededly lawful traffic stop that reveals no information other than the location of a substance that no individual has any right to possess does not violate the Fourth Amendment.

Caballes, 543 U.S. at 409–10, 125 S.Ct. 834.

B. Two Additional Federal Cases

In two additional cases, the United States Supreme Court has addressed Fourth Amendment issues that are relevant here. First, in *United States v. Jacobsen,* 466 U.S. 109, 104 S.Ct. 1652, 80 L.Ed.2d 85 (1984), the Court addressed the issue of whether police, without a showing of probable cause, could temporarily seize and inspect a small portion of the contents of a package, which had been damaged in transit and was being held by a private shipping company, and then subject the contents to a field test for cocaine. After employees of a private freight carrier discovered a suspicious white powder in a damaged package and notified federal agents, the agents conducted a field chemical test on the powder and determined that it was cocaine. The federal district court denied Jacobsen's motion to suppress, and the court of appeals reversed. The United States Supreme Court reversed, reasoning as follows:

> A chemical test that merely discloses whether or not a particular substance is cocaine does not compromise any legitimate interest in privacy. This conclusion is not dependent on the result of any particular test. It is probably safe to assume that virtually all of the tests conducted under circumstances comparable to those disclosed by this record would result in a positive finding; in such cases, no legitimate interest has been compromised. But even if the results are negative — merely disclosing that the substance is something other than cocaine — such a result reveals nothing of special interest. Congress has decided — and there is no question about its power to do so — to treat the interest in "privately" possessing cocaine as illegitimate; thus governmental conduct that can reveal whether a substance is cocaine, and no other arguably "private" fact, compromises no legitimate privacy interest.

> This conclusion is dictated by *United States v. Place,* 462 U.S. 696 [103 S.Ct. 2637, 77 L.Ed.2d 110] (1983), in which the Court held that subjecting luggage to a "sniff test" by a trained narcotics detection dog was not a "search" within the meaning of the Fourth Amendment. . . .

> Here, as in *Place,* the likelihood that official conduct of the kind disclosed by the record will actually compromise any legitimate interest in privacy

7 · THE DECLARATION OF RIGHTS AND THE TAKING OF PROPERTY   783

seems much too remote to characterize the testing as a search subject to the Fourth Amendment.

Jacobsen, 466 U.S. at 123–24 [104 S.Ct. 1652] (footnote omitted).

And second, in *Kyllo v. United States,* 533 U.S. 27, 121 S.Ct. 2038, 150 L.Ed.2d 94 (2001), the United States Supreme Court addressed the issue of whether police, without a warrant, could use a thermal-imaging device to scan a private home to determine if the amount of heat generated by the home was consistent with the use of high-intensity lamps used in growing marijuana. After federal agents became suspicious that Kyllo was growing marijuana in his home, agents scanned the outside of the triplex with a thermal-imaging device, which showed that the garage roof and side of the residence were inordinately warm. The agents obtained a warrant and searched the residence and found live marijuana plants inside. The federal district court denied Kyllo's motion to suppress, and the circuit court affirmed. The United States Supreme Court reversed, reasoning as follows:

> The *Katz* test — whether the individual has an expectation of privacy that society is prepared to recognize as reasonable — has often been criticized as circular, and hence subjective and unpredictable. While it may be difficult to refine *Katz* when the search of areas such as telephone booths, automobiles, or even the curtilage and uncovered portions of residences is at issue, in the case of the search of the interior of homes — the prototypical and hence most commonly litigated area of protected privacy — there is a ready criterion, with roots deep in the common law, of the minimal expectation of privacy that *exists,* and that is acknowledged to be *reasonable.* To withdraw protection of this minimum expectation would be to permit police technology to erode the privacy guaranteed by the Fourth Amendment. We think that obtaining by sense-enhancing technology any information regarding the interior of the home that could not otherwise have been obtained without physical "intrusion into a constitutionally protected area" constitutes a search — at least where (as here) the technology in question is not in general public use. This assures preservation of that degree of privacy against government that existed when the Fourth Amendment was adopted. On the basis of this criterion, the information obtained by the thermal imager in this case was the product of a search.

> . . . .

> We have said that the Fourth Amendment draws "a firm line at the entrance to the house." That line, we think, must be not only firm but also bright — which requires clear specification of those methods of surveillance that require a warrant. While it is certainly possible to conclude from the videotape of the thermal imaging that occurred in this case that no "significant" compromise of the homeowner's privacy has occurred, we must take the long view, from the original meaning of the Fourth Amendment forward.

"The Fourth Amendment is to be construed in the light of what was deemed an unreasonable search and seizure when it was adopted, and in a manner which will conserve public interests as well as the interests and rights of individual citizens." *Carroll v. United States,* 267 U.S. 132, 149 [45 S.Ct. 280, 69 L.Ed. 543] (1925).

Where, as here, the Government uses a device that is not in general public use, to explore details of the home that would previously have been unknowable without physical intrusion, the surveillance is a "search" and is presumptively unreasonable without a warrant.

Kyllo, 533 U.S. at 34–40, 121 S.Ct. 2038 (citations omitted) (quoting *Silverman,* 365 U.S. at 512, 81 S.Ct. 679; *Payton v. New York,* 445 U.S. 573, 590, 100 S.Ct. 1371, 63 L. Ed.2d 639 (1980)).

III. Analysis

As noted above, the issue raised in the present case is twofold: (i) whether a "sniff test" by a drug detection dog conducted at the front door of a private residence is a "search" under the Fourth Amendment and, if so, (ii) whether the evidentiary showing of wrongdoing that the government must make prior to conducting such a search is probable cause or reasonable suspicion.

A. The Federal "Dog Sniff" Cases Are Inapplicable to the Home

For reasons explained below, we conclude that the analysis used in the above federal "dog sniff" cases is inapplicable to a "sniff test" conducted at a private home. First, we recognize that the United States Supreme Court has ruled that because a "sniff test" conducted by a drug detection dog is "sui generis," or unique, in the sense that it is minimally intrusive and is designed to detect only illicit drugs and nothing more, *Place,* 462 U.S. at 707, 103 S.Ct. 2637, a dog "sniff test" does not implicate Fourth Amendment rights when employed in the following settings: (i) when conducted on luggage that has been seized at an airport based on reasonable suspicion of unlawful activity, where the luggage has been separated from its owner and the "sniff test" is conducted in a public place, *see Place,* 462 U.S. 696, 103 S.Ct. 2637; (ii) when conducted on the exterior of a vehicle that has been stopped in a dragnet-style stop at a drug interdiction checkpoint, *see Edmond,* 531 U.S. 32, 121 S.Ct. 447; and (iii) when conducted on the exterior of a vehicle that has been subjected to a lawful traffic stop. *See Caballes,* 543 U.S. 405, 125 S.Ct. 834. Further, the United States Supreme Court has applied a similar analysis to a chemical "field test" for drugs when conducted on the contents of a package that has been damaged in transit and is being held by a private shipping company. *See Jacobsen,* 466 U.S. 109, 104 S.Ct. 1652.

We note, however, that in each of the above cases, the United States Supreme Court was careful to tie its ruling to the particular facts of the case. *See Place,* 462 U.S. at 707, 103 S.Ct. 2637 ("[W]e conclude that the particular course of investigation that the agents intended to pursue here — exposure of respondent's luggage, which was located in a public place, to a trained canine — did not constitute a 'search' within the meaning of the Fourth Amendment."); *Edmond,* 531 U.S. at 40, 121 S. Ct. 447 ("The fact that officers walk a narcotics-detection dog around the exterior of each car at the Indianapolis checkpoints does not transform the seizure into a search."); *Caballes,* 543 U.S. at 409, 125 S.Ct. 834 ("In this case, the dog sniff was performed on the exterior of respondent's car while he was lawfully seized for a traffic violation. Any intrusion on respondent's privacy expectations does not rise to the level of a constitutionally cognizable infringement."); *Jacobsen,* 466 U.S. at 123, 104 S.Ct. 1652 ("It is probably safe to assume that virtually all of the tests conducted under circumstances comparable to those disclosed by this record would result in a positive finding; in such cases, no legitimate interest has been compromised."). Nothing in the above cases indicates that the same analysis would apply to a dog "sniff test" conducted at a private residence.

Significantly, all the sniff and field tests in the above cases were conducted in a minimally intrusive manner upon objects—luggage at an airport in *Place,* vehicles on the roadside in *Edmond* and *Caballes,* and a package in transit in *Jacobsen*— that warrant no special protection under the Fourth Amendment. All the tests were conducted in an impersonal manner that subjected the defendants to no untoward level of public opprobrium, humiliation or embarrassment. There was no public link between the defendants and the luggage as it was being tested in *Place* or the package as it was being tested in *Jacobsen,* and the defendants retained a degree of anonymity during the roadside testing of their vehicles in *Edmond* and *Caballes.* Further, and more important, under the particular circumstances of each of the above cases, the tests were not susceptible to being employed in a discriminatory or arbitrary manner—the luggage in *Place* had been seized based on reasonable suspicion; the vehicle in *Edmond* had been seized in a dragnet-style stop; the vehicle in *Caballes* had been seized pursuant to a lawful traffic stop; and the contents of the package in *Jacobsen* had been seized after the package had been damaged in transit by a private carrier. All these objects were seized and tested in an objective and nondiscriminatory manner, and there was no evidence of overbearing or harassing government conduct. There was no need for Fourth Amendment protection. As explained below, however, such is not the case with respect to a dog "sniff test" conducted at a private residence.

B. "Sniff Test" at a Private Home

As noted above, the United States Supreme Court has held that "wherever an individual may harbor a reasonable 'expectation of privacy,' he is entitled to be free from unreasonable government intrusion." *Terry,* 392 U.S. at 9, 88 S.Ct. 1868 (quoting *Katz,* 389 U.S. at 351, 88 S.Ct. 507 (Harlan, J., concurring)). Nowhere is this right more resolute than in the private home: "'At the very core' of the Fourth Amendment 'stands the right of a man to retreat into his own home and there be free from unreasonable governmental intrusion.'" *Kyllo,* 533 U.S. at 31, 121 S.Ct. 2038 (quoting *Silverman v. United States,* 365 U.S. 505, 511, 81 S.Ct. 679, 5 L.Ed.2d 734 (1961)). . . .

* * *

Although police generally may initiate a "knock and talk" encounter at the front door of a private residence without any prior showing of wrongdoing, *see State v. Morsman,* 394 So.2d 408, 409 (Fla.1981) ("Under Florida law it is clear that one does not harbor an expectation of privacy on a front porch where salesmen or visitors may appear at any time."), a dog "sniff test" is a qualitatively different matter. Contrary to popular belief, a "sniff test" conducted at a private residence is not necessarily a casual affair in which a canine officer and dog approach the front door and the dog then performs a subtle "sniff test" and signals an "alert" if drugs are detected. Quite the contrary. In the present case, for instance, on the morning of December 5, 2006, members of the Miami-Dade Police Department, Narcotics Bureau, and agents of the Drug Enforcement Administration (DEA), United States Department of Justice, conducted a surveillance of Jardines' home. As Detectives Pedraja and Bartlet and the drug detection dog, Franky, approached the residence, Sergeant Ramirez and Detective Donnelly of the Miami-Dade Police Department established perimeter positions around the residence and federal DEA agents assumed stand-by positions as backup units.

The "sniff test" conducted by the dog handler and his dog was a vigorous and intensive procedure. . . .

* * *

After the "sniff test" was completed, Detective Bartlet and Franky left the scene to assist in another case. Detective Pedraja, after waiting at the residence for fifteen or twenty minutes, also left the scene to prepare a search warrant and to submit it to a magistrate. Federal DEA agents, however, remained behind to maintain surveillance of Jardines' home. Pedraja obtained a search warrant later that day and returned to the scene. About an hour later, members of the Miami-Dade Police Department, Narcotics Bureau, and DEA agents executed the warrant by gaining entry to Jardines' home through the front door. As agents entered the front door, Jardines exited through a sliding glass door at the rear of the house. He was apprehended by Special Agent Wilson of the DEA and was turned over to the Miami-Dade Police Department. He was charged with trafficking in marijuana and theft of electricity.

Based on the foregoing, we conclude that the dog "sniff test" that was conducted here was an intrusive procedure. The "sniff test" was a sophisticated undertaking that was the end result of a sustained and coordinated effort by various law enforcement departments. On the scene, the procedure involved multiple police vehicles, multiple law enforcement personnel, including narcotics detectives and other officers, and an experienced dog handler and trained drug detection dog engaged in a vigorous search effort on the front porch of the residence. Tactical law enforcement personnel from various government agencies, both state and federal, were on the scene for surveillance and backup purposes. The entire on-the-scene government activity — i.e., the preparation for the "sniff test," the test itself, and the aftermath, which culminated in the full-blown search of Jardines' home — lasted for hours. The "sniff test" apparently took place in plain view of the general public. There was no anonymity for the resident.

Such a public spectacle unfolding in a residential neighborhood will invariably entail a degree of public opprobrium, humiliation and embarrassment for the resident, whether or not he or she is present at the time of the search, for such dramatic government activity in the eyes of many-neighbors, passers-by, and the public at large-will be viewed as an official accusation of crime. *Cf. Place*, 462 U.S. at 707, 103 S.Ct. 2637 (explaining that the dog "sniff test" in that case was not a "search" within the meaning of the Fourth Amendment because it was limited in scope and was anonymous and did not subject the individual to "embarrassment and inconvenience"). And if the resident happens to be present at the time of the "sniff test," such an intrusion into the sanctity of his or her home will generally be a frightening and harrowing experience that could prompt a reflexive or unpredictable response.

Further, all the underlying circumstances that were present in the above federal "dog sniff" and "field test" cases that guaranteed objective, uniform application of those tests — i.e., the temporary seizure of luggage based on reasonable suspicion of criminal activity in *Place;* the temporary seizure of a vehicle in a dragnet-style stop at a drug interdiction checkpoint in *Edmond;* the temporary seizure of a vehicle based on a lawful traffic stop in *Caballes;* and the temporary seizure of a portion of the contents of a package that had been damaged in transit in *Jacobsen* — are absent from a warrantless "sniff test" conducted at a private residence. Unlike the objects in those cases, a private residence is not susceptible to being seized beforehand based on objective criteria. Thus, if government agents can conduct a dog "sniff test" at a private residence without any prior evidentiary showing of wrongdoing, there is simply nothing to prevent the agents from applying the procedure in an arbitrary or discriminatory manner, or based on whim and fancy, at the home of any citizen. *Cf. Camara v. Mun. Court of City & Cnty. of S. F.,* 387 U.S. 523, 528, 87 S.Ct. 1727, 18 L. Ed.2d 930 (1967) ("The basic purpose of [the Fourth] Amendment, as recognized in countless decisions of this Court, is to safeguard the privacy and security of individuals against arbitrary invasions by governmental officials."). Such an open-ended policy invites overbearing and harassing conduct.[7]

In sum, a "sniff test" by a drug detection dog conducted at a private residence does not *only* reveal the presence of contraband, as was the case in the federal "sui generis" dog sniff cases discussed above, but it also constitutes an intrusive

---

7. There is little doubt, however, that a dragnet-style sweep of an entire residential neighborhood or of a multi-unit residential dwelling, conducted without any individualized suspicion of wrongdoing, would be impermissible. *Cf. City of Indianapolis v. Edmond,* 531 U.S. at 41, 121 S.Ct. 447 ("We have never approved a checkpoint program whose primary purpose was to detect evidence of ordinary criminal wrongdoing. Rather, our checkpoint cases have recognized only limited exceptions to the general rule that a seizure must be accompanied by some measure of individualized suspicion.").

procedure that may expose the resident to public opprobrium, humiliation and embarrassment, and it raises the specter of arbitrary and discriminatory application. Given the special status accorded a citizen's home under the Fourth Amendment, we conclude that a "sniff test," such as the test that was conducted in the present case, is a substantial government intrusion into the sanctity of the home and constitutes a "search" within the meaning of the Fourth Amendment. As such, it warrants the safeguards that inhere in that amendment — specifically, the search must be preceded by an evidentiary showing of wrongdoing. . . .

C. The Requirement of Probable Cause

* * *

We agree with the above analyses and note that the parties in the present case have failed to point to a single case in which the United States Supreme Court has indicated that a search for evidence for use in a criminal prosecution, absent special needs beyond the normal need of law enforcement, may be based on anything other than probable cause. We assume that this is because, as noted in the commentary above, all that Court's precedent in this area indicates just the opposite. And that precedent, we recognize, applies with extra force where the sanctity of the home is concerned. Accordingly, we conclude that probable cause, not reasonable suspicion, is the proper evidentiary showing of wrongdoing that the government must make under the Fourth Amendment prior to conducting a dog "sniff test" at a private residence.

* * *

V. Conclusion

"We have said that the Fourth Amendment draws 'a firm line at the entrance to the house.' That line, we think, must be not only firm but also bright — which requires clear specification of those methods of surveillance that require a warrant." *Kyllo,* 533 U.S. at 40, 121 S.Ct. 2038 (citation omitted) (quoting *Payton,* 445 U.S. at 590, 100 S.Ct. 1371). Given the special status accorded a citizen's home in Anglo-American jurisprudence, we hold that the warrantless "sniff test" that was conducted at the front door of the residence in the present case was an unreasonable government intrusion into the sanctity of the home and violated the Fourth Amendment.

We quash the decision in *Jardines* and approve the result in *Rabb.*

It is so ordered.

PARIENTE, LEWIS, QUINCE, and LABARGA, JJ., concur.

LEWIS, J., specially concurs with an opinion, in which PARIENTE and LABARGA, JJ., concur.

POLSTON, J., dissents with an opinion, in which CANADY, C.J., concurs.

[The concurring opinion of Justice Lewis and the dissenting opinion of Justice Polston are omitted.]

J. Administrative Penalties

Fla. Const. art. I, § 18

Administrative Penalties. — No administrative agency, except the Department of Military Affairs in an appropriately convened court-martial action as provided by law, shall impose a sentence of imprisonment, nor shall it impose any other penalty except as provided by law.

Florida Elections Commission v. Davis

44 So. 3d 1211 (Fla. 1st Dist. Ct. App. 2010)

BENTON, Judge.

On this appeal from an administrative law judge's corrected final order, the Florida Elections Commission asks us to reverse, insofar as the order declines — citing a lack of statutory authority — to levy a civil penalty against a former candidate found guilty of five violations of the election code. We affirm.

Until the Legislature enacted chapter 2007-30, section 48, Laws of Florida, the Florida Elections Commission had the option under section 106.25(5), Florida Statutes (2006), of hearing matters itself, after probable cause was determined, or of referring them for formal hearing at the Division of Administrative Hearings (just as the Administrative Procedure Act still provides in the case of most other executive branch agencies.) But chapter 2007-30, section 48, Laws of Florida, effected the following changes:

> (5) ~~Unless~~ When there are disputed issues of material fact in a proceeding conducted under ss. 120.569 and 120.57, a person alleged by the Elections Commission to have committed a violation of this chapter or chapter 104 ~~elects~~ may elect, within 30 days after the date of the filing of the commission's allegations, to have a *formal or informal hearing conducted before the commission, or elects to resolve the complaint by consent order, such person shall be entitled to a formal administrative* hearing conducted by an administrative law judge in the Division of Administrative Hearings. *The administrative law judge in such proceedings shall enter a final order subject to appeal as provided in s. 120.68.*

(Language added by chapter 2007-30 is underscored; language deleted by chapter 2007-30 is struck-through.) For one thing, the amendment made a formal administrative hearing at the Division of Administrative Hearings the default procedure. For another — and central to the present controversy — it conferred some sort of final order authority on the administrative law judge. But it does not specify the nature or scope of the authority, and therein lies the rub.

On April 18, 2006, the Commission received a sworn complaint alleging that Mr. Davis, who tried unsuccessfully to qualify as a candidate for Congress before campaigning for a seat in the Legislature, had violated certain election laws. After an investigation, the Commission entered its order of probable cause charging five violations of provisions in chapter 106, Florida Statutes. Because he did not request a hearing before the Commission, or elect to resolve the matter by a consent order, the matter was referred to the Division of Administrative Hearings for a formal administrative hearing. After hearing evidence on February 15 and May 18, 2009, the administrative law judge entered a final order on June 30, 2009, finding Mr. Davis had violated the election code as alleged in the order of probable cause, and concluded that Mr. Davis should pay a civil penalty of $5,000 ($1,000 for each violation) within 30 days, without specifying where, or to whom the penalty should be paid.

The Commission filed a motion for clarification of final order, requesting that Mr. Davis be ordered to remit the penalty directly to the Commission or, at least, to provide the Commission with verification that he had paid the penalty. Purportedly granting the motion for clarification, the administrative law judge entered the corrected final order under review, finding the same violations as before but imposing no penalties. The administrative law judge disavowed any authority to impose a civil penalty: The corrected final order invited the Commission to levy civil penalties on the basis of the fact finding at the Division of Administrative Hearings, but took the position that the administrative law judge lacked any power to impose civil penalties.

Until chapter 2007-30, section 48, Laws of Florida, took effect, administrative law judges' involvement in Commission cases (if any) ended with entry of a recommended order containing findings of fact, conclusions of law, and a recommendation as to penalty. Even where election code violations were proven, the administrative law judge had no authority to impose any penalty. Imposition of penalties fell to the Commission. The Commission could follow the administrative law judge's recommendation as to penalty — or not, after review of the entire record, *see* §120.57(1) (*l*), Fla. Stat. (2006) — once the case returned to the Commission from the Division of Administrative Hearings, and after due deliberation concerning "the gravity of each act or omission" found by the administrative law judge to constitute a violation. *Celestin v. Florida Elections Com'n,* 858 So.2d 382, 383 (Fla. 3d DCA 2003). *See also McGann v. Florida Elections Com'n,* 803 So.2d 763, 766 (Fla. 1st DCA 2001). The amendment to section 106.25(5) that chapter 2007-30, section 48 enacted changed this procedure without mentioning penalties.

Both before and after the amendment, the Commission's statutory authority to levy civil penalties has been clear:

> The commission is authorized upon the finding of a violation of this chapter [Chapter 106] or chapter 104 to impose civil penalties in the form of fines not to exceed $1,000 per count.

§106.265(1), Fla. Stat. (2006). At issue is whether an administrative law judge has comparable statutory authority.

Only the Legislature can confer on executive branch entities the power to levy civil penalties. Explicitly and in no uncertain terms, the Florida Constitution requires statutory authorization for such power:

> *No administrative agency,* except the Department of Military Affairs in an appropriately convened court-martial action as provided by law, shall impose a sentence of imprisonment, nor *shall* it *impose any* other *penalty except as provided by law.*

Art. I, § 18, Fla. Const. (Emphasis supplied.) Section 106.265(1), Florida Statutes (2006), authorizes the Commission, but not the Division of Administrative Hearings or administrative law judges, to levy civil penalties for election code violations.

We do not find such authorization in section 120.574, Florida Statutes (2006), governing summary hearings, set out in pertinent part in the margin. [Footnote omitted.] This provision confers authority on administrative law judges to impose "a fine or penalty, if applicable," as part of a final order *in summary proceedings.* § 120.574(2)(f) 3., Fla. Stat. (2006).

But summary hearings require the agreement of all (original) parties to the proceeding, which would mean here the agreement not only of the Commission, but of Mr. Davis, as well.[2] *See* § 120.574(1), Fla. Stat. (2006). As provided by section 106.25(5), the present case ended up at the Division of Administrative Hearings because of Mr. Davis's inaction, not because of his agreement. Once there, moreover, the statute directed that "a formal administrative hearing conducted by an administrative law judge in the Division of Administrative Hearings" take place. § 106.25(5), Fla. Stat. (2007). A formal administrative hearing contemplates "the formal adjudicatory process described in s. 120.57(1)," not summary proceedings. § 120.574(2)(a) 5, Fla. Stat. (2007).

If administrative law judges' authority to sanction candidates for election code violations is not inferred, the Commission contends, clear violations will go unpunished despite the (Commission's) statutory authority to impose sanctions. The Commission relies heavily on the proposition that statutes on the same subject should be construed *in pari materia,* citing *Forsythe v. Longboat Key Beach Erosion Control District,* 604 So.2d 452, 455 (Fla.1992).[3] The Commission rejects the suggestion that it impose sanctions for election code violations itself, after the administrative law

---

2. We assume for purposes of decision that, if the Commission and Mr. Davis had agreed to proceed under section 120.574, Florida Statutes (2006), the agreement would have conferred authority on the administrative law judge to impose a civil penalty, if appropriate. (Mr. Davis would not, in any event, have been in a position to complain.)

3. It is axiomatic that all parts of a statute must be read *together* in order to achieve a consistent whole. *See, e.g., Marshall v. Hollywood, Inc.,* 224 So.2d 743, 749 (Fla. 4th DCA 1969), *writ discharged,* 236 So.2d 114 (Fla.), *cert. denied,* 400 U.S. 964, 91 S.Ct. 366, 27 L.Ed.2d 384 (1970). Where possible, courts must give full effect to *all* statutory provisions and construe related statutory provisions in harmony with one another. *E.g., Villery v. Florida Parole & Probation Comm'n,* 396 So.2d 1107, 1111 (Fla.1980). *Forsythe v. Longboat Key Beach Erosion Control Dist.,* 604 So.2d 452, 455 (Fla.1992).

judge rules, as unworkable, and in any event at odds with the statutory directive that the administrative law judge "shall enter a final order." § 106.25(5), Fla. Stat. (2007). But the fact remains that no statute authorizes administrative law judges to "impose civil penalties in the form of fines." Only the Commission is so authorized: "The *commission* is authorized . . . to impose civil penalties in the form of fines not to exceed $1,000 per count." § 106.265(1), Fla. Stat. (2006) (emphasis supplied).

The Legislature well knows how to confer on administrative law judges the power to levy administrative penalties as part of the administrative law judge's final order authority. *See* § 379.502(2)(d), Fla. Stat. (2009) (providing, in the event of administrative proceedings instituted by the Florida Fish and Wildlife Conservation Commission for violations of section 379.501, "the administrative law judge shall issue a final order on all matters including the imposition of an administrative penalty"); § 403.121(2)(d), Fla. Stat. (2009) (listing remedies available for violations of chapter 403, and conferring final order authority on administrative law judges, expressly including the ability to impose administrative penalties, in administrative actions in which the Department of Environmental Protection requests imposition of administrative penalties); Ch. 2010-100, § 10, Laws of Fla., creating section 556.116(3)(c), Florida Statutes (conferring final order authority under the Underground Facility Damage Prevention and Safety Act to determine whether an "incident" has occurred and providing that the Division of Administrative Hearings "may impose a fine against a violator"). The Legislature conferred no such authority on administrative law judges in the event of violations of the provisions of chapters 104 or 106. *Inclusio unius est exclusio alterius.*

* * *

Affirmed.

THOMAS and ROWE, JJ., concur.

K. Access to Courts

Fla. Const. art. I, § 21

Access to courts. — The courts shall be open to every person for redress of any injury, and justice shall be administered without sale, denial or delay.

This provision is commonly referred to as the Access to Courts clause of the Florida Constitution. Literally applied, this section would bar the use of filing fees, court costs, and statutes of limitation. Generally, the courts have concluded that the Access to Courts clause is not violated if such restrictions are reasonable.[32] However,

---

32. *See Carter v. Sparkman*, 335 So. 2d 802, 805 (Fla. 1976).

7 · THE DECLARATION OF RIGHTS AND THE TAKING OF PROPERTY   793

where court costs or fees have created an inaccessible barrier, they have been invalidated.[33] Also, statutes of limitation that have operated to bar a cause of action before its accrual also have been invalidated.[34] The Florida Supreme Court has held that the requirement of the payment of a bond to appeal a decision of a medical review board violates the Access to Courts clause.[35] However, a statute requiring indigent non-resident plaintiffs to post a one-hundred dollar bond before commencing an action in a Florida court is not a deprivation of access to the courts.[36] Similarly, a statute prohibiting "vexatious litigants" who may be indigent from maintaining a lawsuit without posting "security" in an amount the court deems appropriate does not violate the Access to Courts clause.[37]

Kluger v. White
281 So. 2d 1 (Fla. 1973)

ADKINS, Justice.

This is an appeal from an order of dismissal entered for defendants and against plaintiff in this property damage action by the Dade County Circuit Court, specifically passing upon the constitutionality of Fla. Stat. § 627.738, F.S.A. We have jurisdiction pursuant to Fla.Const., art. V, § 3(b)(1), F.S.A.

The cause of action arose from an automobile collision between a car owned by appellant, and driven by her son, and one owned by appellee, and driven by another person. The amended complaint filed by appellant alleged that the driver of appellee's car was negligent and had been formally charged with failure to yield the right of way; that there were no personal injuries; that there were damages to appellant's car to the extent of $774.95; and that the fair market value of the car was $250.00.

Appellant was insured with appellee, Manchester Insurance and Indemnity Company, but the policy did not provide for "basic or full" property damage coverage. Appellant alleged that the Manchester agent had not specifically explained to her the possible results of failing to include property damage coverage.

Fla.Stat. § 627.738, F.S.A., provides, in effect, that the traditional right of action in tort for property damage arising from an automobile accident is abolished, and one must look to property damage with one's own insurer, unless the plaintiff is one who

(1) has chosen not to purchase property damage insurance, and

(2) has suffered property damage in excess of $550.00.

* * *

---

33. *G.B.B. Investments, Inc. v. Hinterkopf,* 343 So. 2d 899 (Fla. 3d Dist. Ct. App. 1977).

34. *Diamond v. E. R. Squibb & Sons, Inc.,* 397 So. 2d 671 (Fla. 1981).

35. *Psychiatric Assocs. v. Siegel,* 610 So. 2d 419 (Fla. 1992).

36. *Achord v. Osceola Farms Co.,* 52 So. 3d 699 (Fla. 4th Dist. Ct. App. 2010), *review denied, Achord v. Osceola Farms Co.,* 67 So. 3d 1049 (Fla. 2011).

37. *Smith v. Fisher,* 965 So. 2d 205 (Fla. 4th Dist. Ct. App. 2007), *review denied, Smith v. Fisher,* 980 So. 2d 490 (Fla. 2008).

The appellant in the case *sub judice* falls into that class of accident victims with no recourse against any person or insurer for loss caused by the fault of another, taking her allegations as true. She did not choose to purchase either "full or basic coverage for accidental property damage" to her automobile, and her damages were the fair market value of her automobile since repair costs cannot be recovered where they exceed the fair market value of the automobile before the collision. Blashfield, Automobile Law, Vol. 15, § 480.1, and 25 C.J.S. Damages § 82.

Appellant has raised numerous constitutional challenges to Fla.Stat. § 627.738, F.S.A. As appellant points out in her brief, the issues are limited to the single statute dealing with property damage, and the remainder of the Florida Automobile Reparations Act is not under consideration in the case *sub judice*.

It is likewise unnecessary for this Court to consider but one of the constitutional issues raised by appellant, for we find, as explained below, that Fla.Stat. § 627.728, F.S.A., fails to comply with a reasonable interpretation of Fla.Const., art. I, § 21, F.S.A., which reads as follows:

> "The courts shall be open to every person for redress of any injury, and justice shall be administered without sale, denial or delay."

This Court has never before specifically spoken to the issue of whether or not the constitutional guarantee of a "redress of any injury" (Fla.Const., art. I, § 21, F.S.A.) bars the statutory abolition of an existing remedy without providing an alternative protection to the injured party.

Corpus Juris Secundum provides:

> "A constitutional provision insuring a certain remedy for all injuries or wrongs does not command continuation of a specific statutory remedy. However, in a jurisdiction wherein the constitutional guaranty applies to the legislature as well as to the judiciary, . . . it has been held that the guaranty precludes the repeal of a statute allowing a remedy where the statute was in force at the time of the adoption of the Constitution. Furthermore, . . . the guaranty also prevents, in some jurisdictions, the total abolition of a common-law remedy." 16A C.J.S. Constitutional Law § 710, pp. 1218–1219.

This Court has held that the Declaration of Rights of the Constitution of the State of Florida does apply to State government and to the Legislature. *Spafford v. Brevard County*, 92 Fla. 617, 110 So. 451 (1926). The right to a cause of action in tort for negligent causation of damage to an automobile in a collision was recognized by statute prior to the adoption of the 1968 Constitution of the State of Florida, as evidenced by the fact that Fla.Stat. § 627.728, F.S.A., the statute under attack, specifically exempts owners and drivers of automobiles from tort liability for such damages. In addition, the cause of action for damage to property by force or violence — trespass *vi et armis* — was one of the earliest causes of action recognized at English Common Law.

It is essential, therefore, that this Court consider whether or not the Legislature is, in fact, empowered to abolish a common law and statutory right of action without providing an adequate alternative.

7 · THE DECLARATION OF RIGHTS AND THE TAKING OF PROPERTY   795

Upon careful consideration of the requirements of society, and the ever-evolving character of the law, we cannot adopt a complete prohibition against such legislative change. Nor can we adopt a view which would allow the Legislature to destroy a traditional and long-standing cause of action upon mere legislative whim, or when an alternative approach is available.

We hold, therefore, that where a right of access to the courts for redress for a particular injury has been provided by statutory law predating the adoption of the Declaration of Rights of the Constitution of the State of Florida, or where such right has become a part of the common law of the State pursuant to Fla.Stat. §2.01, F.S.A., the Legislature is without power to abolish such a right without providing a reasonable alternative to protect the rights of the people of the State to redress for injuries, unless the Legislature can show an overpowering public necessity for the abolishment of such right, and no alternative method of meeting such public necessity can be shown.

It is urged that this Court has previously approved action by the Legislature which violated the rule which we have laid down. We disagree.

In *McMillan v. Nelson*, 149 Fla. 334, 5 So.2d 867 (1942), this Court approved the so-called "Guest Statute" which merely changed the degree of negligence necessary for a passenger in an automobile to maintain a tort action against the driver. It did not abolish the right to sue, and does not come under the rule which we have promulgated.

Workmen's compensation abolished the right to sue one's employer in tort for a job-related injury, but provided adequate, sufficient, and even preferable safeguards for an employee who is injured on the job, thus satisfying one of the exceptions to the rule against abolition of the right to redress for an injury.

The Legislature in 1945 enacted Fla.Stat. Ch. 771, F.S.A., which abolishes the rights of action to sue for damages for alienation of affections, criminal conversation, seduction or breach of promise. This Court upheld the validity of the chapter in *Rotwein v. Gersten*, 160 Fla. 736, 36 So.2d 419 (1948). The Court opined:

> "The causes of action proscribed by the act under review were a part of the common law and have long been a part of the law of the country. They have no doubt served a good purpose, but *when they become an instrument of extortion and blackmail, the legislature has the power to, and may, limit or abolish them.*" (Emphasis supplied.) (p. 421)

Thus, in abolishing the right of action for alienation of affections, etc., the Legislature showed the public necessity required for the total abolition of a right to sue.

The Legislature has not presented such a case in relation to the abolition of the right to sue an automotive tortfeasor for property damage. Nor has alternative protection for the victim of the accident been provided, as evidenced by the facts here before the Court.

Had the Legislature chosen to require that appellant be insured against property damage loss — as is, in effect, required by Fla.Stat. §627.733, F.S.A., with respect to other possible damages — the issues would be different. A reasonable alternative to an action in tort would have been provided and the issue would have been whether or not the requirement of insurance for all motorists was reasonable. That issue is not before us.

Retaining the right of action for damages over $550.00 (Fla.Stat. §627.738(5), F.S.A.) does not correct the constitutional infirmity, but merely gives rise to another argument, that appellant has been deprived of the equal protection of the law solely on the basis of the value of her automobile in violation of Fla.Const., art. I, §2, F.S.A., and U.S.Const., amend. XIV, §1. It is unnecessary to reach the merits of this contention because the statute under consideration has already failed constitutional muster on other grounds.

Accordingly, the decision of the trial court holding Fla.Stat. §627.738, F.S.A., to be constitutional and denying appellant a cause of action against appellee is reversed, and the cause is remanded for further proceedings not inconsistent herewith.

It is so ordered.

ROBERTS, ERVIN and McCAIN, JJ., concur.

BOYD, J., dissents with opinion.

CARLTON, C. J., and DEKLE, J., dissent and concur with BOYD, J.

[The dissenting opinion of Justice Boyd is omitted.]

———————

A violation or potential violation of Fla. Const. art. I, §21, necessitating the application of the *Kluger* formula, can take many forms.[38] Although the Florida Supreme Court rejected a constitutional challenge to the workers' compensation law based on access to courts in *Kluger*, the court must consider whether subsequent changes to the workers' compensation law remain a reasonable alternative to tort litigation. The following case is illustrative.

———————

38. *See Weaver v. Myers*, 229 So. 3d 1118 (Fla. 2017); *Warren v. State Farm Mut. Auto. Ins. Co.*, 899 So. 2d 1090 (Fla. 2005); *Kennedy v. Guarantee Mgmt. Servs., Inc.*, 667 So. 2d 1013 (Fla. 3d Dist. Ct. App. 1996).

Westphal v. City of St. Petersburg

194 So. 3d 311 (Fla. 2016)

PARIENTE, J.

[For the facts of this case, see page 75 of this text.]

B. Denial of Access to Courts

Article I, section 21, of the Florida Constitution, part of our state constitutional "Declaration of Rights" since 1968, guarantees every person access to the courts and ensures the administration of justice without denial or delay: "The courts shall be open to every person for redress of any injury, and *justice shall be administered without sale, denial or delay.*" Art. I, § 21, Fla. Const. (emphasis added). This important state constitutional right has been construed liberally in order to "guarantee broad accessibility to the courts for resolving disputes." *Psychiatric Assocs. v. Siegel,* 610 So.2d 419, 424 (Fla.1992), *receded from on other grounds by Agency for Health Care Admin. v. Associated Indus. of Fla., Inc.,* 678 So.2d 1239 (Fla.1996).

In *Kluger,* this Court explained the meaning of the access to courts provision and the necessary showing for demonstrating a constitutional violation based on access to courts:

> [W]here a right of access to the courts for redress for a particular injury has been provided by statutory law predating the adoption of the Declaration of Rights of the Constitution of the State of Florida, or where such right has become a part of the common law of the State pursuant to Fla. Stat. § 2.01, F.S.A., the Legislature is without power to abolish such a right without providing a reasonable alternative to protect the rights of the people of the State to redress for injuries, unless the Legislature can show an overpowering public necessity for the abolishment of such right, and no alternative method of meeting such public necessity can be shown.

281 So.2d at 4.

Prior to 1968, when the access to courts provision was adopted, the Legislature had already abolished the common-law tort remedy for injured workers and enacted a workers' compensation law "as administrative legislation to be simple, expeditious, and inexpensive so that the injured employee, his family, or society generally, would be relieved of the economic stress resulting from work-connected injuries, and place the burden on the industry which caused the injury." *Lee Eng'g & Constr. Co. v. Fellows,* 209 So.2d 454, 456 (Fla.1968). The workers' compensation law "abolishes the right to sue one's employer and substitutes the right to receive benefits under the compensation scheme." *Sasso v. Ram Prop. Mgmt.,* 452 So.2d 932, 933 (Fla.1984).

Nevertheless, the fact that workers' compensation was created prior to 1968 as a non-judicial statutory scheme of no fault benefits intended to provide full medical care and wage-loss payments does not mean that changes to the workers' compensation law to reduce or eliminate benefits are immune from a constitutional attack based on access to courts. In fact, this Court in *Kluger* specifically discussed the alternative remedy of workers' compensation, explaining that "[w]orkmen's compensation abolished the right to sue one's employer in tort for a job-related injury, *but provided adequate, sufficient, and even preferable safeguards for an employee who is injured on the job,* thus satisfying one of the exceptions to the rule against abolition of the right to redress for an injury." *Kluger,* 281 So.2d at 4 (emphasis added). In other words, as *Kluger* held, workers' compensation constitutes a "reasonable alternative" to tort litigation — and therefore does not violate the access to courts provision — so long as it provides adequate and sufficient safeguards for the injured employee. *Id.*

This Court has applied the *Kluger* analysis in subsequent cases that have raised constitutional challenges to the workers' compensation law based on access to courts. Citing to *Kluger,* this Court in *Martinez* explained that in order to be upheld as constitutional, the workers' compensation law must continue to provide a "reasonable alternative to tort litigation." *Martinez,* 582 So.2d at 1171–72; *see also Mahoney v. Sears, Roebuck & Co.,* 440 So.2d 1285, 1286 (Fla.1983) ("Workers' compensation, therefore, still stands as a reasonable litigation alternative.").

In *Martinez,* this Court noted that it "previously has rejected claims that workers' compensation laws violate access to courts by failing to provide a reasonable alternative to common-law tort remedies." *Martinez,* 582 So.2d at 1171 (citing *Kluger,* 281 So.2d at 4). Although the 1990 amendment addressed by the Court in *Martinez* "undoubtedly reduce[d] benefits to eligible workers," by reducing the administration of temporary total disability benefits from 350 weeks to 260 weeks, this Court concluded at that time that "the workers' compensation law *remains a reasonable alternative* to tort litigation." *Id.* at 1171–72 (emphasis added). But this conclusion was premised on the holding that the workers' compensation scheme as a whole continued to provide "injured workers with full medical care and wage-loss payments for total or partial disability regardless of fault and without the delay and uncertainty of tort litigation." *Id.* at 1172. That is, under the *Kluger* analysis, the law at the time of *Martinez,* which provided for 260 weeks for temporary total disability, continued to provide adequate and sufficient safeguards for injured employees.

Therefore, although this Court has rejected constitutional challenges to the workers' compensation law in the past, our precedent clearly establishes that, when confronted with a constitutional challenge based on access to courts, we must determine whether the law "remains a reasonable alternative to tort litigation." *Acton v. Fort Lauderdale Hosp.,* 440 So.2d 1282, 1284 (Fla.1983). However, because the workers' compensation law had already been adopted in 1968, the question in this case is whether the workers' compensation law with regard to the 104–week limitation remains a "system of compensation without contest," *Mullarkey,* 268 So.2d at 366, that provides *"full medical care and wage-loss payments for total or partial disability regardless of fault,"* *Martinez,* 582 So.2d at 1172 (emphasis added).

The 104–week limitation on temporary total disability benefits and the statutory gap must therefore be viewed through the analytical paradigm of *Kluger,* asking whether the workers' compensation law continues to provide adequate and sufficient safeguards for the injured worker and thus constitutes a constitutional, reasonable alternative to tort litigation. *Kluger,* 281 So.2d at 4. The "reasonable alternative" test is then the linchpin and measuring stick, and this Court has undoubtedly upheld as constitutional many limitations on workers' compensation benefits as benefits have progressively been reduced over the years and the statutory scheme changed to the detriment of the injured worker.

But, there must eventually come a "tipping point," where the diminution of bene- fits becomes so significant as to constitute a *denial* of benefits — thus creating a con- stitutional violation. We accordingly must review what has occurred to the workers' compensation system since the 1968 adoption of the access to courts provision, as it relates to providing "full medical care and wage-loss payments for total or partial disability regardless of fault," *Martinez,* 582 So.2d at 1172, in order to determine whether we have now reached that constitutional "tipping point."

As applied to Westphal, the current workers' compensation statutory scheme does not just reduce the amount of benefits he would receive, which was the issue we addressed in *Martinez,* but in fact completely cuts off his ability to receive any disability benefits at all. It does so even though there is no dispute that Westphal remained a severely injured and disabled firefighter under active treatment by doc- tors the City selected for him. As stated in the First District's original panel opinion:

> Under this law, the City — not Westphal — had the right to select and, if appropriate, de-select, the doctors who would treat his work-related inju- ries. Through this statutory system of recovery, the City had the right to meet and confer with their selected doctors without Westphal's involve- ment, and obtain otherwise- confidential medical information — whether or not Westphal consented to such communications. And the City had the right to make decisions as to whether it would authorize the medical treat- ment recommended by the doctors of its choosing. For his part, Westphal, removed from his otherwise inherent right to select his medical provid- ers and make unfettered decisions about his medical care, was required to follow the recommendations of the doctors authorized by his employer. Should he fail to do so, he risked losing entitlement to his workers' compen- sation benefits, his only legal remedy.

> As part of his medical care, Westphal required multiple surgical procedures, culminating in a five-level fusion of the lumbar spine. Under chapter 440, Westphal was then required to refrain from working *and go without disabil- ity pay or wages* — and *wait.* Westphal had to wait until the [City's] autho- rized doctors opined that he had reached maximum medical improvement, with no guarantee that such a day would ever come. But, even once he fully recovered, Westphal could not, under normal circumstances, recover dis- ability benefits for the indeterminate waiting period.

Westphal v. City of St. Petersburg/City of St. Petersburg Risk Mgmt., No. 1D12–3563, op. at 315–16 (Fla. 1st DCA Feb. 28, 2013) (footnote omitted) (emphasis added), *opinion withdrawn and superseded on rehearing en banc by Westphal*, 122 So.3d 440. In other words, even though doctors chosen by the City had performed multiple surgical procedures culminating in a five-level spinal fusion, because those same doctors did not render an opinion that Westphal had reached maximum medical improvement — that is, that he had reached the end of his medical recovery and would improve no further — Westphal was not yet eligible for permanent total disability benefits. And there was no way to know when those doctors would determine that he had reached maximum medical improvement, leaving Westphal without disability benefits for an indefinite amount of time while he was still totally disabled and incapable of working.

In comparing the rights of a worker such as Westphal injured on the job today with those of a worker injured in 1968, the extent of the changes in the workers' compensation system is dramatic. A worker injured in 1968 was entitled to receive temporary total disability benefits for up to 350 weeks. *See* § 440.15(2), Fla. Stat. (1967). In 1990, the Legislature reduced the availability of temporary total disability benefits from 350 to 260 weeks — a 25.7% reduction of two years. *See* ch. 90–201, § 20, Laws of Fla. Then, in 1993, the Legislature again reduced the availability of temporary total disability benefits, this time from 260 weeks to 104 weeks — a 60% reduction. *See* ch. 93–415, § 20, Laws of Fla. This means that an injured worker such as Westphal is now eligible to receive only 104 weeks of temporary total disability benefits — a massive 70% reduction when compared to the temporary total disability benefits available in 1968.

It is uncontroverted that decreasing substantially the period of payments from 350 weeks to 104 weeks, standing alone, results in a dramatic reduction from almost seven years of disability benefits down to two years. Whereas almost seven years or even five years post-accident should be a reasonable period for an injured worker to achieve maximum medical improvement, clearly two years is not for the most severely injured of workers, like Westphal, who might be in need of multiple surgical interventions.

Currently, at the conclusion of the 104–week limit, temporary total disability benefits cease, regardless of the condition of the injured worker. Therefore, rather than receive "full medical care and wage-loss payments" for a continuing disability, as the workers' compensation law was intended, an injured worker's full medical care and wage-loss payments are eliminated after 104 weeks if the worker falls into the statutory gap. This is true even if the worker remains incapable of working for an indefinite period of time, based on the advice of the employer-selected doctors.

Recognizing the constitutional implications of such a statutory scheme, Judge Van Nortwick, in his dissent in *Hadley,* cogently noted:

> [I]n the case of a totally disabled claimant whose rights to temporary disability benefits has expired, but who is prohibited from receiving permanent

disability benefits, the elimination of disability benefits may reach a point where the claimant's cause of action has been effectively eliminated. In such a case, the courts might well find that the benefits under the Workers' Compensation Law are no longer a reasonable alternative to a tort remedy and that, as a result, workers have been denied access to courts.

78 So.3d at 634 (Van Nortwick, J., dissenting). We have now reached that point at which "the claimant's cause of action has been effectively eliminated" — the constitutional "tipping point" of which Judge Van Nortwick forewarned.

We conclude that the 104–week limitation on temporary total disability benefits, as applied to a worker like Westphal, who falls into the statutory gap at the conclusion of those benefits, does not provide a "reasonable alternative" to tort litigation. Under the current statute, workers such as Westphal are denied their constitutional right of access to the courts. We agree with the point our colleague, Justice Lewis, makes in his concurring in result opinion that:

> Under the plain language of the statute, many hardworking Floridians who become injured in the course of employment are denied the benefits necessary to pay their bills and survive on a day-to-day basis. The inequitable impact of this statute is patent because it provides permanent total disability benefits to the disabled worker who reaches maximum medical improvement quickly, but arbitrarily and indefinitely terminates benefits to other disabled workers — i.e., until the employee proves that he or she is permanently and totally disabled once maximum medical improvement is attained, *even where there is no dispute that the employee is totally disabled at the time the temporary benefits expire, and even if maximum medical improvement will occur in the future.*

Concurring in result op. of Lewis, J., at 329-30 (footnote omitted) (emphasis in original).

* * *

Thus, under the access to courts analysis articulated in *Kluger,* the only way to avoid a holding of unconstitutionality under these circumstances would be to demonstrate an overwhelming public necessity to justify the Legislature's elimination of temporary total disability benefits after 104 weeks for our most injured workers. *See Kluger,* 281 So.2d at 4. We conclude that this showing has not been made. The statute is unconstitutional as applied.

* * *

III. Conclusion

For all the reasons explained in this opinion, we hold section 440.15(2)(a), Florida Statutes (2009), unconstitutional as applied to Westphal and all others similarly situated, as a denial of access to courts under article I, section 21, of the Florida Constitution. The statute deprives a severely injured worker of disability benefits at a critical time, when the worker cannot return to work and is totally disabled, but the worker's doctors — chosen by the employer — determine that the worker has not reached maximum medical improvement.

Such a significant diminution in the availability of benefits for severely injured workers, particularly when considered in conjunction with the totality of changes to the workers' compensation law from 1968, when the access to courts provision was added to our Constitution, to the present, is unconstitutional under our precedent. Accordingly, we quash the First District's en banc decision in *Westphal* and remand this case to the First District for further proceedings consistent with this opinion.

It is so ordered.

LABARGA, C.J., and QUINCE, and PERRY, JJ., concur.

LEWIS, J., concurs in result with an opinion. [The concurring opinion of Justice Lewis is omitted.]

CANADY, J., dissents with an opinion, in which POLSTON, J., concurs.

CANADY, J., dissenting.

... I would reject Westphal's argument that the statutory limitation on the period of eligibility for temporary total disability benefits violates the right of access to courts provided for in article I, section 21 of the Florida Constitution.

In the foundational case of *Kluger v. White,* 281 So.2d 1, 4 (Fla.1973) (emphasis added), we set forth the test for determining whether an access- to-courts violation has occurred:

> [W]here a right of access to the courts for redress for a particular injury has been provided by statutory law predating the adoption of the Declaration of Rights of the [1968] Constitution of the State of Florida, or where such right has become a part of the common law of the State pursuant to [section 2.01, Florida Statutes], the Legislature is without power to *abolish such a right* without providing a reasonable alternative to protect the rights of the people of the State to redress for injuries, unless the Legislature can show an overpowering public necessity for the abolishment of such right, and no alternative method of meeting such public necessity can be shown.

(Emphasis added.) The threshold question in evaluating an access-to-courts claim therefore is whether the Legislature has abolished a right of redress that was in existence when the access to courts provision was incorporated into the 1968 Constitution.

Here, the challenged statutory provision restructures an existing right of redress. It does not abolish that right. The State argues persuasively that "today's workers' compensation system allowed Westphal substantially greater temporary total disability benefits than any 1968 statutory right provided" and that "[t]he amendment limiting temporary total disability benefits to 104 weeks, therefore, did not 'abolish' any pre- existing right." State's Answer Brief at 14. Westphal does not dispute the State's assertion that the aggregate compensation paid to him for temporary total disability benefits substantially exceeded the aggregate compensation for such benefits that would have been available under the pre–1968 law, even when the pre–1968 benefits are adjusted for inflation. Instead, he contends that "[t]his case is about weeks, not about dollars." Petitioner's Reply Brief at 9. But the decision to substantially increase weekly compensation for temporary total disability and to reduce the number of weeks that such benefits are paid is a trade-off that is a matter of policy within the province of the Legislature. The Legislature — rather than this Court — has the institutional competence and authority to make such policy judgments.

* * *

L. Privacy

1. In General

Fla. Const. art. I, § 23

Right of privacy. — Every natural person has the right to be let alone and free from governmental intrusion into the person's private life except as otherwise provided herein. This section shall not be construed to limit the public's right of access to public records and meetings as provided by law.

This provision was added to the Florida Constitution in 1980. It is assuming a preeminent role in state constitutional law adjudication. The Florida Supreme Court explained that the right of privacy in the Florida Constitution is broader in scope than the right of privacy under the Federal Constitution.[39] The Florida Supreme Court also has held that the right of privacy in the Florida Constitution that attaches to the life of a citizen "is not retroactively destroyed by death."[40] In the following case, the Florida Supreme Court identified the right of privacy as a fundamental right. As a fundamental right, it is subject to particularly rigorous protection by the judiciary.

---

39. *Weaver v. Myers*, 229 So. 3d 1118, 1125–1126 (Fla. 2017).
40. *Id.* at 1141–1142.

Winfield v. Division of Pari-Mutuel Wagering, Department of Business Regulation

477 So. 2d 544 (Fla. 1985)

ADKINS, Justice.

This cause is before us for review of two questions certified by the Fourth District Court of Appeal to be of great public importance. *Division of Pari-Mutuel Wagering, Department of Business Regulation v. Winfield*, 443 So.2d 455 (Fla. 4th DCA 1984). We have jurisdiction. Art. V, § 3(b)(4), Fla. Const.

The Department of Business Regulation and the Division of Pari-Mutuel Wagering, respondents, issued subpoenas duces tecum to various banking institutions to obtain banking records of the accounts of Nigel Winfield and Malcolm Winfield, petitioners. Respondents gave no notice of the subpoenas to petitioners and asked the banks not to inform petitioners of the investigation.

Petitioners filed for declaratory and injunctive relief against the subpoenas duces tecum alleging that the subpoenas were facially invalid, that they violated petitioners' constitutional right to privacy and due process, and that maintenance of the records as public records in the respondent's files constituted an additional violation of their constitutional right to privacy. The circuit court found that respondents had probable cause to institute the investigation, and that it had acted within its authority. The court nevertheless granted petitioners relief on the grounds that their constitutional privacy rights would be violated if the subpoenaed records became public records in the hands of respondents pursuant to chapter 119, Florida Statutes. The court thereupon confirmed a previous interlocutory order in effect restraining respondents from inspecting, copying or using the records or the information contained in them, and directing that the records be maintained under court seal. Appeal was taken to the district court which ruled in favor of respondents and certified the following questions to this Court as being of great public importance:

> I. Does article I, section 23 of the Florida Constitution prevent the Division of Pari-Mutuel Wagering from subpoenaing a Florida citizen's bank records without notice?

> II. Does the subpoenaing of *all* of a citizen's bank records under the facts of this case constitute an impermissible and unbridled exercise of legislative power?

443 So.2d at 457. We answer both questions in the negative and approve the decision of the district court.

The concept of privacy or right to be let alone is deeply rooted in our heritage and is founded upon historical notions and federal constitutional expressions of ordered liberty. Justice Brandeis, sometimes called the father of the idea of privacy, recognized this fundamental right of privacy when he wrote:

> The makers of our Constitution undertook to secure conditions favorable to the pursuit of happiness. They recognized the significance of man's spiritual

nature, of his feelings and of his intellect. . . . They sought to protect Americans in their beliefs, their thoughts, their emotions and their sensations. They conferred, as against the Government, the right to be let alone — the most comprehensive of rights and the right most valued by civilized men.

Olmstead v. United States, 277 U.S. 438, 478, 48 S.Ct. 564, 572, 72 L.Ed. 944 (1928) (Brandeis, J., dissenting).

The United States Supreme Court has fashioned a right of privacy which protects the decision-making or autonomy zone of privacy interests of the individual. The Court's decisions include matters concerning marriage, procreation, contraception, family relationships and child rearing, and education. *Roe v. Wade*, 410 U.S. 113, 152–53, 93 S.Ct. 705, 726–27, 35 L.Ed.2d 147 (1973). Other privacy interests enunciated by the Court in *Nixon v. Administrator of General Services*, 433 U.S. 425, 97 S. Ct. 277, 53 L.Ed.2d 867 (1977), and *Whalen v. Roe*, 429 U.S. 589, 97 S.Ct. 869, 51 L. Ed.2d 64 (1976), involve one's interest in avoiding the public disclosure of personal matters. However, *Nixon*, *Whalen*, and those cases involving the autonomy zone of privacy are not directly applicable to the case at bar.

Likewise, the decision of the Third District Court of Appeal in *Milohnich v. First National Bank*, 224 So.2d 759 (Fla. 3d DCA 1969), does not apply to the case before us. In that case, the court held that the complaint was sufficient to state a cause of action for breach by a bank of an implied contractual duty to its depositor by negligently, intentionally, willfully or maliciously disclosing information concerning a depositor's accounts to a private third party. *Id.* at 762. In *Milohnich*, the court clearly stated that it was dealing with the bank's liability only and not with disclosures required by the government or under compulsion of law. *Id.*

In formulating privacy interests, the Supreme Court has given much of the responsibility to the individual states. *Katz v. United States*, 389 U.S. 347, 350–351, 88 S.Ct. 507, 511, 19 L.Ed.2d 576 (1967). Thus, on November 4, 1980, the voters of Florida approved article I, section 23, thereby adding a new privacy provision to the Florida Constitution. Article I, section 23 provides:

> Right of privacy. — Every natural person has the right to be let alone and free from governmental intrusion into his private life except as otherwise provided herein. This section shall not be construed to limit the public's right of access to public records and meetings as provided by law.

Heretofore, we have not enunciated the appropriate standard of review in assessing a claim of unconstitutional governmental intrusion into one's privacy rights under article I, section 23. Since the privacy section as adopted contains no textual standard of review, it is important for us to identify an explicit standard to be applied in order to give proper force and effect to the amendment. The right of privacy is a fundamental right which we believe demands the compelling state interest standard. This test shifts the burden of proof to the state to justify an intrusion on privacy. The burden can be met by demonstrating that the challenged regulation serves a compelling state interest and accomplishes its goal through the use of the least intrusive means. *See Roe v. Wade*, 410 U.S. 113, 93 S.Ct. 705, 35 L.Ed.2d 147 (1973); *In re Estate of Greenberg*, 390 So.2d 40 (Fla. 1980).

Although we choose a strong standard to review a claim under article I, section 23, "this constitutional provision was not intended to provide an absolute guarantee against all governmental intrusion into the private life of an individual." *Florida Board of Bar Examiners Re: Applicant*, 443 So.2d 71, 74 (Fla.1983). The right of privacy does not confer a complete immunity from governmental regulation and will yield to compelling governmental interests.

However, before the right of privacy is attached and the delineated standard applied, a reasonable expectation of privacy must exist. Thus, implicit within the question of whether article I, section 23 of the Florida Constitution prevents the Division of Pari-Mutuel Wagering from subpoenaing a Florida citizen's bank records [without] notice, is the threshold question of whether the law recognizes an individual's legitimate expectation of privacy in financial institution records.

The United States Supreme Court addressed the threshold question in *United States v. Miller*, 425 U.S. 435, 96 S.Ct. 1619, 48 L.Ed.2d 71 (1976), where it held that bank records, subpoenaed by the government without notice to a depositor under investigation, did not fall within a protected zone of privacy and were not "private papers" protected by the Fourth Amendment. *Id.* at 440, 96 S.Ct. at 1622–23. In reaching its conclusion, the Court further noted that there is no legitimate "expectation of privacy" in the contents of original checks and deposit slips in the possession of a bank. *Id.* at 442, 96 S.Ct. at 1623–24. However, as previously noted, the United States Supreme Court has also made it absolutely clear that the states, not the federal government, are responsible for the protection of personal privacy: "the protection of a person's general right to privacy — his right to be let alone by other people — is, like the protection of his property and of his very life, left largely to the law of the individual States." *Katz v. United States*, 389 U.S. 347, 350–51, 88 S.Ct. 507, 511, 19 L. Ed.2d 576 (1967). This Court accepted that responsibility of protecting the privacy interests of Florida citizens when we stated that "the citizens of Florida, through their state constitution, may provide themselves with more protection from governmental intrusion than that afforded by the United States Constitution." *State v. Sarmiento*, 397 So.2d 643, 645 (1981).

The citizens of Florida opted for more protection from governmental intrusion when they approved article I, section 23, of the Florida Constitution. This amendment is an independent, freestanding constitutional provision which declares the fundamental right to privacy. Article I, section 23, was intentionally phrased in strong terms. The drafters of the amendment rejected the use of the words "unreasonable" or "unwarranted" before the phrase "governmental intrusion" in order to make the privacy right as strong as possible. Since the people of this state exercised their prerogative and enacted an amendment to the Florida Constitution which expressly and succinctly provides for a strong right of privacy not found in the United States Constitution, it can only be concluded that the right is much broader in scope than that of the Federal Constitution.

This is a case of first impression in the state of Florida; therefore, it is within the discretion of this Court to decide the limitations and latitude afforded article I, section 23. We believe that the amendment should be interpreted in accordance with the intent of its drafters. Thus, we find that the law in the state of Florida recognizes an individual's legitimate expectation of privacy in financial institution records. However, we further find that the state's interest in conducting effective investigations in the pari-mutuel industry is a compelling state interest and that the least intrusive means was employed to achieve that interest. We also note that predisclosure notification by a bank to its customers should not be and is not mandated by article I, section 23. Thus, we hold that article I, section 23, of the Florida Constitution does not prevent the Division of Pari-Mutuel wagering from subpoenaing a Florida citizen's bank records without notice.

Concerning the second certified question, we believe that the information sought by the government was essential to its inquiry. To ensure that it has all of the information necessary for a complete investigation, the agency rather than the bank or depositor must calculate what is and what is not relevant. The subpoenas in question were reasonably calculated to obtain information relevant to a state investigation. There is nothing in the record to support a contrary finding. Thus, we hold that the subpoenaing of all of a citizen's bank records under the facts of this case does not constitute an impermissible and unbridled exercise of legislative power.

It is so ordered.

BOYD, C.J., and OVERTON, EHRLICH and SHAW, JJ., concur.

McDONALD, J., concurs in result only.

2. The Existence of a Reasonable Expectation of Privacy

As stated by the Florida Supreme Court in *Winfield*, before the protections of Fla. Const. art. I, §23 apply to a person, that person must have a reasonable expectation of privacy in the circumstances into which the government has intruded. The boundaries of this reasonable expectation were discussed by the Fourth District Court of Appeal in *State v. Conforti*.[41] The context was an obscene[42] performance by the appellee.

> ... The United States Supreme Court has recognized that the federal right encompasses and protects "the personal intimacies of the home, the family, marriage, motherhood, procreation, and child rearing." *Id.* Florida's right of privacy "embraces more privacy interests, and extends more protection to the individual in those interests, than does the federal Constitution." *In re T.W.*, 551 So.2d 1186, 1192, (Fla.1989); *accord Mozo v. State*, 632 So.2d 623, 632–33 (Fla. 4th DCA 1994), aff'd, 655 So.2d 1115 (Fla. 1995).

---

41. 688 So. 2d 350, 357–359 (Fla. 4th Dist. Ct. App. 1997).
42. The court found that the appellees' activity was not protected by freedom of speech.

The supreme court first considered article I, section 23 in *Winfield*, where it held that privacy is a fundamental right subject to the compelling state interest standard of review. 477 So.2d at 547. If the right attaches to a claimed privacy interest, the burden of proof shifts to the state to prove that a governmental intrusion on privacy both serves a compelling state interest and accomplishes its goal through the least intrusive means. *Id.* Before the right to privacy attaches and the compelling state interest standard is applied, there must be a "legitimate" expectation of privacy. *City of North Miami v. Kurtz*, 653 So.2d 1025, 1028 (Fla. 1995), *cert. denied*, ___ U.S. ___, 116 S.Ct. 701, 133 L.Ed.2d 658 (1996); *Stall v. State*, 570 So.2d 257, 260 (Fla.1990), *cert. denied sub nom., Long v. Florida*, 501 U.S. 1250, 111 S. Ct. 2888, 115 L.Ed.2d 1054 (1991); *Winfield*, 477 So.2d at 547. "Determining whether an individual has a legitimate expectation of privacy in any given case must be made by considering all the circumstances, especially objective manifestations of that expectation." *Stall*, 570 So.2d at 260 (quoting *Shaktman v. State*, 553 So.2d 148, 153 (Ehrlich, C.J., concurring)); *City of North Miami*, 653 So.2d at 1028. Delineating the zone of privacy protected by the constitution begins with the subjective expectations of the individual, which are protected "provided they are not spurious or false." *Mozo*, 632 So.2d at 634.

* * *

... Florida's right to privacy is broad and deep, but it is not a guarantee against all intrusion into the private life of an individual. *Kurtz*, 653 So.2d at 1027–28; *Stall*, 570 So.2d at 262. Although a person's subjective expectation of privacy is one consideration in deciding whether a constitutional right attaches, the final determination of an expectation's legitimacy takes a more global view, placing the individual in the context of a society and the values that the society seeks to foster. [Footnote omitted.] The right to privacy has not made each person a solipsistic island of self-determination. Florida's constitutional right to privacy is not implicated in this case.

City of North Miami v. Kurtz

653 So. 2d 1025 (Fla. 1995)

OVERTON, Justice.

We have for review *Kurtz v. City of North Miami*, 625 So.2d 899 (Fla. 3d DCA 1993). After the district court issued that decision, it certified, in a separate order, the following question as one of great public importance:

DOES ARTICLE I, SECTION 23 OF THE FLORIDA CONSTITUTION PROHIBIT A MUNICIPALITY FROM REQUIRING JOB APPLICANTS TO REFRAIN FROM USING TOBACCO OR TOBACCO PRODUCTS FOR ONE YEAR BEFORE APPLYING FOR, AND AS A CONDITION FOR BEING CONSIDERED FOR EMPLOYMENT, EVEN WHERE THE

USE OF TOBACCO IS NOT RELATED TO JOB FUNCTION IN THE POSITION SOUGHT BY THE APPLICANT?

This question involves the issue of whether applicants seeking government employment have a reasonable expectation of privacy under article I, section 23, as to their smoking habits.[1] We have jurisdiction. Art. I, § 3(b)(4), Fla. Const. For the reasons expressed, we answer the certified question in the negative, finding that Florida's constitutional privacy provision does not afford Arlene Kurtz, the job applicant in this case, protection under the circumstances presented.

The record establishes the following unrefuted facts. To reduce costs and to increase productivity, the City of North Miami adopted an employment policy designed to reduce the number of employees who smoke tobacco. In accordance with that policy decision, the City issued Administrative Regulation 1-46, which requires all job applicants to sign an affidavit stating that they have not used tobacco or tobacco products for at least one year immediately preceding their application for employment. The intent of the regulation is to gradually reduce the number of smokers in the City's work force by means of natural attrition. Consequently, the regulation only applies to job applicants and does not affect current employees. Once an applicant has been hired, the applicant is free to start or resume smoking at any time. Evidence in the record, however, reflects that a high percentage of smokers who have adhered to the one year cessation requirement are unlikely to resume smoking.

Additional evidence submitted by the City indicates that each smoking employee costs the City as much as $4,611 per year in 1981 dollars over what it incurs for non-smoking employees. The City is a self-insurer and its taxpayers pay for 100% of its employees' medical expenses. In enacting the regulation, the City made a policy decision to reduce costs and increase productivity by eventually eliminating a substantial number of smokers from its work force. Evidence presented to the trial court indicated that the regulation would accomplish these goals.

The respondent in this case, Arlene Kurtz, applied for a clerk-typist position with the City. When she was interviewed for the position, she was informed of Regulation 1-46. She told the interviewer that she was a smoker and could not truthfully sign an affidavit to comply with the regulation. The interviewer then informed Kurtz that she would not be considered for employment until she was smoke-free for one year. Thereafter, Kurtz filed this action seeking to enjoin enforcement of the regulation and asking for a declaratory judgment finding the regulation to be unconstitutional.

In ruling on a motion for summary judgment, the trial judge recognized that Kurtz has a fundamental right of privacy under article I, section 23 of the Florida Constitution. The trial judge noted that Kurtz had presented the issue in the narrow

---

1. Notably, because Florida's constitutional privacy provision applies only to government action, the provision would not be implicated if a job applicant was applying for a position with a private employer.

context of whether she has a right to smoke in her own home. While he agreed that such a right existed, he concluded that the true issue to be decided was whether the City, as a government entity, could regulate smoking through employment. Because he found that there is no expectation of privacy in employment and that the regulation did not violate any provision of either the Florida or the federal constitutions, summary judgment was granted in favor of the City.

The Third District Court of Appeal reversed. The district court first determined that Kurtz' privacy rights are involved when the City requires her to refrain from smoking for a year prior to being considered to employment. The district court then found that, although the City does have an interest in saving taxpayers money by decreasing insurance costs and increasing productivity, such interest is insufficient to outweigh the intrusion into Kurtz' right of privacy and has no relevance to the performance of the duties involved with a clerk-typist. Consequently, the district court concluded that the regulation violated Kurtz's privacy rights under article I, section 23, of the Florida Constitution. We disagree.

Florida's constitutional privacy provision, which is contained in article I, section 23, provides as follows:

> Right of privacy. — Every natural person has the right to be let alone and free from governmental intrusion into his private life except as otherwise provided herein. This section shall not be construed to limit the public's right of access to public records and meetings as provided by law.

This right to privacy protects Florida's citizens from the government's uninvited observation of or interference in those areas that fall within the ambit of the zone of privacy afforded under this provision. *Shaktman v. State*, 553 So.2d 148 (Fla.1989). Unlike the implicit privacy right of the federal constitution, Florida's privacy provision is, in and of itself, a fundamental one that, once implicated, demands evaluation under a compelling state interest standard. *Winfield v. Division of Pari-Mutuel Wagering*, 477 So.2d 544 (Fla.1985). The federal privacy provision, on the other hand, extends only to such fundamental interests as marriage, procreation, contraception, family relationships, and the rearing and educating of children. *Carey v. Population Serv. Int'l*, 431 U.S. 678, 97 S.Ct. 2010, 52 L.Ed.2d 675 (1977).

Although Florida's privacy right provides greater protection than the federal constitution, it was not intended to be a guarantee against all intrusion into the life of an individual. *Florida Bd. of Bar Examiners re Applicant*, 443 So.2d 71 (Fla.1983). First, the privacy provision applies only to government action, and the right provided under that provision is circumscribed and limited by the circumstances in which it is asserted. *Id.* Further, "[d]etermining 'whether an *individual* has a legitimate expectation of privacy in any given case must be made by considering all the circumstances, especially objective manifestations of that expectation.'" *Stall v. State*, 570 So.2d 257, 260 (Fla.1990) (alteration in original) (quoting *Shaktman*, 553 So.2d at 153 (Fla. 1989) (Ehrlich, C.J., concurring)), *cert. denied*, 501 U.S. 1250, 111 S.Ct. 2888, 115 L.Ed.2d 1054 (1991). Thus, to determine whether Kurtz, as a job applicant, is entitled to protection under article I, section 23, we must first determine whether a governmental entity is intruding into an aspect of Kurtz's life in which she has a "legitimate expectation of privacy." If we find in the affirmative, we must then look to whether a compelling interest exists to justify that intrusion and, if so, whether the least intrusive means is being used to accomplish the goal.

In this case, we find that the City's action does not intrude into an aspect of Kurtz' life in which she has a legitimate expectation of privacy. In today's society, smokers are constantly required to reveal whether they smoke. When individuals are seated in a restaurant, they are asked whether they want a table in a smoking or non-smoking section. When individual rent hotel or motel rooms, they are asked if they smoke so that management may ensure that certain rooms remain free from the smell of smoke odors. Likewise, when individuals rent cars, they are asked if they smoke so that rental agencies can make proper accommodations to maintain vehicles for non-smokers. Further, employers generally provide smoke-free areas for non-smokers, and employees are often prohibited from smoking in certain areas. Given that individuals must reveal whether they smoke in almost every aspect of life in today's society, we conclude that individuals have no reasonable expectation of privacy in the disclosure of that information when applying for a government job and, consequently, that Florida's right of privacy is not implicated under these unique circumstances.

In reaching the conclusion that the right to privacy is not implicated in this case, however, we emphasize that our holding is limited to the narrow issue presented. Notably, we are not addressing the issue of whether an applicant, once hired, could be compelled by a government agency to stop smoking. Equally as important, neither are we holding today that a governmental entity can ask any type of information it chooses of prospective job applicants.

* * *

For the reasons expressed, we answer the question in the negative, finding that Florida's constitutional privacy provision does not afford the applicant, Arlene Kurtz, protection because she has no reasonable expectation of privacy under the circumstances of this case. Accordingly, we quash the district court's decision, and we remand this case with directions that the district court of appeal affirm the trial court judgment.

It is so ordered.

GRIMES, C.J., and HARDING, WELLS and ANSTEAD, JJ., concur.

KOGAN, J., dissents with an opinion, in which SHAW, J., concurs.

[Justice Kogan's dissent is omitted.]

Green v. Alachua County

323 So. 3d 246 (Fla. 1st Dist. Ct. App. 2021)

Tanenbaum, J.[1]

From May 2020 until around mid-May 2021, anyone residing in or visiting Alachua County has found himself under the yoke of a mask mandate, accomplished through a series of emergency orders from the chair of the board of county commissioners. Under these fiats, any person in the county had to wear a government- approved face-covering to patronize a restaurant, grocery store, or retail establishment; visit or work on a construction site; or use public transit. The diktats also required that a person cover his face in any location "where social distancing measures are not possible." One consequence for being caught without a mask was a fine. Another consequence was being subjected to whispering informants, impelled by county-designed publicity . . .

The threat of government-sponsored shaming was not an idle one. The chairman who issued the original mask mandate stated publicly that "masks are the only outwardly visible signal that you are contributing to the solution," and that "masks are also a sign of respect that you recognize [essential workers'] risk and are doing something to lower it." Justin Green sued the county to challenge the mask mandate, which until recently seemed like it might never end.[2] Green argues, among other

---

1. Judge Tanenbaum substituted in for Judge Makar after oral argument had taken place in this case, but he has viewed the recording of that argument — and of course has considered the briefs — in full.

2. Green recently suggested this matter is now moot, but we disagree. At the beginning of May, the Governor issued another COVID-19-emergency executive order, this one Executive Order 21-102. That order purports to "eliminate[ ] and supersede[ ] all local COVID-19 restrictions and mandates on individuals and businesses." Fla. Exec. Order 21-102 § 1 (May 3, 2021); *see also id.* § 2 (purporting to eliminate and supersede any local emergency order or ordinance that imposes "restrictions or mandates upon businesses or individuals due to the COVID-19 emergency"); § 3 (prohibiting local governments from renewing or enacting any such "restrictions or mandates"). While the State seemingly continues to be governed more by a flurry of state and local orders, and less by statutes and ordinances, this opinion offers no comment on the effect the Governor's order may have on local mandates like the one at issue here.

Still, Green advises that the county recently failed to renew (one more time, at least, after many previous renewals) its continuing local state of emergency. Even though the latest mask mandate was to stay in effect "until Alachua County no longer has a local state of emergency," Alachua Cnty. Emergency Order 2021-13, § 5 (March 22, 2021), the latest gubernatorial executive order expressly does *not* preclude the county from enacting an actual ordinance, "pursuant to regular enactment procedures," containing the same mask mandate, provided the enacted mandate is not "based on a local state of emergency or on emergency enactment procedures due to the COVID-19 emergency." Fla. Exec. Order 21-102, § 4.

Because of the nature of the various emergency orders that we have seen and the county's continued commitment to public mask-wearing, we are not convinced that this is the last that we will see of this issue. We conclude, then, that this case fits within the exception to the mootness doctrine, which is "for controversies that are capable of repetition, yet evading review." *Morris Publ'g Grp., LLC v. State* , 136 So. 3d 770, 776 (Fla. 1st DCA 2014) (internal quotation omitted); *cf. Tandon*

points, that the county's command that he wear something on his face violated his fundamental right to privacy. He moved for an emergency temporary injunction, and after a hearing, the trial court denied the request. Green appeals that order denying the injunction. We reverse because the trial court did not apply the strict scrutiny that the supreme court specifically requires for this type of constitutional challenge. We remand so the trial court can apply the correct analysis, if there is any extant mask mandate for Green to challenge.

* * *

II.

A.

When we look at the proceeding before the trial court through the lens of *Gainesville Woman Care*, then, we must initially consider whether the trial court reached the right conclusion about whether the mask mandate implicated a privacy right. The trial court did not subject the mask mandate to strict-scrutiny analysis, because the court concluded at the threshold that there was no cognizable constitutional right in play. As the trial court put it in its order, "[t]here is no recognized constitutional right *not* to wear a facial covering in *public* locations or to expose other citizens of the county to a contagious and potentially lethal virus during a declared pandemic emergency."

The trial court, though, did not assess Florida law to consider Green's asserted right of privacy. Indeed, it never discussed or even referenced the Florida Constitution's express guarantee of privacy. It instead relied heavily on a case from a federal appellate court that considered a challenge to Florida's motorcycle helmet law under the United States Constitution. *Cf. Picou v. Gillum*, 874 F.2d 1519, 1521–22 (11th Cir. 1989). In *Picou*, the Eleventh Circuit stated that "there is no broad legal or constitutional 'right to be let alone' by government," which the trial court quoted in its order. *Id.* at 1521. The trial court later backtracked by seemingly acknowledging there is a right to be let alone, but it still concluded that the right "is no more precious than the corresponding right of his fellow citizens not to become infected by that person and potentially hospitalized."

We cannot reconcile this analysis of the trial court with the express privacy guarantee found in the Florida Constitution, as it has been characterized and interpreted by our supreme court. The trial court simply looked at the right asserted by Green too narrowly, relying on the wrong privacy jurisprudence. The right to be let alone by government does exist in Florida, as part of a right of privacy that our supreme court has declared to be fundamental. *See, e.g.*, *Winfield*, 477 So. 2d at 547. As we

---

v. Newsom , —— U.S. ——, 141 S. Ct. 1294, 1297, 209 L.Ed.2d 355 (2021) (per curiam) (noting that "even if the government withdraws or modifies a COVID restriction in the course of litigation, that does not necessarily moot the case," so long as a petitioner remains" 'under a constant threat' that government officials will use their power to reinstate the challenged restrictions" (quoting *Roman Catholic Diocese of Brooklyn v. Cuomo* , —— U.S. ——, 141 S. Ct. 63, 75, 208 L.Ed.2d 206 (2020))).

are about to explain, the supreme court has construed this fundamental right to be so broad as to include the complete freedom of a person to control his own body. Under this construction, a person reasonably can expect not to be forced by the government to put something on his own face against his will. Florida's constitutional right to privacy, then, necessarily is implicated by the nature of the county's mask mandate. This means the trial court had to apply the single-prong, strict-scrutiny mode of analysis set out in *Gainesville Woman Care*. Because of its erroneous treatment of Green's asserted right, the trial court did not do so. That is the error we correct by reversing the order currently on review.

B.

A person's "right to be let alone by other people" is "left largely to the law of the individual States" and is not contained in the Fourth Amendment of the U.S. Constitution. *Katz v. United States*, 389 U.S. 347, 350, 88 S.Ct. 507, 19 L.Ed.2d 576 (1967); *see also State v. Sarmiento*, 397 So. 2d 643, 645 (Fla. 1981) ("[T]he citizens of Florida, through their state constitution, may provide themselves with more protection from governmental intrusion than that afforded by the United States Constitution."). Florida's citizens later secured for themselves a broader state right of privacy, including an explicit right to be let alone, by adding section 23 to the Florida Constitution's Declaration of Rights, which states in pertinent part as follows: "Every natural person has *the right to be let alone* and free from governmental intrusion into the person's private life except as otherwise provided herein." Art. I, § 23, Fla. Const. (emphasis supplied); *see Winfield*, 477 So. 2d at 548 (characterizing amendment as "an independent, freestanding constitutional provision which declares the fundamental right to privacy," and as one "intentionally phrased in strong terms"); *cf. id.* ("The drafters of the amendment rejected the use of the words 'unreasonable' or 'unwarranted' before the phrase 'governmental intrusion' in order to make the privacy right as strong as possible.").

* * *

Although the constitutional text is silent on the point, the supreme court has explained repeatedly that within the right to be let alone is "a fundamental right to the *sole control* of his or her person." *In re Guardianship of Browning*, 568 So. 2d 4, 10 (Fla. 1990) (emphasis supplied) (quoting *Schloendorff v. Soc'y of New York Hosp.*, 211 N.Y. 125, 105 N.E. 92, 93 (1914) ("Every human being of adult years and sound mind has a right to determine what shall be done with his own body. . . .")); *Burton v. State*, 49 So. 3d 263, 265 (Fla. 1st DCA 2010). This right ostensibly covers "an individual's control over or the autonomy of the intimacies of personal identity" and a "physical and psychological zone within which an individual has the right to be free from intrusion or coercion, whether by government or by society at large." *Browning*, 568 So. 2d at 10 (quotations and citations omitted). The supreme court has applied the principle to state that a person cannot be forced to receive unwanted medical treatment, *Id.* at 11–12 ; or be forced to devote her body to the carrying of a child to term, *see In re T.W.* , 551 So. 2d at 1196 ; *cf. Shevin v. Byron, Harless, Schaffer, Reid & Assocs., Inc.* , 379 So. 2d 633, 636 (Fla. 1980) (characterizing the right of privacy as also protecting one's right to "decisional autonomy" in "various types of important personal" matters).

As defined by the supreme court, article I, section 23's guarantee of bodily and personal inviolability—which we are asked to follow—must include the inviolability of something so intimate as one's own face. A person then reasonably can expect to be free from governmental coercion regarding what he puts on it. *Cf. State v. Presidential Women's Ctr.*, 937 So. 2d 114, 116 (Fla. 2006) ("Under a free government, at least, the free citizen's first and greatest right, which underlies all others [is] the right to the inviolability of his person; in other words, the right to himself. . . ." (quoting *Chambers v. Nottebaum*, 96 So. 2d 716, 719 (Fla. 3d DCA 1957))); *id.* at 117; *Gainesville Woman Care*, 210 So. 3d at 1262 (reiterating well-understood "concepts of bodily autonomy and integrity" (quotation and citation omitted)).

III.

* * *

Based on what the supreme court has told us about the scope of article I, section 23, Green (and anyone else in Alachua County) reasonably could expect autonomy over his body, including his face, which means that he was correct to claim an entitlement to be let alone and free from intrusion by Alachua County's commission chairman. The mask mandate, then, implicated the right of privacy. According to *Gainesville Woman Care*, the mask mandate was *presumptively* unconstitutional as a result.[5] Because the trial court reached the opposite legal conclusion, it did not subject the mask mandate to the strict scrutiny analysis that *Gainesville Woman Care* requires for consideration of a temporary injunction motion when privacy is implicated. . . .

REVERSED and REMANDED for further proceedings. CONFLICT CERTIFIED.

LONG, J., concurs with opinion, in which TANENBAUM, J., joins. [The concurring opinion of Judge Long is omitted.]

LEWIS, J., dissents with opinion.

LEWIS, J., dissenting.

* * *

. . . In order for the right of privacy to be implicated, and for the attendant strict scrutiny standard to apply, "a reasonable expectation of privacy must exist." *Winfield v. Div. of Pari- Mutuel Wagering, Dep't of Bus. Regulation*, 477 So. 2d 544, 547 (Fla. 1985). Florida's privacy right "is circumscribed and limited by the circumstances in which it is asserted." *Kurtz*, 653 So. 2d at 1028. In determining whether an individual has a legitimate expectation of privacy, "all the circumstances" must be considered, "especially objective manifestations of that expectation." *Id.*; *see also*

---

5. *But see Machovec v. Palm Beach County*, 310 So. 3d 941 (Fla. 4th DCA 2021) (reaching a different legal conclusion). We certify conflict with the Fourth District on this issue.

Fla. Bd. of Bar Examiners Re: Applicant, 443 So. 2d 71, 74 (Fla. 1983) ("The extent of his privacy right, however, must be considered in the context in which it is asserted and may not be considered wholly independent of those circumstances.").

The majority's conclusion that "a person reasonably can expect not to be forced by the government to put something on his own face against his will" completely fails to consider the circumstances in which the right is asserted, *i.e.*, that the mask mandate was Alachua County's response to "a clear and present threat to the lives, health, welfare, and safety" of its people posed by a contagious, airborne virus during a global pandemic. The majority's decision to ignore the circumstances in which Appellant asserts the right of privacy renders its analysis fatally flawed. The conclusion that the right of privacy is not implicated in this case does not authorize the government to force a person to wear a facial covering for no reason at all or for any reason other than to curtail the spread of a potentially deadly virus during a global pandemic.

Of further significance is that the Florida Constitution provides for "the right to be let alone and free from government intrusion into **the person's private life**." Art. I, § 23, Fla. Const. (emphasis added). The County's mask mandate does not require a person to wear a mask in his or her own home; rather, it requires the use of a facial covering only when a person might come into contact with members of the public in order to reduce the spread of COVID-19. The fact that the mask mandate does not infringe on a person's private or home life further indicates that it does not implicate Florida's right of privacy. Although the majority makes the conclusory statement that the mask mandate "potentially reached into the privacy of one's home," that supposition is not supported by the language of the mandate. Additionally, Appellant is not raising an as- applied constitutional challenge, nor is he arguing that the mask mandate reaches into his home.

Moreover, the majority's conclusion that the mask mandate implicates the right to privacy is based on its conclusory and faulty reasoning that because Florida's right of privacy guarantees the freedom of a person to control his own body, a person can reasonably expect not to be forced to put something on his face. But the majority does not explain how requiring a person to wear a mask when interacting with the public during a pandemic is the equivalent of controlling the person's body. In fact, the case law the majority relies upon is distinguishable and its application to this case would be far-fetched.

The majority primarily relies on *Gainesville Woman Care, LLC*, where the supreme court held that the Mandatory Delay Law — which "impedes a woman's ability to terminate her pregnancy for at least an additional twenty-four hours and requires the woman to make a second, medically unnecessary trip, which adds additional costs and delay" — infringed on the right to privacy and "turn[ed] informed consent on its head, placing the State squarely between a woman who has already made her decision to terminate her pregnancy and her doctor who has decided that the procedure is appropriate for his or her patient." 210 So. 3d at 1246, 1258 (explaining the potential consequences of such an unnecessary delay, including the possibility that it might push women past the gestational limit for medication abortion and, thus, force them to undergo a riskier surgical abortion). Because the challenged law implicated Florida's right of privacy, strict scrutiny applied. *Id.* at 1254. The court explained that its precedent establishes that "Florida's constitutional right of privacy encompasses a woman's right to choose to end her pregnancy," and "[t]his right would have little substance if it did not also include the woman's right to effectuate her decision to end her pregnancy." *Id.* at 1253–54. It would be irrational, and downright repugnant, to liken a woman's fundamental right to choose to end her pregnancy or an unnecessary interference with that right, which is indisputably a deeply personal decision and involves bodily integrity and personal autonomy, to a requirement that a person wear a facial covering when interacting with members of the public during a pandemic so as to curtail the spread of a contagious virus.

In *In re Guardianship of Browning*, the supreme court concluded that the constitutional right of privacy includes the right to choose or refuse medical treatment and extends to all relevant decisions concerning one's health for competent and incompetent persons alike and that the right may be exercised by proxies or surrogates. 568 So. 2d 4, 11, 13 (Fla. 1990). Accordingly, the court answered in the affirmative the certified question of "[w]hether the guardian of a patient who is incompetent but not in a permanent vegetative state and who suffers from an incurable, but not terminal condition, may exercise the patient's right of self-determination to forego sustenance provided artificially by a nasogastric tube," and explained that "[t]he right of privacy requires that we must safeguard an individual's right to chart his or her own medical course in the event of later incapacity." *Id.* at 7–8, 13. Curiously, the majority relies on *Browning* in support of its conclusion, yet it does not find that the mask mandate is the equivalent of compelled medical treatment — a conclusion that would, indeed, be both bizarre and unsupported by case law.

. . .

Nor is the majority's conclusion supported by *Winfield*, where the supreme court found that "the law in the state of Florida recognizes an individual's legitimate expectation of privacy in financial institution records"; accordingly, the right of privacy was implicated and the strict scrutiny standard applied to the question of whether the Division could subpoena a citizen's bank records without notice. 477 So. 2d at 547–48. The court noted that the United States Supreme Court has held that the right of privacy "protects the decision-making or autonomy zone of privacy interests of the individual" in "matters concerning marriage, procreation, contraception, family relationships and child rearing, and education," as well as "one's interest in avoiding the public disclosure of personal matters." *Id.* at 546. None of those privacy interests are at issue here, and the mask mandate does not bear even a remote resemblance to those important and limited privacy rights. The majority does not draw any parallels, and there are none, between a person's legitimate expectation of privacy in his or her own financial records and a person's interest in not wearing a mask during a pandemic for the protection of others (and him/herself).

* * *

As these cases demonstrate, a person's privacy right is not absolute and is not to be considered in isolation, without regard for the circumstances under which the right is asserted. When a person chooses to be around fellow citizens, his or her decisions and actions affect others. Persons who are unwilling to be subject to any inconvenience, however minimal, for the protection of others around them may choose to remain in the privacy of their own home, free from any government intrusion. As the trial court aptly stated, a person's right to be let alone is no more precious than his fellow citizen's right not to become infected by him with a contagious, airborne, and potentially fatal virus. The mask mandate is in no way an attempt by the government to control a person's body, as found by the majority. The mask mandate is not compelled medical treatment, and the wearing of facial covering does not alter one's physical person. Rather, the mask mandate is a temporary and *de minimus* interference with a person's public interactions in response to a global pandemic. I agree with the trial court that the " [t]he County's need to take measures to control the spread of COVID-19 clearly outweighs [Appellant's] private interest in not wearing a mask in the limited circumstances required by the county's emergency order; and, an injunction in this situation would disserve the public interest."

* * *

3. Privacy and Public Trials

Barron v. Florida Freedom Newspapers, Inc.

531 So. 2d 113 (Fla. 1988)

OVERTON, Justice.

This is a petition to review *Florida Freedom Newspapers, Inc. v. Sirmons*, 508 So.2d 462 (Fla. 1st DCA 1987), which reversed a trial court order sealing a substantial portion of the court file in a dissolution proceeding between Dempsey J. Barron, a state senator, and Louverne Barron. The district court acknowledged conflict with *Sentinel Communications Co. v. Smith*, 493 So.2d 1048 (Fla. 5th DCA 1986), *review denied*, 503 So.2d 328 (Fla.1987). We find the district court expressly construed article I, section 23, of the Florida Constitution, agree there is conflict, and accept jurisdiction.*

We hold that *all* trials, civil and criminal, are public events and there is a strong presumption of public access to these proceedings and their records, subject to certain narrowly defined exceptions. We have articulated principles that govern these exceptions and, after applying them to this case, we find no basis to seal the file. Although we disagree in part with the district court's reasoning, we approve the result.

* * *

---

* Art. V, § 3(b)(3), Fla.Const.

Public Access to Civil Court Proceedings

At the outset we hold that both civil and criminal court proceedings in Florida are public events and adhere to the well established common law right of access to court proceedings and records. In *Craig v. Harney*, 331 U.S. 367, 374, 67 S.Ct. 1249, 1254, 91 L.Ed. 1546 (1947), the United States Supreme Court held: "A trial is a public event. What transpires in the court room is public property. . . . There is no special perquisite of the judiciary which enables it, as distinguished from other institutions of democratic government, to suppress, edit, or censor events which transpire in proceedings before it." In *Richmond Newspapers, Inc. v. Virginia*, 448 U.S. 555, 580 n. 17, 100 S.Ct. 2814, 2829 n. 17, 65 L.Ed.2d 973 (1980), Chief Justice Burger stated: "Whether the public has a right to attend trials of civil cases is a question not raised by this case, but we note that historically both civil and criminal trials have been presumptively open." In a concurring opinion, Justice Stewart expressed that "the first and fourteenth amendments clearly give the press and public a right of access to trials themselves, civil as well as criminal." *Id.* at 599, 100 S.Ct. at 2839. *See also Publicker Industries, Inc. v. Cohen*, 733 F.2d 1059 (3d Cir.1984); *Brown & Williamson Tobacco Corp. v. Federal Trade Comm'n*, 710 F.2d 1165 (6th Cir.1983), *cert. denied*, 465 U.S. 1100, 104 S.Ct. 1595, 80 L.Ed.2d 127 (1984); *In re Astri Investment, Management & Securities Corp.*, 88 B.R. 730 (D.Md.1988).

While this Court has recognized the common law right of access to criminal proceedings in *Bundy v. State*, 455 So.2d 330 (Fla.1984), *cert. denied*, 476 U.S. 1109, 106 S.Ct. 1958, 90 L.Ed.2d 366 (1986), and *Miami Herald Publishing Co. v. Lewis*, 426 So.2d (Fla.1982), we have not expressly done so in civil proceedings. The reason for openness is basic to our form of government. Public trials are essential to the judicial system's credibility in a free society. The Supreme Court of California, in *In re Shortridge*, 99 Cal. 526, 530–31, 34 P. 227, 228–29 (1893), justified the public's right to know what transpires in both civil and criminal courtrooms and stated:

> In this country it is a first principle that the people have the right to know what is done in their courts. The old theory of government which invested royalty with an assumed perfection, precluding the possibility of wrong, and denying the right to discuss its conduct of public affairs, is opposed to the genius of our institutions, in which the sovereign will of the people is the paramount idea; and the greatest publicity to the acts of those holding positions of public trust, and the greatest freedom in the discussion of the proceedings of public tribunals that is consistent with truth and decency, are regarded as essential to the public welfare. Therefore, when it is claimed that this right has in any manner been abridged, such claim must find its support, if any there be, in some limitation expressly imposed by the lawmaking power, or the right to exercise the authority claimed must be necessarily implied as essential to the execution of the powers expressly conferred.

Wigmore also articulated reasons for public access to *all* court proceedings, explaining:

> The publicity of a judicial proceeding is a requirement of much broader bearing than its mere effect upon the quality of testimony. . . . Nevertheless, it plays an important part as a security for testimonial trustworthiness. . . .
>
> (1) Its operation in tending to *improve the quality of testimony* is twofold. Subjectively, it produces in the witness' mind a disinclination to falsify; first, by stimulating the instinctive responsibility to public opinion, symbolized in the audience, and ready to scorn a demonstrated liar; and next, by inducing the fear of exposure of subsequent falsities through disclosure by informed persons who may chance to be present or to hear of the testimony from others present. Objectively, it secures the presence of those who by possibility may be able to furnish testimony in chief or to contradict falsifiers and yet may not have been known beforehand to the parties to possess any information.
>
> . . . .
>
> (2) The other reasons . . . for requiring publicity are of three distinct sorts:
>
> (a) Subjectively, a wholesome effect is produced, analogous to that secured for witnesses, upon all the officers of the court, in particular, upon judge, jury, and counsel. In acting under the public gaze, they are more strongly moved to a strict conscientiousness in the performance of duty. In all experience, secret tribunals have exhibited abuses which have been wanting in courts whose procedure was public.
>
> (b) Persons not called as parties to the suits before the court may nevertheless be affected, or think themselves likely to be affected, by pending litigation. They should have the opportunity of learning whether they are thus affected, and of protecting themselves accordingly; they have "a right to be present for the purpose of hearing what is going on."
>
> (c) The educative effect of public attendance is a material advantage. Not only is respect for the law increased and intelligent acquaintance acquired with the methods of government, but a strong confidence in judicial remedies is secured which could never be inspired by a system of secrecy. . . .

6 Wigmore, Evidence §1834 (Chadbourn rev. 1976) (emphasis in original; footnotes omitted). We fully approve the reasoning of *Shortridge* and Wigmore.

While a strong presumption of openness in judicial proceedings exists, the law has established numerous exceptions to protect competing interests. These exceptions fall into two categories: the first includes those necessary to ensure order and dignity in the courtroom and the second deals with the content of the information. We address only the second category in this case. Because of the strong openness presumption, a closure order must be drawn with particularity and narrowly applied.

In *Miami Herald Publishing Co. v. Lewis*, we modified the Fourth District's test regarding closure of criminal proceedings. We directed that trial judges apply the following three-pronged test when considering closure of criminal court proceedings:

1. Closure is necessary to prevent a serious and imminent threat to the administration of justice;

2. No alternatives are available, other than a change of venue, which would protect the defendant's right to a fair trial; and

3. Closure would be effective in protecting the rights of the accused, without being broader than necessary to accomplish this purpose.

426 So.2d at 6. This test, derived primarily because of first amendment contentions, was designed to address the problems of prejudicial pretrial publicity and the competing constitutional rights to a fair trial by an impartial jury for criminal defendants. The test was not conceived or drawn to address closure in civil proceedings.

In *State ex rel. Gore Newspaper Co. v. Tyson*, the Fourth District addressed the closure of a dissolution proceeding. The court reversed a closure order and stated that it could not permit closure "solely upon the wishes of the parties to the litigation, absent cogent reasons." 313 So.2d at 788. The court recognized the trial court's authority to close civil proceedings, stating:

The court, under its inherent power, may for cogent reasons exclude the public and press from any judicial proceeding to protect the rights of the litigants and to otherwise further the administration of justice;

In determining the restrictions to be placed upon access to judicial proceedings, the court must balance the rights and interests of the parties to the litigation with those of the public and press;

The type of civil proceeding, the nature of the subject matter and the status of the participants are factors to be considered when evaluating the cogent reasons for excluding the public and press from access to the courts.

Id. at 787. We are in general agreement with this holding, recognizing that trial courts may exercise their power to close all or part of a proceeding in limited circumstances. In this regard, we feel that a definitive statement by this Court is necessary to assist judicial officers in this sensitive area. We conclude that the following factors must be considered to determine a request for closure of a civil proceeding.

First, a strong presumption of openness exists for all court proceedings. A trial is a public event, and the filed records of court proceedings are public records available for public examination.

Second, both the public and news media shall have standing to challenge any closure order. The burden of proof in these proceedings shall always be on the party seeking closure.

Third, closure of court proceedings or records should occur only when necessary (a) to comply with established public policy set forth in the constitution, statutes, rules, or case law; (b) to protect trade secrets; (c) to protect a compelling governmental interest [e.g., national security; confidential informants]; (d) to obtain evidence to properly determine legal issues in a case; (e) to avoid substantial injury to innocent third parties [e.g., to protect young witnesses from offensive testimony; to protect children in a divorce]; or (f) to avoid substantial injury to a party by disclosure of matters protected by a common law or privacy right not generally inherent in the specific type of civil proceeding sought to be closed. We find that, under appropriate circumstances, the constitutional right of privacy established in Florida by the adoption of article I, section 23, could form a constitutional basis for closure under (e) or (f). In this regard, we disagree with the district court in the instant case. Further, we note that it is generally the content of the subject matter rather than the status of the party that determines whether a privacy interest exists and closure should be permitted. However, a privacy claim may be negated if the content of the subject matter directly concerns a position of public trust held by the individual seeking closure.

Fourth, before entering a closure order, the trial court shall determine that no reasonable alternative is available to accomplish the desired result, and, if none exists, the trial court must use the least restrictive closure necessary to accomplish its purpose.

Fifth, the presumption of openness continues through the appellate review process, and the party seeking closure continues to have the burden to justify closure. This heavy burden is placed on the party seeking closure not only because of the strong presumption of openness but also because those challenging the order will generally have little or no knowledge of the specific grounds requiring closure.

We find no justification to give dissolution proceedings special consideration, as advocated by Dempsey Barron. The parties seeking a dissolution of their marriage are not entitled to a private court proceeding just because they are required to utilize the judicial system. Dissolution proceedings are regulated by statute and are unique because the state is considered an interested third party to protect the public welfare. *See, e.g., Perez v. Perez*, 164 So.2d 561 (Fla. 3d DCA 1964); *Harman v. Harman*, 128 So.2d 164 (Fla. 3d DCA 1961). While Florida, as a matter of public policy, has expressly made certain civil proceedings confidential (adoptions, § 63.162, Fla.Stat. (1987); paternity, § 742.031, Fla.Stat. (1987); juvenile proceedings, § 39.09 and 39.408, Fla.Stat. (1987)) and some states have enacted legislation limiting public access to divorce proceedings (Cal. [Civ.] Code § 4360 (Deering 1984); Del.Code Ann. tit. 13, § 1516 (1981)), the Florida Legislature has chosen not to do so. We conclude that dissolution proceedings must be treated similar to other civil proceedings, and thus the presumption of openness applies.

In *Sentinel Communications*, the Fifth District held that parents and children in a dissolution proceeding had privacy rights that justified closure of the court file. We disapprove that decision to the extent it implies that parties to *all* dissolution proceedings involving minor children have an absolute privacy right to seal the file. We also disapprove that portion placing the burden of proof on the challenging party rather than the party seeking closure. We agree with the closure in *Sentinel Communications* because of the express finding of injury to an innocent third party. In that proceeding, the trial judge determined that a minor child had been adversely affected by the litigation and that continued publicity would in all likelihood be "highly detrimental" to that child. That factual finding makes it distinguishable from the instant case.

The Instant Case

After thoroughly reviewing the sealed and unsealed portions of the instant case and applying the principles outlined above, we conclude that the sealed portion of this file does not contain protected information. The undisclosed matter primarily concerns medical reports regarding one party's physical condition. That party asserted the condition to justify certain actions and conduct. Although generally protected by one's privacy right, medical reports and history are no longer protected when the medical condition becomes an integral part of the civil proceeding, particularly when the condition is asserted as an issue by the party seeking closure. The sealed findings of fact here clearly establish that the medical records were an integral part of this case. This medical information is similar to that presented in personal injury actions, workers' compensation proceedings, and other dissolution of marriage proceedings. In dissolution proceedings, it is not unusual for a party's medical condition to be relevant in determining appropriate alimony, child support, or property disposition. Accordingly, we conclude that the medical information is an inherent part of these proceedings and cannot be utilized as a proper basis for closure. In view of this holding, it is unnecessary to determine whether the public positions held by Dempsey Barron and Terri Jo Kennedy create an additional basis to open these proceedings.

For the reasons expressed, we agree with the district court that there was no justifiable basis for closure. Upon this opinion's becoming final, the order sealing the file will be vacated and the entire file will be open and available for examination in the same manner as any other court file.

It is so ordered.

SHAW, GRIMES and KOGAN, JJ., concur.

EHRLICH, C.J., concurs in the result only with an opinion.

BARKETT, J., concurs specially with an opinion.

McDONALD, J., dissents with an opinion.

[The opinions of Justices Ehrlich, Barkett, and McDonald are omitted.]

In *Bainter v. League of Women's Voters of Florida*,[43] the Florida Supreme Court affirmed its commitment to the principle that "all trials, civil and criminal, are

---

43. 150 So. 3d 1115 (Fla. 2014).

public events and there is a strong presumption of public access to these proceedings and their records." In *Bainter*, several voting rights groups sought the production of documents from Pat Bainter and other nonparties as circumstantial evidence of their claim that Bainter and other political consultants engaged in "a parallel redistricting process" to produce an unconstitutional "partisan map favoring Republicans and incumbents."[44] After the trial court ordered Bainter and other nonparties to produce 538 pages of "relevant" documents, Bainter asserted that the documents the trial court ordered him to produce were privileged under the First Amendment. In response to the trial court's order which permitted the documents to remain confidential and prohibited public disclosure of the documents at that time, Bainter and the other nonparties produced the documents. However, in a subsequent order, the trial court denied Bainter's and the other nonparties' motion to close the courtroom to the public during use of the documents at trial.[45] Bainter and the other nonparties appealed the trial court's ruling. "In accordance with the overriding public interest in openness to judicial proceedings and records," the Florida Supreme Court ordered the sealed portion of the trial transcript, as well as the documents themselves, unsealed.[46]

4. Privacy and Abortion

On June 24, 2022, the United States Supreme Court abandoned decades of precedent and paved the way for states to ban abortions when it overturned *Roe v. Wade*,[47] the seminal case establishing a constitutional right to an abortion. In *Dobbs v. Jackson Women's Health Organization*,[48] the United States Supreme Court held the federal constitution does not provide a right to abortion, and authority to regulate abortion must be returned to the people and their elected representatives. In anticipation of the *Dobbs* decision, the Florida Legislature enacted law prohibiting abortions if the gestational age of the fetus is more than 15 weeks unless the procedure is necessary to (1) save the pregnant woman's life, (2) prevent serious physical injury to the pregnant woman, or (3) if the fetus has a fatal abnormality.[49] This law became effective July 1, 2022.

In *State v. Planned Parenthood of Southwest and Central Florida*,[50] several abortion clinics and a medical doctor challenged Florida's new abortion law as violative of article I, section 23 of the Florida Constitution. In reversing the trial court's non-final order granting a temporary injunction prohibiting enforcement of the new abortion law, the First District Court of Appeal held that the abortion clinics

---

44. *Id.* at 1118.
45. *Id.* at 1126.
46. *Id.* at 1133.
47. 93 S.Ct. 705 (1973).
48. 142 S.Ct. 2228 (2022).
49. *See* § 390.0111, Florida Statutes (2022).
50. ___ So.3d ___ (Fla. 1st Dist. Ct. App. 2022).

7 · THE DECLARATION OF RIGHTS AND THE TAKING OF PROPERTY 825

and doctor could not assert they would suffer irreparable harm because their claims did not allege that they themselves may be prohibited from obtaining an abortion after a certain time.[51] Notably, no pregnant woman asserted any claim in the *Planned Parenthood* lawsuit. Therefore, whether Florida's new abortion law violates Florida's broad constitutional right to privacy which provides more protection than the federal privacy right is yet to be determined. The following cases were decided before enactment of Florida's new abortion law.

In re T.W.

551 So. 2d 1186 (Fla. 1989)

SHAW, Justice.

We have on appeal *In re T.W.*, 543 So.2d 837 (Fla. 5th DCA 1989), which declared unconstitutional section 390.001(4)(a), Florida Statutes (Supp.1988), the parental consent statute. We have jurisdiction. Art. V, § 3(b)(1), Fla. Const. We approve the opinion of the district court and hold the statute invalid under the Florida Constitution.

I.

The procedure that a minor must follow to obtain an abortion in Florida is set out in the parental consent statute [footnote omitted] and related rules. [Footnote omitted.] Prior to undergoing an abortion, a minor must obtain parental consent or, alternatively, must convince a court that she is sufficiently mature to make the decision herself or that, if she is immature, the abortion nevertheless is in her best interests. Pursuant to this procedure, T.W., a pregnant, unmarried, fifteen-year-old, petitioned for a waiver of parental consent under the judicial bypass provision on the alternative grounds that (1) she was sufficiently mature to give an informed consent to the abortion, (2) she had a justified fear of physical or emotional abuse if her parents were requested to consent, and (3) her mother was seriously ill and informing her of the pregnancy would be an added burden. The trial court, after appointing counsel for T.W. and separate counsel as guardian ad litem for the fetus, conducted a hearing within twenty-four hours of the filing of the petition.

The relevant portions of the hearing consisted of T.W.'s uncontroverted testimony that she was a high-school student, participated in band and flag corps, worked twenty hours a week, baby-sat for her mother and neighbors, planned on finishing high school and attending vocational school or community college, had observed an instructional film on abortion, had taken a sex education course at school, would not put her child up for adoption, and had discussed her plans with the child's father and obtained his approval. She informed the court that due to her mother's illness, she had assumed extra duties at home caring for her sibling and that if she told her mother about the abortion, "it would kill her." Evidence was introduced showing that the pregnancy was in the first trimester.

---

51. *Id.*

The guardian ad litem was accorded standing and allowed to argue that the judicial bypass portion of the statute was unconstitutionally vague and that parental consent must therefore be required in every instance where a minor seeks to obtain an abortion. The trial court ruled that the judicial bypass provision of the statute was unconstitutional because it failed to make sufficient provision for challenges to its validity, was vague, and made no provision for testimony to controvert that of the minor. The court denied the petition for waiver and required T.W. to obtain parental consent under the remaining provisions of the statute.

The district court found that the statute's judicial alternative to parental consent was unconstitutionally vague, permitting arbitrary denial of a petition, and noted the following defects: failure to provide for a record hearing, lack of guidelines relative to admissible evidence, a brief forty-eight-hour time limit, and failure to provide for appointed counsel for an indigent minor. The court declared the entire statute invalid, quashed the trial court's order requiring parental consent, and ordered the petition dismissed. The guardian ad litem appealed to this Court. The Florida Attorney General was granted permission to appear as amicus curiae. The guardian filed a number of motions to block the abortion but was unsuccessful and T.W. lawfully ended her pregnancy, which would normally moot the issue of parental consent.

Because the questions raised are of great public importance and are likely to recur, we accept jurisdiction despite T.W.'s abortion. *See Holly v. Auld*, 450 So.2d 217 (Fla.1984). Preliminarily, we find that the appointment of a guardian ad litem for the fetus was clearly improper. The attorney general alone has standing to pursue this appeal.[3]

> It cannot be doubted that the constitutional integrity of the laws of Florida is a matter in which the State has great interest, or that the State is a proper, but not necessary, party to any determination of the constitutionality of any state statute. Since many constitutional challenges are raised in a trial court which can be simply disposed of as obviously meritless, it would be futile for the Attorney General to defend each statute against all constitutional challenges at the trial level. However, where the trial court finds a statute to be unconstitutional, it is proper that the Attorney General appear on appeal to defend the statute.

State ex rel. Shevin v. Kerwin, 279 So.2d 836, 837–38 (Fla.1973).

The seminal case in United States abortion law is *Roe v. Wade*, 410 U.S. 113, 93 S. Ct. 705, 35 L.Ed.2d 147 (1973). There, the Court ruled that a right to privacy implicit in the fourteenth amendment embraces a woman's decision concerning abortion.

---

3. We are compelled to comment on the trial judge's finding that the court, "as the only entity otherwise involved [i]n the proceeding which could possibly protect the state's interest," could have standing to challenge the constitutionality of the statute. Under no circumstances is a trial judge permitted to argue one side of a case as though he were a litigant in the proceedings. The survival of our system of justice depends on the maintenance of the judge as an independent and impartial decisionmaker. A judge who becomes an advocate cannot claim even the pretense of impartiality.

Autonomy to make this decision constitutes a fundamental right and states may impose restrictions only when narrowly drawn to serve a compelling state interest. The Court recognized two important state interests, protecting the health of the mother and the potentiality of life in the fetus, and ruled that these interests become compelling at the completion of the first trimester of pregnancy and upon viability of the fetus (approximately at the end of the second trimester), respectively. Thus, during the first trimester, states must leave the abortion decision to the woman and her doctor; during the second trimester, states may impose measures to protect the mother's health; and during the period following viability, states may possibly forbid abortions altogether. Although the workability of the trimester system and the soundness of *Roe* itself have been seriously questioned in *Webster v. Reproductive Health Services*, ___ U.S. ___, 109 S.Ct. 3040, 106 L.Ed.2d 410 (1989), the decision for now remains the federal law. Subsequent to *Roe*, the Court issued several decisions dealing directly with the matter of parental consent for minors seeking abortions. *See Planned Parenthood Ass'n v. Ashcroft*, 462 U.S. 476, 103 S.Ct. 2517, 76 L.Ed.2d 733 (1983); *City of Akron v. Akron Center for Reproductive Health Inc.*, 462 U.S. 416, 103 S. Ct. 2481, 76 L.Ed.2d 687 (1983); *Bellotti v. Baird*, 443 U.S. 622, 99 S.Ct. 3035, 61 L. Ed.2d 797 (1979) (plurality opinion); *Planned Parenthood v. Danforth*, 428 U.S. 52, 96 S.Ct. 2831, 49 L.Ed.2d 788 (1976).

To be held constitutional, the instant statute must pass muster under both the federal and state constitutions. Were we to examine it solely under the federal Constitution, our analysis necessarily would track the decisions noted above. However, Florida is unusual in that it is one of at least four states having its own express constitutional provision guaranteeing an independent right to privacy, *see* Note, *Toward a Right of Privacy as a Matter of State Constitutional Law*, 5 Fla.St.U.L. Rev. 632, 691 (1977) (others include Alaska, California, and Montana),[4] and we opt to examine the statute first under the Florida Constitution. If it fails here, then no further analysis under federal law is required.

As we noted in *Winfield v. Division of Pari-Mutuel Wagering*, 477 So.2d 544 (Fla.1985), the essential concept of privacy is deeply rooted in our nation's political and philosophical heritage. Justice Brandeis in *Olmstead v. United States*, 277 U.S. 438, 478, 48 S.Ct. 564, 572, 72 L.Ed. 944 (1928) (Brandeis, J., dissenting), eloquently expressed the fundamental and wide-ranging "right to be let alone":

> The makers of our Constitution undertook to secure conditions favorable to the pursuit of happiness. They recognized the significance of man's spiritual nature, of his feelings and of his intellect. . . . They sought to protect Americans in their beliefs, their thoughts, their emotions and their sensations.

---

4. *See* Alaska Const. art. I, §22; Cal. Const. art. I, §1; Mont. Const. art. II, §10. A second group of states has incorporated the privacy right into a constitutional provision dealing with additional matters. *See* Ariz. Const art. II, §8; Haw. Const. art. I, §§6, 7; Ill. Const. art. I, §§6, 12; La. Const. art. I, §5; S.C. Const. art. I, §10; Wash. Const. art. I, §7.

They conferred, as against the government, the right to be let alone — the most comprehensive of rights and the right most valued by civilized men.

Pursuant to this principle, the United States Supreme Court has recognized a privacy right that shields an individual's autonomy in deciding matters concerning marriage, procreation, contraception, family relationships, and child rearing and education. *Roe*, 410 U.S. at 152–53, 93 S.Ct. at 726–27. It is this general right to privacy that protects against the public disclosure of private matters. *Nixon v. Administrator of General Servs.*, 433 U.S. 425, 97 S.Ct. 2777, 53 L.Ed.2d 867 (1977); *Whalen v. Roe*, 429 U.S. 589, 97 S.Ct. 869, 51 L.Ed.2d 64 (1977). The Court, however, has made it clear that the states, not the federal government, are the final guarantors of personal privacy: "But the protection of a person's *general* right to privacy — his right to be let alone by other people — is, like the protection of his property and of his very life, left largely to the law of the individual States." *Katz v. United States*, 389 U.S. 347, 350–51, 88 S.Ct. 507, 510–511, 19 L.Ed.2d 576 (1967) (footnotes omitted; emphasis in original). While the federal Constitution traditionally shields enumerated and implied individual liberties from encroachment by state or federal government, the federal Court has long held that state constitutions may provide even greater protection. *See, e.g., Pruneyard Shopping Center v. Robins*, 447 U.S. 74, 81, 100 S.Ct. 2035, 2040, 64 L.Ed.2d 741 (1980) ("Our reasoning . . . does not *ex proprio vigore* limit the authority of the State to exercise its police power or its sovereign right to adopt in its own Constitution individual liberties more expansive than those conferred by the Federal Constitution.").

> State constitutions, too, are a font of individual liberties, their protections often extending beyond those required by the Supreme Court's interpretation of federal law. The legal revolution which has brought federal law to the fore must not be allowed to inhibit the independent protective force of state law — for without it, the full realization of our liberties cannot be guaranteed.

W. Brennan, *State Constitutions and the Protection of Individual Rights*, 90 Harv. L. Rev. 489, 491 (1977).

In 1980, Florida voters by general election amended our state constitution to provide:

> Section 23. Right of privacy. — Every natural person has the right to be let alone and free from governmental intrusion into his private life except as otherwise provided herein. This section shall not be construed to limit the public's right of access to public records and meetings as provided by law.

Art. I, § 23, Fla. Const. This Court in *Winfield* described the far-reaching impact of the Florida amendment:

> The citizens of Florida opted for more protection from governmental intrusion when they approved article I, section 23, of the Florida Constitution. This amendment is an independent, freestanding constitutional provision which declares the fundamental right to privacy. Article I, section 23, was intentionally phrased in strong terms. The drafters of the amendment

rejected the use of the words "unreasonable" or "unwarranted" before the phrase "governmental intrusion" in order to make the privacy right as strong as possible. Since the people of this state exercised their prerogative and enacted an amendment to the Florida Constitution which expressly and succinctly provides for a strong right of privacy not found in the United States Constitution, it can only be concluded that the right is much broader in scope than that of the Federal Constitution.

Winfield, 477 So.2d at 548. In other words, the amendment embraces more privacy interests, and extends more protection to the individual in those interests, than does the federal Constitution.

Consistent with this analysis, we have said that the amendment provides "an explicit textual foundation for those privacy interests inherent in the concept of liberty which may not otherwise be protected by specific constitutional provisions." [Footnote omitted.] *Rasmussen v. South Fla. Blood Serv.*, 500 So.2d 533, 536, (Fla.1987) (footnote omitted). We have found the right implicated in a wide range of activities dealing with the public disclosure of personal matters. *See Barron v. Florida Freedom Newspapers*, 531 So.2d 113 (Fla.1988) (closure of court proceedings and records); *Rasmussen* (confidential donor information concerning AIDS-tainted blood supply); *Winfield* (banking records); *Florida Bd. of Bar Examiners re: Applicant*, 443 So.2d 71 (Fla.1983) (bar application questions concerning disclosure of psychiatric counselling). Florida courts have also found the right involved in a number of cases dealing with personal decision-making. *See Public Health Trust v. Wons*, 541 So.2d 96 (Fla.1989) (refusal of blood transfusion that is necessary to sustain life); *Corbett v. D'Alessandro*, 487 So.2d 368 (Fla. 2d DCA), *review denied*, 492 So.2d 1331 (Fla.1986) (removal of nasogastric feeding tube from adult in permanent vegetative state); *In re Guardianship of Barry*, 445 So.2d 365 (Fla. 2d DCA 1984) (removal of life support system from brain-dead infant); *see also Satz v. Perlmutter*, 379 So.2d 359 (Fla.1980) (removal of respirator from competent adult, decided prior to passage of privacy amendment under general right of privacy).

The privacy section contains no express standard of review for evaluating the lawfulness of a government intrusion into one's private life, and this Court when called upon, adopted the following standard:

Since the privacy section as adopted contains no textual standard of review, it is important for us to identify an explicit standard to be applied in order to give proper force and effect to the amendment. The right of privacy is a fundamental right which we believe demands the compelling state interest standard. This test shifts the burden of proof to the state to justify an intrusion on privacy. The burden can be met by demonstrating that the challenged regulation serves a compelling state interest and accomplishes its goal through the use of the least intrusive means.

Winfield, 477 So.2d at 547. When this standard was applied in disclosural cases, government intrusion generally was upheld as sufficiently compelling to overcome the individual's right to privacy. We reaffirm, however, that this is a highly stringent standard, emphasized by the fact that no government intrusion in the personal decision-making cases cited above has survived.

Florida's privacy provision is clearly implicated in a woman's decision of whether or not to continue her pregnancy. We can conceive of few more personal or private decisions concerning one's body that one can make in the course of a lifetime, except perhaps the decision of the terminally ill in their choice of whether to discontinue necessary medical treatment. *See Wons; Perlmutter.*

> Of all decisions a person makes about his or her body, the most profound and intimate relate to two sets of ultimate questions: first, whether, when, and how one's body is to become the vehicle for another human being's creation; second, when and how — this time there is no question of "whether" — one's body is to terminate its organic life.

L. Tribe, *American Constitutional Law* 1337–38 (2d ed. 1988). The decision whether to obtain an abortion is fraught with specific physical, psychological, and economic implications of a uniquely personal nature for each woman. *See Roe*, 410 U.S. at 153, 93 S.Ct. at 727. The Florida Constitution embodies the principle that "[f]ew decisions are more personal and intimate, more properly private, or more basic to individual dignity and autonomy, than a woman's decision . . . whether to end her pregnancy. A woman's right to make that choice freely is fundamental." *Thornburgh v. American College of Obstetricians and Gynecologists*, 476 U.S. 747, 106 S.Ct. 2169, 2185, 90 L.Ed.2d 779 (1986).

The next question to be addressed is whether this freedom of choice concerning abortion extends to minors. We conclude that it does, based on the unambiguous language of the amendment: The right of privacy extends to "[e]very natural person." Minors are natural persons in the eyes of the law and "[c]onstitutional rights do not mature and come into being magically only when one attains the state-defined age of majority. Minors, as well as adults, . . . possess constitutional rights." *Danforth*, 428 U.S. at 74, 96 S.Ct. at 2843. *See also Ashcroft; City of Akron; H.L. v. Matheson*, 450 U.S. 398, 101 S.Ct. 1164, 67 L.Ed.2d 388 (1981); and *Bellotti.*

II.

Common sense dictates that a minor's rights are not absolute; in order to overcome these constitutional rights, a statute must survive the stringent test announced in *Winfield:* The state must prove that the statute furthers a compelling state interest through the least intrusive means. The *Roe* Court recognized two state interests implicated in the abortion decision: the health of the mother and the potentiality of life in the fetus. Under *Roe*, the health of the mother does not become a compelling state interest until immediately following the end of the first trimester because until that time, "mortality in abortion may be less than mortality in normal childbirth." *Roe*, 410 U.S. at 163, 93 S.Ct. at 731. Due to technological developments in second-trimester abortion procedures, the point at which abortions are safer than childbirth may have been extended into the second trimester. *See City of Akron*,

7 · THE DECLARATION OF RIGHTS AND THE TAKING OF PROPERTY 831

462 U.S. at 429 n. 11, 103 S.Ct. at 2492. n. 11. We nevertheless adopt the end of the first trimester as the time at which the state's interest in maternal health becomes compelling under Florida law because it is clear that prior to this point no interest in maternal health could be served by significantly restricting the manner in which abortions are performed by qualified doctors whereas after this point the matter becomes a genuine concern. *See id.* Under Florida law, prior to the end of the first trimester, the abortion decision must be left to the woman and may not be significantly restricted by the state. Following this point, the state may impose significant restrictions only in the least intrusive manner designed to safeguard the health of the mother.[6] Insignificant burdens during either period must substantially further important state interests. *Compare id.* at 430, 103 S.Ct. at 2492 ("Certain regulations that have no significant impact on the woman's exercise of her right may be permissible where justified by important state health objectives.").

Under *Roe*, the potentiality of life in the fetus becomes compelling at the point in time when the fetus becomes viable, which the Court defined as the time at which the fetus becomes capable of meaningful life outside the womb, albeit with artificial aid. *Roe*, 410 U.S. at 160, 163, 93 S.Ct. at 730, 731. Under our Florida Constitution, the state's interest becomes compelling upon viability, as defined below. Until this point, the fetus is a highly specialized set of cells that is entirely dependent upon the mother for sustenance. No other member of society can provide this nourishment. The mother and fetus are so inextricably intertwined that their interests can be said to coincide. Upon viability, however, society becomes capable of sustaining the fetus, and its interest in preserving its potential for life thus becomes compelling.[7] *See Web-*

---

6. Restrictions to protect the state's interest in the potentiality of life, as explained *infra*, also may be imposed, but only after viability, as defined *infra*, is reached.

7. As to the argument that the state's interest in the potentiality of life is compelling throughout pregnancy, Justice Stevens has noted:

> I should think it obvious that the state's interest in the protection of an embryo — even if that interest is defined as "protecting those who will be citizens," — increases progressively and dramatically as the organism's capacity to feel pain, to experience pleasure, to survive, and to react to its surroundings increased day by day. The development of a fetus — and pregnancy itself — are not static conditions, and the assertion that the government's interest is static simply ignores this reality.
>
> Nor is it an answer to argue that life itself is not a static condition, and that "there is no nonarbitrary line separating a fetus from a child, or indeed, an adult human being." For, unless the religious view that a fetus is a "person" is adopted ... there is a fundamental and well-recognized difference between a fetus and a human being; indeed, if there is not such a difference, the permissibility of terminating the life of a fetus could scarcely be left to the will of the state legislatures. And if distinctions may be drawn between a fetus and a human being in terms of the state interest in their protection — even though the fetus represents one of "those who will be citizens" — it seems to me quite odd to argue that distinctions may not also be drawn between the state interest in protecting the freshly fertilized egg and the state interest in protecting the 9-month-gestated, fully sentient fetus on the eve of birth. Recognition of this distinction is supported not only by logic, but also by history and by our shared experiences.

Thornburgh, 106 S.Ct. at 2188 (Stevens, J., concurring) (footnotes and citations omitted).

ster, 109 S.Ct. at 3075 (Blackmun, J., concurring/dissenting). Viability under Florida law occurs at that point in time when the fetus becomes capable of meaningful life outside the womb through standard medical measures. Under current standards, this point generally occurs upon completion of the second trimester. *See id.* at 3075 n. 9 (no medical evidence exists indicating that technological improvements will move viability forward beyond twenty-three to twenty-four weeks gestation within the foreseeable future due to the anatomic threshold of fetal development). Following viability, the state may protect its interest in the potentiality of life by regulating abortion, provided that the mother's health is not jeopardized.

III.

The challenged statute fails because it intrudes upon the privacy of the pregnant minor from conception to birth. Such a substantial invasion of a pregnant female's privacy by the state for the full term of the pregnancy is not necessary for the preservation of maternal health or the potentiality of life. However, where parental rights over a minor child are concerned, society has recognized additional state interests — protection of the immature minor and preservation of the family unit. For reasons set out below, we find that neither of these interests is sufficiently compelling under Florida law to override Florida's privacy amendment.

In evaluating the validity of parental consent and notice statutes, the federal Court has taken into consideration the state's interests in the well-being of the immature minor, *see Ashcroft; City of Akron; Matheson; Bellotti; Danforth*, and in the integrity of the family, *see Matheson; Bellotti*. In *Bellotti*, the Court set forth three reasons justifying the conclusion that states can impose more restrictions on the right of minors to obtain abortions than they can impose on the right of adults: "[T]he peculiar vulnerability of children; their inability to make critical decisions in an informed, mature manner; and the importance of the parental role in child rearing." *Bellotti*, 443 U.S. at 634, 99 S.Ct. at 3043. The Court pointed out that "during the formative years of childhood and adolescence, minors often lack the experience, perspective, and judgement to recognize and avoid choices that could be detrimental to them," *id.* at 635, 99 S.Ct. at 3044, and that the role of parents in "teaching, guiding, and inspiring by precept and example is essential to the growth of young people into mature, socially responsible citizens," *id.* at 638, 99 S.Ct. at 3045. In assessing the validity of parental consent statutes, the federal Court applied a relaxed standard; the state interest need only be "significant," not "compelling," to support the intrusion.[8]

---

8. *See City of Akron v. Akron Center for Reproductive Health, Inc.*, 462 U.S. 416, 427 n. 10, 103 S. Ct. 2481, 2491 n. 10, 76 L.Ed.2d 687 (1983) ("[T]he Court has repeatedly recognized that, in view of the unique status of children under the law, the States have a 'significant' interest in certain abortion regulations aimed at protecting children 'that is not present in the case of an adult.' "); *H.L. v. Matheson*, 450 U.S. 398, 441 n. 32, 101 S.Ct. 1164, 1188 n. 32, 67 L.Ed.2d 388 (1981) (Marshall, J., dissenting) ("Although it may seem that the minor's privacy right is somehow less fundamental because it may be overcome by a 'significant state interest,' the more sensible view is that state interests inapplicable to adults may justify burdening the minor's right.").

We agree that the state's interest in protecting minors and in preserving family unity are worthy objectives. Unlike the federal Constitution, however, which allows intrusion based on a "significant" state interest, the Florida Constitution requires a "compelling" state interest in all cases where the right to privacy is implicated. *Winfield*. We note that Florida does not recognize these two interests as being sufficiently compelling to justify a parental consent requirement where procedures other than abortion are concerned. Section 743.065, Florida Statutes (1987), provides:

> 743.065 Unwed pregnant minor or minor mother, consent to medical services for minor or minor's child valid. —
>
> (1) An unwed pregnant minor may consent to the performance of medical or surgical care or services relating to her pregnancy by a hospital or clinic or by a physician licensed under chapter 458 or chapter 459, and such consent is valid and binding as if she had achieved her majority.
>
> (2) An unwed minor mother may consent to the performance of medical or surgical care or services for her child by a hospital or clinic or by a physician licensed under chapter 458 or chapter 459, and such consent is valid and binding as if she had achieved her majority.
>
> (3) Nothing in this act shall affect the provisions of s. 390.001 [the abortion statute].

Under this statute, a minor may consent, without parental approval, to any medical procedure involving her pregnancy or her existing child — no matter how dire the possible consequences — except abortion. Under *In re Guardianship of Barry*, 445 So.2d 365 (Fla. 2d DCA 1984) (parents permitted to authorize removal of life support system from infant in permanent coma), this could include authority in certain circumstances to order life support discontinued for a comatose child. In light of this wide authority that the state grants an unwed minor to make life-or-death decisions concerning herself or an existing child without parental consent, we are unable to discern a special compelling interest on the part of the state under Florida law in protecting the minor only where abortion is concerned. We fail to see the qualitative difference in terms of impact on the well-being of the minor[9] between allowing the life of an existing child to come to an end and terminating a pregnancy, or between undergoing a highly dangerous medical procedure on oneself and undergoing a far less dangerous procedure to end one's pregnancy. If any qualitative difference exists, it certainly is insufficient in terms of state interest. Although the state does have an interest in protecting minors, "the selective approach employed by the legislature evidences the limited nature of the . . . interest being furthered by these provisions." *Ivey v. Bacardi Imports Co.*, 541 So.2d 1129, 1139 (Fla.1989). We note that the state's adoption act similarly contains no

---

9. Having already examined the state's interest in the potentiality of life in the fetus, we are concerned here only with the state's interest in the well-being of the minor.

requirement that a minor obtain parental consent prior to placing a child up for adoption, even though this decision clearly is fraught with intense emotional and societal consequences. *See* ch. 63, Fla.Stat. (1987).

The parental consent statute also fails the second prong of the *Winfield* standard, i.e., it is not the least intrusive means of furthering the state interest. Any inquiry under this prong must consider procedural safeguards relative to the intrusion. As pointed out by the district court below, although the instant statute does provide for a judicial bypass procedure, it makes no provision for a lawyer for the minor or for a record hearing. In *In re D.B. and D.S.*, 385 So.2d 83 (Fla.1980), we recognized that an individual's interest in preserving the family unit and raising children is fundamental, and that in any proceeding involving permanent termination of parental rights, counsel for the affected party is constitutionally required. As noted above, we have determined that a woman's right to decide whether or not to continue her pregnancy constitutes a fundamental constitutional right and this right extends to minors. "[T]here are few situations in which denying a minor the right to make an important decision will have consequences so grave and indelible." *Bellotti*, 443 U.S. at 642, 99 S.Ct. at 3047. In proceedings wherein a minor can be wholly deprived of authority to exercise her fundamental right to privacy, counsel is required under our state constitution. Examining a comparable statute under federal law, the United States Court of Appeals, Seventh Circuit, pointed out:

> If the waiver procedure . . . simply involved speaking to the judge in order to demonstrate maturity, counsel might not seem essential. But no legal proceeding is that simple. A minor, completely untrained in the law, needs legal advice to help her understand how to prepare her case, what papers to file, and how to appeal if necessary. Requiring an indigent minor to handle her case all alone is to risk deterring many minors from pursuing their rights because they are unable to understand how to navigate the complicated court system on their own or because they are too intimidated by the seeming complexity to try.

Indiana Planned Parenthood Affiliates Ass'n v. Pearson, 716 F.2d 1127, 1138 (7th Cir.1983). We note that even the state in *Pearson* conceded that "'[t]here can be no doubt that in a case dealing with the abortion decision, refusal to assign counsel to an indigent minor would be reversible error.'" *Id.*

Without a record hearing to memorialize a trial judge's reasons for denying a petition for waiver of parental consent, appellate review is meaningless. *See In re: J.V., a child*, 548 So.2d 749 (Fla. 4th DCA 1989) (without record hearing, appellate review is "illusory and meaningless"); *In re: E.B.L., a minor*, 544 So.2d 333 (Fla. 2d DCA 1989) (appellate court constrained to reverse denial of petition where record non-existent). Without a record, the appellate court will be unable to determine whether the denial was lawful or was simply based on the trial judge's moral, religious, or political beliefs. Additionally, we note that the statute fails to make any exception for emergency or therapeutic abortions, procedures clearly no different, in terms of impact upon the minor, from other medical procedures that a minor can unilaterally authorize under section 743.065. Accordingly, we conclude that the statute fails to provide adequate procedural safeguards.

Based on the foregoing analysis of our state law, we hold that section 390.001(4)(a), Florida Statutes (Supp.1988), violates the Florida Constitution. Accordingly, no further analysis under federal law is required. We expressly decide this case on state law grounds and cite federal precedent only to the extent that it illuminates Florida law. We approve the district court's decision.

It is so ordered.

BARKETT and KOGAN, JJ., concur.

EHRLICH, C.J., concurs specially with an opinion.

OVERTON, J., concurs in part and dissents in part with an opinion with which GRIMES, J., concurs.

GRIMES, J., concurs in part and dissents in part with an opinion.

McDONALD, J., dissents with an opinion.

[The Ehrlich, Overton, Grimes and McDonald opinions are omitted.]

In 2004, Florida voters adopted Fla. Const. art. X, § 22 of the Florida Constitution which authorizes the Legislature to require parental notice before termination of a minor's pregnancy. Arguably, this constitutional amendment was in direct response to the Florida Supreme Court's decision in *In re T.W.* In 2005, the Legislature enacted Fla. Stat. § 390.01114 which requires a physician to notify a parent or legal guardian within 48 hours of performing or inducing the termination of a minor's pregnancy. The statute also provides a judicial bypass process for waiver of the notice requirement for minors who can establish that they are mature enough to decide whether to terminate their pregnancy. Notably, unlike the statute in *In re T.W.*, Fla. Stat. § 390.01114 requires *notice* and not *parental consent*.

Gainesville Woman Care, LLC v. State

210 So. 3d 1243 (Fla. 2017)

PARIENTE, J.

The issue in this case is whether the trial court properly applied strict scrutiny when reviewing the Mandatory Delay Law, which imposes an additional twenty-four hour waiting period on women seeking to terminate their pregnancies. See ch. 2015–118 § 1, Laws of Fla. (codified at § 390.0111(3), Fla. Stat. (2015)) ("Mandatory Delay Law"). The Mandatory Delay Law implicates the Florida Constitution's express right of privacy. In Florida, any law that implicates the fundamental right of privacy, regardless of the activity, is subject to strict scrutiny and, therefore, presumptively unconstitutional. Accordingly, we hold that the trial court correctly applied strict scrutiny in reviewing the Mandatory Delay Law's constitutionality.

* * *

Florida's Mandatory Delay Law

Florida's general informed consent law requires that, for a patient to give valid, informed consent to any medical treatment in Florida, the health care professional must conform to "an accepted standard of medical practice among members of the medical profession" and provide information conveying three things: (1) the nature of the procedure, (2) the medically acceptable alternatives to the procedure, and (3) the procedure's substantial risks. § 766.103(3)(a)1.–2., Fla. Stat. (2016). In addition, in 1997, the Florida Legislature passed the "Woman's Right to Know Act," an informed consent statute specific to procedures involving the termination of pregnancies. Ch. 97–151, Laws of Fla. This Court upheld the Woman's Right to Know Act in 2006, only after the State conceded to a limiting interpretation of the law and this Court interpreted the law to require physicians to discuss only medical risks of either terminating or continuing the pregnancy and that the scope of the advice was patient-driven. See *State v. Presidential Women's Ctr.*, 937 So.2d 114, 120 (Fla. 2006).

The Woman's Right to Know Act requires the physician to inform the patient of "[t]he nature and risks of undergoing or not undergoing" the termination of pregnancy procedure, "[t]he probable gestational age of the fetus," and some other, additional information. See § 390.0111(3) (a), Fla. Stat. (2015). In 2015, the Florida Legislature amended the Woman's Right to Know Act to require that a woman be given the statutorily required information at least twenty-four hours prior to the termination of pregnancy procedure. Ch. 2015–118 § 1, Laws of Fla. (codified at § 390.0111(3)). These amendments constitute the Mandatory Delay Law. [Footnote omitted.]

The Mandatory Delay Law does not require a woman to receive any new information beyond what the Woman's Right to Know Act requires.

* * *

Analysis

Fundamental Right of Privacy

Article I, section 23, of the Florida Constitution, added by Florida voters in 1980, has remained unchanged since it was adopted. See art. I, § 23, Fla. Const. (1980). This Court has broadly interpreted that right, stating:

> The citizens of Florida opted for more protection from governmental intrusion when they approved article I, section 23, of the Florida Constitution. This amendment is an independent, freestanding constitutional provision which declares the fundamental right to privacy. Article I, section 23, was intentionally phrased in strong terms. The drafters of the amendment rejected the use of the words "unreasonable" or "unwarranted" before the phrase "governmental intrusion" in order to make the privacy right as strong as possible. Since the people of this state exercised their prerogative and enacted an amendment to the Florida Constitution which expressly and succinctly provides for a strong right of privacy not found in the United

States Constitution, it can only be concluded that the right is much broader in scope than that of the Federal Constitution.

Winfield, 477 So.2d at 548. In *Winfield*, the Court applied a strict scrutiny test in reviewing an attempt by the Pari–Mutuel Wagering Department of the Florida Department of Business and Professional Regulation to subpoena individuals' financial records because, the Court reasoned, subpoenaing the records intruded upon an individual's legitimate expectation of privacy as a matter of law. Id. The Court explained:

> The right of privacy is a fundamental right which we believe demands the compelling state interest standard. This test shifts the burden of proof to the state to justify an intrusion on privacy. The burden can be met by demonstrating that the challenged regulation serves a compelling state interest and accomplishes its goal through the use of the least intrusive means.

Id. at 547; see *State v. J.P.*, 907 So.2d 1101, 1109 (Fla. 2004) ("When a statute or ordinance operates to the disadvantage of a suspect class or impairs the exercise of a fundamental right, then the law must pass strict scrutiny."). Thus, while the Federal Constitution, at the very least, requires the recognition and protection of an implicit right of privacy, Florida voters have clearly opted for a broader, explicit protection of their right of privacy. Indeed, Florida voters rejected a constitutional amendment in 2012 that would have interpreted Florida's explicit constitutional right of privacy as being no broader than the implicit federal constitutional right of privacy.[4]

* * *

... [A]ny law that implicates Florida's right of privacy will be subject to strict scrutiny review. Florida's constitutional right of privacy encompasses a woman's right to choose to end her pregnancy. This right would have little substance if it did not also include the woman's right to effectuate her decision to end her pregnancy. As this Court demonstrated in *T.W.* and *North Florida Women's*, laws that place the State between a woman, or minor, and her choice to end her pregnancy clearly implicate the right of privacy. For instance, the law at issue in *T.W.* prevented a minor from terminating her pregnancy without either parental consent or satisfying a judicial bypass procedure. 551 So.2d at 1189. However, the law did not completely forbid minors from terminating their pregnancies; it merely placed an additional obstacle in a minor's way, causing the minor additional hardship and delay in effectuating her decision. Similarly, the law at issue in *North Florida Women's* required a minor to notify her parents prior to terminating her pregnancy, or convince a court that she need not do so. 866 So.2d at 615. Again, this law only imposed additional requirements before a minor could terminate her pregnancy, but did not prevent the minor from undergoing the actual procedure for any period of time. Moreover, a

---

4. *See Initiative Information: Prohibition on Public Funding of Abortions; Construction of Abortion Rights*, Fla. Dep't of State, Division of Elections, http://dos.elections.myflorida.com/initiatives /initdetail.asp?account=10&seqnum=82 (last visited Feb. 1, 2017).

petitioner need not present additional evidence that the law intrudes on her right of privacy if it is evident on the face of the law that it implicates this right. Indeed, this Court has repeatedly applied strict scrutiny to laws that intrude upon an individual's fundamental right of privacy without first requiring in-depth factual findings about the extent of the burden imposed by the law. See, e.g. , *T.M. v. State*, 784 So.2d 442, 443–44 (Fla. 2001) (agreeing that strict scrutiny applies to juvenile curfew ordinances without any discussion of the percentage of juveniles who would be exempt from the curfew or whether those juveniles who were subject to the curfew would in fact be harmed by six- or seven-hour restrictions on travel); *Beagle*, 678 So.2d at 1275 ("Certainly the imposition, by the State, of grandparental visitation rights implicates the privacy rights of the Florida Constitution."); *Winfield*, 477 So.2d at 548 (applying strict scrutiny to administrative subpoena of financial records without any discussion of the potential burden posed by their release because subpoenaing the records intruded upon an individual's legitimate expectation of privacy as a matter of law).

Whether Strict Scrutiny Review Requires that the Challenger Establish a Significant Restriction

Although this Court has made clear that those who challenge laws implicating the fundamental right of privacy are not first required to establish an undue burden or significant restriction, the parties dispute whether there is a threshold requirement applicable only to challenges to laws involving the decision to terminate a pregnancy that the law operate as a "significant restriction" on that right before strict scrutiny applies. The First District held and the State maintains that the trial court must "make sufficient factually-supported findings about the existence of a significant restriction on a woman's right to seek an abortion." *Gainesville Woman Care*, 187 So.3d at 282 (emphasis added).

To support its argument, the First District and the State primarily rely on language from a discussion in *T.W.* regarding when the State's interest in maternal health becomes compelling. In that discussion, this Court stated:

> We nevertheless adopt the end of the first trimester as the time at which the state's interest in maternal health becomes compelling under Florida law because it is clear that prior to this point no interest in maternal health could be served by significantly restricting the manner in which abortions are performed by qualified doctors, whereas after this point the matter becomes a genuine concern. Under Florida law, prior to the end of the first trimester, the abortion decision must be left to the woman and may not be significantly restricted by the state. Following this point, the state may impose significant restrictions only in the least intrusive manner designed to safeguard the health of the mother. Insignificant burdens during either period must substantially further important state interests.

T.W., 551 So.2d at 1193 (footnote omitted) (citations omitted). To the extent the Court used the term "significant restriction," it was borrowing from the United States

Supreme Court opinion in *City of Akron v. Akron Center for Reproductive Health, Inc.*, 462 U.S. 416, 103 S.Ct. 2481, 76 L.Ed.2d 687 (1983), which provided that medical record-keeping and neutral informed consent laws would have "no significant impact" on a woman's right to choose. Id. at 430–31, 103 S.Ct. 2481. This Court was merely clarifying that prior to the end of the first trimester, the State was not permitted to restrict a woman's right to choose to terminate her pregnancy. Put into the appropriate context, it is clear that *T.W.* in no way created a threshold requirement that a challenger must prove through sufficient, factually supported findings that a law imposes a significant restriction on a woman's right of privacy before the law is reviewed under strict scrutiny.

Likewise, the Court has not required an additional evidentiary prerequisite before strict scrutiny applies in other cases implicating the right of privacy, or any other context where strict scrutiny is appropriate. To single out the instance in which a woman chooses to end her pregnancy to apply this additional evidentiary burden would contradict our precedent emphasizing the importance of Florida's fundamental right of privacy.

Finally, the significant restriction requirement that the State maintains is appropriate would equate the Florida constitutional inquiry in the termination of pregnancy context to the federal "undue burden" test. See Casey, 505 U.S. at 877, 112 S.Ct. 2791. This cannot be. As explained above, this Court explicitly rejected the federal standard in *North Florida Women's*, which requires that a petitioner prove that a regulation has the purpose of placing a substantial obstacle in the path of a woman seeking to terminate her pregnancy. Casey, 505 U.S. at 877, 112 S.Ct. 2791; 866 So.2d at 634–35. Clearly, we did not endorse substantially the same standard, disguised as a threshold requirement, in the same case where we specifically rejected the federal "undue burden" standard.

To the extent there is any doubt or confusion regarding our precedent, we clarify that there is no threshold requirement that a petitioner must show by "sufficient factual findings" that a law imposes a significant restriction on a woman's right of privacy before strict scrutiny applies to laws that implicate the right of privacy. Any law that implicates the right of privacy is presumptively unconstitutional, and the burden falls on the State to prove both the existence of a compelling state interest and that the law serves that compelling state interest through the least restrictive means. *Winfield*, 477 So.2d at 547.

* * *

Having concluded that the trial court was correct that the law implicated the right of privacy, we turn to review whether the trial court erred in finding that the Mandatory Delay Law would be unlikely to survive strict scrutiny review. . . .

Because the Mandatory Delay Law, which impedes Florida women's exercise of their fundamental rights, implicates the right of privacy, the trial court was correct to conclude that strict scrutiny applies to this challenge. The case law is clear: "A legislative act impinging on [the right of privacy] is presumptively unconstitutional unless proved valid by the State." *N. Fla. Women's*, 866 So.2d at 626. Thus, after the trial court made the threshold inquiry that the Mandatory Delay Law implicated a woman's fundamental right of privacy, the burden in this case shifted to the State to prove that the law furthered a compelling state interest in the least restrictive way.

* * *

As stated above, the trial court properly placed the burden on the State in this case to prove that the Mandatory Delay Law furthered a compelling state interest through the least restrictive means. The trial court stated numerous times that the State failed to provide any evidence of a compelling state interest that would be furthered by enhancing the informed consent statute. The First District's statement that the trial court failed "to make any findings regarding the State's compelling interests in support of this statute" is clearly in error. *Gainesville Woman Care*, 187 So.3d at 282. The trial court found that the State failed to offer evidence of a compelling state interest in treating a woman who has chosen to terminate her pregnancy, unlike any other patient, as unable to determine for herself when she is ready to make an informed decision about her medical care; and this differential treatment undermines any purported state interest in ensuring that women are adequately informed. It would make no sense to require a trial court to make factual findings regarding a state's compelling interest, as the First District would require, when the State presented no evidence from which a trial court could make such findings.

The Mandatory Delay Law impacts only those women who have already made the choice to end their pregnancies. Indeed, under Florida's pre-existing informed consent law, a woman can already take all of the time she needs to decide whether to terminate her pregnancy, both before she arrives at the clinic and after she receives the required counseling information. The State presented no evidence to indicate that the prior, neutral informed consent statute that this Court approved in *Presidential Women's Center* is inadequate and requires the revisions enacted by the Legislature. Nor are there any legislative findings explaining the compelling state interests at stake or indicating why the Legislature was compelled to amend the statute in order to support those interests.

Moreover, despite the State's contention that women will not be required to make two trips to the clinic by the new law because they can receive the information from their referring physician, the law, in fact, requires women to make a second trip to their health care provider at least twenty-four hours after their first visit. See § 390.0111, Fla. Stat. Even if the woman receives the required information from her referring doctor, as the State contends, she must still make two trips: one to the referring physician and one to the abortion clinic at least twenty-four hours later. The challengers presented evidence that requiring a woman to make a second trip increases the likelihood that her choice to terminate her pregnancy will not remain confidential, which is particularly important, as amici assert, in the domestic violence and human trafficking context. Further, the delay is, at a minimum, twenty-four hours, but it may be considerably more if the doctor is not available or the date falls on a weekend. No other medical procedure, even those with greater health consequences, requires a twenty-four hour waiting period in the informed consent process.

Next, we also conclude that the First District erred when it admonished the trial court for failing to make findings regarding the State's compelling interests. The First District stated:

> The court failed to make any findings regarding the State's compelling interests in support of this statute, which the State has argued include compelling interests in providing women a short time to reflect privately after receiving required relevant information, in maintaining the integrity of the medical profession by making that post-informed reflective time free from influence by a physician or clinic personnel, in protecting the unique potentiality of human life, in protecting the organic law of Florida from interpretations and impacts never contemplated or approved by Floridians or their elected representatives, and in protecting the viability of a duly-enacted state law.

Gainesville Woman Care, 187 So.3d at 282. This Court has never recognized that the State might have a compelling interest in "protecting the organic law of Florida from interpretations and impacts never contemplated or approved by Floridians or their elected representatives" and in "protecting the viability of a duly-enacted state law." Id. Accordingly, the First District's holding that the trial court erred in failing to issue findings on such an interest would render the highest level of judicial review toothless in almost all cases because the State could be deemed to have a compelling interest in upholding any law, no matter how patently unconstitutional it may be.

The First District compounded this error by requiring that the trial court first consider what it referred to as the State's compelling interests in "providing women a short time to reflect privately after receiving required relevant information, in maintaining the integrity of the medical profession by making that post-informed reflective time free from influence by a physician or clinic personnel" and in "protecting the viability of a duly-enacted state law." The Mandatory Delay Law does not differentiate between stages of pregnancy in its application. Instead, it broadly operates any time that a woman is intending to terminate a pregnancy after conception. As to the "unique potentiality of human life," and the concern regarding the integrity of the medical profession, this law is part of the medical informed consent law that this Court has already held was a statute designed to inform the patient of only the medical risks of continuing or not continuing the pregnancy. This Court made clear in *Presidential Women's Center* that "[t]he doctrine of medical informed consent is rooted in the concepts of bodily autonomy and integrity . . . and it is logical that physicians be required to inform the patient only and exclusively of the medical risks of terminating or not terminating a pregnancy." 937 So.2d at 119 (emphasis added). Such social and moral concerns have no place in the concept of informed consent.

Finally, in light of the discussion above, it was also error for the First District to insinuate that the voters in any way overruled our decision in *North Florida*

Women's when they added article X, section 22, to the Florida Constitution in 2004. *Gainesville Woman Care*, 187 So.3d at 282 (faulting trial court for not addressing "the evidence of voter intent reflected in the 2004 adoption of article X, section 22, of the Florida Constitution, which in effect overruled *North Florida Women's* and authorized a requirement of parental notice of termination of a minor's pregnancy"). Article X, section 22, of the Florida Constitution is an extremely limited provision of the constitution, which deals solely with the issue of parental notification in the context of a minor choosing to terminate her pregnancy. It was not added to the Declaration of Rights, nor did it amend the right of privacy in article I, section 23, of the Florida Constitution. See art. X, § 22, Fla. Const. In article X, section 22, the voters in no way altered this Court's core holding in *North Florida Women's* — laws that implicate the right of privacy are subject to strict scrutiny — and it was error for the First District to improperly insinuate such a notion.

* * *

Conclusion

... Today we make clear, in Florida, any law that implicates the fundamental right of privacy, regardless of the activity, is subject to strict scrutiny and is presumptively unconstitutional. In this case, the State failed to present any evidence that the Mandatory Delay Law serves any compelling state interest, much less through the least restrictive means, and, therefore, the trial court correctly concluded that there is a substantial likelihood that the Mandatory Delay Law is unconstitutional. Accordingly, we quash the decision of the First District below and remand this case back to the First District for instructions not inconsistent with this opinion.

It is so ordered.

LABARGA, C.J., and LEWIS, and QUINCE, JJ., concur.

CANADY, J., dissents with an opinion, in which POLSTON, J., concurs. [The dissenting opinion of Justice Canady is omitted.]

LAWSON, J., did not participate.

5. Privacy and the Refusal of Medical Treatment

In re Guardianship of Browning
568 So. 2d 4 (Fla. 1990)

BARKETT, Justice.

We have for review *In re Guardianship of Browning*, 543 So.2d 258 (Fla. 2d DCA 1989), in which the district court certified the following question as one of great public importance:

Whether the guardian of a patient who is incompetent but not in a permanent vegetative state and who suffers from an incurable, but not terminal condition, may exercise the patient's right of self-determination to forego sustenance provided artificially by a nasogastric tube?

Id. at 274.[1] We answer the question in the affirmative as qualified in this opinion.

I. The Facts

On November 19, 1985, a competent Estelle Browning executed a declaration that provides, in part:

If at any time I should have a terminal condition and if my attending physician has determined that there can be no recovery from such condition and that my death is imminent, I direct that life-prolonging procedures be withheld or withdrawn when the application of such procedures would serve only to prolong artificially the process of dying.

In addition, Mrs. Browning stipulated that she desired not to have "nutrition and hydration (food and water) provided by gastric tube or intravenously."[2]

At eighty-six years of age, Mrs. Browning suffered a stroke. She was admitted to the hospital on November 9, 1986, where her treating physician diagnosed a massive hemorrhage in the left parietal region of the brain, the portion that controls cognition. Because Mrs. Browning was unable to swallow, she underwent a gastrostomy on November 20 during which a feeding tube was inserted directly into her stomach.

The following day, she was discharged from the hospital and transferred to a nursing home where she remained bedridden and required total care. Mrs. Browning's second cousin and only living relative, Doris Herbert, eighty, was then appointed guardian of the person and property of Mrs. Browning.

During the course of her stay in the nursing home, Mrs. Browning was plagued with physical difficulties, including complications with her feeding tube, which

---

1. We have jurisdiction. Art. V, § 3(b)(4), Fla. Const. Estelle Browning died on July 16, 1989, at the age of 89. Although the claim is moot, we accept jurisdiction because the issue raised is of great public importance and likely to recur. *In re T.W.*, 551 So.2d 1186, 1189 (Fla. 1989); *Holly v. Auld*, 450 So.2d 217, 218, n. 1 (Fla. 1984).

2. The entire form is reproduced in the appendix of the district court's opinion. *In re Guardianship of Browning*, 543 So.2d 258, 275 (Fla. 2d DCA 1989).

became dislodged.[3] The gastrostomy tube was replaced by a nasogastric tube on May 19, 1988.[4]

Nearly two years after Mrs. Browning suffered a stroke, her guardian filed a petition in circuit court to terminate the nasogastric feeding based upon Mrs. Browning's living will. At the evidentiary hearing, the guardian presented additional evidence of Mrs. Browning's wishes. The evidence reflected that a predecessor living will, written in 1980, contained the same provisions for rejection of medical treatment at issue as the one presently before the Court. Believing that the death of a witness to the 1980 will might have rendered the will invalid, she executed the 1985 document. Neighbors also testified that Mrs. Browning had expressed her wishes orally in this regard several times. Mrs. Rose Kings, a close personal friend of Mrs. Browning since 1965, witnessed Mrs. Browning execute the 1985 document. She testified that Mrs. Browning signed the declaration about two days after visiting patients in a nursing home and had said, "'Oh Lord, I hope this never happens to me . . . thank God I've got this taken care of. I can go in peace when my time comes.'" Mrs. Kings' husband added that Mrs. Browning had a friend in the hospital on life-support and remarked that she "'never want[ed] to be that way.'"

The guardian, Mrs. Herbert, who had lived with Mrs. Browning from 1982 to 1986, testified that she had discussed the withdrawal of life-prolonging measures with Mrs. Browning following the death of Mrs. Browning's husband in 1978. According to Mrs. Herbert, Mrs. Browning said that she did not want to be maintained through artificial life-support mechanisms.

The consensus of the medical evidence indicated that the brain damage caused by the hemorrhage was major and permanent and that there was virtually no chance of recovery. Death would occur within seven to ten days were the nasogastric feeding tube removed. However, Mrs. Browning's life could have been prolonged up to one year as long as she was maintained on the feeding tube and assuming the absence of infection.

At the same time, the medical evidence reflected that Mrs. Browning was not comatose. Although she was noncommunicative, she "appeared alert and would follow [a visitor] with her eyes." However, she "would not blink in any consistent pattern when asked to respond to simple questions[,] . . . would not follow any simple commands [, and] . . . would not look to the right or to the left on command." A

---

3. The ailments included numerous episodes of vomiting; numerous bed sores, some of which evidenced profuse drainage; bruises and blisters on extremities; swelling of the hands, feet, and ankles; ingrown toenails; sporadic vaginal bleeding; and rectal discharge. The complications included leakage from the tube; drainage from the incision around the tube; plugging of the catheter bulb, which required frequent replacement and insertion; and leakage from the catheter. Like the district court, we are distressed at the need to discuss the details of Mrs. Browning's condition.

4. Gastrostomy and nasogastric tubes are two means of supplying nutrition and hydration to the patient. The former is surgically placed into the stomach through the abdomen, and the latter is placed into the stomach through the nose and esophagus.

nurse testified that Mrs. Browning had attempted to say a word on a few occasions, although she conceded that the words had not been clear and the speech was garbled.

Dr. James Barnhill, a neurologist, described Mrs. Browning as noncommunicative and essentially existing only by virtue of fluid and nutrition supplied by the feeding tube. Dr. Barnhill opined that she was in a persistent vegetative state, which he defined as the absence of cognitive behavior and inability to communicate or interact purposefully with the environment.

The trial court found that Mrs. Browning could continue to live for an indeterminate time with artificial sustenance but that death would result within four to nine days without it. Construing Florida's "Life-Prolonging Procedure Act," sections 765.01–.15, Florida Statutes (1987), the trial court concluded that death was not imminent, and it denied the petition.

The district court affirmed the trial court's decision that the termination of this treatment was not permitted by the statute. However, the district court held that Mrs. Browning was entitled to relief under our state constitution, which expressly recognized every citizen's basic right of privacy. *Browning*, 543 So.2d at 261. The district court then authorized the guardian to make the decision in accordance with procedures established in the opinion.

II. A Competent Person's Right Of Privacy

We agree with the district court that chapter 765 of the Florida Statutes (1987) is not applicable to Mrs. Browning's situation.[5] We also agree with the district court that Mrs. Browning's fundamental right of self-determination, commonly expressed as the right of privacy, controls this case.

Because the word "privacy" generally has been used in common parlance in its informational or disclosural sense, its broader meaning has been somewhat ignored. However, the concept of privacy encompasses much more than the right to control the disclosure of information about oneself. "Privacy" has been used interchangeably with the common understanding of the notion of "liberty," and both imply a fundamental right of self-determination subject only to the state's compelling and overriding interest. For example, privacy has been defined as an individual's "control over or the autonomy of the intimacies of personal identity," Gerety, *Redefining Privacy*, 12 Harv.C.R.-C.L.L. Rev. 233, 281 (1977); or as a "physical and psychological zone within which an individual has the right to be free from intrusion or coercion,

---

5. Section 765.04(1) of the Florida Statutes (1987) permits competent adults to order the withholding or withdrawal of "life-prolonging procedures" under certain conditions. Section 765.03(3) of the Florida Statutes (1987) specifically excludes the provision of sustenance from the term "life-prolonging procedure." We note that the legislature has since expanded the definition of "life-prolonging procedure" to include the provision of sustenance. Effective October 1, 1990, a patient may authorize the withholding or withdrawal of nutrition or hydration under certain circumstances. Ch. 90-223, Laws of Fla.

846   7 · THE DECLARATION OF RIGHTS AND THE TAKING OF PROPERTY

whether by government or by society at large." Cope, *To Be Let Alone: Florida's Proposed Right of Privacy*, 6 Fla.St.U.L.Rev. 671, 677 (1978).

These components of privacy are the same as those encompassed in the concept of freedom, and, as recognized in *In re T.W.*, 551 So.2d 1186 (Fla.1989), are deeply rooted in our nation's philosophical and political heritage. *See also Winfield v. Division of Pari-Mutuel Wagering*, 477 So.2d 544 (Fla.1985). In Florida, we have recognized that this fundamental right of privacy has been expressly enumerated in article I, section 23 of the Florida Constitution, which provides "an explicit textual foundation for those privacy interests inherent in the concept of liberty." *Rasmussen v. South Fla. Blood Serv., Inc.*, 500 So.2d 533, 536 (Fla.1987).

Thus, we begin with the premise that everyone has a fundamental right to the sole control of his or her person. As Justice Cardozo noted seventy-six years ago:

> Every human being of adult years and sound mind has a right to determine what shall be done with his own body. . . .

Schloendorff v. Society of New York Hosp., 211 N.Y. 125, 129–130, 105 N.E. 92, 93 (1914). An integral component of self-determination is the right to make choices pertaining to one's health, including the right to refuse unwanted medical treatment. "We can conceive of few more personal or private decisions concerning one's body that one can make in the course of a lifetime . . . [than] the decision of the terminally ill in their choice of whether to discontinue necessary medical treatment." *In re T.W.*, 551 So.2d at 1192; *see Public Health Trust v. Wons*, 541 So.2d 96 (Fla.1989).

Recognizing that one has the inherent right to make choices about medical treatment, we necessarily conclude that this right encompasses all medical choices. A competent individual has the constitutional right to refuse medical treatment regardless of his or her medical condition. *Wons; accord Cruzan ex rel. Cruzan v. Director, Mo. Dep't of Health*, ___ U.S. ___, 110 S.Ct. 2841, 2852, 111 L.Ed.2d 224 (1990) ("for the purposes of this case, we assume that the United States Constitution would grant a competent person a constitutionally protected right to refuse lifesaving hydration and nutrition"). The issue involves a patient's right of self-determination and does not involve what is thought to be in the patient's best interests.

> More is involved in respect for self-determination than just the belief that each person knows what's best for him- or herself. . . . Even if it could be shown that an expert (or a computer) could do the job better, the worth of the individual, as acknowledged in Western ethical traditions and especially in Anglo-American law, provides an independent — and more important — ground for recognizing self-determination as a basic principle in human relations, particularly when matters as important as those raised by health care are at stake.

President's Commission for the Study of Ethical Problems in Medicine and Biomedical and Behavioral Research, I *Making Health Care Decisions* 44–45 (1982).

* * *

We conclude that a competent person has the constitutional right to choose or refuse medical treatment, and that right extends to all relevant decisions concerning one's health.[6] Courts overwhelmingly have held that a person may refuse or remove artificial life-support, whether supplying oxygen by a mechanical respirator[7] or supplying food and water through a feeding tube.[8] We agree and find no significant legal distinction between these artificial means of life-support.

---

6. We see no reason to qualify that right on the basis of the denomination of a medical procedure as major or minor, ordinary or extraordinary, life-prolonging, life-maintaining, life-sustaining, or otherwise. Although research disclosed no cases that sought to distinguish these terms in the context of the rights of a competent patient, as opposed to an incompetent patient, courts generally are agreed that the terms are legally indistinguishable. *See, e.g., Cruzan ex rel. Cruzan v. Director, Mo. Dep't of Health*, ___ U.S. ___, 110 S.Ct. 2841, 2853, 111 L.Ed.2d 224 (1990) (addressing the issue as the refusal of "life-sustaining medical treatment"); *Corbett v. D'Alessandro*, 487 So.2d 368, 371 (Fla. 2d DCA) ("We are unable to distinguish on a legal, scientific, or a moral basis between those artificial measures that sustain life—whether by means of 'forced' sustenance or 'forced' continuance of vital functions—of the vegetative, comatose patient who would soon expire without use of those artificial means."), *review denied*, 492 So.2d 1331 (Fla.1986); *Brophy v. New England Sinai Hosp., Inc.*, 398 Mass 417, 437, 497 N.E.2d 626, 637 (1986) ("[w]hile we believe that the distinction between extraordinary and ordinary care is a factor to be considered the use of such a distinction as the sole, or major, factor of decision tends, in a case such as this, [is] to create a distinction without meaning"); *In re Hier*, 18 Mass.App.Ct. 200, 207, 464 N.E.2d 959, 964, *review denied*, 392 Mass. 1102, 465 N.E.2d 261 (1984) (rejecting distinction between nutrition and treatment); *In re Gardner*, 534 A.2d 947, 954 (Me.1987) (nutrition and hydration indistinguishable from other life-sustaining procedures); *In re Conroy*, 98 N.J. 321, 367–70, 486 A.2d 1209, 1233–34 (1985) ("[W]e reject the distinction . . . between actively hastening death by terminating treatment and passively allowing a person to die of a disease. . . . [and] also reject any distinction between withholding and withdrawing life-sustaining treatment."); *In re Guardianship of Grant*, 109 Wash.2d 545, 563, 747 P.2d 445, 454 (1987) (the right to withhold life-sustaining procedures extends to "all artificial procedures which serve only to prolong the life of a terminally-ill patient"); *Gray ex rel. Gray v. Romeo*, 697 F. Supp. 580, 588 n. 4 (D.R.I. 1988) (no analytical difference between withholding and withdrawing medical treatment).

7. *See John F. Kennedy Memorial Hosp., Inc. v. Bludworth*, 452 So.2d 921 (Fla.1984); *Satz v. Perlmutter*, 379 So.2d 359 (Fla.1980); *State v. McAfee*, 259 Ga. 579, 385 S.E.2d 651 (1989); *In re Quinlan*, 70 N.J. 10, 355 A.2d 647, *cert. denied*, 429 U.S. 922, 97 S.Ct. 319, 50 L.Ed.2d 289 (1976); *In re Colyer*, 99 Wash.2d 114, 660 P.2d 738 (1983).

8. *Cruzan ex rel. Cruzan v. Director, Mo. Dep't of Health*, ___ U.S. ___, 110 S.Ct. 2841, 111 L. Ed.2d 224 (1990); *Rasmussen ex rel. Mitchell v. Fleming*, 154 Ariz. 207, 741 P.2d 674 (1987); *Conservatorship of Drabick*, 200 Cal.App.3d 185, 245 Cal.Rptr. 840 (Ct.App.), *cert. denied*, 488 U.S. 958, 109 S. Ct. 399, 102 L.Ed.2d 387 (1988); *Bouvia v. Superior Court*, 179 Cal.App.3d 1127, 225 Cal.Rptr. 297 (Ct. App.), *review denied* (June 5, 1986); *Corbett v. D'Alessandro*, 487 So.2d 368 (Fla. 2d DCA), *review denied*, 492 So.2d 1331 (Fla.1986); *In re Gardner*, 534 A.2d 947 (Me. 1987); *In re Estate of Longeway*, 133 Ill.2d 33, 139 Ill.Dec. 780, 549 N.E.2d 292 (1989); *Brophy v. New England Sinai Hosp., Inc.*, 398 Mass. 417, 497 N.E.2d 626 (1986); *In re Hier*, 18 Mass.App. 200, 464 N.E.2d 959, *review denied*, 392 Mass. 1102, 465 N.E.2d 261 (1984); *In re Jobes*, 108 N.J. 394, 529 A.2d 434 (1987); *In re Requena*, 213 N.J.Super. 475, 517 A.2d 886 (Ch.Div.), *aff'd*, 213 N.J.Super. 443, 517 A.2d 869 (App.Div.1986); *Delio v. Westchester County Medical Center*, 129 A.D.2d 1, 516 N.Y.S.2d 677 (App.Div.1987); *Gray ex rel. Gray v. Romero*, 697 F.Supp. 580 (D.R.I. 1988).

848   7 · THE DECLARATION OF RIGHTS AND THE TAKING OF PROPERTY

III. An Incompetent Person'S Right Of Privacy

Having determined that a competent person has the constitutionally protected right to choose or reject medical treatment, we consider whether this right is lost or diminished by virtue of physical or mental incapacity or incompetence.[9] We previously determined that it is not. In *John F. Kennedy Memorial Hospital, Inc. v. Bludworth*, 452 So.2d 921, 923 (Fla.1984), this Court held that an incompetent person has the same right to refuse medical treatment as a competent person. Thus, our cases have recognized no basis for drawing a constitutional line between the protections afforded to competent persons and incompetent persons. Indeed, the right of privacy would be an empty right were it not to extend to competent and incompetent persons alike. *In re Guardianship of Barry*, 445 So.2d 365, 370 (Fla. 2d DCA 1984). As we have already stated:

> The primary concern . . . is that this valuable right should not be lost because the noncognitive and vegetative condition of the patient prevents a conscious exercise of the choice to refuse further extraordinary treatment.

Bludworth, 452 So.2d at 924. *Accord Cruzan ex rel. Cruzan v. Director, Mo. Dep't of Health*, 110 S.Ct. at 2852 (1990) (fourteenth amendment due process liberty interest).

IV. Another May Exercise The Incompetent'S Right To Forego Medical Treatment

The real issue before us is an extension of the one presented in *Bludworth*. When a person is unable to personally and directly express his or her desires for health care because of physical and mental incapacity,[10] "[t]he question is who will exercise this right and what parameters will limit them in the exercise of this right." *Bludworth*, 452 So.2d at 924–25. In *Bludworth*, the question related to a comatose patient. Mrs. Browning, in comparison, was not in a total comatose state. However, we fail to see a significant legal distinction. As we previously noted, the right involved here is one of self-determination that cannot be qualified by the condition of the patient. In this case, as in *Bludworth*, the patient was unable to personally or directly exercise

---

9. Recent statutory changes that have taken effect since the decision of the court below require some explanation of the use of the terms "incompetent" and "incapacitated" in this opinion. The term "incompetent" as used here refers to a status classification valid under applicable sections of the Florida Guardianship Law, chapter 744 of the Florida Statutes (1987). The Florida Guardianship Law was substantially revised effective October 1, 1989. Ch. 89-96, Laws of Fla. The reform legislation makes the word "incompetent" obsolete and replaces the "incompetency" concept with "incapacity," a term defined in the statute to recognize varying levels of capacity among persons who need surrogate decision-making by guardians. As used here, the terms "incompetent" and "incapacitated" mean those individuals unable to make medical decisions on their own behalf. Obviously, persons of limited capacity, who have retained the legal right pursuant to court order to make their own medical treatment decisions, will be "competent" to make those decisions.

10. This opinion addresses only those persons who are mentally *and* physically incapacitated and are being sustained by artificial means. We do not address those who are mentally incapacitated but physically are in good health.

the right to refuse medical treatment. Significantly, the patients in both cases, while competent, had executed written documents expressing their wishes.

We find that the district court correctly followed the principles underlying *Bludworth*. We hold that, because Mrs. Browning was unable to exercise her constitutional right of privacy by reason of her medical condition, her guardian was authorized to exercise it for her. As in *Bludworth*, we do not limit the ability to exercise this right only to a legally appointed guardian, but recognize that it may be exercised by proxies or surrogates such as close family members or friends.[11] We emphasize and caution that when the patient has left instructions regarding life-sustaining treatment, the surrogate must make the medical choice that the patient, if competent, would have made, and not one that the surrogate might make for himself or herself, or that the surrogate might think is in the patient's best interests. . . .

The state argues that we should not permit the enforcement of Mrs. Browning's expressed wish because we can never know whether Mrs. Browning may have changed her mind. A critical problem regarding the exercise of an incompetent's choice is sometimes posed by the inability of the incompetent to express his or her immediate wishes. Unfortunately, human limitations preclude absolute knowledge of the wishes of someone in Mrs. Browning's condition. However, we cannot avoid making a decision in these circumstances, for even the failure to act constitutes a choice. That choice must be the patient's choice whenever possible. The right of privacy requires that we must safeguard an individual's right to chart his or her own medical course in the event of later incapacity.

V. Compelling State Interest

The state has a duty to assure that a person's wishes regarding medical treatment are respected.[12] That obligation serves to protect the rights of the individual from intrusion by the state unless the state has a compelling interest great enough to override this constitutional right. The means to carry out any such compelling state interest must be narrowly tailored in the least intrusive manner possible to safeguard the rights of the individual.

Cases decided by this Court have identified state interests in the preservation of life, the protection of innocent third parties, the prevention of suicide, and maintenance of the ethical integrity of the medical profession, and have balanced them against an individual's right to refuse medical treatment.

---

11. We note that in its most recent session, the legislature passed legislation relating to the appointment of health care surrogates and the creation of a durable power of attorney. Ch. 90-232, §§ 11–24, Laws of Fla.

12. As Justice Stevens observed, "[o]ur Constitution is born of the proposition that all legitimate governments must secure the equal right of every person to 'Life, Liberty, and the pursuit of Happiness.'" *Cruzan ex rel., Cruzan v. Director, Mo. Dep't of Health*, 110 S.Ct. at 2878 (1990) (Stevens, J., dissenting).

The state's interest in the preservation of life generally is considered the most significant state interest. However, "'there is a substantial distinction in the State's insistence that human life be saved where the affliction is curable, as opposed to the State interest where, as here, the issue is not whether, but when, for how long and at what cost to the individual [his] [or her] life may be briefly extended.'" *Satz v. Perlmutter*, 362 So.2d 160, 162 (Fla. 4th DCA 1978) (quoting *Superintendent of Belchertown State School v. Saikewicz*, 373 Mass. 728, 740–44, 370 N.E.2d 417, 425–26 (1977)), *adopted*, 379 So.2d 359 (Fla.1980). Hence in *Satz*, we determined that a competent person suffering from an incurable affliction could refuse medical treatment. *See also Wons*. Likewise, in *Bludworth*, the state interests were insufficient to override the decision of a guardian or close family members carrying out the wishes of an incompetent patient not to be kept alive through the use of life-sustaining measures. *Bludworth*, 452 So.2d at 926.

Two other asserted state interests do not merit much discussion. First, there is no issue in this case pertaining to third parties. Second, suicide is not an issue when, as here, the discontinuation of life support "in fact will merely result in [her] death, if at all, from natural causes." *Satz*, 362 So.2d at 162.

The last and least significant of the aforementioned state interests is the maintenance of ethical integrity of the medical profession. However, "[r]ecognition of the right to refuse necessary treatment in appropriate circumstances is consistent with existing medical mores; such a doctrine does not threaten either the integrity of the medical profession, the proper role of hospitals in caring for such patients[,] or the State's interest in protecting the same." *Satz*, 362 So.2d at 163 (quoting *Saikewicz*, 373 Mass. At 742–45, 370 N.E.2d at 426–27). "Given the fundamental nature of the constitutional rights involved, protection of the ethical integrity of the medical profession alone could never override those rights." *Wons*, 541 So.2d at 101 (Ehrlich, C.J., concurring specially).

As we noted in *Wons*, the state interests discussed above are "by no means a brightline test, capable of resolving every dispute regarding the refusal of medical treatment. Rather, they are intended merely as factors to be considered while reaching the difficult decision of when a compelling state interest may override the basic constitutional right[] of privacy." *Wons*, 541 So.2d at 97.[13] We are satisfied that the state's interests do not outweigh the right of the individual to forego life-sustaining measures.

VI. Procedures For The Decision-Maker

The state argues that its interests are substantial enough to require more procedural protections than those provided in the district court's opinion. The state urges

---

13. For example, the state may have *parens patriae* interests in protecting an incompetent from an abusive or erroneous decision, *see Cruzan*, 110 S.Ct. at 2853, in avoiding unwanted medical care, *see id*. at 2851, or in "safe-guarding the accuracy" of determining the person's wishes. *Id*. at 2871 (Brennan, J., dissenting).

us to quash that section of the district court's opinion that permits a surrogate to make this life-or-death decision in a "private setting." Instead, the state suggests that we implement a judicial procedure requiring the surrogate to obtain prior court approval, giving an opportunity for the state or interested parties to be heard.

We cannot ignore the possibility that a surrogate might act contrary to the wishes of the patient. Yet, we are loath to impose a cumbersome legal proceeding at such a delicate time in those many cases where the patient neither needs nor desires additional protection. The decision to terminate artificial life-sustaining measures is being made over and over in nursing homes, hospitals, and private homes in this nation. It is being made painfully by loving family members, concerned guardians, or surrogates, in conjunction with the advice of ethical and caring physicians or other health care providers. It is being made when the only alternative to a natural death is to artificially maintain a bare existence. *See In re Guardianship of Barry*, 445 So.2d 365, 371 (Fla. 2d DCA 1984).

We are persuaded that when the patient has taken the time and the trouble to specifically express his or her wishes for future health care in the event of later incapacity, the surrogate need not obtain prior judicial approval to carry out those wishes. This applies whether the patient has expressed his or her desires in a "living will," through oral declarations, or by the written designation of a proxy to make all health care decisions in these circumstances.[14] We recognize that instructions evinced in the form of a "living will" or other written or oral statements may not have designated a decision-maker to carry out those instructions. In instances when a patient has left instructions, the patient may designate, orally or in writing, the decision-maker who is to carry out those instructions; but the patient need not do so.[15] However, when the patient has not expressed instructions, but has merely delegated full responsibility to a proxy, the designation of the proxy must have been made in writing.

A surrogate must take great care in exercising the patient's right of privacy, and must be able to support that decision with clear and convincing evidence. Before

---

14. As Justice O'Connor observed in *Cruzan*,

[f]ew individuals provide explicit oral or written instructions regarding their intent to refuse medical treatment should they become incompetent. States which decline to consider any evidence other than such instructions may frequently fail to honor a patient's intent. Such failures might be avoided if the State considered an equally probative source of evidence: the patient's appointment of a proxy to make health care decisions on her behalf. Delegating the authority to make medical decisions to a family member or friend is becoming a common method of planning for the future. See, *e.g.*, Areen, The Legal Status of Consent Obtained from Families of Adult Patients to Withhold or Withdraw Treatment, 258 JAMA 229, 230 (1987).

Cruzan, 110 S.Ct. at 2857 (O'Connor, J., concurring) (footnote omitted).

15. As we noted earlier, when a decision-maker has not been designated, a close family member or friend may carry out the patient's instructions.

exercising the incompetent's right to forego treatment, the surrogate must satisfy the following conditions:

1. The surrogate must be satisfied that the patient executed any document knowingly, willingly, and without undue influence, and that the evidence of the patient's oral declarations is reliable;

2. The surrogate must be assured that the patient does not have a reasonable probability of recovering competency so that the right could be exercised directly by the patient; and

3. The surrogate must take care to assure that any limitations or conditions expressed either orally or in the written declaration have been carefully considered and satisfied.

Likewise, when a proxy has been designated to make the decision without explicit instructions from the patient, the proxy must satisfy the following conditions:

1. The proxy must be satisfied that the patient executed the written designation of proxy knowingly, willingly, and without undue influence; and

2. The proxy must be assured that the patient does not have a reasonable probability of recovering competency so that the right could be exercised directly by the patient.

In determining whether the patient may recover competency or whether a medical condition or limitation referred to in the declaration exists, the surrogate or proxy must obtain, and may rely upon, certificates[16] from the patient's "primary treating physician" and "at least two other physicians with specialties relevant to the patient's condition." *Bludworth*, 452 So.2d at 926.

VII. Challenges To The Decision

We emphasize, as did the district court, that courts are always open to adjudicate legitimate questions pertaining to the written or oral instructions.[17] First, the surrogate or proxy may choose to present the question to the court for resolution. Second, interested parties may challenge the decision of the proxy or surrogate.

---

16. By certificates, we mean affidavits, sworn statements, or depositions. *In re Guardianship of Browning*, 543 So.2d 258, 272 (Fla. 2d DCA 1989).

17. We request the Probate and Guardianship Committee of The Florida Bar to submit to the Court within six months a proposed rule establishing procedures for *expedited* judicial intervention as required herein. The experience of numerous patients who died during the course of burdensome litigation underscores the importance of rules that provide such patients with certain access to the courts and the ability to swiftly resolve their claims when nonlegal means prove unsuccessful. *See, e.g., John F. Kennedy Memorial Hosp. v. Bludworth*, 452 So.2d 921 (Fla.1984); *In re Guardianship of Browning*, 543 So.2d 258 (Fla. 2d DCA 1989); *Corbett v. D'Alessandro*, 487 So.2d 368 (Fla. 2d DCA), *review denied*, 492 So.2d 1331 (Fla.1986); *Rasmussen ex rel. Mitchell v. Fleming*, 154 Ariz. 207, 741 P.2d 674 (1987); *Superintendent of Belchertown State School v. Saikewicz*, 373 Mass. 728, 370 N.E.2d 417 (1977); *In re Farrell*, 108 N.J. 335, 529 A.2d 404 (1987); *In re Conroy*, 98 N.J. 321, 486 A.2d 1209 (1985); *In re Storar*, 52 N.Y.2d 363, 420 N.E.2d 64, 438 N.Y.S.2d 266, *cert. denied*, 454 U.S. 858, 102 S.Ct. 309, 70 L.Ed.2d 153 (1981).

When the decision of a proxy or surrogate is challenged, a written declaration or designation of proxy, in the absence of any evidence of intent to the contrary, establishes a rebuttable presumption that constitutes clear and convincing evidence of the patient's wishes. Evidence of the physicians' certificates establishing the existence of any medical condition required by the declaration likewise establishes a rebuttable presumption that these conditions have been satisfied.

Although a surrogate may rely on oral statements made by the incompetent, while competent, to exercise the incompetent's wishes to forego life-sustaining treatment, the presumption of clear and convincing evidence that attaches to a written declaration does not attach to purely oral declarations. Oral evidence, considered alone, may constitute clear and convincing evidence. However, the surrogate would bear the burden of proof if a decision based on purely oral evidence is challenged.

Because the only issue before the court is a determination of the patient's wishes, challenges generally would be limited to that issue. For example, there may be challenges to claims that the declaration was not executed knowingly, willingly, and without undue influence; that the patient had changed his or her mind after executing the declaration; that the declaration was ambiguous; that the conditions or limitations contained in the declaration were not satisfied; that the surrogate or proxy was the one actually designated; and, of course, that there was a reasonable probability that the patient would regain competency. When the only evidence of intent is an oral declaration, the accuracy and reliability of the declarant's oral expression of intent also may be challenged.

For example, Mrs. Browning made a written declaration. Had Mrs. Browning merely indicated in her written document that she wanted to refuse any and all efforts to artificially prolong her life, viable challenges to her guardian's decision to implement those wishes would have included: that Mrs. Browning changed her mind; that she executed the document unknowingly, unwillingly, or under undue influence; or that there existed a reasonable probability that she would regain competency. Evidence on other issues generally would have been irrelevant to the only issue to be decided — the patient's wishes.

In this instance, however, Mrs. Browning's wishes were conditional. She indicated that her decision to refuse treatment was limited to a time when she had a "terminal condition" from which her attending physician determined that there could be "no recovery" and that "death [was] imminent." Thus, in a case like this one, the surrogate's conclusions as to those matters could become additional bases of challenge. We are satisfied in this case that the surrogate's conclusions were correct. No one questioned that the declaration was executed by Mrs. Browning knowingly, willingly, and without undue influence. Nor was there any question that Mrs. Browning was beyond hope of regaining her competency and making the decision herself. Thus, the only question was whether the conditions established by Mrs. Browning in her declaration were satisfied.

The trial court found that death would occur within four to nine days after removal of the nasogastric tube. Therefore, Mrs. Browning's life could only have been sustained beyond that time by the administration of artificial, intrusive medical measures. Under those circumstances, Mrs. Browning's death was imminent as we construe her express written intent. In addition, all the doctors agreed that Mrs. Browning suffered permanent brain damage and the medical testimony established that there was no hope that she would recover from her condition. We are satisfied that clear and convincing evidence existed to support a finding that Mrs. Browning suffered from a terminal condition. Under these circumstances, the surrogate was correct in instructing Mrs. Browning's health care providers to discontinue all life-sustaining procedures in accordance with Mrs. Browning's wishes.

VIII. Conclusion

We have previously held that competent and incompetent persons have the right to determine for themselves the course of their medical treatment. Today we hold that, without prior judicial approval, a surrogate or proxy, as provided here, may exercise the constitutional right of privacy for one who has become incompetent and who, while competent, expressed his or her wishes orally or in writing. We also determine that there is no legal distinction between gastrostomy or nasogastric feeding and any other means of life support. This case resolves a question of an individual's constitutional right of self-determination. We are hopeful that this decision will encourage those who want their wishes to be followed to express their wishes clearly and completely.

For the reasons expressed above, we answer the certified question in the affirmative as qualified here and approve the decision of the district court.

It is so ordered.

SHAW, C.J., and EHRLICH, GRIMES and KOGAN, JJ., concur.

McDONALD, J., concurs with an opinion.

OVERTON, J., concurs in part and dissents in part with an opinion.

[The McDonald and Overton opinions are omitted.]

In *In re Dubreuil*,[52] the Florida Supreme Court discussed in detail the state's interest in individual medical decisions where the interests of dependent minors might be affected by the decision. The following case addresses the state's interest in a pregnant woman's refusal of medical treatment necessary for the survival of her unborn fetus.

---

52. 629 So. 2d 819 (Fla. 1993).

Burton v. State

49 So. 3d 263 (Fla. 1st Dist. Ct. App. 2010)

CLARK, J.

This is an appeal of a circuit court order compelling a pregnant woman to submit to any medical treatment deemed necessary by the attending obstetrician, including detention in the hospital for enforcement of bed rest, administration of intra-venous medications, and anticipated surgical delivery of the fetus. The action was initiated in the circuit court by the State Attorney under the procedure described in *In re Dubreuil*, 629 So.2d 819 (Fla.1994). As provided in *Dubreuil*, after the State Attorney received notification from a health care provider that a patient refused medical treatment, the State Attorney exercised his discretion to determine that a sufficient state interest was at stake to justify legal action.

This appeal is moot with regard to Appellant because, as ordered, she submitted to the hospital confinement, medical treatment and surgical delivery. Two days after entry of the order, Appellant's deceased fetus was delivered by Cesarean section. Thus, the justiciable controversy between these parties has expired. However, mootness does not preclude appellate jurisdiction if the issue is "capable of repetition yet evading review," as in the case of medical issues which require immediate resolution. *See Roe v. Wade*, 410 U.S. 113, 93 S.Ct. 705, 35 L.Ed.2d 147 (1973); *Matter of Dubreuil*, 629 So.2d 819 (Fla.1993); *Holly v. Auld*, 450 So.2d 217, n. 1 (Fla.1984); Philip Padovano, *Florida Appellate Practice*, §1.4, p. 9 (2007-8 ed.).

The situation presented to the trial court in this case is capable of repetition yet evading review. Florida case precedent has addressed the right to privacy where a patient seeks to discontinue life-sustaining medical treatment, refuse a life-saving medical procedure, and as applied to statutory regulation of a minor's decision whether or not to continue her pregnancy. *In re Guardianship of Browning*, 568 So.2d 4 (Fla.1990); *In re Dubreuil*, 629 So.2d 819 (Fla.1994); *In re T.W.*, 551 So.2d 1186 (Fla.1989). However, case precedent governing the use of a *Dubreuil* proceeding to compel a pregnant woman to undergo medical confinement, treatment and procedures against her wishes for the benefit of her unborn fetus is not found in Florida's jurisprudence. In an effort to assist trial courts and counsel involved in these expedited, if not emergency proceedings, we exercise our discretionary authority to address this appeal. *See In re T.A.C.P.*, 609 So.2d 588 (Fla.1992); *Harrell v. St. Mary's Hospital*, 678 So.2d 455 (Fla. 4th DCA 1996).

The trial court found that the appellant had failed to follow the doctor's instructions and recommendations, rendering her pregnancy "high-risk," and found a "substantial and unacceptable" risk of severe injury or death to the unborn child if the appellant continued to fail to follow the recommended course of treatment. The trial court stated the rule that "as between parent and child, the ultimate welfare of the child is the controlling factor," and concluded that the State's interests in the matter "override Ms. Burton's privacy interests at this time." The court ordered Samantha Burton to comply with the physician's orders "including, but not limited to" bed rest, medication to postpone labor and prevent or treat infection, and eventual performance of a cesarean section delivery.

The law in Florida is clear: Every person has the right "to be let alone and free from government intrusion into the person's private life." Art. I, sec. 23, Fla. Const. This fundamental right to privacy encompasses a person's "right to the sole control of his or her person" and the "right to determine what shall be done with his own body." *In re Guardianship of Browning,* 568 So.2d 4, 10 (Fla.1990). The Florida Supreme Court has specifically recognized that "a competent person has the constitutional right to choose or refuse medical treatment, and that right extends to all relevant decisions concerning one's health." *Browning,* 568 So.2d at 11.

A patient's fundamental constitutional right to refuse medical intervention "can only be overcome if the state has a compelling state interest great enough to override this constitutional right." *Singletary v. Costello,* 665 So.2d 1099, 1105 (Fla. 4th DCA 1996). Thus, the threshold issue in this situation is whether the state established a compelling state interest sufficient to trigger the court's consideration and balance of that interest against the appellant's right to refuse to submit to the medical intervention the obstetrician prescribed. The state's interest in the potentiality of life of an unborn fetus becomes compelling "at the point in time when the fetus becomes viable," defined as "the time at which the fetus becomes capable of meaningful life outside the womb, albeit with artificial aid." *Roe v. Wade,* 410 U.S. 113, 163, 93 S. Ct. 705, 35 L.Ed.2d 147 (1973); *In re T.W.,* 551 So.2d 1186, 1193 (Fla.1989). The Legislature has defined "viability" as "that stage of fetal development when the life of the unborn child may with a reasonable degree of medical probability be continued indefinitely outside the womb." § 390.0111(4), Fla. Stat. No presumption of viability is provided in the statute.

Because there is no statutory or precedential presumption of viability, in terms of the stage of pregnancy or otherwise, there must be some evidence of viability via testimony or otherwise. Only after the threshold determination of viability has been made may the court weigh the state's compelling interest to preserve the life of the fetus against the patient's fundamental constitutional right to refuse medical treatment.

Even if the State had made the threshold showing of viability and the court had made the requisite determination, the legal test recited in the order on appeal was a misapplication of the law. The holding in *M.N. v. Southern Baptist Hosp. of Florida,* 648 So.2d 769 (Fla. 1st DCA 1994), "that as between parent and child, the ultimate welfare of the child is the controlling factor," does not apply to this case. Unlike this case, in *M.N.,* the parents refused consent for a blood transfusion and chemotherapy for their 8-month-old infant. No privacy rights of a pregnant woman were involved.

The test to overcome a woman's right to refuse medical intervention in her pregnancy is whether the state's compelling state interest is sufficient to override the pregnant woman's constitutional right to the control of her person, including her right to refuse medical treatment. *Dubreuil,* 629 So.2d 819; *Browning,* 568 So.2d 4;

Public Health Trust of Dade County v. Wons, 541 So.2d 96 (Fla.1989). In addition, where the state does establish a compelling state interest and the court has found the state's interest sufficient to override a pregnant patient's right to determine her course of medical treatment, the state must then show that the method for pursuing that compelling state interest is "narrowly tailored in the least intrusive manner possible to safeguard the rights of the individual." *Browning,* 568 So.2d at 14.

REVERSED.

VAN NORTWICK, J., Concurs with Written Opinion, and BERGER, WENDY, Associate Judge, Dissents with Written Opinion.

[The concurring and dissenting opinions are omitted.]

6. Privacy and Physician Assisted Suicide

Krischer v. McIver

697 So. 2d 97 (Fla. 1997)

GRIMES, Justice.

We have on appeal a judgment of the trial court certified by the Fourth District Court of Appeal to be of great public importance and to require immediate resolution by this Court. We have jurisdiction under article V, section 3(b)(5) of the Florida Constitution.

Charles E. Hall and his physician, Cecil McIver, M.D., filed suit for a declaratory judgment that section 782.08, Florida Statutes (1995), which prohibits assisted suicide, violated the Privacy Clause of the Florida Constitution and the Due Process and Equal Protection Clauses of the Fourteenth Amendment to the United States Constitution. [Footnote omitted.] They sought an injunction against the state attorney from prosecuting the physician for giving deliberate assistance to Mr. Hall in committing suicide. After a six-day bench trial, the trial court issued a final declaratory judgment and injunctive decree responding to the "question of whether a competent adult, who is terminally ill, immediately dying and acting under no undue influence, has a constitutional right to hasten his own death by seeking and obtaining from his physician a fatal dose of prescription drugs and then subsequently administering such drugs to himself." The court concluded that section 782.08 could not be constitutionally enforced against the appellees and enjoined the state attorney from enforcing it against Dr. McIver should he assist Mr. Hall in committing suicide. The court based its conclusion on Florida's privacy provision and the federal Equal Protection Clause but held that there was no federal liberty interest in assisted suicide guaranteed by the federal Due Process Clause.

Mr. Hall is thirty-five years old and suffers from acquired immune deficiency syndrome (AIDS) which he contracted from a blood transfusion. The court found that Mr. Hall was mentally competent and that he was in obviously deteriorating health, clearly suffering, and terminally ill. The court also found that it was

858   7 · THE DECLARATION OF RIGHTS AND THE TAKING OF PROPERTY

Dr. McIver's professional judgment that it was medically appropriate and ethical to provide Mr. Hall with the assistance he requests at some time in the future.

Dr. McIver had testified that he would assist Mr. Hall in committing suicide by intravenous means. In granting the relief sought by the respondents, the court held that "the lethal medication must be self administered only after consultation and determination by both physician and patient that Mr. Hall is (1) competent, (2) imminently dying, and (3) prepared to die." The court explained that Mr. Hall must state that he subjectively believes that his time to die has come because he has no hope for further life of satisfactory quality and would die soon in any event "and that at that time, Dr. McIver must conclude that Mr. Hall's belief—and his chosen option—is objectively reasonable at the time."

The state attorney appealed. The trial court then set aside the automatic stay imposed by Florida Rule of Appellate Procedure 9.310(b)(2). When this Court assumed jurisdiction of the case, we reinstated the stay and provided for expedited review.

At the outset, we note that the United States Supreme Court recently issued two decisions on the subject of whether there is a right to assisted suicide under the United States Constitution. In *Washington v. Glucksberg*, ___ U.S. ___, 117 S.Ct. 2258, 138 L.Ed.2d 772 (1997), the Court reversed a decision of the Ninth Circuit Court of Appeals which had held that the State of Washington's prohibition against assisted suicide violated the Due Process Clause. Like the trial court's decision in the instant case, the Court reasoned that the asserted "right" to assistance in committing suicide was not a fundamental liberty interest protected by the Due Process Clause.

In the second decision, the Court upheld New York's prohibition on assisted suicide against the claim that it violated the Equal Protection Clause. *Vacco v. Quill*, ___ U.S. ___, 117 S.Ct. 2293, 138 L.Ed.2d 834 (1997). In reversing the Second Circuit Court of Appeals, the Court held that there was a logical and recognized distinction between the right to refuse medical treatment and assisted suicide and concluded that there were valid and important public interests which easily satisfied the requirement that a legislative classification bear a rational relation to some legitimate end. Thus, the Court's decision in *Vacco* rejected one of the two bases for the trial court's ruling in the instant case.

The remaining issue is whether Mr. Hall has the right to have Dr. McIver assist him in committing suicide under Florida's guarantee of privacy contained in our constitution's declaration of rights. Art. I, § 23, Fla. Const. Florida has no law against committing suicide.[2] However, Florida imposes criminal responsibility on those who assist others in committing suicide. Section 782.08, Florida Statutes (1995), which

---

2. At common law committing suicide was a criminal offense which resulted in the forfeiture of the suicide's goods and chattels. These sanctions were later abolished in recognition of the unfairness of penalizing the suicide's family. *See Washington*.

was first enacted in 1868, provides in pertinent part that "every person deliberately assisting another in the commission of self murder shall be guilty of manslaughter." *See also* §§ 765.309, 458.326(4), Fla. Stat. (1995) (disapproving mercy killing and euthanasia). Thus, it is clear that the public policy of this state as expressed by the legislature is opposed to assisted suicide.

Florida's position is not unique. Forty-five states that recognize the right to refuse treatment or unwanted life support have expressed disapproval of assisted suicide. Edward R. Grant & Paul Benjamin Linton, *Relief or Reproach?: Euthanasia Rights in the Wake of Measure 16*, 74 Or. L.Rev. 449, 462–63 (1995). As of 1994, thirty-four jurisdictions had statutes which criminalized such conduct. *People v. Kevorkian*, 447 Mich. 436, 527 N.W.2d 714 (1994).[3] Since that date, at least seventeen state legislatures have rejected proposals to legalize assisted suicide. *Washington*.

The only case in the nation in which a court has considered whether assisted suicide is a protected right under the privacy provision of its state's constitution is *Donaldson v. Lungren*, 2 Cal.App.4th 1614, 4 Cal.Rptr.2d 59, 63 (1992), which held: "We cannot expand the nature of Donaldson's right of privacy to provide a protective shield for third persons who end his life." The court reasoned:

> In such a case, the state has a legitimate competing interest in protecting society against abuses. This interest is more significant than merely the abstract interest in preserving life no matter what the quality of that life is. Instead, it is the interest of the state to maintain social order through enforcement of the criminal law and to protect the lives of those who wish to live no matter what their circumstances. This interest overrides any interest Donaldson possesses in ending his life through the assistance of a third person in violation of the state's penal laws.

Id. See Kevorkian v. Arnett, 939 F.Supp. 725 (C.D.Cal.1996) (there is no persuasive authority to believe that the California Supreme Court would hold contrary to *Donaldson* when directly presented with the issue).

* * *

We have previously refused to allow the state to prohibit affirmative medical intervention, such as the case with the right to an abortion before viability of the fetus, only because the state's interests in preventing the intervention were not compelling. *In re T.W.*, 551 So.2d 1186 (Fla.1989) (state's interest in prohibiting abortion is compelling after fetus reaches viability). This is because, under our privacy provision, once a privacy right has been implicated, the state must establish a compelling interest to justify intruding into the privacy rights of an individual. *Winfield v. Division of Pari-Mutuel Wagering*, 477 So.2d 544 (Fla.1985).

---

3. Iowa and Rhode Island have subsequently enacted statutes against assisted suicide. Iowa Code Ann. §§ 707A.2, 707A.3 (Supp.1997); R.I. Gen. Laws §§ 11-60-1, 11-60-3 (Supp.1996).

860   7 · THE DECLARATION OF RIGHTS AND THE TAKING OF PROPERTY

This Court has also rendered several prior decisions declaring in various contexts that there is a constitutional privacy right to refuse medical treatment. Those cases recognized the state's legitimate interest in (1) the preservation of life, (2) the protection of innocent third parties, (3) the prevention of suicide, and (4) the maintenance of the ethical integrity of the medical profession. However, we held that these interests were not sufficiently compelling to override the patient's right of self-determination to forego life-sustaining medical treatment.

The respondents successfully convinced the trial court that there was no meaningful difference between refusing medical treatment and obtaining a physician's assistance in committing suicide. We cannot agree that there is no distinction between the right to refuse medical treatment and the right to commit physician-assisted suicide through self-administration of a lethal dose of medication. The assistance sought here is not treatment in the traditional sense of that term. It is an affirmative act designed to cause death — no matter how well-grounded the reasoning behind it. Each of our earlier decisions involved the decision to refuse medical treatment and thus allow the natural course of events to occur. *In re Dubreuil*, 629 So.2d 819 (Fla.1993) (due to religious beliefs, individual wanted to refuse blood transfusion); *In re Guardianship of Browning*, 568 So.2d 4 (Fla.1990) (surrogate asserted right of woman who was vegetative but not terminally ill to remove nasogastric feeding tube); *Public Health Trust v. Wons*, 541 So.2d 96 (Fla.1989) (same facts as *Dubreuil*); *Satz v. Perlmutter*, 379 So.2d 359 (Fla.1980) (individual suffering from Lou Gehrig's disease sought to remove artificial respirator needed to keep him alive).

In the instant case, Mr. Hall seeks affirmative medical intervention that will end his life on his timetable and not in the natural course of events. There is a significant difference between these two situations. As explained by the American Medical Association:

> When a life-sustaining treatment is declined, the patient dies primarily because of an underlying disease. The illness is simply allowed to take its natural course. With assisted suicide, however, death is hastened by the taking of a lethal drug or other agent. Although a physician cannot force a patient to accept a treatment against the patient's will, even if the treatment is life-sustaining, it does not follow that a physician ought to provide a lethal agent to the patient. The inability of physicians to prevent death does not imply that physicians are free to help cause death.

AMA Council on Ethical and Judicial Affairs, Report I-93-8, at 2.

Measured by the criteria employed in our cases addressing the right to refuse medical treatment, three of the four recognized state interests are so compelling as to clearly outweigh Mr. Hall's desire for assistance in committing suicide.[4] First, the state has an unqualified interest in the preservation of life. *Cruzan v. Director,*

---

4. There was no evidence introduced to demonstrate the effect of Mr. Hall's suicide upon innocent third parties.

Missouri Department of Health, 497 U.S. 261, 110 S.Ct. 2841, 111 L.Ed.2d 224 (1990). The opinion we adopted in *Perlmutter* included the caveat that suicide was not at issue because the discontinuation of life support would "merely result in [the patient's] death, if at all, from natural causes." *Satz v. Perlmutter*, 362 So.2d 160, 162 (Fla. 4th DCA 1978); *accord Browning*, 568 So.2d at 14. Although the constitutional privacy provision was not involved, in Mr. Perlmutter's case a sharp distinction was drawn between disconnecting a respirator that would result in his death from "natural causes" (i.e., the inability to breathe on his own) and an "unnatural death by means of a 'death producing agent.'" *Perlmutter*, 362 So.2d at 162. It is the second scenario that we encounter in the instant case. Mr. Hall will not die from the complications of his illness. Rather, a physician will assist him in administering a "death producing agent" with the intent of causing certain death. The state has a compelling interest in preventing such affirmative destructive act and in preserving Mr. Hall's life.

The state also has a compelling interest in preventing suicide. As the United States Supreme Court explained in *Washington*:

> Those who attempt suicide—terminally ill or not—often suffer from depression or other mental disorders. See New York Task Force 13–22, 126–128 (more than 95% of those who commit suicide had a major psychiatric illness at the time of death; among the terminally ill, uncontrolled pain is a "risk factor" because it contributes to depression); Physician-Assisted Suicide and Euthanasia in the Netherlands: A Report of Chairman Charles T. Canady to the Subcommittee on the Constitution of the House Committee on the Judiciary, 104th Cong., 2d Sess., 10–11 (Comm. Print 1996); cf. Back, Wallace, Starts, & Pearlman, Physician-Assisted Suicide and Euthanasia in Washington State, 275 JAMA 919, 924 (1996) ("[I]ntolerable physical symptoms are not the reason most patients request physician-assisted suicide or euthanasia"). Research indicates, however, that many people who request physician-assisted suicide withdraw that request if their depression and pain are treated. H. Hendin, Seduced by Death: Doctors, Patients and the Dutch Cure 24–25 (1997) (suicidal, terminally ill patients "usually respond well to treatment for depressive illness and pain medication and are then grateful to be alive"); New York Task Force 177–178. The New York Task Force, however, expressed its concern that, because depression is difficult to diagnose, physicians and medical professionals often fail to respond adequately to seriously ill patients' needs. *Id.*, at 175. Thus, legal physician-assisted suicide could make it more difficult for the State to protect depressed or mentally ill persons, or those who are suffering from untreated pain, from suicidal impulses.

Washington, ___ U.S. at ___, 117 S.Ct. at 2273.

Finally, the state also has a compelling interest in maintaining the integrity of the medical profession. While not all health care providers agree on the issue, the leading health care organizations are unanimous in their opposition to legalizing

862   7 · THE DECLARATION OF RIGHTS AND THE TAKING OF PROPERTY

assisted suicide. The American Medical Association, which represents 290,000 physicians, as late as June of 1996 overwhelmingly endorsed a recommendation to reaffirm the ethical ban on physician-assisted suicide. American Medical Association, Press Release, "AMA Soundly Reaffirms Policy Opposing Physician-Assisted Suicide" (June 24, 1996). The same position is endorsed by the Florida Medical Association, the Florida Society of Internal Medicine, the Florida Society of Thoracic and Cardiovascular Surgeons, the Florida Osteopathic Medical Association, the Florida Hospices, Inc., and the Florida Nurses Association. Who would have more knowledge of the dangers of legalizing assisted suicide than those intimately charged with maintaining the patient's well-being?

In addition, the *Code of Medical Ethics*, § 2.211, states that physician-assisted suicide is "fundamentally incompatible with the physician's role as healer, would be difficult or impossible to control, and would pose serious societal risks." Even the Hippocratic Oath itself states that a physician "will neither give a deadly drug to anybody if asked for it, nor . . . make a suggestion to this effect." Physician-assisted suicide directly contradicts these ethical standards and compromises the integrity of the medical profession and the role of hospitals in caring for patients.

We do not hold that a carefully crafted statute authorizing assisted suicide would be unconstitutional. Nor do we discount the sincerity and strength of the respondents' convictions. However, we have concluded that this case should not be decided on the basis of this Court's own assessment of the weight of the competing moral arguments. By broadly construing the privacy amendment to include the right to assisted suicide, we would run the risk of arrogating to ourselves those powers to make social policy that as a constitutional matter belong only to the legislature. *See* Art. II, § 3, Fla. Const. (separation of powers).[5]

We reverse the judgment of the trial court and uphold the constitutionality of section 782.08.

It is so ordered.

SHAW and WELLS, JJ., concur.

OVERTON and HARDING, JJ., concur with an opinion. [These opinions are omitted.]

KOGAN, C.J., dissents with an opinion.

ANSTEAD, J., recused.

* * *

KOGAN, Chief Justice, dissenting.

---

5. In *Shands Teaching Hospital & Clinics, Inc. v. Smith*, 497 So.2d 644, 646 (Fla.1986), we acknowledged that:

[O]f the three branches of government, the judiciary is the least capable of receiving public input and resolving broad public policy questions based on a societal consensus.

7 · THE DECLARATION OF RIGHTS AND THE TAKING OF PROPERTY   863

The notion of "dying by natural causes" contrasts neatly with the word "suicide," suggesting two categories readily distinguishable from one another. How nice it would be if today's reality were so simple. No doubt there once was a time when, for all practical purposes, the distinction was clear enough to all. But that was a time before today, before technology had crept into medicine, when dying was a far more inexorable process. Medicine now has pulled the aperture separating life and death far enough apart to expose a limbo unthinkable fifty years ago, for which the law has no easy description. Dying no longer falls into the neat categories our ancestors knew. In today's world, we demean the hard reality of terminal illness to say otherwise.

Even the evolution of the legal term "suicide" shows the change forced upon us. At common law in both England and the United States, "suicide" was any action *or inaction* causing one's own death even if intended "to avoid those ills which [people] had not the fortitude to endure." 4 William Blackstone, Commentaries. The duty imposed by this law on the dying was especially rigorous:

> The life of those to whom life has become a burden — of those who are hopelessly diseased or fatally wounded — nay, even the lives of criminals condemned to death, are under the protection of the law, equally as lives of those who are in the full tide of life's enjoyment, and anxious to continue to live.

Blackburn v. State, 23 Ohio St. 146, 163 (1872). If this law were in effect today, there could be no question about Mr. Hall's case: He would be forced to endure his final agony. Perhaps that notion made sense in the medieval age that invented it, before the most basic processes of disease were understood. Today it reflects a cruelty we cannot take lightly.

The ability of medicine to intrude so profoundly into the act of dying has prompted a rising emphasis on the right of privacy, with its deep concern with self-determination. Since being added to the state Constitution in 1980, Florida's privacy right unquestionably has subtracted certain death-inducing actions from the category of "suicide" as defined at common law. Thus, in *Satz v. Perlmutter*, 379 So.2d 359, 360 (Fla.1980), we upheld the decision of an individual suffering Lou Gehrig's disease to cease artificial respiration needed to keep him alive. In *Public Health Trust v. Wons*, 541 So.2d 96, 97–98 (Fla.1989), we upheld an individual's right to refuse a blood transfusion needed to save her life even though she had children, where refusal was based on religious beliefs. On similar facts, we reached the same conclusion *In re Dubreuil*, 629 So.2d 819, 827–28 (Fla.1993), where the State failed to establish the unfitness of the other parent to assume custody of the children. [Footnote omitted.] *In re Guardianship of Browning*, 568 So.2d 4, 17 (Fla.1990), we found that the right to refuse treatment could be asserted by a surrogate on behalf of a woman who was vegetative but not terminally ill, but who previously had indicated she wanted life support removed in such circumstances. All of these acts would have been suicide at common law, and the assistance provided by physicians would have been homicide. Today they are not.

Once Florida had set itself adrift from the common law definition, the problem that immediately arose — that has vexed our courts ever since — is where to draw the new dividing line between improper "suicide" and the emerging "right of self-determination" without simultaneously authorizing involuntary euthanasia. This is no simple task. And until today, no Florida court had attempted it. The majority tries to fix the mark through scrutinizing the *means* by which dying occurs: Suicide thus is "active" death caused by a "death producing agent," whereas Floridians have a right to choose "passive" death through "natural causes." While language in our prior opinions can be read to support this view, I am not convinced this language can be stretched beyond the differing facts we previously faced. All of these earlier cases dealt with the refusal of medical treatment needed *if life was to continue*. The present case asks a far different question: How must Charles Hall die, given the fact an agonizing death is both imminent and inevitable? Principles developed in these earlier cases were not intended to, and to my mind cannot properly, resolve the very different and very troubling legal issues surrounding an unstoppable, painful death.

Indeed, the majority's "sharp" distinction between active and passive dying may cause substantial mischief. The price could be, on one hand, agony forced upon dying patients by physicians who simply do not know what else they can lawfully do, or on the other hand, a legally questionable medical hypocrisy that distorts the "active" versus "passive" distinction in an effort to be humane. Until today, for example, many people viewed *Browning* as letting patients make an advance refusal of nasogastric feeding and hydration effective whenever they became incompetent, no matter how incompetency came about. This was true even if a conscious patient voluntarily requested complete sedation to relieve otherwise unquenchable pain of a terminal illness. Given the majority's means-based analysis, I am at a loss to explain what now must happen in this situation, because it is here that the distinction between "active death" and "passive death" breaks down. Honoring the patient's request is very hard to distinguish from the assistance Mr. Hall requests, since both involve the "active" administration of a drug with intent to produce a more rapid death. As Florida's own living will statute indicates, physicians are not authorized "to permit any affirmative or deliberate act *or omission* to end life other than to permit the natural process of dying." §765.309(1), Fla. Stat. (1995) (emphasis added). Yet, I for one have great difficulty saying that, privacy notwithstanding, the law must force Mr. Hall to suffer his agony as best he can or else must force nasogastric support on him until AIDS finally takes him away. This is little more than a retreat to the common law rule developed in Europe's Dark Ages.

One might argue that the two situations are distinguishable because in the latter the drug is not actually the "death producing agent" — starvation and dehydration are — whereas in Mr. Hall's case the drug itself would cause death. Yet the distinction is unworkable, as demonstrated in another hypothetical: Suppose, for example, that the person asking to be permanently sedated is *not* terminally ill but merely suffers chronic, irreversible pain. Would it be an illegal assisted suicide if the attending physician agreed to narcotize the patient to allow starvation and dehydration? And what if the patient is an adult of sound mind who simply feels life no longer worth-while? Can the physician also sedate and starve this one? Under a means-based test, any one of these hypotheticals must be suicide if any other is. And while I might agree that the latter two examples are questionable, I am utterly unwilling to suggest that Mr. Hall's case also might be. When his pain becomes unbearable, which one of us on this Court will be at his bedside telling him to be brave and bear it?

The issue is different here. In cases of this type, we simply cannot focus on the means by which death occurs, but on the fact that the patient at the time in question has reached the death bed. That is the fact unique in this case that was not present in the earlier cases, and it is the reason why we must use a different analysis. A means-based test works well in the context of refusing medical treatment where life other-wise will continue. It does not work where there is no question death must occur, and must occur painfully.

To my mind, the right of privacy attaches with unusual force at the death bed. This conclusion arises in part from the privacy our society traditionally has afforded the death bed, but also from the very core of the right of privacy — the right of self-determination even in the face of majoritarian disapproval. *See Shaktman v. State*, 553 So.2d 148, 151 (Fla.1989). What possible interest does society have in saving life when there is nothing of life to save but a final convulsion of agony? The state has no business in this arena. Terminal illness is not a portrait in blacks and whites, but unending shades of gray, involving the most profound of personal, moral, and reli-gious questions. Many people can and do disagree over these questions, but the fact remains that it is the dying person who must resolve them in the particular case. And while we certainly cannot ignore the slippery-slope problem, we previously have established fully adequate standards to police the exercise of privacy rights in this context to ensure against abuse.[8]

Finally, I cannot ignore the majority's statement that the issues in this case must be left to the legislature. Such a statement ignores fundamental tenets of our law. Constitutional rights must be enforced by courts even against the legislature's pow-ers, and privacy in particular must be enforced even against majoritarian sentiment. *Shaktman*. Indeed, the overarching purpose of the Florida Declaration of Rights along with its privacy provision is to "protect each individual within our borders from the unjust encroachment of state authority — from whatever official source — into his or her life." *Traylor v. State*, 596 So.2d 957, 963 (Fla.1992).

At a fundamental level, the role of the Justices and judges of Florida is to guaran-tee and enforce the protection afforded by these basic rights. This is at once a judge's greatest calling and heaviest burden. It is an obligation we shoulder by our oath of

---

8. In *Dubreuil*, 629 So.2d at 823–24, we held that any physician concerned about a patient's deci-sion must immediately provide notice to the appropriate state attorney and to interested third par-ties known to the physician. As a practical matter, notification must always be given in cases of this type.

office, binding ourselves to enforce individual liberty even in the face of public or official opposition. To shield the liberties of the individual from encroachment is uniquely the task of courts. In that sense, we are obliged to give sanctuary against the overreaches of government.

* * *

Florida's express right of privacy[16] clearly forms a major component of the protections afforded by the Declaration of Rights. Codified in the Constitution in 1980,[17] it is a fundamental right that protects the people's "legitimate expectations of privacy." *Winfield v. Division of Pari-Mutuel Wagering*, 477 So.2d 544, 547 (Fla.1985). The legitimacy of such expectations are defined neither by consensus nor majoritarian sentiment, *Shaktman v. State*, 553 So.2d 148, 151 (Fla.1989), but by reference to the historical development of the Anglo-American concept of "ordered liberty." *Winfield*, 477 So.2d at 546. Put another way, our right of privacy is both general and comprehensive. It guarantees to individuals, as against government, the broadest possible personal autonomy and freedom from disclosures of personal information that are consistent with an ordered society.[18] As we have stated:

> [T]he concept of privacy encompasses much more than the right to control the disclosure of information about oneself. "Privacy" has been used interchangeably with the common understanding of the notion of "liberty," and both imply a fundamental right of self-determination subject only to the state's compelling and overriding interest. For example, privacy has been defined as an individual's "control over or the autonomy of the intimacies of personal identity," Gerety, *Redefining Privacy*, 12 Harv. C.R.C.L.L.Rev. 233, 281 (1977); or as a "physical and psychological zone within which an individual has the right to be free from intrusion or coercion, whether by government or by society at large." Cope, *To Be Let Alone: Florida's Proposed Right of Privacy*, 6 Fla. St. U.L.Rev. 671, 677 (1978).

In re Guardianship of Browning, 568 So.2d 4, 9–10 (Fla.1990). In sum, privacy protects at a minimum both a "nondisclosure interest" and an "autonomy interest."[19]

---

16. Article I, section 23, of the Florida Constitution provides in pertinent part that "[e]very natural person has the right to be let alone and free from governmental intrusion into his private life."

17. A right of privacy had existed prior to its codification in the Constitution, *see Satz v. Perlmutter*, 379 So.2d 359 (Fla.1980), though there is no doubt the amendment also broadened the right's scope. Florida also recognizes a civil form of privacy protecting individuals from unwarranted intrusions by other private individuals. *Cason v. Baskin*, 155 Fla. 198, 20 So.2d 243 (1944).

18. It is important to distinguish this broader concept of "ordered liberty" from the narrower "liberty interests" protected by due process, with their different contexts and contrasting burdens of proof. *Compare Department of Law Enforcement v. Real Property*, 588 So.2d 957 (Fla.1991) (due process guarantees inherent fairness; government can infringe property right only upon clear and convincing evidence) with *In re Guardianship of Browning*, 568 So.2d 4 (Fla. 1990) (privacy guarantees personal autonomy; state can justify infringements only for "compelling" interest enforced through least intrusive means).

19. There are, of course, cases in which a claim of privacy is made for acts not genuinely private in nature. Such claims must be denied. For example, building a fence around one's property in

Judicial analysis can differ according to which interest is at stake. The difference in analysis arises to the extent that one person's privacy interest is in conflict with other basic rights possessed by separate individuals. This can occur, for example, where enforcement of one person's nondisclosure interests will undermine freedom of the press or the right to a fair trial. When such conflict exists, the Court has used a balancing test to resolve the competing constitutional claims.

Autonomy interests, by contrast, typically involve personal decisions about one's own body, home, or private life. Intrusion is inherently less justifiable to the extent the state is acting solely in its regulatory capacity. Because privacy exists precisely to protect individuals from overuse of state powers, the general interest in regulating society does not in itself prevail against a valid privacy claim, without more. Rather, the state must establish a special or *compelling* interest justifying the intrusion into privacy. Otherwise privacy prevails.

Our case law illustrates the distinction between nondisclosure cases and cases involving personal autonomy. We have held that the privacy amendment does not shield public records from disclosure, *State v. Hume*, 512 So.2d 185, 188 (Fla.1987), although it can in certain instances require quashal of a subpoena aimed at private records containing personal information. This was true, for example, where the information sought could harm third parties by identifying them as potential carriers of HIV, at least where that information was not genuinely essential to a fair trial. *Rasmussen v. South Fla. Blood Serv. Inc.*, 500 So.2d 533, 537–38 (Fla.1987). In reaching this conclusion, the Court weighed the interest in nondisclosure against the information's relevance to the proceedings. *Id.; accord Times Publishing Co. v. A.J.*, 626 So.2d 1314, 1315–16 (Fla.1993).

A similar balancing test has been applied in at least one case where closure of court proceedings and records was sought to preserve alleged privacy interests. *Barron v. Florida Freedom Newspapers, Inc.*, 531 So.2d 113, 118–19 (Fla.1988). There, the Court emphasized the need to balance the privacy interest against the right to freedom of information. *Id.* Thus, the latter outweighed privacy interests of a Florida politician who sought closure of divorce records containing his personal medical records.[20] *See id.* at 120 (Barkett, J., specially concurring).

---

a manner contrary to state environmental law and policy is not a private act entitled to protection under article I, section 23. *Department of Community Affairs v. Moorman*, 664 So.2d 930, 933 (Fla.1995), *cert. denied*, ___ U.S. ___, 117 S.Ct. 79, 136 L.Ed.2d 37 (1996). Privacy likewise does not authorize parents to donate the organs of their living child, thereby killing it, merely because it was born with a severe birth defect. *In re T.A.C.P.*, 609 So.2d 588, 593 n. 9 (Fla.1992). Nor does it protect individuals from a governmental employer's decision not to hire them because they smoke cigarettes. *City of North Miami v. Kurtz*, 653 So.2d 1025, 1028 (Fla.1995).

20. It deserves great stress that both *Rasmussen* and *Barron* involved private parties asserting their own personal rights about a governmental process to permit or restrain disclosures sought by *other* private parties. *Accord Times Publishing Co.*, 626 So.2d at 1315. The result would not be the same where only the government's regulatory interests, not the basic rights of other persons, are the single justification for disclosure of otherwise private information.

868   7 · THE DECLARATION OF RIGHTS AND THE TAKING OF PROPERTY

Autonomy cases — of which the present controversy is one — involve issues of a wholly different magnitude. Generally, they ask not how to balance competing rights of individuals, but how far government in its regulatory capacity may intrude into personal decision-making. Wherever a legitimate expectation of privacy exists, governmental intrusion into that expectation must be based on a special or "*compelling*" interest. Interests are compelling if they lie at the core of government's ability to maintain order and protect the rights or well-being of others. Moreover, the means used to advance the compelling interest must be narrowly tailored through use of the least intrusive means available. *Browning*, 568 So.2d at 14.

We have held, for example, that privacy forbids governmental intrusion into parenting decisions, absent a compelling state interest such as a threat of harm to the child. *Beagle v. Beagle*, 678 So.2d 1271, 1275–76 (Fla.1996). In broad terms, the intimacies of home life, the relation of parent and child, and the decision how to structure one's private life fall within the guarantee of article I, section 23, subject only to the state's compelling interests.

Yet our cases clearly establish two other autonomy interests of great magnitude. They arise from life's two most personal and private experiences — procreation and death. In 1989, this Court noted that the voters of Florida approved the privacy amendment at a time when the concept of privacy clearly was understood to give women control of their own bodies in making reproductive decisions, within certain limits. *In re T.W.*, 551 So.2d 1186 (Fla.1989). Likewise, we have found that health-care decision-making in general — most especially when confronting death — is a protected interest. This is so in part because privacy gives people inherent control over decisions affecting their own bodies. *E.g.*, *Browning*, 568 So.2d at 11; *Public Health Trust v. Wons*, 541 So.2d 96 (Fla.1989). Thus,

> a competent person has the constitutional right to choose or refuse medical treatment, *and that right extends to all relevant decisions concerning one's health.*

Browning, 568 So.2d at 11 (emphasis added).

There is no doubt that the state has an interest in preserving life. *Id.* at 14. In the vast majority of cases, that interest also is compelling. None of our case law assumes otherwise. But as our cases clearly show, there are rare instances when the state's interest falls below the mark of "compelling." Indeed, the issue before us today as in our earlier cases is the

> 'substantial distinction in the State's insistence that human life be saved where the affliction is curable, as opposed to the State interest where, as here, the issue is not whether, but when, for how long and at what cost to the individual [his][or her] life may be briefly extended.'

Browning, 568 So.2d at 14 (quoting *Satz v. Perlmutter*, 362 So.2d 160, 162 (Fla. 4th DCA 1978) (quoting *Superintendent of Belchertown State School v. Saikewicz*, 373 Mass. 728, 740–44, 370 N.E.2d 417, 425–26 (1977)), *approved*, 379 So.2d 359 (Fla.1980)). Because Mr. Hall's case involves this same critical distinction, the right of privacy clearly attaches to the decisions he is confronting with the help of his physician. I cannot in good conscience say that the state's interest is compelling, given the fact that Mr. Hall's life no longer can be saved. Here, the state is vouchsafing nothing but indignity and suffering — hardly "compelling" interests. I further believe that the rule established by the majority is not merely unworkable but rests on concerns of an era that, however much we may regret it, no longer exists. A sharp dividing line once separated life from death. Today there stretches a chasm of ambiguities. Because the confrontation of these ambiguities is inherently a personal decision, I am unwilling to remove from Mr. Hall's control the way in which he confronts his own personal fate.

I respectfully dissent.

In 2020, for the first time in Florida's history, a bill titled the Florida Death with Dignity Act was introduced in the Florida Legislature that would have allowed terminally ill Florida residents aged 18 or older to request life-ending medication from a physician. The bill died in the Senate.[53]

7. Privacy, Statutory Rape, and Sexual Misconduct with a Minor

J.A.S. v. State

705 So. 2d 1381 (Fla. 1998)

ANSTEAD, Justice.

We have for review the decision in *State v. J.A.S.*, 686 So.2d 1366 (Fla. 5th DCA 1997). We accepted jurisdiction to answer the following question certified to be of great public importance:

> WHETHER THE POTENTIAL PENALTY FOR VIOLATION OF SECTION 800.04, FLORIDA STATUTES, BY A MINOR UNDER THE AGE OF SIXTEEN FURTHERS A COMPELLING STATE INTEREST THROUGH THE LEAST INTRUSIVE MEANS?

Id. at 1370. We have jurisdiction. Art. V, § 3(b)(4), Fla. Const. For the reasons expressed below, we answer the certified question in the affirmative, approve the decision under review, and hold that under the factual circumstances presented herein section 800.04, Florida Statutes (1993), furthers the State's compelling interest in protecting minors from harmful sexual conduct through the least intrusive means.

---

53. S.B. 1800, 122d Reg. Sess. (Fla. 2020).

Material Facts And Procedure Below[1]

The trial court dismissed statutory rape charges against two fifteen-year-old boys, J.A.S. and J.L.R., who engaged in "consensual" sex with two twelve-year-old girls. One of the boys had sixty-five prior referrals to HRS with thirty-five adjudications. He was on community control when charged and had previously engaged in sex with the victim's thirteen-year-old sister. The other boy had eight prior juvenile referrals and four adjudications. *Id.* at 1368. The trial judge found section 800.04, Florida Statutes (1993),[2] unconstitutional as applied to the boys because it violated their rights to privacy and equal protection, and the harsh adult sanctions would constitute cruel and unusual punishments if the boys were charged as adults in a felony criminal prosecution.[3]

The district court vacated the dismissal. First, the court found that the trial judge inappropriately relied on his own personal experience as a juvenile judge to conclude that "the boys are always charged by the state" whenever sexual misconduct is alleged between juveniles. The court stated that this was an inadequate evidentiary basis to support such a claim of discrimination and that a prosecutor's absolute discretion to charge only some offenders "is not a ground for a claim of denial of equal protection." Second, the district court found that the potential penalties for juveniles if sentenced as adults was not the proper test in determining whether cruel and unusual punishment was imposed.[4]

Finally, the district court considered whether application of the statute invaded the boys' privacy rights. After analyzing the legislative intent behind the statute and our opinion in *B.B. v. State*, 659 So.2d 256 (Fla. 1995), the district court concluded that "[w]hatever rights of privacy a minor under sixteen may have, surely it does not extend to an absolute and unregulated right to engage in recreational sex with a minor also under that age." 686 So.2d at 1369. Accordingly, the court refused to

---

1. The following facts are taken from the district court's opinion. *J.A.S.*, 686 So.2d at 1367–70.

2. The trial court specifically found subsection (4) unconstitutional as applied. The first three subsections of section 800.04 deal with sexual assault or sexual battery. Subsection (4) provides:

A person who:

. . . .

(4) Knowingly commits any lewd or lascivious act in the presence of any child under the age of 16 years, without committing the crime of sexual battery, commits a felony of the second degree, punishable as provided in s. 775.082, s. 775.083, or s. 775.084. Neither the victim's lack of chastity nor the victim's consent is a defense to the crime proscribed by this section.

3. The trial court then certified a question of great public importance to that effect to the Fifth District. The district court declined to answer the question, finding no provision for a certified question from a trial court and determining that the equal protection and cruel and unusual punishment issues were premature.

4. As to the severity of the sanction attached, the court also noted that the "legislature seemed to be content with the potential punishment involved, as reflected by its unwillingness to change the statutory prohibitions and penalties . . . during their 1996 session, although fully acknowledging that it was aware of the problem." 686 So.2d at 1369.

7 · THE DECLARATION OF RIGHTS AND THE TAKING OF PROPERTY   871

"eliminate by judicial fiat whatever restraint section 800.04 provides in prohibiting sexual activity by minors in furtherance of the State's compelling interest in preventing such conduct and its consequences." *Id.*

Law And Analysis

This case presents policy questions similar to the ones we addressed in *B.B. v. State*, 659 So.2d 256 (Fla.1995), and *Jones v. State*, 640 So.2d 1084 (Fla.1994).

In *Jones*, we upheld the constitutionality of the specific statute at issue in this case, section 800.04.[5] There, the issue was whether Florida's statutory rape law as defined in section 800.04 was constitutional in criminalizing consensual sexual intercourse by an adult with a person under the age of sixteen. *Id.* at 1086. *Jones* involved separate cases, wherein three adult males, ages eighteen, nineteen, and twenty, were charged with violating the statute's prohibition against sexual intercourse with "any child under the age of 16 years." In each case the female victim consented to sexual intercourse with the defendant. Jones, the eighteen-year-old, was convicted and sentenced to four and one-half years' imprisonment. However, in separate cases involving the other defendants, a different trial judge dismissed the charges, declared section 800.04 unconstitutional as applied and held that the statute constituted an unreasonable restriction on the consenting victims' right of privacy. The Fifth District reversed on the constitutional issue, and certified the constitutional privacy issue to this Court as one of great public importance.

On review in *Jones* we approved the district court's decision, noting that the legislature had enacted numerous statutes to protect minors from harmful sexual conduct, and that those laws clearly invoke a policy that "any type of sexual conduct involving a child constitutes an intrusion upon the rights of that child, whether or not the child consents . . . [therefore] society has a compelling interest in intervening to stop such misconduct." *Id.* at 1086 (quoting *Schmitt v. State*, 590 So.2d 404, 410–11 (Fla.1991)). Emphasizing the primacy of the child protection policies implicit in the laws, we determined that "neither the level of intimacy nor the degree of harm are relevant when an adult and a child under the age of sixteen engage in sexual intercourse." *Id.* We noted that neither the child's maturity or lack of chastity could override these concerns because "sexual activity with a child opens the door to sexual exploitation, physical harm, and sometimes psychological damage." *Jones*, 640 So.2d at 1086. We also refused to extend a minor's privacy rights involving abortion as confirmed in *In re T.W.*, 551 So.2d 1186 (Fla.1989), to include a right to initiate consensual sexual relationships with adults. We noted that "*T.W.* did not transform a minor into an adult for all purposes." Finally, we concluded that whatever the extent

---

5. Although both cases construe section 800.04, *Jones* addressed the 1991 statute, while *J.A.S.* interpreted the 1993 statute. There are slight differences between the statutes, although none are material. Specifically, "Any person" is now "A person"; "makes an assault upon any child" is now "assaults any child"; and a final sentence was added in 1993: "A mother's breastfeeding of her baby does not under any circumstance violate this section." Ch. 93-4, § 5 Laws of Fla. (1993).

of a minor's privacy rights, those rights "do not vitiate the legislature's efforts and authority to protect [minors] from conduct of others." *Jones*, 640 So.2d at 1087.

Justice Kogan wrote separately in *Jones*, noting that our decision on minors' abortion rights in *In re T.W.*, 551 So.2d 1186 (Fla.1989), "did not directly or indirectly address the propriety of teens engaging in sexual activities." *Id.* at 1087 n. 5. He opined that "sex in early adolescence is a dangerous folly that the state clearly does not condone; but once a girl is pregnant, very different issues and dangers of a completely different magnitude arise. *T.W.*, in sum, does *not* create a right for young adolescents to 'consent' to sex." *Id.* Justice Kogan also feared that "an uncritical acceptance of the notion of youths 'consenting' to sexual activity will merely create a convenient smoke screen for a predatory exploitation of children and young adolescents." *Id.* at 1088. As evidence of the genuineness of these concerns, Justice Kogan cited copious social science research detailing the resulting psychological costs to the exploited individual, and the increase in criminal activity connected to the childhood sexual abuse of the perpetrators, thereby affecting society as a whole. *Id.* at 1088–89.

B.B. v. State

Subsequently, in *B.B. v. State*, 659 So.2d 256 (Fla.1995), upon review of a certified question,[6] we found section 794.05, Florida Statutes (1991),[7] unconstitutional *as applied* to the unique facts of that case, including the fact that both the charged defendant and the alleged consenting victim were aged sixteen. We cast the issue in *B.B.* as "whether a minor who engages in 'unlawful' carnal intercourse with an unmarried minor of previous chaste character can be adjudicated delinquent of a felony of the second degree in light of the minor's right to privacy guaranteed by the Florida Constitution." 659 So.2d at 258. After noting that other intimate acts fall within the zone of privacy recognized by the United States Constitution, and in light of our decision in *T.W.* finding abortion rights to be within a minor's privacy interest, we concluded that "Florida's clear constitutional mandate in favor of privacy is implicated in B.B., a sixteen-year-old, engaging in carnal intercourse." *Id.* at

---

6. "Whether Florida's privacy amendment, Article I, section 23 of the Florida Constitution, renders section 794.05, Florida Statutes (1991), unconstitutional as it pertains to a minor's consensual sexual activity?" *Id.* at 257. The trial court granted B.B.'s motion to declare the statute unconstitutional, relying on *T.W.* for the proposition that B.B.'s privacy rights under the Florida Constitution outweighed the State's interest in protecting the other consenting sixteen-year-old from her own consensual sexual conduct. *Id.* at 258.

7. Section 794.05 provided that:

(1) Any person who has unlawful sexual intercourse with any unmarried person, of previous chaste character, who at the time of such intercourse is under the age of 18 years, shall be guilty of a felony of the second degree. . . .

(2) It shall not be a defense to a prosecution under this section that the prosecuting witness was not of previous chaste character at the time of the act when the lack of previous chaste character in the prosecuting witness was caused solely by previous intercourse between the defendant and the prosecuting witness.

7 · THE DECLARATION OF RIGHTS AND THE TAKING OF PROPERTY   873

259. Thereafter, we applied the "stringent test"[8] to the statute, the standard whereby the State "must prove that the statute furthers a compelling state interest through the least intrusive means." *Id.* at 259 (quoting *T.W.*, 551 So.2d at 1193), and found that the State's interest fell short of that measure in its attempt to punish one sixteen-year-old for consenting to having sex with another sixteen-year-old.

We distinguished *B.B.* from *Jones* by pointing out material distinctions between both the statutes, the issues under review, and especially the specific factual circumstances involved of two consenting sixteen-year-olds. We specifically distinguished the State's interest that we found compelling in *Jones*. We noted that *Jones* implicated an adult-minor situation where "the crux of the State's interest . . . [was] the prevention of exploitation of the minor by the adult." *Id.* In contrast, "in this minor-minor situation, the crux of the State's interest is in protecting the minor from the sexual activity itself for reasons of health and quality of life." *Id.*

We also explored the ancient roots of the statute in an attempt to determine "why the statute protected only unmarried minors who were chaste." *Id.* Finally, after agreeing with a Fourth District opinion[9] that the statute's apparent purpose was "to protect minors from sex acts imposed by adults," we held that section 794.05 was unconstitutional as applied to sixteen-year-old B.B., since in his case it was "being used as a weapon to adjudicate a minor delinquent," rather than "being utilized as a shield to protect a minor." *Id.* at 260.[10] Hence, we held, in essence, that the State could not single out, solely on the basis of chastity, one of two consenting sixteen-year-old minors for criminal prosecution.[11]

---

8. This test was first established in *Winfield v. Division of Pari-Mutuel Wagering*, 477 So.2d 544 (Fla.1985).

9. *Victor v. State*, 566 So.2d 354, 356 (Fla. 4th DCA 1990).

10. As in *Jones*, Justice Kogan filed a separate concurrence and decried the selectivity of section 794.05, writing that this "singularly odd state of affairs indicates that the real objective of this statute is not to protect children as a class, but to prevent the loss of chastity of those not already 'despoiled.'" *Id.* Justice Kogan found section 794.05 "inherently questionable" since it "purports to grant special status to a favored group of children over all others," thus violating the fundamental legal principle that "[l]aws should protect everyone, not merely a favored subgroup." *Id.* at 261. Justice Kogan also urged the legislature to either modernize section 794.05 or at least "decide if it is genuinely necessary in light of the variety of other statutes more than adequately protecting children from sexual predation." *Id.*

11. We note that in apparent response to our decision in *B.B.*, the legislature completely revised section 794.05 in 1996. Ch. 96-409, §1, Laws of Fla. The most significant change is reflected in subsection (1), which provides that:

> A person 24 years of age or older who engages in sexual activity with a person 16 or 17 years of age commits a felony of the second degree. . . . As used in this section, "sexual activity" means oral, anal, or vaginal penetration by, or union with, the sexual organ of another; however, sexual activity does not include an act done for a bona fide medical purpose.

§794.05, Fla. Stat. (1997). Hence, section 794.05 no longer exists in the same form we considered in *B.B.*

874   7 · THE DECLARATION OF RIGHTS AND THE TAKING OF PROPERTY

Policy Choices

In the present case, in considering an "as applied" constitutional challenge, we are again faced with difficult, competing policy choices, in a situation involving minors as defendants and victims. In *B.B.*, we concluded that the purpose of section 794.05(1) was "to protect minors from sex acts imposed by adults." 659 So.2d at 260 (quoting *Victor v. State*, 566 So.2d 354, 356 (Fla. 4th DCA 1990)), and, accordingly, we found the statute unconstitutional as applied in singling out one of two consenting sixteen-year-olds because it was "not being utilized as a shield to protect a minor." *Id.* We find *B.B.* clearly distinguishable because while both "defendant" and "victim" were sixteen in that case, here we have two fifteen year-old boys engaging in sexual activity with two twelve-year-old girls.[12] As J.A.S.'s counsel acknowledged at oral argument, and we reaffirm here, twelve-year-old children are entitled to considerable protection by the State, even when some of them resist its extension to them.

Fundamentally, our inquiry here involves weighing the State's legitimate interest in either regulating or forbidding the challenged conduct of the minors involved herein against the minors' privacy rights under article I, section 23 of the Florida Constitution.[13] Consistent with that approach, and with our prior analysis in *Jones* upholding the same statute, we find that as to the "as applied" challenge here, the scales clearly tip in favor of the State's compelling interest in protecting children from harmful sexual conduct. *See Jones*, 640 So.2d at 1086 ("The State has the prerogative to safeguard its citizens, particularly children, from potential harm when such harm outweighs the interests of the individual.") (citing *Griffin v. State*, 396 So.2d 152 (Fla.1981)).

Our conclusion is consistent with our particularized approach to similar privacy issues in *B.B.* and in *Jones*. We recognized in *Jones* that the Florida Legislature, "[a]s evidenced by the number and breadth of the statutes concerning minors and sexual exploitation . . . has established an unquestionably strong policy interest in protecting minors from harmful sexual conduct." 640 So.2d at 1085. Moreover, "[the] rights of privacy that have been granted to minors do not vitiate the legislature's efforts and authority to protect [them] from conduct of others." *Id.* at 1087. Although applied in the adult-minor context, our reasoning in *Jones* is equally applicable here in recognizing the State's compelling interest in protecting twelve-year-olds from older teenagers and from their own immaturity in choosing to participate in harmful activity. 640 So.2d at 1087 (finding that the State "has an obligation and

---

12. Neither are we faced here with a statute that selectively protects only a favored sub-group of minors such as was decried by Justice Kogan in *B.B.* 659 So.2d at 260–61 (finding inexplicable a statute "that seems to regard unchaste minors as being somehow less deserving of the state's protection than those who are otherwise").

13. "Every natural person has the right to be let alone and free from governmental intrusion into his private life except as otherwise provided herein. This section shall not be construed to limit the public's right of access to public records and meetings as provided by law." Art. I, § 23, Fla. Const.

a compelling interest in protecting children from 'sexual activity and exploitation before their minds and bodies have sufficiently matured to make it appropriate, safe, and healthy for them' ") (quoting *Jones v. State*, 619 So.2d 418, 424 (Fla. 5th DCA 1993) (Sharp, J., concurring specially)).

On the other hand, we reasoned in *B.B.* that the statute was "not being utilized as a shield to protect a minor, but rather, it [was] being used as a weapon to adjudicate a minor delinquent." *B.B.*, 659 So.2d at 260. In contrast, under the circumstances presented here, we conclude that section 800.04 is being primarily utilized as a shield to protect the twelve-year-old girls, rather than a weapon to arbitrarily adjudicate the fifteen-year-old boys as delinquents. While we agree that the trial court, based upon its actual experience, has identified a potential legitimate concern in the observation that "the boys are always charged by the state" when sexual misconduct is alleged involving minors, we do not find that concern implicated or determinative here. As already repeatedly noted, the facts here are clearly distinguishable from those in *B.B.* where such a concern may have merited further exploration.

Further, in accord with our reasoning in *T.W.*, 551 So.2d at 1193, that "a minor's rights are not absolute," we again decline to find that a minor has an open-ended privacy right in carnal intercourse with another minor, of any age, that shields the minor from adjudication as a delinquent. Counterposed against respect for the privacy rights of "[e]very natural person," including minors, is the legislature's legitimate concern with the social problems engendered by minors' sexual activity. On that subject, we agree, for example, that the statute evinces a policy that "sex in early adolescence is a dangerous folly that the state clearly does not condone." *Jones*, 640 So.2d at 1087 n. 5 (Kogan, J., concurring).[14]

We conclude that whatever privacy interest a fifteen-year-old minor has in carnal intercourse is clearly outweighed by the State's interest in protecting twelve-year-old children from harmful sexual conduct, irrespective of whether the twelve-year-old "consented" to the sexual activity. We simply cannot ignore the State's weighty interest in protecting the twelve-year-old girls from harmful sexual conduct "for reasons of health and quality of life," *B.B.*, 659 So.2d at 259, and from possible sexual exploitation by the older minors. *See J.A.S.*, 686 So.2d at 1369 (reasoning that minors under sixteen have no unfettered right to engage in recreational sex with others under sixteen because the "costs and risks to society and the children involved are far too great").

---

14. This Court has consistently acknowledged the legitimacy of such a policy. "We do say that if our decision was what should be taught and reasoned to minors, the unequivocal text of our message would be abstinence." *B.B.*, 659 So.2d at 260 (majority opinion). "Persons under the age of eighteen are still considered minors, and as this Court held in *Jones*, the legislature has a strong policy interest in protecting minors from harmful sexual conduct." *Id.* at 261–62 (Grimes, C.J., dissenting with Shaw, J., concurring). "The facts of this case make its resolution troublesome . . . [where] [t]wo persons, both minors, agreed to engage in sexual intercourse." *Id.* at 262 (Harding, J., dissenting).

876   7 · THE DECLARATION OF RIGHTS AND THE TAKING OF PROPERTY

Therefore, we conclude that section 800.04, as applied herein, furthers the compelling interest of the State in the health and welfare of its children, through the least intrusive means, by prohibiting such conduct and attaching reasonable sanctions through the rehabilitative juvenile justice system.[15] *See P.W.G. v. State*, 702 So.2d 488, 491 (Fla.1997) ("Given the different goals of the juvenile delinquency and the adult criminal systems, and the former's emphasis on rehabilitation as the principal means by which to achieve the goal of preventing delinquent children from becoming adult offenders, we believe that it is constitutionally permissible for the trial court to impose whatever treatment plan it concludes is most likely to be effective for a particular child, as long as that plan does not pose a significant threat to the health or well-being of the child."). While education and counseling are obvious means of addressing the State's concerns, we do not find it unreasonable for the State to include the invocation of juvenile sanctions in particular instances such as the ones presented here as an additional means of protecting children. Stated another way, the more compelling the interest under the particular circumstances, the more leeway the State will be afforded.

We recognize that it would simplify privacy analysis if we could fashion a precise equation by which all could easily determine which interest should prevail in whatever context a privacy right is asserted. In cases like this, all interested parties legitimately seek bright-line rules in determining whether the disputed conduct is sanctionable in the juvenile or criminal justice systems, or whether the activity falls within the constitutionally-protected zone of privacy established for certain forms of intimate human conduct. However, the human experience is not so easily categorized or quantified and no single formula can be crafted for deciding issues which implicate the most personal and intimate forms of conduct and privacy, especially where children are involved. If we blinded ourselves to the unique facts of each case, we would render decisions in a vacuum with no thought to the serious consequences of our decisions for the affected parties and society in general.

Conclusion

In summary, we hold that section 800.04, Florida Statutes (1993), as applied in the circumstances presented here, furthers the State's compelling interest in protecting

---

15. In *P.W.G. v. State*, 702 So.2d 488 (Fla.1997), we adopted the opinion of the First District which in turn relied extensively upon our previous decision in *In re C.J.W.*, 377 So.2d 22, 24 (Fla.1979), wherein we declared:

> A child offender, even after being adjudged delinquent, is never held to be a criminal, even if the act would be considered a crime if committed by an adult. The key to this difference in approach lies in the juvenile justice system's ultimate aims. Juveniles are considered to be rehabilitatable. They do not need punishment. Their need lies in the area of treatment.

As J.A.S. notes in his brief, a minor convicted of a second-degree felony (if charged as an adult), potentially faces a maximum fifteen-year prison sentence. However, as counsel conceded at oral argument, such a severe sanction is an impossibility in this case since both minors remain within the juvenile justice system and have not been charged as adults.

minors from harmful sexual conduct through the least intrusive means. Accordingly, we answer the certified question in the affirmative and, in accord with the reasoning set out above, approve the Fifth District's decision.

It is so ordered.

KOGAN, C.J., OVERTON, SHAW, HARDING and WELLS, J.J., and GRIMES, Senior Justice concur.

A.H. v. State

949 So. 2d 234 (Fla. 1st Dist. Ct. App. 2007)

WOLF, J.

A.H. challenges her adjudication of delinquency for producing, directing or promoting a photograph or representation that she knew included sexual conduct of a child in violation of section 827.071(3), Florida Statutes. She filed a motion to dismiss the charges alleging that the statute was [unconstitutional] as applied to her. She contended that, because the photographs were not actually distributed to a third party and the other participant in the sexual act was an older minor, her right to privacy was implicated and that criminal prosecution was not the least intrusive means of furthering a compelling state interest. The trial court ruled that there was a compelling state interest in preventing the production of these photographs and criminal prosecution was the least intrusive means of furthering the State's compelling interest. We agree with this analysis and further determine that the privacy provision of the state constitution does not protect the behavior of appellant. We, thus, affirm.

By Amended Petition of Delinquency, 16-year-old appellant, A.H., and her 17-year-old boyfriend, J.G.W., were charged as juveniles under the child pornography laws. The charges were based on digital photos A.H. and J.G.W. took on March 25, 2004, of themselves naked and engaged in sexual behavior. The State alleged that, while the photos were never shown to a third party, A.H. and J.G.W. emailed the photos to another computer from A.H.'s home. A.H. and J.G.W. were each charged with one count of producing, directing or promoting a photograph or representation that they knew to include the sexual conduct of a child, in violation of section 827.071(3), Florida Statutes.[1]

A.H. filed a motion to dismiss on October 24, 2005, arguing that section 827.071(3), Florida Statutes, was unconstitutional as applied to her. She contended that her privacy interests were implicated in the charges, that she was actually younger than her alleged victim, J.G.W., and that criminal prosecution was not the least intrusive means of furthering a compelling state interest. A hearing was held on the motion

---

1. J.G.W. was also charged with one count of possession of child pornography under section 827.071(5), Florida Statutes (2005).

878   7 · THE DECLARATION OF RIGHTS AND THE TAKING OF PROPERTY

to dismiss on November 30, 2005, after which the trial court issued an order denying the motion. The order included the following conclusions:

> Assuming that the child's right to privacy is implicated, the standard for evaluating whether the State may regulate the sexual conduct of minors, articulated in *B.B. v. State,* 659 So.2d 256, 258–59 (Fla.1995), requires the State to show both that it has a compelling interest and that it is furthering this interest in the least intrusive manner.

> As to the first prong of the test, whether the State has a compelling interest in regulating the sexual behavior of minors, this Court recognizes a compelling state interest in protecting children from sexual exploitation, particularly the form of sexual exploitation involved in this case. This compelling interest exists whether the person sexually exploiting the child is an adult or a minor and is certainly triggered by the production of 117 photographs of minors engaging in graphic sexual acts. *State v. A.R.S.,* 684 So.2d 1383, 1387 (Fla. 1st DCA 1996).

> The Court further finds that prosecuting the child under the statute in question is the least intrusive means of furthering the State's compelling interest. Not prosecuting the child would do nothing to further the State's interest. Prosecution enables the State to prevent future illegal, exploitative acts by supervising and providing any necessary counseling to the child. The Court finds that the State has shown that Section 827.071(3), Florida Statutes, as applied to the child, is the least intrusive means of furthering the State's compelling interest in preventing the sexual exploitation of children, rendering the statute constitutional.

A.H. argues that the trial court erred in denying her motion to dismiss below because the statute is unconstitutional as applied to her. She relies, in part, on the 1995 Florida Supreme Court decision in *B.B. v. State,* 659 So.2d 256 (Fla.1995), in which she alleges the court held that a child's privacy interests under article I, section 23 of the Florida Constitution are triggered by engaging in sexual conduct.

According to A.H., given the lack of a significant age difference or of any allegation that the pictures were shown to a third party, the only compelling state interest that could be involved here was the protection of the co-defendants from engaging in sexual behavior until their minds and bodies had matured. A.H. argues that prosecuting her for the second-degree felony of promoting a sexual performance by a child was not the least intrusive means of furthering this interest. Therefore, she maintains that section 827.071(3), Florida Statutes, is unconstitutional as applied to her, and the trial court's ruling to the contrary must be reversed.

Implicit in A.H.'s argument is that article I, section 23 protects a minor's right to have sexual intercourse and that this right of privacy extends to situations where the minor memorializes the act through pictures or video. We cannot accept this argument.

In *State v. A.R.S.*, 684 So.2d 1383 (Fla. 1st DCA 1996), we addressed the constitutionality of section 827.071(3), Florida Statutes, the same statute at issue in this case. In that case, the court assumed "that a minor's privacy interests were implicated." *Id.* The court went on to hold that the State had a compelling interest "to protect minors from exploitation by anyone who induces them to appear in a sexual performance and shows that performance to other people." *Id.* at 1387.

The question before us is, even assuming that the privacy provision of article I, section 23 of the Florida Constitution extends to minors having sexual intercourse, whether that right extends to them memorializing that activity through photographs.

"Florida's right to privacy is a fundamental right that requires evaluation under a compelling state interest standard. However, before the right to privacy attaches and the standard is applied, a reasonable expectation of privacy must exist." *Bd. of County Comm'rs of Palm Beach County v. D.B.*, 784 So.2d 585, 588 (Fla. 4th DCA 2001). Whether an individual has a legitimate expectation of privacy is determined by considering all the circumstances, especially objective manifestations of that expectation. *City of N. Miami v. Kurtz*, 653 So.2d 1025, 1028 (Fla.1995).

A number of factors lead us to conclude that there is no reasonable expectation of privacy under these circumstances.

First, the decision to take photographs and to keep a record that may be shown to people in the future weighs against a reasonable expectation of privacy. *See Four Navy Seals v. Associated Press*, 413 F.Supp.2d 1136 (S.D.Cal.2005) (holding active duty military members who allowed photographs to be taken of prisoner abuse did not have reasonable expectation of privacy under state constitution).

Second, the photographs which were taken were shared by the two minors who were involved in the sexual activities. Neither had a reasonable expectation that the other would not show the photos to a third party. Minors who are involved in a sexual relationship, unlike adults who may be involved in a mature committed relationship, have no reasonable expectation that their relationship will continue and that the photographs will not be shared with others intentionally or unintentionally. One motive for revealing the photos is profit. Unfortunately, the market for child pornography in this country, according to news reports, appears to be flourishing. *See, e.g.,* "Child porn ring busted, 27 face charges," March 15, 2006, http://www.msnbc.msn.com/id/11839832; Jeremy W. Peters, *Another Arrest in Webcam Pornography Case*, N.Y. Times, May 16, 2006, available at http://www.nytimes.com (search the NYT Archive since 1981 for "Webcam Pornography Case," then click on title). These 117 sexually explicit photographs would undoubtedly have market value.

In addition, a number of teenagers want to let their friends know of their sexual prowess. Pictures are excellent evidence of an individual's exploits. A reasonably prudent person would believe that if you put this type of material in a teenager's hands that, at some point either for profit or bragging rights, the material will be disseminated to other members of the public.

Distribution of these types of photos is likely, especially after the relationship has ended. It is not unreasonable to assume that the immature relationship between the co-defendants would eventually end. The relationship has neither the sanctity of law nor the stability of maturity or length. The subjective belief of these co-defendants that the photos might not be shared is not dispositive. In fact, the defendant in this case expressed her concern to law enforcement that her co-defendant might do something disagreeable with the photographs.

The mere fact that the defendant may have subjectively believed that the pictures would remain private does not control; it is whether society is willing to recognize an objective expectation.

As this court previously stated in *State v. Conforti*, 688 So.2d 350, 358–59 (Fla. 4th DCA 1997):

> Although a person's subjective expectation of **privacy** is one consideration in deciding whether a constitutional right attaches, the final determination of an expectation's legitimacy takes a more global view, placing the individual in the context of a society and the values that the society seeks to foster. The right to **privacy** has not made each person a solipsistic island of self-determination.

Bd. of County Comm'rs of Palm Beach County v. D.B., 784 So.2d 585, 590 (Fla. 4th DCA 2001).

The fact that these photographs may have or may not have been shown in no way affects the minor's reasonable expectation that there was a distinct and real possibility that the other teenager involved would at some point make these photos public.

Even assuming, arguendo, that a reasonable expectation of privacy existed, the statute in the instant case serves a compelling state interest. In *A.R.S.*, 684 So.2d at 1387, this court addressed the statute in question where a minor had videotaped himself involved in sexual conduct with a female minor and played the videotape for a third party.

> Assuming that a minor's privacy interests are implicated in the instant case, we recognize that the state's compelling interest in section 827.071 is different. The statute is not limited to protecting children only from sexual exploitation by adults, nor is it intended to protect minors from engaging in sexual intercourse. The state's purpose in this statute is to protect minors from exploitation by anyone who induces them to appear in a sexual performance and shows that performance to other people. *See Schmitt v. State*, 590 So.2d 404, 412 (Fla.1991) (stating that the "obvious purpose" of section 827.071 "is to prohibit certain forms of child exploitation"), *cert. denied*, 503 U.S. 964, 112 S.Ct. 1572, 118 L.Ed.2d 216 (1992). The State's interest in protecting children from exploitation in this statute is the same regardless of whether the person inducing the child to appear in a sexual performance and then promoting that performance is an adult or a minor.

Id.

7 · THE DECLARATION OF RIGHTS AND THE TAKING OF PROPERTY   881

Appellant asserts that the State only has a compelling interest when the photograph or video is shown to a third party. The Legislature has, however, recognized a compelling interest in seeing that the videotape or picture including "sexual conduct by a child of less than 18 years of age" is never produced. § 827.071(3), Fla. Stat.

As previously stated, the reasonable expectation that the material will ultimately be disseminated is by itself a compelling state interest for preventing the production of this material. In addition, the statute was intended to protect minors like appellant and her co-defendant from their own lack of judgment.

Without either foresight or maturity, appellant engaged in the conduct at issue, then expressed concern to law enforcement personnel that her co-defendant may do something inappropriate, i.e., disseminate sexually explicit photos that were lodged on his computer. Appellant was simply too young to make an intelligent decision about engaging in sexual conduct and memorializing it. Mere production of these videos or pictures may also result in psychological trauma to the teenagers involved.

Further, if these pictures are ultimately released, future damage may be done to these minors' careers or personal lives. These children are not mature enough to make rational decisions concerning all the possible negative implications of producing these videos.

In addition, the two defendants placed the photos on a computer and then, using the internet, transferred them to another computer. Not only can the two computers be hacked, but by transferring the photos using the net, the photos may have been and perhaps still are accessible to the provider and/or other individuals. Computers also allow for long-term storage of information which may then be disseminated at some later date. The State has a compelling interest in seeing that material which will have such negative consequences is never produced.

The decision of the trial court is affirmed.

THOMAS, J., concurs; PADOVANO, J., dissents with opinion.

PADOVANO, J. dissenting.

Section 827.071(3) Florida Statutes was designed to protect children from abuse by others, but it was used in this case to punish a child for her own mistake. In my view, the application of this criminal statute to the conduct at issue violates the child's right to privacy under Article 1, Section 23 of the Florida Constitution. For this reason, I would reverse.

The supreme court held in *B.B. v. State*, 659 So.2d 256 (Fla.1995), that a statute prohibiting unlawful carnal intercourse is unconstitutional as applied to a minor. In support of this holding, the court reasoned that the citizens of Florida had issued a "clear constitutional mandate in favor of privacy" by adopting Article 1, Section 23 of the Florida Constitution. *B.B.* 659 So.2d at 259. The court went on to say that the right of privacy is not limited to adults, but that it applies to children, as well.

I am not able to reconcile the supreme court's holding in *B.B.* with the court's decision in this case. The majority points out that the child in *B.B.* was charged with unlawful sexual intercourse while the child in this case was charged with photographing an act of sexual intercourse, but I think this a distinction without a difference. As in *B.B.*, the child in this case had sex with another minor. The only additional fact is that, in this case, the two took photographs of themselves and shared the photos with each other. There is no indication that the photos were intended to be any less private than the act itself. Consequently, I am unable to conclude that Article 1, Section 23 is inapplicable or that it somehow offers the child in this case less protection.

The majority is correct to say that *B.B.* involved a prosecution under a different statute. However, the principle of constitutional law articulated in the opinion is not one that applies only to a particular statute. To the contrary, it is a principle that would apply to any statute that is used in a way that violates the right of privacy. If a minor cannot be criminally prosecuted for having sex with another minor, as the court held in *B.B.*, it follows that a minor cannot be criminally prosecuted for taking a picture of herself having sex with another minor. Although I do not condone the child's conduct in this case, I cannot deny that it is private conduct. Because there is no evidence that the child intended to show the photographs to third parties, they are as private as the act they depict.

The majority relies on the decision of this court in *State v. A.R.S.*, 684 So.2d 1383 (Fla. 1st DCA 1996), but that case does not support the decision the court has made here. In *A.R.S.*, the child made a videotape of himself and a younger female child engaging in a sexual activity and then played the videotape to a third person at a time when the female was not present. The act of displaying the videotape was the main reason the court gave for its decision. As the court explained, "The state's purpose in [section 827.071] is to protect minors from exploitation by anyone who induces them to appear in a sexual performance *and shows that performance to other people*." *A.R.S.*, 684 So.2d at 1387. In contrast, the child in this case did not show the photographs to anyone. Nor has she been charged with doing so. She stands accused of nothing more than taking photographs of herself and her boyfriend.

The fact that the delinquent child in *A.R.S.* showed the videotape to a third party is significant for the reasons given by the court and for another reason not mentioned in the opinion. The voluntary publication of the videotape to a third party completely undermined the delinquent child's claim of privacy. Unlike the accused child in this case, A.R.S. was not in a good position to claim that his actions were protected by the constitutional right of privacy. Whatever privacy rights he had in the videotape he made of himself and another child engaging in an intimate act, he gave up entirely when she showed the tape to another person.

The critical point in this case is that the child intended to keep the photographs private. She did not attempt to exploit anyone or to embarrass anyone. I think her expectation of privacy in the photographs was reasonable. Certainly, an argument could be made that she was foolish to expect that, but the expectation of a sixteen year old cannot be measured by the collective wisdom of appellate judges who have no emotional connection to the event. Perhaps if the child had as much time to reflect on these events, she would have eventually concluded, as the majority did, that there were ways in which these photos might have been unintentionally disclosed. That does not make her expectation of privacy unreasonable.

For these reasons, I believe the court has committed a serious error. The statute at issue was designed to protect children, but in this case the court has allowed the state to use it against a child in a way that criminalizes conduct that is protected by constitutional right of privacy. In the process, the court has rendered a decision that expressly and directly conflicts with the decision of the Florida Supreme Court in *B.B.* on the same point of law. The child in that case was prosecuted under a different statute, but the constitutional principles are the same and they should be applied in the same way in this case.

8. Privacy and Grandparent Visitation Statutes

In *Beagle v. Beagle*,[54] the Florida Supreme Court provided an overview of the historical development of grandparent visitation statutes in Florida:

> First, in 1978, the legislature modified section 61.13(2)(b) of the Florida Statutes. The relevant language read:
>
>> The court may award the grandparents visitation rights of a minor children [sic] if it is deemed by the court to be in the child's best interest. Nothing in this section shall be construed to require that grandparents be made parties or given notice of dissolution pleadings or proceedings, nor shall such grandparents have legal standing as "contestants" as defined in s. 61.1306.
>
> § 61.13(2)(b), Fla. Stat. (Supp.1978). The modification quoted above was not the only action concerning grandparental visitation rights taken by the legislature in 1978. The following, contained in section 68.08, was also enacted:
>
>> Any court of this state which is competent to decide child custody matters shall have jurisdiction to award the grandparents of a minor child or minor children visitation rights of the minor child or children upon the death of or desertion by one of the minor child's parents if it is deemed by the court to be in the minor child's best interest.
>
> § 68.08, Fla. Stat. (Supp.1978).
>
> Second, in 1984 the legislature consolidated the grandparental visitation provisions in chapter 752 of the Florida Statutes. That chapter was titled "Grandparental Visitation Rights." It included a procedure for the granting of grandparental visitation rights in situations: (1) where one or both parents of the child are deceased,[1] (2) where the marriage of the child's parents

---

54. 678 So. 2d 1271 (Fla. 1996).

1. § 752.01(1)(a), Fla. Stat. (Supp.1984).

884   7 · THE DECLARATION OF RIGHTS AND THE TAKING OF PROPERTY

has been dissolved,[2] or (3) where a parent of the child has deserted the child.[3] Further, the legislature explicitly limited the chapter by refusing to extend its scope to situations in which a child is adopted unless the adoption is by a stepparent.[4]

Third, in 1990, the legislature added guidelines with which the courts might determine the best interest of the child.[5] In that same year, the legislature added a section that requires mediation, if such services are available in a given circuit, in cases where families cannot internally resolve their differences and a petition for grandparental visitation rights is filed.[6]

Finally, in 1993, ... [a] paragraph was added authorizing the award of grandparental visitation rights in situations where the child lives within an intact family.[7] For a full understanding of the [statute], we set forth subsection one in its entirety ...

> (1) The court shall, upon petition filed by a grandparent of a minor child, award reasonable visitation rights of visitation to the grandparent with respect to the child when it is in the best interest of the minor child if:
>
> (a) One or both parents of the child are deceased;
>
> (b) The marriage of the parents of the child has been dissolved;
>
> (c) A parent of the child has deserted the child;
>
> (d) The minor child was born out of wedlock and not later determined to be a child born within wedlock as provided in s. 742.091; or
>
> (e) The minor is living with both natural parents who are still married to each other whether or not there is a broken relationship between either or both parents of the minor child and the grandparents, and either or both parents have used their parental authority to prohibit a relationship between the minor child and the grandparents.

752.01(1), Fla. Stat. (1995).

In *Beagle*, the Florida Supreme Court considered the constitutionality of the provision allowing grandparent visitation when the child was living with both natural parents who were married to each other. In finding the provision unconstitutional, the Court held that a judge could not impose grandparent visitation over the express wishes of at least one parent in an intact family absent demonstrated harm to the

---

2. §752.01(1)(b), Fla. Stat. (Supp.1984).
3. §752.01(1)(c), Fla. Stat. (Supp.1984).
4. §752.01(2), Fla. Stat. (Supp.1984).
5. §752.01(2), Fla. Stat. (Supp.1990).
6. §752.015, Fla. Stat. (Supp.1990).
7. §752.01(1)(e), Fla. Stat. (1993).

child because doing so would violate a parent's fundamental right of privacy to raise his or her children free from government intrusion.[55]

In subsequent decisions, the Florida Supreme Court and Florida appellate courts extended the same privacy protection to parents who were not in intact families.[56] These decisions essentially rendered Florida's then-existing grandparent visitation statute unconstitutional as violative of parents' fundamental privacy right to rear their children without interference from the government.

In 2015, the Florida Legislature enacted Fla. Stat. §752.0111, a limited grandparent visitation statute, that allows grandparents and great-grandparents of minor children to petition the courts for visitation when the minor child's parents are deceased, missing, or in a persistent vegetative state, or when one of the minor child's parents is deceased, missing, or in a persistent vegetative state and the other parent has been convicted of a felony or a violent offense evincing behavior that poses a substantial threat of harm to the child's health or welfare. In 2022, the Florida Legislature enacted a law that grants grandparents whose child is deceased reasonable visitation with that child's children if the court finds the other parent has been held criminally or civilly liable for the death of the deceased parent.[57] The Florida Supreme Court has not yet considered the constitutionality of these statutes.

Although grandparent visitation statutes for the most part have been held unconstitutional as violative of Florida's right of privacy, under the Full Faith and Credit Clause of the United States Constitution, Florida courts are required to enforce orders of sister states granting grandparent visitation with minor children in accordance with that state's law. The following case is illustrative.

Ledoux-Nottingham v. Downs

210 So. 3d 1217 (Fla. 2017)

CANADY, J.

In this case we consider whether the Full Faith and Credit Clause of the United States Constitution requires enforcement of a sister state's judgment ordering grandparent visitation with minor children despite the fact that the right of privacy set forth in article I, section 23 of the Florida Constitution protects the right of parents to raise their children free from unwarranted governmental interference. We have for review *LeDoux–Nottingham v. Downs*, 163 So.3d 560 (Fla. 5th DCA 2015), in which the Fifth District Court of Appeal rejected the argument that a Colorado judgment ordering grandparent visitation is unenforceable as a matter of Florida law and public policy because it violates "childrearing autonomy" guaranteed to

---

55. 678 So. 2d at 1276.

56. *See Saul v. Brunetti*, 753 So. 2d 26 (Fla. 2000); *Von Eiff v. Azicri*, 720 So. 2d 510 (Fla. 1998); *Belair v. Drew*, 776 So. 2d 1105 (Fla. 5th Dist. Ct. App. 2001); *Lonon v. Ferrell*, 739 So. 2d 650 (Fla. 2d Dist. Ct. App. 1999).

57. *See* Grandparent Visitation Rights, H.R. 1119, 90th H., 124th Reg. Sess. (Fla. 2022).

parents under article I, section 23 of the Florida Constitution. The Fifth District held that under "the Full Faith and Credit Clause [of the United States Constitution], trial courts are required, without discretion, to give recognition to final judgments of another state when applicable," and certified conflict with *M.S. v. D.C.*, 763 So.2d 1051, 1055 (Fla. 4th DCA 1999), in which the Fourth District held that the Full Faith and Credit Clause does not trump Florida's overriding public policy of a guaranteed fundamental right of privacy in childrearing autonomy. *LeDoux–Nottingham*, 163 So.3d at 563–65. We have jurisdiction. See art. V, § 3(b) (4), Fla. Const.

For the reasons we explain, we approve the Fifth District's decision in *LeDoux–Nottingham* and disapprove the Fourth District's decision in *M.S.* We also disapprove the decision of the Second District in *Fazzini v. Davis*, 98 So.3d 98 (Fla. 2d DCA 2012), to the extent that it holds that Florida's public policy may provide an exception to the full faith and credit due judgments of sister states.

I. Background

Petitioner, Ruth D. LeDoux–Nottingham, and the father of her two minor children were divorced in Colorado in 2010. *LeDoux–Nottingham*, 163 So.3d at 561. The father died in 2011 in Colorado. *Id.* Immediately after the funeral, LeDoux—Nottingham and her minor children moved to Florida. *Id.* Respondents, Jennifer Joy Downs and William Glen Downs (hereinafter "the Grandparents"), timely initiated a proceeding in Colorado seeking visitation with the children. *Id.* LeDoux–Nottingham then filed a separate action in Florida to register the Colorado final judgment dissolving her marriage and for a judicial determination that the Grandparents have no legal right to timesharing with her minor children. *Id.* In October 2012, the Colorado court issued a final judgment awarding the Grandparents visitation with the children (hereinafter "the Colorado order"). *Id.* at 562. LeDoux–Nottingham then amended her petition in Florida and sought to both domesticate and modify the Colorado order, arguing, in relevant part, that under Florida law, enforcement of a grandparent visitation order is unconstitutional and against public policy. *Id.* After a trial, the Florida court entered a final order which registered and domesticated the Colorado order, stated that it was enforceable in Florida, and denied LeDoux–Nottingham's request for modification. *Id.*

LeDoux–Nottingham appealed the Florida trial court's order, arguing that the Colorado order was unenforceable as a matter of Florida law and public policy because it violates childrearing autonomy guaranteed to parents under article I, section 23 of the Florida Constitution, which states that "[e]very natural person has the right to be let alone and free from governmental intrusion into the person's private life except as otherwise provided herein." *Id.* (alteration in original). In rejecting LeDoux–Nottingham's argument, the Fifth District relied on the decision of the United States Supreme Court in *Baker v. General Motors Corp.*, 522 U.S. 222, 118 S. Ct. 657, 139 L.Ed.2d 580 (1998), which the district court concluded "makes clear that the public policy of one state has no effect on whether the state must give full faith and credit to judgments, rather than law, of another state," and held that under "the Full Faith and Credit Clause, trial courts are required, without discretion, to give recognition to final judgments of another state when applicable." 163 So.3d at 563. The district court concluded that the trial court properly enforced the Colorado order granting the Grandparents visitation, reasoning as follows:

> Since the Colorado order was a final judgment and emanated from a "child custody proceeding" within the meaning of section 61.503(4), Florida Statutes (2013),[N.2] it became enforceable in Florida pursuant to the Full Faith and Credit Clause as well as section 61.526, Florida Statutes. *See [Baker,* 522 U.S. at 232–33, 118 S.Ct. 657];§ 61.526(1), Fla. Stat. (2013) ("A court of this state shall recognize and enforce a child custody determination of a court of another state if the latter court exercised jurisdiction in substantial conformity with this part or the determination was made under factual circumstances meeting the jurisdictional standards of this part and the determination has not been modified in accordance with this part.").

Id.

The Fifth District also affirmed the trial court's decision that modification of the Colorado order was not warranted because there had not been a subsequent substantial and material change in circumstances. *Id.* at 564. And the Fifth District certified conflict with *M.S.,* in which the Fourth District reversed an order granting a motion for visitation filed by grandparents based on a Connecticut divorce and custody decree that provided for grandparent visitation. The Fourth District in *M.S.* stated:

> We have considered the argument that the Connecticut [grandparent] visitation order is entitled to full faith and credit. However, a visitation provision such as this, while entitled to our respect on comity principles, does not prevent the application of an overriding provision of our law, applying a paramount public policy. As our supreme court has recognized, few policies in the state are more paramount than enforcement of an exercise of a recognized constitutional right to privacy.

763 So.2d at 1055 (citations omitted).

II. Analysis

In the analysis that follows, we first consider whether final judgments entered by sister states relating to child custody and visitation are entitled to full faith and credit or subject to the principles of comity. Because we conclude that such judgments are entitled to full faith and credit, we then consider whether the Full Faith and Credit Clause mandates enforcement of the Colorado order in Florida even if such enforcement would violate LeDoux–Nottingham's right of privacy under the Florida Constitution or whether there is a public policy exception to the Full Faith

---

[N.2] § 61.504(4), Fla. Stat. (2013) (defining "child custody proceeding" as "a proceeding in which legal custody, physical custody, residential care, or visitation with respect to a child is an issue").

888   7 · THE DECLARATION OF RIGHTS AND THE TAKING OF PROPERTY

and Credit Clause. We conclude that there is no public policy exception to the Full Faith and Credit Clause, and the Colorado order is enforceable in Florida.

A. Comity vs. the Full Faith and Credit Clause

Because the Fourth District in *M.S.* held that a grandparent visitation order from a sister state was entitled to "respect on comity principles," 763 So.2d at 1055, while the Fifth District below held that under "the Full Faith and Credit Clause, trial courts are required, without discretion, to give recognition to final judgments of another state when applicable," 163 So.3d at 563, we first consider whether child custody and visitation orders entered by a sister state are entitled to full faith and credit or merely subject to the principles of comity.

The Full Faith and Credit Clause of the United States Constitution provides that "Full Faith and Credit shall be given in each State to the public Acts, Records, and judicial Proceedings of every other State." Art. IV, §1, U.S. Const. The clause was intended to replace the earlier rule of comity with a constitutional duty of states to honor the laws and judgments of sister states. *Estin v. Estin*, 334 U.S. 541, 546, 68 S. Ct. 1213, 92 L.Ed. 1561 (1948) (noting that the Full Faith and Credit Clause "substituted a command for the earlier principles of comity and thus basically altered the status of the States as independent sovereigns"). The clause contains implementing language that gives Congress the power "by general Laws [to] prescribe the Manner in which such Acts, Records and Proceedings shall be proved, and the Effect thereof." Art. IV, §1, U.S. Const. Congress adopted such a law with regard to custody determinations when it enacted the Parental Kidnaping Prevention Act of 1980 (PKPA). Pub. L. 96–611, §§6–10, 96 Stat. 3568 (1980).

The PKPA requires "every State [to] enforce according to its terms . . . any custody determination or visitation determination made consistently with the provisions of this section[1] by a court of another State." 28 U.S.C. §1738A(a) (2012). In *Thompson v. Thompson*, 484 U.S. 174, 183, 108 S.Ct. 513, 98 L.Ed.2d 512 (1988), the United States Supreme Court explained that "Congress' chief aim in enacting the PKPA was to extend the requirements of the Full Faith and Credit Clause to custody determinations" and that "the PKPA is a mandate directed to state courts to respect the custody decrees of sister States." Thus, there is no doubt that custody determinations of a sister state are entitled to full faith and credit.

LeDoux–Nottingham acknowledges that custody determinations are entitled to full faith and credit under the PKPA and she does not contend that the Colorado

---

1. Consistency with section 1738A has been described as follows:
   In order for a state court's custody decree to be consistent with the provisions of the Act, the State must have jurisdiction under its own local law and one of five conditions set out in §1738A(c) (2) must be met. Briefly put, these conditions authorize the state court to enter a custody decree if the child's home is or recently has been in the State, if the child has no home State and it would be in the child's best interest for the State to assume jurisdiction, or if the child is present in the State and has been abandoned or abused.
   Thompson v. Thompson, 484 U.S. 174, 176–77, 108 S.Ct. 513, 98 L.Ed.2d 512 (1988).

court did not have jurisdiction to enter the visitation order. Even so, she contends that the PKPA does not apply here because "this is not a custody issue" and the PKPA applies only to parents. This contention is untenable.

The PKPA was amended in 1998 to include any "visitation determination" in addition to "any custody determination." See Enforcement of Child Custody and Visitation Orders, Pub. L No. 105–374, 112 Stat. 3383 (1998) ("Section 1738A(a) of title 28, United States Code, is amended by striking 'subsection (f) of this section, any child custody determination' and inserting 'subsections (f), (g), and (h) of this section, any custody determination or visitation determination.'"). The 1998 amendment also modified the definition of a "contestant" in subsection (b)(2) from "a person, including a parent, who claims a right to custody of a child" to "a person, including a parent or grandparent, who claims a right to custody or visitation of a child." Id. (emphasis added).

Because the PKPA explicitly applies to "any custody determination or visitation determination," including those in which a grandparent claims a right to visitation of a child, the Colorado order — which was entered in compliance with the PKPA — is by the express terms of the PKPA subject to the commands of the Full Faith and Credit Clause. And to the extent that the PKPA conflicts with Florida law, the PKPA — as federal law — controls under the Supremacy Clause of the United States Constitution. *Yurgel v. Yurgel*, 572 So.2d 1327, 1329 (Fla. 1990) ("Under the supremacy clause of the [United States] Constitution, the PKPA supersedes any and all inconsistent state laws." (citing *Thompson*)); see art. VI, cl. 2, U.S. Const. ("This Constitution, and the Laws of the United States which shall be made in Pursuance thereof; and all Treaties made, or which shall be made, under the Authority of the United States, shall be the supreme Law of the Land; and the Judges in every State shall be bound thereby, any Thing in the Constitution or Laws of any State to the Contrary notwithstanding.").[2]

B. Whether a Public Policy Exception to the Full Faith and Credit Clause Exists

We next consider whether a public policy exception to the Full Faith and Credit Clause exists that would prevent enforcement of the Colorado order in Florida. LeDoux — Nottingham asserts that enforcement of the Colorado order is not required in Florida because it would offend the right of privacy as articulated in article I, section 23 of the Florida Constitution and there is a public policy exception to the Full Faith and Credit Clause. While the Florida Constitution does protect the right of parents to raise their children free from unwarranted governmental interference, *see Richardson v. Richardson*, 766 So.2d 1036, 1043 (Fla. 2000), that state right is subordinate to the directives of the Federal Constitution under the Supremacy Clause, and the United States Supreme Court has made it clear that there is no

---

2. LeDoux–Nottingham has not challenged the constitutional authority of Congress to enact the PKPA.

public policy exception to the full faith and credit due final judgments of a sister state.

As explained by the Supreme Court, the Full Faith and Credit Clause "requires each State to recognize and give effect to valid judgments rendered by the courts of its sister States." *V.L. v. E.L.*, —— U.S. ——, 136 S.Ct. 1017, 1020, 194 L.Ed.2d 92 (2016). It serves "to alter the status of the several states as independent foreign sovereignties, each free to ignore obligations created under the laws or by the judicial proceedings of the others, and to make them integral parts of a single nation." *Milwaukee County v. M.E. White Co.*, 296 U.S. 268, 277, 56 S.Ct. 229, 80 L.Ed. 220 (1935); *see also Magnolia Petroleum Co. v. Hunt*, 320 U.S. 430, 439, 64 S.Ct. 208, 88 L.Ed. 149 (1943) (noting that "the clear purpose of the full faith and credit clause" was to establish the principle that "a litigation once pursued to judgment shall be as conclusive of the rights of the parties in every other court as in that where the judgment was rendered"); *Pac. Employers Ins. Co. v. Indus. Accident Comm'n*, 306 U.S. 493, 501, 59 S.Ct. 629, 83 L. Ed. 940 (1939) ("[T]he purpose of [the Full Faith and Credit Clause] was to preserve rights acquired or confirmed under the public acts and judicial proceedings of one state by requiring recognition of their validity in other states. . . ."). As authorized by the Full Faith and Credit Clause, Congress has prescribed:

> Such Acts, records and judicial proceedings or copies thereof, so authenticated, shall have the same full faith and credit in every court within the United States and its Territories and Possessions as they have by law or usage in the courts of such State, Territory or Possession from which they are taken.

28 U.S.C. § 1738.

In interpreting the Full Faith and Credit Clause, the Supreme Court stated in *Baker*, "Regarding judgments . . . the full faith and credit obligation is exacting. A final judgment in one State, if rendered by a court with adjudicatory authority over the subject matter and persons governed by the judgment, qualifies for recognition throughout the land." 522 U.S. at 233, 118 S.Ct. 657. There is "no roving 'public policy exception' to the full faith and credit due judgments." Id. (citing *Estin*, 334 U.S. at 546, 68 S.Ct. 1213 (stating that the Full Faith and Credit Clause "ordered submission by one State even to hostile policies reflected in the judgment of another State, because the practical operation of the federal system, which the Constitution designed, demanded it"), and *Fauntleroy v. Lum*, 210 U.S. 230, 237, 28 S.Ct. 641, 52 L. Ed. 1039 (1908) (holding that judgment of Missouri court was entitled to full faith and credit in Mississippi even if Missouri judgment rested on a misapprehension of Mississippi law)).

Last year, the Court reiterated these principles, stating:

> With respect to judgments, "the full faith and credit obligation is exacting." *Baker v. General Motors Corp.*, 522 U.S. 222, 233, 118 S.Ct. 657, 139 L. Ed.2d 580 (1998). "A final judgment in one State, if rendered by a court with adjudicatory authority over the subject matter and persons governed by the

judgment, qualifies for recognition throughout the land." *Ibid.* A State may not disregard the judgment of a sister State because it disagrees with the reasoning underlying the judgment or deems it to be wrong on the merits. On the contrary, "the full faith and credit clause of the Constitution precludes any inquiry into the merits of the cause of action, the logic or consistency of the decision, or the validity of the legal principles on which the judgment is based." *Milliken v. Meyer*, 311 U.S. 457, 462, 61 S.Ct. 339, 85 L.Ed. 278 (1940).

V.L., 136 S.Ct. at 1020. The Supreme Court thus continues to reject any notion that a state may elevate its own public policy over the policy behind a sister state's judgment and thereby disregard the command of the Full Faith and Credit Clause.

Although we have previously held unconstitutional numerous Florida statutes providing for grandparent visitation as violative of Florida's right of privacy,[3] the question presented here is not whether the Grandparents are entitled to visitation under Florida law, but whether Florida is required to enforce the Colorado order despite the fact that entry of a similar judgment by a Florida court under the same circumstances would be prohibited by the Florida Constitution[4] and the answer is yes.

III. Conclusion

For the reasons explained above, we approve the decision of the Fifth District in *LeDoux–Nottingham* and disapprove the decision of the Fourth District in *M.S.* to the extent that it applied comity principles to an out-of-state visitation order rather than the Full Faith and Credit Clause and concluded that Florida's public policy can override the requirement to provide full faith and credit to judgments entered by a sister state. We also disapprove the decision of the Second District in *Fazzini* to the extent that it holds that the public policy of Florida may provide an exception to the full faith and credit due to judgments entered by a sister state.

It is so ordered.

---

3. *See Sullivan v. Sapp*, 866 So.2d 28, 37 (Fla. 2004); *Richardson v. Richardson*, 766 So.2d 1036, 1043 (Fla. 2000); *Saul v. Brunetti*, 753 So.2d 26, 29 (Fla. 2000); *Von Eiff v. Azicri*, 720 So.2d 510, 517 (Fla. 1998); *Beagle v. Beagle*, 678 So.2d 1271, 1276 (Fla. 1996). We have not considered the constitutionality of the current limited grandparent visitation provision, section 752.011, Florida Statutes (2015).

4. Entry of a similar judgment by a Florida court under the same circumstances would undoubtedly be prohibited by the Florida Constitution. Colorado law provides for grandparent visitation in the case of a divorce or a deceased parent based on the best interests of the child without first requiring proof of demonstrable harm to the child, see section 19–1–117, Colorado Revised Statutes, and the Colorado court here indeed ordered visitation based on the children's best interests alone, but we held in *Von Eiff*, 720 So.2d at 516–17, that Florida's right of privacy was violated by section 752.01(1)(a), Florida Statutes (1993), which mandated that if one or both parents are deceased, a court shall order grandparent visitation when in the best interest of the minor child, without first requiring proof of demonstrable harm to the child.

LABARGA, C.J., and PARIENTE, QUINCE, and POLSTON, JJ., concur.
LEWIS, J., concurs in result. LAWSON, J., did not participate.

M. The Taking of Property

Fla. Const. art. X, § 6[58]

Eminent domain. —

(a) No private property shall be taken except for a public purpose and with full compensation therefore paid to each owner or secured by deposit in the registry of the court and available to the owner.

(b) Provision may be made by law for the taking of easements, by like proceedings, for the drainage of the land of one person over or through the land of another.

(c) Private property taken by eminent domain pursuant to a petition to initiate condemnation proceedings filed on or after January 2, 2007, may not be conveyed to a natural person or private entity except as provided by general law passed by a three-fifths vote of the membership of each house of the Legislature.

In 2006, the eminent domain provision of the Florida Constitution was amended to prohibit the taking of property by eminent domain and conveying it to a natural person or private entity without a three-fifths vote of the Legislature. In that same year, the Florida Legislature enacted statutes to reinforce the constitutional restriction that private property be taken only for public purposes. Specifically, the Florida Legislature created §§ 73.013 and 73.014, Florida Statutes. Section 73.013 restricts the ability of condemning authorities to transfer property acquired by eminent domain to private parties, and § 73.014 prohibits the taking of private property to abate a public nuisance or to prevent or eliminate slum or blight conditions. Section 73.014 also specifically declares that the taking of private property for the purpose of preventing or eliminating nuisance, slum, or blight conditions is not a public purpose for which eminent domain may be used.

These constitutional amendments and statutory enactments were in direct response to the United States Supreme Court's decision in *Kelo v. City of New London*.[59] In *Kelo*, the United States Supreme Court found economic development

---

58. This is not part of the Declaration of Rights but is considered here because of its similarity to those guarantees found in the Declaration of Rights.

59. 545 U.S. 469 (2005).

7 · THE DECLARATION OF RIGHTS AND THE TAKING OF PROPERTY

to be a valid public use for eminent domain purposes.[60] To ensure that private property would not be taken for economic development purposes in Florida, the above-referenced constitutional and statutory changes were made by the Florida electorate and the Florida Legislature. In making these changes, Florida voters and the Legislature may have eliminated a local government's ability to redevelop blighted areas. Consider the following case and whether the outcome would be different in light of the constitutional and statutory changes discussed above.

City of Hollywood Community Redevelopment Agency v. 1843, LLC[61]

980 So. 2d 1138 (Fla. 4th Dist. Ct. App. 2008)

TAYLOR, J.

The City of Hollywood Community Redevelopment Agency (CRA) appeals an order denying its request for an order of taking and dismissing its petition in eminent domain. The CRA sought to take the subject property, a lot with a one-story commercial building owned by the Mach family, as part of its community redevelopment plan. The trial court found that there was no necessity for the taking. Because the CRA presented some evidence of the reasonable necessity for the taking, the trial court was required to defer to the CRA's determination that the property was necessary for the redevelopment and uphold that decision. We thus reverse the trial court's order.

A Broward County resolution allowing the City of Hollywood to create a community redevelopment agency (CRA) was passed on April 3, 1979. In 1979, the City established the CRA by resolution. As part of the resolution, certain statutory blight factors were identified, such as inefficient traffic flow, inappropriate platting patterns, diversity of ownership, and inappropriately-mixed land uses.

In 1981, the City adopted a community redevelopment plan for the Central City Area to restore and redevelop the City's downtown commercial district. The plan identified its priority as redeveloping the center or core of the area and then working towards the perimeter. The subject parcel is located within the core or central area of the redevelopment area.

The plat which includes the subject property was recorded in 1921. The plat contains a series of extremely small lots that do not provide for any type of internal circulation, parking, or landscape buffers. The lots are only twenty-five feet wide. Block 40 contains Young Circle, which City of Hollywood Mayor Mara Giulianti describes as arguably the most important feature of their downtown. In Block 40, the majority

---

60. In *Kelo*, property was acquired through eminent domain for the purpose of leasing it to a private developer for a nominal amount for a ninety-nine-year term.

61. This case was not decided under the current version of the eminent domain statutes enacted in 2006 as those statutes were not retroactive.

of the buildings face the historic, three-story Great Southern Hotel. The parcel at issue in this case, the Mach parcel, is Lot 1 in Block 40. Located on this parcel is a single narrow building, which houses four small businesses. The northern edge of the Mach parcel is separated from the southern edge of the Great Southern Hotel by a public alley thirteen feet wide.

In 1985, the community redevelopment plan was amended by ordinance and made more specific. It identifies six redevelopment sites surrounding Young Circle in the central business district. Those are priority areas where redevelopment efforts were to be targeted to generate the best impact. Block 40 was identified as a target area. The redevelopment plan called for the restoration of the Great Southern Hotel, if "structurally and economically feasible."

The final amendment to the redevelopment plan was made by a 1995 ordinance, which added more detail regarding the Harrison Street streetscape and sought to accommodate sidewalk cafes and pedestrian access points. It identified the entire Block 40 as a redevelopment site, which would include the subject property.

Developer Chip Abele has been able to assemble 13 of the 14 lots in Block 40. He proposes to build on that property the "Young Circle Commons" project. The bottom floor will be retail, with six floors of parking above that. Above the parking area is a common amenity floor with a recreation room, swimming pool, and social room. Above that are more than a dozen floors of residential condominiums.

John Fullerton and his firm are the architects for the project. Very early on, they considered demolishing 15 or 16 feet of the Great Southern facade adjacent to the alley for the residents' entry. However, they never presented this as an option to the CRA. Instead, they first publicly presented the "Harrison Street option." This design was to have an entrance/exit area for the parking garage off Harrison Street. This option would not have impacted the façade of the Great Southern Hotel and would not have required acquisition of the Mach parcel. The developer submitted the original plan sometime in November 2002.

This development will generate 4,000 trips per day, several hundred in the peak hour. Miguel Santibanez is a traffic engineer for the City. He reviewed the plan for compliance with the technical requirements within the Code of the City. Santibanez found that the Harrison Street garage entrance was too close to the 19th Avenue intersection. There were significant problems for ingress and egress. The exit lane from the garage would have been very close to the crosswalk and there would have been several safety impacts on pedestrian and vehicular traffic based on the location of the driveway. According to Robert Rawls, the head of the City's building and engineering services department, the plan would have ended up with gridlock, with cars trying to make left turns into the garage through stopped traffic at the light. The planners looked at other access points more mid-block on Harrison, but it was still a major pedestrian corridor as contrasted with 19th Avenue. There was still the gridlock scenario. None of the options worked well on Harrison. All of the traffic considerations brought them back to 19th Avenue. They explored ingress and egress on Hollywood Boulevard and Young Circle also, but did not find that they were viable options.

The plan was then changed, moving the entrance to the parking garage over to 19th Avenue. The entrance/exit of the garage is now approximately mid-block, which offers cars a better chance of finding a gap to be able to get out of the garage. 19th Avenue is wider and much more conducive for access and egress as opposed to Harrison Street. It was undisputed that this plan is the safest design for access to the site. It had the least impact on pedestrian movements and the least impact on vehicular movements. The garage entrance needed to be mid-block on 19th Avenue. Architect Fullerton, who designed the original Harrison entrance, testified that the new design "very definitely . . . is a better solution than what we had originally."

With this design the planners were also able to preserve the entire western façade of the Great Southern Hotel. However, this design required the taking of the Mach property, because seventeen feet of the thirty foot garage entrance is now to be situated on the Mach property. Land Planner Keller testified that there would be a detrimental planning impact if the project is designed around the Mach parcel, stating, "Unfortunately, if you do that, you are left with a narrow 25-foot parcel that is right there on the corner of one of your key commercial blocks in the downtown that's going to be surrounded on all sides by a high-rise structure with far more intense use; and for it to remain in its current condition, it is not going to be consistent with that; and if it's ever removed then you are going to have a remnant parcel that will have virtually no functional utility to it."

Architect Tamara Peacock is a member of the Broward Trust for Historic Preservation and the chair of the Hollywood Preservation Board. She testified that the original plan was to restore the Great Southern Hotel, which had been shut down by fire officials in 1991. However, it became apparent that the whole building could not be saved. Both the state and federal governments have expressed concern about even the partial demolition of the Great Southern. Under the current proposal, the developer will do a façade restoration. The proposal is to completely preserve the north façade, the west façade, and a portion of the east. Those facades have the significant fenestration and architectural detail. The primary windows with the large arches and striped awnings will be restored along that façade to create the original streetscape. They will bring it back to the original façade of the 1920s. It is necessary to acquire the Mach property in order to save a portion of the west façade. Without the Mach property, from 16 to 25 feet of the west façade would be lost. The west façade will be completely restored if the Mach property is acquired.

In June 2005, the City Commission voted to condemn the Mach parcel. On August 5, 2005, the CRA brought its petition in eminent domain, seeking to take the subject property.

The trial court denied the requested order of taking and dismissed the petition in eminent domain. The court found that the CRA had "demonstrated a valid public purpose, i.e., the redevelopment of a blighted area." However, it went on to find, "[b]ased upon the totality of the testimony and evidence presented, as weighed and considered by the Court, the Petitioner did not prove by competent, substantial evidence that the condemnation of Respondent-Owner's property is reasonably necessary for the public purpose alleged in this case."

The term "blight" is borrowed from science and connotes an organism that promotes disease. *City of Norwood v. Horney,* 110 Ohio St.3d 353, 853 N.E.2d 1115, 1134–35 (2006). It has become synonymous with urban decay. *Id.* "Urban renewal, through the force of eminent domain, became the treatment for saving the body politic from the spread of blight. . . ." *Id.* at 1135. Florida's Community Redevelopment Act of 1969 provided for the creation of community redevelopment agencies and vested in them the power of eminent domain. *See* § 163.330-375, Fla. Stat. (1979).

A "two-tiered" model is applied in determining whether a condemning authority has met its burden of proving reasonable necessity for a taking. *City of Jacksonville v. Griffin,* 346 So.2d 988, 990 (Fla.1977). First, the condemning authority must show a reasonable necessity for the condemnation. *Id.* If such proof is presented, the exercise of the condemning authority's discretion should not be disturbed in the absence of illegality, bad faith or gross abuse of discretion. *Id.*

In order to meet its initial burden, the condemning authority need present only "some evidence" of reasonable necessity. *Id.; Broward County v. Ellington,* 622 So.2d 1029, 1031 (Fla. 4th DCA 1993). Thus, the critical question posed by this appeal is whether the CRA presented "some evidence" of reasonable necessity. This "some evidence" inquiry is similar to questions appellate courts face in reviewing summary judgments and motions for directed verdict. Like those, the question here concerns a matter of law subject to *de novo* review.

The condemning authority is required to show only some evidence of a *reasonable* necessity for the taking, not an absolute necessity. *See Canal Auth. v. Litzel,* 243 So.2d 135, 137–38 (Fla.1970); *Canal Auth. v. Miller,* 243 So.2d 131, 134 (Fla.1970); *Ellington,* 622 So.2d at 1031. In this case, the CRA showed that it considered alternative plans, but that they were unsuitable. The CRA also pointed out that, as a matter of long-range planning, it made no sense to have the tiny Mach parcel remain, surrounded by a high-rise complex, with the likelihood of it becoming an unusable remnant parcel when the current building outlived its usefulness.

The condemning authority need not present evidence pinpointing the need for the particular property sought to be condemned. *Griffin,* 346 So.2d at 991. Broad discretion is vested in the condemning authority to determine what property and how much is necessary to condemn for public purposes, and the trial court may not refuse the application on such concerns absent a clear abuse of discretion. *Id.; Cordones v. Brevard County,* 781 So.2d 519, 522 (Fla. 5th DCA 2001). A landowner cannot complain simply because some other location might have been made or some other property obtained which would have been suitable for the purpose. *Pasco County v. Franzel,* 569 So.2d 877, 879 (Fla. 2d DCA 1990) (quoting *Wilton v. St. Johns County,* 98 Fla. 26, 123 So. 527, 535 (1929)).

There were only three options presented for the entrance site to the parking garage: 1) the Harrison Street option, which was unsafe; 2) the Great Southern option, which destroyed a significant portion of the western façade of the historic hotel; and 3) the Mach option, which required the taking of the subject parcel. Historic preservation is a legitimate basis upon which to disqualify an alternative site plan. The Community Redevelopment Act of 1969 recognizes that community redevelopment projects may include "rehabilitation and conservation in a community redevelopment area." *See* § 163.340(9), Fla. Stat. (1979). The CRA argues that this language encompasses the concept of historic preservation. We agree.

The power of eminent domain has been granted to government to preserve areas of historic interest. *Devon-Aire Villas Homeowners Ass'n. v. Americable Assocs., Ltd.,* 490 So.2d 60, 62 n. 6 (Fla. 3d DCA 1985); *see also Lubelle v. City of Rochester,* 145 A.D.2d 954, 536 N.Y.S.2d 325 (N.Y.App.Div.1988) ("there is no dispute that historic preservation serves a public purpose").

If a government can take property solely for historical purposes, it follows that it can refuse to consider development alternatives which would destroy historic property, even in part.

The trial court never reached the second-tier question as to whether the CRA's condemnation of the subject property was the product of fraud, bad faith, or an abuse of discretion. Although in some instances we might direct the trial court to consider this question on remand, having reviewed the complete record in this case, we can safely conclude that there is no competent, substantial evidence in the record to support a finding of fraud, bad faith or abuse of discretion. We therefore reverse and remand for entry of an order of taking and such further proceedings as are necessary upon entry of the order. We have considered the cross-appeal and find it to be without merit.

Reversed and Remanded

FARMER, J., concurs.

DAVIDSON, LISA, Associate Judge, concurs in part and dissents in part with opinion.

[The concurring and dissenting opinion of Judge Davidson is omitted.]

Chapter 8

Homestead

Fla. Const. art. X, § 4

Homestead; exemptions. —

(a) There shall be exempt from forced sale under process of any court, and no judgment, decree or execution shall be a lien thereon, except for the payment of taxes and assessments thereon, obligations contracted for the purchase, improvement or repair thereof, or obligations contracted for house, field or other labor performed on the realty, the following property owned by a natural person:

(1) a homestead, if located outside a municipality, to the extent of one hundred sixty acres of contiguous land and improvements thereon, which shall not be reduced without the owner's consent by reason of subsequent inclusion in a municipality; or if located within a municipality, to the extent of one-half acre of contiguous land, upon which the exemption shall be limited to the residence of the owner or his family;

(2) personal property to the value of one thousand dollars.

(b) These exemptions shall inure to the surviving spouse or heirs of the owner.

(c) The homestead shall not be subject to devise if the owner is survived by spouse or minor child, except the homestead may be devised to the owner's spouse if there be no minor child. The owner of homestead real estate, joined by the spouse if married, may alienate the homestead by mortgage, sale or gift and, if married, may by deed transfer the title to an estate by the entirety with the spouse. If the owner or spouse is incompetent, the method of alienation or encumbrance shall be as provided by law.

———

A. Introduction

The Florida Constitution has contained provisions exempting homesteads from the claims of most creditors for over a hundred years. The Florida Supreme Court has interpreted these provisions to promote the stability and welfare of the state by securing to the owner of the homestead and the owner's heirs, protection from financial misfortune.[1] This policy of preserving the home and protecting the owner's family is so strong that it overrides the otherwise just claims of creditors.[2] Thus, the homestead provisions are liberally construed in order to achieve the beneficial purpose for which they were created, but not to promote fraud or a means of escaping honest debts.[3]

B. Establishment of a Homestead

Once a parcel of real property attains homestead status, it is exempt from forced sale and other judicial process and is generally not subject to liens until the owner abandons the homestead, validly transfers it, or the owner's interest in the homestead terminates.[4] Due to the legal consequences of homestead status, it is extremely important to define precisely the requisite elements for real property to qualify as a homestead. There are four basic requirements that must be satisfied:

1. The real property must be owned by a "*natural person*."

2. The person claiming the exemption must be a Florida resident who establishes that he or she made, or intended to make, the real property his or her "*permanent residence*."

3. The person claiming the exemption must establish that he or she is the "*owner*" of the property.

4. The property claimed as the homestead must satisfy the "*size and contiguity*" requirements of the constitution.

1. Natural Person Requirement

First, the real property must be owned by a "natural person." Prior to 1985, homestead protection from forced sale was made available only to owners who were the "head of a family." An individual was the "head of a family" if he or she satisfied one of two tests:

> ... Whether a person qualifies as head of a family is a factual determination that may be found in either of two ways: (1) a legal duty to support that arises out of a family relationship — "family in law," or (2) continued communal living by at least two individuals in such circumstances that one is regarded as being in charge — "family in fact." [Citation omitted.][5]

---

1. *Pub. Health Trust of Dade Cnty. v. Lopez*, 531 So. 2d 946 (Fla. 1988).
2. *Frase v. Branch*, 362 So. 2d 317 (Fla. 2d Dist. Ct. App. 1978).
3. *Id.*
4. *Wilson v. Fla. Nat'l Bank & Trust Co. at Miami*, 64 So. 2d 309 (Fla. 1953).
5. *Flannery v. Green*, 482 So. 2d 400, 402 (Fla. 2d Dist. Ct. App. 1985).

In the 1984 general election, the Florida Constitution was amended and the phrase "head of a family" was changed to "a natural person." This amendment expanded the class of persons who could benefit from the homestead protections and, for the first time, included single persons.

2. Permanent Residence Requirement

Second, real property can only qualify as a homestead if the owner establishes that he or she made, or intended to make, the real property his or her family's permanent "residence."[6] Only owners (or family members of owners residing at the claimed homestead property) who have permanent resident status in the United States can formulate an intent to the make the real property his or her family's permanent residence.[7]

Prior to the 1984 amendment, the "head of a family" requirement limited homestead protection only to heads of family who actually resided in the state *and* who intended to make the property the family's permanent residence. As a result of the 1984 amendment, the actual residence test has been eliminated.[8]

3. Owner Requirement

Third, the person claiming the homestead exemption must establish that he or she is the "owner" of the property.[9] An individual need not hold legal or fee simple title to the property to meet this requirement.[10] Homestead status may be derived from any equitable or beneficiary interest in real property.[11] Although the constitution places size limits on real property that may qualify as a homestead, it does not limit the types of estates eligible for homestead status. Thus, not only a fee simple title, but a freehold estate is eligible for homestead status.[12] Similarly, undivided interests in property, such as a tenancy in common, are eligible for homestead status.[13] Additionally, an individual's interest in his or her residence as the beneficiary of a revocable trust will qualify for homestead protection.[14]

Nonetheless, the legal or equitable ownership interests must be possessory for homestead status to attach. As a result, a remainder interest in property will

---

6. *In re Estate of Van Meter*, 214 So. 2d 639 (Fla. 2d Dist. Ct. App. 1968), *approved*, 231 So. 2d 524 (Fla. 1970).

7. *Grisolia v. Pfeffer*, 77 So. 3d 732 (Fla. 3d Dist. Ct. App. 2012).

8. *In re Cooke*, 412 So. 2d 340 (Fla. 1982).

9. *Raulerson v. Peeples*, 81 So. 271 (Fla. 1919).

10. *Bessemer Props., Inc. v. Gamble*, 27 So. 2d 832, 833 (Fla. 1946).

11. *Id.*; *Heiman v. Capital Bank*, 438 So. 2d 932 (Fla. 3d Dist. Ct. App. 1983).

12. *Menendez v. Rodriguez*, 143 So. 223 (Fla. 1932).

13. *Hill v. First Nat'l Bank of Marianna*, 75 So. 614 (Fla. 1917).

14. *Engelke v. Estate of Engelke*, 921 So. 2d 693 (Fla. 4th Dist. Ct. App. 2006).

not qualify as homestead property,[15] but a life estate[16] and a long-term leasehold interest will.[17]

4. Size and Contiguity Requirements

Fourth, the property must satisfy the size and contiguity requirements of the Constitution. The quantity of property that is eligible for homestead status depends on the location of the property. If the property is located within a municipality, the homestead is limited to one-half acre of contiguous land upon which the homestead is limited to the residence of the owner or his or her family. If the real property is located outside a municipality, the homestead can extend to one hundred and sixty acres of contiguous land and improvements thereon, which cannot be reduced without the owner's consent by reason of subsequent inclusion in a municipality.

C. Duration of and Protection Afforded to a Homestead

Once a natural person establishes the existence of a homestead, the Florida Constitution operates to protect the homestead from forced sale to satisfy the debts, and most other obligations, of the owner. Further, no judgment, decree, or execution shall be a lien on the homestead except for certain exceptions discussed in the following section.

1. Duration of Protection from Creditors

For the homestead exemption to protect the property, the homestead must have been established before the judgment is recorded or before the seizure for forfeiture. Once established, the protection continues while the owner or owner's family is alive and continues to occupy the home. The homestead exemption terminates upon the death of the owner[18] or upon the abandonment or transfer of the homestead.

---

15. *Aetna Ins. Co. v. LaGasse*, 223 So. 2d 727 (Fla. 1969).

16. *Smith v. Unkefer*, 515 So. 2d 757 (Fla. 2d Dist. Ct. App. 1987).

17. *Geraci v. Sunstar EMS*, 93 So. 3d 384 (Fla. 2d Dist. Ct. App. 2012).

18. *See Wilson v. Fla. Nat'l Bank & Trust Co. at Miami*, 64 So. 2d 309 (Fla. 1953). But see section E, *infra* discussing inured exemptions and section I of this chapter discussing termination of homesteads.

Yost-Rudge v. A to Z Props., Inc.

263 So. 3d 95 (Fla. 4th Dist. Ct. App. 2019)

LEVINE, J.

In this case, the husband sold the property, claimed by appellant ("wife") to be protected by homestead, without the wife's agreement or signature on the warranty deed. Appellee ("buyer") claims that municipal violations regarding the safety of that property resulted in an injunction prohibiting the wife and her husband from occupying the property which, in turn, resulted in their abandonment of the property. The Buyer claims further that if the property was abandoned, then the property lost its homestead protection, obviating the buyer's need to obtain the wife's written consent to her husband's sale of the property.

We find, consistent with the Florida Constitution, that the wife must agree to the sale of the property and that her being prevented from returning to the property due to an injunction for municipal violations was not an abandonment that destroyed the homestead protections of the property.

* * *

Article X, section 4 of the Florida Constitution applies homestead protection "to the residence of the owner or the owner's family." Fla. Const., art. X, § 4 (a)(1). As a result, the married owner of a homestead property may not alienate the property without joinder or consent of his or her spouse. *Vera v. Wells Fargo Bank, N.A.*, 178 So.3d 517, 519 n.1 (Fla. 4th DCA 2015). The protections of homestead are limited to the residence of the owner and generally require the owner's occupancy of the home with the intent to remain there. *Law v. Law*, 738 So.2d 522, 524 (Fla. 4th DCA 1999).

The homestead is accorded special status under Florida law and, as such, the Florida Constitution's homestead provisions are construed liberally. *See JBK Assocs. v. Sill Bros., Inc.*, 160 So.3d 94, 96 (Fla. 4th DCA 2015) ("Homestead exemption laws should be liberally applied to the end that the family shall have shelter and shall not be reduced to absolute destitution.") (quoting *Orange Brevard Plumbing & Heating Co. v. La Croix*, 137 So.2d 201, 204 (Fla. 1962)).

It is clear, however, that once homestead is established, it still can be lost due to abandonment. "Once homestead status is acquired, it continues until the homestead is abandoned or alienated in the manner provided by law. To show abandonment, both the owner and his family must have abandoned the property." *Coy v. Mango Bay Prop. and Invs., Inc.*, 963 So.2d 873, 878 (Fla. 4th DCA 2007) (citation omitted). Consistent with the special status of Florida homestead, a finding of abandonment requires a "strong showing" of intent not to return to the homestead. *In re Herr*, 197 B.R. 939, 941 (Bankr. S.D. Fla. 1996).

Whether a property has been abandoned and thus lost its homestead protections is determined, case by case, in light of the totality of circumstances. *Beensen v. Burgess*, 218 So.2d 517, 519 (Fla. 4th DCA 1969). Only in light of the totality of circumstances, with all doubts resolved against the moving party, can it be determined that the owner has abandoned the property and abandoned its homestead protections.

Florida courts have consistently held that a property is not abandoned for the purposes of homestead protection when the owner involuntarily ceases to reside on the property. *In re Estate of Melisi* , 440 So.2d 584, 585 (Fla. 4th DCA 1983). For example, the Florida Supreme Court held in *Stokes v. Whidden*, 97 Fla. 1057, 122 So. 566 (1929), that a homestead was not abandoned even though the owner of the property had been adjudged insane and committed to a state institution. In that case, unlike this one, the owner's family continued to live on the property. *Id.* at 566; *see also Dean v. Heimbach*, 409 So.2d 157 (Fla. 1st DCA 1982) (finding homestead not abandoned when father had to leave county as condition of bail but intended to return and family continued to live on property).

Still, courts have also upheld homestead protections even when a property has been left completely unoccupied, as is the case here. One such case is *Crain v. Putnam*, 687 So.2d 1325 (Fla. 4th DCA 1997). There, the homeowner had been absent from the homestead property for around two years after being placed in a nursing home in a vegetative state; nothing was done with the property during this period. *Id.* at 1326. However, the homeowner's furniture, clothing, and most of her possessions remained on the property, she received mail at the property, and, given her condition, she could not "communicate any intention regarding her residence" or her plans to maintain it as a homestead. *Id.* This court was asked to determine whether the article VII homestead tax exemption still applied to the property in light of this absence. *Id.* We concluded that, under the circumstances, the property retained its homestead character. *Id.* In doing so, we noted that Florida's homestead protections are not subject to a physical presence requirement, nor are they forfeited when a homeowner involuntarily changes his or her residence. *Id.*

Another factually similar and persuasive case is *In re Herr*. In *Herr*, the owner's home was destroyed by a hurricane and the property was rendered uninhabitable after the city demolished the remaining structures on the property. 197 B.R. at 941. The property languished for three years without any action by the debtor, but the debtor maintained that he was planning on selling the property and using the proceeds to purchase a new homestead. *Id.* Because Florida law requires a "strong showing of a debtor's intent not to return to his residence" before the homestead can be considered abandoned, the court held that the property retained its homestead protections. *Id.*

Here, the trial court decided the homestead issue on summary judgment. As discussed above, abandonment turns on intent and is necessarily a fact-intensive inquiry. *See Beensen*, 218 So.2d at 519 ("The question of whether there has been an abandonment of a homestead so as to deprive it of its status as such under the constitution should be determined by consideration of all of the pertinent facts and circumstances of each case."). The information available to the court at summary judgment gave rise to a genuine issue of material fact. Although the wife did not submit an affidavit in response to the motion for summary judgment or raise affirmative defenses, she did affirmatively deny the allegations of the complaint. Further, the record does contain some evidence indicating there was a conflict of material fact as to whether the wife abandoned the property.

For one, the wife maintained in her answer that the family was involuntarily "forced off" the property and generally asserted a continuing homestead interest in the property. Additionally, the wife attached to her answer in denial evidence indicating that, after being removed from the property, she was making efforts to remediate it with the intention of returning. These attachments included a 2011 letter from an engineering consultant reflecting that the husband had the property inspected in June 2010 for structural issues with the home. Another 2011 letter indicated that the husband tried to contact the city commission regarding his attempts to bring the property up to code and to "determine the facts concerning my building, on my property." Further, an invoice indicated that the husband paid for waste disposal on the property as late as January 2011. Finally, numerous court filings from the wife indicated that she was fighting to retain the property until at least 2012, supporting her argument that she did not intend to abandon the property.

The trial court erred in granting summary judgment, since the question of the wife's intent relating to the alleged abandonment of the homestead was still in dispute.

In conclusion, due to the material conflict of facts and the special status accorded to the protection of the homestead property, we reverse and remand for further proceedings consistent with this opinion.

Reversed and remanded for further proceedings.

WARNER and CIKLIN, JJ., concur.

The proceeds from the sale or destruction of a homestead are protected from the owner's creditors for a "reasonable" period of time. When an insured homestead is destroyed or damaged, any insurance proceeds intended to restore the property are also constitutionally protected from the owner's creditors.[19]

---

19. *Kohn v. Coats*, 138 So. 760 (Fla. 1931); *Orange Brevard Plumbing & Heating Co. v. La Croix*, 137 So. 2d 201 (Fla. 1962).

Orange Brevard Plumbing & Heating Co. v. La Croix

137 So. 2d 201 (Fla. 1962)

HOBSON, Justice.

On May 22, 1959, the appellant, who was the plaintiff in the action below, obtained and recorded a judgment in the circuit court for Orange County, Florida against the appellees in the sum of $5,972.18. At the time the judgment was rendered and for some three and one-half years prior thereto the appellees owned as tenants by the entirety and occupied as their homestead certain real property in Orange County, Florida. On July 22, 1959, the appellees sold this homestead property. The attorneys for the purchaser, having discovered the aforementioned judgment of record, withheld from the appellees $6,000.00 of the purchase price of the property pending a determination that it was homestead property as of the date of sale.

While the attorneys for the purchaser were thus holding the sum of $6,000.00 the appellant caused to be issued by the Circuit Court of Orange County in September 1959 a writ of garnishment against the attorneys. Thereafter the garnishees filed their answer in which they admitted holding the sum of $6,000.00 for and on behalf of the appellees. Subsequently the appellees filed a motion to dissolve the writ of garnishment on the ground that the sum of $6,000.00 held by the garnishees was exempt from forced levy, since that sum represented proceeds of the sale of homestead property. . . .

A hearing was held before the circuit court on the motion to dissolve the writ of garnishment, and it was agreed by the parties that the issues should be determined on the basis of the affidavit of Henry J. La Croix. Thereafter the court entered an order dissolving the writ of garnishment and finding that the sum of $6,000.00 held by the garnishees was exempt from forced levy under the Constitution and laws of the State of Florida.

The appellant then appealed to the District Court of Appeal, Second District. The district court, however, noting that the circuit court in its order had construed a controlling provision of the Constitution and that therefore exclusive jurisdiction of the appeal rested with the Supreme Court, ordered the appeal transferred to this court pursuant to Rule 2.1, subd. a(5) (d), Florida Appellate Rules, 31 F.S.A.

The question with which we are faced, therefore, is whether the exemption of homestead property from forced sale which is accorded by Article X, Section 1 of the Florida Constitution, F.S.A., extends also to the proceeds of a voluntary sale of a homestead when it is intended in good faith that such proceeds are to be reinstated in a new homestead.

* * *

After a full consideration of the applicable authorities representing both views on the issue before us, and in recognition of the liberal interpretation of the homestead exemption to which this court is committed, we hold the proceeds of a voluntary sale of a homestead to be exempt from the claims of creditors just as the homestead itself is exempt, if, and only if, the vendor shows, by a preponderance of the evidence an abiding good faith intention prior to and at the time of the sale of the homestead to reinvest the proceeds thereof in another homestead within a reasonable time. Moreover, only *so much* of the proceeds of the sale as are intended to be reinvested in another homestead may be exempt under this holding. Any surplus over and above that amount should be treated as general assets of the debtor. We further hold that in order to satisfy the requirements of the exemption the funds must not be commingled with other monies of the vendor but must be kept separate and apart and held for the sole purpose of acquiring another home. The proceeds of the sale are not exempt if they are not reinvested in another homestead in a reasonable time or if they are held for the general purposes of the vendor.

The homestead exemption provision was not placed in our Constitution for the purpose of tying the owner thereof and his family to a particular home, once established, for the remaining period of their natural lives. It is a protection which should remain inviolate so long as the head of the family who is indebted acts in good faith and with reasonable diligence in converting one homestead into another. In our modern peripatetic society it often becomes necessary for a family to give up its former homestead and move to a new home out of economic necessity or for other compelling reasons. To hold other than we have in the instant case would be to deny to a family finding itself in such circumstances the full benefit of the homestead exemption provision of our Constitution and would be inimical to our declared policy of a liberal construction thereof.

We have considered the early case of Drucker v. Rosenstein, 19 Fla. 191, wherein it was held that the *intent* of the owner of a parcel of land to build a home thereon and to occupy it as his homestead is not sufficient to invest such land with the character of a homestead and thus put it beyond the reach of creditors. Our present holding is by no means inconsistent with that case. We adhere to the rule that intent *alone* is not a sufficient basis for the establishment of a homestead. There must first be, as there unquestionably was in this case, property which meets the constitutional requirements of a homestead. In the *Drucker* case there was *never* any real property to which the homestead exemption could attach. In the instant case, on the other hand, the appellees had established and maintained a homestead up until the time of the sale. Having done so, the funds realized from such sale enjoy an exempt status *provided* the other requirements for such exemption as herein set forth are fully met.

* * *

It is not for the courts to fix in a case such as this an iron clad inflexible period of time and thereby define reasonable period of time. The question whether funds received from the sale of a homestead are invested in another homestead within a *reasonable time* must be determined from the facts and circumstances of each case.

* * *

In order that all the facts may be fully developed and that a decision may be reached in harmony with the views expressed herein, the judgment below is reversed

908   8 · HOMESTEAD

and the cause remanded in the interest of simple justice, for further proceedings in accordance with this opinion.

It is so ordered.

ROBERTS, C. J., and TERRELL and THORNAL, JJ., concur.

THOMAS and DREW, JJ., and ODOM, C.J., dissent. [The dissenting opinion is omitted.]

In *JBK Associates, Inc. v. Sill Bros., Inc.*,[20] the Florida Supreme Court reaffirmed its decision in *Orange Brevard Plumbing & Heating Company v. La Croix* when it held that proceeds from the sale of homestead property placed in an investment account did not lose homestead protection when the owner manifested his intent to reinvest the sale proceeds into a new homestead by designating the investment account his "homestead account."

2. Extent of Protection from Creditors

Homestead provisions have been liberally construed by the courts in the interest of protecting the family home. The Florida Constitution specifically protects a validly established homestead from forced sale and other judicial process, including forfeiture proceedings authorized by state racketeering statutes.[21] Homestead protection extends not only to debts voluntarily incurred by the owner of the homestead, but to other financial obligations as well. The Florida Supreme Court reaffirmed this principle in the context of homestead property purchased with specific intent to hinder, delay, or defraud creditors.

Havoco of America, LTD v. Hill

790 So. 2d 1018 (Fla. 2001)

SHAW, Justice.

We have for review the following question of Florida law certified by the United States Court of Appeals for the Eleventh Circuit that is determinative of a cause pending in the federal courts and for which there appears to be no controlling precedent:

> Does Article X, Section 4 of the Florida Constitution exempt a Florida homestead, where the debtor acquired the homestead using non-exempt funds with the specific intent of hindering, delaying, or defrauding creditors in violation of Fla. Stat. §726.105 or Fla. Stat. §§222.29 and 222.30?

---

20. 191 So. 3d 879 (Fla. 2016).
21. *See Butterworth v. Caggiano*, 605 So. 2d 56 (Fla. 1992).

Havoco of America, Ltd. v. Hill, 197 F.3d 1135, 1144 (11th Cir.1999). We have jurisdiction. Art. V, § 3(b)(6), Fla. Const. For the reasons that follow we answer the certified question in the affirmative.

Facts

On July 22, 1992, Elmer Hill filed a voluntary Chapter 7 bankruptcy petition in which he claimed that real property located in Destin, Florida, (Destin Property) was exempt as his homestead under article X, section 4 of the Florida Constitution.[1] Havoco objected, arguing that Hill converted nonexempt assets into the homestead with the intent to hinder, delay, or defraud his creditors. The dealings between the parties which precipitated the instant action, as stated by the Eleventh Circuit in its opinion, are as follows:

> In 1981, Havoco filed suit against Hill claiming damages for fraud, conspiracy, tortuous [sic] interference with contractual relations, and breach of fiduciary duty. Havoco alleged that Hill conspired to eliminate Havoco as a principal under its ten year contract to supply coal to the Tennessee Valley Authority. The jury found for Havoco on all its claims against Hill and awarded Havoco $15,000,000 in damages. The district court entered judgment in accordance with the jury verdict on December 19, 1990, and the judgment became enforceable on January 2, 1991.
>
> Hill purchased the Destin property on December 30, 1990. Although he was a long-time resident of Tennessee, Hill claims that he intended to make the Destin property his retirement home. He paid approximately $650,000 in cash for the Destin property.

Havoco, 197 F.3d at 1137 (footnote omitted).

The bankruptcy court held an evidentiary hearing in which Havoco attempted to present evidence of other transfers of nonexempt assets by Hill to demonstrate that the purchase of the Destin property was part of a larger scheme to defraud Hill's creditors via bankruptcy. The bankruptcy court deemed the evidence irrelevant and denied Havoco the opportunity to present the evidence in support of its claim. Thereafter, the bankruptcy court overruled Havoco's objections to Hill's homestead claims, concluding that Havoco had not proven by a preponderance of the evidence that Hill acted with the specific intent to defraud his creditors when he purchased the Destin property.

On appeal, the district court reversed, finding error in the bankruptcy court's supposition that a debtor's specific intent to defraud his creditors could provide a ground to deny the homestead exemption. The district court ordered the bankruptcy

---

1. Hill also claimed that household furnishings in the Destin property worth approximately $75,000 were exempt because he owned the furnishings in tenancy by the entireties with his wife. Hill purchased the furnishings shortly before moving into the Destin property with funds drawn from a Florida bank account held jointly with his wife and from Hill's individual accounts in Florida and Tennessee.

court on remand "to determine whether and under what circumstances Florida law prevented debtors in 1990 and 1991 from converting nonexempt property to exempt property." *Havoco,* 197 F.3d at 1138. Further, the district court ordered the bankruptcy court to conduct an evidentiary hearing during which Havoco would be allowed to present evidence of Hill's other transfers of nonexempt assets if it determined that Hill's homestead claim was limited under Florida law.

On remand, the bankruptcy court, relying upon *Bank Leumi Trust Co. v. Lang,* 898 F.Supp. 883 (S.D.Fla.1995), and *Butterworth v. Caggiano,* 605 So.2d 56 (Fla.1992), held that Florida law did not prohibit Hill from converting nonexempt assets into a homestead, even if done with the intent to place those assets beyond the reach of his creditors. *Havoco,* 197 F.3d at 1138. The bankruptcy court further concluded that Florida's fraudulent conveyance statute did not "affect the debtor's right to the homestead exemption." *Id.* The district court affirmed the bankruptcy court's decision.

The Eleventh Circuit, detailing the inconsistent treatment of the issue in the bankruptcy courts stemming from this Court's application of the homestead exemption, certified the instant question to this Court. [Footnote omitted.]

The Homestead Exemption

Florida's homestead exemption provides, in pertinent part:

> There shall be exempt from forced sale under process of any court, and no judgment, decree or execution shall be a lien thereon, except for the payment of taxes and assessments thereon, obligations contracted for the purchase, improvement or repair thereof, or obligations contracted for house, field or other labor performed on the realty, the following property owned by a natural person:
>
> (1) a homestead. . . .

Art. X, § 4(a)(1), Fla. Const. This Court has long emphasized that the homestead exemption is to be liberally construed in the interest of protecting the family home. *See, e.g., Milton v. Milton,* 63 Fla. 533, 58 So. 718, 719 (1912) ("Organic and statutory provisions relating to homestead exemptions should be liberally construed in the interest of the family home."). However, in the same breath we have similarly cautioned that the exemption is not to be so liberally construed as to make it an instrument of fraud or imposition upon creditors: "[T]he [homestead exemption] should not be so applied as to make it an instrument of fraud or imposition upon creditors." *Id.* The petitioner and amici curiae[3] seize upon this latter language to argue that the transfer of nonexempt assets into an exempt homestead with the intent to defraud creditors cannot receive constitutional sanction. While we are certainly loathe to provide constitutional sanction to the conduct alleged by the petitioner

---

3. An amicus brief in support of Havoco was filed on behalf of the Florida Bankers Association, Florida Retail Federation, NACM of Florida, Inc., and NACM Florida Gulf Coast Unit, Inc.

8 · HOMESTEAD

and implicated by the certified question, this Court is powerless to depart from the plain language of article X, section 4.[4]

Treatment of the Exemption

As previously mentioned, this Court's homestead exemption jurisprudence has long been guided by a policy favoring the liberal construction of the exemption: "Organic and statutory provisions relating to homestead exemptions should be liberally construed in the interest of the family home." *Milton,* 58 So. at 719. A concomitant in harmony with this rule of liberal construction is the rule of strict construction as applied to the exceptions. *See, e.g., Quigley v. Kennedy & Ely Ins., Inc.,* 207 So.2d 431, 432 (Fla.1968).[5] Indeed, this strict construction of the exceptions proved paramount in our most recent inquiries into the homestead exemption in the context of civil and criminal forfeitures.

The Forfeiture Cases

In *Butterworth v. Caggiano,* 605 So.2d 56 (Fla.1992), the State sought civil forfeiture of Caggiano's residence following Caggiano's conviction on one count of racketeering in violation of the Florida Racketeer Influenced and Corrupt Organization Act and fifteen counts of bookmaking. The State sought forfeiture of Caggiano's homestead on the grounds that the property was used by Caggiano in the course of racketeering activity. *Id.*

This Court, in rejecting the State's attempted distinction between forfeitures and the constitution's reference to "forced sale[s]," held that article X, section 4 prohibited the forfeiture of Caggiano's homestead:

> Consequently, in light of the historical prejudice against forfeiture, the constitutional sanctity of the home, and the rules of construction requiring a liberal, nontechnical interpretation of the homestead exemption and a strict construction of the exceptions to that exemption, we hold that article X, section 4 of the Florida Constitution prohibits civil or criminal forfeiture of homestead property.

---

4. As similarly noted by the Southern District in confronting a similar claim by a creditor: "[A]lthough this Court is reluctant to place its imprimatur upon conduct which, beyond question, was an effort to delay, hinder, or defraud, it is obligated to follow Article X, Section 4(a) of the Florida Constitution." *Bank Leumi Trust Co. v. Lang,* 898 F.Supp. 883, 889 (S.D.Fla.1995).

5. In *Olesky v. Nicholas,* 82 So.2d 510, 513 (Fla.1955), this Court stated: "We find no difficulty in holding that the Florida constitutional exemption of homesteads protects the homestead against every type of claim and judgment except those specifically mentioned in the constitutional provision itself. . . ."

Id. at 61. While our conclusion was influenced by the legally disfavored status of forfeitures,[6] paramount in our reasoning was the plain language of the homestead provision and the strict construction of the exceptions enumerated therein:

> *Most significantly, article X, section 4 expressly provides for three exceptions to the homestead exemption. Forfeiture is not one of them.* According to the plain and unambiguous wording of article X, section 4, a homestead is *only* subject to forced sale for (1) the payment of taxes and assessments thereon; (2) obligations contracted for the purchase, improvement or repair thereof; or (3) obligations contracted for house, field or other labor performed on the realty. Under the rule "expressio unius est exclusio alterious" — the expression of one thing is the exclusion of another — forfeitures are not excluded from the homestead exemption because they are not mentioned, either expressly or by reasonable implication, in the three exceptions that are expressly stated.

Id. at 60 (first emphasis added). Notably, we rejected the State's attempt to imply an exception for homesteads acquired through criminal or immoral conduct:

> The homestead provision of our Constitution sets forth the exceptions and provides the method of waiving the homestead rights attached to the residence. *These exceptions are unqualified. They create no personal qualifications touching the moral character of the resident nor do they undertake to exclude the vicious, the criminal, or the immoral from the benefits so provided.* The law provides for punishment of persons convicted of illegal acts, but this forfeiture of homestead rights guaranteed by our Constitution is not part of the punishment.

Id. at 60 (alteration in original) (quoting *State ex rel. Apt v. Mitchell,* 194 Kan. 463, 399 P.2d 556, 558 (1965)). We were again faithful to our strict construction of the exceptions to the exemption five years later in *Tramel v. Stewart,* 697 So.2d 821 (Fla.1997).

In *Tramel,* the Stewarts faced forfeiture of their homestead under the Florida Contraband Forfeiture Act after they were arrested for selling marijuana and a search of their home revealed drugs, drug paraphernalia, and a sophisticated marijuana growing operation.[7] The State thus sought forfeiture of the Stewarts' real and personal property, claiming that the property was either being used as an instrumentality of the drug operation or that the property was acquired with funds obtained from the drug activity. Consistent with *Caggiano,* we held:

---

6. "Forfeitures are considered harsh penalties that are historically disfavored in law and equity, and courts have long followed a policy of strictly construing such statutes." *Butterworth v. Caggiano,* 605 So.2d at 58.

7. In *Tramel,* the First District certified the following question to this Court: "Whether article X, section 4, Fla. Const., prohibits civil forfeiture of homestead property pursuant to sections 932.701– .702, Fla. Stat., when the proceeds of illegal activity are invested in or used to purchase the property?" *Tramel,* 697 So.2d at 822.

As we found in respect to the Florida RICO Act in *Caggiano,* we find that article X, section 4, does not provide an exception for the forfeiture of homestead property for a violation of the Forfeiture Act. The homestead guarantee uses broad language protecting the homestead from involuntary divestiture by the courts. *The constitutional protection of homesteads has not changed since our discussion in Caggiano to include forfeiture as one of the enumerated exceptions. In the absence of such a provision, this court cannot judicially create one.*

Tramel, 697 So.2d at 824 (citation omitted) (emphasis added).[8] Indeed, it is on the strength of our decisions in *Caggiano* and *Tramel* that several federal courts have rejected attempts by creditors to enforce claims against homestead property.

* * *

Nevertheless, the petitioner and amici curiae argue that this Court has not hesitated to reach beyond the literal language of the exemption to allow the imposition of equitable liens against homestead property used as an "instrument of fraud or imposition upon creditors." *Milton,* 58 So. at 719. Admittedly, we have strayed from the literal language of the exemption where the equities have demanded it; however, we have done so rarely and always with due regard to the exceptions provided in article X, section 4.

Fishbein and the Equitable Lien Cases

In *Palm Beach Savings & Loan Ass'n v. Fishbein,* 619 So.2d 267 (Fla.1993), this Court allowed an equitable lien against homestead property in favor of a lender, where the debtor husband fraudulently obtained a loan and used the loan to satisfy three preexisting mortgages on the homestead property. Specifically, in March of 1998, Mr. Fishbein borrowed $1.2 million from a Palm Beach bank, securing the debt with a mortgage on the house he owned with his wife. Prior to his marriage, Mr. Fishbein owned the house subject to two mortgages. Following their marriage,

---

8. This Court referred the issue raised by *Tramel* to the Constitutional Revision Commission, stating:

> Certainly, there are compelling reasons to support the forfeiture of homestead property "acquired or improved" with funds obtained through felonious criminal activity or homestead property used in the commission of felonious criminal activity. As well, the homestead protection should not be used to shield fraud or reprehensible conduct. However, to permit the State to forfeit a homestead based upon this criminal activity in Florida requires a constitutional revision. We call this to the attention of the Constitutional Revision Commission.

Tramel, 697 So.2d at 824 (citation and footnote omitted). Such an amendment was considered by the 1997–98 Constitutional Revision Commission, as was an amendment to article X, section 4, which would have provided:

> "The homestead exemption in this section does not apply to any property to the extent that it is acquired with the intent to defraud creditors." *Journal of the 1997–1998 Florida Constitutional Revision Commission,* Proposal 70, Amendment 7. That amendment was rejected by the Commission by a 24 to 7 vote.

Mr. and Mrs. Fishbein received a third mortgage in which they acknowledged the existence of the prior mortgages.

In securing the $1.2 million loan, Mr. Fishbein, while engaged in dissolution proceedings with his wife, forged his wife's signature on the mortgage. Mr. Fishbein used approximately $930,000 of the loan to satisfy the three existing mortgages and taxes on the property. In August of 1998, the Fishbeins entered into a property settlement, in which Mr. Fishbein agreed to buy his wife a $275,000 home and pay her $225,000 in exchange for her relinquishment of any interest in the Palm Beach house. As collateral, Mr. Fishbein gave his wife's attorney a quitclaim deed conveying the Palm Beach house to his wife and himself. Mr. Fishbein represented that the house was clear of all liens except for those claimed by his mother and sister. He failed to comply with the property settlement agreement, and the Palm Beach house went into default. After the bank initiated foreclosure proceedings, Mrs. Fishbein moved back into the house. Mrs. Fishbein was awarded the house *nunc pro tunc* after the judge in the dissolution proceeding set aside the property settlement agreement for fraud in the procurement.

In the foreclosure proceeding the trial judge allowed an equitable lien on the property to the extent that the loan proceeds were used to satisfy the existing mortgages and property taxes. On appeal, the Fourth District held that the bank was not entitled to an equitable lien because Mrs. Fishbein was not guilty of fraudulent or egregious conduct.

We agreed with the trial court and allowed the bank an equitable lien against Mrs. Fishbein's homestead, accepting the bank's argument that although it could not foreclose on the mortgage under the literal language of the exemption it should be entitled to a lien under the doctrine of equitable subrogation as its loan proceeds were used to satisfy the prior liens against the home. *Fishbein,* 619 So.2d at 269. Stated differently, we allowed the Palm Beach bank to stand in the shoes of the prior mortgagees who would have been entitled to proceed against the Fishbeins' homestead under the express terms of article X, section 4.

As we emphasized in *Fishbein,* the imposition of an equitable lien in circumstances suggesting the use of fraud in the acquisition of the homestead was not a remedy of recent vintage: "[W]here equity demands it this Court has not hesitated to permit equitable liens to be imposed on homesteads beyond the literal language of article X, section 4." *Fishbein,* 619 So.2d at 270.

* * *

The petitioner argues that this Court through its equitable lien jurisprudence has created a fourth exception to the homestead exemption excepting homesteads claimed in the furtherance of fraud from the protection of article X, section 4. The petitioner is not alone in this belief. *See In re Tabone,* 247 B.R. 541, 544 (Bkrtcy.M.D.Fla.2000) ("[T]he Florida Supreme Court has already engrafted an exception to the homestead provision in the Florida Constitution in order to prevent unjust enrichment."); *In re Lazin,* 221 B.R. 982, 988 (Bkrtcy.M.D.Fla.1998) (reading *Fishbein* to create fourth exception where nonexempt funds are fraudulently obtained and used to acquire a homestead or pay off a mortgage on the homestead).

In fact, several bankruptcy courts have relied on *Fishbein* and the cases preceding it to deny homestead claims or impose equitable liens where the evidence established that the transfer of assets to the homestead was accomplished with the intent to shield assets from creditors or with fraudulently obtained assets. . . .

* * *

Nevertheless, in *Caggiano* we cautioned that our equitable lien jurisprudence should not be read too broadly:

> All of the cases cited by the State where a court has actually imposed a lien on the homestead in question, however, are either factually or legally inapposite. Virtually all of the relevant cases involve situations that fell within one of the three stated exceptions to the homestead provision. Most of those cases involve equitable liens that were imposed where proceeds from fraud or reprehensible conduct were used to invest in, purchase, or improve the homestead. *See, e.g., Jones v. Carpenter,* 90 Fla. 407, 415, 106 So. 127, 130 (1925); *La Mar,* 135 Fla. 703, 711, 185 So. 833, 836. Other relevant cases cited involve situations where an equitable lien was necessary to secure to an owner the benefit of his or her interest in the property. *See, e.g., Tullis v. Tullis,* 360 So.2d 375, 377 (Fla.1978) ("We hold, with the First District, that our constitutional provisions allow the partition and forced sale of homestead property upon suit by one of the owners of that property, if such partition and forced sale is necessary to protect the beneficial enjoyment of the owners in common to the extent of their interest in the property."). In particular, *Tullis* involved a marital situation with joint homestead property. In no other case has this Court imposed a lien on a homestead beyond one of the three stated exceptions in the constitutional provision. The Court in *Bessemer [v. Gersten]* specifically did not address the issue of whether the lien came within one of the stated exceptions to the homestead exemption. 381 So.2d [1344] at 1347 n. 1 [(Fla.1980)].

Caggiano, 605 So.2d at 60 n. 5. We reiterated that position in *Tramel* in rejecting the State's attempts to extend our holding in *Fishbein* to allow the forfeiture of homestead property and do so again today. *Tramel,* 697 So.2d at 824; *see also Smith v. Smith,* 761 So.2d 370, 373 (Fla. 5th DCA 2000) ("[T]he supreme court has limited the exception allowing an equitable lien on homestead to those cases where the owner of the property has used the proceeds from fraud or reprehensible conduct to either invest in, purchase, or improve the homestead.").

Moreover, although we have not had the occasion to answer the precise question before us today, we have previously intimated that the use of the homestead exemption to shield assets from the claims of creditors is not conduct sufficient in and of itself to forfeit the exemption under the express terms of article X, section 4.

* * *

In sum, we conclude that we must answer the certified question in the affirmative. The transfer of nonexempt assets into an exempt homestead with the intent to hinder, delay, or defraud creditors is not one of the three exceptions to the homestead exemption provided in article X, section 4. Nor can we reasonably extend our equitable lien jurisprudence to except such conduct from the exemption's protection. We have invoked equitable principles to reach beyond the literal language of the exceptions only where funds obtained through fraud or egregious conduct were used to invest in, purchase, or improve the homestead.[12]

* * *

Conclusion

Accordingly, we answer the certified question in the affirmative, holding that a homestead acquired by a debtor with the specific intent to hinder, delay, or defraud creditors is not excepted from the protection of article X, section 4. Having answered the certified question, we return this case to the United States Court of Appeals for the Eleventh Circuit for further proceedings.

It is so ordered.

WELLS, C.J., and HARDING, PARIENTE, LEWIS and QUINCE, JJ., concur.

ANSTEAD, J., dissents without an opinion.

In response to the very liberal homestead exemptions in several states, including Florida, in 2005, Congress enacted the Bankruptcy Abuse Prevention and Consumer Act of 2005 which, in part, provides that the value of investment proceeds placed in a homestead with the intent to hinder, delay, or defraud a creditor within ten years of filing bankruptcy are recoverable by the trustee in a bankruptcy proceeding.[22] By virtue of the Supremacy Clause, Florida's homestead exemption that allows the purchase of homestead property with the specific intent to hinder, delay, or defraud creditors will be preempted by this federal law in bankruptcy proceedings.

---

12. We recognize that several District Courts have allowed equitable liens beyond the exceptions provided under article X, section 4 where a husband has used the homestead exemption to avoid his alimony and child support obligations. *See Brose v. Brose,* 750 So.2d 717 (Fla. 2nd DCA 2000); *Rosenblatt v. Rosenblatt,* 635 So.2d 132 (Fla. 3d DCA 1994); *Radin v. Radin,* 593 So.2d 1231 (Fla. 3d DCA 1992); *Gepfrich v. Gepfrich,* 582 So.2d 743 (Fla. 4th DCA 1991); *cf. Smith v. Smith,* 761 So.2d 370 (Fla. 5th DCA 2000); *Isaacson v. Isaacson,* 504 So.2d 1309 (Fla. 1st DCA 1987). We express no opinion as to the validity of this approach.

22. 11 U.S.C. § 522(o).

D. Exceptions to Homestead Exemption

The Florida Constitution recognizes three instances in which the homestead exemption does not protect otherwise qualifying property from forced sale, judicial process, or liens. First, the homestead exemption does not extend to obligations contracted for the purchase, improvement, or repair of the homestead. This exception exists to prevent an individual from borrowing funds to acquire, improve, or repair a home and then refusing repayment using the homestead exemption to defeat collection efforts. Few lenders would be willing to lend money for the purpose of acquiring, improving, or repairing a home if the homestead exemption effectively made repayment by the debtor optional.

Second, and for similar reasons, obligations contracted for labor performed on the homestead are excepted from homestead protections. Thus, individuals or entities that have enhanced the value of the homestead by the value of services rendered are permitted a collection remedy not available to other creditors.

Third, the homestead exemption is not applicable to taxes and assessments made on the homestead property. Even though federal taxes are not taxes "thereon" the homestead, the Supremacy Clause of the United States Constitution overrides the homestead exemption, permitting the federal government to sell, if necessary, the homestead of a delinquent taxpayer to satisfy a federal tax obligation.[23]

The exception to the homestead exemption for state taxes and assessments applies only to taxes and assessments on the homestead itself. Thus, a lien created as a result of an administrative fine imposed by a code enforcement board is not eligible for the exception.[24]

Although it is rare, courts have been known to exercise their equitable lien jurisdiction and impose liens on homestead property beyond the three specified constitutional exceptions. For example, courts have allowed an equitable lien on homestead property in cases where the owner of the property has used the proceeds from fraud or reprehensible conduct to invest in, purchase, or improve the homestead.[25] Additionally, some courts have allowed equitable liens where a former spouse has used the homestead exemption to avoid alimony and child support obligations.[26] Lastly, courts have imposed liens on homestead property when an owner has failed to pay homeowners' association assessments and the owner had actual or constructive notice of a covenant in the declaration that stated that failure to pay assessments would result in a continuing lien on the property.[27]

---

23. *Weitzner v. United States*, 309 F.2d 45 (5th Cir. 1962).

24. *Mathieu v. City of Lauderdale Lakes*, 961 So. 2d 363 (Fla. 4th Dist. Ct. App. 2007).

25. *Palm Beach Savings & Loan Ass'n v. Fishbein*, 619 So. 2d 267, 270 (Fla. 1993).

26. *Anderson v. Anderson*, 44 So. 2d 652 (Fla. 1950); *Partridge v. Partridge*, 912 So. 2d 649 (Fla. 4th Dist. Ct. App. 2005), *review denied*, 942 So. 2d 413 (Fla. 2006).

27. *Zerquera v. Centennial Homeowners' Ass'n, Inc.*, 752 So. 2d 694 (Fla. 3d Dist. Ct. App. 2000).

E. Inured Homestead Exemptions — Who Is an Heir?

The legal complexities generated by the homestead provisions arise from the concept of the "inured" homestead exemption created by the Florida Constitution. On the one hand, lawyers and judges frequently — and accurately — assert that a homestead terminates with the death of the owner. However, these same individuals are also frequently — and accurately — heard to assert that the homestead exemption which terminates on the owner's death inures to the spouse and/or heirs of the deceased owner. Not surprisingly, this distinction is lost on almost all laymen, and many lawyers.

This constitutional sleight of hand is occasioned by the language of Fla. Const. art. X, § 4(b). A homestead exemption which was created by an owner of property inures to the surviving spouse or heirs of the owner upon the owner's death. In other words, when the owner of a homestead dies, the homestead property passes directly to the surviving spouse or heir free of claims of the owner's creditors. Even though the homestead status of the property terminates upon the owner's death, the deceased owner's creditors cannot force the sale of the homestead. Simply stated, although the homestead terminates upon the death of the owner, the homestead exemption protecting the property from the deceased owner's creditors survives the owner's death if the homestead is distributed to the deceased owner's surviving spouse or heirs.

The operation of these provisions is perhaps best illustrated by example. Assume that Aaron and Ann Adams are a married couple without children. They reside in a home in Florida titled solely in Ann's name. Assume further that all other requirements of the law have been satisfied and the property qualifies as the couple's homestead. One of Ann's creditors has reduced a claim against Ann to a judgment. The judgment was rendered following the creation of the couple's homestead.

During Ann's life, her judgment creditor will be unable to execute the judgment against the homestead. Assume Ann dies leaving the title to the homestead to Aaron. Immediately upon Ann's death, the title to the homestead will vest in Aaron, but Ann's homestead will terminate. Despite the termination of the homestead, Ann's judgment creditor will be unable to execute the judgment against the property because Ann's homestead exemption will inure to the benefit of her surviving spouse, Aaron.

Further, a new homestead may be created when Aaron receives title to the property. This newly created homestead will also create an exemption protecting the property from most of Aaron's creditors.

The Florida Supreme Court has had frequent occasion to interpret the inured exemption provision in a variety of contexts.

Public Health Trust of Dade County v. Lopez

531 So. 2d 946 (Fla. 1988)

BARKETT, Justice.

We review the conflicting decisions of *Lopez v. Public Health Trust of Dade County*, 509 So.2d 1286 (Fla. 3d DCA 1987), and *In re Estate of Taylor*, 516 So.2d 322 (Fla. 2d DCA 1987). In so doing, we answer in the affirmative the following question posed in *Lopez*:

> Whether article X, section 4 of the Constitution of Florida, as amended, serves to exempt a decedent's homestead property from forced sale for the benefit of the decedent's creditors, where the decedent is not survived by a dependent spouse or children? [Footnote omitted.]

We have jurisdiction. Art. V, §§ 3(b)(3) and (4), Fla. Const.

The principal facts are not in dispute. In *Lopez*, the decedent homeowner, Nereida Lopez, at the time of her death, was residing in the home with her three adult children. The decedent's personal representatives petitioned the probate court to have the property set aside as homestead under article X, section 4 of the Florida Constitution. [Footnote omitted.] The petition was opposed by Public Health Trust, to whom the decedent was indebted. The trial court denied the petition based upon its finding that the decedent's heirs, her three adult children, were not dependent on her at the time of her death.

* * *

On this appeal, Public Health Trust, Gessler Clinic, and Winter Haven Hospital ("creditors") argue that article X, section 4(b), extending the homestead exemption to the "surviving spouse or heirs of the owner," must be construed to apply only to minor or dependent heirs. To support this interpretation, the creditors assert that under prior case law,[3] Florida's homestead exemption was not available to adult heirs of a decedent unless the heirs had been dependent on the decedent. They point to the history of the 1985 amendment as evidence that the legislature never intended to eliminate this requirement. The creditors also argue that a literal interpretation of section 4(b) would provide a windfall for financially independent heirs at the expense of the decedent's creditors, distorting the historical purpose of homestead laws to protect dependents in need of shelter.

In addition, Public Health Trust questions whether the amended provision protects the homes of all single persons and suggests that it applies only to those single persons who are surviving widows or divorced parents.

---

3. *E.g., Brown & Hutch*, 156 So.2d 683 (Fla. 2d DCA 1963), *cert. denied*, 162 So.2d 665 (Fla.1964); *Dana Bank v. Wilson & Toomer Fertilizer Co.*, 127 Fla. 45, 172 So. 476 (1937); *Whidden v. Abbott*, 124 Fla. 293, 168 So. 253 (1936); *In re Wilder's Estate*, 240 So.2d 514 (Fla. 1st DCA 1970); *In re Noble's Estate*, 73 So.2d 873 (Fla.1954); *Brady v. Brady*, 55 So.2d 907 (Fla.1950).

The personal representatives, on the other hand, argue that the language of the homestead exemption is clear and unambiguous; that the cases relied upon by the creditors are inapposite; and that the precise question presented already has been answered in their favor in *Miller v. Finegan*, 26 Fla. 29, 7 So. 140 (1890); *Scull v. Beatty*, 27 Fla. 426, 9 So. 4 (1891); and *Cumberland & Liberty Mills v. Keggin*, 139 Fla. 133, 190 So. 492 (1939).

For the reasons advanced by the personal representatives, we reject the creditors' position. For over a century, Florida has by constitutional provision made the homeplace exempt from the claims of creditors. *See Baker v. State*, 17 Fla. 406 (1879) (construing homestead provision of the Florida Constitution of 1868). As a matter of public policy, the purpose of the homestead exemption is to promote the stability and welfare of the state by securing to the householder a home, so that the homeowner and his or her heirs may live beyond the reach of financial misfortune and the demands of creditors who have given credit under such law. *See Bigelow v. Dunphe*, 143 Fla. 603, 197 So. 328 (1940).

Until 1985, the homestead protection was limited to those persons who qualified under the constitutionally designated term "head of a family." *See* art. X, § 4, Fla. Const. (1983). In 1984, however, the people of Florida approved an amendment changing the term "head of a family" to "a natural person." The amendment thus expanded the class of persons who can take advantage of the homestead provision and its protections.

As an initial matter, we reject Public Health Trust's suggestion that "natural person," when applied to single persons, means only widows and divorced parents. Such an interpretation is contrary to the language, logic and history of the amendment. As Representative Hawkins, who sponsored the amendment in the House of Representatives, explained, the purpose of the revision was "to give protection against forced sale for the homestead of a single person, a divorced person, any person who has a homestead, rather than just a head of a family." House Judiciary Full Committee Meeting, March 29, 1983.

The 1985 amendment thus made the homestead protection available to *any* natural person. Accordingly, the property and residences in question clearly fit within the definition of "homestead" under section 4(a)(1), as amended.

We turn then to the principal issue before us, the meaning and application of article X, section 4(b). The language of this provision is indeed plain and unambiguous. As the district court in *Lopez* noted:

> The amended section serves to exempt all homestead property from forced sale for the benefit of the decedent's heirs, regardless of whether the decedent was the head of a household prior to his or her death. As such, whether the decedent had dependent heirs at the time of her death is immaterial under the new amendment. Once it was established that the decedent owned and resided in the property at the time of her death, her estate was entitled to have the property set aside as homestead.

509 So.2d at 1286–87 (citations omitted).

As the creditors themselves point out, legislative intent controls construction of statutes in Florida.[4] Moreover, "that intent is determined primarily from the language of the statute [and] . . . [t]he plain meaning of the statutory language is the first consideration." *St. Petersburg Bank and Trust Co. v. Hamm*, 414 So.2d 1071, 1073 (Fla.1982) (citation omitted). . . .

The constitutional provision at issue is clear, reasonable and logical in its operation. Section 4(b) states, without any qualification, that the benefits "inure to the surviving spouse or heirs of the owner." There are no words suggesting that the heirs or surviving spouse had to have been dependent on the homeowner to enjoy this protection. Consequently, the creditors are not asking us merely to construe or interpret the amendment but rather to graft onto it something that is not there. This we cannot do. We are not permitted to attribute to the legislature an intent beyond that expressed, *see Bill Smith, Inc. v. Cox*, 166 So.2d 497, 498 (Fla. 2d DCA 1964), or to speculate about what should have been intended. *Tropical Coach Line v. Carter*, 121 So.2d 779, 782 (1960). Nor may we insert words or phrases in a constitutional provision, or supply an omission that was not in the minds of the people when the law was enacted. *See Brooks v. Anastasia Mosquito Control Dist.*, 148 So.2d 64, 66 (Fla. 1st DCA 1963). The legislature, and in this case, the people who adopted the amendment, must be held to have intended what was so plainly expressed.

We are fortified in our conclusion by the legislative history of the amendment. We have examined the materials submitted by the parties and find nothing in them even remotely suggesting that the legislature intended "surviving spouse or heirs" to mean "dependent spouse or heirs." Nor can we say that the people of Florida had any such limitation in mind. The Ballot Summary upon which the people voted said:

> EXEMPTION OF HOMESTEAD AND PERSONAL PROPERTY FROM FORCED SALE — Provides that the exemption of a homestead and of personal property to the value of $1,000 from forced sale and certain liens shall extend to any natural person, not just head of a family.

We conclude that neither the language nor the legislative history of the amendment supports the creditors' position.

* * *

Lastly, we reject the creditors' argument that a literal interpretation of section 4(b) will provide a windfall for financially independent heirs at the expense of the just demands of creditors. Even if we were free to ignore the plain language of the constitution, we would not be persuaded by this argument. The homestead protection has never been based upon principles of equity, *see Bigelow*, but always has

---

4. The principles governing constitution of statutes are generally applicable to the construction of constitutions. *City of Jacksonville v. Continental Can Co.*, 113 Fla. 168 171, 151 So. 488, 489 (1933); *State ex. rel. Moodie v. Bryan*, 50 Fla. 293, 385, 39 So. 929, 958 (1905).

been extended to the homesteader and, after his or her death, to the heirs whether the homestead was a twenty-two room mansion or a two-room hut and whether the heirs were rich or poor.

In sum, we conclude that the homestead exemption formerly only enjoyed by a head of a family can now be enjoyed by any natural person. The exemption continues after the homesteader's death without regard to whether the heirs were dependent on the homestead owner. Thus, the homestead descends directly to the spouse or heirs [footnote omitted] free and clear of creditor's claims.

* * *

It is so ordered.

OVERTON, EHRLICH, SHAW, and KOGAN, JJ., concur.

McDONALD, C.J., concurs in part and dissents in part with an opinion. [The opinion of Chief Justice McDonald is omitted.]

Snyder v. Davis

699 So. 2d 999 (Fla. 1997)

OVERTON, Justice.

We have for review the decision of the Second District Court of Appeal in *Davis v. Snyder*, 681 So.2d 1191 (Fla. 2d DCA 1996). The district court held that the testator could not both devise her homestead property to her granddaughter and preserve its exemption from creditors. The court found that while the homestead could be devised, the constitutional exemption from creditors would follow the homestead only if it were devised to the person or persons who would have actually taken the homestead had the testator died intestate. In this case the granddaughter would not have taken the homestead under the intestacy statutes because the testator's natural son was still alive at the death of the testator. *See* § 732.103, Fla. Stat. (1995). The court then certified the following question to be of great public importance:

> WHETHER ARTICLE X, SECTION 4, OF THE FLORIDA CONSTITU-
> TION EXEMPTS FROM FORCED SALE A DEVISE OF A HOMESTEAD
> BY A DECEDENT NOT SURVIVED BY A SPOUSE OR MINOR CHILD
> TO A LINEAL DESCENDANT WHO IS NOT AN HEIR UNDER THE
> DEFINITION IN SECTION 731.201(18), FLORIDA STATUTES (1993).

Id. at 1193. We have jurisdiction. Art. V, § 3(b)(4), Fla. Const.

For the reasons expressed, we answer the certified question in the affirmative and quash the district court's decision. We find that in these circumstances the word "heirs," when determining entitlement to the homestead protections against creditors, is not limited to only the person or persons who would actually take the homestead by law in intestacy on the death of the decedent. Instead, we hold that the constitution must be construed to mean that a testator, when drafting a will prior to death, may devise the homestead (if there is no surviving spouse or minor children)

8 · HOMESTEAD

to any of that class of persons categorized in section 732.103 (the intestacy statute). To hold otherwise would mean that a testator, when making an effort to avoid intestacy by drafting a will, would have to *guess* who his or her actual heirs[1] would be on the date of death in order to maintain the homestead's constitutional protections against creditors.

Facts

Betty Snyder died testate on February 15, 1995. In her will, she made the following dispositions:

> First, the expenses of my funeral, burial, or other disposition of my remains I may have directed, my just debts, and the costs of administering my estate shall be paid out of the residue of my estate.

> Second, I give, devise and make special provisions as follows:

> a. The sum of $3,000 to my son, MILO SNYDER, provided he survives me.

> b. The sum of $2,000 to my friends, JOE BEDRIN and BARBARA BEDRIN, or to the survivor of them.

> Third, I give and devise all the rest, residue, and remainder of my property of every kind and wherever situated, as follows: All to my granddaughter, KELLI SNYDER.

Betty Snyder was not survived by a spouse. She was, however, survived by her only son, Milo Snyder and his only daughter, Kelli Snyder. Both Milo and Kelli are adults.

Kent W. Davis, the personal representative of Betty Snyder's estate, sought to sell the homestead property to satisfy creditors' claims, to fund specific bequests, and to pay the costs of administration. Kelli Snyder, the residuary beneficiary, asserted that the testator's homestead passed to her free of claims because she was protected by article X, section 4, of the Florida Constitution (the homestead provision). The homestead provision reads, in relevant part, as follows:

> (a) There shall be exempt from forced sale under process of any court, and no judgment, decree, or execution shall be a lien thereon, except for the payment of taxes and assessments thereon, obligations contracted for the purchase, improvement or repair thereof, or obligations contracted for house, field or other labor performed on the realty, the following property owned by a natural person:

> (1) a homestead. . . .

> . . . .

---

1. Actual heirs are only determined upon death.

(b) These exemptions shall inure to the surviving spouse or *heirs of the owner.*

Art. X, § 4, Fla. Const. (emphasis added).

There is no dispute in this case that Betty Snyder's home was homestead property for the purpose of distribution or that said property was properly devised in the residuary clause of her will. The sole issue is whether Kelli Snyder, as the granddaughter, may be properly considered an heir under the homestead provision, qualifying her for protection from the forced sale of the homestead property when her father, the next-in-line heir under statutory intestate succession, is still living.

The personal representative argues that, had Betty Snyder died intestate, Kelli Snyder would not have qualified as an heir under the intestacy statute. He asserts that Milo Snyder, as the testator's son, would have been the sole taker of the homestead under the intestacy statute and, consequently, the homestead was not devised to an heir by Betty Snyder's will. Accordingly, he argues that the homestead property is not protected by the homestead provision and is subject to creditors' claims.

The trial judge disagreed with these assertions and found that the homestead provision protected the homestead from creditors in this case. The district court reversed, finding that because Milo Snyder would have been the sole heir had there been intestacy, Kelli Snyder is precluded from benefiting from the homestead provision's protections against creditors. In so finding, the district court explained its position as follows:

> Section 731.201(18) defines "heirs" as "those persons, including the surviving spouse, who are entitled under the statutes of intestate succession to the property of a decedent." While Kelli Snyder is a lineal descendant of her grandmother, the decedent's adult son, Milo Snyder, is the only member of the next generation of "lineal descendant." A reference to "heirs" is generally considered as referring to those who inherit under the laws of intestate succession. *See, e.g., Arnold v. Wells,* 100 Fla. 1470, 131 So. 400 (1930). If Betty Snyder had died *intestate,* Milo Snyder would have inherited everything as her "heir," i.e., next lineal descendant in line, and Kelli Snyder, under any construction of section 732.103, would have inherited nothing. This would be so because inheritance in Florida is "per stirpes." § 732.104, Fla. Stat. (1993). Because Milo Snyder survived, Kelli Snyder is not an intestate "heir" of her grandmother. Therefore, for purposes of the homestead exemption inuring to "the heir of the decedent," as defined by intestate succession, the exemption cannot inure to Kelli Snyder.

681 So.2d at 1193. We granted review in order to answer the certified question. We note, though, that we have an additional basis for jurisdiction because this district court opinion expressly and directly conflicts with *Walker v. Mickler,* 687 So.2d 1328 (Fla. 1st DCA 1997), *review granted,* No. 89,922, 696 So.2d 343 (Fla. June 12, 1997).

The circumstances under which a homestead may be devised while still retaining its protections against creditors present a significant issue for both the legal

8 · HOMESTEAD

profession and the public in general. All Floridians need to fully understand how their homestead property might be properly devised while still maintaining its protections against creditors (when there are no surviving spouses or minor children).[2]

The Homestead Provision

The homestead provision has been characterized as "our legal chameleon."[3] Our constitution protects Florida homesteads in three distinct ways. First, a clause, separate and apart from the homestead provision applicable in this case, provides homesteads with an exemption from taxes.[4] Second, the homestead provision protects the homestead from forced sale by creditors.[5] Third, the homestead provision delineates the restrictions a homestead owner faces when attempting to alienate or devise the homestead property.[6] This case involves the second and third protections described above.

Homestead law in the United States has evolved over time and it is strictly an American innovation. In Florida, moreover, our case law surrounding the homestead provision has its own contours and legal principles. As a result, it is not susceptible to comparisons with similar provisions in other jurisdictions. Importantly, our courts have emphasized that, in Florida, the homestead provision is in place to protect and preserve the interest of the family in the family home. We recently reaffirmed that general policy by stating:

> As a matter of public policy, the purpose of the homestead exemption is to promote the stability and welfare of the state by securing to the householder a home, so that the homeowner and his or her heirs may live beyond the reach of financial misfortune and the demands of creditors who have given credit under such law.

Public Health Trust v. Lopez, 531 So.2d 946, 948 (Fla.1988). Further, it is clear that the homestead provision is to be liberally construed in favor of maintaining the homestead property. *See Butterworth v. Caggiano*, 605 So.2d 56 (Fla.1992); *Hubert v. Hubert*, 622 So.2d 1049 (Fla. 4th DCA 1993); *Moore v. Rote*, 552 So.2d 1150 (Fla. 3d DCA 1989); *In re Estate of Skuro*, 467 So.2d 1098 (Fla. 4th DCA 1985), *approved*, 487

---

2. The issue was addressed in a recent publication from the Real Property, Probate, and Trust Law Section of the Florida Bar. Carlos A. Rodriguez, *Inurement of the Real Property Homestead Exemption to Devisees of the Owner*, XX Actionline 4 (April–May 1997).

3. Harold B. Crosby & George John Miller, *Our Legal Chameleon, the Florida Homestead Exemption: I–III*, 2 U. Fla. L.Rev. 12 (1949); Harold B. Crosby & George John Miller, *Our Legal Chameleon, the Florida Homestead Exemption: IV*, 2 U. Fla. L.Rev. 219 (1949); Harold B. Crosby & George John Miller, *Our Legal Chameleon, the Florida Homestead Exemption: V*, 2 U. Fla. L.Rev. 346 (1949); J. Allen Maines & Donna Litman Maines, *Our Legal Chameleon Revisited: Florida's Homestead Exemption* 30 U. Fla. L.Rev. 227 (1978); Donna Litman Seiden, *An Update on the Legal Chameleon: Florida's Homestead Exemption and Restrictions*, 40 U. Fla. L.Rev. 919 (1988).

4. *See* art. VII, § 6, Fla. Const.

5. *See id.* art. X, § 4(a)-(b).

6. *See id.* art. X, § 4(c).

So.2d 1065 (Fla.1986). As a matter of policy as well as construction, our homestead protections have been interpreted broadly.[7]

In addition, in 1984, the people further expanded homestead provision to substantially broaden the class of people eligible to take advantage of our homestead protections. While those protections had been previously limited to the "head of a family," they are now available to any "natural person." *Compare* art. X, § 4(a), Fla. Const.(1972) ("There shall be exempt from forced sale under process of any court ... the following property owned by the head of a family") *with* art. X, § 4(a), Fla. Const. ("There shall be exempt from forced sale under process of any court ... the following property owned by a natural person").

Finally, it is important to note that creditors are aware of the homestead provision and its inherent protections. As we discussed in *Public Health Trust*, we will not narrowly interpret the homestead provision simply because "financially independent heirs" may receive a windfall. 531 So.2d at 950. There we wrote:

> The homestead protection has never been based on principles of equity, *see Bigelow* [*v. Dunphe*, 143 Fla. 603, 197 So. 328 (1940)], but always has been extended to the homesteader and, after his or her death, to the heirs whether the homestead was a twenty-two room mansion or a two-room hut and whether the heirs were rich or poor.

Id. Creditors have been on notice for many years that the plain language of the constitution protects homestead property from most creditors.

It is with these policy considerations in mind that we address the two major issues in this case.

Devisees of a Homestead may be Entitled to the Homestead Provision's Protections Against Creditors

The first question we must resolve is whether the protection against creditors found in the homestead provision can be transferred, with a will, to a devisee. This Court has never addressed whether the term "heirs" in the homestead provision includes devisees.

Under the common law, an heir was a person designated to inherit in the event of intestacy at the death of the decedent. Now, however, "the term is frequently used in a popular sense to designate a successor to property either by will or by law." *Black's Law Dictionary* 724 (6th ed. 1990) ("Word 'heirs' is no longer limited to designated character of estate as at common law.") If we define the term "heirs" in the homestead provision by its strict common-law definition, the very act of devising the homestead would abolish the homestead protections against creditors. We refuse to construe the homestead provision in such a narrow way. In reaching this conclusion,

---

7. *See Tramel v. Stewart*, 697 So.2d 821 (Fla.1997) (liberally construing homestead provision in the face of a[n] [sic.] attempted forfeiture action against homestead property).

we are persuaded by the reasoning of the Third District Court of Appeal, sitting en banc, in *Bartelt v. Bartelt*, 579 So.2d 282 (Fla. 3d DCA 1991). That court addressed the situation in which the decedent, who died without a surviving spouse but with two surviving adult children, a son and a daughter, devised his homestead only to his son. There, the district court held that the homestead exemption passed to the devisee through the will even though the omitted child would have been entitled to an equal share of the homestead had the decedent died intestate. In so holding, the *Bartelt* court stated:

> When the decedent's homestead is devised to his son — a member of the class of persons who are the decedent's "heirs" — the constitutional exemption from forced sale by the decedent's creditors found in Article X, Section 4(b) of the Florida Constitution, inures to that son. The test is not how title was devolved, but rather to whom it passed. . . .
>
> The personal representative argues that, although "heirs" may avail themselves of the constitutional protection from creditors, "devisees" may not. Section 731.201(18), Florida Statutes (1989), defines heirs or heirs at law as "those persons . . . who are entitled under the statutes of intestate succession to the property of a decedent." Devisees are defined in section 731.201(9) as persons "designated in a will to receive a devise." According to the personal representative, a devisee cannot be an heir because a devisee takes by will and an heir takes only where there is no will. We disagree. Heirs, as defined in section 731.201(18), are simply those persons *entitled* to receive property under the laws of intestacy; the decedent's son, as his lineal descendant, is a member of that class. §732.103(1), Fla. Stat. (1989). The class designated as "heirs" does not *exclude* those who, *but for* the decedent's foresight in executing a will, would have taken by the laws of intestate succession. . . . Article X, section 4 of the Florida Constitution defines the class of persons to whom the decedent's exemption from forced sale of homestead property inures; it does not mandate the technique by which the qualified person must receive title.

Id. at 283–84. An academic commentator on this subject writes approvingly of the result reached by that district court:

> This author supports the *Bartelt* decision. The constitutional exemption from forced sale by creditors, as found in article X, §4(b) of the Florida Constitution, inures to the surviving spouse or heirs of the owner. *Bartelt* includes within the term "heirs" devisees who but for the will would have been heirs. It properly takes a broad gauged approach to the constitutional terminology. It places substance over form. The persons involved as takers are the same whether there is a will or there is not a will. The court points out that without such a determination, with respect to homestead, Florida residents would be discouraged from making wills and would be encouraged to let the property in issue pass by intestate succession. Such a result would be an anathema.

1 David T. Smith, *Florida Probate Code Manual* §4.05, at 29–30 (1995).

We agree that, in cases in which there is no surviving spouse or minor children, the protections against creditors found in the homestead provision may inure to the benefit of the person to whom the homestead property is devised by will. As explained below, though, the class of persons to which such protections may be devised is limited.

The Class of Devisees to Which the Protections Against Creditors Found in the Homestead Provision may be Devised

Having found that the protections against creditors found in the homestead provision may be devised by will, we now must define the scope of the class of persons to which those protections may be so devised. The *Davis* court and the *Walker* court present us with two alternatives. First, the *Davis* court defined the word "heirs" narrowly and found that, in order to preserve the protection against creditors, a devisee had to be entitled to inherit the homestead property under the intestacy statute. The *Walker* court applied a broader definition of the term "heirs." It held that the protections against creditors could be devised to any of the class of potential heirs under the intestacy statute. It found no occasion to require that a testator leave the homestead property to the actual person or persons who would have actually inherited under the intestacy statute. These two views of the term "heirs" can be characterized as the "entitlement definition" and the "class definition," respectively.

We are persuaded by the *Walker* court's view. In a situation almost identical to that in this *Davis* case, the First District Court held that a decedent's grandson was entitled to the homestead protection even though the grandson was not the closest consanguine heir. In doing so, the court found that any person categorized in the intestacy statute was an heir for the purpose of the homestead provision. In particular, it wrote:

> Article X, section 4(b) of the Florida Constitution provides that the exemptions and protections established for homestead property under article X, section 4(a) "shall inure to the surviving spouse or heirs of the owner." As this court explained in *State Department of Health and Rehabilitative Services v. Trammell*, 508 So.2d 422 (Fla. 1st DCA 1987), the term "heir" under article X, section 4(b) means "those who may under the laws of the state inherit from the owner of the homestead." *Id.* at 423, *quoting Shone v. Bellmore*, 75 Fla. 515, 78 So. 605, 607 (Fla.1918). Because Bavle, as the decedent's grandson, was a lineal descendent of the decedent, he is a member of the class of persons entitled to receive property under the laws of intestacy, *see* sections 732.103(1) and 732.401(1), Florida Statutes (1993), and accordingly, is an "heir" for the purposes of article X, section 4(b). *See, Bartelt v. Bartelt*, 579 So.2d 282, 283–4 [84] (Fla. 3d DCA 1991). A remainderman is entitled to claim a homestead exemption. *Hubert v. Hubert*, 622 So.2d 1049 (Fla. 4th DCA 1993), *rev. denied*, 634 So.2d 624 (Fla.1994).

687 So.2d at 1329.

The *Walker* court expressly rejected the holding of the *Davis* court. It wrote:

We find the *Davis* opinion contrary to the purpose of the homestead exemption from forced sale. We start with the well-established principle that the laws regarding homestead exemption are to be liberally construed. *Jetton Lumber Co. v. Hall*, 67 Fla. 61, 64 So. 440 (1914); and *In re Estate of Skuro*, 467 So.2d 1098 (Fla. 4th DCA 1985), *aff'd*, 487 So.2d 1065 (Fla.1986). Although the constitution is silent as to the intent of the drafters with respect to the rights of creditors of estates, we conclude that, as amended in 1984, article V, section 4(b), however, does reflect the intent that the exemption is to inure to whomever the homestead property passes.

Id. at 1330. The *Walker* court grounded its conclusion on the following policy consideration:

It seems clear to us that the intent of the homestead exemption is to protect the decedent's homestead from the decedent's creditors for the benefit of the decedent's heirs. To deny the exemption for a homestead property simply because the person chosen by the decedent to receive the property under the will, even though that person is within the class of persons entitled to take under the laws of intestate succession, is not the closest consanguine heir, is contrary to that constitutional intent.

Id. at 1331.

The *Walker* court, it seems to us, announces the correct view of our homestead provision. Indeed, the approach used by the *Davis* court would force a testator to guess as to his or her survivors in order to successfully devise, by will, the homestead property with the protections against creditors intact. That reading of our constitution is, in our view, unreasonable. If a severe limitation is to be placed on the ability of Floridians to keep the homestead within the family, it should not be done by a narrow judicial construction of the homestead provision.

We are reinforced in our view when the ramifications of the alternative position are considered. Under the *Davis* court's reasoning, an attorney would be faced with giving the following illogical advice to a potential testator with no surviving spouse or minor children:

You have two bad choices. You can devise your homestead to any person you choose. If you do, though, the homestead provision's protections against creditors will be inapplicable and your homestead may be subject to forced sale. On the other hand, you can guess as to which family members will survive you. After we have established the list of your guesses, I can tell you which of those family members would inherit under our intestacy statute. If you leave your homestead to those family members and they really do survive you, the homestead provision's protections against creditors will remain intact. If you guess incorrectly, though, the protections against creditors will be inapplicable. The point is this: If you want to ensure protection of the homestead property against creditors under our constitution, you have no choice as to which family member might best maintain your homestead property. The law requires that in order to utilize the homestead provision's protections against creditors, the homestead property must pass to the person or persons dictated by the intestacy statute.

Creating a system, by engaging a narrow judicial construction of the homestead provision, in which this type of advice must be given is unreasonable. Will-making, in these circumstances, becomes an act of prophecy. Clearly, as a policy matter, we should not be encouraging intestacy as a means of distributing one's property. In many instances where there is no surviving spouse or minor children, the homestead property is the most significant part of a testator's estate. If a testator loses control over the disposition of his or her homestead property, the need for a will is effectively eliminated. Such an approach takes away from the testator any ability to make a choice as to which family member will best preserve and maintain the family homestead. Instead, it promotes absolute adherence to the strict priorities found in the intestacy statute without paying any respect to the needs of individual testators and their families.

The whole purpose of the homestead provision is to protect and maintain the family homestead. The testator is likely in the best position to know which family member is most likely to need or to properly maintain the homestead. A plain reading of the homestead provision establishes that it only prohibits devising the homestead property when the testator is survived by a spouse or minor children. There is no prohibition against devising the homestead property to any of that class of persons who could potentially receive the homestead property under the intestacy statute. We must emphasize, however, that today's ruling does not authorize a testator to devise homestead property to any person not categorized by our intestacy statute with any expectation that the protections against creditors will survive such a devise. *See State Dep't of Health & Rehabilitative Servs. v. Trammell*, 508 So.2d 422 (Fla. 1st DCA 1987) (holding that a devise of homestead to a good friend does not qualify for the homestead exemption).

Conclusion

We have consistently made it clear that the homestead provision must be given a broad and liberal construction. In the context of this case, we reject the narrow entitlement definition of the term "heirs" that includes only those people who would inherit under the intestacy statute at the death of the decedent. Instead, we hold that the homestead provision allows a testator with no surviving spouse or minor children to choose to devise, in a will, the homestead property, with its accompanying protection from creditors, to any family member within the class of persons categorized in our intestacy statute.

Accordingly, we answer the certified question in the affirmative, quash the decision of the district court in *Davis*, and approve the district court's opinion in *Walker*.

It is so ordered.

KOGAN, C.J., and SHAW, WELLS and ANSTEAD, JJ., concur.

GRIMES, J., dissents with an opinion in which HARDING, J., concurs.

HARDING, J., dissents with an opinion.

[The dissenting opinions are omitted.]

In *McKean v. Warburton*,[28] a homestead owner died testate and was not survived by a spouse or minor children. In his will, the deceased homestead owner devised a large cash gift to his nephew. In the residuary clause of his will, the deceased homeowner left the "rest, residue and remainder" of his property to his four half-brothers. The cash assets of the estate were insufficient to satisfy the specific cash gift to the nephew. The nephew argued that the proceeds from the sale of the homestead should be used to satisfy the cash gift to him. The four half-brothers argued that the homestead property passed through the residuary clause of the will to them. The Florida Supreme Court held that because the deceased homeowner did not direct that the homestead be sold and the proceeds be made a part of the general estate, the homestead property passed through the residuary clause to the decedent's heirs, his four half-brothers, and was protected from forced sale to satisfy the cash devise to the nephew.

Because the decedent homeowner in *McKean* devised his homestead property to family members included in the class of persons under Florida's intestacy statute, i.e., his brothers, the homestead property was protected from the decedent's creditors. Had the deceased homeowner devised his property to someone not categorized in the intestacy statute, the homestead property would have lost its protected status.

F. Restrictions on Inter Vivos Transfers of Homestead Property

The Florida Constitution restricts the manner in which homestead property can be conveyed and encumbered. It is this provision which caused one appellate court to characterize a Florida homestead as a "sacred cow" that cannot be alienated contrary to the interests of those protected by the homestead.[29]

Under this provision, a married owner of homestead property may only alienate the homestead by mortgage, sale, or gift if his or her spouse joins in the alienation. The only exception to this rule is where the owner transfers by deed the title to the homestead to an estate by the entirety with his or her spouse. The following cases are illustrative.

---

28. 919 So. 2d 341 (Fla. 2005).

29. *Daniels v. Katz*, 237 So. 2d 58 (Fla. 3d Dist. Ct. App. 1970).

Jameson v. Jameson

387 So. 2d 351 (Fla. 1980)

OVERTON, Justice.

This case is before us on direct appeal from a decision of the Third District Court of Appeal, reported at 369 So.2d 436 (Fla.3d DCA 1979), which held that the Florida Constitution requires the spouse of a homestead owner to join in an interspousal conveyance of the homestead to the husband and wife as tenants by the entirety. In its opinion, the district court directly construed article X, section 4(c), of the Florida Constitution, to require spouse joinder and declared section 689.11(1), Florida Statutes, unconstitutional to the extent it would allow interspousal conveyance of the homestead without joinder. We have jurisdiction, article V, section 3(b)(1), and reverse.

We hold that article X, section 4(c), does not require joinder in an interspousal conveyance of solely owned homestead property to the husband and wife as tenants by the entirety, and find that section 689.11(1) is consistent with the constitutional provision as we construe it.

The relevant facts reflect that in 1974 Louis Jameson conveyed homestead property owned in his sole name to his wife, Martha Jameson, and himself as tenants by the entirety. Martha Jameson, the appellant, did not join in the conveyance. After Louis Jameson's death, his son, Edward, the appellee, filed a declaratory action seeking to have the conveyance declared null and void on grounds that there is a constitutional requirement of joinder in such a conveyance by the spouse. The circuit court agreed with this contention and entered a summary judgment voiding the deed. The district court affirmed and held that article X, section 4(c), "clearly requires joinder of the wife where there is an attempt to alienate homestead property." 369 So.2d at 437. Referring to the facts in the instant case, the district court stated:

> Here, the husband (by a deed not joined in by the wife) attempted to alienate his solely-owned homestead by creating in the parties a tenancy by the entireties. . . . [S]uch attempt collides with the homestead provisions of the Constitution by depriving the heirs of the husband of their constitutional right to take upon his demise. . . . [T]he provisions of the Constitution requiring joinder by the spouse should be required where there is an interspousal alienation of solely-owned homestead property.

Id. In reaching this conclusion, the district court determined such a holding was required by the "implied rationale" of our opinion in *Williams v. Foerster*, 335 So.2d 810 (Fla.1976).

The predecessor language to the present article X, section 4(c), was contained in the 1885 amendment to the constitution of the State of Florida in sections 1 and 4 of article X, which read as follows:

> SECTION 1. Exemption of homestead; extent. — A homestead to the extent of one hundred and sixty acres of land, or the half of one acre within the

limits of any incorporated city or town, owned by the head of a family residing in this State, together with one thousand dollars worth of personal property, and the improvements on the real estate, shall be exempt from forced sale under process of any court, and the real estate shall not be alienable without the joint consent of husband and wife, when that relation exists.

SECTION 4. Homestead may be alienated by husband and wife. — Nothing in this Article shall be construed to prevent the holder of a homestead from alienating his or her homestead so exempted by deed or mortgage duly executed by himself or herself, and by husband and wife, if such relation exists. . . .

These constitutional provisions were so construed as to prohibit the instant conveyance. *Byrd v. Byrd*, 73 Fla. 322, 74 So. 313 (1917); *see* Crosby and Miller, *Our Legal Chameleon, The Florida Homestead Exemption*, 2 U.Fla.L.Rev. 12, 64–67 (1949). Article X was changed in the constitutional revision of 1968, and section 4(c) was amended to read as follows:

The homestead shall not be subject to devise if the owner is survived by spouse or minor child. *The owner of homestead real estate, joined by the spouse if married, may alienate the homestead by mortgage, sale or gift and, if married, may by deed transfer the title to an estate by the entirety with the spouse.* If the owner or spouse is incompetent, the method of alienation or encumbrance shall be as provided by law. [Emphasis supplied.]

In 1972, this section was again amended, although the applicable sentence to the issue before us for decision remains the same as it was in the 1968 revision. The present section 4(c), as amended in 1972, reads as follows:

The homestead shall not be subject to devise if the owner is survived by spouse or minor child, except the homestead may be devised to the owner's spouse if there be no minor child. *The owner of homestead real estate, joined by the spouse if married, may alienate the homestead by mortgage, sale or gift and, if married, may by deed transfer the title to an estate by the entirety with the spouse.* If the owner or spouse is incompetent, the method of alienation or encumbrance shall be as provided by law. [Emphasis supplied.]

The critical language is the emphasized sentence, which we have not expressly construed in any prior case. The issue is whether this provision allows a husband who is the sole owner of the homestead to convey that homestead property to his wife and himself as a tenancy by the entireties without joinder by the wife as a grantor in the conveyance.

In its July 20, 1968, analysis of the instant provision, the Legislative Reference Bureau wrote that under the revision "the right of a married owner to directly transfer by deed the title of the homestead to himself and his spouse as an estate by the entirety would be given constitutional status." Similarly, two articles have expressed the view that the new provision no longer requires spousal joinder as a grantor in interspousal transfers of solely owned homestead property. One author has stated:

> The new constitution allows a gratuitous transfer of the homestead regardless of the grantee's status. Presumably, since no reference is made to the existence of children, this factor was not intended to impose a limitation on the provision. This conclusion is supported by: (1) the Florida supreme court's indication that under the 1885 constitution the existence of children was immaterial as to whether the requirement of consideration should be imposed in an intra-family conveyance, and (2) the court's rejection of the idea that the homesteader's children obtained a vested interest in the homestead.
>
> * * *
>
> The new constitution contains substantial changes regarding the joinder of husband and wife in transferring their homestead. The 1885 constitution's requirements of "joint consent of husband and wife" and that the "deed or mortgage [be] duly executed by himself or herself, and by husband and wife" do not appear in the new constitution. The 1968 constitution simply requires that the owner of the homestead be "joined by the spouse if married." While it is clear that both must join in a conveyance of a homestead owned by one spouse to a third party, the difficult question remains whether the grantee-spouse must join in an interspousal conveyance.
>
> Interspousal transfers commonly take two forms. The husband conveys his fee simple title either to the wife in fee simple or to himself and his wife as tenants by the entirety. The 1968 constitution provides:
>
>> The owner of homestead real estate, joined by the spouse if married, may alienate the homestead by mortgage, sale or gift and, if married, may by deed transfer the title to an estate by the entirety with the spouse.
>
> The section's meaning is unclear, but it seems to convey two separate thoughts: (1) the owner of homestead real estate, joined by the spouse if married, may alienate and (2) the owner of homestead real estate, if married, may by deed transfer the title to an estate by the entirety with the spouse.
>
> This interpretation appears to eliminate the requirement of joinder in a transfer by the owner of the homestead to himself and his wife as tenants by the entirety. [Footnotes omitted.]

Note, *Our Legal Chameleon is a Sacred Cow: Alienation of Homestead under the 1968 Constitution*, 24 U.Fla.L.Rev. 701, 705–07 (1972).

In the *Star Project Commentary* submitted to the 1978 Constitution Revision Commission, the portion pertaining to section 4(c) of article X states in part as follows:

> However, where homestead property is conveyed from a sole owner, not to a third party, but to the owner's spouse in fee simple, or where the sole owner

seeks to transfer to an estate by the entireties with the spouse, the present language may be read so as to eliminate the requirement for the signature of the non-owning spouse. Since the non-owning spouse is a party to the transaction (grantee) the spouse has effectively "joined" in the transfer by acquiescence and participation, although no formal execution was made. Furthermore, the structure of Subsection 4(c) leaves considerable doubt as to whether the phrase "joined by the spouse" is intended to apply to the remainder of the sentence, including transfers to estates by the entireties or merely alienations by mortgage sale or gift. The question is whether joinder means due execution in *all* transfers.

Background Papers in 1978 Constitution Revision Commission, Record Group 5, Series 263, Box 3, Florida State Archives. *See* Maines & Maines, *Our Legal Chameleon Revisited: Florida's Homestead Exemption,* 30 U.Fla.L.Rev. 227, 265–69 (1978).

The appellee in the instant case contends that joinder is required by the wife both to alienate the homestead by mortgage, sale, or gift, and to transfer the property from sole title in the husband to the husband and wife as tenants by the entirety. The district court of appeal agreed with this contention and interpreted the phrase "joined by the spouse" as applying to both the first and second clauses of the subject constitutional provision. We disagree. In our opinion the provision is more logically and reasonably interpreted if the joinder requirement is applied only to the alienation clause. In our view, a requirement of spousal joinder when that spouse is the grantee was not intended by the constitutional drafters, and is neither rational nor necessary to protect the homestead heirs.

The district court of appeal decision relies upon our decision in *Williams v. Foerster,* 335 So.2d 810 (Fla.1976). In that case the present constitutional provision was considered only inferentially because (1) the subject property was at the time of the conveyance owned by the husband and wife as tenants by the entireties and (2) the conveyance was made at a time when the 1885 constitutional provision was applicable. We held that the 1885 constitutional provision did not apply to an estate by the entireties occupied as a home of the parties, citing *Denham v. Sexton,* 48 So.2d 416 (Fla.1950). In so doing, we stated:

> The provisions of Article X, Section 4, of the 1885 Constitution, which Justice Sebring was construing, were in effect at the time the deed was made in the instant case. The same basic requirements are in our present constitutional provision. All the cases cited in the District Court opinion concern homestead property owned *solely* by the head of the household.

335 So.2d at 812. Much reliance was placed by the district court on this portion of our opinion, particularly the sentence stating that the same requirements are in our present constitutional provision. To eliminate any mistaken impression concerning our intent, we explain that this paragraph concluded there was no change between the 1885 constitutional provision and the 1972 constitutional provision *concerning the disposal of property which is held as a tenancy by the entirety.* By our *Williams*

decision we did not intend to adopt a rationale which would require joinder by the spouse where there is interspousal alienation of solely owned homestead property by conveyance to the spouses as a tenancy by the entirety.

Our construction and interpretation of the constitutional provision is in complete harmony with section 689.11, Florida Statutes. The legislature in its interpretation of the constitutional provision obviously believed that joinder is not constitutionally required in circumstances such as those in the instant case. Our conclusion is also in accordance with the authors of *Our Legal Chameleon* (1972) and the *Star Project Report* to the Constitution Revision Commission.

The decision of the district court of appeal is reversed and remanded with directions that the trial court vacate summary judgment and enter a judgment in accordance with the views expressed in this opinion.

It is so ordered.

SUNDBERG, C.J., and ADKINS, BOYD, ENGLAND, ALDERMAN, and McDONALD, JJ., concur.

Clemons v. Thornton

993 So. 2d 1054 (Fla. 1st Dist. Ct. App. 2008)

BENTON, Judge.

Ruth Clemons, the widow of W.C. Clemons, Jr., and her grandson, Lloyd Gilpin, Jr., appeal part of a summary judgment in favor of Joyce M. Thornton, a daughter of the late Mr. Clemons and his first wife, who is also deceased. At issue is whether a deed Mr. Clemons executed on February 23, 1993, after his marriage to Ruth, succeeded in conveying a remainder interest in the homestead he occupied with Ruth at the time. We reverse the summary judgment insofar as it declares the purported grant of the remainder interest effective, and remand for further proceedings.

The preprinted form warranty deed Mr. Clemons executed described the homestead property and named himself and "Ruth Clemons his wife" as grantees. But the deed contained a typewritten provision immediately following the property description, entitled "Addition to This Instrument," which stated:

> The parties of the second part, W.C. Clemons Jr. and Ruth Clemons Witness that the death of the last surviving party of the second part [sic] shall be cause to convey and confirm and assign forever all that certain parcel of land described above to Joyce M. Thornton.

Mr. Clemons died intestate some seven years later, survived by his widow and lineal descendants, including Joyce M. Thornton. By deed dated January 6, 2004, Mrs. Clemons purported to convey the property to herself and Lloyd Gilpin, Jr., her grandson. Ms. Thornton then sued for declaratory and other relief.

In the summary judgment under review, the trial court found that Mr. Clemons intended the deed to convey a life estate to himself and his wife, as tenants by the entireties, with, upon the death of the survivor of them, the remainder over to Joyce M. Thornton. This construction takes into account the language of the deed as a whole, and is the only plausible reading of the instrument considered in its entirety. *See Bronstein v. Bronstein,* 83 So.2d 699, 701 (Fla.1955) ("[I]f a contrary intention does appear in the deed then the fee simple character of the title conveyed is limited and controlled by the expressed contrary intention of the grantor."); *Sanderson v. Sanderson,* 70 So.2d 364, 366 (Fla.1954) (holding that in construing an instrument, "any apparently conflicting expressions should be reconciled, if possible, so as to give full effect to all provisions contained in the instrument"); *Loveland v. CSX Transp., Inc.,* 622 So.2d 1120, 1121 (Fla. 3d DCA 1993) (holding that, if there is only one construction that will permit all parts of the deed to be given effect, it should be followed). We perceive no basis on which to disturb the learned trial judge's construction of the deed as reflecting that "Mr. Clemons . . . intended to convey to himself and Mrs. Clemons a life estate in the property, and intended to convey to [Ms. Thornton] the vested remainder upon the death of the survivor of Mr. and Mrs. Clemons."

Mr. Clemons's grant of a life estate to himself and Mrs. Clemons as tenants by the entireties was a valid conveyance. *See Matthews v. McCain,* 125 Fla. 840, 170 So. 323, 325 (1936) (holding husband and wife may hold life estates as tenants by the entireties). Like the provision on the books today, section 689.11, Florida Statutes (1993), allowed conveyances of real property, including homestead property, between spouses, and did not require the grantee spouse to join in such conveyances. The summary judgment correctly confirms the existence of a life estate in Ruth Clemons, widow of her erstwhile cotenant by the entireties.

But Mr. Clemons's attempt to convey the remainder interest to Joyce M. Thornton was ineffective without Mrs. Clemons's joinder. Florida's Constitution requires that both spouses join in alienating homestead property in favor of any third party. *See* Art. X, § 4(c), Fla. Const. Interpreting the constitutional provision, our supreme court has noted that "it is clear that both [spouses] must join in a conveyance of a homestead owned by one spouse to a third party." *Jameson v. Jameson,* 387 So.2d 351, 353 (Fla.1980) (quoting Note, *Our Legal Chameleon is a Sacred Cow: Alienation of Homestead under the 1968 Constitution,* 24 U. Fla. L.Rev. 701, 705–07 (1972)). A purported transfer of the homestead, not in compliance with constitutional requirements, is void. *See Robbins v. Robbins,* 360 So.2d 10, 11–12 (Fla. 2d DCA 1978), *appeal dismissed,* 365 So.2d 714 (Fla.1978); *Gotshall v. Taylor,* 196 So.2d 479, 481 (Fla. 4th DCA 1967), *cert. denied,* 201 So.2d 558 (Fla.1967). Mr. Clemons's attempt to convey the remainder interest in the homestead to Ms. Thornton by the deed he executed on February 23, 1993, did not succeed, because Mrs. Clemons did not sign the deed.

The fate of the intended grant of the remainder interest has no bearing on the validity of the grant of the life estate. *See generally* W.W. Allen, Annotation, *Prior estate as affected by remainder void for remoteness,* 168 A.L.R. 321, 322 (1947) ("[P]rovisions of a . . . deed, valid in themselves, are as matter of course to be given effect notwithstanding the invalidity of other provisions, unless . . . to permit the valid to take effect without the invalid would produce results presumably objectionable to . . . [the] grantor."); *see also Leffler v. Leffler,* 151 Fla. 455, 10 So.2d 799, 804 (1942) (en banc) ("Where the will provides for successive estates the invalidity of one may not affect the others as for example, the invalidity of a trust in remainder may not affect the validity of a trust for the life tenant. . . .") (quoting Schouler on Wills, Executors and Administrators, Vol. 2, 6th ed., par. 902, pp. 1039–41).

Mr. Clemons retained the remainder interest as his sole property, because the deed was ineffective to convey it. The failure of Mr. Clemons's attempt to convey the remainder interest to Ms. Thornton redounded to the benefit, not of Mrs. Clemons, but of Mr. Clemons's lineal descendants, including Ms. Thornton. Only if Ms. Thornton (and her descendants, if any, *see* § 732.104, Fla. Stat. (2000) ("Descent shall be per stirpes. . . .")) had been Mr. Clemons's sole survivor(s), would the summary judgment be affirmable *in toto* — and she has pleaded the existence of other survivors. Upon his death, the remainder vested in his lineal descendants, per stirpes, pursuant to sections 732.104 and 732.401(1), Florida Statutes (2000).

Accordingly, we reverse the summary judgment insofar as it gives effect to the attempted conveyance of the remainder interest to Joyce M. Thornton by deed, and remand for a determination of Mr. Clemons's descendants in being at the time of his death, and for the grant of declaratory relief that takes their interest in the homestead property into account.

Reversed and remanded for further proceedings consistent with this opinion.

WEBSTER and POLSTON, JJ., concur.

The constitutional restriction requiring both spouses to join in the alienation of homestead property by mortgage, sale, or gift cannot be used to circumvent specific performance of a contract to sell homestead property where both spouses jointly executed the contract.[30]

G. Restrictions on the Devise of Homestead Property

The Florida Constitution also contains provisions restricting how homestead property may be devised. Under these provisions, if the owner of the homestead is survived by a spouse, or minor child, the property is not subject to devise.[31] However, if the owner is survived by a spouse but no minor children, the owner may devise the property to the surviving spouse.[32] Any such devise must be of the full property

------

30. *Mirzataheri v. FM East Developers, LLC,* 193 So. 3d 19 (Fla. 3d Dist. Ct. App. 2016).
31. Fla. Const. art. X, § 4(c).
32. *Id.*

interest of the homestead owner, with no limitations as to quality or quantity of the devised estate. Homestead property may be freely devised to anyone when the owner is not survived by a spouse or minor children.[33]

These constitutional provisions are supplemented by detailed statutory provisions. In fact, it is difficult to comprehend the application of the constitutional provisions without consideration of these supplemental statutes. To assist in the presentation, the alternative constitutional provisions will be discussed separately.

1. Homestead Owner Is Survived by Spouse and Minor Children

If the owner of homestead property dies and is survived by both a spouse and minor children, the constitution deprives the owner of the power to devise the property. Rather, the property will be distributed pursuant to the provisions of statute. Under Fla. Stat. § 732.401, if a decedent dies owning homestead property and is survived by a spouse and lineal descendants, the surviving spouse can elect to take a life estate in the homestead, with the lineal descendants of the deceased owner in being at the time of the decedent's death taking a vested remainder interest in the homestead. Alternatively, in lieu of a life estate, the surviving spouse may elect to take an undivided one-half interest in the homestead as a tenant in common, with the lineal descendants taking the remaining one-half undivided interest. This right of election for the surviving spouse is the result of an amendment to Fla. Stat. § 732.401 that became effective October 1, 2010. Prior to the effective date of the statutory amendment, the surviving spouse had no right of election and under the statute was required to take a life estate with the lineal descendants in being at the time of decedent's death taking a vested remainder.

2. Homestead Owner Is Survived by Spouse and No Minor Children

Fla. Const. art. X, § 4(c) permits the owner of a homestead to devise the homestead to the owner's spouse if there are no surviving children at the time of the owner's death. As in the preceding subsection, pervasive statutory supplementation of the constitutional provision renders the constitutional provision confusing unless it is considered in conjunction with these statutes. Under Florida law, where a deceased homestead owner is survived by a spouse, but no lineal descendants, the surviving spouse becomes the fee simple title holder of the property either by devise or operation of law.

This statement warrants closer examination. Assume that a homestead owner dies and is survived by a spouse, but no lineal descendants. First, assume that the

---

33. *City Nat'l Bank of Fla. v. Tescher*, 578 So. 2d 701, 703 (Fla. 1991).

homestead owner dies intestate. By operation of Fla. Stat. §732.102(1), the surviving spouse will become the fee simple title owner of the homestead as the sole intestate heir.

Next, assume that the deceased homestead owner dies having devised the property to the surviving spouse. Pursuant to Fla. Stat. §732.4015(1), the devise will be valid and the surviving spouse will become the fee simple title owner of the homestead by devise.

Finally, assume that the deceased homestead owner does not devise the homestead to a surviving spouse. Assume the homestead is devised to the owner's best friend. Because the deceased homestead owner is survived by a spouse, the devise to the friend is invalid under Fla. Const. art. X, §4(c), and Fla. Stat. §732.4015(1). Because the devise is invalid, the homestead will be distributed as intestate property under Fla. Stat. §732.401. As the deceased homestead owner died without lineal descendants, the surviving spouse will become the fee simple title owner of the property pursuant to Fla. Stat. §732.102(1).

One question that previously arose about this provision was whether a fee simple title had to be conveyed to satisfy the constitutional requirement, or whether a partial interest in property qualified. The following case resolved this issue.

In re Estate of Finch

401 So. 2d 1308 (Fla. 1981)

ADKINS, Justice.

We are asked to review the decision of the Fourth District Court of Appeal, reported at 383 So.2d 755, which passed on the validity and the compatibility of article X, section 4(c), of the Florida Constitution, and sections 732.4015 and 732.401(1), Florida Statutes (1977), relating to the devise of homestead property. We have jurisdiction. Art. V, §3(b)(3), Fla.Const. We affirm.

The parties involved concede that the real estate in question was homestead property and that the descent of such property is governed by article X, section 4(c) of the Florida Constitution. At the time of his death, decedent, John W. Finch, was survived by his spouse and his two adult daughters, petitioner and her half-sister. His will devised his condominium in Boca Raton, Florida, to his wife, Madeline F. Finch, for life with a vested remainder interest to petitioner, Judy Lynn Finch.

Mrs. Finch, respondent herein, moved to set aside the devise as homestead real estate. Her petition alleged that the property in question was homestead, that decedent was survived by a spouse and lineal descendants, and that the property should descend as provided in section 732.401(1), Florida Statutes . . .

* * *

Similarly, section 732.4015, Florida Statutes (1977), states:

> As provided by the Florida Constitution, the homestead shall not be subject to devise if the owner is survived by a spouse or minor child, except

that the homestead may be devised to the owner's spouse if there is no minor child.

If a devise violates the Florida Probate Code and constitution, it descends by way of intestate succession, pursuant to section 732.401(1), Florida Statutes . . .

* * *

The trial court considered the petition to set aside homestead and granted it over the objection of petitioner. On appeal, the district court affirmed.

Petitioner contends that the intent of the testator was to provide his wife with a life estate and the daughter of his choosing with a vested fee simple remainder interest, and that neither the statutes nor the constitution should frustrate this expressed intent. Furthermore, petitioner argues that neither the Florida Constitution, article X, section 4(c), nor section 732.4015, Florida Statutes, requires that the devise to the surviving spouse must be in fee simple absolute. We disagree with both of these contentions and adopt the position of the district court as our own. We hold, therefore:

> [W]here a testator dies leaving a surviving spouse and adult children, the property may not be devised by leaving less than a fee simple interest to the surviving spouse. The Constitution states, ". . . *except* the homestead may be devised to the owner's spouse if there be no minor children." This exception is exclusive and prohibits the testator from devising less than a fee simple interest to his surviving spouse under the circumstances presented herein. Since the devise here was not a permitted one under the Constitution, the property passed in accordance with section 732.401(1), Florida Statutes (1977).

383 So.2d at 757.

The opinion of the district court is approved.

We overrule the decision of the fifth district in *In Re Estate of Ritz*, 385 So.2d 1102 (Fla. 5th DCA 1980).

It is so ordered.

SUNDBERG, C.J., and BOYD, OVERTON, ENGLAND, ALDERMAN, and McDONALD, JJ., concur.

———————

In *Estate of Murphy*,[34] a deceased homestead owner was survived by a spouse and lineal descendants. The decedent's will did not specifically devise the homestead to the surviving spouse. The lineal descendants argued that because the homestead was not specifically devised to the surviving spouse, the homestead descended by operation of statute. The surviving spouse argued that the Constitution permitted the homestead to be devised to the surviving spouse, and that this was accomplished

———————

34. 340 So. 2d 107 (Fla. 1976).

by a residuary clause in favor of the surviving spouse. The Florida Supreme Court agreed with the surviving spouse.

Which law applies to a testator who executes a will containing a provision invalid under the homestead law existing at the time the will was drafted, but which provision is valid under the homestead law existing at the time the testator dies? In *Jones v. Jones*,[35] a Florida District Court of Appeal applied the traditional rule that the law in effect at the time of the testator's death was controlling.

Although the law does not favor the relinquishment of homestead rights, the courts have recognized that a surviving spouse could either disclaim his or her interest in the property or waive it pursuant to an antenuptial agreement.[36]

3. Homestead Owner Is Not Survived by Spouse or Minor Children

When a homestead owner is not survived by a spouse or minor children, the owner may freely devise the property to anyone. Should the homestead owner devise the property to someone other than an heir, the property loses homestead protection and becomes subject to the administrative expenses and claims of the owner's estate.

Webb v. Blue

243 So. 3d 1054 (Fla. 1st Dist. Ct. App. 2018)

JAY, J.

I.

On August 21, 2016, the decedent, Herbert Otis Daniell, died testate with no surviving spouse or children. The decedent's last will and testament, executed on February 26, 2013, named Judith D. Blue ("Appellee") as the personal representative and sole beneficiary. The will included the following provision: "My entire estate is all property I own at my death that is subject to this will. I leave my entire estate to Judith D. Blue."

On October 4, 2016, Appellee filed a petition for administration. The petition and an inventory listed two estate assets: (1) the decedent's non-exempt homestead (valued at $136,236.00); and (2) the decedent's truck (valued at $12,000.00).

On February 9, 2017, relatives of the decedent ("Appellants") filed a Petition to Determine Homestead Status of Real Property. The petition asserted the real property was the decedent's homestead and descended to the decedent's legitimate heirs where there was no specific intent in the will to pass the homestead property to

---

35. 412 So. 2d 387 (Fla. 2d Dist. Ct. App. 1982).

36. *See City Nat'l Bank of Fla. v. Tescher*, 578 So. 2d 701 (Fla. 1991); *In re Estate of Cleeves*, 509 So. 2d 1256 (Fla. 2d Dist. Ct. App. 1987).

Appellee, who was at most a friend rather than legal heir of the decedent. Appellee objected to the petition on the ground that the decedent claimed a homestead exemption for ad valorem taxation purposes, but devised the property without homestead protection. Appellants responded that the will was prepared by a non-attorney and did not contain the language required to include homestead property into the estate.

On March 15, 2017, the trial court rendered an order that, among other things, denied the Petition to Determine Homestead Status of Real Property. Specifically, the court found that the decedent was not survived by a spouse or minor child and that the decedent could freely devise his homestead to anyone. The court further found that the decedent's will very clearly stated his intention to leave his entire estate, including his homestead, to Appellee. This appeal followed.

II.

Article X, section 4(c) of the Florida Constitution provides in pertinent part:

(c) The homestead shall not be subject to devise if the owner is survived by spouse or minor child, except the homestead may be devised to the owner's spouse if there be no minor child.

This constitutional provision "'is designed to protect two classes of persons only: surviving spouses and minor children.'" *City Nat'l Bank of Fla. v. Tescher*, 578 So.2d 701, 703 (Fla. 1991) (quoting *Wadsworth v. First Union Nat'l Bank of Fla.*, 564 So.2d 634, 636 (Fla. 5th DCA 1990)). Moreover, this "restraint on the right of an individual to devise property at death should not be extended beyond that expressly allowed by the constitution." *Id.*

As a result, "[w]hen there are no surviving minor children and the surviving spouse has waived her homestead rights, there is no constitutional restriction on the devise of the homestead." *Stone v. Stone*, 157 So.3d 295, 304 (Fla. 4th DCA 2014). In *Stone*, because there were no minor children and because the wife waived her homestead rights, the decedent's adult son was not entitled to seek the protection of the homestead devise restrictions and the decedent was free to devise his interest in the homestead property — without any constitutional restriction — to his adult daughter. *Id.*

Similarly, here, because the decedent was not survived by a spouse or by minor children, there was no constitutional restriction on the devise of the homestead. Thus, the homestead could be devised to heirs — the class of persons who could be a beneficiary under the laws of intestacy — in order to maintain the homestead's protections against creditors. *Snyder v. Davis*, 699 So.2d 999, 1003–05 (Fla. 1997). Alternatively, the homestead could be devised to someone other than an heir, which would render the homestead a general asset of the estate subject to administrative expenses and claims. *Id.* at 1005 (citing *State, Dep't of Health & Rehab. Servs. v. Trammell*, 508 So.2d 422 (Fla. 1st DCA 1987)); *see also In re Estate of Hamel*, 821 So.2d 1276, 1279 (Fla. 2d DCA 2002) ("Florida courts have continued to hold that homestead does not become part of the probate estate unless a testamentary disposition is permitted and is made to someone other than an heir, i.e., a person to whom the benefit of homestead protection could not inure.").

"It is an elementary principle that a person can dispose of his or her property by will as he or she pleases so long as that person's intent is not contrary to any principle of law or public policy." *McKean v. Warburton*, 919 So.2d 341, 344 (Fla. 2005). "[O]nce the intent of the testator is ascertained, the entire will should be considered and construed liberally to effectuate the testator's intent." *Id.* The testator's intent to devise a homestead is "'that which is manifest, either expressly or by necessary implication, from the language of the will, as viewed, in case of ambiguity, in the light of the situation of the testator and the circumstances surrounding him at the time it was executed, although technical words are not used[.]'" *Pajares v. Donahue*, 33 So.3d 700, 702–03 (Fla. 4th DCA 2010) (quoting *Rewis v. Rewis* , 79 Fla. 126, 84 So. 93, 94 (1920)).

In this case, the decedent's will succinctly states: "My entire estate is all property I own at my death that is subject to this will. I leave my entire estate to Judith D. Blue." The first sentence simply means that the decedent's estate consists of all devisable property that the decedent owned at his death. Since it is undisputed that the decedent had no surviving spouse or minor children, the decedent's homestead constituted devisable property that the decedent owned at his death, rendering it part of the decedent's estate. Accordingly, the second sentence devised all of the decedent's estate — including his homestead — to Appellee.

Contrary to Appellants' assertions, there is no constitutional, statutory, or common law requirement that the decedent specifically devise his homestead to Appellee where the decedent is survived by heirs. Moreover, there is nothing in the decedent's will — or in the record — expressing the decedent's intent to leave his homestead to Appellants. Because it is undisputed that Appellee was merely a friend of the decedent, Appellee did not qualify as an heir under the laws of intestacy. *See Trammell*, 508 So.2d at 424 (holding that the decedent's "good friend" was not recognized as an heir under Florida law and was not entitled to the protection of the constitutional homestead provisions that exempt the decedent's property from forced sale). Thus, the trial court correctly concluded that the decedent's homestead became a part of the probate estate where a testamentary disposition was permitted and was made to someone other than an heir, i.e., a person to whom the benefit of homestead protection would not inure.

III.

Because the decedent's will expressed a clear intent to devise his homestead to Appellee, a non- heir, the homestead became part of the probate estate where the devise was permitted under article X, section 4(c). Accordingly, we affirm the trial court's denial of the Petition to Determine Homestead Status of Real Property as well as the court's other rulings challenged on appeal.

AFFIRMED.

B.L. THOMAS, C.J., and BILBREY, J., concur.

H. Jointly Held Property

The restrictions on the devise of homestead property do not apply to real property owned as tenants by the entireties or as joint tenants with right of survivorship because such property is not considered homestead property.[37] Real property owned as tenancy by the entireties or as joint tenants with the right of survivorship passes automatically to the surviving tenant by operation of property law upon the death of one tenant. Such property is, however, eligible for protection as homestead property from forced sale.

So far, this chapter has assumed a homestead owner possesses the right to either alienate his property during life or devise the same by will. The latter is, of course, only effective upon death. This fundamental assumption does not apply if an individual dies owning property with another cotenant subject to a right of survivorship. For example, assume that Mr. Williams and Mr. Clark own a parcel of property as joint tenants with a right of survivorship. Further assume that Mr. Williams resides on the property and the property qualifies as a homestead to Mr. Williams and his family. Under basic real property concepts, Mr. Williams will have a one-half interest in the property which will be homestead and eligible for the homestead exemption from Mr. Williams' creditors. However, upon Mr. Williams' death, with Mr. Clark surviving, Mr. Clark, by operation of law, will become the fee simple title owner of the property. The homestead restriction on devising homestead will not apply to Mr. Williams' estate because Mr. Williams' interest in the homestead is extinguished at his death.

The following case illustrates these points.

Marger v. DeRosa

57 So. 3d 866 (Fla. 2d Dist. Ct. App. 2011)

ALTENBERND, Judge.

Bruce Marger, as Administrator ad Litem for the Estate of Francis A. De Rosa, appeals the trial court's order determining that a house owned by the decedent as a joint tenant with the right of survivorship was not homestead property for purposes of the administration of his estate. We affirm.

In 1995, Mr. De Rosa and his mother, Harriet S. De Rosa, purchased a home in Largo, Florida. The warranty deed to the house states that Mr. De Rosa and his mother own it as "joint tenants with full right of survivorship and not as tenants in common." At the time of the conveyance, Mr. De Rosa had two minor children. When he died intestate in 2008, he had no surviving spouse, but he did have two minor children and one adult child.

---

37. Fla. Stat. § 731.201(33).

Harriet S. De Rosa claimed title to the property when her son died. Mr. Marger forcefully argues that the house should have homestead status for the benefit of the children. We conclude that the trial court correctly applied our precedent in *Ostyn v. Olympic,* 455 So.2d 1137 (Fla. 2d DCA 1984), in holding that the house was not homestead and became the sole property of Harriet S. De Rosa at the instant of her son's death.

In *Ostyn,* the decedent was unmarried when he executed a deed conveying his home to himself and three other family members as joint tenants with the right of survivorship. *Id.* at 1138. When he died eleven years later, he was survived by a niece who was the sole surviving joint tenant. He was also survived by a wife. The couple had lived in the home as husband and wife for seven years prior to his death. The trial court held that the wife was entitled to a life estate in the property because the property was homestead. Accordingly, the trial court ruled that the niece's interest in the property as a joint tenant was subject to the wife's life estate. *Id.*

This court reversed the trial court, "discern[ing] no basis for the trial judge's ruling." *Id.* We held that upon the decedent's death, his interest in the property terminated and that there was no property interest then owned by him to which a homestead interest could attach for the benefit of his wife.

Mr. Marger attempts to distinguish *Ostyn* on the basis that the decedent in *Ostyn* had no family when he took title to the property. He points out that when Mr. De Rosa took title to the house along with his mother, Mr. De Rosa had minor children. He argues that because Mr. De Rosa had children, the property was homestead when they took title to it. According to him, Mr. De Rosa and his mother's acquiring the property as joint tenants with right of survivorship was "a future devise of the homestead upon his death to a third party" — which the Florida Constitution prohibits. He further argues that because holding property as a joint tenant with right of survivorship cannot overcome the constitutional protection provided to homestead property, the deed at issue here was invalid. Under his theory, the constitution would prohibit a person with minor children from acquiring some types of real property as a joint tenant with the right of survivorship. We disagree.

Article X, section 4(c), of the Florida Constitution provides that "[t]he homestead shall not be subject to devise if the owner is survived by spouse or minor child." This language does not restrict the type of interests in real property a person may acquire or how a person may title his or her property. Instead, it restricts a person's attempt to devise property he or she owns when homestead status has attached to that property. Thus, even though Mr. De Rosa had children who were eligible for homestead protection at the time he purchased this property along with his mother, he was free to take the property as a joint tenant with the right of survivorship. In so doing, the property did not become homestead property when he and his mother purchased it. Thus, when Mr. De Rosa died, his interest in the property terminated, and it became the sole property of his mother as the surviving joint tenant without any life estate for the benefit of his children. If the circumstances had been reversed and Harriett S. De Rosa had died first, under the facts of this case, it would appear that homestead status would have attached to Mr. De Rosa's interest in the property at the instant of his mother's death. But those are not the facts of this case. Accordingly, we affirm the trial court's decision that this property was not a part of Mr. De Rosa's probate estate.

Affirmed.

DAVIS and MORRIS, JJ., Concur.

———————

The same basic principle will apply where a husband and wife own otherwise qualifying property as tenants by the entirety. During the couple's joint lives, the property will be eligible for protection from both spouses' creditors pursuant to the homestead exemption. However, upon the death of one spouse, the property will immediately descend to the surviving spouse by operation of law. As a result, the property will not be treated as homestead property for purposes of the limitations on the devise of homestead property.[38]

The same basic principle applies where property is held by tenants in common. Assume two individuals own property as tenants in common. One of the tenants resides on the property. The property otherwise qualifies as the resident tenant's homestead. The resident tenant's one-half interest in the homestead is protected from the resident tenant's creditors by the homestead exemption. Unlike property held with a right of survivorship upon the death of the resident tenant, the deceased's interest in the property is subject to the restriction on the devise of homestead property, because it does not pass by operation of law upon the death of the resident tenant.

Nonetheless, the nonresident tenant retains his or her property rights in the property, including the right to partition the property if necessary. This is true even though the property qualifies as homestead property to the resident tenant.[39]

I. Termination of Homestead

Once property acquires homestead status, the status continues until the homestead is either abandoned, validly devised, alienated, or otherwise legally transferred.[40] Continuous, uninterrupted, physical presence is not required to create or maintain a homestead.[41] Rather, a homestead is abandoned when the claimant has relinquished possession and has formed the intention of no longer using the property as a homestead.[42] In order for abandonment to occur, both the owner and the

———————

38. *See* Fla. Stat. § 731.201(33).

39. *See Tullis v. Tullis*, 360 So. 2d 375 (Fla. 1978).

40. *M.O. Logue Sod Serv., Inc. v. Logue*, 422 So. 2d 71 (Fla. 2d Dist. Ct. App. 1982).

41. *Id.*

42. *Brown v. Lewis*, 520 F. Supp. 1114 (M.D. Fla. 1981).

owner's family must have abandoned the homestead.[43] Abandonment is an issue of fact which must be determined from all evidence and inferences.[44]

In re Estate of Scholtz

543 So. 2d 219 (Fla. 1989)

GRIMES, Justice.

We review *In re Estate of Scholtz*, 525 So.2d 516 (Fla. 4th DCA 1988), in which the district court of appeal certified a question to be of great public importance. Our jurisdiction is predicated upon article V, section 3(b)(4), of the Florida Constitution.

John and Alice Scholtz were married in 1928. In 1956 they separated and have lived apart ever since. During their separation, John bought a piece of residential property which was titled solely in his name. He lived there until he moved to a nursing home shortly before his death. John left surviving his wife and one daughter. The trial court determined that the residential property was John's homestead. Relying upon its prior decision of *In re Estate of Boyd*, 519 So.2d 692 (Fla. 4th DCA), *review dismissed*, 525 So.2d 876 (Fla.1988), the district court of appeal affirmed and certified the following question to this Court:

> IS THE CONCEPT OF ABANDONMENT AS SET OUT IN BARLOW V. BARLOW STILL VIABLE IN VIEW OF THE 1985 AMENDMENT OF THE HOMESTEAD PROVISIONS OF THE FLORIDA CONSTITUTION?

525 So.2d at 517.

* * *

Prior to the 1985 amendment, Florida courts had held that under certain circumstances the surviving spouse would be deemed to have abandoned the homestead, thereby permitting the owner to devise the property despite the constitutional proscription. Thus, in *Barlow v. Barlow*, 156 Fla. 458, 23 So.2d 723 (1945), the wife left the home that was owned by her husband while his death was imminent. At the time she left, she told others that she had no intention of returning. After leaving she engaged counsel to procure a divorce. This Court held that the wife had abandoned the homestead and could not make a claim against it after her husband had died. The question before us is whether the concept of abandonment has survived the elimination of the head of the family language in article X, section 4.

In *Public Health Trust v. Lopez*, 531 So.2d 946 (Fla.1988), this Court addressed the effect of the 1985 amendment on the exemption of the homestead from forced sale provided in article X, section 4(a). The creditors argued that under case law prior to the amendment, the homestead exemption was not available to the adult heirs of a decedent unless the heirs were dependent upon the decedent. The creditors contended that a literal interpretation of the constitution would provide a windfall

---

43. *Beltran v. Kalb*, 63 So. 3d 783, 787 (Fla. 3d Dist. Ct. App. 2011).
44. *McGann v. Halker*, 530 So. 2d 440 (Fla. 3d Dist. Ct. App. 1988).

for financially independent heirs at the expense of the decedent's creditors, thereby distorting the historical purpose of the homestead laws to protect dependents in need of shelter. This Court ruled against the creditors, finding that the constitutional provision at issue was clear, reasonable, and logical in its operation. The Court said that it was fortified in its conclusion by the legislative history of the amendment. Finally, we concluded that homestead property always descended free of the claims of creditors without regard to whether the heirs were dependents. The Court pointed out that the cases relied upon by the creditors were ones in which it had been decided that the owner was not the head of the family at the time of his death.

Unlike the situation in *Lopez*, there is no legislative history surrounding the amendment to illustrate what its proponents had in mind with respect to the devise of homesteads. However, it is significant that effective upon the adoption of the 1985 amendment, the legislature repealed section 222.19(1), Florida Statutes (1983), which had provided that it was the declared intention of the legislature that the purpose of the constitutional exemption of the homestead was to shelter the family and the surviving spouse. At the same time, section 732.401, Florida Statutes (1985), which provides the means by which homesteads shall descend, remained unchanged.

Notwithstanding, the petitioner, who is the decedent's nephew, argues that the rationale for the prohibition against the devise of homestead property is for the protection of the surviving family and that when the family no longer resides together in the household, the reason for the prohibition no longer exists. Thus, petitioner argues that the concept of abandonment remains applicable despite the 1985 amendment. In response to such a contention, the district court of appeal in *In re Estate of Boyd* stated:

> It appears that the abandonment concept set out in *Barlow* and other cases was inextricably tied to the "head of household" requirement of the prior constitutional homestead scheme. The abandonment concept appears to be predicated on two possible bases. The first is that a homeowner whose spouse abandons him and sets up her own residence elsewhere with no intent of returning cannot be a "head of household" because there is no longer a family residing with him in the home. In that case, the property loses its homestead status by definition and the surviving spouse has no claim simply because there is no homestead. A second possible basis for *Barlow's* holding is the court's concern that it would be inequitable to allow a spouse who has "abandoned" the homestead to come back and claim it when her spouse dies. This equitable concern would also appear to be tied to the family unit definition of homestead. Even if it is not, however, we do not believe the courts have the authority to act upon such concerns no matter what the equities may be, in view of the clear and unequivocal language to the contrary in the constitutional and statutory homestead scheme.

519 So.2d at 692 (footnotes omitted).

We are compelled to agree with the district court of appeal. The concepts of abandonment and inequity that were part of the cases predating the 1985 amendment all related to the definition of homestead which contemplated a "head of the family." The constitution no longer contains these words and refers only to ownership of the property by a natural person.

Article X, section 4, must be read in its entirety. This Court has previously rejected the argument that the term homestead should be given a different definition under subparagraph (c) than that under subparagraphs (a) and (b). *Holden v. Estate of Gardner*, 420 So.2d 1082 (Fla.1982). While we may have some doubt about whether the proponents of the amendment considered its effect as related to the prohibition against the devise of homesteads, we are unable to state with any certainty that they did not intend the surviving spouse and the children to receive the homestead regardless of whether the family unit continued to exist at the time of the owner's death. In any event, the language of article X, section 4, is clear and unambiguous. The homestead may not be devised if the owner is survived by a spouse or minor child. Because John Scholtz died leaving a spouse, the descent of his property is controlled by section 732.401(1), Florida Statutes (1987).

We approve the decision of the district court of appeal.

It is so ordered.

SHAW, BARKETT, and KOGAN, JJ., concur.

McDONALD, J., concurs specially with an opinion.

EHRLICH, C.J., dissents with an opinion, in which OVERTON, J., concurs.

[These concurring and dissenting opinions are omitted.]

In *Dean v. Heimbach*,[45] the owner of homestead property was arrested on criminal charges. As a condition of his bail, he was required to stay outside the county where his homestead was located. After the resolution of his criminal problem, he intended to return to the homestead. The court concluded the homestead had not been abandoned because the owner's absence was temporary and he intended to return.

J. Homestead Summary

The convoluted world of Florida homestead law is perhaps best conceptualized graphically. A prominent Florida practitioner[46] has reduced the complexities of this area of law to a chart. This chart, which is reproduced on the following page, reorganizes the substantive points of law discussed in the preceding sections and may assist in a proper understanding of the subtleties of the homestead exemption.

---

45. 409 So. 2d 157 (Fla. 1st Dist. Ct. App. 1982).

46. The authors wish to thank Rohan Kelley of Fort Lauderdale, Florida, for permission to include "Kelley's Homestead Paradigm" in this publication.

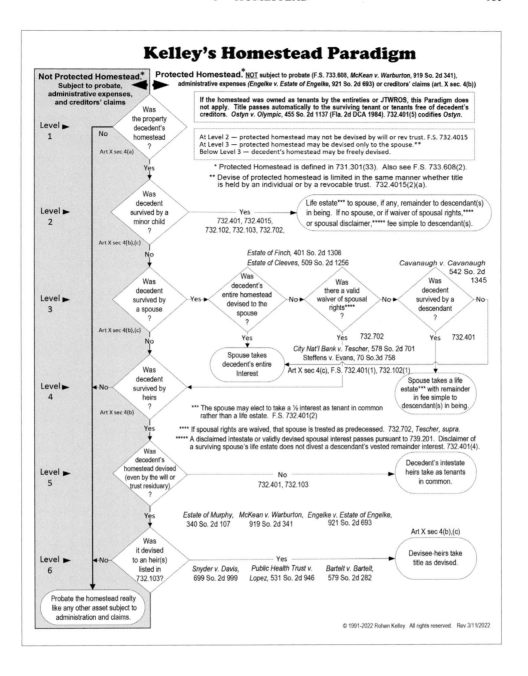

Constitution of the State of Florida

AS REVISED IN 1968 AND SUBSEQUENTLY AMENDED

The Constitution of the State of Florida as revised in 1968 consisted of certain revised articles as proposed by three joint resolutions which were adopted during the special session of June 24-July 3, 1968, and ratified by the electorate on November 5, 1968, together with one article carried forward from the Constitution of 1885, as amended. The articles proposed in House Joint Resolution 1-2X constituted the entire revised constitution with the exception of Articles V, VI, and VIII. Senate Joint Resolution 4-2X proposed Article VI, relating to suffrage and elections. Senate Joint Resolution 5-2X proposed a new Article VIII, relating to local government. Article V, relating to the judiciary, was carried forward from the Constitution of 1885, as amended.

Sections composing the 1968 revision have no history notes. Subsequent changes are indicated by notes appended to the affected sections. The indexes appearing at the beginning of each article, notes appearing at the end of various sections, and section and subsection headings are added editorially and are not to be considered as part of the constitution.

PREAMBLE

We, the people of the State of Florida, being grateful to Almighty God for our constitutional liberty, in order to secure its benefits, perfect our government, insure domestic tranquility, maintain public order, and guarantee equal civil and political rights to all, do ordain and establish this constitution.

ARTICLE I

DECLARATION OF RIGHTS

ARTICLE II

GENERAL PROVISIONS

ARTICLE III

LEGISLATURE

ARTICLE IV

EXECUTIVE

ARTICLE V

JUDICIARY

CONSTITUTION OF THE STATE OF FLORIDA

ARTICLE VI

SUFFRAGE AND ELECTIONS

ARTICLE VII

FINANCE AND TAXATION

ARTICLE VIII

LOCAL GOVERNMENT

ARTICLE IX

EDUCATION

ARTICLE X

MISCELLANEOUS

ARTICLE XI

AMENDMENTS

ARTICLE XII

SCHEDULE

ARTICLE I
DECLARATION OF RIGHTS

SECTION 1.

Political power.

SECTION 2.

Basic rights.

SECTION 3.

Religious freedom.

SECTION 4.

Freedom of speech and press.

SECTION 5.

Right to assemble.

SECTION 6.

Right to work.

SECTION 7.

Military power.

SECTION 8.

Right to bear arms.

SECTION 9.

Due process.

CONSTITUTION OF THE STATE OF FLORIDA

SECTION 10.

Prohibited laws.

SECTION 11.

Imprisonment for debt.

SECTION 12.

Searches and seizures.

SECTION 13.

Habeas corpus.

SECTION 14.

Pretrial release and detention.

SECTION 15.

Prosecution for crime; offenses committed by children.

SECTION 16.

Rights of accused and of victims.

SECTION 17.

Excessive punishments.

SECTION 18.

Administrative penalties.

SECTION 19.

Costs.

SECTION 20.

Treason.

SECTION 21.

Access to courts.

SECTION 22.

Trial by jury.

SECTION 23.

Right of privacy.

SECTION 24.

Access to public records and meetings.

SECTION 25.

Taxpayers' Bill of Rights.

SECTION 26.

Claimant's right to fair compensation.

SECTION 27.

Marriage defined.[1]

SECTION 1. Political power. — All political power is inherent in the people. The enunciation herein of certain rights shall not be construed to deny or impair others retained by the people.

SECTION 2. Basic rights. — All natural persons, female and male alike, are equal before the law and have inalienable rights, among which are the right to enjoy and defend life and liberty, to pursue happiness, to be rewarded for industry, and to acquire, possess and protect property. No person shall be deprived of any right because of race, religion, national origin, or physical disability.

History. — Am. S.J.R. 917, 1974; adopted 1974; Am. proposed by Constitution Revision Commission, Revision No. 9, 1998, filed with the Secretary of State May 5, 1998; adopted 1998; Am. proposed by Constitution Revision Commission, Revision No. 6, 2018, filed with the Secretary of State May 9, 2018; adopted 2018.

SECTION 3. Religious freedom. — There shall be no law respecting the establishment of religion or prohibiting or penalizing the free exercise thereof. Religious freedom shall not justify practices inconsistent with public morals, peace or safety. No revenue of the state or any political subdivision or agency thereof shall ever be taken from the public treasury directly or indirectly in aid of any church, sect, or religious denomination or in aid of any sectarian institution.

SECTION 4. Freedom of speech and press. — Every person may speak, write and publish sentiments on all subjects but shall be responsible for the abuse of that right. No law shall be passed to restrain or abridge the liberty of speech or of the press. In all criminal prosecutions and civil actions for defamation the truth may be given in evidence. If the matter charged as defamatory is true and was published with good motives, the party shall be acquitted or exonerated.

History. — Am. proposed by Constitution Revision Commission, Revision No. 13, 1998, filed with the Secretary of State May 5, 1998; adopted 1998.

SECTION 5. Right to assemble. — The people shall have the right peaceably to assemble, to instruct their representatives, and to petition for redress of grievances.

SECTION 6. Right to work. — The right of persons to work shall not be denied or abridged on account of membership or non-membership in any labor union or labor organization. The right of employees, by and through a labor organization, to bargain collectively shall not be denied or abridged. Public employees shall not have the right to strike.

SECTION 7. Military power. — The military power shall be subordinate to the civil.

SECTION 8. Right to bear arms. —

---

1. This provision has been ruled unconstitutional. *See Brenner v. Scott*, 999 F. Supp. 2d 1278 (N.D. Fla. 2014).

CONSTITUTION OF THE STATE OF FLORIDA 957

(a) The right of the people to keep and bear arms in defense of themselves and of the lawful authority of the state shall not be infringed, except that the manner of bearing arms may be regulated by law.

(b) There shall be a mandatory period of three days, excluding weekends and legal holidays, between the purchase and delivery at retail of any handgun. For the purposes of this section, "purchase" means the transfer of money or other valuable consideration to the retailer, and "handgun" means a firearm capable of being carried and used by one hand, such as a pistol or revolver. Holders of a concealed weapon permit as prescribed in Florida law shall not be subject to the provisions of this paragraph.

(c) The legislature shall enact legislation implementing subsection (b) of this section, effective no later than December 31, 1991, which shall provide that anyone violating the provisions of subsection (b) shall be guilty of a felony.

(d) This restriction shall not apply to a trade in of another handgun.

History. — Am. C.S. for S.J.R. 43, 1989; adopted 1990.

SECTION 9. Due process. — No person shall be deprived of life, liberty or property without due process of law, or be twice put in jeopardy for the same offense, or be compelled in any criminal matter to be a witness against oneself.

History. — Am. proposed by Constitution Revision Commission, Revision No. 13, 1998, filed with the Secretary of State May 5, 1998; adopted 1998.

SECTION 10. Prohibited laws. — No bill of attainder, ex post facto law or law impairing the obligation of contracts shall be passed.

SECTION 11. Imprisonment for debt. — No person shall be imprisoned for debt, except in cases of fraud.

SECTION 12. Searches and seizures. — The right of the people to be secure in their persons, houses, papers and effects against unreasonable searches and seizures, and against the unreasonable interception of private communications by any means, shall not be violated. No warrant shall be issued except upon probable cause, supported by affidavit, particularly describing the place or places to be searched, the person or persons, thing or things to be seized, the communication to be intercepted, and the nature of evidence to be obtained. This right shall be construed in conformity with the 4th Amendment to the United States Constitution, as interpreted by the United States Supreme Court. Articles or information obtained in violation of this right shall not be admissible in evidence if such articles or information would be inadmissible under decisions of the United States Supreme Court construing the 4th Amendment to the United States Constitution.

History. — Am. H.J.R. 31-H, 1982; adopted 1982.

SECTION 13. Habeas corpus. — The writ of habeas corpus shall be grantable of right, freely and without cost. It shall be returnable without delay, and shall never be suspended unless, in case of rebellion or invasion, suspension is essential to the public safety.

SECTION 14. **Pretrial release and detention.** — Unless charged with a capital offense or an offense punishable by life imprisonment and the proof of guilt is evident or the presumption is great, every person charged with a crime or violation of municipal or county ordinance shall be entitled to pretrial release on reasonable conditions. If no conditions of release can reasonably protect the community from risk of physical harm to persons, assure the presence of the accused at trial, or assure the integrity of the judicial process, the accused may be detained.

History. — Am. H.J.R. 43-H, 1982; adopted 1982.

SECTION 15. **Prosecution for crime; offenses committed by children.** —

(a) No person shall be tried for capital crime without presentment or indictment by a grand jury, or for other felony without such presentment or indictment or an information under oath filed by the prosecuting officer of the court, except persons on active duty in the militia when tried by courts martial.

(b) When authorized by law, a child as therein defined may be charged with a violation of law as an act of delinquency instead of crime and tried without a jury or other requirements applicable to criminal cases. Any child so charged shall, upon demand made as provided by law before a trial in a juvenile proceeding, be tried in an appropriate court as an adult. A child found delinquent shall be disciplined as provided by law.

SECTION 16. **Rights of accused and of victims.** —

(a) In all criminal prosecutions the accused shall, upon demand, be informed of the nature and cause of the accusation, and shall be furnished a copy of the charges, and shall have the right to have compulsory process for witnesses, to confront at trial adverse witnesses, to be heard in person, by counsel or both, and to have a speedy and public trial by impartial jury in the county where the crime was committed. If the county is not known, the indictment or information may charge venue in two or more counties conjunctively and proof that the crime was committed in that area shall be sufficient; but before pleading the accused may elect in which of those counties the trial will take place. Venue for prosecution of crimes committed beyond the boundaries of the state shall be fixed by law.

(b) To preserve and protect the right of crime victims to achieve justice, ensure a meaningful role throughout the criminal and juvenile justice systems for crime victims, and ensure that crime victims' rights and interests are respected and protected by law in a manner no less vigorous than protections afforded to criminal defendants and juvenile delinquents, every victim is entitled to the following rights, beginning at the time of his or her victimization:

(1) The right to due process and to be treated with fairness and respect for the victim's dignity.

(2) The right to be free from intimidation, harassment, and abuse.

(3) The right, within the judicial process, to be reasonably protected from the accused and any person acting on behalf of the accused. However, nothing contained

CONSTITUTION OF THE STATE OF FLORIDA

herein is intended to create a special relationship between the crime victim and any law enforcement agency or office absent a special relationship or duty as defined by Florida law.

(4) The right to have the safety and welfare of the victim and the victim's family considered when setting bail, including setting pretrial release conditions that protect the safety and welfare of the victim and the victim's family.

(5) The right to prevent the disclosure of information or records that could be used to locate or harass the victim or the victim's family, or which could disclose confidential or privileged information of the victim.

(6) A victim shall have the following specific rights upon request:

a. The right to reasonable, accurate, and timely notice of, and to be present at, all public proceedings involving the criminal conduct, including, but not limited to, trial, plea, sentencing, or adjudication, even if the victim will be a witness at the proceeding, notwithstanding any rule to the contrary. A victim shall also be provided reasonable, accurate, and timely notice of any release or escape of the defendant or delinquent, and any proceeding during which a right of the victim is implicated.

b. The right to be heard in any public proceeding involving pretrial or other release from any form of legal constraint, plea, sentencing, adjudication, or parole, and any proceeding during which a right of the victim is implicated.

c. The right to confer with the prosecuting attorney concerning any plea agreements, participation in pretrial diversion programs, release, restitution, sentencing, or any other disposition of the case.

d. The right to provide information regarding the impact of the offender's conduct on the victim and the victim's family to the individual responsible for conducting any presentence investigation or compiling any presentence investigation report, and to have any such information considered in any sentencing recommendations submitted to the court.

e. The right to receive a copy of any presentence report, and any other report or record relevant to the exercise of a victim's right, except for such portions made confidential or exempt by law.

f. The right to be informed of the conviction, sentence, adjudication, place and time of incarceration, or other disposition of the convicted offender, any scheduled release date of the offender, and the release of or the escape of the offender from custody.

g. The right to be informed of all postconviction processes and procedures, to participate in such processes and procedures, to provide information to the release authority to be considered before any release decision is made, and to be notified of any release decision regarding the offender. The parole or early release authority shall extend the right to be heard to any person harmed by the offender.

h. The right to be informed of clemency and expungement procedures, to provide information to the governor, the court, any clemency board, and other authority in these procedures, and to have that information considered before a clemency or expungement decision is made; and to be notified of such decision in advance of any release of the offender.

(7) The rights of the victim, as provided in subparagraph (6)a., subparagraph (6) b., or subparagraph (6)c., that apply to any first appearance proceeding are satisfied by a reasonable attempt by the appropriate agency to notify the victim and convey the victim's views to the court.

(8) The right to the prompt return of the victim's property when no longer needed as evidence in the case.

(9) The right to full and timely restitution in every case and from each convicted offender for all losses suffered, both directly and indirectly, by the victim as a result of the criminal conduct.

(10) The right to proceedings free from unreasonable delay, and to a prompt and final conclusion of the case and any related postjudgment proceedings.

a. The state attorney may file a good faith demand for a speedy trial and the trial court shall hold a calendar call, with notice, within fifteen days of the filing demand, to schedule a trial to commence on a date at least five days but no more than sixty days after the date of the calendar call unless the trial judge enters an order with specific findings of fact justifying a trial date more than sixty days after the calendar call.

b. All state-level appeals and collateral attacks on any judgment must be complete within two years from the date of appeal in non-capital cases and within five years from the date of appeal in capital cases, unless a court enters an order with specific findings as to why the court was unable to comply with this subparagraph and the circumstances causing the delay. Each year, the chief judge of any district court of appeal or the chief justice of the supreme court shall report on a case-by-case basis to the speaker of the house of representatives and the president of the senate all cases where the court entered an order regarding inability to comply with this subparagraph. The legislature may enact legislation to implement this subparagraph.

(11) The right to be informed of these rights, and to be informed that victims can seek the advice of an attorney with respect to their rights. This information shall be made available to the general public and provided to all crime victims in the form of a card or by other means intended to effectively advise the victim of their rights under this section.

(c) The victim, the retained attorney of the victim, a lawful representative of the victim, or the office of the state attorney upon request of the victim, may assert and seek enforcement of the rights enumerated in this section and any other right afforded to a victim by law in any trial or appellate court, or before any other

CONSTITUTION OF THE STATE OF FLORIDA 961

authority with jurisdiction over the case, as a matter of right. The court or other authority with jurisdiction shall act promptly on such a request, affording a remedy by due course of law for the violation of any right. The reasons for any decision regarding the disposition of a victim's right shall be clearly stated on the record.

(d) The granting of the rights enumerated in this section to victims may not be construed to deny or impair any other rights possessed by victims. The provisions of this section apply throughout criminal and juvenile justice processes, are self-executing, and do not require implementing legislation. This section may not be construed to create any cause of action for damages against the state or a political subdivision of the state, or any officer, employee, or agent of the state or its political subdivisions.

(e) As used in this section, a "victim" is a person who suffers direct or threatened physical, psychological, or financial harm as a result of the commission or attempted commission of a crime or delinquent act or against whom the crime or delinquent act is committed. The term "victim" includes the victim's lawful representative, the parent or guardian of a minor, or the next of kin of a homicide victim, except upon a showing that the interest of such individual would be in actual or potential conflict with the interests of the victim. The term "victim" does not include the accused. The terms "crime" and "criminal" include delinquent acts and conduct.

History. — Am. S.J.R. 135, 1987; adopted 1988; Am. proposed by Constitution Revision Commission, Revision No. 13, 1998, filed with the Secretary of State May 5, 1998; adopted 1998; Am. proposed by Constitution Revision Commission, Revision No. 1, 2018, filed with the Secretary of State May 9, 2018; adopted 2018.

SECTION 17. Excessive punishments. — Excessive fines, cruel and unusual punishment, attainder, forfeiture of estate, indefinite imprisonment, and unreasonable detention of witnesses are forbidden. The death penalty is an authorized punishment for capital crimes designated by the legislature. The prohibition against cruel or unusual punishment, and the prohibition against cruel and unusual punishment, shall be construed in conformity with decisions of the United States Supreme Court which interpret the prohibition against cruel and unusual punishment provided in the Eighth Amendment to the United States Constitution. Any method of execution shall be allowed, unless prohibited by the United States Constitution. Methods of execution may be designated by the legislature, and a change in any method of execution may be applied retroactively. A sentence of death shall not be reduced on the basis that a method of execution is invalid. In any case in which an execution method is declared invalid, the death sentence shall remain in force until the sentence can be lawfully executed by any valid method. This section shall apply retroactively.

History. — Am. H.J.R. 3505, 1998; adopted 1998; Am. H.J.R. 951, 2001; adopted 2002.

SECTION 18. Administrative penalties. — No administrative agency, except the Department of Military Affairs in an appropriately convened court-martial action as provided by law, shall impose a sentence of imprisonment, nor shall it impose any other penalty except as provided by law.

History. — Am. proposed by Constitution Revision Commission, Revision No. 13, 1998, filed with the Secretary of State May 5, 1998; adopted 1998.

SECTION 19. Costs. — No person charged with crime shall be compelled to pay costs before a judgment of conviction has become final.

SECTION 20. Treason. — Treason against the state shall consist only in levying war against it, adhering to its enemies, or giving them aid and comfort, and no person shall be convicted of treason except on the testimony of two witnesses to the same overt act or on confession in open court.

SECTION 21. Access to courts. — The courts shall be open to every person for redress of any injury, and justice shall be administered without sale, denial or delay.

SECTION 22. Trial by jury. — The right of trial by jury shall be secure to all and remain inviolate. The qualifications and the number of jurors, not fewer than six, shall be fixed by law.

SECTION 23. Right of privacy. — Every natural person has the right to be let alone and free from governmental intrusion into the person's private life except as otherwise provided herein. This section shall not be construed to limit the public's right of access to public records and meetings as provided by law.

History. — Added, C.S. for H.J.R. 387, 1980; adopted 1980; Am. proposed by Constitution Revision Commission, Revision No. 13, 1998, filed with the Secretary of State May 5, 1998; adopted 1998.

SECTION 24. Access to public records and meetings. —

(a) Every person has the right to inspect or copy any public record made or received in connection with the official business of any public body, officer, or employee of the state, or persons acting on their behalf, except with respect to records exempted pursuant to this section or specifically made confidential by this Constitution. This section specifically includes the legislative, executive, and judicial branches of government and each agency or department created thereunder; counties, municipalities, and districts; and each constitutional officer, board, and commission, or entity created pursuant to law or this Constitution.

(b) All meetings of any collegial public body of the executive branch of state government or of any collegial public body of a county, municipality, school district, or special district, at which official acts are to be taken or at which public business of such body is to be transacted or discussed, shall be open and noticed to the public and meetings of the legislature shall be open and noticed as provided in Article III, Section 4(e), except with respect to meetings exempted pursuant to this section or specifically closed by this Constitution.

(c) This section shall be self-executing. The legislature, however, may provide by general law passed by a two-thirds vote of each house for the exemption of records

CONSTITUTION OF THE STATE OF FLORIDA 963

from the requirements of subsection (a) and the exemption of meetings from the requirements of subsection (b), provided that such law shall state with specificity the public necessity justifying the exemption and shall be no broader than necessary to accomplish the stated purpose of the law. The legislature shall enact laws governing the enforcement of this section, including the maintenance, control, destruction, disposal, and disposition of records made public by this section, except that each house of the legislature may adopt rules governing the enforcement of this section in relation to records of the legislative branch. Laws enacted pursuant to this subsection shall contain only exemptions from the requirements of subsections (a) or (b) and provisions governing the enforcement of this section, and shall relate to one subject.

(d) All laws that are in effect on July 1, 1993 that limit public access to records or meetings shall remain in force, and such laws apply to records of the legislative and judicial branches, until they are repealed. Rules of court that are in effect on the date of adoption of this section that limit access to records shall remain in effect until they are repealed.

History. — Added, C.S. for C.S. for H.J.R.'s 1727, 863, 2035, 1992; adopted 1992; Am. S.J.R. 1284, 2002; adopted 2002.

[1]**SECTION 25. Taxpayers' Bill of Rights.** — By general law the legislature shall prescribe and adopt a Taxpayers' Bill of Rights that, in clear and concise language, sets forth taxpayers' rights and responsibilities and government's responsibilities to deal fairly with taxpayers under the laws of this state. This section shall be effective July 1, 1993.

History. — Proposed by Taxation and Budget Reform Commission, Revision No. 2, 1992, filed with the Secretary of State May 7, 1992; adopted 1992.

[1]**Note.** — This section, originally designated section 24 by Revision No. 2 of the Taxation and Budget Reform Commission, 1992, was redesignated section 25 by the editors in order to avoid confusion with section 24 as contained in H.J.R.'s 1727, 863, 2035, 1992.

SECTION 26. Claimant's right to fair compensation. —

(a) Article I, Section 26 is created to read "Claimant's right to fair compensation." In any medical liability claim involving a contingency fee, the claimant is entitled to receive no less than 70% of the first $250,000.00 in all damages received by the claimant, exclusive of reasonable and customary costs, whether received by judgment, settlement, or otherwise, and regardless of the number of defendants. The claimant is entitled to 90% of all damages in excess of $250,000.00, exclusive of reasonable and customary costs and regardless of the number of defendants. This provision is self-executing and does not require implementing legislation.

(b) This Amendment shall take effect on the day following approval by the voters.

History. — Proposed by Initiative Petition filed with the Secretary of State September 8, 2003; adopted 2004.

964   CONSTITUTION OF THE STATE OF FLORIDA

SECTION 27. Marriage defined. — Inasmuch as marriage is the legal union of only one man and one woman as husband and wife, no other legal union that is treated as marriage or the substantial equivalent thereof shall be valid or recognized.[2]

History. — Proposed by Initiative Petition filed with the Secretary of State February 9, 2005; adopted 2008.

ARTICLE II
GENERAL PROVISIONS

SECTION 1.

State boundaries.

SECTION 2.

Seat of government.

SECTION 3.

Branches of government.

SECTION 4.

State seal and flag.

SECTION 5.

Public officers.

SECTION 6.

Enemy attack.

SECTION 7.

Natural resources and scenic beauty.

SECTION 8.

Ethics in government.

SECTION 9.

English is the official language of Florida.

SECTION 1. State boundaries. —

(a) The state boundaries are: Begin at the mouth of the Perdido River, which for the purposes of this description is defined as the point where latitude 30°16'53" north and longitude 87°31'06" west intersect; thence to the point where latitude 30°17'02" north and longitude 87°31'06" west intersect; thence to the point where latitude 30°18'00" north and longitude 87°27'08" west intersect; thence to the point where the center line of the Intracoastal Canal (as the same existed on June 12, 1953) and longitude 87°27'00" west intersect; the same being in the middle of the Perdido River; thence up the middle of the Perdido River to the point where it intersects

---

2. This provision has been ruled unconstitutional. *See Brenner v. Scott*, 999 F. Supp. 2d 1278 (N.D. Fla. 2014).

CONSTITUTION OF THE STATE OF FLORIDA   965

the south boundary of the State of Alabama, being also the point of intersection of the middle of the Perdido River with latitude 31°00'00" north; thence east, along the south boundary line of the State of Alabama, the same being latitude 31°00'00" north to the middle of the Chattahoochee River; thence down the middle of said river to its confluence with the Flint River; thence in a straight line to the head of the St. Marys River; thence down the middle of said river to the Atlantic Ocean; thence due east to the edge of the Gulf Stream or a distance of three geographic miles whichever is the greater distance; thence in a southerly direction along the edge of the Gulf Stream or along a line three geographic miles from the Atlantic coastline and three leagues distant from the Gulf of Mexico coastline, whichever is greater, to and through the Straits of Florida and westerly, including the Florida reefs, to a point due south of and three leagues from the southernmost point of the Marquesas Keys; thence westerly along a straight line to a point due south of and three leagues from Loggerhead Key, the westernmost of the Dry Tortugas Islands; thence westerly, northerly and easterly along the arc of a curve three leagues distant from Loggerhead Key to a point due north of Loggerhead Key; thence northeast along a straight line to a point three leagues from the coastline of Florida; thence northerly and westerly three leagues distant from the coastline to a point west of the mouth of the Perdido River three leagues from the coastline as measured on a line bearing south 0°01'00" west from the point of beginning; thence northerly along said line to the point of beginning. The State of Florida shall also include any additional territory within the United States adjacent to the Peninsula of Florida lying south of the St. Marys River, east of the Perdido River, and south of the States of Alabama and Georgia.

(b) The coastal boundaries may be extended by statute to the limits permitted by the laws of the United States or international law.

SECTION 2. Seat of government. — The seat of government shall be the City of Tallahassee, in Leon County, where the offices of the governor, lieutenant governor, cabinet members and the supreme court shall be maintained and the sessions of the legislature shall be held; provided that, in time of invasion or grave emergency, the governor by proclamation may for the period of the emergency transfer the seat of government to another place.

SECTION 3. Branches of government. — The powers of the state government shall be divided into legislative, executive and judicial branches. No person belonging to one branch shall exercise any powers appertaining to either of the other branches unless expressly provided herein.

SECTION 4. State seal and flag. — The design of the great seal and flag of the state shall be prescribed by law.

SECTION 5. Public officers. —

(a) No person holding any office of emolument under any foreign government, or civil office of emolument under the United States or any other state, shall hold any office of honor or of emolument under the government of this state. No person shall hold at the same time more than one office under the government of the state and the counties and municipalities therein, except that a notary public or military officer may hold another office, and any officer may be a member of a constitution revision commission, taxation and budget reform commission, constitutional convention, or statutory body having only advisory powers.

(b) Each state and county officer, before entering upon the duties of the office, shall give bond as required by law, and shall swear or affirm:

"I do solemnly swear (or affirm) that I will support, protect, and defend the Constitution and Government of the United States and of the State of Florida; that I am duly qualified to hold office under the Constitution of the state; and that I will well and faithfully perform the duties of _(title of office)_ on which I am now about to enter. So help me God.", and thereafter shall devote personal attention to the duties of the office, and continue in office until a successor qualifies.

(c) The powers, duties, compensation and method of payment of state and county officers shall be fixed by law.

History. — Am. H.J.R. 1616, 1988; adopted 1988; Am. proposed by Constitution Revision Commission, Revision No. 13, 1998, filed with the Secretary of State May 5, 1998; adopted 1998.

SECTION 6. Enemy attack. — In periods of emergency resulting from enemy attack the legislature shall have power to provide for prompt and temporary succession to the powers and duties of all public offices the incumbents of which may become unavailable to execute the functions of their offices, and to adopt such other measures as may be necessary and appropriate to insure the continuity of governmental operations during the emergency. In exercising these powers, the legislature may depart from other requirements of this constitution, but only to the extent necessary to meet the emergency.

SECTION 7. Natural resources and scenic beauty. —

(a) It shall be the policy of the state to conserve and protect its natural resources and scenic beauty. Adequate provision shall be made by law for the abatement of air and water pollution and of excessive and unnecessary noise and for the conservation and protection of natural resources.

(b) Those in the Everglades Agricultural Area who cause water pollution within the Everglades Protection Area or the Everglades Agricultural Area shall be primarily responsible for paying the costs of the abatement of that pollution. For the purposes of this subsection, the terms "Everglades Protection Area" and "Everglades Agricultural Area" shall have the meanings as defined in statutes in effect on January 1, 1996.

(c) To protect the people of Florida and their environment, drilling for exploration or extraction of oil or natural gas is prohibited on lands beneath all state waters which have not been alienated and that lie between the mean high water line and the outermost boundaries of the state's territorial seas. This prohibition does not apply

CONSTITUTION OF THE STATE OF FLORIDA

to the transportation of oil and gas products produced outside of such waters. This subsection is self-executing.

History. — Am. by Initiative Petition filed with the Secretary of State March 26, 1996; adopted 1996; Am. proposed by Constitution Revision Commission, Revision No. 5, 1998, filed with the Secretary of State May 5, 1998; adopted 1998; Am. proposed by Constitution Revision Commission, Revision No. 4, 2018, filed with the Secretary of State May 9, 2018; adopted 2018.

[1]**SECTION 8. Ethics in government.** — A public office is a public trust. The people shall have the right to secure and sustain that trust against abuse. To assure this right:

(a) All elected constitutional officers and candidates for such offices and, as may be determined by law, other public officers, candidates, and employees shall file full and public disclosure of their financial interests.

(b) All elected public officers and candidates for such offices shall file full and public disclosure of their campaign finances.

(c) Any public officer or employee who breaches the public trust for private gain and any person or entity inducing such breach shall be liable to the state for all financial benefits obtained by such actions. The manner of recovery and additional damages may be provided by law.

(d) Any public officer or employee who is convicted of a felony involving a breach of public trust shall be subject to forfeiture of rights and privileges under a public retirement system or pension plan in such manner as may be provided by law.

(e) No member of the legislature or statewide elected officer shall personally represent another person or entity for compensation before the government body or agency of which the individual was an officer or member for a period of two years following vacation of office. No member of the legislature shall personally represent another person or entity for compensation during term of office before any state agency other than judicial tribunals. Similar restrictions on other public officers and employees may be established by law.

(f) There shall be an independent commission to conduct investigations and make public reports on all complaints concerning breach of public trust by public officers or employees not within the jurisdiction of the judicial qualifications commission.

(g)(1) A code of ethics for all state employees and nonjudicial officers prohibiting conflict between public duty and private interests shall be prescribed by law.

(2) A public officer or public employee shall not abuse his or her public position in order to obtain a disproportionate benefit for himself or herself; his or her spouse, children, or employer; or for any business with which he or she contracts; in which he or she is an officer, a partner, a director, or a proprietor; or in which he or she owns an interest. The Florida Commission on Ethics shall, by rule in accordance with statutory procedures governing administrative rulemaking, define the term "disproportionate benefit" and prescribe the requisite intent for finding a violation

of this prohibition for purposes of enforcing this paragraph. Appropriate penalties shall be prescribed by law.

(h) This section shall not be construed to limit disclosures and prohibitions which may be established by law to preserve the public trust and avoid conflicts between public duties and private interests.

(i) Schedule — On the effective date of this amendment and until changed by law:

(1) Full and public disclosure of financial interests shall mean filing with the custodian of state records by July 1 of each year a sworn statement showing net worth and identifying each asset and liability in excess of $1,000 and its value together with one of the following:

a. A copy of the person's most recent federal income tax return; or

b. A sworn statement which identifies each separate source and amount of income which exceeds $1,000. The forms for such source disclosure and the rules under which they are to be filed shall be prescribed by the independent commission established in subsection (f), and such rules shall include disclosure of secondary sources of income.

(2) Persons holding statewide elective offices shall also file disclosure of their financial interests pursuant to subsection (i)(1).

(3) The independent commission provided for in subsection (f) shall mean the Florida Commission on Ethics.

History. — Proposed by Initiative Petition filed with the Secretary of State July 29, 1976; adopted 1976; Ams. proposed by Constitution Revision Commission, Revision Nos. 8 and 13, 1998, filed with the Secretary of State May 5, 1998; adopted 1998; Am. proposed by Constitution Revision Commission, Revision No. 7, 2018, filed with the Secretary of State May 9, 2018; adopted 2018.

[1]**Note.** — Section 38, Art. XII, State Constitution, provides in part that "[t]he amendments to Section 8 of Article II and Section 13 of Article V shall take effect December 31, 2022; except that the amendments to Section 8(h) [currently s. 8(g)] of Article II shall take effect December 31, 2020." The amendments to s. 8, Art. II, which take effect December 31, 2022, include the addition of a new subsection (f), which will result in the redesignation of subsequent subsections. **Effective December 31, 2022, s. 8, Art. II, State Constitution, will read:**

SECTION 8. Ethics in government. — A public office is a public trust. The people shall have the right to secure and sustain that trust against abuse. To assure this right:

(a) All elected constitutional officers and candidates for such offices and, as may be determined by law, other public officers, candidates, and employees shall file full and public disclosure of their financial interests.

(b) All elected public officers and candidates for such offices shall file full and public disclosure of their campaign finances.

CONSTITUTION OF THE STATE OF FLORIDA

(c) Any public officer or employee who breaches the public trust for private gain and any person or entity inducing such breach shall be liable to the state for all financial benefits obtained by such actions. The manner of recovery and additional damages may be provided by law.

(d) Any public officer or employee who is convicted of a felony involving a breach of public trust shall be subject to forfeiture of rights and privileges under a public retirement system or pension plan in such manner as may be provided by law.

(e) No member of the legislature or statewide elected officer shall personally represent another person or entity for compensation before the government body or agency of which the individual was an officer or member for a period of two years following vacation of office. No member of the legislature shall personally represent another person or entity for compensation during term of office before any state agency other than judicial tribunals. Similar restrictions on other public officers and employees may be established by law.

(f)(1) For purposes of this subsection, the term "public officer" means a statewide elected officer, a member of the legislature, a county commissioner, a county officer pursuant to Article VIII or county charter, a school board member, a superintendent of schools, an elected municipal officer, an elected special district officer in a special district with ad valorem taxing authority, or a person serving as a secretary, an executive director, or other agency head of a department of the executive branch of state government.

(2) A public officer shall not lobby for compensation on issues of policy, appropriations, or procurement before the federal government, the legislature, any state government body or agency, or any political subdivision of this state, during his or her term of office.

(3) A public officer shall not lobby for compensation on issues of policy, appropriations, or procurement for a period of six years after vacation of public position, as follows:

a. A statewide elected officer or member of the legislature shall not lobby the legislature or any state government body or agency.

b. A person serving as a secretary, an executive director, or other agency head of a department of the executive branch of state government shall not lobby the legislature, the governor, the executive office of the governor, members of the cabinet, a department that is headed by a member of the cabinet, or his or her former department.

c. A county commissioner, a county officer pursuant to Article VIII or county charter, a school board member, a superintendent of schools, an elected municipal officer, or an elected special district officer in a special district with ad valorem taxing authority shall not lobby his or her former agency or governing body.

(4) This subsection shall not be construed to prohibit a public officer from carrying out the duties of his or her public office.

(5) The legislature may enact legislation to implement this subsection, including, but not limited to, defining terms and providing penalties for violations. Any such law shall not contain provisions on any other subject.

(g) There shall be an independent commission to conduct investigations and make public reports on all complaints concerning breach of public trust by public officers or employees not within the jurisdiction of the judicial qualifications commission.

(h)(1) A code of ethics for all state employees and nonjudicial officers prohibiting conflict between public duty and private interests shall be prescribed by law.

(2) A public officer or public employee shall not abuse his or her public position in order to obtain a disproportionate benefit for himself or herself; his or her spouse, children, or employer; or for any business with which he or she contracts; in which he or she is an officer, a partner, a director, or a proprietor; or in which he or she owns an interest. The Florida Commission on Ethics shall, by rule in accordance with statutory procedures governing administrative rulemaking, define the term "disproportionate benefit" and prescribe the requisite intent for finding a violation of this prohibition for purposes of enforcing this paragraph. Appropriate penalties shall be prescribed by law.

(i) This section shall not be construed to limit disclosures and prohibitions which may be established by law to preserve the public trust and avoid conflicts between public duties and private interests.

(j) Schedule — On the effective date of this amendment and until changed by law:

(1) Full and public disclosure of financial interests shall mean filing with the custodian of state records by July 1 of each year a sworn statement showing net worth and identifying each asset and liability in excess of $1,000 and its value together with one of the following:

a. A copy of the person's most recent federal income tax return; or

b. A sworn statement which identifies each separate source and amount of income which exceeds $1,000. The forms for such source disclosure and the rules under which they are to be filed shall be prescribed by the independent commission established in subsection (g), and such rules shall include disclosure of secondary sources of income.

(2) Persons holding statewide elective offices shall also file disclosure of their financial interests pursuant to paragraph (1).

(3) The independent commission provided for in subsection (g) shall mean the Florida Commission on Ethics.

SECTION 9. English is the official language of Florida. —

(a) English is the official language of the State of Florida.

(b) The legislature shall have the power to enforce this section by appropriate legislation.

CONSTITUTION OF THE STATE OF FLORIDA 971

History. — Proposed by Initiative Petition filed with the Secretary of State August 8, 1988; adopted 1988.

ARTICLE III
LEGISLATURE

SECTION 1.

Composition.

SECTION 2.

Members; officers.

SECTION 3.

Sessions of the legislature.

SECTION 4.

Quorum and procedure.

SECTION 5.

Investigations; witnesses.

SECTION 6.

Laws.

SECTION 7.

Passage of bills.

SECTION 8.

Executive approval and veto.

SECTION 9.

Effective date of laws.

SECTION 10.

Special laws.

SECTION 11.

Prohibited special laws.

SECTION 12.

Appropriation bills.

SECTION 13.

Term of office.

SECTION 14.

Civil service system.

SECTION 15.

Terms and qualifications of legislators.

SECTION 16.

Legislative apportionment.

SECTION 17.

Impeachment.

SECTION 18.

Conflict of Interest.

SECTION 19.

State Budgeting, Planning and Appropriations Processes.

SECTION 20.

Standards for establishing congressional district boundaries.

SECTION 21.

Standards for establishing legislative district boundaries.

SECTION 1. Composition. — The legislative power of the state shall be vested in a legislature of the State of Florida, consisting of a senate composed of one senator elected from each senatorial district and a house of representatives composed of one member elected from each representative district.

SECTION 2. Members; officers. — Each house shall be the sole judge of the qualifications, elections, and returns of its members, and shall biennially choose its officers, including a permanent presiding officer selected from its membership, who shall be designated in the senate as President of the Senate, and in the house as Speaker of the House of Representatives. The senate shall designate a Secretary to serve at its pleasure, and the house of representatives shall designate a Clerk to serve at its pleasure. The legislature shall appoint an auditor to serve at its pleasure who shall audit public records and perform related duties as prescribed by law or concurrent resolution.

SECTION 3. Sessions of the legislature. —

(a) ORGANIZATION SESSIONS. On the fourteenth day following each general election the legislature shall convene for the exclusive purpose of organization and selection of officers.

(b) REGULAR SESSIONS. A regular session of the legislature shall convene on the first Tuesday after the first Monday in March of each odd-numbered year, and on the second Tuesday after the first Monday in January of each even-numbered year.

(c) SPECIAL SESSIONS.

(1) The governor, by proclamation stating the purpose, may convene the legislature in special session during which only such legislative business may be transacted as is within the purview of the proclamation, or of a communication from the governor, or is introduced by consent of two-thirds of the membership of each house.

CONSTITUTION OF THE STATE OF FLORIDA

(2) A special session of the legislature may be convened as provided by law.

(d) LENGTH OF SESSIONS. A regular session of the legislature shall not exceed sixty consecutive days, and a special session shall not exceed twenty consecutive days, unless extended beyond such limit by a three-fifths vote of each house. During such an extension no new business may be taken up in either house without the consent of two-thirds of its membership.

(e) ADJOURNMENT. Neither house shall adjourn for more than seventy-two consecutive hours except pursuant to concurrent resolution.

(f) ADJOURNMENT BY GOVERNOR. If, during any regular or special session, the two houses cannot agree upon a time for adjournment, the governor may adjourn the session sine die or to any date within the period authorized for such session; provided that, at least twenty-four hours before adjourning the session, and while neither house is in recess, each house shall be given formal written notice of the governor's intention to do so, and agreement reached within that period by both houses on a time for adjournment shall prevail.

History. — Am. C.S. for S.J.R. 380, 1989; adopted 1990; Am. S.J.R. 2606, 1994; adopted 1994; Am. proposed by Constitution Revision Commission, Revision No. 13, 1998, filed with the Secretary of State May 5, 1998; adopted 1998; Am. proposed by Constitution Revision Commission, Revision No. 5, 2018, filed with the Secretary of State May 9, 2018; adopted 2018.

SECTION 4. Quorum and procedure. —

(a) A majority of the membership of each house shall constitute a quorum, but a smaller number may adjourn from day to day and compel the presence of absent members in such manner and under such penalties as it may prescribe. Each house shall determine its rules of procedure.

(b) Sessions of each house shall be public; except sessions of the senate when considering appointment to or removal from public office may be closed.

(c) Each house shall keep and publish a journal of its proceedings; and upon the request of five members present, the vote of each member voting on any question shall be entered on the journal. In any legislative committee or subcommittee, the vote of each member voting on the final passage of any legislation pending before the committee, and upon the request of any two members of the committee or subcommittee, the vote of each member on any other question, shall be recorded.

(d) Each house may punish a member for contempt or disorderly conduct and, by a two-thirds vote of its membership, may expel a member.

(e) The rules of procedure of each house shall provide that all legislative committee and subcommittee meetings of each house, and joint conference committee meetings, shall be open and noticed to the public. The rules of procedure of each house shall further provide that all prearranged gatherings, between more than two members of the legislature, or between the governor, the president of the senate, or the speaker of the house of representatives, the purpose of which is to agree upon formal legislative action that will be taken at a subsequent time, or at which formal legislative action is taken, regarding pending legislation or amendments, shall be reasonably open to the public. All open meetings shall be subject to order and decorum. This section shall be implemented and defined by the rules of each house, and such rules shall control admission to the floor of each legislative chamber and may, where reasonably necessary for security purposes or to protect a witness appearing before a committee, provide for the closure of committee meetings. Each house shall be the sole judge for the interpretation, implementation, and enforcement of this section.

History. — Am. S.J.R.'s 1990, 2, 1990; adopted 1990.

SECTION 5. Investigations; witnesses. — Each house, when in session, may compel attendance of witnesses and production of documents and other evidence upon any matter under investigation before it or any of its committees, and may punish by fine not exceeding one thousand dollars or imprisonment not exceeding ninety days, or both, any person not a member who has been guilty of disorderly or contemptuous conduct in its presence or has refused to obey its lawful summons or to answer lawful questions. Such powers, except the power to punish, may be conferred by law upon committees when the legislature is not in session. Punishment of contempt of an interim legislative committee shall be by judicial proceedings as prescribed by law.

SECTION 6. Laws. — Every law shall embrace but one subject and matter properly connected therewith, and the subject shall be briefly expressed in the title. No law shall be revised or amended by reference to its title only. Laws to revise or amend shall set out in full the revised or amended act, section, subsection or paragraph of a subsection. The enacting clause of every law shall read: "Be It Enacted by the Legislature of the State of Florida:".

SECTION 7. Passage of bills. — Any bill may originate in either house and after passage in one may be amended in the other. It shall be read in each house on three separate days, unless this rule is waived by two-thirds vote; provided the publication of its title in the journal of a house shall satisfy the requirement for the first reading in that house. On each reading, it shall be read by title only, unless one-third of the members present desire it read in full. On final passage, the vote of each member voting shall be entered on the journal. Passage of a bill shall require a majority vote in each house. Each bill and joint resolution passed in both houses shall be signed by the presiding officers of the respective houses and by the secretary of the senate and the clerk of the house of representatives during the session or as soon as practicable after its adjournment sine die.

History. — Am. S.J.R. 1349, 1980; adopted 1980.

SECTION 8. Executive approval and veto. —

(a) Every bill passed by the legislature shall be presented to the governor for approval and shall become a law if the governor approves and signs it, or fails to veto it within seven consecutive days after presentation. If during that period or on the seventh day the legislature adjourns sine die or takes a recess of more than

CONSTITUTION OF THE STATE OF FLORIDA

thirty days, the governor shall have fifteen consecutive days from the date of presentation to act on the bill. In all cases except general appropriation bills, the veto shall extend to the entire bill. The governor may veto any specific appropriation in a general appropriation bill, but may not veto any qualification or restriction without also vetoing the appropriation to which it relates.

(b) When a bill or any specific appropriation of a general appropriation bill has been vetoed, the governor shall transmit signed objections thereto to the house in which the bill originated if in session. If that house is not in session, the governor shall file them with the custodian of state records, who shall lay them before that house at its next regular or special session, whichever occurs first, and they shall be entered on its journal. If the originating house votes to re-enact a vetoed measure, whether in a regular or special session, and the other house does not consider or fails to re-enact the vetoed measure, no further consideration by either house at any subsequent session may be taken. If a vetoed measure is presented at a special session and the originating house does not consider it, the measure will be available for consideration at any intervening special session and until the end of the next regular session.

(c) If each house shall, by a two-thirds vote, re-enact the bill or reinstate the vetoed specific appropriation of a general appropriation bill, the vote of each member voting shall be entered on the respective journals, and the bill shall become law or the specific appropriation reinstated, the veto notwithstanding.

History. — Ams. proposed by Constitution Revision Commission, Revision Nos. 8 and 13, 1998, filed with the Secretary of State May 5, 1998; adopted 1998.

SECTION 9. Effective date of laws. — Each law shall take effect on the sixtieth day after adjournment sine die of the session of the legislature in which enacted or as otherwise provided therein. If the law is passed over the veto of the governor it shall take effect on the sixtieth day after adjournment sine die of the session in which the veto is overridden, on a later date fixed in the law, or on a date fixed by resolution passed by both houses of the legislature.

SECTION 10. Special laws. — No special law shall be passed unless notice of intention to seek enactment thereof has been published in the manner provided by general law. Such notice shall not be necessary when the law, except the provision for referendum, is conditioned to become effective only upon approval by vote of the electors of the area affected.

SECTION 11. Prohibited special laws. —

(a) There shall be no special law or general law of local application pertaining to:

(1) election, jurisdiction or duties of officers, except officers of municipalities, chartered counties, special districts or local governmental agencies;

(2) assessment or collection of taxes for state or county purposes, including extension of time therefor, relief of tax officers from due performance of their duties, and relief of their sureties from liability;

(3) rules of evidence in any court;

(4) punishment for crime;

(5) petit juries, including compensation of jurors, except establishment of jury commissions;

(6) change of civil or criminal venue;

(7) conditions precedent to bringing any civil or criminal proceedings, or limitations of time therefor;

(8) refund of money legally paid or remission of fines, penalties or forfeitures;

(9) creation, enforcement, extension or impairment of liens based on private contracts, or fixing of interest rates on private contracts;

(10) disposal of public property, including any interest therein, for private purposes;

(11) vacation of roads;

(12) private incorporation or grant of privilege to a private corporation;

(13) effectuation of invalid deeds, wills or other instruments, or change in the law of descent;

(14) change of name of any person;

(15) divorce;

(16) legitimation or adoption of persons;

(17) relief of minors from legal disabilities;

(18) transfer of any property interest of persons under legal disabilities or of estates of decedents;

(19) hunting or fresh water fishing;

(20) regulation of occupations which are regulated by a state agency; or

[1](21) any subject when prohibited by general law passed by a three-fifths vote of the membership of each house. Such law may be amended or repealed by like vote.

(b) In the enactment of general laws on other subjects, political subdivisions or other governmental entities may be classified only on a basis reasonably related to the subject of the law.

[1]**Note.** — *See* the following for prohibited subject matters added under the authority of this paragraph:

s. 112.67, F.S. (Pertaining to protection of public employee retirement benefits).

s. 121.191, F.S. (Pertaining to state-administered or supported retirement systems).

s. 145.16, F.S. (Pertaining to compensation of designated county officials).

s. 189.031(2), F.S. (Pertaining to independent special districts).

s. 190.049, F.S. (Pertaining to the creation of independent special districts having the powers enumerated in two or more of the paragraphs of s. 190.012, F.S.).

s. 215.845, F.S. (Pertaining to the maximum rate of interest on bonds).

s. 298.76(1), F.S. (Pertaining to the grant of authority, power, rights, or privileges to a water control district formed pursuant to ch. 298, F.S.).

s. 373.503(2)(b), F.S. (Pertaining to allocation of millage for water management purposes).

s. 1011.77, F.S. (Pertaining to taxation for school purposes and the Florida Education Finance Program).

s. 1013.37(5), F.S. (Pertaining to the "State Uniform Building Code for Public Educational Facilities Construction").

SECTION 12. Appropriation bills. — Laws making appropriations for salaries of public officers and other current expenses of the state shall contain provisions on no other subject.

SECTION 13. Term of office. — No office shall be created the term of which shall exceed four years except as provided herein.

SECTION 14. Civil service system. — By law there shall be created a civil service system for state employees, except those expressly exempted, and there may be created civil service systems and boards for county, district or municipal employees and for such offices thereof as are not elected or appointed by the governor, and there may be authorized such boards as are necessary to prescribe the qualifications, method of selection and tenure of such employees and officers.

SECTION 15. Terms and qualifications of legislators. —

(a) SENATORS. Senators shall be elected for terms of four years, those from odd-numbered districts in the years the numbers of which are multiples of four and those from even-numbered districts in even-numbered years the numbers of which are not multiples of four; except, at the election next following a reapportionment, some senators shall be elected for terms of two years when necessary to maintain staggered terms.

(b) REPRESENTATIVES. Members of the house of representatives shall be elected for terms of two years in each even-numbered year.

(c) QUALIFICATIONS. Each legislator shall be at least twenty-one years of age, an elector and resident of the district from which elected and shall have resided in the state for a period of two years prior to election.

(d) ASSUMING OFFICE; VACANCIES. Members of the legislature shall take office upon election. Vacancies in legislative office shall be filled only by election as provided by law.

SECTION 16. Legislative apportionment. —

(a) SENATORIAL AND REPRESENTATIVE DISTRICTS. The legislature at its regular session in the second year following each decennial census, by joint resolution, shall apportion the state in accordance with the constitution of the state and of the United States into not less than thirty nor more than forty consecutively numbered senatorial districts of either contiguous, overlapping or identical territory, and into not less than eighty nor more than one hundred twenty consecutively numbered representative districts of either contiguous, overlapping or identical territory. Should that session adjourn without adopting such joint resolution, the governor by proclamation shall reconvene the legislature within thirty days in special apportionment session which shall not exceed thirty consecutive days, during which no other business shall be transacted, and it shall be the mandatory duty of the legislature to adopt a joint resolution of apportionment.

(b) FAILURE OF LEGISLATURE TO APPORTION; JUDICIAL REAPPORTIONMENT. In the event a special apportionment session of the legislature finally adjourns without adopting a joint resolution of apportionment, the attorney general shall, within five days, petition the supreme court of the state to make such apportionment. No later than the sixtieth day after the filing of such petition, the supreme court shall file with the custodian of state records an order making such apportionment.

(c) JUDICIAL REVIEW OF APPORTIONMENT. Within fifteen days after the passage of the joint resolution of apportionment, the attorney general shall petition the supreme court of the state for a declaratory judgment determining the validity of the apportionment. The supreme court, in accordance with its rules, shall permit adversary interests to present their views and, within thirty days from the filing of the petition, shall enter its judgment.

(d) EFFECT OF JUDGMENT IN APPORTIONMENT; EXTRAORDINARY APPORTIONMENT SESSION. A judgment of the supreme court of the state determining the apportionment to be valid shall be binding upon all the citizens of the state. Should the supreme court determine that the apportionment made by the legislature is invalid, the governor by proclamation shall reconvene the legislature within five days thereafter in extraordinary apportionment session which shall not exceed fifteen days, during which the legislature shall adopt a joint resolution of apportionment conforming to the judgment of the supreme court.

(e) EXTRAORDINARY APPORTIONMENT SESSION; REVIEW OF APPORTIONMENT. Within fifteen days after the adjournment of an extraordinary apportionment session, the attorney general shall file a petition in the supreme court of the state setting forth the apportionment resolution adopted by the legislature, or if none has been adopted reporting that fact to the court. Consideration of the validity of a joint resolution of apportionment shall be had as provided for in cases of such joint resolution adopted at a regular or special apportionment session.

(f) JUDICIAL REAPPORTIONMENT. Should an extraordinary apportionment session fail to adopt a resolution of apportionment or should the supreme court determine that the apportionment made is invalid, the court shall, not later than sixty days after receiving the petition of the attorney general, file with the custodian of state records an order making such apportionment.

History. — Am. proposed by Constitution Revision Commission, Revision No. 8, 1998, filed with the Secretary of State May 5, 1998; adopted 1998.

CONSTITUTION OF THE STATE OF FLORIDA

SECTION 17. Impeachment. —

(a) The governor, lieutenant governor, members of the cabinet, justices of the supreme court, judges of district courts of appeal, judges of circuit courts, and judges of county courts shall be liable to impeachment for misdemeanor in office. The house of representatives by two-thirds vote shall have the power to impeach an officer. The speaker of the house of representatives shall have power at any time to appoint a committee to investigate charges against any officer subject to impeachment.

(b) An officer impeached by the house of representatives shall be disqualified from performing any official duties until acquitted by the senate, and, unless impeached, the governor may by appointment fill the office until completion of the trial.

(c) All impeachments by the house of representatives shall be tried by the senate. The chief justice of the supreme court, or another justice designated by the chief justice, shall preside at the trial, except in a trial of the chief justice, in which case the governor shall preside. The senate shall determine the time for the trial of any impeachment and may sit for the trial whether the house of representatives be in session or not. The time fixed for trial shall not be more than six months after the impeachment. During an impeachment trial senators shall be upon their oath or affirmation. No officer shall be convicted without the concurrence of two-thirds of the members of the senate present. Judgment of conviction in cases of impeachment shall remove the offender from office and, in the discretion of the senate, may include disqualification to hold any office of honor, trust or profit. Conviction or acquittal shall not affect the civil or criminal responsibility of the officer.

History. — Am. S.J.R. 459, 1987; adopted 1988; Am. proposed by Constitution Revision Commission, Revision No. 13, 1998, filed with the Secretary of State May 5, 1998; adopted 1998.

[1]**SECTION 18. Conflict of Interest.** — A code of ethics for all state employees and nonjudicial officers prohibiting conflict between public duty and private interests shall be prescribed by law.

History. — Am. proposed by Constitution Revision Commission, Revision No. 13, 1998, filed with the Secretary of State May 5, 1998; adopted 1998.

[1]**Note.** — This section was repealed effective January 5, 1999, by Am. proposed by Constitution Revision Commission, Revision No. 13, 1998, filed with the Secretary of State May 5, 1998; adopted 1998. *See* s. 5(e), Art. XI, State Constitution, for constitutional effective date. Identical language to s. 18, Art. III, State Constitution, was enacted in s. 8(g), Art. II, State Constitution, by Revision No. 13, 1998.

SECTION 19. State Budgeting, Planning and Appropriations Processes. —

(a) ANNUAL BUDGETING.

(1) General law shall prescribe the adoption of annual state budgetary and planning processes and require that detail reflecting the annualized costs of the state budget and reflecting the nonrecurring costs of the budget requests shall accompany

state department and agency legislative budget requests, the governor's recommended budget, and appropriation bills.

(2) Unless approved by a three-fifths vote of the membership of each house, appropriations made for recurring purposes from nonrecurring general revenue funds for any fiscal year shall not exceed three percent of the total general revenue funds estimated to be available at the time such appropriation is made.

(3) As prescribed by general law, each state department and agency shall be required to submit a legislative budget request that is based upon and that reflects the long-range financial outlook adopted by the joint legislative budget commission or that specifically explains any variance from the long-range financial outlook contained in the request.

(4) For purposes of this section, the terms department and agency shall include the judicial branch.

(b) APPROPRIATION BILLS FORMAT. Separate sections within the general appropriation bill shall be used for each major program area of the state budget; major program areas shall include: education enhancement "lottery" trust fund items; education (all other funds); human services; criminal justice and corrections; natural resources, environment, growth management, and transportation; general government; and judicial branch. Each major program area shall include an itemization of expenditures for: state operations; state capital outlay; aid to local governments and nonprofit organizations operations; aid to local governments and nonprofit organizations capital outlay; federal funds and the associated state matching funds; spending authorizations for operations; and spending authorizations for capital outlay. Additionally, appropriation bills passed by the legislature shall include an itemization of specific appropriations that exceed one million dollars ($1,000,000.00) in 1992 dollars. For purposes of this subsection, "specific appropriation," "itemization," and "major program area" shall be defined by law. This itemization threshold shall be adjusted by general law every four years to reflect the rate of inflation or deflation as indicated in the Consumer Price Index for All Urban Consumers, U.S. City Average, All Items, or successor reports as reported by the United States Department of Labor, Bureau of Labor Statistics or its successor. Substantive bills containing appropriations shall also be subject to the itemization requirement mandated under this provision and shall be subject to the governor's specific appropriation veto power described in Article III, Section 8.

(c) APPROPRIATIONS PROCESS.

(1) No later than September 15 of each year, the joint legislative budget commission shall issue a long-range financial outlook setting out recommended fiscal strategies for the state and its departments and agencies in order to assist the legislature in making budget decisions. The long-range financial outlook must include major workload and revenue estimates. In order to implement this paragraph, the joint legislative budget commission shall use current official consensus estimates and may request the development of additional official estimates.

CONSTITUTION OF THE STATE OF FLORIDA

(2) The joint legislative budget commission shall seek input from the public and from the executive and judicial branches when developing and recommending the long-range financial outlook.

(3) The legislature shall prescribe by general law conditions under which limited adjustments to the budget, as recommended by the governor or the chief justice of the supreme court, may be approved without the concurrence of the full legislature.

(d) SEVENTY-TWO HOUR PUBLIC REVIEW PERIOD. All general appropriation bills shall be furnished to each member of the legislature, each member of the cabinet, the governor, and the chief justice of the supreme court at least seventy-two hours before final passage by either house of the legislature of the bill in the form that will be presented to the governor.

(e) FINAL BUDGET REPORT. A final budget report shall be prepared as prescribed by general law. The final budget report shall be produced no later than the 120th day after the beginning of the fiscal year, and copies of the report shall be furnished to each member of the legislature, the head of each department and agency of the state, the auditor general, and the chief justice of the supreme court.

(f) TRUST FUNDS.

(1) No trust fund of the State of Florida or other public body may be created or re-created by law without a three-fifths vote of the membership of each house of the legislature in a separate bill for that purpose only.

(2) State trust funds shall terminate not more than four years after the effective date of the act authorizing the initial creation of the trust fund. By law the legislature may set a shorter time period for which any trust fund is authorized.

(3) Trust funds required by federal programs or mandates; trust funds established for bond covenants, indentures, or resolutions, whose revenues are legally pledged by the state or public body to meet debt service or other financial requirements of any debt obligations of the state or any public body; the state transportation trust fund; the trust fund containing the net annual proceeds from the Florida Education Lotteries; the Florida retirement trust fund; trust funds for institutions under the management of the Board of Governors, where such trust funds are for auxiliary enterprises and contracts, grants, and donations, as those terms are defined by general law; trust funds that serve as clearing funds or accounts for the chief financial officer or state agencies; trust funds that account for assets held by the state in a trustee capacity as an agent or fiduciary for individuals, private organizations, or other governmental units; and other trust funds authorized by this Constitution, are not subject to the requirements set forth in paragraph (2) of this subsection.

(4) All cash balances and income of any trust funds abolished under this subsection shall be deposited into the general revenue fund.

(g) BUDGET STABILIZATION FUND. Subject to the provisions of this subsection, an amount equal to at least 5% of the last completed fiscal year's net revenue collections for the general revenue fund shall be retained in the budget stabilization fund. The budget stabilization fund's principal balance shall not exceed an amount equal to 10% of the last completed fiscal year's net revenue collections for the general revenue fund. The legislature shall provide criteria for withdrawing funds from the budget stabilization fund in a separate bill for that purpose only and only for the purpose of covering revenue shortfalls of the general revenue fund or for the purpose of providing funding for an emergency, as defined by general law. General law shall provide for the restoration of this fund. The budget stabilization fund shall be comprised of funds not otherwise obligated or committed for any purpose.

(h) LONG-RANGE STATE PLANNING DOCUMENT AND DEPARTMENT AND AGENCY PLANNING DOCUMENT PROCESSES. General law shall provide for a long-range state planning document. The governor shall recommend to the legislature biennially any revisions to the long-range state planning document, as defined by law. General law shall require a biennial review and revision of the long-range state planning document and shall require all departments and agencies of state government to develop planning documents that identify statewide strategic goals and objectives, consistent with the long-range state planning document. The long-range state planning document and department and agency planning documents shall remain subject to review and revision by the legislature. The long-range state planning document must include projections of future needs and resources of the state which are consistent with the long-range financial outlook. The department and agency planning documents shall include a prioritized listing of planned expenditures for review and possible reduction in the event of revenue shortfalls, as defined by general law.

(i) GOVERNMENT EFFICIENCY TASK FORCE. No later than January of 2007, and each fourth year thereafter, the president of the senate, the speaker of the house of representatives, and the governor shall appoint a government efficiency task force, the membership of which shall be established by general law. The task force shall be composed of members of the legislature and representatives from the private and public sectors who shall develop recommendations for improving governmental operations and reducing costs. Staff to assist the task force in performing its duties shall be assigned by general law, and the task force may obtain assistance from the private sector. The task force shall complete its work within one year and shall submit its recommendations to the joint legislative budget commission, the governor, and the chief justice of the supreme court.

(j) JOINT LEGISLATIVE BUDGET COMMISSION. There is created within the legislature the joint legislative budget commission composed of equal numbers of senate members appointed by the president of the senate and house members appointed by the speaker of the house of representatives. Each member shall serve at the pleasure of the officer who appointed the member. A vacancy on the commission shall be filled in the same manner as the original appointment. From November of each odd-numbered year through October of each even-numbered year, the chairperson of the joint legislative budget commission shall be appointed by the president

CONSTITUTION OF THE STATE OF FLORIDA

of the senate and the vice chairperson of the commission shall be appointed by the speaker of the house of representatives. From November of each even-numbered year through October of each odd-numbered year, the chairperson of the joint legislative budget commission shall be appointed by the speaker of the house of representatives and the vice chairperson of the commission shall be appointed by the president of the senate. The joint legislative budget commission shall be governed by the joint rules of the senate and the house of representatives, which shall remain in effect until repealed or amended by concurrent resolution. The commission shall convene at least quarterly and shall convene at the call of the president of the senate and the speaker of the house of representatives. A majority of the commission members of each house plus one additional member from either house constitutes a quorum. Action by the commission requires a majority vote of the commission members present of each house. The commission may conduct its meetings through teleconferences or similar means. In addition to the powers and duties specified in this subsection, the joint legislative budget commission shall exercise all other powers and perform any other duties not in conflict with paragraph (c)(3) and as prescribed by general law or joint rule.

History. — Proposed by Taxation and Budget Reform Commission, Revision No. 1, 1992, filed with the Secretary of State May 7, 1992; adopted 1992; Ams. proposed by Constitution Revision Commission, Revision Nos. 8 and 13, 1998, filed with the Secretary of State May 5, 1998; adopted 1998; Am. C.S. for S.J.R. 2144, 2005; adopted 2006.

SECTION 20. Standards for establishing congressional district boundaries. — In establishing congressional district boundaries:

(a) No apportionment plan or individual district shall be drawn with the intent to favor or disfavor a political party or an incumbent; and districts shall not be drawn with the intent or result of denying or abridging the equal opportunity of racial or language minorities to participate in the political process or to diminish their ability to elect representatives of their choice; and districts shall consist of contiguous territory.

(b) Unless compliance with the standards in this subsection conflicts with the standards in subsection [1](a) or with federal law, districts shall be as nearly equal in population as is practicable; districts shall be compact; and districts shall, where feasible, utilize existing political and geographical boundaries.

(c) The order in which the standards within subsections [1](a) and (b) of this section are set forth shall not be read to establish any priority of one standard over the other within that subsection.

History. — Proposed by Initiative Petition filed with the Secretary of State September 28, 2007; adopted 2010.

[1]**Note.** — The subsections of section 20, as it appeared in Amendment No. 6, proposed by Initiative Petition filed with the Secretary of State September 28, 2007, and

adopted in 2010, were designated (1)-(3); the editors redesignated them as (a)-(c) to conform to the format of the State Constitution.

SECTION 21. Standards for establishing legislative district boundaries. — In establishing legislative district boundaries:

(a) No apportionment plan or district shall be drawn with the intent to favor or disfavor a political party or an incumbent; and districts shall not be drawn with the intent or result of denying or abridging the equal opportunity of racial or language minorities to participate in the political process or to diminish their ability to elect representatives of their choice; and districts shall consist of contiguous territory.

(b) Unless compliance with the standards in this subsection conflicts with the standards in subsection [1](a) or with federal law, districts shall be as nearly equal in population as is practicable; districts shall be compact; and districts shall, where feasible, utilize existing political and geographical boundaries.

(c) The order in which the standards within subsections [1](a) and (b) of this section are set forth shall not be read to establish any priority of one standard over the other within that subsection.

History. — Proposed by Initiative Petition filed with the Secretary of State September 28, 2007; adopted 2010.

[1]**Note.** — The subsections of section 21, as it appeared in Amendment No. 5, proposed by Initiative Petition filed with the Secretary of State September 28, 2007, and adopted in 2010, were designated (1)-(3); the editors redesignated them as (a)-(c) to conform to the format of the State Constitution.

ARTICLE IV

EXECUTIVE

SECTION 1.

Governor.

SECTION 2.

Lieutenant governor.

SECTION 3.

Succession to office of governor; acting governor.

SECTION 4.

Cabinet.

SECTION 5.

Election of governor, lieutenant governor and cabinet members; qualifications; terms.

SECTION 6.

Executive departments.

CONSTITUTION OF THE STATE OF FLORIDA   985

SECTION 7.

Suspensions; filling office during suspensions.

SECTION 8.

Clemency.

SECTION 9.

Fish and wildlife conservation commission.

SECTION 10.

Attorney General.

SECTION 11.

Department of Veterans' Affairs.

SECTION 12.

Department of Elderly Affairs.

SECTION 13.

Revenue Shortfalls.

SECTION 1. Governor. —

(a) The supreme executive power shall be vested in a governor, who shall be commander-in-chief of all military forces of the state not in active service of the United States. The governor shall take care that the laws be faithfully executed, commission all officers of the state and counties, and transact all necessary business with the officers of government. The governor may require information in writing from all executive or administrative state, county or municipal officers upon any subject relating to the duties of their respective offices. The governor shall be the chief administrative officer of the state responsible for the planning and budgeting for the state.

(b) The governor may initiate judicial proceedings in the name of the state against any executive or administrative state, county or municipal officer to enforce compliance with any duty or restrain any unauthorized act.

(c) The governor may request in writing the opinion of the justices of the supreme court as to the interpretation of any portion of this constitution upon any question affecting the governor's executive powers and duties. The justices shall, subject to their rules of procedure, permit interested persons to be heard on the questions presented and shall render their written opinion not earlier than ten days from the filing and docketing of the request, unless in their judgment the delay would cause public injury.

(d) The governor shall have power to call out the militia to preserve the public peace, execute the laws of the state, suppress insurrection, or repel invasion.

(e) The governor shall by message at least once in each regular session inform the legislature concerning the condition of the state, propose such reorganization of the executive department as will promote efficiency and economy, and recommend measures in the public interest.

(f) When not otherwise provided for in this constitution, the governor shall fill by appointment any vacancy in state or county office for the remainder of the term of an appointive office, and for the remainder of the term of an elective office if less than twenty-eight months, otherwise until the first Tuesday after the first Monday following the next general election.

History. — Am. proposed by Taxation and Budget Reform Commission, Revision No. 1, 1992, filed with the Secretary of State May 7, 1992; adopted 1992; Am. proposed by Constitution Revision Commission, Revision No. 13, 1998, filed with the Secretary of State May 5, 1998; adopted 1998.

SECTION 2. Lieutenant governor. — There shall be a lieutenant governor, who shall perform such duties pertaining to the office of governor as shall be assigned by the governor, except when otherwise provided by law, and such other duties as may be prescribed by law.

History. — Am. proposed by Constitution Revision Commission, Revision No. 13, 1998, filed with the Secretary of State May 5, 1998; adopted 1998.

SECTION 3. Succession to office of governor; acting governor. —

(a) Upon vacancy in the office of governor, the lieutenant governor shall become governor. Further succession to the office of governor shall be prescribed by law. A successor shall serve for the remainder of the term.

(b) Upon impeachment of the governor and until completion of trial thereof, or during the governor's physical or mental incapacity, the lieutenant governor shall act as governor. Further succession as acting governor shall be prescribed by law. Incapacity to serve as governor may be determined by the supreme court upon due notice after docketing of a written suggestion thereof by three cabinet members, and in such case restoration of capacity shall be similarly determined after docketing of written suggestion thereof by the governor, the legislature or three cabinet members. Incapacity to serve as governor may also be established by certificate filed with the custodian of state records by the governor declaring incapacity for physical reasons to serve as governor, and in such case restoration of capacity shall be similarly established.

History. — Ams. proposed by Constitution Revision Commission, Revision Nos. 8 and 13, 1998, filed with the Secretary of State May 5, 1998; adopted 1998.

SECTION 4. Cabinet. —

(a) There shall be a cabinet composed of an attorney general, a chief financial officer, and a commissioner of agriculture. In addition to the powers and duties specified herein, they shall exercise such powers and perform such duties as may be prescribed by law. In the event of a tie vote of the governor and cabinet, the side on which the governor voted shall be deemed to prevail.

CONSTITUTION OF THE STATE OF FLORIDA

(b) The attorney general shall be the chief state legal officer. There is created in the office of the attorney general the position of statewide prosecutor. The statewide prosecutor shall have concurrent jurisdiction with the state attorneys to prosecute violations of criminal laws occurring or having occurred, in two or more judicial circuits as part of a related transaction, or when any such offense is affecting or has affected two or more judicial circuits as provided by general law. The statewide prosecutor shall be appointed by the attorney general from not less than three persons nominated by the judicial nominating commission for the supreme court, or as otherwise provided by general law.

(c) The chief financial officer shall serve as the chief fiscal officer of the state, and shall settle and approve accounts against the state, and shall keep all state funds and securities.

(d) The commissioner of agriculture shall have supervision of matters pertaining to agriculture except as otherwise provided by law.

(e) The governor as chair, the chief financial officer, and the attorney general shall constitute the state board of administration, which shall succeed to all the power, control, and authority of the state board of administration established pursuant to Article IX, Section 16 of the Constitution of 1885, and which shall continue as a body at least for the life of Article XII, Section 9(c).

(f) The governor as chair, the chief financial officer, the attorney general, and the commissioner of agriculture shall constitute the trustees of the internal improvement trust fund and the land acquisition trust fund as provided by law.

(g) The governor as chair, the chief financial officer, the attorney general, and the commissioner of agriculture shall constitute the agency head of the Department of Law Enforcement. The Office of Domestic Security and Counterterrorism is created within the Department of Law Enforcement. The Office of Domestic Security and Counterterrorism shall provide support for prosecutors and federal, state, and local law enforcement agencies that investigate or analyze information relating to attempts or acts of terrorism or that prosecute terrorism, and shall perform any other duties that are provided by law.

History. — Am. H.J.R. 435, 1983; adopted 1984; Am. H.J.R. 386, 1985; adopted 1986; Ams. proposed by Constitution Revision Commission, Revision Nos. 8 and 13, 1998, filed with the Secretary of State May 5, 1998; adopted 1998; Am. proposed by Constitution Revision Commission, Revision No. 5, 2018, filed with the Secretary of State May 9, 2018; adopted 2018.

SECTION 5. Election of governor, lieutenant governor and cabinet members; qualifications; terms. —

(a) At a state-wide general election in each calendar year the number of which is even but not a multiple of four, the electors shall choose a governor and a lieutenant governor and members of the cabinet each for a term of four years beginning on the first Tuesday after the first Monday in January of the succeeding year. In primary elections, candidates for the office of governor may choose to run without a lieutenant governor candidate. In the general election, all candidates for the offices of governor and lieutenant governor shall form joint candidacies in a manner prescribed by law so that each voter shall cast a single vote for a candidate for governor and a candidate for lieutenant governor running together.

(b) When elected, the governor, lieutenant governor and each cabinet member must be an elector not less than thirty years of age who has resided in the state for the preceding seven years. The attorney general must have been a member of the bar of Florida for the preceding five years. No person who has, or but for resignation would have, served as governor or acting governor for more than six years in two consecutive terms shall be elected governor for the succeeding term.

History. — Am. proposed by Constitution Revision Commission, Revision No. 11, 1998, filed with the Secretary of State May 5, 1998; adopted 1998.

SECTION 6. Executive departments. — All functions of the executive branch of state government shall be allotted among not more than twenty-five departments, exclusive of those specifically provided for or authorized in this constitution. The administration of each department, unless otherwise provided in this constitution, shall be placed by law under the direct supervision of the governor, the lieutenant governor, the governor and cabinet, a cabinet member, or an officer or board appointed by and serving at the pleasure of the governor, except:

(a) When provided by law, confirmation by the senate or the approval of three members of the cabinet shall be required for appointment to or removal from any designated statutory office.

(b) Boards authorized to grant and revoke licenses to engage in regulated occupations shall be assigned to appropriate departments and their members appointed for fixed terms, subject to removal only for cause.

SECTION 7. Suspensions; filling office during suspensions. —

(a) By executive order stating the grounds and filed with the custodian of state records, the governor may suspend from office any state officer not subject to impeachment, any officer of the militia not in the active service of the United States, or any county officer, for malfeasance, misfeasance, neglect of duty, drunkenness, incompetence, permanent inability to perform official duties, or commission of a felony, and may fill the office by appointment for the period of suspension. The suspended officer may at any time before removal be reinstated by the governor.

(b) The senate may, in proceedings prescribed by law, remove from office or reinstate the suspended official and for such purpose the senate may be convened in special session by its president or by a majority of its membership.

(c) By order of the governor any elected municipal officer indicted for crime may be suspended from office until acquitted and the office filled by appointment for the period of suspension, not to extend beyond the term, unless these powers are vested elsewhere by law or the municipal charter.

History. — Ams. proposed by Constitution Revision Commission, Revision Nos. 8 and 13, 1998, filed with the Secretary of State May 5, 1998; adopted 1998.

SECTION 8. Clemency. —

(a) Except in cases of treason and in cases where impeachment results in conviction, the governor may, by executive order filed with the custodian of state records, suspend collection of fines and forfeitures, grant reprieves not exceeding sixty days and, with the approval of two members of the cabinet, grant full or conditional pardons, restore civil rights, commute punishment, and remit fines and forfeitures for offenses.

(b) In cases of treason the governor may grant reprieves until adjournment of the regular session of the legislature convening next after the conviction, at which session the legislature may grant a pardon or further reprieve; otherwise the sentence shall be executed.

(c) There may be created by law a parole and probation commission with power to supervise persons on probation and to grant paroles or conditional releases to persons under sentences for crime. The qualifications, method of selection and terms, not to exceed six years, of members of the commission shall be prescribed by law.

History. — Am. proposed by Constitution Revision Commission, Revision No. 8, 1998, filed with the Secretary of State May 5, 1998; adopted 1998.

SECTION 9. Fish and wildlife conservation commission. — There shall be a fish and wildlife conservation commission, composed of seven members appointed by the governor, subject to confirmation by the senate for staggered terms of five years. The commission shall exercise the regulatory and executive powers of the state with respect to wild animal life and fresh water aquatic life, and shall also exercise regulatory and executive powers of the state with respect to marine life, except that all license fees for taking wild animal life, fresh water aquatic life, and marine life and penalties for violating regulations of the commission shall be prescribed by general law. The commission shall establish procedures to ensure adequate due process in the exercise of its regulatory and executive functions. The legislature may enact laws in aid of the commission, not inconsistent with this section, except that there shall be no special law or general law of local application pertaining to hunting or fishing. The commission's exercise of executive powers in the area of planning, budgeting, personnel management, and purchasing shall be as provided by law. Revenue derived from license fees for the taking of wild animal life and fresh water aquatic life shall be appropriated to the commission by the legislature for the purposes of management, protection, and conservation of wild animal life and fresh water aquatic life. Revenue derived from license fees relating to marine life shall be appropriated by the legislature for the purposes of management, protection, and conservation of marine life as provided by law. The commission shall not be a unit of any other state agency and shall have its own staff, which includes management, research, and enforcement. Unless provided by general law, the commission shall have no authority to regulate matters relating to air and water pollution.

History. — Am. C.S. for H.J.R. 637, 1973; adopted 1974; Am. proposed by Constitution Revision Commission, Revision No. 5, 1998, filed with the Secretary of State May 5, 1998; adopted 1998.

SECTION 10. Attorney General. — The attorney general shall, as directed by general law, request the opinion of the justices of the supreme court as to the validity of any initiative petition circulated pursuant to Section 3 of Article XI. The justices shall, subject to their rules of procedure, permit interested persons to be heard on the questions presented and shall render their written opinion no later than April 1 of the year in which the initiative is to be submitted to the voters pursuant to Section 5 of Article XI.

History. — Added, H.J.R. 71, 1986; adopted 1986; Am. S.J.R. 2394, 2004; adopted 2004.

SECTION 11. Department of Veterans' Affairs. — The legislature, by general law, shall provide for a Department of Veterans' Affairs and prescribe its duties. The head of the department is the governor and cabinet.

History. — Added, C.S. for H.J.R. 290, 1988; adopted 1988; Am. proposed by Constitution Revision Commission, Revision No. 5, 2018, filed with the Secretary of State May 9, 2018; adopted 2018.

SECTION 12. Department of Elderly Affairs. — The legislature may create a Department of Elderly Affairs and prescribe its duties. The provisions governing the administration of the department must comply with Section 6 of Article IV of the State Constitution.

History. — Added, C.S. for H.J.R. 290, 1988; adopted 1988.

SECTION 13. Revenue Shortfalls. — In the event of revenue shortfalls, as defined by general law, the governor and cabinet may establish all necessary reductions in the state budget in order to comply with the provisions of Article VII, Section 1(d). The governor and cabinet shall implement all necessary reductions for the executive budget, the chief justice of the supreme court shall implement all necessary reductions for the judicial budget, and the speaker of the house of representatives and the president of the senate shall implement all necessary reductions for the legislative budget. Budget reductions pursuant to this section shall be consistent with the provisions of Article III, Section 19(h).

History. — Proposed by Taxation and Budget Reform Commission Revision No. 1, 1992, filed with the Secretary of State May 7, 1992; adopted 1992.

ARTICLE V
JUDICIARY

<u>SECTION 1.</u>

Courts.

<u>SECTION 2.</u>

Administration; practice and procedure.

CONSTITUTION OF THE STATE OF FLORIDA

SECTION 3.

Supreme court.

SECTION 4.

District courts of appeal.

SECTION 5.

Circuit courts.

SECTION 6.

County courts.

SECTION 7.

Specialized divisions.

SECTION 8.

Eligibility.

SECTION 9.

Determination of number of judges.

SECTION 10.

Retention; election and terms.

SECTION 11.

Vacancies.

SECTION 12.

Discipline; removal and retirement.

SECTION 13.

Prohibited activities.

SECTION 14.

Funding.

SECTION 15.

Attorneys; admission and discipline.

SECTION 16.

Clerks of the circuit courts.

SECTION 17.

State attorneys.

SECTION 18.

Public defenders.

SECTION 19.

Judicial officers as conservators of the peace.

SECTION 20.

Schedule to Article V.

SECTION 21.

Judicial interpretation of statutes and rules.

SECTION 1. Courts. — The judicial power shall be vested in a supreme court, district courts of appeal, circuit courts and county courts. No other courts may be established by the state, any political subdivision or any municipality. The legislature shall, by general law, divide the state into appellate court districts and judicial circuits following county lines. Commissions established by law, or administrative officers or bodies may be granted quasi-judicial power in matters connected with the functions of their offices. The legislature may establish by general law a civil traffic hearing officer system for the purpose of hearing civil traffic infractions. The legislature may, by general law, authorize a military court-martial to be conducted by military judges of the Florida National Guard, with direct appeal of a decision to the District Court of Appeal, First District.

History. — S.J.R. 52-D, 1971; adopted 1972; Am. H.J.R. 1608, 1988; adopted 1988; Am. proposed by Constitution Revision Commission, Revision No. 13, 1998, filed with the Secretary of State May 5, 1998; adopted 1998.

SECTION 2. Administration; practice and procedure. —

(a) The supreme court shall adopt rules for the practice and procedure in all courts including the time for seeking appellate review, the administrative supervision of all courts, the transfer to the court having jurisdiction of any proceeding when the jurisdiction of another court has been improvidently invoked, and a requirement that no cause shall be dismissed because an improper remedy has been sought. The supreme court shall adopt rules to allow the court and the district courts of appeal to submit questions relating to military law to the federal Court of Appeals for the Armed Forces for an advisory opinion. Rules of court may be repealed by general law enacted by two-thirds vote of the membership of each house of the legislature.

(b) The chief justice of the supreme court shall be chosen by a majority of the members of the court; shall be the chief administrative officer of the judicial system; and shall have the power to assign justices or judges, including consenting retired justices or judges, to temporary duty in any court for which the judge is qualified and to delegate to a chief judge of a judicial circuit the power to assign judges for duty in that circuit.

(c) A chief judge for each district court of appeal shall be chosen by a majority of the judges thereof or, if there is no majority, by the chief justice. The chief judge shall be responsible for the administrative supervision of the court.

(d) A chief judge in each circuit shall be chosen from among the circuit judges as provided by supreme court rule. The chief judge shall be responsible for the administrative supervision of the circuit courts and county courts in his circuit.

CONSTITUTION OF THE STATE OF FLORIDA

History. — S.J.R. 52-D, 1971; adopted 1972; Am. proposed by Constitution Revision Commission, Revision No. 13, 1998, filed with the Secretary of State May 5, 1998; adopted 1998.

SECTION 3. Supreme court. —

(a) ORGANIZATION. — The supreme court shall consist of seven justices. Of the seven justices, each appellate district shall have at least one justice elected or appointed from the district to the supreme court who is a resident of the district at the time of the original appointment or election. Five justices shall constitute a quorum. The concurrence of four justices shall be necessary to a decision. When recusals for cause would prohibit the court from convening because of the requirements of this section, judges assigned to temporary duty may be substituted for justices.

(b) JURISDICTION. — The supreme court:

(1) Shall hear appeals from final judgments of trial courts imposing the death penalty and from decisions of district courts of appeal declaring invalid a state statute or a provision of the state constitution.

(2) When provided by general law, shall hear appeals from final judgments entered in proceedings for the validation of bonds or certificates of indebtedness and shall review action of statewide agencies relating to rates or service of utilities providing electric, gas, or telephone service.

(3) May review any decision of a district court of appeal that expressly declares valid a state statute, or that expressly construes a provision of the state or federal constitution, or that expressly affects a class of constitutional or state officers, or that expressly and directly conflicts with a decision of another district court of appeal or of the supreme court on the same question of law.

(4) May review any decision of a district court of appeal that passes upon a question certified by it to be of great public importance, or that is certified by it to be in direct conflict with a decision of another district court of appeal.

(5) May review any order or judgment of a trial court certified by the district court of appeal in which an appeal is pending to be of great public importance, or to have a great effect on the proper administration of justice throughout the state, and certified to require immediate resolution by the supreme court.

(6) May review a question of law certified by the Supreme Court of the United States or a United States Court of Appeals which is determinative of the cause and for which there is no controlling precedent of the supreme court of Florida.

(7) May issue writs of prohibition to courts and all writs necessary to the complete exercise of its jurisdiction.

(8) May issue writs of mandamus and quo warranto to state officers and state agencies.

(9) May, or any justice may, issue writs of habeas corpus returnable before the supreme court or any justice, a district court of appeal or any judge thereof, or any circuit judge.

(10) Shall, when requested by the attorney general pursuant to the provisions of Section 10 of Article IV, render an advisory opinion of the justices, addressing issues as provided by general law.

(c) CLERK AND MARSHAL. — The supreme court shall appoint a clerk and a marshal who shall hold office during the pleasure of the court and perform such duties as the court directs. Their compensation shall be fixed by general law. The marshal shall have the power to execute the process of the court throughout the state, and in any county may deputize the sheriff or a deputy sheriff for such purpose.

History. — S.J.R. 52-D, 1971; adopted 1972; Am. C.S. for S.J.R.'s 49, 81, 1976; adopted 1976; Am. S.J.R. 20-C, 1979; adopted 1980; Am. H.J.R. 71, 1986; adopted 1986; Am. proposed by Constitution Revision Commission, Revision No. 13, 1998, filed with the Secretary of State May 5, 1998; adopted 1998.

SECTION 4. District courts of appeal. —

(a) ORGANIZATION. — There shall be a district court of appeal serving each appellate district. Each district court of appeal shall consist of at least three judges. Three judges shall consider each case and the concurrence of two shall be necessary to a decision.

(b) JURISDICTION. —

(1) District courts of appeal shall have jurisdiction to hear appeals, that may be taken as a matter of right, from final judgments or orders of trial courts, including those entered on review of administrative action, not directly appealable to the supreme court or a circuit court. They may review interlocutory orders in such cases to the extent provided by rules adopted by the supreme court.

(2) District courts of appeal shall have the power of direct review of administrative action, as prescribed by general law.

(3) A district court of appeal or any judge thereof may issue writs of habeas corpus returnable before the court or any judge thereof or before any circuit judge within the territorial jurisdiction of the court. A district court of appeal may issue writs of mandamus, certiorari, prohibition, quo warranto, and other writs necessary to the complete exercise of its jurisdiction. To the extent necessary to dispose of all issues in a cause properly before it, a district court of appeal may exercise any of the appellate jurisdiction of the circuit courts.

(c) CLERKS AND MARSHALS. — Each district court of appeal shall appoint a clerk and a marshal who shall hold office during the pleasure of the court and perform such duties as the court directs. Their compensation shall be fixed by general law. The marshal shall have the power to execute the process of the court throughout the territorial jurisdiction of the court, and in any county may deputize the sheriff or a deputy sheriff for such purpose.

History. — S.J.R. 52-D, 1971; adopted 1972.

CONSTITUTION OF THE STATE OF FLORIDA

SECTION 5. Circuit courts. —

(a) ORGANIZATION. — There shall be a circuit court serving each judicial circuit.

(b) JURISDICTION. — The circuit courts shall have original jurisdiction not vested in the county courts, and jurisdiction of appeals when provided by general law. They shall have the power to issue writs of mandamus, quo warranto, certiorari, prohibition and habeas corpus, and all writs necessary or proper to the complete exercise of their jurisdiction. Jurisdiction of the circuit court shall be uniform throughout the state. They shall have the power of direct review of administrative action prescribed by general law.

History. — S.J.R. 52-D, 1971; adopted 1972.

SECTION 6. County courts. —

(a) ORGANIZATION. — There shall be a county court in each county. There shall be one or more judges for each county court as prescribed by general law.

(b) JURISDICTION. — The county courts shall exercise the jurisdiction prescribed by general law. Such jurisdiction shall be uniform throughout the state.

History. — S.J.R. 52-D, 1971; adopted 1972.

SECTION 7. Specialized divisions. — All courts except the supreme court may sit in divisions as may be established by general law. A circuit or county court may hold civil and criminal trials and hearings in any place within the territorial jurisdiction of the court as designated by the chief judge of the circuit.

History. — S.J.R. 52-D, 1971; adopted 1972.

SECTION 8. Eligibility. — No person shall be eligible for office of justice or judge of any court unless the person is an elector of the state and resides in the territorial jurisdiction of the court. No justice or judge shall serve after attaining the age of seventy-five years except upon temporary assignment. No person is eligible for the office of justice of the supreme court or judge of a district court of appeal unless the person is, and has been for the preceding ten years, a member of the bar of Florida. No person is eligible for the office of circuit judge unless the person is, and has been for the preceding five years, a member of the bar of Florida. Unless otherwise provided by general law, no person is eligible for the office of county court judge unless the person is, and has been for the preceding five years, a member of the bar of Florida. Unless otherwise provided by general law, a person shall be eligible for election or appointment to the office of county court judge in a county having a population of 40,000 or less if the person is a member in good standing of the bar of Florida.

History. — S.J.R. 52-D, 1971; adopted 1972; Am. H.J.R. 37, 1984; adopted 1984 (effective July 1, 1985); Am. proposed by Constitution Revision Commission, Revision No. 13, 1998, filed with the Secretary of State May 5, 1998; adopted 1998; Am. proposed by Constitution Revision Commission, Revision No. 1, 2018, filed with the Secretary of State May 9, 2018; adopted 2018.

SECTION 9. Determination of number of judges. — The supreme court shall establish by rule uniform criteria for the determination of the need for additional judges except supreme court justices, the necessity for decreasing the number of judges and for increasing, decreasing or redefining appellate districts and judicial circuits. If the supreme court finds that a need exists for increasing or decreasing the number of judges or increasing, decreasing or redefining appellate districts and judicial circuits, it shall, prior to the next regular session of the legislature, certify to the legislature its findings and recommendations concerning such need. Upon receipt of such certificate, the legislature, at the next regular session, shall consider the findings and recommendations and may reject the recommendations or by law implement the recommendations in whole or in part; provided the legislature may create more judicial offices than are recommended by the supreme court or may decrease the number of judicial offices by a greater number than recommended by the court only upon a finding of two-thirds of the membership of both houses of the legislature, that such a need exists. A decrease in the number of judges shall be effective only after the expiration of a term. If the supreme court fails to make findings as provided above when need exists, the legislature may by concurrent resolution request the court to certify its findings and recommendations and upon the failure of the court to certify its findings for nine consecutive months, the legislature may, upon a finding of two-thirds of the membership of both houses of the legislature that a need exists, increase or decrease the number of judges or increase, decrease or redefine appellate districts and judicial circuits.

History. — S.J.R. 52-D, 1971; adopted 1972.

SECTION 10. Retention; election and terms. —

(a) Any justice or judge may qualify for retention by a vote of the electors in the general election next preceding the expiration of the justice's or judge's term in the manner prescribed by law. If a justice or judge is ineligible or fails to qualify for retention, a vacancy shall exist in that office upon the expiration of the term being served by the justice or judge. When a justice or judge so qualifies, the ballot shall read substantially as follows: "Shall Justice (or Judge) _(name of justice or judge)_ of the _(name of the court)_ be retained in office?" If a majority of the qualified electors voting within the territorial jurisdiction of the court vote to retain, the justice or judge shall be retained for a term of six years. The term of the justice or judge retained shall commence on the first Tuesday after the first Monday in January following the general election. If a majority of the qualified electors voting within the territorial jurisdiction of the court vote to not retain, a vacancy shall exist in that office upon the expiration of the term being served by the justice or judge.

(b)(1) The election of circuit judges shall be preserved notwithstanding the provisions of subsection (a) unless a majority of those voting in the jurisdiction of that circuit approves a local option to select circuit judges by merit selection and retention rather than by election. The election of circuit judges shall be by a vote of the qualified electors within the territorial jurisdiction of the court.

CONSTITUTION OF THE STATE OF FLORIDA

(2) The election of county court judges shall be preserved notwithstanding the provisions of subsection (a) unless a majority of those voting in the jurisdiction of that county approves a local option to select county judges by merit selection and retention rather than by election. The election of county court judges shall be by a vote of the qualified electors within the territorial jurisdiction of the court.

(3)a. A vote to exercise a local option to select circuit court judges and county court judges by merit selection and retention rather than by election shall be held in each circuit and county at the general election in the year 2000. If a vote to exercise this local option fails in a vote of the electors, such option shall not again be put to a vote of the electors of that jurisdiction until the expiration of at least two years.

b. After the year 2000, a circuit may initiate the local option for merit selection and retention or the election of circuit judges, whichever is applicable, by filing with the custodian of state records a petition signed by the number of electors equal to at least ten percent of the votes cast in the circuit in the last preceding election in which presidential electors were chosen.

c. After the year 2000, a county may initiate the local option for merit selection and retention or the election of county court judges, whichever is applicable, by filing with the supervisor of elections a petition signed by the number of electors equal to at least ten percent of the votes cast in the county in the last preceding election in which presidential electors were chosen. The terms of circuit judges and judges of county courts shall be for six years.

History. — S.J.R. 52-D, 1971; adopted 1972; Am. C.S. for S.J.R.'s 49, 81, 1976; adopted 1976; Ams. proposed by Constitution Revision Commission, Revision Nos. 7 and 13, 1998, filed with the Secretary of State May 5, 1998; adopted 1998.

SECTION 11. Vacancies. —

(a) Whenever a vacancy occurs in a judicial office to which election for retention applies, the governor shall fill the vacancy by appointing for a term ending on the first Tuesday after the first Monday in January of the year following the next general election occurring at least one year after the date of appointment, one of not fewer than three persons nor more than six persons nominated by the appropriate judicial nominating commission.

(b) The governor shall fill each vacancy on a circuit court or on a county court, wherein the judges are elected by a majority vote of the electors, by appointing for a term ending on the first Tuesday after the first Monday in January of the year following the next primary and general election occurring at least one year after the date of appointment, one of not fewer than three persons nor more than six persons nominated by the appropriate judicial nominating commission. An election shall be held to fill that judicial office for the term of the office beginning at the end of the appointed term.

(c) The nominations shall be made within thirty days from the occurrence of a vacancy unless the period is extended by the governor for a time not to exceed thirty days. The governor shall make the appointment within sixty days after the nominations have been certified to the governor.

(d) There shall be a separate judicial nominating commission as provided by general law for the supreme court, each district court of appeal, and each judicial circuit for all trial courts within the circuit. Uniform rules of procedure shall be established by the judicial nominating commissions at each level of the court system. Such rules, or any part thereof, may be repealed by general law enacted by a majority vote of the membership of each house of the legislature, or by the supreme court, five justices concurring. Except for deliberations of the judicial nominating commissions, the proceedings of the commissions and their records shall be open to the public.

History. — S.J.R. 52-D, 1971; adopted 1972; Am. C.S. for S.J.R.'s 49, 81, 1976; adopted 1976; Am. H.J.R. 1160, 1984; adopted 1984; Am. C.S. for S.J.R. 978, 1996; adopted 1996; Ams. proposed by Constitution Revision Commission, Revision Nos. 7 and 13, 1998, filed with the Secretary of State May 5, 1998; adopted 1998.

SECTION 12. Discipline; removal and retirement. —

(a) JUDICIAL QUALIFICATIONS COMMISSION. — A judicial qualifications commission is created.

(1) There shall be a judicial qualifications commission vested with jurisdiction to investigate and recommend to the Supreme Court of Florida the removal from office of any justice or judge whose conduct, during term of office or otherwise occurring on or after November 1, 1966, (without regard to the effective date of this section) demonstrates a present unfitness to hold office, and to investigate and recommend the discipline of a justice or judge whose conduct, during term of office or otherwise occurring on or after November 1, 1966 (without regard to the effective date of this section), warrants such discipline. For purposes of this section, discipline is defined as any or all of the following: reprimand, fine, suspension with or without pay, or lawyer discipline. The commission shall have jurisdiction over justices and judges regarding allegations that misconduct occurred before or during service as a justice or judge if a complaint is made no later than one year following service as a justice or judge. The commission shall have jurisdiction regarding allegations of incapacity during service as a justice or judge. The commission shall be composed of:

a. Two judges of district courts of appeal selected by the judges of those courts, two circuit judges selected by the judges of the circuit courts and two judges of county courts selected by the judges of those courts;

b. Four electors who reside in the state, who are members of the bar of Florida, and who shall be chosen by the governing body of the bar of Florida; and

c. Five electors who reside in the state, who have never held judicial office or been members of the bar of Florida, and who shall be appointed by the governor.

(2) The members of the judicial qualifications commission shall serve staggered terms, not to exceed six years, as prescribed by general law. No member of the commission except a judge shall be eligible for state judicial office while acting as a

member of the commission and for a period of two years thereafter. No member of the commission shall hold office in a political party or participate in any campaign for judicial office or hold public office; provided that a judge may campaign for judicial office and hold that office. The commission shall elect one of its members as its chairperson.

(3) Members of the judicial qualifications commission not subject to impeachment shall be subject to removal from the commission pursuant to the provisions of Article IV, Section 7, Florida Constitution.

(4) The commission shall adopt rules regulating its proceedings, the filling of vacancies by the appointing authorities, the disqualification of members, the rotation of members between the panels, and the temporary replacement of disqualified or incapacitated members. The commission's rules, or any part thereof, may be repealed by general law enacted by a majority vote of the membership of each house of the legislature, or by the supreme court, five justices concurring. The commission shall have power to issue subpoenas. Until formal charges against a justice or judge are filed by the investigative panel with the clerk of the supreme court of Florida all proceedings by or before the commission shall be confidential; provided, however, upon a finding of probable cause and the filing by the investigative panel with said clerk of such formal charges against a justice or judge such charges and all further proceedings before the commission shall be public.

(5) The commission shall have access to all information from all executive, legislative and judicial agencies, including grand juries, subject to the rules of the commission. At any time, on request of the speaker of the house of representatives or the governor, the commission shall make available all information in the possession of the commission for use in consideration of impeachment or suspension, respectively.

(b) PANELS. — The commission shall be divided into an investigative panel and a hearing panel as established by rule of the commission. The investigative panel is vested with the jurisdiction to receive or initiate complaints, conduct investigations, dismiss complaints, and upon a vote of a simple majority of the panel submit formal charges to the hearing panel. The hearing panel is vested with the authority to receive and hear formal charges from the investigative panel and upon a two-thirds vote of the panel recommend to the supreme court the removal of a justice or judge or the involuntary retirement of a justice or judge for any permanent disability that seriously interferes with the performance of judicial duties. Upon a simple majority vote of the membership of the hearing panel, the panel may recommend to the supreme court that the justice or judge be subject to appropriate discipline.

(c) SUPREME COURT. — The supreme court shall receive recommendations from the judicial qualifications commission's hearing panel.

(1) The supreme court may accept, reject, or modify in whole or in part the findings, conclusions, and recommendations of the commission and it may order that the justice or judge be subjected to appropriate discipline, or be removed from office with termination of compensation for willful or persistent failure to perform judicial

duties or for other conduct unbecoming a member of the judiciary demonstrating a present unfitness to hold office, or be involuntarily retired for any permanent disability that seriously interferes with the performance of judicial duties. Malafides, scienter or moral turpitude on the part of a justice or judge shall not be required for removal from office of a justice or judge whose conduct demonstrates a present unfitness to hold office. After the filing of a formal proceeding and upon request of the investigative panel, the supreme court may suspend the justice or judge from office, with or without compensation, pending final determination of the inquiry.

(2) The supreme court may award costs to the prevailing party.

(d) The power of removal conferred by this section shall be both alternative and cumulative to the power of impeachment.

(e) Notwithstanding any of the foregoing provisions of this section, if the person who is the subject of proceedings by the judicial qualifications commission is a justice of the supreme court of Florida all justices of such court automatically shall be disqualified to sit as justices of such court with respect to all proceedings therein concerning such person and the supreme court for such purposes shall be composed of a panel consisting of the seven chief judges of the judicial circuits of the state of Florida most senior in tenure of judicial office as circuit judge. For purposes of determining seniority of such circuit judges in the event there be judges of equal tenure in judicial office as circuit judge the judge or judges from the lower numbered circuit or circuits shall be deemed senior. In the event any such chief circuit judge is under investigation by the judicial qualifications commission or is otherwise disqualified or unable to serve on the panel, the next most senior chief circuit judge or judges shall serve in place of such disqualified or disabled chief circuit judge.

(f) SCHEDULE TO SECTION 12. —

(1) Except to the extent inconsistent with the provisions of this section, all provisions of law and rules of court in force on the effective date of this article shall continue in effect until superseded in the manner authorized by the constitution.

(2) After this section becomes effective and until adopted by rule of the commission consistent with it:

a. The commission shall be divided, as determined by the chairperson, into one investigative panel and one hearing panel to meet the responsibilities set forth in this section.

b. The investigative panel shall be composed of:

1. Four judges,

2. Two members of the bar of Florida, and

3. Three non-lawyers.

c. The hearing panel shall be composed of:

1. Two judges,

2. Two members of the bar of Florida, and

CONSTITUTION OF THE STATE OF FLORIDA

3. Two non-lawyers.

d. Membership on the panels may rotate in a manner determined by the rules of the commission provided that no member shall vote as a member of the investigative and hearing panel on the same proceeding.

e. The commission shall hire separate staff for each panel.

f. The members of the commission shall serve for staggered terms of six years.

g. The terms of office of the present members of the judicial qualifications commission shall expire upon the effective date of the amendments to this section approved by the legislature during the regular session of the legislature in 1996 and new members shall be appointed to serve the following staggered terms:

1. Group I. — The terms of five members, composed of two electors as set forth in s. 12(a)(1)c. of Article V, one member of the bar of Florida as set forth in s. 12(a)(1)b. of Article V, one judge from the district courts of appeal and one circuit judge as set forth in s. 12(a)(1)a. of Article V, shall expire on December 31, 1998.

2. Group II. — The terms of five members, composed of one elector as set forth in s. 12(a)(1)c. of Article V, two members of the bar of Florida as set forth in s. 12(a)(1) b. of Article V, one circuit judge and one county judge as set forth in s. 12(a)(1)a. of Article V shall expire on December 31, 2000.

3. Group III. — The terms of five members, composed of two electors as set forth in s. 12(a)(1)c. of Article V, one member of the bar of Florida as set forth in s. 12(a)(1) b., one judge from the district courts of appeal and one county judge as set forth in s. 12(a)(1)a. of Article V, shall expire on December 31, 2002.

h. An appointment to fill a vacancy of the commission shall be for the remainder of the term.

i. Selection of members by district courts of appeal judges, circuit judges, and county court judges, shall be by no less than a majority of the members voting at the respective courts' conferences. Selection of members by the board of governors of the bar of Florida shall be by no less than a majority of the board.

j. The commission shall be entitled to recover the costs of investigation and prosecution, in addition to any penalty levied by the supreme court.

k. The compensation of members and referees shall be the travel expenses or transportation and per diem allowance as provided by general law.

History. — S.J.R. 52-D, 1971; adopted 1972; Am. H.J.R. 3911, 1974; adopted 1974; Am. H.J.R. 1709, 1975; adopted 1976; Am. C.S. for S.J.R. 978, 1996; adopted 1996; Am. proposed by Constitution Revision Commission, Revision No. 7, 1998, filed with the Secretary of State May 5, 1998; adopted 1998.

[1]**SECTION 13. Prohibited activities.** — All justices and judges shall devote full time to their judicial duties. They shall not engage in the practice of law or hold office in any political party.

History. — S.J.R. 52-D, 1971; adopted 1972; Am. proposed by Constitution Revision Commission, Revision No. 7, 2018, filed with the Secretary of State May 9, 2018; adopted 2018.

[1]**Note.** — Section 38, Art. XII, State Constitution, provides in part that "[t]he amendments to Section 8 of Article II and Section 13 of Article V shall take effect December 31, 2022; except that the amendments to Section 8(h) of Article II shall take effect December 31, 2020." **Effective December 31, 2022, s. 13, Art. V, as amended by Constitution Revision Commission, Revision No. 7 (2018), will read:**

SECTION 13. Ethics in the judiciary. —

(a) All justices and judges shall devote full time to their judicial duties. A justice or judge shall not engage in the practice of law or hold office in any political party.

(b) A former justice or former judge shall not lobby for compensation on issues of policy, appropriations, or procurement before the legislative or executive branches of state government for a period of six years after he or she vacates his or her judicial position. The legislature may enact legislation to implement this subsection, including, but not limited to, defining terms and providing penalties for violations. Any such law shall not contain provisions on any other subject.

SECTION 14. Funding. —

(a) All justices and judges shall be compensated only by state salaries fixed by general law. Funding for the state courts system, state attorneys' offices, public defenders' offices, and court-appointed counsel, except as otherwise provided in subsection (c), shall be provided from state revenues appropriated by general law.

(b) All funding for the offices of the clerks of the circuit and county courts performing court-related functions, except as otherwise provided in this subsection and subsection (c), shall be provided by adequate and appropriate filing fees for judicial proceedings and service charges and costs for performing court-related functions as required by general law. Selected salaries, costs, and expenses of the state courts system may be funded from appropriate filing fees for judicial proceedings and service charges and costs for performing court-related functions, as provided by general law. Where the requirements of either the United States Constitution or the Constitution of the State of Florida preclude the imposition of filing fees for judicial proceedings and service charges and costs for performing court-related functions sufficient to fund the court-related functions of the offices of the clerks of the circuit and county courts, the state shall provide, as determined by the legislature, adequate and appropriate supplemental funding from state revenues appropriated by general law.

(c) No county or municipality, except as provided in this subsection, shall be required to provide any funding for the state courts system, state attorneys' offices, public defenders' offices, court-appointed counsel or the offices of the clerks of the circuit and county courts performing court-related functions. Counties shall be required to fund the cost of communications services, existing radio systems,

CONSTITUTION OF THE STATE OF FLORIDA

existing multi-agency criminal justice information systems, and the cost of construction or lease, maintenance, utilities, and security of facilities for the trial courts, public defenders' offices, state attorneys' offices, and the offices of the clerks of the circuit and county courts performing court-related functions. Counties shall also pay reasonable and necessary salaries, costs, and expenses of the state courts system to meet local requirements as determined by general law.

(d) The judiciary shall have no power to fix appropriations.

History. — S.J.R. 52-D, 1971; adopted 1972; Am. proposed by Constitution Revision Commission, Revision No. 7, 1998, filed with the Secretary of State May 5, 1998; adopted 1998.

SECTION 15. Attorneys; admission and discipline. — The supreme court shall have exclusive jurisdiction to regulate the admission of persons to the practice of law and the discipline of persons admitted.

History. — S.J.R. 52-D, 1971; adopted 1972.

SECTION 16. Clerks of the circuit courts. — There shall be in each county a clerk of the circuit court who shall be selected pursuant to the provisions of Article VIII section 1. Notwithstanding any other provision of the constitution, the duties of the clerk of the circuit court may be divided by special or general law between two officers, one serving as clerk of court and one serving as ex officio clerk of the board of county commissioners, auditor, recorder, and custodian of all county funds. There may be a clerk of the county court if authorized by general or special law.

History. — S.J.R. 52-D, 1971; adopted 1972.

SECTION 17. State attorneys. — In each judicial circuit a state attorney shall be elected for a term of four years. Except as otherwise provided in this constitution, the state attorney shall be the prosecuting officer of all trial courts in that circuit and shall perform other duties prescribed by general law; provided, however, when authorized by general law, the violations of all municipal ordinances may be prosecuted by municipal prosecutors. A state attorney shall be an elector of the state and reside in the territorial jurisdiction of the circuit; shall be and have been a member of the bar of Florida for the preceding five years; shall devote full time to the duties of the office; and shall not engage in the private practice of law. State attorneys shall appoint such assistant state attorneys as may be authorized by law.

History. — S.J.R. 52-D, 1971; adopted 1972; Am. H.J.R. 386, 1985; adopted 1986; Am. proposed by Constitution Revision Commission, Revision No. 13, 1998, filed with the Secretary of State May 5, 1998; adopted 1998.

SECTION 18. Public defenders. — In each judicial circuit a public defender shall be elected for a term of four years, who shall perform duties prescribed by general law. A public defender shall be an elector of the state and reside in the territorial jurisdiction of the circuit and shall be and have been a member of the Bar of Florida for the preceding five years. Public defenders shall appoint such assistant public defenders as may be authorized by law.

1004 CONSTITUTION OF THE STATE OF FLORIDA

History. — S.J.R. 52-D, 1971; adopted 1972; Am. proposed by Constitution Revision Commission, Revision No. 13, 1998, filed with the Secretary of State May 5, 1998; adopted 1998.

SECTION 19. Judicial officers as conservators of the peace. — All judicial officers in this state shall be conservators of the peace.

History. — S.J.R. 52-D, 1971; adopted 1972.

SECTION 20. Schedule to Article V. —

(a) This article shall replace all of Article V of the Constitution of 1885, as amended, which shall then stand repealed.

(b) Except to the extent inconsistent with the provisions of this article, all provisions of law and rules of court in force on the effective date of this article shall continue in effect until superseded in the manner authorized by the constitution.

(c) After this article becomes effective, and until changed by general law consistent with sections 1 through 19 of this article:

(1) The supreme court shall have the jurisdiction immediately theretofore exercised by it, and it shall determine all proceedings pending before it on the effective date of this article.

(2) The appellate districts shall be those in existence on the date of adoption of this article. There shall be a district court of appeal in each district. The district courts of appeal shall have the jurisdiction immediately theretofore exercised by the district courts of appeal and shall determine all proceedings pending before them on the effective date of this article.

(3) Circuit courts shall have jurisdiction of appeals from county courts and municipal courts, except those appeals which may be taken directly to the supreme court; and they shall have exclusive original jurisdiction in all actions at law not cognizable by the county courts; of proceedings relating to the settlement of the estate of decedents and minors, the granting of letters testamentary, guardianship, involuntary hospitalization, the determination of incompetency, and other jurisdiction usually pertaining to courts of probate; in all cases in equity including all cases relating to juveniles; of all felonies and of all misdemeanors arising out of the same circumstances as a felony which is also charged; in all cases involving legality of any tax assessment or toll; in the action of ejectment; and in all actions involving the titles or boundaries or right of possession of real property. The circuit court may issue injunctions. There shall be judicial circuits which shall be the judicial circuits in existence on the date of adoption of this article. The chief judge of a circuit may authorize a county court judge to order emergency hospitalizations pursuant to Chapter 71-131, Laws of Florida, in the absence from the county of the circuit judge and the county court judge shall have the power to issue all temporary orders and temporary injunctions necessary or proper to the complete exercise of such jurisdiction.

(4) County courts shall have original jurisdiction in all criminal misdemeanor cases not cognizable by the circuit courts, of all violations of municipal and county

CONSTITUTION OF THE STATE OF FLORIDA

ordinances, and of all actions at law in which the matter in controversy does not exceed the sum of two thousand five hundred dollars ($2,500.00) exclusive of interest and costs, except those within the exclusive jurisdiction of the circuit courts. Judges of county courts shall be committing magistrates. The county courts shall have jurisdiction now exercised by the county judge's courts other than that vested in the circuit court by subsection (c)(3) hereof, the jurisdiction now exercised by the county courts, the claims court, the small claims courts, the small claims magistrates courts, magistrates courts, justice of the peace courts, municipal courts and courts of chartered counties, including but not limited to the counties referred to in Article VIII, sections 9, 10, 11 and 24 of the Constitution of 1885.

(5) Each judicial nominating commission shall be composed of the following:

a. Three members appointed by the Board of Governors of The Florida Bar from among The Florida Bar members who are actively engaged in the practice of law with offices within the territorial jurisdiction of the affected court, district or circuit;

b. Three electors who reside in the territorial jurisdiction of the court or circuit appointed by the governor; and

c. Three electors who reside in the territorial jurisdiction of the court or circuit and who are not members of the bar of Florida, selected and appointed by a majority vote of the other six members of the commission.

(6) No justice or judge shall be a member of a judicial nominating commission. A member of a judicial nominating commission may hold public office other than judicial office. No member shall be eligible for appointment to state judicial office so long as that person is a member of a judicial nominating commission and for a period of two years thereafter. All acts of a judicial nominating commission shall be made with a concurrence of a majority of its members.

(7) The members of a judicial nominating commission shall serve for a term of four years except the terms of the initial members of the judicial nominating commissions shall expire as follows:

a. The terms of one member of category a. b. and c. in subsection (c)(5) hereof shall expire on July 1, 1974;

b. The terms of one member of category a. b. and c. in subsection (c)(5) hereof shall expire on July 1, 1975;

c. The terms of one member of category a. b. and c. in subsection (c)(5) hereof shall expire on July 1, 1976;

(8) All fines and forfeitures arising from offenses tried in the county court shall be collected, and accounted for by clerk of the court, and deposited in a special trust account. All fines and forfeitures received from violations of ordinances or misdemeanors committed within a county or municipal ordinances committed within a municipality within the territorial jurisdiction of the county court shall be paid monthly to the county or municipality respectively. If any costs are assessed and collected in connection with offenses tried in county court, all court costs shall be

paid into the general revenue fund of the state of Florida and such other funds as prescribed by general law.

(9) Any municipality or county may apply to the chief judge of the circuit in which that municipality or county is situated for the county court to sit in a location suitable to the municipality or county and convenient in time and place to its citizens and police officers and upon such application said chief judge shall direct the court to sit in the location unless the chief judge shall determine the request is not justified. If the chief judge does not authorize the county court to sit in the location requested, the county or municipality may apply to the supreme court for an order directing the county court to sit in the location. Any municipality or county which so applies shall be required to provide the appropriate physical facilities in which the county court may hold court.

(10) All courts except the supreme court may sit in divisions as may be established by local rule approved by the supreme court.

(11) A county court judge in any county having a population of 40,000 or less according to the last decennial census, shall not be required to be a member of the bar of Florida.

(12) Municipal prosecutors may prosecute violations of municipal ordinances.

(13) Justice shall mean a justice elected or appointed to the supreme court and shall not include any judge assigned from any court.

(d) When this article becomes effective:

(1) All courts not herein authorized, except as provided by subsection (d)(4) of this section shall cease to exist and jurisdiction to conclude all pending cases and enforce all prior orders and judgments shall vest in the court that would have jurisdiction of the cause if thereafter instituted. All records of and property held by courts abolished hereby shall be transferred to the proper office of the appropriate court under this article.

(2) Judges of the following courts, if their terms do not expire in 1973 and if they are eligible under subsection (d)(8) hereof, shall become additional judges of the circuit court for each of the counties of their respective circuits, and shall serve as such circuit judges for the remainder of the terms to which they were elected and shall be eligible for election as circuit judges thereafter. These courts are: civil court of record of Dade county, all criminal courts of record, the felony courts of record of Alachua, Leon and Volusia Counties, the courts of record of Broward, Brevard, Escambia, Hillsborough, Lee, Manatee and Sarasota Counties, the civil and criminal court of record of Pinellas County, and county judge's courts and separate juvenile courts in counties having a population in excess of 100,000 according to the 1970 federal census. On the effective date of this article, there shall be an additional number of positions of circuit judges equal to the number of existing circuit judges and the number of judges of the above named courts whose term expires in 1973. Elections to such offices shall take place at the same time and manner as elections to other

CONSTITUTION OF THE STATE OF FLORIDA

state judicial offices in 1972 and the terms of such offices shall be for a term of six years. Unless changed pursuant to section nine of this article, the number of circuit judges presently existing and created by this subsection shall not be changed.

(3) In all counties having a population of less than 100,000 according to the 1970 federal census and having more than one county judge on the date of the adoption of this article, there shall be the same number of judges of the county court as there are county judges existing on that date unless changed pursuant to section 9 of this article.

(4) Municipal courts shall continue with their same jurisdiction until amended or terminated in a manner prescribed by special or general law or ordinances, or until January 3, 1977, whichever occurs first. On that date all municipal courts not previously abolished shall cease to exist. Judges of municipal courts shall remain in office and be subject to reappointment or reelection in the manner prescribed by law until said courts are terminated pursuant to the provisions of this subsection. Upon municipal courts being terminated or abolished in accordance with the provisions of this subsection, the judges thereof who are not members of the bar of Florida, shall be eligible to seek election as judges of county courts of their respective counties.

(5) Judges, holding elective office in all other courts abolished by this article, whose terms do not expire in 1973 including judges established pursuant to Article VIII, sections 9 and 11 of the Constitution of 1885 shall serve as judges of the county court for the remainder of the term to which they were elected. Unless created pursuant to section 9, of this Article V such judicial office shall not continue to exist thereafter.

(6) By March 21, 1972, the supreme court shall certify the need for additional circuit and county judges. The legislature in the 1972 regular session may by general law create additional offices of judge, the terms of which shall begin on the effective date of this article. Elections to such offices shall take place at the same time and manner as election to other state judicial offices in 1972.

(7) County judges of existing county judge's courts and justices of the peace and magistrates' court who are not members of bar of Florida shall be eligible to seek election as county court judges of their respective counties.

(8) No judge of a court abolished by this article shall become or be eligible to become a judge of the circuit court unless the judge has been a member of bar of Florida for the preceding five years.

(9) The office of judges of all other courts abolished by this article shall be abolished as of the effective date of this article.

(10) The offices of county solicitor and prosecuting attorney shall stand abolished, and all county solicitors and prosecuting attorneys holding such offices upon the effective date of this article shall become and serve as assistant state attorneys for the circuits in which their counties are situate for the remainder of their terms, with

1008 CONSTITUTION OF THE STATE OF FLORIDA

compensation not less than that received immediately before the effective date of this article.

(e) LIMITED OPERATION OF SOME PROVISIONS. —

(1) All justices of the supreme court, judges of the district courts of appeal and circuit judges in office upon the effective date of this article shall retain their offices for the remainder of their respective terms. All members of the judicial qualifications commission in office upon the effective date of this article shall retain their offices for the remainder of their respective terms. Each state attorney in office on the effective date of this article shall retain the office for the remainder of the term.

(2) No justice or judge holding office immediately after this article becomes effective who held judicial office on July 1, 1957, shall be subject to retirement from judicial office because of age pursuant to section 8 of this article.

(f) Until otherwise provided by law, the nonjudicial duties required of county judges shall be performed by the judges of the county court.

[1](g) All provisions of Article V of the Constitution of 1885, as amended, not embraced herein which are not inconsistent with this revision shall become statutes subject to modification or repeal as are other statutes.

(h) The requirements of section 14 relative to all county court judges or any judge of a municipal court who continues to hold office pursuant to subsection (d)(4) hereof being compensated by state salaries shall not apply prior to January 3, 1977, unless otherwise provided by general law.

(i) DELETION OF OBSOLETE SCHEDULE ITEMS. — The legislature shall have power, by concurrent resolution, to delete from this article any subsection of this section 20 including this subsection, when all events to which the subsection to be deleted is or could become applicable have occurred. A legislative determination of fact made as a basis for application of this subsection shall be subject to judicial review.

(j) EFFECTIVE DATE. — Unless otherwise provided herein, this article shall become effective at 11:59 o'clock P.M., Eastern Standard Time, January 1, 1973.

History. — S.J.R. 52-D, 1971; adopted 1972; Am. proposed by Constitution Revision Commission, Revision No. 13, 1998, filed with the Secretary of State May 5, 1998; adopted 1998.

[1]**Note.** — All provisions of Art. V of the Constitution of 1885, as amended, considered as statutory law, were repealed by ch. 73-303, Laws of Florida.

SECTION 21. Judicial interpretation of statutes and rules. — In interpreting a state statute or rule, a state court or an officer hearing an administrative action pursuant to general law may not defer to an administrative agency's interpretation of such statute or rule, and must instead interpret such statute or rule de novo.

History. — Proposed by Constitution Revision Commission, Revision No. 1, 2018, filed with the Secretary of State May 9, 2018; adopted 2018.

ARTICLE VI
SUFFRAGE AND ELECTIONS

SECTION 1.

Regulation of elections.

SECTION 2.

Electors.

SECTION 3.

Oath.

SECTION 4.

Disqualifications.

SECTION 5.

Primary, general, and special elections.

SECTION 6.

Municipal and district elections.

SECTION 7.

Campaign spending limits and funding of campaigns for elective state-wide office.

SECTION 1. Regulation of elections. — All elections by the people shall be by direct and secret vote. General elections shall be determined by a plurality of votes cast. Registration and elections shall, and political party functions may, be regulated by law; however, the requirements for a candidate with no party affiliation or for a candidate of a minor party for placement of the candidate's name on the ballot shall be no greater than the requirements for a candidate of the party having the largest number of registered voters.

History. — Am. proposed by Constitution Revision Commission, Revision No. 11, 1998, filed with the Secretary of State May 5, 1998; adopted 1998.

SECTION 2. Electors. — Only a citizen of the United States who is at least eighteen years of age and who is a permanent resident of the state, if registered as provided by law, shall be an elector of the county where registered.

History. — Am. proposed by Constitution Revision Commission, Revision No. 11, 1998, filed with the Secretary of State May 5, 1998; adopted 1998; Am. by Initiative Petition filed with the Secretary of State November 28, 2018; adopted 2020.

SECTION 3. Oath. — Each eligible citizen upon registering shall subscribe the following: "I do solemnly swear (or affirm) that I will protect and defend the Constitution of the United States and the Constitution of the State of Florida, and that I am qualified to register as an elector under the Constitution and laws of the State of Florida."

1010 CONSTITUTION OF THE STATE OF FLORIDA

SECTION 4. Disqualifications. —

(a) No person convicted of a felony, or adjudicated in this or any other state to be mentally incompetent, shall be qualified to vote or hold office until restoration of civil rights or removal of disability. Except as provided in subsection (b) of this section, any disqualification from voting arising from a felony conviction shall terminate and voting rights shall be restored upon completion of all terms of sentence including parole or probation.

(b) No person convicted of murder or a felony sexual offense shall be qualified to vote until restoration of civil rights.

(c) No person may appear on the ballot for re-election to any of the following offices:

(1) Florida representative,

(2) Florida senator,

(3) Florida Lieutenant governor,

(4) any office of the Florida cabinet,

(5) U.S. Representative from Florida, or

(6) U.S. Senator from Florida

if, by the end of the current term of office, the person will have served (or, but for resignation, would have served) in that office for eight consecutive years.

History. — Am. by Initiative Petition filed with the Secretary of State July 23, 1992; adopted 1992; Am. by Initiative Petition filed with the Secretary of State October 31, 2014; adopted 2018.

SECTION 5. Primary, general, and special elections. —

(a) A general election shall be held in each county on the first Tuesday after the first Monday in November of each even-numbered year to choose a successor to each elective state and county officer whose term will expire before the next general election and, except as provided herein, to fill each vacancy in elective office for the unexpired portion of the term. A general election may be suspended or delayed due to a state of emergency or impending emergency pursuant to general law. Special elections and referenda shall be held as provided by law.

(b) If all candidates for an office have the same party affiliation and the winner will have no opposition in the general election, all qualified electors, regardless of party affiliation, may vote in the primary elections for that office.

History. — Am. S.J.R. 162, 1992; adopted 1992; Am. proposed by Constitution Revision Commission, Revision No. 11, 1998, filed with the Secretary of State May 5, 1998; adopted 1998.

SECTION 6. Municipal and district elections. — Registration and elections in municipalities shall, and in other governmental entities created by statute may, be provided by law.

CONSTITUTION OF THE STATE OF FLORIDA

SECTION 7. Campaign spending limits and funding of campaigns for elective state-wide office. — It is the policy of this state to provide for state-wide elections in which all qualified candidates may compete effectively. A method of public financing for campaigns for state-wide office shall be established by law. Spending limits shall be established for such campaigns for candidates who use public funds in their campaigns. The legislature shall provide funding for this provision. General law implementing this paragraph shall be at least as protective of effective competition by a candidate who uses public funds as the general law in effect on January 1, 1998.

History. — Proposed by Constitution Revision Commission, Revision No. 11, 1998, filed with the Secretary of State May 5, 1998; adopted 1998.

ARTICLE VII
FINANCE AND TAXATION

SECTION 1.

Taxation; appropriations; state expenses; state revenue limitation.

SECTION 2.

Taxes; rate.

SECTION 3.

Taxes; exemptions.

SECTION 4.

Taxation; assessments.

SECTION 5.

Estate, inheritance and income taxes.

SECTION 6. Homestead exemptions.

SECTION 7.

Allocation of pari-mutuel taxes.

SECTION 8.

Aid to local governments.

SECTION 9.

Local taxes.

SECTION 10.

Pledging credit.

SECTION 11.

State bonds; revenue bonds.

SECTION 12.

Local bonds.

SECTION 13.

Relief from illegal taxes.

SECTION 14.

Bonds for pollution control and abatement and other water facilities.

SECTION 15.

Revenue bonds for scholarship loans.

SECTION 16.

Bonds for housing and related facilities.

SECTION 17.

Bonds for acquiring transportation right-of-way or for constructing bridges.

SECTION 18.

Laws requiring counties or municipalities to spend funds or limiting their ability to raise revenue or receive state tax revenue.

SECTION 19.

Supermajority vote required to impose, authorize, or raise state taxes or fees.

SECTION 1. Taxation; appropriations; state expenses; state revenue limitation. —

(a) No tax shall be levied except in pursuance of law. No state ad valorem taxes shall be levied upon real estate or tangible personal property. All other forms of taxation shall be preempted to the state except as provided by general law.

(b) Motor vehicles, boats, airplanes, trailers, trailer coaches and mobile homes, as defined by law, shall be subject to a license tax for their operation in the amounts and for the purposes prescribed by law, but shall not be subject to ad valorem taxes.

(c) No money shall be drawn from the treasury except in pursuance of appropriation made by law.

(d) Provision shall be made by law for raising sufficient revenue to defray the expenses of the state for each fiscal period.

(e) Except as provided herein, state revenues collected for any fiscal year shall be limited to state revenues allowed under this subsection for the prior fiscal year plus an adjustment for growth. As used in this subsection, "growth" means an amount equal to the average annual rate of growth in Florida personal income over the most recent twenty quarters times the state revenues allowed under this subsection for the prior fiscal year. For the 1995–1996 fiscal year, the state revenues allowed under this subsection for the prior fiscal year shall equal the state revenues collected for the 1994–1995 fiscal year. Florida personal income shall be determined by the legislature, from information available from the United States Department of Commerce or its successor on the first day of February prior to the beginning of the fiscal year. State revenues collected for any fiscal year in excess of this limitation shall be transferred to the budget stabilization fund until the fund reaches the maximum balance specified in Section 19(g) of Article III, and thereafter shall be refunded to taxpayers as provided by general law. State revenues allowed under this subsection for any fiscal year may be increased by a two-thirds vote of the membership of each house of the legislature in a separate bill that contains no other subject and that sets forth the dollar amount by which the state revenues allowed will be increased. The vote may not be taken less than seventy-two hours after the third reading of the bill. For purposes of this subsection, "state revenues" means taxes, fees, licenses, and charges for services imposed by the legislature on individuals, businesses, or agencies outside state government. However, "state revenues" does not include: revenues that are necessary to meet the requirements set forth in documents authorizing the issuance of bonds by the state; revenues that are used to provide matching funds for the federal Medicaid program with the exception of the revenues used to support the Public Medical Assistance Trust Fund or its successor program and with the exception of state matching funds used to fund elective expansions made after July 1, 1994; proceeds from the state lottery returned as prizes; receipts of the Florida Hurricane Catastrophe Fund; balances carried forward from prior fiscal years; taxes, licenses, fees, and charges for services imposed by local, regional, or school district governing bodies; or revenue from taxes, licenses, fees, and charges for services required to be imposed by any amendment or revision to this constitution after July 1, 1994. An adjustment to the revenue limitation shall be made by general law to reflect the fiscal impact of transfers of responsibility for the funding of governmental functions between the state and other levels of government. The legislature shall, by general law, prescribe procedures necessary to administer this subsection.

History. — Am. H.J.R. 2053, 1994; adopted 1994.

SECTION 2. Taxes; rate. — All ad valorem taxation shall be at a uniform rate within each taxing unit, except the taxes on intangible personal property may be at different rates but shall never exceed two mills on the dollar of assessed value; provided, as to any obligations secured by mortgage, deed of trust, or other lien on real estate wherever located, an intangible tax of not more than two mills on the dollar may be levied by law to be in lieu of all other intangible assessments on such obligations.

SECTION 3. Taxes; exemptions. —

(a) All property owned by a municipality and used exclusively by it for municipal or public purposes shall be exempt from taxation. A municipality, owning property outside the municipality, may be required by general law to make payment to the taxing unit in which the property is located. Such portions of property as are used predominantly for educational, literary, scientific, religious or charitable purposes may be exempted by general law from taxation.

(b) There shall be exempt from taxation, cumulatively, to every head of a family residing in this state, household goods and personal effects to the value fixed by general law, not less than one thousand dollars, and to every widow or widower or person who is blind or totally and permanently disabled, property to the value fixed by general law not less than five hundred dollars.

(c) Any county or municipality may, for the purpose of its respective tax levy and subject to the provisions of this subsection and general law, grant community and economic development ad valorem tax exemptions to new businesses and expansions of existing businesses, as defined by general law. Such an exemption may be granted only by ordinance of the county or municipality, and only after the electors of the county or municipality voting on such question in a referendum authorize the county or municipality to adopt such ordinances. An exemption so granted shall apply to improvements to real property made by or for the use of a new business and improvements to real property related to the expansion of an existing business and shall also apply to tangible personal property of such new business and tangible personal property related to the expansion of an existing business. The amount or limits of the amount of such exemption shall be specified by general law. The period of time for which such exemption may be granted to a new business or expansion of an existing business shall be determined by general law. The authority to grant such exemption shall expire ten years from the date of approval by the electors of the county or municipality, and may be renewable by referendum as provided by general law.

(d) Any county or municipality may, for the purpose of its respective tax levy and subject to the provisions of this subsection and general law, grant historic preservation ad valorem tax exemptions to owners of historic properties. This exemption may be granted only by ordinance of the county or municipality. The amount or limits of the amount of this exemption and the requirements for eligible properties must be specified by general law. The period of time for which this exemption may be granted to a property owner shall be determined by general law.

[1](e) By general law and subject to conditions specified therein:

(1) Twenty-five thousand dollars of the assessed value of property subject to tangible personal property tax shall be exempt from ad valorem taxation.

(2) The assessed value of solar devices or renewable energy source devices subject to tangible personal property tax may be exempt from ad valorem taxation, subject to limitations provided by general law.

[2](f) There shall be granted an ad valorem tax exemption for real property dedicated in perpetuity for conservation purposes, including real property encumbered by perpetual conservation easements or by other perpetual conservation protections, as defined by general law.

(g) By general law and subject to the conditions specified therein, each person who receives a homestead exemption as provided in section 6 of this article; who was a member of the United States military or military reserves, the United States Coast Guard or its reserves, or the Florida National Guard; and who was deployed during the preceding calendar year on active duty outside the continental United States, Alaska, or Hawaii in support of military operations designated by the legislature shall receive an additional exemption equal to a percentage of the taxable value of his or her homestead property. The applicable percentage shall be calculated as the number of days during the preceding calendar year the person was deployed

CONSTITUTION OF THE STATE OF FLORIDA   1015

on active duty outside the continental United States, Alaska, or Hawaii in support of military operations designated by the legislature divided by the number of days in that year.

History. — Am. S.J.R.'s 9-E, 15-E, 1980; adopted 1980; Am. C.S. for S.J.R.'s 318, 356, 1988; adopted 1988; Am. S.J.R. 152, 1992; adopted 1992; Am. H.J.R. 969, 1997; adopted 1998; Am. C.S. for S.J.R. 2-D, 2007; adopted 2008; Ams. proposed by Taxation and Budget Reform Commission, Revision Nos. 3 and 4, 2008, filed with the Secretary of State April 28, 2008; adopted 2008; Am. H.J.R. 833, 2009; adopted 2010; Am. C.S. for H.J.R. 193, 2016; adopted 2016.

[1]**Note.** — Section 34, Art. XII, State Constitution, provides in part that "the amendment to subsection (e) of Section 3 of Article VII authorizing the legislature, subject to limitations set forth in general law, to exempt the assessed value of solar devices or renewable energy source devices subject to tangible personal property tax from ad valorem taxation . . . shall take effect on January 1, 2018, and shall expire on December 31, 2037. Upon expiration, this section shall be repealed and the text of subsection (e) of Section 3 of Article VII . . . shall revert to that in existence on December 31, 2017, except that any amendments to such text otherwise adopted shall be preserved and continue to operate to the extent that such amendments are not dependent upon the portions of text which expire pursuant to this section." Effective December 31, 2037, s. 3(e), Art. VII, State Constitution, will read:

(e) By general law and subject to conditions specified therein, twenty-five thousand dollars of the assessed value of property subject to tangible personal property tax shall be exempt from ad valorem taxation.

[2]**Note.** — This subsection, originally designated (g) by Revision No. 4 of the Taxation and Budget Reform Commission, 2008, was redesignated (f) by the editors to conform to the redesignation of subsections by Revision No. 3 of the Taxation and Budget Reform Commission, 2008.

SECTION 4. Taxation; assessments. — By general law regulations shall be prescribed which shall secure a just valuation of all property for ad valorem taxation, provided:

(a) Agricultural land, land producing high water recharge to Florida's aquifers, or land used exclusively for noncommercial recreational purposes may be classified by general law and assessed solely on the basis of character or use.

(b) As provided by general law and subject to conditions, limitations, and reasonable definitions specified therein, land used for conservation purposes shall be classified by general law and assessed solely on the basis of character or use.

(c) Pursuant to general law tangible personal property held for sale as stock in trade and livestock may be valued for taxation at a specified percentage of its value, may be classified for tax purposes, or may be exempted from taxation.

(d) All persons entitled to a homestead exemption under Section 6 of this Article shall have their homestead assessed at just value as of January 1 of the year following the effective date of this amendment. This assessment shall change only as provided in this subsection.

(1) Assessments subject to this subsection shall be changed annually on January 1st of each year; but those changes in assessments shall not exceed the lower of the following:

a. Three percent (3%) of the assessment for the prior year.

b. The percent change in the Consumer Price Index for all urban consumers, U.S. City Average, all items 1967 = 100, or successor reports for the preceding calendar year as initially reported by the United States Department of Labor, Bureau of Labor Statistics.

(2) No assessment shall exceed just value.

(3) After any change of ownership, as provided by general law, homestead property shall be assessed at just value as of January 1 of the following year, unless the provisions of paragraph (8) apply. Thereafter, the homestead shall be assessed as provided in this subsection.

(4) New homestead property shall be assessed at just value as of January 1st of the year following the establishment of the homestead, unless the provisions of paragraph (8) apply. That assessment shall only change as provided in this subsection.

(5) Changes, additions, reductions, or improvements to homestead property shall be assessed as provided for by general law; provided, however, after the adjustment for any change, addition, reduction, or improvement, the property shall be assessed as provided in this subsection.

(6) In the event of a termination of homestead status, the property shall be assessed as provided by general law.

(7) The provisions of this amendment are severable. If any of the provisions of this amendment shall be held unconstitutional by any court of competent jurisdiction, the decision of such court shall not affect or impair any remaining provisions of this amendment.

(8)a. A person who establishes a new homestead as of January 1 and who has received a homestead exemption pursuant to Section 6 of this Article as of January 1 of any of the three years immediately preceding the establishment of the new homestead is entitled to have the new homestead assessed at less than just value. The assessed value of the newly established homestead shall be determined as follows:

1. If the just value of the new homestead is greater than or equal to the just value of the prior homestead as of January 1 of the year in which the prior homestead was abandoned, the assessed value of the new homestead shall be the just value of the new homestead minus an amount equal to the lesser of $500,000 or the difference between the just value and the assessed value of the prior homestead as of January 1 of the year in which the prior homestead was abandoned. Thereafter, the homestead shall be assessed as provided in this subsection.

CONSTITUTION OF THE STATE OF FLORIDA

2. If the just value of the new homestead is less than the just value of the prior homestead as of January 1 of the year in which the prior homestead was abandoned, the assessed value of the new homestead shall be equal to the just value of the new homestead divided by the just value of the prior homestead and multiplied by the assessed value of the prior homestead. However, if the difference between the just value of the new homestead and the assessed value of the new homestead calculated pursuant to this sub-subparagraph is greater than $500,000, the assessed value of the new homestead shall be increased so that the difference between the just value and the assessed value equals $500,000. Thereafter, the homestead shall be assessed as provided in this subsection.

b. By general law and subject to conditions specified therein, the legislature shall provide for application of this paragraph to property owned by more than one person.

(e) The legislature may, by general law, for assessment purposes and subject to the provisions of this subsection, allow counties and municipalities to authorize by ordinance that historic property may be assessed solely on the basis of character or use. Such character or use assessment shall apply only to the jurisdiction adopting the ordinance. The requirements for eligible properties must be specified by general law.

(f) A county may, in the manner prescribed by general law, provide for a reduction in the assessed value of homestead property to the extent of any increase in the assessed value of that property which results from the construction or reconstruction of the property for the purpose of providing living quarters for one or more natural or adoptive grandparents or parents of the owner of the property or of the owner's spouse if at least one of the grandparents or parents for whom the living quarters are provided is 62 years of age or older. Such a reduction may not exceed the lesser of the following:

(1) The increase in assessed value resulting from construction or reconstruction of the property.

(2) Twenty percent of the total assessed value of the property as improved.

(g) For all levies other than school district levies, assessments of residential real property, as defined by general law, which contains nine units or fewer and which is not subject to the assessment limitations set forth in subsections (a) through (d) shall change only as provided in this subsection.

(1) Assessments subject to this subsection shall be changed annually on the date of assessment provided by law; but those changes in assessments shall not exceed ten percent (10%) of the assessment for the prior year.

(2) No assessment shall exceed just value.

(3) After a change of ownership or control, as defined by general law, including any change of ownership of a legal entity that owns the property, such property shall be assessed at just value as of the next assessment date. Thereafter, such property shall be assessed as provided in this subsection.

(4) Changes, additions, reductions, or improvements to such property shall be assessed as provided for by general law; however, after the adjustment for any change, addition, reduction, or improvement, the property shall be assessed as provided in this subsection.

(h) For all levies other than school district levies, assessments of real property that is not subject to the assessment limitations set forth in subsections (a) through (d) and (g) shall change only as provided in this subsection.

(1) Assessments subject to this subsection shall be changed annually on the date of assessment provided by law; but those changes in assessments shall not exceed ten percent (10%) of the assessment for the prior year.

(2) No assessment shall exceed just value.

(3) The legislature must provide that such property shall be assessed at just value as of the next assessment date after a qualifying improvement, as defined by general law, is made to such property. Thereafter, such property shall be assessed as provided in this subsection.

(4) The legislature may provide that such property shall be assessed at just value as of the next assessment date after a change of ownership or control, as defined by general law, including any change of ownership of the legal entity that owns the property. Thereafter, such property shall be assessed as provided in this subsection.

(5) Changes, additions, reductions, or improvements to such property shall be assessed as provided for by general law; however, after the adjustment for any change, addition, reduction, or improvement, the property shall be assessed as provided in this subsection.

[1](i) The legislature, by general law and subject to conditions specified therein, may prohibit the consideration of the following in the determination of the assessed value of real property:

(1) Any change or improvement to real property used for residential purposes made to improve the property's resistance to wind damage.

(2) The installation of a solar or renewable energy source device.

[2](j)

(1) The assessment of the following working waterfront properties shall be based upon the current use of the property:

a. Land used predominantly for commercial fishing purposes.

b. Land that is accessible to the public and used for vessel launches into waters that are navigable.

c. Marinas and drystacks that are open to the public.

d. Water-dependent marine manufacturing facilities, commercial fishing facilities, and marine vessel construction and repair facilities and their support activities.

CONSTITUTION OF THE STATE OF FLORIDA

(2) The assessment benefit provided by this subsection is subject to conditions and limitations and reasonable definitions as specified by the legislature by general law.

History. — Am. S.J.R. 12-E, 1980; adopted 1980; Am. H.J.R. 214, 1987; adopted 1988; Am. by Initiative Petition filed with the Secretary of State August 3, 1992; adopted 1992; Am. H.J.R. 969, 1997; adopted 1998; Am. proposed by Constitution Revision Commission, Revision No. 13, 1998, filed with the Secretary of State May 5, 1998; adopted 1998; Am. C.S. for H.J.R. 317, 2002; adopted 2002; Am. C.S. for S.J.R. 2-D, 2007; adopted 2008; Ams. Proposed by Taxation and Budget Reform Commission, Revision Nos. 3, 4, and 6, 2008, filed with the Secretary of State April 28, 2008; adopted 2008; Am. C.S. for H.J.R. 193, 2016; adopted 2016; Am. H.J.R. 369, 2020; adopted 2020.

[1]**Note.** —

A. This subsection, originally designated (h) by Revision No. 3 of the Taxation and Budget Reform Commission, 2008, was redesignated (i) by the editors to conform to the redesignation of subsections by Revision No. 4 of the Taxation and Budget Reform Commission, 2008.

B. Section 34, Art. XII, State Constitution, provides in part that "the amendment to subsection (i) of Section 4 of Article VII authorizing the legislature, by general law, to prohibit the consideration of the installation of a solar device or a renewable energy source device in determining the assessed value of real property for the purpose of ad valorem taxation shall take effect on January 1, 2018, and shall expire on December 31, 2037. Upon expiration, this section shall be repealed and the text of . . . subsection (i) of Section 4 of Article VII shall revert to that in existence on December 31, 2017, except that any amendments to such text otherwise adopted shall be preserved and continue to operate to the extent that such amendments are not dependent upon the portions of text which expire pursuant to this section." Effective December 31, 2037, s. 4(i), Art. VII, State Constitution, will read:

(i) The legislature, by general law and subject to conditions specified therein, may prohibit the consideration of the following in the determination of the assessed value of real property used for residential purposes:

(1) Any change or improvement made for the purpose of improving the property's resistance to wind damage.

(2) The installation of a renewable energy source device.

[2]**Note.** — This subsection, originally designated (h) by Revision No. 6 of the Taxation and Budget Reform Commission, 2008, was redesignated (j) by the editors to conform to the redesignation of subsections by Revision No. 4 of the Taxation and Budget Reform Commission, 2008, and the creation of a new (h) by Revision No. 3 of the Taxation and Budget Reform Commission, 2008.

SECTION 5. Estate, inheritance and income taxes. —

(a) NATURAL PERSONS. No tax upon estates or inheritances or upon the income of natural persons who are residents or citizens of the state shall be levied by the state, or under its authority, in excess of the aggregate of amounts which may be allowed to be credited upon or deducted from any similar tax levied by the United States or any state.

(b) OTHERS. No tax upon the income of residents and citizens other than natural persons shall be levied by the state, or under its authority, in excess of 5% of net income, as defined by law, or at such greater rate as is authorized by a three-fifths (3/5) vote of the membership of each house of the legislature or as will provide for the state the maximum amount which may be allowed to be credited against income taxes levied by the United States and other states. There shall be exempt from taxation not less than five thousand dollars ($5,000) of the excess of net income subject to tax over the maximum amount allowed to be credited against income taxes levied by the United States and other states.

(c) EFFECTIVE DATE. This section shall become effective immediately upon approval by the electors of Florida.

History. — Am. H.J.R. 7-B, 1971; adopted 1971.

SECTION 6. Homestead exemptions. —

(a) Every person who has the legal or equitable title to real estate and maintains thereon the permanent residence of the owner, or another legally or naturally dependent upon the owner, shall be exempt from taxation thereon, except assessments for special benefits, up to the assessed valuation of twenty-five thousand dollars and, for all levies other than school district levies, on the assessed valuation greater than fifty thousand dollars and up to seventy-five thousand dollars, upon establishment of right thereto in the manner prescribed by law. The real estate may be held by legal or equitable title, by the entireties, jointly, in common, as a condominium, or indirectly by stock ownership or membership representing the owner's or member's proprietary interest in a corporation owning a fee or a leasehold initially in excess of ninety-eight years. The exemption shall not apply with respect to any assessment roll until such roll is first determined to be in compliance with the provisions of section 4 by a state agency designated by general law. This exemption is repealed on the effective date of any amendment to this Article which provides for the assessment of homestead property at less than just value.

(b) Not more than one exemption shall be allowed any individual or family unit or with respect to any residential unit. No exemption shall exceed the value of the real estate assessable to the owner or, in case of ownership through stock or membership in a corporation, the value of the proportion which the interest in the corporation bears to the assessed value of the property.

(c) By general law and subject to conditions specified therein, the Legislature may provide to renters, who are permanent residents, ad valorem tax relief on all ad valorem tax levies. Such ad valorem tax relief shall be in the form and amount established by general law.

[1](d) The legislature may, by general law, allow counties or municipalities, for the purpose of their respective tax levies and subject to the provisions of general law, to grant either or both of the following additional homestead tax exemptions:

(1) An exemption not exceeding fifty thousand dollars to a person who has the legal or equitable title to real estate and maintains thereon the permanent residence of the owner, who has attained age sixty-five, and whose household income, as defined by general law, does not exceed twenty thousand dollars; or

(2) An exemption equal to the assessed value of the property to a person who has the legal or equitable title to real estate with a just value less than two hundred and fifty thousand dollars, as determined in the first tax year that the owner applies and is eligible for the exemption, and who has maintained thereon the permanent residence of the owner for not less than twenty-five years, who has attained age sixty-five, and whose household income does not exceed the income limitation prescribed in paragraph (1).

The general law must allow counties and municipalities to grant these additional exemptions, within the limits prescribed in this subsection, by ordinance adopted in the manner prescribed by general law, and must provide for the periodic adjustment of the income limitation prescribed in this subsection for changes in the cost of living.

(e)(1) Each veteran who is age 65 or older who is partially or totally permanently disabled shall receive a discount from the amount of the ad valorem tax otherwise owed on homestead property the veteran owns and resides in if the disability was combat related and the veteran was honorably discharged upon separation from military service. The discount shall be in a percentage equal to the percentage of the veteran's permanent, service-connected disability as determined by the United States Department of Veterans Affairs. To qualify for the discount granted by this paragraph, an applicant must submit to the county property appraiser, by March 1, an official letter from the United States Department of Veterans Affairs stating the percentage of the veteran's service-connected disability and such evidence that reasonably identifies the disability as combat related and a copy of the veteran's honorable discharge. If the property appraiser denies the request for a discount, the appraiser must notify the applicant in writing of the reasons for the denial, and the veteran may reapply. The Legislature may, by general law, waive the annual application requirement in subsequent years.

(2) If a veteran who receives the discount described in paragraph (1) predeceases his or her spouse, and if, upon the death of the veteran, the surviving spouse holds the legal or beneficial title to the homestead property and permanently resides thereon, the discount carries over to the surviving spouse until he or she remarries or sells or otherwise disposes of the homestead property. If the surviving spouse sells or otherwise disposes of the property, a discount not to exceed the dollar amount granted from the most recent ad valorem tax roll may be transferred to the surviving spouse's new homestead property, if used as his or her permanent residence and he or she has not remarried.

(3) This subsection is self-executing and does not require implementing legislation.

(f) By general law and subject to conditions and limitations specified therein, the Legislature may provide ad valorem tax relief equal to the total amount or a portion of the ad valorem tax otherwise owed on homestead property to:

(1) The surviving spouse of a veteran who died from service-connected causes while on active duty as a member of the United States Armed Forces.

(2) The surviving spouse of a first responder who died in the line of duty.

(3) A first responder who is totally and permanently disabled as a result of an injury or injuries sustained in the line of duty. Causal connection between a disability and service in the line of duty shall not be presumed but must be determined as provided by general law. For purposes of this paragraph, the term "disability" does not include a chronic condition or chronic disease, unless the injury sustained in the line of duty was the sole cause of the chronic condition or chronic disease.

As used in this subsection and as further defined by general law, the term "first responder" means a law enforcement officer, a correctional officer, a firefighter, an emergency medical technician, or a paramedic, and the term "in the line of duty" means arising out of and in the actual performance of duty required by employment as a first responder.

History. — Am. S.J.R. 1-B, 1979; adopted 1980; Am. S.J.R. 4-E, 1980; adopted 1980; Am. H.J.R. 3151, 1998; adopted 1998; Am. proposed by Constitution Revision Commission, Revision No. 13, 1998, filed with the Secretary of State May 5, 1998; adopted 1998; Am. H.J.R. 353, 2006; adopted 2006; Am. H.J.R. 631, 2006; adopted 2006; Am. C.S. for S.J.R. 2-D, 2007; adopted 2008; Am. S.J.R. 592, 2011; adopted 2012; Am. H.J.R. 93, 2012; adopted 2012; Am. H.J.R. 169, 2012; adopted 2012; Am. C.S. for H.J.R. 275, 2016; adopted 2016; Am. C.S. for H.J.R. 1009, 2016; adopted 2016; Am. H.J.R. 877, 2020; adopted 2020.

[1]**Note.** — Section 36, Art. XII, State Constitution, provides in part that "the amendment to Section 6 of Article VII revising the just value determination for the additional ad valorem tax exemption for persons age sixty-five or older shall take effect January 1, 2017, . . . and shall operate retroactively to January 1, 2013, for any person who received the exemption under paragraph (2) of Section 6(d) of Article VII before January 1, 2017."

SECTION 7. Allocation of pari-mutuel taxes. — Taxes upon the operation of pari-mutuel pools may be preempted to the state or allocated in whole or in part to the counties. When allocated to the counties, the distribution shall be in equal amounts to the several counties.

SECTION 8. Aid to local governments. — State funds may be appropriated to the several counties, school districts, municipalities or special districts upon such conditions as may be provided by general law. These conditions may include the use of relative ad valorem assessment levels determined by a state agency designated by general law.

History. — Am. S.J.R. 4-E, 1980; adopted 1980.

CONSTITUTION OF THE STATE OF FLORIDA

SECTION 9. Local taxes. —

(a) Counties, school districts, and municipalities shall, and special districts may, be authorized by law to levy ad valorem taxes and may be authorized by general law to levy other taxes, for their respective purposes, except ad valorem taxes on intangible personal property and taxes prohibited by this constitution.

(b) Ad valorem taxes, exclusive of taxes levied for the payment of bonds and taxes levied for periods not longer than two years when authorized by vote of the electors who are the owners of freeholds therein not wholly exempt from taxation, shall not be levied in excess of the following millages upon the assessed value of real estate and tangible personal property: for all county purposes, ten mills; for all municipal purposes, ten mills; for all school purposes, ten mills; for water management purposes for the northwest portion of the state lying west of the line between ranges two and three east, 0.05 mill; for water management purposes for the remaining portions of the state, 1.0 mill; and for all other special districts a millage authorized by law approved by vote of the electors who are owners of freeholds therein not wholly exempt from taxation. A county furnishing municipal services may, to the extent authorized by law, levy additional taxes within the limits fixed for municipal purposes.

History. — Am. S.J.R. 1061, 1975; adopted 1976.

SECTION 10. Pledging credit. — Neither the state nor any county, school district, municipality, special district, or agency of any of them, shall become a joint owner with, or stockholder of, or give, lend or use its taxing power or credit to aid any corporation, association, partnership or person; but this shall not prohibit laws authorizing:

(a) the investment of public trust funds;

(b) the investment of other public funds in obligations of, or insured by, the United States or any of its instrumentalities;

(c) the issuance and sale by any county, municipality, special district or other local governmental body of (1) revenue bonds to finance or refinance the cost of capital projects for airports or port facilities, or (2) revenue bonds to finance or refinance the cost of capital projects for industrial or manufacturing plants to the extent that the interest thereon is exempt from income taxes under the then existing laws of the United States, when, in either case, the revenue bonds are payable solely from revenue derived from the sale, operation or leasing of the projects. If any project so financed, or any part thereof, is occupied or operated by any private corporation, association, partnership or person pursuant to contract or lease with the issuing body, the property interest created by such contract or lease shall be subject to taxation to the same extent as other privately owned property.

(d) a municipality, county, special district, or agency of any of them, being a joint owner of, giving, or lending or using its taxing power or credit for the joint ownership, construction and operation of electrical energy generating or transmission facilities with any corporation, association, partnership or person.

History. — Am. H.J.R. 1424, 1973; adopted 1974.

CONSTITUTION OF THE STATE OF FLORIDA

SECTION 11. State bonds; revenue bonds. —

(a) State bonds pledging the full faith and credit of the state may be issued only to finance or refinance the cost of state fixed capital outlay projects authorized by law, and purposes incidental thereto, upon approval by a vote of the electors; provided state bonds issued pursuant to this subsection may be refunded without a vote of the electors at a lower net average interest cost rate. The total outstanding principal of state bonds issued pursuant to this subsection shall never exceed fifty percent of the total tax revenues of the state for the two preceding fiscal years, excluding any tax revenues held in trust under the provisions of this constitution.

(b) Moneys sufficient to pay debt service on state bonds as the same becomes due shall be appropriated by law.

(c) Any state bonds pledging the full faith and credit of the state issued under this section or any other section of this constitution may be combined for the purposes of sale.

(d) Revenue bonds may be issued by the state or its agencies without a vote of the electors to finance or refinance the cost of state fixed capital outlay projects authorized by law, and purposes incidental thereto, and shall be payable solely from funds derived directly from sources other than state tax revenues.

(e) Bonds pledging all or part of a dedicated state tax revenue may be issued by the state in the manner provided by general law to finance or refinance the acquisition and improvement of land, water areas, and related property interests and resources for the purposes of conservation, outdoor recreation, water resource development, restoration of natural systems, and historic preservation.

(f) Each project, building, or facility to be financed or refinanced with revenue bonds issued under this section shall first be approved by the Legislature by an act relating to appropriations or by general law.

History. — Am. C.S. for C.S. for S.J.R. 612, 1984; adopted 1984; Am. proposed by Constitution Revision Commission, Revision No. 5, 1998, filed with the Secretary of State May 5, 1998; adopted 1998.

SECTION 12. Local bonds. — Counties, school districts, municipalities, special districts and local governmental bodies with taxing powers may issue bonds, certificates of indebtedness or any form of tax anticipation certificates, payable from ad valorem taxation and maturing more than twelve months after issuance only:

(a) to finance or refinance capital projects authorized by law and only when approved by vote of the electors who are owners of freeholds therein not wholly exempt from taxation; or

(b) to refund outstanding bonds and interest and redemption premium thereon at a lower net average interest cost rate.

SECTION 13. Relief from illegal taxes. — Until payment of all taxes which have been legally assessed upon the property of the same owner, no court shall grant relief from the payment of any tax that may be illegal or illegally assessed.

CONSTITUTION OF THE STATE OF FLORIDA

SECTION 14. Bonds for pollution control and abatement and other water facilities. —

(a) When authorized by law, state bonds pledging the full faith and credit of the state may be issued without an election to finance the construction of air and water pollution control and abatement and solid waste disposal facilities and other water facilities authorized by general law (herein referred to as "facilities") to be operated by any municipality, county, district or authority, or any agency thereof (herein referred to as "local governmental agencies"), or by any agency of the State of Florida. Such bonds shall be secured by a pledge of and shall be payable primarily from all or any part of revenues to be derived from operation of such facilities, special assessments, rentals to be received under lease-purchase agreements herein provided for, any other revenues that may be legally available for such purpose, including revenues from other facilities, or any combination thereof (herein collectively referred to as "pledged revenues"), and shall be additionally secured by the full faith and credit of the State of Florida.

(b) No such bonds shall be issued unless a state fiscal agency, created by law, has made a determination that in no state fiscal year will the debt service requirements of the bonds proposed to be issued and all other bonds secured by the pledged revenues exceed seventy-five per cent of the pledged revenues.

(c) The state may lease any of such facilities to any local governmental agency, under lease-purchase agreements for such periods and under such other terms and conditions as may be mutually agreed upon. The local governmental agencies may pledge the revenues derived from such leased facilities or any other available funds for the payment of rentals thereunder; and, in addition, the full faith and credit and taxing power of such local governmental agencies may be pledged for the payment of such rentals without any election of freeholder electors or qualified electors.

(d) The state may also issue such bonds for the purpose of loaning money to local governmental agencies, for the construction of such facilities to be owned or operated by any of such local governmental agencies. Such loans shall bear interest at not more than one-half of one per cent per annum greater than the last preceding issue of state bonds pursuant to this section, shall be secured by the pledged revenues, and may be additionally secured by the full faith and credit of the local governmental agencies.

(e) The total outstanding principal of state bonds issued pursuant to this section 14 shall never exceed fifty per cent of the total tax revenues of the state for the two preceding fiscal years.

History. — C.S. for H.J.R.'s 3853, 4040, 1970; adopted 1970; Am. H.J.R. 1471, 1980; adopted 1980.

SECTION 15. Revenue bonds for scholarship loans. —

(a) When authorized by law, revenue bonds may be issued to establish a fund to make loans to students determined eligible as prescribed by law and who have been admitted to attend any public or private institutions of higher learning, junior colleges, health related training institutions, or vocational training centers, which are recognized or accredited under terms and conditions prescribed by law. Revenue bonds issued pursuant to this section shall be secured by a pledge of and shall be payable primarily from payments of interest, principal, and handling charges to such fund from the recipients of the loans and, if authorized by law, may be additionally secured by student fees and by any other moneys in such fund. There shall be established from the proceeds of each issue of revenue bonds a reserve account in an amount equal to and sufficient to pay the greatest amount of principal, interest, and handling charges to become due on such issue in any ensuing state fiscal year.

(b) Interest moneys in the fund established pursuant to this section, not required in any fiscal year for payment of debt service on then outstanding revenue bonds or for maintenance of the reserve account, may be used for educational loans to students determined to be eligible therefor in the manner provided by law, or for such other related purposes as may be provided by law.

History. — Added, H.J.R. 46-D, 1971; adopted 1972.

SECTION 16. Bonds for housing and related facilities. —

(a) When authorized by law, revenue bonds may be issued without an election to finance or refinance housing and related facilities in Florida, herein referred to as "facilities."

(b) The bonds shall be secured by a pledge of and shall be payable primarily from all or any part of revenues to be derived from the financing, operation or sale of such facilities, mortgage or loan payments, and any other revenues or assets that may be legally available for such purposes derived from sources other than ad valorem taxation, including revenues from other facilities, or any combination thereof, herein collectively referred to as "pledged revenues," provided that in no event shall the full faith and credit of the state be pledged to secure such revenue bonds.

(c) No bonds shall be issued unless a state fiscal agency, created by law, has made a determination that in no state fiscal year will the debt service requirements of the bonds proposed to be issued and all other bonds secured by the same pledged revenues exceed the pledged revenues available for payment of such debt service requirements, as defined by law.

History. — Added, S.J.R. 6-E, 1980; adopted 1980.

SECTION 17. Bonds for acquiring transportation right-of-way or for constructing bridges. —

(a) When authorized by law, state bonds pledging the full faith and credit of the state may be issued, without a vote of the electors, to finance or refinance the cost of acquiring real property or the rights to real property for state roads as defined by law, or to finance or refinance the cost of state bridge construction, and purposes incidental to such property acquisition or state bridge construction.

CONSTITUTION OF THE STATE OF FLORIDA

(b) Bonds issued under this section shall be secured by a pledge of and shall be payable primarily from motor fuel or special fuel taxes, except those defined in Section 9(c) of Article XII, as provided by law, and shall additionally be secured by the full faith and credit of the state.

(c) No bonds shall be issued under this section unless a state fiscal agency, created by law, has made a determination that in no state fiscal year will the debt service requirements of the bonds proposed to be issued and all other bonds secured by the same pledged revenues exceed ninety percent of the pledged revenues available for payment of such debt service requirements, as defined by law. For the purposes of this subsection, the term "pledged revenues" means all revenues pledged to the payment of debt service, excluding any pledge of the full faith and credit of the state.

History. — Added, C.S. for C.S. for S.J.R. 391, 1988; adopted 1988.

SECTION 18. Laws requiring counties or municipalities to spend funds or limiting their ability to raise revenue or receive state tax revenue. —

(a) No county or municipality shall be bound by any general law requiring such county or municipality to spend funds or to take an action requiring the expenditure of funds unless the legislature has determined that such law fulfills an important state interest and unless: funds have been appropriated that have been estimated at the time of enactment to be sufficient to fund such expenditure; the legislature authorizes or has authorized a county or municipality to enact a funding source not available for such county or municipality on February 1, 1989, that can be used to generate the amount of funds estimated to be sufficient to fund such expenditure by a simple majority vote of the governing body of such county or municipality; the law requiring such expenditure is approved by two-thirds of the membership in each house of the legislature; the expenditure is required to comply with a law that applies to all persons similarly situated, including the state and local governments; or the law is either required to comply with a federal requirement or required for eligibility for a federal entitlement, which federal requirement specifically contemplates actions by counties or municipalities for compliance.

(b) Except upon approval of each house of the legislature by two-thirds of the membership, the legislature may not enact, amend, or repeal any general law if the anticipated effect of doing so would be to reduce the authority that municipalities or counties have to raise revenues in the aggregate, as such authority exists on February 1, 1989.

(c) Except upon approval of each house of the legislature by two-thirds of the membership, the legislature may not enact, amend, or repeal any general law if the anticipated effect of doing so would be to reduce the percentage of a state tax shared with counties and municipalities as an aggregate on February 1, 1989. The provisions of this subsection shall not apply to enhancements enacted after February 1, 1989, to state tax sources, or during a fiscal emergency declared in a written joint proclamation issued by the president of the senate and the speaker of the house of representatives, or where the legislature provides additional state-shared revenues which are anticipated to be sufficient to replace the anticipated aggregate loss of state-shared revenues resulting from the reduction of the percentage of the state tax shared with counties and municipalities, which source of replacement revenues shall be subject to the same requirements for repeal or modification as provided herein for a state-shared tax source existing on February 1, 1989.

(d) Laws adopted to require funding of pension benefits existing on the effective date of this section, criminal laws, election laws, the general appropriations act, special appropriations acts, laws reauthorizing but not expanding then-existing statutory authority, laws having insignificant fiscal impact, and laws creating, modifying, or repealing noncriminal infractions, are exempt from the requirements of this section.

(e) The legislature may enact laws to assist in the implementation and enforcement of this section.

History. — Added, C.S. for C.S. for C.S. for C.S. for H.J.R.'s 139, 40, 1989; adopted 1990.

SECTION 19. Supermajority vote required to impose, authorize, or raise state taxes or fees. —

(a) SUPERMAJORITY VOTE REQUIRED TO IMPOSE OR AUTHORIZE NEW STATE TAX OR FEE. No new state tax or fee may be imposed or authorized by the legislature except through legislation approved by two-thirds of the membership of each house of the legislature and presented to the Governor for approval pursuant to Article III, Section 8.

(b) SUPERMAJORITY VOTE REQUIRED TO RAISE STATE TAXES OR FEES. No state tax or fee may be raised by the legislature except through legislation approved by two-thirds of the membership of each house of the legislature and presented to the Governor for approval pursuant to Article III, Section 8.

(c) APPLICABILITY. This section does not authorize the imposition of any state tax or fee otherwise prohibited by this Constitution, and does not apply to any tax or fee imposed by, or authorized to be imposed by, a county, municipality, school board, or special district.

(d) DEFINITIONS. As used in this section, the following terms shall have the following meanings:

(1) "Fee" means any charge or payment required by law, including any fee for service, fee or cost for licenses, and charge for service.

(2) "Raise" means:

a. To increase or authorize an increase in the rate of a state tax or fee imposed on a percentage or per mill basis;

b. To increase or authorize an increase in the amount of a state tax or fee imposed on a flat or fixed amount basis; or

c. To decrease or eliminate a state tax or fee exemption or credit.

CONSTITUTION OF THE STATE OF FLORIDA

(e) SINGLE-SUBJECT. A state tax or fee imposed, authorized, or raised under this section must be contained in a separate bill that contains no other subject.

History. — Added, H.J.R. 7001, 2018; adopted 2018.

ARTICLE VIII
LOCAL GOVERNMENT

SECTION 1.

Counties.

SECTION 2.

Municipalities.

SECTION 3.

Consolidation.

SECTION 4.

Transfer of powers.

SECTION 5.

Local option.

SECTION 6.

Schedule to Article VIII.

SECTION 1. Counties. —

(a) POLITICAL SUBDIVISIONS. The state shall be divided by law into political subdivisions called counties. Counties may be created, abolished or changed by law, with provision for payment or apportionment of the public debt.

(b) COUNTY FUNDS. The care, custody and method of disbursing county funds shall be provided by general law.

(c) GOVERNMENT. Pursuant to general or special law, a county government may be established by charter which shall be adopted, amended or repealed only upon vote of the electors of the county in a special election called for that purpose.

[1](d) COUNTY OFFICERS. There shall be elected by the electors of each county, for terms of four years, a sheriff, a tax collector, a property appraiser, a supervisor of elections, and a clerk of the circuit court. Unless otherwise provided by special law approved by vote of the electors or pursuant to Article V, section 16, the clerk of the circuit court shall be ex officio clerk of the board of county commissioners, auditor, recorder and custodian of all county funds. Notwithstanding subsection 6(e) of this article, a county charter may not abolish the office of a sheriff, a tax collector, a property appraiser, a supervisor of elections, or a clerk of the circuit court; transfer the duties of those officers to another officer or office; change the length of the four-year term of office; or establish any manner of selection other than by election by the electors of the county.

(e) COMMISSIONERS. Except when otherwise provided by county charter, the governing body of each county shall be a board of county commissioners composed of five or seven members serving staggered terms of four years. After each decennial census the board of county commissioners shall divide the county into districts of contiguous territory as nearly equal in population as practicable. One commissioner residing in each district shall be elected as provided by law.

(f) NON-CHARTER GOVERNMENT. Counties not operating under county charters shall have such power of self-government as is provided by general or special law. The board of county commissioners of a county not operating under a charter may enact, in a manner prescribed by general law, county ordinances not inconsistent with general or special law, but an ordinance in conflict with a municipal ordinance shall not be effective within the municipality to the extent of such conflict.

(g) CHARTER GOVERNMENT. Counties operating under county charters shall have all powers of local self-government not inconsistent with general law, or with special law approved by vote of the electors. The governing body of a county operating under a charter may enact county ordinances not inconsistent with general law. The charter shall provide which shall prevail in the event of conflict between county and municipal ordinances.

(h) TAXES; LIMITATION. Property situate within municipalities shall not be subject to taxation for services rendered by the county exclusively for the benefit of the property or residents in unincorporated areas.

(i) COUNTY ORDINANCES. Each county ordinance shall be filed with the custodian of state records and shall become effective at such time thereafter as is provided by general law.

(j) VIOLATION OF ORDINANCES. Persons violating county ordinances shall be prosecuted and punished as provided by law.

(k) COUNTY SEAT. In every county there shall be a county seat at which shall be located the principal offices and permanent records of all county officers. The county seat may not be moved except as provided by general law. Branch offices for the conduct of county business may be established elsewhere in the county by resolution of the governing body of the county in the manner prescribed by law. No instrument shall be deemed recorded until filed at the county seat, or a branch office designated by the governing body of the county for the recording of instruments, according to law.

History. — Am. H.J.R. 1907, 1973; adopted 1974; Am. H.J.R. 452, 1984; adopted 1984; Am. H.J.R. 125, 1998; adopted 1998; Am. proposed by Constitution Revision Commission, Revision No. 8, 1998, filed with the Secretary of State May 5, 1998; adopted 1998; Am. proposed by Constitution Revision Commission, Revision No. 5, 2018, filed with the Secretary of State May 9, 2018; adopted 2018.

[1]**Note.** — Section 6(g), Art. VIII, State Constitution, provides that:

CONSTITUTION OF THE STATE OF FLORIDA 1031

(g) SELECTION AND DUTIES OF COUNTY OFFICERS.

(1) Except as provided in this subsection, the amendment to Section 1 of this article, relating to the selection and duties of county officers, shall take effect January 5, 2021, but shall govern with respect to the qualifying for and the holding of the primary and general elections for county constitutional officers in 2020.

(2) For Miami-Dade County and Broward County, the amendment to Section 1 of this article, relating to the selection and duties of county officers, shall take effect January 7, 2025, but shall govern with respect to the qualifying for and the holding of the primary and general elections for county constitutional officers in 2024.

Prior to the amendment of s. 1, Art. VIII, State Constitution, by Constitution Revision Commission, Revision No. 5 (2018), s. 1(d), Art. VIII, read:

(d) COUNTY OFFICERS. There shall be elected by the electors of each county, for terms of four years, a sheriff, a tax collector, a property appraiser, a supervisor of elections, and a clerk of the circuit court; except, when provided by county charter or special law approved by vote of the electors of the county, any county officer may be chosen in another manner therein specified, or any county office may be abolished when all the duties of the office prescribed by general law are transferred to another office. When not otherwise provided by county charter or special law approved by vote of the electors, the clerk of the circuit court shall be ex officio clerk of the board of county commissioners, auditor, recorder and custodian of all county funds.

SECTION 2. Municipalities. —

(a) ESTABLISHMENT. Municipalities may be established or abolished and their charters amended pursuant to general or special law. When any municipality is abolished, provision shall be made for the protection of its creditors.

(b) POWERS. Municipalities shall have governmental, corporate and proprietary powers to enable them to conduct municipal government, perform municipal functions and render municipal services, and may exercise any power for municipal purposes except as otherwise provided by law. Each municipal legislative body shall be elective.

(c) ANNEXATION. Municipal annexation of unincorporated territory, merger of municipalities, and exercise of extra-territorial powers by municipalities shall be as provided by general or special law.

SECTION 3. Consolidation. — The government of a county and the government of one or more municipalities located therein may be consolidated into a single government which may exercise any and all powers of the county and the several municipalities. The consolidation plan may be proposed only by special law, which shall become effective if approved by vote of the electors of the county, or of the county and municipalities affected, as may be provided in the plan. Consolidation shall not extend the territorial scope of taxation for the payment of pre-existing debt except to areas whose residents receive a benefit from the facility or service for which the indebtedness was incurred.

SECTION 4. Transfer of powers. — By law or by resolution of the governing bodies of each of the governments affected, any function or power of a county, municipality or special district may be transferred to or contracted to be performed by another county, municipality or special district, after approval by vote of the electors of the transferor and approval by vote of the electors of the transferee, or as otherwise provided by law.

SECTION 5. Local option. —

(a) Local option on the legality or prohibition of the sale of intoxicating liquors, wines or beers shall be preserved to each county. The status of a county with respect thereto shall be changed only by vote of the electors in a special election called upon the petition of twenty-five per cent of the electors of the county, and not sooner than two years after an earlier election on the same question. Where legal, the sale of intoxicating liquors, wines and beers shall be regulated by law.

(b) Each county shall have the authority to require a criminal history records check and a 3 to 5-day waiting period, excluding weekends and legal holidays, in connection with the sale of any firearm occurring within such county. For purposes of this subsection, the term "sale" means the transfer of money or other valuable consideration for any firearm when any part of the transaction is conducted on property to which the public has the right of access. Holders of a concealed weapons permit as prescribed by general law shall not be subject to the provisions of this subsection when purchasing a firearm.

History. — Am. proposed by Constitution Revision Commission, Revision No. 12, 1998, filed with the Secretary of State May 5, 1998; adopted 1998.

SECTION 6. Schedule to Article VIII. —

(a) This article shall replace all of Article VIII of the Constitution of 1885, as amended, except those sections expressly retained and made a part of this article by reference.

(b) COUNTIES; COUNTY SEATS; MUNICIPALITIES; DISTRICTS. The status of the following items as they exist on the date this article becomes effective is recognized and shall be continued until changed in accordance with law: the counties of the state; their status with respect to the legality of the sale of intoxicating liquors, wines and beers; the method of selection of county officers; the performance of municipal functions by county officers; the county seats; and the municipalities and special districts of the state, their powers, jurisdiction and government.

(c) OFFICERS TO CONTINUE IN OFFICE. Every person holding office when this article becomes effective shall continue in office for the remainder of the term if that office is not abolished. If the office is abolished the incumbent shall be paid adequate compensation, to be fixed by law, for the loss of emoluments for the remainder of the term.

(d) ORDINANCES. Local laws relating only to unincorporated areas of a county on the effective date of this article may be amended or repealed by county ordinance.

CONSTITUTION OF THE STATE OF FLORIDA 1033

(e) CONSOLIDATION AND HOME RULE. Article VIII, Sections [1]9, [2]10, [3]11 and [4]24, of the Constitution of 1885, as amended, shall remain in full force and effect as to each county affected, as if this article had not been adopted, until that county shall expressly adopt a charter or home rule plan pursuant to this article. All provisions of the Metropolitan Dade County Home Rule Charter, heretofore or hereafter adopted by the electors of Dade County pursuant to [3]Article VIII, Section 11, of the Constitution of 1885, as amended, shall be valid, and any amendments to such charter shall be valid; provided that the said provisions of such charter and the said amendments thereto are authorized under said [3]Article VIII, Section 11, of the Constitution of 1885, as amended.

(f) DADE COUNTY; POWERS CONFERRED UPON MUNICIPALITIES. To the extent not inconsistent with the powers of existing municipalities or general law, the Metropolitan Government of Dade County may exercise all the powers conferred now or hereafter by general law upon municipalities.

(g) SELECTION AND DUTIES OF COUNTY OFFICERS. —

(1) Except as provided in this subsection, the amendment to Section 1 of this article, relating to the selection and duties of county officers, shall take effect January 5, 2021, but shall govern with respect to the qualifying for and the holding of the primary and general elections for county constitutional officers in 2020.

(2) For Miami-Dade County and Broward County, the amendment to Section 1 of this article, relating to the selection and duties of county officers, shall take effect January 7, 2025, but shall govern with respect to the qualifying for and the holding of the primary and general elections for county constitutional officers in 2024.

(h) DELETION OF OBSOLETE SCHEDULE ITEMS. The legislature shall have power, by joint resolution, to delete from this article any subsection of this Section 6, including this subsection, when all events to which the subsection to be deleted is or could become applicable have occurred. A legislative determination of fact made as a basis for application of this subsection shall be subject to judicial review.

History. — Am. proposed by Constitution Revision Commission, Revision No. 5, 2018, filed with the Secretary of State May 9, 2018; adopted 2018.

[1]**Note.** — Section 9 of Art. VIII of the Constitution of 1885, as amended, reads as follows:

SECTION 9. Legislative power over city of Jacksonville and Duval County. — The Legislature shall have power to establish, alter or abolish, a Municipal corporation to be known as the City of Jacksonville, extending territorially throughout the present limits of Duval County, in the place of any or all county, district, municipal and local governments, boards, bodies and officers, constitutional or statutory, legislative, executive, judicial, or administrative, and shall prescribe the jurisdiction, powers, duties and functions of such municipal corporation, its legislative, executive, judicial and administrative departments and its boards, bodies and officers; to divide the territory included in such municipality into subordinate districts, and to prescribe a just and reasonable system of taxation for such municipality and districts; and to fix the liability of such municipality and districts. Bonded and other indebtedness, existing at the time of the establishment of such municipality, shall be enforceable only against property theretofore taxable therefor. The Legislature shall, from time to time, determine what portion of said municipality is a rural area, and a homestead in such rural area shall not be limited as if in a city or town. Such municipality may exercise all the powers of a municipal corporation and shall also be recognized as one of the legal political divisions of the State with the duties and obligations of a county and shall be entitled to all the powers, rights and privileges, including representation in the State Legislature, which would accrue to it if it were a county. All property of Duval County and of the municipalities in said county shall vest in such municipal corporation when established as herein provided. The offices of Clerk of the Circuit Court and Sheriff shall not be abolished but the Legislature may prescribe the time when, and the method by which, such offices shall be filled and the compensation to be paid to such officers and may vest in them additional powers and duties. No county office shall be abolished or consolidated with another office without making provision for the performance of all State duties now or hereafter prescribed by law to be performed by such county officer. Nothing contained herein shall affect Section 20 of Article III of the Constitution of the State of Florida, except as to such provisions therein as relate to regulating the jurisdiction and duties of any class of officers, to summoning and impanelling grand and petit jurors, to assessing and collecting taxes for county purposes and to regulating the fees and compensation of county officers. No law authorizing the establishing or abolishing of such Municipal corporation pursuant to this Section, shall become operative or effective until approved by a majority of the qualified electors participating in an election held in said County, but so long as such Municipal corporation exists under this Section the Legislature may amend or extend the law authorizing the same without referendum to the qualified voters unless the Legislative act providing for such amendment or extension shall provide for such referendum.

History. — Added, S.J.R. 113, 1933; adopted 1934.

[2]**Note.** — Section 10, Art. VIII of the Constitution of 1885, as amended, reads as follows:

SECTION 10. Legislative power over city of Key West and Monroe county. — The Legislature shall have power to establish, alter or abolish, a Municipal corporation to be known as the City of Key West, extending territorially throughout the present limits of Monroe County, in the place of any or all county, district, municipal and local governments, boards, bodies and officers, constitutional or statutory, legislative, executive, judicial, or administrative, and shall prescribe the jurisdiction, powers, duties and functions of such municipal corporation, its legislative, executive, judicial and administrative departments and its boards, bodies and officers; to divide the territory included in such municipality into subordinate districts, and to prescribe a just and reasonable system of taxation for such municipality and districts; and to fix the liability of such municipality and districts. Bonded and other

CONSTITUTION OF THE STATE OF FLORIDA   1035

indebtedness, existing at the time of the establishment of such municipality, shall be enforceable only against property theretofore taxable therefor. The Legislature shall, from time to time, determine what portion of said municipality is a rural area, and a homestead in such rural area shall not be limited as if in a city or town. Such municipality may exercise all the powers of a municipal corporation and shall also be recognized as one of the legal political divisions of the State with the duties and obligations of a county and shall be entitled to all the powers, rights and privileges, including representation in the State Legislature, which would accrue to it if it were a county. All property of Monroe County and of the municipality in said county shall vest in such municipal corporation when established as herein provided. The offices of Clerk of the Circuit Court and Sheriff shall not be abolished but the Legislature may prescribe the time when, and the method by which, such offices shall be filled and the compensation to be paid to such officers and may vest in them additional powers and duties. No county office shall be abolished or consolidated with another office without making provision for the performance of all State duties now or hereafter prescribed by law to be performed by such county officer. Nothing contained herein shall affect Section 20 of Article III of the Constitution of the State of Florida, except as to such provisions therein as relate to regulating the jurisdiction and duties of any class of officers, to summoning and impanelling grand and petit juries, to assessing and collecting taxes for county purposes and to regulating the fees and compensation of county officers. No law authorizing the establishing or abolishing of such Municipal corporation pursuant to this Section shall become operative or effective until approved by a majority of the qualified electors participating in an election held in said County, but so long as such Municipal corporation exists under this Section the Legislature may amend or extend the law authorizing the same without referendum to the qualified voters unless the Legislative Act providing for such amendment or extension shall provide for such referendum.

History. — Added, S.J.R. 429, 1935; adopted 1936.

[3]**Note.** — Section 11 of Art. VIII of the Constitution of 1885, as amended, reads as follows:

SECTION 11. Dade County, home rule charter. — (1) The electors of Dade County, Florida, are granted power to adopt, revise, and amend from time to time a home rule charter of government for Dade County, Florida, under which the Board of County Commissioners of Dade County shall be the governing body. This charter:

(a) Shall fix the boundaries of each county commission district, provide a method for changing them from time to time, and fix the number, terms and compensation of the commissioners, and their method of election.

(b) May grant full power and authority to the Board of County Commissioners of Dade County to pass ordinances relating to the affairs, property and government of Dade County and provide suitable penalties for the violation thereof; to levy and collect such taxes as may be authorized by general law and no other taxes, and to do everything necessary to carry on a central metropolitan government in Dade County.

(c) May change the boundaries of, merge, consolidate, and abolish and may provide a method for changing the boundaries of, merging, consolidating and abolishing from time to time all municipal corporations, county or district governments, special taxing districts, authorities, boards, or other governmental units whose jurisdiction lies wholly within Dade County, whether such governmental units are created by the Constitution or the Legislature or otherwise, except the Dade County Board of County Commissioners as it may be provided for from time to time by this home rule charter and the Board of Public Instruction of Dade County.

(d) May provide a method by which any and all of the functions or powers of any municipal corporation or other governmental unit in Dade County may be transferred to the Board of County Commissioners of Dade County.

(e) May provide a method for establishing new municipal corporations, special taxing districts, and other governmental units in Dade County from time to time and provide for their government and prescribe their jurisdiction and powers.

(f) May abolish and may provide a method for abolishing from time to time all offices provided for by Article VIII, Section 6, of the Constitution or by the Legislature, except the Superintendent of Public Instruction and may provide for the consolidation and transfer of the functions of such offices, provided, however, that there shall be no power to abolish or impair the jurisdiction of the Circuit Court or to abolish any other court provided for by this Constitution or by general law, or the judges or clerks thereof although such charter may create new courts and judges and clerks thereof with jurisdiction to try all offenses against ordinances passed by the Board of County Commissioners of Dade County and none of the other courts provided for by this Constitution or by general law shall have original jurisdiction to try such offenses, although the charter may confer appellate jurisdiction on such courts, and provided further that if said home rule charter shall abolish any county office or offices as authorized herein, that said charter shall contain adequate provision for the carrying on of all functions of said office or offices as are now or may hereafter be prescribed by general law.

(g) Shall provide a method by which each municipal corporation in Dade County shall have the power to make, amend or repeal its own charter. Upon adoption of this home rule charter by the electors this method shall be exclusive and the Legislature shall have no power to amend or repeal the charter of any municipal corporation in Dade County.

(h) May change the name of Dade County.

(i) Shall provide a method for the recall of any commissioner and a method for initiative and referendum, including the initiation of and referendum on ordinances and the amendment or revision of the home rule charter, provided, however, that the power of the Governor and Senate relating to the suspension and removal of officers provided for in this Constitution shall not be impaired, but shall extend to all officers provided for in said home rule charter.

(2) Provision shall be made for the protection of the creditors of any governmental unit which is merged, consolidated, or abolished or whose boundaries are changed or functions or powers transferred.

(3) This home rule charter shall be prepared by a Metropolitan Charter Board created by the Legislature and shall be presented to the electors of Dade County for ratification or rejection in the manner provided by the Legislature. Until a home rule charter is adopted the Legislature may from time to time create additional Charter Boards to prepare charters to be presented to the electors of Dade County for ratification or rejection in the manner provided by the Legislature. Such Charter, once adopted by the electors, may be amended only by the electors of Dade County and this charter shall provide a method for submitting future charter revisions and amendments to the electors of Dade County.

(4) The County Commission shall continue to receive its pro rata share of all revenues payable by the state from whatever source to the several counties and the state of Florida shall pay to the Commission all revenues which would have been paid to any municipality in Dade County which may be abolished by or in the method provided by this home rule charter; provided, however, the Commission shall reimburse the comptroller of Florida for the expense incurred if any, in the keeping of separate records to determine the amounts of money which would have been payable to any such municipality.

(5) Nothing in this section shall limit or restrict the power of the Legislature to enact general laws which shall relate to Dade County and any other one or more counties in the state of Florida or to any municipality in Dade County and any other one or more municipalities of the State of Florida, and the home rule charter provided for herein shall not conflict with any provision of this Constitution nor of any applicable general laws now applying to Dade County and any other one or more counties of the State of Florida except as expressly authorized in this section nor shall any ordinance enacted in pursuance to said home rule charter conflict with this Constitution or any such applicable general law except as expressly authorized herein, nor shall the charter of any municipality in Dade County conflict with this Constitution or any such applicable general law except as expressly authorized herein, provided however that said charter and said ordinances enacted in pursuance thereof may conflict with, modify or nullify any existing local, special or general law applicable only to Dade County.

(6) Nothing in this section shall be construed to limit or restrict the power of the Legislature to enact general laws which shall relate to Dade County and any other one or more counties of the state of Florida or to any municipality in Dade County and any other one or more municipalities of the State of Florida relating to county or municipal affairs and all such general laws shall apply to Dade County and to all municipalities therein to the same extent as if this section had not been adopted and such general laws shall supersede any part or portion of the home rule charter provided for herein in conflict therewith and shall supersede any provision of any ordinance enacted pursuant to said charter and in conflict therewith, and

1038   CONSTITUTION OF THE STATE OF FLORIDA

shall supersede any provision of any charter of any municipality in Dade County in conflict therewith.

(7) Nothing in this section shall be construed to limit or restrict the power and jurisdiction of the Railroad and Public Utilities Commission or of any other state agency, bureau or commission now or hereafter provided for in this Constitution or by general law and said state agencies, bureaus and commissions shall have the same powers in Dade County as shall be conferred upon them in regard to other counties.

(8) If any section, subsection, sentence, clause or provisions of this section is held invalid as violative of the provisions of Section 1 Article XVII of this Constitution the remainder of this section shall not be affected by such invalidity.

(9) It is declared to be the intent of the Legislature and of the electors of the State of Florida to provide by this section home rule for the people of Dade County in local affairs and this section shall be liberally construed to carry out such purpose, and it is further declared to be the intent of the Legislature and of the electors of the State of Florida that the provisions of this Constitution and general laws which shall relate to Dade County and any other one or more counties of the State of Florida or to any municipality in Dade County and any other one or more municipalities of the State of Florida enacted pursuant thereto by the Legislature shall be the supreme law in Dade County, Florida, except as expressly provided herein and this section shall be strictly construed to maintain such supremacy of this Constitution and of the Legislature in the enactment of general laws pursuant to this Constitution.

History. — Added, H.J.R. 858, 1941; adopted 1942; Am. S.J.R. 1046, 1955; adopted 1956.

[4]**Note.** — Section 24 of Art. VIII of the Constitution of 1885, as amended, reads as follows:

SECTION 24. Hillsborough County, home rule charter. —

(1) The electors of Hillsborough county are hereby granted the power to adopt a charter for a government which shall exercise any and all powers for county and municipal purposes which this constitution or the legislature, by general, special or local law, has conferred upon Hillsborough county or any municipality therein. Such government shall exercise these powers by the enactment of ordinances which relate to government of Hillsborough county and provide suitable penalties for the violation thereof. Such government shall have no power to create or abolish any municipality, except as otherwise provided herein.

(2) The method and manner by which the electors of Hillsborough county shall exercise this power shall be set forth in a charter for the government of Hillsborough county which charter shall be presented to said electors by any charter commission established by the legislature. The legislature may provide for the continuing existence of any charter commission or may establish a charter commission or commissions subsequent to any initial commission without regard to any election or elections held upon any charter or charters theretofore presented. A charter shall

become effective only upon ratification by a majority of the electors of Hillsborough county voting in a general or special election as provided by law.

(3) The number, qualifications, terms of office and method of filling vacancies in the membership of any charter commission established pursuant to this section and the powers, functions and duties of any such commission shall be provided by law.

(4) A charter prepared by any commission established pursuant to this section shall provide that:

(a) The governments of the city of Tampa and the county of Hillsborough shall be consolidated, and the structure of the new local government shall include:

1. An executive branch, the chief officer of which shall be responsible for the administration of government.

2. An elected legislative branch, the election to membership, powers and duties of which shall be as provided by the charter.

3. A judicial branch, which shall only have jurisdiction in the enforcement of ordinances enacted by the legislative branch created by this section.

(b) Should the electors of the municipalities of Plant City or Temple Terrace wish to consolidate their governments with the government hereinabove created, they may do so by majority vote of the electors of said municipality voting in an election upon said issue.

(c) The creditors of any governmental unit consolidated or abolished under this section shall be protected. Bonded or other indebtedness existing at the effective date of any government established hereunder shall be enforceable only against the real and personal property theretofore taxable for such purposes.

(d) Such other provisions as might be required by law.

(5) The provisions of such charter and ordinances enacted pursuant thereto shall not conflict with any provision of this constitution nor with general, special or local laws now or hereafter applying to Hillsborough county.

(6) The government established hereunder shall be recognized as a county, that is one of the legal political subdivisions of the state with the powers, rights, privileges, duties and obligations of a county, and may also exercise all the powers of a municipality. Said government shall have the right to sue and be sued.

(7) Any government established hereunder shall be entitled to receive from the state of Florida or from the United States or from any other agency, public or private, funds and revenues to which a county is, or may hereafter be entitled, and also all funds and revenues to which an incorporated municipality is or may hereafter be entitled, and to receive the same without diminution or loss by reason of any such government as may be established. Nothing herein contained shall preclude such government as may be established hereunder from receiving all funds and revenues from whatever source now received, or hereinafter received provided by law.

1040

CONSTITUTION OF THE STATE OF FLORIDA

(8) The board of county commissioners of Hillsborough county shall be abolished when the functions, duties, powers and responsibilities of said board shall be transferred in the manner to be provided by the charter to the government established pursuant to this section. No other office provided for by this constitution shall be abolished by or pursuant to this section.

(9) This section shall not restrict or limit the legislature in the enactment of general, special or local laws as otherwise provided in this constitution.

History. — Added, C.S. for H.J.R. 1987, 1965; adopted 1966.

ARTICLE IX
EDUCATION

SECTION 1.

Public education.

SECTION 2.

State board of education.

SECTION 3.

Terms of appointive board members.

SECTION 4.

School districts; school boards.

SECTION 5.

Superintendent of schools.

SECTION 6.

State school fund.

SECTION 7.

State University System.

SECTION 8.

State College System.

SECTION 1. Public education. —

(a) The education of children is a fundamental value of the people of the State of Florida. It is, therefore, a paramount duty of the state to make adequate provision for the education of all children residing within its borders. Adequate provision shall be made by law for a uniform, efficient, safe, secure, and high quality system of free public schools that allows students to obtain a high quality education and for the establishment, maintenance, and operation of institutions of higher learning and other public education programs that the needs of the people may require. To assure that children attending public schools obtain a high quality education, the legislature shall make adequate provision to ensure that, by the beginning of the 2010 school year, there are a sufficient number of classrooms so that:

CONSTITUTION OF THE STATE OF FLORIDA   1041

(1) The maximum number of students who are assigned to each teacher who is teaching in public school classrooms for prekindergarten through grade 3 does not exceed 18 students;

(2) The maximum number of students who are assigned to each teacher who is teaching in public school classrooms for grades 4 through 8 does not exceed 22 students; and

(3) The maximum number of students who are assigned to each teacher who is teaching in public school classrooms for grades 9 through 12 does not exceed 25 students.

The class size requirements of this subsection do not apply to extracurricular classes. Payment of the costs associated with reducing class size to meet these requirements is the responsibility of the state and not of local schools districts. Beginning with the 2003–2004 fiscal year, the legislature shall provide sufficient funds to reduce the average number of students in each classroom by at least two students per year until the maximum number of students per classroom does not exceed the requirements of this subsection.

(b) Every four-year old child in Florida shall be provided by the State a high quality pre-kindergarten learning opportunity in the form of an early childhood development and education program which shall be voluntary, high quality, free, and delivered according to professionally accepted standards. An early childhood development and education program means an organized program designed to address and enhance each child's ability to make age appropriate progress in an appropriate range of settings in the development of language and cognitive capabilities and emotional, social, regulatory and moral capacities through education in basic skills and such other skills as the Legislature may determine to be appropriate.

(c) The early childhood education and development programs provided by reason of subparagraph (b) shall be implemented no later than the beginning of the 2005 school year through funds generated in addition to those used for existing education, health, and development programs. Existing education, health, and development programs are those funded by the State as of January 1, 2002 that provided for child or adult education, health care, or development.

History. — Am. proposed by Constitution Revision Commission, Revision No. 6, 1998, filed with the Secretary of State May 5, 1998; adopted 1998; Ams. by Initiative Petitions filed with the Secretary of State July 30, 2002, and August 1, 2002; adopted 2002.

SECTION 2. State board of education. — The state board of education shall be a body corporate and have such supervision of the system of free public education as is provided by law. The state board of education shall consist of seven members appointed by the governor to staggered 4-year terms, subject to confirmation by the senate. The state board of education shall appoint the commissioner of education.

History. — Am. proposed by Constitution Revision Commission, Revision No. 8, 1998, filed with the Secretary of State May 5, 1998; adopted 1998.

SECTION 3. Terms of appointive board members. — Members of any appointive board dealing with education may serve terms in excess of four years as provided by law.

SECTION 4. School districts; school boards. —

(a) Each county shall constitute a school district; provided, two or more contiguous counties, upon vote of the electors of each county pursuant to law, may be combined into one school district. In each school district there shall be a school board composed of five or more members chosen by vote of the electors in a nonpartisan election for appropriately staggered terms of four years, as provided by law.

(b) The school board shall operate, control and supervise all free public schools within the school district and determine the rate of school district taxes within the limits prescribed herein. Two or more school districts may operate and finance joint educational programs.

History. — Am. proposed by Constitution Revision Commission, Revision No. 11, 1998, filed with the Secretary of State May 5, 1998; adopted 1998.

SECTION 5. Superintendent of schools. — In each school district there shall be a superintendent of schools who shall be elected at the general election in each year the number of which is a multiple of four for a term of four years; or, when provided by resolution of the district school board, or by special law, approved by vote of the electors, the district school superintendent in any school district shall be employed by the district school board as provided by general law. The resolution or special law may be rescinded or repealed by either procedure after four years.

History. — Am. proposed by Constitution Revision Commission, Revision No. 13, 1998, filed with the Secretary of State May 5, 1998; adopted 1998.

SECTION 6. State school fund. — The income derived from the state school fund shall, and the principal of the fund may, be appropriated, but only to the support and maintenance of free public schools.

SECTION 7. State University System. —

(a) PURPOSES. In order to achieve excellence through teaching students, advancing research and providing public service for the benefit of Florida's citizens, their communities and economies, the people hereby establish a system of governance for the state university system of Florida.

(b) STATE UNIVERSITY SYSTEM. There shall be a single state university system comprised of all public universities. A board of trustees shall administer each public university and a board of governors shall govern the state university system.

(c) LOCAL BOARDS OF TRUSTEES. Each local constituent university shall be administered by a board of trustees consisting of thirteen members dedicated to the purposes of the state university system. The board of governors shall establish the powers and duties of the boards of trustees. Each board of trustees shall consist of six citizen members appointed by the governor and five citizen members appointed by the board of governors. The appointed members shall be confirmed by the senate and serve staggered terms of five years as provided by law. The chair of the faculty senate, or the equivalent, and the president of the student body of the university shall also be members.

(d) STATEWIDE BOARD OF GOVERNORS. The board of governors shall be a body corporate consisting of seventeen members. The board shall operate, regulate, control, and be fully responsible for the management of the whole university system. These responsibilities shall include, but not be limited to, defining the distinctive mission of each constituent university and its articulation with free public schools and community colleges, ensuring the well-planned coordination and operation of the system, and avoiding wasteful duplication of facilities or programs. The board's management shall be subject to the powers of the legislature to appropriate for the expenditure of funds, and the board shall account for such expenditures as provided by law. The governor shall appoint to the board fourteen citizens dedicated to the purposes of the state university system. The appointed members shall be confirmed by the senate and serve staggered terms of seven years as provided by law. The commissioner of education, the chair of the advisory council of faculty senates, or the equivalent, and the president of the Florida student association, or the equivalent, shall also be members of the board.

(e) FEES. Any proposal or action of a constituent university to raise, impose, or authorize any fee, as authorized by law, must be approved by at least nine affirmative votes of the members of the board of trustees of the constituent university, if approval by the board of trustees is required by general law, and at least twelve affirmative votes of the members of the board of governors, if approval by the board of governors is required by general law, in order to take effect. A fee under this subsection shall not include tuition.

History. — Proposed by Initiative Petition filed with the Secretary of State August 6, 2002; adopted 2002; Am. proposed by Constitution Revision Commission, Revision No. 2, 2018, filed with the Secretary of State May 9, 2018; adopted 2018.

SECTION 8. State College System. —

(a) PURPOSES. In order to achieve excellence and to provide access to undergraduate education to the students of this state; to originate articulated pathways to a baccalaureate degree; to ensure superior commitment to teaching and learning; and to respond quickly and efficiently to meet the demand of communities by aligning certificate and degree programs with local and regional workforce needs, the people hereby establish a system of governance for the state college system of Florida.

(b) STATE COLLEGE SYSTEM. There shall be a single state college system comprised of all public community and state colleges. A local board of trustees shall govern each state college system institution and the state board of education shall supervise the state college system.

(c) LOCAL BOARDS OF TRUSTEES. Each state college system institution shall be governed by a local board of trustees dedicated to the purposes of the state college system. A member of a board of trustees must be a resident of the service delivery area of the college. The powers and duties of the boards of trustees shall be provided by law. Each member shall be appointed by the governor to staggered 4-year terms, subject to confirmation by the senate.

(d) ROLE OF THE STATE BOARD OF EDUCATION. The state board of education shall supervise the state college system as provided by law.

History. — Proposed by Constitution Revision Commission, Revision No. 2, 2018, filed with the Secretary of State May 9, 2018; adopted 2018.

ARTICLE X
MISCELLANEOUS

SECTION 1.

Amendments to United States Constitution.

SECTION 2.

Militia.

SECTION 3.

Vacancy in office.

SECTION 4.

Homestead; exemptions.

SECTION 5.

Coverture and property.

SECTION 6.

Eminent domain.

SECTION 7.

Lotteries.

SECTION 8.

Census.

SECTION 9.

Repeal of criminal statutes.

SECTION 10.

Felony; definition.

SECTION 11.

Sovereignty lands.

SECTION 12.

Rules of construction.

CONSTITUTION OF THE STATE OF FLORIDA

SECTION 13.

Suits against the state.

SECTION 14.

State retirement systems benefit changes.

SECTION 15.

State operated lotteries.

SECTION 16.

Limiting marine net fishing.

SECTION 17.

Everglades Trust Fund.

SECTION 18.

Disposition of conservation lands.

SECTION 19.

[Repealed]

SECTION 20.

Workplaces without tobacco smoke or vapor.

SECTION 21.

Limiting cruel and inhumane confinement of pigs during pregnancy.

SECTION 22.

Parental notice of termination of a minor's pregnancy.

SECTION 23.

Slot machines.

SECTION 24.

Florida minimum wage.

SECTION 25.

Patients' right to know about adverse medical incidents.

SECTION 26.

Prohibition of medical license after repeated medical malpractice.

SECTION 27.

Comprehensive Statewide Tobacco Education And Prevention Program.

SECTION 28.

Land Acquisition Trust Fund.

SECTION 29.

Medical marijuana production, possession and use.

SECTION 30.

Voter control of gambling in Florida.

SECTION 31.

Death benefits for survivors of first responders and military members.

SECTION 32.

Prohibition on racing of and wagering on greyhounds or other dogs.

SECTION 1. Amendments to United States Constitution. — The legislature shall not take action on any proposed amendment to the constitution of the United States unless a majority of the members thereof have been elected after the proposed amendment has been submitted for ratification.

SECTION 2. Militia. —

(a) The militia shall be composed of all ablebodied inhabitants of the state who are or have declared their intention to become citizens of the United States; and no person because of religious creed or opinion shall be exempted from military duty except upon conditions provided by law.

(b) The organizing, equipping, housing, maintaining, and disciplining of the militia, and the safekeeping of public arms may be provided for by law.

(c) The governor shall appoint all commissioned officers of the militia, including an adjutant general who shall be chief of staff. The appointment of all general officers shall be subject to confirmation by the senate.

(d) The qualifications of personnel and officers of the federally recognized national guard, including the adjutant general, and the grounds and proceedings for their discipline and removal shall conform to the appropriate United States army or air force regulations and usages.

SECTION 3. Vacancy in office. — Vacancy in office shall occur upon the creation of an office, upon the death, removal from office, or resignation of the incumbent or the incumbent's succession to another office, unexplained absence for sixty consecutive days, or failure to maintain the residence required when elected or appointed, and upon failure of one elected or appointed to office to qualify within thirty days from the commencement of the term.

History. — Am. proposed by Constitution Revision Commission, Revision No. 13, 1998, filed with the Secretary of State May 5, 1998; adopted 1998.

SECTION 4. Homestead; exemptions. —

(a) There shall be exempt from forced sale under process of any court, and no judgment, decree or execution shall be a lien thereon, except for the payment of taxes and assessments thereon, obligations contracted for the purchase, improvement or repair thereof, or obligations contracted for house, field or other labor performed on the realty, the following property owned by a natural person:

CONSTITUTION OF THE STATE OF FLORIDA

(1) a homestead, if located outside a municipality, to the extent of one hundred sixty acres of contiguous land and improvements thereon, which shall not be reduced without the owner's consent by reason of subsequent inclusion in a municipality; or if located within a municipality, to the extent of one-half acre of contiguous land, upon which the exemption shall be limited to the residence of the owner or the owner's family;

(2) personal property to the value of one thousand dollars.

(b) These exemptions shall inure to the surviving spouse or heirs of the owner.

(c) The homestead shall not be subject to devise if the owner is survived by spouse or minor child, except the homestead may be devised to the owner's spouse if there be no minor child. The owner of homestead real estate, joined by the spouse if married, may alienate the homestead by mortgage, sale or gift and, if married, may by deed transfer the title to an estate by the entirety with the spouse. If the owner or spouse is incompetent, the method of alienation or encumbrance shall be as provided by law.

History. — Am. H.J.R. 4324, 1972; adopted 1972; Am. H.J.R. 40, 1983; adopted 1984; Am. proposed by Constitution Revision Commission, Revision No. 13, 1998, filed with the Secretary of State May 5, 1998; adopted 1998.

SECTION 5. Coverture and property. — There shall be no distinction between married women and married men in the holding, control, disposition, or encumbering of their property, both real and personal; except that dower or curtesy may be established and regulated by law.

SECTION 6. Eminent domain. —

(a) No private property shall be taken except for a public purpose and with full compensation therefor paid to each owner or secured by deposit in the registry of the court and available to the owner.

(b) Provision may be made by law for the taking of easements, by like proceedings, for the drainage of the land of one person over or through the land of another.

(c) Private property taken by eminent domain pursuant to a petition to initiate condemnation proceedings filed on or after January 2, 2007, may not be conveyed to a natural person or private entity except as provided by general law passed by a three-fifths vote of the membership of each house of the Legislature.

History. — Am. H.J.R. 1569, 2006; adopted 2006.

SECTION 7. Lotteries. — Lotteries, other than the types of pari-mutuel pools authorized by law as of the effective date of this constitution, are hereby prohibited in this state.

SECTION 8. Census. —

(a) Each decennial census of the state taken by the United States shall be an official census of the state.

1048 CONSTITUTION OF THE STATE OF FLORIDA

(b) Each decennial census, for the purpose of classifications based upon population, shall become effective on the thirtieth day after the final adjournment of the regular session of the legislature convened next after certification of the census.

SECTION 9. Repeal of criminal statutes. — Repeal of a criminal statute shall not affect prosecution for any crime committed before such repeal.

History. — Am. proposed by Constitution Revision Commission, Revision No. 6, 2018, filed with the Secretary of State May 9, 2018; adopted 2018.

SECTION 10. Felony; definition. — The term "felony" as used herein and in the laws of this state shall mean any criminal offense that is punishable under the laws of this state, or that would be punishable if committed in this state, by death or by imprisonment in the state penitentiary.

SECTION 11. Sovereignty lands. — The title to lands under navigable waters, within the boundaries of the state, which have not been alienated, including beaches below mean high water lines, is held by the state, by virtue of its sovereignty, in trust for all the people. Sale of such lands may be authorized by law, but only when in the public interest. Private use of portions of such lands may be authorized by law, but only when not contrary to the public interest.

History. — Am. H.J.R. 792, 1970; adopted 1970.

SECTION 12. Rules of construction. — Unless qualified in the text the following rules of construction shall apply to this constitution.

(a) "Herein" refers to the entire constitution.

(b) The singular includes the plural.

(c) The masculine includes the feminine.

(d) "Vote of the electors" means the vote of the majority of those voting on the matter in an election, general or special, in which those participating are limited to the electors of the governmental unit referred to in the text.

(e) Vote or other action of a legislative house or other governmental body means the vote or action of a majority or other specified percentage of those members voting on the matter. "Of the membership" means "of all members thereof."

(f) The terms "judicial office," "justices" and "judges" shall not include judges of courts established solely for the trial of violations of ordinances.

(g) "Special law" means a special or local law.

(h) Titles and subtitles shall not be used in construction.

SECTION 13. Suits against the state. — Provision may be made by general law for bringing suit against the state as to all liabilities now existing or hereafter originating.

SECTION 14. State retirement systems benefit changes. — A governmental unit responsible for any retirement or pension system supported in whole or in part by public funds shall not after January 1, 1977, provide any increase in the benefits to the members or beneficiaries of such system unless such unit has made or

CONSTITUTION OF THE STATE OF FLORIDA

concurrently makes provision for the funding of the increase in benefits on a sound actuarial basis.

History. — Added, H.J.R. 291, 1975; adopted 1976.

SECTION 15. State operated lotteries. —

(a) Lotteries may be operated by the state.

(b) If any subsection or subsections of the amendment to the Florida Constitution are held unconstitutional for containing more than one subject, this amendment shall be limited to subsection (a) above.

(c) This amendment shall be implemented as follows:

(1) Schedule — On the effective date of this amendment, the lotteries shall be known as the Florida Education Lotteries. Net proceeds derived from the lotteries shall be deposited to a state trust fund, to be designated The State Education Lotteries Trust Fund, to be appropriated by the Legislature. The schedule may be amended by general law.

History. — Proposed by Initiative Petition filed with the Secretary of State June 10, 1985; adopted 1986.

SECTION 16. Limiting marine net fishing. —

(a) The marine resources of the State of Florida belong to all of the people of the state and should be conserved and managed for the benefit of the state, its people, and future generations. To this end the people hereby enact limitations on marine net fishing in Florida waters to protect saltwater finfish, shellfish, and other marine animals from unnecessary killing, overfishing and waste.

(b) For the purpose of catching or taking any saltwater finfish, shellfish or other marine animals in Florida waters:

(1) No gill nets or other entangling nets shall be used in any Florida waters; and

(2) In addition to the prohibition set forth in (1), no other type of net containing more than 500 square feet of mesh area shall be used in nearshore and inshore Florida waters. Additionally, no more than two such nets, which shall not be connected, shall be used from any vessel, and no person not on a vessel shall use more than one such net in nearshore and inshore Florida waters.

(c) For purposes of this section:

(1) "gill net" means one or more walls of netting which captures saltwater finfish by ensnaring or entangling them in the meshes of the net by the gills, and "entangling net" means a drift net, trammell net, stab net, or any other net which captures saltwater finfish, shellfish, or other marine animals by causing all or part of heads, fins, legs, or other body parts to become entangled or ensnared in the meshes of the net, but a hand thrown cast net is not a gill net or an entangling net;

(2) "mesh area" of a net means the total area of netting with the meshes open to comprise the maximum square footage. The square footage shall be calculated

using standard mathematical formulas for geometric shapes. Seines and other rectangular nets shall be calculated using the maximum length and maximum width of the netting. Trawls and other bag type nets shall be calculated as a cone using the maximum circumference of the net mouth to derive the radius, and the maximum length from the net mouth to the tail end of the net to derive the slant height. Calculations for any other nets or combination type nets shall be based on the shapes of the individual components;

(3) "coastline" means the territorial sea base line for the State of Florida established pursuant to the laws of the United States of America;

(4) "Florida waters" means the waters of the Atlantic Ocean, the Gulf of Mexico, the Straits of Florida, and any other bodies of water under the jurisdiction of the State of Florida, whether coastal, intracoastal or inland, and any part thereof; and

(5) "nearshore and inshore Florida waters" means all Florida waters inside a line three miles seaward of the coastline along the Gulf of Mexico and inside a line one mile seaward of the coastline along the Atlantic Ocean.

(d) This section shall not apply to the use of nets for scientific research or governmental purposes.

(e) Persons violating this section shall be prosecuted and punished pursuant to the penalties provided in section 370.021(2)(a),(b),(c)6. and 7., and (e), Florida Statutes (1991), unless and until the legislature enacts more stringent penalties for violations hereof. On and after the effective date of this section, law enforcement officers in the state are authorized to enforce the provisions of this section in the same manner and authority as if a violation of this section constituted a violation of Chapter 370, Florida Statutes (1991).

(f) It is the intent of this section that implementing legislation is not required for enforcing any violations hereof, but nothing in this section prohibits the establishment by law or pursuant to law of more restrictions on the use of nets for the purpose of catching or taking any saltwater finfish, shellfish, or other marine animals.

(g) If any portion of this section is held invalid for any reason, the remaining portion of this section, to the fullest extent possible, shall be severed from the void portion and given the fullest possible force and application.

(h) This section shall take effect on the July 1 next occurring after approval hereof by vote of the electors.

History. — Proposed by Initiative Petition filed with the Secretary of State October 2, 1992; adopted 1994.

SECTION 17. Everglades Trust Fund. —

(a) There is hereby established the Everglades Trust Fund, which shall not be subject to termination pursuant to Article III, Section 19(f). The purpose of the Everglades Trust Fund is to make funds available to assist in conservation and protection of natural resources and abatement of water pollution in the Everglades Protection

Area and the Everglades Agricultural Area. The trust fund shall be administered by the South Florida Water Management District, or its successor agency, consistent with statutory law.

(b) The Everglades Trust Fund may receive funds from any source, including gifts from individuals, corporations or other entities; funds from general revenue as determined by the Legislature; and any other funds so designated by the Legislature, by the United States Congress or by any other governmental entity.

(c) Funds deposited to the Everglades Trust Fund shall be expended for purposes of conservation and protection of natural resources and abatement of water pollution in the Everglades Protection Area and Everglades Agricultural Area.

(d) For purposes of this subsection, the terms "Everglades Protection Area," "Everglades Agricultural Area" and "South Florida Water Management District" shall have the meanings as defined in statutes in effect on January 1, 1996.

History. — Proposed by Initiative Petition filed with the Secretary of State March 26, 1996; adopted 1996.

SECTION 18. Disposition of conservation lands. — The fee interest in real property held by an entity of the state and designated for natural resources conservation purposes as provided by general law shall be managed for the benefit of the citizens of this state and may be disposed of only if the members of the governing board of the entity holding title determine the property is no longer needed for conservation purposes and only upon a vote of two-thirds of the governing board.

History. — Proposed by Constitution Revision Commission, Revision No. 5, 1998, filed with the Secretary of State May 5, 1998; adopted 1998.

SECTION 19. [Repealed] —

History. — Proposed by Initiative Petition filed with the Secretary of State September 3, 1999; adopted 2000; Am. proposed by Initiative Petition filed with the Secretary of State February 18, 2004; adopted 2004; Am. proposed by Constitution Revision Commission, Revision No. 6, 2018, filed with the Secretary of State May 9, 2018; adopted 2018.

SECTION 20. Workplaces without tobacco smoke or vapor. —

(a) PROHIBITION. As a Florida health initiative to protect people from the health hazards of second-hand tobacco smoke and vapor, tobacco smoking and the use of vapor-generating electronic devices are prohibited in enclosed indoor workplaces. This section does not preclude the adoption of ordinances that impose more restrictive regulation on the use of vapor-generating electronic devices than is provided in this section.

(b) EXCEPTIONS. As further explained in the definitions below, tobacco smoking and the use of vapor-generating electronic devices may be permitted in private residences whenever they are not being used commercially to provide child care, adult care, or health care, or any combination thereof; and further may be permitted in retail tobacco shops, vapor-generating electronic device retailers, designated smoking guest rooms at hotels and other public lodging establishments; and stand-alone bars. However, nothing in this section or in its implementing legislation or regulations shall prohibit the owner, lessee, or other person in control of the use of an enclosed indoor workplace from further prohibiting or limiting smoking or the use of vapor-generating electronic devices therein.

(c) DEFINITIONS. For purposes of this section, the following words and terms shall have the stated meanings:

(1) "Smoking" means inhaling, exhaling, burning, carrying, or possessing any lighted tobacco product, including cigarettes, cigars, pipe tobacco, and any other lighted tobacco product.

(2) "Second-hand smoke," also known as environmental tobacco smoke (ETS), means smoke emitted from lighted, smoldering, or burning tobacco when the smoker is not inhaling; smoke emitted at the mouthpiece during puff drawing; and smoke exhaled by the smoker.

(3) "Work" means any person's providing any employment or employment-type service for or at the request of another individual or individuals or any public or private entity, whether for compensation or not, whether full or part-time, whether legally or not. "Work" includes, without limitation, any such service performed by an employee, independent contractor, agent, partner, proprietor, manager, officer, director, apprentice, trainee, associate, servant, volunteer, and the like.

(4) "Enclosed indoor workplace" means any place where one or more persons engages in work, and which place is predominantly or totally bounded on all sides and above by physical barriers, regardless of whether such barriers consist of or include uncovered openings, screened or otherwise partially covered openings; or open or closed windows, jalousies, doors, or the like. This section applies to all such enclosed indoor workplaces without regard to whether work is occurring at any given time.

(5) "Commercial" use of a private residence means any time during which the owner, lessee, or other person occupying or controlling the use of the private residence is furnishing in the private residence, or causing or allowing to be furnished in the private residence, child care, adult care, or health care, or any combination thereof, and receiving or expecting to receive compensation therefor.

(6) "Retail tobacco shop" means any enclosed indoor workplace dedicated to or predominantly for the retail sale of tobacco, tobacco products, and accessories for such products, in which the sale of other products or services is merely incidental.

(7) "Designated smoking guest rooms at public lodging establishments" means the sleeping rooms and directly associated private areas, such as bathrooms, living rooms, and kitchen areas, if any, rented to guests for their exclusive transient occupancy in public lodging establishments including hotels, motels, resort condominiums, transient apartments, transient lodging establishments, rooming houses,

boarding houses, resort dwellings, bed and breakfast inns, and the like; and designated by the person or persons having management authority over such public lodging establishment as rooms in which smoking may be permitted.

(8) "Stand-alone bar" means any place of business devoted during any time of operation predominantly or totally to serving alcoholic beverages, intoxicating beverages, or intoxicating liquors, or any combination thereof, for consumption on the licensed premises; in which the serving of food, if any, is merely incidental to the consumption of any such beverage; and that is not located within, and does not share any common entryway or common indoor area with, any other enclosed indoor workplace including any business for which the sale of food or any other product or service is more than an incidental source of gross revenue.

(9) "Vapor-generating electronic device" means any product that employs an electronic, a chemical, or a mechanical means capable of producing vapor or aerosol from a nicotine product or any other substance, including, but not limited to, an electronic cigarette, electronic cigar, electronic cigarillo, electronic pipe, or other similar device or product, any replacement cartridge for such device, and any other container of a solution or other substance intended to be used with or within an electronic cigarette, electronic cigar, electronic cigarillo, electronic pipe, or other similar device or product.

(10) "Vapor-generating electronic device retailer" means any enclosed indoor workplace dedicated to or predominantly for the retail sale of vapor-generating electronic devices and components, parts, and accessories for such products, in which the sale of other products or services is merely incidental.

(d) LEGISLATION. In the next regular legislative session occurring after voter approval of this section or any amendment to this section, the legislature shall adopt legislation to implement this section and any amendment to this section in a manner consistent with its broad purpose and stated terms, and having an effective date no later than July 1 of the year following voter approval. Such legislation shall include, without limitation, civil penalties for violations of this section; provisions for administrative enforcement; and the requirement and authorization of agency rules for implementation and enforcement. This section does not preclude the legislature from enacting any law constituting or allowing a more restrictive regulation of tobacco smoking or the use of vapor-generating electronic devices than is provided in this section.

History. — Proposed by Initiative Petition filed with the Secretary of State May 10, 2002; adopted 2002; Am. proposed by Constitution Revision Commission, Revision No. 4, 2018, filed with the Secretary of State May 9, 2018; adopted 2018.

[1]**SECTION 21. Limiting cruel and inhumane confinement of pigs during pregnancy.** — Inhumane treatment of animals is a concern of Florida citizens. To prevent cruelty to certain animals and as recommended by The Humane Society of the United States, the people of the State of Florida hereby limit the cruel and inhumane confinement of pigs during pregnancy as provided herein.

(a) It shall be unlawful for any person to confine a pig during pregnancy in an enclosure, or to tether a pig during pregnancy, on a farm in such a way that she is prevented from turning around freely.

(b) This section shall not apply:

(1) when a pig is undergoing an examination, test, treatment or operation carried out for veterinary purposes, provided the period during which the animal is confined or tethered is not longer than reasonably necessary.

(2) during the prebirthing period.

(c) For purposes of this section:

(1) "enclosure" means any cage, crate or other enclosure in which a pig is kept for all or the majority of any day, including what is commonly described as the "gestation crate."

(2) "farm" means the land, buildings, support facilities, and other appurtenances used in the production of animals for food or fiber.

(3) "person" means any natural person, corporation and/or business entity.

(4) "pig" means any animal of the porcine species.

(5) "turning around freely" means turning around without having to touch any side of the pig's enclosure.

(6) "prebirthing period" means the seven day period prior to a pig's expected date of giving birth.

(d) A person who violates this section shall be guilty of a misdemeanor of the first degree, punishable as provided in s. 775.082(4)(a), Florida Statutes (1999), as amended, or by a fine of not more than $5000, or by both imprisonment and a fine, unless and until the legislature enacts more stringent penalties for violations hereof. On and after the effective date of this section, law enforcement officers in the state are authorized to enforce the provisions of this section in the same manner and authority as if a violation of this section constituted a violation of Section 828.13, Florida Statutes (1999). The confinement or tethering of each pig shall constitute a separate offense. The knowledge or acts of agents and employees of a person in regard to a pig owned, farmed or in the custody of a person, shall be held to be the knowledge or act of such person.

(e) It is the intent of this section that implementing legislation is not required for enforcing any violations hereof.

(f) If any portion of this section is held invalid for any reason, the remaining portion of this section, to the fullest extent possible, shall be severed from the void portion and given the fullest possible force and application.

(g) This section shall take effect six years after approval by the electors.

History. — Proposed by Initiative Petition filed with the Secretary of State August 5, 2002; adopted 2002.

CONSTITUTION OF THE STATE OF FLORIDA

1055

[1]**Note.** — This section, originally designated section 19 by Amendment No. 10, 2002, proposed by Initiative Petition filed with the Secretary of State August 5, 2002, adopted 2002, was redesignated section 21 by the editors in order to avoid confusion with already existing section 19, relating to the high speed ground transportation system, and section 20, relating to prohibiting workplace smoking, as contained in Amendment No. 6, proposed by Initiative Petition filed with the Secretary of State May 10, 2002, and adopted in 2002.

SECTION 22. Parental notice of termination of a minor's pregnancy. — The Legislature shall not limit or deny the privacy right guaranteed to a minor under the United States Constitution as interpreted by the United States Supreme Court. Notwithstanding a minor's right of privacy provided in Section 23 of Article I, the Legislature is authorized to require by general law for notification to a parent or guardian of a minor before the termination of the minor's pregnancy. The Legislature shall provide exceptions to such requirement for notification and shall create a process for judicial waiver of the notification.

History. — Added, H.J.R. 1, 2004; adopted 2004.

[1]**SECTION 23. Slot machines.** —

(a) After voter approval of this constitutional amendment, the governing bodies of Miami-Dade and Broward Counties each may hold a county-wide referendum in their respective counties on whether to authorize slot machines within existing, licensed parimutuel facilities (thoroughbred and harness racing, greyhound racing, and jai-alai) that have conducted live racing or games in that county during each of the last two calendar years before the effective date of this amendment. If the voters of such county approve the referendum question by majority vote, slot machines shall be authorized in such parimutuel facilities. If the voters of such county by majority vote disapprove the referendum question, slot machines shall not be so authorized, and the question shall not be presented in another referendum in that county for at least two years.

(b) In the next regular Legislative session occurring after voter approval of this constitutional amendment, the Legislature shall adopt legislation implementing this section and having an effective date no later than July 1 of the year following voter approval of this amendment. Such legislation shall authorize agency rules for implementation, and may include provisions for the licensure and regulation of slot machines. The Legislature may tax slot machine revenues, and any such taxes must supplement public education funding statewide.

(c) If any part of this section is held invalid for any reason, the remaining portion or portions shall be severed from the invalid portion and given the fullest possible force and effect.

(d) This amendment shall become effective when approved by vote of the electors of the state.

History. — Proposed by Initiative Petition filed with the Secretary of State May 28, 2002; adopted 2004.

¹**Note.** — This section, originally designated section 19 by Amendment No. 4, 2004, proposed by Initiative Petition filed with the Secretary of State May 28, 2002, adopted 2004, was redesignated section 23 by the editors in order to avoid confusion with already existing section 19, relating to the high speed ground transportation system.

SECTION 24. Florida minimum wage. —

(a) PUBLIC POLICY. All working Floridians are entitled to be paid a minimum wage that is sufficient to provide a decent and healthy life for them and their families, that protects their employers from unfair low-wage competition, and that does not force them to rely on taxpayer-funded public services in order to avoid economic hardship.

(b) DEFINITIONS. As used in this amendment, the terms "Employer," "Employee" and "Wage" shall have the meanings established under the federal Fair Labor Standards Act (FLSA) and its implementing regulations.

(c) MINIMUM WAGE. Employers shall pay Employees Wages no less than the Minimum Wage for all hours worked in Florida. Six months after enactment, the Minimum Wage shall be established at an hourly rate of $6.15. Effective September 30th, 2021, the existing state Minimum Wage shall increase to $10.00 per hour, and then increase each September 30th thereafter by $1.00 per hour, until the Minimum Wage reaches $15.00 per hour on September 30th, 2026. On September 30th of 2027 and on each following September 30th, the state Agency for Workforce Innovation shall calculate an adjusted Minimum Wage rate by increasing the current Minimum Wage rate by the rate of inflation during the twelve months prior to each September 1st using the consumer price index for urban wage earners and clerical workers, CPI-W, or a successor index as calculated by the United States Department of Labor. Each adjusted Minimum Wage rate calculated shall be published and take effect on the following January 1st. For tipped Employees meeting eligibility requirements for the tip credit under the FLSA, Employers may credit towards satisfaction of the Minimum Wage tips up to the amount of the allowable FLSA tip credit in 2003.

(d) RETALIATION PROHIBITED. It shall be unlawful for an Employer or any other party to discriminate in any manner or take adverse action against any person in retaliation for exercising rights protected under this amendment. Rights protected under this amendment include, but are not limited to, the right to file a complaint or inform any person about any party's alleged noncompliance with this amendment, and the right to inform any person of his or her potential rights under this amendment and to assist him or her in asserting such rights.

(e) ENFORCEMENT. Persons aggrieved by a violation of this amendment may bring a civil action in a court of competent jurisdiction against an Employer or person violating this amendment and, upon prevailing, shall recover the full amount of any back wages unlawfully withheld plus the same amount as liquidated damages, and shall be awarded reasonable attorney's fees and costs. In addition, they shall be entitled to such legal or equitable relief as may be appropriate to remedy the violation including, without limitation, reinstatement in employment and/or injunctive relief. Any Employer or other person found liable for willfully violating this amendment shall also be subject to a fine payable to the state in the amount of $1000.00 for each violation. The state attorney general or other official designated by the state legislature may also bring a civil action to enforce this amendment. Actions to enforce this amendment shall be subject to a statute of limitations of four years or, in the case of willful violations, five years. Such actions may be brought as a class action pursuant to Rule 1.220 of the Florida Rules of Civil Procedure.

(f) ADDITIONAL LEGISLATION, IMPLEMENTATION AND CONSTRUCTION. Implementing legislation is not required in order to enforce this amendment. The state legislature may by statute establish additional remedies or fines for violations of this amendment, raise the applicable Minimum Wage rate, reduce the tip credit, or extend coverage of the Minimum Wage to employers or employees not covered by this amendment. The state legislature may by statute or the state Agency for Workforce Innovation may by regulation adopt any measures appropriate for the implementation of this amendment. This amendment provides for payment of a minimum wage and shall not be construed to preempt or otherwise limit the authority of the state legislature or any other public body to adopt or enforce any other law, regulation, requirement, policy or standard that provides for payment of higher or supplemental wages or benefits, or that extends such protections to employers or employees not covered by this amendment. It is intended that case law, administrative interpretations, and other guiding standards developed under the federal FLSA shall guide the construction of this amendment and any implementing statutes or regulations.

(g) SEVERABILITY. If any part of this amendment, or the application of this amendment to any person or circumstance, is held invalid, the remainder of this amendment, including the application of such part to other persons or circumstances, shall not be affected by such a holding and shall continue in full force and effect. To this end, the parts of this amendment are severable.

History. — Proposed by Initiative Petition filed with the Secretary of State August 7, 2003; adopted 2004; Am. by Initiative Petition filed with the Secretary of State January 10, 2018; adopted 2020.

[1]**SECTION 25. Patients' right to know about adverse medical incidents. —**

(a) In addition to any other similar rights provided herein or by general law, patients have a right to have access to any records made or received in the course of business by a health care facility or provider relating to any adverse medical incident.

(b) In providing such access, the identity of patients involved in the incidents shall not be disclosed, and any privacy restrictions imposed by federal law shall be maintained.

(c) For purposes of this section, the following terms have the following meanings:

(1) The phrases "health care facility" and "health care provider" have the meaning given in general law related to a patient's rights and responsibilities.

(2) The term "patient" means an individual who has sought, is seeking, is undergoing, or has undergone care or treatment in a health care facility or by a health care provider.

(3) The phrase "adverse medical incident" means medical negligence, intentional misconduct, and any other act, neglect, or default of a health care facility or health care provider that caused or could have caused injury to or death of a patient, including, but not limited to, those incidents that are required by state or federal law to be reported to any governmental agency or body, and incidents that are reported to or reviewed by any health care facility peer review, risk management, quality assurance, credentials, or similar committee, or any representative of any such committees.

(4) The phrase "have access to any records" means, in addition to any other procedure for producing such records provided by general law, making the records available for inspection and copying upon formal or informal request by the patient or a representative of the patient, provided that current records which have been made publicly available by publication or on the Internet may be "provided" by reference to the location at which the records are publicly available.

History. — Proposed by Initiative Petition filed with the Secretary of State April 1, 2003; adopted 2004.

[1]**Note.** —

A. This section, originally designated section 22 by Amendment No. 7, 2004, proposed by Initiative Petition filed with the Secretary of State April 1, 2003, adopted 2004, was redesignated section 25 by the editors in order to avoid confusion with section 22, relating to parental notice of termination of a minor's pregnancy, as contained in Amendment No. 1, 2004, added by H.J.R. 1, 2004, adopted 2004.

B. Amendment No. 7, 2004, proposed by Initiative Petition filed with the Secretary of State April 1, 2003, adopted 2004, published "[f]ull [t]ext" consisting of a statement and purpose, the actual amendment "inserting the following new section at the end [of Art. X]," and an effective date and severability provision not specifically included in the amendment text. The effective date and severability provision reads:

3) Effective Date and Severability:

This amendment shall be effective on the date it is approved by the electorate. If any portion of this measure is held invalid for any reason, the remaining portion of this measure, to the fullest extent possible, shall be severed from the void portion and given the fullest possible force and application.

[1]**SECTION 26. Prohibition of medical license after repeated medical malpractice.** —

(a) No person who has been found to have committed three or more incidents of medical malpractice shall be licensed or continue to be licensed by the State of Florida to provide health care services as a medical doctor.

CONSTITUTION OF THE STATE OF FLORIDA   1059

(b) For purposes of this section, the following terms have the following meanings:

(1) The phrase "medical malpractice" means both the failure to practice medicine in Florida with that level of care, skill, and treatment recognized in general law related to health care providers' licensure, and any similar wrongful act, neglect, or default in other states or countries which, if committed in Florida, would have been considered medical malpractice.

(2) The phrase "found to have committed" means that the malpractice has been found in a final judgment of a court of law, final administrative agency decision, or decision of binding arbitration.

History. — Proposed by Initiative Petition filed with the Secretary of State April 7, 2003; adopted 2004.

[1]**Note.** —

A. This section, originally designated section 20 by Amendment No. 8, 2004, proposed by Initiative Petition filed with the Secretary of State April 7, 2003, adopted 2004, was redesignated section 26 by the editors in order to avoid confusion with already existing section 20, relating to prohibiting workplace smoking.

B. Amendment No. 8, 2004, proposed by Initiative Petition filed with the Secretary of State April 7, 2003, adopted 2004, published "[f]ull [t]ext" consisting of a statement and purpose, the actual amendment "inserting the following new section at the end [of Art. X]," and an effective date and severability provision not specifically included in the amendment text. The effective date and severability provision reads:

c) Effective Date and Severability:

This amendment shall be effective on the date it is approved by the electorate. If any portion of this measure is held invalid for any reason, the remaining portion of this measure, to the fullest extent possible, shall be severed from the void portion and given the fullest possible force and application.

SECTION 27. Comprehensive Statewide Tobacco Education And Prevention Program. — In order to protect people, especially youth, from health hazards of using tobacco, including addictive disorders, cancer, cardiovascular diseases, and lung diseases; and to discourage use of tobacco, particularly among youth, a portion of the money that tobacco companies pay to the State of Florida under the Tobacco Settlement each year shall be used to fund a comprehensive statewide tobacco education and prevention program consistent with recommendations of the U.S. Centers for Disease Control and Prevention (CDC), as follows:

(a) PROGRAM. The money appropriated pursuant to this section shall be used to fund a comprehensive statewide tobacco education and prevention program consistent with the recommendations for effective program components in the 1999 *Best Practices for Comprehensive Tobacco Control Programs* of the CDC, as such *Best Practices* may be amended by the CDC. This program shall include, at a minimum, the following components, and may include additional components that are also contained within the CDC *Best Practices*, as periodically amended, and that are effective at accomplishing the purpose of this section, and that do not undermine the effectiveness of these required minimum components:

(1) an advertising campaign to discourage the use of tobacco and to educate people, especially youth, about the health hazards of tobacco, which shall be designed to be effective at achieving these goals and shall include, but need not be limited to, television, radio, and print advertising, with no limitations on any individual advertising medium utilized; and which shall be funded at a level equivalent to one-third of each total annual appropriation required by this section;

(2) evidence-based curricula and programs to educate youth about tobacco and to discourage their use of it, including, but not limited to, programs that involve youth, educate youth about the health hazards of tobacco, help youth develop skills to refuse tobacco, and demonstrate to youth how to stop using tobacco;

(3) programs of local community-based partnerships that discourage the use of tobacco and work to educate people, especially youth, about the health hazards of tobacco, with an emphasis on programs that involve youth and emphasize the prevention and cessation of tobacco use;

(4) enforcement of laws, regulations, and policies against the sale or other provision of tobacco to minors, and the possession of tobacco by minors; and

(5) publicly-reported annual evaluations to ensure that moneys appropriated pursuant to this section are spent properly, which shall include evaluation of the program's effectiveness in reducing and preventing tobacco use, and annual recommendations for improvements to enhance the program's effectiveness, which are to include comparisons to similar programs proven to be effective in other states, as well as comparisons to CDC *Best Practices*, including amendments thereto.

(b) FUNDING. In every year beginning with the calendar year after voters approve this amendment, the Florida Legislature shall appropriate, for the purpose expressed herein, from the total gross funds that tobacco companies pay to the State of Florida under the Tobacco Settlement, an amount equal to fifteen percent of such funds paid to the State in 2005; and the appropriation required by this section shall be adjusted annually for inflation, using the Consumer Price Index as published by the United States Department of Labor.

(c) DEFINITIONS. "Tobacco" includes, without limitation, tobacco itself and tobacco products that include tobacco and are intended or expected for human use or consumption, including, but not limited to, cigarettes, cigars, pipe tobacco, and smokeless tobacco. The "Tobacco Settlement" means that certain Settlement Agreement dated August 25, 1997, entered into in settlement of the case styled as *State of Florida, et al. v. American Tobacco Company, et al.*, Case No. 95-1466 AH (Fla. 15th Cir. Ct.), as amended by Stipulation of Amendment dated September 11, 1998; and includes any subsequent amendments and successor agreements. "Youth" includes minors and young adults.

CONSTITUTION OF THE STATE OF FLORIDA

(d) EFFECTIVE DATE. This amendment shall become effective immediately upon approval by the voters.

History. — Proposed by Initiative Petition filed with the Secretary of State July 20, 2005; adopted 2006.

SECTION 28. Land Acquisition Trust Fund. —

(a) Effective on July 1 of the year following passage of this amendment by the voters, and for a period of 20 years after that effective date, the Land Acquisition Trust Fund shall receive no less than 33 percent of net revenues derived from the existing excise tax on documents, as defined in the statutes in effect on January 1, 2012, as amended from time to time, or any successor or replacement tax, after the Department of Revenue first deducts a service charge to pay the costs of the collection and enforcement of the excise tax on documents.

(b) Funds in the Land Acquisition Trust Fund shall be expended only for the following purposes:

(1) As provided by law, to finance or refinance: the acquisition and improvement of land, water areas, and related property interests, including conservation easements, and resources for conservation lands including wetlands, forests, and fish and wildlife habitat; wildlife management areas; lands that protect water resources and drinking water sources, including lands protecting the water quality and quantity of rivers, lakes, streams, springsheds, and lands providing recharge for groundwater and aquifer systems; lands in the Everglades Agricultural Area and the Everglades Protection Area, as defined in Article II, Section 7(b); beaches and shores; outdoor recreation lands, including recreational trails, parks, and urban open space; rural landscapes; working farms and ranches; historic or geologic sites; together with management, restoration of natural systems, and the enhancement of public access or recreational enjoyment of conservation lands.

(2) To pay the debt service on bonds issued pursuant to Article VII, Section 11(e).

(c) The moneys deposited into the Land Acquisition Trust Fund, as defined by the statutes in effect on January 1, 2012, shall not be or become commingled with the general revenue fund of the state.

History. — Proposed by Initiative Petition filed with the Secretary of State September 17, 2012; adopted 2014.

SECTION 29. Medical marijuana production, possession and use. —

(a) PUBLIC POLICY.

(1) The medical use of marijuana by a qualifying patient or caregiver in compliance with this section is not subject to criminal or civil liability or sanctions under Florida law.

(2) A physician shall not be subject to criminal or civil liability or sanctions under Florida law solely for issuing a physician certification with reasonable care to a person diagnosed with a debilitating medical condition in compliance with this section.

(3) Actions and conduct by a Medical Marijuana Treatment Center registered with the Department, or its agents or employees, and in compliance with this section and Department regulations, shall not be subject to criminal or civil liability or sanctions under Florida law.

(b) DEFINITIONS. For purposes of this section, the following words and terms shall have the following meanings:

(1) "Debilitating Medical Condition" means cancer, epilepsy, glaucoma, positive status for human immunodeficiency virus (HIV), acquired immune deficiency syndrome (AIDS), post-traumatic stress disorder (PTSD), amyotrophic lateral sclerosis (ALS), Crohn's disease, Parkinson's disease, multiple sclerosis, or other debilitating medical conditions of the same kind or class as or comparable to those enumerated, and for which a physician believes that the medical use of marijuana would likely outweigh the potential health risks for a patient.

(2) "Department" means the Department of Health or its successor agency.

(3) "Identification card" means a document issued by the Department that identifies a qualifying patient or a caregiver.

(4) "Marijuana" has the meaning given cannabis in Section 893.02(3), Florida Statutes (2014), and, in addition, "Low-THC cannabis" as defined in Section 381.986(1)(b), Florida Statutes (2014), shall also be included in the meaning of the term "marijuana."

(5) "Medical Marijuana Treatment Center" (MMTC) means an entity that acquires, cultivates, possesses, processes (including development of related products such as food, tinctures, aerosols, oils, or ointments), transfers, transports, sells, distributes, dispenses, or administers marijuana, products containing marijuana, related supplies, or educational materials to qualifying patients or their caregivers and is registered by the Department.

(6) "Medical use" means the acquisition, possession, use, delivery, transfer, or administration of an amount of marijuana not in conflict with Department rules, or of related supplies by a qualifying patient or caregiver for use by the caregiver's designated qualifying patient for the treatment of a debilitating medical condition.

(7) "Caregiver" means a person who is at least twenty-one (21) years old who has agreed to assist with a qualifying patient's medical use of marijuana and has qualified for and obtained a caregiver identification card issued by the Department. The Department may limit the number of qualifying patients a caregiver may assist at one time and the number of caregivers that a qualifying patient may have at one time. Caregivers are prohibited from consuming marijuana obtained for medical use by the qualifying patient.

(8) "Physician" means a person who is licensed to practice medicine in Florida.

(9) "Physician certification" means a written document signed by a physician, stating that in the physician's professional opinion, the patient suffers from a debilitating medical condition, that the medical use of marijuana would likely outweigh the

potential health risks for the patient, and for how long the physician recommends the medical use of marijuana for the patient. A physician certification may only be provided after the physician has conducted a physical examination and a full assessment of the medical history of the patient. In order for a physician certification to be issued to a minor, a parent or legal guardian of the minor must consent in writing.

(10) "Qualifying patient" means a person who has been diagnosed to have a debilitating medical condition, who has a physician certification and a valid qualifying patient identification card. If the Department does not begin issuing identification cards within nine (9) months after the effective date of this section, then a valid physician certification will serve as a patient identification card in order to allow a person to become a "qualifying patient" until the Department begins issuing identification cards.

(c) LIMITATIONS.

(1) Nothing in this section allows for a violation of any law other than for conduct in compliance with the provisions of this section.

(2) Nothing in this section shall affect or repeal laws relating to non-medical use, possession, production, or sale of marijuana.

(3) Nothing in this section authorizes the use of medical marijuana by anyone other than a qualifying patient.

(4) Nothing in this section shall permit the operation of any vehicle, aircraft, train or boat while under the influence of marijuana.

(5) Nothing in this section requires the violation of federal law or purports to give immunity under federal law.

(6) Nothing in this section shall require any accommodation of any on-site medical use of marijuana in any correctional institution or detention facility or place of education or employment, or of smoking medical marijuana in any public place.

(7) Nothing in this section shall require any health insurance provider or any government agency or authority to reimburse any person for expenses related to the medical use of marijuana.

(8) Nothing in this section shall affect or repeal laws relating to negligence or professional malpractice on the part of a qualified patient, caregiver, physician, MMTC, or its agents or employees.

(d) DUTIES OF THE DEPARTMENT. The Department shall issue reasonable regulations necessary for the implementation and enforcement of this section. The purpose of the regulations is to ensure the availability and safe use of medical marijuana by qualifying patients. It is the duty of the Department to promulgate regulations in a timely fashion.

(1) Implementing Regulations. In order to allow the Department sufficient time after passage of this section, the following regulations shall be promulgated no later than six (6) months after the effective date of this section:

a. Procedures for the issuance and annual renewal of qualifying patient identification cards to people with physician certifications and standards for renewal of such identification cards. Before issuing an identification card to a minor, the Department must receive written consent from the minor's parent or legal guardian, in addition to the physician certification.

b. Procedures establishing qualifications and standards for caregivers, including conducting appropriate background checks, and procedures for the issuance and annual renewal of caregiver identification cards.

c. Procedures for the registration of MMTCs that include procedures for the issuance, renewal, suspension and revocation of registration, and standards to ensure proper security, record keeping, testing, labeling, inspection, and safety.

d. A regulation that defines the amount of marijuana that could reasonably be presumed to be an adequate supply for qualifying patients' medical use, based on the best available evidence. This presumption as to quantity may be overcome with evidence of a particular qualifying patient's appropriate medical use.

(2) Identification cards and registrations. The Department shall begin issuing qualifying patient and caregiver identification cards, and registering MMTCs no later than nine (9) months after the effective date of this section.

(3) If the Department does not issue regulations, or if the Department does not begin issuing identification cards and registering MMTCs within the time limits set in this section, any Florida citizen shall have standing to seek judicial relief to compel compliance with the Department's constitutional duties.

(4) The Department shall protect the confidentiality of all qualifying patients. All records containing the identity of qualifying patients shall be confidential and kept from public disclosure other than for valid medical or law enforcement purposes.

(e) LEGISLATION. Nothing in this section shall limit the legislature from enacting laws consistent with this section.

(f) SEVERABILITY. The provisions of this section are severable and if any clause, sentence, paragraph or section of this measure, or an application thereof, is adjudged invalid by a court of competent jurisdiction other provisions shall continue to be in effect to the fullest extent possible.

History. — Proposed by Initiative Petition filed with the Secretary of State January 9, 2015; adopted 2016.

SECTION 30. Voter control of gambling in Florida. —

(a) This amendment ensures that Florida voters shall have the exclusive right to decide whether to authorize casino gambling in the State of Florida. This amendment requires a vote by citizens' initiative pursuant to Article XI, section 3, in order for casino gambling to be authorized under Florida law. This section amends this Article; and also affects Article XI, by making citizens' initiatives the exclusive method of authorizing casino gambling.

CONSTITUTION OF THE STATE OF FLORIDA 1065

(b) As used in this section, "casino gambling" means any of the types of games typically found in casinos and that are within the definition of Class III gaming in the Federal Indian Gaming Regulatory Act, 25 U.S.C. ss. 2701 et seq. ("IGRA"), and in 25 C.F.R. s. 502.4, upon adoption of this amendment, and any that are added to such definition of Class III gaming in the future. This includes, but is not limited to, any house banking game, including but not limited to card games such as baccarat, chemin de fer, blackjack (21), and pai gow (if played as house banking games); any player-banked game that simulates a house banking game, such as California black jack; casino games such as roulette, craps, and keno; any slot machines as defined in 15 U.S.C. s. 1171(a)(1); and any other game not authorized by Article X, section 15, whether or not defined as a slot machine, in which outcomes are determined by random number generator or are similarly assigned randomly, such as instant or historical racing. As used herein, "casino gambling" includes any electronic gambling devices, simulated gambling devices, video lottery devices, internet sweepstakes devices, and any other form of electronic or electromechanical facsimiles of any game of chance, slot machine, or casino-style game, regardless of how such devices are defined under IGRA. As used herein, "casino gambling" does not include pari-mutuel wagering on horse racing, dog racing, or jai alai exhibitions. For purposes of this section, "gambling" and "gaming" are synonymous.

(c) Nothing herein shall be deemed to limit the right of the Legislature to exercise its authority through general law to restrict, regulate, or tax any gaming or gambling activities. In addition, nothing herein shall be construed to limit the ability of the state or Native American tribes to negotiate gaming compacts pursuant to the Federal Indian Gaming Regulatory Act for the conduct of casino gambling on tribal lands, or to affect any existing gambling on tribal lands pursuant to compacts executed by the state and Native American tribes pursuant to IGRA.

(d) This section is effective upon approval by the voters, is self-executing, and no Legislative implementation is required.

(e) If any part of this section is held invalid for any reason, the remaining portion or portions shall be severed from the invalid portion and given the fullest possible force and effect.

History. — Proposed by Initiative Petition filed with the Secretary of State October 26, 2015; adopted 2018.

SECTION 31. Death benefits for survivors of first responders and military members. —

(a) A death benefit shall be paid by the employing agency when a firefighter; a paramedic; an emergency medical technician; a law enforcement, correctional, or correctional probation officer; or a member of the Florida National Guard, while engaged in the performance of their official duties, is:

(1) Accidentally killed or receives accidental bodily injury which results in the loss of the individual's life, provided that such killing is not the result of suicide and that such bodily injury is not intentionally self-inflicted; or

(2) Unlawfully and intentionally killed or dies as a result of such unlawful and intentional act or is killed during active duty.

(b) A death benefit shall be paid by funds from general revenue when an active duty member of the United States Armed Forces is:

(1) Accidentally killed or receives accidental bodily injury which results in the loss of the individual's life, provided that such killing is not the result of suicide and that such bodily injury is not intentionally self-inflicted; or

(2) Unlawfully and intentionally killed or dies as a result of such unlawful and intentional act or is killed during active duty.

(c) If a firefighter; a paramedic; an emergency medical technician; a law enforcement, correctional, or correctional probation officer; or an active duty member of the Florida National Guard or United States Armed Forces is accidentally killed as specified in paragraphs (a)(1) and (b)(1), or unlawfully and intentionally killed as specified in paragraphs (a)(2) and (b)(2), the state shall waive certain educational expenses that the child or spouse of the deceased first responder or military member incurs while obtaining a career certificate, an undergraduate education, or a post-graduate education.

(d) An eligible first responder must have been working for the State of Florida or any of its political subdivisions or agencies at the time of death. An eligible military member must have been a resident of this state or his or her duty post must have been within this state at the time of death.

(e) The legislature shall implement this section by general law.

(f) This section shall take effect on July 1, 2019.

History. — Proposed by Constitution Revision Commission, Revision No. 2, 2018, filed with the Secretary of State May 9, 2018; adopted 2018.

SECTION 32. Prohibition on racing of and wagering on greyhounds or other dogs. — The humane treatment of animals is a fundamental value of the people of the State of Florida. After December 31, 2020, a person authorized to conduct gaming or pari-mutuel operations may not race greyhounds or any member of the *Canis Familiaris* subspecies in connection with any wager for money or any other thing of value in this state, and persons in this state may not wager money or any other thing of value on the outcome of a live dog race occurring in this state. The failure to conduct greyhound racing or wagering on greyhound racing after December 31, 2018, does not constitute grounds to revoke or deny renewal of other related gaming licenses held by a person who is a licensed greyhound permitholder on January 1, 2018, and does not affect the eligibility of such permitholder, or such permitholder's facility, to conduct other pari-mutuel activities authorized by general law. By general law, the legislature shall specify civil or criminal penalties for violations of this section and for activities that aid or abet violations of this section.

History. — Proposed by Constitution Revision Commission, Revision No. 8, 2018, filed with the Secretary of State May 9, 2018; adopted 2018.

CONSTITUTION OF THE STATE OF FLORIDA

ARTICLE XI
AMENDMENTS

SECTION 1.

Proposal by legislature.

SECTION 2.

Revision commission.

SECTION 3.

Initiative.

SECTION 4.

Constitutional convention.

SECTION 5.

Amendment or revision election.

SECTION 6.

Taxation and budget reform commission.

SECTION 7.

Tax or fee limitation.

SECTION 1. Proposal by legislature. — Amendment of a section or revision of one or more articles, or the whole, of this constitution may be proposed by joint resolution agreed to by three-fifths of the membership of each house of the legislature. The full text of the joint resolution and the vote of each member voting shall be entered on the journal of each house.

SECTION 2. Revision commission. —

(a) Within thirty days before the convening of the 2017 regular session of the legislature, and each twentieth year thereafter, there shall be established a constitution revision commission composed of the following thirty-seven members:

(1) the attorney general of the state;

(2) fifteen members selected by the governor;

(3) nine members selected by the speaker of the house of representatives and nine members selected by the president of the senate; and

(4) three members selected by the chief justice of the supreme court of Florida with the advice of the justices.

(b) The governor shall designate one member of the commission as its chair. Vacancies in the membership of the commission shall be filled in the same manner as the original appointments.

(c) Each constitution revision commission shall convene at the call of its chair, adopt its rules of procedure, examine the constitution of the state, hold public hearings, and, not later than one hundred eighty days prior to the next general election, file with the custodian of state records its proposal, if any, of a revision of this constitution or any part of it.

History. — Am. H.J.R. 1616, 1988; adopted 1988; Am. S.J.R. 210, 1996; adopted 1996; Ams. proposed by Constitution Revision Commission, Revision Nos. 8 and 13, 1998, filed with the Secretary of State May 5, 1998; adopted 1998.

SECTION 3. Initiative. — The power to propose the revision or amendment of any portion or portions of this constitution by initiative is reserved to the people, provided that, any such revision or amendment, except for those limiting the power of government to raise revenue, shall embrace but one subject and matter directly connected therewith. It may be invoked by filing with the custodian of state records a petition containing a copy of the proposed revision or amendment, signed by a number of electors in each of one half of the congressional districts of the state, and of the state as a whole, equal to eight percent of the votes cast in each of such districts respectively and in the state as a whole in the last preceding election in which presidential electors were chosen.

History. — Am. H.J.R. 2835, 1972; adopted 1972; Am. by Initiative Petition filed with the Secretary of State August 3, 1993; adopted 1994; Am. proposed by Constitution Revision Commission, Revision No. 8, 1998, filed with the Secretary of State May 5, 1998; adopted 1998.

SECTION 4. Constitutional convention. —

(a) The power to call a convention to consider a revision of the entire constitution is reserved to the people. It may be invoked by filing with the custodian of state records a petition, containing a declaration that a constitutional convention is desired, signed by a number of electors in each of one half of the congressional districts of the state, and of the state as a whole, equal to fifteen per cent of the votes cast in each such district respectively and in the state as a whole in the last preceding election of presidential electors.

(b) At the next general election held more than ninety days after the filing of such petition there shall be submitted to the electors of the state the question: "Shall a constitutional convention be held?" If a majority voting on the question votes in the affirmative, at the next succeeding general election there shall be elected from each representative district a member of a constitutional convention. On the twenty-first day following that election, the convention shall sit at the capital, elect officers, adopt rules of procedure, judge the election of its membership, and fix a time and place for its future meetings. Not later than ninety days before the next succeeding general election, the convention shall cause to be filed with the custodian of state records any revision of this constitution proposed by it.

History. — Am. proposed by Constitution Revision Commission, Revision No. 8, 1998, filed with the Secretary of State May 5, 1998; adopted 1998.

SECTION 5. Amendment or revision election. —

(a) A proposed amendment to or revision of this constitution, or any part of it, shall be submitted to the electors at the next general election held more than ninety

CONSTITUTION OF THE STATE OF FLORIDA   1069

days after the joint resolution or report of revision commission, constitutional convention or taxation and budget reform commission proposing it is filed with the custodian of state records, unless, pursuant to law enacted by the affirmative vote of three-fourths of the membership of each house of the legislature and limited to a single amendment or revision, it is submitted at an earlier special election held more than ninety days after such filing.

(b) A proposed amendment or revision of this constitution, or any part of it, by initiative shall be submitted to the electors at the general election provided the initiative petition is filed with the custodian of state records no later than February 1 of the year in which the general election is held.

(c) The legislature shall provide by general law, prior to the holding of an election pursuant to this section, for the provision of a statement to the public regarding the probable financial impact of any amendment proposed by initiative pursuant to section 3.

(d) Once in the tenth week, and once in the sixth week immediately preceding the week in which the election is held, the proposed amendment or revision, with notice of the date of election at which it will be submitted to the electors, shall be published in one newspaper of general circulation in each county in which a newspaper is published.

(e) Unless otherwise specifically provided for elsewhere in this constitution, if the proposed amendment or revision is approved by vote of at least sixty percent of the electors voting on the measure, it shall be effective as an amendment to or revision of the constitution of the state on the first Tuesday after the first Monday in January following the election, or on such other date as may be specified in the amendment or revision.

History. — Am. H.J.R. 1616, 1988; adopted 1988; Am. proposed by Constitution Revision Commission, Revision No. 8, 1998, filed with the Secretary of State May 5, 1998; adopted 1998; Am. H.J.R. 571, 2001; adopted 2002; Am. S.J.R. 2394, 2004; adopted 2004; Am. H.J.R. 1723, 2005; adopted 2006.

SECTION 6. Taxation and budget reform commission. —

(a) Beginning in 2007 and each twentieth year thereafter, there shall be established a taxation and budget reform commission composed of the following members:

(1) eleven members selected by the governor, none of whom shall be a member of the legislature at the time of appointment.

(2) seven members selected by the speaker of the house of representatives and seven members selected by the president of the senate, none of whom shall be a member of the legislature at the time of appointment.

(3) four non-voting ex officio members, all of whom shall be members of the legislature at the time of appointment. Two of these members, one of whom shall be a member of the minority party in the house of representatives, shall be selected by the speaker of the house of representatives, and two of these members, one of whom

shall be a member of the minority party in the senate, shall be selected by the president of the senate.

(b) Vacancies in the membership of the commission shall be filled in the same manner as the original appointments.

(c) At its initial meeting, the members of the commission shall elect a member who is not a member of the legislature to serve as chair and the commission shall adopt its rules of procedure. Thereafter, the commission shall convene at the call of the chair. An affirmative vote of two thirds of the full commission shall be necessary for any revision of this constitution or any part of it to be proposed by the commission.

(d) The commission shall examine the state budgetary process, the revenue needs and expenditure processes of the state, the appropriateness of the tax structure of the state, and governmental productivity and efficiency; review policy as it relates to the ability of state and local government to tax and adequately fund governmental operations and capital facilities required to meet the state's needs during the next twenty year period; determine methods favored by the citizens of the state to fund the needs of the state, including alternative methods for raising sufficient revenues for the needs of the state; determine measures that could be instituted to effectively gather funds from existing tax sources; examine constitutional limitations on taxation and expenditures at the state and local level; and review the state's comprehensive planning, budgeting and needs assessment processes to determine whether the resulting information adequately supports a strategic decisionmaking process.

(e) The commission shall hold public hearings as it deems necessary to carry out its responsibilities under this section. The commission shall issue a report of the results of the review carried out, and propose to the legislature any recommended statutory changes related to the taxation or budgetary laws of the state. Not later than one hundred eighty days prior to the general election in the second year following the year in which the commission is established, the commission shall file with the custodian of state records its proposal, if any, of a revision of this constitution or any part of it dealing with taxation or the state budgetary process.

History. — Added, H.J.R. 1616, 1988; adopted 1988; Ams. proposed by Constitution Revision Commission, Revision Nos. 8 and 13, 1998, filed with the Secretary of State May 5, 1998; adopted 1998.

SECTION 7. Tax or fee limitation. — Notwithstanding Article X, Section 12(d) of this constitution, no new State tax or fee shall be imposed on or after November 8, 1994 by any amendment to this constitution unless the proposed amendment is approved by not fewer than two-thirds of the voters voting in the election in which such proposed amendment is considered. For purposes of this section, the phrase "new State tax or fee" shall mean any tax or fee which would produce revenue subject to lump sum or other appropriation by the Legislature, either for the State general revenue fund or any trust fund, which tax or fee is not in effect on November 7, 1994 including without limitation such taxes and fees as are the subject of proposed constitutional amendments appearing on the ballot on November 8, 1994. This section shall apply to proposed constitutional amendments relating to State taxes or fees which appear on the November 8, 1994 ballot, or later ballots, and any such proposed amendment which fails to gain the two-thirds vote required hereby shall be null, void and without effect.

History. — Proposed by Initiative Petition filed with the Secretary of State March 11, 1994; adopted 1996.

ARTICLE XII
SCHEDULE

SECTION 1.

Constitution of 1885 superseded.

SECTION 2.

Property taxes; millages.

SECTION 3.

Officers to continue in office.

SECTION 4.

State commissioner of education.

SECTION 5.

Superintendent of schools.

SECTION 6.

Laws preserved.

SECTION 7.

Rights reserved.

SECTION 8.

Public debts recognized.

SECTION 9.

Bonds.

SECTION 10.

Preservation of existing government.

SECTION 11.

Deletion of obsolete schedule items.

SECTION 12.

Senators.

SECTION 13.

Legislative apportionment.

SECTION 14.

Representatives; terms.

SECTION 15.

Special district taxes.

SECTION 16.

Reorganization.

SECTION 17.

Conflicting provisions.

SECTION 18.

Bonds for housing and related facilities.

SECTION 19.

Renewable energy source property.

SECTION 20.

Access to public records.

SECTION 21.

State revenue limitation.

SECTION 22.

Historic property exemption and assessment.

SECTION 23.

Fish and wildlife conservation commission.

SECTION 24.

Executive branch reform.

SECTION 25.

Schedule to Article V amendment.

SECTION 26.

Increased homestead exemption.

SECTION 27.

Property tax exemptions and limitations on property tax assessments.

SECTION 28.

Property tax exemption and classification and assessment of land used for conservation purposes.

SECTION 29.

Limitation on the assessed value of real property used for residential purposes.

SECTION 30.

Assessment of working waterfront property.

SECTION 31.

Additional ad valorem tax exemption for certain members of the armed forces deployed on active duty outside of the United States.

SECTION 32.

Veterans disabled due to combat injury; homestead property tax discount.

SECTION 33.

Ad valorem tax relief for surviving spouses of veterans who died from service-connected causes and first responders who died in the line of duty.

SECTION 34.

Solar devices or renewable energy source devices; exemption from certain taxation and assessment.

SECTION 35.

Tax exemption for totally and permanently disabled first responders.

SECTION 36.

Additional ad valorem exemption for persons age sixty-five or older.

SECTION 37.

Eligibility of justices and judges.

SECTION 38.

Prohibitions regarding lobbying for compensation and abuse of public position by public officers and public employees.

SECTION 39.

Prohibition on racing of or wagering on greyhounds or other dogs.

SECTION 40.

Transfer of the accrued benefit from specified limitations on homestead property tax assessments; increased portability period.

SECTION 41.

Ad valorem tax discount for surviving spouses of certain permanently disabled veterans.

SECTION 1. Constitution of 1885 superseded. — Articles I through IV, VII, and IX through XX of the Constitution of Florida adopted in 1885, as amended from time to time, are superseded by this revision except those sections expressly retained and made a part of this revision by reference.

SECTION 2. Property taxes; millages. — Tax millages authorized in counties, municipalities and special districts, on the date this revision becomes effective, may be continued until reduced by law.

SECTION 3. Officers to continue in office. — Every person holding office when this revision becomes effective shall continue in office for the remainder of the term if that office is not abolished. If the office is abolished the incumbent shall be paid adequate compensation, to be fixed by law, for the loss of emoluments for the remainder of the term.

SECTION 4. State commissioner of education. — The state superintendent of public instruction in office on the effective date of this revision shall become and, for the remainder of the term being served, shall be the commissioner of education.

SECTION 5. Superintendent of schools. —

(a) On the effective date of this revision the county superintendent of public instruction of each county shall become and, for the remainder of the term being served, shall be the superintendent of schools of that district.

(b) The method of selection of the county superintendent of public instruction of each county, as provided by or under the Constitution of 1885, as amended, shall apply to the selection of the district superintendent of schools until changed as herein provided.

SECTION 6. Laws preserved. —

(a) All laws in effect upon the adoption of this revision, to the extent not inconsistent with it, shall remain in force until they expire by their terms or are repealed.

(b) All statutes which, under the Constitution of 1885, as amended, apply to the state superintendent of public instruction and those which apply to the county superintendent of public instruction shall under this revision apply, respectively, to the state commissioner of education and the district superintendent of schools.

SECTION 7. Rights reserved. —

(a) All actions, rights of action, claims, contracts and obligations of individuals, corporations and public bodies or agencies existing on the date this revision becomes effective shall continue to be valid as if this revision had not been adopted. All taxes, penalties, fines and forfeitures owing to the state under the Constitution of 1885, as amended, shall inure to the state under this revision, and all sentences as punishment for crime shall be executed according to their terms.

(b) This revision shall not be retroactive so as to create any right or liability which did not exist under the Constitution of 1885, as amended, based upon matters occurring prior to the adoption of this revision.

SECTION 8. Public debts recognized. — All bonds, revenue certificates, revenue bonds and tax anticipation certificates issued pursuant to the Constitution of 1885, as amended by the state, any agency, political subdivision or public corporation of the state shall remain in full force and effect and shall be secured by the same sources of revenue as before the adoption of this revision, and, to the extent necessary to effectuate this section, the applicable provisions of the Constitution of 1885, as amended, are retained as a part of this revision until payment in full of these public securities.

CONSTITUTION OF THE STATE OF FLORIDA

SECTION 9. Bonds. —

(a) ADDITIONAL SECURITIES.

(1) [1]Article IX, Section 17, of the Constitution of 1885, as amended, as it existed immediately before this Constitution, as revised in 1968, became effective, is adopted by this reference as a part of this revision as completely as though incorporated herein verbatim, except revenue bonds, revenue certificates or other evidences of indebtedness hereafter issued thereunder may be issued by the agency of the state so authorized by law.

(2) That portion of [2]Article XII, Section 9, Subsection (a) of this Constitution, as amended, which by reference adopted [3]Article XII, Section 19 of the Constitution of 1885, as amended, as the same existed immediately before the effective date of this amendment is adopted by this reference as part of this revision as completely as though incorporated herein verbatim, for the purpose of providing that after the effective date of this amendment all of the proceeds of the revenues derived from the gross receipts taxes, as therein defined, collected in each year shall be applied as provided therein to the extent necessary to comply with all obligations to or for the benefit of holders of bonds or certificates issued before the effective date of this amendment or any refundings thereof which are secured by such gross receipts taxes. No bonds or other obligations may be issued pursuant to the provisions of [3]Article XII, Section 19, of the Constitution of 1885, as amended, but this provision shall not be construed to prevent the refunding of any such outstanding bonds or obligations pursuant to the provisions of this subsection (a)(2).

Subject to the requirements of the first paragraph of this subsection (a)(2), beginning July 1, 1975, all of the proceeds of the revenues derived from the gross receipts taxes collected from every person, including municipalities, as provided and levied pursuant to the provisions of chapter 203, Florida Statutes, as such chapter is amended from time to time, shall, as collected, be placed in a trust fund to be known as the "public education capital outlay and debt service trust fund" in the state treasury (hereinafter referred to as "capital outlay fund"), and used only as provided herein.

The capital outlay fund shall be administered by the state board of education as created and constituted by Section 2 of Article IX of the Constitution of Florida as revised in 1968 (hereinafter referred to as "state board"), or by such other instrumentality of the state which shall hereafter succeed by law to the powers, duties and functions of the state board, including the powers, duties and functions of the state board provided in this subsection (a)(2). The state board shall be a body corporate and shall have all the powers provided herein in addition to all other constitutional and statutory powers related to the purposes of this subsection (a)(2) heretofore or hereafter conferred by law upon the state board, or its predecessor created by the Constitution of 1885, as amended.

State bonds pledging the full faith and credit of the state may be issued, without a vote of the electors, by the state board pursuant to law to finance or refinance capital projects theretofore authorized by the legislature, and any purposes appurtenant or incidental thereto, for the state system of public education provided for in Section 1 of Article IX of this Constitution (hereinafter referred to as "state system"), including but not limited to institutions of higher learning, community colleges, vocational technical schools, or public schools, as now defined or as may hereafter be defined by law. All such bonds shall mature not later than thirty years after the date of issuance thereof. All other details of such bonds shall be as provided by law or by the proceedings authorizing such bonds; provided, however, that no bonds, except refunding bonds, shall be issued, and no proceeds shall be expended for the cost of any capital project, unless such project has been authorized by the legislature.

Bonds issued pursuant to this subsection (a)(2) shall be primarily payable from such revenues derived from gross receipts taxes, and shall be additionally secured by the full faith and credit of the state. No such bonds shall ever be issued in an amount exceeding ninety percent of the amount which the state board determines can be serviced by the revenues derived from the gross receipts taxes accruing thereafter under the provisions of this subsection (a)(2), and such determination shall be conclusive.

The moneys in the capital outlay fund in each fiscal year shall be used only for the following purposes and in the following order of priority:

a. For the payment of the principal of and interest on any bonds due in such fiscal year;

b. For the deposit into any reserve funds provided for in the proceedings authorizing the issuance of bonds of any amounts required to be deposited in such reserve funds in such fiscal year;

c. For direct payment of the cost or any part of the cost of any capital project for the state system theretofore authorized by the legislature, or for the purchase or redemption of outstanding bonds in accordance with the provisions of the proceedings which authorized the issuance of such bonds, or for the purpose of maintaining, restoring, or repairing existing public educational facilities.

(b) REFUNDING BONDS. Revenue bonds to finance the cost of state capital projects issued prior to the date this revision becomes effective, including projects of the Florida state turnpike authority or its successor but excluding all portions of the state highway system, may be refunded as provided by law without vote of the electors at a lower net average interest cost rate by the issuance of bonds maturing not later than the obligations refunded, secured by the same revenues only.

(c) MOTOR VEHICLE FUEL TAXES.

(1) A state tax, designated "second gas tax," of two cents per gallon upon gasoline and other like products of petroleum and an equivalent tax upon other sources of energy used to propel motor vehicles as levied by [4]Article IX, Section 16, of the Constitution of 1885, as amended, is hereby continued. The proceeds of said tax shall be placed monthly in the state roads distribution fund in the state treasury.

CONSTITUTION OF THE STATE OF FLORIDA

(2) [4]Article IX, Section 16, of the Constitution of 1885, as amended, is adopted by this reference as a part of this revision as completely as though incorporated herein verbatim for the purpose of providing that after the effective date of this revision the proceeds of the "second gas tax" as referred to therein shall be allocated among the several counties in accordance with the formula stated therein to the extent necessary to comply with all obligations to or for the benefit of holders of bonds, revenue certificates and tax anticipation certificates or any refundings thereof secured by any portion of the "second gas tax."

(3) No funds anticipated to be allocated under the formula stated in [4]Article IX, Section 16, of the Constitution of 1885, as amended, shall be pledged as security for any obligation hereafter issued or entered into, except that any outstanding obligations previously issued pledging revenues allocated under said [4]Article IX, Section 16, may be refunded at a lower average net interest cost rate by the issuance of refunding bonds, maturing not later than the obligations refunded, secured by the same revenues and any other security authorized in paragraph (5) of this subsection.

(4) Subject to the requirements of paragraph (2) of this subsection and after payment of administrative expenses, the "second gas tax" shall be allocated to the account of each of the several counties in the amounts to be determined as follows: There shall be an initial allocation of one-fourth in the ratio of county area to state area, one-fourth in the ratio of the total county population to the total population of the state in accordance with the latest available federal census, and one-half in the ratio of the total "second gas tax" collected on retail sales or use in each county to the total collected in all counties of the state during the previous fiscal year. If the annual debt service requirements of any obligations issued for any county, including any deficiencies for prior years, secured under paragraph (2) of this subsection, exceeds the amount which would be allocated to that county under the formula set out in this paragraph, the amounts allocated to other counties shall be reduced proportionately.

(5) Funds allocated under paragraphs (2) and (4) of this subsection shall be administered by the state board of administration created under Article IV, Section 4. The board shall remit the proceeds of the "second gas tax" in each county account for use in said county as follows: eighty per cent to the state agency supervising the state road system and twenty per cent to the governing body of the county. The percentage allocated to the county may be increased by general law. The proceeds of the "second gas tax" subject to allocation to the several counties under this paragraph (5) shall be used first, for the payment of obligations pledging revenues allocated pursuant to [4]Article IX, Section 16, of the Constitution of 1885, as amended, and any refundings thereof; second, for the payment of debt service on bonds issued as provided by this paragraph (5) to finance the acquisition and construction of roads as defined by law; and third, for the acquisition and construction of roads and for road maintenance as authorized by law. When authorized by law, state bonds pledging the full faith and credit of the state may be issued without any election: (i) to refund obligations secured by any portion of the "second gas tax" allocated to a

county under [4]Article IX, Section 16, of the Constitution of 1885, as amended; (ii) to finance the acquisition and construction of roads in a county when approved by the governing body of the county and the state agency supervising the state road system; and (iii) to refund obligations secured by any portion of the "second gas tax" allocated under paragraph 9(c)(4). No such bonds shall be issued unless a state fiscal agency created by law has made a determination that in no state fiscal year will the debt service requirements of the bonds and all other bonds secured by the pledged portion of the "second gas tax" allocated to the county exceed seventy-five per cent of the pledged portion of the "second gas tax" allocated to that county for the preceding state fiscal year, of the pledged net tolls from existing facilities collected in the preceding state fiscal year, and of the annual average net tolls anticipated during the first five state fiscal years of operation of new projects to be financed, and of any other legally available pledged revenues collected in the preceding state fiscal year. Bonds issued pursuant to this subsection shall be payable primarily from the pledged tolls, the pledged portions of the "second gas tax" allocated to that county, and any other pledged revenue, and shall mature not later than forty years from the date of issuance.

(d) SCHOOL BONDS.

(1) [5]Article XII, Section 9, Subsection (d) of this constitution, as amended, (which, by reference, adopted [6]Article XII, Section 18, of the Constitution of 1885, as amended) as the same existed immediately before the effective date of this amendment is adopted by this reference as part of this amendment as completely as though incorporated herein verbatim, for the purpose of providing that after the effective date of this amendment the first proceeds of the revenues derived from the licensing of motor vehicles as referred to therein shall be distributed annually among the several counties in the ratio of the number of instruction units in each county, the same being coterminus with the school district of each county as provided in Article IX, Section 4, Subsection (a) of this constitution, in each year computed as provided therein to the extent necessary to comply with all obligations to or for the benefit of holders of bonds or motor vehicle tax anticipation certificates issued before the effective date of this amendment or any refundings thereof which are secured by any portion of such revenues derived from the licensing of motor vehicles.

(2) No funds anticipated to be distributed annually among the several counties under the formula stated in [5]Article XII, Section 9, Subsection (d) of this constitution, as amended, as the same existed immediately before the effective date of this amendment shall be pledged as security for any obligations hereafter issued or entered into, except that any outstanding obligations previously issued pledging such funds may be refunded by the issuance of refunding bonds.

(3) Subject to the requirements of paragraph (1) of this subsection (d) beginning July 1, 1973, the first proceeds of the revenues derived from the licensing of motor vehicles (hereinafter called "motor vehicle license revenues") to the extent necessary to comply with the provisions of this amendment, shall, as collected, be placed

CONSTITUTION OF THE STATE OF FLORIDA 1079

monthly in the school district and community college district capital outlay and debt service fund in the state treasury and used only as provided in this amendment. Such revenue shall be distributed annually among the several school districts and community college districts in the ratio of the number of instruction units in each school district or community college district in each year computed as provided herein. The amount of the first motor vehicle license revenues to be so set aside in each year and distributed as provided herein shall be an amount equal in the aggregate to the product of six hundred dollars ($600) multiplied by the total number of instruction units in all the school districts of Florida for the school fiscal year 1967-68, plus an amount equal in the aggregate to the product of eight hundred dollars ($800) multiplied by the total number of instruction units in all the school districts of Florida for the school fiscal year 1972-73 and for each school fiscal year thereafter which is in excess of the total number of such instruction units in all the school districts of Florida for the school fiscal year 1967-68, such excess units being designated "growth units." The amount of the first motor vehicle license revenues to be so set aside in each year and distributed as provided herein shall additionally be an amount equal in the aggregate to the product of four hundred dollars ($400) multiplied by the total number of instruction units in all community college districts of Florida. The number of instruction units in each school district or community college district in each year for the purposes of this amendment shall be the greater of (1) the number of instruction units in each school district for the school fiscal year 1967-68 or community college district for the school fiscal year 1968-69 computed in the manner heretofore provided by general law, or (2) the number of instruction units in such school district, including growth units, or community college district for the school fiscal year computed in the manner heretofore or hereafter provided by general law and approved by the state board of education (hereinafter called the state board), or (3) the number of instruction units in each school district, including growth units, or community college district on behalf of which the state board has issued bonds or motor vehicle license revenue anticipation certificates under this amendment which will produce sufficient revenues under this amendment to equal one and twelve-hundredths (1.12) times the aggregate amount of principal of and interest on all bonds or motor vehicle license revenue anticipation certificates issued under this amendment which will mature and become due in such year, computed in the manner heretofore or hereafter provided by general law and approved by the state board.

(4) Such funds so distributed shall be administered by the state board as now created and constituted by Section 2 of Article IX of the State Constitution as revised in 1968, or by such other instrumentality of the state which shall hereafter succeed by law to the powers, duties and functions of the state board, including the powers, duties and functions of the state board provided in this amendment. For the purposes of this amendment, said state board shall be a body corporate and shall have all the powers provided in this amendment in addition to all other constitutional and statutory powers related to the purposes of this amendment heretofore or hereafter conferred upon said state board.

(5) The state board shall, in addition to its other constitutional and statutory powers, have the management, control and supervision of the proceeds of the first motor vehicle license revenues provided for in this subsection (d). The state board shall also have power, for the purpose of obtaining funds for the use of any school board of any school district or board of trustees of any community college district in acquiring, building, constructing, altering, remodeling, improving, enlarging, furnishing, equipping, maintaining, renovating, or repairing of capital outlay projects for school purposes to issue bonds or motor vehicle license revenue anticipation certificates, and also to issue such bonds or motor vehicle license revenue anticipation certificates to pay, fund or refund any bonds or motor vehicle license revenue anticipation certificates theretofore issued by said state board. All such bonds or motor vehicle license revenue anticipation certificates shall bear interest at not exceeding the rate provided by general law and shall mature not later than thirty years after the date of issuance thereof. The state board shall have power to determine all other details of the bonds or motor vehicle license revenue anticipation certificates and to sell in the manner provided by general law, or exchange the bonds or motor vehicle license revenue anticipation certificates, upon such terms and conditions as the state board shall provide.

(6) The state board shall also have power to pledge for the payment of the principal of and interest on such bonds or motor vehicle license revenue anticipation certificates, including refunding bonds or refunding motor vehicle license revenue anticipation certificates, all or any part from the motor vehicle license revenues provided for in this amendment and to enter into any covenants and other agreements with the holders of such bonds or motor vehicle license revenue anticipation certificates at the time of the issuance thereof concerning the security thereof and the rights of the holders thereof, all of which covenants and agreements shall constitute legally binding and irrevocable contracts with such holders and shall be fully enforceable by such holders in any court of competent jurisdiction.

(7) No such bonds or motor vehicle license revenue anticipation certificates shall ever be issued by the state board, except to refund outstanding bonds or motor vehicle license revenue anticipation certificates, until after the adoption of a resolution requesting the issuance thereof by the school board of the school district or board of trustees of the community college district on behalf of which the obligations are to be issued. The state board of education shall limit the amount of such bonds or motor vehicle license revenue anticipation certificates which can be issued on behalf of any school district or community college district to ninety percent (90%) of the amount which it determines can be serviced by the revenue accruing to the school district or community college district under the provisions of this amendment, and shall determine the reasonable allocation of the interest savings from the issuance of refunding bonds or motor vehicle license revenue anticipation certificates, and such determinations shall be conclusive. All such bonds or motor vehicle license revenue anticipation certificates shall be issued in the name of the state board of education but shall be issued for and on behalf of the school board of the school district or board of

trustees of the community college district requesting the issuance thereof, and no election or approval of qualified electors shall be required for the issuance thereof.

(8) The state board shall in each year use the funds distributable pursuant to this amendment to the credit of each school district or community college district only in the following manner and in order of priority:

a. To comply with the requirements of paragraph (1) of this subsection (d).

b. To pay all amounts of principal and interest due in such year on any bonds or motor vehicle license revenue anticipation certificates issued under the authority hereof, including refunding bonds or motor vehicle license revenue anticipation certificates, issued on behalf of the school board of such school district or board of trustees of such community college district; subject, however, to any covenants or agreements made by the state board concerning the rights between holders of different issues of such bonds or motor vehicle license revenue anticipation certificates, as herein authorized.

c. To establish and maintain a sinking fund or funds to meet future requirements for debt service or reserves therefor, on bonds or motor vehicle license revenue anticipation certificates issued on behalf of the school board of such school district or board of trustees of such community college district under the authority hereof, whenever the state board shall deem it necessary or advisable, and in such amounts and under such terms and conditions as the state board shall in its discretion determine.

d. To distribute annually to the several school boards of the school districts or the boards of trustees of the community college districts for use in payment of debt service on bonds heretofore or hereafter issued by any such school boards of the school districts or boards of trustees of the community college districts where the proceeds of the bonds were used, or are to be used, in the acquiring, building, constructing, altering, remodeling, improving, enlarging, furnishing, equipping, maintaining, renovating, or repairing of capital outlay projects in such school districts or community college districts and which capital outlay projects have been approved by the school board of the school district or board of trustees of the community college district, pursuant to the most recent survey or surveys conducted under regulations prescribed by the state board to determine the capital outlay needs of the school district or community college district. The state board shall have power at the time of issuance of any bonds by any school board of any school district or board of trustees of any community college district to covenant and agree with such school board or board of trustees as to the rank and priority of payments to be made for different issues of bonds under this subparagraph d., and may further agree that any amounts to be distributed under this subparagraph d. may be pledged for the debt service on bonds issued by any school board of any school district or board of trustees of any community college district and for the rank and priority of such pledge. Any such covenants or agreements of the state board may be enforced by any holders of such bonds in any court of competent jurisdiction.

e. To pay the expenses of the state board in administering this subsection (d), which shall be prorated among the various school districts and community college districts and paid out of the proceeds of the bonds or motor vehicle license revenue anticipation certificates or from the funds distributable to each school district and community college district on the same basis as such motor vehicle license revenues are distributable to the various school districts and community college districts.

f. To distribute annually to the several school boards of the school districts or boards of trustees of the community college districts for the payment of the cost of acquiring, building, constructing, altering, remodeling, improving, enlarging, furnishing, equipping, maintaining, renovating, or repairing of capital outlay projects for school purposes in such school district or community college district as shall be requested by resolution of the school board of the school district or board of trustees of the community college district.

g. When all major capital outlay needs of a school district or community college district have been met as determined by the state board, on the basis of a survey made pursuant to regulations of the state board and approved by the state board, all such funds remaining shall be distributed annually and used for such school purposes in such school district or community college district as the school board of the school district or board of trustees of the community college district shall determine, or as may be provided by general law.

(9) Capital outlay projects of a school district or community college district shall be eligible to participate in the funds accruing under this amendment and derived from the proceeds of bonds and motor vehicle license revenue anticipation certificates and from the motor vehicle license revenues, only in the order of priority of needs, as shown by a survey or surveys conducted in the school district or community college district under regulations prescribed by the state board, to determine the capital outlay needs of the school district or community college district and approved by the state board; provided that the priority of such projects may be changed from time to time upon the request of the school board of the school district or board of trustees of the community college district and with the approval of the state board; and provided, further, that this paragraph (9) shall not in any manner affect any covenant, agreement or pledge made by the state board in the issuance by said state board of any bonds or motor vehicle license revenue anticipation certificates, or in connection with the issuance of any bonds of any school board of any school district or board of trustees of any community college district.

(10) The state board shall have power to make and enforce all rules and regulations necessary to the full exercise of the powers herein granted and no legislation shall be required to render this amendment of full force and operating effect. The legislature shall not reduce the levies of said motor vehicle license revenues during the life of this amendment to any degree which will fail to provide the full amount necessary to comply with the provisions of this amendment and pay the necessary expenses of administering the laws relating to the licensing of motor vehicles, and shall not enact any law having the effect of withdrawing the proceeds

CONSTITUTION OF THE STATE OF FLORIDA

of such motor vehicle license revenues from the operation of this amendment and shall not enact any law impairing or materially altering the rights of the holders of any bonds or motor vehicle license revenue anticipation certificates issued pursuant to this amendment or impairing or altering any covenant or agreement of the state board, as provided in such bonds or motor vehicle license revenue anticipation certificates.

(11) Bonds issued by the state board pursuant to this subsection (d) shall be payable primarily from said motor vehicle license revenues as provided herein, and if heretofore or hereafter authorized by law, may be additionally secured by pledging the full faith and credit of the state without an election. When heretofore or hereafter authorized by law, bonds issued pursuant to [6]Article XII, Section 18 of the Constitution of 1885, as amended prior to 1968, and bonds issued pursuant to Article XII, Section 9, subsection (d) of the Constitution as revised in 1968, and bonds issued pursuant to this subsection (d), may be refunded by the issuance of bonds additionally secured by the full faith and credit of the state.

(e) DEBT LIMITATION. Bonds issued pursuant to this Section 9 of Article XII which are payable primarily from revenues pledged pursuant to this section shall not be included in applying the limits upon the amount of state bonds contained in Section 11, Article VII, of this revision.

History. — Am. H.J.R. 1851, 1969; adopted 1969; Am. C.S. for S.J.R. 292, 1972, and Am. C.S. for H.J.R. 3576, 1972; adopted 1972; Am. C.S. for H.J.R.'s 2289, 2984, 1974; adopted 1974; Am. S.J.R. 824, 1980; adopted 1980; Am. S.J.R. 1157, 1984; adopted 1984; Am. proposed by Taxation and Budget Reform Commission, Revision No. 1, 1992, filed with the Secretary of State May 7, 1992; adopted 1992; Am. S.J.R. 2-H, 1992; adopted 1992; Am. proposed by Constitution Revision Commission, Revision No. 8, 1998, filed with the Secretary of State May 5, 1998; adopted 1998.

[1]**Note.** — Section 17 of Art. IX of the Constitution of 1885, as amended, reads as follows:

SECTION 17. Bonds; land acquisition for outdoor recreation development. — The outdoor recreational development council, as created by the 1963 legislature, may issue revenue bonds, revenue certificates or other evidences of indebtedness to acquire lands, water areas and related resources and to construct, improve, enlarge and extend capital improvements and facilities thereon in furtherance of outdoor recreation, natural resources conservation and related facilities in this state; provided, however, the legislature with respect to such revenue bonds, revenue certificates or other evidences of indebtedness shall designate the revenue or tax sources to be deposited in or credited to the land acquisition trust fund for their repayment and may impose restrictions on their issuance, including the fixing of maximum interest rates and discounts.

The land acquisition trust fund, created by the 1963 legislature for these multiple public purposes, shall continue from the date of the adoption of this amendment for a period of fifty years.

In the event the outdoor recreational development council shall determine to issue bonds for financing acquisition of sites for multiple purposes the state board of administration shall act as fiscal agent, and the attorney general shall handle the validation proceedings.

All bonds issued under this amendment shall be sold at public sale after public advertisement upon such terms and conditions as the outdoor recreational development council shall provide and as otherwise provided by law and subject to the limitations herein imposed.

History. — S.J.R. 727, 1963; adopted 1963.

[2]**Note.** — Prior to its amendment by C.S. for H.J.R.'s 2289, 2984, 1974, subsection (a) read as follows:

(a) ADDITIONAL SECURITIES. Article IX, Section 17, of the Constitution of 1885, as amended, as it existed immediately before this Constitution, as revised in 1968, became effective, is adopted by this reference as a part of this revision as completely as though incorporated herein verbatim, except revenue bonds, revenue certificates or other evidences of indebtedness hereafter issued thereunder may be issued by the agency of the state so authorized by law.

Article XII, Section 19, of the Constitution of 1885, as amended, as it existed immediately before this revision becomes effective, is adopted by this reference as a part of this revision as completely as though incorporated herein verbatim, except bonds or tax anticipation certificates hereafter issued thereunder may bear interest not in excess of five percent (5%) per annum or such higher interest as may be authorized by statute passed by a three-fifths (3/5) vote of each house of the legislature. No revenue bonds or tax anticipation certificates shall be issued pursuant thereto after June 30, 1975.

[3]**Note.** — Section 19 of Art. XII of the Constitution of 1885, as amended, reads as follows:

SECTION 19. Institutions of higher learning and junior college capital outlay trust fund bonds. — (a) That beginning January 1, 1964, and for fifty years thereafter, all of the proceeds of the revenues derived from the gross receipts taxes collected from every person, including municipalities, receiving payment for electricity for light, heat or power, for natural or manufactured gas for light, heat or power, for use of telephones and for the sending of telegrams and telegraph messages, as now provided and levied as of the time of adoption of this amendment in Chapter 203, Florida Statutes (hereinafter called "Gross Receipts Taxes"), shall, as collected be placed in a trust fund to be known as the "Institutions of Higher Learning and Junior Colleges Capital Outlay and Debt Service Trust Fund" in the State Treasury (hereinafter referred to as "Capital Outlay Fund"), and used only as provided in this Amendment.

Said fund shall be administered by the State Board of Education, as now created and constituted by Section 3 of Article XII [now s. 2, Article IX] of the Constitution of Florida (hereinafter referred to as "State Board"). For the purpose of this Amendment, said State Board, as now constituted, shall continue as a body corporate during the life of this Amendment and shall have all the powers provided in this Amendment in addition to all other constitutional and statutory powers related to the purposes of this Amendment heretofore or hereafter conferred by law upon said State Board.

(b) The State Board shall have power, for the purpose of obtaining funds for acquiring, building, constructing, altering, improving, enlarging, furnishing or equipping capital outlay projects theretofore authorized by the legislature and any purposes appurtenant or incidental thereto, for Institutions of Higher Learning or Junior Colleges, as now defined or as may be hereafter defined by law, and for the purpose of constructing buildings and other permanent facilities for vocational technical schools as provided in chapter 230 Florida Statutes, to issue bonds or certificates, including refunding bonds or certificates to fund or refund any bonds or certificates theretofore issued. All such bonds or certificates shall bear interest at not exceeding four and one-half per centum per annum, and shall mature at such time or times as the State Board shall determine not exceeding, in any event, however, thirty years from the date of issuance thereof. The State Board shall have power to determine all other details of such bonds or certificates and to sell at public sale, after public advertisement, such bonds or certificates, provided, however, that no bonds or certificates shall ever be issued hereunder to finance, or the proceeds thereof expended for, any part of the cost of any capital outlay project unless the construction or acquisition of such capital outlay project has been theretofore authorized by the Legislature of Florida. None of said bonds or certificates shall be sold at less than ninety-eight per centum of the par value thereof, plus accrued interest, and said bonds or certificates shall be awarded at the public sale thereof to the bidder offering the lowest net interest cost for such bonds or certificates in the manner to be determined by the State Board.

The State Board shall also have power to pledge for the payment of the principal of and interest on such bonds or certificates, and reserves therefor, including refunding bonds or certificates, all or any part of the revenue to be derived from the said Gross Receipts Taxes provided for in this Amendment, and to enter into any covenants and other agreements with the holders of such bonds or certificates concerning the security thereof and the rights of the holders thereof, all of which covenants and agreements shall constitute legally binding and irrevocable contracts with such holders and shall be fully enforceable by such holders in any court of competent jurisdiction.

No such bonds or certificates shall ever be issued by the State Board in an amount exceeding seventy-five per centum of the amount which it determines, based upon the average annual amount of the revenues derived from said Gross Receipts Taxes during the immediately preceding two fiscal years, or the amount of the revenues derived from said Gross Receipts Taxes during the immediately preceding fiscal year, as shown in a certificate filed by the State Comptroller with the State Board prior to the issuance of such bonds or certificates, whichever is the lesser, can be serviced by the revenues accruing thereafter under the provisions of this Amendment; nor shall the State Board, during the first year following the ratification of this amendment, issue bonds or certificates in excess of seven times the anticipated revenue from said Gross Receipts Taxes during said year, nor during each succeeding year, more than four times the anticipated revenue from said Gross Receipts Taxes during such year. No election or approval of qualified electors or freeholder electors shall be required for the issuance of bonds or certificates hereunder.

After the initial issuance of any bonds or certificates pursuant to this Amendment, the State Board may thereafter issue additional bonds or certificates which will rank equally and on a parity, as to lien on and source of security for payment from said Gross Receipts Taxes, with any bonds or certificates theretofore issued pursuant to this Amendment, but such additional parity bonds or certificates shall not be issued unless the average annual amount of the revenues derived from said Gross Receipts Taxes during the immediately preceding two fiscal years, or the amount of the revenues derived from said Gross Receipts Taxes during the immediately preceding fiscal year, as shown in a certificate filed by the State Comptroller with the State Board prior to the issuance of such bonds or certificates, whichever is the lesser, shall have been equal to one and one-third times the aggregate amount of principal and interest which will become due in any succeeding fiscal year on all bonds or certificates theretofore issued pursuant to this Amendment and then outstanding, and the additional parity bonds or certificates then proposed to be issued. No bonds, certificates or other obligations whatsoever shall at any time be issued under the provisions of this Amendment, except such bonds or certificates initially issued hereunder, and such additional parity bonds or certificates as provided in this paragraph. Notwithstanding any other provision herein no such bonds or certificates shall be authorized or validated during any biennium in excess of fifty million dollars, except by two-thirds vote of the members elected to each house of the legislature; provided further that during the biennium 1963–1965 seventy-five million dollars may be authorized and validated pursuant hereto.

(c) Capital outlay projects theretofore authorized by the legislature for any Institution of Higher Learning or Junior College shall be eligible to participate in the funds accruing under this Amendment derived from the proceeds of bonds or certificates and said Gross Receipts Taxes under such regulations and in such manner as shall be determined by the State Board, and the State Board shall use or transmit to the State Board of Control or to the Board of Public Instruction of any County authorized by law to construct or acquire such capital outlay projects, the amount of the proceeds of such bonds or certificates or Gross Receipts Taxes to be applied to or used for such capital outlay projects. If for any reason any of the proceeds of any bonds or certificates issued for any capital outlay project shall not be expended for such capital outlay project, the State Board may use such unexpended proceeds for any other capital outlay project for Institutions of Higher Learning or Junior Colleges and vocational technical schools, as defined herein, as now defined or as may be hereafter defined by law, theretofore authorized by the State Legislature. The holders of bonds or certificates issued hereunder shall not have any responsibility whatsoever for the application or use of any of the proceeds derived from the sale of said bonds or certificates, and the rights and remedies of the holders of such bonds or certificates and their right to payment from said Gross Receipts Taxes in the manner provided herein shall not be affected or impaired by the application or use of such proceeds.

The State Board shall use the moneys in said Capital Outlay Fund in each fiscal year only for the following purposes and in the following order of priority:

(1) For the payment of the principal of and interest on any bonds or certificates maturing in such fiscal year.

(2) For the deposit into any reserve funds provided for in the proceedings authorizing the issuance of said bonds or certificates, of any amounts required to be deposited in such reserve funds in such fiscal year.

(3) After all payments required in such fiscal year for the purposes provided for in (1) and (2) above, including any deficiencies for required payments in prior fiscal years, any moneys remaining in said Capital Outlay Fund at the end of such fiscal year may be used by the State Board for direct payment of the cost or any part of the cost of any capital outlay project theretofore authorized by the legislature or for the purchase of any bonds or certificates issued hereunder then outstanding upon such terms and conditions as the State Board shall deem proper, or for the prior redemption of outstanding bonds or certificates in accordance with the provisions of the proceedings which authorized the issuance of such bonds or certificates.

The State Board may invest the moneys in said Capital Outlay Fund or in any sinking fund or other funds created for any issue of bonds or certificates, in direct obligations of the United States of America or in the other securities referred to in Section 344.27, Florida Statutes.

(d) The State Board shall have the power to make and enforce all rules and regulations necessary to the full exercise of the powers herein granted and no legislation shall be required to render this Amendment of full force and operating effect on and after January 1, 1964. The Legislature, during the period this Amendment is in effect, shall not reduce the rate of said Gross Receipts Taxes now provided in said Chapter 203, Florida Statutes, or eliminate, exempt or remove any of the persons, firms or corporations, including municipal corporations, or any of the utilities, businesses or services now or hereafter subject to said Gross Receipts Taxes, from the levy and collection of said Gross Receipts Taxes as now provided in said Chapter 203, Florida Statutes, and shall not enact any law impairing or materially altering the rights of the holders of any bonds or certificates issued pursuant to this Amendment or impairing or altering any covenants or agreements of the State Board made hereunder, or having the effect of withdrawing the proceeds of said Gross Receipts Taxes from the operation of this Amendment.

The State Board of Administration shall be and is hereby constituted as the Fiscal Agent of the State Board to perform such duties and assume such responsibilities under this Amendment as shall be agreed upon between the State Board and such State Board of Administration. The State Board shall also have power to appoint such other persons and fix their compensation for the administration of the provisions of this Amendment as it shall deem necessary, and the expenses of the State Board in administering the provisions of this Amendment shall be paid out of the proceeds of bonds or certificates issued hereunder or from said Gross Receipts Taxes deposited in said Capital Outlay Fund.

(e) No capital outlay project or any part thereof shall be financed hereunder unless the bill authorizing such project shall specify it is financed hereunder and shall be approved by a vote of three-fifths of the elected members of each house.

History. — S.J.R. 264, 1963; adopted 1963.

[4]**Note.** — Section 16 of Art. IX of the Constitution of 1885, as amended, reads as follows:

SECTION 16. Board of administration; gasoline and like taxes, distribution and use; etc. — (a) That beginning January 1st, 1943, and for fifty (50) years thereafter, the proceeds of two (2¢) cents per gallon of the total tax levied by state law upon gasoline and other like products of petroleum, now known as the Second Gas Tax, and upon other fuels used to propel motor vehicles, shall as collected be placed monthly in the 'State Roads Distribution Fund' in the State Treasury and divided into three (3) equal parts which shall be distributed monthly among the several counties as follows: one part according to area, one part according to population, and one part according to the counties' contributions to the cost of state road construction in the ratio of distribution as provided in Chapter 15659, Laws of Florida, Acts of 1931, and for the purposes of the apportionment based on the counties' contributions for the cost of state road construction, the amount of the contributions established by the certificates made in 1931 pursuant to said Chapter 15659, shall be taken and deemed conclusive in computing the monthly amounts distributable according to said contributions. Such funds so distributed shall be administered by the State Board of Administration as hereinafter provided.

(b) The Governor as chairman, the State Treasurer, and the State Comptroller shall constitute a body corporate to be known as the 'State Board of Administration,' which board shall succeed to all the power, control and authority of the statutory Board of Administration. Said Board shall have, in addition to such powers as may be conferred upon it by law, the management, control and supervision of the proceeds of said two (2¢) cents of said taxes and all moneys and other assets which on the effective date of this amendment are applicable or may become applicable to the bonds of the several counties of this state, or any special road and bridge district, or other special taxing district thereof, issued prior to July 1st, 1931, for road and bridge purposes. The word 'bonds' as used herein shall include bonds, time warrants, notes and other forms of indebtedness issued for road and bridge purposes by any county or special road and bridge district or other special taxing district, outstanding on July 1st, 1931, or any refunding issues thereof. Said Board shall have the statutory powers of Boards of County Commissioners and Bond Trustees and of any other authority of special road and bridge districts, and other special taxing districts thereof with regard to said bonds, (except that the power to levy ad valorem taxes is expressly withheld from said Board), and shall take over all papers, documents and records concerning the same. Said Board shall have the power from time to time to issue refunding bonds to mature within the said fifty (50) year period, for any of said outstanding bonds or interest thereon, and to secure them by a pledge of anticipated receipts from such gasoline or other fuel taxes to be distributed to such county as herein provided, but not at a greater rate of interest than said bonds now bear; and to issue, sell or exchange on behalf of any county or unit for the sole purpose of retiring said bonds issued by such county, or special road and bridge district, or other special taxing district thereof, gasoline or other fuel tax anticipation certificates bearing interest at not more than three (3) per cent per annum in such denominations and maturing at such time within the fifty (50) year period as the board may determine. In addition to exercising the powers now provided by statute for the investment of sinking funds, said Board may use the sinking funds created for said bonds of any county or special road and bridge district, or other unit hereunder, to purchase the matured or maturing bonds participating herein of any other county or any other special road and bridge district, or other special taxing district thereof, provided that as to said matured bonds, the value thereof as an investment shall be the price paid therefor, which shall not exceed the par value plus accrued interest, and that said investment shall bear interest at the rate of three (3) per cent per annum.

(c) The said board shall annually use said funds in each county account, first, to pay current principal and interest maturing, if any, of said bonds and gasoline or other fuel tax anticipation certificates of such county or special road and bridge district, or other special taxing district thereof; second, to establish a sinking fund account to meet future requirements of said bonds and gasoline or other fuel tax anticipation certificates where it appears the anticipated income for any year or years will not equal scheduled payments thereon; and third, any remaining balance out of the proceeds of said two (2¢) cents of said taxes shall monthly during the year be remitted by said board as follows: Eighty (80%) per cent to the State Road Department for the construction or reconstruction of state roads and bridges within the county, or for the lease or purchase of bridges connecting state highways within the county, and twenty (20%) per cent to the Board of County Commissioners of such county for use on roads and bridges therein.

(d) Said board shall have the power to make and enforce all rules and regulations necessary to the full exercise of the powers hereby granted and no legislation shall be required to render this amendment of full force and operating effect from and after January 1st, 1943. The Legislature shall continue the levies of said taxes during the life of this Amendment, and shall not enact any law having the effect of withdrawing the proceeds of said two (2¢) cents of said taxes from the operation of this amendment. The board shall pay refunding expenses and other expenses for services rendered specifically for, or which are properly chargeable to, the account of any county from funds distributed to such county; but general expenses of the board for services rendered all the counties alike shall be prorated among them and paid out of said funds on the same basis said tax proceeds are distributed among the several counties; provided, report of said expenses shall be made to each Regular Session of the Legislature, and the Legislature may limit the expenses of the board.

History. — Added, S.J.R. 324, 1941; adopted 1942.

[5]**Note.** — Prior to its amendment by C.S. for H.J.R. 3576, 1972, subsection (d) read as follows:

(d) SCHOOL BONDS. Article XII, Section 18, of the Constitution of 1885, as amended, as it existed immediately before this revision becomes effective is adopted by this reference as part of this revision as completely as though incorporated herein verbatim, except bonds or tax anticipation certificates hereafter issued thereunder may bear interest not in excess of five per cent per annum or such higher interest as may be authorized by statute passed by a three-fifths vote of each house of the legislature. Bonds issued pursuant to this subsection (d) shall be payable primarily from revenues as provided in Article XII, Section 18, of the Constitution of 1885, as amended, and if authorized by law, may be additionally secured by pledging the full faith and credit of the state without an election. When authorized by law, bonds issued pursuant to Article XII, Section 18, of the Constitution of 1885, as amended, and bonds issued pursuant to this subsection (d), may be refunded by the issuance of bonds additionally secured by the full faith and credit of the state only at a lower net average interest cost rate.

[6]**Note.** — Section 18, Art. XII of the Constitution of 1885, as amended, reads as follows:

SECTION 18. School bonds for capital outlay, issuance. —

(a) Beginning January 1, 1965 and for thirty-five years thereafter, the first proceeds of the revenues derived from the licensing of motor vehicles to the extent necessary to comply with the provisions of this amendment, shall, as collected, be placed monthly in the county capital outlay and debt service school fund in the state treasury, and used only as provided in this amendment. Such revenue shall be distributed annually among the several counties in the ratio of the number of instruction units in each county in each year computed as provided herein. The amount of the first revenues derived from the licensing of motor vehicles to be so set aside in each year and distributed as provided herein shall be an amount equal in the aggregate to the product of four hundred dollars multiplied by the total number of instruction units in all the counties of Florida. The number of instruction units in each county in each year for the purposes of this amendment shall be the greater of (1) the number of instruction units in each county for the school fiscal year 1951-52 computed in the manner heretofore provided by general law, or (2) the number of instruction units in such county for the school fiscal year computed in the manner heretofore or hereafter provided by general law and approved by the state board of education (hereinafter called the state board), or (3) the number of instruction units in each county on behalf of which the state board of education has issued bonds or motor vehicle tax anticipation certificates under this amendment which will produce sufficient revenues under this amendment to equal one and one-third times the aggregate amount of principal of and interest on such bonds or motor vehicle tax anticipation certificates which will mature and become due in such year, computed in the manner heretofore or hereafter provided by general law and approved by the state board.

Such funds so distributed shall be administered by the state board as now created and constituted by Section 3 of Article XII [now s. 2, Article IX] of the Constitution of Florida. For the purposes of this amendment, said state board, as now constituted, shall continue as a body corporate during the life of this amendment and shall have all the powers provided in this amendment in addition to all other constitutional and statutory powers related to the purposes of this amendment heretofore or hereafter conferred upon said board.

(b) The state board shall, in addition to its other constitutional and statutory powers, have the management, control and supervision of the proceeds of the first part of the revenues derived from the licensing of motor vehicles provided for in subsection (a). The state board shall also have power, for the purpose of obtaining funds for the use of any county board of public instruction in acquiring, building, constructing, altering, improving, enlarging, furnishing, or equipping capital outlay projects for school purposes, to issue bonds or motor vehicle tax anticipation certificates, and also to issue such bonds or motor vehicle tax anticipation certificates to pay, fund or refund any bonds or motor vehicle tax anticipation certificates theretofore issued by said state board. All such bonds shall bear interest at not exceeding four and one-half per centum per annum and shall mature serially in annual installments commencing not more than three years from the date of issuance thereof and ending not later than thirty years from the date of issuance or January 1, 2000, A.D., whichever is earlier. All such motor vehicle tax anticipation certificates shall bear interest at not exceeding four and one-half per centum per annum and shall mature prior to January 1, 2000, A.D. The state board shall have power to determine all other details of said bonds or motor vehicle tax anticipation certificates and to sell at public sale after public advertisement, or exchange said bonds or motor vehicle tax anticipation certificates, upon such terms and conditions as the state board shall provide.

The state board shall also have power to pledge for the payment of the principal of and interest on such bonds or motor vehicle tax anticipation certificates, including refunding bonds or refunding motor vehicle tax anticipation certificates, all or any part from the anticipated revenues to be derived from the licensing of motor vehicles provided for in this amendment and to enter into any covenants and other agreements with the holders of such bonds or motor vehicle tax anticipation certificates at the time of the issuance thereof concerning the security thereof and the rights of the holders thereof, all of which covenants and agreements shall constitute legally binding and irrevocable contracts with such holders and shall be fully enforceable by such holders in any court of competent jurisdiction.

No such bonds or motor vehicle tax anticipation certificates shall ever be issued by the state board until after the adoption of a resolution requesting the issuance thereof by the county board of public instruction of the county on behalf of which such obligations are to be issued. The state board of education shall limit the amount of such bonds or motor vehicle tax anticipation certificates which can be issued on behalf of any county to seventy-five per cent of the amount which it determines can be serviced by the revenue accruing to the county under the provisions of this amendment, and such determination shall be conclusive. All such bonds or motor vehicle tax anticipation certificates shall be issued in the name of the state board of education but shall be issued for and on behalf of the county board of public instruction requesting the issuance thereof, and no election or approval of qualified electors or freeholders shall be required for the issuance thereof.

(c) The State Board shall in each year use the funds distributable pursuant to this Amendment to the credit of each county only in the following manner and order of priority:

(1) To pay all amounts of principal and interest maturing in such year on any bonds or motor vehicle tax anticipation certificates issued under the authority hereof, including refunding bonds or motor vehicle tax anticipation certificates, issued on behalf of the Board of Public Instruction of such county; subject, however, to any covenants or agreements made by the State Board concerning the rights between holders of different issues of such bonds or motor vehicle tax anticipation certificates, as herein authorized.

(2) To establish and maintain a sinking fund or funds to meet future requirements for debt service, or reserves therefor, on bonds or motor vehicle tax anticipation certificates issued on behalf of the Board of Public Instruction of such county, under the authority hereof, whenever the State Board shall deem it necessary or advisable, and in such amounts and under such terms and conditions as the State Board shall in its discretion determine.

(3) To distribute annually to the several Boards of Public Instruction of the counties for use in payment of debt service on bonds heretofore or hereafter issued by any such Board where the proceeds of the bonds were used, or are to be used, in the construction, acquisition, improvement, enlargement, furnishing, or equipping of capital outlay projects in such county, and which capital outlay projects have been approved by the Board of Public Instruction of the county, pursuant to a survey or surveys conducted subsequent to July 1, 1947 in the county, under regulations prescribed by the State Board to determine the capital outlay needs of the county.

The State Board shall have power at the time of issuance of any bonds by any Board of Public Instruction to covenant and agree with such Board as to the rank and priority of payments to be made for different issues of bonds under this

CONSTITUTION OF THE STATE OF FLORIDA

Subsection (3), and may further agree that any amounts to be distributed under this Subsection (3) may be pledged for the debt service on bonds issued by any Board of Public Instruction and for the rank and priority of such pledge. Any such covenants or agreements of the State Board may be enforced by any holders of such bonds in any court of competent jurisdiction.

(4) To distribute annually to the several Boards of Public Instruction of the counties for the payment of the cost of the construction, acquisition, improvement, enlargement, furnishing, or equipping of capital outlay projects for school purposes in such county as shall be requested by resolution of the County Board of Public Instruction of such county.

(5) When all major capital outlay needs of a county have been met as determined by the State Board, on the basis of a survey made pursuant to regulations of the State Board and approved by the State Board, all such funds remaining shall be distributed annually and used for such school purposes in such county as the Board of Public Instruction of the county shall determine, or as may be provided by general law.

(d) Capital outlay projects of a county shall be eligible to participate in the funds accruing under this Amendment and derived from the proceeds of bonds and motor vehicle tax anticipation certificates and from the motor vehicle license taxes, only in the order of priority of needs, as shown by a survey or surveys conducted in the county under regulations prescribed by the State Board, to determine the capital outlay needs of the county and approved by the State Board; provided, that the priority of such projects may be changed from time to time upon the request of the Board of Public Instruction of the county and with the approval of the State Board; and provided further, that this Subsection (d) shall not in any manner affect any covenant, agreement, or pledge made by the State Board in the issuance by said State Board of any bonds or motor vehicle tax anticipation certificates, or in connection with the issuance of any bonds of any Board of Public Instruction of any county.

(e) The State Board may invest any sinking fund or funds created pursuant to this Amendment in direct obligations of the United States of America or in the bonds or motor vehicle tax anticipation certificates, matured or to mature, issued by the State Board on behalf of the Board of Public Instruction of any county.

(f) The State Board shall have power to make and enforce all rules and regulations necessary to the full exercise of the powers herein granted and no legislation shall be required to render this Amendment of full force and operating effect from and after January 1, 1953. The Legislature shall not reduce the levies of said motor vehicle license taxes during the life of this Amendment to any degree which will fail to provide the full amount necessary to comply with the provisions of this Amendment and pay the necessary expenses of administering the laws relating to the licensing of motor vehicles, and shall not enact any law having the effect of withdrawing the proceeds of such motor vehicle license taxes from the operation of this Amendment and shall not enact any law impairing or materially altering the rights of the holders of any bonds or motor vehicle tax anticipation certificates issued pursuant to this Amendment or impairing or altering any covenant or agreement of the State Board, as provided in such bonds or motor vehicle tax anticipation certificates.

The State Board shall have power to appoint such persons and fix their compensation for the administration of the provisions of this Amendment as it shall deem necessary, and the expenses of the State Board in administering the provisions of this Amendment shall be prorated among the various counties and paid out of the proceeds of the bonds or motor vehicle tax anticipation certificates or from the funds distributable to each county on the same basis as such motor vehicle license taxes are distributable to the various counties under the provisions of this Amendment. Interest or profit on sinking fund investments shall accrue to the counties in proportion to their respective equities in the sinking fund or funds.

History. — Added, S.J.R. 106, 1951; adopted 1952; (a), (b) Am. S.J.R. 218, 1963; adopted 1964.

[1]**SECTION 10. Preservation of existing government.** — All provisions of Articles I through IV, VII and IX through XX of the Constitution of 1885, as amended, not embraced herein which are not inconsistent with this revision shall become statutes subject to modification or repeal as are other statutes.

[1]**Note.** — *See* table in Volume 6 of the Florida Statutes tracing various provisions of the Constitution of 1885, as amended, into the Florida Statutes.

SECTION 11. Deletion of obsolete schedule items. — The legislature shall have power, by joint resolution, to delete from this revision any section of this Article XII, including this section, when all events to which the section to be deleted is or could become applicable have occurred. A legislative determination of fact made as a basis for application of this section shall be subject to judicial review.

SECTION 12. Senators. — The requirements of staggered terms of senators in Section 15(a), of Article III of this revision shall apply only to senators elected in November, 1972, and thereafter.

SECTION 13. Legislative apportionment. — The requirements of legislative apportionment in Section 16 of Article III of this revision shall apply only to the apportionment of the legislature following the decennial census of 1970, and thereafter.

SECTION 14. Representatives; terms. — The legislature at its first regular session following the ratification of this revision, by joint resolution, shall propose to the electors of the state for ratification or rejection in the general election of 1970 an amendment to Article III, Section 15(b), of the constitution providing staggered terms of four years for members of the house of representatives.

SECTION 15. Special district taxes. — Ad valorem taxing power vested by law in special districts existing when this revision becomes effective shall not be abrogated by Section 9(b) of Article VII herein, but such powers, except to the extent necessary to pay outstanding debts, may be restricted or withdrawn by law.

SECTION 16. **Reorganization.** — The requirement of Section 6, Article IV of this revision shall not apply until July 1, 1969.

SECTION 17. **Conflicting provisions.** — This schedule is designed to effect the orderly transition of government from the Constitution of 1885, as amended, to this revision and shall control in all cases of conflict with any part of Article I through IV, VII, and IX through XI herein.

SECTION 18. **Bonds for housing and related facilities.** — Section 16 of Article VII, providing for bonds for housing and related facilities, shall take effect upon approval by the electors.

History. — Added, S.J.R. 6-E, 1980; adopted 1980.

[1]SECTION 19. **Renewable energy source property.** — The amendment to Section 3 of Article VII, relating to an exemption for a renewable energy source device and real property on which such device is installed, if adopted at the special election in October 1980, shall take effect January 1, 1981.

History. — Added, S.J.R. 15-E, 1980; adopted 1980.

[1]**Note.** —

A. This section, originally designated section 18 by S.J.R. 15-E, 1980, was redesignated section 19 by the editors in order to avoid confusion with section 18 as contained in S.J.R. 6-E, 1980.

B. The amendment to section 3 of Article VII, relating to an exemption for renewable energy source property, was repealed effective November 4, 2008, by Am. proposed by the Taxation and Budget Reform Commission, Revision No. 3, 2008, filed with the Secretary of State April 28, 2008; adopted 2008.

SECTION 20. **Access to public records.** — Section 24 of Article I, relating to access to public records, shall take effect July 1, 1993.

History. — Added, C.S. for C.S. for H.J.R.'s 1727, 863, 2035, 1992; adopted 1992.

SECTION 21. **State revenue limitation.** — The amendment to Section 1 of Article VII limiting state revenues shall take effect January 1, 1995, and shall first be applicable to state fiscal year 1995–1996.

History. — Added, H.J.R. 2053, 1994; adopted 1994.

SECTION 22. **Historic property exemption and assessment.** — The amendments to Sections 3 and 4 of Article VII relating to ad valorem tax exemption for, and assessment of, historic property shall take effect January 1, 1999.

History. — Added, H.J.R. 969, 1997; adopted 1998.

[1]SECTION 23. **Fish and wildlife conservation commission.** —

(a) The initial members of the commission shall be the members of the game and fresh water fish commission and the marine fisheries commission who are serving on those commissions on the effective date of this amendment, who may serve the remainder of their respective terms. New appointments to the commission shall not be made until the retirement, resignation, removal, or expiration of the terms of the initial members results in fewer than seven members remaining.

(b) The jurisdiction of the marine fisheries commission as set forth in statutes in effect on March 1, 1998, shall be transferred to the fish and wildlife conservation commission. The jurisdiction of the marine fisheries commission transferred to the commission shall not be expanded except as provided by general law. All rules of the marine fisheries commission and game and fresh water fish commission in effect on the effective date of this amendment shall become rules of the fish and wildlife conservation commission until superseded or amended by the commission.

(c) On the effective date of this amendment, the marine fisheries commission and game and fresh water fish commission shall be abolished.

(d) This amendment shall take effect July 1, 1999.

History. — Proposed by Constitution Revision Commission, Revision No. 5, 1998, filed with the Secretary of State May 5, 1998; adopted 1998.

[1]**Note.** — This section, originally designated section 22 by Revision No. 5 of the Constitution Revision Commission, 1998, was redesignated section 23 by the editors in order to avoid confusion with section 22 as created in H.J.R. 969, 1997.

[1]**SECTION 24. Executive branch reform. —**

(a) The amendments contained in this revision shall take effect January 7, 2003, but shall govern with respect to the qualifying for and the holding of primary elections in 2002. The office of chief financial officer shall be a new office as a result of this revision.

(b) In the event the secretary of state is removed as a cabinet office in the 1998 general election, the term "custodian of state records" shall be substituted for the term "secretary of state" throughout the constitution and the duties previously performed by the secretary of state shall be as provided by law.

History. — Proposed by Constitution Revision Commission, Revision No. 8, 1998, filed with the Secretary of State May 5, 1998; adopted 1998.

[1]**Note.** — This section, originally designated section 22 by Revision No. 8 of the Constitution Revision Commission, 1998, was redesignated section 24 by the editors in order to avoid confusion with section 22 as created in H.J.R. 969, 1997.

[1]**SECTION 25. Schedule to Article V amendment. —**

(a) Commencing with fiscal year 2000–2001, the legislature shall appropriate funds to pay for the salaries, costs, and expenses set forth in the amendment to Section 14 of Article V pursuant to a phase-in schedule established by general law.

(b) Unless otherwise provided herein, the amendment to Section 14 shall be fully effectuated by July 1, 2004.

History. — Proposed by Constitution Revision Commission, Revision No. 7, 1998, filed with the Secretary of State May 5, 1998; adopted 1998.

CONSTITUTION OF THE STATE OF FLORIDA 1097

[1]**Note.** — This section, originally designated section 22 by Revision No. 7 of the Constitution Revision Commission, 1998, was redesignated section 25 by the editors in order to avoid confusion with section 22 as created in H.J.R. 969, 1997.

SECTION 26. Increased homestead exemption. — The amendment to Section 6 of Article VII increasing the maximum additional amount of the homestead exemption for low-income seniors shall take effect January 1, 2007.

History. — Added, H.J.R. 353, 2006; adopted 2006.

SECTION 27. Property tax exemptions and limitations on property tax assessments. —

(a) The amendments to Sections 3, 4, and 6 of Article VII, providing a $25,000 exemption for tangible personal property, providing an additional $25,000 homestead exemption, authorizing transfer of the accrued benefit from the limitations on the assessment of homestead property, and this section, if submitted to the electors of this state for approval or rejection at a special election authorized by law to be held on January 29, 2008, shall take effect upon approval by the electors and shall operate retroactively to January 1, 2008, or, if submitted to the electors of this state for approval or rejection at the next general election, shall take effect January 1 of the year following such general election. The amendments to Section 4 of Article VII creating subsections (g) and (h) of that section, creating a limitation on annual assessment increases for specified real property, shall take effect upon approval of the electors and shall first limit assessments beginning January 1, 2009, if approved at a special election held on January 29, 2008, or shall first limit assessments beginning January 1, 2010, if approved at the general election held in November of 2008.

(b) The amendment to subsection (a) abrogating the scheduled repeal of subsections (g) and (h) of Section 4 of Article VII of the State Constitution as it existed in 2017, shall take effect January 1, 2019.

History. — Added, C.S. for S.J.R. 2-D, 2007; adopted 2008; Am., C.S. for H.J.R. 21, 2017; adopted 2018.

SECTION 28. Property tax exemption and classification and assessment of land used for conservation purposes. — The amendment to Section 3 of Article VII requiring the creation of an ad valorem tax exemption for real property dedicated in perpetuity for conservation purposes, and the amendment to Section 4 of Article VII requiring land used for conservation purposes to be classified by general law and assessed solely on the basis of character or use for purposes of ad valorem taxation, shall take effect upon approval by the electors and shall be implemented by January 1, 2010. This section shall take effect upon approval of the electors.

History. — Proposed by Taxation and Budget Reform Commission, Revision No. 4, 2008, filed with the Secretary of State April 28, 2008; adopted 2008.

SECTION 29. Limitation on the assessed value of real property used for residential purposes. —

(a) The repeal of the renewable energy source property tax exemption in Section 3 of Article VII shall take effect upon approval by the voters.

(b) The amendment to Section 4 of Article VII authorizing the legislature to prohibit an increase in the assessed value of real property used for residential purposes as the result of improving the property's resistance to wind damage or installing a renewable energy source device shall take effect January 1, 2009.

History. — Proposed by Taxation and Budget Reform Commission, Revision No. 3, 2008, filed with the Secretary of State April 28, 2008; adopted 2008.

SECTION 30. Assessment of working waterfront property. — The amendment to Section 4 of Article VII providing for the assessment of working waterfront property based on current use, and this section, shall take effect upon approval by the electors and shall first apply to assessments for tax years beginning January 1, 2010.

History. — Proposed by Taxation and Budget Reform Commission, Revision No. 6, 2008, filed with the Secretary of State April 28, 2008; adopted 2008.

SECTION 31. Additional ad valorem tax exemption for certain members of the armed forces deployed on active duty outside of the United States. — The amendment to Section 3 of Article VII providing for an additional ad valorem tax exemption for members of the United States military or military reserves, the United States Coast Guard or its reserves, or the Florida National Guard deployed on active duty outside of the United States in support of military operations designated by the legislature and this section shall take effect January 1, 2011.

History. — Added, H.J.R. 833, 2009; adopted 2010.

SECTION 32. Veterans disabled due to combat injury; homestead property tax discount. — The amendment to subsection (e) of Section 6 of Article VII relating to the homestead property tax discount for veterans who became disabled as the result of a combat injury shall take effect January 1, 2013.

History. — Added, S.J.R. 592, 2011; adopted 2012.

[1]**SECTION 33. Ad valorem tax relief for surviving spouses of veterans who died from service-connected causes and first responders who died in the line of duty.** — This section and the amendment to Section 6 of Article VII permitting the legislature to provide ad valorem tax relief to surviving spouses of veterans who died from service-connected causes and first responders who died in the line of duty shall take effect January 1, 2013.

History. — Added, H.J.R. 93, 2012; adopted 2012.

[1]**Note.** — This section, originally designated section 32 by H.J.R. 93, 2012, was redesignated section 33 by the editors in order to avoid confusion with section 32 as created in S.J.R. 592, 2011.

CONSTITUTION OF THE STATE OF FLORIDA

SECTION 34. Solar devices or renewable energy source devices; exemption from certain taxation and assessment. — This section, the amendment to subsection (e) of Section 3 of Article VII authorizing the legislature, subject to limitations set forth in general law, to exempt the assessed value of solar devices or renewable energy source devices subject to tangible personal property tax from ad valorem taxation, and the amendment to subsection (i) of Section 4 of Article VII authorizing the legislature, by general law, to prohibit the consideration of the installation of a solar device or a renewable energy source device in determining the assessed value of real property for the purpose of ad valorem taxation shall take effect on January 1, 2018, and shall expire on December 31, 2037. Upon expiration, this section shall be repealed and the text of subsection (e) of Section 3 of Article VII and subsection (i) of Section 4 of Article VII shall revert to that in existence on December 31, 2017, except that any amendments to such text otherwise adopted shall be preserved and continue to operate to the extent that such amendments are not dependent upon the portions of text which expire pursuant to this section.

History. — Added, C.S. for H.J.R. 193, 2016; adopted 2016.

SECTION 35. Tax exemption for totally and permanently disabled first responders. — The amendment to Section 6 of Article VII relating to relief from ad valorem taxes assessed on homestead property for first responders, who are totally and permanently disabled as a result of injuries sustained in the line of duty, takes effect January 1, 2017.

History. — Added, C.S. for H.J.R. 1009, 2016; adopted 2016.

SECTION 36. Additional ad valorem exemption for persons age sixty-five or older. — This section and the amendment to Section 6 of Article VII revising the just value determination for the additional ad valorem tax exemption for persons age sixty-five or older shall take effect January 1, 2017, following approval by the electors, and shall operate retroactively to January 1, 2013, for any person who received the exemption under paragraph (2) of Section 6(d) of Article VII before January 1, 2017.

History. — Added, C.S. for H.J.R. 275, 2016; adopted 2016.

SECTION 37. Eligibility of justices and judges. — The amendment to Section 8 of Article V, which increases the age at which a justice or judge is no longer eligible to serve in judicial office except upon temporary assignment, shall take effect July 1, 2019.

History. — Proposed by Constitution Revision Commission, Revision No. 1, 2018, filed with the Secretary of State May 9, 2018; adopted 2018.

SECTION 38. Prohibitions regarding lobbying for compensation and abuse of public position by public officers and public employees. — The amendments to Section 8 of Article II and Section 13 of Article V shall take effect December 31, 2022; except that the amendments to Section 8(h) of Article II shall take effect December 31, 2020, and:

(a) The Florida Commission on Ethics shall, by rule, define the term "disproportionate benefit" and prescribe the requisite intent for finding a violation of the prohibition against abuse of public position by October 1, 2019, as specified in Section 8(h) of Article II.

(b) Following the adoption of rules pursuant to subsection (a), the legislature shall enact implementing legislation establishing penalties for violations of the prohibition against abuse of public position to take effect December 31, 2020.

History. — Proposed by Constitution Revision Commission, Revision No. 7, 2018, filed with the Secretary of State May 9, 2018; adopted 2018.

SECTION 39. Prohibition on racing of or wagering on greyhounds or other dogs. — The amendment to Article X, which prohibits the racing of or wagering on greyhound and other dogs, and the creation of this section, shall take effect upon the approval of the electors.

History. — Proposed by Constitution Revision Commission, Revision No. 8, 2018, filed with the Secretary of State May 9, 2018; adopted 2018.

SECTION 40. Transfer of the accrued benefit from specified limitations on homestead property tax assessments; increased portability period. — This section and the amendment to Section 4 of Article VII, which extends to three years the time period during which the accrued benefit from specified limitations on homestead property tax assessments may be transferred from a prior homestead to a new homestead, shall take effect January 1, 2021.

History. — Added, H.J.R. 369, 2020; adopted 2020.

SECTION 41. Ad valorem tax discount for surviving spouses of certain permanently disabled veterans. — The amendment to Section 6 of Article VII, relating to the ad valorem tax discount for spouses of certain deceased veterans who had permanent, combat-related disabilities, and this section shall take effect January 1, 2021.

History. — Added, H.J.R. 877, 2020; adopted 2020.

Index

A

abortion, 816–817, 824–828, 830–834, 838, 840, 871–872,

access to courts, 76, 117–118, 406, 731, 758, 792–793, 796–799, 801–802, 955, 962

ad valorem taxation exemption, 552, 555, 557, 566, 579

ad valorem taxation, 425, 484, 489, 494, 506, 509, 511, 524–530, 533, 535–537, 541, 544–547, 550, 552, 555, 557, 566, 568, 572–573, 579, 605, 642–645, 648, 652–653, 655–659, 943, 1013–1015, 1019, 1024, 1026, 1097, 1099

adequate and independent state grounds, 671

administrative penalties, 789, 792, 955, 961

administrative review, 258–264, 268–273, 277, 290, 298, 313, 315, 318, 320–322, 324, 367, 994–995

advisory opinions, 10, 13, 22, 32, 35, 181, 339, 349, 543, 560, 592, 595, 600, 677, 992, 994

all writs necessary, 242, 248–249, 251–253, 318, 320, 324, 993, 995

allocating power, 9, 11–12

amendment by constitutional convention, 18, 19, 716, 966, 1067–1069

amendment by initiative petition, 19, 22–23, 30, 963–964, 967–968, 971, 983–984, 990, 1009–1010, 1019, 1043, 1049–1051, 1053–1055, 1057–1059, 1061, 1064–1065, 1068–1069, 1071

amendment by interpretation, 38

amendment by legislative proposal, 17, 1067

amendment by revision commission, 17–19, 386, 481, 484, 934–936, 956–957, 961–962, 966–968, 973, 975, 978–979, 983, 986–990, 992–998, 1001–1004, 1008–1011, 1019, 1022, 1024, 1030–1033, 1041–1044, 1046–1048, 1051, 1053, 1066–1070, 1096, 1099–1100

amendment by taxation and budget reform commission, 19–20, 46, 52, 963, 966, 983, 986, 990, 1015, 1019, 1067, 1069, 1083, 1095, 1097–1098

amendments, 13, 21, 34–36, 46–49, 51–52, 58, 73, 87, 89, 112, 117, 138–139, 141, 145, 186, 191, 194, 196, 198, 200, 227, 232, 235, 240, 242–243, 251, 259, 264, 326, 329, 331–335, 373, 383, 386–387, 412, 443, 450–451, 509, 592, 731, 819, 954, 968, 974, 1001–1002, 1015, 1019, 1033, 1037, 1044, 1046, 1060, 1067, 1071, 1095–1097, 1099

annexation, 146–147, 388, 391, 395, 400, 404–411, 445–447, 492, 1031

appeal as a matter of right, 198, 258, 274

appeals, 68, 103, 112, 114, 127, 162, 178, 187–188, 190–191, 194, 197–198, 200, 238–242, 251, 255–256, 258–260, 262–266, 270–271, 274–276, 278, 291, 295, 300–301, 303–308, 314, 318, 320, 324, 337–338, 397, 412, 419, 427, 499, 548, 567, 575, 577, 581, 607, 620, 654

appropriation bills, 148, 177, 971, 975, 977, 980–981

arbitrage bonds, 660, 662

assessment, 20, 48, 51, 151, 167, 239, 298, 359–360, 385, 393, 396–397, 455, 460–472, 478, 494–522, 537–542, 546, 551, 553–555, 564, 572, 585–598, 612, 629–630, 635, 647, 688, 862, 975, 1004, 1016–1020, 1022, 1063, 1070, 1072–1073, 1095, 1097–1099

associational standing, 366

B

ballot summaries, 13, 22–23, 27–34, 921

ballots and single subject requirement, 22–27

ballots, 122, 1071

basic rights, 85, 667, 674, 677, 681–683, 865, 867, 954, 956

bills of attainder, 605, 715, 957

bonds, 35–37, 102, 198, 353, 359, 371–374, 380, 393, 396, 402–403, 412–413, 415–416, 421, 424, 471, 476, 479–480, 487, 489, 527, 532–534, 563, 611–663, 976, 993, 1011–1013, 1023–1027, 1061, 1071–1072, 1074–1095

bond validation, 36, 347, 413, 418, 471, 487, 613, 620, 629, 632, 635, 649, 654, 658, 661–662

branches of government, 25–27, 63–64, 66, 90, 98, 105, 120, 662, 862, 962, 964–965

C

case or controversy, 338, 343

certiorari, 39, 103–104, 110, 199–208, 211–212, 217, 220, 229, 246, 250–251, 258, 260–281, 288–327, 331, 334–339, 362, 405–406, 409, 411, 444, 513, 994

charter counties, 369–371, 376, 378, 381, 383, 385–386, 448, 451, 536

circuit courts, 8, 185–186, 243, 254–255, 257–261, 263, 268–271, 279, 283, 287–288, 291, 302, 307–310, 315, 318–322, 324, 338, 610, 689, 691, 979, 991–992, 994–995, 998, 1003–1004

citizen standing, 343, 362, 364

common law certiorari, 199–200, 250, 268–269, 273, 288–292, 294–295, 297–301, 303–306, 308, 310–313, 320–322, 326, 335

consolidation, 219, 251, 401, 403, 441–447, 605, 1029, 1031, 1033, 1036

constitutional certiorari, 199, 306

constitutional convention, 18–19, 716, 966, 1067–1069

constitutional interpretation, 6, 14, 485, 570, 573, 582, 592, 594, 599–600

constitutional language, 9–11, 47, 161, 172, 582, 621

constitutional provisions, 10, 12, 14–16, 34–35, 38–39, 47, 49, 53–54, 58–59, 62, 64, 98, 146, 185, 347, 351, 364, 369, 385, 465, 474, 476, 492, 594–595, 600, 615, 659, 666–667, 672, 683, 717, 829, 915, 933, 939

counties, 8, 10, 26, 85, 101, 151, 157, 160, 161, 163, 166–167, 173, 175, 281, 319, 341, 343–344, 352, 366, 369–373, 376–378, 381, 383, 385–386, 396, 416, 418, 424–425, 430–431, 435, 448, 450–451, 460, 472, 474, 476–477, 479, 482–485, 487, 491, 496, 506, 512–514, 526, 529–536, 539, 544, 565, 601–602, 604–606, 611, 616, 642–643, 653, 661, 958, 962, 966, 975, 985, 1002, 1005–1007, 1012, 1017, 1020–1024, 1027–1030, 1032, 1037–1038, 1042, 1055, 1073, 1077–1078, 1088, 1090, 1092–1094

county courts, 185, 258, 289, 310, 318–320, 324, 979, 991–992, 995, 997–998, 1002, 1004, 1007

courts, 6, 8, 10–16, 38, 40, 42, 47, 59–60, 66–68, 71, 73, 75–76, 79, 82–84, 86, 89, 91, 93, 99, 103–105, 107, 111–112, 114–118, 121, 125, 127, 129, 148, 152, 158–159, 164, 168, 174, 182, 185–368, 376, 382, 385, 394, 406–407, 413, 416, 418, 426, 433–434, 455–456, 459–460,

464, 467–468, 472, 478, 499, 504, 517, 525, 547, 555, 557, 579, 605–607, 610, 619, 635, 637, 640, 666–668, 671–673, 678, 685–687, 689–691, 694, 700, 706, 708, 723, 725, 731, 734, 741, 743, 757–758, 763, 765–768, 773, 776, 778, 791–799, 801–802, 819–821, 829, 847, 852, 855, 864–866, 884–886, 888, 890, 896, 904, 907–908, 910, 912–913, 915–917, 925, 942–943, 948–949, 955, 958, 962, 979, 990–995, 997–998, 1001–1008, 1036, 1048

D

debt service, 374, 380, 480, 612, 638, 641–642, 648, 652, 656, 660, 981, 1024–1027, 1061, 1075, 1077–1079, 1081, 1084, 1090, 1092–1093

declaration of rights, 283, 378, 665–897, 953–954

delegation of power, 119, 127, 402

Dillon's Rule, 392, 394

discretionary review, 193–197, 199, 222–225, 261, 301, 305, 307–308

district courts of appeal, 13, 69, 129, 182, 185–186, 191, 193, 196–197, 205, 209, 211–212, 222–224, 227–228, 233, 243, 249, 251, 255, 258–259, 262–263, 268, 270–271, 277–279, 282–284, 287–289, 294, 300–302, 304–305, 308–309, 313, 317, 672, 734, 768, 979, 991–994, 998, 1001, 1004

due process, 261–262, 264, 266–267, 272–276, 293, 296–297, 314, 318, 325, 377, 390, 401–402, 444, 492, 508, 512, 626, 674, 683, 685, 693, 695, 707, 714–715, 737–738, 741, 743–747, 749–750, 752–753, 756–762, 764–767, 770, 772, 804, 848, 857–858, 866, 954, 957–958, 989

E

effective date of laws, 180, 971, 975

ejusdem generis, 53, 55

eminent domain, 249, 355, 360, 397–399, 420, 433–434, 438, 892–897, 1044, 1047

encroachment, 66, 84, 95, 103, 106, 109, 112, 666–667, 669, 677, 758, 766, 828, 865–866

equal protection, 70–71, 146, 159, 160, 163, 307, 309, 368, 377, 390, 401, 407, 492, 508, 512, 626, 674, 676, 681–683, 685–686, 692–699, 701, 703–704, 706, 738, 757–758, 770, 772, 796, 857–858, 870

ex post facto law, 733–737

executive encroachment on the judicial branch, 109–111

executive encroachment on the legislative branch, 95–103

executive power, 107, 181, 985

expressio unius est exclusio alterius, 9, 11, 56–57, 712, 912

F

federal courts, 82, 89, 91, 114, 118, 667, 725, 908, 913

finance, 8, 35, 52, 254, 350, 373, 396, 411, 417, 421, 455–611, 618–663, 954, 977, 1011, 1023–1026, 1042, 1061, 1075–1078, 1085, 1088

Florida Supreme Court, 4, 6, 9–10, 12, 21, 38, 65–67, 69, 112, 117, 128, 137, 142, 158, 163, 181, 185–187, 191–192, 198, 200, 204–205, 208–209, 214–215, 220, 222, 225, 227, 232, 234–236, 240–242, 245, 248–250, 252, 254–255, 257–258, 265, 267–268, 275, 277, 285–286, 289–290, 310, 340, 354–355, 361, 367, 386, 405, 421, 441, 455, 460, 468, 472–473, 475, 485–486, 503, 507, 557, 560–561, 607, 613–616, 620, 623, 627, 649, 651, 671–673, 676, 680–681, 685, 692, 707, 713, 725, 728, 743, 775–776, 793, 796, 803, 807, 823–824, 854, 856, 878, 883–885, 899, 904, 908, 914, 918, 931, 942

G

general laws, 150, 153, 158 442, 447, 888, 976, 1037–1038

general laws of local application, 150, 152, 160, 163–164

general obligation bond, 371–373, 612–613, 641–642, 657

governor's veto power, 176, 179–180,

grandparent visitation, 883–888, 891

H

habeas corpus, 160, 242, 255–258, 288, 318, 320, 324, 490, 493, 955, 957, 993–995

head of family, 523, 546, 571, 894, 900–901, 907, 920–922, 926, 933, 935, 948–949–950, 1013

head of household, 949

heirs, 899, 918–931, 942–944, 948–949, 1047

home rule, 36, 370–373, 377, 382, 385, 392–397, 412, 430–431, 437, 456, 537, 611, 1033, 1035–1038

home rule power, 373, 392, 395–397, 412, 431

homestead abandonment, 902–905, 947–950

homestead conveyance, 932–938

homestead devise, 943

homestead establishment, 495, 522, 585, 593–594, 596–598, 900, 907, 1016

homestead exceptions, 902, 917

homestead exemption, 36–37, 494–495, 519–521, 524, 564, 566–568, 571, 573, 577–580, 585–586, 589, 591–598, 902–903, 906–907, 909–920, 924–925, 927–930, 933, 935, 943, 945, 947–948, 950, 1014–1016, 1072, 1097

homestead partition, 915, 947

homestead termination, 495, 520, 585, 593, 900, 902, 918, 947, 1016

homestead, 36–37, 465, 494–496, 518–522, 524, 564–568, 570–574, 577–598, 605, 679, 899–951, 1011, 1014–1017, 1020–1022, 1034–1035, 1044, 1046–1047, 1072–1073, 1097–1100

household goods and personal effects, 523, 544–547, 1013

I

illegal tax, 377, 455, 460, 1012, 1024

impact fees, 455–456, 459–460

impairment of contract rights, 724, 728–733

imprisonment for debt, 768, 773, 955, 957

income tax exemption, 534, 614, 618, 1023

inherency doctrine, 191, 200

inherent state power, 6–7, 10–12, 155

initiative petition, 963–964, 967–968, 971, 983–984, 990, 1009–1010, 1019, 1043, 1049–1051, 1053–1054, 1057–1059, 1061, 1064–1065, 1068–1069, 1071

injury-in-fact, 341–342

inter vivos, 567, 931

interlocutory orders, 199, 250, 258, 277, 289, 301–302, 306–308

J

jointly-held property, 208, 945

judicial delegation, 124

judicial encroachment on the executive branch, 103–106

judicial encroachment on the legislative branch, 66–94

judicial power, 10, 45, 51, 75, 78, 80–81, 86, 135–136, 183, 220, 246, 256, 259, 765

jurisdiction, 7, 12–13, 22, 39, 47, 51, 59, 68–69, 80, 88, 97–98, 100–101, 104, 106, 109, 118–120, 129, 137, 143, 145–146, 151, 153, 164, 167, 174, 185–187, 190–218, 220–236, 238–240, 242–256, 258–259, 261–265, 268–271, 275, 277–278, 280–285, 288–293, 297, 300–303, 305, 308–311, 314–315, 318–322, 324–326,

INDEX 1105

328, 330–331, 334, 336, 338–339, 347–349, 352, 355, 362, 368, 371, 380–381, 383, 389–390, 393, 401, 412–414, 423, 435, 442, 446, 450–452, 461, 474, 478, 482, 487, 491–493, 495–496, 500, 507, 515, 525, 537, 539–540, 544, 553–554, 559, 561, 568, 585–589, 591, 593, 602, 613, 620, 623, 625, 628, 643, 647, 649, 651, 660, 667–668, 671–673, 675, 679, 682, 684–685, 693, 696, 714, 716, 726, 727, 733–734, 736, 744, 747, 768, 776, 793–794, 804, 809, 818, 825–826, 843, 855, 857–859, 869, 883, 886–889, 906, 909, 917, 919, 922, 924, 925, 932, 940, 948, 961, 967, 970, 975, 987, 992–999, 1003–1007, 1016–1017, 1032–1036, 1038–1039, 1050, 1056, 1064, 1080–1081, 1085, 1092–1093, 1096

just valuation, 375, 377, 380–381, 383, 389–390, 393, 397, 400, 414, 419, 445, 447, 784

justiciable questions, 256, 263

L

legislative delegation, 119, 146

legislative encroachment on the executive branch, 106–109

legislative encroachment on the judicial branch, 112–118

legislative powers, 377, 436

legislative proposal, 20

life support, 829, 833, 850, 854, 859, 861, 863

limitations on taxation, 20, 48–49, 461, 1070

local bonds, 489, 642, 653, 1011, 1024

local government, 12, 20, 22–31, 33, 35, 48, 151, 162, 164, 167, 171, 268, 318, 327, 330–331, 333–334, 337, 369, 370, 378, 382, 386, 396, 411–412, 414, 416, 418, 421–422, 424–425, 428, 430–432, 446–447, 452–453, 455–456, 460–461, 473–477, 479–481, 484, 488, 529,

532, 534, 537, 539, 611–612, 614, 618, 635, 642–644, 646, 649, 651, 653, 658, 710–713, 812, 893, 953–954, 975, 980, 1011, 1022–1025, 1027, 1029, 1033–1034, 1039, 1070

local-local relationships, 441

M

mandamus, 85, 106, 109, 242, 253–254, 258, 288, 318, 320, 324, 356–357, 561, 641–642, 993–995

merger, 388, 395, 400, 401, 403, 447, 1031

mootness, 338–342, 344, 812, 855

municipal corporations, 352, 369, 387, 392, 394, 396, 400, 404, 407, 410, 421–424, 432, 434, 442, 445, 457, 1036, 1087

municipal home rule power, 392, 394–395, 397, 437

municipal purpose, 372, 376, 388, 391, 394–395, 398–399, 432, 437, 457, 482–485, 491, 539, 661–663, 1023, 1031, 1038

municipal service taxing unit, 371–373, 418, 462, 482–484, 486, 655

municipalities, 11, 85, 151, 167, 281, 370, 381, 385–388, 390, 392–396, 398–403, 405, 409, 417–418, 424–425, 432, 435–437, 441–444, 446–449, 452–453, 460, 462, 471–472, 474–475, 483–487, 492, 496, 512, 529, 531–533, 535–539, 541, 544, 565, 598–599, 601–608, 610, 642–643, 653, 662–663, 718, 962, 966, 975, 1010, 1012, 1017, 1020–1025, 1027–1034, 1037–1039, 1073, 1075, 1084

N

natural persons, 558, 560–562, 674, 677, 682–682, 685, 698, 775, 803, 805, 810, 814, 828, 830, 866, 874–875, 886, 892, 899, 900–902, 910, 920–923, 926, 950, 956, 962, 1019–1020, 1046–1047, 1054

necessary writs, 248

non-charter counties, 369–371, 374, 376, 386, 391

non-justiciable questions, 338, 347

non-preemption, 432

non-recourse bonds, 615, 627

non-self-executing and self-executing, 13

O

owner requirement, 901

P

permanent residence, 564–565, 566–584, 589, 593, 900–901, 1010, 1020–1021

physician assisted suicide, 857–858

pledging public credit, 614–615, 618–620, 623, 625–627, 629–630

pledging state credit, 613–614, 617, 624, 638–642, 1026

population acts, 162–164, 394

preemption, 26, 383–384, 386–387, 405, 427–430, 432, 448, 451–452

privacy, 367–368, 665–666, 685–687, 689–691, 775–776, 778–779, 781–783, 785–787, 803–811, 813–818, 822–830, 832–840, 842–843, 845–846, 848–851, 854–872, 874–887, 889, 891, 955, 962, 1055, 1057

procedural due process, 261–262, 264, 266–267, 272–276, 296–297, 314, 318, 766–767

procedural law, 113, 127, 204

prohibited laws, 715, 955, 957

prohibition, 6, 9, 34, 46, 60, 65–66, 86, 120–121, 127–128, 171, 242–247, 258, 276, 288, 318, 320, 324, 410, 560, 562–563, 578, 615, 618, 623, 630, 712–713, 717, 721, 724, 733–737, 740–742, 745, 747, 795, 837, 858, 870–871, 930, 949–950, 961, 966, 968, 970, 993–995, 1032, 1045–1046, 1049, 1051, 1058, 1066, 1073, 1099–1100

protection from creditors, 902, 908, 927, 930

public trials, 818–819

Q

quasi-executive, 324

quasi-judicial,108, 185–186, 246, 253, 268, 279, 291, 297–298, 320–322, 324–326, 328–331, 334–337, 992

quasi-legislative, 322, 324–325

quo warranto, 95, 102, 242, 253–255, 258, 288, 318, 320, 324, 389, 402, 404–406, 993–995

R

rate of taxation, 491–492, 494, 653

rational basis test, 689, 691, 694, 696, 698–699, 703–707, 757–758

reasonable basis test, 162, 408, 757, 761–762

refusal of medical treatment, 843, 850, 854, 864

revenue bonds, 373, 380, 402, 412, 416, 421, 479, 487, 532, 534, 612, 614–627, 629, 632, 636, 638, 641, 646, 649–650, 652–653, 660–661, 1011–1012, 1023–1026, 1074–1076, 1083–1084

revision commission, 17–20, 86, 385–386, 481, 484, 641, 659, 684, 913, 934–936, 956–957, 961–962, 966–968, 973, 975, 978–979, 983, 986–990, 992–995, 997–998, 1001–1004, 1008–1011, 1019, 1022, 1024, 1030–1033, 1042–1044, 1046–1048, 1051, 1053, 1066–1070, 1083, 1096–1097, 1099–1100

right to assemble, 707, 954, 956

right to bargain collectively, 175, 707, 711, 714

right to privacy, 666, 689–691, 775, 804, 806, 808, 810–811, 813–814, 816, 825–828, 830, 833–834, 855–856, 872, 877–881, 887

right to work, 707–708, 954, 956

ripeness, 338, 340, 343–344

INDEX

rules of construction, 49, 59, 911, 1044, 1048

S

search and seizure, 774–776, 778, 784

self-executing and non-self-executing, 13

separation of powers, 63–66, 84, 88, 90–91, 93–94, 98–100, 102–105, 107–108, 112, 116, 119–120, 123, 127, 179–180, 242, 244, 264, 338, 728, 758, 862

single subject limitation, 128, 136, 145

size and contiguity requirement, 902

special assessment, 37, 372, 393, 396–397, 455, 458, 460–471, 509, 612, 630, 647, 655, 1025

special laws, 146, 150–155, 158–159, 164, 166, 170, 172–174, 381, 386, 405, 407, 414, 476–479, 971, 975

special taxing districts, 350, 423–425, 487–489, 1036, 1088–1089

standing to challenge administrative action, 367

state and local aid to private sector, 614

state court, 6, 10, 99, 223, 241, 319, 666–668, 671–673, 888, 1002–1003, 1008

state-local relationships, 426

statutory certiorari, 199, 320–322

statutory rape and sexual exploitation/misconduct, 869–871, 874–875, 878, 880

substantive due process, 674, 685, 707, 737, 743–744, 757–758, 766–767

substantive law, 112–113, 127, 150, 200, 264, 268, 271

T

taking of property, 665, 674,759, 892

tax exemption, 23, 523–525, 537–538, 542, 552, 556–557, 565, 568–579, 581, 584, 589, 594, 904, 1014, 1020, 1022, 1072–1073, 1095, 1097–1099

tax increment financing, 488, 650–651, 655, 658–659

taxation and budget reform commission, 19–20, 46, 52, 963, 966, 983, 986, 990, 1015, 1019, 1067

taxation, 8, 19–20, 33, 36–37, 48–52, 359, 393, 425, 441, 455, 461, 468, 472–478, 481, 483–486, 489,494, 506, 509, 511, 514, 517, 523–547, 549–555, 557–559, 561–564, 566–568, 570, 572–573, 579, 582, 585–586, 588, 591, 593, 597–605, 607–608, 611–612, 614, 617–618, 642–645, 648, 652–659, 943, 963, 966–967, 983, 986, 990, 1011–1015, 1019–1020, 1023–1024, 1026, 1030–1031, 1034, 1067, 1069–1070, 1073, 1083, 1095, 1097–1099

taxpayer standing, 338, 350–354, 361, 364

third party standing, 367–368

time-share estate, 507–511

title requirement, 128, 146, 152

U

unincorporated areas, 323, 375, 379, 381, 401–403, 431, 445, 449, 467, 484, 485–486, 539, 598–603, 605–611, 1030, 1052

United States Supreme Court, 4, 34, 72–73, 91, 97, 114–115, 117, 188, 223, 241, 284, 563, 665, 670, 682–684, 686, 716–717, 721, 724–725, 731, 764, 770, 772, 774–776, 778–785, 788, 805–807, 817, 819, 824, 828, 858, 861, 886, 888–889, 957, 961, 1055

user services charges, 456

V

vacant property owned by city, 537

valuation, 355, 471, 491–492, 494, 498–499, 501–503, 507–510, 512–514, 516, 520, 522, 541, 546, 554, 562, 564, 586–587, 590, 592–593, 597, 652, 1015, 1020

1108 INDEX

veto power of governor, 176–180

W

window period, 136, 138, 139, 141, 142, 143, 145

writs, 39, 85–86, 95, 102–103, 106, 109–110, 160, 186, 196, 201–204, 206–208, 221–222, 242–258, 260–262, 266, 269–272, 274–276, 278–280, 288–295, 297–301, 303–310, 312–315, 318, 320–324, 326, 335–336, 356–357, 389, 404, 406, 490, 561, 642, 791, 906, 957, 993–995